WHAT DO I READ NEXT?

Nonfiction 2005–2010

A Reader's Guide to Current Nonfiction

- Arts & Humanities
- Biographies & Memoirs
- Business
- Health & Wellness
- History
- Pop Culture
- Science
- Social Sciences

ISSN 1052-2212

WHAT DO I READ NEXT?

Nonfiction 2005–2010

A Reader's Guide to Current Nonfiction

- Arts & Humanities
- Biographies & Memoirs
- Business
- Health & Wellness
- History
- Pop Culture
- Science
- Social Sciences

ANITA CAMPBELL

DR. LAURA J. CATALDO

RYAN FISCHER-HARBAGE

HOLLY HIBNER

KELLY HOWES

MARY KELLY

NICOLE STEEVES

GALE
CENGAGE Learning™

Detroit • New York • San Francisco • New Haven, Conn • Waterville, Maine • London

GALE
CENGAGE Learning™

What Do I Read Next? Nonfiction, 2005-2010

Project Editors: Dana Ferguson, Michelle Kazensky

Composition and Electronic Prepress: Gary Leach, Evi Seoud

Manufacturing: Cynde Lentz, Rita Wimberley

For product information and technology assistance, contact us at
Gale Customer Support, 1-800-877-4253.
For permission to use material from this text or product,
submit all requests online at **www.cengage.com/permissions.**
Further permissions questions can be emailed to
permissionrequest@cengage.com

While every effort has been made to ensure the reliability of the information presented in this publication, Gale, a part of Cengage Learning, does not guarantee the accuracy of the data contained herein. Gale accepts no payment for listing; and inclusion in the publication of any organization, agency, institution, publication, service, or individual does not imply endorsement of the editors or publisher. Errors brought to the attention of the publisher and verified to the satisfaction of the publisher will be corrected in future editions.

Gale
27500 Drake Rd.
Farmington Hills, MI, 48331-3535

LIBRARY OF CONGRESS CATALOGING-IN-PUBLICATION DATA

What do I read next? Nonfiction, 2005-2010 : a reader's guide to current nonfiction / Laura J. Cataldo ... [et al.].
    p. cm.
   Includes bibliographical references and indexes.
   ISBN 978-1-4144-4847-3
   1. Books and reading--United States--History--21st century. 2. Popular literature--United States--Bibliography. 3. Books--United States--Reviews--Bibliography. 4. Public libraries--United States--Book lists. 5. Readers' advisory services--United States. 6. Reading interests--United States. I. Cataldo, Laura J.

Z1003.2.W48 2011
025.5'4--dc22   2010051690

ISBN-13: 978-1-4144-4847-3
ISBN-10: 1-4144-4847-3

ISSN: 1052-2212

Printed in Mexico
1 2 3 4 5 6 7 15 14 13 12 11

Contents

Introduction

Over the past five years, there has been a marked increase in the popularity of nonfiction books with general readers. While, in the past, the term "nonfiction" might conjure up images of dry, factual tomes most suited to students or researchers, more recently, there has been resurgence in both the appeal and the variety of nonfiction titles being released by major publishers. In the world of readers advisory, terms like "narrative nonfiction" and "readable nonfiction" have become increasingly prevalent as titles such as *Freakonomics*, by Steven D. Levitt and Stephen J. Dubner, *Outliers* by Malcolm Gladwell, *Dress Your Family in Corduroy and Denim* by David Sedaris, and *The Immortal Life of Henrietta Lacks* by Rebecca Skloot, among many others, have become international best-sellers, with the sales and resulting cultural impact to challenge even the most popular genre fiction titles.

Given the huge variety of nonfiction titles available each year, added to the numbers from previous years, readers can be forgiven if they're stumped by the question "What do I read next?" And that's where this book comes in. Designed as a tool to assist in the exploration of recent readable nonfiction, between the years 2005 and 2010, *What Do I Read Next?: Nonfiction* guides the reader to both current and classic recommendations in eight widely read "genres" of nonfiction: Arts and Humanities, Biographies and Memoirs, Business, Health and Wellness, History, Pop Culture, Science, and Social Sciences. *What Do I Read Next?* allows readers quick and easy access to specific data on recent titles in these popular nonfiction genres. Plus, each entry provides alternate reading selections, thus coming to the rescue of librarians and booksellers, who are often unfamiliar with a genre, yet must answer the question frequently posed by their patrons and customers, "What do I read next?"

Details on Titles

This edition of *What Do I Read Next?: Nonfiction* contains entries for titles published between 2005 and 2010. These entries are divided into sections for Arts and Humanities, Biographies and Memoirs, Business, Health and Wellness, History, Pop Culture, Science, and Social Sciences. Experts in each field compile the entries for their respective genres. The experts also discuss topics relevant to nonfic-

tion genres and the art of recommending nonfiction titles in essays that appear at the beginning of this volume. The criteria for inclusion of specific titles vary somewhat from genre to genre. In genres such as Biography and History, where large numbers of titles are published each year, the inclusion criteria are more selective, with the experts attempting to select the recently published books that they consider best. In genres such as Social Sciences, where the amount of new material is relatively smaller, a broader range of titles is represented, including many titles published by small or independent houses. The entries are listed alphabetically by main author in each genre section. Most provide the following information:

- **Author or editor's** name and real name if a pseudonym is used. Co-authors, co-editors, and illustrators are also listed where applicable.
- **Book title.**
- **Date and place of publication; name of publisher. Subject(s):** Gives the subject matter covered by the title.
- **What the book is about:** A brief overview of the title.
- **Where it's reviewed:** Citations to reviews of the book, including the source of the review, date of the source, and the page on which the review appears. Reviews are included from genre-specific sources as well as more general reviewing sources such as *Booklist* and *Publishers Weekly*.
- **Other books by the author:** Titles and publication dates of other books the author has written, useful for those wanting to read more by a particular author.
- **Other books you might like:** Titles by other authors written on a similar theme or in a similar style. These titles further the reader's exploration of the genre.

Indexes Answer Readers Questions

The three indexes in *What Do I Read Next?: Nonfiction* used separately or in conjunction with each other, create many pathways to the featured titles, answering general questions or locating specific titles. For example:

"What has Malcolm Gladwell written recently?"

The AUTHOR INDEX contains the names of all

viii • Introduction

What Do I Read Next? Nonfiction 2005 • 2010

authors featured in the entries and those listed under "Other books you might like."

The TITLE INDEX includes all main entry titles and all titles recommended under "Other books by the author" and "Other books you might like" in one alphabetical listing. Thus a reader can find a specific title, new or old, then go to that entry to find out what new titles are similar.

"I'm interested in books that depict military life."

The SUBJECT INDEX is an alphabetical listing of all the subjects covered by the main entry titles.

The indexes can also be used together to narrow down or broaden choices. And with the AUTHOR and TITLE indexes, which include all books listed under "Other books by the author" and "Other books you might like," it is easy to compile an extensive list of recommended reading, beginning with a recently published title or a classic from the past.

Also Available Online

The entries in this book can also be found online in Gale's new *Books & Authors* database. This electronic product encompasses over 200,000 books, including genre fiction, mainstream fiction, and nonfiction. All the books included in the online version are recommended by librarians or other experts, award winners, or appear on bestseller lists. The user-friendly functionality allows users to refine their searching by using several criteria, while making it easy to identify similar titles for further research and reading. *Books & Authors* is updated with new information weekly. For more information about *Books & Authors*, please visit Gale online at gale.cengage.com.

Suggestions Are Welcome

The editors welcome any comments and suggestions for enhancing and improving What Do I Read Next? Please address correspondence to the Editor, *What Do I Read Next?*, at the following address:

Gale, Cengage Learning

27500 Drake Rd.

Farmington Hills, MI 48331-3535

Phone: 248-699-GALE

Toll-free: 800-347-GALE

Fax: 248-699-8054

About the Genre Experts

Anita Campbell (Business): As publisher of several online media properties and syndicated content, Anita reaches over 1,000,000 small business owners and entrepreneurs annually. She is the founder and Editor-in-Chief of SmallBizTrends.com, an award-winning online publication noted and praised by Forbes and MSNBC, among others. SmallBizTrends.com is home of the annual Small Business Book Awards, and features weekly in-depth reviews of books for entrepreneurs and small business owners. Her media properties also include BizSugar.com, a popular social media site specifically for businesspeople and entrepreneurs. Anita was a contributing expert source to the original Intuit Future of Small Business Report. Anita is a prolific writer and speaker on the topic of small business. In addition to her own online publications, her articles and columns are published at numerous places such as Business.gov, Inc Technology, BNet, PayPal's Online Merchant Network, the American Express OPEN Forum, and *Success Magazine*. Prior to starting her own business, Anita held a variety of senior executive positions in the corporate world, including Senior Vice President of Bell & Howell Publishing Services, culminating in the role of CEO of an information technology subsidiary of Bell & Howell. She currently serves or previously served on a variety of Boards, including the NorTech Advisory Board; Center for Information Technology and eBusiness (CITe) at the University of Akron; Advisory Board for "http://www.neosa.org/" NEOSA (the Northeast Ohio Software Association); and the Network Solutions Social Media Advisory Board. She has a B.A. in English from Duquesne University, and a J.D. from the University of Akron Law School. Anita is the co-author of the upcoming book *Visual Marketing* (Wiley, Fall 2011).

Dr. Laura J. Cataldo (Health and Wellness; Science): Dr. Cataldo is a nurse, speaker, and educator. She holds extensive medical experience as a clinician in critical care healthcare arenas, leadership and technical expertise as a system administrator, and consultant experience as a medical advisor. In addition to the field of nursing, she has a background in business, educational technology, and program development, and is an adjunct faculty member teaching business and leadership courses to adult learn-

ers. She is experienced in curriculum development and program design for both in-classroom and online environments. Dr. Cataldo works as an advisor, editor, and contributor for a variety of medical and manuscript businesses in the field of publication.

Ryan Fischer-Harbage (Biographies and Memoirs): Ryan is a literary agent at The Fischer-Harbage Agency. Previously he worked as a book editor at Little, Brown & Company, Simon & Schuster and Penguin Group (USA). He graduated from Kalamazoo College, The Radcliffe Publishing Course and the MFA program in writing and literature at Bennington College. He has worked with numerous bestselling and prizewinning authors.

Holly Hibner (Social Sciences): Holly manages the Adult Services department at a public library in Michigan. She received an MLIS degree from Wayne State University in 1999. Since that time, she has published and spoken on a variety of topics, and received the 2007 Loleta Fyan award from the Michigan Library Association for innovation in library service. She loves all things techie and the challenge of a good reference question. Together with Mary Kelly, Holly created the popular blog "Awful Library Books," which led to an appearance on *Jimmy Kimmel Live,* and has also co-authored the book *Making a Collection Count: A Holistic Approach to Library Collection Management.*

Mary Kelly (Social Sciences): Mary is a Youth Services Librarian at the Lyon Township Public Library in Michigan. She has worked in a variety of library jobs for more than ten years. Mary has published and presented on topics such as computer instruction, reader's advisory, and providing tech support. She received both an MBA and an MLIS from Wayne State University. Mary is passionate about collection quality and technology. Together with Holly Hibner, Mary created the popular blog "Awful Library Books," which led to an appearance on *Jimmy Kimmel Live,* and has also co-authored the book *Making a Collection Count: A Holistic Approach to Library Collection Management.*

Kelly Howes (History): Kelly is the author of eight literary and historical reference books, including *The War*

x • About the Genre Experts

What Do I Read Next? Nonfiction 2005 • 2010

of 1812, The Reconstruction Era, and *The Roaring Twenties.* She was a guest speaker on the Harlem Renaissance at the American Cultural Center in Taipei, Taiwan, and on cultural diversity in the United States at ICANA (Instituto Cultural Argentino Norteamericano) in Buenos Aires, Argentina. She is also a teacher who has worked in a variety of educational settings around the world, and with elementary and middle school students as well as adults.

Nicole Steeves (Arts and Humanities; Pop Culture): Nicole is a librarian at Chicago Public Library's Harold Washington Library Center, specializing in newspapers and general periodicals. A 2010 Librarian of the Year finalist, she is also a leader in CPL's bibliographic instruction, both one-on-one and with groups of students from junior high through college, including an annual course for History Fair students. She has also enjoyed editing a system-wide Reference Services newsletter, creating a departmental intranet, and orchestrating a massive inventory of CPL's historical newspaper microfilm collection. Her love of pop culture led her to appearances on *Jeopardy!* and *USA Today*'s Pop Candy podcast.

Pop Culture Nonfiction Titles for the Literary Fiction Reader
by
Nicole Steeves

Readers' advisory can feel like a treacherous road, full of potholes and wrong turns, when librarian and patron can't find themselves in agreement. In one particularly painful instance, after a patron declined a dozen movies (Not. Exaggerating.) similar to Drew Barrymore's last movie that she'd loved, I ended up literally reading her our library's entire romantic comedy DVD list before finding one movie that hit.

So when I do recommend something that clicks for a patron or friend, it feels like a little Christmas present. To my great pleasure, the genre that has delivered the most success in this area has been pop culture non-fiction. It's not the best known subset of publishing, but the great titles in the group can stand with the elite of literary fiction. In fact, I have found that lovers of literary fiction are ripe for trying out pop culture non-fiction, often coming to the reference desk saying that they love reading novels but would like to take a chance with some non-fiction, not having read any since college.

Enter Bill Bryson, Sarah Vowell, and Michael Chabon. I am an unabashed believer that everyone should love these authors, and readers who are hesitant about non-fiction should find all three of them rewarding guides into a new realm of publishing. They exemplify today's version of renaissance men—because they are smart, interesting people with that inexhaustible thirst for knowledge, they naturally turn out smart, interesting writing on a multitude of subjects. Their curiosity rubs off on the reader as we follow their journey of discovery about whatever it is that has captured their interest.

With popular writer Bill Bryson, travel writing becomes more than a bulleted list of best restaurants and museum discount days. His journeys around England and America reflect on why we travel, what we hope to find, why we need to leave home, and why it is so satisfying to return. I don't know that I would use *Notes from a Small Island* to plan a trip around England—starting with the fact that I will NEVER walk ten miles in a day for the sake of a great view—but I will undoubtedly go to far-flung parts of that country knowing that Bryson has given me the eyes to find something special

anywhere I go. Or the willingness to move on if something is just a frightful dump. That lesson also appears in *A Walk in the Woods*, as Bryson cheerfully rewrites plan after plan during his hike of the Appalachian Trail. (Sidebar: If your friend has read this one already—quite possible since it was such a huge best-seller—try suggesting the lesser known *Neither Here nor There: Travels in Europe*. The same tragicomic travel companion appears in both books.) We also get to know Bryson's love of the curious scientific in *Walk in the Woods*, as he explores the dramatic environmental changes America's wilderness has undergone in the past century. If that aspect of his writing lights up your reader's eyes, his titles not on travel but on his forays into amateur science and historiography will be great options—*A Short History of Nearly Everything, At Home: A Short History of Private Life*, or *The Mother Tongue: English and How It Got that Way*.

Another unlettered but endlessly entertaining history writer is Sarah Vowell. Where Bill Bryson is pop culture largely because of word of mouth and good sales, Sarah Vowell's pop culture cachet existed first outside her writing career. As *consigliere* to Ira Glass on *This American Life*, frequent contributor to McSweeney's, and voice of Violet in *The Incredibles*, Vowell has crept into our consciousness as a presence in her own right and parlayed that into creating a niche in history writing for the non-academic reader. As I write, it is Thanksgiving weekend—perfect timing for a rereading of *The Wordy Shipmates*, Vowell's book on the other buckles-and-breeches New Englanders, the Puritans of Boston (and eventual founders of Harvard). While promoting this book, Vowell came back again and again to a list of supplies created by the colony's governor, a man who was also captivated by the ideal "city on a hill." Vowell loved that someone in government could pursue something so lofty while remaining grounded in the daily realities of keeping a state, a colony, a household functioning. Such a figure must have especially appealed to the writer of *The Partly Cloudy Patriot*, in which Vowell shares her tears and hopes in the wake of the 2000 election debacle, where the practical nerd was somehow trounced by a cowboy unlikely to wax rhapsodic about citizenship nor create a practical plan to feed his people. Things presidential are also the focus of *Assassination Vacation*, in which Vowell chronicles the classic American road trip taken not to classic destinations such as the Grand Canyon or Niagara Falls but instead to the sites of presidential murders. Readers of this book can delight in endless minutiae about the murdered, the murderers, and the social conditions that bred the atmosphere leading to each assassination—perhaps a nice counterpoint to Bryson for your reader who likes unique travel writers. I very much look forward to her next book about the taking of Hawaii in the nineteenth century, the research for which she discussed in a speaking engagement I was lucky to catch in early 2010 (and something I would tell any reader to watch for in her city if Vowell's writing appeals to her).

Michael Chabon also has a reputation for captivating his live audiences with effortless wit and buoyant storytelling, and seeing him is high on my to-do list. Until then, I will keep devouring his masterful essays that show him to be a great lover of pop culture—a fanboy who became the subject of fervent fandom. Many of your readers may know and love Chabon for his fiction, especially the Pulitzer-Prize-winning *The Amazing Adventures of Kavalier & Clay*. Happily, that should make it especially easy to sell his books of non-fiction. I know that it worked for me—my love of *Kavalier & Clay* led me straight to the related comic book series *Michael Chabon Presents: The Amazing Adventures of the Escapist*, and thanks to the quirks of Library of Congress shelving, that selection also brought my attention to Chabon's beautiful collection of essays, *Maps and Legends: Reading and Writing along the Borderlands*. And here Chabon elevates pop culture non-fiction straight out of any imaginable genre ghetto, right to the top of my list of any kind of writing. He transcends and transforms pop culture, writing about the subject's most arcane ephemera even as he looks into the most monumental of questions: why we read, why characters become our friends, why genre literature must be given equal stature with the literary fiction that would do its best to stigmatize genre and make it "other." This book, then, may be the best piece you can hand to the reader nervous about letting go of a novel; Chabon seduces us into a world of comic books and detectives and sci fi and kiddie lit and memoir. Readers will find that loving literature means loving it all, and Chabon's charisma makes us wonder why we ever thought otherwise. Once you've got your reader hooked, don't let her leave the library without Chabon's follow-up collection, *Manhood for Amateurs: The Pleasures and Regrets of a Husband, Father, and Son*. Here he not only celebrates pop culture staples such as *Doctor Who* and suburban coming-of-age, but he reminds us that somehow, everything in our lives—grocery shopping, depression, being bored in grandma's basement—is popular culture, because pop culture is built on touchstones anyone and everyone can share.

And that is the core of my readers' advisory advice: Pop culture is a spectacular way to connect with readers. It is fun and easy to read without being dumb or any less thoughtful than any literary fiction out there. It is a joy to discuss, a pleasure to recommend, and a reliable bridge into non-fiction, making a huge section of publishing suddenly safe for the novel reader to explore. So seek it out, read it yourself, make a display (the iconic imagery makes displays a cinch for even those of us utterly devoid of craft skill). Your fiction readers will thank you—and even better, trust your future recommendations without a catalog recitation!

Contemporary Pop Culture Nonfiction Writing by Women: Intimacy with Strangers
by
Nicole Steeves

In college, my girlfriends and I, like all college girlfriends do, had many inside jokes. In fact, we did not call them inside jokes—instead, we referred to them as MCBs. One of our number was a philosophy major and had learned about MCBs—mutual contextual beliefs—in one of her seminars. Basically, they are phrases that act as shorthand: two or three words that invoke a shared experience, story, belief. In short (too late!), an inside joke. And though I may besmirch the memory of MCBs by giving such a lengthy description for something that embodies brevity, I am tickled to get to bring more folks into the MCB circle. Once you know about them, you see their usefulness—and in much of contemporary pop culture writing by women, they exemplify the writing style that seems so casual and yet so crystal clear in these ladies' addictive works. We readers feel like we are in on the joke, like we know that story, and suddenly, authors feel like friends.

This surprising intimacy plays out on my favorite pop culture blog, Go Fug Yourself (http://gofugyourself. com/), a site dedicated to eviscerating celebrities who have too much money and too many handlers to go out in public looking as ridiculous as they often do. From comparisons to specific outfits worn by tertiary characters on single episodes of long-forgotten 80s sitcoms to heartrending coming-of-age moments in the lesser-read later volumes of the Anne of Green Gables series, the Fug Girls (Jessica Morgan and Heather Cox) drop obscure pop-culture references left and right. Scarcely a day goes when they don't mention something I had thought was unique to my own experience; it's like I am reading a Facebook message from my own best friend rather than a blog entry for the world to read. That intimacy defines their writing style and helps create their loyal following, Fug Nation. They successfully transfer that dynamic to their book, *Go Fug Yourself: The Fug Awards*. The awards in the book, such as the Sag Award for mishandling the coverage of breasts and the Tanorexia Award for the person most addicted to bronzer are giggle-inducing snapshots of the Fug Girls' ongoing battle against celebrity fashion crimes for longtime and first-time readers alike. For any reader who is looking for a laugh, particularly a laugh like the kind she gets from a night out with the girls, you can't go wrong with this book.

Before the Fug Girls claimed their own territory on the internet, they were a part of the granddaddy of TV-episode-recap sites known as Television Without Pity, affectionately abbreviated as TWoP (http://www. televisionwithoutpity.com/). TWoP founders Tara Ariano and Sarah Bunting created a world where all of the comments you yelled at the TV set with your girlfriends were shared and drawn out into 12-page recaps of every episode of the covered shows. Hated what Buffy wore to fight in the sewer one week? So did the recapper. Couldn't believe that the show is about Dawson and his forehead instead of Jen, Jack, and Grams? So believed these writers. By sharing the same shorthand jokes as girlfriends in their living rooms for a Sunday-night viewing of *Sex and the City* did, the TWoP brigade fostered a tight-knit online community of real friends, both shaping and responding to a certain sense of humor that could only exist as a response to pop culture television. Like the Fug Girls, Ariano and Bunting synthesized their site's vibe into a book to be read by fans and newbies alike. *Television Without Pity: 752 Things We Love to Hate (and Hate to Love) about TV* addresses the good, bad, hilarious, and infuriating tropes of television: canned laughter, theme songs, William Shatner, and more. Their very specific viewpoint about what makes television so great—and sometimes SO STUPID—is encapsulated here for any TV fan to enjoy. Sadly, the founders have since moved on to greener pastures, selling the TWoP site to NBC and departing for good in 2008. But their style of love-hating TV and loquaciously recapping it live on at The AV Club (http://www.avclub.com/) and Vulture (http://nymag.com/daily/entertainment/).

Any lover of television and pop culture has probably enjoyed a hearty, snorting laugh at the VERY SERIOUS reporting of Samantha Bee on *The Daily Show*. I love her, and when her book *I Know I Am, but What Are You?* came out in 2010, I snapped it up. I wasn't disappointed. Every chapter covers some painfully awkward event in Bee's childhood and teen years, told in such a funny way that only the least self-conscious should dare to read it in public, because readers will certainly make spectacles of themselves raucously laughing. Like the Fug Girls and the TWoP folks, Bee uses pop culture touchstones to evoke a specific time and place. Unlike those writers, though, Bee makes no bones about being "just like you!" Instead, she presents her young-adult life as the worst-case scenario, the nightmare that most suburban girls (and their mothers) dread—all while being side-splittingly funny and just barely side-stepping of actual tragedy. You once flirted with a much older stranger on the bus when you were a teen? When Bee did that, she was so oblivious to danger that she went right ahead and took up his offer to come to his apartment and "talk about music." You had a goofy summer job? Bee spent summers touring rural Canada dressed as Sailor Moon in a not-quite-legitimate live-action play of a Japanese comic unknown to Canadians. No genuine harm comes to Bee in these stories, other than minor psychological trauma. But her experience isn't just like yours, either. Instead of being the friend who thinks like you and likes the same things, Bee is the one who gives you perspective on all the vagaries of life. That is, your childhood will look a lot better after reading about hers.

Reading Marjane Satrapi's *Embroideries* might be a nice palate cleanser after Bee, because these stories of women talking together put us firmly back in the camp of mirroring our own lives. Best known for her *Persepolis* graphic novels and the Academy-Award-nominated film based on them, Satrapi has a reputation for drawing and telling stark stories of children in war. Not here: These are women's stories—fading beauty, "handling" husbands and lovers, drinking with mothers, gossiping with aunts, grandmothers, neighbors. Despite taking place in the Middle East, these could just as easily be your own memories of late nights after Thanksgiving dinners as a young woman being welcomed into the female adult world. Women can know Satrapi's world even from thousands of miles away, just as well as they know the Fug Girls' pop-culture-rich upbringing—without even a single mention of Brenda Walsh's love of men's ties.

Non-Fiction Reader Advisory: Tips, Tricks, and Techniques
by
Holly Hibner

Non-fiction reader advisory is similar in many ways to any other kind of reader advisory: matching people to titles they may enjoy. Included here are some tips, tricks, and techniques specific to non-fiction that may help advisors find more choices to offer to readers.

When asked for a good book, reader advisors need to keep non-fiction in mind. When considered holistically, library and bookstore collections have a wide variety of collections and formats available, and appeal factors run across those collections. The first tip for non-fiction reader advisory, then, is to offer subject-based reader advisory rather than genre-based, age-based, or format-based.

Subject-based reader advisory might include titles in fiction, non-fiction, DVD, and audio, and span youth, teen, and adult collections. For example, a reader who loved the baseball aspect of Stephen King's *Blockade Billy* might be interested in a non-fiction book about baseball scandals, such as *Game of Shadows* by Mark Fainaru-Wada that discusses the dark underbelly of steroid use in baseball. There is also the Ken Burns documentary called (simply) *Baseball*. Any item that falls under the general category of baseball might be suggested to a reader who was interested in that one aspect of the book they started with.

To be fair, offering such a plethora of options to readers who ask for "something similar" can be overwhelming. They may want only one simple suggestion. Still, various collections and formats should be considered. Pairing non-fiction choices with well-loved fiction titles is a scaled-back way to approach reader advisory. Setting, theme, subject, character type—all can be taken into consideration.

To give a simpler example, a reader who enjoys historical fiction may enjoy a non-fiction book about a particular time period. In this way, you can pair fiction titles with non-fiction titles. Because many libraries and bookstores separate fiction from non-fiction geographically, readers are less likely to find and pair these titles on their own. A lover of a classic fiction title such as Nathaniel Hawthorne's *The Scarlet Letter* might enjoy the non-fiction title *The Wordy Shipmates* by Sarah Vowell.

Some other ideas for pairings between fiction and non-fiction can start with genre-based suggestions and branch out into non-fiction. For example, women's fiction (chick lit) authors like Sophie Kinsella or Helen Fielding pair interestingly with non-fiction books such as *See Jane Write: A Girl's Guide to Writing Chick Lit* by Sarah Mlynowski or *Flirting with Pride and Prejudice: Fresh Perspectives on the Original Chick-Lit Masterpiece* edited by Jennifer Crusie and Glenn Yeffeth. Together, these books talk about how to write chick lit, what inspires authors of chick lit, and actual chick lit novels.

To give an example from a different genre, readers of supernatural fiction by authors such as Laurell K. Hamilton and John Saul pair with a book like Stephen Asma's *On Monsters: An Unnatural History of Our Worst Fears*. It discusses both literary monsters such as Dracula and Frankenstein's monster and real-life monsters such as Adolf Hitler, and then analyzes human nature's abhorrence of frightening, monster-like behavior, and the lengths people will go to protect and defend even at the risk of becoming a monster themselves. Taken together, supernatural fiction puts a monster in an imaginative story, often terrorizing people and places, and then the non-fiction book takes it a bit farther and asks the reader to consider what makes one a monster.

Geography is another way to pair fiction with non-fiction. Take a fiction title with an interesting setting and pair it with a book about that place. Examples are *The Lost Tiki Palaces of Detroit* by Michael Zadoorian or *Middlesex* by Jeffrey Eugenides paired with non-fiction books about Detroit such as *Detroit Then and Now by Cheri Gay* or *Detroit: A Postcard Album* by Richard Bak. Any fiction book with a strong sense of place could be paired with a non-fiction book about that place: a travelogue, a historical profile, or even a book about a landmark in that location.

Another very useful non-fiction reader advisory technique is to compare subject interests to magazines. When asked for a reading suggestion, the reader advisor might ask what magazines the reader enjoys. This provides a very broad subject to work with, which the reader might not come up with or identify clearly if simply asked what subjects he or she finds interesting. A reader of *Popular Mechanics* might enjoy a blue-collar, do-it-yourself non-fiction book such as Matthew Crawford's *Shop Class as Soul Craft*. The author posits that this thinker of this generation, educated for the "knowledge revolution," don't know how to work with their hands. The book discusses the value of hard, physical work and hand-made items. Those who read *Redbook*, *Ladies Home Journal*, or *More* magazines are likely to be mature women. They may enjoy the *Sweet Potato Queens* series by Jill Conner Browne or *The Girls from Ames: A Story of Women and a Forty-Year Friendship* by Jeffrey Zaslow. These are books that speak to the interests and issues of the demographic who also read these magazines. *National Geographic* readers might enjoy adventure and exotic settings such as those in books such as *The Lost City of Z* by David Grann or Greg Mortenson's *Stones into Schools* or *Three Cups of Tea*.

Along the same lines of asking about magazines that readers enjoy, advisors could ask what movies they like. Someone who likes a Sherlock Holmes-type *who done it* might enjoy a historical true crime book such as *The Suspicions of Mr. Whicher, or the Murder at Road Hill House* by Kate Summerscale. Adventure movie buffs could try Susan Wels' book *Amelia Earhart: The Thrill of It* as a companion to the movie *Amelia* starring Hillary Swank. Those who prefer comedies could browse through the book *Monty Python Live* by Graham Chapman et al. Something scary? How about *Seeking Spirits: The Lost Cases of the Atlantic Paranormal Society* by Jason Hawes and Grant Wilson (stars of the television show *Ghost Hunters*). Foreign films? There's *The Boy That Harnessed the Wind* by William Kamkwamba. This is a relatively easy way to match books to people because lots of people watch movies and television and can more easily describe movies and shows they watch than describe books they read. They're likely to leave out whole categories of non-fiction if simply asked what kinds of books they like, non-fiction that very well could appeal to them upon discovery. This technique finds success quickly and easily with reader advisors because it is something with which most people can identify.

Along the same lines, everyone has jobs, kids, parents, in-laws, a to-do list, stress, pets, money problems, food issues, etc., in their lives. These are topics of common ground among most people. Starting a conversation with someone about any one of these topics could get the ball rolling toward non-fiction reader advisory. Go with the moment! If a reader volunteers conversation about anything, an advisor can suggest a book on that subject. Books such as *Working with You is Killing Me: Freeing Yourself from Emotional Traps at Work* by Katherine Crowley and Kathi Elster or *Type Talk at Work: How the 16 Personality Types Determine Your Success on the Job* by Otto Kroeger are both funny and interesting to people

who have jobs. There is *Too Much of a Good Thing* by Dan Kindlon for people with children, grandchildren, or noisy neighbor kids. Martha Stout's *The Sociopath Next Door* will make anyone look at their friends, neighbors, family, and co-workers in a whole different light! These are books on subjects we can all identify with, as they are part of everyday life. A reader didn't necessarily show up looking for these books, but will leave perfectly satisfied and entertained with such choices. They appeal to the general curiosity in people of all backgrounds.

Reader advisors should be as personal as they are comfortable with. They should share stories and interests with readers and simply talk about books they have enjoyed themselves. This personal touch creates a relationship that leads to trust and mutual interest. Readers will feel comfortable asking for reading suggestions across collections because they know the reader advisor can match them with something about whatever they are going through. Find common ground and create the relationship using those innocuous subjects listed above, and then go deeper as you get to know the readers better.

Embrace the trashy, the junky, and the funky! Readers advisors don't judge; they simply listen and match interests to titles. It is a great ice breaker to suggest a funny book such as *Five People Who Died during Sex: and 100 Other Terribly Tasteless Lists* by Karl Shaw or *The Zombie Survival Guide* by Max Brooks. Of course, it is imperative to know one's audience before suggesting titles they might find off-color, inappropriate, or even offensive. Once that relationship is established and a sense of humor is judged, these are some fun books that have broad appeal. They are the kinds of books few people come looking for specifically, but that anyone can enjoy browsing through leisurely.

You can judge a book by its cover! A flashy, pretty, interesting cover catches the eye of readers. Display non-fiction books face-forward whenever and wherever possible. Put a pile of books on your desk that have "eye appeal." Readers will notice them and ask about them, which leads to instant reader advisory! Look for cover art that is bright and colorful, such as DK's *Eyewitness* books that have encyclopedic formats and wonderful photographs and illustrations. The book *Why Can't You Shut Up: How We Ruin Relationships—How Not To* by Anthony Wolf is a great example of an interesting cover. It features a huge open mouth with teeth and a word bubble. Combined with its provocative title, it's a sure winner!

Think about the mood or the tone of a book, not just its subject matter. There are lots of books that appeal to a mood that might be about a subject the reader thought they had no interest in. For example, *The Prison Angel* by Mary Jordan is about woman who grew up privileged in Beverly Hills, who suffered divorces and general unhappiness. She becomes "Mother Angelica" and gives her life in service to those incarcerated in Mexican jails. In fact, she lives among them in a jail cell! One does not need to be Catholic or interested in jails or Mexico to enjoy this book. It is filled with stories with such inspiration, but in a setting so out of the ordinary that it breeds curiosity, that general readers can enjoy it. It becomes less about the subject matter and more about the mood and feeling one gets from reading it. Good writing trumps topic! The *Monty Python Live* book listed above is a great example of a book that cam make readers laugh out loud and feel genuinely happy without ever having heard of Monty Python.

Teens require another set of techniques where non-fiction reader advisory is concerned. Teenagers who bother to ask for reader advisory assistance often fall in one of three categories. First, they are good readers, interested in books and reading, and are just looking for a good book. Second, they have an assignment to do for school that they just want to finish; they don't really care about the book itself. Third, they are bored and don't know what they want but can become interested in a number of subjects. It is important to approach teens with a helpful air. They may assume that a reader advisor is going to insist that they read something "important," literary, or academic. The reader advisor can use words such as *browse* instead of *read* and talk about the cover. They can add a creep-out factor by giving teens books such as *Stiff: The Secret Life of Human Cadavers* by Mary Roach. This makes reading fun and encourages teens to ask for reading suggestions again later. Again, once a relationship is established between reader advisor and teen, the more easily difficult and important questions can be dealt with over time. Being approachable so that they will ask is the most important part! Break down barriers and stereotypes so that teens see reader advisors as interesting people they can relate to through books.

Create a go-to list of non-fiction books. Start at the beginning of the Dewey decimal range and find a few titles in each area that are interesting and fun to talk about. When caught off-guard by a reader looking for a "good book," the advisor will have a ready list of favorite standbys. Going back to the idea of having a pile of books with eye appeal on the desk, the pile can be filled with books from the advisor's go-to list. The list should be updated as new books come out, maybe a few times per year, but it is still reasonable to include backlist titles that are perennial favorites. The list should be short—maybe just a page long—so that it can be consulted at a glance. It is not meant to take the place of reader advisory books and databases, but only put a few titles in the advisor's mind when they need them. If you've ever been put on the spot trying to remember a great book you loved but you can't grasp the title or author, you will appreciate having a quick list handy!

In closing, non-fiction reader advisory can be approached holistically. That is, various genres, subjects, authors, and settings have appeal factors across collections, age groups, and formats. Finding titles of interest to readers can be as easy as striking up a conversation and talking about everyday things such as family and work, magazines, and movies. Once a relationship is established between reader and advisor, deeper conversations and more personal suggestions can be made. Non-fiction has mass appeal to people who might not ever have considered it. Matching interests across collections increases collection awareness and broad readership, and may even ignite new interests!

Gender Appeal in Non-Fiction
by
Holly Hibner

It may seem like a gross generalization to say that males and females have different reading tastes. Why wouldn't they, though? Their brains are biologically different, so it stands to reason that they may have different reading preferences (http://www.scientificamerican.com/article.cfm?id=girl-brain-boy-brain). Of course, circumstances and life experiences may have a lot to do with personal choice as well, so we are not suggesting that men and women never enjoy the same books. The purpose of this essay is to recommend non-fiction categories and titles that may have broad appeal to one gender or the other, as well as provide reader advisory tips to "sell" just about any book to either gender in ways they can identify with. In the end, reader advisors will suggest books that match whatever appeal factors readers identify, whether they are "women's literature" or "men's literature."

The suggestions here do generalize preferences based on gender, but only as a path from which both readers and advisors can understand and work. They should be approached as a starting point for discussion and identification of reader tastes, not hard-and-fast rules for gender-biased reader advisory. The appeal factors here have been derived from studies on reading and gender, combined with various works on reader advisory techniques. For further study of those topics, please refer to authors such as Joyce Sericks, Nancy Pearl, Sarah Statz Cords, Neal Wyatt, Michael Sullivan, and Patrick Jones.

Katherine Husser's non-fiction genre study (http://sites.google.com/site/nonfictiongenrestudy) defines four appeal characteristics of non-fiction: characterization, pace, frame (such as time and place), and storyline. These characteristics are not intrinsically gender-based, but can be used to describe the draw that men and women may have toward certain types of non-fiction.

It is no leap of faith to say that the subject-specific nature of non-fiction draws readers to books on subjects in which they have an interest. Baseball fans will find interest in books about baseball. Crafters will enjoy books about crafts. Books about music will appeal to musicians. However, there are certainly sub-genres within non-fiction that could take the broader subject of baseball, crafts, and music and break them down to books with more specific gender appeal.

For example, studies show that males gravitate to biographies. Men who are excited about sports may enjoy biographies of players (such as *Sweet Thunder: The Life and Times of Sugar Ray Robinson* by Wil Haygood or *Zero Regret: Be Greater Than Yesterday* by Apolo Anton Ohno) and coaches/managers (such as *Red and Me: My Coach, My Lifelong Friend* by Bill Russell or *I Live for This: Baseball's Last True Believer*, a biography of Tommy LaSorda written by Bill Plaschke).

Women, on the other hand, are more inclined toward fiction and leisure reading. Women interested in sports might enjoy a more narrative book of non-fiction such as *Fathers & Daughters & Sports* by Jim Craig, et. al, which is a book of essays written by sports journalists, athletes, and writers. The essays are inspirational and emotional, which is also said to appeal more to women than men (or, perhaps, a "feminine sensibility," whether biologically male or female.) Other narrative-type sports books that may catch the interest of women include *On the Right Track: From Olympic Downfall to Finding Forgiveness and the Strength to Overcome and Succeed* by Marion Jones, *Rowing the Atlantic: Lessons Learned on the Open Ocean* by Roz Savage, or *The U.S. Women's Soccer Team: An American Success Story* by Clemente A. Lisi.

Men are also said to prefer magazines and newspapers to books. There are many books with magazine and newspaper-like formats, like the very entertaining *Headless Body in Topless Bar: The Best Headlines from America's Favorite Newspaper* by the staff of the New York Post. Another great book with this format is *Page One: One Hundred Years of Headlines as Presented in the New York Times*, edited by the New York Times. Men are more likely to be browsers than readers, so books with encyclopedic and visual formats are also appealing to them. A good example of this is *National Geographic Visual History of the World*. These books give snippets of storyline, frame, and character at a fast pace.

As said above, women are more inclined toward fiction and leisure reading. Non-fiction that reads like fiction has more appeal for them. Books like *Mom: A Celebration of Mothers from StoryCorps* by Dave Isay, *Kabul Beauty School: An American Woman Goes behind the Veil* by Deborah Rodriguez, and *Making Toast: A Family Story* by Roger Rosenblatt have more narrative styles that women may enjoy. These books have strong storylines and characterization, as well as a frame (time/place) that is important to the story, but at a slower pace that women can savor.

Women also typically like reading about other women. Strong women who defy convention are very appealing to today's female non-fiction readers. *Amelia Earhart: The Thrill of It* by Susan Wels is one example, as well as *America's Women: 400 Years of Dolls, Drudges, Helpmates, and Heroines* by Gail Collins. Men will appreciate books about men, such as *Where Men Win Glory: The Odyssey of Pat Tillman* by Jon Krakauer or *Life*, the memoir by Keith Richards.

Let's now consider how to sell the same non-fiction title to each gender. We will start with the example *Ice Bound: A Doctor's Incredible Battle for Survival at the South Pole* by Jerri Nielsen. If we follow what the experts say are the gender appeals, women will sympathize with Dr. Nielsen's emotional state as she battles breast cancer. They will appreciate her strength and

determination. They will read the book as a novel, cover to cover. Men, according to the experts' suggestions about male reading habits, will be captivated by the medicine itself—Dr. Nielsen operated on herself! Men will appreciate the harshness of the setting. They will recognize Dr. Neilsen's never-give-up attitude and the pure gutsiness of actually performing surgery in such conditions.

Let's look at the gender appeals of another title. This time we will use Greg Mortenson's *Three Cups of Tea*. Its exotic and, again, "harsh" setting appeals to men, as well as the male character and his affinity for mountain climbing. Men can also be sold on the adventure of the story and the variety of people the author meets along the way, including con artists, swindlers, and village elders. Women will identify with the personal relationships formed between the author and the people of Korphe in Pakistan. They will feel for the children in the story and their future prospects, thanks to Mortenson's efforts.

Reader advisors do not have to shy away from using gender as a technique toward finding reading suggestions. If approached as one piece of the advisory puzzle, it can help both parties define appeal factors. Once again, we caution anyone from relying solely on gender in a reader advisory transaction, just as we caution relying on any one technique. It is simply a tool to help define what it is about books that readers enjoy. There is research to back these generalizations, which gives more credence to this idea.

Welcoming Adults Back to Leisure Reading
by
Holly Hibner

There are a number of reasons why adults fall out of the habit of reading. It does not mean that they aren't inherently readers or book lovers; only that circumstances deemed that they put their attention elsewhere for some amount of time. Once those circumstances change, they may find themselves yearning to read again. Where does one begin when one has not read much in several years' time? How can library staff and programs help adults rediscover reading?

One of the reasons people may stop reading is because of their children. Children require a lot of time and attention, leaving only moments here and there for pleasure reading. Once children go to school full time or perhaps years later when they grow up and leave home, adults may find time to read again. There is a good chance that their interests have changed over the years, so simply to pick up with the authors and series they used to enjoy might not do the trick (although that is certainly one strategy!). They may have spent years reading about parenting and child development, so one possibility is to use their familiarity with that subject and transfer it over to pleasure reading. An easy-reading fiction book such as Danielle Steel's *Family Ties* would be a quick, low-effort way to introduce a fiction book about parenting. Other good choices would be *The Atlas of Love* by Laurie Frankel or *Man of the House* by Ad Hudler. All three of these books are about parenting and families and all make for simple forays into reading. As readers develop new reading habits, they may start to look for more complicated stories. More literary titles or non-fiction titles could then be suggested, such as *The Mercy Rule* by Perri Klass or *Waiting for Christopher* by Louise Hawes (both are novels about children and families) or *Making Toast*, a non-fiction book about grandparents as parents by Roger Rosenblatt.

Another reason people may stop reading is job-related. Depending on the job and the industry in which one works, there may not be a lot of time or energy left at the end of the day for leisure reading. Some people work long hours, leaving them with only a little time to enjoy their families and homes (and to sleep!). Others spend their days reading at work, making reading a dif-ficult activity to see as "leisure." In these economic times, there are more and more layoffs, company re-organizations, and forced retirements, leaving many people who used to fill their days with work with time for other things—like reading. Those who are between jobs may be interested in books about work life, such as *The Man Who Mistook His Job for a Life: A Chronic Overachiever Finds the Way Home* by Jonathon Lazear or *The Cat's Meow* by Emily Carmichael (both about workaholism) or *Company* by Max Barry (a satire novel about corporate America).

This strategy can be applied to just about any subject. Pinpoint the circumstances that got in the way of someone's reading and re-introduce them to reading fun books that have something to do with that subject—children, work, illness, school, or whatever the roadblock. If they've focused their attention on that subject for any length of time, it is familiar to them. It's a way to ease back into reading with a familiar subject. Of course, this strategy is only a gateway into re-introducing reading for pleasure to adults. Over time, many readers will move away from familiar subjects and crave new ideas.

The exact opposite may be true, and should also be acknowledged: People who have spent years thinking about children, work, or school may want a completely new subject to focus on. They may want to read about anything *but* what has been familiar to them. The trick in this case is to find something simple that won't overwhelm a return-reader, on a subject of interest, and with which he or she can have a successful reading experience. Traditional reader advisory techniques apply here, matching suggested appeal factors with potential titles. The focus is high interest, low effort reading!

Summer reading programs are another great way for adults to rediscover reading. Many libraries have adult reading programs that challenge people to read new genres, to read as a family, or to try new formats such as audio books. Librarians can encourage adults to become good reading role models for their children by spending family time reading together—or at least in the same time and place if not the same books. Adults will find themselves immersed in the reading, reintroduced to the pleasure of the activity. A challenge to read certain types of books, a certain number of books, or even spend certain amount of time reading, might give them just the push they need to get started.

Adults who read to their children may also find themselves excited about reading children's books they loved when they were young, as well as discovering new children's books their children want to read. It does not matter *what* one reads, only that the reading is enjoyed. Librarians can encourage adults to read aloud to their families, which keeps them in the habit of pleasure reading, introduces that simple pleasure to their children, and may even ignite their own interest in reading more for fun. As the children get older and pass through higher grades in school, adults may find themselves re-reading classics that they didn't understand when they were forced to read them in high school. As adults, they may experience a new appreciation for those titles, which in turn could persuade further reading of classic literature.

Book discussion groups are yet another way to re-introduce adults to reading. It is a supportive setting with other book lovers and readers, with a purpose and a set title. There is no frustration or stress over choosing a book because the group often either chooses it together or the facilitator provides the reading choice. Someone sliding back into reading may find all the choices overwhelming. So many books have been published over the years, talked about on TV, and reviewed in newspapers, that returning readers don't know where to start! They may also find themselves trying to read like they did in high school or college, looking for hidden meanings and themes, and then frustrated that their analytic thinking is rusty. A book club would enable return-readers to listen and talk about a book honestly and simply, sharing and observing without having to wonder if they are "right" or "getting it" on their own. Feedback is helpful in re-learning how to read critically.

Librarians can encourage those re-discovering reading to read books about books. That is, returning readers can read about what to read! Books such as *100 One-Night Reads: A Book Lover's Guide* by David Major, *You've Got to Read This Book: 55 People Tell the Story of the Book That Changed Their Life* edited by Jack Canfield (of *Chicken Soup for the Soul* fame), or *1001 Books for Every Mood* by Hallie Ephron are wonderful annotated lists of books to get adults thinking about what kinds of books they might like to try.

Adults who claim they don't have time to read can be treated as reluctant readers, just as children and teens are often described. Those who have gotten away from reading for fun may have lots of excuses as to the reasons, but librarians can encourage them to get back into it by using some of the techniques used on reluctant readers of other ages. They can suggest magazines and newspapers (which certainly count as reading!) or encyclopedia-type books with short passages of interest on any subject, such as Rosemary Guiley's *Encyclopedia of Vampires and Warewolves* or the *National Geographic Visual History of the World*. These books are browsable, but interesting enough to pique a reader's curiosity about a subject and lead to other books on the same subject or in the same style that the reader finds enjoyable.

Finally, technology has made reading a new kind of experience. Adults who love technology might prefer pleasure reading on an eBook reader, or listening to an audio book downloaded to an mp3 player. Portable devices have the advantage of making reading more accessible. People might get on the reading bandwagon more readily if shown these technology-driven options.

Adults who are interested in getting back into pleasure reading may have been one-time readers in their lives. Before college, before children, before their careers, they enjoyed a good book, and for a variety of reasons they have time again for reading. Librarians need to welcome these adults back and help them rediscover the joy of reading through good reader advisory methods such as those outlined above. Imagine how overwhelming all the choices are to a returning reader! Librarians can take away that frustration through various collections, programs, and services and help them be successful and avid readers once again.

Arts and Humanities

1

STACEY ABBOTT

Angel

(Detroit, Michigan: Wayne State University Press, 2009)

Subject(s): Television; Criticism; Television programs

Summary: In *Angel*, Stacey Abbott presents a scholarly critique of the television show of the same name, which featured a character named Angel—a vampire with a soul. *Angel* was a spin-off of the popular *Buffy the Vampire Slayer* television show. Unlike *Buffy*, however, *Angel* was a completely different program, intended for adult viewers. In the book, Abbot discusses the show in relationship to topics such as feminism, gender, the horror genre, and television itself. She also discusses the show's creative aspects, including its visual presentation and its writing team.

Where it's reviewed:
Booklist, August 2005, page 1982
Reference & Research Book News, August 2009

Other books by the same author:
Falling in Love Again, 2009
Celluloid Vampires, 2007
Reading Angel, 2005

Other books you might like:
Stacey Abbott, *Celluloid Vampires*, 2007
Stacey Abbott, *Reading Angel*, 2005
Tamy Burnett, *The Literary Angel: Essays on Influences and Traditions Reflected in the Joss Whedon Series*, 2010
    Amijo Comeford, co-author
Kevin K. Durand, *Buffy Meets the Academy: Essays on the Episodes and Scripts as Texts*, 2009
Erin B. Waggoner, *Sexual Rhetoric in the Works of Joss Whedon: New Essays*, 2010

2

FRANCES PAYNE ADLER
DEBRA BUSMAN , Co-Editor
DIANA GARCIA , Co-Editor

Fire and Ink: An Anthology of Social Action Writing

(Tucson, Arizona: University of Arizona Press, 2009)

Subject(s): Social conditions; Law; Short stories

Summary: Compiled by Frances Payne Adler, Debra Busman, and Diana Garcia, *Fire and Ink: An Anthology of Social Action Writing* is a collection of fiction and nonfiction pieces focused on the theme of social justice. The collection features short stories, essays, interviews, and poetry from well-known writers such as Martin Espada, June Jordan, Patricia Smith, Gloria Anzaldua, Sharon Olds, Arundhati Roy, Sonia Sanchez, Carolyn Forche, Chitra Banerjee Divakaruni, Alice Walker, Linda Hogan, Gary Soto, Kim Blaeser, Minnie Bruce Pratt, Li-Young Lee, and Jimmy Santiago Baca. Divided into ten sections, each piece included in *Fire and Ink* addresses a specific social issue such as identity, sexuality and gender, war, peace, and the environment.

Where it's reviewed:
The Progressive, September 2009, page 42
Publishers Weekly, August 10, 2009, page 47
Reference & Research Book News, May 2010
Tikkun, November-December 2009, page 81

Other books by the same author:
The Making of A Matriot, 2003
When the Bough Breaks: Pregnancy and the Legacy of Addiction, 1994
Raising the Tents, 1993

Other books you might like:
S.E. Anderson, *In Defense of Mumia*, 1996
D. Stanley Eitzen, *Solutions to Social Problems from the Bottom Up: Successful Social Movements*, 2006
Martin Espada, *Poetry Like Bread*, 2000
June Jordan, *Some of Us Did Not Die: New and Selected Essays*, 2003
Grant H. Kester, *Conversation Pieces: Community and Communication in Modern Art*, 2004

Kenneth Stewart, *Solutions to Social Problems from the Bottom Up: Successful Social Movements*, 2006

3

KATHLEEN ALCALA

The Desert Remembers My Name: On Family and Writing

(Tucson, Arizona: University of Arizona Press, 2007)

Subject(s): Family; Culture; Family history

Summary: *The Desert Remembers My Name: On Family and Writing* is a collection of candid autobiographical essays from author Kathleen Alcala. Growing up as a Mexican American in California, Alcala embraced her family's heritage as well as her new way of life. In *The Desert Remembers My Name*, she offers insights, musings, and personal anecdotes about her life, heritage, upbringing, and the world at large. Her intimate essays cover everything from digging into her family background to uncovering shocking family secrets to contemplating national news cases, like a mother who killed her own children. The collection is honest, moving, and authentic, shedding light on Alcala's own life and encouraging readers to dig into their own family histories as well.

Where it's reviewed:
Publishers Weekly, January 29, 2007, page 56
Reference & Research Book News, November 2007

Other books by the same author:
Treasures in Heaven, 2003
The Flower in the Skull, 1999
Spirits of the Ordinary, 1998

Other books you might like:
Kathleen Alcala, *The Flower in the Skull*, 1998
Kathleen Alcala, *Mrs. Vargas and the Dead Naturalist*, 1992
Kathleen Alcala, *Spirits of the Ordinary*, 1997
Kathleen Alcala, *Treasures in Heaven*, 2003
Tom Kealey, *Creative Writing MFA Handbook: A Guide for Prospective Graduate Students*, 2008

4

TAMAR ALEXANDER-FRIZER

The Heart Is a Mirror: The Sephardic Folktale

(New York: Wayne State University Press, 2008)

Subject(s): History; Jewish history; Jews

Summary: In *The Heart Is a Mirror: The Sephardic Folktale*, Tamar Alexander-Frizer presents a critical examination of the more than 4,000 folktales told by Sephardic Jews, a Judeo-Spanish people exiled from Spain in 1492. Despite their hardships, the Sephardic Jews succeeded in preserving their culture, identity, and language, known as Ladino. The folktales these people told over many generations provide important information about their history. The author divides this book into three sections to discuss the folktales and their significance. The first section discusses the connection between the tales and the history of the Sephardic Jews. The second section examines the different types of folktales, while the third section focuses on the tradition of storytelling and its role in shaping the Sephardic folktales.

Where it's reviewed:
Reference & Research Book News, February 2008

Other books you might like:
Victor Ambrus, *The Little House: A Jewish Folk Tale*, 1991
Victor Ambrus, *The Rabbi's Wisdom: A Jewish Folk Tale from Eastern Europe*, 1991
Adele Geras, *My Grandmother's Stories: A Collection of Jewish Folk Tales*, 1990
Erica Gordon, *The Little House: A Jewish Folk Tale*, 1991
Erica Gordon, *The Rabbi's Wisdom: A Jewish Folk Tale from Eastern Europe*, 1991
Leo Pavlat, *Jewish Folk Tales*, 1986
Margot Zemach, *It Could Always Be Worse: A Yiddish Folk Tale*, 1976

5

RAY ALLEN

Gone to the Country: The New Lost City Ramblers and the Folk Music Revival

(Urbana: University of Illinois Press, 2010)

Subject(s): Music; Musicians; Southern United States

Summary: *Gone to the Country: The New Lost City Ramblers and the Folk Music Revival* is a detailed biography on the urban folk trio the New Lost City Ramblers from author Ray Allen. During the 1950s and the 1960s, the folk trio, comprised of Mike Seeger, John Cohen, and Tom Paley, helped lead the charge for the resurgence of folk music. Despite the fact that the band was made up of northern city dwellers, the New Lost City Ramblers helped pave the way for Southern-style music. In *Gone to the Country*, Allen recounts the band's humble beginnings in New York, its rise to fame, and the surrounding controversy. He also chronicles the folk revival and how the New Lost City Ramblers helped bridge the gap between folk fans and urban audiences.

Where it's reviewed:
Library Journal, September 1, 2010, page 109

Other books by the same author:
Singing in the Spirit, 1991

Other books you might like:
Alan Lomax, *American Ballads and Folk Songs*, 1994
Alan Lomax, *Our Singing Country: Folk Songs and Ballads*, 2000
John A. Lomax, *American Ballads and Folk Songs*, 1994

John A. Lomax, *Our Singing Country: Folk Songs and Ballads*, 2000
Jean Ritchie, *The Dulcimer Book*, 1992
Jean Ritchie, *Folk Songs of the Southern Appalachians as Sung by Jean Ritchie*, 1997
Carl Sandburg, *The American Songbag*, 1990

6

JAY ALLISON
DAN GEDIMAN , Co-Editor

This I Believe: The Personal Philosophies of Remarkable Men and Women

(New York: Henry Holt and Co., 2006)

Subject(s): Conduct of Life; Ethics; Faith

Summary: During the 1950s, Edward R. Murrow hosted a radio series titled "This I Believe." The program asked Americans to explain their most important beliefs in a brief essay. In 2005, National Public Radio re-created this series beginning with a weekly segment. Allison and Gediman, host and executive producer of the series, respectively, have collected 80 essays from both the 1950s program and the current series. Essay contributors include well-known personalities such as Helen Keller, Eleanor Roosevelt, Newt Gingrich, John Updike, Isabel Allende, Bill Gates, and Colin Powell; however, ordinary citizens are also represented: a surgeon, a part-time hospital clerk, a teenager, a lawyer, and a Burmese immigrant are among the many contributors.

Where it's reviewed:
Booklist, September 1, 2006, page 23
Books (Chicago Tribune), April 1, 2007, page 2
Library Journal, October 1, 2006, page 80
Publishers Weekly, August 14, 2006, page 201

Other books by the same author:
This I Believe II: More Personal Philosophies of Remarkable Men and Women, 2006
The Life Stories Collection, 2001
Animals and Other Stories, 2000

Other books you might like:
Jay Allison, *This I Believe II: More Personal Philosophies of Remarkable Men and Women*, 2008
Dave Eggers, *Zeitoun*, 2009
Dan Gediman, *Edward R. Murrow's This I Believe: Selections from the 1950s Radio Series*, 2009
Dan Gediman, *This I Believe II: More Personal Philosophies of Remarkable Men and Women*, 2008
Mary Jo Gediman, *Edward R. Murrow's This I Believe: Selections from the 1950s Radio Series*, 2009
John Gregory, co-author
Dave Isay, *Mom: A Celebration of Mothers from StoryCorps*, 2010
Steve Lopez, *The Soloist: A Lost Dream, an Unlikely Friendship, and the Redemptive Power of Music*, 2008

7

E.N. ANDERSON

Everyone Eats: Understanding Food and Culture

(New York: New York University Press, 2005)

Subject(s): Food; Biology; Culture

Summary: *Everyone Eats: Understanding Food and Culture* is a biological and cultural examination of eating, from author E.N. Anderson. It's an understood and accepted thing that everyone needs to eat, but Anderson gives readers a greater understanding of why humans need to eat and why individuals around the world eat certain foods. *Everyone Eats* explains the biological need to eat, the nutritional reasons behind eating, and the cultural significance of certain foods. Anderson explains the connection between food and religion, food and medicine, and food and ethnicity, while also offering details about the globalization of food and suggestions on how to end world hunger, malnutrition, and starvation.

Where it's reviewed:
Booklist, July 2005

Other books by the same author:
The Pursuit of Ecotopia, 2010
Ecologies of the Heart, 1996
The Food of China, 1990

Other books you might like:
Melissa L. Caldwell, *The Cultural Politics of Food and Eating*, 2005
Carole Counihan, *Food and Culture: A Reader*, 2007
Erik Millstone, *The Atlas of Food: Who Eats What, Where and Why*, 2008
Sidney W. Mintz, *Sweetness and Power: The Place of Sugar in Modern History*, 1986
Massimo Montanari, *Food Is Culture*, 2006
James L. Watson, *The Cultural Politics of Food and Eating*, 2005

8

LYNNE CHRISTY ANDERSON

Breaking Bread: Recipes and Stories from Immigrant Kitchens

(Berkeley, California: University of California Press, 2010)

Subject(s): Food; Cooking; Immigrants

Summary: In *Breaking Bread: Recipes and Stories from Immigrant Kitchens*, author Lynne Christy Anderson explores the American immigrant experience through the foods and recipes of various cultures. From this perspective, Anderson's study provides an intensely personal and powerful look at how immigrants struggled to integrate into American society while still holding onto the traditions and, of course, the cuisine of their homelands. Blending biography, cookbook, and cultural commentary, this volume celebrates the vibrant diversity of America's kitchens. With photography by Robin Radin, *Breaking Bread* includes a foreword by food writer Corby Kummer.

Where it's reviewed:
Library Journal, May 15, 2010, page 89

Other books you might like:
William Alexander, *52 Loaves: One Man's Relentless Pursuit of Truth, Meaning, and a Perfect Crust*, 2010
Arlene Voski Avakian, *From Betty Crocker to Feminist Food Studies: Critical Perspectives on Women and Food*, 2005
  Barbara Haber, co-author
Sherrie A. Inness, *Dinner Roles: American Women and Culinary Culture*, 2001
Laura Schenone, *A Thousand Years over a Hot Stove: A History of American Women Told through Food, Recipes, and Remembrances*, 2003
Jane Ziegelman, *97 Orchard: An Edible History of Five Immigrant Families in One New York Tenement*, 2010

9

STEVE ANKER
KATHY GERITZ , Co-Editor
STEVE SEID , Co-Editor

Radical Light: Alternative Film and Video in the San Francisco Bay Area, 1945-2000

(Berkeley: University of California Press, 2010)

Subject(s): Movie industry; Movies; United States

Summary: In *Radical Light: Alternative Film and Video in the San Francisco Bay Area, 1945-2000*, editors Steve Anker, Kathy Geritz, and Steve Seid compile a diverse assortment of essays examining the city by the bay's unique contributions to the world of experimental filmmaking. The editors include interviews, photographs, and artwork to further illustrate the San Francisco movie scene and its evolution from the mid-20th century to the present. This volume illuminates the cutting-edge styles and powerful impact of one American city's approach to creating movie magic. *Radical Light* contains a bibliography and an index.

Other books you might like:
Ken Dancyger, *Alternative Scriptwriting, Fourth Edition: Rewriting the Hollywood Formula*, 2006
Courtney Lehmann, *The Reel Shakespeare: Alternative Cinema and Theory*, 2002
Scott MacDonald, *Adventures of Perception: Cinema as Exploration*, 2009
Scott MacDonald, *Canyon Cinema: The Life and Times of an Independent Film Distributor*, 2008
Jeff Rush, *Alternative Scriptwriting, Fourth Edition: Rewriting the Hollywood Formula*, 2006
Rebecca Solnit, *River of Shadows: Eadweard Muybridge and the Technological Wild West*, 2003
Lisa S. Starks, *The Reel Shakespeare: Alternative Cinema and Theory*, 2002

10

ARAB AMERICAN NATIONAL MUSEUM

Telling Our Story: The Arab American National Museum

(Dearborn, Michigan: Wayne State University Press, 2007)

Subject(s): United States; Museums; Middle East

Summary: Written by the Arab American National Museum in Dearborn, Michigan, *Telling Our Story: The Arab American National Museum* is a historical examination of Arab American life and the origin of the museum. The authoritative narrative includes fascinating details about the history of Arabs in America, the way of life for the Arab American community, and the cultural differences this group experiences. Relying on several unique perspectives, the book discusses the origins of the Arab American National Museum and takes readers inside its doors with a detailed account of many of its major exhibits.

Where it's reviewed:
Skipping Stones, March-April 2008, page 33

Other books you might like:
Sheila S. Blair, *Prisse d'Avennes: Arab Art*, 2010
  Jonathan S. Bloom, co-author
Saeb Eigner, *Art of the Middle East: Modern and Contemporary Art of the Arab World and Iran*, 2010
  Zaha Hadid, co-author
Andrew Hammond, *Pop Culture Arab World!: Media, Arts, and Lifestyle*, 2004
Fran Lloyd, *Contemporary Arab Women's Art: Dialogues of the Present*, 2002
Nada M. Shabout, *Modern Arab Art: Formation of Arab Aesthetics*, 2007

11

MELANIE BALES
REBECCA NETTL-FIOL , Co-Editor

The Body Eclectic: Evolving Practices in Dance Training

(Urbana, Illinois: University of Illinois Press, 2008)

Subject(s): Dance; Art; Teaching

Summary: Edited by Melanie Bales and Rebecca Nettl-Fiol, *The Body Eclectic: Evolving Practices in Dance Training* is a collection of essays and interviews examining the development and progression of dance training over the past five decades. The contributors analyze modern dance techniques, choreography styles, dancer participation, and dance training. The book examines the various ways that training methods, styles, and approaches influence dance trends and art forms. In addition to essays by contributors such as Glenna Batson, Joshua Monten, and Martha Myers, *The Body Eclectic* also includes interviews with dance professionals such as David Dorfman, Ralph Lemon, and Bebe Miller.

Where it's reviewed:
Dance Magazine, June 2008, page 62

Other books you might like:
Lynne Anne Blom, *The Intimate Act Of Choreography*, 1982

Curtis J. Bonk, *The World Is Open: How Web Technology Is Revolutionizing Education*, 2009

Jo Butterworth, *Contemporary Choreography: A Critical Reader*, 2009

L. Tarin Chaplin, *The Intimate Act Of Choreography*, 1982

Jan Erkert, *Harnessing the Wind: the Art of Teaching Modern Dance*, 2003

Richard Shusterman, *Body Consciousness: A Philosophy of Mindfulness and Somaesthetics*, 2008

Liesbeth Wildschut, *Contemporary Choreography: A Critical Reader*, 2009

12

JAMES L. BAUGHMAN

The Republic of Mass Culture: Journalism, Filmmaking, and Broadcasting in America Since 1941

(Baltimore: Johns Hopkins University Press, 1992)

Subject(s): Television; Movies; Journalism

Summary: The history of media is the focus of this all-encompassing study by author and journalism professor James L. Baughman. *The Republic of Mass Culture: Journalism, Filmmaking, and Broadcasting in America Since 1941* looks first at how the invention of movies and television revolutionized mass media. Baughman discusses the obstacles the new media faced and the media's ever-changing priorities. The book offers readers an exploration of the industry's past, present, and future. *The Republic of Mass Culture* includes a bibliography and an index.

Where it's reviewed:
Journal of Popular Film & Television, Spring 2007, page 47

Other books by the same author:
Same Time, Same Station, 2007

Other books you might like:
Andrew Chadwick, *Internet Politics: States, Citizens, and New Communication Technologies*, 2006

David Copeland, *The Media's Role in Defining the Nation: The Active Voice*, 2009

Ralph E. Hanson, *Mass Communication: Living in a Media World*, 2010

George R. Rodman, *Mass Media in a Changing World*, 2009

Paul Starr, *The Creation of the Media: Political Origins of Modern Communication*, 2005

13

CHRISTOPHER BEACH

The Films of Hal Ashby

(Detroit, Michigan: Wayne State University Press, 2009)

Subject(s): Movies; History; Criticism

Summary: In *The Films of Hal Ashby*, Christopher Beach considers the work of the Academy Award-winning film-maker, who during the 1970s directed a string of successful and critically acclaimed films. Beach turns a critical eye to Ashby's work, focusing on his first seven films in particular—*The Landlord*, *Harold and Maude*, *The Last Detail*, *Shampoo*, *Bound for Glory*, *Coming Home*, and *Being There*. Beach begins with a history of Ashby's career, then discusses common themes found in many of his films. He considers the manner in which the military is represented in Ashby's films as well as the importance of the musical scores in many of his works. Beach concludes by elucidating reasons Ashby's career as a director steadily declined after his 1979 film, *Being There*.

Where it's reviewed:
Reference & Research Book News, November 2009

Other books by the same author:
Class, Language, and American Film Comedy, 2001
Poetic Culture, 1999
ABC of Influence, 1992

Other books you might like:
Peter Biskind, *Easy Riders, Raging Bulls: How the Sex-Drugs-and-Rock 'n' Roll Generation Saved Hollywood*, 1998

Nick Dawson, *Being Hal Ashby: Life of a Hollywood Rebel*, 2009

Nick Dawson, *Hal Ashby: Interviews*, 2010

Daniel Gerould, *American Melodrama*, 2001

Peter Lev, *American Films of the 70s: Conflicting Visions*, 2000

14

SANDRA L. BECKETT

Red Riding Hood for All Ages: A Fairy-Tale Icon in Cross-Cultural Contexts

(Detroit, Michigan: Wayne State University Press, 2008)

Subject(s): Literature; Fairy tales; Sociology

Summary: In *Red Riding Hood for All Ages: A Fairy-Tale Icon in Cross-Cultural Contexts*, author Sandra L. Beckett looks at one of the most popular fairy tale characters in literary history. In the text, Beckett ruminates on the appearance of dozens of Red Riding Hood-like characters in contemporary literature and describes how such characters transcend genres, appearing in both adult and children's fiction. The author offers a unique collection that includes retellings of the classic tale from countries around the world. Beckett also organizes these adaptations by theme, categorizing some of tales as coming-of-age stories and others as instructive tales designed to keep children out of trouble. She then contemplates the lasting appeal of this character and considers what this reveals about modern society.

Where it's reviewed:
Folklore, August 2010, page 238
Marvels & Tales, April 2010, page 176

Other books by the same author:
Crossover Fiction, 2010
Recycling Red Riding Hood, 2009

Other books you might like:
M.T. Anderson, *The Astonishing Life of Octavian Nothing, Traitor to the Nation, Volume One: The Pox Party*, 2006
Stephen Benson, *Contemporary Fiction and the Fairy Tale*, 2008
Ruth B. Bottigheimer, *Fairy Tales: A New History*, 2009
Maria Tatar, *Enchanted Hunters: The Power of Stories in Childhood*, 2008
Catherynne M. Valente, *In the Night Garden*, 2006

15

VALERIA BELLETTI

Adventures of a Hollywood Secretary: Her Private Letters from Inside the Studios of the 1920s

(Berkeley: University of California Press, 2006)

Subject(s): Letters (Correspondence); Movie industry; Movies

Summary: Valeria Belletti never intended to become an insider into the world of 1920s Hollywood; she was only seeking employment when she became secretary to iconic movie mogul Samuel Goldwyn. But, as illustrated in Cari Beauchamp's *Adventures of a Hollywood Secretary: Her Private Letters from Inside the Studios of the 1920s*, Belletti was offered a prime, front-row seat to the inside workings of the early years of the motion-picture industry. This chronicle is brimming with Belletti's Tinseltown experiences as she hobnobs with stars and star-makers, directors and producers, and aspiring hopefuls desperate for their big break. Sam Goldwyn, Jr., provides a foreword to this volume.

Where it's reviewed:
Kirkus Reviews, March 15, 2006, page 270

Other books you might like:
Samantha Barbas, *The First Lady of Hollywood: A Biography of Louella Parsons*, 2005
Cari Beauchamp, *Without Lying Down: Frances Marion and the Powerful Women of Early Hollywood*, 1998
Marion Davies, *The Times We Had: Life with William Randolph Hearst*, 1985
James Parish, *The Hollywood Book of Scandals: The Shocking, Often Disgraceful Deeds and Affairs of Over 100 American Movie and TV Idols*, 2004
Joshua Zeitz, *Flapper: A Madcap Story of Sex, Style,*

Celebrity, and the Women Who Made America Modern, 2006

16

JOSHUA DAVID BELLIN

Framing Monsters: Fantasy Film and Social Alienation

(Carbondale, Illinois: Southern Illinois University Press, 2005)

Subject(s): Movies; Criticism; Fantasy

Summary: Are fantasy movies anything more than a harmless way to pass the time? According to author and expert Joshua David Bellin, fantasy films are rich in social commentary and hold great importance as emblems of the era in which they were produced. *Framing Monsters: Fantasy Film and Social Alienation* looks at this subject in depth, focusing on various trends in fantasy filmmaking. Among the movies discussed are *King Kong*, *The Wizard of Oz*, *Edward Scissorhands*, and the *Lord of the Rings* films. *Framing Monsters* includes photos, a filmography, notes on the text, a bibliography, and an index.

Where it's reviewed:
Journal of Popular Film and Television, Spring 2009, page 46

Other books by the same author:
Medicine Bundle, 2007
The Demon of the Continent, 2000

Other books you might like:
Stephen Asma, *On Monsters: An Unnatural History of Our Worst Fears*, 2009
Jeffrey Jerome Cohen, *Monster Theory: Reading Culture*, 1996
Neil Coombs, *Studying Surrealist and Fantasy Cinema*, 2008
David D. Gilmore, *Monsters: Evil Beings, Mythical Beasts, and All Manner of Imaginary Terrors*, 2009
Richard Kearney, *Strangers, Gods and Monsters: Interpreting Otherness*, 2002

17

CATHERINE L. BENAMOU

It's All True: Orson Welles's Pan-American Odyssey

(Berkeley, California: University of California Press, 2007)

Subject(s): Movies; Movie industry; Criticism

Summary: In the early 1940s, legendary director, writer, and actor Orson Welles devoted his lifeblood to the making of a film that was never completed. Catherine L. Benamou's *It's All True: Orson Welles's Pan-American Odyssey* shares the story of the making of that film and the people, personalities, and events that shaped its fate. Benamou uses previously untapped resources to provide an all-encompassing look at the behind-the-scenes world of Welles's unfinished masterpiece, as well as its important place in American cinema.

Where it's reviewed:
Michigan Quarterly Review, Winter 2009, pages 141-146

Other books you might like:
Simon Callow, *Orson Welles, Volume 1: The Road to Xanadu*, 1995
Simon Callow, *Orson Welles, Volume 2: Hello Americans*, 2006
Chris Welles Feder, *In My Father's Shadow: A Daughter Remembers Orson Welles*, 2009
David Thomson, *Rosebud: The Story of Orson Welles*, 1996
Orson Welles, *This Is Orson Welles*, 1998

18

STEPHEN BENSON

Contemporary Fiction and the Fairy Tale

(Detroit, Michigan: Wayne State University Press, 2008)

Subject(s): Fairy tales; Literature; Writing

Summary: In *Contemporary Fiction and the Fairy Tale*, editor Stephen Benson provides a collection of perspectives on modern fiction writers' fascination with fairy tales. In this collection, Benson shows readers that fairy tales, which once served as cautionary stories for children, have the power to inspire stories for all ages about the very nature of humanity. The scholarly essays in this text focus on the ways that classic fairy tales influence contemporary writers, including Margaret Atwood and Salman Rushdie. Several of the contributing authors also present an analysis of the scholarly criticism concerning the position that fairy tales occupy in modern literature. Stephen Benson is also the author of *Cycles of Influence: Fiction, Folktale, Theory* and *Literary Music: Writing Music in Contemporary Fiction*.

Other books by the same author:
Cycles of Influence: Fiction, Folktale, Theory, 2003
Literary Music: Writing Music in Contemporary Fiction, 2003

Other books you might like:
M.T. Anderson, *The Astonishing Life of Octavian Nothing, Traitor to the Nation, Volume One: The Pox Party*, 2006
Sandra L. Beckett, *Red Riding Hood for All Ages: A Fairy-Tale Icon in Cross-Cultural Contexts*, 2008
Ruth B. Bottigheimer, *Fairy Tales: A New History*, 2009
Maria Tatar, *Enchanted Hunters: The Power of Stories in Childhood*, 2008
Catherynne M. Valente, *In the Night Garden*, 2006

19

KATE BERNHEIMER

Brothers and Beasts: An Anthology of Men on Fairy Tales

(Detroit, Michigan: Wayne State University Press, 2007)

Subject(s): Literature; Criticism; Folklore

Summary: *Brothers and Beasts: An Anthology of Men on Fairy Tales* is a collection edited by Kate Bernheimer. It includes 23 essays from male writers on their perspectives on various fairy tales, the ways the tales have influenced their own work, and the emotional attachments they still experience to the stories well past childhood. The essays are personal and sometimes autobiographical in nature, but add additional perspectives and literary criticisms to well-known fairy tales. Contributors to this anthology include Steve Almond, Christopher Barzak, Eric Kraft, Norman Lock, Vijay Seshadri, and Willy Vlautin. *Brothers and Beasts* is the follow-up to Bernheimer's *Mirror, Mirror on the Wall: Women Writers Explore Their Favorite Fairy Tales*.

Where it's reviewed:
Marvels & Tales, October 2009, page 413

Other books you might like:
M.T. Anderson, *The Astonishing Life of Octavian Nothing, Traitor to the Nation, Volume One: The Pox Party*, 2006
Stephen Benson, *Contemporary Fiction and the Fairy Tale*, 2008
Ruth B. Bottigheimer, *Fairy Tales: A New History*, 2009
Maria Tatar, *Enchanted Hunters: The Power of Stories in Childhood*, 2008
Catherynne M. Valente, *In the Night Garden*, 2006

20

MYKEL BOARD

Even A Daughter Is Better Than Nothing

(New Orleans, Louisiana: Garrett County Press, LLC, 2005)

Subject(s): Mongols; Travel; Humor

Summary: In *Even a Daughter is Better than Nothing*, author Mykel Board recounts the trip he took to Mongolia, where he taught linguistics for a year. In the book, Board discusses the country's landscape, culture, traditions, and people. Although Board enjoyed his journey through Mongolia, he describes the country as being extremely inefficient. According to the Board, neither the electricity nor the government work well there. While on his trip, Board completely immersed himself in the culture and took part in many traditional Mongolian events.

Where it's reviewed:
Publishers Weekly, September 26, 2005, page 77

Other books by the same author:
Good Advice for Young Trendy People of All Ages, 2005

I A, Me-ist or The Portable Mykel Board, 2005

Other books you might like:
Mykel Board, *I A, Me-ist or The Portable Mykel Board*, 2005
Dan Savage, *The Commitment: Love, Sex, Marriage, and My Family*, 2005
Dan Savage, *Skipping Towards Gomorrah: The Seven Deadly Sins and the Pursuit of Happiness in America*, 2002
George Tabb, *Playing Right Field: A Jew Grows in Greenwich*, 2004
George Tabb, *Surfing Armageddon: Fishnets, Fascists, and Body Fluids in Florida*, 2006

21

KEVIN ALEXANDER BOON

Script Culture and the American Screenplay

(Detroit, Michigan: Wayne State University Press, 2008)

Subject(s): Literature; Criticism; Movies

Summary: In *Script Culture and the American Screenplay*, Kevin Alexander Boon considers the art of writing a screenplay separately from the film in which it will be produced. Boon argues that the screenplay is a type of literature and can be read critically as such, using theories of literary criticism to evaluate it. The author begins with a brief discussion of the history of the screenplay, followed by examinations of particular screenplays and the ways in which the adaptation of a screenplay can be analyzed, focusing most intently on the themes found in the various works.

Other books by the same author:
The Human Genome Project, 2002
An Interpretive Reading of Virginia Woolf's the Waves, 1998

Other books you might like:
Dsvid Herman, *The Cambridge Companion to Narrative*, 2007
Pauline Kael, *5001 Nights at the Movies*, 1991
Jonathan Rosenbaum, *Essential Cinema: On the Necessity of Film Canons*, 2008
David Thomson, *"Have You Seen . . . ?": A Personal Introduction to 1,000 Films*, 2008
David Thomson, *The Whole Equation: A History of Hollywood*, 2004

22

DAVID BORDWELL

The Way Hollywood Tells It: Story and Style in Modern Movies

(Berkeley: University of California Press, 2006)

Subject(s): Movie industry; Movies; Storytelling

Summary: Film expert David Bordwell studies the story-telling legacy left by the once-flourishing Hollywood studio system and how this legacy has shaped and defined modern movies. *The Way Hollywood Tells It: Story and Style in Modern Movies* chronicles the rich heritage of the films made by the big studios during the golden age of Hollywood. Throughout the book Bordwell relates past and present to show readers how classic story and style have formed modern approaches to moviemaking.

Where it's reviewed:
Journal of Popular Film & Television, Fall 2007, page 144

Other books by the same author:
Film Art: An Introduction, 2009
Film History: An Introduction, 2009
Film Art, 2006

Other books you might like:
Steven Bach, *Final Cut: Art, Money, and Ego in the Making of Heaven's Gate, the Film That Sank United Artists*, 1999
David Bordwell, *On the History of Film Style*, 1998
J.J. Murphy, *Me and You and Memento and Fargo: How Independent Screenplays Work*, 2007
Jennifer Van Sijll, *Cinematic Storytelling: The 100 Most Powerful Film Conventions Every Filmmaker Must Know*, 2005
Kristin Thompson, *Storytelling in the New Hollywood: Understanding Classical Narrative Technique*, 1999

23

LESLEY BRILL

Crowds, Power and Transformation in Cinema

(Detroit, Michigan: Wayne State University Press, 2006)

Subject(s): Criticism; Movies; Popular culture

Summary: In *Crowds, Power and Transformation in Cinema*, Lesley Brill considers the symbolism behind the use of crowds in various films, and the way a crowd is nearly always found in opposition to whatever or whomever happens to be in power at the time. She states that understanding this concept helps one to understand the capability of film to transform. Brill considers examples from films such as *The Battleship Potemkin*, *Intolerance*, *Citizen Kane*, *North by Northwest*, and *Silence of the Lambs*. Brill presents the image of the crowd as a predatory pack, arguing that transformation by those in power is always the necessary key to escape.

Other books by the same author:
John Huston's Filmmaking, 1997
The Hitchcock Romance, 1991

Other books you might like:
Elias Canetti, *Crowds and Power*, 1962
Gustave Le Bon, *The Crowd: A Study of the Popular Mind*, 2010
Charles Mackay, *Extraordinary Popular Delusions & the Madness of Crowds*, 1841
James Surowiecki, *The Wisdom of Crowds: Why the*

Many Are Smarter than the Few and How Collective Wisdom Shapes Business, Economies, Societies and Nations, 2004

Michael Tratner, *Crowd Scenes: Movies and Mass Politics*, 2008

24

BILL BRYSON

Shakespeare: The World as Stage

(New York: Atlas Books/HarperCollins, 2007)

Subject(s): Literature; England; English literature, 1558-1603 (Elizabethan)

Summary: Bill Bryson, well-known travel writer, turns his exploratory nature to the life of William Shakespeare. His account investigates the other biographies that have been written about the bard and also provides humorous anecdotes from his travels to research the subject. Bryson uses previous scholarship and literary criticism to give a fresh look at Shakespeare's life and the times in which he lived. The final chapter reflects on the numerous conspiracy theories that suggest that Shakespeare was not the author of the great literary canon that bears his name. The book also provides interesting facts and trivia, including a story about P.T. Barnum, who wanted to have Shakespeare's birthplace shipped to America so he could incorporate it into a traveling show. *Shakespeare: The World as Stage* is part of the Eminent Lives series.

Where it's reviewed:
Booklist, November 15, 2007, page 14
The Bookseller, December 14, 2007, page 11
Publishers Weekly, September 3, 2007, page 47
Reference and Research Book News, February 2008
Tennessee Bar Journal, February 2009, page 35

Other books by the same author:
At Home: A Short History of Private Life, 2010
A Short History of Nearly Everything: Special Illustrated Edition, 2010
A Walk in the Woods: Rediscovering America on the Appalachian Trail, 2006

Other books you might like:
Bill Bryson, *At Home: A Short History of Private Life*, 2010
Bill Bryson, *Bryson's Dictionary of Troublesome Words*, 2002
Bill Bryson, *The Mother Tongue: English & How It Got That Way*, 1990

25

ANDREA J. BUCHANAN
MIRIAM PESKOWITZ , Co-Author

The Daring Book for Girls

(New York: HarperCollins, 2007)

Subject(s): Childhood; Growing Up

Summary: Andrea J. Buchanan and Miriam Peskowitz of-fer this book as a companion to Conn and Hal Iggulden's *The Dangerous Book for Boys*. It will appeal to the nostalgia of adult readers, but it also contains a kind of compendium of useful information for girls. Topics range from short biographical sketches of famous women, to games and activities, to sports, to projects, to information on changing a tire, pitching a tent and building a fire, book recommendations, self-defense, stocks and shares, and even negotiating a salary. The book targets a range of ages, but some activities and projects may require adult participation.

Where it's reviewed:
Newsweek, December 3, 2007, page 16

Other books by the same author:
The Double-Daring Book for Girls, 2009
The Pocket Daring Book for Girls: Wisdom & Wonder, 2008

Other books you might like:
Suzanne Collins, *The Hunger Games*, 2008
Conn Iggulden, *The Dangerous Book for Boys*, 2007
    Hal Iggulden, co-author
Kara Jesella, *How Sassy Changed My Life: A Love Letter to the Greatest Teen Magazine of All Time*, 2007
    Marisa Meltzer, co-author
Jennifer O'Connell, *Everything I Needed to Know About Being a Girl I Learned from Judy Blume*, 2007
Lizzie Skurnick, *Shelf Discovery: The Teen Classics We Never Stopped Reading*, 2009

26

JOY H. CALICO

Brecht at the Opera

(Berkeley: University of California Press, 2008)

Subject(s): Operas; Music; Writers

Summary: Joy H. Calico's *Brecht at the Opera* investigates the famed playwright Bertolt Brecht's love-hate relationship with the opera. Calico shows how Brecht's youthful appreciation of the art form slowly evolved into disgust. However, throughout his life, the playwright wrote several operas, including the legendary *Threepenny Opera*. In her scrutiny of Brecht's obvious contradiction regarding the genre, Calico provides an intimate peek into the complex mind of a great artist. *Brecht at the Opera* includes notes on the text, a bibliography, and an index. First book.

Where it's reviewed:
Opera, March 2009, pages 364-365
Opera News, December 2008, page 77

Other books you might like:
Eric Bentley, *Brecht-Eisler Song Book*, 1992
Thomas Desi, *The New Music Theater: Seeing the Voice, Hearing the Body*, 2008
John Fuegi, *Brecht and Co.: Sex, Politics, and the Making of the Modern Drama*, 2002
Michael John Tyler Gilbert, *Bertolt Brecht's Striving for Reason, Even in Music: A Critical Assessment*, 1989

Stephen Hinton, *Kurt Weill: The Threepenny Opera*, 1990

Eric Salzman, *The New Music Theater: Seeing the Voice, Hearing the Body*, 2008

27

BRETT CALLWOOD

MC5: Sonically Speaking: A Tale of Revolution and Rock 'n' Roll

(Detroit, Michigan: Wayne State University Press, 2010)

Subject(s): Music; Biographies; Bands (Music)

Summary: In *MC5: Sonically Speaking: A Tale of Revolution and Rock 'n' Roll*, Brett Callwood presents a biography of the band MC5, which existed from 1964 to 1972. The original members of the band were Rob Tyner, Wayne Kramer, Fred "Sonic" Smith, Michael Davis, and Dennis Thompson. Tyner and Smith both passed away in the 1990s. Callwood interviewed the remaining members of the band and people who worked with them for this biography. Formed in Detroit and becoming active in the revolutionary White Panther Party, MC5 was often seen as one of the first true punk rock bands. Callwood tells the personal stories of the band members, including the challenges they faced and the successes they had.

Other books you might like:

LeRoy Barnett, *Makin' Music: Michigan's Rock and Roll Legacy*, 2002

Brett Callwood, *The Stooges: A Journey Through the Michigan Underworld*, 2008

David A. Carson, *Grit, Noise and Revolution: The Birth of Detroit Rock 'n' Roll*, 2006

Carolyn Damstra, *Makin' Music: Michigan's Rock and Roll Legacy*, 2002

Robert Matheu, *The Stooges: The Authorized and Illustrated Story*, 2009

Denise Sullivan, *The White Stripes: Sweethearts of the Blues*, 2004

28

KERMIT E. CAMPBELL

Gettin' Our Groove On: Rhetoric, Language, and Literacy for the Hip Hop Generation

(Detroit: Wayne State University Press, 2005)

Subject(s): African Americans; Popular culture; Literacy

Summary: What is the relationship between African American dialect and hip hop music? This is the question professor Kermit E. Campbell sets out to answer in *Gettin' Our Groove On: Rhetoric, Language, and Literacy for the Hip Hop Generation*. Campbell studies the vernacular within traditional African oral storytelling traditions and how this use of language has inspired and influenced generations of rhetoric, including the language

of modern hip hop. This volume also explores the role of the African American vernacular in contemporary society, its importance, and the challenges it faces. *Gettin' Our Groove On* includes a bibliography and an index. First book.

Where it's reviewed:

CHOICE: Current Reviews for Academic Libraries, February 2006, page 1011

Other books you might like:

Jane Bolgatz, *Talking Race In The Classroom*, 2005

Marc Lamont Hill, *Beats, Rhymes, and Classroom Life: Hip-Hop Pedagogy and the Politics of Identity*, 2009

Studs Terkel, *Race: How Blacks and Whites Think and Feel about the American Obsession*, 1992

Vershawn Ashanti Young, *Your Average Nigga: Performing Race, Literacy, and Masculinity*, 2007

29

CHARLOTTE M. CANNING

The Most American Thing in America: Circuit Chautauqua as Performance

(Iowa City, Iowa: University of Iowa Press, 2005)

Story type: Historical
Subject(s): Rural life; Theater; History

Summary: In *The Most American Thing in America: Circuit Chautauqua as Performance*, author Charlotte M. Canning examines the cultural impact of the Circuit Chautauquas, a performance group that toured America in the early 20th century. From 1904 until the Great Depression, the Circuit Chautauquas visited rural American towns each summer and performed a wide variety of pieces, including music, orations, lectures, readings, dramatic presentations, and children's programs. Many theater historians have overlooked or discounted the cultural impact that the Circuit Chautauquas had because they were unconventional and didn't create original material or techniques. In *The Most American Thing in America*, Canning evaluates the efforts and significance of the performers and contends that they were responsible for uniting and educating rural residents of the United States.

Other books by the same author:

Feminist Theatres in the USA, 2005

Other books you might like:

Burton J. Bledstein, *The Middling Sorts: Explorations in the History of the American Middle Class*, 2001

Victoria Case, *We Called It Culture: The Story Of Chautauqua*, 2007

Robert D. Johnston, *The Middling Sorts: Explorations in the History of the American Middle Class*, 2001

Andrew Chamberlin Rieser, *The Chautauqua Moment: Protestants, Progressives, and the Culture of Modern Liberalism, 1874-1920*, 2003

Jeffrey Simpson, *Chautauqua*, 1999

John E. Tapia, *Circuit Chautauqua: From Rural*

Education to Popular Entertainment in Early Twentieth Century America, 2008

30

ANDREI CODRESCU

New Orleans, Mon Amour: Twenty Years of Writings from the City
(Chapel Hill, North Carolina: Algonquin Books of Chapel Hill, 2006)

Subject(s): United States; Americana; Southern United States

Summary: New Orleans is one of the most colorful cities in the world. In *New Orleans, Mon Amour: Twenty Years of Writings from the City*, author and radio commentator Andrei Codrescu reflects on his two decades of living in New Orleans. Codrescu describes the city as a unique one full of flamboyant and creative personalities. He also addresses dark parts of its history, particularly its near-destruction during Hurricane Katrina and the slow, painful recovery.

Where it's reviewed:
Books (Chicago Tribune), February 19, 2006, page 3
Southern Living, February 2006, page 147

Other books by the same author:
The Poetry Lesson, 2010
The Posthuman Dada Guide, 2009
The Blood Countess, 2008

Other books you might like:
Dan Baum, *Nine Lives: Mystery, Magic, Death, and Life in New Orleans*, 2009
Jed Horne, *Breach of Faith: Hurricane Katrina and the Near Death of a Great American City*, 2006
Tom Piazza, *City of Refuge: A Novel*, 2008
Tom Piazza, *Why New Orleans Matters*, 2008
Chris Rose, *1 Dead in Attic: After Katrina*, 2007

31

JOHN R. COOK
PETER WRIGHT , Co-Author

British Science Fiction Television: A Hitchhiker's Guide
(New York; London: I.B. Tauris, 2006)

Subject(s): Television programs; Criticism; Science fiction

Summary: British television has been a trailblazing force in the production of top-quality, highly memorable works of science fiction. In *British Science Fiction Television: A Hitchhiker's Guide*, authors John R. Cook and Peter Wright offer a comprehensive exploration of UK television's contributions to the sci-fi genre. The authors look at individual programs to point out how British science fiction has made a unique and enduring impact not only on the creation of quality television series but also on the entire science fiction industry. This volume

includes a list of further reading resources and an index.

Where it's reviewed:
Journal of Popular Film and Television, Spring 2009, pages 44-45

Other books by the same author:
The Passion of Dennis Potter: International Collected Essays, 2000
Dennis Potter: A Life on Screen, 1998

Other books you might like:
Benjamin Cook, *Doctor Who: The Writer's Tale*, 2010
Russell T. Davies, co-author
Jan Johnson-Smith, *American Science Fiction TV: Star Trek, Stargate, and Beyond*, 2005
Tara O'Shea, *Chicks Dig Time Lords: A Celebration of Doctor Who by the Women Who Love It*, 2010
Brian J. Robb, *Timeless Adventures: How Doctor Who Conquered TV*, 2010
Lynne M. Thomas, *Chicks Dig Time Lords: A Celebration of Doctor Who by the Women Who Love It*, 2010
Steve Tribe, *Doctor Who: The TARDIS Handbook*, 2010

32

CHARLES L. CROW

History of the Gothic: American Gothic
(Cardiff, Wales: University of Wales Press, 2009)

Subject(s): Literature; Criticism; Gothic novels

Summary: Author Charles L. Crow discusses the gothic tradition in American literature and its place in history and popular culture. *History of the Gothic: American Gothic* studies the work of a diverse cross-section of authors, including Edgar Allan Poe, William Faulker, and Toni Morrison, to illustrate the enduring appeal of the genre and the opportunities it offers for social commentary and the tackling of sensitive topics. Crow also points out the relationship of gothic literature to the evolution of the country's larger intellectual history.

Where it's reviewed:
Journal of Popular Culture, June 2010, pages 657-659

Other books by the same author:
Maxine Hong Kingston, 2004
American Gothic: An Anthology 1787-1916, 1999
Janet Lewis, 1980

Other books you might like:
Charles L. Crow, *American Gothic: An Anthology 1787-1916*, 1999
Justin D. Edwards, *Gothic Passages: Racial Ambiguity and the American Gothic*, 2002
Markman Ellis, *The History of Gothic Fiction*, 2001
Dennis R. Perry, *Poe, "The House of Usher," and the American Gothic*, 2009
Allan Lloyd Smith, *American Gothic Fiction: An Introduction*, 2004

33

STEVE CUSHING

Blues Before Sunrise: The Radio Interviews

(Urbana, Illinois: University of Illinois Press, 2010)

Subject(s): Music; Musicians; Radio

Summary: Compiled by Steve Cushing, *Blues Before Sunrise: The Radio Interviews* is a collection of interviews with prominent blues musicians, producers, singers, and deejays. The interviews come from Cushing's long-running and hugely popular radio program, "Blues Before Sunrise," which was dedicated to early blues and R&B music. The interviews in this collection showcase the careers, history, and successes of key leaders and innovators in the musical genre, such as African-American singer Alberta Hunter and prominent record producer Ralph Bass. The individuals highlighted in *Blues Before Sunrise* are predominantly musicians from the 1930s, 1940s, and 1950s who played a vital role in the formation of blues music.

Other books you might like:
Stephen Calt, *Barrelhouse Words: A Blues Dialect Dictionary*, 2009
William Ferris, *Give My Poor Heart Ease: Voices of the Mississippi Blues*, 2009
Alan Govenar, *Lightnin' Hopkins: His Life and Blues*, 2010
George Lipsitz, *Midnight at the Barrelhouse: The Johnny Otis Story*, 2010
Patrick A. Roberts, *Give 'Em Soul, Richard!: Race, Radio, and Rhythm and Blues in Chicago*, 2010
Richard E. Stamz, co-author

34

HAMID DABASHI

Makhmalbaf at Large: The Making of a Rebel Filmmaker

(New York: I.B. Tauris, 2008)

Subject(s): Movies; Movie industry; Biographies

Summary: Mohsen Makhmalbaf has long been regarded as the most visionary force in Iranian filmmaking. In *Makhmalbaf at Large: The Making of a Rebel Filmmaker*, cultural commentator, historian, and Makhmalbaf's close friend Hamid Dabashi delves into the rich life and career of the movie maestro. Dabashi takes special interest in how Makhmalbaf's films—including *The Street Vendor*, *The Bicyclist*, and *Kandahar*—not only mark breakthroughs in inventive filmed storytelling but also signify changes and evolutions in the director's own life. *Makhmalbaf at Large* includes notes on the text, an index, and a foreword by the director himself.

Where it's reviewed:
Sight & Sound, October 2008, page 101

Other books by the same author:

Iran: A People Interrupted, 2008
Post-Orientalism: Knowledge and Power in Time of Terror, 2008
Dreams of a Nation: On Palestinian Cinema, 2006

Other books you might like:
Hamid Dabashi, *Conversations with Mohsen Makhmalbaf*, 2010
AW Azhar Dehlvi, *Revolution and Creativity: A Survey of Iranian Literature, Films and Art in the Post Revolutionary Era*, 2006
Eric Egan, *Films of Makhmalbaf: Cinema, Politics and Culture in Iran*, 2005
Mohsen Makhmalbaf, *Conversations with Mohsen Makhmalbaf*, 2010
Hamid Reza Sadr, *Iranian Cinema: A Political History*, 2006
Azarmi Dukht Safawi, *Revolution and Creativity: A Survey of Iranian Literature, Films and Art in the Post Revolutionary Era*, 2006
Saeed Zeydabadi-Nejad, *The Politics of Iranian Cinema: Film and Society in the Islamic Republic*, 2009

35

JESSICA MILNER DAVIS

Understanding Humor in Japan

(Detroit, Michigan: Wayne State University Press, 2006)

Subject(s): Japanese (Asian people); Criticism; Humor

Summary: In *Understanding Humor in Japan*, editor Jessica Milner Davis compiles a detailed explanation of Japanese humor, often misunderstood or completely missed by Western visitors to the country. She first examines the history of humor in Japan, examining ancient traditions, and then brings the discussion to present-day methods of stand-up comedy, joke-telling, and the subtle humor often found in wordplay and Japanese newspapers. Davis also considers censorship in Japan, and how it has affected the communication of Japanese humor. She also considers television programs and film to determine the role of humor in Japanese popular culture, among other topics, and provides specific examples for reference.

Other books by the same author:
Farce, 2002

Other books you might like:
Roger J. Davies, *The Japanese Mind: Understanding Contemporary Japanese Culture*, 2002
Patrick W. Galbraith, *The Otaku Encyclopedia: An Insider's Guide to the Subculture of Cool Japan*, 2009
Osamu Ikeno, *The Japanese Mind: Understanding Contemporary Japanese Culture*, 2002
Roland Kelts, *Japanamerica: How Japanese Pop Culture Has Invaded the U.S.*, 2007
Mark W. Macwilliams, *Japanese Visual Culture: Explorations in the World of Manga and Anime*, 2008

Susan J. Napier, *Anime from Akira to Howls Moving Castle, Updated Edition: Experiencing Contemporary Japanese Animation*, 2005

36

GUERRIC DEBONA

Film Adaptation in the Hollywood Studio Era

(Urbana, Illinois: University of Illinois Press, 2010)

Story type: Arts
Subject(s): Movie industry; Movies; Books

Summary: Written by author Guerric DeBona, *Film Adaptation in the Hollywood Studio Era* is a critical examination of film adaptations during the 1930s, '40s, and '50s. DeBona examines the many factors that contribute to a film adaptation, including the original source, social climate, audience expectations and responses, cultural influences, and industry standards. In *Film Adaptation in the Hollywood Studio Era*, he examines four British and American books that were turned into films between 1935 and 1951. DeBona analyzes how the film versions of *David Copperfield, Heart of Darkness, The Long Voyage Home*, and *The Red Badge of Courage* were translated and altered, resulting in new expectations and standards for the adaptations of literary works into movies following World War II.

Other books by the same author:
Preaching Effectively, Revitalizing Your Church, 2009
Praying With the Benedictines, 2007
Fulfilled In Our Hearing, 2005

Other books you might like:
Linda Hutcheon, *A Theory of Adaptation*, 2006
Thomas M. Leitch, *Film Adaptation and Its Discontents: From Gone with the Wind to The Passion of the Christ*, 2009
James Naremore, *Film Adaptation*, 2000
Alessandra Raengo, *Literature and Film: A Guide to the Theory and Practice of Film Adaptation*, 2004
Linda Seger, *The Art of Adaptation: Turning Fact and Fiction Into Film*, 1992
Robert Stam, *Literature and Film: A Guide to the Theory and Practice of Film Adaptation*, 2004

37

EDUARDO R. DEL RIO

One Island, Many Voices: Conversations with Cuban-American Writers

(Tucson, Arizona: University of Arizona Press, 2008)

Story type: Ethnic
Subject(s): Cuban Americans; Writers; Writing

Summary: In *One Island, Many Voices: Conversations with Cuban-American Writers*, Eduardo R. del Rio selected twelve prominent Cuban-American authors for insightful and candid interviews. Each of the writers featured in the book were born in Cuba but have lived in the United States for a significant amount of time. Although their writing styles and genres vary greatly, each author is known for writing about themes important to Cuban-American literature like duality, identity, memory, and exile. The interviews reveal the unique ways that each writer's Cuban heritage has influenced his or her writing, personal style, motives, history, values, and identity. *One Island, Many Voices* includes interviews with Nilo Cruz, Roberto Fernandez, Cristina Garcia, Carolina Hospital, Eduardo Machado, Dionisio Martinez, Pablo Medina, Achy Obejas, Ricardo Pau-Llosa, Gustavo Perez Firmat, Dolores Prida, and Virgil Suarez.

Where it's reviewed:
Reference & Research Book News, February 2009

Other books by the same author:
The Prentice Hall Anthology of Latino Literature, 2001

Other books you might like:
Madeline Camara Betancourt, *Cuban Women Writers: Imagining a Matria*, 2008
Peter Bush, *The Voice of the Turtle: An Anthology of Cuban Literature*, 1998
Jorge Cantera, *A Century of Cuban Writers in Florida*, 2002
David Frye, *Cuban Women Writers: Imagining a Matria*, 2008
Carolina Hospital, *A Century of Cuban Writers in Florida*, 2002
Linda S. Howe, *Transgression and Conformity: Cuban Writers and Artists after*, 2004
Antonio Jose Ponte, *Tales from the Cuban Empire*, 2002

38

CELESTINO DELEYTO
MARIA DEL MAR AZCONA , Co-Author

Alejandro Gonzalez Inarritu

(Urbana, Illinois: University of Illinois Press, 2010)

Story type: Arts
Subject(s): Movie industry; Movies; Mexicans

Summary: Written by film professors Celestino Deleyto and Maria del Mar Azcona, *Alejandro Gonzalez Inarritu* is a critical examination and detailed study of the Mexican filmmaker. As a movie director, Alejandro Gonzalez Inarritu helped reshape the medium with his groundbreaking films and unique approach to creating. His experimental films contributed to the evolution of Mexican filmmaking by encouraging filmmakers to focus on wider global themes rather than national political agendas. Deleyto and Azcona examine Inarritu's films and highlight the common themes among them, such as suffering, redemption, luck, and accidental encounters.

Other books you might like:
Ernesto R. Acevedo-Munoz, *Bunuel and Mexico: The Crisis of National Cinema*, 2003

Armida De la Garza, *Mexico On Film: National identity and International Relations*, 2006

Carl J. Mora, *Mexican Cinema: Reflections of a Society, 1896-1980*, 1990

Andrea Noble, *Mexican National Cinema*, 2005

Masha Salazkina, *In Excess: Sergei Eisenstein's Mexico*, 2009

39

FRANK DONOGHUE

The Last Professors: The Corporate University and the Fate of the Humanities

(New York: Fordham University Press, 2008)

Subject(s): Education; Economics; Teachers

Summary: In *The Last Professors: The Corporate University and the Fate of the Humanities*, Frank Donoghue discusses the current state of higher education in America. In this text, Donoghue examines the reasons why the number of humanities professors has steadily decreased in recent decades. As college admission rates continue to soar, Donoghue fears that American universities may experience a shortage of art, English, and language professors in the years to come. The author believes that many colleges are too focused on the business side of maintaining a university to truly appreciate the value of liberal arts professors. Therefore, when budgets need slashing, liberal arts programs and educators often fall by the wayside. Donoghue uses this book to remind readers why humanities professors are still an important part of higher education.

Where it's reviewed:
Booklist, April 15, 2008, page 9
Comparatist, May 2010, pages 175-179
Library Journal, July 1, 2008, page 90

Other books by the same author:
The Fame Machine: Book Reviewing and Eighteenth-Century Literary Careers, 2000

Other books you might like:
Claudia Dreifus, *Higher Education?: How Colleges Are Wasting Our Money and Failing Our Kids—and What We Can Do About It*, 2010
Andrew Hacker, co-author
Alex Nicholls, *Social Entrepreneurship: New Models of Sustainable Social Change*, 2008
Martha C. Nussbaum, *Cultivating Humanity: A Classical Defense of Reform in Liberal Education*, 1997
Robert E. Quinn, *Change the World : How Ordinary People Can Achieve Extraordinary Results*, 2000
Mark C. Taylor, *Crisis on Campus: A Bold Plan for Reforming Our Colleges and Universities*, 2010

40

ROBERT M. DOWLING

Slumming in New York: From the Waterfront to Mythic Harlem

(Urbana, Illinois: University of Illinois Press, 2007)

Subject(s): History; Neighborhoods; Cultural identity

Summary: Professor and author Robert M. Dowling's *Slumming in New York: From the Waterfront to Mythic Harlem* is an examination of the gritty underworld of New York City between 1880 and 1930. Dowling paints a portrait of the life and culture of Manhattan during this 50-year period, creating vivid pictures of the distinct neighborhoods and subcultures that existed during the era. Relying on written works of the time such as Stephen Crane's Bowery tales and Carl Van Vechten's *Nigger Heaven*, Dowling showcases how much the city's unique communities influenced creativity and art. *Slumming in New York* highlights the diverse styles of writers from neighborhoods like the East Side waterfront, the Bowery, "Black Bohemia," the Jewish Lower East Side, and mythic Harlem.

Where it's reviewed:
Journal of American Culture, September 2008, page 320

Other books by the same author:
Critical Companion to Eugene O'Neill, 2009

Other books you might like:
Jim Carroll, *The Basketball Diaries*, 1978
Jim Carroll, *Forced Entries: The Downtown Diaries: 1971-1973*, 1987
Chad Heap, *Slumming: Sexual and Racial Encounters in American Nightlife, 1885-1940*, 2009
Justin Spring, *Secret Historian: The Life and Times of Samuel Steward, Professor, Tattoo Artist, and Sexual Renegade*, 2010
Edmund White, *City Boy: My Life in New York During the 1960s and 1970s*, 2010

41

PAUL DUNCAN
BENGT WANSELIUS , Co-Editor

The Ingmar Bergman Archives

(Los Angeles: Taschen America LLC., 2008)

Subject(s): Biographies; Movie industry; Entertainment industry

Summary: In *The Ingmar Bergman Archives*, editors Paul Duncan and Bengt Wanselius examine the complete life of famed Swedish film director Ingmar Bergman, creator of such pieces as *Through a Glass Darkly* and *The Virg Spring*. Before his death in 2007, Bergman granted Taschen America LLC., this book's publisher, permission for and access to his entire archive collection, which includes interviews and writings that had been previously unpublished. This book includes an introduction by Swedish actor Erland Josephson, more than 1,000 scenes from Bergman's films, and images of the director at work as well as a chronology, filmography, and bibliography.

Where it's reviewed:
Entertainment Weekly, October 10, 2008, page 76
Spectator, November 1, 2008, page 54
Variety, October 20, 2008, page 19

Other books by the same author:
The Art of Bollywood, 2010
The Godfather Family Album, 2010
Cinema Now, 2007

Other books you might like:
Alison Castle, *The Stanley Kubrick Archives*, 2008
Federico Fellini, *Federico Fellini The Book of Dreams*, 2008
Raphael Shargel, *Ingmar Bergman: Interviews*, 2007
Irving Singer, *Ingmar Bergman, Cinematic Philosopher: Reflections on His Creativity*, 2009
Birgitta Steene, *Ingmar Bergman: A Reference Guide*, 2006

42

DAVID M. EARLE

Re-Covering Modernism: Pulps, Paperbacks, and the Prejudice of Form

(Farnham, United Kingdom; Burlington, Vermont: Ashgate, 2009)

Subject(s): Literature; Criticism; Publishing industry

Summary: In *Re-Covering Modernism: Pulps, Paperbacks, and the Prejudice of Form*, author and English professor David M. Earle chronicles and analyzes the roots of modernist literature and its publication history. Many modernist works were published for literary audiences, but still more found their way to publication as pulp novels or as stories in gaudy magazines. Yet still, modernist literature remains a highbrow concept, and it is this concept that Earle studies in this wide-ranging work of literary scholarship. *Re-Covering Modernism* includes a bibliography and an index. First book.

Where it's reviewed:
Journal of Popular Culture, June 2010, pages 649-650

Other books by the same author:
All Man!: Hemingway, 1950s Men's Magazines, and the Masculine Persona, 2009

Other books you might like:
Chet Dembeck, *Sci-Fi Pulp Before PC: The Real Stuff*, 2009
Katherine V. Forrest, *Lesbian Pulp Fiction: The Sexually Intrepid World of Lesbian Paperback Novels, 1950-1965*, 2005
Maxim Jakubowski, *The Mammoth Book of Pulp Fiction*, 1996
Gary Lovisi, *The Dames, Dolls and Delinquents: A*

Collector's Guide to Sexy Pulp Fiction Paperbacks, 2009
Otto Penzler, *The Black Lizard Big Book of Pulps*, 2007

43

MICHAEL R. FEDERSPIEL

Picturing Hemingway's Michigan

(Detroit, Michigan: Wayne State University Press, 2010)

Subject(s): History; Photography; Writers

Summary: Compiled by Michael R. Federspiel, *Picturing Hemingway's Michigan* is a collection of photographs and excerpts from Ernest Hemingway's life, writings, and era. When working on short stories, famed American novelist Ernest Hemingway would spend a great deal of time in Michigan's Little Traverse Bay area in the early 20th century. In *Picturing Hemingway's Michigan*, Federspiel gives readers a peek at the small lumbering town turned tourist destination with photographs taken during the early 1900s, accompanied by captions and commentaries. The book also includes excerpts of Hemingway's writings as well as his own personal family photographs to give readers a better understanding of this legendary author, his writing style, and the inspiration he drew from his time in Michigan.

Other books you might like:
Donald F. Bouchard, *Hemingway: So Far from Simple*, 2010
Mark Cirino, *Ernest Hemingway and the Geography of Memory*, 2010
Ernest Hemingway, *The Nick Adams Stories*, 1972
Donald Lystra, *Season of Water and Ice*, 2009
Mark P. Ott, *Ernest Hemingway and the Geography of Memory*, 2010
Catherine Reef, *Ernest Hemingway: A Writer's Life*, 2009

44

JAIMEY FISHER
BRAD PRAGER , Co-Editor

The Collapse of the Conventional: German Film and Its Politics at the Turn of the Twenty-First Century

(Detroit, Michigan: Wayne State University Press, 2010)

Subject(s): Movie industry; Movies; Criticism

Summary: *The Collapse of the Conventional: German Film and Its Politics at the Turn of the Twenty-First Century* is a collection of scholarly essays, edited by Jaimey Fisher and Brad Prager. The essays examine the history of German filmmaking, beginning with films that address the Nazis as part of German history. The second section explores the subject of the reunification of Germany as shown in specific films. The remainder of the book is devoted to contemporary German filmmaking, examining films made after the end of the Cold War and elucidating the global themes that are often depicted through German cinematography.

Other books by the same author:
Spatial Turns: Space, Place, and Mobility in German Literary and Visual Culture. (Amsterdamer Beitrage zur Neueren Germanistik), 2010
Disciplining Germany: Youth, Reeducation, and Reconstruction After the Second World War (Kritik: German Literary Theory and Cultural Studies), 2007
Critical Theory: Current State and Future Prospects, 2002

Other books you might like:
David N. Coury, *The Return Of Storytelling In Contemporary German Literature And Film: Peter Hanke And Win Wenders*, 2004
Mila Ganeva, *Women in Weimar Fashion: Discourses and Displays in German Culture, 1918-1933*, 2008
Alison Guenther-Pal, *German Essays on Film*, 2004
Siegfried Kracauer, *From Caligari to Hitler: A Psychological History of the German Film*, 2004
Richard McCormick, *German Essays on Film*, 2004
Victoria Sturtevant, *A Great Big Girl Like Me: The Films of Marie Dressler*, 2009

45

SONDRA FRALEIGH

Butoh: Metamorphic Dance and Global Alchemy

(Urbana, Illinois: University of Illinois Press, 2010)

Story type: Arts; Historical
Subject(s): Dance; Japanese (Asian people); Philosophy

Summary: Written by dance professor Sondra Fraleigh, *Butoh: Metamorphic Dance and Global Alchemy* is a detailed history of the origins, evolution, and growth of Butoh, a Japanese style of dance. The art form originated in the wake of World War II as a response to the bombings of Hiroshima and Nagasaki and as an objection to Western values and philosophy. Since its creation, butoh has grown in popularity as a dance form and a means of promoting certain political and philosophical messages. Fraleigh chronicles the history of butoh, from its bleak beginnings to its eventual acceptance, and showcases key artists and performances of the past six decades.

Other books by the same author:
Dancing Into Darkness: Butoh, Zen, and Japan, 2010
Hijikata Tatsumi and Ohno Kazuo, 2006
Researching Dance: Evolving Modes of Inquiry, 1999

Other books you might like:
Stephen Barber, *Hijikata: Revolt of the Body*, 2010
Sondra Horton Fraleigh, *Dancing Into Darkness: Butoh, Zen, and Japan*, 2010
Sondra Fraleigh, *Hijikata Tatsumi and Ohno Kazuo*, 2006
Lorna Marshall, *The Body Speaks: Performance and Expression*, 2002

Tamah Nakamura, *Hijikata Tatsumi and Ohno Kazuo*, 2006
Kazuo Ohno, *Kazuo Ohno's World: From Without and Within*, 2004
Yoshito Ohno, co-author

46

JOSH FRANK
CHARLIE BUCKHOLTZ , Co-Author

In Heaven Everything Is Fine: The Unsolved Life of Peter Ivers and the Lost History of the New Wave Theatre

(New York: Free Press, 2008)

Subject(s): Musicians; Murder; Popular culture
Summary: Josh Franks blends nonfiction crime narrative with pop-culture history in this recounting of the life and mysterious death of musician Peter Ivers. *In Heaven Everything Is Fine: The Unsolved Life of Peter Ivers and the Lost History of the New Wave Theatre* charts Ivers's contributions to the worlds of punk music and stand-up comedy, which began with his cult-hit television show *New Wave Theatre*. His show gave Ivers the platform to marry cutting-edge music and experimental comedy in fresh new ways, but his endeavors were cut short when he was murdered in his apartment. Franks and co-author Charlie Buckholtz investigate the case of Ivers's death as well as his lasting impact on popular culture.

Where it's reviewed:
Library Journal, July 1, 2008, page 81

Other books you might like:
Stevie Chick, *Spray Paint the Walls: The Story of Black Flag*, 2009
Joshua Frank, *Fool the World: The Oral History of a Band Called Pixies*, 2006
Caryn Ganz, co-author
Robert Hofler, *Party Animals: A Hollywood Tale of Sex, Drugs, and Rock 'n' Roll Starring the Fabulous Allan Carr*, 2010
Ben Sisario, *The Pixies' Doolittle (33 1/3)*, 2006
Dave Stimson, *Touch and Go: The Complete Hardcore Punk Zine '79-'83*, 2010
Tesco Vee, co-author

47

MARY GARRETT
HEIDI GOTTFRIED , Co-Editor
SANDRA F. VANBURKLEO , Co-Editor

Remapping the Humanities: Identity, Community, Memory, (Post)Modernity

(Detroit, Michigan: Wayne State University, 2007)

Subject(s): Human behavior; Education; Literature
Summary: In *Remapping the Humanities: Identity, Com-*

munity, Memory, (Post)Modernity, editors Mary Garrett, Heidi Gottfried, and Sandra F. VanBurkleo offer a collection of essays that represent the wide range of humanist disciplines. The writings in this book cover such diverse areas of study as English, political science, history, languages, and rhetoric. Together, these essays strive to explain how the study of humanities continues to change. Published by Wayne State University in Detroit, Michigan, this compilation was created to celebrate the Humanities Center's tenth anniversary.

Where it's reviewed:
Reference and Research Book News, May 2008

Other books you might like:
Claudia Dreifus, *Higher Education?: How Colleges Are Wasting Our Money and Failing Our Kids—and What We Can Do About It*, 2010
Andrew Hacker, co-author
Alex Nicholls, *Social Entrepreneurship: New Models of Sustainable Social Change*, 2008
Martha C. Nussbaum, *Cultivating Humanity: A Classical Defense of Reform in Liberal Education*, 1997
Robert E. Quinn, *Change the World : How Ordinary People Can Achieve Extraordinary Results*, 2000
Mark C. Taylor, *Crisis on Campus: A Bold Plan for Reforming Our Colleges and Universities*, 2010

48

FRANCES GATEWARD
MURRAY POMERANCE , Co-Editor

Where the Boys Are: Cinemas of Masculinity and Youth

(Detroit: Wayne State University Press, 2005)

Subject(s): Movies; Men; Criticism

Summary: Sociologist Murray Pomerance and film studies professor Frances Gateward present a series of essays examining the subjects of masculinity and boyhood in film. The pieces that comprise *Where the Boys Are: Cinemas of Masculinity and Youth* tackle the theme from a variety of perspectives, including ruminations on archetypes, identity, social interaction, and emotional makeup. The editors include a diverse cross-section of films in their wide-ranging investigation. *Where the Boys Are* includes a bibliography and an index.

Where it's reviewed:
Quarterly Review of Film and Video, January-March 2009, page 80

Other books by the same author:
Popping Culture: 4th Edition, 2009
Cinema and Modernity, 2006
From Hobbits to Hollywood: Essays on Peter Jackson's Lord of the Rings, 2006

Other books you might like:
Dennis Bingham, *Acting Male: Masculinities in the Films of James Stewart, Jack Nicholson, and Clint Eastwood*, 1994
Sergio de la Mora, *Cinemachismo: Masculinities and*

Sexuality in Mexican Film, 2006
Robert T. Eberwein, *Armed Forces: Masculinity and Sexuality in the American War Film*, 2007
Peter Lehman, *Masculinity: Bodies, Movies, Culture*, 2001
Peter Lehman, *Running Scared: Masculinity and the Representation of the Male Body*, 2007

49

CAROLE GERSTER
LAURA W. ZLOGAR , Co-Editor

Teaching Ethnic Diversity with Film: Essays and Resources for Educators in History, Social Studies, Literature and Film Studies

(Jefferson, North Carolina: McFarland & Co., 2006)

Subject(s): Minorities; Movies; Teaching

Summary: Editors Carole Gerster and Laura W. Zlogar offer a series of essays examining the various roles of minorities in films, as well as the best ways to teach this multifaceted subject to students. *Teaching Ethnic Diversity with Film: Essays and Resources for Educators in History, Social Studies, Literature and Film Studies* probes the contributions of African Americans, Asian Americans, Hispanic Americans, and American Indians to the film industry, most notably the ways minority moviemakers have managed to tailor their cultural experiences to fit their personal journeys in order to tell an entertaining story. *Teaching Ethnic Diversity with Film* includes resources for teachers looking to educate students on this subject. First book.

Where it's reviewed:
Journal of Popular Film & Television, Fall 2009, page 148

Other books you might like:
Lila Abu-Lughod, *Media Worlds: Anthropology on New Terrain*, 2002
Howard Gardner, *Changing Minds: The Art and Science of Changing Our Own and Other People's Minds*, 2004
Faye D. Ginsburg, *Media Worlds: Anthropology on New Terrain*, 2002
Brian Larkin, co-author
Thomas L. McPhail, *Development Communication: Reframing the Role of the Media*, 2009
Michelle Stewart, *Global Indigenous Media: Cultures, Poetics, and Politics*, 2008
Pamela Wilson, co-author
Houston Wood, *Native Features: Indigenous Films from Around the World*, 2008

50

RAY GONZALEZ

Renaming the Earth: Personal Essays

(Tucson, Arizona: University of Arizona Press, 2008)

Story type: Collection
Subject(s): Deserts; Childhood; United States

Summary: *Renaming the Earth: Personal Essays* is a collection of honest and emotional essays about the American Southwest from author, poet, novelist, and anthologist, Ray Gonzalez. Although Gonzalez has spent many years living elsewhere, he was raised in the American Southwest, a special place to him because of the influential role it played in shaping him. In *Renaming the Earth*, Gonzalez reflects on this region, its landscape, and the unique cultures that it brings together. The essays are filled with nostalgia for childhood, frustration at the current political issues plaguing the area, sadness over the loss of loved ones, and appreciation for the natural beauty of the land.

Where it's reviewed:
Booklist, September 15, 2008, page 23
Reference & Research Book News, February 2009

Other books by the same author:
Faith Run, 2009
The Religion of Hands, 2005
Memory Fever, 1999

Other books you might like:
Eula Biss, *Notes from No Man's Land: American Essays*, 2009
Judith Butler, *Gender Trouble: Feminism and the Subversion of Identity*, 1990
Don DeLillo, *Point Omega: A Novel*, 2010
Evan Lavender-Smith, *From Old Notebooks*, 2010
Carmen Gimenez Smith, *Odalisque in Pieces*, 2009

51

RIGOBERTO GONZALEZ

Camino del Sol: Fifteen Years of Latina and Latino Writing

(Tucson, Arizona: University of Arizona Press, 2010)

Subject(s): Hispanic Americans; Writers; Writing

Summary: Edited by Rigoberto Gonzalez, *Camino del Sol: Fifteen Years of Latina and Latino Writing* is a collection of memorable writings from Latina and Latino authors. Since 1994, prominent and talented Latina and Latino writers and poets have been featured in the Camino del Sol series. In honor of its 15th anniversary, *Camino del Sol* brings together some of the series' greatest, most moving, and most memorable pieces. The collection includes everything from poetry to short fiction to nonfiction and features Latina and Latino authors such as Richard Blanco, Diana Garcia, Luis Alberto Urrea,

Pat Mora, Kathleen Alcala, Sergio Troncoso, and Kathleen de Azevedo.

Where it's reviewed:
Library Journal, July 2010, page 88

Other books by the same author:
The Mariposa Club, 2009
Butterfly Boy, 2006
So Often the Pitcher Goes to Water Until It Breaks, 1999

Other books you might like:
Eula Biss, *Notes from No Man's Land: American Essays*, 2009
Judith Butler, *Gender Trouble: Feminism and the Subversion of Identity*, 1990
Don DeLillo, *Point Omega: A Novel*, 2010
Evan Lavender-Smith, *From Old Notebooks*, 2010
Carmen Gimenez Smith, *Odalisque in Pieces*, 2009

52

LEWIS L. GOULD

Helen Taft: Our Musical First Lady

(Lawrence, Kansas: University Press of Kansas, 2010)

Story type: Historical
Subject(s): United States; Art; Biographies

Summary: Lewis L. Gould's *Helen Taft: Our Musical First Lady* is a comprehensive biography on the former First Lady and her contributions to the White House and the United States as a whole. Part of the Modern First Ladies series, *Helen Taft* presents a vivid portrait of the first lady and her commitment to the arts. When the Tafts came to the White House in 1909, "Nellie" was determined to turn Washington, D.C., into a hub of culture for the nation. Unfortunately, she suffered a stroke later that same year, which debilitated her and ruined her plans. Gould challenges previous biographies on Helen Taft by revealing new information about her passion for the arts, commitment to providing outlets for brilliant musicians and performers, and unfulfilled goals for broadening artistic understanding and appreciation in the United States.

Other books by the same author:
The Modern American Presidency, 2009
The William Howard Taft Presidency, 2009
The Most Exclusive Club: A History Of The Modern United States Senate, 2006

Other books you might like:
Carl Sferrazza Anthony, *Nellie Taft: The Unconventional First Lady of the Ragtime Era*, 2006
Peri E. Arnold, *Remaking the Presidency: Roosevelt, Taft, and Wilson, 1901-1916*, 2009
Lewis L. Gould, *The William Howard Taft Presidency*, 2009
Judith E. Greenberg, *Helen Herron Taft: 1861-1943*, 2000
Cormac O'Brien, *Secret Lives of the First Ladies: What Your Teachers Never Told You About the Women of The White House*, 2009

53

GARY GRAFF
TOM WESCHLER , Co-Author

Travelin' Man: On the Road and Behind the Scenes with Bob Seger

(Detroit, Michigan: Wayne State University Press, 2010)

Subject(s): Music; Biographies; Photography

Summary: Gary Graff and Tom Weschler's *Travelin' Man: On the Road and Behind the Scenes with Bob Seger* is look at the early career of the legendary musician. During the late 1960s and early 1970s, Weschler worked as a tour manager and photographer for Seger. He knew Seger before and after the singer became famous. This book is primarily composed of behind-the-scenes photographs from Weschler's years with Seger, accompanied by memories, stories, and reflections of the singer. Graff, a music journalist, provides additional anecdotes about the songs and concerts that defined Seger's career during this time. The text includes art from Seger's albums and an introduction from musician John Mellencamp.

Other books by the same author:
Neil Young: Long May You Run, 2010
Musichound Rock: The Essential Album Guide, 1998
Musichound Country: The Essential Album Guide, 1997

Other books you might like:
LeRoy Barnett, *Makin' Music: Michigan's Rock and Roll Legacy*, 2002
David A. Carson, *Grit, Noise and Revolution: The Birth of Detroit Rock 'n' Roll*, 2006
Carolyn Damstra, *Makin' Music: Michigan's Rock and Roll Legacy*, 2002
Eminem, *The Way I Am*, 2008
Bob Harris, *Motor City Rock and Roll: The 1960's and 1970's*, 2008
Sacha Jenkins, *The Way I Am*, 2008
John Douglas Peters, *Motor City Rock and Roll: The 1960's and 1970's*, 2008
Denise Sullivan, *The White Stripes: Sweethearts of the Blues*, 2004

54

LEON GRANDIN

A Parisienne in Chicago: Impressions of the World's Columbian Exposition

(Urbana, Illinois: University of Illinois Press, 2010)

Story type: Historical
Subject(s): Women; World's Columbian Exposition, Chicago, Illinois, 1893; History

Summary: *A Parisienne in Chicago: Impressions of the World's Columbian Exposition* is a travelogue from French native Madame Leon Grandin written during her ten-month visit to Chicago in 1893. Grandin visited America and spend nearly a year living in Chicago because her husband was involved with the World's Columbia Exposition. During her stay, Grandin documented her observations, thoughts, and opinions about America's culture, people, and places. *A Parisienne in Chicago* recounts Grandin's fascination with the amount of freedom and culture she witnessed in America and her views on life during the late 19th century.

Other books you might like:
Karen Abbott, *Sin in the Second City: Madams, Ministers, Playboys, and the Battle for America's Soul*, 2007
Norman Bolotin, *The World's Columbian Exposition: The Chicago World's Fair of 1893*, 2002
Julie K. Brown, *Contesting Images: Photography and the World's Columbian Exposition*, 1994
Perry R. Duis, *Challenging Chicago: Coping with Everyday Life, 1837-1920*, 2006
Christine Laing, *The World's Columbian Exposition: The Chicago World's Fair of 1893*, 2002
Erik Larson, *The Devil in the White City: Murder, Magic, and Madness at the Fair That Changed America*, 2003

55

BARRY KEITH GRANT

Britton on Film: The Complete Film Criticism of Andrew Britton

(Detroit, Michigan: Wayne State University Press, 2008)

Subject(s): Criticism; Movies; Movie industry

Summary: *Britton on Film: The Complete Film Criticism of Andrew Britton*, edited by Barry Keith Grant, is a collection of 28 essays by Andrew Britton about various films from the 1960s and 1970s. Britton considered both European films and those coming out of Hollywood at the time, composing scholarly critiques that discussed theory, theme, and subjects found in various films from different genres, including *Jaws*, *The Exorcist*, and *Meet Me in St. Louis*, among many others. Britton focused on topics including formalism, camp, feminism, and more and occasionally discussed the filmmakers behind the films as well.

Where it's reviewed:
Cineaste, Fall 2009, page 67
Reference & Research Book News, May 2009

Other books you might like:
Andrew Britton, *Katharine Hepburn: Star as Feminist*, 2004
Manny Farber, *Farber on Film: The Complete Film Writings of Manny Farber*, 2009
Robin Wood, *Hitchcock's Films Revisited*, 2002
Robin Wood, *Hollywood from Vietnam to Reagan...and Beyond*, 2003
Robin Wood, *Personalviews: Explorations in Film*, 2006

56

BARRY KEITH GRANT

Shadows of Doubt: Negotiations of Masculinity in American Genre Films

(Detroit, Michigan: Wayne State University Press, 2010)

Subject(s): Criticism; Men; Movies

Summary: In *Shadows of Doubt: Negotiations of Masculinity in American Genre Films*, Barry Keith Grant explores the portrayal of men in films throughout history, arguing that changing perceptions of masculinity in American culture are evident through these portrayals. He explores films from different genres to prove his thesis, including comedies, dramas, horror films, science fiction movies, action films, and westerns. He considers specific titles such as *Broken Blossoms* (1919), *2001: A Space Odyssey* (1968), *Night of the Living Dead* (1968), and *The Hurt Locker* (2008), stating that some films offer an opposing viewpoint to the current American image of masculinity, while others reinforce the idea. Grant keeps the discussion of each film within its cultural contexts, considering popular culture, literature, television, and music at the time the film was produced.

Other books by the same author:
Invasion of the Body Snatchers, 2011
Schirmer Encyclopedia of Film, 2006
Voyages of Discovery, 1992

Other books you might like:
Dennis Bingham, *Acting Male: Masculinities in the Films of James Stewart, Jack Nicholson, and Clint Eastwood*, 1994
Sergio de la Mora, *Cinemachismo: Masculinities and Sexuality in Mexican Film*, 2006
Frances Gateward, *Where the Boys Are: Cinemas of Masculinity and Youth*, 2005
Peter Lehman, *Masculinity: Bodies, Movies, Culture*, 2001
Murray Pomerance, *Where the Boys Are: Cinemas of Masculinity and Youth*, 2005

57

BILL HARRIS

Birth of a Notion; Or, the Half Ain't Never Been Told: A Narrative Account with Entertaining Passages of the State of Minstrelsy and of America and the True Relation Thereof

(Detroit, Michigan: Wayne State University Press, 2010)

Subject(s): African Americans; Storytelling; Literature

Summary: In *Birth of a Notion; Or, the Half Ain't Never Been Told: A Narrative Account with Entertaining Pas-*

sages of the State of Minstrelsy and of America and the True Relation Thereof, Bill Harris writes in a combination of poetry and standard prose to offer a critical examination of African American identity. Harris looks back through American history, beginning with the 1830s, to focus on the development of prejudice and the perception of blacks in American culture. He focuses on notable events in early American history, such as abolition, Reconstruction, and the Industrial Revolution, and events of the late nineteenth and early twentieth centuries, such as the publication of *Uncle Tom's Cabin* and the World's Fair in Chicago, that had a significant impact on the way blacks are regarded in the United States.

Other books by the same author:
The Ringmaster's Array, 1997
Yardbird Suite: Side One : 1920-1940, 1997

Other books you might like:
Annemarie Bean, *Inside the Minstrel Mask: Readings in Nineteenth-Century Blackface Minstrelsy*, 1996
Bill Harris, *The Ringmaster's Array*, 1997
Bill Harris, *Yardbird Suite: Side One : 1920-1940*, 1997
Eric Lott, *Love and Theft: Blackface Minstrelsy and the American Working Class*, 1993
Arnold Shaw, *Black Popular Music in America: From the Spirituals, Minstrels, and Ragtime to Soul, Disco, and Hip-Hop*, 1986

58

CLINTON HEYLIN

Despite the System: Orson Welles Versus the Hollywood Studios

(Chicago, Illinois: Chicago Review Press, 2005)

Subject(s): Movie industry; Movies; Criticism

Summary: Throughout his storied career, famed director Orson Welles was involved in notorious battles with Hollywood's rigid studio system. In *Despite the System: Orson Welles Versus the Hollywood Studios*, author Clinton Heylin probes the details surrounding the director's legendary struggles to find support, financing, distribution, and artistic integrity within the confines of Tinseltown hierarchies. Through an in-depth examination of Welles's canon of films, Heylin paints a vivid portrait of a man who, despite popular belief, was not wracked with personal demons but was instead caught in a tug-of-war with studio bigwigs. *Despite the System* includes a bibliography, a filmography, and an index.

Where it's reviewed:
Michigan Quarterly Review, Winter 2009, pages 141-146

Other books by the same author:
So Long as Men Can Breathe, 2010
Revolution in the Air, 2009
Bob Dylan: Behind the Shades Revisited, 2003

Other books you might like:
Simon Callow, *Orson Welles, Volume 1: The Road to Xanadu*, 1995

Simon Callow, *Orson Welles, Volume 2: Hello Americans*, 2006

Chris Welles Feder, *In My Father's Shadow: A Daughter Remembers Orson Welles*, 2009

David Thomson, *Rosebud: The Story of Orson Welles*, 1996

Orson Welles, *This Is Orson Welles*, 1998

59

CRISTOPHER HOLLINGSWORTH

Alice Beyond Wonderland: Essays for the Twenty-First Century

(Iowa City, Iowa: University of Iowa Press, 2009)

Subject(s): Literature; Criticism; Culture

Summary: Editor Cristopher Hollingsworth brings together a series of essays exploring the lasting impact of Lewis Carroll's work on literature and culture in the new millennium. *Alice Beyond Wonderland: Essays for the Twenty-First Century* takes on the characters, storylines, and subjects Carroll made famous in his iconic writings and considers how these literary elements fit into modern society. From the relationship between Carroll's Wonderland and the worlds of algebra and geometry to the similarities between Carroll and Dante, this all-encompassing work blends literary analysis with cultural commentary. *Alice Beyond Wonderland* includes a foreword by playwright and author Karoline Leach.

Where it's reviewed:
Choice, May 2010, page 1683

Other books by the same author:
Poetics of the Hive: Insect Metaphor in Literature, 2001

Other books you might like:
Richard Brian Davis, *Alice in Wonderland and Philosophy: Curiouser and Curiouser*, 2010
William Irwin, co-author

Bernard M. Patten, *The Logic of Alice: Clear Thinking in Wonderland*, 2009

Daniel Doen Silberberg, *Wonderland: The Zen of Alice*, 2009

Robin Wilson, *Lewis Carroll in Numberland: His Fantastical Mathematical Logical Life*, 2008

Jenny Woolf, *The Mystery of Lewis Carroll: Discovering the Whimsical, Thoughtful, and Sometimes Lonely Man Who Created "Alice in Wonderland"*, 2010

60

NICK HORNBY

Shakespeare Wrote for Money

(San Francisco, California: McSweeney's, 2008)

Subject(s): Writing; Biographies; Journalism

Summary: *Shakespeare Wrote for Money* is the third compilation of Nick Hornby's columns, all of which originally appeared in the *Believer* magazine. Best noted for his novels *About a Boy* and *High Fidelity*, Hornby's magazine column, Stuff I've Been Reading, is basically a collection of notes about his reading habits. In the column, Hornby often examines the ways that books affect people's lives. This collection includes 15 of Hornby's columns as well as an introduction by Sarah Vowell, author of *The Wordy Shipmates*. Nick Hornby is also the author of *How to Be Good* and *Juliet, Naked*.

Other books by the same author:
High Fidelity, 2005
Fever Pitch, 1998

Other books you might like:
Nick Hornby, *Housekeeping vs. the Dirt*, 2006
Nick Hornby, *Juliet, Naked*, 2009
Nick Hornby, *Not a Star*, 2009
Nick Hornby, *The Polysyllabic Spree*, 2004
Nick Hornby, *Speaking with the Angel*, 2001

61

AMY HOROWITZ

Mediterranean Israeli Music and the Politics of the Aesthetic

(Detroit, Michigan: Wayne State University Press, 2010)

Subject(s): Music; Culture; Politics

Summary: In *Mediterranean Israeli Music and the Politics of the Aesthetic*, Amy Horowitz discusses the new Mizrahi identity and the music that resulted from the cultural blending that occurred when Jews from northern Africa and Middle Eastern countries moved to Israel in the 1950s and '60s. Communities began to form, and though they were often transitory and impoverished, they began attempting to create a new sense of identity and legitimacy. In many cases, this was most successful through the creation and recording of a new style of music, eventually bringing the community both international and political recognition. Horowitz lived in the community in order to write this text, and the author has chosen to focus a great deal of the work on three individuals: Avihu Medina, Zohar Argov, and Zehava Ben.

Where it's reviewed:
Reference & Research Book News, August 2010
Xpress Reviews, April 30, 2010

Other books you might like:
Philip V. Bohlmann, *Israeli Folk Music: Songs of the Early Pioneers*, 1995

Benjamin Elon Brinner Brinner, *Playing Across a Divide: Israeli-Palestinian Musical Encounters*, 2009

Robert Jay Fleisher, *Twenty Israeli Composers: Voices of a Culture*, 1997

Hans Nathan, *Israeli Folk Music: Songs of the Early Pioneers*, 1995

Motti Regev, *Popular Music and National Culture in Israel*, 2004
Edwin Seroussi, co-author

Na'ama Sheffi, *The Ring of Myths: The Israelis, Wagner and the Nazis*, 2000

62

JULIE HUBBERT

Celluloid Symphonies: Texts and Contexts in Film Music History

(Berkeley: University of California Press, 2011)

Subject(s): Music; Movies; Criticism

Summary: The music of film takes the spotlight in this collection of essays written by the composers and musicians who helped make an art form of the modern movie soundtrack. Compiled by author and music professor Julie Hubbert, *Celluloid Symphonies: Texts and Contexts in Film Music History* includes insightful, critical analyses from such legendary movie music icons as Elmer Bernstein, Max Steiner, and Henry Mancini. This volume charts the evolution of music in film and analyzes how issues of technology, popular trends, and commercialization have impacted the craft. *Celluloid Symphonies* includes a bibliography and a full index.

Other books you might like:

Doug Adams, *The Music of The Lord of the Rings Films: A Comprehensive Account of Howard Shore's Scores*, 2010
Richard Dyer, *Nino Rota: Music, Film and Feeling*, 2010
Roger Hickman, *Reel Music: Exploring 100 Years of Film Music*, 2010
Pauline Reay, *Music in Film: Soundtracks and Synergy*, 2004

63

DARNELL M. HUNT

Channeling Blackness: Studies on Television and Race in America

(New York: Oxford University Press, 2005)

Subject(s): African Americans; Television; Criticism

Summary: In *Channeling Blackness: Studies on Television and Race in America*, editor Darnell M. Hunt offers an in-depth analysis of African Americans on television. This study includes essays by some of the foremost academics in the fields of race, media, and popular culture, illustrating the evolution and ideologies behind black characters on American television programs. *Channeling Blackness* includes a bibliography and an index.

Where it's reviewed:

Journal of Popular Film and Television, Summer 2005, pages 126-127

Other books by the same author:

O. J. Simpson Facts and Fictions, 1999

Other books you might like:

Christine Acham, *Revolution Televised: Prime Time and the Struggle for Black Power*, 2005
Gail Dines, *Gender, Race, and Class in Media: A Text-Reader*, 2002
Herman Gray, *Watching Race: Television and the Struggle for Blackness*, 2004
Jean McMahon Humez, *Gender, Race, and Class in Media: A Text-Reader*, 2002
Laurie Ouellette, *Reality TV: Remaking Television Culture*, 2008
Sasha Torres, *Living Color: Race and Television in the United States*, 1998

64

JOHN DIXON HUNT
DAVID LOMAS , Co-Author
MICHAEL CORRIS , Co-Author

Art, Word and Image: 2,000 Years of Visual/Textual Interaction

(London, England: Reaktion, 2010)

Story type: Arts
Subject(s): Art; Painting (Art); Artists

Summary: *Art, Word and Image: 2,000 Years of Visual/ Textual Interaction* is a collection of critical essays from scholars John Dixon Hunt, David Lomas, and Michael Corris about the significance of language in art. In their chronological essays, Hunt, Lomas, and Corris reflect on art throughout history and highlight the importance of artists using words in their paintings. *Art, Word and Image* examines artists in every era from Classical Greece to the Middle Ages through the Renaissance leading up to the present day to understand the use and impact of language. In addition to the essays, the book includes over 300 images of art from prominent artists such as Picasso, Max Ernst, Andy Warhol, and Jasper Johns.

Other books by the same author:

The Italian Garden: Art, Design and Culture, 2007
Gardens and the Picturesque: Studies in the History of Landscape Architecture, 1994
Garden History: Issues, Approaches, Methods, 1992

Other books you might like:

Mary Ann Caws, *Manifesto: A Century of Isms*, 2000
Denis Dutton, *The Art Instinct: Beauty, Pleasure, and Human Evolution*, 2008
Charles Harrison, *Art in Theory 1900-2000: An Anthology of Changing Ideas*, 2002
Michael Kammen, *Visual Shock: A History of Art Controversies in American Culture*, 2006
Nadine Monem, *Art and Text*, 2009
Paul J. Wood, *Art in Theory 1900-2000: An Anthology of Changing Ideas*, 2002

65

SHARON IRISH

Suzanne Lacy: Spaces Between
(Minneapolis, Minnesota: University of Minnesota Press, 2010)

Story type: Arts
Subject(s): Artists; Women; Art

Summary: In *Suzanne Lacy: Spaces Between*, author Sharon Irish examines the history and impact of the shocking and controversial artist. Lacy uses a variety of mediums to spread awareness about social issues such as feminism and racism. Lacy uses her graphic work, which includes videos, performances, and multi-sensory productions, to promote a message or increase awareness about an issue. In *Suzanne Lacy*, Irish examines the artist's work from 1972 to the present, highlighting her more memorable pieces or performances, and analyzes the impact Lacy has made in the art world.

Where it's reviewed:
Reference & Research Book News, May 2010

Other books by the same author:
Cass Gilbert, Architect, 1999

Other books you might like:
Tom Finkelpearl, *Dialogues in Public Art*, 2001
Ronald Lee Fleming, *The Art of Placemaking: Interpreting Community Through Public Art and Urban Design*, 2007
Arlene Goldbard, *New Creative Community: The Art of Cultural Development*, 2006
Cher Krause Knight, *Public Art: Theory, Practice and Populism*, 2008
Suzanne Lacy, *Mapping the Terrain: New Genre Public Art*, 1994

66

MATTHEW FRYE JACOBSON
GASPAR GONZALEZ , Co-Author

What Have They Built You To Do?: The Manchurian Candidate and Cold War America
(Minneapolis: University of Minnesota Press, 2006)

Subject(s): Movies; Criticism; Cold War, 1945-1991

Summary: Authors Matthew Frye Jacobson and Gaspar Gonzalez investigate the impact of the famed 1962 film *The Manchurian Candidate* and how its messages and meaning have remained relevant for more than four decades. *What Have They Built You To Do?: The Manchurian Candidate and Cold War America* looks at how this movie, which was directed by John Frankenheimer and starred Frank Sinatra, offers a timeless, disturbing examination of power, politics, and greed in the ever-changing landscape of America. This volume includes notes on the text and a full index.

Where it's reviewed:
Film International, 2009, pages 89-91

Other books by the same author:
Roots Too, 2006
Barbarian Virtues, 2001
Whiteness of a Different Color, 1999

Other books you might like:
Gregory D. Black, *Hollywood Goes to War: How Politics, Profits and Propaganda Shaped World War II Movies*, 1990
Richard Condon, *The Manchurian Candidate*, 1959
Glenn Hendler, *Keywords for American Cultural Studies*, 2007
Clayton R. Koppes, *Hollywood Goes to War: How Politics, Profits and Propaganda Shaped World War II Movies*, 1990
Fred Turner, *From Counterculture to Cyberculture: Stewart Brand, the Whole Earth Network, and the Rise of Digital Utopianism*, 2008
Simon Winder, *The Man Who Saved Britain: A Personal Journey into the Disturbing World of James Bond*, 2007

67

DEBORAH JERMYN

Sex and the City
(Detroit, Michigan: Wayne State University Press, 2009)

Subject(s): Criticism; Television; Popular culture

Summary: In *Sex and the City*, Deborah Jermyn offers a critical examination of the popular television show of the same name, which aired for six seasons on HBO. In this text, Jermyn analyzes how the show fits into a post-feminist world as it addresses questions of sexuality, female friendships, and consumerism. Jermyn also considers how the slightly surreal aspects of the show impacted its reception and determines why the show's characters continue to resonate with both fans and critics. The author also examines specific episodes to study the ways the show addresses various social issues. The text includes anecdotes from the actresses who starred on the show, as well as information about the fandom that surrounds *Sex and the City*.

Other books by the same author:
Prime Suspect, 2010

Other books you might like:
Candace Bushnell, *The Carrie Diaries*, 2010
Candace Bushnell, *Four Blondes*, 2000
Candace Bushnell, *Lipstick Jungle*, 2005
Candace Bushnell, *Sex and the City*, 2002
Robb Pearlman, *The Q Guide to Sex and the City: Stuff You Didn't Even Know You Wanted to Know...about Carrie, Samantha, Miranda, and Charlotte...and Cosmos*, 2010

68

KATHERINE JOSLIN

Jane Addams, A Writer's Life

(Urbana, Illinois: University of Illinois Press, 2009)

Story type: Literary
Subject(s): Writers; Women; History

Summary: Written by Katherine Joslin, *Jane Addams, A Writer's Life* is an examination of the written works of the prominent reformer and philosopher. Addams is best known as the founder of the Hull House and the first American woman to win a Nobel Peace Prize for her humanitarian efforts, but in this book, Joslin highlights her role as an important literary figure through her nonfiction pieces. *Jane Addams, A Writer's Life* examines all of Addams's written works to help readers understand her personal style, growth as a writer, and methods for communication and persuasion. Joslin compares Addams to other Chicago writers of her time, including Upton Sinclair and Harriet Monroe, to showcase Addams's unique voice.

Where it's reviewed:
Legacy: A Journal of American Women Writers, June 2005, page 205

Other books by the same author:
Edith Wharton and the Making of Fashion, 2009
Edith Wharton, 1994

Other books you might like:
Susan B. Anthony, *Failure Is Impossible: Susan B. Anthony in Her Own Words*, 1996
Allen F. Davis, *American Heroine: The Life and Legend of Jane Addams*, 2000
Louise W. Knight, *Citizen: Jane Addams and the Struggle for Democracy*, 2006
Louise W. Knight, *Jane Addams: Spirit in Action*, 2010
Louis Menand, *The Marketplace of Ideas: Reform and Resistance in the American University*, 2010

69

DALIA JUDOVITZ

Drawing on Art: Duchamp and Company

(Minneapolis, Minnesota: University of Minnesota Press, 2010)

Story type: Arts
Subject(s): Art; Artists; History

Summary: In *Drawing on Art: Duchamp and Company*, professor and author Dalia Judovitz examines the contributions that Marcel Duchamp made to the art world and the critical conversations that his work inspired. In the early 20th century, Duchamp was known for his "readymades," a collection of objects or artwork that he altered. One of his most famous readymades was L.H.O.O.Q, a reproduction of the Mona Lisa with a mustache and goatee. Duchamp's controversial art and work from the Dada and Surrealist periods, spurred discussion about defining and valuing art. In *Drawing on Art*, Judovitz

examines the work of Duchamp, his colleagues, and his successors and explains how they changed the definition of art, creation, and collaboration.

Where it's reviewed:
Reference & Research Book News, August 2010

Other books by the same author:
The Culture of the Body, 2001
Unpacking Duchamp, 1998
Subjectivity and Representation in Descartes, 1988

Other books you might like:
Wayne Andersen, *Marcel Duchamp: The Failed Messiah*, 2010
Hans Belting, *Looking through Duchamp's Door*, 2010
Marcel Duchamp, *Marcel Duchamp: Works, Writings, Interviews*, 2009
Herbert Molderings, *Duchamp and the Aesthetics of Chance: Art as Experiment*, 2010
Gloria Moure, *Marcel Duchamp: Works, Writings, Interviews*, 2009
Michael R. Taylor, *Marcel Duchamp: Etant Donnes*, 2009

70

ROZ KAVENEY

From Alien to the Matrix: Reading Science Fiction Film

(New York: I.B. Tauris, 2005)

Subject(s): Movies; Criticism; Science fiction

Summary: Science fiction films often possess elaborate worlds, complex characters, and turbulent storylines. In *From Alien to the Matrix: Reading Science Fiction Film*, sci-fi guru Roz Kaveney guides readers through the sometimes-daunting world of science fiction films. Kaveney explores a vast array of topics, including the history and mythology of the genre, storytelling styles, technology and special effects, and the commercialization of this once-ignored movie form.

Where it's reviewed:
Journal of Popular Film & Television, Winter 2009, page 199

Other books by the same author:
Teen Dreams, 2006

Other books you might like:
Ximena Gallardo-C., *Alien Woman: The Making of Lt. Ellen Ripley*, 2006
Lincoln Geraghty, *American Science Fiction Film and Television*, 2009
Geoff King, *Science Fiction Cinema: From Outerspace to Cyberspace*, 2001
Tanya Krzywinska, co-author
Gregg Rickman, *The Science Fiction Film Reader*, 2004
Jason Smith, *Alien Woman: The Making of Lt. Ellen Ripley*, 2006
Vivian Sobchack, *Screening Space: The American Science Fiction Film*, 1997

71

HENRY KELLERMAN

Greedy, Cowardly, and Weak: Hollywood's Jewish Stereotypes

(Fort Lee, New Jersey: Barricade Books, 2009)

Subject(s): Jews; Movies; Criticism

Summary: In *Greedy, Cowardly, and Weak: Hollywood's Jewish Stereotypes*, author Henry Kellerman examines the stereotypes perpetuated in movies and what these stereotypes say about modern culture. Kellerman explores many films in his comprehensive study of Jewish stereotypes, including *A Walk in the Sun*, *Saving Private Ryan*, *Dracula*, *Scarface*, and *Pretty Woman*.

Where it's reviewed:
Journal of Popular Culture, June 2010, pages 647-648

Other books by the same author:
Haggadah: A Passover Seder for the Rest of Us, 2005

Other books you might like:
Daniel Bar-Tal, *Stereotypes and Prejudice in Conflict: Representations of Arabs in Israeli Jewish Society*, 2005
Helen Epstein, *Swimming Against Stereotype: The Story of a Twentieth Century Jewish Athlete*, 2006
Chiara Francesca Ferrari, *Since When Is Fran Drescher Jewish?: Dubbing Stereotypes in The Nanny, The Simpsons, and The Sopranos*, 2011
Danusha V. Goska, *Bieganski: The Brute Polak Stereotype in Polish-Jewish Relations and American Popular Culture*, 2010
Yona Teichman, *Stereotypes and Prejudice in Conflict: Representations of Arabs in Israeli Jewish Society*, 2005
Anat Zajdman, *Semites and Stereotypes: Characteristics of Jewish Humor*, 1993
Avner Ziv, co-editor

72

DENIS KITCHEN
PAUL BUHLE , Co-Author

The Art of Harvey Kurtzman: The Mad Genius of Comics

(New York: Abrams ComicArts, 2009)

Subject(s): Comic books; Artists; Criticism

Summary: Artist Harvey Kurtzman was an innovative and controversial figure in the world of comics, and his unique style made him an icon of the genre. In *The Art of Harvey Kurtzman: The Mad Genius of Comics*, authors Denis Kitchen and Paul Buhle present a critical biography of the legendary illustrator, who was also renowned as a writer, humorist, and editor. His work drew him the acclaim of powerful figures, and his unstinting eye led to the discovery of several major artistic talents. The authors examine his unprecedented contributions and the wild, unpredictable course of his life and work. *The Art of Harvey Kurtzman* includes a foreword by actor and comedian Harry Shearer.

Where it's reviewed:
Booklist, July 1, 2009, page 46
Library Journal, September 1, 2009, page 112

Other books by the same author:
The Oddly Compelling Art of Denis Kitchen, 2010

Other books you might like:
Will Eisner, *Will Eisner's Shop Talk*, 2001
Harvey Kurtzman, *The EC Archives: Frontline Combat*, 2008
Harvey Kurtzman, *Humbug*, 2009
Harvey Kurtzman, *Inside Mad: Mad Reader, Volume 3*, 2002
Greg Sadowski, *The Comics Journal Library Vol. 7: Harvey Kurtzman*, 2006

73

YEKHEZKEL KOTIK

Journey to a Nineteenth-Century Shtetl: The Memoirs of Yekhezkel Kotik

(Detroit, Michigan: Wayne State University Press, 2008)

Subject(s): Autobiographies; History; Jews

Summary: *Journey to a Nineteenth-Century Shtetl: The Memoirs of Yekhezkel Kotik* is a memoir, originally written in Hebrew by Yekhezkel Kotik and published in Warsaw in 1913. This version is translated into English and includes a foreword and numerous annotations by David Assaf. Kotik grew up in a shtetl in Poland known as Kamieniec Litewski, a significant place in Jewish history. He shares personal stories about himself and his family, friends and neighbors, discussing the many colorful characters who came in and out of his life. Kotik also discusses political topics such as interactions between the Jewish population and the Russian and Polish governments and the rule of Tsar Nicholas I. The annotations provide additional information about certain terms, names, and Jewish customs mentioned in the book.

Where it's reviewed:
CHOICE: Current Reviews for Academic Libraries, April 2003, page 1421

Other books you might like:
Jonathan Boyarin, *From a Ruined Garden, Second Expanded Edition: The Memorial Books of Polish Jewry*, 1998
Gluckel, *The Memoirs of Gluckel of Hameln*, 1987
Elizabeth Herzog, *Life Is with People: The Culture of the Shtetl*, 2006
Gershon David Hundert, *Jews in Poland-Lithuania in the Eighteenth Century: A Genealogy of Modernity*, 2006
Jack Kugelmass, *From a Ruined Garden, Second Expanded Edition: The Memorial Books of Polish Jewry*, 1998

Jeffrey Shandler, *Awakening Lives: Autobiographies of Jewish Youth in Poland before the Holocaust*, 2002

Mark Zborowski, *Life Is with People: The Culture of the Shtetl*, 2006

74

NICOLE LAPORTE

The Men Who Would Be King: An Almost Epic Tale of Moguls, Movies and a Company Called DreamWorks

(New York: Houghton Mifflin Harcourt, 2010)

Subject(s): Entertainment industry; Business

Summary: In *The Men Who Would Be King: An Almost Epic Tale of Moguls, Movies and a Company Called DreamWorks*, entertainment journalist Nicole LaPorte, a former reporter for *Variety* magazine, takes an inside look at the rise and fall of DreamWorks. Started in 1994 by movie production tycoons David Geffen, Jeffrey Katzenberg, and Steven Spielberg, the company promised to mesh business savvy with creativity for an innovative approach to entertainment production. Instead, according to LaPorte, the egos of each entrepreneur conflicted to the detriment of the company.

Where it's reviewed:
Booklist, May 1, 2010, page 4
Entertainment Weekly, May 7, 2010, pages 373-376
Kirkus Reviews, May 1, 2010
Maclean's, June 14, 2010, page 86
New York Times Book Review, June 28, 2010, page 69

Other books you might like:
Peter Biskind, *Star: How Warren Beatty Seduced America*, 2010
Rich Cohen, *When I Stop Talking, You'll Know I'm Dead: Useful Stories from a Persuasive Man*, 2010
Michael Deeley, *Blade Runners, Deer Hunters, and Blowing the Bloody Doors Off: My Life in Cult Movies*, 2009
Sarah Ellison, *War at the Wall Street Journal: Inside the Struggle To Control an American Business Empire*, 2010
Robert Hofler, *Party Animals: A Hollywood Tale of Sex, Drugs, and Rock 'n' Roll Starring the Fabulous Allan Carr*, 2010
Jerry Weintraub, *When I Stop Talking, You'll Know I'm Dead: Useful Stories from a Persuasive Man*, 2010

75

MAUD LAVIN

The Oldest We've Ever Been: Seven True Stories of Midlife Transitions

(Tucson, Arizona: University of Arizona Press, 2008)

Subject(s): Short stories; Friendship; Marriage

Summary: Edited by Maud Lavin, *The Oldest We've Ever Been: Seven True Stories of Midlife Transitions* is a collection of nonfiction essays about the challenges, surprises, and struggles of the middle-aged. The seven contributors—Kim Larsen, Calvin Forbes, Ellen McMahon, Allan deSouza, Peggy Shinner, William Davies King, and Maud Lavin (with help from Locke Bowman)—recount their personal experiences during midlife transitions. The candid and emotional tales in the book cover a broad range of topics and issues, including illness, divorce, parenting, death, love, dating, and friendship. *The Oldest We've Ever Been* is an anthology of honest and straightforward experiences, struggles, and triumphs about life, love, hardship, and family.

Where it's reviewed:
Chicago Tribune, June 14, 2008, page 4
Publishers Weekly, January 14, 2008, page 50

Other books by the same author:
Push Comes to Shove, 2010
Clean New World, 2002
Cut with the Kitchen Knife, 1993

Other books you might like:
Pamela D. Blair, *The Next Fifty Years: A Guide for Women at Midlife and Beyond*, 2005
Army Ferris, *Marrying George Clooney: Confessions from a Midlife Crisis*, 2009
Maud Lavin, *Push Comes to Shove: New Images of Aggressive Women*, 2010
Ani Liggett, *Endings. Beginnings... When Midlife Women Leave Home in Search Authenticity*, 2010
Linda Nochlin, *Global Feminisms: New Directions in Contemporary Art*, 2007
Maura Reilly, co-author

76

JIM LEACH

Doctor Who

(Detroit, Michigan: Wayne State University Press, 2009)

Subject(s): Criticism; Television; Television programs

Summary: In *Doctor Who*, Jim Leach presents an examination of the television show of the same name, which first aired on the BBC in 1963 and ran for twenty-six subsequent seasons. It went off the air in 1989 and returned once again in 2005. Over the years, the title character has been played by seven different actors, and Leach considers how each of the actors portrayed the character. He considers the show's impact on popular culture, and he discusses the way the show effectively combines science fiction, horror, and fantasy. Leach also explores seven of the original episodes in detail.

Where it's reviewed:
Reference & Research Book News, August 2009

Other books by the same author:
Film in Canada, 2006
British Film, 2004
A Possible Cinema, 1995

Other books you might like:

Benjamin Cook, *Doctor Who: The Writer's Tale*, 2010
  Russell T. Davies, co-author

Tara O'Shea, *Chicks Dig Time Lords: A Celebration of Doctor Who by the Women Who Love It*, 2010

Brian J. Robb, *Timeless Adventures: How Doctor Who Conquered TV*, 2010

Lynne M. Thomas, *Chicks Dig Time Lords: A Celebration of Doctor Who by the Women Who Love It*, 2010

Steve Tribe, *Doctor Who: Companions And Allies*, 2009

Steve Tribe, *Doctor Who: The TARDIS Handbook*, 2010

77

PETER LEHMAN

Running Scared: Masculinity and the Representation of the Male Body

(Detroit, Michigan: Wayne State University Press, 2007)

Subject(s): Criticism; Sexuality; Movies

Summary: In *Running Scared: Masculinity and the Representation of the Male Body*, Peter Lehman considers the representation of the male body in different forms of art, including films, literature, music, paintings, and photos. In the book the author contends that the lack of sexuality related to the male body says something about the American culture. According to Lehman, this "maintains the male mystique and preserves the power of the phallus." Lehman considers specific films and works of literature, as well as broader topics such as pornography and homophobia. He argues that the culture generally presents men as either a hero or a "vulnerable failure."

Other books by the same author:
Thinking About Movies, 2008

Roy Orbison: Invention of an Alternative Rock Masculinity, 2003

Other books you might like:
Dennis Bingham, *Acting Male: Masculinities in the Films of James Stewart, Jack Nicholson, and Clint Eastwood*, 1994

Sergio de la Mora, *Cinemachismo: Masculinities and Sexuality in Mexican Film*, 2006

Robert T. Eberwein, *Armed Forces: Masculinity and Sexuality in the American War Film*, 2007

Frances Gateward, *Where the Boys Are: Cinemas of Masculinity and Youth*, 2005

Peter Lehman, *Masculinity: Bodies, Movies, Culture*, 2001

Murray Pomerance, *Where the Boys Are: Cinemas of Masculinity and Youth*, 2005

78

PAUL LOPES

Demanding Respect: The Evolution of the American Comic Book

(Philadelphia: Temple University Press, 2009)

Subject(s): Comic books; Popular culture; Criticism

Summary: Sociology professor Paul Lopes explores the advancement of the comic book in popular culture, chronicling the genre's journey from outsider status to esteemed source of popular movies, books, and video games. *Demanding Respect: The Evolution of the American Comic Book* looks at the intricacies of comic book culture, delving into the contributions of authors, artists, publishers, and, of course, the zealous readership. This array of perspectives provides an all-encompassing, revealing study of the American comic book as it has risen higher and higher in the public regard. *Demanding Respect* includes notes on the text and an index.

Where it's reviewed:
Journal of Popular Culture, April 2010, pages 421-422

Other books by the same author:
The Rise of a Jazz Art World, 2002

Other books you might like:
Randy Duncan, *The Power of Comics: History, Form and Culture*, 2009

Thierry Groensteen, *The System of Comics*, 2009

Mike Madrid, *The Supergirls: Fashion, Feminism, Fantasy, and the History of Comic Book Heroines*, 2009

Matthew J. Smith, *The Power of Comics: History, Form and Culture*, 2009

Douglas Wolk, *Reading Comics: How Graphic Novels Work and What They Mean*, 2008

Bradford W. Wright, *Comic Book Nation: The Transformation of Youth Culture in America*, 2001

79

SCOTT MACDONALD

Canyon Cinema: The Life and Times of an Independent Film Distributor

(Berkeley: University of California Press, 2008)

Subject(s): Movies; Movie industry; United States

Summary: Experimental film expert Scott MacDonald studies a trailblazing movement in early avant-garde filmmaking and how it made a lasting impression on the entire movie industry. *Canyon Cinema: The Life and Times of an Independent Film Distributor* chronicles the history of the San Francisco-based movie company, which began in the 1960s and soon developed a cult following. In the ensuing years, the films distributed by Canyon Cinema became renown for their bold style and powerful storytelling, influencing the ever-growing popularity of independent cinema. *Canyon Cinema* includes a bibliography and an index.

Where it's reviewed:
Film Comment, March-April 2008, page 79

Other books by the same author:
Adventures of Perception: Cinema as Exploration, 2009
The Garden in the Machine, 2001
Avant-Garde Film: Motion Studies, 1993

Other books you might like:
Steve Anker, *Radical Light: Alternative Film and Video in the San Francisco Bay Area, 1945-2000*, 2010
Ken Dancyger, *Alternative Scriptwriting, Fourth Edition: Rewriting the Hollywood Formula*, 2006
Kathy Geritz, *Radical Light: Alternative Film and Video in the San Francisco Bay Area, 1945-2000*, 2010
Courtney Lehmann, *The Reel Shakespeare: Alternative Cinema and Theory*, 2002
Scott MacDonald, *Adventures of Perception: Cinema as Exploration*, 2009
Jeff Rush, *Alternative Scriptwriting, Fourth Edition: Rewriting the Hollywood Formula*, 2006
Steve Seid, *Radical Light: Alternative Film and Video in the San Francisco Bay Area, 1945-2000*, 2010
Rebecca Solnit, *River of Shadows: Eadweard Muybridge and the Technological Wild West*, 2003
Lisa S. Starks, *The Reel Shakespeare: Alternative Cinema and Theory*, 2002

80

ALLISTER MACTAGGART

The Film Paintings of David Lynch: Challenging Film Theory

(Chicago, Illinois: Intellect, 2010)

Subject(s): Movie industry; Movies; Criticism

Summary: Written by Allister Mactaggart, *The Film Paintings of David Lynch: Challenging Film Theory* is a critical examination of filmmaker David Lynch's unique approach to directing. Lynch—a legendary movie director whose work includes *The Elephant Man*, *Blue Velvet*, *Mulholland Drive*, and *Inland Empire*—first approached filmmaking as an extension of fine art. In *The Film Paintings of David Lynch*, Mactaggart contrasts Lynch's body of work to other films in an effort to show readers the connections between the director's films and avant-garde art, cinematic theory, and psychology.

Other books you might like:
Richard A. Barney, *David Lynch: Interviews*, 2009
Dietmar Dath, *David Lynch: Dark Splendor*, 2010
Patrice Forest, *David Lynch: Lithos*, 2010
   David Lynch, co-author
   Dominique Paini, co-author
Chris Rodley, *Lynch on Lynch, Revised Edition*, 2005
Peter-Klaus Schuster, *David Lynch: Dark Splendor*, 2010
   Werner Spies, co-author
Mark Stewart, *David Lynch Decoded*, 2008

81

JULIE MALNIG

Ballroom, Boogie, Shimmy Sham, Shake: A Social and Popular Dance Reader

(Urbana, Illinois: University of Illinois Press, 2008)

Subject(s): Dance; History; Recreation

Summary: Compiled by Julie Malnig, *Ballroom, Boogie, Shimmy Sham, Shake: A Social and Popular Dance Reader* is a collection of essays from 20 contributors about social dance styles. Social dance includes any type of dance performed or participated in by the public in communal areas such as ballrooms and dance halls. The book examines the history of social dance throughout different eras and in different regions around the globe. The contributors use ethnography, anthropology, gender studies, and critical race theory to examine social dance and its history.

Where it's reviewed:
Society for American Music Bulletin, Spring 2010, page 29

Other books by the same author:
Dancing Till Dawn: A Century of Exhibition Ballroom Dance, 1995

Other books you might like:
Jan Erkert, *Harnessing the Wind: the Art of Teaching Modern Dance*, 2003
Brenda Dixon Gottschild, *The Black Dancing Body: A Geography from Coon to Cool*, 2005
Julie Malnig, *Dancing Till Dawn: A Century of Exhibition Ballroom Dance*, 1995
Maureen Needham, *I See America Dancing: Selected Readings, 1685-2000*, 2002
Jean Stearns, *Jazz Dance: The Story Of American Vernacular Dance*, 1994
   Marshall Stearns, co-author

82

JOE MCELHANEY

The Death of Classical Cinema: Hitchcock, Lang, Minnelli

(Albany: State University of New York Press, 2006)

Subject(s): Movie industry; Movies; Criticism

Summary: During the early part of the 1960s, American dramatic filmmaking was undergoing a drastic change from sterile black-and-white melodramas to edgy, hard-hitting, and artistically driven portraits of people and places. This evolution in movies had a major impact on three of the era's most popular directors—Alfred Hitchcock, Fritz Lang, and Vincente Minnelli, who each tried his hand at making a film blending the old and new ways of filmmaking. In *The Death of Classical Cinema: Hitchcock, Lang, Minnelli*, film studies professor Joe

McElhaney looks at the three films made by these directors during this period and shows how—despite their reception at the time—these movies have endured as important, inspired works of cinematic art. First book.

Where it's reviewed:
Journal of Popular Film and Television, Spring 2008, pages 46-47

Other books by the same author:
Albert Maysles, 2009
Vincente Minnelli: The Art of Entertainment, 2009

Other books you might like:
David A. Gerstner, *Authorship and Film*, 2002
Barry Keith Grant, *Auteurs and Authorship: A Film Reader*, 2008
Tom Gunning, *D.W. Griffith and the Origins of American Narrative Film*, 1993
Emanuel Levy, *Vincente Minnelli: Hollywood's Dark Dreamer*, 2009
Janet Staiger, *Authorship and Film*, 2002
Virginia Wright Wexman, *Film and Authorship*, 2002

83

JOE MCELHANEY

Vincente Minnelli: The Art of Entertainment

(Detroit, Michigan: Wayne State University Press, 2009)

Subject(s): Criticism; Movies; Popular culture

Summary: In *Vincente Minnelli: The Art of Entertainment*, editor Joe McElhaney brings together 50 years' worth of criticism for filmmaker Vincente Minnelli's body of work. Minnelli is well known for directing films such as *Meet Me in St. Louis*, *An American in Paris*, and *Father of the Bride*, to name a few, though critical assessment of his films was somewhat lacking, at least in English. This collection compiles essays written by critics around the world, including North America, Europe, and Australia, many of which have been translated in English. The book is divided into four sections to discuss Minnelli's oeuvre chronologically, placing the films into historical, cultural, and aesthetic contexts, considering common topics of film theory.

Where it's reviewed:
Cineaste, Winter 2009, page 84
Library Journal, January 1, 2009, page 93

Other books by the same author:
Albert Maysles, 2009
The Death of Classical Cinema (Suny Series, Horizons of Cinema), 2006

Other books you might like:
David A. Gerstner, *Authorship and Film*, 2002
Barry Keith Grant, *Auteurs and Authorship: A Film Reader*, 2008
Tom Gunning, *D.W. Griffith and the Origins of American Narrative Film*, 1993
Emanuel Levy, *Vincente Minnelli: Hollywood's Dark Dreamer*, 2009

Janet Staiger, *Authorship and Film*, 2002
Virginia Wright Wexman, *Film and Authorship*, 2002

84

JOHN MCGOWAN

American Liberalism: An Interpretation for Our Time

(Chapel Hill, North Carolina: The University of North Carolina Press, 2007)

Subject(s): Political campaigns; United States; Politics

Summary: In *American Liberalism: An Interpretation for Our Time*, John McGowan provides readers with an overview of liberalism and explains how it has influenced the United States over time. The author explains that liberalism is often frowned upon today by members of both the Democratic and Republican parties. But McGowan defends liberalism and explains its value to American citizens by describing the various liberal principles that the Founding Fathers tried to incorporate into the nation's foundation. McGowan is also the author of *Democracy's Children: Intellectuals and the Rise of Cultural Politics*, *Postmodernism and Its Critics*, and *Hannah Arendt: An Introduction*.

Where it's reviewed:
Booklist, October 15, 2007, page 7

Other books by the same author:
Democracy's Children, 2002
Hannah Arendt: An Introduction, 1997
Postmodernism and Its Critics, 1991

Other books you might like:
Patrick Allitt, *The Conservatives: Ideas and Personalities Throughout American History*, 2009
Peter Berkowitz, *Varieties of Conservatism in America*, 2004
Bryan-Paul Frost, *History of American Political Thought*, 2003
Russell Kirk, *The Conservative Mind: From Burke to Eliot*, 1986
Sam Tanenhaus, *The Death of Conservatism*, 2009

85

BARBRA A. MEEK

We Are Our Language: An Ethnography of Language Revitalization in a Northern Athabascan Community

(Tucson, Arizona: University of Arizona Press, 2010)

Subject(s): Indigenous peoples; Education; Speech

Summary: In *We Are Our Language: An Ethnography of Language Revitalization in a Northern Athabascan Community*, anthropology and linguistics professor Barbra A. Meek argues for the importance of language revitalization for indigenous peoples around the world. According to Meek, many indigenous languages are in danger of going extinct if language preservation is not initiated. In *We Are Our Language*, Meek uses the story of Kaska, a threatened language in the Yukon, to make her argument. She contends that if an endangered language is to be saved, it will take a complete social transformation including a change in government policies, teaching practices, and unity within the linguistics field.

Other books you might like:

Rachel Corr, *Ritual and Remembrance in the Ecuadorian Andes*, 2009

Monica Diaz, *Indigenous Writings from the Convent: Negotiating Ethnic Autonomy in Colonial Mexico*, 2010

Malinda Maynor Lowery, *Lumbee Indians in the Jim Crow South: Race, Identity, and the Making of a Nation*, 2010

Claude Clayton Smith, *The Way of Kinship: An Anthology of Native Siberian Literature*, 2010
Alexander Vaschenko, co-author

Michael J. Zogry, *Anetso, the Cherokee Ball Game: At the Center of Ceremony and Identity*, 2010

86

DENIS MEIKLE

The Ring Companion

(London: Titan Books, 2005)

Subject(s): Movies; Horror; Criticism

Summary: Film writer Denis Meikle studies the far-ranging influence and unique storytelling structure of the now-classic Japanese horror film *Ringu* and its American remake, *The Ring*. *The Ring Companion* takes readers into the story of these movies and how they employ the use of classic mythology mixed with a thrilling new style of horror filmmaking. Meikle also looks at the novels on which the movies are based, the strikingly original narrative, and the draw of *The Ring* for audiences around the world.

Where it's reviewed:

Journal of Popular Film and Television, Fall 2007, pages 143-144

Other books by the same author:

A History of Horrors: The Rise and Fall of the House of Hammer, 2009

Johnny Depp: A Kind of Illusion, 2009

Vincent Price: The Art of Fear, 2006

Other books you might like:

Colette Balmain, *Introduction to Japanese Horror Film*, 2009

Laurence Bush, *Asian Horror Encyclopedia: Asian Horror Culture in Literature, Manga, and Folklore*, 2001

Patrick Galloway, *Asia Shock: Horror and Dark Cinema from Japan, Korea, Hong Kong, and Thailand*, 2006

David Kalat, *J-Horror: The Definitive Guide to The Ring, The Grudge and Beyond*, 2007

Jay McRoy, *Japanese Horror Cinema*, 2005

87

WALTER METZ

Bewitched

(Detroit, Michigan: Wayne State University Press, 2007)

Subject(s): Criticism; Television; Television programs

Summary: In *Bewitched*, Walter Metz provides critical commentary on the beloved television show that aired for eight years from 1964 to 1972. Metz considers the historical and cultural contexts in which the show aired, and the ways in which some events and viewpoints were reflected in the themes of the show. For instance, Samantha and her husband Darrin Stephens are constantly worried that her true identity as a witch will be revealed, which may have mirrored the fears of many during the "postwar surveillance culture." The show also addressed feminist themes, domesticity, politics, and ideas surrounding television itself when television programs could be shown in color rather than black and white. Metz considers the entire series in his discussions, pointing out that the show can be interpreted in many different ways when individual episodes are considered.

Where it's reviewed:

Film Quarterly, Summer 2008, page 80

Historical Journal of Film, Radio and Television, March 2009, page 150

Other books by the same author:

Engaging Film Criticism, 2004

Other books you might like:

Gregory Branson-Trent, *Bewitched: The Complete Episode Guide*, 2009

Marion Gibson, *Witchcraft Myths in American Culture*, 2007

Lynn Kear, *Agnes Moorehead: A Bio-Bibliography*, 1992

Gina Meyers, *The Magic of Bewitched Trivia and More*, 2004

Bernice Murphy, *The Suburban Gothic in American Popular Culture*, 2009

88

ELIZABETH CAROLYN MILLER

Framed: The New Woman Criminal in British Culture at the Fin de Siecle

(Ann Arbor: University of Michigan Press, 2008)

Subject(s): Literature; Detective fiction; Women

Summary: In fin de siecle British literature, female criminals were consistently conveyed as seductive and sexy, while their male counterparts were typically unattractive or unlikable. In *Framed: The New Woman Criminal in British Culture at the Fin de Siecle*, English professor Elizabeth Carolyn Miller explores this unusual trend, studying the literature and films of late 19th- and early 20th century British culture. The author shows how this portrayal of the female criminal ultimately impacted everything from consumerism to popular fashion. First book.

Where it's reviewed:
Victorian Studies, Winter 2010, pages 310-312

Other books you might like:
Clemens F. Bartollas, *Women and the Criminal Justice System*, 2010
Lynne Goodstein, *Women, Crime, and Criminal Justice: Original Feminist Readings*, 2003
Francine Hornberger, *Mistresses of Mayhem: The Book of Women Criminals*, 2002
Susan Ehrlich Martin, *Doing Justice, Doing Gender: Women in Law and Criminal Justice Occupations*, 1996
Barbara Raffel Price, *The Criminal Justice System and Women: Offenders, Prisoners, Victims and Workers*, 2003
Claire Renzetti, *Women, Crime, and Criminal Justice: Original Feminist Readings*, 2003
Natalie Sokoloff, *The Criminal Justice System and Women: Offenders, Prisoners, Victims and Workers*, 2003
Katherine Stuart van Wormer, *Women and the Criminal Justice System*, 2010

89

CHANA MLOTEK
MARK SLOBIN , Co-Editor

Yiddish Folksongs from the Ruth Rubin Archive

(Detroit, Michigan: Wayne State University Press, 2007)

Subject(s): Music; Folklore; History

Summary: *Yiddish Folksongs from the Ruth Rubin Archive* is a collection edited by Chana Mlotek and Mark Slobin. This collection contains more than 2,000 authentic Yiddish folksongs that Rubin collected from Yiddish-speaking immigrants who moved to North America during the 1900s. Although many of these songs were passed down through an oral tradition, Rubin provides sheet music for each folksong in addition to the Yiddish text. Because Rubin died before the book's completion, academics Mlotek and Slobin provide additional commentary on various songs. The book comes with an audio CD of selected Yiddish folksongs.

Where it's reviewed:
Shofar, Fall 2008, page 207

Other books by the same author:
Pearls of Yiddish Poetry, 2010

Other books you might like:
M. Beregovski, *Old Jewish Folk Music: The Collections and Writings of Moshe Beregovski*, 2001

Jack Gottlieb, *Funny, It Doesn't Sound Jewish: How Yiddish Songs and Synagogue Melodies Influenced Tin Pan Alley, Broadway and Hollywood*, 2004
Seth Rogovoy, *The Essential Klezmer: A Music Lover's Guide to Jewish Roots and Soul Music, from the Old World to the Jazz Age to the Downtown Avant Garde*, 2000
Rose Rubin, *A Treasury of Jewish Folksong*, 1987
Ruth Rubin, *Voices of a People*, 2000

90

ANDREW MOOR

Powell and Pressburger: A Cinema of Magic Spaces

(New York: I.B. Tauris, 2005)

Subject(s): Movies; Movie industry; Criticism

Summary: Film lecturer Andrew Moor studies the pioneering films of visionary moviemakers Michael Powell and Emeric Pressburger. In *Powell and Pressburger: A Cinema of Magic Spaces*, Moor delves into the canon of the great team's work, from *The Spy in Black* to the iconic *The Red Shoes*. This volume further explores the contributions of Powell and Pressburger by illustrating the symbols and messages within their movies, which range from explorations of identity to the relationship between reality and fantasy. *Powell and Pressburger* includes photographs, notes on the text, a bibliography, and an index.

Where it's reviewed:
Journal of Popular Film and Television, Winter 2007, pages 189-190

Other books by the same author:
Colours of Architecture, 2006
Architectural Glass Art, 1998
Architectural Glass, 1989

Other books you might like:
Ian Christie, *Michael Powell: International Perspectives on an English Filmmaker*, 2008
Mark Connelly, *The Red Shoes*, 2005
Stella Hockenhull, *Neo-Romantic Landscapes: An Aesthetic Approach to the Films of Powell and Pressburger*, 2008
Andrew Moor, *Michael Powell: International Perspectives on an English Filmmaker*, 2008
Michael Powell, *A Life in Movies: An Autobiography*, 2001
Sarah Street, *Black Narcissus*, 2005

91

JULIA R. MYERS

Energy: Charles McGee at Eighty-Five

(Ypsilanti, Michigan: Eastern Michigan University, 2009)

Subject(s): Biographies; Art; Culture
Summary: *Energy: Charles McGee at Eighty-Five*, by

biographer Julia R. Myers, is a look into the life and times of Detroit-based artist Charles McGee, from his experience as a U.S. Marine to his establishment of the Charles McGee School of Art. Written to complement an exhibition at Eastern Michigan University consisting of more than six decades of McGee's work, this book looks at McGee's impact in the African American community in Detroit as well as his influence in the art world.

Other books by the same author:
Completing the Circle, 2007

Other books you might like:
Dan Austin, *Lost Detroit: Stories Behind the Motor City's Majestic Ruins*, 2010
Cynthia Davis, *Detroit: Hand-Altered Polaroid Photographs*, 2005
Linda Bank Downs, *Diego Rivera: The Detroit Industry Murals*, 1999
    Frida Kahlo, co-author
Mason Klein, *Alias Man Ray: The Art of Reinvention*, 2009
Dennis Alan Nawrocki, *Art in Detroit Public Places: Third Edition*, 2008
Diego Rivera, *Diego Rivera: The Detroit Industry Murals*, 1999

92

GARY PAUL NABHAN

Arab/American: Landscape, Culture, and Cuisine in Two Great Deserts

(Tucson, Arizona: University of Arizona Press, 2008)

Subject(s): Middle East; United States; Deserts

Summary: Written by Arab American ecologist Gary Paul Nabhan, *Arab/American: Landscape, Culture, and Cuisine in Two Great Deserts* is a collection of essays about the commonalities between the United States and the Middle East. In a time when many Arabs and Americans do everything possible to distance themselves from each other and draw distinctions about their unique cultures, Nabhan has devoted himself to finding common ground between the two civilizations. In *Arab/American*, Nabhan crosses cultural boundaries to locate the geographic, ethnic, linguistic, and gastronomic similarities between the Middle East and the desert regions of the southwestern United States.

Where it's reviewed:
Booklist, March 1, 2008, page 44
Reference & Research Book News, May 2008
Utne Reader, July-August 2008, page 31

Other books by the same author:
Where Our Food Comes From: Retracing Nikolay Vavilov's Quest to End Famine, 2008
Natural Beekeeping: Organic Approaches to Modern Apiculture, 2007
Why Some Like It Hot: Food, Genes, and Cultural Diversity, 2006

Other books you might like:
Sarah Gualtieri, *Between Arab and White: Race and Ethnicity in the Early Syrian American Diaspora*, 2009
Pierrette Hondagneu-Sotelo, *Domestica: Immigrant Workers Cleaning and Caring in the Shadows of Affluence*, 2007
Alixa Naff, *Becoming American: The Early Arab Immigrant Experience*, 1993
Nina Revoyr, *Southland*, 2003
George J. Sanchez, *Becoming Mexican American: Ethnicity, Culture and Identity in Chicano Los Angeles, 1900-1945*, 1995

93

OLGA NAJERA-RAMIREZ
NORMA E. CANTU , Co-Editor
BRENDA M. ROMERO , Co-Editor

Dancing across Borders: Danzas y Bailes Mexicanos

(Urbana, Illinois: University of Illinois Press, 2009)

Story type: Collection
Subject(s): Dance; Mexicans; Mexican Americans

Summary: Edited by Olga Najera-Ramirez, Norma E. Cantu, and Brenda M. Romero, *Dancing Across Borders: Danzas y Bailes Mexicanos* is an examination of traditional and popular Mexican dance styles that are practiced in Mexico and the United States. The book includes works written by scholars and that analyze different aspects of Mexican dance, including its aesthetics, interpretations, authenticity, performance, and methodologies. The book includes written works from 20 contributors including Susan Cashion, Renee de la Torre Castellanos, Peter J. Garcia, Shakina Nayfack, and Russell Rodriguez.

Other books by the same author:
Chicana Feminisms: A Critical Reader, 2003
Chicana Traditions, 2002
La fiesta de los tastoanes: Critical Encounters in Mexican Festival Performance, 1998

Other books you might like:
Harold Augenbraum, *The Latino Reader: An American Literary Tradition from 1542 to the Present*, 1997
Debbie Cavalier, *Mexican Folk Dances*, 1994
    Maria Arias Cruz, co-author
Juan Gonzalez, *Harvest of Empire: A History of Latinos in America*, 2000
Reyna Grande, *Dancing with Butterflies*, 2009
Carlos Francisco Jackson, *Chicana and Chicano Art: ProtestArte*, 2009
E. B. Jurey, *Mexican Folk Dances*, 1994
Margarite Fernandez Olmos, *The Latino Reader: An American Literary Tradition from 1542 to the Present*, 1997

94

LAWRENCE NAPPER

British Cinema and Middlebrow Culture in the Interwar Years

(Exeter, United Kingdom: University of Exeter Press, 2009)

Subject(s): Movies; Movie industry; England

Summary: Written by Lawrence Napper, *British Cinema and Middlebrow Culture in the Interwar Years* is a critical examination of British filmmaking between the years of 1928 and 1939. While many have written off the interwar era as a weak period in British filmmaking history, Napper reevaluates the films produced between the First and Second World Wars and shows how the British film companies attempted to differentiate their movies from the ones produced in Hollywood. *British Cinema and Middlebrow Culture in the Interwar Years* shows how the scope of movies was broadened to target the growing middle class.

Other books you might like:
Justine Ashby, *British Cinema, Past and Present*, 2000
Christine Gledhill, *Nationalising Femininity: Culture, Sexuality and British Cinema in the Second World War*, 2010
Andrew Higson, *British Cinema, Past and Present*, 2000
Sue Longhurst, *Keeping the British End Up: Four Decades of Saucy Cinema*, 2010
Robert Murphy, *The British Cinema Book*, 2009
Amy Sargeant, *British Cinema: A Critical History*, 2008
Simon Sheridan, *Keeping the British End Up: Four Decades of Saucy Cinema*, 2010
Gillian Swanson, *Nationalising Femininity: Culture, Sexuality and British Cinema in the Second World War*, 2010
Johnny Vegas, *Keeping the British End Up: Four Decades of Saucy Cinema*, 2010

95

DENNIS ALAN NAWROCKI

Art in Detroit Public Places: Third Edition

(Detroit, Michigan: Wayne State University Press, 2008)

Subject(s): Art; Urban life; Parks

Summary: Written by Dennis Alan Nawrocki, *Art in Detroit Public Places: Third Edition* is a guide for natives and tourists alike to the 150 pieces of artwork that can be found in public areas throughout greater Detroit. Impressive pieces of art can be spotted all across metropolitan Detroit in public parks, hospitals, libraries, and schools. *Art in Detroit Public Places* includes information on each piece of art and divides the city into six districts, detailing the artwork's locations accordingly.

A detailed street map is featured in the book, making it easy for tourists or art enthusiasts to coordinate walking or driving tours of the city to spot these impressive pieces of art.

Where it's reviewed:
Internet Bookwatch, December 2008

Other books you might like:
John Gallagher, *AIA Detroit: The American Institute of Architects Guide to Detroit Architecture*, 2002
John Gallagher, *Great Architecture of Michigan*, 2008
Greg Grandin, *Fordlandia: The Rise and Fall of Henry Ford's Forgotten Jungle City*, 2009
Eric J. Hill, *AIA Detroit: The American Institute of Architects Guide to Detroit Architecture*, 2002
Andrew Moore, *Andrew Moore: Detroit Disassembled*, 2010
Robert Sharoff, *American City: Detroit Architecture, 1845-2005*, 2005

96

MAGGIE NELSON

Women, the New York School, and Other True Abstractions

(Iowa City, Iowa: University of Iowa Press, 2007)

Subject(s): Women; Writing; Writers

Summary: Author Maggie Nelson discusses gender, literature, and education in *Women, the New York School, and Other True Abstractions*. In this work, Nelson describes the contributions of the women who were part of the New York School of Poets from the mid-20th century to the present. Nelson discusses the works of a number of celebrated female authors who were involved in the school, including Bernadette Mayer, Alice Notley, and Barbara Guest. The author also discusses the work of many male writers who were associated with the school from a feminist perspective. Maggie Nelson is also the author of *The Red Parts: A Memoir*.

Where it's reviewed:
London Review of Bookbs, Decemer 3, 2009, page 33

Other books by the same author:
Something Bright, Then Holes, 2007
The Latest Winter, 2003
Shiner, 2001

Other books you might like:
Eileen Myles, *Chelsea Girls*, 1994
Maggie Nelson, *Bluets*, 2009
Alice Notley, *Alma, or The Dead Women*, 2006
Alice Notley, *The Descent of Alette*, 1996
Alice Notley, *Grave of Light: New and Selected Poems, 1970-2005*, 2006

97

ALEXANDER NEMEROV

Acting in the Night: Macbeth and the Places of the Civil War

(Berkeley: University of California Press, 2010)

Subject(s): United States Civil War, 1861-1865; Theater; Shakespeare, William

Summary: In *Acting in the Night: Macbeth and the Places of the Civil War*, art history professor Alexander Nemerov uses a 1863 performance of Shakespeare's classic play to illustrate the American political turbulence of the era. The play was produced in Washington, D.C., with Abraham Lincoln in the audience, in the hopes that the performance would open eyes and raise questions about the nature of war, politics, and greed. With America on the brink of the Civil War, this one play valiantly attempted to provoke and generate discussion in a time of great fear and uncertainty. Nemerov's chronicle shows how art tries—and sometimes fails—to change the world. *Acting in the Night* includes a bibliography and a full index.

Other books by the same author:
Icons of Grief: Val Lewton's Home Front Pictures, 2005
Frederic Remington: The Color of Night, 2003
The Body of Raphaelle Peale: Still Life and Selfhood, 1812-1824, 2001

Other books you might like:
Nancy K. Anderson, *Frederic Remington: The Color of Night*, 2003
Martin A. Berger, *Man Made: Thomas Eakins and the Construction of Gilded Age Manhood*, 2000
Rachael Ziady DeLue, *George Inness and the Science of Landscape*, 2007
Alexander Nemerov, *Icons of Grief: Val Lewton's Home Front Pictures*, 2005

98

GIDEON NISBET

Ancient Greece in Film and Popular Culture

(Exeter, Devon, United Kingdom: Bristol Phoenix, 2006)

Subject(s): Ancient Greek civilization; Movie industry; Popular culture

Summary: From big budget Hollywood epics to Sunday morning cartoon strips, the world of Ancient Greece has served as a powerful setting for historical storytelling. In *Ancient Greece in Film and Popular Culture*, author Gideon Nisbet looks at the history of the ancient Greek world—not through conventional historical recounting but through the lens of 20th-century pop culture. Nisbet examines the numerous ways modern storytellers have reshaped, reused, and reimagined some of the most legendary figures and events in Greek history and what this says about contemporary audiences. *Ancient Greece*

in Film and Popular Culture includes a bibliography and a full index.

Where it's reviewed:
Film & History, Fall 2009, pages 85-86

Other books by the same author:
Epigram: Volume 38, 2010
Rome On Film: A Reader, 2010
Greek Epigram in the Roman Empire: Martial's Forgotten Rivals, 2004

Other books you might like:
John Camp, *The World of the Ancient Greeks*, 2010
Paul Cartledge, *Alexander the Great*, 2005
Paul Cartledge, *The Spartans: The World of the Warrior-Heroes of Ancient Greece*, 2004
Elizabeth Fisher, *The World of the Ancient Greeks*, 2010
Herodotus, *The Histories*, 2003
Xenophon Xenophon, *The Persian Expedition*, 1950

99

VORRIS L. NUNLEY

Keepin' It Hushed: The Barbershop and African American Hush Harbor Rhetoric

(Detroit, Michigan: Wayne State University Press, 2010)

Subject(s): African Americans; Blacks; Cultural identity

Summary: In *Keepin' It Hushed: The Barbershop and African American Hush Harbor Rhetoric*, author Vorris L. Nunley explores the significance of the barbershop within African American culture. Long known as a symbol of unity and camaraderie amongst urban men, the barbershop has also served, according to Nunley, as a hush harbor, a safe haven for free speech and freedom of expression in African American communities. The author looks at popular culture's representation of these symbols as well as evidence of the barbershop's role in political, civil rights, and social platforms.

Other books you might like:
Jane Bolgatz, *Talking Race In The Classroom*, 2005
Kermit E. Campbell, *Gettin' Our Groove On: Rhetoric, Language, and Literacy for the Hip Hop Generation*, 2005
Marc Lamont Hill, *Beats, Rhymes, and Classroom Life: Hip-Hop Pedagogy and the Politics of Identity*, 2009
Studs Terkel, *Race*, 1992
Vershawn Ashanti Young, *Your Average Nigga: Performing Race, Literacy, and Masculinity*, 2007

100

MARTHA NUSSBAUM

Not for Profit: Why Democracy Needs the Humanities

(Princeton, New Jersey: Princeton University Press, 2010)

Subject(s): Education; Politics; Educational environment

Summary: In *Not for Profit: Why Democracy Needs the*

Arts and Humanities

Humanities, Martha Nussbaum discusses the liberal arts and educational policies in our society. Her main point throughout the piece is that the liberal arts should be taught at every level. While Nussbaum understands that students need to learn about current events, math, and science, she also believes that they should not lose touch with the liberal arts. Although the liberal arts may not help expand a student's knowledge of historical events, programs in art, theater, and music do help students to grow as individuals, allowing them to view the world from a different perspective. Nussbaum argues that students need the arts to become democratic citizens, and it's the job of educators and politics to keep the liberal arts alive in our nation's schools.

Where it's reviewed:
Booklist, May 1, 2010, page 61
New York Times Book Review, July 26, 2010, page 77
Publishers Weekly, April 26, 2010, page 104

Other books by the same author:
For Love of Country?, 2002
Women and Human Development, 2001
Cultivating Humanity, 1998

Other books you might like:
Claudia Dreifus, *Higher Education?: How Colleges Are Wasting Our Money and Failing Our Kids—-and What We Can Do About It*, 2010
    Andrew Hacker, co-author
Alex Nicholls, *Social Entrepreneurship: New Models of Sustainable Social Change*, 2008
Martha C. Nussbaum, *Cultivating Humanity: A Classical Defense of Reform in Liberal Education*, 1997
Mark C. Taylor, *Crisis on Campus: A Bold Plan for Reforming Our Colleges and Universities*, 2010

101

DIOG O'CONNELL

New Irish Storytellers: Narrative Strategies in Film

(Wilmington, North Carolina: Intellect, 2010)

Subject(s): Movie industry; Movies; Storytelling

Summary: *New Irish Storytellers: Narrative Strategies in Film* is a critical examination of Irish filmmaking from author Diog O'Connell. In 1993, after a seven-year hiatus, the Irish Film Board was reestablished, ushering in a new era of filmmaking for Ireland. In *New Irish Storytellers*, O'Connell examines the style and techniques for storytelling used in Irish films from 1993 to the present day. O'Connell identifies unique narrative and filmmaking patterns among Irish directors and compares them to their British and American contemporaries, noting the ways that filmmaking has served as a creative outlet for the Irish to express social tensions and frustrations.

Other books you might like:
Ruth Barton, *Keeping it Real: Irish Film and Television*, 2004
Michael Patrick Gillespie, *The Myth of an Irish*

Cinema: Approaching Irish-Themed Films, 2008
Rosa Gonzalez, *Cinema on the Periphery: Contemporary Irish and Spanish Film*, 2010
John Hill, *National Cinemas And World Cinema (Studies in Irish Film)*, 2006
Conn Holohan, *Cinema on the Periphery: Contemporary Irish and Spanish Film*, 2010
Martin McLoone, *Irish Film: The Emergence of a Contemporary Cinema*, 2008
Harvey O'Brien, *Keeping it Real: Irish Film and Television*, 2004
Kevin Rockett, *National Cinemas And World Cinema (Studies in Irish Film)*, 2006

102

MIKELLE S. OMARI-TUNKARA

Manipulating the Sacred: Yoruba Art, Ritual,and Resistance in Brazilian Candomble

(Detroit, Michigan: Wayne State University Press, 2005)

Subject(s): Art; Anthropology; Rituals

Summary: In *Manipulating the Sacred: Yoruba Art, Ritual, and Resistance in Brazilian Candomble*, author Mikelle S. Omari-Tunkara offers an anthropological perspective on the art, customs, and culture of Brazil. In the text, Omari-Tunkara focuses on the Bahai region's candomble, a type of temple devoted to the African-rooted spiritual ideology that unites cultural beliefs from several religions. Omari-Tunkara immersed herself in the local culture to obtain a complete understanding of the people who populate this unique region. The author also explores how traditional European-based cultures are eschewed in favor of African culture.

Where it's reviewed:
African Arts, Summer 2007, pages 94-95

Other books you might like:
Patrick Bellegarde-Smith, *Haitian Vodou: Spirit, Myth, and Reality*, 2006
David H. Brown, *Santeria Enthroned: Art, Ritual, and Innovation in an Afro-Cuban Religion*, 2003
Paul Christopher Johnson, *Secrets, Gossip, and Gods: The Transformation of Brazilian Candomble*, 2005
Jacob K. Olupona, *Orisa Devotion as World Religion: The Globalization of Yoruba Religious Culture*, 2008
Lizabeth Paravisini-Gebert, *Creole Religions of the Caribbean: An Introduction from Vodou and Santeria to Obeah and Espiritismo*, 2003
Terry Rey, *Orisa Devotion as World Religion: The Globalization of Yoruba Religious Culture*, 2008

103

ANNE-MARIE OOMEN

An American Map

(Detroit, Michigan: Wayne State University Press, 2010)

Subject(s): Travel; Adventure; Writing

Summary: *An American Map* is a collection of essays by Anne-Marie Oomen. In the essays, Oomen chronicles her travels across America, in an attempt to get over her writer's block and rediscover a sense of adventure after spending many years at home in Michigan. She travels to both urban and rural locations, each time considering how her experiences and lessons in these places could be applied to the larger, cultural American experience. For instance, during a visit to the Smoky Mountains, she considers how the mountains might offer a new perspective on the war in Iraq; a broken-down military tank makes her consider ways to help endangered turtles. This deeply personal collection of essays provides new insight into the American landscape.

Where it's reviewed:
ForeWord, May 19, 2010

Other books by the same author:
House of Fields, 2006
Uncoded Woman: Poems, 2006
Pulling Down the Barn, 2004

Other books you might like:
Bill Bryson, *Bill Bryson's African Diary*, 2002
Bill Bryson, *I'm a Stranger Here Myself: Notes on Returning to America After 20 Years Away*, 1999
Bill Bryson, *Neither Here nor There: Travels in Europe*, 1990
Bill Bryson, *A Walk in the Woods*, 1998
Bonnie Jo Campbell, *American Salvage: Stories*, 2009

104

GREGORY ORFALEA

Angeleno Days: An Arab American Writer on Family, Place, and Politics

(Tucson, Arizona: University of Arizona Press, 2009)

Subject(s): Autobiographies; United States; Teaching

Summary: *Angeleno Days: An Arab American Writer on Family, Place, and Politics* is a collection of emotional essays from author Gregory Orfalea. The pieces included in this book were originally published in the *Los Angeles Times Magazine* and are compiled together here for the first time. Orfalea, an Arab American man, recounts his experiences in Los Angeles, where he onced lived as a child. As an adult, Orfalea returned to LA to become a teacher. In *Angeleno Days*, he recounts the challenges and obstacles he must overcome in Los Angeles as he creates a new life for himself and comes to terms with his shocking, painful past.

Other books by the same author:
The Man Who Guarded the Bomb, 2010
The Arab Americans: A History, 2006
Messengers of the Lost Battalion, 1999

Other books you might like:
Sarah Gualtieri, *Between Arab and White: Race and Ethnicity in the Early Syrian American Diaspora*, 2009
Pierrette Hondagneu-Sotelo, *Domestica: Immigrant*

Workers Cleaning and Caring in the Shadows of Affluence, 2007
Alixa Naff, *Becoming American: The Early Arab Immigrant Experience*, 1993
Nina Revoyr, *Southland*, 2003
George J. Sanchez, *Becoming Mexican American: Ethnicity, Culture and Identity in Chicano Los Angeles, 1900-1945*, 1995

105

PETER ORNER

Underground America: Narratives of Undocumented Lives

(San Francisco, California: McSweeney's, 2008)

Subject(s): Work environment; Working conditions; United States

Summary: *Underground America: Narratives of Undocumented Lives* tells the stories of numerous illegal aliens living in the United States. In the book, 25 illegal aliens tell stories about their experiences in the United States. These people are from numerous countries, and they describe what their lives and living conditions are like in the U.S. Many of the aliens work in dangerous, tedious jobs. They often get paid less than other workers, and they are denied the benefits that most full-time workers receive. *Underground America* helps tell the story of people who usually do not have a voice in the media.

Where it's reviewed:
The Houston Chronicle, July 27, 2008, page 14

Other books by the same author:
The Second Coming of Mavala Shikongo: A Novel, 2007
Esther Stories, 2001

Other books you might like:
Dave Eggers, *Surviving Justice: America's Wrongfully Convicted and Exonerated*, 2005
Clare Howell, *GenderQueer: Voices From Beyond the Sexual Binary*, 2002
Sonja Linden, *I Have Before Me a Remarkable Document Given To Me By a Young Lady From Rwanda*, 2005
Joan Nestle, *GenderQueer: Voices From Beyond the Sexual Binary*, 2002
Lola Vollen, *Surviving Justice: America's Wrongfully Convicted and Exonerated*, 2005
Lola Vollen, *Voices from the Storm: The People of New Orleans on Hurricane Katrina and Its Aftermath*, 2006
Craig Walzer, *Out of Exile: Narratives from the Abducted and Displaced People of Sudan*, 2009
Riki Wilchins, *GenderQueer: Voices From Beyond the Sexual Binary*, 2002
Chris Ying, *Voices from the Storm: The People of New Orleans on Hurricane Katrina and Its Aftermath*, 2006

106

DAVID L. PIKE

Metropolis on the Styx: The Underworlds of Modern Urban Culture, 1800-2001

(Ithaca, New York: Cornell University Press, 2007)

Subject(s): Sociology; Modern Life; Literature

Summary: The world of the underground is the focus of this critical analysis by author and literature professor David L. Pike. *Metropolis on the Styx: The Underworlds of Modern Urban Culture, 1800-2001* illuminates the ways underground areas have shaped perspectives on big city life, charting the subterranean constructions of such cities as London and Paris. Pike points out how these spaces have had lasting influences not only on popular viewpoints of urban existence but also on the areas of art, literature, sociology, and psychology. *Metropolis on the Styx* includes illustrations, notes on the text, and an index.

Where it's reviewed:
Nineteenth-Century French Studies, Spring/Summer 2010, pages 281-282

Other books by the same author:
Literature: A World of Writing Stories, Poems, Plays, and Essays, 2010
The Longman Anthology of World Literature, 2008
Passage Through Hell, 1997

Other books you might like:
Neil Gaiman, *Neverwhere*, 1997
Mark Ovenden, *Paris Underground: The Maps, Stations, and Design of the Metro*, 2009
Liza Picard, *Victorian London: The Tale of a City 1840—1870*, 2007
David Pike, *Subterranean Cities: The World Beneath Paris and London, 1800-1945*, 2005
Donald Reid, *Paris Sewers and Sewermen: Realities and Representations*, 1991

107

PHIL POWRIE
ROBYNN STILWELL , Co-Editor

Changing Tunes: The Use of Pre-existing Music in Film

(Burlington, Vermont: Ashgate, 2006)

Subject(s): Music; Movies; Criticism

Summary: In *Changing Tunes: The Use of Pre-existing Music in Film*, editors Phil Powrie and Robynn Stilwell present a series of essays examining music—not specifically recorded for film—that is used in soundtracks for a range of movies. Twelve music and film experts contribute pieces to this all-encompassing collection, which tackles instrumental, classical, opera, and popular music and how these styles fit into the storylines and atmo-

spheres of various films. *Changing Tunes* includes musical examples, a filmography, a bibliography, and an index.

Where it's reviewed:
Music, Sound, and the Moving Image, Autumn 2007, pages 193-199

Other books by the same author:
The Trouble with Men: Masculinities in European and Hollywood Cinema, 2004
French Cinema: A Student's Guide, 2002
French Cinema in the 1990s: Continuity and Difference, 2000

Other books you might like:
Doug Adams, *The Music of The Lord of the Rings Films: A Comprehensive Account of Howard Shore's Scores*, 2010
Mervyn Cooke, *A History of Film Music*, 2008
Richard Dyer, *Nino Rota: Music, Film and Feeling*, 2010
Roger Hickman, *Reel Music: Exploring 100 Years of Film Music*, 2010
Pauline Reay, *Music in Film: Soundtracks and Synergy*, 2004

108

BRIAN PRICE
JOHN DAVID RHODES , Co-Editor

On Michael Haneke

(Detroit, Michigan: Wayne State University Press, 2010)

Subject(s): Movies; Movie industry; Criticism

Summary: *On Michael Haneke* is a collection of essays, edited by Brian Price and John David Rhodes. Each of the essays features Austrian filmmaker Michael Haneke as the subject. Haneke is considered to be one of the most influential contemporary filmmakers, whose stylistic films address important social questions. The essays presented in this book are scholarly critiques of Haneke's films and work. The book is divided into three sections: "Violence and Play," where the violence often seen in Haneke's films is discussed symbolically; "Style and Media," which discusses Haneke's own style and his influences; and "Culture and Conflict," which explores historical and cultural issues that are often represented in the films.

Other books you might like:
Peter Brunette, *Michael Haneke*, 2010
Roy Grundmann, *A Companion to Michael Haneke*, 2010
Alexander D. Ornella, *Fascinatingly Disturbing: Interdisciplinary Perspectives on Michael Haneke's Cinema*, 2010
Oliver C. Speck, *Funny Frames: The Filmic Concepts of Michael Haneke*, 2010
Catherine Wheatley, *Michael Haneke Cinema: The Ethic of the Image*, 2009

109

DAVID A. PRICE

The Pixar Touch

(New York: Alfred A. Knopf, 2008)

Subject(s): Animation (Cinematography); Cartoons; Entertainment industry

Summary: In *The Pixar Touch*, author David A. Price provides a detailed look at the history of Pixar, the studio known for transforming animated films in the late 1990s and early 2000s with movies such as *Toy Story* and *A Bug's Life*. Price gives readers a behind-the-scenes look at the studio that grew from a small computer division at Lucasfilm and eventually became a huge corporation in its own right. The author also provides a glimpse at the studio's founder, Ed Catmull, and his dealings throughout the years with Apple's Steve Jobs and animator John Lasseter. Price is also the author of *Love and Hate in Jamestown: John Smith, Pocahontas, and the Start of a New Nation*.

Where it's reviewed:
New York Times Book Review, June 22, 2008

Other books by the same author:
Love and Hate in Jamestown, 2005

Other books you might like:
John Lasseter, *Toy Story The Art and Making of the Animated Film*, 2009
Karen Paik, *To Infinity and Beyond!: The Story of Pixar Animation Studios*, 2007

110

HILARY RADNER
ALISTAIR FOX , Co-Editor
IRENE BESSIERE , Co-Editor

Jane Campion: Cinema, Nation, Identity

(Detroit, Michigan: Wayne State University Press, 2009)

Subject(s): Criticism; Movies; Women

Summary: *Jane Campion: Cinema, Nation, Identity* is a collection of essays edited by Hilary Radner, Alistair Fox, and Irene Bessiere. All of the essay focus on New Zealand filmmaker Jane Campion. These are critical, scholarly essays examining Campion's films and the manner in which she chooses to direct. The book is divided into three sections. The first section focuses on some of her films specifically, considering the points of view of her characters and the way Campion explores the theme of identity. The second section is concentrated on Campion's influences, from her love of literature to her relationship with New Zealand. The third and final section discusses the feminist themes often found in Campion's work and the way the physical settings of the films are often symbolically representative of larger ideas.

Where it's reviewed:
Reference & Research Book News, November 2009

Other books by the same author:
Neo-Feminist Cinema: Girly Films, Chick Flicks, and Consumer Culture, 2010
Cinema Genre, 2008
Siegfried Sassoon: The Journey From The Trenches, A Biography (1918-1967), 2004

Other books you might like:
Jane Campion, *Jane Campion: Interviews*, 1999
Jane Campion, *The Piano*, 1994
Kathleen McHugh, *Jane Campion*, 2007
    Dana B. Polan, co-author
Kate Pullinger, *The Piano*, 1994
Estella Tincknell, *Viewing Jane Campion: Angels, Demons and Unsettling Voices*, 2010

111

JOHN RAEBURN

A Staggering Revolution: A Cultural History of Thirties Photography

(Chicago: University of Illinois Press, 2006)

Subject(s): Photography; Criticism; History

Summary: Author John Raeburn examines the vibrant history and lasting influence of the photography of the 1930s. *A Staggering Revolution: A Cultural History of Thirties Photography* explores this energetic era in the evolution of photography as an art form, which saw radical changes in the way photos were shot. From studies of Edward Steichen and his images of celebrities to the photos-as-documents of Margaret Bourke White, this volume celebrates a period in photography that revitalized and revolutionized the art form.

Where it's reviewed:
The Art Bulletin, September 2007, pages 601-604

Other books by the same author:
Ben Shahn's American Scene, 2010
Fame Became of Him, 1984

Other books you might like:
James Agee, *Let Us Now Praise Famous Men: Three Tenant Families*, 1939
Erskine Caldwell, *You Have Seen Their Faces*, 1995
Susan Sontag, *On Photography*, 1977
William Stott, *Documentary Expression and Thirties America*, 1986
Alan Trachtenberg, *Reading American Photographs: Images As History, Mathew Brady to Walker Evans*, 1990

112

SONYA RAMSEY

Reading, Writing, and Segregation: A Century of Black Women Teachers in Nashville

(Urbana, Illinois: University of Illinois Press, 2008)

Subject(s): Teachers; African Americans; Southern United States

Summary: Written by Sonya Ramsey, *Reading, Writing, and Segregation: A Century of Black Women Teachers in Nashville* is an examination of the experiences of African American educators living and working in the Southern United States during the segregation and integration of schools. Ramsey chronicles the history of black teachers in Nashville, Tennessee, from the establishment of segregated schooling in 1867 through the desegregation efforts and subsequent fallout that lasted until 1983. Relying on interviews with both black and white teachers, Ramsey paints a comprehensive picture of life, education, and family of African American educators during this century of tumultuous social change.

Where it's reviewed:
The Journal of African American History, Spring 2009, page 299

Other books you might like:
John Blake, *Children of the Movement*, 2007
Steve Estes, *I Am a Man!: Race, Manhood, and the Civil Rights Movement*, 2005
Adam Fairclough, *A Class of Their Own: Black Teachers in the Segregated South*, 2007
Devin Fergus, *Liberalism, Black Power, and the Making of American Politics, 1965-1980*, 2009
Troy Jackson, *Becoming King: Martin Luther King Jr. and the Making of a National Leader*, 2008

113

ROBERT D. RICHARDSON

First We Read, Then We Write: Emerson on the Creative Process

(Iowa City, Iowa: University of Iowa Press, 2009)

Subject(s): Books and reading; Writing; Writers

Summary: The life and work of 19th century writer and philosopher Ralph Waldo Emerson was devoted to the world of words. In *First We Read, Then We Write: Emerson on the Creative Process*, award-winning author Robert D. Richardson probes the artistic practices of the great writer, focusing specifically on his fascination with the powerful link between reading and the crafting of good writing. Drawing from Emerson's own diaries, Richardson takes readers deep into the brilliant mind of the legendary figure, showing how reading and writing informed and shaped nearly every aspect of his adult life. *First We Read, Then We Write* includes a bibliography and an index.

Where it's reviewed:
Colorado Review, Spring 2010, page 150

Other books by the same author:
William James: In the Maelstrom of American Modernism, 2006
Emerson: The Mind on Fire, 1996
Henry Thoreau: A Life of the Mind, 1988

Other books you might like:
Brooks Atkinson, *The Essential Writings of Ralph Waldo Emerson*, 2000
Ralph Waldo Emerson, co-author
Lyndall Gordon, *Lives Like Loaded Guns: Emily Dickinson and her Family's Feuds*, 2010
Robert D. Richardson Jr., *Henry Thoreau: A Life of the Mind*, 1986
Robert D. Richardson, *Emerson: The Mind on Fire*, 1995
Robert D. Richardson, *William James: In the Maelstrom of American Modernism*, 2006

114

GILLIAN M. RODGER

Champagne Charlie and Pretty Jemima: Variety Theater in the Nineteenth Century

(Urbana, Illinois: University of Illinois Press, 2010)

Story type: Historical
Subject(s): Entertainment industry; Theater; History

Summary: In *Champagne Charlie and Pretty Jemima: Variety Theater in the Nineteenth Century*, professor and author Gillian M. Rodger presents a detailed history of the origins and popularity of variety theater. During the mid-19th century, variety musical theater emerged as a means of hilarious, creative, and bawdy entertainment and social commentary. Variety entertained audiences while also making observations on gender differences, sexuality, racism, and class divisions. Rodger examines the birth of this entertainment medium, its far-reaching popularity, its key players and performers, and how it ultimately paved the way for 20th-century entertainment, such as vaudeville and comedy performances on radio and television.

Other books you might like:
Susan G. Davis, *Parades and Power: Street Theatre in Nineteenth-Century Philadelphia*, 1988
Tracy C. Davis, *The Performing Century: Nineteenth-Century Theatre's History*, 2010
David Thatcher Gies, *The Theatre in Nineteenth-Century Spain*, 2005
Peter Holland, *The Performing Century: Nineteenth-Century Theatre's History*, 2010
John McCormick, *Popular Theatres of Nineteenth Century France*, 1993
Philip Sadgrove, *The Egyptian Theatre in the Nineteenth Century (1799-1882)*, 2007

115

IVAN SANCHEZ
LUIS "DJ DISCO WIZ" CEDENO , Co-Author

It's Just Begun: The Epic Journey of DJ Disco Wiz, Hip Hop's First Latino DJ

(Brooklyn: powerHouse Books, 2009)

Subject(s): Music; Popular culture; Hispanic Americans

Summary: Deejay Luis "DJ Disco Wiz" Cedeno teams up with author Ivan Sanchez to tell the story of his turbulent life and the pivotal role hip hop music played in his eventual rescue. *It's Just Begun: The Epic Journey of DJ Disco Wiz, Hip Hop's First Latino DJ* looks at Cedeno's early years growing up in the poorest sections of New York City, struggling to deal with an alcoholic father and a terminally ill mother. Though he found escape in deejaying during the inaugural years of hip hop, the pull of the streets eventually landed Cedeno in prison on a murder rap. This is the story of one man's road to acceptance—and the potholes and speed bumps he encountered along the way to become a defining voice in hip hop culture. First book.

Where it's reviewed:
Journal of Popular Culture, April 2010, pages 424-425

Other books by the same author:
Next Stop: Growing Up Wild-Style in the Bronx, 2008

Other books you might like:
Iesha Brown, *The Story Of The Beginning and End Of The First Hip Hop Female MC...Luminary Icon Sha-Rock*, 2010
KRS-One KRS-One, *The Gospel of Hip Hop: The First Instrument*, 2009
Johan Kugelberg, *Born in the Bronx: A Visual Record of the Early Days of Hip Hop*, 2007
Sha Rock, *The Story Of The Beginning and End Of The First Hip Hop Female MC...Luminary Icon Sha-Rock*, 2010
Ivan Sanchez, *Next Stop: Growing Up Wild-Style in the Bronx*, 2008
Sheri Sher, *Mercedes Ladies*, 2008

116

STEVEN SANDERS

Miami Vice

(Detroit, Michigan: Wayne State University Press, 2010)

Subject(s): Popular culture; Television; Criticism

Summary: In *Miami Vice*, Steven Sanders explores the history of the popular television show from a critical perspective, considering the themes found throughout the show as well as its influences and impact on popular culture. Sanders argues that *Miami Vice* was inspired by classic film noir and neo-noir, classifying the program itself as a type of "TV noir." He identifies the themes of alienation, redemption, and personal identity as well as existentialist and postmodern motifs in a number of episodes. Sanders also considers the setting of Miami Beach as a character in itself, and he examines other topics surrounding the production of the popular television show and the ways in which it impacted future television programs.

Other books by the same author:
The Philosophy of Science Fiction Film (The Philosophy of Popular Culture), 2009
The Philosophy of TV Noir (The Philosophy of Popular Culture), 2008
Five Fists of Science, 2006

Other books you might like:
Thomas Foltyn, *Unofficial "Miami Vice" Episode Guide*, 2009
Stephen Grave, *Miami Vice #1: The Florida Burn*, 1985
Stephen Grave, *Miami Vice #2: Vengence Game*, 1985
Trish Janeshutz, *Making of Miami Vice*, 1986
John-Paul Trutnau, *A One-Man Show? The Construction and Deconstruction of a Patriarchal Image in the Reagan Era: Reading the Audio-Visual Poetics of Miami Vice*, 2005

117

CIA SAUTTER

The Miriam Tradition: Teaching Embodied Torah

(Urbana, Illinois: University of Illinois Press, 2010)

Story type: Historical; Religious
Subject(s): Dance; Religion; Values (Philosophy)

Summary: Written by author Cia Sautter, *The Miriam Tradition: Teaching Embodied Torah* is an examination of the use of dance to promote and instruct personal or religious values and beliefs. In the book, Sautter contends that movement is crucial in the formation of religious values. *The Miriam Tradition* examines the practices of the Sephardic Jews who followed the example of Miriam, the prophetess, and used ritualistic dances to celebrate Jewish events. These women—who were known as tanyaderas—used dance, movement, and music to teach other people about Judaism.

Other books you might like:
Maggie Anton, *Rashi's Daughters, Book II: Miriam: A Novel of Love and the Talmud in Medieval France*, 2007
Michael Berg, *The Way: Using the Wisdom of Kabbalah for Spiritual Transformation and Fulfillment*, 2001
Ellen Frankel, *Five Books of Miriam: A Woman Commentary on the Torah*, 1997
Daniel C. Matt, *The Essential Kabbalah: The Heart of Jewish Mysticism*, 1996
Miriam Millhauser, *Inner Torah: Where Consciousness and Kedushah Meet*, 2004

118

MARLIS SCHWEITZER

When Broadway Was the Runway: Theater, Fashion and American Culture

(Philadelphia: University of Pennsylvania Press, 2009)

Subject(s): Theater; Fashion; Popular culture

Summary: Theater expert Marlis Schweitzer investigates the rich relationship between fashion, consumerism, and the world of the American theater. *When Broadway Was the Runway: Theater, Fashion and American Culture* chronicles the history of theater as a springboard for emerging cultural trends. In an era before Hollywood premieres and Tinseltown starlets set standards for fashion and style, the Great White Way was the definitive starting point for the showcasing of these elements. Schweitzer charts this largely forgotten history, illuminating another aspect of theater's vital place in American society. *When Broadway Was the Runway* includes a bibliography and an index. First book.

Where it's reviewed:
Journal of Popular Culture, February 2010, pages 201-203

Other books you might like:
Pamela Golbin, *Madeleine Vionnet*, 2009
Amy de la Haye, *Lucile: London, Paris, New York and Chicago*, 2009
Lucy Johnston, *Nineteenth Century Fashion in Detail*, 2009
Valerie D. Mendes, *Lucile: London, Paris, New York and Chicago*, 2009
Valerie D. Mendes, *Twentieth-Century Fashion in Detail*, 2009
Caroline Weber, *Queen of Fashion: What Marie Antoinette Wore to the Revolution*, 2006
Claire Wilcox, *Twentieth-Century Fashion in Detail*, 2009

119

BONNIE KIME SCOTT

Gender in Modernism: New Geographies, Complex Intersections

(Urbana, Illinois: University of Illinois Press, 2007)

Story type: Collection
Subject(s): Feminism; Modern Life; Writers

Summary: Edited by Bonnie Kime Scott, *Gender in Modernism: New Geographies, Complex Intersections* is a collection of the best essays and texts dealing with feminism and modernism from the past fifteen years. The book is intended to be a sequel to Scott's *The Gender of Modernism*, released in 1990. The written pieces included in this sequel are divided into 21 thematic sections dealing with issues as diverse as suffrage, sex wars, lesbian politics, left-wing writers, and

modern art forms such as dance, drama, film, and painting. Contributors include Ann Ardis, Nancy Berke, Barbara Green, Suzette A. Henke, Claire M. Tylee, and Gay Wachman.

Other books by the same author:
Refiguring Modernism, Volume 1: Women of 1928, 1995
The Gender of Modernism: A Critical Anthology, 1990
New Alliances in Joyce Studies: When Its Aped to Foul a Dephian, 1988

Other books you might like:
Djuna Barnes, *Nightwood*, 2006
Richard Begam, *Modernism and Colonialism: British and Irish Literature, 1899[e28026]ldquo;1939*, 2007
Mary Lynn Broe, *The Gender of Modernism: A Critical Anthology*, 1990
Rita Felski, *The Gender of Modernity*, 1995
Michael Valdez Moses, *Modernism and Colonialism: British and Irish Literature, 1899[e28026]ldquo;1939*, 2007
Jean Rhys, *Voyage in the Dark*, 1994

120

TIM JON SEMMERLING

"Evil" Arabs in American Popular Film: Orientalist Fear

(Austin, Texas: University of Texas Press, 2006)

Subject(s): Movies; Ethnicity; Criticism

Summary: In *"Evil" Arabs in American Popular Film: Orientalist Fear*, author Tim Jon Semmerling blasts apart a commonly held stereotype and a frequent moviemaking device: Arabs as "the bad guys." This volume blends social commentary and film criticism to delve into the subject, shedding light on the numerous ways the American public has been misled about the true nature of Arab peoples. Semmerling's study contains examinations of six films, including *The Exorcist*, *Rules of Engagement*, and *South Park: Bigger, Longer & Uncut*, as well as a CNN documentary on the 9/11 attacks. *"Evil" Arabs in American Popular Film* includes a bibliography and an index.

Other books by the same author:
Israeli and Palestinian Postcards, 2004

Other books you might like:
Amaney Jamal, *Race and Arab Americans Before and After 9/11: From Invisible Citizens to Visible Subjects*, 2007
Lina Khatib, *Filming the Modern Middle East: Politics in the Cinemas of Hollywood and the Arab World*, 2006
Nadine Naber, *Race and Arab Americans Before and After 9/11: From Invisible Citizens to Visible Subjects*, 2007
Sheila J. Petty, *Contact Zones: Memory, Origin, and Discourses in Black Diasporic Cinema*, 2008
Jack G. Shaheen, *Guilty: Hollywood's Verdict on Arabs After 9/11*, 2008

Jack Shaheen, *Reel Bad Arabs: How Hollywood Vilifies a People*, 2009

121

DAN SICKO

Techno Rebels: The Renegades of Electronic Funk

(Detroit, Michigan: Wayne State University Press, 2010)

Subject(s): Music; Biographies; Musicians

Summary: *Techno Rebels: The Renegades of Electronic Funk* is a comprehensive history on techno music, from author Dan Sicko. Techno, or electronica, music has its origins in Detroit, Michigan. What started out as a mistake eventually become one of the most unique, celebrated, and popular genres of music in the late 20th century. Sicko gives readers a thorough background on this different style of music and how it came to be created and spread to the masses. He highlights the key people involved with the birth and development of techno music and what social circumstances helped propel it to greater success and acceptance. *Techno Rebels* is an authoritative examination on an unusual but important style of musical expression.

Where it's reviewed:
California Bookwatch, May 2010
Reference & Research Book News, August 2010

Other books you might like:
Bill Brewster, *Last Night a DJ Saved My Life: The History of the Disc Jockey*, 2000
   Frank Broughton, co-author
Matthew Collin, *Altered State, Updated Edition: The Story of Ecstasy Culture and Acid House*, 1998
   John Godfrey, co-author
Simon Reynolds, *Generation Ecstasy : Into the World of Techno and Rave Culture*, 1999
Peter Shapiro, *Modulations: A History of Electronic Music: Throbbing Words on Sound*, 2000
Timothy D. Taylor, *Strange Sounds: Music, Technology and Culture*, 2001

122

CARMEN GIMENEZ SMITH

Bring Down the Little Birds: On Mothering, Art, Work and Everything Else

(Tucson, Arizona: University of Arizona Press, 2010)

Subject(s): Autobiographies; Mother-daughter relations; Mothers

Summary: *Bring Down the Little Birds: On Mothering, Art, Work and Everything Else* is a moving memoir about life, parenting, creativity, and illness from author Carmen Gimenez Smith. As a poet, an editor, a professor, and a mother to one child, Smith was already struggling to find balance between her professional career and her family life. Pregnant with a second baby, Smith received news that her mother was suffering from a brain tumor and Alzheimer's. In *Bring Down the Little Birds*, she shares her personal thoughts, feelings, and challenges as she tried to balance the various roles and responsibilities in her life. Ultimately, this memoir is an emotional and insightful examination of motherhood, pregnancy, illness, art, and work.

Other books by the same author:
Odalisque in Pieces, 2009
David Smith: A Centennial, 2006

Other books you might like:
Eula Biss, *Notes from No Man's Land: American Essays*, 2009
Judith Butler, *Gender Trouble: Feminism and the Subversion of Identity*, 1990
Don DeLillo, *Point Omega: A Novel*, 2010
Evan Lavender-Smith, *From Old Notebooks*, 2010
Carmen Gimenez Smith, *Odalisque in Pieces*, 2009

123

MATTHEW SOLOMON

Disappearing Tricks: Silent Film, Houdini, and the New Magic of the Twentieth Century

(Urbana, Illinois: University of Illinois Press, 2010)

Story type: Historical
Subject(s): Movie industry; Movies; Magic

Summary: Matthew Solomon's *Disappearing Tricks: Silent Film, Houdini, and the New Magic of the Twentieth Century* is an examination of how professional magicians shaped the early development of cinema. Solomon revisits the silent film era to showcase the pivotal role that professional illusionists played in the creation of movies from 1895 to 1929. Presenting a detailed history of the origins of cinema in the United States and France, *Disappearing Tricks* highlights the works of Harry Houdini and Georges Melies, two men who utilized theatrical magic to create special effects and groundbreaking entertainment that helped boost film's appeal.

Other books you might like:
Mike Caveney, *Magic 1400s-1950s*, 2009
Glen David Gold, *Carter Beats the Devil*, 2001
Harry Houdini, *On Deception*, 2009
Ricky Jay, *Magic 1400s-1950s*, 2009
William Kalush, *The Secret Life of Houdini: The Making of America's First Superhero*, 2007
Brooke Kamin Rapaport, *Houdini: Art and Magic*, 2010
Larry Sloman, *The Secret Life of Houdini: The Making of America's First Superhero*, 2007
Jim Steinmeyer, *Magic 1400s-1950s*, 2009

124

JORDAN SOMMERS
JUSTYN BARNES , Co-Editor

The Official Michael Jackson Opus

(London: OPUS Media Group, 2009)

Subject(s): Entertainment industry; Music; Popular culture

Summary: *The Official Michael Jackson Opus* is a commemorative, leather-bound book that was designed as a tribute to entertainer Michael Jackson, known to popular music fans as the King of Pop. This book is the only book officially approved and issued by Michael Jackson's estate. *The Official Michael Jackson Opus* contains more than 400 pages of photographs and essays about one of the most famous artists of the 20th century, as well as illustrations by Nate Giorgio and David Nordahl. This book was edited by biographer Jordan Sommers and sports historian Justyn Barnes.

Where it's reviewed:
Entertainment Weekly, December 18, 2009, page 87

Other books by the same author:
The New War, 2008

Other books you might like:
EBONY Magazine, *Ebony Special Tribute: Michael Jackson In His Own Words*, 2009
Nelson George, *Thriller: The Musical Life of Michael Jackson*, 2010
Todd Gray, *Michael Jackson: Before He Was King*, 2009
Henry Leutwyler, *Neverland Lost: A Portrait of Michael Jackson*, 2010
Chris Roberts, *Michael Jackson: The King of Pop 1958-2009*, 2010

125

SHEILA A. SPECTOR

Byron and the Jews

(Detroit, Michigan: Wayne State University Press, 2010)

Subject(s): Poetry; Criticism; Jews

Summary: In *Byron and the Jews*, Sheila A. Spector provides a scholarly examination of Lord Byron's poetry and explains why his poetry seemed to resonate with Jewish readers. In this text, Spector analyses the relationship between Byron and the Jewish population. Many of Byron's works were translated into Hebrew and Yiddish, a fact that sets him apart from many other British poets of his era. Spector describes the spiritual meaning that many of Byron's poems held for Jewish readers. However, the author notes that many of these readers may have ascribed religious meaning to the Hebrew and Yiddish translations of Byron's poems, even though this was not what the poet originally intended. Spector also includes various translations of Byron's work, which are often very difficult to find.

Other books by the same author:
Glorious Incomprehensible, 2001
Wonders Divine, 2001

Other books you might like:
George Gordon Byron, *Lord Byron: The Major Works*, 2008
Benita Eisler, *Byron: Child of Passion, Fool of Fame*, 2000
John Galt, *The Life of Lord Byron*, 2010
Fiona MacCarthy, *Byron: Life and Legend*, 2004
Thomas Moore, *Life of Lord Byron, Vol. 1: With His Letters and Journals*, 2010

126

LYNN SPIGEL

TV by Design: Modern Art and the Rise of Network Television

(Chicago: University Of Chicago Press, 2008)

Subject(s): Television; Art; Popular culture

Summary: In *TV by Design: Modern Art and the Rise of Network Television*, author and professor Lynn Spigel sheds light on the often overlooked relationship between television and the visual arts during the mid-20th century. Spigel points out the ways television shows introduced a vast section of the American viewing audience to the latest developments, movements, and styles in the world of modern art and design. This volume looks at the television representations of contemporary architecture, abstract art, and pop art—to name just a few—and how these art forms educated and illuminated the television-watching masses. *TV by Design* includes notes on the text and an index.

Where it's reviewed:
Journal of Popular Culture, April 2010, pages 434-436

Other books by the same author:
Welcome to the Dreamhouse, 2001
Make Room for TV: Television and the Family Ideal in Postwar America, 1992

Other books you might like:
James L. Baughman, *Same Time, Same Station: Creating American Television, 1948-1961*, 2007
Aniko Bodroghkozy, *Groove Tube: Sixties Television and the Youth Rebellion*, 2001
Lynn Spigel, *Make Room for TV: Television and the Family Ideal in Postwar America*, 1992
Jinna Tay, *Television Studies After TV: Understanding Television in the Post-Broadcast Era*, 2009
Graeme Turner, co-author
Raymond Williams, *Television: Technology and Cultural Form*, 2003

127

MICHAEL SRAGOW

Victor Fleming: An American Movie Master

(New York: Pantheon Books, 2008)

Subject(s): Movie industry; Entertainment industry; Biographies

Summary: In *Victor Fleming: An American Movie Master*, biographer Michael Sragow celebrates the life and films of Hollywood director Victor Fleming. Fleming is noted for making some of the most influential and well-known films of the mid-20th century, including *Gone with the Wind*, *The Virginian*, and *Dr. Jekyll and Mr. Hyde*. Sragow also delves deeper into the director's inner psyche, giving readers a glimpse at the director's personal life, which included romances with Ingrid Bergman and Clara Bow. Movie critic Michael Sragow has also contributed to the *New Yorker*, *Salon*, and *Rolling Stone*.

Where it's reviewed:
The Atlantic, March 2009, page 104
Booklist, December 1, 2008, page 12
Entertainment Weekly, December 19, 2008, page 67
Library Journal, November 15, 2008, page 74
Los Angeles Magazine, December 2008, page 112

Other books you might like:
Scott Eyman, *Lion of Hollywood: The Life and Legend of Louis B. Mayer*, 2005
Molly Haskell, *Frankly, My Dear: "Gone with the Wind" Revisited*, 2009
Jessica Rains, *Claude Rains: An Actor's Voice*, 2008
David J. Skal, co-author
Mark A. Vieira, *Hollywood Dreams Made Real: Irving Thalberg and the Rise of M-G-M*, 2009
Mark A. Vieira, *Irving Thalberg: Boy Wonder to Producer Prince*, 2009

128

SHARON MCKENZIE STEVENS

A Place for Dialogue: Language, Land Use, and Politics in Southern Arizona

(Iowa City, Iowa: University of Iowa Press, 2007)

Subject(s): United States; Politics; Ecology

Summary: The politics of land use take center stage in Sharon McKenzie Stevens's study of the rhetoric, reality, and relationships that make up Southern Arizona life. *A Place for Dialogue: Language, Land Use, and Politics in Southern Arizona* examines the alliances and incongruities inherent in the public land administration and shows how the vagaries of language have stunning implications on the subject. Stevens also explores the delicate relationships between environmental activists, ranchers, and a series of other diverse individuals who must work together for the efficient management of public lands.

Other books you might like:
Gary J. Hausladen, *Western Places, American Myths: How We Think About The West*, 2006
Robert T. Hayashi, *Haunted by Waters: A Journey through Race and Place in the American West*, 2007
William M. Keith, *The Essential Guide to Rhetoric*, 2008
Richard Lanham, *The Electronic Word: Democracy, Technology, and the Arts*, 1993

Andrea A. Lunsford, *Everything's an Argument*, 2010
John J. Ruszkiewicz, co-author
Keith Walters, co-author

129

KAY STONE

Some Day Your Witch Will Come

(Detroit, Michigan: Wayne State University Press, 2008)

Subject(s): Folklore; Fairy tales; Literature

Summary: *Some Day Your Witch Will Come* is a collection of essays written by Kay Stone, an English professor, who has produced a sizable body of scholarly work and literary criticism based largely on folklore and fairy tales. This book, which elucidates the continued importance and value of fairy tales to adults as well as children, is divided into three sections. In the first section, Stone focuses on the role and treatment of women in folklore. The second is devoted to the ways in which traditional fairy tales are retold in contemporary times, and the third section considers the ways that dreams and folk tales can be seen and compared as artistic expressions.

Where it's reviewed:
Reference & Research Book News, November 2008

Other books by the same author:
The Golden Woman, 2004
Burning Brightly, 1998

Other books you might like:
M.T. Anderson, *The Astonishing Life of Octavian Nothing, Traitor to the Nation, Volume One: The Pox Party*, 2006
Stephen Benson, *Contemporary Fiction and the Fairy Tale*, 2008
Ruth B. Bottigheimer, *Fairy Tales: A New History*, 2009
Maria Tatar, *Enchanted Hunters: The Power of Stories in Childhood*, 2008
Catherynne M. Valente, *In the Night Garden*, 2006

130

SARAH STREET

Black Narcissus

(New York: I.B. Tauris, 2005)

Subject(s): Movies; Movie industry; Criticism

Summary: When it was released in 1947, the film *Black Narcissus* created a sensation with its candid portrayal of nuns battling their demons in a remote Himalayan convent. In this critical study, author and film professor Sarah Street presents a comprehensive analysis of *Black Narcissus*. Street delves into the rampant symbolism in the movie and answers long-perplexing questions about the filmmaking process, the casting, and the back story of the classic film. This volume includes notes on the text and a bibliography.

Where it's reviewed:
Journal of Popular Film and Television, Winter 2007, pages 188-189

Other books by the same author:
Film Architecture and the Transnational Imagination: Set Design in 1930s European Cinema, 2007
European Cinema: An Introduction, 2001
Cinema and State: The Film Industry and the British Government 1927-1984, 1985

Other books you might like:
Ian Christie, _Michael Powell: International Perspectives on an English Filmmaker,_ 2008
Mark Connelly, _The Red Shoes,_ 2005
Stella Hockenhull, _Neo-Romantic Landscapes: An Aesthetic Approach to the Films of Powell and Pressburger,_ 2008
Andrew Moor, _Michael Powell: International Perspectives on an English Filmmaker,_ 2008
Andrew Moor, _Powell and Pressburger: A Cinema of Magic Spaces,_ 2005
Michael Powell, _A Life in Movies: An Autobiography,_ 2001

131

JUAN A. SUAREZ

Pop Modernism: Noise and the Reinvention of the Everyday
(Urbana, Illinois: University of Illinois Press, 2007)

Subject(s): Art; History; Artists

Summary: In _Pop Modernism: Noise and the Reinvention of the Everyday,_ Juan A. Suarez examines the various forms of experimental art prevalent in the beginning of the 20th century. The book includes a collection of essays written by Suarez, critiquing popular and experimental films, paintings, poems, photographs, and music in an effort to understand the origins, purpose, and motivation of modernism in the United States, much of which was grounded in repurposing everyday items. To explain the history of popular modernism in America, Suarez explores a wide range of materials and individuals, including the work of surrealist artist Joseph Cornell; the film _Manhatta_; and the contributions of Vachel Lindsay, Charles Henri Ford, and Helen Levitt.

Where it's reviewed:
American Literature, September 2009, pages 626-628

Other books by the same author:
Jim Jarmusch, 2007
Bike Boys, Drag Queens, and Superstars: Avant-Garde, Mass Culture, and Gay Identities in the 1960s Underground Cinema, 1996

Other books you might like:
Chad Heap, _Slumming: Sexual and Racial Encounters in American Nightlife, 1885-1940,_ 2009
Andreas Huyssen, _After The Great Divide: Modernism, Mass Culture, Postmodernism,_ 2008
Bonnie Kime Scott, _Gender in Modernism: New

Geographies, Complex Intersections, 2007
P. Adams Sitney, _Eyes Upside Down: Visionary Filmmakers and the Heritage of Emerson,_ 2008
Shane Vogel, _The Scene of Harlem Cabaret: Race, Sexuality, Performance,_ 2009

132

CAROLINE SUMPTER

The Victorian Press and the Fairy Tale
(Basingstoke, United Kingdom; New York: Palgrave Macmillan, 2008)

Subject(s): Fairy tales; Criticism; Literature

Summary: English professor and author Caroline Sumpter analyzes the role of the fairy tale and its place in popular and literary culture. _The Victorian Press and the Fairy Tale_ looks specifically at the publication of fairy tales in periodical volumes during the 19th century, which helped to redefine the genre for changing audiences. Sumpter further explores the topic by delving into the social, political, and sexual implications of fairy tales and how they are often retailored to fit the sensibilities of their readerships. This volume includes illustrations, notes on the text, a bibliography, and an index.

Where it's reviewed:
Victorian Studies, Summer 2009, pages 738-740

Other books you might like:
Nina Auerbach, _Forbidden Journeys: Fairy Tales and Fantasies by Victorian Women Writers,_ 1992
U. C. Knoepflmacher, _Ventures into Childland: Victorians, Fairy Tales, and Femininity,_ 2000
Cynthia Demarcus Manson, _The Fairy-Tale Literature of Charles Dickens, Christina Rossetti and George MacDonald: Antidotes to the Victorian Spiritual Crisis,_ 2008
Maria Tatar, _Off with Their Heads! Fairy Tales and the Culture of Childhood,_ 1993
Jack Zipes, _Fairy Tales and the Art of Subversion: The Classical Genre for Children and the Process of Civilization,_ 2006

133

MEGHAN SUTHERLAND

The Flip Wilson Show
(Detroit, Michigan: Wayne State University Press, 2008)

Subject(s): Television; Television programs; Criticism

Summary: Meghan Sutherland's _The Flip Wilson Show_ is a comprehensive, scholarly study of the television show of the same name. The television show aired in the 1970s, a period in United States history that was rife with racial discord. Flip Wilson was an African American comedian who became a star after NBC started airing his variety show in 1970. In the text, Sutherland considers Wilson's success and analyzes the characters he created within the social context of the 1970s. She also explains how Wilson laid the groundwork for future black comedians and describes how the show changed the way politics and other socially sensitive subjects were discussed on television.

Other books you might like:

Anthony Bozza, *I Am the New Black*, 2009

Thomas Braun, *On Stage: Flip Wilson*, 1976

Hal Erickson, *"From Beautiful Downtown Burbank": A Critical History of Rowan and Martin's Laugh-In, 1968-1973*, 2009

James A. Hudson, *Flip Wilson Close Up*, 1971

Darryl Littleton, *Black Comedians on Black Comedy: How African-Americans Taught Us to Laugh*, 2008

Tracy Morgan, *I Am the New Black*, 2009

134

ALISON SWAN

Fresh Water: Women Writing on the Great Lakes

(East Lansing, Michigan: Michigan State University Press, 2006)

Subject(s): United States; Americana; United States history

Summary: *Fresh Water: Women Writing on the Great Lakes* is a compilation of nonfiction essays by female authors. All of these writings in this collection focus on life around the Great Lakes of North America. Editor Alison Swan compiles the work of more than 35 authors, including Rachael Perry, Judith Strasser, Linda Loomis, Linda Nemec Foster, Annick Smith, and Teresa Jordon. *Fresh Water: Women Writing on the Great Lakes* was awarded the Michigan Notable Book Award in 2007 for its representation of Michigan's cultural heritage. Alison Swan has also written for many literary journals, including the *Red Cedar Review* and the *Detroit MetroTimes*.

Where it's reviewed:

Internet Bookwatch, November 2006

Reference and Research Book News, May 2007

Other books by the same author:

The Saugatuck Dunes: Artists Respond to a Freshwater Landscape, 2009

Other books you might like:

Bill Bryson, *A Walk in the Woods*, 1998

Timothy Egan, *The Worst Hard Time: The Untold Story of Those Who Survived the Great American Dust Bowl*, 2005

Steven Hopp, *Animal, Vegetable, Miracle: A Year of Food Life*, 2007
   Barbara Kingsolver, co-author
   Camille Kingsolver, co-author

Bill McKibben, *American Earth: Environmental Writing Since Thoreau*, 2008

Thomas Springer, *Looking for Hickories: The Forgotten Wildness of the Rural Midwest*, 2008

135

KRISTIN THOMPSON

The Frodo Franchise: The Lord of the Rings and Modern Hollywood

(Berkeley: University of California Press, 2007)

Subject(s): Movies; Movie industry; Commerce

Summary: What is the relationship between filmmaking and commercialization? This is the question author Kristin Thompson sets out to answer in *The Frodo Franchise: The Lord of the Rings and Modern Hollywood*, centering her study on the landmark films based on the books of J.R.R. Tolkien. Thompson's in-depth investigation brings readers into the inner circle of the iconic *Lord of the Rings* franchise, offering first-person accounts from the people, the country, and the industry that made the movie series legendary. This volume sheds light on how moviemaking professionals, industry insiders, and even everyday people can come together to not only make great art—but also make great are that *sells*.

Other books by the same author:

Film History: An Introduction, 2009

Film Art: An Introduction, 2006

The Classical Hollywood Cinema, 1985

Other books you might like:

J. W. Braun, *The Lord of the Films: The Unofficial Guide to Tolkien's Middle-Earth on the Big Screen*, 2009

Janet Brennan Croft, *Tolkien on Film: Essays on Peter Jackson's the Lord of the Rings*, 2005

Andy Serkis, *Gollum: A Behind the Scenes Guide of the Making of Gollum*, 2003

Brian Sibley, *The Lord of the Rings: The Making of the Movie Trilogy*, 2002

Brian Sibley, *Peter Jackson: A Film-Maker's Journey*, 2006

136

JESSICA TIFFIN

Marvelous Geometry: Narrative and Metafiction in Modern Fairy Tale

(Detroit, Michigan: Wayne State University Press, 2009)

Subject(s): Fairy tales; Literature; Mathematics

Summary: In *Marvelous Geometry: Narrative and Metafiction in Modern Fairy Tale*, author Jessica Tiffin examines the ways that modern fairy tale authors present an awareness of the roles their stories play in contemporary literature and popular culture. The author focuses on the works of James Thurber, Angela Carter, and A.S. Byatt as she determines the presence of cultural critical theories in modern and postmodern literature. Tiffin doesn't limit herself to the written word; she also examines fairy tales on television and in movies and explains what these stories and adaptations reveal about modern values. Jes-

Arts and Humanities

sica Tiffin is a native of Zimbabwe and a lecturer at the University of Cape Town.

Where it's reviewed:
Reference and Research Book News, August 2009

Other books you might like:
M.T. Anderson, *The Astonishing Life of Octavian Nothing, Traitor to the Nation, Volume One: The Pox Party*, 2006
Stephen Benson, *Contemporary Fiction and the Fairy Tale*, 2008
Maria Tatar, *Enchanted Hunters: The Power of Stories in Childhood*, 2008
Catherynne M. Valente, *In the Night Garden*, 2006

137

JAMES W. TOTTIS

The Guardian Building: Cathedral of Finance

(Detroit, Michigan: Wayne State University Press, 2008)

Subject(s): History; Buildings; Architecture

Summary: Written by James W. Tottis, *The Guardian Building: Cathedral of Finance* is a historical account of the creation and construction of the Union Trust Building in downtown Detroit. The Union Trust Building, now known as the Guardian Building, is one of the most significant and beautiful skyscrapers gracing the Detroit skyline. Designed and constructed by architect Wirt C. Rowland, the art deco skyscraper is one of the greatest of its type in the world. Tottis begins his narrative with an in-depth look at Rowland's life, career, and inspiration for the Union Trust Building. In addition to historical facts, *The Guardian Building* also tells the skyscraper's story using rich, detailed photographs.

Where it's reviewed:
Internet Bookwatch, November 2008

Other books you might like:
John Gallagher, *AIA Detroit: The American Institute of Architects Guide to Detroit Architecture*, 2002
John Gallagher, *Great Architecture of Michigan*, 2008
Greg Grandin, *Fordlandia: The Rise and Fall of Henry Ford's Forgotten Jungle City*, 2009
Eric J. Hill, *AIA Detroit: The American Institute of Architects Guide to Detroit Architecture*, 2002
Andrew Moore, *Andrew Moore: Detroit Disassembled*, 2010
Robert Sharoff, *American City: Detroit Architecture, 1845-2005*, 2005

138

ARIANA TRAILL

Women and the Comic Plot in Menander

(Cambridge, United Kingdom: Cambridge University Press, 2008)

Subject(s): Drama; Criticism; Women

Summary: The Greek dramatist Menander often used mistaken identity as a storytelling device in his classic works of comedy. In *Women and the Comic Plot in Menander*, classics professor Ariana Traill dissects this trend in the great playwright's work, illustrating the ways Menander used language and character development to address issues of gender and comedy. Through examples and critical analysis, Traill sheds light on Menander's trend-setting efforts to transform human unawareness into comedy. *Women and the Comic Plot in Menander* includes a bibliography and an index.

Where it's reviewed:
The Classical World, Winter 2010, pages 274-275

Other books you might like:
Aristophanes Aristophanes, *Classical Comedy*, 2007
Katrina Cawthorn, *Becoming Female: The Male Body in Greek Tragedy*, 2008
Casey Due, *The Captive Woman's Lament in Greek Tragedy*, 2009
Nicole Loraux, *The Mourning Voice: An Essay on Greek Tragedy*, 2002
Menander Menander, *Classical Comedy*, 2007
Menander Menander, *The Plays and Fragments*, 2008
Plautus Plautus, *Classical Comedy*, 2007
Terence Terence, co-author

139

JOHN TULLOCH

Shakespeare and Chekhov in Production and Reception: Theatrical Events and Their Audiences

(Iowa City, Iowa: University of Iowa Press, 2005)

Subject(s): Theater; Art; Shakespeare, William

Summary: In *Shakespeare and Chekhov in Production and Reception: Theatrical Events and Their Audiences*, professor and author John Tulloch presents new ideas for studying theatrical performances and productions based on case studies of successful performances around the globe. Tulloch spent a decade in Australia, England, and America compiling studies of popular performances that were hailed by critics and audiences to offer a new approach to examining and understanding theater history, productions, and audiences. Relying heavily on the works of Shakespeare and Chekhov, Tulloch examines audience members' responses and experiences to help readers better understand what makes a successful "theatrical event."

Where it's reviewed:
Choice, July-August 2005, page 1998
Comparative Drama, Fall 2006, page 383

Other books by the same author:
Risk and Everyday Life, 2003
Watching Television Audiences, 2000
Doctor Who: The Unfolding Text, 1984

Other books you might like:

Richard C. Beacham, *The Roman Theatre and Its Audience*, 1996

Susan Bennett, *Theatre Audiences*, 1997

Faye E. Dudden, *Women in the American Theatre: Actresses and Audiences, 1790-1870*, 2009

Helen Freshwater, *Theatre and Audience*, 2009

Mayo Simon, *The Audience and The Playwright: How to Get the Most Out of Live Theatre*, 2003

140

RICHARD MARGGRAF TURLEY
DAMIAN WALFORD DAVIES , Co-Editor

The Monstrous Debt: Modalities of Romantic Influence in Twentieth-Century Literature

(Detroit, Michigan: Wayne State University Press, 2006)

Subject(s): Literature; Writing; Authorship

Summary: *The Monstrous Debt: Modalities of Romantic Influence in Twentieth-Century Literature* is a critical review of reoccurring themes of romanticism contained within 20th-century literature. Edited by Damian Walford Davies and Richard Marggraf Turley, with a foreword by Lucy Newlyn, this book draws from critical theory and comparisons between such authors as Virginia Woolf and Mary Wollstonecraft, Dylan Thomas and William Blake, and William Wordsworth and Seamus Heaney, to elucidate how the contemporary authors borrowed from themes written in earlier works. The book includes critiques by Harriet Devine Jump, Hugh Haughton, John Beer, and Emma Mason.

Where it's reviewed:
CHOICE: Current Reviews for Academic Libraries, April 2007, page 1343

Other books by the same author:
Romanticism, History, Historicism: Essays on an Orthodoxy, 2008

Wales and the Romantic Imagination, 2006

Presences that Disturb: Models of Romantic Self-Definition in the Culture and Literature of the 1790s, 2002

Other books you might like:
Damian Walford Davies, *Echoes to the Amen: Essays After R.S. Thomas*, 2009

Damian Walford Davies, *Presences that Disturb: Models of Romantic Self-Definition in the Culture and Literature of the 1790s*, 2002

Damian Walford Davies, *Romanticism, History, Historicism: Essays on an Orthodoxy*, 2008

Damian Walford Davies, *Saints and Stones*, 2002

Damian Walford Davies, *Wales and the Romantic Imagination*, 2006

141

VENDELA VIDA

"The Believer" Book of Writers Talking to Writers: Revised and Expanded

(San Francisco, California: McSweeny's, 2008)

Subject(s): Writers; Authorship; Interpersonal relations

Summary: *"The Believer" Book of Writers Talking to Writers: Revised and Expanded* is a collection of interviews from *The Believer*, an American literary magazine. Originally published in 2005, the book was updated with previously unpublished material in 2008. The 23 interviews in this collection allow writers from various generations to speak with the authors who inspired them. Although the act of writing comes up in many interviews, the authors discuss a variety of topics, including religion, politics, and love. Entries include discussions between Zadie Smith and Ian McEwan, Julie Orringer and Tobias Wolff, and Dave Eggers and Joan Didion.

Where it's reviewed:
Review of Contemporary Fiction, Spring 2006, pages 153-154

Other books by the same author:
The Lovers, 2010
Let the Northern Lights Erase Your Name, 2008
And Now You Can Go, 2004

Other books you might like:
Marie Arana, *The Writing Life: Writers on How They Think and Work*, 2003

The New York Times, *Writers on Writing, Volume II: More Collected Essays from The New York Times*, 2004

The Paris Review, *The Paris Review Interviews, III*, 2008

The Paris Review, *The Paris Review Interviews, I*, 2006

142

JANS B. WAGER

Dames in the Driver's Seat: Rereading Film Noir

(Austin, Texas: University of Texas Press, 2005)

Subject(s): Movies; Movie industry; Criticism

Summary: Author and professor Jans B. Wager delves into the sociology, politics, and artistic importance of the movie genre known as film noir. In *Dames in the Driver's Seat: Rereading Film Noir*, Wager explores this unique filmmaking style—which was popular in the 1940s and 50s—and what it says about society during that period. Wager points out how classic film noir elements are actually emblematic of an evolving social landscape, and they offer a dynamic commentary on the racial, sexual, and financial challenges of the era. *Dames in the Driver's Seat* includes a bibliography and an index.

Where it's reviewed:
Journal of Popular Film & Television, 2007, page 94

Other books by the same author:
Dangerous Dames, 1999

Other books you might like:
Helen Hanson, *Hollywood Heroines: Women in Film Noir and the Female Gothic Film*, 2008

Foster Hirsch, *The Dark Side of the Screen: Film Noir*, 2008

E. Ann Kaplan, *Women in Film Noir*, 2008

Eddie Muller, *Dark City Dames: The Wicked Women of Film Noir*, 2002

James Naremore, *More than Night: Film Noir in Its Contexts*, 2008

143

ELIJAH WALD

How the Beatles Destroyed Rock 'n Roll: An Alternative History of American Popular Music

(New York: Oxford University Press, 2009)

Subject(s): Rock music; History; Criticism

Summary: Author and musician Elijah Wald turns conventional rock and roll history on its ear by providing another perspective of the genre's evolution. *How the Beatles Destroyed Rock N Roll: An Alternative History of American Popular Music* introduces readers to the people, personalities, and events that shaped the industry. These are not, however, the typical names mentioned in rock and roll biographies; they are the outsiders, the rebels who worked on the fringes of the movement and managed to leave an indelible impression on it—no matter how forgotten they are today. This is the story of those defining moments that are seldom discussed, concerts and performances and gatherings that ultimately changed the trajectory of American rock and roll music. *How the Beatles Destroyed Rock N Roll* includes notes on the text, a bibliography, and an index.

Where it's reviewed:
Journal of Popular Culture, April 2010, pages 408-409

Other books by the same author:
The Blues, 2010
The Mayor of MacDougal Street, 2006
Escaping the Delta, 2004

Other books you might like:
Glenn C. Altschuler, *All Shook Up: How Rock 'n' Roll Changed America*, 2004

Bakari Kitwana, *Why White Kids Love Hip Hop: Wankstas, Wiggers, Wannabes, and the New Reality of Race in America*, 2006

Bill C. Malone, *Singing Cowboys and Musical Mountaineers: Southern Culture and the Roots of Country Music*, 2003

Greg Milner, *Perfecting Sound Forever: An Aural History of Recorded Music*, 2009

Elijah Wald, *Escaping the Delta: Robert Johnson and the Invention of the Blues*, 2004

144

IRENE WALT
GRACE SERRA , Co-Editor

The Healing Work of Art: From the Collection of Detroit Receiving Hospital

(Detroit, Michigan: Detroit Receiving Hospital, 2007)

Subject(s): Art; Hospitals; Artists

Summary: Edited by Irene Walt and Grace Serra, *The Healing Work of Art: From the Collection of Detroit Receiving Hospital* is an examination of the impressive art collection lining the halls of Detroit Receiving Hospital. In the late 1960s, the Detroit Receiving Hospital began accepting pieces of art from local artists and donors to start the first hospital art collection in the United States. The goal was to line the hospital's walls with lively and colorful pieces of art to improve the moods and attitudes of hospital patients, doctors, staff, visitors, and families. Over the years, the collection continued to grow to include more than 1,000 pieces of artwork. Walt and Serra detail the hospital's amazing collection, which includes sculptures, painting, tapestries, African beadwork, photo murals, and a tile water fountain.

Other books by the same author:
Art In The Stations: The Detroit People Mover, 2004

Other books you might like:
Tony Blee, *The Arts in Health Care: A Palette of Possibilities*, 1996
Charles Kaye, co-author

Ellen G. Levine, *Foundations of Expressive Arts Therapy: Theoretical and Clinical Perspective*, 1999
Stephen K. Levine, co-author

Shaun McNiff, *Art as Medicine*, 1992

Shaun McNiff, *Art Heals: How Creativity Cures the Soul*, 2004

Bernie Warren, *Using the Creative Arts in Therapy and Healthcare: A Practical Introduction*, 1993

145

EUGENE Y. WANG

Shaping the Lotus Sutra: Buddhist Visual Culture in Medieval China

(Seattle: University of Washington Press, 2007)

Subject(s): Art; Buddhism; Criticism

Summary: For thousands of years, the Buddhist text known as the Lotus Sutra has served as the inspiration for countless works of visual art. In *Shaping the Lotus Sutra: Buddhist Visual Culture in Medieval China*, art history professor Eugene Y. Wang investigates the rich artistic legacy that has been influenced by this classic work of Buddhist scholarship. Wang's all-encompassing study goes beyond the sutras of Buddhism to show how religious art has always fascinated the public and how it has often been infused with social, religious, and political messages. *Shaping the Lotus Sutra* includes a bibliography and an index.

Where it's reviewed:
The Art Bulletin, September 2008, pages 487-489

Other books you might like:
Sarah Fraser, *Performing the Visual: The Practice of Buddhist Wall Painting in China and Central Asia, 618-960*, 2003
Amy McNair, *Donors of Longmen: Faith, Politics, And Patronage in Medieval Chinese Buddhist Sculpture*, 2007
Erwin Panofsky, *Perspective as Symbolic Form*, 1993
Ning Qiang, *Art, Religion, and Politics in Medieval China: The Dunhuang Cave of the Zhai Family*, 2004
Dorothy C. Wong, *Chinese Steles: Pre-Buddhist and Buddhist Use of a Symbolic Form*, 2004

146

NAGUEYALTI WARREN

Margaret, Circa 1834-1858
(Detroit, Michigan: Lotus Press, 2008)

Subject(s): African Americans; Blacks; Slavery

Summary: In *Margaret, Circa 1834-1858*, author Nagueyalti Warren tells through poetry the true story of Margaret Garner. Born into slavery, Garner was so devastated by the cruelty and viciousness of the institution that she murdered her young daughter, rather than allow her child to bear the same burden that she had. Garner's tale was later represented in the painting *The Modern Medea*, created by Thomas Satterwhite Noble. Now, Warren portrays Garner's life through verse and prose. This book was awarded the 2008 Naomi Long Madgett Poetry Award. Warren is also the author of *Southern Mothers* and *Temba Tupu*.

Other books by the same author:
An Intellectual Biography of W.E.B. Du Bois, Initiator of Black Studies in the University, 2010
Temba Tupu!/Walking Naked: Africana Women's Poetic Self-portrait, 2005
Southern Mothers: Fact and Fictions in Southern Women's Writing, 2000

Other books you might like:
Delores P. Aldridge, *An Intellectual Biography of W.E.B. Du Bois, Initiator of Black Studies in the University*, 2010
Nikki Giovanni, *The Collected Poetry of Nikki Giovanni, 1968-1998*, 2003
Nagueyalti Warren, *An Intellectual Biography of W.E.B. Du Bois, Initiator of Black Studies in the University*, 2010
Nagueyalti Warren, *Lodestar and Other Night Lights/Poems*, 1992

Nagueyalti Warren, *Southern Mothers: Fact and Fictions in Southern Women's Writing*, 2000
Nagueyalti Warren, *Temba Tupu!/Walking Naked: Africana Women's Poetic Self-portrait*, 2005

147

ELWOOD WATSON

Pimps, Wimps, Studs, Thugs and Gentlemen: Essays on Media Images of Masculinity
(Jefferson, North Carolina: McFarland & Co., 2009)

Subject(s): Men; Sex roles; Criticism

Summary: In *Pimps, Wimps, Studs, Thugs and Gentlemen: Essays on Media Images of Masculinity*, editor Elwood Watson presents a collection of pieces exploring the role of masculinity in modern media. The essays of this volume cover the topic from a variety of angles, from the images of masculinity portrayed in reality television and film to the portrayal of men in literature and sports. A number of entries focus specifically on racial issues and masculinity, including the stereotypes perpetuated by the mass media. *Pimps, Wimps, Studs, Thugs and Gentlemen* includes a bibliography and a full index.

Where it's reviewed:
Journal of Popular Culture, June 2010, pages 665-667

Other books by the same author:
The Oprah Phenomenon, 2009
Outsiders Within: Black Women in the Legal Academy After Brown v. Board, 2009
"There She Is, Miss America": The Politics of Sex, Beauty, and Race in America's Most Famous Pageant, 2004

Other books you might like:
Dennis Bingham, *Acting Male: Masculinities in the Films of James Stewart, Jack Nicholson, and Clint Eastwood*, 1994
Sergio de la Mora, *Cinemachismo: Masculinities and Sexuality in Mexican Film*, 2006
Robert T. Eberwein, *Armed Forces: Masculinity and Sexuality in the American War Film*, 2007
Frances Gateward, *Where the Boys Are: Cinemas of Masculinity and Youth*, 2005
Peter Lehman, *Masculinity: Bodies, Movies, Culture*, 2001
Murray Pomerance, *Where the Boys Are: Cinemas of Masculinity and Youth*, 2005

148

JEFFREY ANDREW WEINSTOCK

Taking South Park Seriously
(Albany: State University of New York Press, 2008)

Subject(s): Television programs; Popular culture; Criticism

Summary: The animated Comedy Central series *South Park* is the focus of this series of scholarly essays edited by Jeffrey Andrew Weinstock. *Taking South Park Seriously* brings together a collection of pieces exploring the style, themes, and impact of the popular television show. Though it may seem like an irreverent, politically incorrect cartoon, *South Park*—according to the authors of the essays assembled here—is actually a revealing commentary on modern society, psychology, religion, and popular culture. *Taking South Park Seriously* includes a complete listing of episodes and an index.

Where it's reviewed:
Journal of Popular Culture, April 2010, pages 418-419

Other books by the same author:
Critical Approaches to the Films of M. Night Shyamalan: Spoiler Warnings, 2010
Scare Tactics: Supernatural Fiction by American Women, 2008
Spectral America: Phantoms and the National Imagination, 2004

Other books you might like:
Robert Arp, *South Park and Philosophy: You Know, I Learned Something Today*, 2006
Richard Hanley, *South Park and Philosophy: Bigger, Longer, and More Penetrating*, 2007
Toni Johnson-Woods, *Blame Canada!: South Park and Contemporary Culture*, 2007
James R. Keller, *The Deep End of South Park: Critical Essays on Television's Shocking Cartoon Series*, 2009
Trey Parker, *South Park Guide to Life*, 2009
Matt Stone, co-author
Leslie Stratyner, *The Deep End of South Park: Critical Essays on Television's Shocking Cartoon Series*, 2009

149

LAWRENCE WESCHLER

Everything That Rises: A Book of Convergences
(San Francisco: McSweeney's, 2006)

Subject(s): Art; Philosophy; Culture

Summary: In *Everything that Rises: A Book of Convergences*, author Lawrence Weschler considers a variety of artistic images that are seemingly in juxtaposition to each other, and discusses their philosophical, cultural, political, and artistic convergences. This presentation of dissimilar yet comparable materials is known as convergence. From artwork and photography to political leaders, Weschler finds subjects that converge and considers that convergence from a philosophical perspective. The book contains interviews with artists and photographers, who discuss the way their work can be compared to works created in very different contexts. For example, the author discusses a photograph taken at Ground Zero in Manhattan with the photographer, Joel Meyerowitz, who compares his image to a Civil War photograph.

Where it's reviewed:
Entertainment Weekly, February 24, 2006, page 67
Kirkus Reviews, December 15, 2005, page 1315
New Statesman, August 24, 2009, page 44
Publishers Weekly, November 28, 2005, page 33

Other books by the same author:
Seeing Is Forgetting the Name of the Thing One Sees, 2009
True to Life: Twenty-Five Years of Conversations with David Hockney, 2009
Mr. Wilson's Cabinet of Wonder: Pronged Ants, Horned Humans, Mice on Toast and Other Marvels..., 1995

Other books you might like:
Alice Munro, *The Love of a Good Woman*, 1998
W. G. Sebald, *The Emigrants*, 1993
Lawrence Weschler, *Mr. Wilson's Cabinet of Wonder: Pronged Ants, Horned Humans, Mice on Toast and Other Marvels...*, 1996
Lawrence Weschler, *Seeing Is Forgetting the Name of the Thing One Sees*, 2009
Lawrence Weschler, *True to Life: Twenty-Five Years of Conversations with David Hockney*, 2009

150

BOB W. WHITE

Rumba Rules: The Politics of Dance Music in Mobutu's Zaire
(Durham, North Carolina: Duke University Press, 2008)

Subject(s): Music; Africa; History

Summary: In *Rumba Rules: The Politics of Dance Music in Mobutu's Zaire*, anthropologist Bob W. White examines the role of popular music in the African nation during the reign of a merciless dictator. Mobutu Sese Seko, who led Zaire from 1965 until his death in 1997, placed great social and political emphasis on the role of the country's indigenous dance music. White illustrates how this music—once reserved for the enjoyment of the country's elite—soon became a centerpiece of Zairians' lives, from the richest of the rich to the most remote, poverty-stricken villagers. In his study of Zaire's music, White offers a rich account of one country's turbulent past and unique culture.

Where it's reviewed:
African Arts, Spring 2010, page 94

Other books you might like:
Kofi Agawu, *Representing African Music: Postcolonial Notes, Queries, Positions*, 2003
J. Lorand Matory, *Sex and the Empire That is no More: Gender and the Politics of Metaphor in Oyo Yoruba Religion*, 2005
Louise Meintjes, *Sound of Africa: Making Music Zulu in a South African Studio*, 2003
Gwendolyn Mikell, *Cocoa and Chaos in Ghana*, 1991
Gary Stewart, *Rumba on the River: A History of the Popular Music of the Two Congos*, 2004

151

MARTIN M. WINKLER

Cinema and Classical Texts: Apollo's New Light

(New York: Cambridge University Press, 2009)

Subject(s): Movies; Literature; Criticism

Summary: Classics professor Martin M. Winkler offers an in-depth study of both film and classic literature, providing a thorough exploration of movies as works of literary art. *Cinema and Classical Texts: Apollo's New Light* investigates the topics of heroes and mythology in literature and film, the role of women, and the standard character archetypes of both art forms. This volume includes photographs, a bibliography, and an index.

Where it's reviewed:
Journal of Popular Culture, June 2010, pages 644-645

Other books by the same author:
The Roman Salute, 2009
The Persona in Three Satires of Juvenal, 1983

Other books you might like:
Paul Cartledge, *Ancient Greece: A History in Eleven Cities*, 2010
Sandra R. Joshel, *Imperial Projections: Ancient Rome in Modern Popular Culture*, 2005
Gideon Nisbet, *Ancient Greece in Film and Popular Culture*, 2006
Elena Theodorakopoulos, *Ancient Rome at the Cinema: Story and Spectacle in Hollywood and Rome*, 2010
Martin M. Winkler, *Classical Myth and Culture in the Cinema*, 2001

152

CHRISTOPHER S. WOOD

Forgery, Replica, Fiction: Temporalities of German Renaissance Art

(Chicago: University of Chicago Press, 2008)

Subject(s): Art; Forgery; Germans

Summary: In *Forgery, Replica, Fiction: Temporalities of German Renaissance Art*, Christopher S. Wood discusses the ways that different people view art. In this text, the author focuses on art in Germany and how the people there appreciate or criticize various works. He reveals that Germans do not adore relics or pieces of art for their age. Instead, they admire pieces that connect them to their roots. Wood, however, believes that viewing art in such a way is risky; forgeries are easy to pass along to buyers when a piece of art isn't connected with its time period. The author examines the ways that forgeries have been created over the years and explains how new areas of study are working to identify fakes.

Where it's reviewed:
CHOICE: Current Reviews for Academic Libraries, May 2009, page 1684
German Studies Review, May 2009, pages 440-441
Renaissance Quarterly, Summer 2009, page 540
Renaissance Studies, June 2009, page 398

Other books by the same author:
Albrecht Altdorfer and the Origins of Landscape, 1993

Other books you might like:
Lorraine Daston, *Things That Talk: Object Lessons from Art and Science*, 2007
Joseph Leo Koerner, *The Reformation of the Image*, 2008
Walter Mignolo, *The Darker Side of the Renaissance: Literacy, Territoriality and Colonization, 2nd Edition*, 2003
Alexander Nagel, *Anachronic Renaissance*, 2010
Erwin Panofsky, *The Life and Art of Albrecht Durer*, 2005
Christopher S. Wood, *Anachronic Renaissance*, 2010

153

J. WOOD

Living Lost: Why We're All Stuck on the Island

(New Orleans, Louisiana: Garrett County Press, LLC, 2006)

Subject(s): Television; Television programs; Current events

Summary: *Living Lost: Why We're All Stuck on the Island* is an exploration how *Lost*, the famous television show of the early 2000s, relates to modern culture and society. In the book, author J. Wood describes the premise of show and recounts some of the show's most thrilling and meaningful moments. Then, Wood compares the events of show with events, such as the war on terror, that occurred in real life during the same time the show aired. The book gives insight into why the show was so popular and why the audience felt a deep connect both to it and its characters.

Where it's reviewed:
Entertainment Weekly, April 4, 2007

Other books you might like:
Sharon Kaye, *Lost and Philosophy: The Island Has Its Reasons*, 2007
David Lavery, *Lost's Buried Treasures, 3E: The Unofficial Guide to Everything Lost Fans Need to Know*, 2010
Marc Oromaner, *The Myth of Lost: Solving the Mysteries and Understanding the Wisdom*, 2008
Christian Piatt, *Lost: A Search for Meaning*, 2006
Lynnette Porter, *Lost's Buried Treasures, 3E: The Unofficial Guide to Everything Lost Fans Need to Know*, 2010
Nikki Stafford, *Finding Lost: The Unofficial Guide*, 2006

Arts and Humanities

154

LISA WOOLFORK

Embodying American Slavery in Contemporary Culture

(Urbana, Illinois: University of Illinois Press, 2008)

Story type: Historical
Subject(s): Slavery; United States history; Art

Summary: Written by professor and author Lisa Woolfork, *Embodying American Slavery in Contemporary Culture* is a critical examination of how the traumatic events of slavery are depicted in modern-day art forms. Woolfork examines the ways in which current films, novels, performances, and reenactments depict American slavery. While many media portray slavery as a distant trauma of the past, Woolfork finds films, books, and performances that bridge the gap between the past and present, depicting a more realistic interpretation of the grueling and horrific nature of slavery in the United States. As a result, these works of art manage to conjure up the emotional and physical significance of American slavery in an effort to inspire and incite audiences.

Where it's reviewed:
Reference & Research Book News, February 2009

Other books you might like:
Cathy Caruth, *Unclaimed Experience: Trauma, Narrative and History*, 1996
Saidiya Hartman, *Lose Your Mother: A Journey Along the Atlantic Slave Route*, 2008
James Oliver Horton, *Slavery and Public History: The Tough Stuff of American Memory*, 2008
  Lois E. Horton, co-author
Michael Rossington, *Theories of Memory: A Reader*, 2007
Rebecca Skloot, *The Immortal Life of Henrietta Lacks*, 2009
Anne Whitehead, *Theories of Memory: A Reader*, 2007

155

MAURICE YACOWAR

Hitchcock's British Films

(Detroit, Michigan: Wayne State University Press, 2010)

Subject(s): Movies; Criticism; England

Summary: *Hitchcock's British Films* by Maurice Yacowar was originally published in 1977 and is an examination of the 23 films that Hitchcock directed in England before he began his career in the United States. Though critics often consider Hitchcock's work from the 1940s to the 1960s to be his best and most "mature" work, Yacowar disagrees, and presents his arguments comprehensively in this text. He takes each film chronologically and deconstructs it, discussing technical issues including staging, shot composition, and verbal effects while also considering more subjective interpretations such as the theme of each film and the sources and inspirations that Hitchcock employed. Yacowar also provides detailed information regarding Hitchcock's appearances in each of his British films.

Other books by the same author:
Sopranos on the Couch, 2006
The Films of Paul Morrissey, 1993
Method in Madness, 1983

Other books you might like:
Paul Jensen, *Hitchcock Becomes Hitchcock: The British Years*, 2009
Tom Ryall, *Alfred Hitchcock and the British Cinema: Second Edition*, 2001
Susan Smith, *Hitchcock: Suspense, Humour and Tone*, 2008
David Sterritt, *The Films of Alfred Hitchcock*, 1993
Robin Wood, *Hitchcock's Films Revisited*, 2002

156

VERSHAWN ASHANTI YOUNG

Your Average Nigga: Performing Race, Literacy, and Masculinity

(Detroit: Wayne State University Press, 2007)

Subject(s): African Americans; Men; Literacy

Summary: In *Your Average Nigga: Performing Race, Literacy, and Masculinity*, author Vershawn Ashanti Young examines the world of African American men and how this world is influenced by matters of language, rhetoric, and literacy. Young relates stories from his own life with an academic analysis of the subject, centering specifically on how society forces black men to abandon their unique dialect if they want to make it in the world of academia. Part cultural commentary, part social study, and part memoir, this volume investigates an often-overlooked topic in modern African American studies.

Where it's reviewed:
CHOICE: Current Reviews for Academic Libraries, November 2007, page 551

Other books you might like:
Jane Bolgatz, *Talking Race In The Classroom*, 2005
Kermit E. Campbell, *Gettin' Our Groove On: Rhetoric, Language, and Literacy for the Hip Hop Generation*, 2005
Marc Lamont Hill, *Beats, Rhymes, and Classroom Life: Hip-Hop Pedagogy and the Politics of Identity*, 2009
Vorris L. Nunley, *Keepin' It Hushed: The Barbershop and African American Hush Harbor Rhetoric*, 2010
Studs Terkel, *Race: How Blacks and Whites Think and Feel about the American Obsession*, 1992

157

LOIS PARKINSON ZAMORA

The Inordinate Eye: New World Baroque and Latin American Fiction

(Chicago: University Of Chicago Press, 2006)

Subject(s): History; Literature; Art

Summary: *The Inordinate Eye: New World Baroque and Latin American Fiction* is a celebration of Latin American art and culture. Written by Lois Parkinson Zamora, this book touches all forms of artistic expression, including painting, writing, and sculpting. Zamora also discusses the history of Latin America and shows how art developed and changed over the years in the area. She also shows how art and writing have helped form the way Latin Americans view the world. Lois Parkinson Zamora is also the author of *Writing the Apocalypse: Historical Vision in Contemporary U.S. and Latin American Fiction*, and *The Usable Past: The Imagination of History in Recent Fiction of the Americas*.

Where it's reviewed:
Comparatist, May 2008, pages 216-218
Comparative Literature Studies, 2008, pages 373-376
Hispanic Review, Autumn 2008, pages 459-461
Modern Language Quarterly, June 2008, pages 310-313
Rocky Mountain Review of Language and Literature, 2007, pages 134-136

Other books by the same author:
The Usable Past, 2008
Writing the Apocalypse, 1993

Other books you might like:
Jorge Luis Borges, *Selected Non-Fictions*, 1999
Alejo Carpentier, *The Kingdom of This World*, 1957
Gabriel Garcia Marquez, *Of Love and Other Demons*, 1995
Elena Garro, *Recollections of Things to Come*, 1969
John Rupert Martin, *Baroque*, 1977

158

YAEL ZARHY-LEVO

The Making of Theatrical Reputations: Studies from the Modern London Theatre

(Iowa City, Iowa: University of Iowa Press, 2008)

Subject(s): Theater; Drama; Criticism

Summary: Literature professor Yael Zarhy-Levo examines the individuals who come together to form the popular regard of contemporary British plays, focusing specifically on how these creative professionals help a theatrical work make its mark on the public's memory. *The Making of Theatrical Reputations: Studies from the Modern London Theatre* looks at four very different scenarios in today's British theater scene, and Zarhy-Levo breaks down each one to show how professionals both in and out of the theater industry have a direct impact on the reputation of a show. Among the situations discussed is an in-depth study of the controversial play *Look Back in Anger* by John Osborne. *The Making of Theatrical Reputations* includes a bibliography and an index.

Where it's reviewed:
Theatre Notebook, February 2009, page 63

Other books by the same author:
The Theatrical Critic as Cultural Agent: Constructing Pinter, Orton and Stoppard as Absurdist Playwrights, 2001

Other books you might like:
John Russell Brown, *The Routledge Companion to Directors' Shakespeare*, 2010
Marjorie Garber, *Shakespeare and Modern Culture*, 2009
Scott Kaiser, *Shakespeare's Wordcraft*, 2007
David L. Rinear, *Stage, Page, Scandals and Vandals: William E. Burton and Nineteenth-Century American Theatre*, 2004

159

THOMAS DE ZENGOTITA

Mediated: How the Media Shapes Our World and the Way We Live in It

(New York: Bloomsbury, 2005)

Subject(s): Culture; Television; Advertising

Summary: Journalist Thomas de Zengotita investigates the influence of the mass media on the individual mind and how this influence has formed collective perspectives on contemporary culture and world affairs. *Mediated: How the Media Shapes Our World and the Way We Live in It* chronicles the ever-growing pressure exerted by the media since the 1960s, illustrating just how egocentric and single-minded the average consumer has become. De Zengotita uses numerous examples to back up his findings, including the death of Princess Diana, the September 11 attacks, and the assassination of JFK.

Where it's reviewed:
Booklist, February 1, 2005, page 921
Kirkus Reviews, January 1, 2005, pages 30-31
Library Journal, February 2005, page 141
Publishers Weekly, February 2005, page 66

Other books you might like:
Jake Halpern, *Fame Junkies: The Hidden Truths Behind America's Favorite Addiction*, 2006
Regina Lynn, *The Sexual Revolution 2.0: Getting Connected, Upgrading Your Sex Life, and Finding True Love — or at Least a Dinner Date — in the Internet Age*, 2005
Jerry Mander, *Four Arguments for the Elimination of Television*, 1977
Neil Postman, *Technopoly: The Surrender of Culture to Technology*, 1992
Martin Rees, *Our Final Hour: A Scientist's Warning: How Terror, Error, and Environmental Disaster Threaten Humanity's Future in This Century*, 2003

160

WENDY I. ZIERLER

And Rachel Stole the Idols: The Emergence of Modern Hebrew Women's Writing

(Detroit, Michigan: Wayne State University Press, 2009)

Subject(s): Literature; Criticism; Jewish history

Summary: At one time, women were not allowed to produce Hebrew literature. In *And Rachel Stole the Idols: The Emergence of Modern Hebrew Women's Writing*, Wendy I. Zierler discusses the process by which women were able to rise up and reclaim Hebrew literature, using themes and symbols of femininity in their writing to assert power. Zierler particularly explores female Hebrew writers from the 19th and early 20th centuries, discussing different expressions of feminism in the texts and various methods of interpreting these texts. Writers discussed in this text include Meinkin Foner, Hava Shapiro, Nechama Pukhachevsky, Rachel Morpurgo, Yokheved Bat-Miriam, Esther Raab, Anda Pinkerfeld-Amir, Shulamit Kalugai, and Leah Goldberg.

Where it's reviewed:
Shofar: An Interdisciplinary Journal of Jewish Studies, Summer 2006, pages 149-151

Other books you might like:
Howard Cooper, *Living a Jewish Life: A Guide for Starting, Learning, Celebrating, and Parenting*, 1991
Anita Diamant, *Choosing a Jewish Life: A Handbook for People Converting to Judaism and for Their Family and Friends*, 1997
Anita Diamant, *Day After Night*, 2009
Anita Diamant, *Living a Jewish Life: A Guide for Starting, Learning, Celebrating, and Parenting*, 1991
Anita Diamant, *Pitching My Tent*, 2005
Anita Diamant, *The Red Tent*, 1997

Biographies and Memoirs

161

ANDRE AGASSI

Open: An Autobiography
(New York: A. Knopf, 2009)

Subject(s): Autobiographies; Tennis; Sports

Summary: In *Open: An Autobiography*, Andre Agassi chronicles his life as a professional tennis player. He recalls his "lost childhood," saying his forced training began when he was a preschooler. His father focused all of his energy on Agassi's skills and sent him all over the world to compete. By the age of 12, he was drinking and taking drugs on a regular basis. He rebelled by wearing his hair in a Mohawk and piercing his ears—a look that would get much attention on the courts. He dropped out of school to concentrate on tennis. Looking back, he says he hates tennis and always had, but had no alternative. Agassi explores his successful career on the court and problematic life off the court, filled with drugs, alcohol, fire, and doomed relationships.

Where it's reviewed:
CHOICE: Current Reviews for Academic Libraries, June 2010, page 1966
Library Journal, March 15, 2010, page p75
The New York Review of Books, June 24, 2010, page p8
The New York Times, Nov 9, 2009, page pC1
Time, Nov 16, 2009, page p59

Other books you might like:
Peter Bodo, *A Champion's Mind: Lessons from a Life in Tennis*, 2008
Brad Gilbert, *Winning Ugly: Mental Warfare in Tennis—Lessons from a Master*, 1993
  Steve Jamison, co-author
James Kaplan, *You Cannot Be Serious*, 2002
  John McEnroe, co-author
Daniel Paisner, *On the Line*, 2009
Pete Sampras, *A Champion's Mind: Lessons from a Life in Tennis*, 2008
Monica Seles, *Getting a Grip: On My Body, My Mind, My Self*, 2009
Serena Williams, *On the Line*, 2009

162

MAYA ANGELOU

Letter to My Daughter
(New York: Random House, 2008)

Subject(s): Autobiographies; Parent-child relations; Adolescence

Summary: Maya Angelou's *Letter to My Daughter* is a collection of short essays about events in her life that played a major role in making her the well-known poet and author she is today. While Angelou never had a daughter, she dedicates this collection to the young woman she feels would have existed had she had more children. Many of Angelou's vignettes tell tales of her childhood and adolescence. She writes about spending time with her grandmother and mother and about her first sexual experience, which later resulted in the birth of her son. Some entries are embarrassing and honest, while others are humorous and light.

Other books by the same author:
Great Food, All Day Long: Cook Splendidly, Eat Smart, 2010
Mother: A Cradle to Hold Me, 2006
Amazing Peace, 2005
A Song Flung Up to Heaven, 2002

Other books you might like:
Eve Ensler, *I Am an Emotional Creature: The Secret Life of Girls Around the World*, 2010
Kate Gosselin, *I Just Want You to Know: Letters to My Kids on Love, Faith, and Family*, 2010

163

DEBBY APPLEGATE

The Most Famous Man in America: The Biography of Henry Ward Beecher
(New York: Doubleday, 2006)

Subject(s): Biographies; Abolition of slavery; Philosophy

Summary: *The Most Famous Man in America: The*

Biography of Henry Ward Beecher by Debby Applegate chronicles the life of a man who was well known in his time as a minister, an intellectual, and an abolitionist, but whose memory has been all but forgotten. Beecher was the brother of Harriet Beecher Stowe, whose book *Uncle Tom's Cabin* sealed her fame in world history. With his sister, Beecher preached ideas that went against the grain of their Calvinist upbringing. The siblings spoke openly against slavery, and Beecher preached about a loving, hopeful, and forgiving God. While his ideas were celebrated, his personal indiscretions threatened to tarnish his reputation, as he was known for his extramarital relationships and was prosecuted publicly for one in particular discussed in this book.

Other books you might like:

Kai Bird, *American Prometheus: The Triumph and Tragedy of J. Robert Oppenheimer*, 2005

Joan Hedrick, *Harriet Beecher Stowe: A Life*, 1994

Jack Miles, *God: A Biography*, 1995

Martin Sherwin, *American Prometheus: The Triumph and Tragedy of J. Robert Oppenheimer*, 2005

Harriet Beecher Stowe, *Life and Letters of Harriet Beecher Stowe*, 1897

Harriet Beecher Stowe, *Life of Harriet Beecher Stowe Compiled from Her Letters and Journals by Her Son, Charles Edward Stowe*, 1897

164

DAVID ARCHULETA

Chords of Strength: A Memoir of Soul, Song and the Power of Perseverance

(New York: Celebra Hardcover, 2010)

Subject(s): Autobiographies; Singing; Music

Summary: In his first book, *Chords of Strength: A Memoir of Soul, Song and the Power of Perseverance*, David Archuleta discusses the role that music, specifically singing, has played in his life since the age of six. Ten years later, in 2007, Archuleta appeared on the television show *American Idol* and gained millions of fans. Despite suffering from vocal chord paralysis when he was younger, Archuleta always knew he would chase a career in the music business. It didn't matter to him that the words he sang didn't sound right at first. In this book, Archuleta explains how he mastered his vocal range with the support and inspiration of his friends and family members.

Other books you might like:

Clay Aiken, *Learning to Sing: Hearing the Music in Your Life*, 2004

Lance Bass, *Out of Sync: A Memoir*, 2007

Fantasia, *Life Is Not a Fairy Tale*, 2005

Allison Glock, *Learning to Sing: Hearing the Music in Your Life*, 2004

Donny Osmond, *Life Is Just What You Make It: My Story So Far*, 1999

Patricia Romanowski, co-author

Britney Spears, *Britney Spears' Heart to Heart*, 2000
Lynne Spears, co-author

165

SHALOM AUSLANDER

Foreskin's Lament: A Memoir

(New York: Riverhead Harcover, 2007)

Subject(s): Family relations; Family history; Judaism

Summary: Author Shalom Auslander is a magazine writer born and raised in New York. *Foreskin's Lament: A Memoir* chronicles his very difficult and traumatic upbringing in a strict, religious household. As Auslander prepares to welcome his son into the world, he faces the decision of whether to have him circumcised or to skip the procedure. The decision weighs on Auslander and takes him back to instance after instance of familial abuse in the name of religion over his lifetime. As is often the case with young men and women, Auslander sought to rebel against the values his parents instilled in him when he became old enough to do so, but his guilt over acts against God have continued to torture him. Despite the subject matter, Auslander's tone is sardonic and full of wit.

Where it's reviewed:
Library Journal, August 1, 2007, page 92
New York Times Book Review, October 21, 2007, page 5
Publishers Weekly, May 28, 2007, page 45

Other books by the same author:
Beware of God: Stories, 2007

Other books you might like:
Elisa Albert, *How This Night Is Different: Stories*, 2006
Saul Bellow, *Herzog*, 1964
Philip Roth, *Portnoy's Complaint*, 1969

166

BLAKE BAILEY

Cheever: A Life

(New York: Alfred A. Knopf, 2009)

Subject(s): Biographies; Authorship; Writers

Summary: In *Cheever: A Life*, author Blake Bailey provides an unprecedented look into the life of American author John Cheever. Bailey studies Cheever's life from his childhood during the Great Depression to his rise to fame. He also looks at Cheever's struggles with bisexuality, alcoholism, and family life, and his relationships with literary friends, such as John Irving, and rivals, such as J.D. Salinger. Aided by Cheever's own family, who granted access to Cheever's journals, Bailey is able to include insightful details and thoughts on Cheever's life. Many personal photos from Cheever's life accompany the text.

Where it's reviewed:
Booklist, Nov 1, 2008, page p4
The Economist, March 14, 2009, page p79

Time, April 6, 2009, page p64
USA Today, March 12, 2009, page p04D

Other books by the same author:
A Tragic Honesty: The Life and Work of Richard Yates, 2004

Other books you might like:
Raymond Carver, *Where I'm Calling From: Selected Stories*, 1988
John Cheever, *The Stories of John Cheever*, 1978
Flannery O'Connor, *The Complete Stories*, 1971
John Updike, *John Updike: The Early Stories*, 2004

167

EVAN L. BALKAN

Vanished!: Explorers Forever Lost
(Birmingham, Alabama: Menasha Ridge Press, 2007)

Subject(s): Biographies; Adventure; Travel

Summary: In *Vanished!: Explorers Forever Lost*, author Evan Balkan presents seven stories of adventure and tragedy about famous explorers who never returned from their final journeys. In "All Good Gringos Go to Heaven When Shot," Balkan writes about journalist Ambrose Bierce, who disappeared in 1913 while covering the revolution in Mexico. "The Honeymooners" chronicles the ill-fated attempt by newlyweds Glen and Bessie Hyde to navigate the Colorado River rapids through the Grand Canyon in 1928. "No Fear of Failure" describes Percy Fawcett's search for the lost city of "Z" in South America in 1925. *Vanished!* also includes stories about Amelia Earhart, Michael Rockefeller, Everett Ruess, and others.

Other books by the same author:
The Best in Tent Camping, 2008
Shipwrecked, 2008

Other books you might like:
David Grann, *The Devil and Sherlock Holmes: Tales of Murder, Madness, and Obsession*, 2010
David Grann, *The Lost City of Z: A Tale of Deadly Obsession in the Amazon*, 2009

168

JULIAN BARNES

Nothing to Be Frightened Of
(New York: Knopf, 2008)

Subject(s): Death; Humor; Philosophy

Summary: "For me, death is the one appalling fact which defines life; unless you are constantly aware of it, you cannot begin to understand what life is about" This statement neatly grasps the intentions of author Julian Barnes in writing *Nothing to Be Frightened Of*. Now in his sixties, Barnes writes about death and searching for the meaning of life. In the act of writing about his observations of the world around him, seeing friends in their last days, thinking up ways to stop obsessing about death, Barnes creates a personal philosophy to take him through the last stages of his life with his sense of humor intact.

Where it's reviewed:
Booklist, August 1, 2008, page p26
The Humanist, May-June 2009, page p44
The Nation, Oct 26, 2009, page p28
New York Times Book Review, Oct 9, 2008, page p38

Other books by the same author:
Arthur & George, 2007
The Lemon Table, 2005
Flaubert's Parrot, 1990

Other books you might like:
Jim Crace, *Being Dead*, 2000
J.E. Malpas, *Death and Philosophy*, 1999
   Robert C. Solomon, co-author

169

LANCE BASS

Out of Sync: A Memoir
(New York: Simon & Schuster, 2007)

Subject(s): Autobiographies; Music; Singing

Summary: Lance Bass, member of the popular boy band NSYNC, comes clean about his life in this candid autobiography. Two years after receiving a life-altering phone call from Justin Timberlake and leaving his small hometown, Bass found himself surrounded by millions of screaming fans. In *Out of Sync: A Memoir*, Bass chronicles his life from growing up in Clinton, Mississippi, to the pressure of being a devout Christian living the life of a pop star. Bass discusses how he felt when the band broke up and during the six months he spent training to go into outer space with the Russian space program. He opens up about his homosexuality and how he tried to hide it from the fans so it didn't impact NSYNC's popularity. He also explains why he decided to go public about his sexuality a few years later. *Out of Sync* provides a fascinating behind-the-scenes look at the life of an infamously private pop sensation.

Other books you might like:
Tyler Gray, *The Hit Charade: Lou Pearlman, Boy Bands, and the Biggest Ponzi Scheme in U.S. History*, 2008
Reichen Lehmkul, *Here's What We'll Say: Growing Up, Coming Out, and the U.S. Air Force Academy*, 2007
Rosie O'Donnell, *Celebrity Detox (The Fame Game)*, 2007
Guy Phillips, *Dancing with the Stars: Jive, Samba, and Tango Your Way into the Best Shape of Your Life*, 2007
Mark Tewksbury, *Inside Out: Straight Talk from a Gay Jock*, 2007

170

ISHMAEL BEAH

A Long Way Gone: Memoirs of a Boy Soldier

(New York: Farrar, Straus and Giroux, 2007)

Subject(s): Children and War; Drug Abuse; Military Life

Summary: *A Long Way Gone: Memoirs of a Boy Soldier* by Ishmael Beah is a first-hand account of the life of a child who survived a brutal civil war in West Africa. At the age of 12, Beah's childhood was destroyed when his family was killed in an attack on his village. After some time trying to survive as a refugee, Beah joined the army, where he was taught to kill and was given ready access to cocaine. Addicted to the killing and the drugs, he spent three years in the army until he was placed in a rehabilitation center supported by UNICEF. He became an advocate and spokesperson for the center, and eventually fled Sierra Leone for the United States.

Where it's reviewed:
New York Times Book Review, February 25, 2007, page 12
The New Yorker, February 12, 2007, page 85
Publishers Weekly, December 18, 2006, page 55
USA Today, August 14, 2008, page 11B

Other books you might like:
Greg Campbell, *Blood Diamonds: Tracing the Deadly Path of the World's Most Precious Stones*, 2001
John Bul Dau, *God Grew Tired of Us: A Memoir*, 2007
Alephonsion Deng, *They Poured Fire on Us from the Sky: The True Story of the Three Lost Boys from Sudan*, 2005
    Benson Deng, co-author
Dave Eggers, *What Is the What*, 2006
P.W. Singer, *Children at War*, 2005
Michael S. Sweeney, *God Grew Tired of Us: A Memoir*, 2007

171

ALISON BECHDEL

Fun Home: A Family Tragicomic

(New York: Mariner, 2006)

Subject(s): Autobiography; Coming-of-Age; Family Life

Summary: The "Fun Home" in the title of this autobiography is what Alison Bechdel and her brothers called the funeral home run by their father. He also worked as a High School English teacher and devoted much of his spare time to renovating and restoring the family's Victorian home. Bechdel's relationship with her father is central to this graphic novel, in which she recounts that books were the best way to gain the attention of her emotionally reserved and distant father. Her father's interests and actions, including a hearing that occurred

because he tried to buy a teenaged boy a beer, overshadowed much of Bechdel's childhood and coming of age, making adolescence that much more difficult. Even in college, when Bechdel came out as a lesbian to her mother, her mother replied that her father, too, was gay, topping Bechdel's declaration

Where it's reviewed:
Booklist, March 15, 2006, page 3
The New York Times, March 29, 2009, page 7
People Weekly, June 12, 2006, page 51
Publishers Weekly, February 27, 2006, page 40
Times Literary Supplement, Nov 17, 2006, page 32

Other books by the same author:
The Essential Dykes to Watch Out For, 2008
Dykes and Sundry Other Carbon-Based Life Forms to Watch Out For, 2003
Hot, Throbbing Dykes to Watch Out for, 1997

Other books you might like:
Phoebe Gloeckner, *A Child's Life and Other Stories*, 2000
Laurie Sandell, *The Impostor's Daughter: A True Memoir*, 2009
Marjane Satrapi, *The Complete Persepolis*, 2007
Adrian Tomine, *Shortcomings*, 2007
Chris Ware, *Jimmy Corrigan: The Smartest Kid on Earth*, 2000

172

VALERIE BERTINELLI

Losing It: And Gaining My Life Back One Pound at a Time

(New York: Free Press, 2008)

Subject(s): Family; Children; Addiction

Summary: Valerie Bertinelli first found fame at age fourteen when she starred in the television show *One Day at a Time*. Spending time in the entertainment spotlight turned Bertinelli's life upside down. After her successful stint on TV, Bertinelli remained in the public eye. In her autobiography, *Losing It: And Gaining My Life Back One Pound at a Time*, Bertinelli shares stories about both the good and the bad times in her life. She is open about her famously dramatic marriage to rock star Eddie Van Halen. She also discusses personal troubles such as a cocaine addiction and her battle with her weight. The actress also discusses the joys and trials of motherhood.

Other books you might like:
Frank Bruni, *Born Round: The Secret History of a Full-Time Eater*, 2009
Mackenzie Phillips, *High on Arrival*, 2009
Tori Spelling, *Uncharted terriTORI*, 2010

173

KAI BIRD
MARTIN SHERWIN , Co-Author

American Prometheus: The Triumph and Tragedy of J. Robert Oppenheimer
(New York: Knopf, 2005)

Subject(s): Biography; McCarthy Era; Nuclear Science

Summary: The life of J. Robert Oppenheimer, known as the father of the atomic bomb, had many milestones. He was head of the Manhattan Project, which brought together hundreds of nuclear physicists to build the first atomic bomb at Los Alamos, New Mexico. Following the bombings of Hiroshima and Nagasaki that lead to the American victory over Japan, Oppenheimer was hailed as a great patriot. When he began to speak in favor of arms control in the 1950s, however, he was branded a communist, and the U.S. government revoked his security clearance. Over twenty-five years of research went into this biography, which begins with Oppenhemier's youth in New York City and follows his career through to his final position directing the Institute for Advanced Study in Princeton, New Jersey. Thirty-two pages of photographs are included.

Where it's reviewed:
American Scientist, January/February 2006, page 68
Foeign Affairs, May/June 2005, page 136
New Republic, October 17, 2005, page 35
New York Times Book Review, September 22, 2005, page 73
Time, May 9, 2005, page 81

Other books by the same author:
A World Destroyed: Hiroshima and Its Legacies, 2003
The Color of Truth: McGeorge Bundy and William Bundy: Brothers in Arms, 2000
Crossing Mandelbaum Gate: Coming of Age Between the Arabs and Israelis, 1956-1978, 2000
The Chairman: John J. McCloy and the Making of the American Establishment, 1992

Other books you might like:
Jeremy Bernstein, *Oppenheimer: Portrait of an Enigma*, 2005
Jennet Conant, *109 East Palace: Robert Oppenheimer and the Secret City of Los Alamos*, 2005
Robert P. Crease, *J. Robert Oppenheimer: A Life*, 2006 Abraham Pais, co-author
Silvan G. Schweber, *Einstein and Oppenheimer: The Meaning of Genius*, 2008
Charles Thorpe, *Oppenheimer: The Tragic Intellect*, 2008

174

JULIA BLACKBURN

The Three of Us: A Family Story
(New York: Pantheon, 2008)

Subject(s): Family relations; Abuse; Addiction

Summary: Julia Blackburn's memoir focuses on the difficult relationships she shared with her eccentric artist parents. As the daughter of Thomas Blackburn, a poet, and Rosalie de Meric, a painter, Blackburn's childhood was anything but normal. Her parents separated when she was young, and she lived with her mother most of the time. Her father, who was an alcoholic and an addict, died early in her life. When she became a teenager, her mother saw her as a threat, sexually. Blackburn had an affair with one of her mother's former lovers, who later committed suicide. She uses excerpts from her personal diaries, her mother's papers, and her father's poetry to reconcile her feelings about the events that took place.

Where it's reviewed:
Booklist, May 15, 2008, page p16
Harper's Magazine, Sept 2008, page p8
New York Times Book Review, August 10, 2008, page p22
Publishers Weekly, April 21, 2008, page p43

Other books by the same author:
Daisy Bates in the Desert: A Woman's Life Among the Aborigines, 1995

Other books you might like:
Julia Blackburn, *With Billie*, 2005
Thomas Blackburn, *Thomas Blackburn: Selected Poems*, 2001
Katie Rophie, *Uncommon Arrangements: Seven Portraits of Married Life in London Literary Circles 1919-1939*, 2007

175

TOMEK BOGACKI

The Champion of Children: The Story of Janusz Korczak
(New York: Farrar Straus Giroux, 2009)

Subject(s): Biographies; Jews; Polish history

Summary: In *The Champion of Children: The Story of Janusz Korczak*, author Tomek Bogacki relates the inspiring story of the Polish doctor, author, and humanitarian who devoted his life to the welfare of Warsaw's poorest children. In 1912, Korczak established an orphanage for Jewish children that would empower its residents by giving them a voice in the organization's governance. After years of success, the orphanage was driven to the city's ghetto by Hitler's growing influence in Poland. Even under the desperate conditions imposed by Nazi rule, Janusz Korczak remained dedicated to his cause, finally losing his life at Treblinka with the beloved children of his orphanage.

Other books by the same author:
Monkeys and Dog Days, 2008
The Turtle and the Hippopotamus, 2002
Five Creatures, 2001
My First Garden, 2000

Other books you might like:
Deborah Durland DeSaix, *The Grand Mosque of Paris:*

A Story of How Muslims Rescued Jews During the Holocaust, 2009

Malka Drucker, *Portraits of Jewish-American Heroes*, 2008

Richard Michelson, *As Good as Anybody: Martin Luther King and Abraham Joshua Heschel's Amazing March Toward Freedom*, 2008

Richard Michelson, *A Is for Abraham: A Jewish Family Alphabet*, 2008

Karen Gray Ruell, *The Grand Mosque of Paris: A Story of How Muslims Rescued Jews During the Holocaust*, 2009

176

H.W. BRANDS

Traitor to His Class: The Privileged Life and Radical Presidency of Franklin Delano Roosevelt

(New York: Doubleday, 2008)

Subject(s): Economics; Politics; Presidents (Government)

Summary: Author, H.W. Brands, sheds new light on the life and accomplishments of FDR both in and out of the White House. It chronicles Roosevelt's early days growing up with a domineering mother, and how from an early age he was driven to succeed in politics. While coping with the onset of polio, Roosevelt saw first hand the effects of poverty at a spa in Warm Springs, GA. This experience led to much of the policies he implemented in Washington D.C., including his "New Deal". It also led to his popularity with the voters, which kept him elected for 12 years making him the longest serving president in American history. Roosevelt's policies had a lasting effect on politics, which can still be felt today.

Where it's reviewed:
The Economist, Nov 1, 2008, page p83
The Economist, July 23, 2005, page p76
Library Journal, Oct 1, 2008, page p77
The New York Review of Books, Feb 12, 2009[a0], page p4
Publishers Weekly, August 18, 2008, page p5

Other books by the same author:
American Colossus: The Triumph of Capitalism, 1865-1900, 2010
Andrew Jackson: His Life and Times, 2006
The Age of Gold: The California Gold Rush and the New American Dream, 2003
The First American: The Life and Times of Benjamin Franklin, 2002

Other books you might like:
H.W. Brands, *Andrew Jackson: His Life and Times*, 2005
H.W. Brands, *The First American: The Life and Times of Benjamin Franklin*, 2000
H.W. Brands, *T.R.: The Last Romantic*, 1997
Jean Edward Smith, *FDR*, 2007

177

DOUGLAS BRINKLEY

The Wilderness Warrior: Theodore Roosevelt and the Crusade for America

(New York: HarperCollins, 2009)

Subject(s): United States history; Presidents (Government); Biographies

Summary: In *The Wilderness Warrior: Theodore Roosevelt and the Crusade for America*, Douglas Brinkley explores the life of the 26th and youngest president of the United States. Our "naturalist" president had a passion for hunting and protecting the environment and wildlife. Brinkley includes information about Roosevelt's hiking trips in college, bird watching adventures, and hunting and ranching trips. He also explores the frequent conflicts Roosevelt had with other naturalists. Roosevelt protected more than 230 million acres of wild land and created 45 national forests. He also helped save animals that were in danger of becoming extinct such as buffalo, manatees, antelope, egrets, and elk.

Where it's reviewed:
American Heritage, Winter 2010, page p98
Library Journal, August 1, 2009, page p90
The New Yorker, August 24, 2009, page p77
Time, August 3, 2009, page p18

Other books by the same author:
The Reagan Diaries, 2009
The Great Deluge: Hurricane Katrina, New Orleans, and the Mississippi Gulf Coast, 2007
The Boys of Pointe du Hoc: Ronald Reagan, D-Day, and the U.S. Army 2nd Ranger Battalion, 2006
Wheels for the World: Henry Ford, His Company, and a Century of Progress, 2004

Other books you might like:
Timothy Egan, *The Big Burn: Teddy Roosevelt and the Fire that Saved America*, 2009
Roderick Nash, *Wilderness and the American Mind: 4th Ed.*, 2001
Amity Shlaes, *The Forgotten Man: A New History of the Great Depression*, 2007
Donald Worster, *A Passion for Nature: The Life of John Muir*, 2008

178

HUGH BROGAN

Alexis de Tocqueville: A Life

(New Haven, Connecticut: Yale University Press, 2007)

Story type: Historical
Subject(s): History; Politics; Social conditions

Summary: Alexis de Tocqueville was a political thinker from France who was best known for publishing multiple works about government, politics, and democracy in both France and America. In *Alexis de Tocqueville: A Life*, author Hugh Brogan provides details about the politician's early life, travels, and writings. Alexis de Tocqueville had many opinions about social injustice, inequality, and Western standards. He has been compared to John Stuart Mill and Karl Marx, and he was an active politician until Napoleon came to power.

Where it's reviewed:
Harper's Magazine, April 2007, page 89
Library Journal, March 1, 2007, page 91
National Review, April 2, 2007, page 46
Publishers Weekly, January 8, 2007, page 44

Other books by the same author:
The Penguin History of the USA, 2001

Other books you might like:
Henry Reeve, *Democracy in America*, 1971
Alexis de Tocqueville, *Letters from America*, 1931
Alexis de Tocqueville, *Democracy in America*, 1971
Cheryl B. Welch, *The Cambridge Companion to Tocqueville*, 2006
Sheldon S. Wolin, *Tocqueville between Two Worlds: The Making of a Political and Theoretical Life*, 2001

179

FREDERICK BROWN
Flaubert: A Biography
(New York: Little, Brown and Co., 2006)

Subject(s): Biographies; History; Writers
Summary: *Flaubert: A Biography,* by Frederick Brown, is a detailed reflection on the life of Gustave Flaubert (1821-1880), author of *Madame Bovary*. Brown focuses on Flaubert's life in Paris and his time in Rouen, Normandy. He discusses the important people in Flaubert's life and their influence on his writing, along with Flaubert's own beliefs and ideals.

Where it's reviewed:
Booklist, February 15, 2006, page 32
Choice, October 2006, page 303
Library Journal, January 2010, page 118

Other books by the same author:
For the Soul of France: Culture Wars in the Age of Dreyfus, 2010
Zola: A Life, 1997

Other books you might like:
Dacia Mariani, *Searching for Emma: Gustave Flaubert and Madame Bovary*, 1998
Francis Steegmuller, *Flaubert and Madame Bovary*, 1939
Geoffrey Wall, *Flaubert: A Life*, 2002

180

TINA BROWN
The Diana Chronicles
(New York: Broadway Books, 2007)

Subject(s): Biography; Heroes and Heroines; Princes and Princesses

Summary: Tina Brown reveals the secrets of the late Princess Diana. Brown shows that the princess di knew how to manipulate the media to her advantage but also takes a closer look at the real Diana. She talks about Diana's difficulties in acting as a dutiful wife and mother as well as her being an outsider as far as the British royal family was concerned.

Where it's reviewed:
The New Republic, August 27, 2007, page 44
New York Times Book Review, June 10, 2007, page 1
Newsweek, June 18, 2007, page 50
USA Today, May 3, 2007, page 06D

Other books you might like:
Paul Burrell, *The Way We Were: Remembering Diana*, 2006
Andrew Morton, *Diana: Her True Story, in Her Own Words*, 1997

181

FRANK BRUNI
Born Round: The Secret History of a Full-Time Eater
(New York: Penguin Press, 2009)

Subject(s): Autobiographies; Journalism; Eating disorders
Summary: *Born Round: The Secret History of a Full-Time Eater* by Frank Bruni is an autobiography focusing on the writer's lifetime struggles with weight. Bruni grew up equating food with love and was constantly fighting to lose weight. He became a bulimic as an adult: binging, sleep eating, and abusing laxatives. Bruni eventually became the restaurant critic for The *New York Times* and began a life of eating at restaurants seven days per week. He writes honestly of his experiences of never being satisfied with his appearance, and the guilt and shame that he felt when he would continue to eat and remain unable to lose the weight, even postponing dates in the hope of just losing a few pounds.

Where it's reviewed:
Library Journal, August 1, 2009, page 102
New York Times, August 26, 2009, page C4
New York Times Book Review, August 19, 2009, page BR7

Other books by the same author:
Italy: The Best Travel Writing from the New York Times, 2005
Ambling Into History: The Unlikely Odyssey of George W. Bush, 2002
A Gospel of Shame: Children, Sexual Abuse, and the Catholic Church, 2002

Other books you might like:
Elizabeth Berg, *The Day I Ate Whatever I Wanted: And Other Small Acts of Liberation*, 2008
Anthony Bourdain, *Kitchen Confidential Updated Edition: Adventures in the Culinary Underbelly*, 2007
Bill Buford, *Heat: An Amateur's Adventures as Kitchen Slave, Line Cook, Pasta-Maker, and Apprentice to a Dante-Quoting Butcher in Tuscany*, 2006

Marya Hornbacher, *Wasted: A Memoir of Anorexia and Bulemia*, 1998

Jeffrey Steingarten, *The Man Who Ate Everything: And Other Gastronomic Feats, Disputes and Pleasurable Pursuits*, 1997

182

JEN BRYANT

A River of Words: The Story of William Carlos Williams

(Grand Rapids, Mich: Eerdmans Books for Young Readers, 2008)

Subject(s): Biographies; Poetry; Writing

Summary: When William Carlos Williams was a child, he often escaped to a river near his New Jersey hometown. "The water went slipping and sliding over/the smooth rocks, then poured in a torrent/over the falls, then quieted again below./The river's music both excited and soothed Willie." This image flows through this biography as Williams, bowing under pressure to become a doctor even though his heart is in his poetry, always responds to an inner need to write his "river of words." Sweet's detailed collages and watercolors add depth, while Bryant's poetic text underscores the love of language and expression that is so much a part of Willams's life.

Other books by the same author:
Kaleidoscope Eyes, 2009
Ringside 1925: Views from the Scopes Trial, 2008

Other books you might like:
Sharon Creech, *Hate That Cat*, 2008
Ted Lewin, *I Was a Teenage Professional Wrestler*, 1993
Leonard Marcus, *Pass It Down! Five Picture-Book Families Make Their Mark*
Joyce Sidman, *This Is Just to Say: Poems of Apology and Forgiveness*, 2007
Jane Yolen, *My Uncle Emily*, 2009

183

MIKA BRZEZINKSI

All Things at Once

(New York: Weinstein, 2010)

Subject(s): Autobiographies; Journalism; Entertainment industry

Summary: In her first book, *All Things at Once*, journalist Mika Brzezinski, co-host of MSNBC's *Morning Joe*, discusses her career and family life. Beginning with her first job as a cub reporter in New England, to her jobs at local affiliate stations in Hartford, Connecticut, and then anchor positions at CBS and MSNBC, Brzezinski describes the trajectory of her life as she manages a career along with raising two daughters.

Other books you might like:
Laura Bush, *Spoken from the Heart*, 2010
Haven Kimmel, *A Girl Named Zippy: Growing Up*

Small in Mooreland, Indiana, 2001
Jenny Sandford, *Staying True*, 2010
Joe Scarborough, *The Last Best Hope: Restoring Conservatism and America's Promise*, 2009
Jeannette Walls, *The Glass Castle: A Memoir*, 2005

184

BILL BUFORD

Heat: An Amateur's Adventures as Kitchen Slave, Line Cook, Pasta-Maker, and Apprentice to a Dante-Quoting Butcher in Tuscany

(New York: Vintage Press, 2006)

Subject(s): Biography; Cooking; Journalism

Summary: Bill Buford is a journalist with the *New Yorker* who wanted to write a profile of celebrity chef and restaurant owner Mario Batali. Rather than just interviewing the famous chef, he conceived the idea of spending time in Batali's kitchen: cooking, prepping, obeying orders, and getting an insider's view of one of New York's most lauded chefs at work. The resultant book explores not just Batali's personality, but also the history and techniques of Italian cuisine, the inner workings of a three-star restaurant, the production of Batali's television shows, and the sweaty, demanding grunt-work of restaurant cooking. Buford also chronicles his own almost constant kitchen mishaps and cooking injuries.

Where it's reviewed:
New Statesman, July 17, 2006, page 56
New York Times Book Review, May 28, 2006, page 9
People Weekly, June 26, 2006, page 49
Restaurant Hospitality, December 2006, page 23

Other books by the same author:
Among the Thugs, 1993

Other books you might like:
Anthony Bourdain, *Kitchen Confidential Updated Edition: Adventures in the Culinary Underbelly*, 2007
M.F.K. Fisher, *The Art of Eating*, 1963
Jeffrey Steingarten, *The Man Who Ate Everything: And Other Gastronomic Feats, Disputes and Pleasurable Pursuits*, 1997

185

ELISABETH BUMILLER

Condoleezza Rice: An American Life: A Biography

(New York: Random House, 2007)

Subject(s): African Americans; Politics; Biographies

Summary: *Condoleezza Rice: An American Life: A Biography* by Elisabeth Bumiller describes the life of Condoleezza Rice. Bumiller's description of Rice's life begins in the late nineteenth century with Rice's great-great grandfather and ends within a year of Rice's last year as Secretary of State. The book chronicles many of Rice's personal achievements. She excelled in Soviet-area studies at the University of Denver and later became provost at Stanford. She worked on George H.W. Bush's staff as a Soviet analyst for the National Security Council. Ultimately, she became the first black female Secretary of State, serving under President George W. Bush. Bullimer's research is based on hundreds of interviews, both with Rice herself and with people close to her including coworkers, friends, and family members. The author does not attempt to cover up Rice's flaws, especially when discussing her time in Washington.

Where it's reviewed:
Foreign Affairs, Nov-Dec 2008, page p166
Library Journal, March 15, 2008, page p104
New York Times Book Review, Jan 27, 2008, page p18

Other books by the same author:
For Women Only, Revised Edition: A Revolutionary Guide to Reclaiming Your Sex Life, 2005
May You Be the Mother of a Hundred Sons: A Journey Among the Women of India, 1991

Other books you might like:
Mary Beth Brown, *Condi: The Life of a Steel Magnolia*, 2008
George W. Bush, *Decision Points*, 2010
Marcus Mabry, *Twice As Good: Condoleezza Rice and Her Path to Power*, 2007
Leslie Montgomery, *The Faith of Condoleezza Rice*, 2007
Joseph Persico, *My American Journey*, 1995
    Colin L. Powell, co-author
Condoleezza Rice, *Extraordinary, Ordinary People: A Memoir of Family*, 2010

186

MICHAEL BURLINGAME

Abraham Lincoln: A Life, Volumes 1 and 2

(Baltimore: The Johns Hopkins University Press, 2008)

Subject(s): Abolition of slavery; United States Civil War, 1861-1865; United States history, 1865-1901

Summary: *Abraham Lincoln: A Life* by Michael Burlingame is a two-volume collection about President Abraham Lincoln's life. Using information by the various Lincoln biographies released in recent years, Burlingame presents a comprehensive account of Lincoln's personal life and career. The first volume includes information about Lincoln's childhood and adolescence, his relationship with his family, and the motivations that led to his interest in law. It ends with his election to Congress in 1840. The second volume focuses on Lincoln's tenure as president, discussing all of the leader's accomplishments and shortcomings. This collection was released in time to honor Lincoln's 200th birthday.

Where it's reviewed:
Journal of American Culture, Sept 2009, page p267
Journal of Southern History, May 2010, page p401

New York Times Book Review, Feb 8, 2009, page p1
Publishers Weekly, Nov 3, 2008, page p50

Other books by the same author:
Abraham Lincoln: The Observations of John G. Nicolay and John Hay, 2007
The Inner World of Abraham Lincoln, 1997

Other books you might like:
Ron Chernow, *Washington: A Life*, 2010
Eric Foner, *The Fiery Trial: Abraham Lincoln and American Slavery*, 2010
Donald Stoker, *The Grand Design: Strategy and the U.S. Civil War*, 2010
Ronald C. White, *A. Lincoln: A Biography*, 2009

187

CAROL BURNETT

This Time Together: Laughter and Reflection

(New York: Harmony Books, 2010)

Subject(s): Autobiographies; Entertainment industry; Television

Summary: *This Time Together: Laughter and Reflection* is famed comedian and actress Carol Burnett's autobiography. Burnett chronicles her life in the entertainment industry, beginning with her first jobs in New York City and her game show appearances, followed by 11 years on *The Carol Burnett Show*. Burnett includes a number of personal anecdotes, including funny interactions with fans and the ways in which various sketches on her show were conceived, as well as stories about her celebrity costars and other friends. This personal examination of her career isn't always humorous, however, as Burnett tells of difficult times and challenging losses in her life.

Other books by the same author:
One More Time: A Memoir, 2003

Other books you might like:
Lucille Ball, *Love, Lucy*, 1996
    Betty Hannah Hoffman, co-author
Steve Martin, *Born Standing Up: A Comic's Life*, 2007
Mary Tyler Moore, *After All*, 1995
Bob Newhart, *I Shouldn't Even Be Doing This and Other Things That Strike Me as Funny*, 2006
Barbara Walters, *Audition: A Memoir*, 2008

188

GEORGE W. BUSH

Decision Points

(New York: Crown, 2010)

Subject(s): Presidents (Government); United States history; Politics

Summary: *Decision Points* is a frank memoir by one of the most controversial figures in 21st-century American politics. George W. Bush, the 43rd president of the United States, looks back on his personal and public lives, focusing on the life-changing decisions he has made. From his childhood of wealth and privilege as son to Texas's royal family to the history-making election that forever altered his destiny, from defense of his political decisions to extolling the joys of being a husband and father, Bush recounts the experiences that have shaped his life and his presidency.

Other books by the same author:

George W. Bush on God and Country: The President Speaks Out About Faith, Principle, and Patriotism, 2004

We Will Prevail: President George W. Bush on War, Terrorism and Freedom, 2003

A Charge to Keep: My Journey to the White House, 1999

Other books you might like:

Laura Bush, *Spoken from the Heart,* 2010

Bill Clinton, *My Life,* 2004

Robert Draper, *Dead Certain: The Presidency of George W. Bush,* 2007

Scott McClellan, *What Happened: Inside the Bush White House and Washington's Culture of Deception,* 2008

Condoleezza Rice, *Extraordinary, Ordinary People: A Memoir of Family,* 2010

189

LAURA BUSH

Spoken from the Heart

(New York: Scribner, 2010)

Subject(s): Autobiographies; Presidents (Government); Marriage

Summary: Laura Bush, nee Welch, grew up in a West Texas oil town; years later, she would become one of the most treasured first ladies of the United States. In her first book, *Spoken from the Heart,* she chronicles her life as the wife of the man who would become the 43rd president of the United States. This book looks at her romance with George W. Bush and their marriage and family. She also discusses the years she spent in the White House as the first lady, and those leading up to that point. Bush is the founder of the National Book Festival and the Texas Book Festival.

Other books you might like:

Barbara Bush, *Barbara Bush: A Memoir,* 1994

George W. Bush, *Decision Points,* 2010

George W. Bush, *A Charge to Keep: My Journey to the White House,* 2001

Hillary Rodham Clinton, *Living History,* 2003

Sarah Palin, *Going Rogue,* 2009

190

TIM BUTCHER

Blood River: A Journey to Africa's Broken Heart

(New York: Grove Press, 2008)

Subject(s): Biographies; History; Africa

Summary: In a first book, *Blood River: A Journey to Africa's Broken Heart,* author and journalist Tim Butcher travels to the African Congo in order to retrace the path that the first western explorer traveled along the Congo River in 1877. What begins as a historical journey becomes a travelogue and investigative report on the current state of the Congo. Butcher's 3,000-kilometer journey exposes him to the brutalities of war in an area that was once the most promising prospect for an African nation. Using explorer Henry Stanley's travelogue, *Through the Dark Continent,* as a guide, Butcher reveals historical and current perspectives on the Congo.

Other books you might like:

Peter Godwin, *When a Crocodile Eats the Sun: A Memoir of Africa,* 2005

Walter Isaacson, *Einstein: His Life and Universe,* 2007

191

PETER CANELLOS

Last Lion: The Fall and Rise of Ted Kennedy

(New York: Simon & Schuster, 2009)

Subject(s): Biographies; Political campaigns; United States history

Summary: In his first book, *Last Lion: The Fall and Rise of Ted Kennedy,* author Peter Canellos provides a comprehensive study of one of the most powerful and influential senators in all of American political history. Compiled from a series of reports from *The Boston Globe,* this biography takes readers down the path of Ted Kennedy's unlikely political career. As the youngest brother of John F. Kennedy, Ted did not often show political ambitions. The few times that he took up the political mantra, he met with personal tragedy. Detailing all aspects of Kennedy's life, Canellos shows the physical and mental obstacles that he had to overcome to reach the position that he holds today.

Other books you might like:

Jill Abramson, *Obama: The Historic Journey,* 2009

The Boston Globe, *Ted Kennedy: Scenes from an Epic Life,* 2009

Vincent Bzdek, *The Kennedy Legacy: Jack, Bobby and Ted and a Family Dream Fulfilled,* 2009

Walter Cronkite, *Reporter's Life,* 1996

Edward M. Kennedy, *True Compass: A Memoir,* 2009

The New York Times, *Obama: The Historic Journey,* 2009

192

DAVID CANNADINE

Mellon: An American Life

(New York: A. A. Knopf, 2006)

Subject(s): United States history; Politics; Business

Summary: In *Mellon: An American Life*—biography of the American entrepreneur Andrew Mellon— author David Cannadine provides great insight on both the man and the business practices that made Mellon a legend. Cannadine starts with Mellon's humble beginnings in Pittsburgh and the lessons he learned from his immigrant father. Mellon put these lessons into practice and had great professional success in many business sectors. Though his personal life was less of a success, Mellon's expertise, and money made him the Treasury Secretary and bought an impressive art collection, now housed in The National Gallery of Art. Mellon's political life was turbulent, having been applauded during the Roaring Twenties and but blamed for the Great Depression. Nevertheless, Cannadine sees Andrew Mellon as one of American's premier businessmen.

Other books you might like:

Ron Chernow, *The House of Morgan: An American Banking Dynasty and the Rise of Modern Finance*, 1990

Ron Chernow, *Titan: The Life of John D. Rockefeller, Sr.*, 1998

Ron Chernow, *The Warburgs*, 1993

David Nasaw, *Andrew Carnegie*, 2006

T.J. Stiles, *The First Tycoon: The Epic Life of Cornelius Vanderbilt*, 2009

193

ROBERT CARO

Master of the Senate: The Years of Lyndon Johnson: Vol. 3

(New York: Vintage Press, 2002)

Series: The Years of Lyndon Johnson
Subject(s): Biography; Careers; Civil Rights

Summary: This biographical account of Lyndon Johnson's years in the United States Senate, from his election in 1949 until his acceptance of the vice-presidential nomination in 1960, examines his skillful acquisition and use of power during those years. Particular attention is given to his strategic work to pass the 1957 Civil Rights Act, legislation he believed would help to propel him toward the presidency.

Where it's reviewed:

Businessweek, May 6, 2002, page p15
Library Journal, May 1, 2002, page p11
New Statesman, Sept 2, 2002, page p35
Publishers Weekly, July 1, 2002, page p34

Other books by the same author:

Means of Ascent, 1991
The Path to Power, 1990

Other books you might like:

Robert Caro, *Means of Ascent*, 1990

Robert Caro, *The Path to Power*, 1999
Robert Caro, *The Power Broker: Robert Moses and the Fall of New York*, 1974
Robert Olfshski, *Agendas and Decisions*, 2008

194

DAVID CARR

The Night of the Gun: A Reporter Investigates the Darkest Story of His Life. His Own.

(New York: Simon & Schuster, 2008)

Subject(s): Addiction

Summary: David Carr is an elegant and insightful writer, a New York Times media columnist, and an ex-junkie. Not content to wallow, as so many before him have, in his own faulty memories of a time when he did crack and beat women, Carr puts his considerable investigative skills to use in constructing a truthful engrossing account of his own downfall. When former drug buddies are interviewed, prison reports are examined and rehab records, obtained, Carr is shocked at the ugliness of his former self. This is illustrated in an incident from which Carr gets the book's title. He is sure that long ago he had a fight with a fellow user and friend during which the friend pulled a gun on him. The gun, it turns out, was in Carr's hand aimed at his friend. The witty, weird story is long and winding, laced with violence, relapse and repercussions. Along the way he has twin daughters, fights cancer, wears a tuxedo to jail, and finally transforms into the single father with a job who meets his responsibilities and pens one riveting junkie memoir.

Where it's reviewed:

New York Times Book Review, August 10, 2008, page p12
The New Yorker, August 4, 2008, page p73
People, August 18, 2008, page p4

Other books you might like:

Augusten Burroughs, *Dry: A Memoir*, 2003
Thomas De Quincey, *Confessions of an English Opium Eater*, 1821
Mary Karr, *The Liars' Club*, 1995
Caroline Knapp, *Drinking: A Love Story*, 1996
David Sheff, *Beautiful Boy: A Father's Journey through His Son's Addiction*, 2008
Koren Zailckas, *Smashed: Story of a Drunken Girlhood*, 2005

195

ARTHUR H. CASH

John Wilkes: The Scandalous Father of Civil Liberty

(Cambridge, Massachusetts: Yale University Press, 2006)

Subject(s): Biographies; Writers; British history, 1714-1815

Summary: In *John Wilkes: The Scandalous Father of Civil Liberty*, author Arthur H. Cash chronicles the life of an extraordinary, though mostly obscure, figure in English history. Wilkes was an 18th-century radical who supported William Pitt and made public his ideas about liberty and freedom, which would influence the Founding Fathers of the United States in their writing of the Constitution. The author also makes a case for Wilkes's influence on the Enlightenment in England. On the personal side, Cash chronicles the life of a libertine, who left his wife for many mistresses, wrote dirty limericks, and was known for not paying his debts.

Where it's reviewed:
Booklist, Jan 1, 2006, page p50
Library Journal, Feb 1, 2006, page p88
New Statesman, March 6, 2006, page p52

Other books by the same author:
Laurence Sterne: The Later Years, 1993

Other books you might like:
Pauline Maier, *From Resistance to Revolution: Colonial Radicals and the Development of American Opposition to Britain, 1765-1776*, 1972
Peter Marshall, *Reformation England 1480-1642*, 2003
David Underdown, *Fire from Heaven: Life in an English Town in the Seventeenth Century*, 1992
Gordon S. Wood, *The Radicalism of the American Revolution*, 1991

196

JUNG CHANG
JON HALLIDAY , Co-Author

Mao: The Unknown Story

(New York: Random House, Anchor, 2005)

Subject(s): Biography; Communism; History

Summary: Authors Chang and Halliday aim to provide evidence that Mao Tse-tung should be remembered only as an ambitious, egotistical leader who was responsible for the deaths of millions of Chinese. The authors researched this biography using archives in China, Russia, and other countries to build a portrait of Mao as a ruthless, power-driven leader. Mao's life and political ambition are recounted in a global context, framed by events such as World War II, the Korean War, the Cultural Revolution, and the Vietnam War.

Where it's reviewed:
The Atlantic, December 2005, page 115
The National Review, February 13, 2006, page 9
The New York Review of Books, November 3, 2005, page 23
The New York Times, January 23, 2006, page A15

Other books by the same author:
Wild Swans : Three Daughters of China, 2003
Madame Sun Yat-Sen: Soong Ching-Ling, 1986

Other books you might like:
Patrick Lescot, *Before Mao: The Untold Story of Li Lisan and the Creation of Communist China*, 2004

Ina Rilke, *Balzac and the Little Chinese Seamstress*, 2001
Dai Sijie, co-author
Gao Wengian, *Zhou Enlai: The Last Perfect Revolutionary*, 2007
Li Zhi-Sui, *The Private Life of Chairman Mao*, 1995

197

DUANE "DOG" CHAPMAN

Where Mercy is Shown, Mercy is Given

(New York: Hyperion Books, 2010)

Subject(s): Autobiographies; Crime; Law enforcement

Summary: Bounty hunter Duane "Dog" Chapman gives a behind-the-scenes look at some of his most challenging cases in *Where Mercy is Shown, Mercy is Given*. Chapman, whose life is featured on an A&E reality television series titled *Dog the Bounty Hunter*, is an expert on fugitive behavior. He is well known for his role as compassionate mentor to the fugitives he chases, offering them the chance to open their eyes and turn their lives around. In this work, Chapman also explores his own past as a fugitive and explains how he uses his past struggles with abuse, addiction, and crime to help others right their lives.

Other books by the same author:
You Can Run but You Can't Hide, 2007

Other books you might like:
Duane "Dog" Chapman, *You Can Run but You Can't Hide*, 2007
Terri Irwin, *Steve and Me*, 2007
Ozzy Osbourne, *I Am Ozzy*, 2009
Jesse Ventura, *I Ain't Got Time to Bleed: Reworking the Body Politic from the Bottom Up*, 1999

198

CHRISTOPHER CICCONE
WENDY LEIGH , Co-Author

Life with My Sister Madonna

(New York: Simon Spotlight Entertainment, 2008)

Subject(s): Betrayal; Family Relations; Family Saga

Summary: Christopher Ciccone, brother to iconic superstar Madonna, chronicles their love-hate relationship from the very beginning. He talks about growing up in Michigan in a large family, and how after Madonna moved to New York City, she invited him along and he witnessed her meteoric rise to stardom. Ciccone flitted in an out of her life, working for her as a back-up dancer, personal assistant, dresser, and even designer. Like any siblings, there was fighting and forgiving. Although Ciccone admits that Madonna treated him badly and kept pushing him away, he always went running back whenever she would snap her fingers. As a sibling to a superstar, Ciccone obviously struggles with living in his older sister's huge shadow. By writing this revealing book not only about his sister and her excess, but also about himself, Ciccone tries to reconcile his bitterness at Madonna's action and his love for his sister.

Where it's reviewed:
Library Journal, October 15, 2008, page 105

Other books you might like:
Kitty Kelley, *Oprah: A Biography*, 2010
Madonna, *The English Roses*, 2003
Madonna, *Sex*, 1992
Andrew Morton, *Angelina: An Unauthorized Biography*, 2010
Andrew Morton, *Tom Cruise: An Unauthorized Biography*, 2008

199

ADRIENNE CLARKSON

Norman Bethune

(Toronto, Ontario, Canada: Penguin Canada, 2009)

Subject(s): Biographies; History; Medical care

Summary: *Norman Bethune* by Adrienne Clarkson is from the Extraordinary Canadians series and is a biography of Canadian doctor and humanitarian Norman Bethune. In the first half of the 20th century, Bethune made many outstanding contributions to the field of medicine, including the development of new surgical tools and mobile blood-transfusion units. Bethune also fought for a public health care plan to provide medical care for all; some viewed this as a communist effort, while others saw it as a humanitarian idea. This biography provides insight into Norman Bethune's personality, background, and his major life accomplishments.

Other books by the same author:
Heart Matters, 2006

Other books you might like:
Mark Kingwell, *Glenn Gould*, 2009
Michael Posner, *The Last Honest Man: Mordecai Richler: an Oral Biography*, 2004
Nino Ricci, *Pierre Elliott Trudeau*, 2009
Jane Urquhart, *L.M. Montgomery*, 2009
William Carlos Williams, *William Carlos Williams: The Doctor Stories*, 1984

200

PAUL CLEMENS

Made in Detroit: A South of 8 Mile Memoir

(New York: Doubleday, 2005)

Subject(s): Race relations; Cultural identity; Childhood

Summary: In *Made in Detroit: A South of 8 Mile Memoir*, Paul Clemens chronicles his life in northeastern Detroit as a white child in an increasingly African American city. Born in 1973, the year that Coleman Young was elected Detroit's first black mayor, Clemens witnessed firsthand the decline of the car manufacturing industry, the dramatic increase in crime, and the phenomenon of white flight. Raised in a small community of whites and educated in Catholic schools, Clemens struggled throughout his life with the concept of racism. Though there is no mistake that Detroit's downturn coincided with Young's 20 years in office, Clemens avoids reducing the city's woes to racism and retains a strong sense of hometown pride.

Where it's reviewed:
Library Journal, July 1, 2005, page 94
The New Yorker, October 10, 2005, page 87
Publishers Weekly, May 30, 2005, page 47

Other books you might like:
Kevin Boyle, *Arc of Justice: A Saga of Race, Civil Rights, and Murder in the Jazz Age*, 2004
Paul Clemens, *Punching Out: One Year in a Closing Auto Plant*, 2011
Susan Messer, *Grand River and Joy: A Novel*, 2009
Upton Sinclair, *The Flivver King*, 1969

201

STEVE COLL

The Bin Ladens: An Arabian Family in the American Century

(New York: Penguin Press, 2008)

Subject(s): Middle East; Islam; History

Summary: The bin Laden family has become world-renowned as of late, due to the actions of its most infamous member. But the family as a whole has a story to tell, and Steven Coll does so with little bias in his book about the Arabian clan. He starts with the patriarch, Mohammed bin Laden, who made his wealth constructing homes and other buildings for the Saudi royal family. He fathered 54 children by many different women and led a life that combined Western and Islamic values. His children, including Osama, were able to attend the best schools in the region and most went into the family construction business after graduating. However, Osama, whom others describe as a timid child, was more interested in the Islamic faith than in good business deals; when the family began negotiating with the United States in the 1980s, he made his radical opinions known. From then on, a rift opened up between Osama and the rest of the bin Laden clan. Coll simultaneously tells the story of an individual and a group, of differing ideals, while at the same time addressing a world tragedy that still affects many today.

Where it's reviewed:
Booklist, April 1, 2008, page p4
The Economist, April 12, 2008, page p93
New York Times Book Review, May 25, 2008, page p11
Publishers Weekly, March 31, 2008, page p54

Other books by the same author:
On the Grand Trunk Road: A Journey into South Asia, 2009

Ghost Wars: The Secret History of the CIA, Afghanistan, and Bin Laden, from the Soviet Invasion to September 10, 2001, 2004

Other books you might like:

Rachel Bronson, *Thicker than Oil: America's Uneasy Partnership with Saudi Arabia,* 2006

Steve Coll, *Ghost Wars: The Secret History of the CIA, Afghanistan, and Bin Laden, from the Soviet Invasion to September 10, 2001,* 2004

Robert Lacey, *Inside the Kingdom: Kings, Clerics, Modernists, Terrorists, and the Struggle for Saudi Arabia,* 2009

Lawrence Wright, *The Looming Tower: Al-Qaeda and the Road to 9/11,* 2006

202

LINDA COLLEY

The Ordeal of Elizabeth Marsh: A Woman in World History

(New York: Random House, Anchor, 2007)

Summary: *A Long Way Gone: Memoirs of a Boy Soldier* by Ishmael Beah is a first-hand account of the life of a child who survived a brutal civil war in West Africa. At the age of 12, Beah's childhood was destroyed when his family was killed in an attack on his village. After some time trying to survive as a refugee, Beah joined the army, where he was taught to kill and was given ready access to cocaine. Addicted to the killing and the drugs, he spent three years in the army until he was placed in a rehabilitation center supported by UNICEF. He became an advocate and spokesperson for the center, and eventually fled Sierra Leone for the United States.

Where it's reviewed:
The Economist, July 14, 2007, page 89
Library Journal, July 1, 2007, page 98
New York Times Book Review, September 23, 2007, page 26
The New Yorker, October 22, 2007, page 175

Other books by the same author:
Britons: Forging the Nation 1707-1837; Revised Edition, 2009
Captives: Britain, Empire, and the World, 1600-1850, 2004

Other books you might like:

Judith Bennett, *A Medieval Life: Cecilia Penifader of Brigstock, c. 1297-1344,* 1998

Susan Butler, *East to the Dawn: The Life of Amelia Earhart,* 1997

Linda Colley, *Captives: Britain, Empire, and the World, 1600-1850,* 2003

Donald Spoto, *Joan: The Mysterious Life of the Heretic Who Became,* 2007

203

BERNARD COOPER

The Bill from My Father: A Memoir

(New York: Simon & Schuster, 2006)

Subject(s): Autobiographies; Father-son relations; Homosexuality

Summary: After his father's death in 2000, author Bernard Cooper was surprised to receive a bill—for every service his father had ever provided him throughout his life. In *The Bill from My Father: A Memoir,* Cooper provides details about the relationship he had with his deceased father, a powerful divorce attorney who practiced until he was 83 years old. Cooper's father appreciated the work ethics of the author's successful, heterosexual brothers more than he ever appreciated the writings of his sole homosexual son. Cooper captures this frustrating relationship within the pages of his memoir. Bernard Cooper is also the author of *Maps to Anywhere.*

Where it's reviewed:
Booklist, February 1, 2006, page 16
Lamda Book Report, Spring 2006, page 22
Publishers Weekly, November 7, 2005, page 66

Other books by the same author:
Guess Again: Short Stories, 2006
Truth Serum: A Memoir, 1997

Other books you might like:

Augusten Burroughs, *Running with Scissors: A Memoir,* 2002

Bernard Cooper, *Maps to Anywhere,* 1990

Kathryn Harrison, *The Kiss,* 1997

Mary Karr, *The Liars' Club,* 1995

Tobias Wolff, *This Boy's Life: A Memoir,* 1989

204

JOHN MILTON COOPER

Woodrow Wilson: A Biography

(New York: Knopf, 2009)

Story type: Historical - World War I
Subject(s): United States history, 1921-1945; World War I, 1914-1918; Presidents (Government)

Summary: In *Woodrow Wilson: A Biography,* John Milton Cooper offers details about the life of the United States' 28th president, Woodrow Wilson. After four consecutive terms served by Republicans in the White House, Wilson took over as a Democrat in 1913. Before he was president, however, he held the position of president of Princeton University and then served two years as governor of New Jersey. Once elected president of the United States, Wilson established the Federal Trade Commission Act, the Federal Reserve Act, and the Clayton Antitrust Act. World War I occurred during his second term in office. In this book, Cooper delves into Wilson's personal, as well as his political, life.

Where it's reviewed:
American Heritage, Winter 2010, page p98
New York Times Book Review, Dec 13, 2009, page p20
Newsweek, Nov 30, 2009, page p54
Publishers Weekly, Sept 14, 2009, page p37

Other books by the same author:
Breaking the Heart of the World: Woodrow Wilson and the Fight for the League of Nations, 2010
Walter Hines Page: The Southerner as American, 1855-1918, 2009

Other books you might like:
Josiah Bunting, *Ulysses S. Grant: The American Presidents Series: The 18th President, 1869-1877*, 2004
Robert Dallek, *Harry S. Truman*, 2008
Lewis L. Gould, *The William Howard Taft Presidency*, 2009
Robert W. Merry, *A Country of Vast Designs: James K. Polk, The Mexican War, and the Conquest of the American Continent*, 2009

◼ 205

SLOANE CROSLEY

How Did You Get This Number

(New York: Riverhead Hardcover, 2010)

Subject(s): Autobiographies; Travel; Humor

Summary: *How Did You Get This Number* is a continuation of Sloane Crosley's *I Was Told There'd Be Cake*. In her first essay collection, Crosley introduced readers to the joys of her life in the Big Apple. Having just moved to New York City from a comfy life in the suburbs, Crosley had encountered difficulties fitting in while balancing parties on the weekends with her entry-level, yet insanely demanding job during the week. In *How Did You Get This Number*, Crosley has settled into her life amidst the hustle and bustle of the big city, but has taken to traveling around the world whenever possible. From attending weddings in Alaska to planning random trips to Portugal, Crosley tells of her experiences along with the tolls they are taking on her relationships with her friends and family members.

Other books by the same author:
I Was Told There'd Be Cake, 2008

Other books you might like:
Samantha Bee, *I Know I Am, but What Are You?*, 2010
Sloane Crosley, *I Was Told There'd Be Cake*, 2008
Jen Lancaster, *My Fair Lazy: One Reality Television Addict's Attempt to Discover If Not Being A Dumb Ass Is the New Black, or, a Culture-Up Manifesto*, 2010
David Sedaris, *Me Talk Pretty One Day*, 2000
David Sedaris, *When You Are Engulfed in Flames*, 2008

◼ 206

JULIE CUMMINS

Sam Patch: Daredevil Jumper

(New York: Holiday House, 2009)

Subject(s): Biographies; Sports; History

Summary: *Sam Patch: Daredevil Jumper* is a biography for kids, written by Julie Cummins and illustrated by Michael Allen Austin. Sam Patch (1807-1829) became world famous in his short life for jumping off various waterfalls, including Passaic Falls and Niagra Falls twice. His final jump was from Genesee Falls into the freezing water below; his body was not found for months. The book also includes a description of his childhood and his early fondness for daredevil jumps.

Other books by the same author:
Women Daredevils: Thrills, Chills, and Frills, 2008
Tomboy of the Air: Daredevil Pilot Blanche Stuart Scott, 2001
The Inside-Outside Book of Libraries, 1996

Other books you might like:
Julie Cummins, *Women Daredevils: Thrills, Chills, and Frills*, 2008
Mordicai Gerstein, *The Man Who Walked between the Towers*, 2003
Emily Arnold McCully, *Mirette on the High Wire*, 1992

◼ 207

ROBERT DALLEK

Harry S. Truman

(New York: Times Books, 2008)

Subject(s): Biographies; Politics; Political campaigns

Summary: Robert Dallek's *Harry S. Truman*, part of The American Presidents series of biographies, explores the life of the United States' 33rd president, Harry S. Truman. Truman was a party politician in Missouri before becoming Franklin Roosevelt's vice president. He became president when Roosevelt unexpectedly died. During his presidency, Truman faced many challenges including ending World War II, establishing the Marshall Plan in Europe, and facing the beginning of the Cold War with Russia. It was Truman who decided to drop the atomic bomb on Japan, and Truman who faced blame for the Communists employed by the federal government and hunted by Joe McCarthy. Truman also won an historic and exciting 1948 election against Thomas Dewey. Dallek argues that these accomplishments, which surprised many of Truman's contemporaries, make him one of the greatest presidents of the 20th century.

Other books by the same author:
The Lost Peace: Leadership in a Time of Horror and Hope, 1945-1953, 2010
Nixon and Kissinger: Partners in Power, 2007

Other books you might like:
Dean Acheson, *Affection and Trust: The Personal*

Correspondence of Harry S. Truman and Dean Acheson, 1953-1971, 2010

John Milton Cooper, *Woodrow Wilson: A Biography*, 2009

Harry S. Truman, *Affection and Trust: The Personal Correspondence of Harry S. Truman and Dean Acheson, 1953-1971*, 2010

208

LEOPOLD DAMROSCH

Jean-Jacques Rousseau: Restless Genius

(Boston: Houghton Mifflin Company, 2005)

Subject(s): Philosophy; Writers; Biographies

Summary: Leopold Damrosch explores the life of 18th-century writer and philosopher Jean-Jacques Rousseau in *Jean-Jacques Rousseau: Restless Genius*. Born in Geneva, Rousseau was influenced by the French and American revolutions and devoted much of his time to political philosophy. In his first major philosophical work, *A Discourse on the Sciences and Arts*, he argued that sciences and arts caused the corruption of virtue and morality. Rosseau believed that human beings are basically good by nature but have been tarnished by society. Damrosch also touches on how Rosseau's beliefs greatly influenced Immanuel Kant's work on ethics.

Where it's reviewed:
Booklist, Novemeber 1, 2005, page 14
Library Journal, October 1, 2005, page 79
Publishers Weekly, August 29, 2005, page 43

Other books by the same author:
Tocqueville's Discovery of America, 2010

Other books you might like:
Leopold Damrosch, *Toqueville's Discovery of America*, 2010

William Doyle, *The Oxford History of the French Revolution*, 1989

Jean-Jacques Rousseau, *Confessions*, 1902

Jean-Jacques Rousseau, *Reveries of the Solitary Walker*, 1980

Jean-Jacques Rousseau, *The Social Contract and Discourses*, 1993

209

EDWIDGE DANTICAT

Brother, I'm Dying

(New York: Random House, 2007)

Subject(s): Biography; Brothers; Emigration and Immigration

Summary: Author Edwidge Danticat recounts the history of her family and her native Haiti through the lives of the men closest to her: her father, Mira, and his brother Joseph. This biography opens with the single day in 2004 on which Danticat learned she was pregnant and that her father was dying of end-stage pulmonary fibrosis. The author then looks back on her childhood in Haiti, where her uncle Joseph raised her while her parents lived and worked in Brooklyn. Danticat finally joined her parents and two younger brothers in New York at age 12, leaving the uncle she loved and her only home. The author describes adjusting to her new life while worrying about the family she left behind in Haiti as political unrest compromises their safety. She concludes her family's story with recent events: the death of her beloved uncle, who, upon fleeing Haiti, was detained by U.S. Customs in Miami and died while in custody, and the birth of her first child, Mira.

Where it's reviewed:
Library Journal, August 1, 2007, page 86
Ms. Magazine, Summer 2007, page 72
People Weekly, September 24, 2007, page 71
Publishers Weekly, July 16, 2007, page 155

Other books by the same author:
Eight Days, 2010
The Dew Breaker, 2005
The Farming of Bones, 1999
Breath, Eyes, Memory, 1998

Other books you might like:
Beverly Bell, *Walking on Fire: Haitian Women's Stories of Survival and Resistance*, 2000

Edwidge Danticat, *Breath, Eyes, Memory*, 1994

Edwidge Danticat, *The Farming of Bones*, 1998

Philipe Girard, *Haiti: The Tumultuous History — From Pearl of the Caribbean to Broken Nation*, 2010

210

TRACY DAUGHERTY

Hiding Man: A Biography of Donald Barthelme

(New York: St. Martin's Press, 2008)

Subject(s): Writers; Writing; Father-son relations

Summary: In *Hiding Man: A Biography of Donald Barthelme*, author Tracy Daugherty describes the life of one of America's most influential postmodern writers. Donald Barthelme was heavily influenced by his past relationship with his father and the works of his closest friends—authors such as Norman Mailer, Thomas Pynchon, and Kurt Vonnegut. He was the author of hundreds of short stories and four full-length novels including *Snow White*, *The Dead Father*, and *Paradise*. Aside from writing fiction, Barthelme was also an editor and a journalist. Daugherty's book is the first biography ever published about Barthelme.

Where it's reviewed:
The Antioch Review, Spring 2010, page p382
Booklist, March 1, 2009, page p14
Library Journal, Dec 1, 2008, page p129
Time, Feb 23, 2009, page p99

Other books by the same author:
One Day the Wind Changed: Stories, 2010

Axeman's Jazz: A Novel, 2003
The Woman in the Oil Field, 1996

Other books you might like:
Donald Barthelme, *Not-Knowing: The Essays and
    Interviews*, 1997
Donald Barthelme, *Sixty Stories*, 1981
Richard Ellmann, *James Joyce*, 1959

211

PORTIA DE ROSSI

Unbearable Lightness: A Story of Loss and Gain

(New York: Simon & Schuster, 2010)

Subject(s): Autobiographies; Actors; Entertainment
industry

Summary: In her first book, *Unbearable Lightness: A Story
of Loss and Gain*, Australian actress Portia de Rossi
chronicles the challenges she's faced in her personal and
professional life. Best known for her role in the television show *Ally McBeal*, de Rossi has battled anorexia
nervosa for years. In addition to her eating disorder, she
also experienced difficulty dealing with her sexuality.
Though briefly married to a man in the late 1990s, de
Rossi knew that she was a lesbian. At first she was
hesitant to reveal herself as gay, but eventually became
more comfortable with her identity, marrying television
talk show host Ellen DeGeneres in 2008.

Other books you might like:
Pat Benatar, *Between a Heart and a Rock Place: A
    Memoir*, 2010
Marlo Thomas, *Growing Up Laughing: My Story and
    the Story of Funny*, 2010

212

JOAN DIDION

The Year of Magical Thinking

(New York: Vintage, 2005)

Subject(s): Autobiography; Death; Grief

Summary: In 2003, writer Joan Didion suffered a painful
double shock. Her husband of 40 years died of a sudden,
massive heart attack. Meanwhile, her daughter was in a
coma, suffering from pneumonia and near to death. In
this memoir, Didion describes how grief propelled her
into a state of what she calls "magical thinking," a period
of utter denial about her loss. She rushed to her
daughter's side in a Los Angeles hospital, bringing with
her memories of her husband, still alive and available
for conversation in her mind. Didion describes her period
of pathological grief, and how she eventually came back
to herself.

Where it's reviewed:
The Christian Century, July 25, 2006, page 34

Library Journal, September 15, 2006, page 60
Newsweek, March 26, 2007, page 82
TLS. Times Literary Supplement, December 23, 2005,
    page 12
Vogue, March 2007, page 564

Other books by the same author:
The White Album: Essays, 2009
Slouching Towards Bethlehem, 2008
Play It as It Lays, 2005

Other books you might like:
Glenda Burgess, *The Geography of Love*, 2009
Patricia Hampl, *The Florist's Daughter*, 2007
Audre Lorde, *The Cancer Journals: Special Edition*,
    2006
Sherwin B. Nuland, *How We Die: Reflections on Life's
    Final Chapter*, 1993
Studs Terkel, *Will the Circle Be Unbroken?: Reflections
    on Death, Rebirth, and Hunger for a Faith*, 2001

213

PHYLLIS DILLER

Like a Lampshade In a Whorehouse: My Life In Comedy

(New York: Tarcher, 2005)

Subject(s): Biographies; Comedy; Culture

Summary: Famous American comedian Phyllis Diller
discusses her personal and professional lives in her
memoir *Like a Lampshade in a Whorehouse: My Life in
Comedy*. In the book, Diller describes her life stories,
including those from her married life and those from her
experiences in the entertainment industry. She talks about
her marriage and the births of her five children as well
as how she broke into the world of comedy when male
comedians dominated the scene. Throughout the biography, she keeps her signature humor and wit, and she
reveals the struggles she endured to find a spot in the
comedy limelight.

Where it's reviewed:
Publishers Weekly, February 7, 2005, page 57

Other books by the same author:
The Joys of Aging, 1981

Other books you might like:
Carol Burnett, *This Time Together: Laughter and
    Reflection*, 2010
Rodney Dangerfield, *It's Not Easy Bein' Me: A Lifetime
    of No Respect but Plenty of Sex and Drugs*, 2004
Valerie Frankel, *Men Are Stupid ... And They Like Big
    Boobs: A Woman's Guide to Beauty Through Plastic
    Surgery*, 2009
Cloris Leachman, *Cloris: My Autobiography*, 2009
Don Rickles, *Rickles' Book: A Memoir*, 2007
    David Ritz, co-author
Joan Rivers, *Men Are Stupid ... And They Like Big*

Boobs: A Woman's Guide to Beauty Through Plastic Surgery, 2009

214

PHILIP DRAY

Capitol Men: The Epic Story of Reconstruction through the Lives of the First Black Congressmen

(New York: Houghton Mifflin Harcourt, 2008)

Subject(s): Civil rights; Law; Ku Klux Klan

Summary: Philip Dray's focus in *Capitol Men: The Epic Story of Reconstruction through the Lives of the First Black Congressmen* is the marginalized history of the first African American congressmen in the United States. The Reconstruction Era, which took place after the Civil War, did little in the way of creating equal rights for African Americans. It wasn't until the 1950s when the Supreme Court decided in *Brown v. The Board of Education* to desegregate public schools and the actions of great men and women like Martin Luther King Jr. and Rosa Parks inspired the country to fight for equality that the divide caused by slavery began to close. Dray's account puts the actions of sixteen African American men who were elected to Congress in context with the progress that came later and the work that still needs to be done.

Where it's reviewed:
Library Journal, July 1, 2008, page p92
The Nation, Nov 3, 2008, page p30
New York Times Book Review, Sept 28, 2008, page p20
The New Yorker, Oct 13, 2008, page p145

Other books by the same author:
There is Power in a Union: The Epic Story of Labor in America, 2010
Stealing God's Thunder: Benjamin Franklin's Lightning Rod and the Invention of America, 2005
At the Hands of Persons Unknown: The Lynching of Black America, 2003

Other books you might like:
Ira Berlin, *Many Thousands Gone: The First Two Centuries of Slavery in North America*, 1998
David W. Blight, *Race and Reunion: The Civil War in American Memory*, 2001
W.E.B. Du Bois, *Black Reconstruction in America*, 1992
Eric Foner, *Reconstruction: America's Unfinished Revolution 1863-1877*, 1988
Jesse J. Holland, *Black Men Built the Capitol: Discovering African-American History In and Around Washington, D.C.*, 2007
Heather Cox Richardson, *West from Appomattox: The Reconstruction of America after the Civil War*, 2007

215

SHIRIN EBADI
AZADEH MOAVENI , Co-Author

Iran Awakening: A Memoir of Revolution and Hope

(New York: Random House, 2006)

Subject(s): Human rights; Islam; Autobiographies

Summary: In *Iran Awakening: A Memoir of Revolution and Hope*, Shirin Ebadi looks back on the oppression of Iranian women, beginning with the 1979 Islamic Revolution. Before then, Ebadi had been one of the premiere judges in Iran—but after the revolution, women were considered second-class citizens and were stripped of any status. Ebadi traces Iranian troubles further back than 1979—to 1953 when a coup led by the United States overthrew Prime Minister Mohammad Mossadegh. Although Ebadi's family left Iran after the 1979 revolution, along with more than 5 million other Iranians, Ebadi was determined to stay behind and fight for the equality of all Iranians. In 2003, Ebadi was awarded a Nobel Peace Prize for her human rights activism. This book is co-authored with Azadeh Moaveni, author of *Lipstick Jihad*.

Where it's reviewed:
Booklist, May 1, 2006, page 56
Library Journal, May 15, 2006, page 10
New York Times Book Review, July 16, 2006, page 14
Publishers Weekly, March 27, 2006, page 74

Other books by the same author:
Honeymoon in Tehran: Two Years of Love and Danger in Iran, 2010
Lipstick Jihad: A Memoir of Growing up Iranian in America and American in Iran, 2006

Other books you might like:
Firoozeh Dumas, *Funny in Farsi: A Memoir of Growing Up Iranian in America*, 2003
Azadeh Moaveni, *Lipstick Jihad: A Memoir of Growing Up Iranian in America and American in Iran*, 2005
Azar Nafisi, *Reading Lolita in Tehran: A Memoir in Books*, 2003
Azar Nafisi, *Things I've Been Silent About: Memories*, 2008
Nahid Rachlin, *Persian Girls: A Memoir*, 2006

216

EMINEM
SACHA JENKINS , Co-Author

The Way I Am

(New York: Dutton Adult, 2008)

Subject(s): Autobiographies; Musicians; Entertainment industry

Summary: *The Way I Am* is an autobiography from rapper Eminem and author Sacha Jenkins. The book includes a collection of personal reflections and photographs. Eminem writes about his life as a superstar, his daughter Hallie, and some of the struggles and challenges he has faced during his years in the spotlight. Private photographs of his home life and some of his drawings, along with numerous pages of never-before-published handwritten song lyrics with commentary from Eminem, fill the book's pages.

Other books by the same author:
Angry Blonde, 2000

Other books you might like:
Pat Benatar, *Between a Heart and a Rock Place: A Memoir*, 2010
Gary Graff, *Travelin' Man: On the Road and Behind the Scenes with Bob Seger*, 2010
  Tom Weschler, co-author

217

GRAHAM FARMELO

The Strangest Man: The Hidden Life of Paul Dirac, Mystic of the Atom

(London: Faber and Faber, 2009)

Subject(s): Physics; Science; Research

Summary: Physics professor Graham Farmelo studies the life and contributions of Paul Dirac, the Nobel Prize-winning physicist whose pioneering work is largely forgotten today. While *The Strangest Man: The Hidden Life of Paul Dirac, Mystic of the Atom* charts the subject's life and times, it takes special interest in Dirac's singular personality and approach. Unusually quiet and reserved and viewed as a man of few words, Paul Dirac has nonetheless created some of the most important discoveries in the field of physics, including an early foundation for what would later become string theory. *The Strangest Man* contains photos, notes on the text, a bibliography, and an index.

Where it's reviewed:
Booklist, Sept 1, 2009, page p19
New York Times Book Review, Sept 13, 2009, page p14
Physics Today, Dec 2009, page p52
Publishers Weekly, June 29, 2009, page p120

Other books you might like:
David C. Cassidy, *Beyond Uncertainty: Heisenberg, Quantum Physics, and The Bomb*, 2009
Graham Farmelo, *It Must Be Beautiful: Great Equations of Modern Science*, 2002
Masha Gessen, *Perfect Rigor: A Genius and the Mathematical Breakthrough of the Century*, 2009

218

PERCY FAWCETT

Exploration Fawcett: Journey to the Lost City of Z

(Beverly Hills, California: Phoenix, 2010)

Subject(s): Biographies; Adventure; Travel

Summary: *Exploration Fawcett: Journey to the Lost City of Z* is a first book by Percy Fawcett that chronicles the South American adventures of Colonel Percival Harrison Fawcett. In the 1920s, Fawcett set out for a lost city, "Z," that he was convinced he would find in the dense terrain of Brazil. A British artillery officer and trained archaeologist, Fawcett had made several expeditions in the region and in 1925, accompanied by his son, Jack, entered the Matto Grosso in search of the legendary city. Percy and Jack never returned, though theories abound regarding their mysterious disappearance. This account was created from Colonel Fawcett's journals and correspondence.

Other books you might like:
Craig Childs, *Finders Keepers: A Tale of Archaeological Plunder and Obsession*, 2010
David Grann, *The Devil and Sherlock Holmes: Tales of Murder, Madness, and Obsession*, 2010
David Grann, *The Lost City of Z: A Tale of Deadly Obsession in the Amazon*, 2009

219

DAVID HACKETT FISCHER

Champlain's Dream

(New York: Simon and Schuster, 2008)

Subject(s): Biographies; History; Travel

Summary: Although Samuel de Champlain is probably best known in the United States as the namesake for a lake, he was an important and often overlooked part of North American history. In the book *Champlain's Dream*, author David Hackett Fischer details the life of this talented captain, explorer, spy, writer, and naturalist. Fischer explains that Champlain explored parts of North America even before the Pilgrims arrived and that he made his way from present-day Philadelphia to Canada. Champlain befriended some groups of Native Americans, but he went to war with others. During a battle with a group of Mohawks, Champlain was shot, but he kept fighting. In addition to covering Champlain's exciting and dangerous journeys, the author also discusses the effects of French settlers in America and in Canada.

Where it's reviewed:
American Heritage, Winter 2009, page p61
Library Journal, Oct 1, 2008, page p82
New York Times Book Review, Nov 9, 2008, page p50
Publishers Weekly, Sept 8, 2008, page p48

Other books by the same author:
Liberty and Freedom: A Visual History of America's Founding Ideas, 2004
The Great Wave: Price Revolutions and the Rhythm of History, 1999
Paul Revere's Ride, 1995

Other books you might like:
Samuel de Champlain, *Voyages of Samuel de Champlain, 1600-1618*, 2001
W.J. Eccles, *The Canadian Frontier, 1534-1760*, 1969
David Hackett Fischer, *Washington's Crossing*, 2004

JOHN HOPE FRANKLIN

Mirror to America: The Autobiography of John Hope Franklin

(New York: Farrar, Straus, and Giroux, 2005)

Subject(s): African Americans; Civil rights; Civil rights movements

Summary: In *Mirror to America: The Autobiography of John Hope Franklin*, Franklin chronicles his remarkable life. In a straightforward unsentimental voice, Franklin describes the incidences of racism that he experienced as a child growing up in the Oklahoma territory in the early 20th century. He then describes the key events of his successful career as an educator and activist, such as serving on committees for Franklin Delano Roosevelt and Bill Clinton, receiving the Presidential Medal of Freedom, and assisting Thurgood Marshall in *Brown vs. Board of Education*. He also shares personal triumphs, such as his refusal to sit at the back of a bus in 1945. Written when Franklin was 90 years old, this autobiography shares the life of a man, but also offers an up close look at a pivotal period of American history.

Where it's reviewed:
America, March 20, 2006, page 23
The Crisis, November-December 2005, page 52
Ebony, December 2005, page 28
New York Times Book Review, January 12, 2006, page 26

Other books by the same author:
From Slavery to Freedom, 2010
In Search of the Promised Land: A Slave Family in the Old South, 2006
Runaway Slaves: Rebels on the Plantation, 2000

Other books you might like:
W.E.B. Du Bois, *The Souls of Black Folk*, 1903
John Hope Franklin, *From Slavery to Freedom*, 1987
Henry Louis Gates Jr., *The Future of the Race*, 1996
    Cornel West, co-author

221

ELIZABETH GILBERT

Committed: A Skeptic Makes Peace with Marriage

(New York: Viking, 2010)

Subject(s): Autobiographies; Marriage; Divorce

Summary: In *Committed: A Skeptic Makes Peace with Marriage*, author Elizabeth Gilbert intertwines her personal story with research on the history of the institution of marriage. At the end of Gilbert's previous memoir *Eat, Pray, Love*, the author found love with Felipe while on her travels through Indonesia. In *Committed*, the two—both of whom suffered painful divorces and have agreed to stay together forever but never marry—

periodically live in the United States or travel to foreign places. On a return trip to the United States, however, Felipe is declined entry into the country, and Gilbert learns that they will have to marry if Felipe ever wants to enter the country again. This event serves as the catalyst for Gilbert's research into historical, contemporary, and multicultural ideas about marriage and divorce, and the starting point for the bumpy road she and Felipe travel to the altar.

Other books by the same author:
Eat, Pray, Love: One Woman's Search for Everything Across Italy, India and Indonesia, 2006
The Last American Man, 2002
Stern Men, 2000

Other books you might like:
Ram Dass, *Still Here: Embracing Aging, Changing, and Dying*, 2000
Elizabeth Fox-Genovese, *Marriage: The Dream That Refuses to Die*, 2008
Elizabeth Gilbert, *Eat, Pray, Love: One Woman's Search for Everything Across Italy, India and Indonesia*, 2006
Anne Lamott, *Operating Instructions: A Journal of My Son's First Year*, 1993
Susan Squire, *I Don't: A Contrarian History of Marriage*, 2008

222

MELISSA GILBERT

Prairie Tale: A Memoir

(New York: Simon Spotlight Entertainment, 2009)

Subject(s): Actors; Autobiographies; Entertainment industry

Summary: In *Prairie Tale: A Memoir*, Melissa Gilbert, one of the stars of the widely acclaimed *Little House on the Prairie* television series, writes a candid memoir that explores the very difficult circumstances of her real life that in no way resembled the life of the little girl she played on screen. Adopted at birth into a show business family, Gilbert discusses her difficult relationship with her adoptive mother, her television personality image, and struggling with perfection. She explores her relationships with Hollywood bad boys, her problems with substance abuse, the failure of her first marriage, and the healing process that helped her to become sober, happy, and able to overcome her past.

Where it's reviewed:
Entertainment Weekly, June 19, 2009, page 64

Other books you might like:
Melissa Anderson, *The Way I See It: A Look Back at My Life on Little House*, 2010
Alison Arngrim, *Confessions of a Prairie Bitch: How I Survived Nellie Oleson and Learned to Love Being Hated*, 2010
James Best, *Best in Hollywood: The Good, the Bad, and the Beautiful*, 2009
    Jim Clark, co-author

Chris Kreski, *Growing Up Brady: I Was a Teenage Greg*, 1992

Mackenzie Phillips, *High on Arrival*, 2009

Barry Williams, *Growing Up Brady: I Was a Teenage Greg*, 1992

223

VICTORIA GLENDINNING

Leonard Woolf: A Biography

(New York: Free Press, 2006)

Subject(s): Biographies; Writers; Marriage

Summary: In *Leonard Woolf: A Biography*, Victoria Glendinning examines the life of the husband of writer Virginia Woolf and explores the odd relationship between the couple. Leonard and Virginia shared a union of minds, but not a bed. Leonard lived a celibate life while his wife carried on with various lesbian affairs. Leonard spent much of his life writing and caring for Virginia when she began to suffer from mental illness. The couple founded the Bloomsbury writing group and helped establish a small printing press they called Hogarth Press.

Where it's reviewed:

The Economist, September 16, 2006, page 94

Harper's Magazine, November 2006, page 81

History Today, February 2007, page 64

New York Times Book Review, December 10, 2006, page 16

Other books by the same author:

Elizabeth Bowen, 2006

Rebecca West: A Life, 1998

Other books you might like:

Virginia Nicholson, *Among the Bohemians: Experiments in Living 1900-1939*, 2004

Leonard Woolf, *Beginning Again: An Autobiography of The Years 1911 to 1918*, 1972

Leonard Woolf, *Downhill All the Way: An Autobiography of the Years 1919 To 1939*, 1967

Leonard Woolf, *The Journey Not the Arrival Matters: An Autobiography of the Years 1939 to 1969*, 1969

Virginia Woolf, *Moments of Being*, 1976

224

PETER GODWIN

When a Crocodile Eats the Sun: A Memoir of Africa

(Johannesburg, South Africa: Pan Macmillan South Africa, 2005)

Subject(s): Biographies; Africa; Family relations

Summary: In *When a Crocodile Eats the Sun: A Memoir of Africa*, journalist Peter Godwin parallels the downfall of Zimbabwe in the late 20th century with his own father's demise. When the author travels to his native country in 1996 to visit his ailing father, he faces the reality of Zimbabwe's troubled political state and surpris-

ing disclosures about his family history. As the author learns, the controversial and often violent tactics instituted by President Mugabe (the titular "crocodile") have made life miserable for both blacks and whites in Zimbabwe. Complicating Godwin's feelings about the ruin of his African homeland is the discovery that his father was not British but a Polish Jew.

Where it's reviewed:

The New Yorker, May 7, 2007, page p74

Other books by the same author:

The Fear: The Last Days of Robert Mugabe, 2010

Mukiwa: A White Boy in Africa, 2004

Other books you might like:

Tim Butcher, *Blood River: A Journey to Africa's Broken Heart*, 2008

Peter Godwin, *Mukiwa: A White Boy in Africa*, 1996

Douglas Rogers, *The Last Resort: A Memoir of Mischief and Mayhem on a Family Farm in Africa*, 2009

Robyn Scott, *Twenty Chickens for a Saddle: The Story of an African Childhood*, 2008

225

BRAD GOOCH

Flannery: A Life of Flannery O'Connor

(New York: Little, Brown and Company, 2009)

Story type: Literary

Subject(s): Biographies; Writing; Writers

Summary: In *Flannery: A Life of Flannery O'Connor*, Brad Gooch provides in-depth information about literary sensation Flannery O'Connor's life. Using letters O'Connor wrote to friends over the years, including Elizabeth Bishop and Betty Hester, Gooch puts together a comprehensive biography of O'Connor's personal and professional life. Gooch includes information about O'Connor's life before and after she achieved literary success. In her lifetime, O'Connor wrote two full novels and more than 30 short stories. Her stories were often set in the southern United States and featured gothic characters who struggled to make moral and ethical decisions.

Where it's reviewed:

The New York Review of Books, April 9, 2009, page p12

The New York Times, Feb 23, 2009, page pC8

The New Yorker, March 23, 2009, page p75

Publishers Weekly, Nov 24, 2008, page p4

Other books by the same author:

Godtalk: Travels in Spiritual America, 2002

City Poet: The Life and Times of Frank O'Hara, 1994

Other books you might like:

Lorraine V. Murray, *The Abbess of Andalusia - Flannery O'Connor's Spiritual Journey*, 2009

Flannery O'Connor, *Flannery O'Connor : Collected Works : Wise Blood / A Good Man Is Hard to Find / The Violent Bear It Away / Everything that Rises Must Converge / Essays & Letters*, 1988

Flannery O'Connor, *The Habit of Being: Letters*, 1979

226

DORIS KEARNS GOODWIN

Team of Rivals: The Political Genius of Abraham Lincoln

(New York: Simon & Schuster, 2005)

Subject(s): American History; Biography; Civil War, U.S.

Summary: This unique biography of Abraham Lincoln focuses on his political choices. Specifically, Goodwin explores Lincoln's decision to include his opponents for the Republican nomination in the 1860 presidential election in his cabinet. At once a detailed look at Lincoln's political career and choices, this work also includes biographical sketches of Lincoln's three rivals: William H. Seward, Edward Bates, and Salmon P. Chase.

Where it's reviewed:
New York Times Book Review, November 6, 2005, page 4
The New Yorker, November 7, 2005, page 126
New Yorker, May 28, 2007, page 30
USA Today, October 20, 2005, page 01D
Washington Monthly, March 2006, page 49

Other books by the same author:
The Fitzgeralds and the Kennedys: An American Saga, 2001
Wait Till Next Year: A Memoir, 1998
No Ordinary Time: Franklin and Eleanor Roosevelt: The Home Front in World War II, 1995
Lyndon Johnson and the American Dream, 1991

Other books you might like:
George Washington Bacon, *The Life and Administration of Abraham Lincoln*, 2010
David Herbert Donald, *Lincoln*, 1996
Philip Shaw Paluden, *The Presidency of Abraham Lincoln*, 1994
Harry Turtledove, *366 Days in Abraham Lincoln's Presidency: The Private, Political, and Military Decisions of America's Greatest President*, 2010
Ronald C. White, *A. Lincoln: A Biography*, 2009
Stephen A. Wynalda, *366 Days in Abraham Lincoln's Presidency: The Private, Political, and Military Decisions of America's Greatest President*, 2010

227

LINDA GORDON

Dorothea Lange: A Life Beyond Limits

(New York: W.W. Norton & Co., 2009)

Subject(s): Biographies; Photography; Great Depression, 1929-1934

Summary: Author Linda Gordon offers a look at the woman who captured the essence of the Great Depression in *Dorothea Lange: A Life Beyond Limits*. While Lange is known mostly for the images she captured, Gordon shows that Lange lived an amazing life filled with triumph and heartbreak. Born in New York City, Lange contracted polio as a child. The disease left her physically disabled. As a young woman, Lange found joy in taking pictures of people and devoted herself to photography. In the 1930s, Lange traveled around the country taking pictures of people affected by the Great Depression. Later parts of the books discuss Lange's marriages, her children, and her work concerning other subjects, such as the interment of Japanese Americans during World War II.

Where it's reviewed:
The New Yorker, Nov 23, 2009, page p113
Newsweek, Nov 16, 2009, page p30
Publishers Weekly, August 24, 2009, page p51
USA Today, Nov 19, 2009, page p04D

Other books by the same author:
Heroes of Their Own Lives: The Politics and History of Family Violence—Boston, 1880-1960, 2002
The Great Arizona Orphan Abduction, 2001

Other books you might like:
Peter Galassi, *Henri Cartier-Bresson: The Modern Century*, 2010
Linda Gordon, *Impounded: Dorothea Lange and the Censored Images of Japanese American Internment*, 2006
Ann Whiston Spirn, *Daring to Look: Dorothea Lange's Photographs and Reports from the Field*, 2008

228

LYNDALL GORDON

Vindication: A Life of Mary Wollstonecraft

(New York: HarperCollins, 2005)

Summary: In this memoir, J.R. Moehringer describes his childhood and upbringing in Manhasset, New York. His mother was a working woman who struggled to raise him on her own; his father was a voice on the other end of a telephone line. One constant in his life was the local drinking establishment: the pub where his Uncle Chas tended bar, and where he hung out from a very tender age. He did not go there to drink—he was too young—but to find steady companionship. Even after he left Manhasset to embark upon his career as a journalist, the bar was always his remembered home. This memoir is as much a love song to the local pub and to its colorful characters as it is a life story.

Where it's reviewed:
American Scholar, Summer 2000, page 138

Other books by the same author:
Lives Like Loaded Guns: Emily Dickinson and Her Family's Feuds, 2010
Virginia Woolf: A Writer's Life, 2001
T.S. Eliot: An Imperfect Life, 1999

Other books you might like:
William Godwin, *Memoirs of the Author of the Vindication of the Rights of Women*, 1798

Lyndall Gordon, *Charlotte Bronte: A Passionate Life*, 1994

Barbara Taylor, *Mary Wollstonecraft and the Feminst Imagination*, 2003

Janet Todd, *Mary Wollstonecraft: A Revolutionary Life*, 2000

Mary Wollstonecraft, *A Vindication of the Rights of Women*, 1792

229

ANNETTE GORDON-REED

The Hemingses of Monticello: An American Family

(New York: W.W. Norton and Co., 2008)

Subject(s): United States history; African Americans; Slavery

Summary: *The Hemingses of Monticello: An American Family* by Annette Gordon-Reed is an in-depth examination of the relationship between Thomas Jefferson and his slave Sally Hemings, along with the rest of the Hemings family. Jefferson allegedly fathered a number of Sally Hemings's children, and this is discussed at length. The lives of those children are discussed, as well as Sally Hemings's siblings, who were also related to Jefferson's wife. Important events serve as the backdrop for the family, including Revolutionary America, Philadelphia in the 1790s, and the revolution in Paris, as well as life at the plantation Monticello. Information about the nature of the slaves' lives is included as well.

Where it's reviewed:
Booklist, August 1, 2008[a0], page p31
Library Journal, August 1, 2008, page p96
New York Review of Books, October 9, 2008, page 15
New York Times Book Review, Oct 5, 2008, page p17
Publishers Weekly, July 14, 2008, page p57

Other books by the same author:
Thomas Jefferson and Sally Hemings: An American Controversy, 1998

Other books you might like:
Tina Andrews, *Sally Hemings: An American Scandal: The Struggle to Tell the Controversial True Story*, 2002

William G. Hyland Jr., *In Defense of Thomas Jefferson: The Sally Hemings Sex Scandal*, 2009

Jan Ellen Lewis, *Sally Hemings and Thomas Jefferson: History, Memory, and Civic Culture*, 1999
Peter S. Onuf, co-author

Lucia C. Stanton, *Slavery at Monticello*, 2002

Clarence E. Walker, *Mongrel Nation: The America Begotten by Thomas Jefferson and Sally Hemings*, 2009

230

DAVID GRANN

The Lost City of Z: A Tale of Deadly Obsession in the Amazon

(New York: Doubleday, 2009)

Subject(s): History; Rain forests; Legends

Summary: The legend of El Dorado has captured the attention of many. Countless lives and dollars have been lost trying to locate the fabled city of gold, and *The Lost City of Z: A Tale of Deadly Obsession in the Amazon* is an account of one such journey. British explorer Percy Fawcett, along with his son and another young man, entered the Amazon jungle in 1925, determined to locate the lost city, which Fawcett called "Z." The party was lost forever, despite several rescue missions and multiple modern searches. To create *The Lost City of Z*, author David Grann meticulously and obsessively researched and collected data on Fawcett, his career, his ambitions, and his previous expeditions. Fawcett's adventure is riveting; one can hardly imagine the hardships he endured. Grann's dedication to his subject continues to astound, however, as he journeyed to the Amazon himself to follow in Fawcett's footsteps. Grann, a born and bred urban New Yorker, chronicles his adventures in the Amazon jungle alongside his research on the Fawcett party, as he seeks to discover the truth behind their fate and finally lay the matter to rest.

Where it's reviewed:
Booklist, November 1, 2008, page 4
Bookmarks, May/June 2009, page 63
Library Journal, November 1, 2008, page 86
Publishers Weekly, October 13, 2008, page 44
Time, March 2, 2009, page 62

Other books by the same author:
The Devil and Sherlock Holmes: Tales of Murder, Madness, and Obsession, 2010

Other books you might like:
Evan L. Balkan, *Vanished!: Explorers Forever Lost*, 2007

Percy Fawcett, *Exploration Fawcett: Journey to the Lost City of Z*, 2010

Joe Jackson, *The Thief at the End of the World: Rubber, Power, and the Seeds of Empire*, 2008

Norman Ollestad, *Crazy for the Storm: A Memoir of Survival*, 2009

Sarah Vowell, *The Wordy Shipmates*, 2008

231

MELISSA FAY GREENE

There Is No Me without You

(New York: Bloomsbury, 2006)

Subject(s): AIDS (Disease); Africa; Orphans

Summary: In her book *There Is No Me without You*, author Melissa Fay Greene explores the AIDS pandemic and its effects on children living in Africa. The book tells the story of Haregewoin Tefarra, an Ethiopian woman who has turned her home into a sanctuary for children who were made orphans by the African AIDS pandemic. After the death of her daughter, Haregewoin took in two AIDS orphans, and more children arrived as word of her care spread. She has expanded her responsibilities and now runs a school, daycare, a shelter for ailing mothers, and an adoption service. Greene uses Tefarra's story to give insight into the most serious pandemic of modern times.

Where it's reviewed:
Booklist, August 1, 20006, page p17
People, Sept 11, 2006, page p55
Publishers Weekly, July 17, 2006, page p148
Sojourner's Magazine, Jan 2007, page p44

Other books by the same author:
Praying for Sheetrock: A Work of Nonfiction, 2006
The Temple Bombing, 2006

Other books you might like:
Josh Bottomly, *Fom Ashes to Africa*, 2009
Russell D. Moore, *Adopted for Life: The Priority of Adoption for Christian Families and Churches*, 2009
Marguerite Wright, *I'm Chocolate, You're Vanilla: Raising Healthy Black and Biracial Children in a Race-Conscious World*, 1998

232

LINDA GREENHOUSE

Becoming Justice Blackmun: Harry Blackmun's Supreme Court Journey

(New York: Henry Holt and Co., 2005)

Subject(s): Biography; Law; Politics

Summary: There is a paradox at the heart of every U.S. Supreme Court justice's position. Although the justices are expected to rule objectively and without regard to politics, they are nominated and confirmed by politicians; the process is inherently a political one. That paradox is explored in this biography of Justice Harry Blackmun by Linda Greenhouse, a Pulitzer Prize-winning journalist with the *New York Times*. She also traces Blackmun's lifelong friendship with Warren Burger (the two men knew one another in kindergarten) and examines how they came to sharply diverge in their political views. Blackmun is perhaps best known for writing the majority opinion of the *Roe v. Wade* ruling.

Where it's reviewed:
The Nation, June 13, 2005, page 28
National Review, August 8, 2005, page 47
New York Times Book Review, May 8, 2005, page BR9
Times Literary Supplement, September 23, 2005, page 11
Washington Monthly, July-August 2005, page 58

Other books you might like:
Fred I. Greenstein, *The Hidden-Hand Presidency: Eisenhower as Leader*, 1982

Jim Newton, *Justice for All: Earl Warren and the Nation He Made*, 2006
William H. Rehnquist, *The Supreme Court*, 2001
Jeffrey Toobin, *The Nine: Inside the Secret World of the Supreme Court*, 2007
Bob Woodward, *The Brethren: Inside the Supreme Court*, 1979

233

GERMAINE GREER

Shakespeare's Wife

(New York: Harper, 2007)

Subject(s): Shakespeare, William; Marriage; English literature, 1558-1603 (Elizabethan)

Summary: Germaine Greer's novel, *Shakespeare's Wife*, uses court records, historical materials, memorabilia, letters, and Shakespearean works in an attempt to piece together a factual account of Anne Hathaway, the playwright's wife. This historical piece allows readers to understand what existence was like during the Elizabethan Age. Greer includes such subjects as dress, women's roles in society, premarital pregnancy, courtship, and survival in 16th-17th century England. Her focus, however, is on Anne Hathaway's life. Hathaway is famous for wedding William Shakespeare, one of the best-known playwrights in world history. Throughout the novel, Greer spotlights the couple's marriage, the social context of this union, and the way past and present day society views this duo. Although other novels tend to depict Hathaway as an unattractive farmer's daughter who tricked Shakespeare into nuptials (some go so far as to imply that she purposefully became pregnant), Greer attempts to show her as a strong-willed, self-sufficient woman and mother. One instance shows how she is capable and resourceful enough to provide food for her children, even though many at the time were dying from malnutrition. In this book, Hathaway is not just the hated spouse left out of her husband's will. She is depicted as a successful wife and mother who, perhaps, loved and missed her husband when he was away writing.

Where it's reviewed:
Booklist, Jan 1, 2008, page p21
Library Journal, April 1, 2008, page p83
The New York Review of Books, April 17, 2008, page p6
Publishers Weekly, Feb 4, 2008, page p46

Other books by the same author:
Shakespeare: A Brief Insight, 2010
The Female Eunuch, 2008
The Whole Woman, 2000

Other books you might like:
Stephen Greenblatt, *Will in the World: How Shakespeare Became Shakespeare*, 2004
Charles Nicholl, *The Lodger Shakespeare: His Life on Silver Street*, 2008
William Shakespeare, *The Complete Pelican Shakespeare*, 1962
James Shapiro, *Contested Will: Who Wrote Shakespeare?*, 2010

James Shapiro, *A Year in the Life of William Shakespeare: 1599*, 2005

234

PETER GURALNICK

Dream Boogie: The Triumph of Sam Cooke

(New York: Little, Brown and Company, 2005)

Story type: Historical
Subject(s): Civil rights movements; Musicians; Biographies
Summary: Peter Guralnick's *Dream Boogie: The Triumph of Sam Cooke* is a biography of the man known as the founder of soul music. Sam Cooke was a singer and songwriter who combined gospel music with pop music to create deep, dramatic songs that impressed the entire nation. Between 1957 and 1964, Cooke produced 29 songs included in the United States' Top 40 list. His success was influential to the ongoing civil rights movement. Cooke was one of the first African Americans to not only write his own lyrics and music, but also manage his own business. Before Cooke's death at 33 years old, he had created a publishing company and a record label. His music inspired many great soul artists such as Aretha Franklin, Stevie Wonder, and James Brown.

Where it's reviewed:
The New York Review of Books, March 9, 2006, page 35
New York Times Book Review, November 20, 2005, page BR10
The New Yorker, November 15, 2005, page 95
Publishers Weekly, December 5, 2005, page 10

Other books by the same author:
Nighthawk Blues: A Novel, 2003
Careless Love: The Unmaking of Elvis Presley, 2000
Last Train to Memphis: The Rise of Elvis Presley, 1995

Other books you might like:
Peter Guralnick, *Careless Love: The Unmaking of Elvis Presley*, 1999
Peter Guralnick, *Last Train to Memphis: The Rise of Elvis Presley*, 1994
Peter Guralnick, *Searching for Robert Johnson: The Life and legend of the King of the Delta Blues Singers*, 1998
Peter Guralnick, *Sweet Soul Music: Rhythm and Blues and the Southern Dream of Freedom*, 1986
Clifton White, *You Send Me: The Life and Times of Sam Cooke*, 1996
Daniel Wolff, co-author

235

BERND HEINRICH

Winter World: The Ingenuity of Animal Survival

(New York: Harper Perennial, 2009)

Subject(s): Animals; Winter; Biology

Summary: In *Winter World: The Ingenuity of Animal Survival*, author Bernd Heinrich explores the survival techniques and tactics employed by animals during the winter season. Heinrich details the manner in which various species behave during colder weather, from those that hibernate to those that burrow, to those that stay awake during the entire season. The author looks at the numerous methods the species detailed in the book use to survive the cold, from biological processes to habitat adjustments. Originally published in 2003, the 2009 edition includes updated material and additional information. Heinrich is also the author of *Mind of the Raven*, which was awarded the John Burroughs Medal for Natural History Writing.

Other books by the same author:
Summer World: A Season of Bounty, 2010

Other books you might like:
Eric Burr, *Ski Trails and Wildlife : Toward Snow Country Restoration*, 2008
Bill Streever, *Cold: Adventures in the World's Frozen Places*, 2009

236

ANNE C. HELLER

Ayn Rand and the World She Made

(New York: Nan A. Talese/Doubleday, 2009)

Subject(s): Writers; Biographies; Philosophy

Summary: Anne C. Heller explores the life of writer and philosopher Ayn Rand in *Ayn Rand and the World She Made*. Russian-American Rand was best known for developing a philosophical system called Objectivism, which is the belief that reality exists independently of consciousness. It holds that the purpose of one's life is the pursuit of one's own happiness. After Rand immigrated to the United States in 1926, she worked as a screenwriter in Hollywood. Her philosophical views were expressed in all aspects of her life, especially in her personal life. In *Ayn Rand and the World She Made*, Heller explores Rand's relationships with her lover, her husband, and her publisher.

Where it's reviewed:
Harper's Magazine, Dec 2009, page p97
Inc., Nov 2009, page p84
Library Journal, Sept 1, 2009, page p116
Washington Monthly, Nov-Dec 2009, page p58

Other books you might like:
Jennifer Burns, *Goddess of the Market: Ayn Rand and the American Right*, 2009
Ayn Rand, *Anthem*, 1953
Ayn Rand, *Atlas Shrugged*, 1957
Ayn Rand, *The Fountainhead*, 1943

237

JOHN HENDRIX

John Brown: His Fight for Freedom

(New York: Abrams Books for Young Readers, 2009)

Subject(s): Biographies; Abolitionists; Slavery

Summary: John Hendrix's *John Brown: His Fight for Freedom* is an illustrated biography about the life of an abolitionist for older children and young adults. The book discusses the life of white abolitionist John Brown, whose fierce passion to end slavery ultimately led to his own end. His most renowned action occurred in Harpers Ferry, Virginia, where he and his followers attempted to raid a U.S. arsenal to arm slaves with weapons and begin a revolt. Though ultimately unsuccessful—the military, under the direction of Robert E. Lee, stopped the raid—the event shed light on the important issue of ending slavery. Hendrix describes Brown's actions—both good and bad—and his words alongside his own vivid pen-and-ink illustrations.

Other books by the same author:
Abe Lincoln Crosses a Creek: A Tall, Thin Tale (Introducing His Forgotten Frontier Friend), 2008
*How to Save Your Tail: *if You Are a Rat Nabbed by Cats Who Really Like Stories about Magic Spoons, Wolves with Snout-warts, Big, Hairy Chimney Trolls . . . and Cookies, Too*, 2007
The Giant Rat of Sumatra: Or Pirates Galore, 2005

Other books you might like:
Janet Halfmann, *Seven Miles to Freedom: The Robert Smalls Story*, 2008
Doreen Rappaport, *Freedom River*, 2000
Anne Rockwell, *Only Passing Through: The Story of Sojourner Truth*, 2000
Carole Boston Weatherford, *Moses: When Harriet Tubman Led Her People to Freedom*, 2006

238

LAURA HILLENBRAND

Unbroken: A World War II Story of Survival, Resilience, and Redemption

(New York: Random House, 2010)

Subject(s): Prisoners of war; World War II, 1939-1945; Survival

Summary: In *Unbroken: A World War II Story of Survival, Resilience, and Redemption*, bestselling author Laura Hillenbrand profiles the extraordinary story of Louis Zamperini, an Army lieutenant and former Olympic athlete who found himself fighting for his life, adrift on the open seas during the Second World War. In May 1943, Zamperini's bomber jet went down in the Pacific, and the young airman somehow—miraculously—managed to survive. But he landed in a wide open expanse of the world's biggest ocean, igniting in him a dogged determination to endure at all costs. *Unbroken* includes a bibliography and an index.

Other books by the same author:
Seabiscuit: An American Legend, 2001

Other books you might like:
James Bradley, *Flyboys: A True Story of Courage*, 2003
Michael Gannon, *Operation Drumbeat: The Dramatic True Story of Germany's First U-boat Attacks Along the American Coast in World War II*, 1990
Richard F. Newcomb, *Abandon Ship!: The Saga of the U.S.S. Indianapolis, the Navy's Greatest Sea Disaster*, 2000
Doug Stanton, *Horse Soldiers: The Extraordinary Story of a Band of US Soldiers Who Rode to Victory in Afghanistan*, 2009
Doug Stanton, *In Harm's Way: The Sinking of the USS Indianapolis and the Extraordinary Story of Its Survivors*, 2001

239

JAMES S. HIRSCH

Willie Mays: The Life, the Legend

(New York: Scribner, 2010)

Subject(s): Biographies; Baseball; African Americans

Summary: *Willie Mays: The Life, the Legend* is an authorized biography written by James S. Hirsch about Willie Mays, considered by many to be the greatest baseball player of all time. The book begins with Mays's start as a teenager playing for the Negro Leagues, then becoming a key player in the Major Leagues. Hirsch also focuses on Mays's actions during the civil rights movement and the way he encouraged reconciliation. Of course, Mays's outstanding records as a player are included as well, in addition to descriptions of the positive way he was received by fans, even when playing in enemy stadiums. This is the first biography that was written with the cooperation of Willie Mays, offering a number of personal accounts from Mays himself, as well as friends, family, and other teammates.

Other books by the same author:
Cheating Destiny: Living with Diabetes, 2007
Hurricane: The Miraculous Journey of Rubin Carter, 2000

Other books you might like:
Jonathan Eig, *Luckiest Man: The Life and Death of Lou Gehrig*, 2005
James S. Hirsch, *Hurricane: The Miraculous Journey of Rubin Carter*, 2000
David Maraniss, *Clemente: The Passion and Grace of Baseball's Last Hero*, 2006
Willie Mays, *Say Hey: The Autobiography of Willie Mays*, 1988
Lou Sahadi, co-author
Larry Tye, *Satchel: The Life and Times of an American Legend*, 2009

240

GEORGINA HOWELL

Gertrude Bell: Queen of the Desert, Shaper of Nations

(New York: Farrar, Straus and Giroux, 2007)

Subject(s): Biographies; Travel; Women

Summary: In *Gertrude Bell: Queen of the Desert, Shaper of Nations*, author Georgina Howell chronicles the life of the Victorian woman who became a central figure in the formation of Iraq. Leaving behind her family's wealthy lifestyle in the late 19th century, Bell read history at Oxford and pursued her interests in archaeology. As her knowledge of the Middle East grew during her extensive travels to the region, Bell became an expert linguist and an invaluable asset to the British military during World War I. So great was her power that Bell—academic, explorer, and spy—was able to influence King Faisal's election and initiate the creation of a new Arab nation.

Where it's reviewed:
Booklist, Feb 15, 2007, page p32
The Nation, July 2, 2007, page p32
The New Yorker, April 16, 2007, page p153
Publishers Weekly, Feb 19, 2007, page p16

Other books by the same author:
Vogue Women, 2001
Diana: Her Life in Fashion, 1999

Other books you might like:
Mary Dearborn, *Mistress of Modernism: The Life of Peggy Guggenheim*, 2004
Jane Fletcher Geniesse, *Passionate Nomad: The Life of Freya Stark*, 1993
Mary Lovell, *A Scandalous Life: The Biography of Jane Digby*, 1995
Janet Wallach, *Desert Queen: The Extraordinary Life of Gertrude Bell: Adventurer, Adviser to Kings, Ally of Lawrence of Arabia*, 1996

241

WALTER ISAACSON

Einstein: The Life of a Genius

(New York: Collins Design, 2009)

Subject(s): Biographies; Science; Research

Summary: In *Einstein: The Life of a Genius*, author Walter Isaacson examines Albert Einstein's contribution to science and many other areas. Using Einstein's personal documents that have only recently been released to the public, Isaacson puts together a book that offers information about Einstein's work with civil rights groups in America, for example. He explains the work Einstein completed that led to the creation of the atomic bomb and takes readers into the scientist's personal life, as well. He describes the relationships he had with his wife and children. Although most think of science when they think of Einstein, Isaacson makes an effort to show that

Einstein was more than a scientific genius.

Where it's reviewed:
Esquire, April 2007, page p56
New York Times Book Review, May 20, 2007, page p16
Publishers Weekly, July 30, 2007, page p79
Science News, May 19, 2007, page p319

Other books by the same author:
American Sketches: Great Leaders, Creative Thinkers, and Heroes of a Hurricane, 2009
Kissinger: A Biography, 2005
The Wise Men: Six Friends and the World They Made, 1997

Other books you might like:
Albert Einstein, *Ideas and Opinions*, 1954
Albert Einstein, *The World As I See It*, 2007
Walter Isaacson, *Benjamin Franklin: An American Life*, 2003

242

WALTER ISAACSON

Einstein: His Life and Universe

(New York: Simon & Schuster, 2007)

Subject(s): Biography; Family Life; History

Summary: Biographer Walter Isaacson takes a look at the life of famed scientist and revolutionary thinker Albert Einstein. He focuses not just on debunking common myths about Einstein—such as he failed in math (which is false: Einstein had mastered calculus by the age of 15)—but also on his family life (Einstein had one illegitimate child and several lovers). The book also explores his scientific theories in everyday terms, with help from numerous prominent scientists.

Where it's reviewed:
Esquire, April 2007, page p56
New York Times Book Review, May 20, 2007, page p16
Publishers Weekly, July 30, 2007, page p79
Science News, May 19, 2007, page p319

Other books by the same author:
American Sketches: Great Leaders, Creative Thinkers, and Heroes of a Hurricane, 2009
Kissinger: A Biography, 2005
The Wise Men: Six Friends and the World They Made, 1997

Other books you might like:
Tim Butcher, *Blood River: A Journey to Africa's Broken Heart*, 2008
Peter Godwin, *Mukiwa: A White Boy in Africa*, 1996
Douglas Rogers, *The Last Resort: A Memoir of Mischief and Mayhem on a Family Farm in Africa*, 2009
Robyn Scott, *Twenty Chickens for a Saddle: The Story of an African Childhood*, 2008

243

DAVID ISAY
STORYCORPS , Co-Author

Listening Is an Act of Love: A Celebration of American Life from the StoryCorps Project

(New York: Penguin, 2007)

Subject(s): Biographies; Storytelling; Social history

Summary: *Listening Is an Act of Love: A Celebration of American Life from the StoryCorps Project* is a collection of stories compiled by Dave Isay. He is the founder of StoryCorps, a nonprofit organization formed to record American oral history. Isay set up recording equipment and invited people to bring their friends and family members to tell stories about their lives. This book contains some of the most memorable stories out of the thousands that Isay collected.

Other books by the same author:
Flophouse: Life on the Bowery, 2000

Other books you might like:
Dave Isay, *Mom: A Celebration of Mothers from StoryCorps*, 2010
Kevin O'Keefe, *Average American: The Extraordinary Search for the Nation's Most Ordinary Citizen*, 2005

244

RHODA JANZEN

Mennonite in a Little Black Dress: A Memoir of Going Home

(New York: Henry Holt and Co., 2009)

Subject(s): Autobiographies; Family; Mennonites

Summary: In Rhoda Janzen's *Mennonite in a Little Black Dress: A Memoir of Going Home*, author Janzen details her return to the religious community of her childhood following a number of setbacks. First Janzen's husband left her—for a man. Then she got into a terrible traffic accident in which she sustained considerable injuries. After that, she moved back home to live with her Mennonite parents, in the tight-knit, faith-based community where she grew up. There, Janzen attempts to reassemble the pieces of her ruptured life and gains a new respect for the lifestyle that once constrained her. Janzen intertwines the tragic stories with enough self-deprecating humor to keep the story of her life light and engaging.

Where it's reviewed:
Entertainment Weekly, October 23, 2009, page 62
New York Times Book Review, Nov 8, 2009, page p12
People, October 26, 2009, page 51
Publishers Weekly, July 13, 2009, page p45
USA Today, Oct 22, 2009, page p07D

Other books by the same author:
Babel's Stair, 2006

Other books you might like:
Elna Baker, *The New York Regional Mormon Singles Halloween Dance: A Memoir*, 2009
Mary-Ann Kirkby, *I Am Hutterite: The Fascinating True Story of a Young Woman's Journey to Reclaim Her Heritage*, 2010
Colm Toibin, *Brooklyn*, 2009
Katie Funk Wiebe, *You Never Gave Me a Name: One Mennonite Woman's Story*, 2009
Diane Wilson, *Holy Roller: Growing Up in the Church of Knock Down, Drag Out; or, How I Quit Loving a Blue-Eyed Jesus*, 2008

245

TIM JEAL

Stanley: The Impossible Life of Africa's Greatest Explorer

(New Haven, Connecticut: Yale University Press, 2007)

Subject(s): Biographies; Discovery and exploration; Travel

Summary: According to author Tim Jeal, Sir Henry Morton Stanley's accomplishments and historical discoveries have been cast aside, or misunderstood. To present factual information and provide readers with insight into the life of the journalist and world explorer, Jeal wrote *Stanley: The Impossible Life of Africa's Greatest Explorer*. In this biography, Jeal examines Stanley's life from his unfortunate, parentless childhood to his independent exploration of Africa and his famous celebrity interviews. Using records, journals, and information that had previously been closed to public, Jeal vividly reconstructs many of the major events in Stanley's life. Jeal is also the author of *Livingstone* and *Baden-Powell: Founder of the Boy Scouts*.

Where it's reviewed:
Booklist, September 15, 2007, page 2
Geographical, April 2007, page 92
History Today, April 2007, page 63
The New York Review of Books, December 6, 2007, page 47

Other books by the same author:
Baden-Powell: Founder of the Boy Scouts, 2007
Swimming with My Father, 2004
Livingstone, 2001

Other books you might like:
Laurence Bergreen, *Over the Edge of the World: Magellan's Terrifying Circumnavigation of the Globe*, 2003
Martin Dugard, *Into Africa: The Epic Adventures of Stanley and Livingstone*, 2003
Dean King, *Skeletons on the Zahara: A True Story of Survival*, 2004
Alan Moorehead, *The White Nile*, 1970
Dan Morrison, *The Black Nile: One Man's Amazing Journey Through Peace and War on the World's Longest River*, 2010

246

WILLIAM KAMKWAMBA
BRYAN MEALER , Co-Author

The Boy Who Harnessed the Wind: Creating Currents of Electricity and Hope

(New York: William Morrow, 2009)

Subject(s): Autobiographies; Famine victims

Summary: *The Boy Who Harnessed the Wind: Creating Currents of Electricity and Hope* is the true story of how a poor Malawian boy changed the lives of his friends and family forever. William Kamkwamba grew up on a farm in Malawi, where electricity and running water were luxuries, not necessities. William dreamed of bringing these Western-world essentials to his family's small farm by earning a science degree at a prestigious boarding school. When famine and drought devastated the country, William was forced to help his family's struggling farm. Determined to make his dream a reality, William used old science textbooks to construct a windmill that brought electricity and water to his family's home. Author Bryan Mealer helps chronicle the amazing story of William's determination to succeed.

Where it's reviewed:
Booklist, March 1, 2010, page p10
Publishers Weekly, October 12, 2009, page 45

Other books you might like:
George Dawson, *Life Is So Good*, 2000
Thomas L. Friedman, *Hot, Flat, and Crowded*, 2008
Richard Glaubman, *Life Is So Good*, 2000
Tracy Kidder, *Strength in What Remains*, 2009
Barbara Kingsolver, *The Poisonwood Bible*, 1998
Christopher Steiner, *$20 Per Gallon: How the Inevitable Rise in the Price of Gasoline Will Change Our Lives for the Better*, 2009

247

MARY KARR

Lit: A Memoir

(New York: Harper, 2009)

Subject(s): Alcoholism; Mental disorders; Family

Summary: In *Lit: A Memoir*, award-winning author Mary Karr takes readers on an intimate tour of her battle with alcoholism and her challenging road to recovery. The daughter of an oil worker father and an artist mother, Karr witnessed firsthand the ravages of alcoholism when her mother fell prey to the bottle. When she herself became a young parent, Karr followed down the only road she knew, drowning her sorrows, fears, and insecurities in alcohol—an act which led to increasing mental instability. *Lit* is also a chronicle of recovery, charting one woman's experiences in getting sober, finding honesty, and becoming whole.

Where it's reviewed:
Library Journal, October 1, 2009, page 77
The New York Review of Books, Feb 25, 2010, page p15
New York Times Book Review, Nov 15, 2009, page p12
The New Yorker, Nov 23, 2009, page p113
Publishers Weekly, August 3, 2009, page p36

Other books by the same author:
Sinners Welcome, 2006
The Liars' Club, 2005
Cherry, 2001
Viper Rum, 2001
The Devil's Tour, 1993

Other books you might like:
Augusten Burroughs, *Dry: A Memoir*, 2003
Maddie Dawson, *The Stuff That Never Happened: A Novel*, 2010
Caroline Knapp, *Drinking: A Love Story*, 1996
David Sedaris, *Holidays on Ice*, 1997

248

KITTY KELLEY

Oprah: A Biography

(New York: Crown Publishers, 2010)

Subject(s): Television; African Americans; Culture

Summary: Best-selling author Kitty Kelley presents an expansive recounting of the life and career of television icon Oprah Winfrey. In *Oprah: A Biography*, Kelley examines Winfrey's upbringing in rural Mississippi, her education and rise to fame, and her role as one of the most trusted personalities in television history. Based on years of tireless research, this volume offers an in-depth look at the woman behind the image: the ambitious student, the spiritual seeker, the determined businessperson, and the cultural legend.

Where it's reviewed:
Booklist, June 1, 2010, page 106
The New Yorker, April 19, 2010, pages 120-121
Publishers Weekly, May 31, 2010, page 45

Other books by the same author:
The Family: The Real Story of the Bush Dynasty, 2004
The Royals, 1997
Nancy Reagan: The Unauthorized Biography, 1991
His Way: The Unauthorized Biography of Frank Sinatra, 1986

Other books you might like:
Bill Adler, *The Uncommon Wisdom of Oprah Winfrey: A Portrait in Her Own Words*, 1997
George Mair, *Oprah Winfrey*, 1994
Robyn Okrant, *Living Oprah: My One-Year Experiment to Walk the Walk of the Queen of Talk*, 2010
Kathleen Rooney, *Reading with Oprah: The Book Club That Changed America*, 2005
Martha Stewart, *The Martha Rules*, 2005

249

ROBIN D.G. KELLEY

Thelonious Monk: The Life and Times of an American Original

(New York: Free Press, 2009)

Subject(s): Jazz; Musicians; Music

Summary: Famed pianist Thelonious Monk took the world of jazz by storm and crafted an enduring legacy in popular music. In *Thelonious Monk: The Life and Times of an American Original*, author and historian Robin D.G. Kelley explores Monk's private and professional lives and the impact his talent has had on the music industry. From a poverty-stricken childhood to the top of the jazz scene, from struggles with mental illness to the many relationships that inspired Monk, this volume traces the phenomenal journey of one man and the unique gift he shared with the world. *Thelonious Monk* includes a discography, filmography, bibliography, and index.

Where it's reviewed:
Booklist, Oct 15, 2009, page p1
Library Journal, Sept 1, 2009, page p118
New York Times Book Review, Oct 18, 2009, page p10
Publishers Weekly, August 24, 2009, page p57

Other books by the same author:
Freedom Dreams: The Black Radical Imagination, 2003
Discourse on Colonialism, 2001
Yo' Mama's Disfunktional !: Fighting the Culture Wars in Urban America, 1998
Hammer and Hoe: Alabama Communists During the Great Depression, 1990

Other books you might like:
Miles Davis, *Miles, the Autobiography*, 1989
Ted Gioia, *The History of Jazz*, 1998
Pannonica de Koenigswarter, *Three Wishes: An Intimate Look at Jazz Greats*, 2008
Terry Teachout, *Pops: A Life of Louis Armstrong*, 2009
Quincy Troupe, *Miles, the Autobiography*, 1989

250

EDWARD M. KENNEDY

True Compass: A Memoir

(New York: Twelve, 2009)

Subject(s): Autobiographies; Politics; United States history

Summary: In *True Compass: A Memoir*, beloved U.S. senator Ted Kennedy recounts both his personal life and his adventures in American politics. A progeny of the adored Kennedy dynasty, Ted was groomed for success early on, but a string of personal tragedies nearly waylaid his political ambitions. Elected to the Senate in 1962, Kennedy had to face a number of challenges: the deaths of two of his brothers, the very public scrutiny he and his family consistently faced, and his own well-

publicized scandals and controversies. In this engaging volume, Kennedy tackles them all with class and dignity, leaving no stone unturned in his quest for total disclosure—and imprinting his own signature on American history.

Where it's reviewed:
The Economist, Sept 19, 2009, page p86
New Statesman, Nov 2, 2009, page p53
The New Yorker, Oct 5, 2009, page p79
People, Sept 28, 2009, page p67

Other books by the same author:
America Back on Track, 2007

Other books you might like:
John Fitzgerald Kennedy, *A Nation of Immigrants*, 2008
John F. Kennedy, *Profiles in Courage*, 1975
Editors of Life, *The Kennedys: End of a Dynasty*, 2009

251

MARK KINGWELL

Glenn Gould

(Toronto, Ontario, Canada: Penguin Canada, 2009)

Subject(s): Biographies; Musicians; Music

Summary: Mark Kingwell's *Glenn Gould* is part of the Extraordinary Canadians series of biographies about accomplished Canadian individuals. Kingwell, a philosophy professor, employs short, unrelated chapters to examine Gould, a world-renowned pianist, from a variety of different perspectives. Gould died at the young age of 50, but that didn't stop him from making a lasting impression on the world of classical music. Though he stopped performing onstage in 1964, he continued to make an impact through other forms of communication including radio, television, and print. In *Glenn Gould*, Kingwell presents a complex portrait of a master musician and an extraordinary Canadian.

Other books by the same author:
Concrete Reveries: Consciousness and the City, 2008
Opening Gambits: Essays on Art and Philosophy, 2008
Nearest Thing to Heaven: The Empire State Building and American Dreams, 2007
Nothing For Granted: Tales of War, Philosophy, and Why the Right Was Mostly Wrong, 2005

Other books you might like:
Kevin Bazzana, *Wondrous Strange: The Life and Art of Glenn Gould*, 2004
J.M. Bumsted, *A History of the Canadian Peoples*, 2007
Adrienne Clarkson, *Norman Bethune*, 2009
Nino Ricci, *Pierre Elliott Trudeau*, 2009
Jane Urquhart, *L.M. Montgomery*, 2009

252

WALTER KIRN

Lost in the Meritocracy: The Undereducation of an Overachiever

(New York: Doubleday, 2009)

Subject(s): Autobiographies; Education; Schools

Summary: Critic and author Walter Kirn chronicles his rise through the American educational system by any means necessary in *Lost in the Meritocracy: The Under-education of an Overachiever*. As an elementary school student, Kirn learned that art is about emotion, not about accurately depicting dinosaurs on paper, which led him to add some squiggly lines—"feelings"—around his dinosaur drawing. From there, Kirn understood that the surest way to advance in life was to do or say whatever the instructor wished to earn the grades. In turn, Kirn thought he would be rewarded with degrees, a job, a girl, and happiness. In high school, Kirn entered any contest he was sure he could win, so as to have one more notch on his college resume. But once he reached Princeton, Kirn felt ashamed of his Minnesota upbringing and attempts to fit in with his classmates fell painfully flat. At Princeton, and later at Oxford, Kirn continued his attempts at kissing up to his teachers and mimicking his cooler classmates, becoming more and more aware that a complete psychic collapse might be looming at the end of his education.

Where it's reviewed:
Booklist, April 15, 2009, page p15
Library Journal, May 1, 2009, page p88
New York Times Book Review, May 24, 2009, page p7
Time, June 8, 2009, page p63

Other books by the same author:
Mission to America: A Novel, 2005
Up in the Air, 2002
Thumbsucker, 1999

Other books you might like:
Peter Elbow, *Being a Writer: A Community of Writers Revisited*, 2002

253

LANG LANG

Lang Lang: Playing with Flying Keys
(New York: Delacorte Books for Young Readers, 2008)

Subject(s): Autobiographies; Musicians; Music

Summary: The extraordinary life and career of world-renowned pianist Lang Lang is recounted for young adult readers in this comprehensive introduction to the man and his music. *Lang Lang: Playing with Flying Keys* chronicles the musician's journey from child prodigy in China to his role as one of the most celebrated artists in contemporary classical music. This volume also explores Lang Lang's personal life, including his relationships with his doting mother and rigid father and a peek into his childhood. The book includes a glossary of Western composers with comments by Lang Lang and a list of the subject's favored interests and pastimes.

Other books by the same author:
Journey of a Thousand Miles: My Story, 2008

Other books you might like:
Li Cunxin, *Dancing to Freedom: The True Story of Mao's Last Dancer*, 2008

Lang Lang, *Journey of a Thousand Miles: My Story*, 2008
David Ritz, co-author
Wladyslaw Szpilman, *The Pianist: The Extraordinary Story of One Man's Survival in Warsaw, 1939-1945*, 1999

254

ROBERT LECKIE

Helmet for My Pillow: From Parris Island to the Pacific
(New York: Bantam Books, 2010)

Subject(s): Autobiographies; World War II, 1939-1945; Wars

Summary: *Helmet for My Pillow: From Parris Island to the Pacific* is an autobiography written by Robert Leckie, a United States Marine who enlisted in 1942, just after the bombing of Pearl Harbor. The book chronicles his entire journey as part of the military, beginning at basic training on Parris Island, South Carolina. From there, Leckie was sent to the Pacific, fighting in the unimaginably brutal battles on Guadalcanal, New Britain, and Peleliu. Leckie also includes stories about life as a Marine on leave, as well as his beliefs on the meaning of war and what people can learn from it.

Other books by the same author:
Conflict: The History of the Korean War, 1950-53, 1996
Okinawa: The Last Battle of World War II, 1996
Ordained, 1969

Other books you might like:
Hugh Ambrose, *The Pacific*, 2010
Sebastian Junger, *War*, 2010

255

HERMIONE LEE

Edith Wharton
(New York: Alfred A. Knopf, 2007)

Subject(s): Biographies; Writers; World War I, 1914-1918

Summary: Hermione Lee's thoroughly researched biography attempts to expel the long-held view of author Edith Wharton as the pretentious product of a wealthy family, and provides new insight into the strong and modern woman who was just as intriguing as the characters she created. Making use of new sources, Lee sheds light on obscure aspects of Wharton's life, embracing the bad traits along with the good. Lee chronicles the author's childhood and upbringing in New York, her early marriage to Teddy Wharton, and her life in France. Highlights of the biography include Wharton's charitable activities during World War I and her friendships with Henry James, Bernard Berenson, and Walter Berry.

Where it's reviewed:
Booklist, February 15, 2007, page 31
New Statesman, February 19, 2007, page 56

People Weekly, January 29, 2007, page 55
Vogue, April 2007, page 281

Other books by the same author:
Willa Cather: A Life Saved Up, 2008
Virginia Woolf's Nose: Essays on Biography, 2007

Other books you might like:
Laura Claridge, *Emily Post: Daughter of the Gilded Age, Mistress of American Manners*, 2008
Kennedy Fraser, *Ornament and Silence: Essays on Women's Lives from Edith Wharton to Germaine Greer*, 1996
R.W.B. Lewis, *Edith Wharton: A Biography*, 1975
Edith Wharton, *A Backward Glance*, 1934

256

STEVE LOPEZ

The Soloist: A Lost Dream, an Unlikely Friendship, and the Redemptive Power of Music

(New York: G.P. Putnam's Sons, 2008)

Subject(s): Mental disorders; Music; Autobiographies

Summary: Steve Lopez's *The Soloist: A Lost Dream, an Unlikely Friendship, and the Redemptive Power of Music* is the real-life story of journalist whose life changed when he met a homeless man with schizophrenia. Lopez, a journalist for the *Los Angeles Times*, first met Nathaniel Ayers when Ayers was playing the violin on the streets. Ayers's abilities amazed Lopez. Soon after their initial meeting, Lopez found out that Ayers was once a music student at Juilliard, but he dropped out due to a mental illness. Ayers's illness made it nearly impossible for him to hold down a steady job, and he—like many other people with mental illnesses—became homeless. Lopez and Ayers formed a friendship, and Lopez tried to improve Ayers's life. Throughout the book, Lopez describes Ayers's talent, the friendship they formed, and the things they taught each other.

Where it's reviewed:
America, June 23, 2008, page p41
Booklist, March 15, 2008, page p14
Library Journal, March 15, 2008, page p74
Publishers Weekly, Feb 18, 2008, page p147

Other books by the same author:
Dreams and Schemes: My Decade of Fun in the Sun, 2010
Land of Giants: Where No Good Deed Goes Unpunished, 1995
Third and Indiana: A Novel, 1995

Other books you might like:
Jay Allison, *This I Believe: The Personal Philosophies of Remarkable Men and Women*, 2006
Dave Eggers, *Zeitoun*, 2009
Dan Gediman, *This I Believe: The Personal*

Philosophies of Remarkable Men and Women, 2006
Sonia Nazario, *Enrique's Journey*, 2006

257

BEN MACINTYRE

Agent Zigzag: A True Story of Nazi Espionage, Love, and Betrayal

(New York: Harmony Books, 2007)

Subject(s): Biographies; History; World War II, 1939-1945

Summary: Ben Macintyre's *Agent Zigzag: A True Story of Nazi Espionage, Love, and Betrayal* is a biography of Eddie Chapman, a man who worked as a double agent during World War II. Chapman was released from an English prison under German command in 1940, at which point he immediately volunteered to become a spy for the Germans. He spent two years in training and then entered England in 1942, theoretically to sabotage an aircraft factory; instead, he immediately surrendered to the government. In return, they trained him as a double spy for MI5 and subsequently used him throughout the war to feed incorrect information to the Germans, such as whether bombs were striking their intended targets. Chapman excelled at this double-agent work, developing friendships with high-ranking German officials and even earning recognition from the Third Reich for his service, all while plotting to assassinate Hitler. Many of Chapman's activities are extensively detailed in this engaging book, based on files obtained from MI5.

Where it's reviewed:
Booklist, September 1, 2007, page 40
New York Times Book Review, October 28, 2007, page 22
Times Literary Supplement, March 9, 2007, page 32

Other books by the same author:
Operation Mincemeat: How a Dead Man and a Bizarre Plan Fooled the Nazis and Assured an Allied Victory, 2010
The Man Who Would Be King: The First American in Afghanistan, 2005
The Napoleon of Crime: The Life and Times of Adam Worth, Master Thief, 1998

Other books you might like:
Nicholas Booth, *Zigzag: The Incredible Wartime Exploits of Double Agent Eddie Chapman*, 2007
James L. Centner, *Codename: Magpie: The Final Nazi Espionage Against the U.S. in WWII*, 2007
Ewen Montagu, *The Man Who Never Was: World War II's Boldest Counter-Intelligence Operation*, 1954
Louis A. Perez Jr., *Hitler's Man in Havana: Heinz Luning and Nazi Espionage in Latin America*, 2008
Thomas D. Schoonover, co-author
Charles Whiting, *Hitler's Secret War: The Nazi Espionage Campaign Against the Allies*, 2000

258

MARGARET MACMILLAN

Extraordinary Canadians: Stephen Leacock

(Toronto: Penguin Books Canada, 2009)

Subject(s): Biographies; Writers; Academia

Summary: In *Extraordinary Canadians: Stephen Leacock*, Margaret MacMillan, author and historian, writes a biography of one of Canada's most celebrated humorists, Stephen Leacock. His book, *Sunshine Sketches of a Little Town*, is a satirical account of Canadian life and culture in the early 20th century from an Anglo-Canadian point of view. MacMillan discusses his early life, which was marked by the fact that he was a difficult student. His teachers did not anticipate him amounting to much, but his determination transformed him from an impoverished academic to an inspired economist, professor, and author, who helped Canadians find humor in their ways of life.

Other books by the same author:
The Uses and Abuses of History, 2008
Nixon and Mao: The Week That Changed the World, 2007
Nixon in China: The Week That Changed the World, 2006
Paris 1919: Six Months That Changed the World, 2002

Other books you might like:
Mark Kingwell, *Glenn Gould*, 2009
Nino Ricci, *Pierre Elliott Trudeau*, 2009

259

BILL MADDEN

Steinbrenner: The Last Lion of Baseball

(New York: Harper, 2010)

Subject(s): Biographies; Baseball; Money

Summary: When George Steinbrenner bought the New York Yankees in 1973, his father dismissed the purchase as unimportant. Managing a professional baseball team was a hobby, not a career, he told his son. More than 35 years later, Steinbrenner has not only made a career out of his Yankees ownership, but also has left a permanent mark on the franchise as a whole. In *Steinbrenner: The Last Lion of Baseball*, author Bill Madden shares the story of Steinbrenner's life before and after he made the Yankees into a billion-dollar team. The text is supported by interviews with everyone from bat boys to field managers.

Other books by the same author:
Zim: A Baseball Life, 2001

Other books you might like:
Les Krantz, *Yankee Stadium: A Tribute: 85 Years of Memories: 1923-2008*, 2008
Kenneth McMillan, *Tales from the Yankee Dugout: A*

Collection of the Greatest Yankee Stories Ever Told, 1999
Bobby Murcer, *Yankee for Life: My 40-Year Journey in Pinstripes*, 2008
Glen Stout, *Yankees Century: 100 Years of New York Yankees Baseball*, 2002
Joe Torre, *The Yankee Years*, 2009
    Tom Verducci, co-author
Glen Waggoner, *Yankee for Life: My 40-Year Journey in Pinstripes*, 2008

260

DAVID MARANISS

Clemente: The Passion and Grace of Baseball's Last Hero

(New York: Simon & Schuster, 2006)

Subject(s): Baseball; Biography; Puerto Rican Americans

Summary: Roberto Clemente is one of the most beloved baseball players of all time. Not only was the Puerto Rican-born player one of the greatest rightfielders of all time, but the manner of his death sealed his fame. He died in a 1972 plane crash, attempting to deliver relief supplies to refugees of a Nicaraguan earthquake. This biography tells the story of Clemente's hard upbringing; his ambition and determination as a baseball player (as well as his famously unique catching style); his struggle with racism and his furious bouts of temper; and the compassion and drive to do good that led to his early death.

Where it's reviewed:
Publishers Weekly, November 9, 2009, page 40

Other books by the same author:
Into the Story: A Writer's Journey through Life, Politics, Sports and Loss, 2010
They Marched Into Sunlight, 2004
When Pride Still Mattered : A Life Of Vince Lombardi, 2000

Other books you might like:
Bruce Markusen, *The Team that Changed Baseball: Roberte Clemente and the 1971 Pittsburgh Pirates*, 2006
Larry Tye, *Satchel: The Life and Times of an American Legend*, 2009

261

DAVID MARGOLICK

Beyond Glory: Joe Louis vs. Max Schmeling and a World on the Brink

(New York: Alfred A. Knopf, 2005)

Subject(s): Sports; Boxing; History

Summary: Author David Margolick analyzes the political

tensions and racial undertones of the historic 1938 boxing match in *Beyond Glory: Joe Louis vs. Max Schmeling and a World on the Brink*. With Nazi Germany at its peak and racial unease rampant in America, the heavyweight title fight between African American Joe Lewis and German Max Schmeling was not just a boxing match, but a showcase for the real drama that was unfolding on the world stage at that time. For spectators around the world, the match was symbolic of the day's struggle—a successful and popular African American in one corner and a so-called Nazi symbol of Aryan racial philosophies in the other. Margolick offers a ringside seat in this compelling look at the famous Louis vs. Schmeling bout.

Where it's reviewed:
The Nation, December 5, 2005, page 17
New York Review of Books, January 12, 2006, page 19
The New York Times, December 3, 2005, page B13
New York Times Book Review, October 2, 2005, page 10
Sports Illustrated, September 19, 2005, page Z6

Other books by the same author:
Strange Fruit: The Biography of a Song, 2001
Undue Influence: The Epic Battle for the Johnson and Johnson Fortune, 2001
At the Bar, 1995

Other books you might like:
Richard Bak, *Joe Louis: The Great Black Hope*, 1998
Lewis A. Erenberg, *The Greatest Fight of Our Generation: Louis Vs. Schmeling*, 2005
Patrick Myler, *Ring of Hate: Joe Louis vs. Max Smeling: The Fight of the Century*, 2005
Randy Roberts, *Joe Louis: Hard Times Man*, 2010
Max Schmeling, *Max Schmeling: An Autobiography*, 1998

262

GERALD MARTIN

Gabriel Garcia Marquez: A Life
(New York: Alfred A. Knopf, 2009)

Subject(s): Biographies; Writing; Writers

Summary: *Gabriel Garcia Marquez: A Life* by Gerald Martin is the first official biography of Noble Prize-winning author Gabriel Garcia Marquez. For this book, Martin interviewed Marquez, his family, friends, and nearly 300 other people to gain an insight into what made the author a literary sensation. Martin takes readers back to Marquez's childhood and adolescence in Colombia. Before his first novel, Marquez studied to be a journalist. At the age of 40, he published *One Hundred Years of Solitude*, a book that international critics claimed had broken ground for other writers who were interested in using magical realism in their work.

Where it's reviewed:
Booklist, May 1, 2009, page p4
The New York Review of Books, July 16, 2009, page p19
New York Times Book Review, June 7, 2009, page p1
USA Today, June 11, 2009, page p05D

Other books you might like:
Gabriel Garcia Marquez, *Collected Stories*, 1984
Gabriel Garcia Marquez, *Memories of My Melancholy Whores*, 2005
Edith Grossman, *Living to Tell the Tale*, 2003
Edith Grossman, *Memories of My Melancholy Whores*, 2005
Gabriel Garcia Marquez, *Living to Tell the Tale*, 2003
Gabriel Garcia Marquez, *The Story of a Shipwrecked Sailor*, 1986

263

MARLEE MATLIN

I'll Scream Later
(New York: Simon Spotlight Entertainment, 2009)

Subject(s): Autobiographies; Movie industry; Entertainment industry

Summary: In *I'll Scream Later*, Marlee Matlin provides insight into her life as a successful, deaf actress. Although she lost her hearing when she was only 18 months old, Matlin would later find that she didn't need to be able to hear to carry on a conversation. Matlin's mother, uncomfortable with her daughter's situation, often refused to communicate with Matlin. Upon entering her teenage years, Matlin turned to drugs to escape her own depression. After a few stays in rehab, she discovered a love of acting. Without any formal training, she moved to Hollywood. In *I'll Scream Later*, Matlin speaks of how her acting career truly changed her life for the better.

Where it's reviewed:
Entertainment Weekly, May 8, 2009, page 6

Other books by the same author:
Leading Ladies, 2007
Nobody's Perfect, 2006
Deaf Child Crossing, 2004

Other books you might like:
Leah Hager Cohen, *Train Go Sorry: Inside a Deaf World*, 1994
Henry Kisor, *What's That Pig Outdoors? A Memoir of Deafness*, 1990
James P. Spradley, *Deaf Like Me*, 1978
    Thomas S. Spradley, co-author
Myron Uhlberg, *Hands of My Father: A Hearing Boy, His Deaf Parents, and the Language of Love*, 2009
Lou Ann Walker, *A Loss for Words: The Story of Deafness in a Family*, 1986

264

JOHN MATTESON

Eden's Outcasts: The Story of Louisa May Alcott and Her Father
(New York: W.W. Norton, 2007)

Subject(s): Biographies; Literature; Writers
Summary: *Eden's Outcasts: The Story of Louisa May Al-*

cott and Her Father by author John Matteson is a biography of famed author Louisa May Alcott and her father Bronson Alcott. Louisa May Alcott and her father shared a unique relationship in that the vast differences in their personalities were what ultimately brought them together as father and daughter. Bronson was a philosopher and a dreamer, whose life work largely resulted in failure and very little income. Louisa, her sister, and her overworked mother had to provide for the family. Both Louisa and her sister Anna were forced to take teaching jobs to keep the family afloat. Although her hardworking and dedicated lifestyle was very different from her father's, Louisa made a steadfast effort to maintain in her own life some of Bronson's ideals. In his first book Matteson tells the story of the Alcott family, with special emphasis on Louisa and Bronson and their special bond.

Other books you might like:

Louisa May Alcott, *The Girlhood Diary of Louisa May Alcott, 1843-1846: Writings of a Young Author*, 2001

Susan Cheever, *Louisa May Alcott: A Personal Biography*, 2010

Megan Marshall, *The Peabody Sisters: Three Women Who Ignited American Romanticism*, 2005

Kelly O'Connor McNees, *The Lost Summer of Louisa May Alcott*, 2010

265

MAUREEN MCCORMICK

Here's the Story: Surviving Marcia Brady and Finding My True Voice

(New York: William Morrow, 2008)

Subject(s): Television programs; Parent-child relations; Drug abuse

Summary: To the world, Marcia Brady was the ideal teenager. She was pretty and smart, boys liked her, and her family was close and always had fun together. While onscreen, Marcia Brady's life was perfect. Offscreen, however, the actress who portrayed the teen was struggling. Maureen McCormick's *Here's the Story: Surviving Marcia Brady and Finding My True Voice* provides detailed, behind-the-scenes information about on-set drama and off-set challenges. She elaborates on her relationships with her co-stars, and provides insight into the drug addiction and depression that resulted after *The Brady Bunch*'s last season came to an end.

Other books you might like:

Melissa Gilbert, *Prairie Tale: A Memoir*, 2009

Chris Kreski, *Growing Up Brady: I Was a Teenage Greg*, 1992

Tatum O'Neal, *A Paper Life*, 2004

Mackenzie Phillips, *High on Arrival*, 2009

Barry Williams, *Growing Up Brady: I Was a Teenage Greg*, 1992

266

FRANK MCCOURT

Teacher Man: A Memoir

(New York: Scribner, 2005)

Subject(s): Autobiography; Education; Irish Americans

Summary: McCourt's third memoir, following *Angela's Ashes* (1996) and *'Tis* (1999), recalls his 30-year teaching career in New York City's public high schools. The author tells how he begins in 1958 at McKee Vocational and Technical, then quickly learns that bureaucracy hampers the system. Later he uncomfortably adjusts to some of the unreasonable demands of administrators but is fired more than once for not deferring to the authorities. He also learns never to underestimate students and how to motivate them through personal storytelling and creative assignments. Additionally, the author asserts his philosophy of teaching, defends the teaching profession, and explains how his experiences in the classroom led to his becoming a writer.

Where it's reviewed:

Library Journal, November 1, 2005, page 86

People Weekly, November 25, 2005, page 57

USA Today, November 15, 2005, page 7D

Other books by the same author:

'Tis: A Memoir, 2000

Angela's Ashes, 1999

Other books you might like:

Brendan Halpin, *Losing My Faculties: A Teacher's Story*, 2003

Alex Kotlowitz, *There Are No Children Here: The Story of Two Boys Growing Up in the Other America*, 1991

Jonathan Kozol, *On Being a Teacher*, 2008

Frank McCourt, *Angela's Ashes*, 1996

Frank McCourt, *'Tis: A Memoir*, 1999

267

ELIZABETH MCCRACKEN

An Exact Replica of a Figment of My Imagination: A Memoir

(London: Little, Brown and Company, 2008)

Subject(s): Birth defects; Pregnancy; Grief

Summary: Novelist Elizabeth McCracken tells a tragic tale of personal loss in her memoir *An Exact Replica of a Figment of My Imagination*. McCracken and her husband, who is also an author, were living and working in France at the time that their first child was supposed to be born. Sadly, at nine months into the pregnancy the baby died and was delivered stillborn. McCracken uses her skills as a storyteller to bring the truth of her agonizing experience to life, as a memento to the son she carried, but who was never born. She uses her dry wit and humor to put the whole experience in context for herself and her audience.

Where it's reviewed:
Booklist, August 1, 2008, page p25
New York Times Book Review, Oct 5, 2008, page p8
Publishers Weekly, July 7, 2008, page p3
Time, Sept 29, 2008, page p64

Other books by the same author:
The Giant's House: A Romance, 2007
Niagara Falls All Over Again, 2002
Here's Your Hat What's Your Hurry: Stories, 1997

Other books you might like:
Lorraine Ash, *Life Touches Life: A Mother's Story of Stillbirth and Healing*, 2004
Deborah L. Davis, *Empty Cradle, Broken Heart, Revised Edition: Surviving the Death of Your Baby*, 1996
Ann Douglas, *Trying Again: A Guide to Pregnancy After Miscarriage, Stillbirth, and Infant Loss*, 2000
Carol Cirulli Lanham, *Pregnancy After a Loss: A Guide to Pregnancy After a Miscarriage, Stillbirth, or Infant Death*, 1999

268

ROBERT MCCRUM

Wodehouse: A Life

(New York: W.W. Norton & Co., 2005)

Subject(s): Biographies; Writers; World War II, 1939-1945

Summary: In *Wodehouse: A Life*, Robert McCrum explores the life of writer P.G. Wodehouse. Over a seventy-year span, Wodehouse wrote humorous short stories, novels, and musical theatre. He lived in England and the United States, but he moved to France to avoid paying taxes near the start of World War II. During his time in France, he was taken prisoner. He entertained fellow prisoners with his witty humor and used this humor as the basis of his 1941 radio broadcasts on Nazi radio. These broadcasts later caused him many problems, including the banning of his books and accusations of treason.

Where it's reviewed:
The Atlantic, November 2004, page 136
Booklist, September 15, 2004, page 194
National Review, December 13, 2004, page 53
The Wilson Quarterly, Winter 2005, page 117

Other books by the same author:
Globish: How the English Language Became the World's Language, 2010
Do You Speak American?, 2005

Other books you might like:
Frances Donaldson, *P.G. Wodehouse: A Biography*, 1984
Robert McCrum, *Globish: How The English Language Became the World's Language*, 2004
P.G. Wodehouse, *The Best of Wodehouse: An Anthology*, 1949
P.G. Wodehouse, *The Most of P.G. Wodehouse*, 1960

269

HEATHER MCDONALD

You'll Never Blue Ball in This Town Again: One Woman's Painfully Funny Quest to Give It Up

(New York: Simon and Schuster, 2010)

Subject(s): Autobiographies; Sexuality; Sexual behavior

Summary: *You'll Never Blue Ball in This Town Again: One Woman's Painfully Funny Quest to Give It Up* is an autobiography written by Heather McDonald, who also works as an actress and stand-up comedienne. This autobiography tells the story of her quest to lose her virginity, even after receiving many offers from wealthy, handsome men. McDonald refused to "give it up," though, even after all of her friends had already lost their virginities. The author, however, would not have sex until she found true love. This is the humorous story of her many misadventures in the search for the perfect guy.

Other books by the same author:
Deal with It!: A Whole New Approach to Your Body, Brain, and Life as a Gurl, 1999

Other books you might like:
Chelsea Handler, *Are You There, Vodka? It's Me, Chelsea*, 2008
Chelsea Handler, *Chelsea Chelsea Bang Bang*, 2010
Chelsea Handler, *My Horizontal Life: A Collection of One-Night Stands*, 2005
Christian Lander, *Stuff White People Like*, 2008
Frank Warren, *PostSecret: Confessions on Life, Death, and God*, 2009

270

JAMES M. MCPHERSON

Abraham Lincoln

(New York: Oxford University Press, 2009)

Subject(s): Biographies; History; United States Civil War, 1861-1865

Summary: *Abraham Lincoln* is a succinct yet comprehensive biography of the sixteenth president of the United States by historian James M. McPherson. McPherson provides a brief background on Lincoln and the events that helped shape his life, such as his childhood, his difficult marriage, and his ongoing battle with depression and discusses his viewpoints on significant issues such as race and slavery. The bulk of the text is spent on Lincoln's politics—his election, his debates with Stephen Douglas, the events surrounding the secession of the Confederate states, and the Civil War. Each significant event in Lincoln's political career is addressed.

Where it's reviewed:
Library Journal, December 2, 2008, page 137

New York Times Book Review, February 15, 2009, page 22

Other books by the same author:
Ordeal by Fire: The Civil War and Reconstruction, 2010
Battle Cry of Freedom: The Civil War Era, 2003
Hallowed Ground: A Walk at Gettysburg, 2003

Other books you might like:
David Donald, *Lincoln,* 1995
Doris Kearns Goodwin, *Team of Rivals: The Political Genius of Abraham Lincoln,* 2005
Stephen B. Oates, *With Malice Toward None: A Life of Abraham Lincoln,* 1994
Ronald C. White, *A. Lincoln: A Biography,* 2009
Garry Wills, *Lincoln at Gettysburg: The Words That Remade America,* 1992

271

JON MEACHAM

American Lion: Andrew Jackson in the White House

(New York: Random House, 2008)

Subject(s): Presidents (Government); Slavery; Indian history

Summary: Jon Meacham utilizes his masterful story telling to breathe fresh air into the history of Andrew Jackson, the seventh President of the United States. Jackson, founder of the Democratic Party, has been a very controversial figure in American history. On the one hand, he made democracy more accessible to the ordinary citizen. On the other hand, he took away land from Native Americans. His tenacity made him a formidable president. To some he was a hero, while to others a villain. His iron will has had a lasting impact on the American presidency. Meacham uses archival papers, some newly discovered, to bring the drama of Jackson's biography to life.

Where it's reviewed:
National Review, Dec 1, 2008, page p53
The New York Review of Books, May 28, 2009, page p35
New York Times Book Review, Nov 16, 2008, page p16
USA Today, Dec 2, 2008, page p02D

Other books by the same author:
American Gospel: God, the Founding Fathers, and the Making of a Nation, 2007
Franklin and Winston: An Intimate Portrait of an Epic Friendship, 2004

Other books you might like:
Jon Butler, *Becoming America: The Revolution Before 1776,* 2000
Andrew Morton, *Diana: Her True Story, in Her Own Words,* 1997
Robert Vincent Remini, *Andrew Jackson,* 1998
    Sean Wilentz, co-author

272

ROBERT W. MERRY

A Country of Vast Designs: James K. Polk, The Mexican War, and the Conquest of the American Continent

(New York: Simon & Schuster, 2009)

Story type: Historical - American Revolution
Subject(s): United States history, 1865-1901; Presidents (Government); Mexican War, 1846-1848

Summary: Robert W. Merry's *A Country of Vast Designs: James K. Polk, The Mexican War, and the Conquest of the American Continent* showcases the accomplishments of the United States' eleventh president. James K. Polk was the Speaker of the House and the governor of Tennessee before he unexpectedly defeated Henry Clay for the presidency in 1844. As president, Polk wished to annex Texas. When Mexico refused, he declared war. After the Mexican-American War, Polk acquired Texas, Arizona, California, and New Mexico for the United States. He oversaw the construction of the Washington Monument, managed the money for the Smithsonian Institution, and issued the first postage stamps in America.

Where it's reviewed:
Library Journal, Oct 1, 2009, page p85
New York Times Book Review, Nov 22, 2009, page p19
Publishers Weekly, Sept 7, 2009, page p38

Other books by the same author:
Sands of Empire: Missionary Zeal, American Foreign Policy, and the Hazards of Global Ambition, 2010
Taking on the World: Joseph and Stewart Alsop, Guardians of the American Century, 1997

Other books you might like:
Ralph Ketchum, *James Madison: A Biography,* 1990
Paul C. Nagel, *John Quincy Adams: A Public Life, a Private Life,* 1997
Harlow Giles Unger, *A Call to Greatness,* 2009

273

DAVID MICHAELIS

Schulz and Peanuts: A Biography

(New York: HarperCollins, 2007)

Subject(s): Biography; Comics; Entertainment

Summary: On October 2, 1950, the first *Peanuts* comic strip appeared in newspapers across America. Charles Schulz, the creator of *Peanuts,* continued to entertain readers for 50 years, until his death in 2000. Michaelis introduces us to the man behind the comics, telling about life events and personality traits that influenced what Schulz drew and that made *Peanuts* such an amazing success.

Where it's reviewed:
CHOICE: Current Reviews for Academic Libraries,
    May 2008, page 1532
Maclean's, October 22, 2007, page 61
The New Yorker, October 22, 2007, page 164
People Weekly, October 22, 2007, page 53
Time, September 3, 2007, page 62

Other books by the same author:
N. C. Wyeth: A Biography, 1998
*The Best of Friends: Profiles of Extraordinary
    Friendship*, 1985

Other books you might like:
Beverly Gherman, *Sparky: The Life and Art of Charles
    Schulz*, 2010
M. Thomas Inge, *Charles M. Schulz: Conversations
    (Conversations with Comic Artists)*, 2000
Rheta Grimsley Johnson, *Good Grief: The Story of
    Charles M. Schultz*, 1989
Charles M. Schulz, *The Complete Peanuts, 1963-1966*,
    2006
Charles Schulz, *My Life with Charlie Brown*, 2010

274

PANKAJ MISHRA

An End to Suffering: The Buddha
in the World

(New York: Farrar, Straus and Giroux, 2004)

Subject(s): Religion; Buddhism

Summary: Author Pankaj Mishra questions Buddha's
relevance in contemporary society in *An End to Suffering: The World Buddha in the World*. The author
describes his own struggle to understand how a peaceful
deity like Buddha could exist in a world where religious
warfare and poverty plague people of all races and
religions. In order to understand Buddha's influence in
the world, Mishra travels to India (his birthplace),
Pakistan, and Afghanistan. The author's own quest mirrors Buddha's struggles with his identity and the idea of
human suffering. Along the way, the author discovers the
true meaning of Buddha's teachings in some of the most
unusual places.

Where it's reviewed:
Michigan Quarterly Review, Spring 2006, page 401
New York Times Book Review, February 26, 2005, page
    BR18
Times Literary Supplement, December 10, 2004, page
    26

Other books by the same author:
*Butter Chicken in Ludhiana: Travels in Small Town
    India*, 2007
*Temptations of the West: How to Be Modern in India,
    Pakistan, Tibet, and Beyond*, 2007
The Romantics: A Novel, 2001

Other books you might like:
Karen Armstrong, *Buddha*, 2001

Karen Armstrong, *Muhammad: A Prophet for Our Time*,
    2006
Marcus J. Borg, *Jesus: Uncovering the Life, Teachings,
    and Relevance of a Religious Revolutionary*, 2006
Glenn Wallis, *The Basic Teachings of the Buddha: A
    New Translation*, 2007

275

J.R. MOEHRINGER

The Tender Bar

(New York: Hyperion, 2005)

Subject(s): Autobiography; Mothers and Sons

Summary: In this memoir, J.R. Moehringer describes his
childhood and upbringing in Manhasset, New York. His
mother was a working woman who struggled to raise
him on her own; his father was a voice on the other end
of a telephone line. One constant in his life was the local
drinking establishment: the pub where his Uncle Chas
tended bar, and where he hung out from a very tender
age. He did not go there to drink—he was too young—
but to find steady companionship. Even after he left
Manhasset to embark upon his career as a journalist, the
bar was always his remembered home. This memoir is
as much a love song to the local pub and to its colorful
characters as it is a life story.

Where it's reviewed:
New York Times Book Review, September 11, 2005,
    page 12
Newsweek, August 29, 2005, page 74
People Weekly, September 19, 2005, page 59
USA Today, September 8, 2005, page 05D

Other books you might like:
Dave Eggers, *A Heartbreaking Work of Staggering
    Genius*, 2000
Barbara Ehrenreich, *Nickel and Dimed: On (Not)
    Getting by in America*, 2001
Nick Flynn, *Another Bullshit Night in Suck City: A
    Memoir*, 2004
Mary Karr, *The Liars' Club*, 1995

276

MANUEL MOLLES

Ecology: Concepts and Applications

(New York: McGraw-Hill, 2009)

Subject(s): Science; Ecology; Astronomy

Summary: *Ecology: Concepts and Applications* by Dr.
Manuel Molles is an educational textbook about ecological theories and principles. In this book, Molles provides
for readers a comprehensive overview of the field of
ecology, as well as applied theories about Earth's natural
history and the stewardship and care of the planet's
ecology. The author also uses supplementary data and
tables to enhance the subject matter. Molles is a professor at the University of New Mexico, where he also

serves as curator of Fishes and Aquatic Invertebrates.

Other books you might like:

Gordon B. Bonan, *Ecological Climatology: Concepts and Applications, Second Edition*, 2008

Brenda C. McComb, *Wildlife Habitat Management: Concepts and Applications in Forestry*, 2007

Michael L. Morrison, *Restoring Wildlife: Ecological Concepts and Practical Applications*, 2009

Fred Van Dyke, *Conservation Biology: Foundations, Concepts, Applications*, 2010

277

CRAIG M. MULLANEY

The Unforgiving Minute: A Soldier's Education

(New York: Penguin Press HC, 2009)

Subject(s): Autobiographies; Military academies; Wars

Summary: In his first book *The Unforgiving Minute: A Soldier's Education*, Craig M. Mullaney, a captain in the United States Armed Forces, chronicles his life as a soldier. Beginning with his education at West Point Military Academy and as a Rhodes Scholar at Oxford University, Mullaney explains what it means to be a "warrior" in modern military training. From there, Mullaney describes his combat experiences in Afghanistan and his guilt and remorse at not being able to save all of his soldiers. The book is dedicated to those men and women. Finally, he discusses his current teaching position and his brother's graduation from West Point, marking another generation of modern warriors.

Other books you might like:

Nathaniel Frank, *Unfriendly Fire: How the Gay Ban Undermines the Military and Weakens America*, 2009

Tom Wiener, *Forever a Soldier: Unforgettable Stories of Wartime Service*, 2005

278

HARUKI MURAKAMI

What I Talk About When I Talk About Running

(New York: Alfred A. Knopf, 2008)

Subject(s): Autobiographies; Writing; Running

Summary: In *What I Talk About When I Talk About Running*, acclaimed writer Haruki Murakami creates an unforgettable memoir that explores the relationship between running and writing. Murakami recounts his experiences training for the New York City marathon and how this event changed his perspectives on both his life and craft. The author looks at the ways his passions for running and writing influence one another, focusing on the concentration and determination each undertaking requires. *What I Talk About When I Talk About Running* is a unique celebration of the powers of the creative

mind and the outlets in which creativity can be discovered.

Other books by the same author:

IQ84, 2009

After Dark, 2007

Blind Willow, Sleeping Woman: 24 Stories, 2006

Kafka on the Shore, 2005

Other books you might like:

Nicola McCloy, *Running Hot*, 2009

Christopher McDougall, *Born to Run: A Hidden Tribe, Superathletes, and the Greatest Race the World Has Never Seen*, 2009

Lisa Tamati, *Running Hot*, 2009

279

DAVID NASAW

Andrew Carnegie

(New York: Penguin Press, 2006)

Subject(s): Industrial Revolution, ca. 1750-1900; Biographies; Business enterprises

Summary: David Nasaw's *Andrew Carnegie* shares the life story of the well-known industrialist. Carnegie was born in a small Scottish village, where his family made a modest living as weavers. His father moved the family to Pittsburgh, Pennsylvania, in the 1840s, when Carnegie was still a boy. From humble beginnings, Carnegie learned early in his career that he was a gifted businessman. Dominating the industrial industry in Pennsylvania, Carnegie became very wealthy. After selling Carnegie Steel Company, which became U.S. Steel, Carnegie dedicated the rest of his life and wealth to philanthropic interests, including education, libraries, science, and world peace. Nasaw covers the significant moments in Carnegie's life and attempts to unravel his puzzling character.

Where it's reviewed:

Business Week, November 27, 2006, page 116

Fortune, October 16, 2006, page 224

The Historian, Fall 2008, page 547

Publishers Weekly, August 7, 2006, page 44

Other books by the same author:

The Gospel of Wealth Essays and Other Writings, 2006

The Chief: The Life of William Randolph Hearst, 2001

Children of the City: At Work and At Play, 1986

Other books you might like:

Andrew Carnegie, *The Autobiography of Andrew Carnegie and The Gospel of Wealth*, 2006

Ron Chernow, *The House of Morgan: An American Banking Dynasty and the Rise of Modern Finance*, 1990

Ron Chernow, *Titan: The Life of John D. Rockefeller, Sr.*, 1998

Charles R. Morris, *The Tycoons: How Andrew Carnegie, John D. Rockefeller, Jay Gould, and J. P. Morgan Invented the American Supereconomy*, 2009

T.J. Stiles, *The First Tycoon: The Epic Life of Cornelius Vanderbilt*, 2009

280

PHILIP NORMAN

John Lennon: The Life
(New York: Ecco, 2008)

Subject(s): Biographies; Musicians; Music

Summary: John Lennon catapulted into stardom as a member of what is arguably the world's most famous band—the Beatles. After his murder in 1980, Lennon became even more famous. Philip Norman—known for writing the Beatles' biography *Shout!: The Beatles in Their Generation*—thoroughly details Lennon's life in a new biography, *John Lennon: The Life*. Although Lennon was an important part of the Beatles, he still looked for more in his life. Often insecure about his work, Lennon always strived for perfection. The book details the musician's early life and his often dysfunctional family. The book also takes a hard look at how Lennon treated those closest to him. The musician divorced his first wife and often behaved cruelly toward the people that he loved. Norman gives an honest and thorough assessment of the idol's life.

Where it's reviewed:
Entertainment Weekly, October 31, 2008, page 65
Library Journal, August 1, 2008, page 87

Other books by the same author:
Shout!: The Beatles in Their Generation, 2006
Rave On, 1996
The Stones, 1994

Other books you might like:
The Beatles, *The Beatles Anthology*, 2000
Peter Ames Carlin, *Paul McCartney: A Life*, 2009
George Harrison, *I, Me, Mine*, 2007
Cynthia Lennon, *John*, 2005
Steve Turner, *A Hard Day's Write: The Stories Behind Every Beatles Song*, 2005

281

SARAH PALIN

Going Rogue
(New York: HarperCollins, 2009)

Subject(s): Presidents (Government); Political campaigns; Politics

Summary: Within the span of a day, Sarah Palin went from a politician largely unknown in the continental United States to one of the most famous people in the world. On that day, she appeared at the Republican National Convention and was introduced as John McCain's presidential running mate. Automatically people knew things had changed. Palin was already known as a reformer in her home state of Alaska, and now she was changing the way people view national politics. She was hardly an insider and spent her time as Alaska's governor fighting the "good ol' boys" as well as being a role model for other working mothers. She showed that anything is possible in America, and tens of thousands of people wanted to see her become vice president. In *Going Rogue*, Sarah Palin tells her own story, not only about her presidential campaign experiences but also about her family, her years in Alaska, and her vision for the future of America.

Other books by the same author:
America by Heart: Reflections on Family, Faith and Flag, 2010

Other books you might like:
Kevin Balfe, *Arguing with Idiots: How to Stop Small Minds and Big Government*, 2009
  Glenn Beck, co-author
Laura Bush, *Spoken from the Heart*, 2010
Richard Kim, *Going Rouge: An American Nightmare*, 2009
Bill O'Reilly, *A Bold Fresh Piece of Humanity*, 2008
Sarah Palin, *America by Heart: Reflections on Family, Faith and Flag*, 2010
Betsy Reed, *Going Rouge: An American Nightmare*, 2009

282

RICK PERLSTEIN

Nixonland: The Rise of a President and the Fracturing of America
(New York: Scribner, 2008)

Subject(s): Presidents (Government); United States; Civil rights

Summary: In *Nixonland: The Rise of a President and the Fracturing of America*, author Rick Perlstein argues that the social and political divides that currently split the country into red and blue states began with Richard Nixon's administration. When he first took office in 1968, Nixon faced a myriad of challenges. The country was embroiled in an often-violent civil rights movement and fighting an increasingly unpopular war in Vietnam. Though such pressures would have broken other politicians, Perlstein shows readers how Nixon used the chaos of the late 1960s to his advantage. While his promise to cure the ills of American society eventually won Nixon reelection, it also created a rift between conservatives and liberals that has yet to mend itself. Perlstein is also the award-winning author of *Before the Storm: Barry Goldwater and the Unmaking of the American Consensus*.

Where it's reviewed:
The Atlantic, May 2008, page 83
National Review, June 16, 2008, page 48
The New Republic, September 8, 2008, page 16
New York Times Book Review, May 11, 2008, page 1
Newsweek, May 10, 2008, page 48

Other books by the same author:
The Stock Ticker and the Super Jumbo: How the Democrats Can Once Again Become America's Dominant Political Party, 2005
Before the Storm: Barry Goldwater and the Unmaking of the American Consensus, 2001

Other books you might like:

Conrad Black, *Richard M. Nixon: A Life in Full*, 2007

Roger Morris, *Richard Milhous Nixon The Rise of an American Politician*, 1989

Richard Nixon, *RN: The Memoirs of Richard Nixon*, 1978

David Pietrusza, *1960: LBJ vs. JFK vs. Nixon: The Epic Campaign That Forged Three Presidencies*, 2008

Richard Reeves, *President Nixon: Alone in the White House*, 2001

283

BARRY PETERSEN

Jan's Story: Love Lost to the Long Goodbye of Alzheimer's

(Lake Forest, California: Behler Publications, 2010)

Subject(s): Biographies; Alzheimer's disease; Journalism

Summary: *Jan's Story: Love Lost to the Long Goodbye of Alzheimer's* is a memoir and first book from CBS News correspondent Barry Petersen. When Barry Petersen's wife, Jan, was just 55 years old, she was diagnosed with early onset Alzheimer's. *Jan's Story* is the heartbreaking and emotional tale of how the disease impacted and altered their lives. Petersen recounts hearing the shocking news, how he and his wife reacted, the things they did and didn't do, and how the disease changed their loving relationship. *Jan's Story* provides a candid and emotional look at the devastation of Alzheimer's disease.

Other books you might like:

Lauren Kessler, *Finding Life in the Land of Alzheimer's: One Daughter's Hopeful Story*, 2008

Scott D. Mendelson, *Beyond Alzheimer's: How to Avoid the Modern Epidemic of Dementia*, 2009

284

DALE PETERSON

Jane Goodall: The Woman Who Redefined Man

(Boston: Houghton Mifflin, 2006)

Subject(s): Biographies; Animals; Chimpanzees

Summary: *Jane Goodall: The Woman Who Redefined Man* by Dale Peterson tells the story of Goodall's life and the effects she has had on modern science. From a young age, Goodall was interested in animals, and she eventually became a scientist. When Goodall was a young woman, she first traveled to Tanzania to study chimpanzees. During her trip, Goodall spent time with these animals and soon learned more about them than anyone else had before. Through her research, Goodall helped changed people's perceptions about the differences between animals and humans. In additional to Goodall's scientific accomplishments, the book also chronicles her personal life and relationships.

Where it's reviewed:

Library Journal, October 1, 2006, page 102

People Weekly, December 4, 2006, page 51

Publishers Weekly, September 11, 2006, page 42

Science News, November 11, 2006, page 31

Other books by the same author:

Eating Apes, 2004

Storyville, USA, 1999

Other books you might like:

Phillip Berman, *Reason for Hope: A Spiritual Journey*, 1999

Carol Flinders, *Enduring Lives: Portraits of Women and Faith in Action*, 2006

Jane Goodall, *Reason for Hope: A Spiritual Journey*, 1999

Sy Montgomery, *Walking with the Great Apes*, 1991

285

MACKENZIE PHILLIPS

High on Arrival

(New York: Simon Spotlight Entertainment, 2009)

Subject(s): Autobiographies; Musicians; Actors

Summary: Actress and musician Mackenzie Phillips presents readers with a harrowing look at her troubled life in the memoir *High on Arrival*. As the daughter of musician John Phillips, young Mackenzie lived a life of unbounded opportunity and unbridled vice. When she was a teenager, she became a star in such films as *American Graffiti* and the television show *One Day at a Time*. But throughout it all, Mackenzie was battling an out-of-control addiction to drugs, a tyrannical father, and a terrifying secret life as a victim of incest. *High on Arrival* is a candid look at the rise and fall of a promising performer who confronts the ghosts of her past and emerges triumphant.

Where it's reviewed:

USA TODAY, October 1, 2009, page D.6.

Other books you might like:

Valerie Bertinelli, *Losing It: And Gaining My Life Back One Pound at a Time*, 2008

Melissa Gilbert, *Prairie Tale: A Memoir*, 2009

Maureen McCormick, *Here's the Story: Surviving Marcia Brady and Finding My True Voice*, 2008

Tatum O'Neal, *A Paper Life*, 2004

Jodie Sweetin, *UnSweetined: A Memoir*, 2009

286

STEVE POIZNER

Mount Pleasant: My Journey from Creating a Billion-Dollar Company to Teaching at a Struggling Public High School

(New York: Portfolio, 2010)

Subject(s): Autobiographies; Business; Teachers

Summary: *Mount Pleasant: My Journey from Creating a*

Billion-Dollar Company to Teaching at a Struggling Public High School is a memoir and first book written by Steve Poizner; as of the publication of this book, Poizner is a Republican candidate in the California gubernatorial race. The topic of this book, however, is not politics—Poizner focuses on the year that he spent teaching and volunteering at Mount Pleasant, a public high school in San Jose, California. He speaks of the challenges he faced and the way he used his business experience to get through to the students and help them become engaged with learning. A great deal of controversy surrounds this book regarding the legitimacy of much of the information Poizner presents as fact.

Other books you might like:
LouAnne Johnson, *Dangerous Minds*, 1993
Robert T. Kiyosaki, *Rich Dad, Poor Dad: What the Rich Teach Their Kids about Money That the Poor and Middle Class Do Not*, 1999
    Sharon L. Lechter, co-author
Frank McCourt, *Teacher Man: A Memoir*, 2005
Greg Mortenson, *Three Cups of Tea: One Man's Mission to Fight Terrorism and Build Nations...One School at a Time*, 2006
    David Oliver Relin, co-author
Paul Tough, *Whatever It Takes: Geoffrey Canada's Quest to Change Harlem and America*, 2009

287

RON POWERS

Mark Twain: A Life

(New York: Free Press, 2005)

Subject(s): Writing; United States history, 1865-1901; Journalism

Summary: In *Mark Twain: A Life*, Ron Powers provides intimate information about the life of Samuel Langhorne Clemens, better known as Mark Twain. As a child, Twain and his family lived in Missouri near the Mississippi River, in a town that would later serve as a model for fictional locations in his novels. At a young age, he got a job as a typesetter at a local newspaper. From there, he went on to draw cartoons and write small articles that appeared in the paper from time to time. As an adult journalist, he covered happenings in the Wild West and wrote the novels for which he became famous, including *The Adventures of Tom Sawyer* and *Adventures of Huckleberry Finn*.

Where it's reviewed:
Booklist, August 2005, page 1982
Library Journal, August 1, 2005, page 86
Publishers Weekly, August 1, 2005, page 60
USA Today, September 8, 2005, page 06D

Other books by the same author:
Last Flag Down: The Epic Journey of the Last Confederate Warship, 2008
Tom and Huck Don't Live Here Anymore, 2001
Flags of Our Fathers, 2000

Other books you might like:
Michael B. Frank, *Autobiography of Mark Twain, Vol. 1*, 2010
Jerome Loving, *Mark Twain: The Adventures of Samuel L. Clemens*, 2010
Leslie Diane Myrick, *Autobiography of Mark Twain, Vol. 1*, 2010
Mark Sheldon, *Mark Twain: Man in White: The Grand Adventure of His Final Years*, 2010
Laura Skandera Trombley, *Mark Twain's Other Woman: The Hidden Story of His Final Years*, 2010
Mark Twain, *The Adventures of Huckleberry Finn*, 1884
Mark Twain, *Autobiography of Mark Twain, Vol. 1*, 2010

288

JOE QUEENAN

Closing Time: A Memoir

(New York: Viking, 2009)

Subject(s): Autobiographies; Childhood; Family

Summary: Joe Queenan is well known for his commentary on the world of pop culture, but in *Closing Time: A Memoir*, he offers commentary on his own childhood growing up in Philadelphia. Queenan's father was an alcoholic and was abusive toward his children, and Queenan describes what it was like to live with him. Queenan used music, movies, and other friends and mentors to hide or escape from this world and eventually move away from it. Queenan's prose can be brutally honest at times but he also speaks with hints of humor and self-deprecation that make this memoir more than just a sad childhood tale.

Where it's reviewed:
Booklist, Feb 1, 2009, page p2
New York Times Book Review, April 26, 2009, page p11
Publishers Weekly, Feb 16, 2009, page p120
USA Today, April 23, 2009, page p08D

Other books by the same author:
Malcontents, 2004
True Believers: The Tragic Inner Life of Sports Fans, 2004
If You're Talking to Me, Your Career Must Be in Trouble: Movies, Mayhem, and Malice, 1999

Other books you might like:
Moustafa Bayoumi, *How Does It Feel to Be a Problem?: Being Young and Arab in America*, 2008
Joe Queenan, *Queenan Country: A Reluctant Anglophile's Pilgrimage to the Mother Country*, 2004
Joe Queenan, *Red Lobster, White Trash and the Blue Lagoon: Joe Queenan's America*, 1998
Joe Queenan, *True Believers: The Tragic Inner Life of Sports Fans*, 2003

289

ARNOLD RAMPERSAD

Ralph Ellison: A Biography

(New York: Knopf, 2007)

Subject(s): Biographies; Writers; Civil rights

Summary: Author Arnold Rampersad offers a detailed biography of one the most influential figures in African American literature in *Ralph Ellison: A Biography*. Ellison was the author of the classic novel *Invisible Man*, an occasionally ironic look at the struggles of African Americans in his time. Rampersad explains how Ellison spent five years constructing his masterpiece. Though critics and scholars praised Ellison, he never published another book. Rampersad uses Ellison's letters to understand the author's personal life and professional relationships. Every detail of Ellison's life is covered: from his childhood to his time at Tuskegee to his political stances during the American Civil Rights Movement.

Where it's reviewed:
Booklist, March 1, 2007, page 37
Library Journal, April 1, 2007, page 90
New York Times Book Review, May 20, 2007, page 18
Publishers Weekly, March 5, 2007, page 5

Other books by the same author:
The Life of Langston Hughes: Volume I: 1902-1941, I, Too, Sing America, 2002
Jackie Robinson: A Biography, 1998

Other books you might like:
Ralph Ellison, *The Collected Essays of Ralph Ellison*, 1995
Ralph Ellison, *Invisible Man*, 1952
Zora Neale Hurston, *Their Eyes Were Watching God*, 1937
John S. Wright, *Shadowing Ralph Ellison*, 2006
Richard Wright, *Black Boy: A Record of Childhood and Youth*, 1945

290

DEBORAH KOGAN RAY

Wanda Gag: The Girl Who Lived to Draw

(New York: Viking Juvenile, 2009)

Subject(s): Biographies; Drawing; Art

Summary: *Wanda Gag: The Girl Who Lived to Draw* by Deborah Kogan Ray is a biography for young readers of artist Wanda Gag. The book begins with Wanda's childhood as the oldest of six children who lived with their German-speaking parents in what is now the Czech Republic until the family moved to Minnesota in the early 1900s. Gag's father loved to paint, and though he passed away when Wanda was 15, he made her promise to attend art school and continue to indulge her passion for drawing. She began to support her family with her artwork and went on to become a successful artist, creat-

ing the children's book *Millions of Cats*, along with many other projects. The text includes numerous direct quotations from Wanda's diaries and other personal writings.

Other books by the same author:
Dinosaur Mountain: Digging into the Jurassic Age, 2010
Flying Eagle, 2009
Down the Colorado: John Wesley Powell, the One-Armed Explorer, 2007
To Go Singing Through the World: The Childhood of Pablo Neruda, 2006

Other books you might like:
M.T. Anderson, *Strange Mr. Satie*, 2003
Wanda Gag, *Millions of Cats*, 1928
Will Hillenbrand, *Louie!*, 2009
Tanya Lee Stone, *Sandy's Circus: A Story About Alexander Calder*, 2008

291

DAVID S. REYNOLDS

Waking Giant: America in the Age of Jackson

(New York: HarperCollins, 2008)

Subject(s): Americana; Social history; Culture

Summary: *Walking Giant* portrays not only the political arena of America, but also the cultural and social aspects of the early to mid 1800s. It was in this atmosphere that Americans chose for their president an uneducated adventurer from Tennessee, Andrew Jackson. America had just ended the war with the British and the frontier boundaries were pushing westward. The economy was booming, making prostitution and alcohol more available in the midst of conservative values. The controversy over slavery was just beginning to brew, as was the movement away from elitism. Author David S. Reynolds gives a colorful description of the era between the British War and the outbreak of the Civil War. While others have written of the time and politics, Reynolds provides a social context to the history that has rarely been explored.

Where it's reviewed:
Booklist, Oct 1, 2008, page p14
Library Journal, July 1, 2008, page p95
The New York Review of Books, Oct 1, 2008, page p14
Publishers Weekly, August 18, 2008, page p55

Other books by the same author:
John Brown, Abolitionist: The Man Who Killed Slavery, Sparked the Civil War, and Seeded Civil Rights, 2006
Walt Whitman's America: A Cultural Biography, 1996

Other books you might like:
Daniel Walker Howe, *What Hath God Wrought: The Transformation of America, 1815-1848*, 2007
Robert Middlekauff, *The Glorious Cause*, 1981
David M. Potter, *Impending Crisis, 1848-1861*
Gordon S. Wood, *Empire of Liberty: A History of the Early Republic, 1789-1815*, 2009

292

NINO RICCI

Pierre Elliott Trudeau

(Toronto, Ontario, Canada: Penguin Canada, 2009)

Subject(s): Biographies; Politics; Social conditions

Summary: Nino Ricci's *Pierre Elliott Trudeau* is part of the Extraordinary Canadians series of biographies about accomplished Canadian individuals. The volume focuses on the life of Trudeau, who served as the prime minister of Canada from 1968-1979 and again from 1980-1984. The biography captures Trudeau's often contradictory nature, and describes the changes that occurred as a result of Trudeau's political policies, which redefined Canada's cultural identity.

Other books by the same author:
The Origin of Species, 2008
Testament, 2003
Where She Has Gone, 1997
In a Glass House: A Novel, 1993
Lives of the Saints, 1990

Other books you might like:
Adrienne Clarkson, *Heart Matters*, 2006
Adrienne Clarkson, *Norman Bethune*, 2009
Mark Kingwell, *Canada: Our Century*, 1999
Mark Kingwell, *Glenn Gould*, 2009
Christopher Moore, *Canada: Our Century*, 1999
Jane Urquhart, *L.M. Montgomery*, 2009

293

KEITH RICHARDS

Life

(New York: Little, Brown and Company, 2010)

Subject(s): Musicians; Rock music; Drugs

Summary: In *Life,* legendary Rolling Stones' guitarist Keith Richards offers fans a backstage pass to the ups and downs of his tumultuous life and career. Co-written with bestselling author James Fox, the book chronicles the famous—and, some might say, infamous—musician's rise to fame with the Stones, his brushes with the law, his drug addiction, and his impassioned relationships with women such as Anita Pallenberg and Patti Hansen. Richards also discusses his friendship with Mick Jagger and the role the Rolling Stones have played in rock-and-roll history.

Other books you might like:
Steven Adler, *My Appetite for Destruction: Sex, and Drugs, and Guns N' Roses*, 2010
Pat Benatar, *Between a Heart and a Rock Place: A Memoir*, 2010
Richard Havers, *Rolling with the Stones*, 2002
Joe Layden, *Mustaine: A Heavy Metal Memoir*, 2010
    Dave Mustaine, co-author
Ozzy Osbourne, *I Am Ozzy*, 2009
Bill Wyman, *Rolling with the Stones*, 2002

294

JOHN RICHARDSON

A Life of Picasso: The Triumphant Years, 1917-1932

(New York: Alfred A. Knopf, 2007)

Subject(s): Artists; Biographies; Art

Summary: John Richardson records the middle years of artist Pablo Picasso in *A Life of Picasso: the Triumphant Years, 1917-1932*. In the third volume in the series, readers learn about Picasso's affair with Russian dancer, Olga Kokhlova, a woman Picasso met during his project for the legendary Ballets Russes ballet company. Richardson provides a glimpse into the fascinating world of Picasso and the life experiences that influenced his work. The biography discusses Picasso's marriage to Kokhlova, their son Paulo, and their life in Paris. It also provides information about Picasso's teenage mistress, who inspired his future artwork.

Where it's reviewed:
The Economist, November 17, 2007, page 99
New York Times Book Review, November 11, 2007, page 1
The New Yorker, November 19, 2007, page 97
Time, September 3, 2007, page 62

Other books by the same author:
A Life of Picasso: The Cubist Rebel, 1907-1916, 2007
A Life of Picasso: The Prodigy, 1881-1906, 2007

Other books you might like:
Francoise Gilot, *Life with Picasso*, 1964
Marilyn McCully, *A Life of Picasso: Volume I: 1881-1906*, 1991
Marilyn McCully, *A Life of Picasso: Volume II: 1907-1917*, 1996
John Richardson, *A Life of Picasso: Volume I: 1881-1906*, 1991
John Richardson, *A Life of Picasso: Volume II: 1907-1917*, 1996
Gertrude Stein, *Picasso*, 1946

295

ANNE ROCKWELL

Big George: How a Shy Boy Became President Washington

(New York: Harcourt Children's Books, 2008)

Subject(s): Biographies; Presidents (Government); Shyness

Summary: As a boy, George Washington was virtually fearless. He had no trouble facing dangerous natives, uncertain times, or wild animals. But young George did possess one fear that profoundly shaped his life: he was scared to talk to people. In *Big George: How a Shy Boy Became President Washington*, young readers learn of the first president's early life and the measures he took to overcome his nearly debilitating shyness. Author Anne

Rockwell eschews the normal historical trivia (the cherry tree, wooden teeth, crossing the Delaware, etc.) to present a fresh take on America's inaugural Commander-in-Chief. Matt Phelan provides the stylish artwork.

Other books by the same author:
What's So Bad About Gasoline?: Fossil Fuels and What They Do, 2009
Clouds, 2008
My Preschool, 2008
Presidents' Day, 2008

Other books you might like:
Deborah Chandra, *George Washington's Teeth*, 2003
    Madeleine Comora, co-author
Cheryl Harness, *George Washington*, 2000
Lane Smith, *John, Paul, George and Ben*, 2006
Judith St. George, *So You Want to Be President? (Revised and Updated Edition)*, 2004
Peggy Thomas, *Farmer George Plants a Nation*, 2008

296

RACHEL VICTORIA RODRIGUEZ

Through Georgia's Eyes
(New York: H. Holt and Co., 2006)

Subject(s): Biographies; Art; Painting (Art)

Summary: *Through Georgia's Eyes* is a biography of Georgia O'Keeffe in picture-book form. The book discusses Georgia's life from when she was a child in Wisconsin, when she first realized that she wanted to be an artist and attend art school, to her time in New York to when she finally settled down in New Mexico. *Through Georgia's Eyes* showcases Georgia's work and the subjects she painted. Though the text in the picture book is limited, a brief account at the end of the book has more detailed biographical information. *Through Georgia's Eyes* was written by Rachel Victoria Rodriguez and illustrated by Julie Paschkis.

Other books by the same author:
Building on Nature, 2009

Other books you might like:
Kathryn Lasky, *Georgia Rises: A Day in the Life of Georgia O'Keeffe*, 2009
Natasha Wing, *An Eye For Color*, 2008

297

ANNE ROIPHE

Epilogue: A Memoir
(New York: Harper, 2008)

Subject(s): Women; Grief; Dating (Social customs)

Summary: Approaching 70 years old, award-winning writer Anne Roiphe was devastated when her beloved husband of nearly 40 years suddenly died of a heart attack. Left on her own for the first time in decades, Roiphe is forced to rebuild her life from the ground up and reacquaint herself with a suddenly empty world. As she makes her way through the grieving process, she begins to piece together the fragments of her life. But when her daughters encourage her to start dating again, Roiphe is unprepared. She hasn't considered any other men beside her late husband, and this new prospect is one that both challenges and invigorates her. *Epilogue: A Memoir* is Roiphe's record of grief and healing.

Where it's reviewed:
Library Journal, August 1, 2008, page p84
Publishers Weekly, June 9, 2008, page p38
USA Today, Oct 9, 2008, page p04D

Other books by the same author:
An Imperfect Lens: A Novel, 2006
Water from the Well: Sarah, Rebekah, Rachel, and Leah, 2006
1185 Park Avenue: A Memoir, 2000

Other books you might like:
Gabriel Garcia Marquez, *The Autumn of the Patriarch*, 1976
William G. Hyland Jr., *In Defense of Thomas Jefferson: The Sally Hemings Sex Scandal*, 2009

298

KARL ROVE

Courage and Consequence: My Life as a Conservative in the Fight
(New York: Threshold Editions, 2010)

Subject(s): Autobiographies; United States; Politics

Summary: *Courage and Consequence: My Life as a Conservative in the Fight* is Karl Rove's autobiography of his time spent in the political spotlight during George W. Bush's presidency. Known as "the Architect," Rove talks about his political views and defends the choices he made while he was at the White House. He explains why Bush chose Dick Cheney as vice president, what really happened when the president was charged with a DUI, and how Bush won in 2000. He explores the decisions that affected the United States after Hurricane Katrina, the attacks of September 11, 2001, and the fighting in Afghanistan and Iraq. Rove also touches on his personal life and talks about his mother's suicide and his father's homosexuality allegations in his first book.

Other books you might like:
George W. Bush, *A Charge to Keep: My Journey to the White House*, 2001
Mark Halperin, *Game Change: Obama and the Clintons, McCain and Palin, and the Race of a Lifetime*, 2010
    John Heilemann, co-author
Dana Milbank, *Smashmouth: Two Years in the Gutter with Al Gore and George W. Bush—Notes from the 2000 Campaign Trail*, 2001
Bill O'Reilly, *A Bold Fresh Piece of Humanity*, 2008
Mitt Romney, *No Apology: The Case for American Greatness*, 2010

299

JENNY SANDFORD

Staying True

(New York: Ballantine Books, 2010)

Subject(s): Autobiographies; Politics; Marriage

Summary: *Staying True* is the autobiography of Jenny Sandford, ex-wife of Mark Sanford, one-time governor of South Carolina who was caught in an affair with an Argentinean woman when he was supposed to be hiking the Appalachian trail. This book tells the story from Jenny's perspective, after she refused to stay married to her husband. The book is a personal account of her marriage, the frequent problems the couple experienced, and the very public demise of their union. Jenny also discusses her friendships, her family, her career, and her unshakable faith in her first book.

Other books you might like:

Mika Brzezinksi, *All Things at Once*, 2010
Laura Bush, *Spoken from the Heart*, 2010
Elizabeth Edwards, *Resilience: Reflections on the Burdens and Gifts of Facing Life's Adversities*, 2009
Elizabeth Edwards, *Saving Graces: Finding Solace and Strength from Friends and Strangers*, 2006
Andrew Young, *The Politician: An Insider's Account of John Edwards's Pursuit of the Presidency and the Scandal That Brought Him Down*, 2010

300

ALICE SCHROEDER

The Snowball: Warren Buffett and the Business of Life

(New York: Bantam Books, 2008)

Subject(s): Business; Biographies; Wealth

Summary: As the richest man in the world and a business mogul, Warren Buffett has long made headlines in newspapers and on television. Despite the extensive media coverage, Buffett declined to give his own account of his life until business professional and author Alice Schroeder decided to write an authorized biography about him. In *The Snowball: Warren Buffett and the Business of Life*, Schroeder gives readers a detailed account of Buffett's life, which she pieced together from interviews with Buffett and his family, coworkers, and friends. The book discusses Buffett's childhood and upbringing and his early business successes. Furthermore, it explores Buffett's relationships and his attitudes about money and society in an open, frank way.

Where it's reviewed:

Businessweek, Oct 13, 2008, page p97
The New York Review of Books, May 28, 2009, page p8
The New Yorker, Oct 13, 2008, page p145
Time, Oct 6, 2008, page p23

Other books you might like:

Benjamin Graham, *The Intelligent Investor*, 2005

Robert G. Hagstrom, *The Warren Buffett Portfolio: Mastering the Power of the Focus Investment Strategy*, 1999
Robert G. Hagstrom, *The Warren Buffett Way, Second Edition*, 2004
Roger Lowenstein, *Buffett: The Making of an American Capitalist*, 1995

301

NICK SCHUYLER
JERE LONGMAN , Co-Author

Not Without Hope

(New York: W. Morrow, 2010)

Subject(s): Autobiographies; Accidents; Friendship

Summary: In their first book *Not Without Hope*, Nick Schuyler and Jere Longman tell the story of an accident that robbed Schuyler of three friends and changed his life forever. In February 2009, Schuyler, a personal trainer, and three of his friends—NFL players Marquis Cooper and Corey Smith and former college football player Will Bleakley—took a fishing trip into the Gulf of Mexico. The four friends planned to do some fishing and return to land before a cold front moved in. The friends' plans went awry, however, when their boat capsized in the water. After the men landed in the water, they had to put on life jackets and cling to the side of the overturned boat. As the men struggled to survive in the cold, rough waters, they shared stories of their loved ones and memories from football. Although all of the men struggled to survive, Marquis, Corey, and Will succumbed to hypothermia. Nick survived for more than 40 hours in the cold water and was eventually rescued by the Coast Guard. In the book, Nick honors his lost friends, and he discusses the psychological impact of the incident on his life.

Other books you might like:

Steven Callahan, *Adrift: Seventy-Six Days Lost at Sea*, 1996
Sebastian Junger, *Perfect Storm: A True Story of Men Against the Sea*, 1997
Jon Krakauer, *Into the Wild*, 1996
Jon Krakauer, *Into Thin Air: A Personal Account of the Mount Everest Disaster*, 1997
Aron Ralston, *Between a Rock and a Hard Place*, 2004

302

DAVID SEDARIS

When You Are Engulfed in Flames

(London: Little, Brown Book Group, 2008)

Subject(s): Love; Family; Satire

Summary: David Sedaris is back with another collection of essays about the inanity of everyday life in *When You Are Engulfed in Flames*. In this volume, he presents twenty-two unique takes on everyday life, commenting on everything from a lover's foibles to an uncomfortable conversation he had while riding with a tow truck driver. Sedaris doesn't claim that all the stories are completely accurate; rather, each contains enough truth to make it "realish." Just as Sedaris seems to be going to the extreme in his rambling, he pulls the stories back on track to deliver a revealing insight into the human condition.

Where it's reviewed:
Booklist, September 15, 2008, page 63
Library Journal, September 1, 2008, page 179
New York Times Book Review, June 15, 2008, page 5L
Publishers Weekly, October 5, 2009, page 3

Other books by the same author:
Squirrel Seeks Chipmunk: A Modest Bestiary, 2010
Me Talk Pretty One Day, 2000
Naked, 1998

Other books you might like:
Chelsea Handler, *Chelsea Chelsea Bang Bang*, 2010
John Hodgman, *The Areas of My Expertise: An Almanac of Complete World Knowledge Compiled with Instructive Annotation and Arranged in Useful Order*, 2005
Eric Spitznagel, *You're a Horrible Person, but I Like You: The Believer Book of Advice*, 2010
Sarah Vowell, *Assassination Vacation*, 2005
Larry Wilmore, *I'd Rather We Got Casinos, and Other Black Thoughts*, 2009

303

MIRANDA SEYMOUR

Thrumpton Hall: A Memoir of Life in My Father's House
(New York: HarperCollins, 2007)

Subject(s): Childhood; Parent-child relations; Homosexuality

Summary: In this memoir, author Miranda Seymour recounts her experiences growing up in England with her eccentric and verbally abusive father, George. Seymour tells of her father's obsessive love with Thrumpton Hall, an elegant house in the Nottinghamshire countryside. While owning the house was just a dream when George wrote a love letter to the house in 1944, he eventually increased his wealth enough to purchase it. Nothing could compete with the house for his love, not even his wife and two children. Throughout her childhood, Miranda is humiliated by George, who once told her she was fat and that her hair was so horrible she should consider wearing a wig. George shocks the world in his senior years when he begins wearing black leather, riding motorcycles, and coveting the affections of young men.

Where it's reviewed:
The New York Review of Books, Sept 25, 2008, page p18
New York Times Book Review, July 27, 2008, page p1
People, August 4, 2008, page p47

Other books by the same author:
Robert Graves: Life on the Edge, 2003
Mary Shelley, 2002

Other books you might like:
Caroline Blackwood, *Dangerous Muse: The Life of Lady Caroline Blackwood*, 2002
Wendy Burden, *Dead End Gene Pool*, 2010
Liza Campbell, *A Charmed Life*, 2008
Anabel Goldsmith, *Anabel: An Unconventional Life*, 2005

304

CAROL SKLENICKA

Raymond Carver: A Writer's Life
(New York: Scribner, 2009)

Subject(s): Biographies; Writing; Father-son relations

Summary: After interviewing more than 100 people who knew Raymond Carver best, Carol Sklenicka penned this biography about Carver's early life—before he became a literary sensation. In *Raymond Carver: A Writer's Life*, Sklenicka brings readers back to the moments before Carver had even decided to be a writer. She includes details about his childhood, including the strong influence his alcoholic father had on his life. In this book, readers learn about the man behind the creative short story collections including *Will You Please Be Quiet, Please* and *What We Talk About When We Talk About Love*.

Where it's reviewed:
Library Journal, Sept 15, 2009, page p60
New York Times Book Review, Nov 22, 2009, page p1
Publishers Weekly, August 31, 2009, page p43
Time, Nov 23, 2009, page p109

Other books by the same author:
D.H. Lawrence and the Child, 1991

Other books you might like:
Raymond Carver, *Call If You Need Me: The Uncollected Fiction and Other Prose*, 2001
Raymond Carver, *Raymond Carver: Collected Stories*, 2009
Maile Meloy, *Both Ways Is the Only Way I Want It*, 2009

305

CHARLES R. SMITH

Twelve Rounds to Glory: The Story of Muhammad Ali
(Somerville, Massachusetts: Candlewick Press, 2007)

Subject(s): Biographies; Boxing; Sports

Summary: In *Twelve Rounds to Glory: The Story of Muhammad Ali*, author Charles R. Smith Jr. uses a rap-like verse to tell the story of the boxer known as "The Greatest." The writing itself has the rhythm of a boxing match, but Smith's book also contains content that is educational and appropriate for young readers. Smith includes information about Ali's milestones as a fighter, such as winning the 1960 Olympic gold medal and beating opponents Sonny Liston and Joe Frazier. However, Smith also gives readers a sense of the athlete's principles and determination outside the ring— challenging racial prejudice and, later, the Vietnam War. He also addresses how Cassius Clay adopted the name Muhammad Ali as part of his Islamic faith. The illustrations, by Bryan Collier, are arranged in a collage format.

Other books by the same author:
Black Jack: The Ballad of Jack Johnson, 2010
My People, 2009
Chameleon, 2008
Winning Words, 2008

Other books you might like:
Ted Lewin, *At Gleason's Gym*, 2007
Robert Lipsyte, *The Contender*, 1967

306

BOB SPITZ

The Beatles: The Biography

(New York: Bloomsbury, 2005)

Subject(s): Biography; Musicians; Popular Culture

Summary: Bob Spitz spent eight years conducting numerous interviews, pouring over articles and books, and reviewing radio programs to piece together this biography of the Beatles. Spitz includes well-known stories such as how John Lennon and Paul McCartney met and the enormous success of their first tour in the United States. He traces the lives of each member from their roots in Liverpool to when the Beatles split up. At the core of this biography is how four young men dealt with becoming the world's first superstars. Thirty-two pages of black and white photographs are included.

Where it's reviewed:
Library Journal, September 15, 2005, page 67
New York Times Book Review, November 27, 2005, page BR23
Publishers Weekly, October 3, 2005, page 64

Other books by the same author:
The Saucier's Apprentice: One Long Strange Trip through the Great Cooking Schools of Europe, 2009
Yeah! Yeah! Yeah!: The Beatles, Beatlemania, and the Music that Changed the World, 2007
Barefoot in Babylon: The Creation of the Woodstock Music Festival, 1969, 1989

Other books you might like:
The Beatles, *The Beatles Anthology*, 2000
George Harrison, *I, Me, Mine*, 2007
John Lennon, *John Lennon: In His Own Write*, 1964
Steve Turner, *A Hard Day's Write: The Stories Behind Every Beatles Song*, 2005

307

AVI STEINBERG

Running the Books: The Adventures of an Accidental Prison Librarian

(New York: Nan A. Talese, 2010)

Subject(s): Autobiographies; Prisoners; Libraries

Summary: With little to show for his college education and Jewish upbringing, Avi Steinberg reaches his turning point, his exact moment of desperation, *Running the Books: The Adventures of an Accidental Prison Librarian*. In need of money and an insurance plan, Steinberg took a job as a prison librarian in Boston a few years after his college career ended. At first, the job seemed simple enough—find books for the convicts, hustlers, strippers, and con men that entered his library every day. As the days passed, however, he became attached to both the job and the inmates who frequently visited him. He learned of their hopes and dreams— some wanted to write their own memoirs while others wished to host television shows—and learned of the crimes they committed in the past and the good deeds they wished to perform once they were released. Aggression, romance, and deceit play a large role in Steinberg's job, however, and soon any comfort and continuity he's found turns to danger and betrayal in his first book.

Other books you might like:
Marilyn Johnson, *This Book Is Overdue!: How Librarians and Cybrarians Can Save Us All*, 2010
Vicki Myron, *Dewey's Nine Lives: The Legacy of the Small-Town Library Cat Who Inspired Millions*, 2010
Bret Witter, co-author

308

DARCEY STEINKE

Easter Everywhere: A Memoir

(New York: Little, Brown, 2007)

Summary: Tina Brown reveals the secrets of the late Princess Diana. Brown shows that the princess di knew how to manipulate the media to her advantage but also takes a closer look at the real Diana. She talks about Diana's difficulties in acting as a dutiful wife and mother as well as her being an outsider as far as the British royal family was concerned.

Where it's reviewed:
Booklist, March 15, 2007, page 15
Library Journal, March 15, 2007, page 74
People Weekly, April 30, 2007, page 49

Other books by the same author:
Suicide Blonde, 2000
Jesus Saves, 1999

Other books you might like:
Barbara Brown Taylor, *Leaving Church: A Memoir of Faith*, 2006

Kathleen Finneran, *The Tender Land: A Family Love Story*, 2000

Anne Lamott, *Traveling Mercies: Some Thoughts on Faith*, 1999

Susanna Sonnenberg, *Her Last Death*, 2008

309

MARK STEVENS
ANNALYN SWAN , Co-Author

de Kooning: An American Master
(New York: Alfred A. Knopf, 2004)

Subject(s): Artists; Biographies

Summary: Authors Mark Stevens and Annalyn Swan present an intimate look at one of the greatest artists of the 20th century in *de Kooning: An American Master*. Born in Holland, Willem de Kooning came to the United States in the 1920s. He settled in New York where he befriended some of the most important artists of the era. Though de Kooning struggled for recognition for many years, he eventually became one of the most revered abstract expressionists of his time. He continued working well into the 1980s, when he was forced to put down his paint brush due to debilitating dementia. This book explores both the life and work of one of America's most productive artists.

Where it's reviewed:
National Review, February 8, 2005, page 54
New York Times Book Review, December 12, 2004, page BR10
The New Yorker, December 20, 2004, page 176
Newsweek, November 22, 2004, page 71

Other books by the same author:
All the Money in the World: How the Forbes 400 Make—and Spend—Their Fortunes, 2008

Other books you might like:
Barbara Hess, *Willem de Koonig: 1904-1997*, 2004
Steven Naifeh, *Jackson Pollock: An American Saga*, 1998
Cecile Shapiro, *Abstract Expressionism: A Critical Record*, 1990
   David Shapiro, co-author
Gregory Smith, *Jackson Pollock: An American Saga*, 1998
Hilary Spurling, *Matisse the Master: A Life of Henri Matisse: The Conquest of Colour, 1909-1954*, 2005

310

RORY STEWART

The Places in Between
(Orlando, Florida, Harcourt, 2005)

Subject(s): Adventure and Adventurers; Current Affairs; Travel

Summary: Not long after the invasion of Afghanistan in 2001, resulting in the 2002 toppling of its Taliban government, a Scotsman named Rory Stewart came to visit. Stewart, a former British Foreign Office staffer, embarked upon an epic on-foot voyage through Pakistan, Iraq, Afghanistan, India, and Nepal; his journey took him from one side of the mountainous, war-torn Afghanistan to the other. In this book, the result of his dangerous 6000-mile journey, Stewart describes the Afghan leg of his trip: the landscape, the weather, and the local cultures and customs he encountered. He also describes Afghanistan's violent history and current political chaos.

Where it's reviewed:
Booklist, April 15, 2006, page 22
Library Journal, April 1, 2007, page 130
The Nation, January 1, 2007, page 2
Publishers Weekly, February 13, 2006, page 7

Other books by the same author:
Occupational Hazards: My Time Governing in Iraq, 2007
The Prince of the Marshes: And Other Occupational Hazards of a Year in Iraq, 2007

Other books you might like:
Farah Ahmadi, *The Story of My Life: An Afghan Girl on the Other Side of the Sky*, 2005
Tamim Ansary, *West of Kabul, East of New York: An Afghan American Story*, 2002
Ingrid Christophersen, *The Bookseller of Kabul*, 2003
Deborah Rodriguez, *Kabul Beauty School: An American Woman Goes Behind the Veil*, 2007
Asne Seierstad, *The Bookseller of Kabul*, 2003

311

T.J. STILES

The First Tycoon: The Epic Life of Cornelius Vanderbilt
(New York: Alfred A. Knopf, 2009)

Subject(s): Entrepreneurship; Business enterprises; Wealth

Summary: Cornelius Vanderbilt was one of America's earliest and greatest tycoons. He was also an American success story, born to humble beginnings and rising to almost incalculable fortunes. Vanderbilt's first great success came in the shipbuilding field, where he was so prominent he was even consulted by President Abraham Lincoln. Later, Vanderbilt turned his attention, energy, and genius to railroads. He became the founder of the Grand Central Railroad which did much to span the young nation. Vanderbilt made himself untold fortunes but more importantly changed the way Americans travel, live, and conduct business. *The First Tycoon: The Epic Life of Cornelius Vanderbilt* by T.J. Stiles is all about this unique American figure.

Where it's reviewed:
American Heritage, October 2009, page 68
Nation, November 2009, page 68
New York Times Book Review, May 17, 2009, page p18
New Yorker, May 25, 2009, page 79

Newsweek, May 4, 2009, page 50

Other books by the same author:
Jesse James: Last Rebel of the Civil War, 2003

Other books you might like:
Stephen Dando-Collins, *Tycoon's War: How Cornelius Vanderbilt Invaded a Country to Overthrow America's Most Famous Military Adventurer*, 2008

Wyn Derbyshire, *Six Tycoons: The Lives of John Jacob Astor, Cornelius Vanderbilt, Andrew Carnegie, John D. Rockefeller, Henry Ford and Joseph P. Kennedy*, 2009

Lewis K. Parker, *Cornelius Vanderbilt and the Railroad Industry*, 2003

Edward J. Renehan, *Commodore: The Life of Cornelius Vanderbilt*, 2007

Arthur T. Vanderbilt, *Fortune's Children: The Fall of the House of Vanderbilt*, 1991

312

TANYA LEE STONE

Elizabeth Leads the Way: Elizabeth Cady Stanton and the Right to Vote

(New York: Henry Holt and Company, 2008)

Subject(s): Biographies; Women; Feminism

Summary: *Elizabeth Leads the Way: Elizabeth Cady Stanton and the Right to Vote* is an inspiring biography for young readers from author Tanya Lee Stone. As a young child in the 19th century, Elizabeth Cady Stanton recognized the injustice that women weren't treated as equals with men. As she grew up, she fought hard to accomplish the same things as her male counterparts, from learning Greek to jumping horses. After going to college, she used her passion and leadership abilities to gather a group of fellow feminists who desired to see women treated more equally. Together, they challenged the United States' government and demanded that women be given the right to vote. Young readers will find this biography fascinating and empowering.

Other books by the same author:
Almost Astronauts: 13 Women Who Dared to Dream, 2009
Sandy's Circus: A Story About Alexander Calder, 2008
A Bad Boy Can Be Good for a Girl, 2006

Other books you might like:
Shana Corey, *Mermaid Queen: The Spectacular True Story of Annette Kellerman, Who Swam Her Way To Fame, Fortune and Swimsuit History!*, 2009

Kelly DiPucchio, *Grace for President*, 2008

Laurie Halse Anderson, *Independent Dames: What You Never Knew About the Women and Girls of the American Revolution*, 2008

Doreen Rappaport, *Eleanor, Quiet No More*, 2009

Lane Smith, *Madame President*, 2008

313

DONALD STURROCK

Storyteller: The Authorized Biography of Roald Dahl

(New York: Simon & Schuster, 2010)

Subject(s): Biographies; Authorship; Literature

Summary: In *Storyteller: The Authorized Biography of Roald Dahl*, Donald Sturrock presents the life story of the children's author best known for the classic work *Charlie and the Chocolate Factory*. An acquaintance of Dahl, Sturrock chronicles the author's life from his early days in British boarding schools to his storied World War II service as an RAF pilot. Married twice and no stranger to personal tragedy, Dahl was a complex character who could be a difficult client for his publishers and agents. But as Sturrock explains, Dahl's unusual stories of "foul things and horrid people" held a unique fascination for young readers and continue to attract followers, even after his death in 1990. First book.

Other books you might like:
Lyndall Gordon, *Lives Like Loaded Guns: Emily Dickinson and her Family's Feuds*, 2010

Michael Maar, *Speak, Nabokov*, 2009

Wendy Moffat, *A Great Unrecorded History: A New Life of E.M. Forster*, 2010

Mary McDonagh Murphy, *Scout, Atticus, and Boo: A Celebration of Fifty Years of To Kill a Mockingbird*, 2010

Michael Sherborne, *H.G. Wells: Another Kind of Life*, 2010

314

YOSHIHIRO TATSUMI

Drifting Life

(Montreal, Quebec, Canada: Drawn and Quarterly, 2009)

Subject(s): Autobiographies; Authorship; Art

Summary: In the autobiography *Drifting Life*, author Yoshihiro Tatsumi relates his life story in the medium that has made him famous: the manga graphic novel. Tatsumi makes good use of his signature style and illustrations to tell his story with pictures and words. Tatsumi begins his story at the age of ten when he first discovered the manga genre after World War II and became inspired by the artform. He goes on to discuss his early successes and the drawbacks he faced on his road to becoming a published author. He also mixes personal bits of his story with the telling of his professional development.

Other books by the same author:
Good-Bye, 2008
Abandon the Old in Tokyo, 2006
The Push Man and Other Stories, 2005

Other books you might like:
David Mazzucchelli, *Asterios Polyp*, 2009

Marjane Satrapi, *Persepolis: The Story of a Childhood*, 2003
David Small, *Stitches: A Memoir*, 2009
Yoshihiro Tatsumi, *Abandon the Old in Tokyo*, 2006
Yoshihiro Tatsumi, *Good-Bye*, 2008

315

TERRY TEACHOUT

Pops: A Life of Louis Armstrong

(Boston: Houghton Mifflin Harcourt, 2009)

Subject(s): Biographies; Jazz; Musicians

Summary: In *Pops: A Life of Louis Armstrong*, drama and culture critic Terry Teachout presents a detailed biography of the celebrated jazz musician. Meticulously researched with information drawn from a vast array of previously untapped sources, this volume chronicles the life and times of the man who became the most influential jazz artist of the 20th century. From Armstrong's childhood in New Orleans to his first forays onto the world stage, from his remarkable craftsmanship to his memorable collaborations, *Pops* provides an intimate look at the life of a legend. This volume includes photographs, notes on the text, a bibliography, and an index.

Where it's reviewed:
Booklist, August 1, 2009, page p6
Library Journal, August 1, 2009, page p83
The Nation, March 1, 2010, page p32
National Review, Dec 31, 2009, page p50

Other books by the same author:
All in the Dances: A Brief Life of George Balanchine, 2004
The Skeptic: A Life of H. L. Mencken, 2003

Other books you might like:
Ted Gioia, *The History of Jazz*, 1998
Pannonica de Koenigswarter, *Three Wishes: An Intimate Look at Jazz Greats*, 2008

316

CLAIRE TOMALIN

Thomas Hardy

(New York: Penguin Books, 2007)

Subject(s): Biography; Poetry; Writing

Summary: Biographer Claire Tomalin presents the story of author and poet Thomas Hardy. Thomas Hardy was born in 1840 in Dorset, England. He grew up modestly in a rural area and went on to write novels consisting of elements such as memory, love, and loss among countless others. Hardy is known for living a simple, quiet life and Tomalin shows us that Hardy is much more than that, delving into his literary works and revealing the complex man that truly is Thomas Hardy.

Where it's reviewed:
The Economist, November 11, 2006, page 96

The New Republic, February 19, 2007, page 29
The New York Review of Books, March 1, 2007, page 21
Newsweek, May 19, 2008, page 9

Other books by the same author:
Samuel Pepys: The Unequalled Self, 2003
Jane Austen: A Life, 1999
The Life and Death of Mary Wollstonecraft, 1992

Other books you might like:
Thomas Hardy, *Thomas Hardy: The Complete Poems*, 1976
Michael Millgate, *Thomas Hardy: A Biography Revisited*, 1982
Ralph Pite, *Thomas Hardy: The Guarded Life*, 2007

317

DANIELLE TRUSSONI

Falling Through the Earth: A Memoir

(New York: Henry Holt and Co., 2006)

Story type: Historical
Subject(s): Vietnam War, 1959-1975; Family; Father-daughter relations

Summary: In *Falling Through the Earth: A Memoir*, Danielle Trussoni recalls how hard she struggled to impress her father, Daniel, throughout her life. As a small child, Trussoni and her siblings simply attempted to stay out of the way of their father after the Vietnam War. When he came home, he was different than they remembered. Soon, their parents divorced and Trussoni chose to live with her father, who she assumed would be lonely without the company. Throughout the years, Trussoni heard her father tell his Vietnam stories again and again. She began to feel as though she needed to travel to the places he had been to understand him. As an adult, she went to Vietnam and began to see her father, and those connected to him, in an entirely different light.

Where it's reviewed:
Booklist, January 1, 2006, page 47
Library Journal, February 15, 2006, page 125
Publishers Weekly, December 19, 2005, page 49

Other books by the same author:
Angelology: A Novel, 2010

Other books you might like:
Tom Bissell, *The Father of All Things: A Father, His Son, and the Legacy of Vietnam*, 2007
Frederick Downs Jr., *The Killing Zone: My Life in the Vietnam War*, 1978
Karl Marlantes, *Matterhorn: A Novel of the Vietnam War*, 2010
Tim O'Brien, *The Things They Carried*, 1990

318

KATHLEEN TURNER

Send Yourself Roses: Thoughts on My Life, Love, and Leading Roles

(New York: Springboard Press, 2008)

Subject(s): Autobiographies; Actors; Acting

Summary: In *Send Yourself Roses: Thoughts on My Life, Love, and Leading Roles,* celebrated actress Kathleen Turner writes about her life, beginning with her vagabond childhood in cities throughout the world. The daughter of a man who worked in the Foreign Service, she talks about the obstacles she faced throughout her youth as she moved with her family to different cities around the globe. Turner, the star of acclaimed movies such as *Body Heat* and *Romancing the Stone,* got her start in acting while a teenager living in London. After her first big break as the lead in the sultry film *Body Heat,* Turner has found success in a variety of roles on both stage and screen. Candidly discussing her personal life, including her marriage, child, and subsequent divorce, Turner provides insight into the choices she has made throughout the years. She discusses her struggles with rheumatoid arthritis and alcohol addiction in addition to what it's like to work with some of the greatest directors and actors in Hollywood today.

Where it's reviewed:
Booklist, December 15, 2007, page 15
Library Journal, January 1, 2008, page 104
Publishers Weekly, January 14, 2008, page 51

Other books you might like:
Aimee Lee Ball, *Cybill Disobedience*, 2000
George Hamilton, *Don't Mind If I Do*, 2008
George Mair, *Under the Rainbow: The Real Liza Minnelli*, 1996
John Nicoletti, *'Tis Herself: A Memoir*, 2004
    Maureen O'Hara, co-author
Darden Asbury Pyron, *Liberace: An American Boy*, 2000
Cybill Shepherd, *Cybill Disobedience*, 2000
William Stadiem, *Don't Mind If I Do*, 2008

319

LARRY TYE

Satchel: The Life and Times of an American Legend

(New York: Random House, 2009)

Subject(s): Biographies; Sports; Baseball

Summary: In *Satchel: The Life and Times of an American Legend,* Larry Tye, author and journalist, writes the first biography of one of the greatest baseball pitchers in both the Negro Leagues and the Major Leagues. Satchel Paige was legendary for his ability to strike out great hitters such as Joe DiMaggio and Ralph Kiner, among others. Tye interviews more than 200 former baseball players who played with Paige to write a detailed profile of the man behind the arm. Tye follows his life from Alabama in the Jim Crow era to the Negro Leagues and finally to a successful career with the Cleveland Indians. He also chronicles the rivalry between Paige and Jackie Robinson.

Where it's reviewed:
Library Journal, May 15, 2009, page p78
New York Times Book Review, July 19, 2009, page p17
Publishers Weekly, April 20, 2009, page p39
USA Today, May 28, 2009, page p03C

Other books by the same author:
Rising from the Rails: Pullman Porters and the Making of the Black Middle Class, 2005
The Father of Spin: Edward L. Bernays and The Birth of Public Relations, 2002
Home Lands: Portraits of the New Jewish Diaspora, 2001

Other books you might like:
William Brashler, *Josh Gibson: A Life in the Negro Leagues*, 1978
Howard Bryant, *The Last Hero: A Life of Henry Aaron*, 2010
Timothy M. Gay, *Satch, Dizzy, and Rapid Robert: The Wild Saga of Interracial Baseball Before Jackie Robinson*, 2010
James S. Hirsch, *Willie Mays: The Life, the Legend*, 2010

320

MELVIN I. UROFSKY

Louis D. Brandeis: A Life

(New York: Pantheon Books, 2009)

Story type: Historical - Mainstream
Subject(s): Biographies; Law; Politics

Summary: In *Louis D. Brandeis: A Life,* Melvin Urofsky discusses the life of one of the most influential Supreme Court justices in American history. Louis Brandeis served as an associate justice from 1916 to 1939. Before that, he came from a humble Jewish family and graduated from Harvard Law School with the highest grade point average in the prestigious school's history. As a lawyer, he fought for the idea of a person's right to privacy and wrote many groundbreaking law reviews. When his family was financially secure, he made an effort to take on pro bono cases. He was called the Robin Hood of the law and even the People's Lawyer. Brandeis was the first lawyer to use expert testimony to support his argument. Much of Urofsky's book focuses on what Brandeis did for the people of the United States before, during, and after his time on the Supreme Court.

Where it's reviewed:
The Economist, Sept 26, 2009, page p86
Library Journal, Sept 15, 2009, page p6
The New York Review of Books, Feb 11, 2010, page p30
The New Yorker, Nov 16, 2009, page p81

Biographies and Memoirs

Other books by the same author:
A March of Liberty: A Constitutional History of the United States Volume II: From 1877 to the Present, 2001
The American Presidents: Critical Essays, 2000

Other books you might like:
Louis D. Brandeis, *Other People's Money and How the Bankers Use It*, 2009
Antonin Scalia, *American Original: The Life and Constitution of Supreme Court Justice Antonin Scalia*, 2009
Jeff Shesol, *Supreme Power: Franklin Roosevelt vs. the Supreme Court*, 2010
G. Edward White, *Justice Oliver Wendell Holmes: Law and the Inner Self*, 1993

321

JANE URQUHART

L.M. Montgomery
(Toronto, Ontario, Canada: Penguin Books Canada, 2009)

Subject(s): Biographies; Writers; Writing

Summary: Jane Urquhart's *L.M. Montgomery* is the biography of Canadian writer Lucy Maud Montgomery (1874-1942). Montgomery was known for her 1908 novel *Anne of Green Gables*, which sparked a series of novels about an orphan named Anne. Many television series and movies based on the books were produced in Canada and the United States, including *Road to Avonlea*. Montgomery spent her early life teaching and writing, publishing more than 100 short stories from 1897-1907. In 1908, she married a Presbyterian minister named Ewan Macdonald, who was said to have suffered from mental illness. She published 20 novels, over 500 stories, a poetry collection, and an autobiography throughout her life. Montgomery's collection of short stories, poems, and vignettes *The Blythes Are Quoted* was published posthumously in 2009 as the ninth book in her Anne of Green Gables series.

Other books by the same author:
Sanctuary Line, 2010
Penguin Book of Canadian Short Stories, 2007
A Map of Glass, 2005

Other books you might like:
Catherine M. Andronik, *Kindred Spirit: A Biography of L.M. Montgomery, Creator of Anne of Green Gables*, 1993
Harry Bruce, *Maud: The Life of L.M. Montgomery*, 1992
Adrienne Clarkson, *Norman Bethune*, 2009
L.M. Montgomery, *Anne of Green Gables*, 1908
L.M. Montgomery, *Anne of Green Gables Series*, 1908

322

NORAH VINCENT

Self-Made Man: One Woman's Journey into Manhood and Back
(New York: Viking, 2006)

Subject(s): Gender Roles; Journalism; Sexism

Summary: Norah Vincent is a former columnist for the *Los Angeles Times*. As an experiment, she disguised herself as a man: short haircut, fake stubble, masculine clothes, and a discreet prosthesis. She posed as a man in a variety of social venues for over a year and a half, and this book is her record of her experiences. She joined a men's bowling league, dated, went to strip clubs, and joined a men's retreat. During these excursions, she made a number of observations about men, their attitudes towards women, and their constant social testing of one another. She also made some unexpected discoveries about women and how they react to men.

Where it's reviewed:
New Statesman, April 24, 2006, page 54
New York Times Book Review, January 22, 2006, page 1
Publishers Weekly, February 6, 2006, page 66
Time, January 30, 2006, page 64

Other books by the same author:
Voluntary Madness: Lost and Found in the Mental Healthcare System, 2009

Other books you might like:
Helen Boyd, *She's Not the Man I Married: My Life with a Transgender Husband*, 2007
Jennifer Finney Boylan, *She's Not There: A Life in Two Genders*, 2003
Veronica Vera, *Miss Vera's Cross-Dress for Success: A Resource Guide for Boys Who Want to Be Girls*, 2002

323

JEANNETTE WALLS

The Glass Castle: A Memoir
(New York: Scribner, 2005)

Subject(s): Alcoholism; Autobiography; Childhood

Summary: As this memoir opens, Jeannette Walls, while riding in a taxi, spots her mother rummaging through garbage in a dumpster. How the author came to live on upscale Park Avenue and her parents to be homeless in New York City is the true tale told here. Alcoholic father Rex, a highly intelligent man who hopes to invent a solar-powered glass house but can't hold down any job for long, and mother Mary Rose, a self-centered artist, raise four children with less-than-benign neglect, always short of cash and moving from place to place. Under their hardly-watchful eyes, the kids endure accidental injuries, cold, hunger, and—when they occasionally attend school—humiliation, though Lori, Jeannette, Brian, and Maureen excel at class work. They learn self-sufficiency, inventiveness, and a sense of adventure from their parents, but the family's situation worsens after a move to West Virginia. As Rex's alcoholism intensifies and Mary Rose's depression deepens, all eventually make their way to New York City and better lives—even the parents, who find shelter in an empty building on the Lower East Side. Having survived such a complex childhood, Jeannette Walls recounts these events matter-of-factly, with little pity for herself and with a mix of affection for and anger toward her parents.

Where it's reviewed:
Booklist, February 1, 2005, page 923
The Christian Century, May 1, 2007, page 3
New York Times Book Review, March 13, 2005, page BR1
Newsweek, March 7, 2005, page 55
The Southern Review, Winter 2006, page 215

Other books by the same author:
Half Broke Horses: A True-Life Novel, 2009
Dish: How Gossip Became the News and the News Became Just Another Show, 2001

Other books you might like:
Augusten Burroughs, *Running with Scissors: A Memoir*, 2002
Mary Karr, *The Liars' Club*, 1995
Frank McCourt, *Angela's Ashes*, 1996
Tim O'Brien, *The Things They Carried*, 1990
Amanda Welch, *The Kids Are All Right: A Memoir*, 2009
   Dan Welch, co-author
   Diana Welch, co-author
   Liz Welch, co-author
William Zinsser, *Writing About Your Life: A Journey into the Past*, 2005

324

BARBARA WALTERS

Audition: A Memoir

(New York: A.A. Knopf, 2008)

Subject(s): Journalism; Modern Life; Autobiographies
Summary: For more than fifty years, Barbara Walters has worked her way through the ranks of journalism and broadcasting to become one of the most well-known interviewers in the world. Walters, however, did not have an easy ascent to the top. In her book *Audition: A Memoir*, Walters gives readers a description of her personal and professional lives. As a young girl, Walters watched her father, Lou, struggle to gain fame. As she grew, she longed to be successful, too. Walters lets readers know about her triumphs and her failures throughout the book. In a chapter titled "The Hardest Chapter to Write," Walters discusses her daughter's struggle with drugs as a teenager. In other chapters, Walters provides insider information about some of her most famous interviewees. She also gives readers insight about how it felt to ask people such tough questions.

Where it's reviewed:
Booklist, April 15, 2008, page 4
Library Journal, May 15, 2008, page 110

New York Times Book Review, June 15, 2008, page p8
People, May 12, 2008, page 61
Publishers Weekly, April 28, 2008, page 129

Other books by the same author:
How to Talk with Practically Anybody about Practically Anything, 1970

Other books you might like:
Julie Andrews, *Home: A Memoir of My Early Years*, 2008
Joy Behar, *When You Need a Lift: But Don't Want to Eat Chocolate, Pay a Shrink, or Drink a Bottle of Gin*, 2007
Carol Burnett, *This Time Together: Laughter and Reflection*, 2010
Larry King, *My Remarkable Journey*, 2009
Cokie Roberts, *We Are Our Mothers' Daughters*, 1998

325

ALISON WEIR

The Lady in the Tower: The Fall of Anne Boleyn

(Toronto, Ontario, Canada: McClelland & Stewart, 2009)

Subject(s): Biographies; English (British people); Royalty
Summary: The story of the rise and fall of Anne Boleyn, the second wife of King Henry VIII of England, has captivated the world for centuries. In the biography *The Lady in the Tower: The Fall of Anne Boleyn*, author Alison Weir attempts to dissect how the queen fell from the king's graces and eventually faced death by beheading. Weir discusses the widely accepted notion that the king, desperate for a male heir whom Anne was unable to produce, may have ordered his most trusted adviser, Thomas Cromwell, to fabricate evidence to destroy Anne's reputation and give him reason to remarry. Weir, however, also puts forth the idea that Cromwell, jealous of Anne's influence on the king, built his own case against the woman. Regardless of what happened, Cromwell's findings led to Anne's arrest for treason. The queen was jailed in the Tower of London and later faced a public trial, during which she was sentenced to death.

Other books by the same author:
The Captive Queen: A Novel of Eleanor of Aquitaine, 2010
The Lady Elizabeth: A Novel, 2008
Innocent Traitor: A Novel of Lady Jane Grey, 2007
Queen Isabella, 2005

Other books you might like:
Philippa Gregory, *The Other Boleyn Girl*, 2002
Francis Hackett, *Queen Anne Boleyn*, 1939
Hilary Mantel, *Wolf Hall*, 2009
David Starkey, *Six Wives: The Queens of Henry VIII*, 2003
Alison Weir, *The Lady Elizabeth: A Novel*, 2008

326

DIANA WELCH
LIZ WELCH, Co-Author

DAN WELCH , Co-Author
AMANDA WELCH , Co-Author

The Kids Are All Right: A Memoir

(New York: Harmony Books, 2009)

Subject(s): Autobiographies; Family; Brothers

Summary: *The Kids are All Right: A Memoir* is a book from the perspectives of Amanda, Dan, Liz, and Diana Welch. With each chapter, one of the four Welch children provides in-depth information about their unusual childhood. In 1983, their perfect family suffered its first loss when their father passed away. Shortly after, their mother was diagnosed with cancer and died in 1984. The children, too young to provide for themselves, were separated and placed with friends of the family. As the oldest, Amanda went to college while the youngest, Liz, was given a new name and became somewhat estranged from her siblings. *The Kids are All Right* tells the story of a family that stuck together despite being physically torn apart.

Other books you might like:

Dave Pelzer, *A Child Called "It": An Abused Child's Journey from Victim to Victor*, 1995
Peter Rock, *My Abandonment*, 2009
David Small, *Stitches: A Memoir*, 2009
Jeannette Walls, *The Glass Castle: A Memoir*, 2005

327

SUZANNE GEORGE WHITAKER

The Daring Miss Quimby

(New York: Holiday House, 2009)

Subject(s): Biographies; Air travel; Women

Summary: In her first book, *The Daring Miss Quimby*, Suzanne George Whitaker tells the story of pioneering female pilot Harriet Quimby. In 1911, when the world of aviation was limited to men, Miss Quimby broke the rules and became the first American woman to get a pilot's license. Quimby's adventures made her famous around the world and she achieved another first by flying across the English Channel. Dressed in her signature purple flight suit, Quimby attracted crowds whenever she appeared in public. Catherine Stock's illustrations capture the excitement of Quimby's ground-breaking life story. A time line of women's accomplishments in aviation highlights the significance of Quimby's contribution.

Other books you might like:

Don Brown, *Ruth Law Thrills a Nation*, 1993
Robert Burleigh, *Flight: The Journey of Charles Lindbergh*, 1991
Bonnie Christensen, *The Daring Nellie Bly: America's Star Reporter*, 2003
Nikki Grimes, *Talkin' about Bessie: The Story of Aviator Elizabeth Coleman*, 2002
Rosemary Wells, *Wingwalker*, 2002

328

EDMUND WHITE

City Boy: My Life in New York During the 1960s and '70s

(New York: Bloomsbury USA, 2009)

Subject(s): Autobiographies; Men; Sexual behavior

Summary: In *City Boy: My Life in New York During the 1960s and '70s*, Edmund White recalls the years he spent living in New York between the 1960s and the 1970s. At the time, New York crawled with two different crowds: the intellectuals and the sexual deviants. White, an adventurous young man, bounced between both groups, chatting about politics and Marxists at one party and soliciting sex at the next. From theaters watching ballet with close friends to the backseats of old cars and trucks with strange women, White takes readers throughout the many New York areas he frequented when he was a young man.

Where it's reviewed:

Booklist, August 1, 2009, page p21
Harper's Magazine, Dec 2009, page p91
The New Yorker, Dec 21, 2009, page p139
Publishers Weekly, August 10, 2009, page p43

Other books by the same author:

A Boy's Own Story: A Novel, 2009
The Flaneur: A Stroll Through the Paradoxes of Paris, 2008
The Farewell Symphony, 1998

Other books you might like:

Edmund White, *A Boy's Own Story*, 1982
Edmund White, *Hotel de Dream*, 2007
Edmund White, *My Lives: An Autobiography*, 2006

329

RONALD C. WHITE

A. Lincoln: A Biography

(New York: Random House, 2009)

Subject(s): Biographies; Abolition of slavery; United States Civil War, 1861-1865

Summary: In *A. Lincoln: A Biography*, Ronald C. White, Jr. examines the 16th President of the United States. The first half of the book focuses on Lincoln's history, his family, and his rise in politics. White not only offers information about Lincoln's ancestors, he also shows how this man became a successful attorney elected to the state legislature by the time he turned 30. Most of the second part of the work explores the challenges that Lincoln faced during his presidency, both in his personal and professional lives. Filled with specific details, maps, and illustrations, White explains that Lincoln was a popular man forced to lead during the most difficult time in American history.

Other books by the same author:
The Eloquent President: A Portrait of Lincoln through His Words, 2005
Lincoln's Greatest Speech: The Second Inaugural, 2002

Other books you might like:
Michael Burlingame, *Abraham Lincoln: A Life, Volumes 1 and 2*, 2008
Ron Chernow, *Washington: A Life*, 2010
Catherine Clinton, *Mrs. Lincoln: A Life*, 2009
Doris Kearns Goodwin, *Team of Rivals: The Political Genius of Abraham Lincoln*, 2005
James M. McPherson, *Abraham Lincoln*, 2009

330

SEAN WILENTZ

Andrew Jackson
(New York: Times Books, 2005)

Story type: Historical
Subject(s): Presidents (Government); United States history; Biographies

Summary: Written by Princeton historian Sean Wilentz, *Andrew Jackson* is a comprehensive biography of the life, political career, accomplishments, and beliefs of the seventh president of the United States of America. Part of the American Presidents series, this book addresses the upbringing, presidency, and political views of Andrew Jackson. Wilentz thoroughly recounts Jackson's life prior to becoming president, including his upbringing and successful military career, before addressing political concerns and dilemmas that faced the leader during his presidency. The biography focuses on the chief issues that Jackson dealt with as a leader, including a battle against the Bank of the United States, South Carolina's nullification of the protective tariff, removing Indians from their land, a scandal involving a Cabinet member's wife, and slavery.

Where it's reviewed:
The American Prospect, November 2005, page 42
The Economist, October 29, 2005, page 89
Publishers Weekly, October 31, 2005, page 42

Other books by the same author:
The Age of Reagan: A History, 1974-2008, 2008
The Rise of American Democracy: Jefferson to Lincoln, 2006

Other books you might like:
H.W. Brands, *Andrew Jackson: His Life and Times*, 2005
Jon Butler, *Becoming America: The Revolution Before 1776*, 2000
Jon Meacham, *American Lion: Andrew Jackson in the White House*, 2008
Robert Vincent Remini, *Andrew Jackson*, 1998

331

ANDREW YOUNG

The Politician: An Insider's Account of John Edwards's Pursuit of the Presidency and the Scandal That Brought Him Down
(New York: Thomas Dunne Books, 2010)

Subject(s): Biographies; Autobiographies; Presidents (Government)

Summary: *The Politician: An Insider's Account of John Edwards's Pursuit of the Presidency and the Scandal That Brought Him Down* is a first book by Andrew Young and is part biography and part autobiography. Young first began working for John Edwards during the Senate race in 1998, and he quickly became Edwards's closest assistant and confidante, truly believing that Edwards would make an outstanding president one day. As Edwards became more powerful and chose to run for president in 2008, Young was frequently given increasingly questionable assignments, finally being asked to cover up Edwards's affair with Rielle Hunter. Young chose instead to reveal the affair and immediately left Edwards's employment, attempting to hide from the press. Edwards continued the run for president, though his career had essentially ended. Young includes personal accounts of the way his work with Edwards changed his beliefs.

Other books you might like:
Bill Clinton, *My Life*, 2004
Elizabeth Edwards, *Resilience: Reflections on the Burdens and Gifts of Facing Life's Adversities*, 2009
Mark Halperin, *Game Change: Obama and the Clintons, McCain and Palin, and the Race of a Lifetime*, 2010
John Heilemann, co-author
Kitty Kelley, *The Family: The Real Story of the Bush Dynasty*, 2004
Jenny Sandford, *Staying True*, 2010

332

MOSAB HASSAN YOUSEF

Son of Hamas: A Gripping Account of Terror, Betrayal, Political Intrigue, and Unthinkable Choices
(Carol Stream, Illinois: SaltRiver, 2010)

Subject(s): Autobiographies; Family; Terror

Summary: In his first book *Son of Hamas: A Gripping Account of Terror, Betrayal, Political Intrigue, and Unthinkable Choices*, Mosab Hassan Yousef tells the story of his life and his experiences as the son of Sheikh Hassan Yousef—a founding member of Hamas. Yousef explains that he was once an important part of the Hamas organization and was even imprisoned in Israel for some of his actions. His father and other leaders of Hamas trained Yousef to become one of the terrorist group's next leaders. After Yousef reached adulthood, however, he turned away from his former life and became a Christian. Yousef had to leave his family and his homeland behind as his newfound faith made him an easy target. Youself tells how his life has changed dramatically over the years and how he believes that the Christian faith could help bring peace to the Middle East.

Other books you might like:
Joe Sacco, *Palestine*, 2001
Edward W. Said, *Out of Place: A Memoir*, 1999
Jonathan Schanzer, *Hamas vs. Fatah: The Struggle for Palestine*, 2008
Sandy Tolan, *The Lemon Tree: An Arab, a Jew, and the Heart of the Middle East*, 2006

333

KOREN ZAILCKAS

Smashed: Story of a Drunken Girlhood

(New York: Penguin Books, 2005)

Subject(s): Adolescence; Alcoholism; Autobiography
Summary: In this memoir, 24-year-old Koren Zailckas lookes back on a decade of heavy drinking. She first began nipping at hard liquor before she entered high school, and throughout her adolescence she abused alcohol constantly, for the specific purpose of getting drunk. During these years she had several experiences that can easily be considered date-rape; as an adult, she confesses that she's not sure how to go about having a sexual relationship without alcohol. Zailckas describes her frightening brushes with alcohol poisoning, violence, and suicidal thoughts. She adds weight to her own experiences by citing statistics about the prevalence and harmfulness of teenaged drinking.

Where it's reviewed:
Booklist, Dec 15, 2004, page p698
Library Journal, Nov 15, 2004, page p77
New York Times Book Review, Feb 27, 2005, page p22
People, Feb 7, 2005, page p49

Other books by the same author:
Fury: A Memoir, 2010
Other books you might like:
Kerry Cohen, *Loose Girl: A Memoir of Promiscuity*, 2008
Caroline Knapp, *Drinking: A Love Story*, 1996
Judith Moore, *Fat Girl: A True Story*, 2005

334

MITCHELL ZUCKOFF

Robert Altman: The Oral Biography

(New York: Alfred A. Knopf, 2009)

Subject(s): Biographies; Movie industry; Movies
Summary: Journalist Mitchell Zuckoff presents a thorough account of the life and career of Academy Award-winning director Robert Altman. *Robert Altman: The Oral Biography* is drawn from a series of interviews Zuckoff conducted with the director before the latter's death in 2006. Detailing Altman's childhood in Kansas City, his World War II service, and his rise to international stardom as a one-of-a-kind director and storyteller, this volume is a celebration of Altman as an artist, a man, and a legend. Containing reminiscences from such stars as Meryl Streep, Warren Beatty, and Paul Newman, *Robert Altman* includes a detailed filmography and a full index.

Other books by the same author:
Ponzi's Scheme: The True Story of a Financial Legend, 2005
Choosing Naia: A Family's Journey, 2002
Other books you might like:
Mike Figgis, *Projections 10: Hollywood Film-Makers on Film-Making*, 2000
Beverly Gray, *Roger Corman: An Unauthorized Biography of the Godfather of Indie Filmmaking*, 2000
Mark Harris, *Pictures at a Revolution: Five Movies and the Birth of the New Hollywood*, 2008
Art Linson, *What Just Happened?: Bitter Hollywood Tales from the Front Line*, 2002
Martin Scorsese, *Scorsese on Scorsese*, 1989

Business

335

KARIN ABARBANEL
BRUCE FREEMAN , Co-Author

Birthing the Elephant: The Woman's Go-For-It! Guide to Overcoming the Big Challenges of Launching a Business

(Berkeley, California: Ten Speed Press, 2008)

Subject(s): Business; Entrepreneurship; Women

Summary: *Birthing the Elephant: The Woman's Go-For-It! Guide to Overcoming the Big Challenges of Launching a Business* by Karin Abarbanel and Bruce Freeman is a collection of advice for female entrepreneurs. In the book, Abarbanel and Freeman present a number of examples of successful female entrepreneurs, and they describe the traits and strategies that helped propel the women to success. The authors also explain that, in order to succeed, female entrepreneurs need to have persistence, determination, courage, the ability to handle setbacks, and the ability to be one's own boss. The volume also includes practical advice about managing money and assets, preventing common business mistakes, finding mentors and support, trusting one's instincts, and maintaining a personal life outside work.

Where it's reviewed:
Publishers Weekly, January 7, 2008, page 48

Other books you might like:
Elizabeth Gordon, *The Chic Entrepreneur: Put Your Business in Higher Heels*, 2008
Nada Jones, *16 Weeks to Your Dream Business: A Weekly Planner for Entrepreneurial Women*, 2008
Emira Mears, *The Boss of You: Everything A Woman Needs to Know to Start, Run, and Maintain Her Own Business*, 2008

336

ALLEN P. ADAMSON

BrandSimple: How the Best Brands Keep It Simple and Succeed

(New York: Palgrave MacMillan, 2006)

Subject(s): Business; Entrepreneurship; Marketing

Summary: In *BrandSimple: How the Best Brands Keep It Simple and Succeed*, author Allen P. Adamson examines successful organizations to determine that those that persevere typically have at least one thing in common: They keep their branding simple. Adamson draws upon his more than two decades of experience in brand development to outline six key principles of a successful brand. The author looks at brands such as FedEx, HBO, American Express, eBay, and others to determine how these organizations have generated continuous success through brand identity. Adamson is also the author of *BrandDigital: Simple Ways Top Brands Succeed in the Digital World*.

Other books by the same author:
BrandDigital: Simple Ways Top Brands Succeed in the Digital World, 2008

Other books you might like:
Tim Calkins, *Kellogg on Branding: The Marketing Faculty of The Kellogg School of Management*, 2005
Alina Wheeler, *Designing Brand Identity: An Essential Guide for the Whole Branding Team*, 2009

337

DAVID ALLEN

Making It All Work: Winning at the Game of Work and Business of Life

(New York: Viking, 2008)

Subject(s): Business; Time; Self help books

Summary: *Making It All Work: Winning at the Game of Work and Business of Life* is a practical resource guide for managing time and life from bestselling author David Allen. The book is a sequel to the bestselling business book *Getting Things Done*. Allen follows up on the same time-management and results-oriented methods introduced in *Getting Things Done* and applies them to all facets of life in *Making It All Work*. The book motivates and educates readers on effective ways to handle all of life's complications and stressors, both big and small. Allen offers tips on everything from selecting a babysitter to organizing a vacation to arranging care for elderly relatives. The book is a useful self-help guide for readers who seek success and efficiency both at the office and at home.

Other books you might like:

Erin R. Doland, *Unclutter Your Life in One Week*, 2009

Neil Fiore, *The Now Habit at Work: Perform Optimally, Maintain Focus, and Ignite Motivation in Yourself and Others*, 2010

Michael Linenberger, *Master Your Workday Now!: Proven Strategies to Control Chaos, Create Outcomes, & Connect Your Work to Who You Really Are*, 2010

338

CHRIS ANDERSON

The Long Tail, Revised and Updated Edition: Why the Future of Business is Selling Less of More

(New York: Hyperion, 2008)

Subject(s): Business; Entrepreneurship; Marketing

Summary: In *The Long Tail, Revised and Updated Edition: Why the Future of Business is Selling Less of More*, author Chris Anderson provides a new-and-improved edition of his 2006 book *The Long Tail*. In the updated book, Anderson examines how businesses in the 21st century are changing by lowering product quantity and increasing product quality. This updated version also includes a new chapter on marketing in the new millennium. *The Long Tail, Revised and Updated Edition* was the recipient of the Gerald Loeb Award for Best Business Book of the Year. Anderson is also the author of *Free: The Future of a Radical Price* and is editor-in-chief of *Wired* magazine.

Other books by the same author:

Free: The Future of a Radical Price, 2009

Other books you might like:

John Battelle, *The Search: How Google and Its Rivals Rewrote the Rules of Business and Transformed Our Culture*, 2005

Jeff Howe, *Crowdsourcing: Why the Power of the Crowd Is Driving the Future of Business*, 2008

Clay Shirky, *Here Comes Everybody: The Power of Organizing Without Organizations*, 2008

339

DAN ARIELY

Predictably Irrational, Revised and Expanded Edition: The Hidden Forces That Shape Our Decisions

(New York: HarperCollins, 2010)

Subject(s): Psychology; Philosophy; Business

Summary: *Predictably Irrational, Revised and Expanded Edition: The Hidden Forces That Shape Our Decisions* is an updated and extended edition of author Dan Ariely's 2009 *New York Times* best seller. In this book, Ariely examines the processes of human thought and how decisions or behaviors that, on the surface, seem illogical are actually part of a behavioral pattern. This revised version includes new information and insight into these behaviors and argues that while we may think our decisions make sense, they are, in fact, unreasonable. Still, the author contends, these decisions are not accidental or arbitrary; rather, they are deliberate, whether we realize it or not. Ariely is the James B. Duke Professor of Psychology and Behavioral Economics at Duke University.

Other books you might like:

Dan Ariely, *The Upside of Irrationality: The Unexpected Benefits of Defying Logic at Work and at Home*, 2010

Jonah Lehrer, *How We Decide*, 2009

Cass R. Sunstein, *Nudge: Improving Decisions about Health, Wealth, and Happiness*, 2009

Richard H. Thaler, co-author

340

PETER ARNELL

Shift: How to Reinvent Your Business, Your Career, and Your Personal Brand

(New York: Broadway Books, 2010)

Subject(s): Advertising; Marketing; Business

Summary: *Shift: How to Reinvent Your Business, Your Career, and Your Personal Brand* is part autobiography, part self-help book, written by advertising guru Peter Arnell. The first half of the book is largely focused on Arnell's personal experiences as a young man, describing his efforts to lose 250 pounds to save his life. Arnell discusses topics such as the projects he is working on, where he travels, and the people who provide him with inspiration. He then provides practical advice for people wanting to make changes in their own lives, whether in the personal or professional realms. Advice on developing one's own "personal brand" is included as well.

Other books you might like:

Catherine Kaputa, *U R a Brand! How Smart People Brand Themselves for Business Success*, 2006

Charlene Li, *Open Leadership: How Social Technology*

Can Transform the Way You Lead, 2010
Dan Schawbel, *Me 2.0, Revised and Updated Edition: 4 Steps to Building Your Future*, 2010

341

MICHAEL A. BANKS

Blogging Heroes: Interviews with 30 of the World's Top Bloggers
(Hoboken, New Jersey: Wiley, 2007)

Subject(s): Internet; Business; Marketing

Summary: Blogging has become one of the most popular forms of publishing one's writing. Over one million blogs exist, but very few of their authors have enjoyed financial success. Bloggers who have reached this level have done so by discovering their niche, writing fascinating content, and learning the ins and outs of Internet marketing. For *Blogging Heroes*, author Michael A. Banks sought out and interviewed 30 of the most successful bloggers in the industry. The bloggers included have been featured in some of the world's most famous magazines and Web sites. Banks's book provides inspirational stories, advice, and insight into how it's possible to turn a blog into a full-time, fulfilling career.

Other books by the same author:
Before Oprah: Ruth Lyons, the Woman Who Created Talk TV, 2009
On the Way to the Web: The Secret History of the Internet and Its Founders, 2008
Crosley: Two Brothers and a Business Empire That Transformed the Nation, 2006

Other books you might like:
Chris Garrett, *ProBlogger: Secrets for Blogging Your Way to a Six-Figure Income*, 2008
Bradley L. Jones, *Web 2.0 Heroes: Interviews with 20 Web 2.0 Influencers*, 2008
Darren Rowse, *ProBlogger: Secrets for Blogging Your Way to a Six-Figure Income*, 2008
Bob Walsh, *Clear Blogging: How People Blogging Are Changing the World and How You Can Join Them*, 2007

342

LOUIS BARAJAS

Small Business, Big Life: Five Steps to Creating a Great Life with Your Own Small Business
(Nashville, Tennessee: Thomas Nelson, 2007)

Subject(s): Business enterprises; Entrepreneurship; Small business

Summary: Financial planner and small business expert Louis Barajas provides a step-by-step guide to establishing a successful small business in his book *Small Business, Big Life: Five Steps to Creating a Great Life with Your Own Small Business*. In this volume, Barajas strives to teach small business owners about how to make their

businesses more productive and lucrative. This book contains financial advice and wisdom that Barajas gained through experience. Barajas acknowledges that owning a small business can sometimes seem overwhelming; however, he believes that if business owners can maintain what he calls the four cornerstones of personal greatness—which he describes as truth, responsibility, awareness, and courage—they can make their endeavors succeed. These elements and their relationships to building a small business are discusses in depth. The book contains four appendixes which offer further explanations.

Other books by the same author:
Overworked, Overwhelmed, and Underpaid: Simple Steps to Go From Stress to Success, 2008

Other books you might like:
Bill Collier, *How to Succeed as a Small Business Owner...and Still Have a Life*, 2006
Tom Gegax, *The Big Book of Small Business: You Don't Have to Run Your Business by the Seat of Your Pants*, 2007

343

JOHN BATTELLE

The Search: How Google and Its Rivals Rewrote the Rules of Business and Transformed Our Culture
(New York: Portfolio, 2005)

Subject(s): Internet; Culture; Technology

Summary: In *The Search: How Google and Its Rivals Rewrote the Rules of Business and Transformed Our Culture*, author John Battelle doesn't just recount the history of Google. Rather, he offers a social critique of search engines and their role in transforming culture. Battelle is an Internet pioneer himself, the creator and editor of two magazines devoted to new technologies. He argues that search engines and databases are indicative of people's intentions and desires. Thus, he believes that they serve as sort of cultural artifacts through which a person can better understand a time and its people.

Other books you might like:
Chris Anderson, *The Long Tail, Revised and Updated Edition: Why the Future of Business is Selling Less of More*, 2008
Ken Auletta, *Googled: The End of the World as We Know It*, 2009
Clay Shirky, *Here Comes Everybody: The Power of Organizing Without Organizations*, 2008

344

SCOTT BELSKY

Making Ideas Happen: Overcoming the Obstacles Between Vision and Reality
(New York: Portfolio, 2010)

Subject(s): Business; Success; Economics

Summary: In *Making Ideas Happen: Overcoming the Obstacles between Vision and Reality*, author Scott Belsky explores the complex process of transforming innovative concepts into real-world solutions. The founder of Behance, an organization devoted to nurturing creativity in business, Belsky is uniquely familiar with the frequent disconnect between vision and reality. In this book, he shares the lessons in creative thinking he's learned first-hand, from the importance of simplicity and the benefits of dissent among teammates to the value of competition—and of sharing. While great ideas abound in industry, the author asserts, few will reach fruition without the necessary organizational tools.

Other books you might like:

Jason Fried, *Rework*, 2010
    David Heinemeier Hansson, co-author
Tony Hsieh, *Delivering Happiness: A Path to Profits, Passion, and Purpose*, 2010
Michael Bungay Stanier, *Do More Great Work. Stop the Busywork, and Start the Work That Matters*, 2010

345

TIM BERRY

The Plan-as-You-Go Business Plan

(Irvine, California: Entrepreneur Press, 2008)

Subject(s): Business; Entrepreneurship; Business enterprises

Summary: *The Plan-as-You-Go Business Plan* is a practical and motivational resource guide for business owners and entrepreneurs from author and business planning expert Tim Berry. In this book, Berry bucks traditional beliefs about business planning and motivates individuals to forgo long-term preparation for in-the-moment inspiration and creativity. His simple and modern approach invites business owners and entrepreneurs to skip the overwhelming process of planning way in advance and instead allow the business to grow and evolve in its own way and at its own pace. *The Plan-as-You-Go Business Plan* allows individuals to start building and growing their businesses immediately and figure out the details as they arise.

Other books by the same author:

3 Weeks to Startup, 2008
Hurdle: The Book on Business Planning, 2006

Other books you might like:

Jason Fried, *Rework*, 2010
    David Heinemeier Hansson, co-author
John Jantsch, *Duct Tape Marketing: The World's Most Practical Small Business Marketing Guide*, 2007
Mike Michalowicz, *The Toilet Paper Entrepreneur: The tell-it-like-it-is guide to cleaning up in business, even if you are at the end of your roll*, 2008

346

ROHIT BHARGAVA

Personality Not Included: Why Companies Lose Their Authenticity and How Great Brands Get It Back

(New York: McGraw-Hill, 2008)

Subject(s): Business; Marketing; Business enterprises

Summary: Award-winning author and marketing guru Rohit Bhargava's *Personality Not Included: Why Companies Lose Their Authenticity and How Great Brands Get It Back* is a business resource guide that highlights the importance of branding and personality. In this book, Bhargava contends that for businesses to attract customers and find success, they must have a compelling and dynamic personality. Using true anecdotes and case studies from real corporations, Bhargava shows the importance of an established and vibrant personality. Divided into two sections, *Personality Not Included* instructs readers on defining the personailty for an organization, marketing myths, effectively communicating a business's personality and products, creating a marketing backstory, and implementing a plan.

Other books you might like:

David Meerman Scott, *The New Rules of Marketing and PR: How to Use News Releases, Blogs, Podcasting, Viral Marketing and Online Media to Reach Buyers Directly*, 2007
Andy Sernovitz, *Word of Mouth Marketing: How Smart Companies Get People Talking, Revised Edition*, 2009
Jerry S. Wilson, *Managing Brand You: 7 Steps to Creating Your Most Successful Self*, 2008

347

KEN BLANCHARD
S. TRUETT CATHY , Co-Author

The Generosity Factor: Discover the Joy of Giving Your Time, Talent, and Treasure

(Grand Rapids, Michigan: Zondervan, 2009)

Subject(s): Business; Gifts; Success

Summary: *The Generosity Factor: Discover the Joy of Giving Your Time, Talent, and Treasure* is an inspirational parable about the importance of giving from best-selling author Ken Blanchard and Chick-fil-a founder S. Truett Cathy. The authors rely on a modern-day allegory to encourage and educate readers on what it means to be truly generous and how giving can impact and bless a person's life. In the story, a young, ambitious broker is desperate to rise to the top and find a sense of purpose and fulfillment in life. Meanwhile, a successful CEO has managed to find true happiness by giving to others. A chance encounter between the two men allows the CEO to impart his principles for living and giving to the broker, changing his life forever.

Other books by the same author:
Eat Mor Chikin: Inspire More People / It's Better to Build Boys Than Mend Men / How Did You Do It, Truett?, 2010
Lead with LUV: A Different Way to Create Real Success (Leading at a Higher Level), 2010
The Mulligan: A Parable of Second Chances, 2010
Leading at a Higher Level, Revised and Expanded Edition: Blanchard on Leadership and Creating High Performing Organizations, 2009
The Secret: What Great Leaders Know — And Do, 2009
Who Killed Change?: Solving the Mystery of Leading People Through Change, 2009
How Did You Do It, Truett?, 2007

Other books you might like:
Randy Alcorn, *The Treasure Principle: Unlocking the Secret of Joyful Giving*, 2005
Barry Moltz, *B-A-M! Bust A Myth: Delivering Customer Service in a Self-Service World*, 2009
John Ortberg, *When the Game is Over, It All Goes Back in the Box*, 2007

348

JEANNE BLISS

I Love You More Than My Dog: Five Decisions That Drive Extreme Customer Loyalty in Good Times and Bad

(New York: Portfolio, 2009)

Subject(s): Business; Economics; Marketing

Summary: In *I Love You More Than My Dog: Five Decisions That Drive Extreme Customer Loyalty in good Times and Bad*, marketing expert Jeanne Bliss shows how businesses of any size can increase profits by improving consumer satisfaction. With customers holding unprecedented potential to communicate a company's good points and bad via the Internet, the author asserts that businesses must learn how to use customer loyalty as a marketing tool. From the user-friendly design of Apple stores to Netflix's preemptory rectification of its delivery policy, Bliss uses real-life examples to demonstrate the importance of cultivating customer loyalty.

Other books by the same author:
Chief Customer Officer : Getting Past Lip Service to Passionate Action, 2006

Other books you might like:
John R. DiJulius, *What's the Secret: To Providing a World-Class Customer Experience*, 2008
Leonardo Inghilleri, *Exceptional Service, Exceptional Profit: The Secrets of Building a Five-Star Customer Service Organization*, 2010

Joseph Jaffe, *Flip the Funnel: How to Use Existing Customers to Gain New Ones*, 2010

349

NEAL BOORTZ
JOHN LINDER , Co-Author

FairTax: The Truth: Answering the Critics

(New York: HarperCollins, 2008)

Subject(s): Politics; Money; Taxation

Summary: Authors Neal Boortz and John Linder published *The Fairtax Book* in 2006. After the book's publication some Americans claimed that the Fairtax is impractical. In their book *FairTax: The Truth: Answering the Critics*, Boortz and Linder return to answer their critics. In the first book, the authors explain why they believe the current tax system is obsolete and present a radical new plan that would eliminate the need for the IRS, while strengthening the economy and creating more jobs. The Fairtax would do away with all the current tax laws and introduce a 23 percent tax on goods and services. The authors argue that the Fairtax plan would eliminate chaos at tax time and increase federal revenue. In *FairTax: The Truth: Answering the Critics*, the authors contradict what they see as falsehoods and misinformation about their plan.

Other books by the same author:
Somebody's Gotta Say It, 2007
The Fair Tax Book: Saying Goodbye to the Income Tax and the IRS, 2005

Other books you might like:
Ken Clark, *The Pocket Idiot's Guide to the FairTax*, 2010
Ken Hoagland, *The FairTax Solution: Financial Justice for All Americans*, 2010
Arthur B. Laffer, *The End of Prosperity: How Higher Taxes Will Doom the Economy—If We Let It Happen*, 2008

350

NORM BRODSKY
BO BURLINGHAM , Co-Author

The Knack: How Street-Smart Entrepreneurs Learn to Handle Whatever Comes Up

(New York: Portfolio, 2008)

Subject(s): Business; Problem solving; Entrepreneurship

Summary: *The Knack: How Street-Smart Entrepreneurs Learn to Handle Whatever Comes Up* is a practical resource guide for small business owners from entrepreneurs and *Inc.* magazine columnists Bo Burlingham and Norm Brodsky. Many new business owners seek formulas to help them accomplish success, but Burlingham and

Brodsky claim that there's no one set of rules that works for everyone. Instead, individuals need to have a certain street-smart mentality known as "the knack" to help them overcome problems and create opportunities. Using true stories of companies overcoming challenges, *The Knack* offers advice on catching problems when they're small, focusing on important goals, and keeping a healthy perspective.

Other books you might like:

Mike Michalowicz, *The Toilet Paper Entrepreneur: The tell-it-like-it-is guide to cleaning up in business, even if you are at the end of your roll*, 2008

Susan Urquhart-Brown, *The Accidental Entrepreneur: The 50 Things I Wish Someone Had Told Me About Starting a Business*, 2008

John Warrillow, *Built to Sell: Turn Your Business Into One You Can Sell*, 2010

351

CHRIS BROGAN
JULIEN SMITH , Co-Author

Trust Agents: Using the Web to Build Influence, Improve Reputation, and Earn Trust

(Hoboken, New Jersey: John WIley & Sons, 2009)

Subject(s): Entrepreneurship; Internet; Business

Summary: *Trust Agents: Using the Web to Build Influence, Improve Reputation, and Earn Trust*, written by Chris Brogan and Julien Smith, is a comprehensive guide for business entrepreneurs to utilizing World Wide Web media for marketing and public relations endeavors. Smith and Brogan show readers through personal anecdotes and interviews how others have successfully used new media marketing tools to promote their brands' exposure. The authors use these examples to offer step-by-step solutions for managing relationships between a brand and its public. Brogan is also the author of *Social Media 101: Tactics and Tips to Develop Your Business Online*. This is Smith's first book.

Other books by the same author:

Social Media 101: Tactics and Tips to Develop Your Business Online, 2010

Other books you might like:

Erik Qualman, *Socialnomics: How Social Media Transforms the Way We Live and Do Business*, 2009

Brian Solis, *Engage: The Complete Guide for Brands and Businesses to Build, Cultivate, and Measure Success in the New Web*, 2010

Tamar Weinberg, *The New Community Rules: Marketing on the Social Web*, 2009

352

ARTHUR C. BROOKS

The Battle: How the Fight Between Free Enterprise and Big Government Will Shape America's Future

(New York: Basic Books, 2010)

Subject(s): Socialism; Business; United States

Summary: *The Battle: How the Fight Between Free Enterprise and Big Government Will Shape America's Future* is an in-depth examination of the role of the U.S. government in business. In the book, Arthur C. Brooks, president of the American Enterprise Institute, contends that a significant battle is taking place in America between free enterprise and social democracy. As the government's power and involvement in business continue to increase, the independence and wealth of the American people are at risk. Brooks highlights the dangers of socialism, the importance of free enterprise, and possible solutions to the problem. He provides a detailed plan of action to defend free enterprise that includes uniting Republicans and Democrats to protect the freedom and rights of American citizens.

Other books by the same author:

Gross National Happiness: Why Happiness Matters for America—and How We Can Get More of It, 2008

Social Entrepreneurship: A Modern Approach to Social Value Creation, 2008

Who Really Cares: The Surprising Truth About Compasionate Conservatism Who Gives, Who Doesn't, and Why It Matters, 2006

Gifts of Time and Money: The Role of Charity in America's Communities, 2005

Other books you might like:

Andrew Bernstein, *The Capitalist Manifesto: The Historic, Economic and Philosophic Case for Laissez-Faire*, 2005

Daniel Hannan, *The New Road to Serfdom: A Letter of Warning to America*, 2010

William Voegeli, *Never Enough: America's Limitless Welfare State*, 2010

353

BOB BURG
JOHN DAVID MANN , Co-Author

The Go-Giver: A Little Story about a Powerful Business Idea

(New York: Portfolio, 2007)

Subject(s): Success; Business

Summary: *The Go-Giver: A Little Story about a Powerful Business Idea* is a business parable told from the point of view of Joe. When Joe needs to land a big deal in order to turn around his dwindling sales record, he seeks the guidance of Pindar. The consultant introduces the eager businessman to five "go-givers." According to Pindar, each of these go-givers represents one of the Five Laws of Stratospheric Success. Pindar uses the five laws—value, compensation, influence, authenticity, and receptivity—to show Joe what his career is missing. Joe learns that stepping on others and calling in favors isn't the way to do business. Rather, Pindar teaches Joe that the only way he can receive the gifts of others is to give of himself first.

Other books you might like:
Og Mandino, *The Greatest Salesman in the World*, 1968
Steve Farber, *Greater Than Yourself: The Ultimate Lesson of True Leadership*, 2009

354

GRANT CARDONE

If You're Not First, You're Last: Sales Strategies to Dominate Your Market and Beat Your Competition
(Hoboken, New Jersey: Wiley, 2010)

Subject(s): Sales; Success; Business

Summary: *If You're Not First, You're Last: Sales Strategies to Dominate Your Market and Beat Your Competition* by Grant Cardone is a guide for both small and large businesses to increase sales, beat the competition, and find success whether the economy is up or down. Cardone offers suggestions for creating new products, increasing market share, finding new opportunities, creating a new financial plan, and, of course, increasing boosting selling.

Other books by the same author:
The Closer's Survival Guide, 2009
Sell To Survive, 2008
Selling: The Secret to Success, 2008

Other books you might like:
Tony Hsieh, *Delivering Happiness: A Path to Profits, Passion, and Purpose*, 2010
John Jantsch, *The Referral Engine: Teaching Your Business to Market Itself*, 2010
Tommy Spaulding, *It's Not Just Who You Know: Transform Your Life (and Your Organization) by Turning Colleagues and Contacts into Lasting, Genuine Relationships*, 2010

355

JAMES E. CHEEKS

Wealth Creation for Small Business Owners: 75 Strategies for Financial Success in Any Economy
(Avon, Massachusetts: Adams Business, 2010)

Subject(s): Wealth; Business; Law

Summary: *Wealth Creation for Small Business Owners: 75 Strategies for Financial Success in Any Economy* is a practical resource guide for entrepreneurs from business

and financial adviser James E. Cheeks. Many small business owners are unaware of the laws and tax cuts available to help them accrue wealth and save money. Cheeks offers 75 practical tips for legal ways to increase assets and extend personal wealth. Readers will learn how to use business laws and tax systems to their advantage to start retirement funds, provide excellent health care and insurance, protect business revenue from tax, allocate business assets, store up and secure family wealth, withdraw business profits when needed, shelter assets from creditors, and more.

Other books you might like:
Tim Berry, *Hurdle: The Book on Business Planning*, 2006
Timothy Ferriss, *The 4-Hour Workweek, Expanded and Updated: Escape 9-5, Live Anywhere, and Join the New Rich*, 2009
John Warrillow, *Built to Sell: Turn Your Business Into One You Can Sell*, 2010

356

DORIS CHRISTOPHER

The Pampered Chef
(New York: Doubleday, 2005)

Subject(s): Business; Business Building; Business Enterprises

Summary: In 1980, Doris Christopher invested $3,000 in a business idea: to sell high-quality kitchen tools and accessories—everything from roasting pans to pretty dishes to ice cream makers and food processors. She used television infomercials to get the word out; later, she utilized the Internet. The business, The Pampered Chef, quickly grew from these humble beginnings into a billion-dollar enterprise; it was recently purchased by Warren Buffet. In this business memoir, Christopher describes her business philosophy, her start up costs and mistakes, and how she handled her company's growth. She shares both her successful strategies and her costly errors, and describes the problems she faced and how she solved them.

Other books you might like:
Laura Klepacki, *Avon, Building The World's Premier Company For Women*, 2006
Bridget Brennan, *Why She Buys: The New Strategy for Reaching the World's Most Poserful Consumers*, 2009

357

ROBERT B. CIALDINI

Influence: The Psychology of Persuasion, 2nd Edition
(New York: Harper Paperbacks, 2006)

Story type: Psychological
Subject(s): Psychology; Human behavior; Human psychological experimentation

Summary: After researching the subject of persuasion for more than 35 years, Dr. Robert B. Cialdini shares what he's discovered in *Influence: The Psychology of Persuasion*. In this book, Cialdini explains why, in his opinion, people are more agreeable in specific situations than they are in others. He proposes that certain aspects of a person's surroundings may make him or her more vulnerable or easily influenced than if those features weren't present. This book offers information as to why some people are more easily persuaded than others are, regardless of the circumstance or the environment. Cialdini also uses findings from a three-year study on persuasion to support his claims.

Other books by the same author:
Yes!: 50 Scientifically Proven Ways to Be Persuasive, 2008

Other books you might like:
Dan Ariely, *Predictably Irrational, Revised and Expanded Edition: The Hidden Forces That Shape Our Decisions*, 2010
Kevin Hogan, *Covert Persuasion: Psychological Tactics and Tricks to Win the Game*, 2006
Marvin Karlins, *What Every BODY is Saying: An Ex-FBI Agent's Guide to Speed-Reading People*, 2008
Joe Navarro, co-author

358

GEORGE CLOUTIER

Profits Aren't Everything, They're the Only Thing: No-Nonsense Rules from the Ultimate Contrarian and Small Business Guru
(New York: HarperBusiness, 2009)

Subject(s): Business; Finance; Success

Summary: In *Profits Aren't Everything, They're the Only Thing: No-Nonsense Rules from the Ultimate Contrarian and Small Business Guru*, George Cloutier offers specific advice for surviving economic downturns and making profits in business. In the book Cloutier states that if a business fails, it is the fault of the business owner, not the economy. Cloutier has 15 Profit Rules that he follows for success in business. These rules emphasize the importance of the business owner rather than the importance of teamwork, and they focus on profits above all else. The author believes in micromanagement and strict rules-based workplaces, arguing these business ideas will lead to greater profits.

Where it's reviewed:
Publishers Weekly, June 22, 2009, page 38

Other books you might like:
Scott Fox, *E-Riches 2.0: Next-Generation Marketing Strategies for Making Millions Online*, 2009
Liam Scanlan, *Web Traffic Magnet: 55 Free Things You Can Do to Drive Traffic to Your Website*, 2008

Lauren Weisberger, *Last Night at Chateau Marmont*, 2010

359

WILLIAM D. COHAN

House of Cards: A Tale of Hubris and Wretched Excess on Wall Street
(New York: Doubleday Publishing, 2009)

Subject(s): Finance; Economic depressions; Economics

Summary: *House of Cards: A Tale of Hubris and Wretched Excess on Wall Street* is an investigation into the 2008-2009 decline of the United States stock market. Written by William Cohen, recipient of the 2007 FT/Goldman Sachs Business Book of the Year Award, this narrative offers an explanation as to what happened to the American economy following the Bear Stearns financial collapse. Most Americans were only able to watch news anchors make prophetic claims that another depression was on its way, but nobody understood why. Cohen traces the roots of the recession back to its start and attempts to explain exactly what happened in a way that can be easily digested.

Other books by the same author:
The Last Tycoons: The Secret History of Lazard Freres & Co., 2007

Other books you might like:
Michael Lewis, *The Big Short: Inside the Doomsday Machine*, 2010
Lawrence G. McDonald, *A Colossal Failure of Common Sense: The Inside Story of the Collapse of Lehman Brothers*, 2009
Patrick Robinson, co-author
Andrew Ross Sorkin, *Too Big to Fail: The Inside Story of How Wall Street and Washington Fought to Save the Financial System from Crisis—and Lost*, 2009

360

CHRISTINE COMAFORD-LYNCH

Rules for Renegades: How to Make More Money, Rock Your Career, and Revel in Your Individuality
(New York: McGraw-Hill, 2007)

Subject(s): Business; Entrepreneurship; Humor

Summary: Multimillionaire Comaford-Lynch has established five companies, served as a board member or advisor for more than 30 start-up companies, and invested in multiple companies, yet never finished high school. She has made and lost millions of dollars and in this book provides advice on how anyone can start a company and become a millionaire. Comaford-Lynch provides step-by-step advice for starting a business and reaching your financial goals quickly. She emphasizes the importance of a business plan, visualization, and self-confidence. She also shares often hilarious anecdotes of her own ups and downs on the road to riches, from hiring a staff before she had a company to working as a Buddhist monk.

Other books you might like:

Chip Conley, *Peak: How Great Companies Get Their Mojo from Maslow*, 2007

Chris Guillebeau, *The Art of Non-Conformity: Set Your Own Rules, Live the Life You Want, and Change the World*, 2010

Chet Holmes, *The Ultimate Sales Machine: Turbocharge Your Business with Relentless Focus on 12 Key Strategies*, 2007

361

STEPHEN M.R. COVEY
REBECCA MERRILL, Co-Author

Speed of Trust: The One Thing That Changes Everything
(New York: Free Press, 2006)

Subject(s): Trust (Psychology); Business; Interpersonal relations

Summary: In *Speed of Trust: The One Thing That Changes Everything*, author Stephen Covey proposes that trust can be a teachable, quantifiable force in the world of commerce. Companies can utilize trust to foster solid relationships with clients and colleagues. Citing anecdotal evidence from his own experience and from various business and government leaders, Covey instructs the reader in ways to create consistent abundance and success in any area of life. The author argues that trust is contagious, spreading out into interpersonal relations and across the entire world. The author describes the processes of engendering and showing respect, repairing lost integrity, and opening new doors.

Other books you might like:

John P. Kotter, *Buy-In: Saving Your Good Idea from Getting Shot Down*, 2010

Dennis S. Reina, *Rebuilding Trust in the Workplace: Seven Steps to Renew Confidence, Commitment, and Energy*, 2010

Cynthia L. Wall, *The Courage To Trust: A Guide To Building Deep And Lasting*, 2005

362

JAMES CRAMER

Jim Cramer's Real Money: Sane Investing in an Insane World
(New York: Simon & Schuster, 2005)

Subject(s): Finance; Money

Summary: Jim Cramer, founder of a daily financial news Web site, co-host of *Kudlow & Cramer*, and experienced trader, explains his investment strategy in simple terms. Arguing that anyone who is willing to put time into learning about investing can do it, Cramer advises that

investors devote at least an hour a week to learning about the stocks they own. He suggests starting with four stocks in diverse sectors and purchasing a fifth stock in a speculative sector. Cramer also outlines his "Ten Commandments of Trading" and "Twenty-Five Rules of Investing."

Other books by the same author:

Jim Cramer's Getting Back to Even, 2009

Jim Cramer's Stay Mad for Life: Get Rich, Stay Rich (Make Your Kids Even Richer), 2007

Jim Cramer's Mad Money: Watch TV, Get Rich, 2006

Other books you might like:

Liz Claman, *The Best Investment Advice I Ever Received: Priceless Wisdom from Warren Buffett, Jim Cramer, Suze Orman, Steve Forbes, and Dozens of Other Top Financial Experts*, 2006

Matt Krantz, *Fundamental Analysis For Dummies*, 2009

James Turk, *The Collapse of the Dollar and How to Profit from It: Make a Fortune by Investing in Gold and Other Hard Assets*, 2008

363

LORI CULWELL

Million Dollar Website: Simple Steps to Help You Compete with the Big Boys - Even on a Small Business Budget
(New York: Prentice Hall Press, 2009)

Subject(s): Internet; Business; Marketing

Summary: For those unfamiliar with web design, the prospect of setting up a website solo may seem like a daunting—and at times terrifying—task. In *Million Dollar Website: Simple Steps to Help You Compete with the Big Boys - Even on a Small Business Budget*, esteemed website consultant Lori Culwell leads small business owners and entrepreneurs through the website-building process. Utilizing her years of experience and a wealth of practical tips, the author explains the critical elements that make a website succeed or fail. Accompanied by an index, *Million Dollar Website* covers such subjects as graphic design fundamentals, the details of search engine optimization, and the importance of blogging.

Where it's reviewed:

Library Journal, June 15, 2009, page 82

Other books by the same author:

Hollywood Car Wash: A Novel, 2009

Other books you might like:

Scott Fox, *E-Riches 2.0: Next-Generation Marketing Strategies for Making Millions Online*, 2009

Liam Scanlan, *Web Traffic Magnet: 55 Free Things You Can Do to Drive Traffic to Your Website*, 2008

Lauren Weisberger, *Last Night at Chateau Marmont*, 2010

364

BOB DENEEN

Betterness In Business: Entrepreneurial Success Guide
(Charleston, South Carolina: BookSurge Publishing, 2010)

Subject(s): Business; Entrepreneurship; Economics

Summary: In *Betterness In Business: Entrepreneurial Success Guide* author Bob Deneen give entrepreneurs insight into developing a successful, profitable business. In the book, the author states that every business owner should follow five particular rules in order to succeed. These rules include long-term planning and making the business more attractive to customers. Deneen suggests that companies achieve these goals by working continuously and identifying areas of success and areas of failure. The book also instructs business owners to look everywhere for new opportunities and to make constant improvements to the business and the products.

Other books by the same author:
Betterness At Investing: The Art of Creating Wealth, 2010
Betterness In Life: Achieve Peak Performance, 2008
Superior Business Performance, 2005

Other books you might like:
Jason Fried, *Rework*, 2010
Brian Halligan, *Inbound Marketing: Get Found Using Google, Social Media, and Blogs*, 2009
David Heinemeier Hansson, *Rework*, 2010
David Meerman Scott, *The New Rules of Marketing and PR: How to Use News Releases, Blogs, Podcasting, Viral Marketing and Online Media to Reach Buyers Directly*, 2007

365

BRYAN EISENBERG
JEFFREY EISENBERG , Co-Author

Call to Action: Secret Formulas to Improve Online Results
(Nashville: Thomas Nelson, 2005)

Subject(s): Commerce; Computers; Internet

Summary: The focus of this book is Internet commerce: how to transform visitors to web sites into actual paying customers. This process is called "conversion" by the authors, Bryan and Jeffrey Eisenberg. Many businesses spend a great deal of time and money trying to get more people to see their web sites. The Eisenbergs argue that simply increasing hits to a web site is useless unless the web site is actually good at persuading viewers to become clients, customers, or members. They give simple steps for increasing a web site's conversion rate, discussing how color, sound, graphics, and text all influence visitors. They describe the principles of persuasion architecture, which is their formula for success at Internet sales.

Other books by the same author:
Always Be Testing: The Complete Guide to Google Website Optimizer, 2008

Waiting for Your Cat to Bark?: Persuading Customers When They Ignore Marketing, 2006

Other books you might like:
Tim Ash, *Landing Page Optimization: The Definitive Guide to Testing and Tuning for Conversions*, 208
Steve Krug, *Don't Make Me Think: A Common Sense Approach to Web Usability, 2nd Editiion*, 2005

366

STEFAN ENGESETH

The Fall of PR & the Rise of Advertising
(Engeseth Publishing, 2009)

Subject(s): Marketing; Advertising; Public relations

Summary: Stefan Engeseth's *The Fall of PR & the Rise of Advertising* was written in response to Al Ries' best-selling *The Fall of Advertising & the Rise of PR*. In 2004, Ries claimed that advertising was no longer doing its job and that it wasn't adapting to what the rest of the world needed. His book shocked and angered advertising agencies everywhere. Ries claimed that public relations was "in" and advertising was no longer needed. Five years after Ries made these claims, Engeseth produced *The Fall of PR & the Rise of Advertising*. In this book, Engeseth shows how advertising is back and better than ever. This time around, PR is the approach that is on its way "out."

Other books by the same author:
ONE: A Consumer Revolution for Business, 2005

Other books you might like:
Chris Brogan, *Trust Agents: Using the Web to Build Influence, Improve Reputation, and Earn Trust*, 2009
David Meerman Scott, *The New Rules of Marketing and PR: How to Use News Releases, Blogs, Podcasting, Viral Marketing and Online Media to Reach Buyers Directly*, 2007
Julien Smith, *Trust Agents: Using the Web to Build Influence, Improve Reputation, and Earn Trust*, 2009
Scott Stratten, *UnMarketing: Stop Marketing. Start Engaging.*, 2010

367

DONNA FENN

Upstarts!: How GenY Entrepreneurs are Rocking the World of Business and 8 Ways You Can Profit from Their Success
(New York: McGraw-Hill, 2009)

Subject(s): Business; Entrepreneurship; Marketing

Summary: In *Upstarts!: How GenY Entrepreneurs are Rocking the World of Business and 8 Ways You Can Profit from Their Success*, author In *Upstarts!: How GenY Entrepreneurs are Rocking the World of Business and 8 Ways You Can Profit from Their Success*, author

Donna Fenn examines the growing phenomenon of Generation Y business owners, and how their success in business has created opportunities for others. Fenn spoke to more than 150 CEOs, all of whom belong to the generation born in the 1980s and 1990s. Those CEOs provided valuable insight into how their observations and inspirations from previous generations have led to their success. Fenn takes that insight and transforms it into key strategies to help any entrepreneur to create a successful business, regardless of their birth date. Fenn is also the author of *Alpha Dogs: How Your Small Business Can Become a Leader of the Pack.*

Other books by the same author:
Alpha Dogs: How Your Small Business Can become a Leader of the Pack, 2005

Other books you might like:
Norm Brodsky, *The Knack: How Street-Smart Entrepreneurs Learn to Handle Whatever Comes Up,* 2008
    Bo Burlingham, co-author
Jason Fried, *Rework,* 2010
    David Heinemeier Hansson, co-author
Mike Michalowicz, *The Toilet Paper Entrepreneur: The tell-it-like-it-is guide to cleaning up in business, even if you are at the end of your roll,* 2008

368

DONNA FENN

Alpha Dogs: How Your Small Business Can Become a Leader of the Pack

(New York: Collins, 2005)

Subject(s): Business; Entrepreneurship; Small business

Summary: *Alpha Dogs: How Your Small Business Can Become a Leader of the Pack* is a practical resource guide for entrepreneurs from author and *Inc.* magazine contributing editor, Donna Fenn. Filled with helpful tips and sage insight, *Alpha Dogs* equips small business owners with the knowledge they need to help their business stand apart from the competition. Fenn profiles eight accomplished entrepreneurs who've made their businesses, ranging from a retail bike shop to an auction house, into major success stories. Each interviewee shares useful advice and practical lessons he or she has learned along the way.

Where it's reviewed:
Publishers Weekly, November 7, 2005, page 69

Other books by the same author:
Upstarts!: How GenY Entrepreneurs are Rocking the World of Business and 8 Ways You Can Profit from Their Success, 2009

Other books you might like:
Robert Spector, *The Mom and Pop Store: How the Unsung Heroes of the American Economy Are Surviving and Thriving,* 2009

369

TIMOTHY FERRISS

The 4-Hour Workweek, Expanded and Updated: Escape 9-5, Live Anywhere, and Join the New Rich

(New York: Crown Publishers, 2009)

Subject(s): Business enterprises; Self help books; Self awareness

Summary: In *The 4-Hour Workweek, Expanded and Updated: Escape 9-5, Live Anywhere, and Join the New Rich,* author, entrepreneur, and world traveler Timothy Ferriss offers readers a detailed road map to living the good life. Packed with practical information, sensible advice, and a trove of insider's tips, this volume shows how anyone can achieve a fulfilling, affluent lifestyle with a bare minimum of toil and trouble. Expanded and updated with new information regarding uneasy economic times and how best to succeed in such a climate, *The 4-Hour Workweek* is a guide to anyone seeking a way out of the 9-5 hamster wheel. First book.

Other books by the same author:
The 4-Hour Body: An Uncommon Guide to Rapid Fat-Loss, Incredible Sex, and Becoming Superhuman, 2010

Other books you might like:
Chris Guillebeau, *The Art of Non-Conformity: Set Your Own Rules, Live the Life You Want, and Change the World,* 2010
David Lindahl, *The Six-Figure Second Income: How To Start and Grow A Successful Online Business Without Quitting Your Day Job,* 2010
Gary Vaynerchuk, *Crush It!: Why NOW Is the Time to Cash In on Your Passion,* 2009

370

JONATHAN FIELDS

Career Renegade: How to Make a Great Living Doing What You Love

(New York: Broadway Books, 2009)

Subject(s): Success; Business enterprises; Employment

Summary: Attorney and entrepreneur Jonathan Fields offers readers a roadmap to finding the job of their dreams. In *Career Renegade: How to Make a Great Living Doing What You Love,* Fields utilizes practical advice and interactive exercises to inspire workers to uncover their vocational passion. He then instructs them on how to use this newfound passion to go into business for themselves, outlining the steps of building a new business and achieving financial success. *Career renegade* includes real-life examples and an appendix. First book.

Other books you might like:
Timothy Ferriss, *The 4-Hour Workweek, Expanded and*

Updated: Escape 9-5, Live Anywhere, and Join the New Rich, 2009

Chris Guillebeau, *The Art of Non-Conformity: Set Your Own Rules, Live the Life You Want, and Change the World*, 2010

Pamela Slim, *Escape From Cubicle Nation: From Corporate Prisoner to Thriving Entrepreneur*, 2009

371

STEPHEN FRIED

Appetite for America: How Visionary Businessman Fred Harvey Built a Railroad Hospitality Empire That Civilized the Wild West

(New York: Bantam, 2010)

Subject(s): Business enterprises; United States history; Restaurants

Summary: Though often overlooked today, Fred Harvey was a prominent figure in 19th century America. In the years following the Civil War, the railroads were expanding across the country, and Harvey — an English-born businessman — saw an opportunity to build a flourishing enterprise. In *Appetite for America: How Visionary Businessman Fred Harvey Built a Railroad Hospitality Empire That Civilized the Wild West*, journalist Stephen Fried chronicles Harvey's extraordinary journey from fledgling entrepreneur to the man who first created chain restaurants and hotels. Fried explores Harvey's personal and professional lives and the legacy he has left on American business.

Other books by the same author:
Husbandry: Sex, Love & Dirty Laundry—Inside the Minds of Married Men, 2007

Other books you might like:
George H. Foster, *The Harvey House Cookbook, 2nd Edition: Memories of Dining Along the Santa Fe Railway*, 2006

Paul Nickens, *Touring the West: With the Fred Harvey Co. & the Santa Fe Railway*, 2008

Joe Welsh, *The Cars of Pullman*, 2010

372

THOMAS L. FRIEDMAN

The World Is Flat: Further Updated and Expanded, Release 3.0: A Brief History of the Twenty-first Century

(New York: Farrar, Straus, and Giroux, 2007)

Subject(s): Modern Life; Business; Technology

Summary: *The World Is Flat: Further Updated and Expanded, Release 3.0: A Brief History of the Twenty-first Century* is a comprehensive examination of globalization from Pulitzer Prize-winning author Thomas L. Friedman. The book analyzes the "flattening" of the world, due to the connectedness of individuals and corporations around the globe and technological advancements that make it possible for instantaneous business transactions and social interaction with billions of individuals. Friedman sheds light on what globalization means for individuals, including an examination of the empowering opportunities it creates and its many environmental, social, and political drawbacks. This revised and updated version includes two new chapters that cover political activism, social entrepreneurship, and privacy issues.

Other books by the same author:
Hot Flat and Crowded- Why We Need a Green Revolution, 2008

Hot, Flat, and Crowded: Why We Need a Green Revolution—and How It Can Renew America, 2008

Other books you might like:
W. Chan Kim, *Blue Ocean Strategy: How to Create Uncontested Market Space and Make Competition Irrelevant*, 2005
  Renee Mauborgne, co-author

Joseph E. Stiglitz, *Making Globalization Work*, 2006

Fareed Zakaria, *The Post-American World*, 2008

373

NEAL GABLER

Walt Disney: The Triumph of the American Imagination

(New York: Knopf, 2006)

Subject(s): Movie industry; Cartoons; Biographies

Summary: Author Neal Gabler is the first biographer of Walt Disney to be granted access to the entire Disney archives, and he used this extensive research to create a full and detailed picture of one of the most influential makers of motion pictures of the 20th century. In *Walt Disney: The Triumph of the American Imagination,* he reveals little-known truths about the man that might come as a surprise to readers, such as his financial difficulties and the years he spent battling depression. Through it all, Disney emerges as a determined man with the highest regard for quality.

Other books you might like:
Michael Barrier, *The Animated Man: A Life of Walt Disney*, 2007

Chad Denver Emerson, *Project Future: The Inside Story Behind the Creation of Disney World*, 2010

James B. Stewart, *DisneyWar*, 2005

374

DAVID SITEMAN GARLAND

Smarter, Faster, Cheaper: Non-Boring, Fluff-Free Strategies for Marketing and Promoting Your Business

(Hoboken, New Jersey: Wiley, 2010)

Subject(s): Business enterprises; Marketing; Entrepreneurship

Summary: When starting one's own business, aspiring entrepreneurs are typically faced with massive overhead costs. In *Smarter, Faster, Cheaper: Non-Boring, Fluff-Free Strategies for Marketing and Promoting Your Business*, start-up business expert David Siteman Garland helps new business owners promote their products or services on a beginner's budget. Garland offers no-nonsense, straightforward, and oftentimes witty advice on how to build clientele, evade common lethal sales tactics, utilize the internet and social media platforms, and much more. First book.

Other books you might like:

Scott Gerber, *Never Get a "Real" Job: How to Dump Your Boss, Build a Business and Not Go Broke*, 2010
Ann Handley, *Content Rules: How to Create Killer Blogs, Podcasts, Videos, Ebooks, Webinars (and More) That Engage Customers and Ignite Your Business*, 2010
Scott Stratten, *UnMarketing: Stop Marketing. Start Engaging.*, 2010

375

CHARLES GASPARINO

Blood on the Street: The Sensational Inside Story of How Wall Street Analysts Duped a Generation of Investors

(New York: Free Press, 2005)

Subject(s): Business; Scandals; Finance

Summary: *Blood on the Street: The Sensational Inside Story of How Wall Street Analysts Duped a Generation of Investors* is an in-depth examination of a Wall Street scam from Pulitzer Prize-nominated author and journalist Charles Gasparino. In *Blood on the Street*, Gasparino, the man who broke the story for the *Wall Street Journal*, takes readers behind the scenes of the scam that costs investors billions of dollars, with never-before-published depositions and documents and e-mail exchanges between Wall Street bigwigs, to recount how the scandal began in the 1990s and the investigative reporting that ultimately brought it to light. Gasparino includes profiles of three key players: Salomon Smith Barney's Jack Grubman, Merrill Lynch's Henry Blodget, and Morgan

Stanley's Mary Meeker. The author also provides a detailed account of New York State attorney general Eliot Spitzer's role in the investigation.

Other books by the same author:

Bought and Paid For: The Unholy Alliance Between Barack Obama and Wall Street, 2010
The Sellout: How Three Decades of Wall Street Greed and Government Mismanagement Destroyed the Global Financial System, 2009
King of the Club: Richard Grasso and the Survival of the New York Stock Exchange, 2007

Other books you might like:

Michael Lewis, *The Big Short: Inside the Doomsday Machine*, 2010
Daniel Reingold, *Confessions of a Wall Street Analyst: A True Story of Inside Information and Corruption in the Stock Market*, 2006
Brian P. Simpson, *Markets Don't Fail!*, 2005

376

SCOTT GERBER

Never Get a "Real" Job: How to Dump Your Boss, Build a Business and Not Go Broke

(Hoboken, New Jersey: Wiley, 2010)

Subject(s): Business; Entrepreneurship; Business enterprises

Summary: *Never Get a "Real" Job: How to Dump Your Boss, Build a Business and Not Go Broke* is a straightforward and practical advice guide for aspiring entrepreneurs from author Scott Gerber. The book provides useful and candid tips about how to successfully turn ideas into a thriving business while avoiding common mistakes and pitfalls made by new business owners. Drawing from his own entrepreneurial experience, Gerber offers honest advice about building a business from the ground up, finding and cultivating contacts, staying focused on the right things, managing time, and focusing business offerings. In addition to step-by-step instruction and sage advice, *Never Get a "Real" Job* provides readers with an assortment of resources including helpful websites, online tools, and checklists.

Other books you might like:

Timothy Ferriss, *The 4-Hour Workweek, Expanded and Updated: Escape 9-5, Live Anywhere, and Join the New Rich*, 2009
David Siteman Garland, *Smarter, Faster, Cheaper: Non-Boring, Fluff-Free Strategies for Marketing and Promoting Your Business*, 2010
Chris Guillebeau, *The Art of Non-Conformity: Set Your Own Rules, Live the Life You Want, and Change the World*, 2010

377

BILL GLAZER

Outrageous Advertising That's Outrageously Successful: Created for the 99% of Small Business Owners Who Are Dissatisfied with the Results They Get from Their Current Advertising

(Garden City, New York: Morgan James Publishing, 2009)

Subject(s): Marketing; Advertising; Business

Summary: In *Outrageous Advertising That's Outrageously Successful: Created for the 99% of Small Business Owners Who Are Dissatisfied with the Results They Get from Their Current Advertising*, author Bill Glazer provides small business entrepreneurs with advice and insight on launching creative marketing campaigns. Glazer uses his own experience as a business owner to examine how outrageous advertising brings small businesses into the spotlight and helps them reach their bottom line. Glazer is also the author of *The Official Get Rich Guide to Information Marketing*.

Other books you might like:

Dan Kennedy, *No B.S. Marketing to the Affluent: The No Holds Barred, Kick Butt, Take No Prisoners Guide to Getting Really Rich*, 2008

Dan S. Kennedy, *The Ultimate Marketing Plan: Find Your Hook. Communicate Your Message. Make Your Mark.*, 2006

Dan S. Kennedy, *The Ultimate Sales Letter: Attract New Customers. Boost Your Sales*, 2006

378

SETH GODIN

Tribes: We Need You to Lead Us

(New York: Portfolio, 2008)

Subject(s): Management; Tribalism; Internet

Summary: Tracing the phenomenon of tribalism to the earliest human civilizations, author Seth Godin presents a thought-provoking study on the modern manifestation of the tribe in *Tribes: We Need You to Lead Us*. Defining a tribe as a group of people of any size associated with a leader and a concept, Godin asserts that the social groups formed on Internet sites qualify as tribes, whether they are based on religious, political, economic, or cultural interests. In that vein, Godin discusses the opportunities for leadership presented by online "tribes" for those dedicated to an idea, interest, or cause. From the Deadheads to Facebook to the Obama campaign, Godin cites examples of contemporary tribes promoting action and leadership.

Other books by the same author:

Meatball Sundae: Is Your Marketing out of Sync?, 2007

Other books you might like:

Chris Brogan, *Trust Agents: Using the Web to Build Influence, Improve Reputation, and Earn Trust*, 2009

Chip Heath, *Made to Stick: Why Some Ideas Survive and Others Die*, 2007

Dan Heath, co-author

Tony Hsieh, *Delivering Happiness: A Path to Profits, Passion, and Purpose*, 2010

Julien Smith, *Trust Agents: Using the Web to Build Influence, Improve Reputation, and Earn Trust*, 2009

379

MARSHALL GOLDSMITH
MARK REITER , Co-Author

What Got You Here Won't Get You There: How Successful People Become Even More Successful

(New York: Hyperion, 2007)

Subject(s): Business; Business Building; Careers

Summary: In *What Got You Here Won't Get You There: How Successful People Become Even More Successful*, executive coach Marshall Goldsmith tells readers how to identify and recover from twenty bad habits that can stop a successful career in its tracks. He also gives tips on how those things can transfer to personal relationships and parenting.

Other books by the same author:

Mojo: How to Get It, How to Keep It, How to Get It Back if You Lose It, 2010

Best Practices in Talent Management: How the World's Leading Corporations Manage, Develop, and Retain Top Talent, 2009

The Final Four of Everything, 2009

The Organization of the Future 2: Visions, Strategies, and Insights on Managing in a New Era, 2009

Succession: Are You Ready? (Memo to the Ceo), 2009

The Enlightened Bracketologist: The Final Four of Everything, 2007

The Leader of the Future 2: Visions, Strategies, and Practices for the New Era, 2006

Other books you might like:

Marshall Goldsmith, *Mojo: How to Get It, How to Keep It, How to Get It Back If You Lose It*, 2003

Joseph Grenny, *Influencer: The Power to Change Anything*, 2007

Chip Heath, *Switch: How to Change Things When Change Is Hard*, 2010

Dan Heath, co-author

Kerry Patterson, *Influencer: The Power to Change Anything*, 2007

380

STEVE GOTTRY

Common Sense Business: Starting, Operating, and Growing Your Small Business—In Any Economy!

(New York: Collins, 2005)

Subject(s): Business; Entrepreneurship; Finance

Summary: In *Common Sense Business: Starting, Operating, and Growing Your Small Business—In Any Economy!* Steve Gottry provides a host of practical advice for successfully starting and running a small business, drawing on his own experiences for material. Gottry's own advertising agency failed after 22 years of success, but he chose to pay off his debts over the next decade rather than declare bankruptcy. In the book, he uses the experiences he had during this challenging time to offer advice to others. Gottry states that each business has a six-stage life cycle and that understanding and working with this life cycle can help to ensure that the business stays afloat.

Where it's reviewed:
Library Journal, July 1, 2005, page 95

Other books you might like:
Paul Hawken, *Growing a Business*, 1988
Jason Fried, *Rework*, 2010

381

RUSSELL GRANGER

The 7 Triggers to Yes: The New Science Behind Influencing People's Decisions

(New York: McGraw-Hill, 2007)

Subject(s): Business; Neurosciences; Self help books

Summary: *The 7 Triggers to Yes: The New Science Behind Influencing People's Decisions* is a helpful guide on mastering the power of persuasion from author Russell Granger. Relying on recent studies in neuroscience, Granger provides readers with seven effective ways to persuade others. New research indicates that a majority of individuals react to emotional responses instead of rational ones. Granger teaches readers to utilize seven key emotional triggers to influence and persuade friends, family, coworkers, employees, and others to get positive results and the answers they want. *The 7 Triggers to Yes* provides readers with a history on persuasion, up-to-date information on scientific and neurological studies and tests, and practical advice for influencing others.

Other books you might like:
Martin Lindstrom, *Buyology: Truth and Lies About Why We Buy*, 2008
Richard Maxwell, *The Elements of Persuasion: Use Storytelling to Pitch Better, Sell Faster & Win More Business*, 2007
Christophe Morin, *Neuromarketing: Understanding the Buy Buttons in Your Customer's Brain*, 2007
Patrick Renvoise, co-author

382

BRUCE C. N. GREENWALD
JUDD KAHN , Co-Author

Competition Demystified: A Radically Simplified Approach to Business Strategy

(New York: Portfolio, 2005)

Subject(s): Business; Business enterprises; Management

Summary: *Competition Demystified: A Radically Simplified Approach to Business Strategy*, by Bruce Greenwald and Judd Kahn, focuses on "potential entrants," one of the principles outlined by author Michael Porter in his classic book *Competitive Strategy*. Filled with suggestions about running a successful business, the authors argue that slashing prices and taking over a single market are advantageous moves. The authors tailor their advice mostly to investors, suggesting that they pinpoint small or local markets that are declining and don't already have entrenched competitors. The authors also debunk the stereotype that conflict and competition are good for business.

Other books by the same author:
Globalization: n. the irrational fear that someone in China will take your job, 2008

Other books you might like:
Michael E. Porter, *Competitive Strategy: Techniques for Analyzing Industries and Competitors*, 1998
Peter Lynch, *One Up On Wall Street: How To Use What You Already Know To Make Money In The Market*, 2000

383

ANDREW GRIFFITHS

Bulletproof Your Business Now

(Crows Nest, New South Wales, Australia: Allen & Unwin, 2010)

Subject(s): Business; Economics; Success

Summary: In *Bulletproof Your Business Now*, author Andrew Griffiths provides 40 ideas for surviving downturns in business. Griffiths advises small business owners to think outside the box when making business decisions and to maintain a fulfilling life outside the office. Having a rewarding personal life is important because businesses have no guarantees and if a business fails, owners and workers will need strong personal relationships to fall back on. Griffiths even states that when businesses fail, entrepreneurs can learn a great deal from their mistakes and can succeed in the future after learning from those mistakes. The book also includes advice about marketing effectively, developing a loyal customer base, making effective decisions, and recognizing potential problems before they become unmanageable.

Where it's reviewed:
Publishers Weekly, May 31, 2010, page 39

Other books by the same author:
*101 Ways to Build a Successful Network Marketing
   Business*, 2010
Me Myth: What do you mean it's not all about me?,
   2009
101 Secrets to Building a Winning Business, 2008
*101 Ways to Market Your Business: Building a
   Successful Business with Creative Marketing*, 2007
*Organizational Change for Corporate Sustainability: A
   Guide for Leaders and Change Agents of the Future
   (Understanding Organizational Change)*, 2007

Other books you might like:
David Meerman Scott, *The New Rules of Marketing and
   PR: How to Use News Releases, Blogs, Podcasting,
   Viral Marketing and Online Media to Reach Buyers
   Directly*, 2007
Andy Sernovitz, *Word of Mouth Marketing: How Smart
   Companies Get People Talking, Revised Edition*,
   2009
Gary Vaynerchuk, *Crush It!: Why NOW Is the Time to
   Cash In on Your Passion*, 2009

384

TIM HARFORD

The Undercover Economist: Exposing Why the Rich Are Rich, the Poor Are Poor—And Why You Can Never Buy a Decent Used Car!

(New York: Oxford University Press, 2006)

Subject(s): Economics; Poverty; Money

Summary: Tim Harford's *The Undercover Economist:
Exposing Why the Rich are Rich, the Poor are Poor—
And Why You Can Never Buy a Decent Used Car!*
explores the world of microeconomics. Using recent
phenomena, such as the price of a coffee at Starbucks
and the cost of rent in London, Harford applies theories
of the past and present to explain the pricing systems
used by today's businesses and corporations. The author
uses other amusing, real world examples to address
methods currently used by government officials, politicians, supermarket owners, and farmers.

Other books by the same author:
*Dear Undercover Economist: Priceless Advice on
   Money, Work, Sex, Kids, and Life's Other
   Challenges*, 2009
*The Logic of Life: The Rational Economics of an
   Irrational World*, 2008

Other books you might like:
Andrew Bernstein, *The Capitalist Manifesto: The
   Historic, Economic and Philosophic Case for
   Laissez-Faire*, 2005
Stephen J. Dubner, *Freakonomics: A Rogue Economist
   Explores the Hidden Side of Everything*, 2005
   Steven D. Levitt, co-author

Charles Wheelan, *Naked Economics: Undressing the
   Dismal Science*, 2010

385

VERNE HARNISH

Mastering the Rockefeller Habits: What You Must Do to Increase the Value of Your Growing Firm

(New York: SelectBooks, 2002)

Subject(s): Business; Entrepreneurship; Success

Summary: Written by business and entrepreneurial expert
Verne Harnish, *Mastering the Rockefeller Habits: What
You Must Do to Increase the Value of Your Growing
Firm* is a collection of secrets to success based on John
D. Rockefeller's personal business philosophy and
strategy. Harnish shares entrepreneurial tips and tactics
for business owners eager for growth and success. *Mastering the Rockefeller Habits* is divided into three sections: Priorities, Data, and Rhythm. Harnish helps readers prioritize their companies' goals and core values,
learn to compile and understand important short-term
and long-term business metrics, make smart and healthy
decisions, find ample financing, and keep employees
accountable.

Other books you might like:
Bradford D. Smart, *Topgrading: How Leading
   Companies Win by Hiring, Coaching, and Keeping
   the Best People, Revised and Updated Edition*, 2005
Geoff Smart, *Who: The A Method for Hiring*, 2008
   Randy Street, co-author
John Warrillow, *Built to Sell: Turn Your Business Into
   One You Can Sell*, 2010

386

MIKE HARRIS

Find Your Lightbulb: How to Make Millions from Apparently Impossible Ideas

(Chichester, United Kingdom: Capstone, 2008)

Subject(s): Entrepreneurship; Inventions; Wealth

Summary: In *Find Your Lightbulb: How to Make Millions
from Apparently Impossible Ideas*, Mike Harris offers
advice for individuals who have great ideas for businesses but aren't quite sure how to get started. Harris
argues that it is not necessary to be a genius to start and
maintain a successful business—even if the idea for the
business seems nearly impossible. The author argues that
the ingredients necessary for success in business include
enthusiasm for the business idea and the ability to pass
along that enthusiasm to others. Harris provides specific
tips and examples from his own experiences as well as
the experiences of the people with whom he's worked.

Other books you might like:
Felix Dennis, *How to Get Rich: One of the World's
   Greatest Entrepreneurs Shares His Secrets*, 2008
Timothy Ferriss, *The 4-Hour Workweek, Expanded and

Updated: Escape 9-5, Live Anywhere, and Join the New Rich, 2009

Brian Halligan, *Inbound Marketing: Get Found Using Google, Social Media, and Blogs*, 2009

387

MELANIE HAWKS

Life-Work Balance

(Chicago, Illinois: Association of College and Research Libraries, 2008)

Subject(s): Business; Management; Work environment

Summary: Author Melanie Hawks provides readers a collection of practical tools to help find that all-important balance between life and work. This volume contains information on how to evaluate one's current level of balance and how to adjust it for maximum comfort and enjoyment. The exercises in *Life-Work Balance* encourage new ways of thinking and approaching situations, inspiring readers to take charge of their work and personal lives on a whole new level. By following Hawks's action plan, one will begin to see a clearer way to one's goals—and how to hold a sense of equanimity on the journey.

Other books by the same author:
Influencing Without Authority, 2009

Other books you might like:
John M. Budd, *The Changing Academic Library: Operations, Culture, Environments*, 2005
Bryan Dodge, *The Good Life Rules: 8 Keys to Being Your Best as Work and at Play*, 2008
Andrea Molloy, *Stop Living Your Job, Start Living Your Life: 85 Simple Strategies to Achieve Work/Life Balance*, 2005

388

RICHARD T. HERMAN
ROBERT L. SMITH , Co-Author

Immigrant, Inc.: Why Immigrant Entrepreneurs Are Driving the New Economy (and how they will save the American worker)

(Hoboken, New Jersey: John Wiley & Sons, 2009)

Subject(s): Immigrants; Economics; Business

Summary: In *Immigrant, Inc.: Why Immigrant Entrepreneurs Are Driving the New Economy (and how they will save the American worker)*, authors Richard T. Herman and Robert L. Smith describe how, in their view, immigrant business owners will be the saving grace of the American economy. The authors look at characteristics of immigrant culture that lead to success in the business world, including work ethic, responsibility to family and community, and the drive for accomplishment. Herman is an immigration attorney based in Cleveland, Ohio;

Smith is a reporter for Cleveland's *Plain Dealer*. First book.

Other books you might like:
Andrew Bernstein, *Capitalism Unbound: The Incontestable Moral Case for Individual Rights*, 2010
Steven V. Roberts, *From Every End of This Earth: 13 Families and the New Lives They Made in America*, 2009
Darrell M. West, *Brain Gain: Rethinking U.S. Immigration Policy*, 2010

389

TONY HSIEH

Delivering Happiness: A Path to Profits, Passion, and Purpose

(New York: Business Plus, 2010)

Subject(s): Business; Management; Entrepreneurship

Summary: In *Delivering Happiness: A Path to Profits, Passion, and Purpose*, Tony Hsieh, the CEO of Zappos, guides readers through his own unique recipe for corporate success. Hsieh drew on a vast array of life lessons to build his empire, and in this volume he shares the secrets that made his company an unprecedented success. From the vital importance of customer service to the imperative role of personal happiness in the workplace, Hsieh offers a distinctive new approach to the corporate business model—an approach that not only improves earnings, but also improves lives. First book.

Other books you might like:
Chip Conley, *Peak: How Great Companies Get Their Mojo from Maslow*, 2007
Halee Fischer-Wright, *Tribal Leadership: Leveraging Natural Groups to Build a Thriving Organization*, 2008
Leonardo Inghilleri, *Exceptional Service, Exceptional Profit: The Secrets of Building a Five-Star Customer Service Organization*, 2010
John King, *Tribal Leadership: Leveraging Natural Groups to Build a Thriving Organization*, 2008
Dave Logan, co-author

390

SHEL ISRAEL

Twitterville: How Businesses Can Thrive in the New Global Neighborhoods

(New York: Portfolio Hardcover, 2009)

Subject(s): Technology; Internet; Business

Summary: In *Twitterville: How Businesses Can Thrive in the New Global Neighborhoods*, social media reporter Shel Israel discusses Twitter's emergence as one of the most popular and instantaneous forms of communication in technological history. In this book, Israel reveals Twitter's constant use by professionals—businessmen and women who work public relations for their companies. They tweet their companies' accomplishments and awards and also publish quotes that may provide comfort to consumers during controversial events. Israel documents how Twitter has brought everyday Internet users into operating rooms, coffee shops, and budget meetings worldwide. Israel is the coauthor of *Naked Conversations: How Blogs Are Changing the Way Businesses Talk with Customers*.

Other books by the same author:
Naked Conversations: How Blogs are Changing the Way Businesses Talk with Customers, 2006

Other books you might like:
Josh Bernoff, *Groundswell: Winning in a World Transformed by Social Technologies*, 2008
    Charlene Li, co-author
Emily Liebert, *Facebook Fairytales: Modern-Day Miracles to Inspire the Human Spirit*, 2010
David Meerman Scott, *The New Rules of Marketing and PR: How to Use News Releases, Blogs, Podcasting, Viral Marketing and Online Media to Reach Buyers Directly*, 2007

391

JOSEPH JAFFE

Flip the Funnel: How to Use Existing Customers to Gain New Ones
(Hoboken, New Jersey: Wiley, 2010)

Subject(s): Business; Marketing; Advertising

Summary: According to Joseph Jaffe, businesses spend more money attracting the attention of new customers via advertising and mass marketing than they make once the customer has been acquired. In *Flip the Funnel: How to Use Existing Customers to Gain New Ones*, Jaffe explains why making a business's current customers feel appreciated will keep old customers while simultaneously gaining new ones. This book offers plenty of tactics business owners can use to gain loyal customers who will surely spread the word about their favorite companies to their closest friends. Jaffe is the president and chief interruptor of Crayon.

Other books by the same author:
Join the Conversation: How to Engage Marketing-Weary Consumers with the Power of Community, Dialogue, and Partnership, 2007
Life After the 30-Second Spot: Energize Your Brand With a Bold Mix of Alternatives to Traditional Advertising, 2005

Other books you might like:
Sally Hogshead, *Fascinate: Your 7 Triggers to Persuasion and Captivation*, 2010
John Jantsch, *The Referral Engine: Teaching Your Business to Market Itself*, 2010
Scott Stratten, *UnMarketing: Stop Marketing. Start Engaging.*, 2010

392

JOHN JANTSCH

The Referral Engine: Teaching Your Business to Market Itself
(New York: Portfolio, 2010)

Subject(s): Business; Marketing; Advertising

Summary: In *The Referral Engine: Teaching Your Business How to Market Itself*, marketing professional John Jantsch presents his innovative method for growing a business through customer recommendations. As expensive, extravagant advertising techniques continue to lose their effectiveness, the author explains, referrals from the end users of a company's products or services have become vital marketing tools. Because consumers respect the opinion of a relative or acquaintance over a television or print ad, business owners can capitalize on loyal customers to market their businesses. The author demonstrates his theory using real-life examples from Southwest Airlines, TerraCycle, and other national companies.

Other books by the same author:
Duct Tape Marketing: The World's Most Practical Small Business Marketing Guide, 2007

Other books you might like:
David Alexander, *Networking Like a Pro: Turning Contacts into Connections*, 2010
    Brian Hilliard, co-author
Joseph Jaffe, *Flip the Funnel: How to Use Existing Customers to Gain New Ones*, 2010
Charlene Li, *Open Leadership: How Social Technology Can Transform the Way You Lead*, 2010
Ivan Misner, *Networking Like a Pro: Turning Contacts into Connections*, 2010
Scott Stratten, *UnMarketing: Stop Marketing. Start Engaging.*, 2010

393

BILL JENSEN
JOSH KLEIN , Co-Author

Hacking Work: Breaking Stupid Rules for Smart Results
(New York: Portfolio Penguin, 2010)

Subject(s): Business; Problem solving; Business enterprises

Summary: *Hacking Work: Breaking Stupid Rules for Smart Results* is a guide to working smarter, not harder, from business consultant Bill Jensen and computer hacker Josh Klein. *Hacking Work* teaches readers how they can bypass and sidestep bureaucratic standards, pointless rules and procedures, and dated technologies to work more efficiently and find greater satisfaction and fulfillment on the job. Jensen and Klein teach readers how to utilize prohibited tools to work around red tape, solve problems, and achieve greater business success. *Hacking*

Work is filled with true anecdotes about unconventional solutions that real employees found to their job dilemmas and how hacking has helped businessmen and women work more effectively and productively at the office.

Other books you might like:
Jason Fried, *Rework*, 2010
Chris Guillebeau, *The Art of Non-Conformity: Set Your Own Rules, Live the Life You Want, and Change the World*, 2010
David Heinemeier Hansson, *Rework*, 2010
John P. Kotter, *Buy-In: Saving Your Good Idea from Getting Shot Down*, 2010

394

MITCH JOEL

Six Pixels of Separation: Everyone Is Connected. Connect Your Business to Everyone
(New York: Business Plus, 2009)

Subject(s): Business; Internet; Marketing

Summary: *Six Pixels of Separation: Everyone Is Connected. Connect Your Business to Everyone* is a practical resource guide for entrepreneurs, executives, and managers from author and digital marketing expert Mitch Joel. With the development of the Internet and the widespread popularity of social networking, business has changed for everyone. The world is so interconnected that businesses have a unique opportunity to easily gather a global audience. In *Six Pixels of Separation*, Joel provides readers with an in-depth knowledge of virtual marketing, social media, business branding, and entrepreneurship and how they can work together to create success and longevity for a company.

Other books you might like:
Chris Brogan, *Trust Agents: Using the Web to Build Influence, Improve Reputation, and Earn Trust*, 2009
Tara Hunt, *The Whuffie Factor: Using the Power of Social Networks to Build Your Business*, 2009
Julien Smith, *Trust Agents: Using the Web to Build Influence, Improve Reputation, and Earn Trust*, 2009
Gary Vaynerchuk, *Crush It!: Why NOW Is the Time to Cash In on Your Passion*, 2009

395

STEVE KAPLAN

Be the Elephant: Build a Bigger, Better Business
(New York, Workman Publishing Co., 2007)

Subject(s): Business; Business Building; Entrepreneurship

Summary: Author Steve Kaplan returns with *Be the Elephant*, the follow-up to *Bag the Elephant*. In this book he teaches readers how to win customers and grow their

businesses. He gives tips on defining objectives, strengthening sales, and how to grow business at the proper rate—not too fast or too slow. The book includes illustrations.

Other books by the same author:
Sell Your Business for the Max!, 2009
Bag the Elephant!: How to Win and Keep Big Customers, 2005

Other books you might like:
Donald R. Keough, *The Ten Commandments for Business Failure*, 2008
David Kord Murray, *Borrowing Brilliance: The Six Steps to Business Innovation by Building on the Ideas of Others*, 2009
Chris Resto, *Recruit or Die: How Any Business Can Beat the Big Guys in the War for Young Talent*, 2007

396

JOSH KAUFMAN

The Personal MBA: Master the Art of Business
(New York: Portfolio Penguin, 2010)

Subject(s): Commerce; Management; Business enterprises

Summary: Is there an art to business? In *The Personal MBA: Master the Art of Business*, business educator Josh Kaufman concludes that there is, and the best way to learn this art is to avoid getting a master's degree and go directly into the workforce. Kaufman advises that hands-on training is the best learning environment in today's ever-changing economic world, and he guides readers through the process of tapping into the art of business for personal, professional, and financial profit. *The Personal MBA* includes a full index. First book.

Other books you might like:
Leo Babauta, *The Power of Less: The Fine Art of Limiting Yourself to the Essential...in Business and in Life*, 2008
Chris Guillebeau, *The Art of Non-Conformity: Set Your Own Rules, Live the Life You Want, and Change the World*, 2010
Mark Levy, *Accidental Genius: Using Writing to Generate Your Best Ideas, Insight, and Content*, 2010

397

GUY KAWASAKI

Reality Check: The Irreverent Guide to Outsmarting, Outmanaging, and Outmarketing Your Competition
(New York: Portfolio, 2008)

Subject(s): Entrepreneurship; Business enterprises; Marketing

Summary: In *Reality Check: The Irreverent Guide to Outsmarting, Outmanaging, and Outmarketing Your Competition*, renowned business expert Guy Kawasaki presents a volume of his unique insights into crafting fail-proof business strategies. Kawasaki draws on his 30-odd years of experience to give readers the benefit of his practical knowledge, which includes advice on how to communicate effectively, how to market one's business, and how to outdo the competition. *Reality Check* contains a full index.

Other books you might like:
Rachel Bridge, *My Big Idea: 30 Successful Entrepreneurs Reveal How They Found Inspiration*, 2006
Jessica Livingston, *Founders at Work: Stories of Startups' Early Days*, 2007
Mike Michalowicz, *The Toilet Paper Entrepreneur: The tell-it-like-it-is guide to cleaning up in business, even if you are at the end of your roll*, 2008

398

KEVIN KELLY

What Technology Wants
(New York: Viking Adult, 2010)

Subject(s): Technology; Social sciences; Engineering

Summary: In *What Technology Wants*, former editor of Wired magazine Kevin Kelly discusses what he refers to as the "technium," the modern global technological evolution. Kelly argues that this technium is similar to biological evolution because it tends towards "self-organizing complexity." He discusses public oppositions to technology, including the anti-technological Amish attitude and lifestyle. Kelly also offers suggestions for viewing technology as a tool rather than a way of life, and he addresses the many impacts of technology on human achievements.

Other books by the same author:
True Films 2.0: 150 Great Documentaries & Factuals, 2006

Other books you might like:
Steve Johnson, *Where Good Ideas Come From: The Natural History of Innovation*, 2010
Clay Shirky, *Cognitive Surplus: Creativity and Generosity in a Connected Age*, 2010
Tim Wu, *The Master Switch: The Rise and Fall of Information Empires*, 2010

399

LOIS KELLY

Beyond Buzz: The Next Generation of Word-of-Mouth Marketing
(New York: AMACOM, 2007)

Subject(s): Business; Sales

Summary: Marketing whiz Lois Kelly explains the ins and

outs of word-of-mouth promotion in the book *Beyond Buzz: The Next Generation of Word-of-Mouth Marketing*. With corporate catchphrases and outdated lingo proving to be unpopular among customers, Kelly maps out the finer points of the word-of-mouth marketing technique, which is fueled by the often-challenging act of simply listening to clients. Chapters cover in detail this delicate art of listening, as well as nine themes that get people talking, ten ways to cultivate "straight talk," and ideas about how to establish a conversation-centered marketing culture. *Beyond Buzz* also cites a wide array of examples, from David and Goliath to McDonald's. An appendix includes checklists, templates, and further informational sources.

Other books by the same author:
Be the Noodle: Fifty Ways to Be a Compassionate, Courageous, Crazy-Good Caregiver, 2010

Other books you might like:
Mark Hughes, *Buzzmarketing: Get People to Talk About Your Stuff*, 2005
David Meerman Scott, *The New Rules of Marketing and PR: How to Use News Releases, Blogs, Podcasting, Viral Marketing and Online Media to Reach Buyers Directly*, 2007
Andy Sernovitz, *Word of Mouth Marketing: How Smart Companies Get People Talking, Revised Edition*, 2009

400

W. CHAN KIM
RENEE MAUBORGNE , Co-Author

Blue Ocean Strategy: How to Create Uncontested Market Space and Make Competition Irrelevant
(Boston: Harvard Business School Press, 2005)

Subject(s): Business; Marketing; Capitalism

Summary: Authors W. Chan Kim and Renee Mauborgne offer corporations a different approach to competition in *Blue Ocean Strategy: How to Create Uncontested Market Space and Make the Competition Irrelevant*. Instead of continuing rivalries to increase profits, the authors recommend making what they call blue oceans, new opportunities for expansion and earnings. With similar businesses fighting for the same market, finding new ways to succeed is often more profitable than trying to compete with other companies. By using these strategic methods, companies can find their niche in the market. Kim and Mauborgne suggest expanding limits, looking for new customers, providing available and easily accessible materials to clients, and following through with plans or ideas. Several companies, including Curves and Starbucks, have used such methods.

Other books you might like:
Thomas L. Friedman, *The World Is Flat: Further Updated and Expanded, Release 3.0: A Brief History of the Twenty-first Century*, 2007

`401`

CHARLES G. KOCH

The Science of Success: How Market-Based Management Built the World's Largest Private Company

(Hoboken, New Jersey: Wiley, 2007)

Subject(s): Business; Business enterprises; Management

Summary: Charles G. Koch is chairman of Koch Industries, a company he inherited from his father and grew into a corporation with revenues greater than Microsoft. In *The Science of Success: How Market Based Management Built the World's Largest Private Company*, Koch shares the techniques he used to turn his oil and gas company into a multi-industry behemoth. Koch's "Market Based Management" is a comprehensive system for seeking out opportunity and rewarding innovation at all levels of management. At the heart of the system is a belief in a set of fixed laws which govern human well-being; hence, Koch also calls his system "the science of human action." Koch argues that study of this science is fundamental to corporate growth, and distills it into five dimensions: vision, virtue and talents, knowledge processes, decision rights, and incentives. Throughout the text, Koch uses case studies from his own business—both successes and failures—to illustrate how these five dimensions are key to success. The focus is on managing efficiently and measuring performance against the ideal, not just the pragmatic.

Other books by the same author:
Market Based Management: The Science of Human Action Applied in the Organization, 2006

Other books you might like:
Luke M. Froeb, *Managerial Economics: A Problem-Solving Approach*, 2009
James D. Gwartney, *Common Sense Economics: What Everyone Should Know About Wealth and Prosperity*, 2010
Russell Roberts, *The Price of Everything: A Parable of Possibility and Prosperity*, 2008

`402`

JILL KONRATH

SNAP Selling: Speed Up Sales and Win More Business with Today's Frazzled Customers

(New York: Portfolio, 2010)

Subject(s): Business; Sales; Self help books

Summary: *SNAP Selling: Speed Up Sales and Win More Business with Today's Frazzled Customers* is a practical guide to selling from sales strategist Jill Konrath. As people grow increasingly busier and have less excess money to spend, selling is growing more and more dif-

ficult for businesses and individuals. In *SNAP Selling*, Konrath provides readers with sage advice, step-by-step instruction, and practical strategies to become a better salesperson and stand out from the competition. The book is broken into four rules for effective selling that teach readers how to simplify their approach; become invaluable, credible, and relevant to the consumer; and understand the customer's priorities, needs, and desires.

Other books by the same author:
Get Back To Work Faster: The Ultimate Job Seeker's Guide, 2009
Selling to Big Companies, 2005

Other books you might like:
Jeb Blount, *People Buy You: The Real Secret to what Matters Most in Business*, 2010
Paul Cherry, *Questions That Sell: The Powerful Process for Discovering What Your Customer Really Wants*, 2006
David Siteman Garland, *Smarter, Faster, Cheaper: Non-Boring, Fluff-Free Strategies for Marketing and Promoting Your Business*, 2010

`403`

JOHN P. KOTTER

A Sense of Urgency

(Boston: Harvard Business Press, 2008)

Subject(s): Finance; Business; Economics

Summary: In *A Sense of Urgency*, author and businessman John P. Kotter presents a look at modern business strategy and offers his opinions and ideas on the subject. Kotter argues that many businesses today have allowed themselves to grow lax by using laid back and nonaggressive business techniques. He says that companies like this need to get aggressive again if they want to pump up their sales. Kotter takes readers inside some of these stalling businesses and points out what's working and what's not. Kotter claims that rather than lamenting over a poor economic state and having a glum outlook, business owners should be motivated by the notion that the world holds a great deal of both opportunity and risk. Kotter highlights some ideas for how to overcome a negative business attitude and provides many examples of real businesses and the success they have found as a result of an improved, positive business strategy.

Other books by the same author:
Buy-In: Saving Your Good Idea from Getting Shot Down, 2010
Our Iceberg Is Melting: Changing and Succeeding Under Any Conditions, 2006

Other books you might like:
Ken Blanchard, *Who Killed Change?: Solving the Mystery of Leading People Through Change*, 2009
Dan S. Cohen, *The Heart of Change Field Guide: Tools and Tactics for Leading Change in Your Organization*, 2005
Vijay Govindarajan, *The Other Side of Innovation: Solving the Execution Challenge*, 2010

404

ALEXANDRA LEVIT

New Job, New You: A Guide to Reinventing Yourself in a Bright New Career

(New York: Ballantine Books Trade Paperbacks, 2009)

Subject(s): Business; Employment; Self help books

Summary: Written by *Wall Street Journal* career columnist Alexandra Levit, *New Job, New You: A Guide to Reinventing Yourself in a Bright New Career* is a practical and inspirational resource for individuals hoping to start a new career. The book offers helpful advice for anyone seeking to start fresh in a new job field, regardless of their motivation. *New Job, New You* is broken into seven sections based on the motivating factors for career changes: family, independence, learning, money, passion, setback, and talent. Levit instructs readers on how to research new career options, stand out among competitors, maintain financial income during job transition, effectively secure an ideal job in a new field, and utilize marketing and networking skills to change career paths.

Other books by the same author:
They Don't Teach Corporate in College: A Twenty-Something's Guide to the Business World, 2009
How'd You Score That Gig?: A Guide to the Coolest Jobs-and How to Get Them, 2008
Success for Hire: Simple Strategies to Find and Keep Outstanding Employees, 2008

Other books you might like:
Andrea Kay, *Life's a Bitch and Then You Change Careers: 9 Steps to Get Out of Your Funk and On to Your Future*, 2006
Lisa Johnson Mandell, *Career Comeback: Repackage Yourself to Get the Job You Want*, 2010
Gretchen Craft Rubin, *The Happiness Project: Or, Why I Spent a Year Trying to Sing in the Morning, Clean My Closets, Fight Right, Read Aristotle, and Generally Have More Fun*, 2009

405

STEVEN D. LEVITT
STEPHEN J. DUBNER , Co-Author

Freakonomics: A Rogue Economist Explores the Hidden Side of Everything. Rev. and Expanded Ed.

(New York: William Morrow, 2006)

Subject(s): Economics; Culture; Current events

Summary: In *Freakonomics: A Rogue Economist Explores the Hidden Side of Everything*, authors Steven Levitt and Stephen Dubner discuss such varied topics as crime rates, whether reading to your children will make them better students, abortion laws, and many other topics that are seemingly unrelated to economics. The authors analyze these topics from an economic perspective. They show how this is possible and what can be divined about the future and understood about current statistical rates from economic theories. The book shows that the study of economics is useful for understanding not only business and finance, but also many other diverse fields.

Other books by the same author:
Superfreakonomics: Global Cooling, Patriotic Prostitutes and Why Suicide Bombers Should Buy Life Insurance, 2009

Other books you might like:
Atul Gawande, *The Checklist Manifesto: How to Get Things Right*, 2009
Malcolm Gladwell, *Outliers*, 2008
Malcolm Gladwell, *The Tipping Point: How Little Things Can Make a Big Difference*, 2000
Madsen Pirie, *How to Win Every Argument: The Use and Abuse of Logic*, 2006
Brian P. Simpson, *Markets Don't Fail!*, 2005

406

CHARLENE LI
JOSH BERNOFF , Co-Author

Groundswell: Winning in a World Transformed by Social Technologies

(Boston, Massachusetts: Harvard Business Press, 2008)

Subject(s): Internet; Business; Technology

Summary: In *Groundswell: Winning in a World Transformed by Social Technologies*, research analysts Charlene Yi and Josh Bernoff examine the ways companies can harness the power of online social networking platforms. As executives at Forrester Research, the authors outline the numerous ways corporations can take full advantage of the benefits offered by new technologies, such as blogs, podcasts, and YouTube. Chapters explore methods of assessing new social technologies as they appear, how to incorporate these practices into one's business for maximum potential, and a fourfold procedure for laying out a strategic plan involving social networking. *Groundswell* includes a list of bibliographical references and indexes.

Other books by the same author:
Empowered: Unleash Your Employees, Energize Your Customers, and Transform Your Business, 2010
Open Leadership: How Social Technology Can Transform the Way You Lead, 2010

Other books you might like:
Shel Israel, *Twitterville: How Businesses Can Thrive in the New Global Neighborhoods*, 2009
Amber Mac, *Power Friending: Demystifying Social Media to Grow Your Business*, 2010
David Meerman Scott, *The New Rules of Marketing and PR: How to Use News Releases, Blogs, Podcasting, Viral Marketing and Online Media to Reach Buyers Directly*, 2007

407

MARTIN LINDSTROM

Buyology: Truth and Lies About Why We Buy
(New York: Doubleday, 2008)

Subject(s): Advertising; Research; Shopping

Summary: *Buyology: Truth and Lies About Why We Buy* by Martin Lindstrom with a foreword by Paco Underhill examines topics such as marketing and advertising, and how neuroscience can illustrate why consumers buy what they buy. Lindstrom discusses how brain-scan studies clearly show what entices consumers to purchase a particular item, and what does not. The text also includes a discussion of why consumers say they do one thing, but in fact behave in the complete opposite way. Various topics regarding advertising, including the effectiveness of subliminal messages, are also discussed.

Other books by the same author:
Brand Sense: Sensory Secrets Behind the Stuff We Buy, 2010

Other books you might like:
Christophe Morin, *Neuromarketing: Understanding the Buy Buttons in Your Customer's Brain,* 2007
    Patrick Renvoise, co-author
Paco Underhill, *Why We Buy: The Science of Shopping—Updated and Revised for the Internet, the Global Consumer, and Beyond,* 2008
Shankar Vedantam, *The Hidden Brain: How Our Unconscious Minds Elect Presidents, Control Markets, Wage Wars, and Save Our Lives,* 2010

408

STEVEN S. LITTLE

The 7 Irrefutable Rules of Small Business Growth
(Hoboken, New Jersey: J. Wiley, 2005)

Subject(s): Business; Business enterprises; Entrepreneurship

Summary: It can be difficult to start a small business and the fact is that many small businesses fail. In *The 7 Irrefutable Rules of Small Business Growth*, author Steve S. Little outlines pragmatic real-life suggestions for making a small business a success story. He provides fact-based anecdotes and creative insights to explain why some businesses work and others fail. The book is designed as a how-to guide for new business owners. The author keeps the book conversational in tone rather than packing it with theory. Some of the rules Little offers range from having a clear purpose to writing a sound business plan.

Other books by the same author:
Duck and Recover: The Embattled Business Owner's Guide to Survival and Growth, 2009
The Milkshake Moment: Overcoming Stupid Systems,

Pointless Policies and Muddled Management to Realize Real Growth, 2008

409

MICHAEL S. MALONE

Bill and Dave: How Hewlett and Packard Built the World's Greatest Company
(New York: Portfolio, 2007)

Subject(s): Business; Management; Biographies

Summary: In *Bill and Dave: How Hewlett and Packard Built the World's Greatest Company*, journalist Michael S. Malone shares the story of the development of the company Hewlett-Packard and the technology that came from it. Hewlett-Packard began in 1938 when Bill Hewlett and Dave Packard—recent Stanford graduates—began working together and created an audio oscillator. After their first invention Hewlett and Packard worked together to develop more innovative technology and create a very successful business. Despite experiencing a few setbacks, HP became an important and influential business. The book also focuses on the management practices known as the "HP Way," emphasizing the importance of the employee and trusting that employees will do the right thing in a given situation. Malone argues that these practices, and others, led HP to become "the world's greatest company."

Other books by the same author:
The Future Arrived Yesterday: The Rise of the Protean Corporation and What It Means for You, 2009
The Everything College Survival Book: From Social Life To Study Skills—All You Need To Fit Right In (Everything: School And Careers), 2005

Other books you might like:
Howard Gardner, *Five Minds for the Future,* 2007
Atul Gawande, *The Checklist Manifesto: How to Get Things Right,* 2009
Chip Heath, *Switch: How to Change Things When Change Is Hard,* 2010
    Dan Heath, co-author

410

JOHN L. MARIOTTI

The Complexity Crisis: Why Too Many Products, Markets, and Customers Are Crippling Your Company—and What To Do about It
(Avon, Massachusetts: Platinum Press, 2008)

Subject(s): Business; Business enterprises; Entrepreneurship

Summary: Written by businessman and entrepreneurial

advisor, John L. Mariotti, *The Complexity Crisis: Why Too Many Products, Markets, and Customers Are Crippling Your Company—and What To Do about It* is a practical and resourceful guide to business owners for simplifying business to increase profits and success. As businesses struggle to stay afloat in troubling economic times, they often complicate matters by increasing products, services, customers, and personnel. Although many of these corporations begin earning more revenue, their complex systems diminish their profits. In *The Complexity Crisis*, Mariotti teaches readers how to streamline their business or organization, identify and reduce complexities, build a simple corporate structure, and increase profits.

Other books by the same author:
The Chinese Conspiracy, 2010
The Power of Partnerships: The Next Step Beyond TQM, Reengineering and Lean Production, 2007
Smart Marketing, 2007
Marketing Express, 2006

Other books you might like:
Tim Brown, *Change by Design: How Design Thinking Transforms Organizations and Inspires Innovation*, 2009
Jim Collins, *How the Mighty Fall: And Why Some Companies Never Give In*, 2009
Stephen A. Wilson, *Waging War on Complexity Costs: Reshape Your Cost Structure, Free Up Cash Flows and Boost Productivity by Attacking Process, Product and Organizational Complexity*, 2009

411

LILLIAN HAYES MARTIN

The Business Devotional: 365 Inspirational Thoughts on Management, Leadership & Motivation

(New York: Sterling Innovation, 2009)

Story type: Inspirational
Subject(s): Business; Self help books; Self confidence

Summary: *The Business Devotional: 365 Inspirational Thoughts on Management, Leadership & Motivation* is an encouraging and uplifting guide for businessmen and women from author Lillian Hayes Martin. The book provides daily words of affirmation, encouragement, and motivation for an entire year, including tips and guidance on every facet of business from making daily decisions to increasing profits to honing and sharpening leadership skills. The brief entries, offered seven days a week, include wisdom, inspiration, and advice from a wide variety of successful business moguls and exceptional leaders such as Oprah Winfrey, Tom Peters, Peter Drucker, Bill Gates, Warren Buffett, Carly Fiorina, and Ken Blanchard.

Other books by the same author:
Talk Less, Say More: Three Habits to Influence Others and Make Things Happen, 2008

Other books you might like:
Connie Dieken, *Talk Less, Say More: Three Habits to Influence Others and Make Things Happen*, 2009
Hugh MacLeod, *Ignore Everybody: And 39 Other Keys to Creativity*, 2009
John C. Maxwell, *The Maxwell Daily Reader: 365 Days of Insight to Develop the Leader Within You and Influence Those Around You*, 2008

412

MATTHEW E. MAY

In Pursuit of Elegance: Why the Best Ideas Have Something Missing

(New York: Doubleday, 2009)

Subject(s): Marketing; Culture; Success

Summary: As consumers and cultures are drawn to certain innovations and indifferent to others, the reasoning behind their reactions can seem hard to pin down. What makes one product more elegant than another? According to Matthew May in *In Pursuit of Elegance: Why the Best Ideas Have Something Missing*, elegance is defined by four characteristics—seduction, subtraction, symmetry, and sustainability. In determining the elegance of a cultural or sporting event, a work of art or a piece of merchandise, humans base their perceptions on these criteria, often with unexpected results. The author argues that it is often what was has been eliminated from a product's design, rather than what is included, that results in its success. May supports his interesting theory with real-world examples ranging from Jackson Pollock to *The Sopranos*.

Other books by the same author:
The Shibumi Strategy: A Powerful Way to Create Meaningful Change, 2010
The Elegant Solution: Toyota's Formula for Mastering Innovation, 2007

Other books you might like:
Scott Berkun, *The Myths of Innovation*, 2007
Hartmut Esslinger, *A Fine Line: How Design Strategies Are Shaping the Future of Business*, 2009
Robin Sharma, *The Leader Who Had No Title: A Modern Fable on Real Success in Business and in Life*, 2010

413

BEN MCCONNELL
JACKIE HUBA , Co-Author

Citizen Marketers: When People Are the Message

(New York: Kaplan Business, 2006)

Subject(s): Business; Internet; Marketing
Summary: In their book *Citizen Marketers: When People*

Are the Message, Ben McConnell and Jackie Huba offer an overview of social media and how it affecting marketing. Social media is a growing network of consumers who communicate with one another regarding experiences with products, businesses, and the like. Social media is enabled by technological advancements, primarily the Internet. The authors point out that consumers have access to tools such as comment boards, blogs, and online videos, which allow them to speak freely about products and services they encounter. In turn, they can mobilize and boycott or praise these items. McConnell and Huba describe four types of citizen marketers. There are filters (collectors of information), fanatics (fans of a product), facilitators (coordinators of action), and firecrackers (short-lived but memorable partakers in a social medium). The text examines and provides examples of the increasing influence of the public on brands, companies, and the world of marketing.

Other books you might like:

Josh Bernoff, *Groundswell: Winning in a World Transformed by Social Technologies*, 2008

Shel Israel, *Naked Conversations: How Blogs Are Changing the Way Businesses Talk with Customers*, 2006

Charlene Li, *Groundswell: Winning in a World Transformed by Social Technologies*, 2008

Robert Scoble, *Naked Conversations: How Blogs Are Changing the Way Businesses Talk with Customers*, 2006

Andy Sernovitz, *Word of Mouth Marketing: How Smart Companies Get People Talking, Revised Edition*, 2009

414

SCOTT MCKAIN

Collapse of Distinction: Stand Out and Move Up While Your Competition Fails

(Nashville, Tennessee: Thomas Nelson, 2009)

Subject(s): Business; Entrepreneurship; Individualism

Summary: *Collapse of Distinction: Stand Out and Move Up While Your Competition Fails* is a helpful and inspirational resource guide for business owners and entrepreneurs from Scott McKain. Business has evolved to the point where uniformity has overtaken the marketplace. Businesses no longer strive to be unique from their competitors. Instead, consumers struggle to see any difference between their options. In *Collapse of Distinction*, McKain instructs readers on the importance of having a business that sets itself apart from other operations in the same field. With the current economic crisis, McKain alleges that the only way a business will survive is by making itself distinct from its contemporaries. He gives readers practical advice and tips on how to stand out in the business world.

Other books by the same author:

What Customers Really Want : How to Bridge the Gap

Between What Your Organization Offers and What Your Clients Crave, 2005

Other books you might like:

Sally Hogshead, *Fascinate: Your 7 Triggers to Persuasion and Captivation*, 2010

John Jantsch, *The Referral Engine: Teaching Your Business to Market Itself*, 2010

John Spence, *Awesomely Simple: Essential Business Strategies for Turning Ideas Into Action*, 2009

415

JOSEPH A. MICHELLI

The Starbucks Experience: 5 Principles for Turning Ordinary into Extraordinary

(New York: McGraw-Hill, 2007)

Subject(s): Business enterprises; Finance

Summary: Since its opening in 1992, the Starbucks coffee and pastry chain has grown and expanded to a staggering size. So what's the secret behind all those steaming hot cups of coffee and sweet flaky treats? How did the company grow so large and successful? And what could other companies learn from Starbucks? These are the questions Joseph Michelli poses in this book. Michelli argues that many factors are responsible for Starbucks's successful rise—such as hiring quality employees, attracting and keeping customers, creating a positive customer experience, and supporting social causes. He explains how these factors can be applied to other companies as well.

Other books by the same author:

The New Gold Standard: 5 Leadership Principles for Creating a Legendary Customer Experience Courtesy of the Ritz-Carlton Hotel Company, 2008

Other books you might like:

Howard Behar, *It's Not About the Coffee: Leadership Principles from a Life at Starbucks*, 2007

Malcolm Gladwell, *What the Dog Saw: And Other Adventures*, 2009

John Moore, *Tribal Knowledge: Business Wisdom Brewed from the Grounds of Starbucks Corporate Culture*, 2006

416

PETER MILLER

The Smart Swarm: How Understanding Flocks, Schools, and Colonies Can Make Us Better at Communicating, Decision Making, and Getting Things Done

(New York: Avery, 2010)

Subject(s): Business; Animals; Communications

Summary: In *The Smart Swarm: How Understanding*

Flocks, Schools, and Colonies Can Make Us Better at Communicating, Decision Making, and Getting Things Done, Peter Miller, reporter for *National Geographic*, examines what humans can learn from ants, bees, fish, and other smart swarms about interdependence. Miller sheds light on what can be learned about organization, communication, collective intelligence, and productivity from observing ant colonies, schools of fish, hives of bees, and groups of other creatures, such as locusts, termites, and birds. *The Smart Swarm* shows readers how colonies of ants inspired computer networks and Southwest Airline's seating methods, how termite behavior is a great model for emergency response, and how fish schools motivated a line of robots created by the United States.

Other books you might like:

Len Fisher, *The Perfect Swarm: The Science of Complexity in Everyday Life*, 2004

Neil Johnson, *Two's Company, Three is Complexity*, 2007

Thomas D. Seeley, *Honeybee Democracy*, 2010

417

IVAN MISNER
DAVID ALEXANDER , Co-Author
BRIAN HILLIARD , Co-Author

Networking Like a Pro: Turning Contacts into Connections
(Irvine, California: Entrepreneur Press, 2010)

Subject(s): Business; Self help books; Success

Summary: *Networking Like a Pro: Turning Contacts into Connections* is a resourceful business guide from best-selling author and networking expert Ivan Misner, with help from Brian Hilliard and David Alexander. The authors offer tips and tricks for successful networking techniques that truly work for businessmen and women to build up their contact lists to increase business. *Networking Like a Pro* provides readers with practical advice on where and how to find new connections and details about online networking opportunities, determining one's target market, succeeding at business events, pitching business ideas to others, building deep relationships, finding referrals, motivating others to network, and tracking success.

Other books by the same author:
Roadmap To Success, 2009
The 29% Solution: 52 Weekly Networking Success Strategies, 2008
Masters of Sales, 2007
Truth or Delusion?: Busting Networking's Biggest Myths, 2006

Other books you might like:
Anne Baber, *Make Your Contacts Count: Networking Know-how for Business And Career Success*, 2007
Harry Beckwith, *You, Inc.: The Art of Selling Yourself*, 2007
Devora Zack, *Networking for People Who Hate*

Networking: A Field Guide for Introverts, the Overwhelmed, and the Underconnected, 2010

418

RAFI MOHAMMED

The 1% Windfall: How Successful Companies Use Price to Profit and Grow
(New York: HarperCollins, 2010)

Subject(s): Business; Finance; Sales

Summary: In *The 1% Windfall: How Successful Companies Use Price to Profit and Grow*, Rafi Mohammed discusses pricing strategies and the way prices can be manipulated to increase profits. Mohammed discusses the ramifications of increasing product prices by 1%, stating that customers will be more willing to pay more for a product they value, regardless of the actual manufacturing costs. Mohammed then uses specific examples from companies, such as Southwest Airlines, and interviews with managers to offer advice to other business owners regarding successful pricing strategies.

Other books by the same author:
The Art of Pricing: How to Find the Hidden Profits to Grow Your Business, 2005

Other books you might like:
Walter L. Baker, *The Price Advantage*, 2010
Reed Holden, *Pricing with Confidence: 10 Ways to Stop Leaving Money on the Table*, 2008
William Poundstone, *Priceless: The Myth of Fair Value (and How to Take Advantage of It)*, 2010

419

BARRY MOLTZ

Bounce!: Failure, Resiliency, and Confidence to Achieve Your Next Great Success
(Hoboken, New Jersey: John Wiley and Sons, 2008)

Subject(s): Business enterprises; Entrepreneurship; Success

Summary: Author and business specialist Barry Moltz analyzes the life cycle that is part and parcel of any business endeavor. In *Bounce!: Failure, Resiliency, and Confidence to Achieve Your Next Great Success*, Moltz uses the elements of this cycle to guide aspiring entrepreneurs to professional and financial prosperity. His wealth of insight on the subject tackles topics as diverse as setting realistic goals, taking risks, and crafting success on individual terms. *Bounce!* contains notes on the text and an index.

Other books by the same author:
B-A-M! Bust A Myth: Delivering Customer Service in a Self-Service World, 2009

Other books you might like:

Norm Brodsky, *The Knack: How Street-Smart Entrepreneurs Learn to Handle Whatever Comes Up*, 2008
Bo Burlingham, co-author

Al Siebert, *The Resiliency Advantage: Master Change, Thrive Under Pressure, and Bounce Back from Setbacks*, 2005

Matthew Syed, *Bounce: Mozart, Federer, Picasso, Beckham, and the Science of Success*, 2010

420

DAVID KORD MURRAY

Borrowing Brilliance: The Six Steps to Business Innovation by Building on the Ideas of Others

(New York: Gotham Publishing, 2009)

Subject(s): Entrepreneurship; Business; Marketing

Summary: In *Borrowing Brilliance: The Six Steps to Business Innovation by Building on the Ideas of Others*, author David Kord Murray discusses how new business ideas can be inspired by existing business plans. Murray contends that making use of such ideas should not be considered stealing but rather an important method of channeling innovation. The author examines how successful people from all walks of life, from Charles Darwin to George Lucas, have become pioneers of their field simply by taking existing ideas to a whole new level. Murray also introduces a system for business entrepreneurs to help them get started on the pathway to innovation and invention.

Other books you might like:

Jeanne Bliss, *I Love You More Than My Dog: Five Decisions That Drive Extreme Customer Loyalty in Good Times and Bad*, 2009

Jeremy Gutsche, *Exploiting Chaos: 150 Ways to Spark Innovation During Times of Change*, 2009

Alexander Osterwalder, *Business Model Generation: A Handbook for Visionaries, Game Changers, and Challengers*, 2009

421

MARTY NEUMEIER

The Brand Gap: Expanded Edition

(Berkeley, California: Peachpit Press, 2005)

Subject(s): Business; Advertising; Self help books

Summary: According to Marty Neumeier, gaps between companies' brand strategies and customer experiences are commonplace. In *The Brand Gap: Expanded Edition*, Neumeier instructs business owners in revamping their brands to make the customer feel appreciated and remain interested in the companies' products. He claims that a set of five disciplines—differentiate, collaborate, innovate, validate, and cultivate—will help any business find the perfect approach to branding their products. Neumeier offers advice about the design of company brands, unique and productive ways to test brands, and how to manage new brands. This book includes a glossary of more than 200 terms.

Other books by the same author:

The Designful Company: How to build a culture of nonstop innovation, 2008

Zag: The Number One Strategy of High-Performance Brands, 2006

Other books you might like:

Allen P. Adamson, *BrandSimple: How the Best Brands Keep It Simple and Succeed*, 2006

David Airey, *Logo Design Love: A Guide to Creating Iconic Brand Identities*, 2009

Alina Wheeler, *Designing Brand Identity: An Essential Guide for the Whole Branding Team*, 2009

422

ADRIAN C. OTT

The 24-Hour Customer: New Rules for Winning in a Time-Starved, Always-Connected Economy

(New York: HarperBusiness, 2010)

Subject(s): Business; Time; Sales

Summary: In *The 24-Hour Customer: New Rules for Winning in a Time-Starved, Always-Connected Economy*, business consultant Adrian C. Ott offers marketing tips and sales strategies for reaching consumers despite their busy and hectic lives. Despite the connectedness of the world, 24/7 commerce opportunities, and multiple communication methods, it's growing increasingly harder for businesses to reach potential customers. People are busier than ever before, trying desperately to find time for anything. In *The 24-Hour Customer*, Ott shows salespeople how to capitalize on the variability of consumers' time and attention to win their business. Utilizing case studies from successful businesses such as Netflix, Zipcar, and Amazon, Ott equips readers with practical advice and in-depth research to help them increase revenue and win new clientele.

Other books you might like:

Alex Bogusky, *Baked In: Creating Products and Businesses That Market Themselves*, 2009

John Jantsch, *The Referral Engine: Teaching Your Business to Market Itself*, 2010

Rick Kash, *How Companies Win: Profiting from Demand-Driven Business Models No Matter What Business You're In*, 2010

423

NATALIE PACE

Put Your Money Where Your Heart Is: Investment Strategies for Lifetime Wealth from a #1 Wall Street Stock Picker

(New York: Vanguard Press, 2008)

Subject(s): Finance; Wealth; Success

Summary: In *Put Your Money Where Your Heart Is: Investment Strategies for Lifetime Wealth from a #1 Wall Street Stock Picker*, Natalie Pace shares her own story of success, from when she was a single mother on the verge of losing her home to becoming the first-ranked Wall Street stock picker. In the book, Pace illustrates the way the same principles can be used over and over again to invest successfully. The author presents a three-step process and six-step process for determining short- and long-term investments. Pace suggests that people rely mostly on their common sense and research when choosing stocks.

Where it's reviewed:
Success, October 2009, page 91

Other books by the same author:
You vs. Wall Street: Grow What You've Got and Get Back What You've Lost, 2009

Other books you might like:
Janet Attwood, *The Passion Test: The Effortless Path to Discovering Your Destiny*, 2007
Jason Kelly, *The Neatest Little Guide to Stock Market Investing*, 2009
Ben Stein, *The Little Book of Bulletproof Investing: Do's and Don'ts to Protect Your Financial Life*, 2010

424

ADAM L. PENENBERG

Viral Loop: From Facebook to Twitter, How Today's Smartest Businesses Grow Themselves

(New York: Hyperion, 2009)

Subject(s): Business; Entrepreneurship; Management

Summary: In *Viral Loop: From Facebook to Twitter, How Today's Smartest Businesses Grow Themselves*, author Adam L. Penenberg explores how social media have impacted the business world. Penenberg takes a comprehensive look at how various web media such as Twitter, Flickr, YouTube, and Facebook—which he terms the "Viral Loop"—have successfully built their brands on the principle of mass exposure. The author also discusses how these web media brands have helped other businesses grow through social media public relations and advertising campaigns. In this book, Penenberg demonstrates how the success of one's business venture can be

no less than a mouse click away. Penenberg is also the author of *Tragic Indifference* and is the co-author, with Marc Barry, of *Spooked: Espionage in Corporate America*.

Other books you might like:
Josh Bernoff, *Groundswell: Winning in a World Transformed by Social Technologies*, 2008
Charlene Li, co-author
David Meerman Scott, *The New Rules of Marketing and PR: How to Use News Releases, Blogs, Podcasting, Viral Marketing and Online Media to Reach Buyers Directly*, 2007
Gabe Zichermann, *Game-Based Marketing: Inspire Customer Loyalty Through Rewards, Challenges, and Contests*, 2010

425

DANIEL H. PINK

A Whole New Mind: Why Right-Brainers Will Rule the Future

(New York: Penguin, 2006)

Subject(s): Business; Careers; Workplace

Summary: Author Daniel Pink feels that the culture of business and the workplace are on the verge of an enormous change. What he calls the "Conceptual Age" is starting to dawn, and Pink explains that creative thinkers, such as artists and inventors, who rely on right brain skills, will succeed in this new age. Pink uses research conducted from around the world to explain the six senses that are central to right-brain thinking: design, story, symphony, empathy, play, and meaning. In describing these critical skills, Pink also describes how to develop them in order to stay competitive, succeed in business, and achieve personal fulfillment.

Other books by the same author:
Drive: The Surprising Truth About What Motivates Us, 2009

Other books you might like:
Howard Gardner, *Five Minds for the Future*, 2007
Atul Gawande, *The Checklist Manifesto: How to Get Things Right*, 2009
Chip Heath, *Switch: How to Change Things When Change Is Hard*, 2010
Dan Heath, co-author

426

RON PLOOF

Read This First: The Executive's Guide to New Media—from Blogs to Social Networks

(Bloomington, Indiana: iUniverse, 2009)

Subject(s): Business; Internet; Marketing

Summary: *Read This First: The Executive's Guide to New*

Media—from Blogs to Social Networks is a resource guide to online marketing and business from author Ron Ploof. With the advancement of technology and new media, businesses now have to worry about their online image and reputation. Ploof provides practical advice and helpful tips for business executives on ways to utilize new media in their companies and corporations. He offers an extensive overview on social media and networking sites, how new media benefits companies, step-by-step instruction on incorporating new media into a company, tips for utilizing free online tools to increase productivity, and ways to measure online success. *Read This First* also features true case studies of companies and corporations using social media.

Other books you might like:
Josh Bernoff, *Groundswell: Winning in a World Transformed by Social Technologies*, 2008
Joseph Jaffe, *Flip the Funnel: How to Use Existing Customers to Gain New Ones*, 2010
Charlene Li, *Groundswell: Winning in a World Transformed by Social Technologies*, 2008
Amber Mac, *Power Friending: Demystifying Social Media to Grow Your Business*, 2010

427

JAMES D. POWER IV
CHRIS DENOVE , Co-Author

Satisfaction: How Every Great Company Listens to the Voice of the Customer
(New York: Portfolio, 2006)

Subject(s): Marketing; Business enterprises; Management

Summary: Almost everyone has heard the common phrase, "the customer is always right." In their book Satisfaction: How Every Great Company Listens to the Voice of the Customer authors Chris Denove and James D. Power argue that, although that old say is not inherently wrong, following it all the time can be nearly impossible. Denove and Power argue that business assessment and strategic planning help businesses best serve their customers. For instance, a thorough investigation into where financial and employee resources are being absorbed may allow for such resources to be reallocated more efficiently. A few angry customers from time to time may be worthwhile when others are so gratified with a given product that they promote that product to their family and friends. In essence, these buyers act as free advertisement. Focus on pleasing the most enthusiastic of consumers, then, far outweighs charming every customer, every time. Also included in the piece is a discussion on measurement tools, vital to gaining perspective on beneficial spending practice, employee work quality, consumer relations and more.

Other books you might like:
Phil Baker, *From Concept to Consumer: How to Turn Ideas Into Money*, 2008
Fred Reichheld, *The Ultimate Question: Driving Good Profits and True Growth*, 2006
Anthony Ulwick, *What Customers Want: Using

Outcome-Driven Innovation to Create Breakthrough Products and Services, 2005

428

ROBERT B. REICH

Aftershock: The Next Economy and America's Future
(New York: Alfred A. Knopf, 2010)

Subject(s): Economics; Social conditions; Business

Summary: In *Aftershock: The Next Economy and America's Future*, economist Robert B. Reich shares his analysis of President Obama's controversial stimulus plan. Having served as Bill Clinton's labor secretary and Barack Obama's economic adviser, Reich possesses unique insights into America's 21st-century economic crisis. Tracing the nation's economic history from the Great Depression of the 1920s to the great prosperity of the 1940s through the 1970s to the contemporary Great Recession, the author discusses how America's spending and credit habits, tax and insurance laws, Medicare and Medicaid have contributed to current economic problems and how those factors will impact the nation's future economy.

Other books by the same author:
Supercapitalism: The Transformation of Business, Democracy, and Everyday Life, 2007

Other books you might like:
Martin Ford, *The Lights in the Tunnel: Automation, Accelerating Technology and the Economy of the Future*, 2009
Brian P. Simpson, *Markets Don't Fail!*, 2005
Matt Taibbi, *Griftopia: Bubble Machines, Vampire Squids, and the Long Con That Is Breaking America*, 2010

429

PATRICK RENVOISE
CHRISTOPHE MORIN , Co-Author

Neuromarketing: Understanding the Buy Buttons in Your Customer's Brain
(Nashville, Tennessee: Thomas Nelson, 2007)

Subject(s): Business; Sales; Marketing

Summary: Written by Christophe Morin and Patrick Renvoise, *Neuromarketing: Understanding the Buy Buttons in Your Customer's Brain* is an examination of the human brain and the factors that influence it to make buying decisions. Morin and Renvoise combine up-to-date studies and research on the brain with marketing experience and proven selling techniques to teach readers how to win over any audience. *Neuromarketing* equips salespeople to tap into the neurological responses in a person's brain to make an effective sale. The book includes a four-step process for selling success, six building blocks for creating a compelling message, and seven impact boosters to make the pitch more powerful.

Other books by the same author:
Neuromarketing: Is There a 'Buy Button' in the Brain? Selling to the Old Brain for Instant Success, 2005

Other books you might like:
Martin Lindstrom, *BRAND sense: Sensory Secrets Behind the Stuff We Buy*, 2005
Martin Lindstrom, *Buyology: Truth and Lies About Why We Buy*, 2008
A.K. Pradeep, *The Buying Brain: Secrets for Selling to the Subconscious Mind*, 2010

430

GLENN REYNOLDS

An Army of Davids: How Markets and Technology Empower Ordinary People to Beat Big Media, Big Government, and Other Goliaths

(Nashville, Tennessee: Thomas Nelson, 2006)

Subject(s): Business; Individualism; Success

Summary: *An Army of Davids: How Markets and Technology Empower Ordinary People to Beat Big Media, Big Government, and Other Goliaths* is an examination of the rise of the individual in the business world from author Glenn Reynolds. In years past, giant organizations and corporations have ruled the marketplace. With the advent of the Internet and the growth of social media, however, individuals now have a louder voice and greater opportunities for success. In *An Army of Davids*, Reynolds shows how the "little guy" is rising in power, influence, and success in every arena, from the music industry to journalism to nanotechnology. Reynolds gives readers an in-depth account of how the world is changing and the growing opportunities being created for individuals.

Other books you might like:
Angelo M. Codevilla, *The Ruling Class: How They Corrupted America and What We Can Do About It*, 2010
Clay Shirky, *Here Comes Everybody: The Power of Organizing Without Organizations*, 2008
Thomas Sowell, *Dismantling America: And Other Controversial Essays*, 2010

431

BARRY RITHOLTZ
BILL FLECKENSTEIN , Co-Author

Bailout Nation: How Greed and Easy Money Corrupted Wall Street and Shook the World Economy

(Hoboken, New Jersey: John Wiley & Sons, 2009)

Subject(s): Business; Finance; Economic depressions

Summary: Written by popular finance blogger Barry Ritholtz, with a foreword by Bill Fleckenstein, *Bailout Nation: How Greed and Easy Money Corrupted Wall Street and Shook the World Economy* is an in-depth account of the U.S. financial crisis in 2008 that included a stock market crash, a real estate catastrophe, and bailouts of major corporations. Ritholtz begins with a concise historical background of financial bailouts, including a look at their common patterns and unexpected results. He then examines the events throughout America's recent history that resulted in the financial collapse of 2008, including specific government interventions in business in the 1970s, '80s, and '90s. Ritholtz combines his insider financial knowledge with historical information to present a comprehensive report of one of the worst economic disasters in history.

Other books by the same author:
Greenspans Bubbles- The Age of Ignorance at the Federal Reserve, 2008

Other books you might like:
Andrew Bernstein, *The Capitalist Manifesto: The Historic, Economic and Philosophic Case for Laissez-Faire*, 2005
John Lanchester, *I.O.U.: Why Everyone Owes Everyone and No One Can Pay*, 2010
R. Christopher Whalen, *Inflated: How Money and Debt Built the American Dream*, 2010

432

DAN ROAM

The Back of the Napkin: Solving Problems and Selling Ideas with Pictures

(New York: Portfolio, 2008)

Subject(s): Business; Art; Drawing

Summary: In *The Back of the Napkin: Solving Problems and Selling Ideas with Pictures*, bestselling author and acclaimed problem solver Dan Roam shows how drawing simple pictures can help individuals find solutions, communicate, and sell ideas. Relying on the latest findings in visual science, Roam alleges that drawing basic illustrations can be one of the most effective tools for sales and problem solving. He highlights the ways that drawing pictures helps individuals clarify thoughts and ideas, work through challenges and setbacks, find logical and effective solutions, and successfully communicate with others. Using true stories and real-life anecdotes of a wide variety of individuals who have used visual drawings to solve problems or make sales, *The Back of the Napkin* encourages the visual thinker in everyone.

Other books by the same author:
Unfolding the Napkin: The Hands-On Method for Solving Complex Problems with Simple Pictures, 2009

Other books you might like:
Nancy Duarte, *Slide:ology: The Art and Science of Creating Great Presentations*, 2008
Dave Gray, *Gamestorming: A Playbook for Innovators,*

Rulebreakers, and Changemakers, 2010
David Sibbet, *Visual Meetings: How Graphics, Sticky Notes and Idea Mapping Can Transform Group Productivity*, 2010

▐433▌

RUSSELL ROBERTS

The Choice: A Fable of Free Trade and Protection, 3rd Edition

(Upper Saddle River, New Jersey: Pearson Prentice Hall, 2005)

Subject(s): Commerce; International relations; Business

Summary: Written by Russell Roberts, *The Choice: A Fable of Free Trade and Protection, 3rd Edition* is a novel designed to teach students about international trade. Designed to simplify complex concepts and terminology related to international trade and trade policy, *The Choice* tells the tale of Ed Johnson, an American television manufacturer seeking protection from his Japanese contemporaries. Economist David Ricardo comes back to life in order to guide Johnson through the complicated and challenging world of international trade. Through their time together, Ricardo explains international trade and trade policy and how it affects individuals, companies, and nations around the globe. To show the positive benefits of international trade and trade policy, Ricardo and Johnson travel through time to see a future America of free trade and an America of self-sufficiency.

Other books by the same author:
Tony Ray-Jones, 2009
The Price of Everything: A Parable of Possibility and Prosperity, 2008

Other books you might like:
Andrew Bernstein, *Capitalism Unbound: The Incontestable Moral Case for Individual Rights*, 2010
James D. Gwartney, *Common Sense Economics: What Everyone Should Know About Wealth and Prosperity*, 2010
Clyde Prestowitz, *Three Billion New Capitalists: The Great Shift of Wealth and Power to the East*, 2005

▐434▌

EMANUEL ROSEN

The Anatomy of Buzz Revisited: Real-Life Lessons in Word-of-Mouth Marketing

(New York: Crown Business, 2009)

Subject(s): Business; Advertising; Public relations

Summary: In *The Anatomy of Buzz*, published in 2000, author Emanuel Rosen explored how word-of-mouth marketing, also known as buzz, generated success for movies, companies, products, books, and more. Now Rosen presents *The Anatomy of Buzz Revisited: Real-Life Lessons in Word-of-Mouth Marketing*, an expanded edition of real-world experiences revised to include buzz campaigns from 2000 through 2009. In this new edition, Rosen explores how social media networks have contributed to buzz and how business leaders and marketers can customize their buzz campaigns toward new media users. Rosen uses interviews, market research, and case studies to examine how buzz remained just as relevant nine years after the publication of his original book.

Other books you might like:
Chip Heath, *Made to Stick: Why Some Ideas Survive and Others Die*, 2007
  Dan Heath, co-author
Andy Sernovitz, *Word of Mouth Marketing: How Smart Companies Get People Talking, Revised Edition*, 2009
Rob Walker, *Buying In: The Secret Dialogue Between What We Buy and Who We Are*, 2008

▐435▌

JEFFREY ROTHFEDER

McIlhenny's Gold: How a Louisiana Family Built the Tabasco Empire

(New York: Collins Business, 2007)

Subject(s): Business enterprises; Family; Entrepreneurship

Summary: In his book *McIlhenny's Gold: How a Louisiana Family Built the Tobasco Empire*, business journalist Jeffrey Rothfeder explores the world of the McIlhenny Tabasco sauce business. This volume charts the tumultuous history of one of the business world's most peculiar families and its unique successes. The book explores the company's unlikely start in post-Civil War Louisiana and its gaining the status as the producer of one of the most distinctive products on the market. Rothfeder also introduces the many members the McIlhenny family who had a part in the company's success. *McIlhenny's Gold* is fully indexed and includes notes on the text.

Other books you might like:
Richard L. Brand, *Inside Larry and Sergey's Brain*, 2009
Mark Kurlansky, *The Big Oyster: History on the Half Shell*, 2006
Julia Flynn Siler, *The House of Mondavi: The Rise and Fall of an American Wine Dynasty*, 2007

▐436▌

DARREN ROWSE
CHRIS GARRETT , Co-Author

ProBlogger: Secrets for Blogging Your Way to a Six-Figure Income

(Hoboken, New Jersey: Wiley, 2008)

Subject(s): Technology; Writing; Internet

Summary: In *ProBlogger: Secrets for Blogging Your Way to a Six-Figure Income*, professional bloggers Darren Rowse and Chris Garrett show readers how to create *successful blogs that will generate definite income. Rowse and Garrett take amateur bloggers through the motions, coaching them on choosing a topic they can continue to write about for years. They help readers figure out their intended audience and then walk them through the stages of finding a site to host their blog and designing a user-friendly page. Users will be prepared for all technical and editorial issues after reading this book. Rowse and Garrett also own ProBlogger.net, a website dedicated to helping out the beginner blogger.*

Other books you might like:

Robert W. Bly, *How to Write & Sell Simple Information for Fun and Profit: Your Guide to Writing and Publishing Books, E-Books, Articles, Special Reports, Audio Programs, DVDs, and Other How-To Content*, 2010

Joel Comm, *KaChing: How to Run an Online Business that Pays and Pays*, 2010

Tara Frey, *Blogging for Bliss: Crafting Your Own Online Journal: A Guide for Crafters, Artists & Creatives of all Kinds*, 2009

437

DAN SCHAWBEL

Me 2.0: Build a Powerful Brand to Achieve Career Success
(New York: Kaplan Publishing, 2009)

Subject(s): Employment; Business; Entrepreneurship

Summary: In *Me 2.0: Build a Powerful Brand to Achieve Career Success*, author Dan Schawbel offers career builders advice on how to achieve their career goals by branding themselves. As Schawbel explains, economic downturns of the early millennium have newly graduated young professionals scrambling to find employment. In this book, Schawbel provides insight on how self-promotion increases exposure for job seekers, thus helping them land that dream job. The author contends that even in the toughest of economies, young professionals who brand themselves stand a great chance of succeeding if they follow his advice.

Other books you might like:

Tom Peters, The Brand You 50: Or : Fify Ways to Transform Yourself from an 'Employee' into a Brand That Shouts Distinction, Commitment, and Passion!, 1999

Harry Beckwith, *You, Inc.: The Art of Selling Yourself*, 2007

438

ROBERT SCOBLE
SHEL ISRAEL , Co-Author

Naked Conversations: How Blogs Are Changing the Way Businesses Talk with Customers
(Hoboken, New Jersey: John Wiley, 2006)

Subject(s): Business; Internet

Summary: Blogs and bloggers have taken over the Internet. Robert Scoble, a Microsoft employee with his own popular blog, and Shel Israel, a technology specialist, want to help businesses harness the power of blogging. Scoble and Israel argue that blogging provides instantaneous and jargon-free communication between companies and clients. In *Naked Conversations: How Blogs Are Changing the Way Businesses Talk with Customers,* they not only provide a history of blogging but also provide many case studies about large and small businesses that have used blogs to successfully interact with their customers. Scoble and Israel also provide a short how-to guide specifically for business blogs.

Other books by the same author:
Twitterville: How Businesses Can Thrive in the New Global Neighborhoods, 2009

Other books you might like:
Josh Bernoff, *Groundswell: Winning in a World Transformed by Social Technologies*, 2008

Chris Brogan, *Trust Agents: Using the Web to Build Influence, Improve Reputation, and Earn Trust*, 2009

Jackie Huba, *Citizen Marketers: When People Are the Message*, 2006

Charlene Li, *Groundswell: Winning in a World Transformed by Social Technologies*, 2008

Ben McConnell, *Citizen Marketers: When People Are the Message*, 2006

Julien Smith, *Trust Agents: Using the Web to Build Influence, Improve Reputation, and Earn Trust*, 2009

439

DAVID MEERMAN SCOTT

The New Rules of Marketing and PR: How to Use News Releases, Blogs, Podcasting, Viral Marketing and Online Media to Reach Buyers Directly
(Hoboken, New Jersey: John Wiley and Sons, 2007)

Subject(s): Marketing; Public relations; Business

Summary: The world of online social media is revolutionizing the industries of marketing and public relations. In *The New Rules of Marketing and PR: How to Use News Releases, Blogs, Podcasting, Viral Marketing and Online Media to Reach Buyers Directly,* respected PR guru David Meerman Scott guides professionals through the ins and outs of this new form of media. Scott's advice sets out to utilize the exposure of the internet for the advancement of marketing and PR businesses large and small, and his professional insights cover everything from blogging and RSS to podcasts and vodcasts. *The New Rules of Marketing and PR* includes a full index.

Other books by the same author:
Marketing Lessons from the Grateful Dead: What Every Business Can Learn from the Most Iconic Band in History, 2010

Real-Time Marketing and PR: How to Instantly Engage Your Market, Connect with Customers, and Create Products that Grow Your Business Now, 2010

World Wide Rave: Creating Triggers that Get Millions

of People to Spread Your Ideas and Share Your Stories, 2009

Cashing In With Content: How Innovative Marketers Use Digital Information to Turn Browsers into Buyers, 2005

Other books you might like:

Brian Halligan, *Inbound Marketing: Get Found Using Google, Social Media, and Blogs*, 2009

Shama Hyder Kabani, *The Zen of Social Media Marketing: An Easier Way to Build Credibility, Generate Buzz, and Increase Revenue*, 2010

Lon Safko, *The Social Media Bible: Tactics, Tools, and Strategies for Business Success*, 2010

440

SCOTT SHANE

Fool's Gold?: The Truth Behind Angel Investing in America

(New York: Oxford University Press USA, 2008)

Subject(s): Business; Economics; Finance

Summary: *Fool's Gold?: The Truth Behind Angel Investing in America* is part of the Financial Management Association Survey and Synthesis series by Oxford University Press. In this book, author Scott Shane explores the phenomenon of angel investing, a practice in which wealthy individuals provide start-up funds for new businesses in exchange for a partnership or stock options. Shane examines the influx of angel investor networks in the 21st century and whether these investors are making smart money or, as Shane describes it, "fool's gold." Shane uses statistics from the Federal Reserve to show strong evidence that many angel investors typically receive little return for their investments. The author also provides valuable advice to assist such investors in bridging the divide between venture capitalist and professional investments.

Other books by the same author:

Born Entrepreneurs, Born Leaders: How Your Genes Affect Your Work Life, 2010

The Illusions of Entrepreneurship: The Costly Myths That Entrepreneurs, Investors, and Policy Makers Live By, 2008

Technology Strategy for Managers and Entrepreneurs, 2008

Entrepreneurship: A Process Perspective, 2007

From Ice Cream to the Internet: Using Franchising to Drive the Growth and Profits of Your Company, 2005

Other books you might like:

David Amis, *Winning Angels: The 7 fundamentals of early stage investing*, 2009

Brad Feld, *Do More Faster: TechStars Lessons to Accelerate Your Startup*, 2010

Alex Wilmerding, *Term Sheets & Valuations - A Line by Line Look at the Intricacies of Venture Capital Term Sheets*, 2006

441

ROBERT SLATER

No Such Thing as Over-Exposure: Inside the Life and Celebrity of Donald Trump

(Upper Saddle River, New Jersey: Financial Times Prentice Hall, 2005)

Subject(s): Real estate; Money; Wealth

Summary: As Donald Trump's *The Apprentice* garnered more attention than ever before with its addition of celebrities and difficult challenges, author Robert Slater sat at Trump's side and took notes diligently. Having convinced Trump to let Slater travel with him to research his biography, Slater was able to sit in on top-secret business meetings and listen in on personal phone calls. Slater combined over 150 interviews with men and women who worked closely with Trump with the events he observed on his own to produce *No Such Thing as Over-Exposure: Inside the Life and Celebrity of Donald T'rump*. This book brings Trump fans information about the billionaire's past, his rise to fame, and his view of his own celebrity status.

Other books by the same author:

Seizing Power: The Grab for Global Oil Wealth, 2010

Soros: The Life, Ideas, and Impact of the World's Most Influential Investor, 2008

Other books you might like:

Donal J. Trump, *Think Big: Make It Happen in Business and Life*, 2008

Ken Lawrence, *The World According to Trump: An Unauthorized Portrait in His Own Words*, 2005

442

PAMELA SLIM

Escape From Cubicle Nation: From Corporate Prisoner to Thriving Entrepreneur

(New York: Portfolio, 2009)

Subject(s): Entrepreneurship; Business; Success

Summary: In *Escape from Cubicle Nation: From Corporate Prisoner to Thriving Entrepreneur*, Pamela Slim, author of a popular blog of the same name, offers advice for leaving a corporate job and becoming a self-employed entrepreneur. Slim discusses the risks and benefits of leaving a corporate job, such as the need to purchase one's own insurance and other benefits, and discusses the realistic downsides behind self-employment and being one's own boss. She also considers the different avenues for self-employment. The book includes tips about creating a successful business plan, finding the right people to work with you, identifying areas in life where finances can be scaled back in order to save money, learning about legal considerations, and more.

Other books by the same author:
Escape From Corporate Hell: Unlock Your Potential and Love Your Work, 2010

Other books you might like:
Norm Brodsky, *The Knack: How Street-Smart Entrepreneurs Learn to Handle Whatever Comes Up*, 2008
    Bo Burlingham, co-author
Jonathan Fields, *Career Renegade: How to Make a Great Living Doing What You Love*, 2009
Chris Guillebeau, *The Art of Non-Conformity: Set Your Own Rules, Live the Life You Want, and Change the World*, 2010

443

DAVID M. SMICK

The World Is Curved: Hidden Dangers to the Global Economy

(New York: Portfolio, 2008)

Subject(s): Finance; Economic depressions; Economics

Summary: In *The World Is Curved: Hidden Dangers to the Global Economy*, esteemed financial strategist David M. Smick exposes the pitfalls of the current global economic landscape and arms readers with the necessary knowledge to circumvent these potentially dangerous roadblocks. Smick goes behind the scenes of the economic crisis to fully illustrate the problems inherent in today's global economy. His findings support the notion that deregulation of business is the key to prosperity, and he advises aspiring entrepreneurs to embark on their dream careers as a catalyst to jumpstarting the economy. *The World Is Curved* includes a bibliography and an index. First book.

Other books you might like:
Gregg Easterbrook, *Sonic Boom: Globalization at Mach Speed*, 2009
Charles R. Morris, *The Trillion Dollar Meltdown: Easy Money, High Rollers, and the Great Credit Crash*, 2008
Joseph E. Stiglitz, *Making Globalization Work*, 2006

444

MICHAEL R. SOLOMON

The Truth about What Customers Want

(Upper Saddle, New Jersey: Financial Times Prentice Hall, 2008)

Subject(s): Marketing; Capitalism; Shopping

Summary: In *The Truth about What Customers Want*, author Michael R. Solomon identifies 50 facts that can help businesses better attract and retain customers. Solomon explains that consumers are always looking for a better experience, that they tend to buy what their neighbors and friends buy, and that businesses need to stay in the consumer's mind long after the purchase is made. Solomon explores many of the newest trends and advances in consumer behavior, such as online shopping,

eco-friendly consumption, and the growth in male beauty products. Gay and lesbian consumer markets and virtual-world marketing strategies are also discussed. Suggestions for further reading and an author's note complement the text.

Other books you might like:
Stephen Ross, *Fundamentals of Corporate Finance Standard Edition*, 2009
Brian D. Till, *The Truth About Creating Brands People Love*, 2008
Rob Walker, *Buying In: The Secret Dialogue Between What We Buy and Who We Are*, 2008

445

JOHN SPENCE

Awesomely Simple: Essential Business Strategies for Turning Ideas Into Action

(San Francisco, California: Jossey-Bass, 2009)

Subject(s): Business; Entrepreneurship; Marketing

Summary: In *Awesomely Simple: Essential Business Strategies for Turning Ideas Into Action*, author John Spence explains how to put into practice specific tactics that will help entrepreneurs succeed in the business world. Spence outlines six key principles to promoting and developing one's business plan. The author also uses case studies, personal anecdotes, interviews, and organizational strategies to help business owners get started. Spence is also the author of *Excellence by Design: Leadership* and *Strategies for Life Success*.

Other books by the same author:
Strategies for Life Success, 2009
Excellence By Design Leadership, 2008

Other books you might like:
Connie Dieken, *Talk Less, Say More: Three Habits to Influence Others and Make Things Happen*, 2009
John Jantsch, *The Referral Engine: Teaching Your Business to Market Itself*, 2010
Simon Sinek, *Start with Why: How Great Leaders Inspire Everyone to Take Action*, 2009

446

NOAH ST. JOHN

The Secret Code of Success: 7 Hidden Steps to More Wealth and Happiness

(New York: HarperCollins Publishers, 2009)

Subject(s): Success; Business; Self help books

Summary: In his motivational book *The Secret Code of Success: 7 Hidden Steps to More Wealth and Happiness*, Noah St. John explains that self-fulfillment cannot be found without getting past certain destructive behavioral patterns. Broken into three "acts," the majority of the book centers around "Act II, The Code." It is here that St. John explains his seven steps for reaching goals quickly. These tips include "Loving Mirrors and Safe Havens," "Goal-Free Zones and Goal Replacement Surgery," and "Find Your No." Each chapter details how to succeed in reaching objectives, both personally and professionally. Topics include making more money, becoming more productive, and feeling better, happier, and more fulfilled. Whether a goal is to lose weight or to be more productive at work, St. John provides the tools necessary to help readers get past emotional barriers to achieve what they set out to accomplish in life and in business.

Other books by the same author:
The Great Little Book of Afformations, 2006

Other books you might like:
Jr. Goi, *How to Attract Money Using Mind Power*, 2007
Madeleine Kay, *Serendipitously Rich: How to Get Delightfully, Delectably, Deliciously Rich (or Anything Else You Want) in 7 Ridiculously Easy Steps*, 2009
Michael Masterson, *The Pledge: Your Master Plan for an Abundant Life*, 2010

447

MICHAEL BUNGAY STANIER

Do More Great Work. Stop the Busywork, and Start the Work That Matters

(New York: Workman Publishers, 2010)

Subject(s): Business; Success; Self help books

Summary: In *Do More Great Work. Stop the Busywork, and Start the Work That Matters*, author Michael Bungay Stanier helps readers find satisfaction and success at work. Many individuals get bogged down at the office doing mindless busywork that's unfulfilling, unrewarding, and time-consuming. When employees are trapped doing "bad work," such as answering e-mails, returning phone calls, or attending meetings, they miss out on opportunities to do "great work" and possibly advance in the company and find happiness in their career. In *Do More Great Work*, Stanier provides readers with a series of brief exercises to help them move beyond tiresome activities on the job and find the work they really love. The book helps individuals come up with new ideas, determine the kind of work they want to do and find ways to do it, manage hectic workloads, and increase prospects for fulfillment on the job.

Other books you might like:
Marshall Goldsmith, *Mojo: How to Get It, How to Keep It, How to Get It Back If You Lose It*, 2003
Chip Heath, *Switch: How to Change Things When Change Is Hard*, 2010
Dan Heath, co-author
M.J. Ryan, *This Year I Will...: How to Finally Change a Habit, Keep a Resolution, or Make a Dream Come True*, 2006

448

SCOTT STRATTEN

UnMarketing: Stop Marketing. Start Engaging.

(Hoboken, New Jersey: Wiley, 2010)

Subject(s): Business; Marketing; Business enterprises

Summary: *UnMarketing: Stop Marketing. Start Engaging.* is a practical resource guide for business owners, managers, and entrepreneurs from marketing expert and author Scott Stratten. As of late, marketing has gotten a bad reputation and has proven to be an ineffective way to win customers, especially with practices such as mass e-mail campaigns, cold calling, and commercials. Stratten challenges business owners to change their marketing methods to a more personable approach. Instead of blind mass marketing, *UnMarketing* encourages business owners, managers, and entrepreneurs to engage potential clients in conversation, truly listen to their needs and desires, and develop a personal relationship with them. The book provides tips and tricks that any business can use and includes advice on relying on social media as a new, effective way to reach customers.

Other books you might like:
Chris Guillebeau, *The Art of Non-Conformity: Set Your Own Rules, Live the Life You Want, and Change the World*, 2010
Ann Handley, *Content Rules: How to Create Killer Blogs, Podcasts, Videos, Ebooks, Webinars (and More) That Engage Customers and Ignite Your Business*, 2010
Brian Solis, *Engage: The Complete Guide for Brands and Businesses to Build, Cultivate, and Measure Success in the New Web*, 2010

449

STEVEN D. STRAUSS

The Small Business Bible: Everything You Need to Know to Succeed in Your Small Business

(Hoboken, New Jersey: Wiley, 2008)

Subject(s): Business; Entrepreneurship; Business enterprises

Summary: *The Small Business Bible: Everything You Need to Know to Succeed in Your Small Business* is a comprehensive resource guide for small business owners from author Steven D. Strauss. This in-depth and straightforward book covers all facets of small business ownership and includes insider tips for success and profit, true stories and anecdotes, and practical advice. Strauss provides readers with detailed information on launching and developing a successful business, from developing the idea to writing a business plan to hiring and firing employees. This updated guide also offers new chapters on key trends and tips for 21st century businesses including e-commerce, green or eco-friendly businesses, online marketing and networking, and technological advances.

Other books by the same author:
The Complete Idiot's Guide to World Conflicts, 2nd Edition, 2006

Other books you might like:
Tim Berry, *3 Weeks to Startup*, 2008
Bill Collier, *How to Succeed as a Small Business Owner ... and Still Have a Life*, 2006
Tom Gegax, *The Big Book of Small Business: You Don't Have to Run Your Business by the Seat of Your Pants*, 2007

450

DON TAPSCOTT
ANTHONY D. WILLIAMS , Co-Author

Wikinomics: How Mass Collaboration Changes Everything
(New York: Penguin, 2006)

Subject(s): Business; Business Enterprises; Economics

Summary: The global collaboration that fuels Internet sites such as Wikipedia and YouTube has become a powerful force that contradicts traditional views on collaboration and intellectual property. If anyone can contribute to an idea, who owns it? While many see this phenomenon as a serious threat to business, CEO Don Tapscott and research director Anthony Williams see it instead as an opportunity. In *Wikinomics*, the authors trace the history of global collaboration and present ways in which the business world can work with and benefit from this new way of generating and sharing ideas.

Other books by the same author:
Macrowikinomics: Rebooting Business and the World, 2010
Grown Up Digital: How the Net Generation is Changing Your World, 2008

Other books you might like:
Dan Ariely, *The Upside of Irrationality: The Unexpected Benefits of Defying Logic at Work and at Home*, 2010
Jeff Howe, *Crowdsourcing: Why the Power of the Crowd Is Driving the Future of Business*, 2008
Clay Shirky, *Here Comes Everybody: The Power of Organizing Without Organizations*, 2008

451

JONATHAN M. TISCH
KARL WEBER , Co-Author

Chocolates on the Pillow Aren't Enough: Reinventing the Customer Experience
(Hoboken, New Jersey: Wiley, 2007)

Subject(s): Business; Work environment; Success

Summary: The head of Loews Hotels, Jonathan M.

Tisch—with the help of writer Karl Weber—presents his expertise in the area of customer service in *Chocolates on the Pillow Aren't Enough: Reinventing the Customer Experience*. In the hotel industry, the patron expects not only spotless rooms and excellent customer service, but also all of the modern amenities. Tisch trains his staff to meet and exceed customers' expectations. Among the fundamentals of successful customer service that Tisch describes are integrating technology without losing human interaction; providing a sense of both "physical and psychological security"; expanding amenities beyond the basics; ensuring that the first area encountered by customers is warm and welcoming; and more. Tisch provides examples of businesses that not only strive to make customer service experiences enjoyable, but also inspire client loyalty. His strategies can be applied to the hotel business, as well as to any other industry that relies on repeat customers for success.

Other books by the same author:
Citizen You: Doing Your Part to Change the World, 2010

Other books you might like:
Danny Meyer, *Setting the Table: The Transforming Power of Hospitality in Business*, 2006
Joseph Michelli, *The New Gold Standard: 5 Leadership Principles for Creating a Legendary Customer Experience Courtesy of the Ritz-Carlton Hotel Company*, 2008
Isadore Sharp, *Four Seasons: The Story of a Business Philosophy*, 2009

452

JOHN H. VANSTON
CARRIE VANSTON , Co-Author

Minitrends: Finding & Profiting from Emerging Business Opportunity Gems
(Austin, Texas: Technology Futures, Inc., 2010)

Subject(s): Business; Finance; Economics

Summary: *Minitrends: Finding & Profiting from Emerging Business Opportunity Gems* by John H. Vanston and Carrie Vanston contains advice for everyone who wants to succeed in business, including investors, entrepreneurs, and business owners. The authors focus on "minitrends," small trends in business and technology that can lead to big rewards, and provide advice on correctly discerning and making use of these trends. The current trends discussed in this text include increasing involvement in social networking and other types of virtual realities, desire for increased privacy and increased website capability, the interest of employees in working from home, and new advances in manufacturing, such as nanotechnology.

Where it's reviewed:
Library Journal, September 1, 2010, page 121

Other books by the same author:
Home Technology Integration: A Technology Forecast, 2007

Mechatronics: A Technology Forecast, 2007
Biotechnology: A Technology Forecast, 2006

Other books you might like:

Scott Belsky, *Making Ideas Happen: Overcoming the Obstacles Between Vision and Reality*, 2010

William Higham, *The Next Big Thing: Spotting and Forecasting Consumer Trends for Profit*, 2009

Richard Watson, *Future Files: The 5 Trends That Will Shape the Next 50 Years*, 2008

453

GARY VAYNERCHUK

Viral Loop: From Facebook to Twitter, How Today's Smartest Businesses Grow Themselves

(New York: HarperBusiness, 2009)

Subject(s): Entrepreneurship; Business; Money

Summary: To entrepreneur Gary Vaynerchuk, passion equals profit. In *Crush It!: Why NOW is the Time to Cash in on Your Passion*, Vaynerchuk encourages readers to decide what they like and then turn it into a big, bustling business. Vaynerchuk supports his assertions with anecdotes about his own experiences. Using blogs, Twitter, Facebook, and other Internet resources, he turned an inherited $4 million liquor business into a $50 million powerhouse.

Other books you might like:/rb

Charlene Li, *Groundswell: Winning in a World Transformed by Social Technologies*, 2008

Josh Bernoff, *Emposered: Unleash Your employees, Energize Your Customers, and Transform Your Business*, 2010

454

TAMAR WEINBERG

The New Community Rules: Marketing on the Social Web

(Sebastopol, California: O'Reilly Media, 2009)

Subject(s): Internet; Business; Marketing

Summary: *The New Community Rules: Marketing on the Social Web*, by Tamar Weinberg, is a guide to business marketing on the Internet and World Wide Web. In this book, Weinberg explains how to properly promote one's business brand via new social media such as Facebook, Twitter, LinkedIn, and other social networks. The author explores how the Internet's global village gives businesses a voice, and how using specific strategies can improve one's brand. Weinberg also looks at how using Web communities such as blogs or message boards can create business name recognition and increase a business's reputation. First book.

Other books you might like:

Lon Safko, *The Social Media Bible: Tactics, Tools, and Strategies for Business Success*, 2010

David Meerman Scott, *The New Rules of Marketing and*

PR: How to Use News Releases, Blogs, Podcasting, Viral Marketing and Online Media to Reach Buyers Directly, 2007

455

JACK WELCH
SUZY WELCH , Co-Author

Winning

(New York: Hyperion, 2005)

Subject(s): Business; Management

Summary: Jack Welch is the near-legendary businessman who transformed General Electric from a big-but-inert power company into one of the most dynamic, powerful, and profitable giants in the world economy. In this book, written after his retirement, he presents the management technique he employed in his four decades helming GE. He discusses a wide range of topics, including business values; organization; motivation and compensation; hiring and firing; crisis management; and overall business strategy. In a section at the end, he answers the most interesting questions asked him in his years of traveling and speaking, including "Do you think you will go to heaven?"

Other books by the same author:

10-10-10: A Fast and Powerful Way to Get Unstuck in Love, at Work, and with Your Family, 2010

Winning: The Answers: Confronting 74 of the Toughest Questions in Business Today, 2006

Winning: The Answers: Confronting 74 of the Toughest Questions in Business Today, 2006

Other books you might like:

Jim Collins, *How the Mighty Fall: And Why Some Companies Never Give In*, 2009

Jeffrey Krames, *Jack Welch and The 4 E's of Leadership: How to Put GE's Leadership Formula to Work in Your Organizaion*, 2005

John C. Maxwell, *The 21 Irrefutable Laws of Leadership: Follow Them and People Will Follow You*, 1998

456

ERIK WESNER

Success Made Simple: An Inside Look at Why Amish Businesses Thrive

(San Francisco, California: Jossey-Bass, 2010)

Subject(s): Amish; Business; Entrepreneurship

Summary: *Success Made Simple: An Inside Look at Why Amish Businesses Thrive* is an in-depth examination of Amish business practices and success from author and Amish expert Erik Wesner. One-half of small businesses end up folding in less than five years. However, businesses opened and run by the Amish have a 95 percent success rate. Wesner examines the phenomenon in *Suc-*

cess Made Simple and provides readers with practical tips that can be learned from Amish business owners. To write the book, Wesner worked and lived with Amish communities across the nation, interviewing more than 50 Amish business owners to find patterns to their success. He shares these secrets in *Success Made Simple*, showing the importance of building strong relationships with employees and clients, maintaining integrity, and planning ahead.

Other books you might like:

Suzanne Woods Fisher, *Amish Peace: Simple Wisdom for a Complicated World*, 2009

Joe Mackall, *Plain Secrets: An Outsider among the Amish*, 2007

Michael H. Shuman, *Small-Mart Revolution: How Local Businesses Are Beating the Global Competition*, 2006

457

ADDISON WIGGIN
KATE INCONTRERA , Co-Author
DORIANNE PERRUCCI , Co-Author

I.O.U.S.A.

(Hoboken, New Jersey: Wiley, 2009)

Subject(s): Economics; United States; Finance

Summary: The United States deficit is running into record highs, and the government keeps writing more checks. As the country sinks further and further into debt, many people worry about how these obligations will be paid. *I.O.U.S.A.*, a book by Addison Wiggin, Kate Incontrera, and Dorianne Perrucci, explores the United States' debt and what can be done about it. The book, which serves as a companion to the documentary film of the same name, contains commentary from well-known figures in the world of finance such as Warren Buffet and Paul O'Neill. The book also aims to convince ordinary American citizens that they have the power to influence their government and reduce the country's massive debt.

Other books by the same author:

The Demise of the Dollar... and Why It's Great For Your Investments, 2005

Other books you might like:

Bill Bonner, *Financial Reckoning Day Fallout: Surviving the Soft Depression of the 21st Century*, 2003

Eileen McGann, *Catastrophe*, 2009
   Dick Morris, co-author

David M. Walker, *Comeback America: Turning the Country Around and Restoring Fiscal Responsibility*, 2010

Addison Wiggin, *Financial Reckoning Day Fallout: Surviving the Soft Depression of the 21st Century*, 2003

458

STEVE WILKINGHOFF

Found Money: Simple Strategies for Uncovering the Hidden Profit and Cash Flow in Your Business

(Hoboken, New Jersey: John Wiley & Sons, 2009)

Subject(s): Business; Economics; Finance

Summary: In *Found Money: Simple Strategies for Uncovering the Hidden Profit and Cash Flow in Your Business*, author Steve Wilkinghoff offers advice and insight on increasing a business's profits by tapping into creative avenues. Wilkinghoff provides key tactics and solutions to unlocking a business's potential, regardless of whether that business is faltering or is already hugely successful. The author is an accountant and business consultant who leads seminars and discussion groups on increasing business revenue. This book also contains a foreword by Michael Gerber, small business entrepreneur and creator of the E-Myth.

Other books you might like:

Michael E. Gerber, *The Most Successful Small Business in The World: The Ten Principles*, 2010

Denise O'Berry, *Small Business Cash Flow: Strategies for Making Your Business a Financial Success*, 2006

John Warrillow, *Built to Sell: Turn Your Business Into One You Can Sell*, 2010

459

MITCHELL ZUCKOFF

Ponzi's Scheme: The True Story of a Financial Legend

(New York: Random House, 2005)

Subject(s): Money; Immigrants; Business

Summary: In *Ponzi's Scheme: The True Story of a Financial Legend*, author and Boston University journalism professor Mitchell Zuckoff presents a spirited biography of notorious con artist Charles Ponzi. After he arrived in America just after the turn of the century, Ponzi recognized the vulnerabilities of the middle class—and promptly set out to skim a profit from those vulnerabilities. His moneymaking scams evolved over the years until he crafted the legendary scheme that is named after him. It was a scheme that brought Ponzi millions of dollars a week...and a place in infamy. *Ponzi's Scheme* includes notes on the text, a bibliography, and an index.

Other books by the same author:
Robert Altman: The Oral Biography, 2009

Other books you might like:

Erin Arvedlund, *Too Good to Be True: The Rise and Fall of Bernie Madoff*, 2010

Frank Partnoy, *The Match King: Ivar Kreuger, The Financial Genius Behind a Century of Wall Street Scandals*, 2009

Health and Wellness

460

ROBERT ABEL JR.

The Eye Care Revolution: Prevent and Reverse Common Vision Problems

(New York: Kensington Books, 2010)

Subject(s): Health; Reference works; Medical care

Summary: In *The Eye Care Revolution: Prevent and Reverse Common Vision Problems*, Robert Abel Jr. takes a holistic approach to preventing and curing various eye conditions and improving vision. The author begins with a discussion of the anatomy of the eye and then provides information about the most common eye diseases, ranging in severity from dry eyes to glaucoma or diabetic retinopathy. Alternative treatments for these conditions, including dietary changes, vitamins, and herbal remedies, among others, fill this volume. *The Eye Care Revolution* also stresses the importance of regular eye exams and the need to examine all medications one takes to determine whether they can damage to the eyes.

Other books by the same author:
Lethal Hindsight, 2010

Other books you might like:
James Compton Burnett, *Curability of Cataract with Medicines*, 2010
Jeffrey S. Heier, *100 Questions and Answers About Macular Degeneration*, 2009
Clyde K. Kitchen, *Fact and Fiction of Healthy Vision: Eye Care for Adults and Children*, 2007
Michael A. Samuel, *Macular Degeneration*, 2008

461

PHYLLIS B. ACOSTA

Nutrition Management of Patients with Inherited Metabolic Diseases

(Sudbury, Massachusetts: Jones and Bartlett Publishers, 2009)

Subject(s): Health; Medicine; Medical care

Summary: In *Nutrition Management of Patients with*
Inherited Metabolic Disorders, nutritionist, editor, and contributor Phyllis B. Acosta presents a guide for health care providers who deal with the treatment of IMDs. Each of the book's 15 chapters—written by leading authorities in the field of nutrition—covers a specific aspect of nutrition management in IMD patients. Topics include newborn screening by mass spectrometry, practical aspects of nutrition management, and nutrition management as it pertains to patients with disorders of aromatic amino acid metabolism, branched-chain amino acid metabolism, sulfur amino acid metabolism, organic acid metabolism, galactose metabolism, mitochondrial fatty acid oxidation, and urea cycle enzymes.

Where it's reviewed:
Medicine and Science in Sports and Exercise, March 2010, page 631

Other books you might like:
Joe T. R. Clarke, *A Clinical Guide to Inherited Metabolic Diseases*, 2006
Steve Hannigan, *Inherited Metabolic Diseases: A Guide to 100 Conditions*, 2007

462

JOHN W. ANDERSON

Stand by Her: A Breast Cancer Guide for Men

(New York: AMACOM, American Management Association, 2009)

Subject(s): Health; Medical care; Medicine

Summary: In *Stand by Her: A Breast Cancer Guide for Men*, John W. Anderson presents a valuable guide for the husbands, sons, brothers, and fathers of breast cancer patients. Having experienced the effects of breast cancer in his own family (wife, mother, and sister), the author is familiar with the unique role the male support system plays in the patient's treatment and recovery. Drawing on his own experiences, Anderson shares advice on supporting a loved one as she deals with diagnosis, surgery, chemotherapy, radiation therapy, related emotional issues, the fear of recurrence, and the joy of complete recovery.

Other books you might like:
Stanley C. Scott, *Surviving Your Wife's Cancer: A Guide For Husbands Whose Wives Have Been*

Diagnosed With Cancer, 2008

Dan Werner, *Real Men Wear Pink: A Man's Guide to Surviving a Loved One's Breast Cancer*, 2007

463

NELSON ANDERSON

A Heart Attack Survivor's Guide to a Long Healthy Life

(Las Vegas, Nevada: HAS Books, 2009)

Subject(s): Health; Heart diseases; Exercise

Summary: Written by Nelson Anderson, *A Heart Attack Survivor's Guide to a Long Healthy Life* is a practical guide for getting fit and staying healthy. After suffering a heart attack, Anderson spent years trying to get into shape and live a healthier lifestyle. Through both trial-and-error and research, he discovered a system of dieting and exercise that truly helped keep him healthy. In *A Heart Attack Survivor's Guide to a Long Healthy Life*, Anderson shares his findings in an effort to help others recover from a heart attack or avoid one altogether. The book includes daily diet plans, exercise regimens, advice on vitamins and supplements, and healthy recipes.

Other books you might like:

Sari Budgazad, *The Cardiac Recovery Cookbook: Heart Healthy Recipes for Life After Heart Attack or Heart Surgery*, 2005
M. Laurel Cutlip, co-author

Patrick J. Fox, *The Widow-Maker Heart Attack At Age 48: Written By A Heart Attack Survivor For A Heart Attack Survivor And Their Loved Ones*, 2009

Paul Kligfield, *The Cardiac Recovery Handbook*, 2006

464

EDWARD BALL

The Genetic Strand: Exploring a Family History Through DNA

(New York: Simon & Schuster, 2007)

Subject(s): Genetics; Genetic research; Genealogy

Summary: When author Edward Ball discovered a few strands of hair inside a long hidden family heirloom container, he seized the opportunity to learn something about his family history by submitting the hairs for genetic DNA testing. The test findings and the resulting consequences encouraged Ball to record his thoughts and experiences in his book *The Genetic Strand: Exploring a Family History Through DNA*. When Ball submitted the hairs, he was looking to uncover whether he, in fact, had African-American blood, as he had long suspected. Ball takes readers along on his journey through numerous DNA laboratories, the science behind genetic testing, and discussions with various genetics experts. As the testing unfolded, the initial results indicated that Ball had some Native American ancestry, which shocked him so much so that he decided to have the test redone at

another lab, where scientists came up with conflicting results. This dramatic turn leads Ball to comment on the reliability of genetic testing and the danger of putting too much importance on science.

Where it's reviewed:
Biography, Winter 2008, page 162
Science Books & Films, Jan-Feb 2008, page 23
Science News, November 17, 2007, page 319

Other books by the same author:
100 Questions and Answers About Leukemia, 2007

Other books you might like:
John C. Avise, *Inside the Human Genome: A Case for Non-Intelligent Design*, 2010
Robin L. Bennett, *The Practical Guide to the Genetic Family History, 2nd Edition*, 2010
Peter S. Harper, *A Short History of Medical Genetics*, 2008
Jon Queijo, *Breakthrough!: How the 10 Greatest Discoveries in Medicine Saved Millions and Changed Our View of the World*, 2010
Doris Teichler-Zallen, *To Test or Not to Test: A Guide to Genetic Screening and Risk*, 2008

465

ARTHUR BANK

Turning Blood Red: The Fight for Life in Cooley's Anemia

(Hackensack, New Jersey: World Scientific, 2008)

Subject(s): Diseases; Medicine; Science

Summary: Physician Arthur Bank presents an all-encompassing exploration of the serious, possibly fatal blood disease known as Cooley's anemia, or beta thalassemia. *Turning Blood Red: The Fight for Life in Cooley's Anemia* offers details on both the clinical and emotional aspects of this disease, highlighting its pathology, the research conducted, and the toll it takes on individuals and families. Bank also examines present and future treatment options, as well as how professionals can utilize data on Cooley's anemia to gain fuller insight into other diseases. *Turning Blood Red* includes a listing of bibliographical references and a full index. First book.

Where it's reviewed:
Journal of Clinical Investigation, March 2009, page 426

Other books you might like:
Onyekachi Ifudu, *Renal Anemia: Conflicts and Controversies*, 2010
Betty Pace, *Renaissance of Sickle Cell Disease Research in the Genome*, 2007
Philip M. Parker, *Sickle Cell Anemia: A Bibliography and Dictionary for Physicians, Patients and Genome Researchers*, 2007
Beth Whitehouse, *Match: 'Savior Siblings' and One Family's Battle to Heal Their Daughter*, 2010
Viroj Wiwanitkit, *Tropical Anemia*, 2006

466

CHARLES BARDES

Pale Faces: The Masks of Anemia

(New York: Bellevue Literary Press, 2008)

Subject(s): Diseases; Medicine; Culture

Summary: Anemia is a common blood disease that has long had profound implications on both medicine and culture. In *Pale Faces: The Masks of Anemia*, Dr. Charles Bardes explores the effects of anemia on these two very different worlds. Bardes looks at the illness from a clinical perspective, charting its history, characteristics, and treatment. He also examines anemia in works of literature, art, and mythology, providing a unique, well-rounded overview of this universal—though often misunderstood—disease. *Pale Faces* includes a bibliography and an index.

Where it's reviewed:
Choice, April 2009, page 1538
Publishers Weekly, April 28, 2008, page 123

Other books you might like:
Onyekachi Ifudu, *Renal Anemia: Conflicts and Controversies*, 2010
Betty Pace, *Renaissance of Sickle Cell Disease Research in the Genome*, 2007
Philip M. Parker, *Sickle Cell Anemia: A Bibliography and Dictionary for Physicians, Patients and Genome Researchers*, 2007
Beth Whitehouse, *Match: 'Savior Siblings' and One Family's Battle to Heal Their Daughter*, 2010
Viroj Wiwanitkit, *Tropical Anemia*, 2006

467

RUSSELL A. BARKLEY

Taking Charge of Adult ADHD

(New York: Guilford Press, 2010)

Subject(s): Health; Medical care; Medicine

Summary: In *Taking Charge of Adult ADHD*, Russell A. Barkley offers a self-help guide for adults suffering from Attention Deficit Hyperactivity Disorder (ADHD). Barkley, an ADHD researcher and clinician, presents his plan in five steps—getting evaluated, changing your mind-set, changing your brain, changing your life, and changing your situation. Through each step, readers learn practical skills to help them deal with daily ADHD issues such as resisting impulses; self-control; medical treatment options (stimulants as well as non-stimulants); making problems external, physical, and manual; and adopting a sense of humor. Barkley gives special attention to the unique issues of adult ADHD, including education, work, money, relationships, driving, drug use, and crime.

Where it's reviewed:
Library Journal, July 2010, page 101

Other books by the same author:
ADHD in Adults, 2009
Assessment of Childhood Disorders, 2009

ADHD and the Nature of Self-Control, 2005
Attention-Deficit Hyperactivity Disorder, Third Edition: A Handbook for Diagnosis and Treatment, 2005

Other books you might like:
Lara Honos-Webb, *The Gift of Adult ADD: How to Transform Your Challenges and Build on Your Strengths*, 2008
Melissa Orlov, *The ADHD Effect on Marriage: Understand and Rebuild Your Relationship in Six Steps*, 2010
Gina Pera, *Is It You, Me, or Adult A.D.D.?*, 2008
Ari Tuckman, *Integrative Treatment for Adult ADHD: A Practical, Easy-to-Use Guide for Clinicians*, 2007
Ari Tuckman, *More Attention, Less Deficit: Success Strategies for Adults with ADHD*, 2009

468

LESLIE BAUMANN

Cosmetic Dermatology: Principles and Practice, 2nd Edition

(New York: McGraw-Hill, 2009)

Story type: Medical
Subject(s): Health; Medical care; Medicine

Summary: *Cosmetic Dermatology: Principles and Practice, 2nd Edition* is a helpful and informative guide for dermatologists on cosmetic treatments and drugs written by author, doctor, and professor Leslie Baumann. In *Cosmetic Dermatology*, Baumann offers a thorough overview of the latest information and research about cosmetic procedures and products for dermatologists who are hoping to understand cosmetic science. The book provides details on issues that affect skin appearance, the effectiveness of topical agents to improve the quality and look of skin, over-the-counter skin care products and their success, and cosmetic dermatological procedures, such as collagen injections, botulinum toxin injections, and chemical peels.

Other books by the same author:
The Skin Type Solution, 2006

Other books you might like:
Zoe Diana Draelos, *Cosmetic Dermatology: Principles and Practice*, 2010
Thomas P. Habif, *Clinical Dermatology*, 2009
Nikhil Yawalkar, *Management of Psoriasis*, 2009

469

ROBIN L. BENNETT

The Practical Guide to the Genetic Family History, 2nd Edition

(Hoboken, New Jersey: Wiley-Blackwell, 2010)

Subject(s): Genetics; Genetic disorders; Health

Summary: Robin L. Bennett's *The Practical Guide to the Genetic Family History, 2nd Edition* is intended for medical professionals and genetic counselors who are attempting to create a family pedigree to determine a patient's risk factors for certain hereditary conditions. The author first provides the reasoning behind the development of a complete family medical history, and then offers specific questions to ask as well as methods to verify that the family history is correct. Methods of interpreting the information and assessing risk are then included, followed by a discussion of any unique circumstances that could affect the information, such as if a patient is adopted. Clinical examples are included for more in-depth study and clarification. Bennett also discusses some of the ethical concerns surrounding genetic research.

Other books you might like:

Edward Ball, *The Genetic Strand: Exploring a Family History Through DNA*, 2007

Myra Vanderpool Gormley, *Family Diseases: Are You at Risk?*, 2009

Peter S. Harper, *A Short History of Medical Genetics*, 2008

Chris Pomery, *Family History in the Genes: Trace Your DNA and Grow Your Family Tree*, 2007

470

LYNN S. BICKLEY

Bates' Pocket Guide to Physical Examination and History Taking, Sixth Edition

(Philadelphia, Pennsylvania: Lippincott Williams & Wilkins, 2009)

Story type: Medical
Subject(s): Medical care; Medicine; Health

Summary: Written by Lynn S. Bickley, *Bates' Pocket Guide to Physical Examination and History Taking, Sixth Edition* is a straightforward and helpful resource guide for medical care professionals on the necessary protocols for conducting physical exams and taking accurate histories. The book features full-color illustrations and a step-by-step guide for medical practitioners to follow during exams and history taking. The information is organized into two columns for ease of use. The left column includes standard examination techniques and procedures while the right column includes information regarding abnormalities and diagnoses. The sixth edition includes expanded chapters and additional details about vital signs, pain assessment, and mental health behaviors.

Other books you might like:

Joseph J. Cipriano, *Photographic Manual of Regional Orthopaedic and Neurologic Tests*, 2010

Jonathan DiLauri, *Physical Therapy Musculoskeletal Examination*, 2009

Jane Schultz Garofano, *SUCCESS! in Massage Therapy*, 2007

A.J. Larner, *A Dictionary of Neurological Signs*, 2010

David K. Miller, *Measurement by the Physical Educator*, 2010

471

WALTER M. BORTZ

Diabetes Danger: What 200 Million Americans at Risk Need to Know

(New York: SelectBooks, 2010)

Story type: Medical
Subject(s): Diseases; Diabetes mellitus; Health

Summary: Written by Walter M. Bortz, *Diabetes Danger: What 200 Million Americans at Risk Need to Know* is a straightforward and thorough guide to understanding the risks associated with diabetes. Bortz addresses diabetics, their family members, and their caregivers in this book, offering useful information about the disease and possible risks. This book provides readers with an explanation of diabetes, how it has grown into such a widespread disease, the dangers facing modern-day Americans, why there is no cure for it, and the treatment limitations. Bortz gives practical tips and advice for readers about ways to prevent the onset of diabetes, strategies for reversing symptoms of the disease, and maintenance tips that healthy individuals should follow.

Where it's reviewed:
The Diabetes Educator, March-April 2007, page 269

Other books by the same author:
The Roadmap to 100: The Breakthrough Science of Living a Long and Healthy Life, 2010
We Live Too Short and Die Too Long: How to Achieve and Enjoy Your Natural 100-Year-Plus Life Span, 2007

Other books you might like:
Richard K. Bernstein, *Dr. Bernstein's Diabetes Solution*, 2007

Riva Greenberg, *50 Diabetes Myths That Can Ruin Your Life: And the 50 Diabetes Truths That Can Save It*, 2009

Elaine Magee, *Tell Me What to Eat If I Have Diabetes*, 2008

David K. McCulloch, *The Diabetes Answer Book: Practical Answers to More than 300 Top Questions*, 2008

Jeff Unger, *Diabetes Management in Primary Care*, 2007

472

JUDITH E. BROWN

Nutrition through the Life Cycle, 3rd Edition

(Belmont, California: Thomson/Wadsworth, 2007)

Subject(s): Health; Nutrition; Children

Summary: In *Nutrition through the Life Cycle, 3rd Edition*, nutrition researcher and author Judith E. Brown updates her text covering the function of nutrition in each phase of life. Beginning with nutrition basics, the text addresses each subsequent topic in two chapters—

one pertaining to normal nutrition and one pertaining to clinical nutrition. Topics include nutrition considerations during preconception, pregnancy, and lactation, as well as nutrition for infants, toddlers, preschoolers, children, adolescents, adults, and older adults. Supplemental information includes growth and body mass indicator charts, as well specific nutritional guidelines for individuals over age 70.

Other books by the same author:
Nutrition Now, 2010

Other books you might like:
Lynn R. Marotz, *Health, Safety, and Nutrition for the Young Child, 7th Edition*, 2008

Janet Henshall Momsen, *Gender and Development*, 2008

473

JARI HOLLAND BUCK

Hospital Stay Handbook: A Guide to Becoming a Patient Advocate for Your Loved Ones

(Woodbury, Minnesota: Llewellyn Publications, 2007)

Subject(s): Hospitals; Family; Health

Summary: Inspired by the time she spent at her ailing husband's bedside, Jari Holland Buck's *Hospital Stay Handbook: A Guide to Becoming a Patient Advocate for Your Loved Ones* is designed to assist family and friends who struggle to care for loved ones residing in hospitals. Without Buck's help—her knowledge of her husband's allergies and past medical conditions, her willingness to ask questions and demand answers, and her around-the-clock vigilant watch for changes in her husband's condition—her husband may not have survived. In this book, Buck provides advice for friends and family members of patients who may need to advocate for better patient care during hospital stays.

Where it's reviewed:
Library Journal, September 1, 2007, page 156

Other books by the same author:
24/7 or Dead: A Handbook for Families with a Loved One in the Hospital, 2006

Other books you might like:
Ann Brandt, *A Caregiver's Story*, 2008

Martine Ehrenclou, *Critical Conditions: The Essential Hospital Guide to Get Your Loved One Out Alive*, 2008

Joshua D. Schor, *The Nursing Home Guide*, 2008

Tom Smith, *A Balanced Life: 9 Strategies for Coping with the Mental Health Problems of a Loved One*, 2008

James Thomas Williams, *The Patient Advocate's Handbook 300 Questions And Answers To Help You Care For Your Loved One At The Hospital And At Home*, 2010

474

BLANDINE CALAIS-GERMAIN

Anatomy of Breathing

(Seattle, Washington: Eastland Press, 2010)

Subject(s): Health; Healing; Biology

Summary: Written by Blandine Calais-Germain, *Anatomy of Breathing* is a thorough overview of the scientific function of breathing, the many variations of it, different breathing techniques, and the ways breathing can enrich and enhance life. Complemented with hundreds of detailed illustrations, the book explains how breathing works; the principles, structures, and organs associated with breathing; and external factors that affect breathing. Calais-Germain then explains the ways in which breathing can be controlled to enrich a person's well-being and enhance his or her regular activities. *Anatomy of Breathing* offers practical tips and helpful practice pages to educate readers on the methods, techniques, and variations of breathing.

Other books by the same author:
Anatomy of Movement: Exercises, 2008
Anatomy of Movement, 2006

Other books you might like:
Anita Ganeri, *Alive: The Living, Breathing, Human Body Book*, 2007

Jen Green, *Breathing (My Healthy Body)*, 2008

475

VANESSA A. CAMILLERI

Healing the Inner City Child: Creative Arts Therapies with At-risk Youth

(Philadelphia: Jessica Kingsley Publishers, 2007)

Subject(s): Psychology; Sociology; Social sciences

Summary: In *Healing the Inner City Child: Creative Arts Therapies with At-risk Youth*, Vanessa A. Camilleri and a number of other contributors consider alternative mental health therapies for working with urban children who may be exceptionally prone to depression and behavioral issues. The nontraditional methods proposed here, which have shown a great deal of promise, include music, dance, art, and drama therapy. The authors of each piece back up their claims with extensive research on proven benefits. This text is intended for psychologists, therapists, educators, or anyone who works with at-risk youth populations.

Where it's reviewed:
Community Practitioner, February 2008, page 38
Music Educators Journal, December 2008, page 34

Other books you might like:
Sharon W. Goodill, *Creative Arts An Introduction to Medical Dance/Movement Therapy: Health Care in Motion*, 2009

Karen D. Goodman, *Music Therapy Groupwork with*

Health and Wellness

Special Needs Children: The Evolving Process, 2007

Daria Halprin, *The Expressive Body in Life, Art, and Therapy: Working with Movement, Metaphor and Meaning*, 2008

Liesl Silverstone, *Art Therapy Exercises: Inspirational and Practical Ideas to Stimulate the Imagination*, 2009

Pamela J. Stack, *Art Therapy Activities: A Practical Guide for Teachers, Therapists And Parents*, 2006

476

ARNALDO CANTANI

Pediatric Allergy, Asthma and Immunology

(New York: Springer, 2008)

Subject(s): Health; Allergy; Children

Summary: *Pediatric Allergy, Asthma and Immunology* by Arnaldo Cantani is a comprehensive text for medical students and professionals. Each of the text's 24 chapters gives in-depth coverage to a different aspect of pediatric immunology, including the neonate risk of atopy, genetic and environmental predisposing, diagnosis of pediatric allergy, atopic dermatitis, allergic skin disorders, food allergy and immunotoxicology, asthma, allergic rhinitis, eye allergy, anaphylaxis, malnutrition and the immune system, specific immunotherapy, pediatric AIDS, and the prevention of allergic disorders. Dr. Arnaldo Cantani is a professor in the University of Rome's Department of Pediatrics, Allergy and Clinical Immunology Division.

Where it's reviewed:
The New England Journal of Medicine, January 1, 2009, page 92

Other books you might like:
Alisa Marie Fleming, *Go Dairy Free*, 2008
Janice M. Vickerstaff Joneja, *Dealing with Food Allergies in Babies and Children*, 2007
Massoud Mahmoudi, *Allergy and Asthma: Practical Diagnosis and Management*, 2007
Kelly Rudnicki, *The Food Allergy Mama's Baking Book: Great Dairy-, Egg-, and Nut-Free Treats for the Whole Family*, 2009

477

LOUIS R. CAPLAN

Caplan's Stroke: A Clinical Approach, Fourth Edition

(Philadelphia, Pennsylvania: Saunders/Elsevier, 2009)

Story type: Medical
Subject(s): Medical care; Health; Stroke

Summary: Written by leading stroke clinician Louis R. Caplan, *Caplan's Stroke: A Clinical Approach, Fourth Edition* is an authoritative guide to diagnosing, evaluating, and treating children and adult stroke patients. Dr.

Caplan, a prominent stroke expert, shares his wisdom and personal experiences in this straightforward, easy-to-read guide. *Caplan's Stroke* covers all facets of stroke management, including the various cerebrovascular diseases that contribute to different types of stroke, symptoms and diagnosis, treatment and rehabilitation methods, preventative measures, and pediatric and adult stroke syndromes. The book also includes detailed artwork, information about imaging and laboratory diagnosing, and case studies.

Where it's reviewed:
JAMA, The Journal of the American Medical Association, December 16, 2009, page 2600

Other books by the same author:
The Effective Clinical Neurologist, 2010
Case Studies in Stroke, 2008
Intracranial Atherosclerosis, 2008
Uncommon Causes of Stroke, 2008
Brain Embolism, 2006

Other books you might like:
Valerie Greene, *Conquering Stroke: How I Fought My Way Back and How You Can Too*, 2008
Peter G. Levine, *Stronger After Stroke: Your Roadmap to Recovery*, 2008
Richard Senelick, *Living with Stroke: A Guide for Families*, 1994
Joel Stein, *Stroke Recovery and Rehabilitation*, 2008
Olajide Williams, *Stroke Diaries: A Guide for Survivors and Their Families*, 2010

478

JEAN CARPER

100 Simple Things You Can Do to Prevent Alzheimer's and Age-Related Memory Loss

(New York: Little, Brown, 2010)

Subject(s): Alzheimer's disease; Aging (Biology); Memory

Summary: In *100 Simple Things You Can Do to Prevent Alzheimer's and Age-Related Memory Loss*, bestselling author Jean Carper offers practical and easy tips and advice on ways to delay the onset of Alzheimer's and dementia. Although most people think that little can be done to prevent Alzheimer's, Carper has discovered 100 preemptive measures that can be taken to postpone or eliminate the illness's onset. The book includes simple and viable steps that anyone can take to strengthen their memory, fortify brain cells, and develop new neurons. The suggestions in the book include taking vitamin B12 (to avoid a shrinking brain), drinking apple juice (to mimic a common Alzheimer's medication), exercising (to increase brain activity), surfing the web (to strengthen brain cells), and meditating regularly (to develop neurons).

Where it's reviewed:
Publishers Weekly, August 16, 2010, page 48

Other books you might like:

Mary Ellen Geist, *Measure of the Heart: Caring for a Parent with Alzheimer's*, 2009

Lauren Kessler, *Finding Life in the Land of Alzheimer's: One Daughter's Hopeful Story*, 2008

Parris M. Kidd, *PS (PhosphatidylSerine) Nature's Brain Booster*, 2007

Scott D. Mendelson, *Beyond Alzheimer's: How to Avoid the Modern Epidemic of Dementia*, 2009

John Zeisel, *I'm Still Here: A Breakthrough Approach to Understanding Someone Living with Alzheimer's*, 2009

479

TINA CASSIDY

Birth: The Surprising History of How We Are Born

(New York: Atlantic Monthly Press, 2007)

Story type: Historical
Subject(s): Pregnancy; Health; Women

Summary: Written by Tina Cassidy, *Birth: The Surprising History of How We Are Born* is a comprehensive guide to pregnancy, labor, and childbirth throughout history. Despite the fact that women have been birthing babies since the dawn of time, new ideas and philosophies about the best way to bring a child into the world constantly arise. Using unusual facts and fascinating personal stories, Cassidy examines the history of childbirth and how it differs by era and culture. *Birth* gives readers a glimpse into how childbirth has evolved and changed throughout time, from the invention of the epidural to the acceptance of midwives to the increase in safety during labor. This book offers a thorough examination on the various methods, beliefs, and philosophies about childbirth around the world.

Where it's reviewed:
Choice, May 2007, page 1564
Entertainment Weekly, October 27, 2006, page 77

Other books by the same author:
Birth: A History, 2007

Other books you might like:

Sheri Bayles, *Laugh and Learn About Childbirth*, 2009

Jennifer Block, *Pushed: The Painful Truth About Childbirth and Modern Maternity Care*, 2007

Denise Spatafora, *Better Birth: The Ultimate Guide to Childbirth from Home Births to Hospitals*, 2009

Giuditta Tornetta, *Painless Childbirth: An Empowering Journey Through Pregnancy and Childbirth*, 2008

Marsden Wagner, *Born in the USA: How a Broken Maternity System Must Be Fixed to Put Women and Children First*, 2006

480

DAVI-ELLEN CHABNER

Medical Terminology: A Short Course, Fifth Edition

(St. Louis, Missouri: Saunders Elsevier, 2008)

Story type: Medical
Subject(s): Medicine; Reference works; Encyclopedias and dictionaries

Summary: In *Medical Terminology: A Short Course, Fifth Edition*, Davi-Ellen Chabner updates her innovative self-teaching guide for the medical terminology student. The easy-to-use program, presented in interactive textbook/workbook format, includes pronunciation guides, review pages, illustrations, and activities that help students navigate the complicated world of medical terminology while gaining an understanding of terms, prefixes, and suffixes. Sample case studies throughout the course demonstrate practical applications of the terms learned. The companion compact disc supplements the text with audio pronunciations, animations, and games that reinforce material covered in the lessons. Additional resources are available on the companion Web site.

Where it's reviewed:
SciTech Book News, June 2003, page 92

Other books by the same author:
Respiratory Physiology: The Essentials, 2008
High Altitude Medicine and Physiology, 2007
Pulmonary Physiology and Pathophysiology, 2007

Other books you might like:
Barbara A. Gylys, *Medical Terminology Systems: A Body Systems Approach, 6th Edition*, 2009
Tina M. Kaufman, *Yes/No Medical Spanish: Comprehensive Handbook of Clinical Spanish*, 2010
Myrna LaFleur-Brooks, *Exploring Medical Language: A Student-Directed Approach*, 2008

481

MICHAEL G. CHEZ

Autism and Its Medical Management: A Guide for Parents and Professionals

(Philadelphia, Pennsylvania: Jessica Kingsley Publishers, 2008)

Story type: Medical
Subject(s): Diseases; Medical care; Health

Summary: Written by Michael G. Chez, *Autism and Its Medical Management: A Guide for Parents and Professionals* is a detailed overview on autistic spectrum disorders (ASDs), available treatment options, and medical care knowledge. The book includes details on different types of ASDs, their associated symptoms, and the ways that autism disorders are diagnosed. Written for both parents of autistic kids and medical care professionals working with children with ASDs, *Autism and Its Medical Management* offers straightforward advice and research on how ASDs develop in children, various treatment options, explanations of medical terminology, and the latest medical developments made in this field.

Other books you might like:

Tara Delaney, *101 Games and Activities for Children With Autism, Aspergers and Sensory Processing Disorders*, 2009

Robert Sears, *The Autism Book: What Every Parent Needs to Know About Early Detection, Treatment, Recovery, and Prevention*, 2008

Barbara Sher, *Early Intervention Games: Fun, Joyful Ways to Develop Social and Motor Skills in Children with Autism Spectrum or Sensory Processing Disorders*, 2009

Chantal Sicile-Kira, *41 Things to Know about Autism*, 2010

William Stillman, *The Autism Answer Book: More Than 300 of the Top Questions Parents Ask*, 2007

482

RACHEL L. CHIN

Emergency Management of Infectious Diseases

(Cambridge, England: Cambridge University Press, 2008)

Story type: Medical
Subject(s): Physicians; Diseases; Medical care

Summary: Edited by doctor and professor Rachel L. Chin, *Emergency Management of Infectious Diseases* is an exhaustive overview for emergency room physicians on the dangers of infectious diseases. Infectious diseases are the second most popular cause for emergency room visits, after trauma, and this book equips doctors and medical professionals with the knowledge to treat and manage patients suffering from a contagious illness. The book provides details on all viral, bacterial, fungal, and parasitic diseases affecting the organs. *Emergency Management of Infectious Diseases* includes detailed photographs, diagnostic tables, and charts of medicinal treatments to assist doctors with the diagnosis and management of infectious diseases.

Where it's reviewed:
JAMA, The Journal of the American Medical Association, April 7, 2010, page 1312

Other books you might like:

Mark S. Dworkin, *Outbreak Investigations Around the World: Case Studies in Infectious Disease Field Epidemiology*, 2009

Jeffrey Lindsey, *Preventing Infectious Diseases*, 2007

Manya Magnus, *Essentials of Infectious Disease Epidemiology*, 2008

Tessa M. Pollard, *Western Diseases: An Evolutionary Perspective*, 2008

Kenneth B. Singleton, *The Lyme Disease Solution*, 2009

483

MARK CICHOCKI

Living with HIV: A Patient's Guide

(Jefferson, North Carolina: McFarland & Co., 2009)

Subject(s): Health; AIDS (Disease); Medical care

Summary: In *Living with HIV: A Patient's Guide*, registered nurse Mark Cichocki presents a comprehensive, accessible guide for recently diagnosed HIV patients, their families, and their caregivers. Drawing on his years of experience working with HIV and AIDS patients, the author discusses a range of related topics including the history of the disease, prevention, testing, selecting a doctor, available medication therapies, and related infections. Cichocki also covers dental care, physical exercise, dietary considerations, drug and alcohol use, and psychological issues. The author emphasizes the importance of treating the HIV patient as a whole, from the unique concerns of the newly diagnosed to those of the individual making end-of-life decisions.

Where it's reviewed:
Library Journal, July 1, 2009, page 117
School Library Journal, Oct 2009, page 144

Other books you might like:

Paul Ashton, *Etched in Hope: A Weekly Journal for Those Living with or Affected by HIV/AIDS*, 2007

Joel E. Gallant, *100 Questions and Answers About HIV and AIDS*, 2009

Brigid M. Kane, *HIV/AIDS Treatment Drugs*, 2008

Venus Perez, *I'm Still Here*, 2009

Alan Whiteside, *HIV/AIDS: A Very Short Introduction*, 2008

484

NANCY CLARK

Nancy Clark's Sports Nutrition Guidebook: 2nd Edition

(Champaign, Illinois: Human Kinetics, 1996)

Subject(s): Cooking; Eating Disorders; Exercise

Summary: *Nancy Clark's Sports Nutrition Guidebook: 2nd Edition* is an in-depth guide to diet and nutrition for athletes of all levels, coaches, trainers, and health professionals from author Nancy Clark. The book provides practical and detailed advice about how nutrition and diet affect health maintenance, sports fitness, and athletics. The second edition provides updated information on scientific findings and medical applications regarding the role of nutrition in fitness training and everyday life. Clark teaches readers how to properly fuel their active lifestyle or ongoing training with the right foods. The exhaustive guide includes details about weight loss and body image, meal planning, nutrition myths, overcoming unhealthy or detrimental dietary habits, food safety, and 51 pages of recipes.

Other books by the same author:

Food Guide for Soccer: Tips & Recipes from the Pros, 2010

Nancy Clark's Food Guide for New Runners: Getting It Right from the Start, 2009

Nancy Clark' s Food Guide for Marathoners: Tips for Everyday Champions, 2007

Other books you might like:

Dan Benardot, *Advanced Sports Nutrition*, 2005

Louise Burke, *Clinical Sports Nutrition*, 2009

Marie Dunford, *Sports Nutrition: A Practice Manual for Professionals*, 2006

Suzanne Girard Eberle, *Endurance Sports Nutrition: 2nd Edition*, 2007

Monique Ryan, *Sports Nutrition for Endurance Athletes*, 2007

485

JOHN D. CLOUGH

The Cleveland Clinic Guide to Arthrits

(New York: Kaplan Publishing, 2009)

Subject(s): Health; Arthritis; Reference works

Summary: In *The Cleveland Clinic Guide to Arthritis*, John D. Clough provides advice to people suffering from arthritis based on his 43 years of experience as an arthritis specialist. Clough suggests changes to patients' diet and exercise habits so they can maintain a high quality of life, and discusses various medications and treatments that may be tried, as well as side effects that can be expected. Clough discusses the different types of arthritis patients suffer from, and he shares stories of individuals who have found relief from their pain after they pursued the proper treatment based on their individual cases. The author also offers practical information regarding what an individual can reasonably expect in the long-term after an arthritis diagnosis.

Other books by the same author:

Arthritis, 2006

To Act as a Unit : The Story of the Cleveland Clinic, 2005

Other books you might like:

Barbara D. Allan, *Conquering Arthritis*, 2009

Grant Cooper, *The Arthritis Handbook*, 2008

Kat Elton, *A Resilient Life: Learning to Thrive, Not Just Survive With Rheumatoid Arthritis*, 2010

Alan Kelton, *The Fit Arthritic: Fighting Knee and Hip Arthritis with Exercise*, 2008

Ann A. Rosenstein, *Water Exercises for Rheumatoid Arthritis: The Effective Way to Reduce Pain and Inflammation While Increasing Flexibility and Mobility*, 2008

486

LEONARD V. CROWLEY

Introduction to Human Disease: Pathology and Pathophysiology Correlations, Eighth Edition: A Student Workbook

(Sudbury, Massachusetts: Jones and Bartlett, 2009)

Subject(s): Health; Diseases; Physiology

Summary: *An Introduction to Human Disease: Pathology and Pathophysiology Correlations, Eighth Edition: A Student Workbook* by Leonard Crowley is a companion to the student nursing text *An Introduction to Human Disease*. Each chapter of the workbook corresponds to the text, providing students with complete outlines, lists of keywords, study questions, pages for notes highlighted with important concepts from the text, and illustrations. Topics include principles of diagnosis, the structure and function of cells and tissues in health and disease, pathogenic microorganisms, congenital and hereditary diseases, abnormalities of blood coagulation, the respiratory system, the urinary system, the gastrointestinal tract, and the musculoskeletal system.

Other books by the same author:

An Introduction to Human Disease: Pathology and Pathophysiology Correlations, 2006

Other books you might like:

Stefan Kaufmann, *The New Plagues: Pandemics and Poverty in a Globalized World*, 2009

Ray M. Merrill, *Environmental Epidemiology: Principles and Methods*, 2007

Tessa M. Pollard, *Western Diseases: An Evolutionary Perspective*, 2008

487

PHILIP E. CRYER

Hypoglycemia in Diabetes: Pathophysiology, Prevalence, and Prevention

(Alexandria, Virginia: American Diabetes Association, 2009)

Subject(s): Health; Diabetes mellitus; Medicine

Summary: In *Hypoglycemia in Diabetes: Pathophysiology, Prevalence, and Prevention*, endocrinologist Philip E. Cryer discusses the clinical issue of hypoglycemia as it pertains to the treatment of diabetes. As the author explains, hypoglycemia (or low blood sugar) can complicate a diabetes patient's condition. In this comprehensive discussion of iatrogenic hypoglycemia, the author covers topics such as the risk factors for hypoglycemia, prevention and treatment, and the physiology and pathophysiology of glucose counterregulation. Dr. Cryer is the Professor of Endocrinology and Metabolism in Medicine at Washington University in St. Louis, Missouri.

Where it's reviewed:
Clinical Diabetes, Summer 2010, page S6

Other books you might like:

Richard K. Bernstein, *Dr. Bernstein's Diabetes Solution*, 2007

Riva Greenberg, *50 Diabetes Myths That Can Ruin Your Life: And the 50 Diabetes Truths That Can Save It*, 2009

Stephanie Kenrose, *The Reactive Hypoglycemia Cookbook*, 2010

David K. McCulloch, *The Diabetes Answer Book: Practical Answers to More than 300 Top Questions*, 2008

Jeff Unger, *Diabetes Management in Primary Care*, 2007

488

LEANNE CURRIE-MCGHEE
Sexually Transmitted Diseases
(San Diego: ReferencePoint Press, 2008)

Story type: Young Adult
Subject(s): Sex education; Diseases; Medical care

Summary: In *Sexually Transmitted Diseases*, author Leanne Currie-McGhee presents young adults with basic facts about sexually transmitted diseases (STDs). This volume discusses an array of topics, including STD identification and prevention and the latest scientific research on the book. Presented in an easy-to-use format, the book allows readers to quickly access important data about various types of STDs and other information. *Sexually Transmitted Diseases* contains a time line, a listing of advocacy organizations, and a bibliography.

Where it's reviewed:
Booklist, October 15, 2008, page 58

Other books by the same author:
Drug Addiction, 2010
AIDS, 2008

Other books you might like:

Lisa Marr, *Sexually Transmitted Diseases: A Physician Tells You What You Need to Know, Second Edition*, 2007

Shana McKibbin, *HealthScouter HPV: Understanding HPV Testing: The Human Papillomavirus Patient Advocate*, 2009

Alexander McMillan, *Sexually Transmissible Infections in Clinical Practice: A Problem-Based Approach*, 2009

Ian Peate, *Manual of Sexually Transmitted Infections*, 2006

Lawrence R. Stanberry, *Understanding Herpes*, 2006

489

ANNE B. CURTIS
Fundamentals of Cardiac Pacing
(Boston: M. Nijhoff Publishers, 2009)

Subject(s): Medical care; Health; Technology

Summary: Cardiac pacemakers are becoming more and more common in healthcare practices throughout the world. In *Fundamentals of Cardiac Pacing*, author Anne B. Curtis provides an introductory overview of pacemakers, specifically geared toward doctors, nurses, and other healthcare professionals. This straightforward manual tackles everything a caregiver needs to know about the proper functioning and operation of cardiac pacing equipment. Topics covered in this volume include a history of cardiac pacing, indications, diagnostics, programming, troubleshooting, and much more. *Fundamentals of Cardiac Pacing* contains an index.

Other books you might like:

Philip Jevon, *Advanced Cardiac Life Support: A Guide for Nurses*, 2009

Mark E. Josephson, *Clinical Cardiac Electrophysiology: Techniques and Interpretations*, 2008

Tom Kenny, *The Nuts and bolts of Paced ECG Interpretation*, 2009

George Stouffer, *Cardiovascular Hemodynamics for the Clinician*, 2007

John Sutherland, *Little Black Book of Cardiology*, 2006

490

M. LAUREL CUTLIP
SARI BUDGAZAD , Co-Author
The Cardiac Recovery Cookbook: Heart Healthy Recipes for Life After Heart Attack or Heart Surgery
(New York: Healthy Living Books/Hatherleigh Press, 2005)

Subject(s): Heart diseases; Health; Cooking

Summary: Heart attack sufferers often have to reevaluate certain aspects of their lives, including their diets. In *The Cardiac Recovery Cookbook: Heart Healthy Recipes for Life After Heart Attack or Heart Surgery*, authors M. Laurel Cutlip and Sari Budgazad present a collection of recipes that heart attack suffers can use to improve the quality of their diets. The more than 100 recipes compiled in this volume, which include everything from appetizers to entrees and side dishes to desserts, are designed to be heart healthy. *The Cardiac Recovery Cookbook* contains a bibliography, an index, and a foreword by doctor Paul Kligfield.

Other books you might like:

Nelson Anderson, *A Heart Attack Survivor's Guide to a Long Healthy Life*, 2009

Dede Bonner, *The 10 Best Questions for Recovering from a Heart Attack: The Script You Need to Take Control of Your Health*, 2009

Larry McConnell, *Cardiac Champs: A Survivor's Guide: How to Live a Healthy, Vigorous, Happy Life After a Heart Attack*, 2010

Stephen T. Sinatra, *The Sinatra Solution: Metabolic Cardiology*, 2008

Morag Thow, *Exercise Leadership in Cardiac*

Rehabilitation for High Risk Groups: An Evidence-Based Approach, 2009

491

GABRIEL M. DANOVITCH

Handbook of Kidney Transplantation: 5th Edition

(Philadelphia: Lippincott Williams & Wilkinson, 2009)

Story type: Medical
Subject(s): Medical care; Transplantation; Health

Summary: Edited by Gabriel M. Danovitch, *Handbook of Kidney Transplantation: 5th Edition* is an informational and practical guide for physicians, surgeons, nurses, and medical professionals working with patients needing a kidney transplant. Complemented by detailed color illustrations, this easy-to-understand book summarizes the chief concerns and complications surrounding the transplant of kidneys and how to ensure success for both short-term and long-term patient care. The fifth edition of *Handbook of Kidney Transplantation* covers a wide range of topics related to renal transplants, including chapters on immunobiology and immunosuppression, surgery, histocompatibility, protocols for transplants, immunosuppressive medications, and post-transplant recovery and treatment.

Where it's reviewed:
Nephrology Nursing Journal, July-August 2005, page 449
SciTech Book News, June 2005, page 105

Other books you might like:
Reg Green, *The Gift that Heals: Stories of Hope, Renewal and Transformation Through Organ and Tissue Donation*, 2007
William L. Henrich, *Principles and Practice of Dialysis, Fourth Edition*, 2009
Chris O'Callaghan, *The Renal System at a Glance*, 2009
Peter Parham, *The Immune System, 3rd Edition*, 2009
Phillip Ruiz, *Transplantation Pathology*, 2009

492

ANN E. DENSMORE

Helping Children with Autism Become More Social: 76 Ways to Use Narrative Play

(Westport, Connecticut: Praeger, 2007)

Subject(s): Interpersonal relations; Social sciences; Psychology

Summary: In *Helping Children with Autism Become More Social: 76 Ways to Use Narrative Play*, therapist Ann E. Densmore shares her innovative methods for encouraging socialization in autistic children. In this guide, Densmore defines narrative play and lists playing methods that expand a child's real-world experiences. As families

affected by autism are aware, the most pervasive aspect of the condition is the seeming absence of social awareness. Throughout the book, Densmore assures readers that the use of narrative play can help many children become social and lead happier, more productive lives.

Where it's reviewed:
Choice, Feburary 2008, page 1009

Other books by the same author:
Your Successful Preschooler: Ten Skills Children Need to Become Confident and Socially Engaged, 2011

Other books you might like:
Tara Delaney, *101 Games and Activities for Children With Autism, Aspergers and Sensory Processing Disorders*, 2009
Temple Grandin, *The Way I See It: A Personal Look at Autism and Asperger's*, 2008
Robert Sears, *The Autism Book: What Every Parent Needs to Know About Early Detection, Treatment, Recovery, and Prevention*, 2008
Barbara Sher, *Early Intervention Games: Fun, Joyful Ways to Develop Social and Motor Skills in Children with Autism Spectrum or Sensory Processing Disorders*, 2009
William Stillman, *The Autism Answer Book: More Than 300 of the Top Questions Parents Ask*, 2007

493

SAMIR P. DESAI

Clinician's Guide to Laboratory Medicine, 3rd Edition

(Houston, Texas: MD2B, 2009)

Story type: Medical
Subject(s): Medical care; Medicine; Health

Summary: Written by Samir P. Desai, *Clinician's Guide to Laboratory Medicine, 3rd Edition* is a comprehensive and practical resource for medical professionals interpreting lab results. The book offers helpful advice and step-by-step instructions for dealing with abnormal test results. *Clinician's Guide to Laboratory Medicine* provides readers with a thorough understanding of the factors that contribute to lab results and helps equip medical practitioners with the knowledge they need to properly interpret them. The book includes information on differing diagnoses, easy-to-follow approaches for interpretation of results, and algorithms to assist in the analysis and understanding of difficult lab work.

Other books by the same author:
The Successful Match: 200 Rules to Succeed in the Residency Match, 2009
250 Biggest Mistakes 3rd Year Medical Students Make And How to Avoid Them, 2006

Other books you might like:
Tracey Hopkins, *LabNotes: Guide to Lab and Diagnostic Tests*, 2009
Wiley D. Jenkins, *Public Health Laboratories*, 2010
A. Laurence Smith Jr., *Integrated Healthcare Information Systems*, 2007

494

UDAY DEVGAN

Cataract Surgery: A Patient's Guide to Cataract Treatment

(Omaha, Nebraska: Addicus Books, 2009)

Story type: Medical

Subject(s): Medical care; Surgery; Health

Summary: Written by ophthalmologist and professor Uday Devgan, *Cataract Surgery: A Patient's Guide to Cataract Treatment* is an educational and helpful guide for patients preparing for cataract surgery. Every year, close to 3 million Americans undergo surgery to remove cataracts. *Cataract Surgery* is a comprehensive overview of the operation to prepare patients for surgery and answer any questions they may have about the procedure. Devgan addresses common inquiries about cataract surgery, including details about the type of lens that is implanted, what kind of anesthesia is used, post-surgery pain management, and expected recovery time. A series of photographs is also included to illustrate how the procedure is performed.

Other books you might like:

James Compton Burnett, *Curability of Cataract with Medicines*, 2010

Jeffrey S. Heier, *100 Questions and Answers About Macular Degeneration*, 2009

Clyde K. Kitchen, *Fact and Fiction of Healthy Vision: Eye Care for Adults and Children*, 2007

Michael A. Samuel, *Macular Degeneration*, 2008

495

ORRIN DEVINSKY

Epilepsy: Patient and Family Guide, 3rd Edition

(New York: Demos Health, 2007)

Story type: Medical

Subject(s): Epilepsy; Health; Medical care

Summary: Written by Orrin Devinsky, one of the nation's leading experts on epilepsy, *Epilepsy: Patient and Family Guide, 3rd Edition* is a comprehensive and straightforward overview of the disease. Epilepsy is the most common neurological disorder affecting children, adults, and the elderly. In this bestselling book, Devinsky offers practical and educational information for individuals living with the disease, including details on how to avoid seizures; factors that cause seizures; updated information on anti-epileptic drugs; medical, surgical, and alternative treatment and therapy options; and legal, financial, and employment concerns. *Epilepsy* provides answers to tough questions about the disease while alleviating fear and anxiety and inspiring patients to become involved in their medical care.

Other books by the same author:

Complementary and Alternative Therapies for Epilepsy, 2005

Other books you might like:

Kathlyn Gay, *Epilepsy: The Ultimate Teen Guide*, 2007

Stuart McCallum, *Beyond My Control*, 2008

Simon D. Shorvon, *Handbook of Epilepsy Treatment*, 2010

Andrew N. Wilner, *Epilepsy: 199 Answers: A Doctor Responds to His Patients' Questions*, 2007

Elaine Wyllie, *The Cleveland Clinic Guide to Epilepsy*, 2010

496

MARK S. DWORKIN

Outbreak Investigations Around the World: Case Studies in Infectious Disease Field Epidemiology

(Sudbury, Massachusetts: Jones & Bartlett Learning, 2009)

Subject(s): Health; Diseases; Medicine

Summary: In *Outbreak Investigations Around the World: Case Studies in Infectious Disease Field Epidemiology*, editor Mark S. Dworkin collects case studies of 19 outbreaks of infectious disease. A chapter on how outbreaks are investigated, written by Dworkin, introduces the book. The case studies, written by the investigators involved, cover both historic and contemporary outbreaks and describe the circumstances and responses to each. The case studies include "The Investigation of Toxic Shock Syndrome in Wisconsin, 1979-1980 and Beyond" by Jeffrey P. Davis, M.D.; "The Early Days of AIDS in the United States: A Personal Perspective" by Harold W. Jaffe, M.D.; and "Tracking a Syphilis Outbreak Through Cyberspace" by Jeffrey D. Klausner, M.D, among others.

Where it's reviewed:

Emerging Infectious Diseases, November 2009, page 1882

JAMA, The Journal of the American Medical Association, January 6, 2010, page 77

Other books by the same author:

Cases in Field Epidemiology: A Global Perspective, 2010

Other books you might like:

Kathleen Meehan Arias, *Outbreak Investigation, Prevention, and Control in Health Care Settings: Critical Issues in Patient Safety*, 2009

Robert H. Friis, *Epidemiology 101*, 2009

Michael Gregg, *Field Epidemiology*, 2008

Lois N. Magner, *A History of Infectious Diseases and the Microbial World*, 2009

William Anton Oleckno, *Epidemiology: Concepts and Methods*, 2008

497

TED EAVES

The Practical Guide to Athletic Training

(Sudbury, Massachusetts: Jones and Bartlett Publishers, 2009)

Subject(s): Sports; Reference works; Medical care

Summary: *The Practical Guide to Athletic Training* by Ted Eaves is a general introduction and overview, intended for the undergraduate student beginning studies in the field of athletic training. Eaves focuses on the most common injuries and issues that athletic trainers see every day rather than more obscure problems that can arise throughout one's career. Symptoms of certain injuries, evaluation techniques, and treatment options are discussed in this text, although the author does not go into extensive detail on taping, wrapping, or padding injuries.

Other books you might like:

Gale Bernhardt, *Training Plans for Multisport Athletes*, 2007

Don Fink, *Be Iron Fit, 2nd: Time-Efficient Training Secrets for Ultimate Fitness*, 2010

Joel Friel, *The Triathlete's Training Bible*, 2009

Mark Hatmaker, *No Holds Barred Fighting: The Ultimate Guide to Conditioning*, 2007

Tom Rodgers, *The Perfect Distance: Training for Long-Course Triathlons*, 2007

498

SUZANNE GIRARD EBERLE

Endurance Sports Nutrition: 2nd Edition

(Champaign, Illinois: Human Kinetics, 2007)

Story type: Medical
Subject(s): Nutrition; Sports; Health

Summary: Written by sports dietician Suzanne Girard Eberle, *Endurance Sports Nutrition: 2nd Edition* is an educational and helpful guide for endurance athletes. The book provides practical nutrition advice and tips for a variety of endurance athletes. Eberle offers straightforward advice on the best foods, drinks, and supplements to help individuals increase training times, decrease length of recovery, avoid injuries, and accomplish exercise and performance goals. Featuring personalized menu plans, profiles and advice from elite endurance athletes, and tactics for avoiding common injuries and dangers, *Endurance Sports Nutrition* provides specific strategies for distance runners, cyclists, duathletes and triathletes, rowers, long-distance swimmers, and skiers.

Where it's reviewed:
Choice, September 2008, page 137

Other books by the same author:

The Pleasure Principal: Can You Really Have Your Cake and Eat It, Too?, 2009

Other books you might like:

Nancy Clark, *Nancy Clark's Sports Nutrition Guidebook: 2nd Edition*, 1996

Monique Ryan, *Sports Nutrition for Endurance Athletes*, 2007

Melvin H. Williams, *Nutrition for Health, Fitness and Sport*, 2009

499

JULIA SCHLAM EDELMAN

Menopause Matters: Your Guide to a Long and Healthy Life

(Baltimore: Johns Hopkins University Press, 2010)

Subject(s): Menopause; Health; Medical care

Summary: Gynecologist Julia Schlam Edelman is a renowned expert in menopause, and in *Menopause Matters: Your Guide to a Long and Healthy Life*, she shares the wisdom she has accumulated during years of study and private practice. This volume addresses the gamut of issues important to women facing this major change of life. Mood changes, hot flashes, sexual problems, lifestyle modifications, and memory problems are among the topics Edelman discusses. *Menopause Matters* includes a listing of bibliographical references and an index.

Where it's reviewed:
Library Journal, December 2009, page 125
Publishers Weekly, November 2, 2009, page 49

Other books you might like:

Amanda McQuade Crawford, *The Natural Menopause Handbook*, 2009

Bernard A. Eskin, *The Menopause: Endocrinologic Basis and Management Options*, 2007

Donna E. Stewart, *Menopause: A Mental Health Practitioner's Guide*, 2005

Nadine Taylor, *Natural Menopause Remedies: Which Drug-Free Cures Really Work*, 2009

Cynthia M. Watson, *User's Guide to Easing Menopause Symptoms Naturally*, 2010

500

MARTINE EHRENCLOU

Critical Conditions: The Essential Hospital Guide to Get Your Loved One Out Alive

(Santa Monica, California: Lemon Grove Press, 2008)

Subject(s): Health; Hospitals; Medicine

Summary: In *Critical Conditions: The Essential Hospital Guide to Getting Your Loved One Out Alive*, patient advocate Martine Ehrenclou offers practical advice on surviving a hospital stay. Having dealt with the complexities of hospitalization during a family member's illness, Ehrenclou realizes the many risks patients face. Through interviews with doctors, nurses, and hospital staff, the author has compiled this guide to help the loved ones of hospital patients navigate the system. Topics covered include how to do your own research, the hazards of secondary infection, accidental falls, medical mistakes, cross-cultural communication, legal issues, and deciding when to move the patient to a different hospital.

Other books you might like:

Sara A. Beazley, *A Brief Guide To The U.S. Health Care Delivery System: Facts, Definitions, and Statistics*, 2010

Jari Holland Buck, *Hospital Stay Handbook: A Guide to Becoming a Patient Advocate for Your Loved Ones*, 2007

Jeffrey L Levine, *Guide to Medical Education in the Teaching Hospital*, 2010

Samuel Steinberg, *The Physician's Survival Guide for the Hospital: Let the Hospital Work for You*, 2008

501

PAMELA ELLSWORTH

100 Q and A About Prostate Cancer, Second Edition

(Sudbury, Massachusetts: Jones and Bartlett, 2008)

Subject(s): Health; Medical care; Medicine

Summary: In *100 Questions and Answers about Prostate Cancer, Second Edition*, Dr. Pamela Ellsworth offers helpful information for prostate cancer patients and their families. Presented in a straightforward question-and-answer format, this valuable resource includes input from physicians as well as patients. Readers first learn the basics of prostate gland physiology and function and the symptoms of enlarged prostate. Additional topics covered include prostate cancer screening and testing, the staging of prostate cancer, the purpose of the bone scan, treatment options, the social aspects of prostate cancer, finding a support group, and considering end of life issues. The appendix provides listings of websites, organizations, and additional resources.

Other books by the same author:

The Little Black Book of Urology, 2006

Questions and Answers about Overactive Bladder and Urinary Incontinence, 2005

Other books you might like:

Arthur Burnett, *Johns Hopkins Patients' Guide to Prostate Cancer*, 2007

Chawnshang Chang, *Prostate Cancer: Basic Mechanisms and Therapeutic Approaches*, 2005

Sheldon Marks, *Prostate and Cancer: A Family Guide to Diagnosis, Treatment, and Survival, Fourth Edition*, 2009

Alan T. Meridith, *Handbook of Prostate Cancer Cell Research: Growth, Signalling and Survival*, 2009

Margaret Rayman, *Healthy Eating for Prostate Care*, 2009

502

ARTHUR T. EVANS

Manual of Obstetrics, Seventh Edition

(Philadelphia, Pennsylvania: Lippincott Williams & Wilkins, 2007)

Story type: Medical
Subject(s): Health; Pregnancy; Medical care

Summary: In *Manual of Obstetrics, Seventh Edition*, Arthur T. Evans presents the revised edition of his comprehensive guide. Organized into six parts—Obstetric Care, Obstetric Complications, Maternal Complications, Fetal Assessment, Fetal Complications, and Neonatal Care—the seventh edition covers such topics as labor, ectopic pregnancy, preeclampsia, respiratory complications, infectious complications, fetal monitoring, and isoimmunization. In addition, it includes updates to information on anesthesia; the use of medications for cardiovascular, neurologic, and endocrine conditions; and gestational diabetes. Information on surgical birth, vaginal birth after cesarean section, and genetic counseling has also been expanded. Additional tables and illustrations supplement the manual's accessible text.

Other books you might like:

Elizabeth Stepp Gilbert, *Manual of High Risk Pregnancy and Delivery*, 2010

Charles W. Hayt, *Obstetrics: A Manual for Students and Practitioners*, 2010

Jo Ann Rosenfeld, *Handbook of Women's Health*, 2009

William Tyler Smith, *A Manual of Obstetrics: Theoretical and Practical*, 2010

Tara A. Solomon, *What Your Gynecologist Never Told You...And Your Mother Didn't Know*, 2008

503

DONNA R. FALVO

Medical and Psychosocial Aspects of Chronic Illness and Disability, Fourth Edition

(Sudbury, Massachusetts: Jones and Bartlett, 2008)

Subject(s): Health; Diseases; Psychology

Summary: In *Medical and Psychosocial Aspects of Illness and Disability, Fourth Edition*, Donna R. Falvo updates her guide for rehabilitative medicine professionals. This revised edition discusses a range of conditions that may be encountered by the rehabilitative medicine practitioner, including conditions of the spinal cord; blindness; deafness; developmental and psychiatric disabilities; substance abuse issues; conditions of the circulatory, gastrointestinal, and pulmonary systems; cancer; and the special issues presented by burns, facial disfigurement, and disorders of the skin. Updates in this edition include new information on conceptualizing chronic illness and disability, intellectual disability, financing rehabilitation, and assistive technology.

Other books by the same author:
Ethics in Rehabilitation Education and Research, 2005

Other books you might like:
Richard M. Cohen, *Strong at the Broken Places: Voices of Illness, a Chorus of Hope*, 2008
Phyllis Porter Dolislager, *Who Hit the Down Button: Life with a Chronic Illness or Disability*, 2008
Renee R. Taylor, *Cognitive Behavioral Therapy for Chronic Illness and Disability*, 2010

504

DEBBIE FEIT

The Parent's Guide to Speech and Language Problems

(New York: McGraw-Hill, 2007)

Subject(s): Speech; Children; Parenthood

Summary: When a child is diagnosed with a speech or language disorder, parents are often at a loss as to where to turn for help. Fortunately, author Debbie Feit has provided a practical guide to treating and dealing with the problems associated with speech and language maladies. *The Parent's Guide to Speech and Language Problems* discusses topics such as early intervention, finding the right doctors, understanding the differences between various therapeutic techniques, and support resources for worried parents. This volume also includes a bibliography and a full index.

Where it's reviewed:
Journal of Developmental & Behavioral Pediatrics, December 2008, page 542

Other books you might like:
Caroline Bowen, *Children's Speech Sound Disorders*, 2009
Susan Howell Brubaker, *Workbook for Cognitive Skills: Exercises for Thought-processing and Word Retrieval*, 2008
Dorothy P. Dougherty, *Teach Me How to Say It Right: Helping Your Child With Articulation Problems*, 2010
Sally K. Gallena, *Voice and Laryngeal Disorders: A Problem-Based Clinical Guide with Voice Samples*, 2006
Patricia McAleer Hamaguchi, *Childhood Speech, Language, and Listening Problems*, 2010

505

AARON G. FILLER

Do You Really Need Back Surgery?: A Surgeon's Guide to Back and Neck Pain and How to Choose Your Treatment

(New York: Oxford University Press, USA, 2007)

Subject(s): Surgery; Health; Medical care

Summary: *Do You Really Need Back Surgery?: A Surgeon's Guide to Back and Neck Pain and How to Choose*

Your Treatment by Dr. Allen Filler helps readers suffering from severe back pain make one of the most important decisions of their lives. Back surgery is often a risky procedure, as simple mistakes near the spinal cord could affect a patient's ability to move for the rest of their lives. This guide provides readers with information about the effects surgeons consider when they recommend back surgery to their patients. It includes information about signs and symptoms of severe back pain that may require surgery in addition to minor back pain that may be treated with rest, exercise, or physical therapy. This book contains more than 80 illustrations that help the reader to further understand their back pain.

Where it's reviewed:
South African Medical Journal, November 2008, page 858

Other books you might like:
Josephine Key, *Back Pain: A Movement Problem*, 2010
Stuart McGill, *Low Back Disorders: Evidence-Based Prevention and Rehabilitation, 2nd Edition*, 2007
Lisa Morrone, *Overcoming Back and Neck Pain: A Proven Program for Recovery and Prevention*, 2008
Rick Olderman, *Fixing You: Back Pain*, 2009
John E. Sarno, *Healing Back Pain: The Mind-Body Connection*, 1991

506

NEIL A. FIORE

Coping with the Emotional Impact of Cancer: Become an Active Patient and Take Charge of Your Treatment

(Point Richmond, California: Bay Tree Publishing, 2009)

Subject(s): Psychology; Health; Cancer

Summary: *Coping with the Emotional Impact of Cancer: Become an Active Patient and Take Charge of Your Treatment* is a helpful resource for cancer sufferers from psychologist and cancer survivor, Neil A. Fiore. In this book, Fiore provides individuals who've been diagnosed with cancer with useful and practical tips about how to control the emotional aspect of the disease. The topics in *Coping with the Emotional Impact of Cancer* include handling the shock of being diagnosed, building collaborative relationships with doctors, sharing news with loved ones, coping with feelings of vulnerability and helplessness, decreasing stress and anxiety, overcoming sadness and depression, preparing for treatment, and finding happiness and satisfaction in life despite the disease.

Other books by the same author:
Awaken Your Strongest Self, 2010
The Now Habit at Work: Perform Optimally, Maintain Focus, and Ignite Motivation in Yourself and Others, 2010

The Now Habit: A Strategic Program for Overcoming Procrastination and Enjoying Guilt-Free Play, 2007

Other books you might like:

Barbara Clark, *The Fight of My Life: The Inspiring Story of a Mother's Fight against Breast Cancer*, 2007

Robin Dye, *Testament: My Survival and Conquest of Breast Cancer*, 2008

Vida Meymand, *Why Not Me?: An Inspiring True Story of Survival*, 2008

Jane Rudden, *If We Must Dance, Then I Will Lead: A Memoir of Breast Cancer Survival*, 2010

Julie K. Silver, *What Helped Get Me Through: Cancer Survivors Share Wisdom and Hope*, 2008

507

NANCY FOLDVARY-SCHAEFER

The Cleveland Clinic Guide to Sleep Disorders

(New York: Kaplan, 2009)

Subject(s): Health; Medicine; Sleep

Summary: In *The Cleveland Clinic Guide to Sleep Disorders*, Nancy Foldvary-Schaefer, director of the Sleep Disorders Center and training program at Cleveland Clinic, presents straightforward information about a range of sleep medicine issues. Stressing the importance of sleep for physical and mental health, the author helps readers assess their own sleep disturbances and explains what happens during a sleep study. The specific sleep disorders discussed include sleep apnea, narcolepsy, restless leg syndrome, psychophysiological insomnia, sleep terrors, rapid eye movement behavior disorder, delayed sleep-phase syndrome, and sleep issues in special populations. Appendices cover how to get a good night's sleep, caffeine, sleep aids, and sleep issues in children and teenagers.

Other books by the same author:

A Case a Week: Sleep Disorders from the Cleveland Clinic, 2010

Other books you might like:

Richard B. Berry, *Positive Airway Pressure Therapy: An Issue of Sleep Medicine Clinics*, 2010

Archibald D. Hart, *Sleep, It Does a Family Good: How Busy Families Can Overcome Sleep Deprivation*, 2010

Barry Krakow, *Sound Sleep, Sound Mind: 7 Keys to Sleeping Through the Night*, 2007

Teofilo L. Lee-Chiong, *Sleep Medicine: Essentials and Review*, 2008

Paul McKenna, *I Can Make You Sleep: Overcome Insomnia Forever and Get the Best Rest of Your Life!*, 2009

508

MELISSA FORD

Navigating the Land of If: Understanding Infertility and Exploring Your Options

(Berkeley, California: Seal Press, 2009)

Subject(s): Health; Medicine; Medical care

Summary: In *Navigating the Land of If: Understanding Infertility and Exploring Your Options*, blogger Melissa Ford presents a guide for women dealing with infertility. Written in a conversational tone and based in part on the author's personal experiences, this practical book leads readers on a journey through the land of infertility (IF, in online language), beginning with an orientation for new (and not-so-new) arrivals. Subsequent chapters address the range of issues and decisions associated with infertility, including treatment options, pregnancy loss, third-party reproduction, and advice for same-sex couples, as well as the emotional aspects of infertility and the prospect of adoption.

Where it's reviewed:

Curve, Jan-Feb 2010, page 15
Library Journal, June 1, 2009, page 116

Other books you might like:

Tertia Loebenberg Albertyn, *So Close: Infertile and Addicted to Hope*, 2009

Ilona Laszlo Higgins, *Creating Life Against the Odds: The Journey from Infertility to Parenthood*, 2006

William Schoolcraft, *If at First You Don't Conceive: A Complete Guide to Infertility from One of the Nation's Leading Clinics*, 2010

Laura S. Scott, *Two Is Enough: A Couple's Guide to Living Childless by Choice*, 2009

Greg Wolfe, *How to Make Love to a Plastic Cup: A Guy's Guide to the World of Infertility*, 2010

509

PATRICK J. FOX

The Widow-Maker Heart Attack At Age 48: Written By A Heart Attack Survivor For A Heart Attack Survivor And Their Loved Ones

(Bloomington, Indiana: AuthorHouse, 2009)

Subject(s): Health; Medicine; Diseases

Summary: In *The Widow-Maker Heart Attack at Age 48: Written by a Heart Attack Survivor for a Heart Attack Survivor and Their Loved Ones*, Patrick J. Fox shares his experiences as the survivor of a severe heart attack. Fox documents the events surrounding his heart attack—the physical symptoms he experienced, the psychological stresses he suffered in the ER and the intensive care unit, and, most remarkably, how he survived after coming back from clinical death six times. The author—a high school teacher, coach, and horse trainer—then goes on to describe the range of challenges he and his family faced during the first year of his recovery.

Where it's reviewed:
Library Journal, January 25, 2010, page 130

Other books you might like:
Nelson Anderson, *A Heart Attack Survivor's Guide to a Long Healthy Life*, 2009
Dede Bonner, *The 10 Best Questions for Recovering from a Heart Attack: The Script You Need to Take Control of Your Health*, 2009
Lawrence D. Chilnick, *The First Year: Heart Disease: An Essential Guide for the Newly Diagnosed*, 2008
Curtis M. Rimmerman, *The Cleveland Clinic Guide to Heart Attack*, 2009
Mike Stone, *Living with Restenosis*, 2007

510

KYM ORSETTI FURNEY

When the Diagnosis Is Multiple Sclerosis: Help, Hope, and Insights from an Affected Physician

(Baltimore, Maryland: John Hopkins University Press, 2009)

Story type: Medical
Subject(s): Multiple sclerosis; Health; Medical care

Summary: In *When the Diagnosis Is Multiple Sclerosis: Help, Hope, and Insights from an Affected Physician*, Kym Orsetti Furney shares her story as a physician and a mother living with multiple sclerosis (MS) and the special challenges she faces as a result of her condition. The author is an advocate for injectable drugs to treat MS, but also briefly discusses concerns that these methods can lead to higher rates of depression, and she elucidates the benefits of supplemental alternative therapies. This book is intended for people who are newly diagnosed with MS and who may be overwhelmed with the information they are receiving about the condition. Furney provides an overview of the diagnosis and offers practical advice for managing the disease while still living a full life.

Where it's reviewed:
Momentum, Winter/Spring 2008, page 5

Other books you might like:
Jeffrey N. Gingold, *Mental Sharpening Stones: Manage the Cognitive Challenges of Multiple Sclerosis*, 2008
Judy Graham, *Managing Multiple Sclerosis Naturally: A Self-help Guide to Living with MS*, 2010
George Jelinek, *Overcoming Multiple Sclerosis*, 2010
Nancy A. Lowenstein, *Fighting Fatigue in Multiple Sclerosis: Practical Ways to Create New Habits and Increase Your Energy*, 2009
Julie Stachowiak, *The Multiple Sclerosis Manifesto: Action to Take, Principles to Live By*, 2010

511

JOEL E. GALLANT

100 Questions and Answers About HIV and AIDS

(Sudbury, Massachusetts: Jones and Bartlett Publishers, 2009)

Subject(s): AIDS (Disease); Medical care; Health

Summary: Joel E. Gallant, a physician at the Johns Hopkins University School of Medicine, tackles a diverse assortment of questions about HIV/AIDS. *100 Questions and Answers About HIV and AIDS* dispels the misconceptions and fear surrounding the disease by addressing practical questions about it. Gallant takes on such issues as the way HIV is diagnosed, symptoms of infection, ways to find the best medical care, the influences of mental health and substance abuse on the disease, and important post-diagnosis lifestyle changes. This volume includes an appendix of additional informational sources.

Other books by the same author:
Johns Hopkins Poc-It Center Hiv Guide 2011, 2011
Medical Management of HIV Infection, 2009
Global HIV/AIDS Medicine, 2007

Other books you might like:
Helen Epstein, *The Invisible Cure: Africa, the West, and the Fight Against AIDS*, 2007
Celia Farber, *Serious Adverse Events: An Uncensored History of AIDS*, 2006
Jay A. Levy, *HIV and the Pathogenesis of AIDS*, 2007
Stephanie Nolen, *28: Stories of AIDS in Africa*, 2007
Randy Shilts, *And the Band Played On: Politics, People, and the AIDS Epidemic*, 1987

512

KANCHAN M. GANDA

Dentist's Guide to Medical Conditions and Complications

(Ames, Iowa: Wiley-Blackwell, 2008)

Story type: Medical
Subject(s): Dentistry; Medical care; Diseases

Summary: Written by Kanchan M. Ganda, *Dentist's Guide to Medical Conditions and Complications* is an informative and helpful resource guide for dentists and dental professionals faced with treating medically ill patients. Ganda presents straightforward and concise information on a wide variety of common conditions to assist and equip dentists needing to individuals who are suffering from an illness or medical condition. *Dentist's Guide to Medical Conditions and Complications* provides dental professionals with everything they need to know for treating ill patients, including details on drug interaction and side effects, protocols for treating individuals with common ailments, and tips for avoiding and managing medical emergencies.

Other books you might like:
Guido Fischer, *Local Anesthesia in Dentistry, with*

Special Reference to the Mucous and Conductive Methods: A Concise Guide for Dentists, Surgeons and Students, 2010

Arthur A. Weiner, *The Fearful Dental Patient: A Guide to Understanding and Managing,* 2011

513

JAN GARAVAGLIA

How Not to Die: Surprising Lessons on Living Longer, Safer, and Healthier from America's Favorite Medical Examiner

(New York: Crown Publishers, 2008)

Subject(s): Health; Medical care; Physicians

Summary: Dr. Jan Garavaglia is a respected medical examiner and the star of her own documentary television show on the Discovery Health network. In *How Not to Die: Surprising Lessons on Living Longer, Safer, and Healthier from America's Favorite Medical Examiner,* Garavaglia, or Dr. G, as she is widely known, uses case studies from her own practice to show the many ways humans inadvertently hurt themselves. Dr. G's findings empower readers with the knowledge to take back their lives and their health, written from a surprisingly fresh and funny perspective. *How Not to Die* includes a bibliography and an index. First book.

Other books you might like:

Dawn Jackson Blatner, *The Flexitarian Diet: The Mostly Vegetarian Way to Lose Weight, Be Healthier, Prevent Disease, and Add Years to Your Life,* 2008

Gary Clark, *Live Forever or Your Money Back: How We Age, How We Die and How Not To! The Ultimate Anti Aging Solution,* 2009

Sanjay Gupta, *Cheating Death: The Doctors and Medical Miracles That Are Saving Lives Against All Odds,* 2009

Bill Hayes, *The Anatomist: A True Story of Gray's Anatomy,* 2009

Jill Bolte Taylor, *My Stroke of Insight: A Brain Scientist's Personal Journey,* 2008

514

CHERYL GARRISON

The Iron Disorders Institute Guide to Anemia, 2nd Edition

(Nashville, Tennessee: Cumberland House, 2009)

Subject(s): Health; Reference works; Diseases

Summary: In *The Iron Disorders Institute Guide to Anemia, 2nd Edition,* Cheryl Garrison provides a wealth of information for people suffering from anemia. Garrison discusses different types of anemia and the causes and symptoms of each type, as it is important to cor-

rectly identify the condition for successful treatment. She also examines different treatment options for anemia and the way dietary changes can affect the severity of the disease. In addition, Garrison identifies information and questions that patients should bring to their doctors to be sure they are getting the best, most comprehensive treatment possible.

Where it's reviewed:
Southern Medical Journal, Nov 2001, page 1132

Other books you might like:
Arthur Bank, *Turning Blood Red: The Fight for Life in Cooley's Anemia,* 2008
Charles Bardes, *Pale Faces: The Masks of Anemia,* 2008
Judy Monroe Peterson, *Sickle Cell Anemia,* 2008

515

JEFFREY N. GINGOLD

Mental Sharpening Stones: Manage the Cognitive Challenges of Multiple Sclerosis

(New York: Demos Medical, 2008)

Subject(s): Multiple sclerosis; Health; Medicine

Summary: For those suffering from multiple sclerosis, the disease presents a series of cognitive obstacles that can seriously prevent healthy intellectual function. In *Mental Sharpening Stones: Manage the Cognitive Challenges of Multiple Sclerosis,* author Jeffrey N. Gingold presents a series of exercises for MS patients to keep their minds strong and healthy. Further advice is offered by such famous names as talk show host Montel Williams and judge Mary Mullarkey, as well as a host of specialists in the field. *Mental Sharpening Stones* includes a bibliography and a full index.

Where it's reviewed:
Momentum, Winter 2008, page 50

Other books by the same author:
Facing the Cognitive Challenges of Multiple Sclerosis, 2010

Other books you might like:
Alfred Anderson, *Achieving Optimal Memory: A Simple Guide To Successfully Sharpening Your Mind With Memory Exercises,* 2010
Alma H. Bond, *Old Age is a Terminal Illness: How I Learned to Age Gracefully and Conquer My Fear of Dying,* 2006
Gary Clark, *Live Forever or Your Money Back: How We Age, How We Die and How Not To! The Ultimate Anti Aging Solution,* 2009
William Matteson, *Stop Memory Loss: How to Fight Forgetfulness over 40,* 2008
Zaldy S. Tan, *Age-Proof Your Mind: Detect, Delay, and Prevent Memory Loss—Before It's Too Late,* 2005

⬛ **516**

CHRISTOPHER G. GOETZ

Textbook of Clinical Neurology, 3rd Edition

(Philadelphia: Saunders Elsevier, 2007)

Subject(s): Neurosciences; Medical care; Reference works

Summary: The *Textbook of Clinical Neurology, 3rd Edition* is edited by Christopher G. Goetz and is intended for those studying and practicing clinical neurology; it is accompanied by a CD-ROM that includes additional information. This volume focuses primarily on analyzing patient symptoms, choosing the correct tests to administer for diagnosis, analyzing the results as well as any other potential hidden causes, and following up with appropriate treatment and management of conditions. This book includes illustrations as well as additional chapters on cutting-edge therapies and new developments in imaging and prescription drugs

Where it's reviewed:
JAMA, The Journal of the American Medical Association, December 3, 2003, page 2865
SciTech Book News, June 2003, page109

Other books by the same author:
Neurology for the Non-Neurologist, 2010

Other books you might like:
Randy W. Beck, *Functional Neurology for Practitioners of Manual Therapy*, 2007
Mary Coleman, *The Neurology of Autism*, 2009
Duane E. Haines, *Neuroanatomy: An Atlas of Structures, Sections, and Systems*, 2007

⬛ **517**

NIECA GOLDBERG

Dr. Nieca Goldberg's Complete Guide to Women's Health

(New York: Ballantine Books, 2009)

Story type: Medical
Subject(s): Women; Health; Medical care

Summary: Written by author, doctor, and professor, Nieca Goldberg, *Dr. Nieca Goldberg's Complete Guide to Women's Health* is a practical and informative health resource for women over the age of 35. Women go through a great deal of changes after the age of 35. In this book, Goldberg addresses the health concerns and issues that females can expect to encounter later in life. She provides details on hormonal issues; treatments of thyroid problems; an overview of fertility, pregnancy, contraceptives, and menopause concerns; tips for breast health and preventative measures for breast cancer; a synopsis of cardiovascular health; strategies for coping with gastrointestinal conditions such as GERD, stomach ulcers, IBS, IBD, gallstones, and colon cancer; facts about sleep apnea and insomnia; advice for overcoming

stress and anxiety; and practical guidance for routine medical exams.

Where it's reviewed:
Publishers Weekly, December 3, 2007, page 65

Other books by the same author:
The Women's Healthy Heart Program: Lifesaving Strategies for Preventing and Healing Heart Disease, 2006

Other books you might like:
Adam Campbell, *The Women's Health Big Book of Exercises*, 2009
Alexa L. Fishback, *Women's Health Daily Fix*, 2008
Tori Hudson, *Womens Encyclopedia of Natural Medicine: Alternative Therapies and Integrative Medicine for Total Health and Wellness*, 2007
Donnica Moore, *Women's Health For Life*, 2009
Christiane Northrup, *Women's Bodies, Women's Wisdom*, 1994

⬛ **518**

KAREN D. GOODMAN

Music Therapy Groupwork with Special Needs Children: The Evolving Process

(Springfield, Illinois: Charles C. Thomas, 2007)

Subject(s): Health; Mental health; Music

Summary: In *Music Therapy Groupwork with Special Needs Children: The Evolving Process*, Karen D. Goodman presents a comprehensive guide for students and professionals in the field of music therapy. An experienced clinician, the author bases this manual on her years of work with children with autism, multiple disabilities, and psychiatric disabilities. As she demonstrates in anecdotes from her own practice, groups comprising children with varying functioning levels, personalities, and musical tastes can be successfully integrated into a unified group that gains therapeutic benefits as a whole. Goodman stresses the importance of the therapist's ability to adjust treatment methods according to the group's needs.

Where it's reviewed:
Australian Journal of Music Therapy, Annual 2008, page 95
Journal of the American Academy of Child and Adolescent Psychiatry, October 2009, page 1043
Nordic Journal of Music Therapy, January 2008, page 83

Other books by the same author:
Music Therapy Education and Training: From Theory to Practice, 2011

Other books you might like:
Vanessa A. Camilleri, *Healing the Inner City Child: Creative Arts Therapies with At-risk Youth*, 2007
Dennis McCarthy, *Speaking About the Unspeakable: Non-Verbal Methods and Experiences in Therapy with Children*, 2008

Edward Podolsky, *Music Therapy*, 2007

Robin Rio, *Connecting Through Music with People with Dementia: A Guide for Caregivers*, 2009

Oliver Sacks, *Musicophilia: Tales of Music and the Brain*, 2007

519

LEON GORDIS

Epidemiology: 4th Edition

(Philadelphia: Elsevier/Saunders, 2008)

Story type: Medical

Subject(s): Medical care; Diseases; Health

Summary: Written by award-winning teacher Leon Gordis, *Epidemiology: 4th Edition* is an educational textbook offering a comprehensive overview of the study of disease origin, development, and spread. The book is divided into three straightforward sections and offers students and physicians an introduction to epidemiology principles, practical uses, and applications in public health and clinical practice, including up-to-date information on identifying the causes of diseases, applying epidemiology to evaluation and policy, and the epidemiological approach to disease and intervention. *Epidemiology* also includes color illustrations, detailed graphs and charts, cartoons, and educational review questions to help readers understand and comprehend the material.

Other books you might like:

Mark S. Dworkin, *Outbreak Investigations Around the World: Case Studies in Infectious Disease Field Epidemiology*, 2009

Robert H. Friis, *Epidemiology 101*, 2009

S. Nassir Ghaemi, *A Clinician's Guide to Statistics and Epidemiology in Mental Health*, 2009

Ray M. Merrill, *Introduction to Epidemiology*, 2000

William Anton Oleckno, *Epidemiology: Concepts and Methods*, 2008

520

ELIZABETH GORDON

Allergy Free Desserts: Gluten-free, Dairy-free, Egg-free, Soy-free and Nut-free Delights

(Hoboken, New Jersey: John Wiley and Sons, 2010)

Subject(s): Allergy; Cooking; Food

Summary: Those who deal with food allergies often find themselves in the unenviable position of having to forgo dessert. They won't, however, for much longer. In *Allergy Free Desserts: Gluten-free, Dairy-free, Egg-free, Soy-free and Nut-free Delights*, author Elizabeth Gordon provides a huge selection of mouthwatering recipes designed to satisfy even the pickiest sweet tooth. Ac-

companied by full-color photos, the 82 recipes in this volume include red velvet cake, fudge, "peanut butter" cookies, pumpkin pie, and much more. *Allergy Free Desserts* contains a full index.

Other books you might like:

Kelly Keough, *Sugar-Free Gluten-Free Baking and Desserts*, 2009

Carol Kicinski, *Simply . . . Gluten-Free Desserts: 150 Delicious Recipes for Cupcakes, Cookies, Pies, and More Old and New Favorites*, 2011

Susan O'Brien, *Gluten-free, Sugar-free Cooking: Over 200 Delicious Recipes to Help You Live a Healthier, Allergy-Free Life*, 2006

Cybele Pascal, *Allergen-Free Baker's Handbook*, 2009

Lori Sandler, *The Divvies Bakery Cookbook: No Nuts. No Eggs. No Dairy. Just Delicious!*, 2010

521

RIVA GREENBERG

50 Diabetes Myths That Can Ruin Your Life: And the 50 Diabetes Truths That Can Save It

(Philadelphia, Pennsylvania: Da Capo Press, 2009)

Subject(s): Health; Medicine; Medical care

Summary: In *50 Diabetes Myths That Can Ruin Your Life: And the 50 Diabetes Truths That Can Save It*, author Riva Greenberg presents an informative guide for individuals diagnosed with diabetes. As a diabetic, Greenberg is familiar with the many misconceptions surrounding the condition that can impede appropriate treatment and quality of life. The author organizes the 50 myths into six categories—common myths, medical myths, food myths, body fitness myths, psych myths, and practical and practices myths. Topics discussed include differences between Type 1 and Type 2 diabetes, diabetes symptoms, weight gain, the effect of diabetes on the body, and insulin injections.

Other books by the same author:

The ABCs of Loving Yourself with Diabetes, 2007

Other books you might like:

Richard K. Bernstein, *Dr. Bernstein's Diabetes Solution*, 2007

Walter M. Bortz, *Diabetes Danger: What 200 Million Americans at Risk Need to Know*, 2010

Philip E. Cryer, *Hypoglycemia in Diabetes: Pathophysiology, Prevalence, and Prevention*, 2009

Dan Hurley, *Diabetes Rising: How a Rare Disease Became a Modern Pandemic, and What to Do About It*, 2010

Jenny Ruhl, *Blood Sugar 101: What They Don't Tell You About Diabetes*, 2009

522

VALERIE GREENE

Conquering Stroke: How I Fought My Way Back and How You Can Too

(Hoboken, New Jersey: Wiley, 2008)

Story type: Medical

Subject(s): Autobiographies; Medical care; Stroke

Summary: In *Conquering Stroke: How I Fought My Way Back and How You Can Too*, author and stroke survivor Valerie Greene shares valuable, first-hand information with readers who have experienced a stroke or whose loved ones have suffered a stroke. At the age of 31, Greene, a determined businesswoman, experienced a stroke that immobilized the left side of her body. Despite warnings from doctors that she may never speak or walk again, Greene accomplished both feats and attained a 90 percent recovery. In this book, Greene recounts her experience and provides advice about warning signs of and treatment options for strokes.

Other books you might like:

Louis R. Caplan, *Caplan's Stroke: A Clinical Approach, Fourth Edition*, 2009

Kinan K. Hreib, *100 Questions and Answers About Stroke*, 2008

Peter G. Levine, *Stronger After Stroke: Your Roadmap to Recovery*, 2008

Dennis C. Tanner, *Family Guide to Surviving Stroke and Communications Disorders*, 2007

Jill Bolte Taylor, *My Stroke of Insight: A Brain Scientist's Personal Journey*, 2008

523

DAVID M. GREER

Acute Ischemic Stroke: An Evidence-Based Approach

(Hoboken, New Jersey: Wiley-Liss, 2007)

Subject(s): Health; Medical care; Stroke

Summary: Compiled by neurologist David M. Greer, *Acute Ischemic Stroke: An Evidence-Based Approach* is an overview of modern medical treatment methods for acute ischemic stroke (AIS). Doctors have struggled to find effective treatment options for acute ischemic stroke for many year. Recently, however, researchers have made a number of advancements in modern medicine and therapy practices to treat AIS. In the book, Greer outlines the biological and clinical research to support current management procedures, and he provides straightforward treatment plans and protocols. *Acute Ischemic Stroke* also provides details on stroke neuroimaging, intravenous thrombolysis, endovascular treatments, surgery options, and more.

Where it's reviewed:

JAMA, The Journal of the American Medical Association, April 23, 2008, page 1958

Other books by the same author:

Pocket Neurology, 2010

Other books you might like:

Louis R. Caplan, *Stroke (What Do I Do Now?)*, 2010

Valerie Greene, *Conquering Stroke: How I Fought My Way Back and How You Can Too*, 2008

Richard Senelick, *Living with Stroke: A Guide for Families*, 1994

Cheryle Sullivan, *Brain Injury Survival Kit: 365 Tips, Tools and Tricks to Deal with Cognitive Function Loss*, 2008

Olajide Williams, *Stroke Diaries: A Guide for Survivors and Their Families*, 2010

524

JILL GRIMES

Seductive Delusions: How Everyday People Catch STDs

(Baltimore: Johns Hopkins University Press, 2008)

Subject(s): Sex education; Diseases; Medicine

Summary: Sexually transmitted diseases (STDs) aren't reserved for the promiscuous; in fact, they are affecting everyday young people and adults at an alarming rate. In *Seductive Delusions: How Everyday People Catch STDs*, physician Jill Grimes examines a series of cases that reveal exactly how STDs are contracted and the clinical and emotional toll they take. Among the diseases discussed in this volume are HIV, cervical cancer, syphilis, gonorrhea, herpes, and the human papilloma virus. *Seductive Delusions* includes a bibliography and an index of symptoms.

Other books by the same author:

The 5-Minute Clinical Consult 2010, 2009

Other books you might like:

Shana McKibbin, *HealthScouter HPV: Understanding HPV Testing: The Human Papillomavirus Patient Advocate*, 2009

Alexander McMillan, *Sexually Transmissible Infections in Clinical Practice: A Problem-Based Approach*, 2009

Ian Peate, *Manual of Sexually Transmitted Infections*, 2006

Lawrence R. Stanberry, *Understanding Herpes*, 2006

Laura Sessions Stepp, *Unhooked: How Young Women Pursue Sex, Delay Love and Lose at Both*, 2008

525

MIMI GUARNERI

The Heart Speaks: A Cardiologist Reveals the Secret Language of Healing

(New York: Simon & Schuster, 2007)

Subject(s): Medical care; Reference works; Health

Summary: In *The Heart Speaks: A Cardiologist Reveals the Secret Language of Healing*, Mimi Guarneri shares her unique holistic approach to treating and preventing heart disease. Guarneri is a successful cardiologist and surgeon, but she began to note that the patients who recovered the best were the ones who practiced alternative therapies such as yoga, meditation, and visualization, among other methods of stress relief. In addition, these patients led a basically healthy lifestyle that included a healthy diet and a regular exercise program. As Guarneri studied the success of these patients, she began to explore other options such as spiritual healing or energy work, the positive effects pets can have on depression and heart disease, and the benefits of a strong support system including friends, family, and faith. Guarneri presents her findings in an accessible style, encouraging people to make these changes in their lives to prevent, or even reverse, heart disease.

Where it's reviewed:
Library Journal, January 1, 2006, page 144
Publishers Weekly, November 21, 2005, page 37

Other books you might like:
Michael Arloski, *Wellness Coaching for Lasting Lifestyle Change*, 2007
Paul Kligfield, *The Cardiac Recovery Handbook*, 2006

526

LEE GUION

Respiratory Management of ALS: Amyotrophic Lateral Sclerosis

(Sudbury, Massachusetts: Jones and Bartlett Publishers, 2010)

Subject(s): Medical care; Diseases; Science

Summary: For patients suffering from ALS, proper respiratory system management is vital, but it can also be a challenge. In the book *Respiratory Management of ALS: Amyotrophic Lateral Sclerosis* author Lee Guion presents a guide for ALS patients, their families, and their caregivers. Guion discusses the effects ALS has on the upper and lower respiratory system. The book also describes possible courses of treatment for the disease. *Respiratory Management of ALS* includes a bibliography and a full index.

Other books you might like:
Richard M. Cohen, *Strong at the Broken Places: Voices of Illness, a Chorus of Hope*, 2008
Roger Hohnsbeen, *Amyotrophic Lateral Sclerosis*, 2008
Hiroshi Mitsumoto, *Amyotrophic Lateral Sclerosis: A Guide for Patients and Families, 3rd Edition*, 2009
Ed Rice, *If They Could Only Hear Me*, 2005
David Tank, *River of Hope: My Journey with Kathy in Search of Healing from Lou Gehrig's Disease*, 2008

527

SANJAY GUPTA

Cheating Death: The Doctors and Medical Miracles That Are Saving Lives Against All Odds

(New York: Wellness Central, 2009)

Subject(s): Health; Medicine; Death

Summary: In *Cheating Death: The Doctors and Medical Miracles That Are Saving Lives Against All Odds*, CNN chief medical correspondent Sanjay Gupta presents true stories of lives saved through the use of innovative medical procedures. In documenting each case, Gupta discusses the treatment that produced the positive outcome. Through therapeutic hypothermia, doctors treating trauma victims gain time by decreasing the body's demand for oxygen. Through in utero surgeries, physicians can correct defects in a fetus before birth. In telling each story of amazing survival, Gupta gives a human side to the miracle medical procedures that save lives every day.

Other books you might like:
Dawn Jackson Blatner, *The Flexitarian Diet: The Mostly Vegetarian Way to Lose Weight, Be Healthier, Prevent Disease, and Add Years to Your Life*, 2008
Gary Clark, *Live Forever or Your Money Back: How We Age, How We Die and How Not To! The Ultimate Anti Aging Solution*, 2009
Jan Garavaglia, *How Not to Die: Surprising Lessons on Living Longer, Safer, and Healthier from America's Favorite Medical Examiner*, 2008
Bill Hayes, *The Anatomist: A True Story of Gray's Anatomy*, 2009
Jill Bolte Taylor, *My Stroke of Insight: A Brain Scientist's Personal Journey*, 2008

528

BARBARA A. GYLYS

Medical Terminology Systems: A Body Systems Approach, 6th Edition

(Philadelphia, Pennsylvania: F. A. Davis Company, 2009)

Story type: Medical
Subject(s): Medical professions; Encyclopedias and dictionaries; Medical care

Summary: Barbara A. Gylys's *Medical Terminology Systems: A Body Systems Approach, 6th Edition* was written with the understanding that medical educators across the country could easily embrace this book in their classrooms. One of the most important approaches to succeeding in medical school is to learn and comprehend all of the terminology medical professionals use on a day-to-day basis. This book breaks these terms into chapters using body systems such as the digestive system, the reproductive system, and the cardiovascular system. The sixth edition, released in 2009, offers software that includes brilliant illustrations, detailed medical cases, and clear audio files.

Other books by the same author:
Medical Terminology Simplified: A Programmed Learning Approach by Body System, 2009

Other books you might like:
Barbara J. Cohen, *Medical Terminology: An Illustrated Guide*, 2010

Dale Pierre Layman, *Medical Terminology Demystified*, 2005

Jane Rice, *Medical Terminology: A Word-Building Approach*, 2007

Donald Venes, *Taber's Cyclopedic Medical Dictionary*, 2009

Marjorie Canfield Willis, *Medical Terminology: A Programmed Learning Approach to the Language of Health Care*, 2007

529

JACQUI GREENE HAAS

Dance Anatomy

(Champaign, Illinois: Human Kinetics, 2010)

Subject(s): Dance; Exercise; Health

Summary: *Dance Anatomy* is a helpful resource guide on dance and exercise from author Jacqui Green Haas. The book provides practical tips and an easy-to-follow guide for becoming a stronger, more graceful dancer. Filled with more than 200 color illustrations, *Dance Anatomy* shows readers the connection between muscle growth and artistic movement in 82 dance exercises. The exercises included in the book are designed to encourage perfect alignment, correct breathing, proper placement, and the avoidance of typical injuries. The illustrations provide step-by-step instructions for each exercise while highlighting the muscles that are used to perform the moves to improve dance quality, relieve muscle tension, and increase flexibility.

Other books you might like:

Karen Clipinger, *Dance Anatomy and Kinesiology*, 2007

Joseph S. Huwyler, *The Dancer's Body: A Medical Perspective on Dance and Dance Training*, 2009

Jo Ann Staugaard-Jones, *The Anatomy of Exercise and Movement: For the Study of Dance, Pilates, Sport and Yoga*, 2010

530

DAVID HABER

Health Promotion and Aging: Practical Applications for Health Professionals

(New York: Springer, 2007)

Subject(s): Aging (Biology); Medical care; Medical professions

Summary: In *Health Promotion and Aging: Practical Applications for Health Professionals*, Dr. David Haber offers health care practitioners sensible advice for dealing with the issues faced by aging patients. With the aim of creating an active, healthy aging populace, Haber sets out to reexamine and reevaluate long-held beliefs about growing older and offers his own wisdom on how medical professionals can best care for older patients. Topics covered include vitamins and supplements, exercise, and

diet and nutrition. *Health Promotion and Aging* includes figures, tables, a bibliography, and an index.

Where it's reviewed:

Family and Community Health, July-September 2009, page 28

Other books you might like:

Nortin M. Hadler, *Worried Sick: A Prescription for Health in an Overtreated America*, 2008

C. Shanthi Johnson, *Health and Aging in the World's Largest Democracy*, 2010

Mary Kay Mitchell, *Nutrition Across the Life Span*, 2008

Staci Nix, *Williams' Basic Nutrition and Diet Therapy, 13th Edition*, 2008

Kay A. Van Norman, *Exercise and Wellness for Older Adults*, 2010

531

NORTIN M. HADLER

The Last Well Person: How to Stay Well Despite the Health-Care System

(Montreal, Quebec, Canada: McGill-Queen's University Press, 2007)

Subject(s): Health; Medicine; Medical care

Summary: In *The Last Well Person: How to Stay Well Despite the Health-Care System*, rheumatologist and microbiology professor Nortin M. Hadler makes a fascinating argument opposing the excessive and unwarranted diagnosis and treatment of illness in America. In the book's first part, "The Methuselah Complex," Hadler examines the current practices used for identifying and treating cardiovascular disease, breast cancer, colon cancer, and prostate cancer, asserting that, statistically speaking, few patients benefit from the often radical surgical remedies performed. In the second part, "Worried Sick," the author criticizes the phenomenon of "medicalization," by which common maladies and the aging process have become categorized as illnesses.

Where it's reviewed:

American Journal of Medical Quality, July-August 2007, page 300

Other books by the same author:

Stabbed in the Back: Confronting Back Pain in an Overtreated Society, 2009

Worried Sick: A Prescription for Health in an Overtreated America, 2008

Other books you might like:

Shannon Brownlee, *Overtreated: Why Too Much Medicine Is Making Us Sicker and Poorer*, 2007

George C. Halvorson, *Health Care Reform Now!: A Prescription for Change*, 2007

George C. Halvorson, *Health Care Will Not Reform Itself: A User's Guide to Refocusing and Reforming American Health Care*, 2009

John E. Sarno, *The Divided Mind: The Epidemic of Mindbody*, 2007

H. Gilbert Welch, *Should I Be Tested for Cancer: Maybe Not and Here's Why*, 2004

532

RICHARD J. HAMILTON

Tarascon Pharmacopoeia 2010 Professional Desk Reference Edition

(Sudbury, Massachusetts: Jones & Bartlett Publishers, 2010)

Subject(s): Health; Reference works; Medicine

Summary: The *Tarascon Pharmacopoeia 2010 Professional Desk Reference Edition* is edited by Richard J. Hamilton and is intended for medical professionals. This desk reference contains detailed information about prescription drugs. The topics covered in the volume include FDA dosing information, approximate prices, potential interactions, generic variations or similar drugs, warnings about metabolism, warnings for pregnant and breastfeeding patients, new dosing information for HIV and AIDS patients. An additional section includes information about herbal supplements as well as other treatment options. Each edition of this guide is peer-reviewed.

Other books by the same author:
Year Book of Emergency Medicine 2010, 2010

Other books you might like:
Joseph Esherick, *Tarascon Primary Care Pocketbook*, 2009
C. P. Panayiotopoulos, *Antiepileptic Drugs, Pharmacopoeia*, 2010

533

STEVE HANNIGAN

Inherited Metabolic Diseases: A Guide to 100 Conditions

(New York: Radcliffe, 2007)

Subject(s): Diseases; Reference works; Health

Summary: Edited by Steve Hannigan, *Inherited Metabolic Diseases: A Guide to 100 Conditions* is designed as an accessible guide for both patients and medical professionals, providing extensive information on metabolic diseases from the ten major groups of disorders. The text serves as a reference for those who are not metabolic specialists, such as general practitioners, nurses, and educators. In addition, the information provided can be useful for patients who suffer from metabolic conditions or for those who care for someone with a condition. Each entry for the 100 conditions listed in the text includes information about causes, symptoms and effects on the body, treatment options, and the different names used for the same condition.

Where it's reviewed:
Archives of Disease in Childhood, January 2008, page 92

Choice, November 2007, page 500
Nursing Standard, October 3, 2007, page 30
Paediatric Nursing, April 2008, page 7

Other books you might like:
Phyllis B. Acosta, *Nutrition Management of Patients with Inherited Metabolic Diseases*, 2009
John C. Avise, *Inside the Human Genome: A Case for Non-Intelligent Design*, 2010
Edward Ball, *The Genetic Strand: Exploring a Family History Through DNA*, 2007
Joe T. R. Clarke, *A Clinical Guide to Inherited Metabolic Diseases*, 2006
Peter S. Harper, *A Short History of Medical Genetics*, 2008

534

GEORG HANSMANN

Neonatal Emergencies

(New York: Cambridge University Press, 2009)

Subject(s): Health; Infants; Medical care

Summary: In *Neonatal Emergencies*, editor Georg Hansmann presents a comprehensive guide for all health care professionals involved in the care of newborns. Obstetricians, emergency medicine professionals, pediatric residents, midwives, neonatal nurses, paramedics, and anesthesiologists will find *Neonatal Emergencies* a valuable resource for treating the critically ill infant from birth through his or her first 72 hours of life. Topics include neonatal transport, respiratory issues, medications and dosages, the decision-making process, and ethical issues—all supported by case studies that demonstrate practical applications of the theory presented. Supplemental materials include tables, diagrams, and algorithms.

Other books you might like:
Cynthia M. Bissell, *Pediatric Tracheostomy Home Care Guide*, 2007
Glenys Boxwell, *Neonatal Intensive Care Nursing*, 2007
Bonnie Urquhart Gruenberg, *Birth Emergency Skills Training*, 2008
Leora Kuttner, *A Child in Pain: What Health Professionals Can Do to Help*, 2010

535

PETER S. HARPER

A Short History of Medical Genetics

(New York: Oxford University Press, 2008)

Subject(s): Health; Medicine; Genetics

Summary: In *A Short History of Medical Genetics*, geneticist Peter S. Harper chronicles the development of the field of genetics. In the first part of the book, Harper discusses the foundations of human and medical genetics, including Mendelism and human inherited disease, as well as the birth of modern genetics and molecular biology. Chapters on human genetics and medical genetics consider such topics as chromosomes, the human gene map, human molecular genetics, and special medical issues of genetic diseases. As Harper examines the history of genetics from Gregor Mendel to the human genome project and beyond, he reveals the brilliant advances as well as the missteps that have defined the field's first centuries.

Where it's reviewed:
Quarterly Review of Biology, September 2009, page 318

Other books by the same author:
First Years of Human Chromosomes: The Beginnings of Human Cytogenetics, 2006

Other books you might like:
Edward Ball, *The Genetic Strand: Exploring a Family History Through DNA*, 2007
Robin L. Bennett, *The Practical Guide to the Genetic Family History, 2nd Edition*, 2010
Jon Queijo, *Breakthrough!: How the 10 Greatest Discoveries in Medicine Saved Millions and Changed Our View of the World*, 2010
Angela Scheuerle, *Understanding Genetics: A Primer for Couples and Families*, 2008
Doris Teichler-Zallen, *To Test or Not to Test: A Guide to Genetic Screening and Risk*, 2008

536

JOANNA HAYDEN

Introduction to Health Behavior Theory

(Sudbury, Massachusetts: Jones and Bartlett, 2008)

Subject(s): Health; Medical care; Psychology

Summary: *Introduction to Health Behavior Theory* by Joanna Hayden provides a basic guide for the undergraduate student of health education. Hayden first explains the definition of health behavior theory and the development of various theories, including such commonly applied theories as the self-efficacy theory, the theory of reasoned action, the theory of planned behavior, the health belief model, the attribution theory, the transtheoretical model, the social cognitive theory, as well as emerging theories and the process of selecting a theory. In discussing each of these theories, Hayden examines pertinent concepts, constructs, and practical applications.

Other books you might like:
Nancy Borkowski, *Organization Behavior in Health Care*, 2009
Mark Cameron Edberg, *Essential Readings in Health Behavior: Theory and Practice*, 2009
Mark Cameron Edberg, *Essentials of Health Behavior*, 2007
David Haber, *Health Promotion and Aging: Practical*

Applications for Health Professionals, 2007
Paul W. O'Neal, *Motivation of Health Behavior*, 2007

537

A. WALLACE HAYES

Principles and Methods of Toxicology, Fifth Edition

(New York: Informa Healthcare, 2007)

Subject(s): Health; Medical care; Science

Summary: In *Principles and Methods of Toxicology, Fifth Edition*, editor A. Wallace Hayes revises his respected text with updated information and the work of new contributors. Organized into three parts—Principles of Toxicology, Agents, and Methods—this comprehensive volume covers the history of toxicology, toxicokinetics, toxicopanomics, the toxicologic assessment of pharmaceutical and biotechnology products, foodborne toxicants, plant and animal toxins, epidemiology for toxicologists, the information infrastructure of toxicology, acute toxicity and eye irritancy, principles of testing for carcinogenic activity, and methods in environmental toxicology. The fifth edition includes four new chapters and an extensive glossary.

Where it's reviewed:
Journal of Toxicology: Clinical Toxicology, November 1994, page 745
SciTech Book News, March 2002, page 89

Other books you might like:
Urs A. Boelsterli, *Mechanistic Toxicology*, 2007
Ernest Hodgson, *A Textbook of Modern Toxicology*, 2008
Curtis D. Klaassen, *Casarett and Doull's Toxicology: The Basic Science of Poisons*, 1986
Ira S. Richards, *Principles and Practice of Toxicology in Public Health*, 2007
John A. Timbrell, *Principles of Biochemical Toxicology*, 2008

538

AMY HENDEL

Fat Families, Thin Families: How to Save Your Family from the Obesity Trap

(Dallas: BenBella Books, 2008)

Subject(s): Weight loss; Family; Nutrition

Summary: The obesity epidemic is plaguing entire families at an alarming rate. In *Fat Families, Thin Families: How to Save Your Family from the Obesity Trap*, author and expert Amy Hendel guides families through the weight loss process by making the system a group effort in which the entire clan can take part. Hendel's plan consists of four parts—Plan Together, Prepare Together, Play Together, and Portion Together—and she explains each in detail, illuminating the variety of ways the family unit can be strengthened and revitalized by the typically daunting weight loss regime. *Fat Families, Thin Families* includes a bibliography. First book.

Where it's reviewed:
Library Journal, June 1, 2008, page 116

Other books you might like:
Elliott M. Blass, *Obesity: Causes, Mechanisms, Prevention, and Treatment*, 2008
Sander L. Gilman, *Obesity: The Biography*, 2010
Zoe Harcombe, *The Obesity Epidemic: What Caused It? How Can We Stop It?*, 2010
Frank B. Hu, *Obesity Epidemiology*, 2008
J. Eric Oliver, *Fat Politics: The Real Story behind America's Obesity Epidemic*, 2006

539

WILLIAM L. HENRICH

Principles and Practice of Dialysis, Fourth Edition

(Philadelphia, Pennsylvania: Lippincott Williams & Wilkins, 2009)

Subject(s): Health; Medical care; Medicine

Summary: In *Principles and Practice of Dialysis, Fourth Edition* author William L. Henrich updates his comprehensive review of a range of topics related to treating the dialysis patient. The text is organized into two parts—the first pertaining to technical issues and the second pertaining to clinical considerations. Topics covered include the selection and use of hemodialysis membranes, anticoagulation strategies, prescribing drugs for dialysis patients, coronary artery disease in end-stage renal patients, endocrine disease, gastrointestinal complications, malnutrition, neurologic complications, and acute dialysis in children. Illustrations, medication charts, and other graphics supplement this revised edition.

Other books you might like:
Shuang Chen, *The Guide to Nutrition and Diet for Dialysis Patients*, 2008
Donna R. Falvo, *Medical and Psychosocial Aspects of Chronic Illness and Disability, Fourth Edition*, 2008
Nina Kolbe, *10 Step Diet and Lifestyle Plan for Healthier Kidneys Avoid Dialysis*, 2009
Sheila Shaw, *5 Simple Steps to doing Peritoneal Dialysis Successfully*, 2007
Lawrence E. Stam, *100 Questions and Answers About Kidney Dialysis*, 2009

540

ROBERT HILL

Dead Men Don't Have Sex: A Guy's Guide to Surviving Prostate Cancer

(Createspace, 2010)

Subject(s): Health; Medical care; Medicine
Summary: In *Dead Men Don't Have Sex: A Guy's Guide*

to Surviving Prostate Cancer, author Robert Hill presents an informative, accessible resource for prostate cancer patients and their families. A prostate cancer survivor, Hill approaches his topic with honesty and wit, organizing his guide into four sections—"The Club You Never Wanted to Join," "Nobody Looks Good in a Hospital Gown," "The New and Improved You—Now with Less Prostate," and "Living Levitra Loca." In each section, Hill discusses everything from diagnosis, surgery, and recovery to sensitive topics such as catheterization, incontinence, and sex after prostate cancer. Through the book's journal format, readers gauge the time line of Hill's experience.

Other books you might like:
Arthur Burnett, *Johns Hopkins Patients' Guide to Prostate Cancer*, 2007
J. Stephen Jones, *The Complete Prostate Book: What Every Man Needs to Know*, 2007
Sheldon Marks, *Prostate and Cancer: A Family Guide to Diagnosis, Treatment, and Survival, Fourth Edition*, 2009
Alan T. Meridith, *Handbook of Prostate Cancer Cell Research: Growth, Signalling and Survival*, 2009
Margaret Rayman, *Healthy Eating for Prostate Care*, 2009

541

TERESA HOLLER

Holler for Your Health: Be the Key to a Healthy Family

(Blue Ridge, Virginia: Healthy Harbor Publications, 2008)

Subject(s): Health; Medicine; Family relations
Summary: In *Holler for Your Health: Be the Key to a Healthy Family*, medical professional, author, and parent Teresa Holler explains how environmental toxins are negatively impacting the lives of American families. Holler examines the variety of toxic substances used in common household products such as toothpaste, toiletries, plastics, pesticides, dental fillings, and even grocery items and drinking water. According to the author, exposure to these pervasive substances has caused a dramatic increase in asthma, autism, Attention Deficit Disorder, and cancer. *Holler for Your Health* goes on to describe simple methods that families can employ to reduce environmental toxins in their homes.

Other books by the same author:
Cardiology Essentials, 2007

Other books you might like:
Christopher Gavigan, *Healthy Child Healthy World: Creating a Cleaner, Greener, Safer Home*, 2009
Amy Hendel, *Fat Families, Thin Families: How to Save Your Family from the Obesity Trap*, 2008
Annabel Karmel, *Lunch Boxes and Snacks: Over 120 healthy recipes from delicious sandwiches and salads to hot soups and sweet treats*, 2007
Ellyn Satter, *Secrets of Feeding a Healthy Family: Orchestrating and Enjoying the Family Meal*, 2008
Charles R. Swindoll, *Parenting: From Surviving to*

Thriving: Building Healthy Families in a Changing World, 2008

542

BETTY DAVIS JONES

Comprehensive Medical Terminology, 3rd Edition

(Florence, Kentucky: Delmar Cengage Learning, 2007)

Subject(s): Encyclopedias and dictionaries; Medical care; Medical professions

Summary: Betty Davis Jones' *Comprehensive Medical Terminology, 3rd Edition* includes more than 20 chapters of medical terms and definitions. Each chapter in the book includes information about a different body system, including the skeletal system, the cardiovascular system, the nervous system, and the reproductive system. The book also includes tips and information about learning basic word parts that are prevalent in medical terminology. The author argues that understanding common roots, prefixes, and suffixes will make learning new terms easier. In this third edition of *Comprehensive Medical Terminology* the author includes more medical scenarios and more discussions about specific disease and ailments.

Other books by the same author:
Workbook for Jones' Comprehensive Medical Terminology, 2010

Other books you might like:
Davi-Ellen Chabner, *Medical Terminology: A Short Course, Fifth Edition*, 2008
Barbara A. Gylys, *Medical Terminology Systems: A Body Systems Approach, 6th Edition*, 2009
Tina M. Kaufman, *Yes/No Medical Spanish: Comprehensive Handbook of Clinical Spanish*, 2010
Myrna LaFleur-Brooks, *Exploring Medical Language: A Student-Directed Approach*, 2008
Donald Venes, *Taber's Cyclopedic Medical Dictionary*, 2009

543

J. STEPHEN JONES

The Complete Prostate Book: What Every Man Needs to Know

(Amherst, New York: Prometheus Books, 2007)

Subject(s): Reference works; Health; Men

Summary: In *The Complete Prostate Book: What Every Man Needs to Know*, urologist J. Stephen Jones provides men with the information they need to understand the importance and maintenance of prostate health. Jones begins with a basic discussion of the anatomy of the prostate and the various methods by which physicians conduct prostate examinations. Jones follows with a discussion of prostate issues that most men will experience at some point, such as an enlarged prostate, and then provides information about more serious problems such as prostate cancer. Diagnoses, treatments, surgical options, and alternative therapies for these conditions are discussed, along with general topics such as sexual activity and maintaining overall prostate health.

Other books by the same author:
Prostate Biopsy: Indications, Techniques, and Complications, 2010

Other books you might like:
J. P. Barral, *Manual Therapy for the Prostate*, 2010
Arthur Burnett, *Johns Hopkins Patients' Guide to Prostate Cancer*, 2007
Robert Hill, *Dead Men Don't Have Sex: A Guy's Guide to Surviving Prostate Cancer*, 2010
Robert J. Marckini, *You Can Beat Prostate Cancer*, 2007
Sheldon Marks, *Prostate and Cancer: A Family Guide to Diagnosis, Treatment, and Survival, Fourth Edition*, 2009

544

BRIGID M. KANE

HIV/AIDS Treatment Drugs

(New York: Chelsea House Publishers, 2008)

Subject(s): AIDS (Disease); Drugs; Medicine

Summary: In *HIV/AIDS Treatment Drugs*, author Brigid M. Kane instructs young readers on the various medications and treatment options available for HIV and AIDS. Kane's extensive, accessible overview includes information on the drugs' histories, how they target the disease, and their rates of effectiveness. This volume also explores HIV/AIDS from a sociological perspective, illustrating the disease's impact on world society. *HIV/AIDS Treatment Drugs* includes diagrams, charts, a bibliography, and a full index.

Other books by the same author:
Drugs: The Straight Facts, 2008
Schizophrenia, 2007
Codeine, 2006

Other books you might like:
S. D. Browne-Umar, *HIV/AIDS Treatment Strategies*, 2010
Salvatore Butera, *HIV Chemotherapy: A Critical Review*, 2005
Ho Mae-Wan, *Unraveling AIDS: The Independent Science and Promising Alternative Therapies*, 2005
Nicholas Seivewright, *Community Treatment of Drug Misuse: More Than Methadone*, 2009
Paul F. Torrence, *Antiviral Drug Discovery for Emerging Diseases and Bioterrorism Threats*, 2005

545

SUNANDA V. KANE

IBD Self-Management: The AGA Guide to Crohn's Disease and Ulcerative Colitis

(Bethesda, Maryland: AGA Press, 2010)

Subject(s): Health; Medical care; Reference works

Summary: In *IBD Self-Management: The AGA Guide to Crohn's Disease and Ulcerative Colitis*, Sunanda V. Kane provides information for sufferers of inflammatory bowel disease (IBD) about what they can do to manage the condition throughout their lives. Kane begins with a discussion of the symptoms of IBD and then considers different treatment options, such as medication and surgery. Kane also provides information for managing the condition through diet and nutritional supplements and discusses specific topics of concern, such as pregnancy and infertility. In addition, Kane addresses ways to ensure that young people with IBD receive satisfactory nutrition for proper development.

Where it's reviewed:
Library Journal, March 15, 2010, page 116

Other books by the same author:
Practical Gastroenterology and Hepatology: Small and Large Intestine and Pancreas, 2010
Pocket Guide to Inflammatory Bowel Disease, 2005

Other books you might like:
David Dahlman, *Why Doesn't My Doctor Know This?*, 2008
Tracie M. Dalessandro, *What to Eat with IBD: A Comprehensive Nutrition and Recipe Guide for Crohn's Disease and Ulcerative Colitis*, 2006
Laura W. Lamps, *Surgical Pathology of the Gastrointestinal System: Bacterial, Fungal, Viral, and Parasitic Infections*, 2009
Gary R. Lichtenstein, *Ulcerative Colitis: The Complete Guide to Medical Management*, 2011
Fred Saibil, *Crohn's Disease and Ulcerative Colitis: Everything You Need to Know, Revised Edition*, 2009

546

STEVEN B. KARCH

Karch's Pathology of Drug Abuse, 4th Edition

(Boca Raton, Florida: CRC Press, 2008)

Subject(s): Drug abuse; Drugs; Medical care

Summary: *Karch's Pathology of Drug Abuse, 4th Edition* by Steven B. Karch is intended for medical professionals, namely forensic pathologists and toxicologists, who are investigating causes of death due to drug abuse or looking for evidence of drug abuse. The text includes more than 160 color photographs, many at the microscopic level, to better facilitate investigation and

understanding. Karch also provides information about advances in the field of molecular biology and genetics and how this new science has contributed to a better understanding of drug abuse and toxicology. The fourth edition also includes a chapter on marijuana. Discussions of individual drugs contain information such as pharmacological data, molecular formula, method of metabolism, volume of distribution, and known drug interactions.

Where it's reviewed:
Anil Aggrawal's Internet Journal of Forensic Medicine and Toxicology, July-Dec 2009, page 5

Other books by the same author:
Forensic Autopsy: A Handbook and Atlas, 2010
Forensic Issues in Alcohol Testing, 2007
Pharmacokinetics and Pharmacodynamics of Abused Drugs, 2007
Postmortem Toxicology of Abused Drugs, 2007

Other books you might like:
Howard Abadinsky, *Drug Use and Abuse: A Comprehensive Introduction*, 2010
Richard Fields, *Drugs in Perspective*, 2009
Philip Robson, *Forbidden Drugs*, 2009
Marc Alan Schuckit, *Drug and Alcohol Abuse: A Clinical Guide to Diagnosis and Treatment*, 2010
Michael E. Winter, *Basic Clinical Pharmacokinetics, Fifth Edition*, 2009

547

STEFAN KAUFMANN

The New Plagues: Pandemics and Poverty in a Globalized World

(London: Haus, 2009)

Subject(s): Medicine; Medical care; Health

Summary: In *The New Plagues: Pandemics and Poverty in a Globalized World*, microbiologist and immunologist Stefan Kaufmann examines the relationship between disease and social class. Kaufmann chronicles the role of infectious diseases throughout human history, by which epidemics have eliminated populations, influenced population movement, and even contributed to the outcome of armed conflicts. With transportation and communication connecting world regions more quickly and closely than ever before, pandemic has become a rising threat. In this book, Kaufmann considers the effect widespread epidemic might have on both affluent and underprivileged populations.

Where it's reviewed:
Nature, October 29, 2009, page 1213
Nature Medicine, February 2010, page 159
Times Higher Education, September 3, 2009, page 53

Other books by the same author:
Immunology of Infection, 2010
AIDS and Tuberculosis: A Deadly Liaison, 2009
Handbook of Tuberculosis: Immunology and Cell Biology, 2008

The Grand Challenge for the Future: Vaccines for Poverty-Related Diseases from Bench to Field, 2005

Other books you might like:

Jon Stuart Abramson, *Inside the 2009 Influenza Pandemic*, 2010

Leonard V. Crowley, *Introduction to Human Disease: Pathology and Pathophysiology Correlations, Eighth Edition: A Student Workbook*, 2009

Dan Hurley, *Diabetes Rising: How a Rare Disease Became a Modern Pandemic, and What to Do About It*, 2010

Dr. Peter Moore, *The Little Book of Pandemics*, 2008

Mary K. Pratt, *Pandemics*, 2011

548

TOM KENNY

The Nuts and Bolts of Cardiac Pacing, Second Edition

(Hoboken, New Jersey: Wiley-Blackwell, 2008)

Story type: Medical
Subject(s): Health; Heart diseases; Medical care

Summary: *The Nuts and Bolts of Cardiac Pacing, Second Edition* by Tom Kenny is specifically written for clinicians or medical professionals who are not cardiologists. It is designed to present information in an easy-to-understand format, and each chapter includes a checklist at the end for self-assessment to be certain that the material is understood. Illustrations and examples from clinical settings are included, presenting a real-life guide on cardiac pacing and defibrillation. Kenny provides information about new technological developments and innovations in the field, including ventricular intrinsic preference and atrial fibrillation (AF) suppression, in addition to the potential dangers of excessive right ventricular (RV) pacing.

Other books by the same author:

The Nuts and bolts of Paced ECG Interpretation, 2009

The Nuts and Bolts of Cardiac Resynchronization Therapy, 2007

The Nuts and Bolts of ICD Therapy, 2005

Other books you might like:

Anthony Y. K. Chan, *Biomedical Device Technology: Principles And Design*, 2007

Anne B. Curtis, *Fundamentals of Cardiac Pacing*, 2009

Mark E. Josephson, *Clinical Cardiac Electrophysiology: Techniques and Interpretations*, 2008

Jo Ann LeQuang, *Pacemaker Owner's Manual: All About Pacemakers for the People Who Have Them*, 2009

Leonard S. Lilly, *Pathophysiology of Heart Disease*, 2006

549

LAUREN KESSLER

Finding Life in the Land of Alzheimer's: One Daughter's Hopeful Story

(New York: Penguin Books, 2008)

Subject(s): Alzheimer's disease; Medical care; Healing

Summary: Journalist Lauren Kessler was haunted by Alzheimer's disease, the illness that took her mother's life, so she set out to find the truth behind this mysterious and terrifying condition. Kessler got a job at an Alzheimer's care facility as an average worker, learning the challenges the residents face and the joys they managed to find. After working in the facility, Kessler reevaluated all she thought she knew about the disease. Her experience finally helped her come to terms with the role the disease played in her mother's life. *Finding Life in the Land of Alzheimer's: One Daughter's Hopeful Story* was previously published as *Dancing with Rose*.

Where it's reviewed:
AudioFile Magazine, Feb-March 2008, page 35

Other books you might like:

Jolene Brackey, *Creating Moments of Joy: A Journal for Caregivers*, 2008

Jean Carper, *100 Simple Things You Can Do to Prevent Alzheimer's and Age-Related Memory Loss*, 2010

Virginia Stem Owens, *Caring for Mother: A Daughter's Long Good-Bye*, 2007

Barry Petersen, *Jan's Story: Love Lost to the Long Goodbye of Alzheimer's*, 2010

Lisa Snyder, *Living Your Best With Early-Stage Alzheimer's: An Essential Guide*, 2010

550

M. GABRIEL KHAN

Rapid ECG Interpretation, Third Edition

(New York: Humana Press, 2007)

Subject(s): Health; Medicine; Medical care

Summary: In *Rapid ECG Interpretation, Third Edition*, M. Gabriel Khan offers a revised edition of his guide to accurate administration and interpretation of the electrocardiogram. This comprehensive guide, written for students and physicians preparing for proficiency testing, first discusses the basics of the ECG, and then takes readers step by step through the process of accurately interpreting results. Topics include P wave abnormalities, bundle branch block, ST segment abnormalities, Q wave abnormalities, atrial and ventricular hypertrophy, T wave abnormalities, electrical axis and fascicular block, and arrhythmias. The included ECG Board assessment quiz gives students the opportunity to evaluate their grasp of the material. Khan is a professor at the University of Ottawa.

Where it's reviewed:
Journal of Intensive Care Medicine, September 2007, page 312

Other books by the same author:
Encyclopedia of Heart Diseases, 2010

Other books you might like:
Peggy Jenkins, *Nurse to Nurse ECG Interpretation*, 2009

Shirley A. Jones, *ECG Notes: Interpretation and Management Guide*, 2009

Shirley A. Jones, *ECG Success: Exercises in ECG Interpretation*, 2007

Tom Kenny, *The Nuts and bolts of Paced ECG Interpretation*, 2009

George A. Stouffer, *Practical ECG Interpretation: Clues to Heart Disease in Young Adults*, 2009

551

CLYDE K. KITCHEN

Fact and Fiction of Healthy Vision: Eye Care for Adults and Children

(New York: Praeger, 2007)

Story type: Medical
Subject(s): Aging (Biology); Medical care; Medicine

Summary: In *Fact and Fiction of Healthy Vision: Eye Care for Adults and Children*, Dr. Clyde K. Kitchen offers information about the eye as it ages. He provides facts about how the eye works, how it is affected by light, and how to know if vision in the eye is weakening. Kitchen believes that many people don't know the truth about their eyes; instead, they follow advice that has been spread through uninformed word-of-mouth. This book offers insight into real diseases that can steal a person's eyesight. Kitchen tells readers about the warning signs of degenerative diseases and then provides information about effective treatment options.

Where it's reviewed:
Choice, October 2007, page 317

Other books you might like:
Lorrie Klosterman, *Vision Disorders*, 2009

Gordon E. Legge, *Psychophysics of Reading in Normal and Low Vision*, 2006

Heather McLannahan, *Visual Impairment: A Global View*, 2008

Daniel L. Roberts, *The First Year: Age-Related Macular Degeneration: An Essential Guide for the Newly Diagnosed*, 2006

Julius Shulman, *No More Glasses: The Complete Guide to Laser Vision Correction*, 2005

552

CURTIS D. KLAASSEN

Casarett and Doull's Toxicology: The Basic Science of Poisons

(New York: Macmillan, 1986)

Subject(s): Science; Medicine; Health

Summary: In *Casarett and Doull's Toxicology: The Basic Science of Poisons*, editor Curtis D. Klaassen presents the quintessential text on the science of toxicology. This expansive volume details the major areas of study on the subject, including the general principles of toxicity, disposition of toxic substances, toxic agents, and environmental toxicology. The foremost scholars in the field provide articles and essays on all aspects of toxicology, making this authoritative tome the definitive go-to guide for those studying the art and science of poison. *Casarett and Doull's Toxicology* includes a full index.

Where it's reviewed:
The Lamp, March 2009, page 42

Other books you might like:
Ernest Hodgson, *A Textbook of Modern Toxicology*, 2008

Moiz Mumtaz, *Principles and Practice of Mixtures Toxicology*, 2010

Kent R. Olson, *Poisoning And Drug Overdose*, 2006

Ira S. Richards, *Principles and Practice of Toxicology in Public Health*, 2007

Adam Woolley, *A Guide to Practical Toxicology: Evaluation, Prediction, and Risk*, 2008

553

ERIC KLEIN

The Cleveland Clinic Guide to Prostate Cancer

(New York: Kaplan Publishing, 2009)

Subject(s): Cancer; Medical care; Health

Summary: Prostate cancer is one of the most prevalent forms of cancer in men. In *The Cleveland Clinic Guide to Prostate Cancer*, Dr. Eric Klein offers practical information on how men can prevent, deal with, and live with the effects of prostate cancer. Dr. Klein helps readers identify the best methods of testing, the best medications to try, and the most successful preventative measures. He also offers advice on shifting one's lifestyle toward health and wellness, as well as a collection of profiles of men who have overcome prostate cancer. *The Cleveland Clinic Guide to Prostate Cancer* includes two appendices and an index.

Other books by the same author:
Prostate Cancer: A Cleveland Clinic Guide, 2008
Operative Urology: At the Cleveland Clinic, 2006

Other books you might like:

Arthur Burnett, *Johns Hopkins Patients' Guide to Prostate Cancer*, 2007

Chawnshang Chang, *Prostate Cancer: Basic Mechanisms and Therapeutic Approaches*, 2005

Sheldon Marks, *Prostate and Cancer: A Family Guide to Diagnosis, Treatment, and Survival, Fourth Edition*, 2009

Alan T. Meridith, *Handbook of Prostate Cancer Cell Research: Growth, Signalling and Survival*, 2009

Margaret Rayman, *Healthy Eating for Prostate Care*, 2009

554

INGRID KOHLSTADT

Food and Nutrients in Disease Management

(Boca Raton, Florida: CRC Press, 2009)

Story type: Medical
Subject(s): Medical care; Diseases; Nutrition

Summary: Written by author and physician nutrition specialist Ingrid Kohlstadt, *Food and Nutrients in Disease Management* is an examination of the importance of diet and food intake in health. In the past, food and nutrients were the most important tools in health maintenance and disease management. With the modern advancements of medicine, nutrition has taken a backseat when it comes to medical care and treatment. In *Food and Nutrients in Disease Management*, Kohlstadt makes an argument for the significance of food and diet in the treatment of illnesses and offers practical advice on how to incorporate food restrictions and dietary recommendations into the medical treatment of conditions, disorders, or diseases.

Where it's reviewed:

JAMA, The Journal of the American Medical Association, December 16, 2009, page 2602

Other books by the same author:

Scientific Evidence for Musculoskeletal, Bariatric, and Sports Nutrition, 2006

Other books you might like:

F. Batmanghelidj, *Your Body's Many Cries for Water*, 2008

James Tad Geiger, *The Sweet Smell of Success*, 2009

David L. Katz, *Nutrition in Clinical Practice: A Comprehensive, Evidence-Based Manual for the Practitioner*, 2008

Staci Nix, *Williams' Basic Nutrition and Diet Therapy, 13th Edition*, 2008

Michael Sharon, *Nutrient A-Z: A User's Guide to Foods, Herbs, Vitamins, Minerals and Supplements*, 2009

555

VICTOR KONSHIN

Beating Gout: A Sufferer's Guide to Living Pain Free, Second Edition

(Williamsville, New York: Ayerware Publishing, 2009)

Story type: Medical
Subject(s): Medical care; Diseases; Medicine

Summary: Written and edited by Victor Konshin, *Beating Gout: A Sufferer's Guide to Living Pain Free, Second Edition* is a comprehensive and practical guide for individuals suffering from gout. A recent study indicates that a vast majority of doctors are treating gout improperly, particularly since it's commonly viewed as a benign disease. In *Beating Gout*, Konshin sheds light on the negative implications that gout can have on a person's health, including a contribution to heart disease, high blood pressure, kidney disease, and stroke. The book provides a thorough overview on the illness, including detailed information about symptoms, progression, diagnosis, and the best and most effective treatments.

Other books you might like:

Casey Adams, *Arthritis — The Botanical Solution: Nature's Answer to Rheumatoid Arthritis, Osteoarthritis, Gout and Other Forms of Arthritis*, 2009

Christine Craggs-Hinton, *Coping with Gout*, 2011

Peebles Cookery Peebles Cookery, *The Ultimate Gout Cookbook*, 2007

Jodi Schneiter, *Gout Hater's Cookbook IV*, 2007

556

MEIR H. KRYGER

Atlas of Clinical Sleep Medicine

(Philadelphia, Pennsylvania: Saunders/Elsevier, 2009)

Subject(s): Health; Medicine; Sleep

Summary: In *Atlas of Clinical Sleep Medicine*, editor Meir H. Kryger presents a comprehensive guide for clinicians on the diagnosis of sleep disorders in children and adults. Opening chapters consider sleep in art and literature and the history of sleep medicine. Subsequent chapters discuss the biology of sleep, normal sleep, and dreaming, as well as descriptions of the physiology and treatment of a full range of sleep disorders including narcolepsy, restless leg syndrome, sleep apnea, and special conditions associated with Parkinson's disease, epilepsy, thyroid disease, pregnancy, and psychiatric disease. Color illustrations throughout the atlas and online access to sleep lab videos supplement the text.

Other books by the same author:

Can't Sleep, Can't Stay Awake: A Woman's Guide to Sleep Disorders, 2007

Principles and Practice of Pediatric Sleep Medicine, 2006

Other books you might like:

Richard B. Berry, *Positive Airway Pressure Therapy: An Issue of Sleep Medicine Clinics*, 2010

Archibald D. Hart, *Sleep, It Does a Family Good: How Busy Families Can Overcome Sleep Deprivation*, 2010

Barry Krakow, *Sound Sleep, Sound Mind: 7 Keys to Sleeping Through the Night*, 2007

Teofilo L. Lee-Chiong, *Sleep Medicine: Essentials and Review*, 2008

John Shneerson, *Sleep Medicine: A Guide to Sleep and its Disorders*, 2005

557

LEORA KUTTNER

A Child in Pain: What Health Professionals Can Do to Help

(Bethel, Connecticut: Crown House Publishing, 2010)

Subject(s): Medical care; Children; Psychology

Summary: Pediatric psychologist Leora Kuttner examines the fragile world of pain as experienced by children and the ways caregivers can best attempt to understand this pain. *A Child in Pain: What Health Professionals Can Do to Help* discusses the physical and mental pain children feel when they undergo medical procedures. Kuttner's findings aim to help medical professionals better understand the stresses faced by their young patients and offers practical advice on how to handle these challenging cases. *A Child in Pain* includes a bibliography and an index.

Where it's reviewed:
Contemporary Pediatrics, Sept 2010, page 8

Other books by the same author:
No Fears, No Tears, 2010
A Child in Pain: How to Help, What to Do, 2008

Other books you might like:
Mary Atkinson, *Healing Touch for Children: Massage, Acupressure and Reflexology Routine for Children Aged 4-12*, 2009

Donna Finando, *Acupoint and Trigger Point Therapy for Babies and Children: A Parent's Healing Touch*, 2008

Helen Garabedian, *Itsy Bitsy Yoga for Toddlers and Preschoolers: 8-Minute Routines to Help Your Child Grow Smarter, Be Happier, and Behave Better*, 2008

Georg Hansmann, *Neonatal Emergencies*, 2009

Lawrence E. Shapiro, *Stopping the Pain: A Workbook for Teens Who Cut and Self-Injure*, 2008

558

EDWARD H. LAUGHLIN

CANCER from A to Z: A Dictionary of Cancer-Related Terms in Easily Understood Language

(Bloomington, Indiana: AuthorHouse, 2008)

Story type: Collection
Subject(s): Cancer; Encyclopedias and dictionaries; Health

Summary: *CANCER from A to Z: A Dictionary of Cancer-Related Terms in Easily Understood Language* is a medical dictionary featuring more than 300 pages of terms medical and their definitions. In the book, author Edward Laughlin includes hundreds of entries as well as numerous essays that explain the stages of cancer, treatment options, and places where cancer patients and their loved ones can find help and support. Essays in this volume include, "Cancer Details," "Prevention and Detection," "Early Warning Signs of Cancer," and "Regular Self and Professional Exams to Detect Early Cancer."

Other books you might like:
Greg Anderson, *Cancer: 50 Essential Things to Do*, 2009

Vickie Girard, *There's No Place Like Hope: A Guide to Beating Cancer in Mind-sized Bites*, 2008

Bill Henderson, *Cancer-Free: Your Guide to Gentle, Non-toxic Healing*, 2007

David Servan-Schreiber, *Anticancer: A New Way of Life*, 2008

Julie K. Silver, *What Helped Get Me Through: Cancer Survivors Share Wisdom and Hope*, 2008

559

TEOFILO L. LEE-CHIONG

Sleep Medicine: Essentials and Review

(New York: Oxford University Press, USA, 2008)

Story type: Medical
Subject(s): Sleep; Medicine; Medical care

Summary: In *Sleep Medicine: Essentials and Review*, Dr. Teofilo L. Lee-Chiong provides information about one of the newest fields in medicine. He examines the growth of the field of sleep medicine over the years and the advances that have been made since it was officially recognized as a specialty in 2007. Today, nearly every medical center has a wing dedicated to sleep studies. In this book, Lee-Chiong advises readers interested in taking the sleep medicine board exam. He includes subjects they should be familiar with and provides practice questions similar to those they will encounter on the exam.

Where it's reviewed:
Medicine and Science in Sports and Exercise, Feburary 2010, page 411
Respiratory Care, June 2009, page 802

Other books by the same author:
Focus on Sleep Medicine: A Self-Assessment, 2009
Sleep Medicine, 2009
Sleep: A Comprehensive Handbook, 2005

Other books you might like:
Sudhansu Chokroverty, *Questions and Answers About Sleep Apnea*, 2008

Matthew Edlund, *The Power of Rest*, 2010

Nancy Foldvary-Schaefer, *The Cleveland Clinic Guide to Sleep Disorders*, 2009

Meir H. Kryger, *Atlas of Clinical Sleep Medicine*, 2009

560

PETER G. LEVINE

Stronger After Stroke: Your Roadmap to Recovery

(New York: Demos Health, 2008)

Subject(s): Health; Medical care; Medicine

Summary: In *Stronger After Stroke: Your Roadmap to Recovery*, Peter G. Levine—an authority on stroke recovery—shares his innovative method for rehabilitation after stroke. Intended for patients recovering from stroke and their caregivers, this accessible volume explains how the stroke survivor can regain skills through physical exercise. Levine promotes the use of mirror and music therapy, the treadmill, rhythm rehab, and weights to alleviate such post-stroke conditions as spasticity, weakness, loss of movement control, and fatigue. *Stronger After Stroke* also includes information on avoiding repeated occurrence of stroke, protecting bones, lifestyle adjustments, and tips for caregivers.

Other books you might like:

Louis R. Caplan, *Caplan's Stroke: A Clinical Approach, Fourth Edition*, 2009
Louis R. Caplan, *Stroke (What Do I Do Now?)*, 2010
Valerie Greene, *Conquering Stroke: How I Fought My Way Back and How You Can Too*, 2008
Richard Senelick, *Living with Stroke: A Guide for Families*, 1994
Olajide Williams, *Stroke Diaries: A Guide for Survivors and Their Families*, 2010

561

MICHAEL G. LEVITZKY

Pulmonary Physiology, 7th Edition

(New York: McGraw-Hill Medical, 2007)

Subject(s): Health; Medicine; Physiology

Summary: In *Pulmonary Physiology, 7th Edition*, Michael G. Levitzky updates his comprehensive text for medical students. Each of the book's 10 chapters covers a different aspect of lung physiology and function. "Mechanics of Breathing" discusses the pressure gradient between atmosphere and alveoli, the interaction of the lungs and the chest wall, and airway resistance. "Diffusion of Gases" discusses the diffusion of oxygen, the diffusion of carbon dioxide, and measurements of diffusing capacity. Other chapters cover the transportation of oxygen and carbon dioxide in the blood, the regulation of acid-base status, and the respiratory system under stress. Each chapter includes a summary of concepts covered.

Where it's reviewed:
Respiratory Care, February 2008, page 252

Other books you might like:

Robert H. Bartlett, *Critical Care Physiology*, 2010
Will Beachey, *Respiratory Care Anatomy and Physiology: Foundations for Clinical Practice*, 2007

Andrew B. Lumb, *Nunn's Applied Respiratory Physiology*, 2010
Gregg L. Ruppel, *Manual of Pulmonary Function Testing*, 2008
John B. West, *Pulmonary Physiology and Pathophysiology: An Integrated, Case-Based Approach*, 2007

562

JOHN LINK

The Breast Cancer Survival Manual: A Step-by-Step Guide for the Woman with Newly Diagnosed Breast Cancer, Fourth Edition

(New York: Henry Holt and Co., 2007)

Subject(s): Alternative Medicine; Cancer; Health

Summary: A crisis manual, designed to help women who have just been diagnosed with breast cancer. Women in this situation are frequently frightened and confused just when they need to be clear-headed and decisive. Dr. John Link wants patients in this situation to know that there is time—usually a week to a month—during which to become educated, get a second opinion, and formulate a plan for treatment. This guide presents the ramifications of many of the decisions a patient might have to make and discusses both mainstream and alternative medicine.

Other books you might like:

Barbara Clark, *The Fight of My Life: The Inspiring Story of a Mother's Fight against Breast Cancer*, 2007
Robin Dye, *Testament: My Survival and Conquest of Breast Cancer*, 2008
Vida Meymand, *Why Not Me?: An Inspiring True Story of Survival*, 2008
Michael J. Michell, *Breast Cancer*, 2010
Jane Rudden, *If We Must Dance, Then I Will Lead: A Memoir of Breast Cancer Survival*, 2010

563

NANCY A. LOWENSTEIN

Fighting Fatigue in Multiple Sclerosis: Practical Ways to Create New Habits and Increase Your Energy

(New York: Demos Health, 2009)

Subject(s): Health; Multiple sclerosis; Medicine

Summary: In *Fighting Fatigue in Multiple Sclerosis: Practical Ways to Create New Habits and Increase Your Energy*, occupational therapist Nancy Lowenstein offers practical advice for MS patients suffering from decreased physical energy. Though individuals with multiple sclerosis sometimes battle the debilitating effects of fatigue with medication, sugar, or caffeine, Lowenstein shows readers how they can apply methods used in occupational therapy to improve their stamina. The author takes readers step-by-step through their day, showing them how to adapt their routine, modify their environment, incorporate exercise, simplify activities and tasks, find time for rejuvenation, and make the changes part of a new lifestyle.

Other books you might like:

Allen C. Bowling, *Complementary and Alternative Medicine and Multiple Sclerosis*, 2006

Jeffrey N. Gingold, *Facing the Cognitive Challenges of Multiple Sclerosis*, 2006

Randall T. Schapiro, *Managing the Symptoms of Multiple Sclerosis*, 2007

Shelley Peterman Schwarz, *Multiple Sclerosis: 300 Tips for Making Life Easier*, 2006

Howard L. Weiner, *Curing MS: How Science Is Solving the Mysteries of Multiple Sclerosis*, 2005

564

GAYLE MACDONALD

Medicine Hands: Massage Therapy for People with Cancer

(Findhorn, Scotland: Findhorn Press, 2007)

Subject(s): Health; Cancer; Healing

Summary: In *Medicine Hands: Massage Therapy for People with Cancer*, Gayle MacDonald offers an informative guide for medical professionals and individuals concerning the role of massage therapy in the treatment of cancer. MacDonald first dispels the misconceptions about massage and cancer, explaining that physical manipulation does not encourage the spread of tumors, as some believe. She then describes the many benefits massage can bring to the cancer patient, providing relief from discomforts associated with chemotherapy and radiation, and even giving stress relief to the caregiver. MacDonald describes applications of massage therapy for the hospitalized or respite care patient as well as the terminally ill.

Where it's reviewed:
Oncology Nursing Forum, Sept-Oct 2008, page 852

Other books you might like:

Mark Beck, *Theory and Practice of Therapeutic Massage*, 2010

William Collinge, *Touch, Caring and Cancer*, 2009

Susan G. Salvo, *Massage Therapy*, 2007

Diana L. Thompson, *Hands Heal*, 2007

Jean M. Wible, *Drug Handbook for Massage Therapists*, 2008

565

MANYA MAGNUS

Essentials of Infectious Disease Epidemiology

(Sudbury, Massachusetts: Jones and Bartlett Publishers, 2008)

Subject(s): Research; Medicine; Diseases

Summary: In *Essentials of Infectious Disease Epidemiology*, author Manya Magnus explores the various modes of studying infectious disease. With certain diseases reaching epidemic proportions, Magnus believes that the need for quality research and reliable study has never been more apparent. In the book, the author explores the ways researchers, doctors, and students can use science and logic to study and research modern diseases. This volume includes a bibliography and an index.

Other books by the same author:
Essential Readings in Infectious Disease Epidemiology, 2008

Other books you might like:

Rachel L. Chin, *Emergency Management of Infectious Diseases*, 2008

Mark S. Dworkin, *Cases in Field Epidemiology: A Global Perspective*, 2010

William Anton Oleckno, *Epidemiology: Concepts and Methods*, 2008

Miquel Porta, *Dictionary of Epidemiology*, 2008

John W.G. Yarnell, *Epidemiology and Prevention: A Systems-Based Approach*, 2007

566

MASSOUD MAHMOUDI

Allergy and Asthma: Practical Diagnosis and Management

(New York: McGraw-Hill Professional, 2007)

Subject(s): Health; Medicine; Allergy

Summary: In *Allergy and Asthma: Practical Diagnosis and Management*, allergy clinician Massoud Mahmoudi presents an informative resource for primary care physicians. Succinct but thorough, this guide covers a broad range of allergy and asthma issues, as well as their causes, diagnosis, and treatment. Allergies of the eye, nose, ears, lung, and skin are discussed, including conjunctivitis, dry eye syndrome, rhinitis, sinusitis, contact sensitivity, Eustachian tube dysfunction, cough, urticaria, and contact dermatitis. Chapters on pediatric and adult asthma consider the effects of occupation and exercise. Later chapters address the timely topics of food allergy, insect allergy, latex allergy, environmental allergy, and sick building syndrome.

Where it's reviewed:
Respiratory Care, February 2009, page 265

Other books by the same author:
Challenging Cases in Allergic and Immunologic Diseases of the Skin, 2010

Challenging Cases in Allergy and Immunology, 2009
Allergy Cure!, 2005

Other books you might like:
Francis V. Adams, *The Asthma Sourcebook*, 2006
Arnaldo Cantani, *Pediatric Allergy, Asthma and Immunology*, 2008
Jordan S. Josephson, *Sinus Relief Now*, 2006
Fred Pescatore, *The Allergy and Asthma Cure: A Complete 8-Step Nutritional Program*, 2008
Gerald W. Volcheck, *Clinical Allergy: Diagnosis and Management*, 2008

567

SHELDON MARKS

Prostate and Cancer: A Family Guide to Diagnosis, Treatment, and Survival, Fourth Edition

(Cambridge, Massachusetts: Da Capo Life Long, 2009)

Subject(s): Health; Medicine; Medical care

Summary: In *Prostate and Cancer: A Family Guide to Diagnosis, Treatment and Survival, Fourth Edition*, prostate cancer specialist Sheldon Marks updates his authoritative guide to one of America's most prevalent cancers. Written for patients and family members, this helpful volume provides in-depth information in accessible language. Topics covered include a broad range of patient concerns, from the anatomy and function of the prostate gland and the symptoms of prostate cancer screening and tests to choosing a physician and treatments options. Marks addresses many of the issues facing the prostate patient, including recovery, follow-up therapy, and potential complications such as incontinence and erectile dysfunction.

Other books you might like:
Arthur Burnett, *Johns Hopkins Patients' Guide to Prostate Cancer*, 2007
Pamela Ellsworth, *100 Q and A About Prostate Cancer, Second Edition*, 2008
Robert Hill, *Dead Men Don't Have Sex: A Guy's Guide to Surviving Prostate Cancer*, 2010
Eric Klein, *The Cleveland Clinic Guide to Prostate Cancer*, 2009
Robert J. Marckini, *You Can Beat Prostate Cancer*, 2007

568

LYNN R. MAROTZ

Health, Safety, and Nutrition for the Young Child, 7th Edition

(Clifton Park, New York: Thomson Delmar Learning, 2008)

Subject(s): Health; Nutrition; Children

Summary: *Health, Safety, and Nutrition for the Young*

Child, 7th Edition by Lynn R. Marotz provides a comprehensive guide to a range of children's health problems. This volume, which includes information about children from infancy through grade school, discusses the direct relationship between children's health and their safety and nutrition. The book also talks about preventing and treating infection, identifying and treating illness, managing injuries, recognizing and responding to abuse, and making nutritious menus for babies, toddlers, and young children. The informative chapters are supplemented with checklists, lessons plans, and suggested activities.

Where it's reviewed:
Childhood Education, Annual 2009, page 326

Other books by the same author:
Developmental Profiles: Pre-birth Through Twelve, 2009

Other books you might like:
Judith E. Brown, *Nutrition through the Life Cycle, 3rd Edition*, 2007
Rosalind Charlesworth, *Understanding Child Development*, 2007
Janet Henshall Momsen, *Gender and Development*, 2008
Barbara Nilsen, *Week by Week: Plans for Documenting Children's Development*, 2010
Terry L. Smith, *Nutrition and Food Safety*, 2010

569

LISA MARR

Sexually Transmitted Diseases: A Physician Tells You What You Need to Know, Second Edition

(Baltimore: The Johns Hopkins University Press, 2007)

Subject(s): Health; Medical care; Sexual behavior

Summary: In *Sexually Transmitted Diseases: A Physician Tells You What You Need to Know, Second Edition* by Lisa Marr, a physician specializing in the treatment of STDs provides a comprehensive guide on understanding, preventing, and treating sexually transmitted diseases. In the first part of the book, "What You Need to Know," Marr shares basic information about male and female genital anatomy, symptoms of STDs, what happens during a medical examination for STDs, and safe sex practices that can prevent the spread of diseases. In the second part, "Encyclopedia of STDs," the author provides an in-depth description of 23 sexually transmitted diseases.

Where it's reviewed:
Choice, January 2008, page 850
Sexually Transmitted Infections, June 2008, page 249

Other books you might like:
Leanne Currie-McGhee, *Sexually Transmitted Diseases*, 2008
Jill Grimes, *Seductive Delusions: How Everyday People Catch STDs*, 2008
Laura Larson, *Sexually Transmitted Diseases: Sourcebook*, 2009

Health and Wellness

Adina Nack, *Damaged Goods?: Women Living With Incurable Sexually Transmitted Diseases*, 2008

David E. Newton, *Sexual Health: A Reference Handbook*, 2009

570

PETER MAZZONE

The Cleveland Clinic Guide to Lung Cancer

(New York: Kaplan Publishing, 2009)

Subject(s): Health; Medical care; Cancer

Summary: *The Cleveland Clinic Guide to Lung Cancer*, written by Peter Mazzone, provides information to people suffering from lung cancer. In the book, Mazzone discusses the different types of lung cancer and its stages of severity. The book also describes the ways cancer can be diagnosed and the types of tests that are run on patients who may have lung cancer. He then discusses different treatment options and new drugs, as well as research about lung cancer and the benefits this research may have in the future. The book includes information on preventing the disease and living a healthy lifestyle through proper diet and exercise before and after one is diagnosed with lung cancer. Stories from people who have survived and recovered from a lung cancer diagnosis are included as well.

Other books you might like:

William Kelley Eidem, *The Doctor Who Cures Cancer*, 2009

Heine Hansen, *Textbook of Lung Cancer*, 2008

Jacqueline Langwith, *Lung Cancer*, 2011

Karen Parles, *100 Questions and Answers About Lung Cancer*, 2008

571

DENNIS MCCARTHY

Speaking About the Unspeakable: Non-Verbal Methods and Experiences in Therapy with Children

(London; Philadelphia: Jessica Kingsley Publishers, 2008)

Subject(s): Speech; Psychology; Children

Summary: Mental health professional Dennis McCarthy edited this volume of essays examining various therapies aimed at non-verbal children. *Speaking About the Unspeakable: Non-Verbal Methods and Experiences in Therapy with Children* discusses a number of beneficial treatments, including dance and movement therapy, play therapy, and utilizing nature as a means of rehabilitation. The essays of this volume also explore ways to penetrate the language barrier and help young patients find their authentic selves when trapped in a world of silence. *Speaking About the Unspeakable* includes a foreword by

psychoanalyst Priscilla Rodgers.

Other books by the same author:

"If You Turned into a Monster": Transformation Through Play: A Body-Centered Approach to Play Therapy, 2007

Other books you might like:

Sharon W. Goodill, *Creative Arts An Introduction to Medical Dance/Movement Therapy: Health Care in Motion*, 2009

Daria Halprin, *The Expressive Body in Life, Art, and Therapy: Working with Movement, Metaphor and Meaning*, 2008

Cathy Malchiodi, *Art Therapy Sourcebook*, 2006

Liesl Silverstone, *Art Therapy Exercises: Inspirational and Practical Ideas to Stimulate the Imagination*, 2009

Pamela J. Stack, *Art Therapy Activities: A Practical Guide for Teachers, Therapists And Parents*, 2006

572

STUART MCGILL

Low Back Disorders: Evidence-Based Prevention and Rehabilitation, 2nd Edition

(Champaign, Illinois: Human Kinetics, 2007)

Subject(s): Medical care; Reference works; Health

Summary: Stuart McGill's *Low Back Disorders: Evidence-Based Prevention and Rehabilitation, 2nd Edition* is intended for medical practitioners or physical therapists who need to assist patients in preventing and treating low back pain of various causes. The text is divided into three sections, each featuring a number of full-color illustrations, charts, and graphs to better communicate the information. The first section focuses on the anatomy of the spine and the common causes of lumbar pain, from poor ergonomics on a daily basis to injuries. The second section of the text is devoted to preventing lower back injury and pain through exercise, proper working environment, and the training of workplace employees to ensure they are moving properly. The third section focuses on rehabilitation—first on diagnosing the problem or injury with various tests and then pursuing the proper course of treatment with specific therapeutic exercises. Step-by-step instructions are provided for more than 50 exercises for the creation of customized rehabilitation programs.

Where it's reviewed:

Choice, September 2008, page139

Other books by the same author:

Low Back Pain: New Research, 2008

Other books you might like:

Aaron G. Filler, *Do You Really Need Back Surgery?: A Surgeon's Guide to Back and Neck Pain and How to Choose Your Treatment*, 2007

Lynne A. Greenberg, *The Body Broken: A Memoir*, 2009

Kerry Levin, *Neck and Low Back Pain: An Issue of Neurologic Clinics*, 2007

Craig Liebenson, *Rehabilitation of the Spine: A Practitioner's Manual*, 2006

Joseph Valdez, *Healing Back and Joint Injuries: A Proven Approach to Ending Chronic Pain and Avoiding Unnecessary Surgery*, 2009

573

SCOTT D. MENDELSON

Beyond Alzheimer's: How to Avoid the Modern Epidemic of Dementia

(Lanham, Maryland: M. Evans, 2009)

Subject(s): Health; Medicine; Medical care

Summary: In *Beyond Alzheimer's: How to Avoid the Modern Epidemic of Dementia*, Scott D. Mendelson presents a ground-breaking guide to preventing and treating dementia. According to the author, Alzheimer's Disease and other dementias are not components of the aging process but conditions that can be prevented and treated through nutrition, physical exercise, and behavioral decisions. In this accessible guide for the lay reader, Mendelson offers dementia patients, caregivers, and those not yet diagnosed advice on dealing with Alzheimer's and related conditions, which the author categorizes as a modern epidemic. Topics include the causes and diagnosis of dementia, medications, and alternative treatments.

Other books by the same author:
Metabolic Syndrome and Psychiatric Illness: Interactions, Pathophysiology, Assessment & Treatment, 2007

Other books you might like:
Jolene Brackey, *Creating Moments of Joy: A Journal for Caregivers*, 2008

Jean Carper, *100 Simple Things You Can Do to Prevent Alzheimer's and Age-Related Memory Loss*, 2010

Virginia Stem Owens, *Caring for Mother: A Daughter's Long Good-Bye*, 2007

Barry Petersen, *Jan's Story: Love Lost to the Long Goodbye of Alzheimer's*, 2010

Lisa Snyder, *Living Your Best With Early-Stage Alzheimer's: An Essential Guide*, 2010

574

RAY M. MERRILL

Environmental Epidemiology: Principles and Methods

(Sudbury, Massachusetts: Jones and Bartlett Publishers, 2007)

Subject(s): Health; Medicine; Science

Summary: In *Environmental Epidemiology: Principles and Methods*, author Ray M. Merrill presents a text for students and professionals in the field of public health.

The first section of the book discusses concepts and methods of environmental epidemiology, including research, exposure, and outcome assessment; monitoring environmental health; study designs; and statistical modeling. The book's second section considers environmental epidemiology according to person, place, and time, including the identification of disease clusters and mapping systems. In the third section, the author discusses applications such as air quality, soil and food contaminants, radiation, and climate change. Ray Merrill, Ph.D., M.P.H., is a professor of biostatistics and epidemiology at Brigham Young University.

Where it's reviewed:
Journal of Occupational and Environmental Medicine, November 2009, page 1349

Other books by the same author:
Principles of Epidemiology Workbook: Exercises and Activities, 2010

Introduction to Epidemiology, 2009

Reproductive Epidemiology: Principles and Methods, 2009

Other books you might like:
Kathleen Meehan Arias, *Outbreak Investigation, Prevention, and Control in Health Care Settings: Critical Issues in Patient Safety*, 2009

Leonard V. Crowley, *Introduction to Human Disease: Pathology and Pathophysiology Correlations, Eighth Edition: A Student Workbook*, 2009

Robert H. Friis, *Epidemiology 101*, 2009

Michael Gregg, *Field Epidemiology*, 2008

William Anton Oleckno, *Epidemiology: Concepts and Methods*, 2008

575

KENNETH D. MILLER

Choices in Breast Cancer Treatment: Medical Specialists and Cancer Survivors Tell You What You Need to Know

(Baltimore, Maryland: Johns Hopkins University Press, 2008)

Story type: Medical
Subject(s): Medical care; Cancer; Health

Summary: Edited by Kenneth D. Miller, *Choices in Breast Cancer Treatment: Medical Specialists and Cancer Survivors Tell You What You Need to Know* is a collection of advice and wisdom for breast cancer sufferers. The book is a thorough examination of various treatment options for women diagnosed with breast cancer. Filled with knowledge, insight, and personal experiences from breast cancer survivors, surgeons, medical oncologists, radiologists, and plastic surgeons, *Choices in Breast Cancer Treatment* educates readers on the types of treatments and medical care available, including detailed descriptions of surgery, radiation, chemotherapy, hormone therapy, and breast reconstruction.

Where it's reviewed:
Choice, September 2008, page 137

Health and Wellness

Publishers Weekly, November 19, 2007, page 54

Other books you might like:
Deann Akande, *How To Fight Breast Cancer And Win!:*
  A Matter Of Life And Health, 2009
Joseph E. Bosiljevac Jr., *Surviving Cancer*, 2010
Judy C. Kneece, *Breast Cancer Treatment Handbook:*
  Understanding the Disease, Treatments, Emotions,
  and Recovery from Breast Cancer, 2009
Vladimir Lange, *Be a Survivor: Your Guide to Breast*
  Cancer, 2009
Jorge R. Pasqualini, *Breast Cancer: Prognosis,*
  Treatment, and Prevention, 2009

576

HIROSHI MITSUMOTO

Amyotrophic Lateral Sclerosis: A Guide for Patients and Families, 3rd Edition

(New York: Demos Health, 2009)

Story type: Medical
Subject(s): Health; Medical care; Diseases

Summary: Compiled by Dr. Hiroshi Mitsumoto, *Amyotrophic Lateral Sclerosis: A Guide for Patients and Families, 3rd Edition* is a comprehensive overview of ALS, also known as Lou Gehrig's disease. Although ALS has no cure, there are many ways to treat it and live with it. In *Amyotrophic Lateral Sclerosis*, Mitsumoto offers straightforward explanations about ALS medical therapy and rehabilitation, clinical trials, medications, the advanced stages of the disease, and dealing with end-of-life concerns and issues. Written for individuals with the disease, their families, and medical providers, the book provides practical advice on dealing with ALS, including info on symptoms, medical care devices, treatments, and finances.

Where it's reviewed:
SciTech Book News, March 2002, page 95

Other books you might like:
Lee Guion, *Respiratory Management of ALS:*
  Amyotrophic Lateral Sclerosis, 2010
Katrina Robinson, *ALS: Lou Gehrig's Disease Patient*
  Advocate, 2009
Morrie Schwartz, *Morrie: In His Own Words*, 2008

577

JANET HENSHALL MOMSEN

Gender and Development

(London; New York: Routledge, 2008)

Subject(s): Sex roles; Women; Sociology

Summary: Geography professor and gender studies specialist Janet Henshall Momsen looks at the issues of gender in a constantly changing world, specifically in developing countries and across Europe. *Gender and*

Development examines its complex subject matter from an array of perspectives, including the relationships between gender and violence, gender and reproduction, gender and the environment, and gender and geographic location. Helpful figures, tables, and boxes accompany the text, along with a list of bibliographical references and an index.

Other books you might like:
Melissa Hines, *Brain Gender*, 2010
Robert V. Kail, *Children and Their Development*, 2006
Elizabeth J. Meyer, *Gender and Sexual Diversity in*
  Schools, 2010
Susan Pinker, *The Sexual Paradox: Men, Women, and*
  the Real Gender Gap, 2008
Leonard Sax, *Why Gender Matters: What Parents and*
  Teachers Need to Know about the Emerging Science
  of Sex Differences by Leonard Sax, 2010

578

JULIA MOOR

Playing, Laughing and Learning with Children on the Autism Spectrum: A Practical Resource of Play Ideas for Parents and Carers

(Philadelphia: Jessica Kingsley Publishers, 2002)

Subject(s): Diseases; Parent-child relations; Health

Summary: When a child is diagnosed with autism or a related spectrum disorder, parents commonly find themselves at a loss for practical resources. In *Playing, Laughing and Learning with Children on the Autism Spectrum: A Practical Resource of Play Ideas for Parents and Carers*, author Julia Moor offers a guide to engaging autistic children in stimulating games. Moor's unique exercises keep children entertained while educating, informing, and preparing them for future learning experiences. Play ideas revolve around themes such as art, music, toys, and even television. *Playing, Laughing and Learning with Children on the Autism Spectrum* includes a bibliography and an index.

Where it's reviewed:
The Exceptional Parent, January 2009, page 141
Journal of Autism and Developmental Disorders, April
  2010, page 520

Other books you might like:
Tracey Beckerleg, *Fun with Messy Play: Ideas and*
  Activities for Children With Special Needs, 2008
Audra Jensen, *When Babies Read: A Practical Guide to*
  Helping Young Children with Hyperlexia, Asperger
  Syndrome and High-Functioning Autism, 2005
Nicole Martin, *Art as an Early Intervention Tool for*
  Children With Autism, 2009
William Stillman, *The Autism Answer Book: More Than*
  300 of the Top Questions Parents Ask, 2007
William Stillman, *Empowered Autism Parenting:*
  Celebrating (and Defending) Your Child's Place in
  the World, 2009

579

LISA MORRONE

Overcoming Back and Neck Pain: A Proven Program for Recovery and Prevention

(Eugene, Oregon: Harvest House Publishers, 2008)

Subject(s): Medical care; Health; Healing

Summary: Lower back pain is one of the most commonly reported everyday aches in the United States. In *Overcoming Back and Neck Pain: A Proven Program for Recovery and Prevention*, author and physical therapist Lisa Morrone offers practical advice on how to deal with aches, pains, and discomfort in the back and neck. This volume details a variety of back and neck conditions and the simple steps people can take to combat them. Morrone's plan includes low-impact exercises, proper nutrition, and restful sleeping habits. *Overcoming Back and Neck Pain* contains notes on the text and a foreword by Dr. John Labiak.

Other books by the same author:
Get Healthy, for Heaven's Sake: 7 Steps to Living Strong, Loving God, and Serving Others, 2011
Diabetes: Are You at Risk? (1 in 3 Adults Are), 2010
Overcoming Overeating: It's Not What You Eat, It's What's Eating You!, 2009
Overcoming Headaches and Migraines: Clinically Proven Cure for Chronic Pain, 2008

Other books you might like:
Aaron G. Filler, *Do You Really Need Back Surgery?: A Surgeon's Guide to Back and Neck Pain and How to Choose Your Treatment*, 2007
Lynne A. Greenberg, *The Body Broken: A Memoir*, 2009
Kerry Levin, *Neck and Low Back Pain: An Issue of Neurologic Clinics*, 2007
Martin T. Taylor, *My Neck Hurts!: Nonsurgical Treatments for Neck and Upper Back Pain*, 2010
Joseph Valdez, *Healing Back and Joint Injuries: A Proven Approach to Ending Chronic Pain and Avoiding Unnecessary Surgery*, 2009

580

BRUCE E. MURDOCH

Acquired Speech and Language Disorders: A Neuroanatomical and Functional Neurological Approach, 2nd Edition

(Chichester, West Sussex, United Kingdom: Wiley-Blackwell, 2010)

Story type: Medical
Subject(s): Speech; Diseases; Health

Summary: Written by Professor Bruce E. Murdoch, *Acquired Speech and Language Disorders: A Neuroanatomical and Functional Neurological Approach, 2nd Edi-* tion is a guide to speech and language disorders that are a result of brain disease or neurological injury. The book provides doctors and health care professionals with detailed descriptions of speech disorders and their causes. The book focuses strictly on disorders—including aphasia, motor speech disorders, Parkinson's disease, right hemisphere damage, closed-head injury, and dementia—that occur due to disease or brain injury. Murdoch also explains the capabilities of brain imaging technologies, such as MRIs and PET scans, and the ways they affect diagnosing speech disorders.

Other books by the same author:
Speech and Language Disorders Associated with Subcortical Pathology, 2009
Dysphagia: Foundation, Theory and Practice, 2006
Speech and Language Disorders in Multiple Sclerosis, 2005

Other books you might like:
Roberta Chapey, *Language Intervention Strategies in Aphasia and Related Neurogenic Communication Disorders*, 2008
Christine A. Dollaghan, *Handbook for Evidence-Based Practice in Communication Disorders*, 2007
Debbie Feit, *The Parent's Guide to Speech and Language Problems*, 2007
Peter Howell, *Recovery from Stuttering*, 2010
Richard G. Schwartz, *Handbook of Child Language Disorders*, 2008

581

ADINA NACK

Damaged Goods?: Women Living With Incurable Sexually Transmitted Diseases

(Philadelphia: Temple University Press, 2008)

Subject(s): Women; Health; Sexuality

Summary: Medical sociologist Adina Nack explores the questions and issues faced by women diagnosed with sexual health problems. *Damaged Goods?: Women Living With Incurable Sexually Transmitted Diseases* examines how modern women reconcile their illnesses with how they view themselves as sexual creatures in a hypersexual society. Drawing from extensive research and more than 40 candid, probing interviews, this volume illustrates how an STD diagnosis can radically transform a woman's life—and her future. *Damaged Goods?* includes three appendices, notes on the text, a glossary, a bibliography, and an index. First book.

Where it's reviewed:
Choice, February 2009, page 1135
The Journal of Sex Research, July-August 2010, page 405

Other books you might like:
Shana McKibbin, *HealthScouter HPV: Understanding HPV Testing: The Human Papillomavirus Patient Advocate*, 2009
Alexander McMillan, *Sexually Transmissible Infections*

in Clinical Practice: A Problem-Based Approach, 2009

Ian Peate, *Manual of Sexually Transmitted Infections*, 2006

Lawrence R. Stanberry, *Understanding Herpes*, 2006

582

DAVID NATHER

The New Health Care System: Everything You Need To Know

(New York: Thomas Dunne Books, 2010)

Subject(s): Medical care; Law; Health

Summary: In *The New Health Care System: Everything You Need to Know*, author David Nather provides an accessible guide to President Obama's 2010 Patient Protection and Affordable Care Act. In this comprehensive handbook, readers learn the basics of health insurance. The author explains how the previous system worked and exposes the flaws the new system aims to correct. Nather then offers in-depth, non-partisan discussion on every facet of the plan, from the requirements of the individual and the role of employers to the terms for long-term care and preventive interventions. Special resources include pertinent Web sites and information about coverage start dates.

Where it's reviewed:
Booklist, July 1, 2010, page 14

Other books you might like:
Phil Bredesen, *Fresh Medicine: How to Fix Reform and Build a Sustainable Health Care System*, 2010
Seth B. Goldsmith, *Principles of Health Care Management*, 2009
Nortin M. Hadler, *The Last Well Person: How to Stay Well Despite the Health-Care System*, 2007
Robert Arthur Levine, *Shock Therapy for the American Health Care System*, 2009
Alan B. Miller, *Health Care Reform that Makes Sense*, 2009

583

DAVID E. NEWTON

Sexual Health: A Reference Handbook

(Santa Barbara: ABC-CLIO, 2009)

Subject(s): Sexual behavior; Sexuality; Adolescence

Summary: In this reference guide for young people, author David E. Newton presents the facts about sex, sexuality, sexually transmitted diseases, and much more information no teen should be without. *Sexual Health: A Reference Handbook* answers the most frequently asked questions regarding sex, covering a diverse assortment of topics and issues young people face. Subjects tackled in this volume include safe sex, pregnancy, abortion, and sex education. The book also includes profiles of notable individuals in the history of human sexuality. *Sexual Health* includes a glossary and an index.

Where it's reviewed:
School Library Journal, June 2010, page 135

Other books by the same author:
Substance Abuse: A Reference Handbook, 2010
DNA Technology: A Reference Handbook, 2009
Chemistry of the Environment, 2008
Food Chemistry, 2007
Forensic Chemistry, 2007

Other books you might like:
Kathy French, *Sexual Health*, 2009
Sandra A. Lawton, *Sexual Health Information for Teens*, 2008
Deborah Mitchell, *The Concise Encyclopedia of Women's Sexual and Reproductive Health*, 2009
Ian Peate, *Men's Sexual Health*, 2005
Chris Sonnex, *Sexual Health and Genital Medicine in Clinical Practice*, 2006

584

STACI NIX

Williams' Basic Nutrition and Diet Therapy, 13th Edition

(St. Louis: Mosby/Elsevier, 2008)

Subject(s): Nutrition; Food; Nursing

Summary: In *Williams' Basic Nutrition and Diet Therapy, 13th Edition*, author Staci Nix presents the ultimate guidebook to nutrition care. Nix relates her findings in a focused, accessible manner, fully illustrating and explaining the various aspects of proper nutrition and diet therapy. Enhanced by case studies and practical, real-life examples, this volume includes a wealth of additional material aimed to help students make the best use of the offered data. Highlighted boxes, questions for self-administered tests, illustrations, appendices, a glossary, and an index are also included. First book.

Other books by the same author:
Nutrition Concepts Online for Nutrition Essentials and Diet Therapy, 2010

Other books you might like:
Nortin M. Hadler, *Worried Sick: A Prescription for Health in an Overtreated America*, 2008
C. Shanthi Johnson, *Health and Aging in the World's Largest Democracy*, 2010
Ingrid Kohlstadt, *Food and Nutrients in Disease Management*, 2009
Ruth A. Roth, *Nutrition and Diet Therapy, Tenth Edition*, 2010
Kay A. Van Norman, *Exercise and Wellness for Older Adults*, 2010

585

CHRISTIANE NORTHRUP

The Secret Pleasures of Menopause
(Carlsbad, California: Hay House, 2008)

Subject(s): Women; Menopause; Sexual behavior

Summary: In her book *The Secret Pleasures of Menopause*, author Christiane Northrup helps women get through menopause. The focus of Northrup's book is on a woman's sexuality before, during, and after menopause. Northrup explains the physiological aspects of a woman's body and how the changes that occur during menopause may actually make it easier for a woman to enjoy sex. She gives hints, tips, and advice for women looking to capitalize on this phenomenon. According to Northrup, nitric oxide plays a key role in a woman's sexual pleasure during this time, and she explains how women can increase their levels of this hormone.

Where it's reviewed:
Library Journal, September 1, 2008, page 149

Other books by the same author:
What's Up Down There?: Questions You'd Only Ask Your Gynecologist If She Was Your Best Friend, 2010
Women's Bodies, Women's Wisdom, 2010
The Wisdom of Menopause Journal, 2007
The Wisdom of Menopause: Creating Physical and Emotional Health and Healing During the Change, 2nd Ed., 2007
Energy Medicine for Women: Aligning Your Body's Energies to Boost Your Health and Vitality, 2005

Other books you might like:
Amanda McQuade Crawford, *The Natural Menopause Handbook*, 2009
Bernard A. Eskin, *The Menopause: Endocrinologic Basis and Management Options*, 2007
Donna E. Stewart, *Menopause: A Mental Health Practitioner's Guide*, 2005
Nadine Taylor, *Natural Menopause Remedies: Which Drug-Free Cures Really Work*, 2009
Cynthia M. Watson, *User's Guide to Easing Menopause Symptoms Naturally*, 2010

586

CHRIS O'CALLAGHAN

The Renal System at a Glance
(Hoboken, New Jersey: Wiley-Blackwell, 2009)

Subject(s): Health; Reference works; Medical care

Summary: *The Renal System at a Glance* by Chris O'Callaghan is a thoroughly illustrated, comprehensive reference guide for medical or nursing students who need to learn about the renal system. General topics include anatomy, embryology, physiology, and pharmacology. Each chapter features case studies, questions for self-assessment, and full-page, full-color diagrams for further illustration of concepts found in the text. This edition includes an additional chapter that provides detailed information for making the determination of chronic kidney disease, as well as other diseases that can impact the kidneys and the renal system.

Where it's reviewed:
Renal Society of Australasia Journal, March 2010, page p41

Other books by the same author:
Practical Paediatric Procedures, 2010

Other books you might like:
Gabriel M. Danovitch, *Handbook of Kidney Transplantation: 5th Edition*, 2009
Tim Eisen, *Renal Cancer*, 2010
William L. Henrich, *Principles and Practice of Dialysis, Fourth Edition*, 2009
Mark S. Slaughter, *Cardiac Surgery in Chronic Renal Failure*, 2007
Lawrence E. Stam, *100 Questions and Answers About Kidney Dialysis*, 2009

587

PAUL A. OFFIT

Autism's False Prophets: Bad Science, Risky Medicine, and the Search for a Cure
(New York: Columbia University Press, 2008)

Subject(s): Medicine; Children

Summary: Since British physician Andrew Wakefield first proposed a connection between autism and the vaccine for measles, mumps, and rubella in 1998, frightened parents have questioned the safety of childhood vaccinations. Though several studies have failed to show a correlation between vaccines and autism, many people now opt against vaccinating their children. In *Autism's False Prophets: Bad Science, Risky Medicine, and the Search for a Cure*, infectious disease and immunology expert Dr. Paul A. Offit explains the dangers of jumping to conclusions when so little is known about autism. Offit argues that vaccines are the only way to prevent many serious infectious diseases and that unvaccinated children put our society at great risk. The doctor also takes the media to task for its sensational coverage of the controversy, while pleading with the scientific community to stop searching for something to blame and start looking for a cure. Dr. Offit is the chief of infectious diseases and the director of the Vaccine Education Center at the Children's Hospital of Philadelphia.

Where it's reviewed:
Archives of Pediatrics & Adolescent Medicine, April 2009, page 396
Journal of Clinical Investigation, April 2009, page 677
Nature Medicine, September 2009, page 992
The New England Journal of Medicine, March 12, 2009, page 1159

Other books by the same author:
Vaccines and Your Child: Separating Fact from Fiction, 2011
Vaccinated: One Man's Quest to Defeat the World's Deadliest Diseases, 2008

Vaccines, 2008

Other books you might like:

Temple Grandin, *Thinking in Pictures: And Other Reports from My Life with Autism*, 1995

Carol Gray, *The New Social Story Book*, 2010

Julia Moor, *Playing, Laughing and Learning with Children on the Autism Spectrum: A Practical Resource of Play Ideas for Parents and Carers*, 2002

Chantal Sicile-Kira, *Autism Life Skills*, 2008

Leeann Whiffen, *A Child's Journey Out of Autism: One Family's Story of Living in Hope and Finding a Cure*, 2009

588

RICK OLDERMAN

Fixing You: Back Pain

(Denver, Colorado: Boone Publishing, 2009)

Subject(s): Health; Medical care; Medicine

Summary: In *Fixing You: Back Pain*, physical therapist Rick Olderman offers an innovative plan for alleviating back pain symptoms. Written in accessible language for readers diagnosed with disk problems, sciatica, stenosis, and other conditions, this manual helps sufferers of back pain identify the cause of their problem and develop a program of exercise to lessen and eventually eliminate pain. Olderman first establishes the connection between mind and body in the healing process, discussing the value of visualization, verbalization, and willpower. Subsequent chapters offer descriptions of the anatomy and physiology of back pain and specific physical exercises designed to correct each condition.

Other books by the same author:

Fixing You: Back Pain During Pregnancy, 2010

Fixing You: Shoulder and Elbow Pain, 2010

Fixing You: Neck Pain and Headaches, 2009

Other books you might like:

Lynne A. Greenberg, *The Body Broken: A Memoir*, 2009

Kerry Levin, *Neck and Low Back Pain: An Issue of Neurologic Clinics*, 2007

John E. Sarno, *Healing Back Pain: The Mind-Body Connection*, 1991

Martin T. Taylor, *My Neck Hurts!: Nonsurgical Treatments for Neck and Upper Back Pain*, 2010

Joseph Valdez, *Healing Back and Joint Injuries: A Proven Approach to Ending Chronic Pain and Avoiding Unnecessary Surgery*, 2009

589

MELISSA ORLOV

The ADHD Effect on Marriage: Understand and Rebuild Your Relationship in Six Steps

(Plantation, Florida: Specialty Press, 2010)

Subject(s): Health; Psychology; Marriage

Summary: In *The ADHD Effect on Marriage: Understand and Rebuild Your Relationship in Six Steps*, author Melissa Orlov presents her proven method for dealing with the issue of Attention Deficit Hyperactivity Disorder in a marital relationship. Drawing on her own experience, Orlov offers personal advice for other spouses of ADHD individuals. The author begins with a discussion on the impact an ADHD diagnosis can have on a marriage, then shares her six-step plan—cultivating empathy for your spouse, addressing obstacle emotions, getting treatment for both parties, improving communication, setting boundaries and finding your own voices, and reigniting romance and having fun. Worksheets and other tools supplement the text.

Where it's reviewed:

Publishers Weekly, January 25, 2010, page 105

Other books by the same author:

Married to Distraction: Restoring Intimacy and Strengthening Your Marriage in an Age of Interruption, 2010

Other books you might like:

Russell A. Barkley, *Taking Charge of Adult ADHD*, 2010

Mimi Handlin, *Living With ADD When You're Not the One Who Has It: A Workbook For Partners*, 2005

Gina Pera, *Is It You, Me, or Adult A.D.D.?*, 2008

Ari Tuckman, *Integrative Treatment for Adult ADHD: A Practical, Easy-to-Use Guide for Clinicians*, 2007

Ari Tuckman, *More Attention, Less Deficit: Success Strategies for Adults with ADHD*, 2009

590

WILLIAM W. ORRISON JR.

Atlas of Brain Function, 2nd Edition

(New York: Thieme, 2008)

Story type: Medical

Subject(s): Neurosciences; Medical care; Health

Summary: Written by William W. Orrison Jr., *Atlas of Brain Function, 2nd Edition* is a comprehensive overview of the structure and function of the brain's different regions. The book carefully explains each area of the brain, its makeup, and its specific functions and uses. The second edition of *Atlas of Brain Function* has been updated to include the latest information about radiologic and neurological imaging, featuring details about 3 Tesla MR technology and MRI studies. High-quality brain images and scans fill the pages of this book, including Sagittal MRI views, Axial MRI views, Coronal MRI views, Fiber-Tracking Diffusion Tensor Imaging, and Three-Dimensional MRI views. Orrison has also included a thorough glossary of terms for readers.

Other books you might like:

Abhilash K. Desa, *Healthy Brain Aging: Evidence Based Methods to Preserve Brain Function and Prevent Dementia*, 2010

David Ferrier, *The Functions of the Brain*, 2010

David A. Sousa, *How the Gifted Brain Learns*, 2003

Cheryle Sullivan, *Brain Injury Survival Kit: 365 Tips,*

Tools and Tricks to Deal with Cognitive Function Loss, 2008

591

PETER PARHAM

The Immune System, 3rd Edition

(New York: Garland Science, 2009)

Subject(s): Medical care; Health; Reference works

Summary: *The Immune System, 3rd Edition* is a textbook by Peter Parham for students of immunology. The book explores concepts such as innate and adaptive immunity and breaks each immune response into its physical, cellular, and molecular levels. Specific immune-response functions and the roles of various cells in the immune system are discussed. Illustrations provide further details of the concepts. The book also examines immunotherapies for treating diseases and concepts such as the immune response in the mucosal tissues and immunological memory. Each chapter typically features a case study, a summary of the concepts covered in the chapter, and questions to assess understanding of the material.

Other books you might like:

William R. Clark, *In Defense of Self: How the Immune System Really Works*, 2008

Theresa Francis-Cheung, *Collins Gem 100 Ways to Boost Your Immune System*, 2008

Beth MacEoin, *Boost Your Immune System Naturally*, 2009

Gary Singh, *How To Boost Your Immune System Naturally?*, 2008

Kyoungho Suk, *Research Focus on Natural Products and the Body's Immune and Inflammatory Systems*, 2007

592

NANCY PEARCE

Inside Alzheimer's: How to Hear and Honor Connections with a Person Who Has Dementia

(Taylors, South Carolina: Forrason Press, 2007)

Subject(s): Health; Alzheimer's disease; Medical care

Summary: In *Inside Alzheimer's: How to Hear and Honor Connections with a Person Who Has Dementia*, geriatric social worker Nancy Pearce shares the methods she has developed for communicating with Alzheimer's patients. Drawing on her 20-plus years' experience in the field, Pearce describes the six principles of connection that she has identified—intend a connection, free yourself of judgment, love, be open to being loved, silence, and thankfulness. By employing these principles, the author explains, relatives, friends, and caregivers can recognize that inside the dementia person is a person worthy of respect and love and that meaningful communication is

possible. Anecdotes, activities, and resources supplement the guide.

Where it's reviewed:
Library Journal, June 15, 2007, page 87

Other books you might like:

Jean Carper, *100 Simple Things You Can Do to Prevent Alzheimer's and Age-Related Memory Loss*, 2010

Mary Ellen Geist, *Measure of the Heart: Caring for a Parent with Alzheimer's*, 2009

Lauren Kessler, *Finding Life in the Land of Alzheimer's: One Daughter's Hopeful Story*, 2008

Scott D. Mendelson, *Beyond Alzheimer's: How to Avoid the Modern Epidemic of Dementia*, 2009

John Zeisel, *I'm Still Here: A Breakthrough Approach to Understanding Someone Living with Alzheimer's*, 2009

593

NANCY J. PECKENPAUGH

Nutrition Essentials and Diet Therapy, 11th Edition

(St. Louis, Missouri: Saunders/Elsevier, 2009)

Subject(s): Health; Nutrition; Medicine

Summary: In *Nutrition Essentials and Diet Therapy, 11th Edition*, author Nancy J. Peckenpaugh updates her text for nursing students. In the book's first section, "The Art and Science of Nutrition in Health and Disease," the author covers the art of nutrition in a social context; the role of carbohydrates, proteins, and fats; the micronutrients of balanced meals; and digestion, absorption, and metabolism. The second section, "Chronic and Acute Illness," deals with conditions such as diabetes, obesity, and cardiovascular disease. The third section, "Life Span and Wellness Concerns in Promoting Health and Managing Illness," discusses maternal, infant, and adult nutritional concerns.

Other books by the same author:

Real Cowboys Eat Beans: For Cowboys and the Women Who Love 'Em, 2005

Other books you might like:

Jane Clarke, *Yummy Baby: The Essential First Nutrition Bible and Cookbook*, 2007

Glen D. Lawrence, *The Fats of Life: Essential Fatty Acids in Health and Disease*, 2010

George Mateljan, *The World's Healthiest Foods, Essential Guide for the Healthiest Way of Eating*, 2007

Ellen Postolowski, *It's Just Personal: A Personal Chef's Essential Guide to Shopping, Cooking, and Eating Smarter*, 2009

Ruth A. Roth, *Nutrition and Diet Therapy, Tenth Edition*, 2010

594

BRENDAN PHIBBS

The Human Heart: A Basic Guide to Heart Disease, 2nd Edition

(Philadelphia, Pennsylvania: Lippincott Willliams & Wilkins, 2007)

Subject(s): Health; Medical care; Reference works

Summary: *The Human Heart: A Basic Guide to Heart Disease, 2nd Edition* by Brendan Phibbs is a basic text intended for use by medical professionals or individuals who simply want to learn more about the anatomy and function of the heart and the ways heart disease is diagnosed and treated. Anatomy and physiology discussions are accessible even to those who have not studied medicine. Phibbs provides information on the treatment of various types of heart disease, including newer, non-invasive treatments for conditions that previously required extensive surgery. Specific cardiovascular treatment options such as defibrillators, coronary arteriography, and prescription drugs are discussed. The author also describes, among a wealth of other topics, methods of resuscitation and cardiovascular stress tests.

Other books by the same author:
Advanced ECG: Boards and Beyond, 2005

Other books you might like:
Arthur Agatston, *The South Beach Heart Health Revolution: Cardiac Prevention That Can Reverse Heart Disease and Stop Heart Attacks and Strokes*, 2008
Lawrence D. Chilnick, *The First Year: Heart Disease: An Essential Guide for the Newly Diagnosed*, 2008
Elaine Magee, *Tell Me What to Eat If I Suffer from Heart Disease*, 2010
Sarah Samaan, *The Smart Woman's Guide to Heart Health: Dr. Sarah's Seven Steps to a Heart-Loving Lifestyle*, 2009
Randall C. Starling, *The Cleveland Clinic Guide to Heart Failure*, 2009

595

TESSA M. POLLARD

Western Diseases: An Evolutionary Perspective

(New York: Cambridge University Press, 2008)

Subject(s): Diseases; Evolution (Biology); Reference works

Summary: Tessa M. Pollard's *Western Diseases: An Evolutionary Perspective* is a textbook for undergraduate or graduate students. The text covers "Western" diseases that have largely evolved due to changing dietary and lifestyle habits. These include type II diabetes, breast cancer, cardiovascular issues, and mental disorders, to name a few. Pollard states that human evolution has not quite caught up to the Western environment, making these diseases much more prevalent in this region of the

world. The author also considers reasons why these diseases are spreading to other regions. The epidemiology, biology, and evolution of these unique diseases are covered from an anthropological perspective in this text.

Where it's reviewed:
American Scientist, Jan-Feb 2009, page 81
Quarterly Review of Biology, June 2009, page 215

Other books you might like:
Jon Stuart Abramson, *Inside the 2009 Influenza Pandemic*, 2010
Michael Bliss, *The Making of Modern Medicine: Turning Points in the Treatment of Disease*, 2011
Leonard V. Crowley, *Introduction to Human Disease: Pathology and Pathophysiology Correlations, Eighth Edition: A Student Workbook*, 2009
J. N. Hays, *The Burdens of Disease: Epidemics and Human Response in Western History*, 2010
Staffan Lindeberg, *Food and Western Disease: Health and Nutrition From an Evolutionary Perspective*, 2010

596

CHRIS POMERY

Family History in the Genes: Trace Your DNA and Grow Your Family Tree

(Kew, London, United Kingdom: National Archives, 2007)

Subject(s): Genetics; Genealogy; Family

Summary: Journalist Chris Pomery instructs readers on how to best utilize DNA testing to successfully trace one's genealogical history. *Family History in the Genes: Trace Your DNA and Grow Your Family Tree* points out the many benefits offered by DNA testing and illustrates the numerous doors it can open for those seeking information about their genealogy. Pomery profiles the various testing methods available and the type of information each test can ascertain. *Family History in the Genes* includes a glossary, a bibliography, and a full index.

Where it's reviewed:
Families, May 2008, page 33

Other books you might like:
Edward Ball, *The Genetic Strand: Exploring a Family History Through DNA*, 2007
Peter S. Harper, *A Short History of Medical Genetics*, 2008
Jon Queijo, *Breakthrough!: How the 10 Greatest Discoveries in Medicine Saved Millions and Changed Our View of the World*, 2010
Angela Scheuerle, *Understanding Genetics: A Primer for Couples and Families*, 2008
Doris Teichler-Zallen, *To Test or Not to Test: A Guide to Genetic Screening and Risk*, 2008

597

JEANETTE M. POTTS

Genitourinary Pain and Inflammation: Diagnosis and Management

(Totowa, New Jersey: Humana Press, 2008)

Subject(s): Health; Medical care; Science

Summary: In *Genitourinary Pain and Inflammation: Diagnosis and Management*, editor Jeanette M. Potts brings together a collection of essays exploring the pathology and treatment of genitourinary (pelvic) pain. This topic has gone largely ignored in current medical studies, but Potts has compiled a revelatory series of articles by some of the most respected scholars in the field, illuminating at last this overlooked condition. Topics are divided by genitourinary issues that are gender-specific and gender-neutral. *Genitourinary Pain and Inflammation* includes a full index.

Other books you might like:

Wendy Cohan, *The Better Bladder Book: A Holistic Approach to Healing Interstitial Cystitis and Chronic Pelvic Pain*, 2010

Harry Rosen, *The Consult Manual of Internal Medicine*, 2008

Daniel A. Shoskes, *Chronic Prostatitis/Chronic Pelvic Pain Syndrome*, 2008

David Wise, *A Headache in the Pelvis: A New Understanding and Treatment for Prostatitis and Chronic Pelvic Pain Syndromes*, 2005

598

DAVID PROUD

The Pulmonary Epithelium in Health and Disease

(Chichester, United Kingdom; Hoboken, New Jersey: John Wiley and Sons, 2008)

Subject(s): Medicine; Science; Diseases

Summary: In *The Pulmonary Epithelium in Health and Disease*, editor David Proud compiles a series of essays examining the identification, pathology, and latest research in the field of the pulmonary epithelium. Some of the world's most respected scholars in the field take on the topic from a variety of angles, from epithelial repair to bacterial infections within the airway epithelium. This all-encompassing reference manual includes information on the contributors and a full index.

Where it's reviewed:
Respiratory Care, September 2009, page 1272

Other books you might like:

Steven H. Abman, *Bronchopulmonary Dysplasia*, 2009

Augustine M. K. Choi, *Acute Respiratory Distress Syndrome*, 2009

Donald E. Gardner, *Toxicology of the Lung*, 2005

Anthony J. Hickey, *Inhalation Aerosols: Physical and Biological Basis for Therapy*, 2006

Stephen K. Tyring, *Mucosal Immunology and Virology*, 2006

599

IRA S. RICHARDS

Principles and Practice of Toxicology in Public Health

(Sudbury, Massachusetts: Jones and Bartlett Publishers, 2007)

Subject(s): Science; Health; Medicine

Summary: Ira S. Richards's *Principles and Practice of Toxicology in Public Health* is geared toward students starting out in the study of toxicology as it relates to public health structures. This volume looks at the principles and practice of toxicology, guiding students through the fundamentals of the science. *Principles and Practice of Toxicology in Public Health* includes a glossary of commonly used terms and a full index.

Where it's reviewed:
JAMA, The Journal of the American Medical Association, December 3, 2008, page 2554
Journal of Environmental Health, October 2008, page 47
Journal of Environmental Health, May 2009, page 59

Other books you might like:

Ernest Hodgson, *A Textbook of Modern Toxicology*, 2008

Curtis D. Klaassen, *Casarett and Doull's Toxicology: The Basic Science of Poisons*, 1986

Moiz Mumtaz, *Principles and Practice of Mixtures Toxicology*, 2010

Kent R. Olson, *Poisoning And Drug Overdose*, 2006

Adam Woolley, *A Guide to Practical Toxicology: Evaluation, Prediction, and Risk*, 2008

600

EDWARD RINGEL

Little Black Book of Pulmonary Medicine

(Sudbury, Massachusetts: Jones and Bartlett Publishers, 2008)

Subject(s): Medicine; Medical care; Diseases

Summary: In *Little Black Book of Pulmonary Medicine*, author Edward Ringel offers respiratory and pulmonary health care providers the definitive go-to guide for all things related to pulmonary health and treatment. Ringel covers a vast field of information in this helpful volume, including advice on assessment and diagnosis, identifying proper testing procedures, and profiles of various lung diseases. *Little Black Book of Pulmonary Medicine* includes a bibliography and a full index.

Other books you might like:

Steven H. Abman, *Bronchopulmonary Dysplasia*, 2009

Augustine M. K. Choi, *Acute Respiratory Distress Syndrome*, 2009

Donald E. Gardner, *Toxicology of the Lung*, 2005

Anthony J. Hickey, *Inhalation Aerosols: Physical and Biological Basis for Therapy*, 2006

Stephen K. Tyring, *Mucosal Immunology and Virology*, 2006

601

ROBIN RIO

Connecting Through Music with People with Dementia: A Guide for Caregivers

(London: Jessica Kingsley Publishers, 2009)

Story type: Medical
Subject(s): Medical care; Music; Memory disorders

Summary: In *Connecting Through Music with People with Dementia: A Guide for Caregivers*, Robin Rio discusses the impact music has on people suffering from dementia. She claims that music is so strong that no matter the mental awareness of a dementia patient, music will reach them. They can speak of the effects of music with fellow listeners and they can critique what they hear, regardless of their knowledge of the piece, its composer, or its beat. The right kind of music can help dementia patients relax and have fun, says Rio. This book is designed for music therapy professionals, nursing students, and musicians interested in working in the medical field.

Where it's reviewed:
Mental Health Practice, February 2010, page 11

Other books you might like:
Karen D. Goodman, *Music Therapy Groupwork with Special Needs Children: The Evolving Process*, 2007

Daniel J. Levitin, *This Is Your Brain on Music: The Science of a Human Obsession*, 2006

Daniel J. Levitin, *The World in Six Songs: How the Musical Brain Created Human Nature*, 2008

Alex Ross, *The Rest Is Noise: Listening to the Twentieth Century*, 2007

Susanna Zaraysky, *Language is Music*, 2009

602

TOM RODGERS

The Perfect Distance: Training for Long-Course Triathlons

(Boulder, Colorado: VeloPress, 2007)

Subject(s): Sports; Running; Swimming

Summary: In *The Perfect Distance: Training for Long-Course Triathlons*, Tom Rodgers provides a comprehensive guide for individuals who wish to compete in long-course triathlons, which include running, biking, and swimming events. Rodgers provides specific exercise plans, workouts, and case studies to prepare for a triath-

lon, with additional focus on choosing quality equipment for workouts. Rodgers stresses the importance of strength training exercises in combination with aerobic conditioning and provides advice for getting the most from indoor workouts as well. Rodgers also offers nutritional advice for staying healthy and increasing muscle mass while in training and devotes a section to preventing and treating injuries that may occur during training.

Other books you might like:
Louise Burke, *Clinical Sports Nutrition*, 2009

Marie Dunford, *Sports Nutrition: A Practice Manual for Professionals*, 2006

Ted Eaves, *The Practical Guide to Athletic Training*, 2009

Suzanne Girard Eberle, *Endurance Sports Nutrition: 2nd Edition*, 2007

Monique Ryan, *Sports Nutrition for Endurance Athletes*, 2007

603

BRENDA ROSCHER

How to Cook for Crohn's and Colitis: More Than 200 Healthy, Delicious Recipes the Whole Family Will Love

(Nashville: Cumberland House, 2007)

Subject(s): Cooking; Food; Diseases

Summary: Crohn's disease and ulcerative colitis are disruptive inflammatory bowel diseases (IBDs) that can seriously impede one's ability to enjoy life. But in *How to Cook for Crohn's and Colitis: More Than 200 Healthy, Delicious Recipes the Whole Family Will Love*, author Brenda Roscher shows readers how IBD sufferers can still enjoy the benefits of delicious foods. Packed with recipes and practical advice (Roscher herself suffers from Crohn's), this volume also contains a list of furthering suggested reading and helpful websites, as well as an easy-to-reference index. First book.

Where it's reviewed:
Library Journal, November 1, 2007, page 92

Other books you might like:
David Dahlman, *Why Doesn't My Doctor Know This?*, 2008

Tracie M. Dalessandro, *What to Eat with IBD: A Comprehensive Nutrition and Recipe Guide for Crohn's Disease and Ulcerative Colitis*, 2006

Laura W. Lamps, *Surgical Pathology of the Gastrointestinal System: Bacterial, Fungal, Viral, and Parasitic Infections*, 2009

Gary R. Lichtenstein, *Ulcerative Colitis: The Complete Guide to Medical Management*, 2011

Mark A. Peppercorn, *Contemporary Diagnosis and Management of Ulcerative Colitis and Proctitis*, 2005

604

RUTH A. ROTH

Nutrition and Diet Therapy, Tenth Edition

(Clifton Park, New York: Delmar Cengage Learning, 2010)

Subject(s): Health; Nutrition; Medical care

Summary: In *Nutrition and Diet Therapy, Tenth Edition*, clinical dietician Ruth A. Roth revises her introductory text on nutrition concepts for nursing students. Organized into three parts—Fundamentals of Nutrition, Maintenance of Health Through Good Nutrition, and Medical Nutritional Therapy—this comprehensive and accessible text covers topics such as the relationships of nutrition and health, planning a healthy diet, food-related illnesses and allergies, diet during all stages of life, and diet as it relates to weight control. The book also discusses conditions such as diabetes, cardiovascular disease, and cancer. The tenth edition has been updated in line with the most recent nutritional guidelines. The companion CD provides supplementary study material.

Other books you might like:

Jack Challem, *The Inflammation Syndrome: Your Nutrition Plan for Great Health, Weight Loss, and Pain-Free Living*, 2010

Jean Fain, *The Self-Compassion Diet*, 2010

Staci Nix, *Williams' Basic Nutrition and Diet Therapy, 13th Edition*, 2008

Nancy J. Peckenpaugh, *Nutrition Essentials and Diet Therapy, 11th Edition*, 2009

Shelia Tucker, *Nutrition and Diet Therapy for Nurses*, 2010

605

KELLY RUDNICKI

The Food Allergy Mama's Baking Book: Great Dairy-, Egg-, and Nut-Free Treats for the Whole Family

(Chicago: Surrey Books, 2009)

Subject(s): Allergy; Cooking; Food

Summary: Author Kelly Rudnicki, the Food Allergy Mama, presents a series of recipes designed for people with food allergies in her book *The Food Allergy Mama's Baking Book: Great Dairy-, Egg-, and Nut-Free Treats for the Whole Family*. This volume contains recipes for everything from quick breads to muffins and pies to cookies. Rudnicki also includes common questions about food allergies and their answers as well as tips and tricks people can use while baking for people with food allergies. *The Food Allergy Mama's Baking Book* contains a full index.

Other books by the same author:

Vegan Baking Classics: Delicious, Easy-to-Make Traditional Favorites, 2010

Other books you might like:

Kelly Keough, *Sugar-Free Gluten-Free Baking and Desserts*, 2009

Carol Kicinski, *Simply . . . Gluten-Free Desserts: 150 Delicious Recipes for Cupcakes, Cookies, Pies, and More Old and New Favorites*, 2011

Susan O'Brien, *Gluten-free, Sugar-free Cooking: Over 200 Delicious Recipes to Help You Live a Healthier, Allergy-Free Life*, 2006

Cybele Pascal, *Allergen-Free Baker's Handbook*, 2009

Lori Sandler, *The Divvies Bakery Cookbook: No Nuts. No Eggs. No Dairy. Just Delicious!*, 2010

606

PHILLIP RUIZ

Transplantation Pathology

(Cambridge, United Kingdom: Cambridge University Press, 2009)

Subject(s): Health; Medicine; Medical care

Summary: In *Transplantation Pathology*, editor Philip Ruiz, M.D., presents a textbook for clinical practitioners and students covering a range of organ transplantation issues. Written by authorities in the discipline, this comprehensive volume offers in-depth discussion of kidney, liver, heart, lung, pancreas, and intestine transplant, as well as the process of stem cell transplantation. Related topics addressed include the immunopathology of organ transplant, dermatological complications in transplant patients, pathology and pathogenesis of post-transplant lymphoproliferative disorders, and the role of the laboratory in transplantation. Dr. Ruiz is professor of pathology and surgery, medical director of transplant laboratories, and director of immunopathology and the University of Miami.

Where it's reviewed:

JAMA, The Journal of the American Medical Association, January 13, 2010, page 176

Other books you might like:

Gabriel M. Danovitch, *Handbook of Kidney Transplantation: 5th Edition*, 2009

Anthony J. Demetris, *Atlas of Transplantation Pathology*, 2011

Susan E. Lederer, *Flesh and Blood: Organ Transplantation and Blood Transfusion in 20th Century America*, 2008

Jay H. Lefkowitch, *Scheuer's Liver Biopsy Interpretation*, 2010

David Petechuk, *Organ Transplantation*, 2006

607

OLIVER SACKS

Musicophilia: Tales of Music and the Brain

(New York: Random House, 2007)

Subject(s): Health; Mental Health; Music

Summary: Neurologist Oliver Sacks examines the many physiological and psychological effects of music on the human brain. Using case studies, he describes both common and uncommon ways that music can influence humans. In one case, he tells about a man who gets struck by lightning and afterward has a sudden love of, and talent for, concert piano music. In another, he shows how music can be used as therapy for patients with various neurological conditions. He discusses why a tune can get caught in our mind and not go away. The tales are of people whose lives have been profoundly affected by music.

Where it's reviewed:
Journal of Chemical Education, July 2009, page 793
The New England Journal of Medicine, May 22, 2008, page 2304
Times Higher Education, November 13, 2008, page 45

Other books by the same author:
The Paradoxical Brain, 2011
Seeing Voices: A Journey Into the World of the Deaf, 2009
Awakenings, 2008
A Journey Round My Skull, 2008
Migraine, 2008

Other books you might like:
Daniel J. Levitin, *This Is Your Brain on Music: The Science of a Human Obsession*, 2006
Daniel J. Levitin, *The World in Six Songs: How the Musical Brain Created Human Nature*, 2008
Justin Locke, *Real Men Don't Rehearse: Adventures in the Secret World of Professional Orchestras*, 2005

608

FRED SAIBIL

Crohn's Disease and Ulcerative Colitis: Everything You Need to Know, Revised Edition

(Buffalo, New York: Firefly Books, 2009)

Story type: Medical
Subject(s): Medical care; Diseases; Health

Summary: In *Crohn's Disease and Ulcerative Colitis: Everything You Need to Know, Revised Edition*, author Fred Saibil offers a thorough explanation of inflammatory bowel disease (IBD) and its two chronic conditions: Crohn's disease and ulcerative colitis. About 1 percent of all Americans suffer from IBD, but most people are often unwilling to openly discuss it. The cause of IBD is unknown and there is currently no cure. In this book, Saibil offers educational and practical information on the conditions, including details on symptoms and side effects, potential complications, diagnosis of the disease, the impact of diet, medications and their effectiveness, how IBD affects children, surgical alternatives, and how IBD affects pregnancy and sexual activity.

Other books you might like:
David Dahlman, *Why Doesn't My Doctor Know This?*, 2008

John O. Hunter, *Inflammatory Bowel Disease*, 2010
Sunanda V. Kane, *IBD Self-Management: The AGA Guide to Crohn's Disease and Ulcerative Colitis*, 2010
Brenda Roscher, *How to Cook for Crohn's and Colitis: More Than 200 Healthy, Delicious Recipes the Whole Family Will Love*, 2007
Andrew Tubesing, *Colitiscope: Living With Crohn's Disease and Ulcerative Colitis*, 2009

609

SARAH SAMAAN

The Smart Woman's Guide to Heart Health: Dr. Sarah's Seven Steps to a Heart-Loving Lifestyle

(Dallas: Brown Books Publishing Group, 2009)

Subject(s): Health; Women; Medicine

Summary: In *The Smart Woman's Guide to Heart Health: Dr. Sarah's Seven Steps to a Heart-Loving Lifestyle*, cardiologist Sarah Samaan shares her holistic approach to cardiovascular health written specifically for women. Presented in a friendly, seven-step format, this guide is designed to inform, empower, and encourage readers to take action against a disease that has become the primary cause of women's death in the United States. Addressing topics such as weight, cholesterol, diet, caffeine, alcohol, tobacco, alternative treatments, exercise, relationships, stress, and hormones, Samaan provides accessible advice for increasing energy and achieving a heart-healthy lifestyle. Readers are also encouraged to help foster heart health in their families.

Other books you might like:
Nelson Anderson, *A Heart Attack Survivor's Guide to a Long Healthy Life*, 2009
Dede Bonner, *The 10 Best Questions for Recovering from a Heart Attack: The Script You Need to Take Control of Your Health*, 2009
Lawrence D. Chilnick, *The First Year: Heart Disease: An Essential Guide for the Newly Diagnosed*, 2008
Curtis M. Rimmerman, *The Cleveland Clinic Guide to Heart Attack*, 2009
Mike Stone, *Living with Restenosis*, 2007

610

MARIE SAVARD

Ask Dr. Marie: What Women Need to Know About Hormones, Libido, and the Medical Problems No One Talks About

(Guilford, Connecticut: Lyons Press, 2010)

Subject(s): Health; Medicine; Women

Summary: In *Ask Dr. Marie: What Women Need to Know*

About Hormones, Libido, and the Medical Problems No One Talks About, ABC News medical contributor Marie Savard presents a comprehensive guide to issues of female sexuality and reproduction. Written for women of all ages, *Ask Dr. Marie* is organized into four parts: "What's Going on Down There," "The Seasons of Your Life," "Is This Normal or Should I Call My Doctor," and "What Happens Down There Doesn't Stay Down There." In an informative but conversational voice, Savard discusses important topics that women can find embarrassing, including female anatomy and physiology, sex, conception, menopause, and the relationship between physical and emotional health.

Other books by the same author:
How to Save Your Own Life: The Eight Steps Only You Can Take to Manage and Control Your Health Care, 2009
Are you an Apple or a Pear?: a Revolutionary Diet Programme for Weight Loss and Optimum Health, 2006
The Body Shape Solution to Weight Loss and Wellness: The Apples & Pears Approach to Losing Weight, Living Longer, and Feeling Healthier, 2006
Apples and Pears: A Revolutionary Diet Programme for Weight Loss and Optimum Health, 2005

Other books you might like:
Michael L. Krychman, *100 Questions and Answers for Women Living with Cancer: A Practical Guide for Survivorship*, 2007
Suzy Lockwood, *Contemporary Issues in Women's Cancers*, 2008
Kathryn R. Simpson, *The Women's Guide to Thyroid Health: Comprehensive Solutions for All Your Thyroid Symptoms*, 2009
Elizabeth A. Stewart, *Uterine Fibroids: The Complete Guide*, 2007
Janet Wright, *Coping with Perimenopause*, 2006

611

WILLIAM SCHOOLCRAFT

If at First You Don't Conceive: A Complete Guide to Infertility from One of the Nation's Leading Clinics

(New York: Rodale Books, 2010)

Subject(s): Health; Pregnancy; Children

Summary: According to the American Society for Reproductive Medicine, more than 7 million American women cannot have children due to infertility complications. Men and women who are told they cannot produce their own children often feel guilty and stressed. In *If at First You Don't Conceive: A Complete Guide to Infertility from One of the Nation's Leading Clinics*, author and physician William Schoolcraft explains why some people cannot get pregnant and why others, even though they are told that it is impossible, can. He provides information about male and female infertility, finding the right

doctors, and embracing alternative techniques.

Other books you might like:
Tertia Loebenberg Albertyn, *So Close: Infertile and Addicted to Hope*, 2009
Kerstin Daynes, *Infertility: Help, Hope, and Healing*, 2010
Melissa Ford, *Navigating the Land of If: Understanding Infertility and Exploring Your Options*, 2009
Constance Hoenk Shapiro, *When You're Not Expecting*, 2010
Pamela Mahoney Tsigdinos, *Silent Sorority: A Barren Woman Gets Busy, Angry, Lost and Found*, 2009

612

ROBERT W. SCHRIER

Disease of the Kidney and Urinary Tract: 8th Edition

(Philadelphia: Wolters Kluwer/Lippincott Williams & Wilkins Health, 2007)

Story type: Medical
Subject(s): Medical care; Health; Diseases

Summary: Edited by Robert W. Schrier, *Disease of the Kidney and Urinary Tract: 8th Edition* is a thorough and comprehensive guide to illnesses and conditions of the kidney and urinary tract. The three-volume set is divided into fourteen sections, each written by prominent doctors and scholars, and targeted towards practicing physicians treating patients suffering from kidney or urinary tract diseases. The book offers practical and helpful information on diagnosing various conditions, addressing symptoms, treatment options, and possible complications. After an overview of renal basic science, the book provides detailed coverage of specific diseases and conditions, such as kidney disease, hypertension, and urologic disorders.

Where it's reviewed:
JAMA, The Journal of the American Medical Association, June 6, 2007, page p2415

Other books by the same author:
Renal and Electrolyte Disorders (Renal and Electrolyte Disorders, 2010
Essential Atlas of Nephrology and Hypertension, 2009
Manual of Nephrology: Diagnosis and Therapy, 2008
The Internal Medicine Casebook: Real Patients, Real Answers, 2007

Other books you might like:
Mark L. Gonzalgo, *Johns Hopkins Patients Guide to Bladder Cancer*, 2009
Elizabeth Kavaler, *A Seat on the Aisle, Please!: The Essential Guide to Urinary Tract Problems in Women*, 2010
Jeanette M. Potts, *Genitourinary Pain and Inflammation: Diagnosis and Management*, 2008
Abhay Rane, *Urinary Tract Infections: Questions and Answers*, 2010

613

DAVID SERVAN-SCHREIBER

Anticancer: A New Way of Life
(New York: Viking, 2008)

Subject(s): Cancer; Health; Alternative medicine

Summary: David Servan-Schreiber describes his own personal experience with brain cancer, which leads him to search for alternatives to help fight the disease. For fifteen years he fought the illness and a relapse to eventually make his way to good health today. What he discovers through years of research is a healthy diet, a healthy lifestyle, and a positive attitude helps reduce the risks of cancer. Among his suggestions are: eliminating household chemicals, not eating unhealthy food such as red meat or processed food, and staying away from unhealthy habits like smoking. He never negates the need for surgery, radiation, chemotherapy, or other modern medicine that helps cancer patients. What he suggests is in addition to what a cancer specialist would recommend.

Where it's reviewed:
Cancer Nursing Practice, March 2009, page 20

Other books by the same author:
Healing without Freud or Prozac: Natural Approaches to Curing Stress, Anxiety and Depression without Drugs and without Psychoanalysis, 2005
The Instinct to Heal: Curing Depression, Anxiety and Stress Without Drugs and Without Talk Therapy, 2004

Other books you might like:
Julia B. Greer, *The Anti-Cancer Cookbook*, 2008
Sotiris Missailidis, *Anticancer Therapeutics*, 2008
Siddhartha Mukherjee, *The Emperor of All Maladies: A Biography of Cancer*, 2010
Michael Pollan, *Food Rules: An Eater's Manual*, 2009
Jodi Buckman Weinstein, *Tell Me What to Eat Before, During, and After Cancer Treatment: Nutritional Guidelines for Patients and Their Loved Ones*, 2010

614

MICHAEL SHARON

Nutrient A-Z: A User's Guide to Foods, Herbs, Vitamins, Minerals and Supplements
(London: Carlton Publishing Group, 2009)

Subject(s): Health; Food; Nutrition

Summary: In *Nutrient A-Z: A User's Guide to Foods, Herbs, Vitamins, Minerals and Supplements*, nutrition consultant Michael Sharon presents a comprehensive guide to understanding and using nutritional health supplements. Presented in dictionary format, *Nutrient A-Z* includes listings of a broad range of foods, herbs, vitamins, minerals, and supplements. Each listing provides a definition, origin, application, and recom-

mended usage. Familiar food products such as bananas, blueberries, carrots, olive oil, and yogurt are discussed, as well as the herb St. John's Wort, the plant guarana, and hundreds of other nutritional items that have been attributed with health benefits.

Where it's reviewed:
Choice, October 2004, page 272

Other books by the same author:
Complete Nutrition: How to Live in Total Health, 2009

Other books you might like:
Paul M. Gross, *Superfruits*, 2009
John Ivy, *Nutrient Timing*, 2009
Ingrid Kohlstadt, *Food and Nutrients in Disease Management*, 2009
James M. Lowrance, *Diagnosing and Treating Common Nutritional Deficiencies*, 2010
Pamela Wartian Smith, *What You Must Know About Vitamins, Minerals, Herbs, and More: Choosing the Nutrients That Are Right for You*, 2008

615

JULIE K. SILVER

What Helped Get Me Through: Cancer Survivors Share Wisdom and Hope
(Atlanta, Georgia: American Cancer Society, 2008)

Subject(s): Cancer; Health; Diseases

Summary: In *What Helped Get Me Through: Cancer Survivors Share Wisdom and Hope*, author Julie K. Silver shares inspirational stories about surviving cancer. This book, which was published by the American Cancer Society, details survivor stories from celebrities such as Lance Armstrong and Carly Simon, as well as Silver's own perspective as a survivor of the disease. The author looks at healthcare issues, wellness advice, and messages of hope from doctors, nurses, and survivors and how they impact those who suffer from the illness. Silver is an oncology rehabilitation specialist and the author of *Super Healing*.

Other books by the same author:
Essentials of Physical Medicine and Rehabilitation, 2008
Super Healing: The Clinically Proven Plan to Maximize Recovery from Illness or Injury, 2007
After Cancer Treatment: Heal Faster, Better, Stronger, 2006

Other books you might like:
Greg Anderson, *Cancer: 50 Essential Things to Do*, 2009
Neil A. Fiore, *Coping with the Emotional Impact of Cancer: Become an Active Patient and Take Charge of Your Treatment*, 2009
Vickie Girard, *There's No Place Like Hope: A Guide to Beating Cancer in Mind-sized Bites*, 2008

Edward H. Laughlin, *CANCER from A to Z: A Dictionary of Cancer-Related Terms in Easily Understood Language*, 2008

Cecil Murphey, *When Someone You Love Has Cancer: Comfort and Encouragement for Caregivers and Loved Ones*, 2008

616

PAMELA WARTIAN SMITH

What You Must Know About Women's Hormones: Your Guide to Natural Hormone Treatments for PMS, Menopause, Osteoporosis, PCOS, and More

(Garden City Park, New York: Square One Publishers, 2010)

Subject(s): Health; Women; Medical care

Summary: *What You Must Know About Women's Hormones: Your Guide to Natural Hormone Treatments for PMS, Menopause, Osteoporosis, PCOS, and More* is written by Pamela Wartian Smith and provides a guide for women going through the change of life. The author considers options for hormone replacement, which she states can be beneficial for menopausal women in a number of ways such as helping to prevent osteoporosis and heart disease as well as managing a healthy weight. Smith explains the way hormones function in the body, the way they change during and after menopause, and the unpleasant symptoms and potential health problems that can arise as a result of this change. Smith elucidates the benefits of natural hormones in comparison to synthetic ones, and explains the benefits of supplements in managing menopause and the effects of aging.

Where it's reviewed:
Library Journal, January 2010, page 130

Other books by the same author:
What You Must Know About Vitamins, Minerals, Herbs, and More: Choosing the Nutrients That Are Right for You, 2008
Demystifying Weight Loss: A Concise Guide for Solving the Weight Loss Puzzle, 2007

Other books you might like:
D. Lindsey Berkson, *Safe Hormones, Smart Women*, 2010
Regina C. Casper, *Women's Health: Hormones, Emotions and Behavior*, 2008
Winnifred Berg Cutler, *Hormones and Your Health*, 2009
Geoffrey Redmond, *It's Your Hormones*, 2006
Sherrill Sellman, *Hormone Heresy What Women Must Know About Their Hormones*, 2009

617

PAMELA WARTIAN SMITH

What You Must Know About Vitamins, Minerals, Herbs, and More: Choosing the Nutrients That Are Right for You

(Garden City Park, New York: Square One Publishers, 2008)

Subject(s): Health; Nutrition

Summary: In *What You Must Know about Vitamins, Minerals, Herbs and More*, Dr. Pamela Wartian Smith presents a guide to using nutrients to improve health. In the first part of the book, Smith introduces readers to a range of nutrients, including vitamins, minerals, fatty acids, amino acids, herbs, and others. The book's second part presents a range of health conditions, from acne, cataracts, lupus, and leaky gut syndrome to balding, premenstrual syndrome, yeast infection, and psoriasis, providing a nutrient treatment for each. Part three addresses the maintenance of health through nutrient uses, covering such topics as diet, weight loss, men's and women's health, and memory enhancement.

Where it's reviewed:
Library Journal, Jan 2010, page 130

Other books by the same author:
What You Must Know About Women's Hormones: Your Guide to Natural Hormone Treatments for PMS, Menopause, Osteoporosis, PCOS, and More, 2009
Demystifying Weight Loss: A Concise Guide for Solving the Weight Loss Puzzle, 2007

Other books you might like:
Benjamin Caballero, *Guide to Nutritional Supplements*, 2009
Jane Clarke, *Yummy Baby: The Essential First Nutrition Bible and Cookbook*, 2007
Glen D. Lawrence, *The Fats of Life: Essential Fatty Acids in Health and Disease*, 2010
George Mateljan, *The World's Healthiest Foods, Essential Guide for the Healthiest Way of Eating*, 2007
Ellen Postolowski, *It's Just Personal: A Personal Chef's Essential Guide to Shopping, Cooking, and Eating Smarter*, 2009

618

TOM SMITH

A Balanced Life: 9 Strategies for Coping with the Mental Health Problems of a Loved One

(Center City, Minnesota: Hazelden Publishing, 2008)

Subject(s): Mental disorders; Psychology; Family

Summary: In *A Balanced Life: 9 Strategies for Coping with the Mental Health Problems of a Loved One*, Tom

Smith provides detailed advice for people who live with loved ones who suffer from mental illness. Smith explains how to help this person cope with the illness and how to prevent stress that can result from it. Smith offers advice for creating a supportive network of friends and family and using this network to help the person suffering from mental illness develop better self-esteem and learn to manage the illness. Strategies for noticing early warning signs that a mental illness is worsening are included, along with advice on what to expect as part of daily life when living with someone with mental illness.

Where it's reviewed:
National Catholic Reporter, November 28, 2008, page 4a

Other books by the same author:
The Tattered Tapestry: A Family's Search for Peace with Bipolar Disorder, 2007

Other books you might like:
Jacqueline M. Atkinson, *Advance Directives in Mental Health: Theory, Practice and Ethics*, 2007
Jari Holland Buck, *Hospital Stay Handbook: A Guide to Becoming a Patient Advocate for Your Loved Ones*, 2007
Donna R. Kemp, *Mental Health in America: A Reference Handbook*, 2007
Jane Matthews, *Carer's Handbook: Essential Information and Support for All Those in a Caring Role*, 2007
Graham Thornicroft, *Shunned: Discrimination against People with Mental Illness*, 2006

619

DAVID A. SOUSA

How the Gifted Brain Learns
(Thousand Oaks, California: Corwin Press, 2003)

Subject(s): Neurosciences; Education; Gifted children

Summary: The fields of education and neuroscience meet in David A. Sousa's *How the Gifted Brain Learns*. This illuminating volume reveals the latest findings in the field of neuroscience and what these revelations divulge about how the brains of gifted individuals operate. Sousa identifies specific talents—from math and science to art and language—and illustrates how they function within the neurological makeup of the brain. For educators, medical professionals, and lay readers, this volume is an enlightening testament to the power of human thought. *How the Gifted Brain Learns* includes a glossary, a bibliography, and an index.

Where it's reviewed:
Choice, February 2010, page 1130

Other books by the same author:
Differentiation and the Brain: How Neuroscience Supports the Learner-Friendly Classroom, 2010
Mind, Brain, and Education: Neuroscience Implications for the Classroom, 2010
How the Brain Learns Mathematics, 2007
How the Special Needs Brain Learns, 2006

How the Brain Learns, 2005

Other books you might like:
Katharine Beals, *Raising a Left-Brain Child in a Right-Brain World: Strategies for Helping Bright, Quirky, Socially Awkward Children to Thrive at Home and at School*, 2009
Karen L. J. Isaacson, *Life in the Fast Brain: Keeping Up With Gifted Minds*, 2007
Eric Jensen, *Enriching the Brain: How to Maximize Every Learner's Potential*, 2008
David Palmer, *Parent's Guide to IQ Testing and Gifted Education*, 2006
Judy Willis, *Inspiring Middle School Minds: Gifted, Creative and Challenging*, 2009

620

JULIE STACHOWIAK

The Multiple Sclerosis Manifesto: Action to Take, Principles to Live By
(New York: Demos Medical, 2010)

Subject(s): Multiple sclerosis; Health; Medical care

Summary: In *The Multiple Sclerosis Manifesto: Action to Take, Principles to Live By*, author, physician, and multiple sclerosis (MS) patient Julia Stachowiak guides fellow patients through the ups and downs of life with this challenging disease. Stachowiak draws on her own experiences to offer readers a manual for tackling everything concerns and for building mental and physical strength. An appendix details resources recommended by the National Multiple Sclerosis Society. This volume also includes a bibliography and an index.

Other books by the same author:
The Diabetes Manifesto: Take Charge of Your Life, 2011

Other books you might like:
Allen C. Bowling, *Complementary and Alternative Medicine and Multiple Sclerosis*, 2006
Jeffrey N. Gingold, *Facing the Cognitive Challenges of Multiple Sclerosis*, 2006
Randall T. Schapiro, *Managing the Symptoms of Multiple Sclerosis*, 2007
Shelley Peterman Schwarz, *Multiple Sclerosis: 300 Tips for Making Life Easier*, 2006
Howard L. Weiner, *Curing MS: How Science Is Solving the Mysteries of Multiple Sclerosis*, 2005

621

STEPHEN M. STAHL

The Prescriber's Guide, 3rd Edition
(New York: Cambridge University Press, 2009)

Subject(s): Health; Drugs; Medical care

Summary: In *The Prescriber's Guide, 3rd Edition*, Stephen

M. Stahl updates his authoritative directory of over 100 psychotrophic drugs. Each drug is listed alphabetically by its generic name—acamprosate to zuclopenthixol—with each entry providing information on the drug's therapeutic applications, use and dosage, related side effects, considerations for specific populations, and pearls. Written as an accessible reference for physicians, Stahl's formulary is comprehensive and easy to use. The third edition includes seven new entries, and provides applicable regulation revisions and indications. Indices include listings by drug name, class, and use, as well as listings of FDA-approved drugs and FDA recommendations for use during pregnancy.

Where it's reviewed:
Journal of Child and Adolescent Psychopharmacology, December 2009, page 795

Other books by the same author:
Stahl's Illustrated Anxiety, Stress, and PTSD, 2010
Stahl's Illustrated Antipsychotics, 2009
Depression and Bipolar Disorder, 2008
Stahl's Essential Psychopharmacology Online: Print and Online, 2008

Other books you might like:
Elaine M. Aldred, *Pharmacology: A Handbook for Complementary Healthcare Professionals*, 2008
Kathleen C. M. Campbell, *Pharmacology and Ototoxicity for Audiologists*, 2006
Barbara H. Roberts, *Treating And Beating Heart Disease: A Consumer's Guide To Cardiac Medicines*, 2008
Jean M. Wible, *Drug Handbook for Massage Therapists*, 2008
Michael E. Winter, *Basic Clinical Pharmacokinetics, Fifth Edition*, 2009

622

RANDALL C. STARLING

The Cleveland Clinic Guide to Heart Failure

(New York: Kaplan, 2009)

Subject(s): Health; Medicine; Medical care

Summary: In *The Cleveland Clinic Guide to Heart Failure*, cardiologist Randall C. Starling offers practical advice for dealing with heart failure and its aftermath. Starling first provides readers with the basics of heart failure, including causes of the condition and available tests and treatments. The book's subsequent chapters consider a range of heart failure scenarios, including heart transplant, the use of beta-blockers, life-support therapy, the Dor procedure, and cardiac resynchronization. In each of these chapters, the author accompanies the medical information related to the topic with a patient's relevant personal story, giving readers solid data as well as encouragement.

Other books you might like:
Susan Elliot-Wright, *Living with Heart Failure*, 2006
Michael McIvor, *Living With Heart Failure: The Patient's Essential Guide*, 2011

Brendan Phibbs, *The Human Heart: A Basic Guide to Heart Disease, 2nd Edition*, 2007
Campion Quinn, *100 Questions and Answers About Congestive Heart Failure*, 2005
David Wilber, *Electrical Therapy for Heart Failure*, 2011

623

ELIZABETH A. STEWART

Uterine Fibroids: The Complete Guide

(Baltimore, Maryland: Johns Hopkins University Press, 2007)

Story type: Medical
Subject(s): Health; Medical care; Women

Summary: *Uterine Fibroids: The Complete Guide* by Elizabeth A. Stewart is a guide for women who are suffering from painful uterine fibroids, benign tumors that can lead to extremely heavy bleeding during menstruation, bloating, severe pain, and even infertility. Stewart explains that although uterine fibroids are not cancerous, often the only treatment plan to remove them in the past was a complete hysterectomy. Stewart states that this does not need to be the case; she first thoroughly discusses what fibroids are— illustrated with diagrams— and then considers alternative treatments to surgery, including uterine artery embolization (UAE), noninvasive focused ultrasound (FUS), and alternative therapies such as hormone treatments. Stewart asserts that women should become informed about the condition and should explore all avenues of treatment possibilities before resorting to hysterectomy.

Where it's reviewed:
Library Journal, Nov 1, 2007, page 90

Other books you might like:
Georgette Maria Delvaux, *A Barefoot Doctors Guide for Women*, 2007
Tori Hudson, *Womens Encyclopedia of Natural Medicine: Alternative Therapies and Integrative Medicine for Total Health and Wellness*, 2007
Christiane Northrup, *Women's Bodies, Women's Wisdom*, 1994
Marie Savard, *Ask Dr. Marie: What Women Need to Know About Hormones, Libido, and the Medical Problems No One Talks About*, 2010
Linda Woolven, *The Smart Woman's Guide to PMS and Pain-Free Periods*, 2008

624

WILLIAM STILLMAN

Empowered Autism Parenting: Celebrating (and Defending) Your Child's Place in the World

(San Francisco, California: Jossey-Bass, 2009)

Story type: Medical
Subject(s): Parent-child relations; Health; Medical care

Summary: Written by author, advocate, and autism expert William Stillman, *Empowered Autism Parenting: Celebrating (and Defending) Your Child's Place in the World* is an educational and inspirational guide for parents of children with autism. In this book, Stillman addresses parents, teachers, and caregivers of autistic children to encourage and inspire them to learn to appreciate and value their autistic child's unique personality and gifts. *Empowered Autism Parenting* is a practical resource that strives to help parents see the intellect and passions of their autistic child, increase and deepen effective communication between parents and child, encourage appreciation and gratefulness for autistic child's behaviors and personality, and dissuade parents from pursuing traditional medical treatments for autism.

Other books by the same author:
The Autism Prophecies, 2010
The Everything Parent's Guide to Children with Asperger's Syndrome, 2010
Demystifying the Autistic Experience, 2009
The Autism Answer Book: More Than 300 of the Top Questions Parents Ask, 2007

Other books you might like:
Temple Grandin, *Thinking in Pictures: And Other Reports from My Life with Autism*, 1995
Carol Gray, *The New Social Story Book*, 2010
Julia Moor, *Playing, Laughing and Learning with Children on the Autism Spectrum: A Practical Resource of Play Ideas for Parents and Carers*, 2002
Chantal Sicile-Kira, *Autism Life Skills*, 2008
Leeann Whiffen, *A Child's Journey Out of Autism: One Family's Story of Living in Hope and Finding a Cure*, 2009

625

KYOUNGHO SUK

Research Focus on Natural Products and the Body's Immune and Inflammatory Systems

(New York: Nova Biomedical Books, 2007)

Subject(s): Biology; Science; Diseases

Summary: In *Research Focus on Natural Products and the Body's Immune and Inflammatory Systems*, editor Kyoungho Suk brings together a series of essays examining the impact of products deemed "all natural" on key systems of the human body. Experts on this subject contribute essays scientific findings the possible therapeutic benefits of natural products. Titles in this volume include "Pharmacological Activity of Natural Products in Vitro and in Animal Models of Parkinson's Disease and Depression," "Oriental Medicine in Cerebral Infarction," and "Anti-allergic Natural Products." *Research Focus on Natural Products and the Body's Immune and Inflammatory Systems* contains a bibliography and an index.

Other books you might like:
Casey Adams, *Oral Probiotics: The Newest Way to*

Prevent Infection, Boost the Immune System and Fight Disease, 2010
Elaine M. Aldred, *Pharmacology: A Handbook for Complementary Healthcare Professionals*, 2008
Elizabeth Lipski, *Digestive Wellness for Children: How to Strengthen the Immune System and Prevent Disease Through Healthy Digestion*, 2006
Joseph C. Maroon, *Fish Oil: The Natural Anti-Inflammatory*, 2010

626

CHERYLE SULLIVAN

Brain Injury Survival Kit: 365 Tips, Tools and Tricks to Deal with Cognitive Function Loss

(New York: Demos Medical, 2008)

Subject(s): Memory disorders; Accidents; Healing

Summary: Traumatic brain injuries have become more and more common in recent years. Despite this fact, research and funding for brain injuries remains shockingly subpar. In *Brain Injury Survival Kit: 365 Tips, Tools and Tricks to Deal with Cognitive Function Loss*, Dr. Cheryle Sullivan guides survivors through the stages of recovery and offers tips, insights, and professional advice on how to reenter the world. As a brain injury survivor herself, Dr. Sullivan is able to provide firsthand knowledge on the subject, as well as a physician's clinical perspective. Topics include time management, handling memory issues, and organization techniques. *Brain Injury Survival Kit* contains a full index.

Other books you might like:
John W. Cassidy, *Mindstorms: Living with Traumatic Brain Injury*, 2009
Norman Doidge, *The Brain That Changes Itself: Stories of Personal Triumph from the Frontiers of Brain Science*, 2007
William W. Orrison Jr., *Atlas of Brain Function, 2nd Edition*, 2008
Richard C. Senelickm, *Living with Brain Injury: A Guide for Families*, 2010
Barbara Zoltan, *Vision, Perception, and Cognition: A Manual for the Evaluation and Treatment of the Adult with Acquired Brain Injury*, 2007

627

GARY TAUBES

Good Calories, Bad Calories: Fats, Carbs, and the Controversial Science of Diet and Health

(New York: Knopf, 2008)

Story type: Medical
Subject(s): Nutrition; Health; Science

Summary: *Good Calories, Bad Calories: Fats, Carbs, and the Controversial Science of Diet and Health* is an informative and comprehensive guide to nutrition and health from award-winning science writer, Gary Taubes. In the book, Taubes argues that good health, fitness, and weight management are the result of the kind of calories consumed, not the number of calories. He explains the difference between good and bad calories, focusing on the benefits of eating natural foods and foods low in carbohydrates, while avoiding foods that are high in sugar, starch, and refined carbs. *Good Calories, Bad Calories* outlines the dangers of unhealthy foods, the keys to losing weight, and the foods that contribute to heart disease, cancer, Alzheimer's, and other chronic conditions.

Where it's reviewed:
Inform, October 2008, page 696
Journal of American Physicians and Surgeons, Fall 2009, page 92

Other books by the same author:
Why We Get Fat: And What to Do About It, 2010
The Diet Delusion: Challenging the Conventional Wisdom on Diet, Weight Loss and Disease, 2008

Other books you might like:
Larry McCleary, *Feed Your Brain Lose Your Belly*, 2010
Barry Sears, *Toxic Fat: When Good Fat Turns Bad*, 2008
Mark Sisson, *The Primal Blueprint*, 2009
Lynn Sonberg, *The Complete Good Fat/ Bad Fat, Carb and Calorie Counter*, 2007

628

JILL BOLTE TAYLOR

My Stroke of Insight: A Brain Scientist's Personal Journey

(New York: Viking, 2008)

Subject(s): Human Behavior; Mothers and Daughters; Rehabilitation

Summary: Harvard-trained brain scientist Jill Bolte Taylor suffered a massive stroke at the age of 37 when a blood vessel ruptured in the left side of her brain. As a neuroanatomist, she had a professional understanding of what was happening inside her brain at the time, and discovered profound differences between the activity taking place in the right and left hemispheres. As the function of the left brain declined, Jill became incapable of speaking, walking, reading, or remembering. As part of her brain was deteriorating, the scientist found that the right hemisphere was capable of creating extraordinary euphoria. With the help of her mother, Jill recovered after eight years of rehabilitation. In *My Stroke of Insight: A Brain Scientist's Personal Journey*, Jill recounts her struggle and recovery. She includes practical advice for those recovering from stroke and motivation for those wishing to tap into the vast amount of power locked inside their brains.

Where it's reviewed:
AudioFile Magazine, Feb-March 2009, page 35

Journal of Psychiatry & Law, Summer-Fall 2009, page 317
The New England Journal of Medicine, December 18, 2008, page 2736
Townsend Letter, June 2009, page 96

Other books you might like:
Jan Garavaglia, *How Not to Die: Surprising Lessons on Living Longer, Safer, and Healthier from America's Favorite Medical Examiner*, 2008
Valerie Greene, *Conquering Stroke: How I Fought My Way Back and How You Can Too*, 2008
Sanjay Gupta, *Cheating Death: The Doctors and Medical Miracles That Are Saving Lives Against All Odds*, 2009
Peter G. Levine, *Stronger After Stroke: Your Roadmap to Recovery*, 2008
Olajide Williams, *Stroke Diaries: A Guide for Survivors and Their Families*, 2010

629

JACOB TEITELBAUM

From Fatigued to Fantastic: A Clinically Proven Program to Regain Vibrant Health and Overcome Chronic Fatigue and Fibromyalgia, 3rd Edition

(New York: Avery, 2007)

Story type: Medical
Subject(s): Medical care; Diseases; Health

Summary: In *From Fatigued to Fantastic: A Clinically Proven Program to Regain Vibrant Health and Overcome Chronic Fatigue and Fibromyalgia, 3rd Edition*, Dr. Jacob Teitelbaum provides readers with a comprehensive and practical guide to understanding and managing fatigue-related illness. Over 25 million Americans suffer from chronic fatigue, fibromyalgia, and other related illnesses. In *From Fatigued to Fantastic*, Teitelbaum draws on his 30+ years of experience to equip individuals with the knowledge to overcome their conditions. He instructs readers on how to assess their symptoms, diagnose their problems and treat their fatigue-related illness. The book provides personalized treatment options, including information on prescription and over-the-counter medicines, nutritional supplements, alternative treatments, and dietary recommendations.

Where it's reviewed:
Total Health, November 2007, page p18
Townsend Letter, Feburary-March 2008, page p114

Other books by the same author:
Pain Free 1-2-3: A Proven Program for Eliminating Chronic Pain Now, 2005

Other books you might like:
Martha E. Kilcoyne, *Defeat Chronic Fatigue Syndrome*, 2007

Deirdre Rawlings, *Food that Helps Win the Battle Against Fibromyalgia*, 2008

630

HOLLY THACKER

The Cleveland Clinic Guide to Menopause

(New York: Kaplan Publishing, 2009)

Subject(s): Menopause; Women; Reference works

Summary: In *The Cleveland Clinic Guide to Menopause*, Holly Thacker provides an accessible, comprehensive guide designed to help women deal with and minimize the symptoms of menopause and ensure their continued good health for the future. Thacker discusses various commonly used treatments for the symptoms of menopause, such as hormone therapy, antidepressants, and herbal supplements, and examines their safety and potential side effects. In addition, Thacker offers tips for improving sleep and increasing both overall energy and sex drive. The guide includes general information for staying healthy before, during, and after menopause, such as maintaining a regular diet and exercise program to prevent osteoporosis, cardiovascular disease, cancer, and other illnesses that often strike post-menopausal women.

Other books by the same author:
Women's Health: Your Body, Your Hormones, Your Choices, 2007

Other books you might like:
Amanda McQuade Crawford, *The Natural Menopause Handbook*, 2009
Julia Schlam Edelman, *Menopause Matters: Your Guide to a Long and Healthy Life*, 2010
Staness Jonekos, *The Menopause Makeover*, 2010
Christiane Northrup, *The Secret Pleasures of Menopause*, 2008
Christiane Northrup, *The Wisdom of Menopause: Creating Physical and Emotional Health and Healing During the Change, 2nd Ed.*, 2007

631

MALCOLM S. THALER

The Only EKG Book You'll Ever Need, Sixth Edition

(Philadelphia, Pennsylvania: Lippincott Williams & Wilkins, 2009)

Story type: Medical
Subject(s): Heart diseases; Medical care; Technology

Summary: *The Only EKG Book You'll Ever Need, Sixth Edition* by Malcolm S. Thaler is written for clinicians using electrocardiography. Using real-world cases and a number of illustrated examples, including 200 printed EKG readouts, Thaler describes how to interpret the information and how to apply that knowledge. Thaler specifically discusses cardiovascular issues such as hy-

pertrophy and enlargement, arrhythmias, conduction blocks, pre-excitation syndromes, and myocardial infarctions, providing examples for the way each will appear on an EKG readout. This book is written in an informal, readable style intended to make the information easily understandable.

Other books you might like:
Peggy Jenkins, *Nurse to Nurse ECG Interpretation*, 2009
Shirley A. Jones, *ECG Notes: Interpretation and Management Guide*, 2009
Shirley A. Jones, *ECG Success: Exercises in ECG Interpretation*, 2007
Tom Kenny, *The Nuts and bolts of Paced ECG Interpretation*, 2009
George A. Stouffer, *Practical ECG Interpretation: Clues to Heart Disease in Young Adults*, 2009

632

GIUDITTA TORNETTA

Painless Childbirth: An Empowering Journey Through Pregnancy and Childbirth

(Nashville, Tennessee: Cumberland House, 2008)

Subject(s): Pregnancy; Labor; Health

Summary: In *Painless Childbirth: An Empowering Journey Through Pregnancy and Childbirth*, respected doula Giuditta Tornetta advises women on the healthiest and most painless ways to carry and deliver a new baby. Tornetta addresses the various obstacles that arise both during pregnancy and during the childbirth process. Her wisdom, gleaned from her own experience and her years as a doula, guides women through the challenges of childbearing to embrace the entire experience with understanding and gratitude. *Painless Childbirth* includes an appendix and notes on the text.

Where it's reviewed:
Midwifery Today, Spring 2009, page 60

Other books you might like:
Tina Cassidy, *Birth: The Surprising History of How We Are Born*, 2007
Mark Sloan, *Birth Day: A Pediatrician Explores the Science, the History, and the Wonder of Childbirth*, 2009
Denise Spatafora, *Better Birth: The Ultimate Guide to Childbirth from Home Births to Hospitals*, 2009
Henry Smith Williams, *Twilight Sleep: A Simple Account of New Discoveries in Painless Childbirth*, 2010
Jacqueline H. Wolf, *Deliver Me from Pain: Anesthesia and Birth in America*, 2009

633

ARI TUCKMAN

Integrative Treatment for Adult ADHD: A Practical, Easy-to-Use Guide for Clinicians

(Oakland, California: New Harbinger Publications, 2007)

Subject(s): Health; Medical care; Psychology

Summary: In *Integrative Treatment for Adult ADHD: A Practical, Easy-to-Use Guide for Clinicians*, psychologist Ari Tuckman presents a valuable resource for mental health professionals. The informative guide covers topics such as the diagnosis of Attention Deficit Disorder in adults, the physiology of ADHD, and special issues related to adult ADHD. Tuckman also describes the range of treatments available to the adult patients, including medication, education, psychotherapy, and coaching. Informative and accessible, *Integrative Treatment for Adult ADHD* is written especially for mental health care providers seeking fast and effective treatment methods. Tuckman, a clinical psychologist, is a recognized authority in the field of ADHD treatment.

Where it's reviewed:
Psychiatric Times, April 2008, page 62

Other books by the same author:
More Attention, Less Deficit: Success Strategies for Adults with ADHD, 2009

Other books you might like:
Russell A. Barkley, *ADHD in Adults*, 2009
Russell A. Barkley, *Taking Charge of Adult ADHD*, 2010
Jennifer Koretsky, *Odd One Out: The Maverick's Guide to Adult ADD*, 2007
Melissa Orlov, *The ADHD Effect on Marriage: Understand and Rebuild Your Relationship in Six Steps*, 2010
Nancy A. Ratey, *The Disorganized Mind: Coaching Your ADHD Brain to Take Control of Your Time, Tasks, and Talents*, 2008

634

BERNARD J. TURNOCK

Essentials of Public Health

(Sudbury, Massachusetts: Jones and Bartlett Publishers, 2007)

Subject(s): Health; Medical professions; Employment

Summary: In *Essentials of Public Health*, Dr. Bernard J. Turnock offers a detailed overview of public health and how it functions. Turnock investigates the typical public health structure and the pivotal roles it plays in the health of society, as well as the responsibilities of government at varying levels. This volume further examines the subject by looking at employment opportunities in this field and how they fit within the framework of the modern healthcare industry. *Essentials of Public Health* includes a glossary and a full index.

Other books by the same author:
Public Health: What It Is and How It Works, 2008
Public Health: Career Choices That Make a Difference, 2006

Other books you might like:
Mark Cameron Edberg, *Essentials of Health Behavior: Social and Behavorial Theory in Public Health*, 2007
Richard K. Riegelman, *Public Health 101: Healthy People - Healthy Populations*, 2010
Mary-Jane Schneider, *Introduction to Public Health*, 2010
Beth Seltzer, *101 Careers in Public Health*, 2010
Richard L. Skolnik, *Essentials of Global Health*, 2007

635

GERALD W. VOLCHECK

Clinical Allergy: Diagnosis and Management

(Totowa, New Jersey: Humana, 2008)

Story type: Medical
Subject(s): Medical care; Allergy; Health

Summary: Written by Gerald W. Volcheck, *Clinical Allergy: Diagnosis and Management* is a comprehensive examination and straightforward resource guide on allergic diseases and disorders. Nearly a quarter of the population suffers from allergic diseases. This book provides a thorough overview of the various types of allergic disorders, including information about the immune system, environmental allergens, and various ways to test for allergies. Common allergic conditions, such as rhinitis and rhinosinusitis, allergic eye disease, asthma, urticaria and angioedema, atopic and contact dermatitis, drug allergy, food allergy, anaphylaxis, and stinging insect allergy, are outlined in detail. *Clinical Allergy* also provides insight and practical advice on diagnosing and treating allergic conditions.

Where it's reviewed:
JAMA, The Journal of the American Medical Association, April 8, 2009, page1486

Other books you might like:
Alisa Marie Fleming, *Go Dairy Free*, 2008
Elizabeth Gordon, *Allergy Free Desserts: Gluten-free, Dairy-free, Egg-free, Soy-free and Nut-free Delights*, 2010
Janice M. Vickerstaff Joneja, *Dealing with Food Allergies in Babies and Children*, 2007
Massoud Mahmoudi, *Allergy and Asthma: Practical Diagnosis and Management*, 2007
Kelly Rudnicki, *The Food Allergy Mama's Baking Book: Great Dairy-, Egg-, and Nut-Free Treats for the Whole Family*, 2009

Health and Wellness

636

MARSDEN WAGNER

Born in the USA: How a Broken Maternity System Must Be Fixed to Put Women and Children First

(Berkeley, California: University of California Press, 2006)

Story type: Medical
Subject(s): Health; Medical care; Pregnancy

Summary: Written by award-winning physician, scientist, and author Marsden Wagner, *Born in the USA: How a Broken Maternity System Must Be Fixed to Put Women and Children First* is a critical examination of hospital care for pregnant women and newborns in America. Wagner analyzes the state of the United States' medical care system for pregnancy and childbirth and raises legitimate concerns over the well-being of women and babies. In *Born in the USA*, Wagner addresses the rise in risky behaviors and prescription drugs, the use of midwives and at-home births, and the processes required to become a doctor. Wagner encourages parents, obstetricians, nurses, midwives, scientists, and insurance agents to regain control over the American maternity system to prevent the continuation of dangerous practices and dire results.

Where it's reviewed:
Feminist Collections: A Quarterly of Women's Studies Resources, Summer-Fall 2008, page 1

Other books by the same author:
Creating Your Birth Plan: The Definitive Guide to a Safe and Empowering Birth, 2006

Other books you might like:
Jennifer Block, *Pushed: The Painful Truth About Childbirth and Modern Maternity Care*, 2007
Tina Cassidy, *Birth: The Surprising History of How We Are Born*, 2007
Melissa Cheyney, *Born at Home: The Biological, Cultural and Political Dimensions of Maternity Care in the United States*, 2010
Nicette Jukelevics, *Understanding the Dangers of Cesarean Birth: Making Informed Decisions*, 2008
Rosemary Mander, *Caesarean: Just Another Way of Birth?*, 2007

637

DANIEL J. WALLACE

The Lupus Book: A Guide for Patients and Their Families, Fourth Edition

(New York: Oxford University Press, 2008)

Story type: Medical
Subject(s): Health; Diseases; Medical care

Summary: *The Lupus Book: A Guide for Patients and Their Families, Fourth Edition* by Daniel J. Wallace

explains the condition and some of the earliest symptoms—which are often misdiagnosed, leading to years of frustration, pain, and often permanent damage to organs before a correct diagnosis is made. Wallace explains the immunological response to lupus in the body and the way it impacts the rest of the body systems, in addition to detailed information regarding potential causes and genetic determinants of lupus, treatment and management options, and anecdotal stories from patients who share information about living a satisfying life with the condition. There are a number of illustrations as well as diagrams and charts provided in this text.

Other books by the same author:
Lupus: The Essential Clinician's Guide, 2008
Dubois' Lupus Erythematosus, 2006
The New Sjogren's Syndrome Handbook, 2006
Fibromyalgia and Other Central Pain Syndromes, 2005

Other books you might like:
Norma J. Bogetto, *Lupus: My View After 35 Years*, 2009
Sara Gorman, *Despite Lupus: How to Live Well with a Chronic Illness*, 2009
Jill Harrington, *The Lupus Recovery Diet*, 2007
Robert G. Lahita, *Systemic Lupus Erythematosus*, 2010
Ana I. Quintero del Rio, *Lupus: A Patient's Guide to Diagnosis, Treatment, and Lifestyle*, 2006

638

STEPHEN WANGEN

Healthier Without Wheat: A New Understanding of Wheat Allergies, Celiac Disease, and Non-Celiac Gluten Intolerance

(Seattle, Washington: Innate Health Publishing, 2009)

Subject(s): Allergy; Food; Health

Summary: *Healthier without Wheat: A New Understanding of Wheat Allergies, Celiac Disease, and Non-Celiac Gluten Intolerance* by Stephen Wangen is an informative resource about wheat and gluten allergies and intolerance. As the text explains, bread, pasta, and other wheat-based foods can cause a range of physical symptoms, including abdominal pain, anemia, diarrhea, constipation, irritable bowel syndrome, fibromyalgia, autoimmune disease, fatigue, depression, and irritability. The author describes the various conditions that precipitate wheat intolerance, including celiac disease, non-celiac gluten intolerance, and wheat allergies. The book also describes the unique characteristics of each ailment. Information on identifying wheat intolerance in babies and young children is also included.

Where it's reviewed:
Library Journal, Feb 15, 2009, page 125

Other books by the same author:
The Irritable Bowel Syndrome Solution: How It's Cured at the IBS Treatment Center, 2006

Other books you might like:
Carol Lee Fenster, *Gluten-Free Quick and Easy*, 2007
Jaqui Karr, *Celiac Disease: Safe/Unsafe Food List and*

Essential Information On Living With A Gluten Free Diet, 2010

Robert M. Landolphi, *Gluten Free Every Day Cookbook*, 2009

Jules E. Dowler Shepard, *The First Year: Celiac Disease and Living Gluten-Free: An Essential Guide for the Newly Diagnosed*, 2008

Kimberly A. Tessmer, *Tell Me What to Eat If I Have Celiac Disease: Nutrition You Can Live With*, 2009

639

ANDREW WEIL

Why Our Health Matters: A Vision of Medicine That Can Transform Our Future

(New York: Hudson Street Press, 2009)

Story type: Medical
Subject(s): Health; Medical care; Politics

Summary: In *Why Our Health Matters: A Vision of Medicine That Can Transform Our Future*, Andrew Weil takes on the current state of health care in the United States, elucidating the areas in which reform needs to take place. Weil states that most people perceive American medicine as some of the best in the world, but in fact the country is ranked 37th among all other nations. He states that training for physicians needs to be adjusted so they can provide better care for patients, and that insurance and pharmaceutical companies are standing in the way of a health care system that could benefit all Americans. Weil proposes a number of solutions for improving health care in America, among them a universal policy subsidized by the government.

Where it's reviewed:
Library Journal, January 2010, page 64

Other books by the same author:
Life Over Cancer: The Block Center Program for Integrative Cancer Treatment, 2009
Healthy Aging: A Lifelong Guide to Your Well-Being, 2007

Other books you might like:
Michael Arloski, *Wellness Coaching for Lasting Lifestyle Change*, 2007
Bernard J. Turnock, *Essentials of Public Health*, 2007

640

ROBIN ELISE WEISS

The Better Way to Breastfeed: The Latest, Most Effective Ways to Feed and Nurture Your Baby with Comfort and Ease

(Minneapolis, Minnesota: Fair Winds Press, 2010)

Subject(s): Infants; Mothers; Parent-child relations
Summary: In *The Better Way to Breastfeed: The Latest,*

Most Effective Ways to Feed and Nurture Your Baby with Comfort and Ease, breastfeeding and child care expert Robin Elise Weiss explains how to properly nurse and nurture babies. With checklists and informative photographs and illustrations, Weiss shows new and experienced mothers alike how to overcome any challenges they may encounter while nursing their young children. These challenges include improper latching, inadequate milk supply, and even sore nipples. Sections of this book titled "Confidence Cues" and "Mama Moments" also provide mothers with important information about forming lasting relationships with their newborns through the breastfeeding process.

Where it's reviewed:
Library Journal, September 1, 2010, page 126

Other books by the same author:
The Complete Illustrated Pregnancy Companion, 2009
Everything Guide to Raising Adolescent Boys, 2008
Guarantee the Sex of Your Baby, 2006

Other books you might like:
Eileen Behan, *Eat Well, Lose Weight, While Breastfeeding*, 2007
Catherine Watson Genna, *Supporting Sucking Skills in Breastfeeding Infants*, 2007
Stacey H. Rubin, *The ABCs of Breastfeeding*, 2008
April Rudat, *Oh Yes You Can Breastfeed Twins!*, 2007
Joan B. Wolf, *Is Breast Best?*, 2011

641

RUTH WERNER

Disease Handbook for Massage Therapists

(Baltimore: Lippincott Williams & Wilkins, 2010)

Story type: Collection
Subject(s): Medical professions; Medical care; Medicine

Summary: The *Disease Handbook for Massage Therapists*, which is edited by Ruth Werner, is a quick reference guide for massage therapists who treat patients with illnesses. When massage therapists treat patients, they have to keep in mind all the patient's other ailments. Because of other ailments or disorders, massage therapists might have to treat their patients differently. This book includes information about hundreds of diseases massage therapists most commonly encounter in their patients. This information includes signs, symptoms, and treatment options for hundreds of diseases and conditions. The information in this book is presented in alphabetical order.

Where it's reviewed:
Massage Therapy Journal, Spring 2010, page 82

Other books by the same author:
A Massage Therapist's Guide to Pathology, 2008

Other books you might like:
Susan G. Salvo, *Massage Therapy*, 2007
Diana L. Thompson, *Hands Heal*, 2007
Jean M. Wible, *Drug Handbook for Massage Therapists*, 2008

642

JOHN B. WEST

Pulmonary Pathophysiology: The Essentials, Seventh Edition

(Philadelphia, Pennsylvania: Lippincott Williams & Wilkins, 2007)

Subject(s): Health; Medical care; Medicine

Summary: In *Pulmonary Pathophysiology: The Essentials, Seventh Edition*, John B. West updates his text on diseases of the lung. Written for medical students and health care professionals, *Pulmonary Pathophysiology* is organized into three parts—Lung Function Tests and What They Mean, Function of the Diseased Lung, and Function of the Failing Lung. The text covers such topics as ventilation, gas exchange, and other pulmonary tests; obstruction, restrictive, and vascular diseases; and respiratory failure, oxygen therapy, and mechanical ventilation. Each chapter contains study questions, with answers provided in the appendix. *Pulmonary Pathophysiology* was written as a companion to *West's Respiratory Physiology*.

Where it's reviewed:
Respiratory Care, July 2008, page 923

Other books by the same author:
Respiratory Physiology: The Essentials, 2008
High Altitude Medicine and Physiology, 2007
Pulmonary Physiology and Pathophysiology, 2007

Other books you might like:
Michael G. Levitzky, *Pulmonary Physiology, 7th Edition*, 2007
Paul Ellis Marik, *Handbook of Evidence-Based Critical Care*, 2010
David Proud, *The Pulmonary Epithelium in Health and Disease*, 2008
Edward Ringel, *Little Black Book of Pulmonary Medicine*, 2008
Anika K. Simonds, *Non Invasive Respiratory Support: A Practical Handbook*, 2007

643

LEEANN WHIFFEN

A Child's Journey Out of Autism: One Family's Story of Living in Hope and Finding a Cure

(Naperville, Illinois: Sourcebooks, Inc., 2009)

Subject(s): Diseases; Family; Medical care

Summary: When Leeann and Sean Whiffen's son Clay was diagnosed with autism, they set out to ensure their son had the best care available and the best life possible. In *A Child's Journey Out of Autism: One Family's Story of Living in Hope and Finding a Cure*, Leeann recounts her family's remarkable story, from their initial denial of Clay's condition to their fearless advocacy and the therapeutic program that eventually changed Clay's life.

The treatment known as Applied Behavior Analysis would, in the end, not only eradicate Clay's diagnosis, but it would also give the entire Whiffen family a new lease on life.

Where it's reviewed:
Booklist, March 1, 2009, page 12
The Exceptional Parent, April 2009, page 10
Publishers Weekly, January 12, 2009, page 38

Other books you might like:
Audra Jensen, *When Babies Read: A Practical Guide to Helping Young Children with Hyperlexia, Asperger Syndrome and High-Functioning Autism*, 2005
Ellen Notbohm, *Ten Things Every Child with Autism Wishes You Knew*, 2005
William Stillman, *The Autism Answer Book: More Than 300 of the Top Questions Parents Ask*, 2007
William Stillman, *Empowered Autism Parenting: Celebrating (and Defending) Your Child's Place in the World*, 2009

644

ALAN WHITESIDE

HIV/AIDS: A Very Short Introduction

(New York: Oxford University Press, 2008)

Subject(s): AIDS (Disease); Health; Medicine

Summary: In *HIV/AIDS: A Very Short Introduction*, professor and HIV/AIDS expert Alan Whiteside addresses the past, present, and future of this tragic epidemic. Whiteside views the subject through a variety of lenses, from the scientific and clinical sides of the disease to its impact on individuals, communities, politics, and the future of civilization. This volume contains illustrations, tables, a bibliography, and an index.

Where it's reviewed:
The Economist, May 3, 2008, page 92

Other books by the same author:
A Decade of HAART: The Development and Global Impact of Highly Active Antiretroviral Therapy, 2008
The HIV Pandemic: Local and Global Implications, 2008
AIDS and Governance, 2007
AIDS in the Twenty-First Century, Fully Revised and Updated Edition: Disease and Globalization, 2006

Other books you might like:
Helen Epstein, *The Invisible Cure: Africa, the West, and the Fight Against AIDS*, 2007
Celia Farber, *Serious Adverse Events: An Uncensored History of AIDS*, 2006
Jay A. Levy, *HIV and the Pathogenesis of AIDS*, 2007
Stephanie Nolen, *28: Stories of AIDS in Africa*, 2007
Randy Shilts, *And the Band Played On: Politics, People, and the AIDS Epidemic*, 1987

645

EELCO F.M. WIJDICKS

The Comatose Patient

(New York: Oxford University Press, USA, 2008)

Story type: Medical
Subject(s): Medical care; Medical professions; Medicine
Summary: In *The Comatose Patient*, Eelco F.M. Wijdicks explains a new approach to treating and examining comatose patients. This approach, called the FOUR Score, allows medical professionals to determine the status of comatose patients using a coma scale. Wijdicks includes information about diagnosing comatose patients using breathing patterns and neuroimaging. He also tackles complicated issues like communicating with comatose patients' family members about end-of-life decisions. This book includes 75 case summaries involving comatose patients, 40 additional cases in which the FOUR Score scale is used, and 200 heavily detailed illustrations.

Where it's reviewed:
Journal of Neuroscience Nursing, December 2008, page 373
Mayo Clinic Proceedings, May/June 2009, page 484
The New England Journal of Medicine, June 12, 2008, page 2653

Other books by the same author:
The Practice of Emergency and Critical Care Neurology, 2010
Neurologic Complications of Critical Illness, 2009
Disorders of Consciousness: Handbook of Clinical Neurology, 2008

Other books you might like:
Jeanne M. Denney, *The Effects of Compassionate Presence on the Dying*, 2008
Kenneth G. Redden, *My Song: Comatose Yet Aware*, 2009
Scott R. Sheaffer, *Comatose Management*, 2009

646

WILLIAM S. WILKE

The Cleveland Clinic Guide to Fibromyalgia

(New York: Kaplan Publishing, 2009)

Subject(s): Health; Reference works; Medical care
Summary: In *The Cleveland Clinic Guide to Fibromyalgia*, William S. Wilke provides a great deal of information for people suffering from fibromyalgia, a condition that is often difficult to diagnose and treat effectively. Wilke describes the disease's symptoms, and he suggests that people who suspect they have fibromyalgia should pursue the correct diagnosis of their condition. He also explains why the disease is so difficult to diagnose. He then discusses various treatment options that may be used from a wide range of sources, and lifestyle changes that can be made to minimize the impact of the disease. In addition, Wilke provides personal stories of people

who have overcome their struggles with fibromyalgia, and he shares information about recent research and promising findings that are currently taking place.

Other books you might like:
Michael C. Hall, *Fibromyalgia Controversy*, 2009
Sharon Ostalecki, *Fibromyalgia: The Complete Guide From Medical Experts and Patients*, 2007
Deirdre Rawlings, *Food that Helps Win the Battle Against Fibromyalgia*, 2008
Shelley Ann Smith, *The Fibromyalgia Cookbook*, 2010
Jacob Teitelbaum, *From Fatigued to Fantastic: A Clinically Proven Program to Regain Vibrant Health and Overcome Chronic Fatigue and Fibromyalgia, 3rd Edition*, 2007

647

OLAJIDE WILLIAMS

Stroke Diaries: A Guide for Survivors and Their Families

(New York: Oxford University Press, 2010)

Subject(s): Health; Medicine; Stroke
Summary: In *Stroke Diaries: A Guide for Survivors and Their Families*, Dr. Olajide Williams offers advice for preventing, surviving, and recovering from stroke. Organized into four parts, "Causes, Prevention, and Emergency Treatment of Stroke," "Unusual and Under-recognized Stroke Syndromes," "Psychosocial and Physical Challenges after Stroke," and "Recovery from Severe Stroke," *Stroke Diaries* features real-life accounts from stroke sufferers and their families, accompanied by relevant clinical comments from the author. Topics include subtypes of stroke, the relationship between drug abuse and stroke, red flag symptoms, the relationship between sleep-disordered breathing and stroke, sex after stroke, stroke in babies, and overcoming caregiver depression.

Other books you might like:
Louis R. Caplan, *Caplan's Stroke: A Clinical Approach, Fourth Edition*, 2009
Valery L. Feigin, *When Lightning Strikes: An Illustrated Guide to Stroke Prevention and Recovery*, 2006
Kinan K. Hreib, *100 Questions and Answers About Stroke*, 2008
Peter G. Levine, *Stronger After Stroke: Your Roadmap to Recovery*, 2008
Jill Bolte Taylor, *My Stroke of Insight: A Brain Scientist's Personal Journey*, 2008

648

MICHAEL E. WINTER

Basic Clinical Pharmacokinetics, Fifth Edition

(Philadelphia, Pennsylvania: Lippincott Williams & Wilkins, 2009)

Story type: Medical
Subject(s): Medical care; Drugs; Medicine
Summary: Written by Michael E. Winter, *Basic Clinical*

Pharmacokinetics, Fifth Edition is a straightforward analysis of pharmacokinetics, the pharmacological field dealing with drug therapy and responses in the body. Written in a case-study format, the book presents clear and concise information about pharmacokinetics intended for medical students, clinical professors, and medical care professionals. The book is broken into two distinct sections. The first part, complete with detailed illustrations and algorithms, provides readers with a thorough understanding of pharmacokinetic principles and terminology. The second part centers on the practical application of these principles and practices, focusing on common clinical issues and problems with drug administration.

Other books you might like:
Larry A. Bauer, *Applied Clinical Pharmacokinetics*, 2008
Andrew Dickman, *Drugs in Palliative Care*, 2010
Steven B. Karch, *Karch's Pathology of Drug Abuse, 4th Edition*, 2008
Stephen M. Stahl, *The Prescriber's Guide, 3rd Edition*, 2009

649

LAWSON R. WULSIN

Treating the Aching Heart: A Guide to Depression, Stress, and Heart Disease

(Nashville, Tennessee: Vanderbilt University Press, 2007)

Subject(s): Heart diseases; Depression (Mood disorder); Medical care

Summary: In *Treating the Aching Heart: A Guide to Depression, Stress, and Heart Disease*, Lawson R. Wulsin considers the links between depression and heart disease; one often begets the other. This book is intended both for medical professionals and for people suffering from heart disease or depression. Wulsin explains how depression makes one more likely to get heart disease, and vice versa, and offers specific tips for patients for who have these problems, helping them become more empowered when speaking with doctors, and requesting complete diagnosis and holistic treatment. Wulsin also discusses the effectiveness of standard and alternative

therapies on heart disease and depression, which might include surgery, medication, light therapy, talk therapy with a psychologist, or stress relief techniques such as exercise or getting a pet. Brief anatomy and physiology facts help to explain certain concepts.

Where it's reviewed:
Library Journal, June 1, 2007, page 142
Publishers Weekly, April 30, 2007, page 149

Other books you might like:
Joseph R. Alila, *Whisper To My Aching Heart*, 2008
Jennifer Brooks, *Embracing An Aching Heart*, 2009
Samuel Hahnemann, *The Chronic Diseases: Their Specific Nature and Homoeopathic Treatment*, 2009

650

NIKHIL YAWALKAR

Management of Psoriasis

(New York: Karger, 2009)

Subject(s): Health; Medicine; Medical care

Summary: In *Management of Psoriasis*, editor Nikhil Yawalkar presents a comprehensive guide to treating psoriasis for dermatologists and other practicing physicians. Written by authorities in the field of dermatology, the text covers a range of issues related to the diagnosis and treatment of psoriasis, including associated comorbitities. Chapters include "Clinical Spectrum and Severity of Psoriasis" by M. Meier and P.B. Sheth; "Practice of Phototherapy in the Treatment of Moderate-to Severe Psoriasis" by T. Nguyen., S. Gatu, R. Pugashetti, and J. Koo; "Therapies for Childhood Psoariasis" by R.M. Trueb; and "Future Perspectives in the Treatment of Psoriasis" by K. Wippel-Slupetzky and G. Stingl.

Other books you might like:
Leslie Baumann, *Cosmetic Dermatology: Principles and Practice, 2nd Edition*, 2009
Charles Camisa, *Handbook of Psoriasis*, 2005
Heather J. Ferris, *Psoriasis Healing from the Inside Out*, 2009
Jerry Johnson, *Healing Your Psoriasis and Psoriatic Arthritis*, 2010
John O. A. Pagano, *Healing Psoriasis: The Natural Alternative*, 2009

History

651

ROSANNE MARION ADDERLEY

New Negroes from Africa: Slave Trade Abolition and Free African Settlement in the Nineteenth-Century Caribbean

(Bloomington, Indiana: Indiana University Press, 2006)

Story type: Historical
Subject(s): Slavery; Abolition of slavery; Colonialism

Summary: *New Negroes from Africa: Slave Trade Abolition and Free African Settlement in the Nineteenth-Century Caribbean* by Rosanne Marion Adderley describes the events that occurred after Britain outlawed slavery in the early 1800s. At the time, many slave ships were heading toward the United States. The ships were either rerouted or the Africans on board were rescued and sent to Britain's Caribbean colonies. As free settlers, they were able to work for pay, become indentured servants, or purchase their own land and have a hand at running their own businesses. Some freed slaves chose to travel to other areas, where they lived among people who had once relied on enslaved Africans to work their lands. In this book, Adderley explains the events that led to the abolition of slavery and what occurred once the slaves were freed.

Where it's reviewed:
American Historical Review, December 2008, page 1587
CHOICE: Current Reviews for Academic Libraries, February 2008, page 1033

Other books you might like:
Kenneth Bilby, *True-Born Maroons*, 2008
Selwyn H.H. Carrington, *The Sugar Industry and the Abolition of Slave Trade, 1775-1810*, 2002
Karla Gottlieb, *The Mother of Us All: A History of Queen Nanny, Leader of the Windward Jamaican Maroons*, 2000
Herbert S. Klein, *African Slavery in Latin America and the Caribbean*, 2007
Rebecca Hartkopf Schloss, *Sweet Liberty: The Final Days of Slavery in Martinique*, 2009

Ben Vinson III, *African Slavery in Latin America and the Caribbean*, 2007

652

LIAQUAT AHAMED

Lords of Finance: The Bankers Who Broke the World

(New York: Penguin Press, 2009)

Subject(s): Finance; Capitalism; Economics

Summary: In *Lords of Finance: The Bankers Who Broke the World*, author Liaquat Ahamed offers a history of difficult pecuniary times in American history. Focusing mainly on the events leading up to the Great Depression, the author singles out the four individuals who contributed to the financial collapse: Mantagu Norman, Amile Moreau, Hjalmar Schacht, and Benjamin Strong. These men were the heads of banks during the 1920s, and their decisions helped to put the United States and the world into economic turmoil. Ahamed looks back on the choices these men made and compares this period in history to the financial state of the world during the early part of the 21st century. Although, in the author's opinion, governments and money depositories have made better decisions than their predecessors did, the world still needs to overcome a large number of hurdles in order to reach financial security.

Where it's reviewed:
Foreign Policy, May-June 2009, page 165

Other books you might like:
Niall Ferguson, *The Ascent of Money: A Financial History of the World*, 2008
Michael Lewis, *The Big Short: Inside the Doomsday Machine*, 2010
Roger Lowenstein, *The End of Wall Street*, 2010
Carmen M. Reinhart, *This Time Is Different: Eight Centuries of Financial Folly*, 2009
  Kenneth Rogoff, co-author
Andrew Ross Sorkin, *Too Big to Fail: The Inside Story of How Wall Street and Washington Fought to Save the Financial System from Crisis—and Lost*, 2009

653

KAREN ARMSTRONG

The Great Transformation: The Beginning of Our Religious Traditions

(New York: Random House, 2006)

Subject(s): Bible; Buddhism; Christianity

Summary: The period between 900 B.C. and 200 B.C. is known to historians as the "axial age." It is the period of time during which the foundations of all the great modern religions were laid. This was the time of the Jewish prophets Elijah and Amos; the time of Confucius; the time of the Buddha; the time of the Greek philosopher Socrates. Karen Armstrong, a scholar of comparative religion, examines this period, describing the cultural upheavals that resulted in the growth of a widely varied group of religious traditions: Judaism, Islam, and Christianity, Hinduism and Buddhism, Taoism and Confucianism. She also examines the things these religions have in common.

Where it's reviewed:
Library Journal, August 1, 2007, page 92

Other books by the same author:
The Case for God, 2009
The Bible: A Biography, 2008
A Short History of Myth, 2006
A History of God: The 4,000-Year Quest of Judaism, Christianity and Islam., 1994

Other books you might like:
Eliza Griswold, *The Tenth Parallel: Dispatches from the Fault Line Between Christianity and Islam*, 2010
Diarmuid McCulloch, *Christ: The First 3,000 Years*, 2010
Stephen R. Prothero, *God Is Not One: The Eight Rival Religions That Run the World—and Why Their Differences Matter*, 2010
James W. Sire, *The Universe Next Door: A Basic Worldview Catalog*, 1997
Huston Smith, *The World's Religions: Our Great Wisdom Traditions*, 1991

654

STEPHEN V. ASH

Firebrand of Liberty: The Story of Two Black Regiments That Changed the Course of the Civil War

(New York: W.W. Norton, 2008)

Subject(s): United States Civil War, 1861-1865; African Americans; Race relations

Summary: Historian Stephen V. Ash tells the story of the First and Second South Carolina regiments, the first all-black brigades in the American Civil War. *Firebrand of Liberty: The Story of Two Black Regiments That Changed the Course of the Civil War* chronicles the formation, combat experiences, and pioneering contributions of these two bands of freed slaves, who rose to defend the nation while dealing with their own marginalized status. This volume includes maps, notes on the text, an appendix, a bibliography, and a full index.

Where it's reviewed:
CHOICE: Current Reviews for Academic Libraries, September 2009, page 2185
Library Journal, April 15, 2008, page 95

Other books by the same author:
Middle Tennessee Society Transformed, 1860-1870: War and Peace in the Upper South, 2006
A Year in the South: 1865: The True Story of Four Ordinary People Who Lived Through the Most Tumultuous Twelve Months in American History, 2004

Other books you might like:
Melvin Claxton, *Uncommon Valor: A Story of Race, Patriotism, and Glory in the Final Battles of the Civil War*, 2005
Dudley Taylor Cornish, *The Sable Arm: Black Troops in the Union Army, 1861-1865*, 1987
Margaret Creighton, *The Colors of Courage: Gettysburg's Forgotten History: Immigrants, Women, and African Americans in the Civil War's Defining Battle*, 2006
Joseph T. Glatthaar, *Forged in Battle: The Civil War Alliance of Black Soldiers and White Officers*, 1990
Mark Puls, *Uncommon Valor: A Story of Race, Patriotism, and Glory in the Final Battles of the Civil War*, 2005
Christian G. Samito, *Becoming American Under Fire: Irish Americans, African Americans, and the Politics of Citizenship During the Civil War Era*, 2009

655

KATHERINE ASHENBURG

The Dirt on Clean: An Unsanitized History

(New York: North Point Press, 2007)

Subject(s): History; Health; Ancient history

Summary: In *The Dirt on Clean: An Unsanitized History*, Katherine Ashenburg explains how views of cleanliness have changed throughout history. In Ancient Rome, people took hour long baths in hot springs, but during the 16th and 17th centuries, men rarely washed their hands, let alone the rest of their bodies. Ashenburg examines what sanitation and hygiene meant to various cultures during different points in time. She compares women's bathing rituals to men's and offers theories as to why people did not support the idea of bathing during certain historical movements. As she describes the sanitation methods and techniques used today, she wonders if perhaps people are now too clean.

Where it's reviewed:
Booklist, November 15, 2007, page 67
Harper's Magazine, April 2008, page 91

Other books by the same author:
The Mourner's Dance: What We Do When People Die, 2003

Other books you might like:
Jean Birrell, *Concepts of Cleanliness: Changing Attitudes in France Since the Middle Ages*, 2008
Emily Cockayne, *Hubbub: Filth, Noise, and Stench in England, 1600-1770*, 2008
Adeline Masquelier, *Dirt, Undress, and Difference: Critical Perspectives on the Body's Surface*, 2005
Virginia Smith, *Clean: A History of Personal Hygiene and Purity*, 2007
Georges Vigarello, *Concepts of Cleanliness: Changing Attitudes in France Since the Middle Ages*, 2008
Fikret K. Yegul, *Bathing in the Roman World*, 2009

656

RICK ATKINSON

The Day of Battle: The War in Sicily and Italy, 1943-1944
(New York: Henry Holt and Co., 2007)

Subject(s): World War II

Summary: In his Liberation Trilogy, Atkinson shows how the U.S. Army changed from a bunch of beginners to a body of well-trained soldiers. In this volume (two), he focuses on the war in Italy, with a special emphasis on the autonomous region of Sicily. Triumphal battles are covered, as well as tragedies caused in great part by mistakes of commanding officers. The author shows how fighting in this area of the Mediterranean, although often overlooked by other scholars, was vital to the Allies' war effort, tying up resources that the Germans would have preferred to use elsewhere.

Where it's reviewed:
Booklist, August 2007, page 26
Library Journal, July 1, 2007, page 102
Publishers Weekly, August 20, 2007, page 35

Other books by the same author:
An Army at Dawn: The War in North Africa, 1942-1943, 2007
In the Company of Soldiers: A Chronicle of Combat, 2005
Crusade: The Untold Story of the Persian Gulf War, 1994

Other books you might like:
Joseph E. Garland, *Unknown Soldiers: Reliving World War II in Europe*, 2008
Ian Gooderson, *A Hard Way to Make a War: The Allied Campaign in Italy in the Second World War*, 2009
Hondon B. Hargrove, *Buffalo Soldiers in Italy: Black Americans in World War II*, 2003
James Holland, *Italy's Sorrow: A Year of War, 1944-1945*, 2008

Edwin Palmer Hoyt, *Backwater War: The Allied Campaign in Italy, 1943-45*, 2007

657

ALAN AXELROD

Patton
(New York: Palgrave Macmillan, 2006)

Subject(s): Biographies; Military science; History

Summary: In *Patton*, historian Alan Axelrod chronicles the personal and military life of General George Patton. Known as "Old Blood and Guts," Patton was as celebrated for his contentious behavior as he was for his military genius. A veteran of World War I and World War II, Patton is credited as the engineer of the critical Battle of the Bulge, but was also reprimanded for his mistreatment of two of his men. In exploring Patton's complex character, Axelrod reveals a military man brilliant in wartime but bored in the absence of conflict. *Patton* is the first book in Palgrave's Great Generals series.

Where it's reviewed:
Booklist, February 1, 2006, page 9
Publishers Weekly, November 28, 2005, page 33

Other books by the same author:
Little-Known Wars of Great and Lasting Impact: The Turning Points in Our History We Should Know More About, 2009
The Real History of the Cold War: A New Look at the Past, 2009
Profiles in Folly: History's Worst Decisions and Why They Went Wrong, 2008
The War Between the Spies: A History of Espionage During the American Civil War, 1992

Other books you might like:
Martin Blumenson, *Patton: The Man Behind the Legend, 1885-1945*, 1994
Terry Brighton, *Patton, Montgomery, Rommel: Masters of War*, 2009
Carlo D'este, *Patton: A Genius for War*, 1996
Ladislas Farago, *Patton: Ordeal and Triumph*, 2005
George Patton, *War as I Knew It*, 1995

658

EIICHIRO AZUMA

Between Two Empires: Race, History, and Transnationalism in Japanese America
(New York: Oxford University Press, 2005)

Subject(s): Japanese Americans; History; Social conditions

Summary: In *Between Two Empires: Race, History, and Transnationalism in Japanese America*, author Eiichiro Azuma examines the complicated issue of Japanese immigration to the United States before World War II. Organized into four parts—"Multiple Beginnings," "Convergences and Divergences," "Pioneers and Successors," and "Complexities of Immigrant Nationalism"—this insightful study discusses the role of early immigrants in American society, the implementation of internment camps, and the complex relationships the Japanese maintained with their motherland and their new country. Azuma reveals a people defined by ancestry and tradition and determined to establish a legitimate place in the culture of America.

Where it's reviewed:
American Historical Review, February 2008, page 194
CHOICE: Current Reviews for Academic Libraries, January 2006, page 915

Other books by the same author:
Before Internment: Essays in Prewar Japanese American History, 2006
In This Great Land of Freedom: The Japanese Pioneers of Oregon, 1993

Other books you might like:
Roger Daniels, *Prisoners Without Trial: Japanese Americans in World War II*, 1993
Lawson Fusao Inada, *Only What We Could Carry: The Japanese American Internment Experience*, 2001
Lon Kurashige, *Japanese American Celebration and Conflict: A History of Ethnic Identity and Festival, 1934-1990*, 2002
Scott Kurashige, *The Shifting Grounds of Race: Black and Japanese Americans in the Making of Multiethnic Los Angeles*, 2010
Paul R. Spickard, *Japanese Americans: The Formation and Transformations of an Ethnic Group*, 2009

659

ZAINAB BAHRANI

Rituals of War: The Body and Violence in Mesopotamia

(New York: Zone Books, 2008)

Subject(s): History; Military science; Social sciences

Summary: In *Rituals of War: The Body and Violence in Mesopotamia*, author Zainab Bahrani explores a range of traditions associated with military conflict in ancient Iraq. In chronicling the region's rituals of violence, the author analyzes the practices of torture, beheading, and disfigurement, as well as the culture's supernatural methods of foretelling battle results and commemorating its war dead through monuments. As Bahrani studies the rituals of war in Mesopotamia from 3000 to 500 B.C.E., she demonstrates their relationship to practices that have persisted to modern-day Iraq, including the validation of violence and ethnic cleansing on religious grounds.

Where it's reviewed:
Times Literary Supplement, October 10, 2008, page 27

Other books by the same author:
The Graven Image: Representation in Babylonia and Assyria, 2003

Women of Babylon: Gender and Representation in Mesopotamia, 2001

Other books you might like:
Peter Heine, *From Mesopotamia to Iraq: A Concise History*, 2009
Gwendolyn Leick, *Mesopotamia*, 2003
Hans J. Nissen, *From Mesopotamia to Iraq: A Concise History*, 2009
A. Leo Oppenheim, *Ancient Mesopotamia: Portrait of a Dead Civilization*, 1977
J.N. Postgate, *Early Mesopotamia: Society and Economy at the Dawn of History*, 1994
Erica Reiner, *Ancient Mesopotamia: Portrait of a Dead Civilization*, 1977
Virginia Schomp, *Ancient Mesopotamia: The Sumerians, Babylonians, and Assyrians*, 2005

660

NICHOLSON BAKER

Human Smoke: The Beginnings of World War II, the End of Civilization

(New York: Simon & Schuster, 2008)

Subject(s): Government; History; Holocaust

Summary: In this work, author Nicholson Baker explores the political and social background that led to World War II. Using research based on newspaper and magazine articles, memoirs, speeches made on radio, and diaries, Baker presents a series of sometimes small, yet critical events from 1892 to 1941. By examining the actions of political leaders—and their dissenters—on all sides, Baker denounces our long-held romantic myths concerning the 1930s and 40s and the notion of World War II as a "good" war.

Where it's reviewed:
The Nation, April 21, 2008, page 9
New Statesman, November 17, 2008, page 46

Other books by the same author:
The Anthologist: A Novel, 2010
Double Fold: Libraries and the Assault on Paper, 2002
The Fermata, 1995

Other books you might like:
Andrew J. Crozier, *The Causes of the Second World War*, 1997
Gordon Martel, *Origins of the Second World War Reconsidered*, 1999
Richard Overy, *The Origins of the Second World War (3rd Edition)*, 2008
A.J.P. Taylor, *The Origins of the Second World War*, 1996
Gerhard L. Weinberg, *Hitler's Foreign Policy 1933-1939: The Road to World War II*, 2004

661

SIMON BAKER

Ancient Rome: The Rise and Fall of an Empire

(London: BBC Worldwide Publishing, 2006)

Subject(s): Ancient Roman civilization; Roman Empire, 30 BC-476 AD; Rome (Ancient state)

Summary: The power, the politics, and the passion of Ancient Rome are vividly retold in author Simon Baker's examination of this crucial period in world history. *Ancient Rome: The Rise and Fall of an Empire* spans some seven centuries as it delves into the history of the region. Baker pays special attention to the powerful individuals who led Rome during this critical time, revealing their unique, oftentimes unsettling minds and the motivations behind their history-defining actions. *Ancient Rome* is based on a BBC television series of the same name.

Other books you might like:

Susan Wise Bauer, *The History of the Ancient World: From the Earliest Accounts to the Fall of Rome*, 2007

Charles Freeman, *Egypt, Greece and Rome: Civilizations of the Ancient Mediterranean*, 2004

P.J. Heather, *The Fall of the Roman Empire: A New History of Rome and the Barbarians*, 2007

Christopher S. Mckay, *Ancient Rome: A Military and Political History*, 2007

Paul A. Zoch, *Ancient Rome: An Introductory History*, 2000

662

ALESSANDRO BARBERO

The Day of the Barbarians: The Battle That Led to the Fall of the Roman Empire

(New York: Walker and Company, 2007)

Subject(s): Ancient Roman civilization; Wars; Roman Empire, 30 BC-476 AD

Summary: In the year 378, Roman troops battled it out with a band of Goths in what would become known as the battle of Adrianople. This conflict, medieval studies professor Alessandro Barbero asserts, was the catalyst for the collapse of the entire Roman state. *The Day of the Barbarians: The Battle That Led to the Fall of the Roman Empire* analyzes this key event, the players involved, and how it heralded the arrival of the Middle Ages. This volume includes a bibliography and a full index.

663

JULIET BARKER

Agincourt: Henry V and the Battle That Made England

(New York: Back Bay Books, 2006)

Subject(s): History; England; Royalty

Summary: In *Agincourt: Henry V and the Battle That Made England*, historian Juliet Barker shares the story of the Battle of Agincourt in October 1415, when a small group of English knights defeated a group of French soldiers. There were six French soldiers for every one English soldier, but the English still emerged victorious. Barker credits this victory to monarch Henry V, spending most of the text discussing the monarch's life, his political attitudes, and his desire to acquire more territory by whatever means necessary. The author focuses on detailed battle preparations and strategic military decisions, explaining why they were ultimately successful.

Where it's reviewed:
Booklist, May 15, 2006, page 18
Library Journal, June 1, 2006, page 135
Publishers Weekly, April 17, 2006

Other books by the same author:
Conquest: The English Kingdom of France 1417-1450, 2009
The Brontes, 2007
Wordsworth: A Life, 2006

Other books you might like:
Matthew Bennett, *Agincourt 1415: Triumph Against the Odds*, 1991
John Keegan, *The Face of Battle*, 1976
Paul Knight, *Henry V and the Conquest of France 1416-53*, 1998
Christopher Rothero, *The Armies of Agincourt*, 1981
Desmond Seward, *The Hundred Years War: The English in France 1337-1453*, 1978

664

BELLA BATHURST

The Wreckers: A Story of Killing Seas and Plundered Shipwrecks, from the 18th-Century to the Present Day

(Boston, Massachusetts: Houghton Mifflin, 2005)

Subject(s): Ships; Shipwrecks; Sea stories

Summary: *The Wreckers: A Story of Killing Seas and Plundered Shipwrecks, from the 18th-Century to the Present Day* is a historical account of the dangerous seas surrounding the British Isles from award-winning author Bella Bathurst. The treacherous waters surrounding Britain have been the cause of many shipwrecks throughout history, and with each accident comes a great deal of goods and treasure to be plundered. Over the years, villagers living along the coastline have viewed these wrecks as a means to gather wealth, improve their way of life, and make ends meet. In *The Wreckers*, Bathurst examines the perils of the British waters and sheds light on the scavengers who have exploited shipwrecks for profit.

Where it's reviewed:
Booklist, July 2005, page 1892
Times Literary Supplement, April 22, 2005, page 32

Other books by the same author:
Special: A Novel, 2002
The Lighthouse Stevensons: The Extraordinary Story of the Building of the Scottish Lighthouses by the Ancestors of Robert Louis Stevenson, 1999

Other books you might like:
Max Hardberger, *Seized: A Sea Captain's Adventures Battling Scoundrels and Pirates While Recovering Stolen Ships in the World's Most Troubled Waters*, 2010
Rebecca Harrison, *Deep, Dark and Dangerous: On the Bottom with the Northwest Salvage Divers*, 2006
Pat Wastell Norris, *High Seas, High Risk: The Story of the Sudburys*, 1999
Dennis Powers, *Sentinel of the Seas: Life and Death at the Most Dangerous Lighthouse Ever Built*, 2009
Dennis M. Powers, *Taking the Sea: Perilous Waters, Sunken Ships, and the True Story of the Legendary Wrecker Captains*, 2009
Ian Tew, *Salvage: A Personal Odyssey*, 2007

665

ANTONY BEEVOR

D-Day: The Battle for Normandy
(New York: Viking, 2009)

Subject(s): World War II, 1939-1945; Military life; History

Summary: In *D-Day: The Battle for Normandy*, bestselling author Antony Beevor presents a detailed look at the history of the legendary D-Day invasion. Chronicling the entire cycle of events that comprised the famed attack, this volume charts the experiences of troops from all over the world: the United States, Great Britain, Canada, Germany, and France. It also traces the tragic repercussions the invasion had on the French people, as well as the events that led to the eventual liberation of Paris. *D-Day* contains illustrations, maps, notes on the text, a bibliography, and a full index, as well as a glossary of commonly used terms.

Where it's reviewed:
American Heritage, Winter 2010, page 98
Foreign Affairs, November/December 2009, page 157
History Today, October 2009, page 68
Library Journal, August 1, 2009, page 93
Publishers Weekly, July 27, 2009

Other books by the same author:
The Mystery of Olga Chekhova, 2005

The Fall of Berlin 1945, 2003
Stalingrad: The Fateful Siege 1942-1943, 1999

Other books you might like:
Stephen E. Ambrose, *D-Day, June 6, 1944: The Climactic Battle of World War II*, 1994
Joseph Balkoski, *Omaha Beach: D-Day, June 6, 1944*, 2004
Dominique Francois, *Normandy: Breaching the Atlantic Wall: From D-Day to the Breakout and Liberation*, 2008
Charles Messenger, *The D-Day Atlas: Anatomy of the Normandy Campaign*, 2004
Hampton Sides, *Ghost Soldiers: The Forgotten Epic Story of World War II's Most Dramatic Mission*, 2001

666

DAVID A. BELL

The First Total War: Napoleon's Europe and the Birth of Warfare as We Know It
(Boston: Houghton Mifflin Company, 2007)

Subject(s): History; Napoleonic Wars, 1800-1815; Wars

Summary: Author and historian David A. Bell traces the roots of modern warfare to the epic battles of Napoleon during the 18th and 19th centuries. *The First Total War: Napoleon's Europe and the Birth of Warfare as We Know It* probes the military action of the notorious leader and how these maneuverings set the stage for all future wars. Bell ties Napoleon's wars—often fought in the name of liberation and freedom—to more recent conflicts and shows readers what can be learned from this bloody history. *The First Total War* includes a bibliography and an index.

Where it's reviewed:
American Historical Review, December 2007, page 1489
Journal of Modern History, December 2008, page 911
The Nation, February 5, 2007, page 82
The New Yorker, February 12, 2007, page 82
World Affairs, Summer 2008, page 98

Other books by the same author:
The Cult of the Nation in France: Inventing Nationalism, 1680-1800, 2003
Lawyers and Citizens: The Making of a Political Elite in Old Regime France, 1994

Other books you might like:
Jeremy Black, *War in the Nineteenth Century: 1800-1914*, 2009
Robert B. Bruce, *Fighting Techniques of the Napoleonic Age 1792-1815: Equipment, Combat Skills, and Tactics*, 2008
Gregory Fremont-Barnes, *The Napoleonic Wars: The Rise and Fall of an Empire*, 2004

Chris McNab, *Napoleon Wars: An Illustrated History*, 2009

Gunther Erich Rothenberg, *The Napoleonic Wars*, 2006

667

WILLIAM J. BENNETT

America: The Last Best Hope, Volumes I and II

(Nashville, Tennessee: Thomas Nelson, 2007)

Subject(s): History; United States history; Reference works

Summary: *America: The Last Best Hope, Volumes I and II* collects the first two volumes in this series, written by William J. Bennett. This version also includes an audio CD, which provides additional discussion and commentary. In these volumes, Bennett provides a comprehensive and interesting discussion of the history of the United States, beginning with Columbus's arrival in the 15th century and continuing through the Cold War in the 20th century. Bennett discusses the major events in U.S. history: the American Revolution, the Civil War, the civil rights movement, and the first missions to space. The author balances these overviews with anecdotes about the people and events that helped shape the country.

Where it's reviewed:
Commentary, December 2006, page 66
Library Journal, June 1, 2007, page 127
Publishers Weekly, March 27, 2006

Other books by the same author:
Why We Fight: Moral Clarity and the War on Terrorism, 2003
The Educated Child: A Parents Guide from Preschool Through Eighth Grade, 2000
The Index of Leading Cultural Indicators: American Society at the End of the 20th Century, 2000

668

PETER L. BERNSTEIN

Wedding of the Waters: The Erie Canal and the Making of a Great Nation

(New York: W.W. Norton & Company, 2005)

Subject(s): History; United States history; Erie Canal

Summary: In *Wedding of the Waters: The Erie Canal and the Making of a Great Nation*, Peter L. Bernstein explores the history and engineering of the Erie Canal. Although plans for the canal were first discussed in 1808, the high cost of the project delayed construction for many years. Work did not begin until 1817, and the canal was finally completed in 1825. The canal, which stretches 363 miles from Buffalo at Lake Erie to the Hudson River, required incredibly challenging human-powered excavation through the Appalachian Mountains. After discussing the construction of the Erie Canal, Bernstein considers the impact it had on American history, agriculture, economy, industrialization, and even global commerce.

Where it's reviewed:
Booklist, November 15, 2004, page 536
Foreign Affairs, March/April 2005, page 158
Library Journal, December 1, 2004, page 134
Publishers Weekly, November 14, 2004, page 47

Other books by the same author:
Capital Ideas: The Improbable Origins of Modern Wall Street, 2005
The Power of Gold: The History of an Obsession, 2004
Against the Odds: The Remarkable Story of Risk, 1998

Other books you might like:
Roger W. Hecht, *The Erie Canal Reader, 1790-1950*, 2003
Gerard T. Koeppel, *Bond of Union: Building the Erie Canal and the American Empire*, 2009
Ronald Shaw, *Erie Water West: A History of the Erie Canal, 1792-1854*, 1966
Carol Sheriff, *The Artificial River: The Erie Canal and the Paradox of Progress, 1817-1862*, 1997
Debbie Daino Stack, *Cruising America's Waterways: The Erie Canal*, 2001

669

KENNETH BILBY

True-Born Maroons

(Gainesville, Florida: University Press of Florida, 2008)

Subject(s): Ethnicity; Identity; Jamaicans

Summary: Author Kenneth Bilby examines the fascinating history and legacy of the Jamaican Maroon people and how they have managed to survive centuries of marginalization. *True-Born Maroons* looks at how this culture—comprised of the descendants of escaped African slaves—has managed to overcome a tumultuous past to form powerful, unique traditions, rituals, and language. Bilby utilizes firsthand, never-before-revealed knowledge about the inner workings of the culture to present an intimate portrait of its people and the challenges they still face today. *True-Born Maroons* includes a bibliography and an index.

Where it's reviewed:
CHOICE: Current Reviews for Academic Libraries, June 2006, page 1885
Times Literary Supplement, July 13, 2007, page 9

Other books by the same author:
The Caribbean as a Musical Region, 1985

Other books you might like:
Rosanne Marion Adderley, *New Negroes from Africa: Slave Trade Abolition and Free African Settlement in the Nineteenth-Century Caribbean*, 2006
Robert Charles Dallas, *The History of the Maroons*,

from Their Origins to the Establishment of Their Chief Tribe at Sierra Leone, 2002

Karla Gottlieb, *The Mother of Us All: A History of Queen Nanny, Leader of the Windward Jamaican Maroons,* 2000

Timothy James Lockley, *Maroon Communities in South Carolina: A Documentary Record,* 2008

Richard Price, *Maroon Societies: Rebel Slave Communities in the Americas,* 1996

670

NED BLACKHAWK

Violence over the Land: Indians and Empires in the Early American West

(Cambridge, Massachusetts: Harvard University Press, 2006)

Subject(s): Native Americans; Native Americans (Mexico); Native American relocation

Summary: In *Violence over the Land: Indians and Empires in the Early American West,* author Ned Blackhawk chronicles the history of the land of New Mexico, Arizona, Colorado, Utah, and Nevada. In this story, Ute, Paiute, and Shoshone tribal peoples figure in the early history, along with the Spanish explorers. Blackhawk discusses the wars between the Spanish, British, and French armies and the wars between the Spanish and the Americans that followed. He chronicles battles, diseases, famines, and the relocation of indigenous peoples, which ravaged the country in its early history. He asserts that the history is an example that reflects the violent nature of the U.S. government's political action.

Where it's reviewed:
Booklist, October 1, 2006, page 21
Library Journal, September 15, 2006, page 71

Other books by the same author:
The Shoshone, 2002

Other books you might like:
Colin G. Calloway, *Our Hearts Fell to the Ground: Plains Indians Views of How the West Was Lost,* 1996

Pekka Hamalainen, *The Comanche Empire,* 2008

Marilynn S. Johnson, *Violence in the West: The Johnson County Range War and Ludlow Massacre,* 2008

Elliott West, *The Contested Plains: Indians, Goldseekers, and the Rush to Colorado,* 1998

Richard White, *"It's Your Misfortune and None of My Own": A New History of the American West,* 1991

671

DAVID W. BLIGHT
WALLACE TURNAGE , Co-Author
JOHN WASHINGTON , Co-Author

A Slave No More: Two Men Who Escaped to Freedom, Including Their Own Narratives of Emancipation

(Orlando, Florida: Harcourt, 2007)

Subject(s): Slavery; Autobiographies; Freedom

Summary: *A Slave No More: Two Men Who Escaped to Freedom, Including Their Own Narratives of Emancipation* is a collection of two previously unpublished slave narratives and accompanying biographical information that further explores the authors' lives. The two narratives were written by slaves Wallace Turnage and John Washington, who eventually escaped the bonds of slavery during the Civil War and found freedom in the North. American history professor David W. Blight provides the additional biographical information about the two men, analyzing their harrowing lives and daring escapes as slaves. Turnage's narrative focuses mainly on his five attempts to flee, while Washington offers a more detailed account of what it was like as a child, an adolescent, and an adult in a slave culture. Blight, using extensive genealogical information, fills in as many holes as possible, explaining the men's participation in the Civil War effort, their reunions with family members, and their lives as free citizens.

Where it's reviewed:
America, February 18, 2008, page 22
Journal of American History, September 2008, page 526
New York Times Book Review, March 20, 2008, page 47
Publishers Weekly, January 28, 2008, page 65

Other books by the same author:
When This Cruel War Is Over, 2009
Race and Reunion: The Civil War in American Memory, 2002
Passages to Freedom: The Underground Railroad in History and Memory, 2001

Other books you might like:
Frederick Douglass, *Narrative of the Life of Frederick Douglass, an American Slave,* 1845

Henry Louis Gates, *The Classic Slave Narratives,* 2005

Harriet Jacobs, *Incidents in the Life of a Slave Girl,* 1861

James Mellon, *Bullwhip Days: The Slaves Remember,* 1989

Norman R. Yetman, *Voices from Slavery: 100 Authentic Slave Narrative,* 1999

672

BENSON BOBRICK

The Fated Sky: Astrology in History

(New York: Simon & Schuster, 2005)

Subject(s): Astrology; Science; History

Summary: In *The Fated Sky: Astrology in History*, historian Benson Bobrick traces the complex history of astrology. Bobrick explains how the often-misunderstood field grew in popularity, despite frequent attempts at discrediting it. He begins with a discussion of the origins of astrology in Mesopotamia and then follows the evolution of the field through biblical literature, the Roman Empire, and the Renaissance, up to contemporary uses and considerations. Bobrick argues that the study of astrology was extremely influential in the fields of astronomy, physics, and chemistry. He also discusses the study's role in major historical events, such as Christopher Columbus's discovery of America.

Where it's reviewed:
Booklist, November 15, 2005, page 7
CHOICE: Current Reviews for Academic Libraries, April 2006, page 1483
Library Journal, October 15, 2005, page 64
New York Times Book Review, February 5, 2006, page 16
Publishers Weekly, September 26, 2005

Other books by the same author:
Master of War: The Life of General George H. Thomas, 2010
Angel in the Whirlwind: The Triumph of the American Revolution, 1998
Knotted Tongues: Stuttering in History and the Quest for a Cure, 1996

Other books you might like:
Nicolas Campion, *History of Western Astrology, Volumes I and II*, 2009
Patrick Curry, *Astrology, Science and Culture: Pulling Down the Moon*, 2004
Thomas K. Dietrich, *The Origin of Culture and Civilization: The Cosmological Philosophy of the Ancient Worldview Regarding Myth, Astrology, Science and Religion*, 2005
James Herschel Holden, *A History of Horoscopic Activity*, 1996
S.J. Tester, *A History of Western Astrology*, 2009
Roy Willis, *Astrology, Science and Culture: Pulling Down the Moon*, 2004

673

FERGUS M. BORDEWICH

Bound for Canaan: The Underground Railroad and the War for the Soul of America

(New York: Amistad, 2005)

Subject(s): Underground Railroad (Slave escape network); Slavery; United States history

Summary: Author and journalist Fergus M. Bordewich presents an in-depth history of the famous African American slave escape route in *Bound for Canaan: The Underground Railroad and the War for the Soul of America*. Bordewich profiles the history of the Underground Railroad from its inception during the Revolutionary War to the Civil War and until 1870, when African Americans first attained voting rights. An assortment of letters, personal writings, government records, and other sources are utilized in an effort to present an accurate and detailed account of this historic piece of American history.

Where it's reviewed:
American Heritage, April-May 2005, page 21
Journal of Southern History, November 2005, page 942
The Nation, May 23, 2005, page 46
New York Times Book Review, July 14, 2005, page 40
Smithsonian, August 2005, page 103

Other books by the same author:
Washington: The Making of the American Capital, 2008
Cathay: A Journey in Search of Old China, 2001
Killing the White Man's Indian: Reinventing Native Americans at the End of the Twentieth Century, 1997

Other books you might like:
David W. Blight, *Passages to Freedom: The Underground Railroad in History and Memory*, 2004
Betty DeRamus, *Forbidden Fruit: Love Stories from the Underground Railroad*, 2005
Raymond G. Dobard, *Hidden in Plain View: A Secret Story of Quilts and the Underground Railroad*, 2000
Wilbur H. Siebert, *Underground Railroad from Slavery to Freedom*, 1874
William Still, *The Underground Railroad: Authentic Narratives and First-Hand Accounts*, 2007
Jacqueline L. Tobin, *Hidden in Plain View: A Secret Story of Quilts and the Underground Railroad*, 2000

674

ELIZABETH BORGWARDT

A New Deal for the World: America's Vision for Human Rights

(Cambridge, Masachussetts: Belknap Press of Harvard University Press, 2005)

Subject(s): International relations; Human rights; History
Summary: In *A New Deal for the World: America's Vision*

for Human Rights, Elizabeth Borgwardt mines one of the foundations of United States foreign policy—human rights. Borgwardt identifies the Atlantic Charter, signed by Franklin Delano Roosevelt and Winston Churchill in 1941, as the moment when protecting human rights became a fundamental goal in international relations. She then describes the diplomatic phases that helped shape and preserve this ideal, including Bretton Woods, the United Nations, and the events at the Nuremberg trials. The text serves not only as historical reference, but also as a lens through which to view current international affairs.

Where it's reviewed:
American Historical Review, February 2008, page 127
Dissent, Summer 2006, page 124
International Affairs, May 2006, page 576
Journal of American History, September 2006, page 583
The Nation, July 3, 2006, page 31

Other books you might like:
Roland Burke, *Decolonization and the Evolution of International Human Rights*, 2010
Michael Haas, *International Human Rights: A Comprehensive Introduction*, 2008
Micheline Ishay, *The Human Rights Reader: Major Political Essays, Speeches and Documents from Ancient Times to the Present, Second Edition*, 2007
Paul Gordon Lauren, *The Evolution of International Human Rights: Visions Seen*, 1998
Samuel Moyn, *The Last Utopia: Human Rights in History*, 2010

675

MARK BOWDEN

Guests of the Ayatollah: The First Battle in America's War with Militant Islam

(New York: Grove Press, 2006)

Subject(s): Current Affairs; International Relations; Islam

Summary: In 1979, a group of student activists took over the United States embassy in Tehran, Iran, holding 66 American citizens hostage for over a year. This was, author Mark Bowden says, America's first skirmish with Islamic militancy; the hostages were the first victims of the War on Terror (a term that Bowden finds inapt). He describes the goals and ideals of the hostage-takers and the culture that produced them. He also looks inside the embassy at the hostages themselves, and at the crisis that occurred within the administration of Jimmy Carter, whose failed attempt at rescuing the hostages almost certainly spelled an end to his presidency.

Where it's reviewed:
Booklist, March 1 2006, page 42
Library Journal, April 15, 2006, page 89
Library Journal, April 15, 2006, page 89
National Review, August 7, 2006, page 45
Publishers Weekly, April 17, 2006, page 174

Other books by the same author:
Black Hawk Down, 2002
Killing Pablo: The Hunt for the World's Greatest Outlaw, 2002
Doctor Dealer: The Rise and Fall of an All-American Boy and His Multimillion-Dollar Cocaine Empire, 2000

Other books you might like:
William J. Daugherty, *In the Shadow of the Ayatollah: A CIA Hostage in Iran*, 2001
David R. Farber, *Taken Hostage: The Iran Hostage Crisis and America's First Encounter with Radical Islam*, 2006
Patrick Houghton, *U.S. Foreign Policy and the Iran Hostage Crisis*, 2001
Laura Ling, *Somewhere Inside: One Sister's Captivity in North Korea and the Other's Fight to Bring Her Home*, 2010
Lisa Ling, co-author
Robert Wright, *Our Man in Tehran: Ken Taylor and the Iran Hostage Crisis*, 2011

676

JAMES BRADLEY

The Imperial Cruise: A Secret History of Empire and War

(New York: Little, Brown and Co., 2009)

Subject(s): United States history; Politics; Presidents (Government)

Summary: In *The Imperial Cruise: A Secret History of Empire and War*, James Bradley exposes America's imperial past and its consequences on the world. In 1905, President Roosevelt sent Secretary of War William Taft, Taft's daughter Alice, and a host of congressmen to Japan, the Philippines, China, and Korea. Roosevelt hoped that they could come up with a U.S.-Japanese agreement that would allow Japan to expand into Korea and China. His plan backfired, however. Bradley explains that this agreement laid the groundwork for World War II, the 1949 Chinese Revolution, and the Korean War. Using letters, documents, and newspaper articles, he reveals Roosevelt's racist attitude and sketchy foreign-policy procedures. Photographs and maps accompany the text.

Where it's reviewed:
Booklist, November 15, 2005, page 42
Booklist, November 15, 2005, page 42
The Christian Century, May 18, 2010, page 41
Library Journal, November 16, 2009, page 71
Publishers Weekly, October 5, 2009, page 42

Other books by the same author:
Flags of Our Fathers, 2003
Flyboys: A True Story of Courage, 2003
What If?, 2001

Other books you might like:
Hugh Ambrose, *The Pacific*, 2010
Stacy A. Cordery, *Alice: Alice Roosevelt Longworth,*

from *White House Princess to Washington Power Broker*, 2007

E. San Juan, *U.S. Imperialism and Revolution in the Philippines*, 2007

Elizabeth M. Norman, *Tears in the Darkness: The Story of the Bataan Death March and Its Aftermath*, 2009 Michael Norman, co-author

Evan Thomas, *The War Lovers: Roosevelt, Lodge, Hearst, and the Rush to Empire, 1898*, 2010

677

TAYLOR BRANCH

At Canaan's Edge: America in the King Years, 1965-1968
(New York: Simon & Schuster, 2006)

Subject(s): American History; Assassination; Civil Rights Movement

Summary: This is the third volume in Taylor Branch's monumental history of America during the Martin Luther King, Jr. years, which began with 1988's *Parting the Waters* and continued in 1998 with *Pillar of Fire*. The three books chronicle the life of Martin Luther King, Jr. and the effect he had on America, politically and socially. This book begins with King's marches for voting rights for blacks in Selma, Alabama. These nonviolent marches—and the violent response they provoked—thrust King onto the national stage. Branch tells the story of King's movement alongside the other great events of the day, such as the Vietnam War and the Watts riots in Los Angeles. He also tells how King's nonviolent leadership was being challenged by those with a more radical agenda, and concludes with the story of King's assassination in Memphis.

Where it's reviewed:
American Scholar, Spring 2006, page 133
Commonwea, February 10, 2006, page 21
Journal of American History, December 2006, page 955
The Nation, March 27, 2006, page 31
New York Times Book Review, April 6, 2006, page 20

Other books by the same author:
The Clinton Tapes: Wrestling History with the President, 2009
Pillar of Fire: America in the King Years 1963-65, 1999
Parting the Waters: America in the King Years, 1954-63, 1989

Other books you might like:
Michael D'Orso, *Walking with the Wind: A Memoir of the Movement*, 1998
Bruce J. Dierenfield, *The Civil Rights Movement: Revised Edition*, 2008
Steve Fayer, *Voices of Freedom: An Oral History of the Civil Rights Movement from the 1950s through the 1980s*, 1990 Henry Hampton, co-author
John R. Lewis, *Walking with the Wind: A Memoir of the Movement*, 1998
Aldon D. Morris, *Origins of the Civil Rights Movements*, 1986

Juan Williams, *Eyes on the Prize: America's Civil Rights Years, 1954-1965*, 1987

678

ALLAN M. BRANDT

The Cigarette Century: The Rise, Fall, and Deadly Persistence of the Product That Defined America
(New York: Basic Books, 2007)

Subject(s): Smoking; Politics; Culture

Summary: In *The Cigarette Century: The Rise, Fall, and Deadly Persistence of the Product That Defined America*, professor Allan M. Brandt examines the product that has caused so much controversy over the last 200 years. From tobacco's humble beginnings to the complications caused by cigarette companies, Brandt explores the strange hold the product has over consumers who are completely aware of the hazards of smoking. The book warns readers that cigarette companies are still going strong, even with a drop in sales over the last few decades. Brandt not only covers the culture surrounding cigarettes, he also investigates the science, politics, and laws governing the industry. At the end of the book, the author explains how the cigarette epidemic is leaving the United States and taking hold of the developing world.

Where it's reviewed:
American Scientist, September/October, 2007, page 444
Journal of Social History, Spring 2009, page 817
The New Yorker, April 2, 2007, page 79
Publishers Weekly, December 31, 2007, page 28
Science, May 4, 2007, page 692

Other books by the same author:
No Magic Bullet: A Social History of Venereal Disease in the United States Since 1880, 1987

Other books you might like:
Martha Derthick, *Up in Smoke: From Legislation to Litigation in Tobacco Politics*, 2004
David Kessler, *A Question of Intent: A Great American Battle with a Deadly Industry*, 2001
Richard Kluger, *Ashes to Ashes: America's Hundred-Year Cigarette War, the Public Health, and the Unabashed Triumph of Philip Morris*, 1996
Jacob Sullum, *For Your Own Good: The Anti-Smoking Crusade and the Tyranny of Public Health*, 1998
Dan Zegart, *Civil Warriors: The Legal Siege on the Tobacco Industry*, 2000

679

DOUGLAS BRINKLEY

The Great Deluge: Hurricane Katrina, New Orleans, and the Mississippi Gulf Coast
(New York: Harper Perennial, 2006)

Subject(s): City and Town Life; Disasters, Natural; Hurricanes

Summary: Douglas Brinkley is a historian and a professor at New Orleans' Tulane University. He stayed in New Orleans during the onslaught of Hurricane Katrina in 2005, and was witness to the total breakdown of services during the weeks thereafter. This book focuses tightly on the events of one week: August 27 through September 3, 2005, during which the city was utterly overwhelmed by the storm. He praises the heroic and compassionate acts of numerous citizens who endangered themselves to help the residents of the beleaguered city. He is also unsparing in his criticism of those who failed to help when the city fell into chaos, and those who attempted to shift the blame afterwards.

Where it's reviewed:
America, September 11, 2006, page 31
Library Journal, August 1, 2006, page 106
National Review, July 17, 2006, page 45
New Republic, August 14, 2006, page 32
Publishers Weekly, May 8, 2006, page 238

Other books by the same author:
Fear and Loathing in America: The Brutal Odyssey of an Outlaw Journalist, 2001

Other books you might like:
Heather Andrews, *That Rough Beast, Its Hour Come Round at Last: A History of Hurricane Katrina*, 2008
Christopher Cooper, *Disaster: Hurricane Katrina and the Failure of Homeland Security*, 2006
Dave Eggers, *Zeitoun*, 2009
Chris Rose, *1 Dead in Attic: After Katrina*, 2007

680

CHRISTOPHER LESLIE BROWN

Moral Capital: Foundations of British Abolitionism

(Chapel Hill, North Carolina: The University of North Carolina Press, 2006)

Subject(s): England; History; Abolition of slavery

Summary: In *Moral Capital: Foundations of British Abolitionism*, Christopher Leslie Brown offers a scholarly examination of the reasons behind the abolition of slavery in Britain in the 18th century, arguing that there was more behind the decision than moral justice. Brown ties the roots of the abolitionist movement to the American Revolution and Britain's need to return to political legitimacy after its defeat in the colonies. The author also examines how new religious teachings and changing attitudes regarding Africa and imperialism contributed to the movement.

Where it's reviewed:
American Historical Review, April 2008, page 578
English Historical Review, June 2007, page 768
Journal of Interdisciplinary History, Winter 2008, page 448
Journal of American History, March 2007, page 1232
Times Literary Supplement, August 17, 2007, page 8

Other books by the same author:
Arming Slaves: From Classical Times to the Modern Age, 2006

Other books you might like:
Brycchan Carey, *British Abolitionism and the Rhetoric of Sensibility: Writing, Sentiment and Slavery, 1760-1807*, 2005
Seymour Drescher, *Capitalism and Antislavery: British Mobilization in Comparative Perspective*, 1987
Julie Roy Jeffrey, *The Great Silent Army of Abolitionism: Ordinary Women in the Antislavery Movement*, 1998
Derek R. Peterson, *Abolitionism and Imperialism in Britain, Africa and the Atlantic*, 2010
C. Peter Ripley, *The Black Abolitionist Papers: Vol. I: The British Isles, 1830-1865*, 1985

681

HOWARD G. BROWN

Ending the French Revolution: Violence, Justice, and Repression from the Terror to Napoleon

(Charlottesville, Virginia: University of Virginia Press, 2006)

Subject(s): French Revolution, 1789; History; Violence

Summary: In *Ending the French Revolution: Violence, Justice, and Repression from the Terror to Napoleon*, Howard G. Brown considers the reasons the French Revolution in 1789 led to a dictatorship, or "security state," under Napoleon, rather than a liberal democracy, which is usually the outcome of a revolution. Brown argues that scholars considering the outcome of the French Revolution focus their attention too much on Paris, ignoring what was going on in the rest of France, including martial law as a number of smaller regions continued to violently revolt, leading to continued repression. Brown uses a great deal of research to back up his analysis, considering his ideas from a number of different theoretical viewpoints.

Where it's reviewed:
American Historical Review, December 2007, page 1487
Canadian Journal of History, Autumn 2007, page 315
Historian, Winter 2009, page 813
Journal of Interdisciplinary History, Winter 2008, page 453
Journal of Modern History, June 2008, page 430

Other books by the same author:
War, Revolution, and the Bureaucratic State: Politics and Army Administration in France, 1791-1799, 1995

Other books you might like:
Bronislaw Baczko, *Ending the Terror:The French Revolution After Robespierre*, 1994
William Doyle, *The Oxford History of the French Revolution*, 1989
Hugh Gough, *The Terror in the French Revolution*, 2010

Peter McPhee, *The French Revolution, 1789-1799*, 2002

R.R. Palmer, *Twelve Who Ruled: The Year of the Terror in the French Revolution*, 2005

Michael Petheram, *Ending the Terror:The French Revolution After Robespierre*, 1994

Isser Woloch, *Twelve Who Ruled: The Year of the Terror in the French Revolution*, 2005

682

LESLIE BROWN

Upbuilding Black Durham: Gender, Class, and the Black Community Development in the Jim Crow South

(Chapel Hill, North Carolina: The University of North Carolina Press, 2008)

Subject(s): Race relations; Racism; Disadvantaged persons

Summary: Leslie Brown's *Upbuilding Black Durham: Gender, Class, and the Black Community Development in the Jim Crow South* explores the history of the African American community in Durham, North Carolina. After the Civil War, the city of Durham was a haven for many blacks, who found a peaceful place to live, work, and thrive. During the Jim Crow era, however, division and conflicts arose in the city's black communities. In the book, Brown claims that, although tensions continued among people in the black community, the city of Durham produced some important figures in the civil rights movement.

Where it's reviewed:
American Historical Review, October 2009, page 1090
Journal of American History, December 2009, page 892
Journal of Social History, Summer 2010, page 1114
Oral History Review, Summer/Fall 2009, page 311
Reviews in American History, June 2009, page 243

Other books you might like:
Jeffrey J. Crow, *History of African Americans in North Carolina*, 2002
    Paul D. Escott, co-author
Glenda Elizabeth Gilmore, *Gender and Jim Crow: Women and the Politics of White Supremacy in North Carolina 1896-1920*, 1996
Christina Greene, *Our Separate Ways: Women and the Black Freedom Movement in Durham, North Carolina*, 2005
Flora J. Hatley, *History of African Americans in North Carolina*, 2002
Angela Hornsby-Gutting, *Black Manhood and Community Building in North Carolina, 1900-1930*, 2009
Jarred Roll, *Spirit of Rebellion: Labor and Religion in the New Cotton South*, 2010

683

HARRY BRUINIUS

Better for All the World: The Secret History of Forced Sterilization and America's Quest for Racial Purity

(New York: Knopf, 2006)

Subject(s): Law; Mental disorders; Evolution (Biology)

Summary: In *Better for All the World: The Secret History of Forced Sterilization and America's Quest for Racial Purity*, Harry Bruinius chronicles the events that led to a Supreme Court Ruling in 1927, which allowed for the forced sterilization of a 21-year-old woman, who was considered to be "feeble-minded" and, therefore, unfit to reproduce. This Supreme Court ruling paved the way for other cases across the country that resulted in the sterilization of 65,000 Americans, many of whom were poverty-stricken young women. Bruinius explores the poeple involved, including advocates such as Charles Davenport and Harry Laughlin, the implications of the Supreme Court ruling, and the effects of eugenics on society.

Where it's reviewed:
Booklist, January 1, 2006, page 32
CHOICE: Current Reviews for Academic Libraries, February 2007, page 1060
National Review, March 27, 2006, page 49
Times Literary Supplement, August 11, 2006, page 29
Wilson Quarterly, Spring 2006, page 115

Other books you might like:
Edwin Black, *War Against the Weak: Eugenics and America's Campaign to Create a Master Race*, 2003
Angela Franks, *Margaret Sanger's Eugenic Legacy: The Control of Female Fertility*, 2008
Rebecca M. Kluchin, *Fit to Be Tied: Sterilization and Reproductive Rights in America, 1950-1980*, 2009
Paul A. Lombardo, *Three Generations, No Imbeciles: Eugenics, the Supreme Court, and Buck vs. Bell*, 2010
Victoria F. Nourse, *In Reckless Hands: Skinner V. Oklahoma and the Near-Triumph of American Eugenics*, 2008

684

PATRICK J. BUCHANAN

Churchill, Hitler and the Unnecessary War: How Britain Lost Its Empire and the West Lost the World

(New York: Three Rivers Press, 2008)

Subject(s): Diplomacy; World War I; World War II

Summary: Patrick Buchanan's impressive resume as advisor to three presidents, author, pundit, and presidential

History

candidate may not be enough to convince readers of his assertion that the two world wars that scarred the first half of the twentieth century were entirely caused by British diplomatic blunders. According to Buchanan, Britain's decision to go to war with Germany should it invade France, in the case of World War I or by pledging to protect Poland, as in the case of World War II, were the impetus for those horrendous conflicts. Buchanan claims that Italy was driven into Hitler's arms by sanctions and not by the ambitions of Mussolini. Buchanan faults Churchill for not recognizing Stalin's true character as well as bowing to American pressure to isolate Japan, thus setting the stage for Pearl Harbor. Buchanan's thesis, which perhaps doesn't give enough credit to the role played by the meticulously assembled Nazi war machine, is a tough sell but provocative nonetheless.

Where it's reviewed:
Booklist, April 15, 2008, page 4
National Review, June 30, 2008, page 43
New York Times Book Review, May 29, 2008, page 4
Newsweek, June 23, 2008, page 26

Other books by the same author:
Day of Reckoning: How Hubris, Ideology, and Greed Are Tearing America Apart, 2009
Where the Right Went Wrong: How Neoconservatives Subverted the Reagan Revolution and Hijacked the Bush Presidency, 2005
The Death of the West: How Dying Populations and Immigrant Invasions Imperil Our Country and Civilization, 2002

Other books you might like:
Simon Berthon, *Warlords: An Extraordinary Re-creation of World War II Through the Eyes and Minds of Hitler, Churchill, Roosevelt and Stalin*, 2007
Max Hastings, *Winston's War: Churchill, 1940-1945*, 2009
Warren F. Kimball, *Forged in War: Roosevelt, Churchill and the Second World War*, 2003
John Lukacs, *The Duel: The Eighty-Day Struggle Between Churchill and Hitler*, 2001
Joanna Potts, *Warlords: An Extraordinary Re-creation of World War II Through the Eyes and Minds of Hitler, Churchill, Roosevelt and Stalin*, 2007
Andrew Roberts, *Hitler and Churchill: Secrets of Leadership*, 2004

685

BRYAN BURROUGH

The Big Rich: The Rise and Fall of the Greatest Texas Oil Fortunes

(New York: Penguin Press HC, 2009)

Subject(s): Business; Wealth; Industries

Summary: *The Big Rich: The Rise and Fall of the Greatest Texas Oil Fortunes* begins with a picture of early 20th century Texas and the many oil prospectors who tried to make a fortune using hunches and luck alone to

strike oil in the otherwise relatively barren country. Four of these oil prospectors rose to the top: H.L. Hunt, Roy Cullen, Clint Murchinson, and Sid Richardson. *Vanity Fair* contributor Bryan Burrough profiles each of these men, their families, and their rise to fortune in the oil industry. Burrough also documents their subsequent decline as Middle Eastern oil became the standard in the 1980s, and their families turned to bitter feuds over what was left of their dynasties.

Where it's reviewed:
Booklist, December 1, 2008, page 6
Business Week, February 9, 2009, page 68
Business Week, December 4, 2009, page 75
Fortune, January 19, 2009, page 12
The New Yorker, March 16, 2009, page 107

Other books by the same author:
Public Enemies: The True Story of America's Greatest Crime Wave, 2004
Barbarians at the Gate: The Fall of RJR Nabisco, 2003
Dragonfly: NASA and the Crisis Aboard Mir, 1998

Other books you might like:
Carmen Bredeson, *The Spindletop Gusher: The Story of the Texas Oil Boom*, 2011
Lawrence Goodwyn, *Texas Oil, American Dreams: A Study of the Texas Independent Producers and Royalty Owners Association*, 1996
Don Graham, *Kings of Texas: The 150-Year Saga of an American Ranching Empire*, 2003
Diana Davids Olien, *Oil in Texas: The Gusher Age, 1895-1945*, 2002
Roger M. Olien, co-author
Roger M. Olien, *Wildcatters: Texas Independent Oilmen*, 1984

686

AUGUSTEN BURROUGHS

A Wolf at the Table: A Memoir of My Father

(New York: St. Martin's Press, 2008)

Subject(s): Child abuse; Father-son relations; Mental health

Summary: While Augusten Burroughs's previous books focused on his bizarre adolescence and the bad choices of early adulthood, *A Wolf at the Table: A Memoir of My Father* delves into his unexplored early childhood. Here, we meet the familiar character of Burroughs's bipolar mother in her early pill-taking career. More importantly we are introduced to the emotionally distant and cruel figure of his father. At first, Burroughs's recollections are of hazy episodes of his father's temper flaring over normal toddler behavior. As he grows older, his father becomes a conflicted figure in his life. Burroughs desperately wants his father's approval, but is unable to get it under any circumstances. Although his mother tries to shelter the young boy by frequently taking him on excursions out of town, she can't completely protect him from his father's physical and emotional brutality. The death of a pet left in the care of his father serves as a turning point in the relationship. Burroughs begins to rethink whether his father is worthy of the love he is trying to give. In reflection, Burroughs realizes that it was ultimately his father's loss that the man was incapable of having a healthy relationship with his son.

Where it's reviewed:
Booklist, March 1, 2008, page 28
People Weekly, May 5, 2008, page 51
Publishers Weekly, March 24, 2008, page 65
USA Today, April 29, 2008, page 9D

Other books by the same author:
Possible Side Effects, 2006
Running with Scissors: A Memoir, 2006
Dry: A Memoir, 2004
Magical Thinking: True Stories, 2004

Other books you might like:
Chelsea Handler, *Chelsea Chelsea Bang Bang*, 2010
David Sedaris, *Barrel Fever: Stories and Essays*, 1994

687

EDWIN G. BURROWS

Forgotten Patriots: The Untold Story of American Prisoners During the Revolutionary War

(New York: Basic Books, 2008)

Subject(s): American Revolution, 1775-1783; Military life; Prisoners of war

Summary: In *Forgotten Patriots: The Untold Story of American Prisoners During the Revolutionary War*, Pulitzer Prize-winning historian Edwin G. Burrows recounts the large number of American soldiers that were taken prisoner during the American Revolution and the deplorable way that most imprisoned soldiers were treated. Burrows elucidates that among the 200,000 men that fought England in the Revolution, nearly 25,000 became prisoners of war, and approximately 18,000 died in prison from starvation or other injuries while living in terribly overcrowded conditions. Using personal accounts expressed through diary entries and private correspondence, Burrows examines the hardships faced by American prisoners of war more than 200 hundred years ago.

Where it's reviewed:
American Heritage, Winter 2009, page 61
CHOICE: Current Reviews for Academic Libraries, September 2009, page 182
Library Journal, October 1, 2008, page 81

Other books by the same author:
Gotham: A History of New York City to 1898, 2002

Other books you might like:
Francis D. Cogliano, *American Maritime Prisoners in the Revolutionary War: The Captivity of William Russell*, 2001
Sheldon S. Cohen, *Yankee Sailors in British Gaols: Prisoners of War at Forton and Mill, 1777-1783*, 1995

Danske Dandridge, *American Prisoners of the Revolution*, 2010
John Ferlin, *Almost a Miracle: The American Victory in the War of Independence*, 2007
Peter A. Lillback, *George Washington's Sacred Fire*, 2006

688

ALEXANDER X. BYRD

Captives and Voyagers: Black Migrants Across the Eighteenth-Century British Atlantic World

(Baton Rouge, Louisiana: Louisiana State University Press, 2008)

Subject(s): Africans; Slavery; England

Summary: In *Captives and Voyagers: Black Migrants Across the Eighteenth-Century British Atlantic World*, historian and professor Alexander X. Byrd considers the process of emigration to and from the New World. Byrd examines the emigration routes of black people from Africa to the British colonies as part of the British slave trade and the routes of free blacks in Britain and the new territories in America to Sierra Leone in West Africa. Byrd considers these two paths back and forth across the Atlantic under the larger themes of slavery and freedom, comparing and contrasting the journeys and the obvious feelings of displacement that followed, and how these feelings of displacement affected settlements and civilizations in the British Empire and beyond.

Where it's reviewed:
American Historical Review, December 2009, page 1419
CHOICE: Current Reviews for Academic Libraries, July 2009, page 2176
Journal of African History, November 2009, page 438
Journal of American History, December 2009, page 819

Other books you might like:
George Reid Andrews, *Afro-Latin America, 1800-2000*, 2004
James T. Campbell, *Middle Passages: African American Journeys to Africa, 1787-2005*, 2006
James Fairhead, *African-American Exploration in West Africa: Four Nineteenth-Century Diaries*, 2003
  Tim Geysbeek, co-editor
  Svend E. Holsoe, co-editor
  Melissa Leach, co-editor
David Northrup, *Crosscurrents in the Black Atlantic, 1770-1965: A Brief History with Documents*, 2007
Richard Price, *Making Empire: Colonial Encounters and the Creation of Imperial Rule in Nineteenth-Century Africa*, 2008

History

689

JAMES T. CAMPBELL

Middle Passages: African American Journeys to Africa, 1787-2005

(New York: Penguin Press, 2006)

Subject(s): Emigration and immigration; Africans; African Americans

Summary: In *Middle Passages: African American Journeys to Africa, 1787-2005*, James T. Campbell takes stories from more than 200 years of history and considers the perspectives of African Americans who have travelled to the continent where many of their ancestors were captured and enslaved. Campbell considers the reasons that individuals have chosen to travel to Africa, which includes a desire to reconnect with one's homeland, among other reasons. Each chapter contains personal stories from people who have made this journey, including Paul Cuffe, Martin Delany, W.E.B. DuBois, Malcolm X, Alice Walker, and Louis Armstrong. Campbell also includes an overview of African sociopolitical history and bibliographical information.

Where it's reviewed:
CHOICE: Current Reviews for Academic Libraries, October 2006, page 349
Journal of American History, June 2007, page 239
Journal of Asian and African Studies, June 2008, page 363
The Nation, September 11, 2006, page 45
New York Times Book Review, September 27, 2007, page 41

Other books by the same author:
Songs of Zion: The African Methodist Episcopal Church in the United States and South Africa, 1995

Other books you might like:
David Birmingham, *Kwame Nkrumah: Father of African Nationalism*, 1998
Alexander X. Byrd, *Captives and Voyagers: Black Migrants Across the Eighteenth-Century British Atlantic World*, 2008
James Fairhead, *African-American Exploration in West Africa: Four Nineteenth-Century Diaries*, 2003
Kevin K. Gaines K. Gaines, *American Africans in Ghana: Black Expatriates and the Civil Rights Era*, 2006
Tim Geysbeek, *African-American Exploration in West Africa: Four Nineteenth-Century Diaries*, 2003
  Svend E. Holsoe, co-editor
  Melissa Leach, co-editor
David Northrup, *Crosscurrents in the Black Atlantic, 1770-1965: A Brief History with Documents*, 2007

690

PAUL CARTLEDGE

Thermopylae: The Battle That Changed the World

(Woodstock, New York: Overlook Press, 2006)

Subject(s): Battle of Thermopylae, 480 BC; History; Ancient Greek civilization

Summary: In *Thermopylae: The Battle That Changed the World*, historian Paul Cartledge provides a detailed history of the battle at Thermopylae, in which 300 Spartans commanded by King Leonidas faced the advancing Persian army, led by Xerxes. Cartledge begins with a discussion of the background of ancient Greek civilization, the Persian Empire, and Sparta. Because only Spartan men with living sons were taken to the dangerous battle, the author believes that the Spartans knew that they were embarking on a suicide mission. The author also considers how the world might be changed if the results of the battle had been different.

Where it's reviewed:
Booklist, November 15, 2006, page 19
History Today, December 2006, page 65
Library Journal, November 1, 2006, page 86
New York Times Book Review, December 6, 2007, page 62

Other books by the same author:
Ancient Greece: A History in Eleven Cities, 2010
The Spartans: The World of the Warrior-Heroes of Ancient Greece, 2005
Alexander the Great, 2004

Other books you might like:
Ernie Bradford, *Thermopylae: The Battle for the West*, 2004
Donald Kagan, *The Peloponnesian War*, 2003
Steven Pressfield, *Gates of Fire: An Epic Novel of the Battle of Thermopylae*, 1998
Barry Strauss, *The Battle of Salamis: The Naval Encounter That Saved Greece—and Western Civilization*, 2005
Barry Strauss, *The Trojan War: A New History*, 2006

691

THURSTON CLARKE

The Last Campaign: Robert F. Kennedy and 82 Days That Inspired America

(New York: Henry Holt and Co., 2008)

Subject(s): Assassination; Politics

Summary: *The Last Campaign* chronicles the events that led to Robert F. Kennedy's decision to run for president and the 82 days he spent on the campaign trail before he was assassinated. With intimate detail, first-hand accounts and thorough research, Clarke gives an insider's view into the man who chose to pick up his brother's torch and lead the country in his own inspired way. Recreating the political arena and the state of the country at the time, Clarke examines how difficult it was for Kennedy to have succeeded as well as he did. Placing Kennedy's words and actions into a historical and modern context, the book explores the significance of the last Kennedy presidential campaign.

Where it's reviewed:
The New Yorker, June 23, 2008, page 83
Politics Magazine, July 2008, page 46
Publishers Weekly, March 31, 2008, page 48
Time, June 16, 2008, page 67

Other books by the same author:
Ask Not: The Inauguration of John F. Kennedy and the Speech That Changed America, 2010
Searching for Paradise: A Grand Tour of the World's Unspoiled Islands, 2002
Pearl Harbor Ghosts: A Journey to Hawaii Then and Now, 1991

Other books you might like:
Marc Aronson, *Robert F. Kennedy: A Twentieth-Century Life*, 2007
Maxwell Taylor Kennedy, *Make Gentle the Life of This World: The Vision of Robert F. Kennedy*, 1998
Joseph A. Palermo, *Robert F. Kennedy and the Death of American Idealism*, 2007
Arthur Schlesinger, *Robert Kennedy and His Times*, 1978
Evan Thomas, *Robert Kennedy: His Life*, 2000

692

DEBORAH COHEN

Household Gods: The British and Their Possessions

(New Haven, Connecticut: Yale University Press, 2006)

Subject(s): England; Shopping; Retail stores

Summary: In *Household Gods: The British and Their Possessions*, Deborah Cohen traces the history of consumerism and materialism in England, beginning in the early 19th century and continuing into the 20th century. Cohen argues that the shift began when people stopped viewing material possessions as sinful and, instead, saw them as a way to express their individual personalities. Possessions were a way to illustrate one's class and good taste, particularly during the Victorian era. Although Cohen examines the way men and women use consumerism to present themselves to the outside world, she specifically focuses on how it relates to the development of a type of feminism.

Where it's reviewed:
American Historical Review, June 2007, page 928
English Historical Review, December 2008, page 1569
Journal of Modern History, June 2009, page 409
Times Literary Supplement, February 9, 2007, page 36
Victorian Studies, Summer 2007, page 721

Other books by the same author:
Braceros: Migrant Citizens and Transnational Subjects in the Postwar United States and Mexico, 2010
The War Come Home: Disabled Veterans in Britain and Germany, 1914-1939, 2001

Other books you might like:
Maxine Berg, *Luxury and Pleasure in Eighteenth-Century Britain*, 2005
David R. Farber, *The Day Before Yesterday: A Photographic Album of Daily Life in Victorian and Edwardian Britain*, 1978
Sally Mitchell, *Daily Life in Victorian England*, 2008
Amanda Vickery, *Behind Closed Doors: At Home in Georgian England*, 2009
Laura Wilson, *Daily Life in a Victorian House*, 1998

693

MATTHEW COUNTRYMAN

Up South: Civil Rights and Black Power in Philadelphia

(Philadelphia, Pennsylvania: University of Pennsylvania Press, 2005)

Subject(s): Civil rights; History; Social sciences

Summary: In *Up South: Civil Rights and Black Power in Philadelphia*, Matthew Countryman considers the civil rights movement as it was seen in Philadelphia, as well as the corresponding Black Power movement. Countryman begins the discussion following World War II, when the development of a new city charter allowed civil rights groups to introduce laws against racial discrimination in the local government. Approximately ten years later, boycotts and protests against racial discrimination were common in schools and neighborhoods. Throughout the text, Countryman disputes the belief that the Black Power movement was detrimental to the civil rights movement, noting the importance of grassroots organizations and individual activism in changing the American political landscape.

Where it's reviewed:
American Historical Review, April 2007, page 536
CHOICE: Current Reviews for Academic Libraries, December 2006, page 701
Diversity Issues in Higher Education, February 8, 2007, page 41
Journal of African American History, Spring 2007, page 314
Journal of American History, December 2006, page 956

Other books you might like:
David A. Canton, *Raymond Pace Alexander: A New Negro Lawyer Fights for Civil Rights in Philadelphia*, 2010
Robert Gregg, *Sparks from the Anvil of Oppression: Philadelphia's African Methodists and Southern Migrants, 1890-1940*, 1998
Peniel E. Joseph, *Waiting Til the Midnight Hour: A Narrative History of Black Power in America*, 2006
David Kairys, *Philadelphia Freedom: Memoir of a Civil Rights Lawyer*, 2008
Florence Mars, *Witness in Philadelphia*, 1989

694

THOMAS J. CRAUGHWELL

Stealing Lincoln's Body

(Cambridge, Massachusetts: Harvard University Press, 2007)

Subject(s): Presidents (Government); History; Crime

Summary: In *Stealing Lincoln's Body*, Thomas J. Craughwell shares the story of the group of criminals who attempted to steal Abraham Lincoln's body on election night in 1876. The men planned to demand $200,000 from the government and the release of a friend from prison for the remains of the 16th president. Although the plan was thwarted, the president's body was then carefully guarded until it could be encased in concrete 25 years later. Craughwell follows Lincoln's body during those 25 years, describing the secret places it was held. When it came time to encase the body in concrete, a number of experts were called in to verify that the authenticity of the remains.

Where it's reviewed:
Booklist, March 1, 2007, page 56
The Historian, Fall 2009, page 594
History, October 2007, page 543
Library Journal, March 1, 2007, page 92
Publishers Weekly, February 19, 2007, page 159

Other books by the same author:
Failures of the Presidents: From the Whiskey Rebellion and War of 1812 to the Bay of Pigs and War in Iraq, 2008
How the Barbarian Invasions Shaped the Modern World, 2008
Saints Behaving Badly: The Cutthroats, Crooks, Trollops, Con Men, and Devil-Worshippers Who Became Saints, 2006

Other books you might like:
Wayne Fanebust, *The Missing Corpse: Grave Robbing a Gilded Age Tycoon*, 2005
David Ralph Johnson, *Illegal Tender: Counterfeiting and the Secret Service in Nineteenth-Century America*, 2000
Philip H. Melanson, *The Secret Service: The Hidden History of an Engimatic Agency*, 2004
Stephen Mihm, *A Nation of Counterfeiters: Capitalists, Con Men and the Making of the United States*, 2007
Bonnie Stahlman Speer, *The Great Abraham Lincoln Hijack*, 1990

695

EMILYE CROSBY

A Little Taste of Freedom: The Black Freedom Struggle in Claiborne County, Mississippi

(Chapel Hill, North Carolina: University of North Carolina Press, 2005)

Subject(s): Civil rights; African Americans; Law

Summary: In *A Little Taste of Freedom: The Black Freedom Struggle in Claiborne County, Mississippi*, Emilye Crosby provides a scholarly analysis of the civil rights movement from the perspective of the citizens of the small, rural community of Claiborne County, Mississippi. Crosby notes that even as national laws were enacted, smaller communities such as this one were often much slower to experience change. It was the actions of the people—such as boycotts, activism, and armed self-defense—that led to real change. Crosby also considers how these small community movements were extremely influential on a national level. A great deal of Crosby's information comes from approximately 100 oral histories taken from people in Claiborne County.

Where it's reviewed:
American Historical Review, February 2008, page 223
Journal of American History, September 2006, page 600
Journal of Southern History, May 2007, page 499
Publishers Weekly, January 23, 2006, page 140
Reviews in American History, September 2006, page 364

Other books you might like:
Kenneth T. Andrews, *Freedom Is a Constant Struggle: The Mississippi Civil Rights Movement and Its Legacy*, 2004
Charles E. Cobb, *Radical Equations: Math Literacy and Civil Rights*, 2001
John Dittmer, *Local People: The Struggle for Civil Rights in Mississippi*, 1994
Steve Fayer, *Voices of Freedom: An Oral History of the Civil Rights Movement from the 1950s through the 1980s*, 1990
Henry Hampton, co-author
Robert P. Moses, *Radical Equations: Math Literacy and Civil Rights*, 2001
Lynne Olson, *Freedom's Daughters: The Unsung Heroines of the Civil Rights Movement from 1830 to 1970*, 2001

696

ROGER CROWLEY

Empires of the Sea: The Siege of Malta, the Battle of Lepanto, and the Contest for the Center of the World

(New York: Random House, 2008)

Subject(s): Wars; Ottoman Empire, ca. 1288-1922; Religion

Summary: *Empires of the Sea: The Siege of Malta, the Battle of Lepanto, and the Contest for the Center of the World* by Roger Crowley explores a number of battles that helped determine the future of Europe during the 16th century. During this time, the Ottoman Empire was extremely powerful and the Christian nations in Europe were weak and vulnerable. When the Turks threatened these Christian nations, however, they banded together to form a united front and fight off their common enemy. In a series of difficult battles, the Christian Europeans fought back the Turks and maintained their dominance in Western Europe.

Where it's reviewed:
Booklist, July 1, 2008, page 30
Publishers Weekly, May 5, 2008, page 53

Other books by the same author:
Empires of the Sea: The Final Battle for the Mediterranean, 1521-1580, 2008
1453: The Holy War for Constantinople and the Clash of Islam and the West, 2006
Constantinople: The Last Great Siege 1453, 2006

Other books you might like:
Ernie Bradford, *The Great Siege: Malta 1565*, 1962
Niccolo Capponi, *Victory of the West: The Great Christian-Muslim Clash at the Battle of Lepanto*, 2007
Angus Konstam, *Lepanto 1571: The Greatest Naval Battle of the Renaissance*, 2005
Jonathan Philips, *Holy Warriors: A Modern History of the Crusades*, 2010
Rodney Stark, *Gods Battalions: The Case for the Crusades*, 2009

697

ROBERT DALLEK

Nixon and Kissinger: Partners in Power

(New York: HarperCollins, 2007)

Subject(s): Political crimes; Politics; Presidents (Government)

Summary: Biographer Robert Dellek's *Nixon and Kissinger: Partners in Power* provides an in-depth look at Richard Nixon and Henry Kissinger's relationship both in and out of the Oval Office. With never-before-heard information from eye witnesses, telephone audio files, and transcripts from the most private of meetings, Dellek paints an extremely detailed portrait of the dynamic duo's reign. He examines the decisions each man made on his own as President of the United States and as Secretary of State respectively, and he also provides information about how they worked together on issues relating to major world events in China, Chile, Vietnam, the Middle East, and Cambodia. Dellek also explores each man's personal history and includes information about the men's personalities, individual strengths, and greatest fears.

Where it's reviewed:
American Historical Review, February 2008, page 225
The Atlantic, June 2007, page 122
Journal of American History, September 2007, page 652
National Review, August 27, 2007, page 36
Newsweek, May 14, 2007, page 47.

Other books by the same author:
John F. Kennedy, 2011
Harry S. Truman, 2008
Lyndon B. Johnson: Portrait of a President, 2005

Other books you might like:
Seymour M. Hersh, *The Price of Power: Kissinger in the Nixon White House*, 1983
Henry Kissinger, *White House Years*, 1979
Frederik Logevall, *Nixon in the World: American Foreign Relations, 1969-1977*, 2008
Clare Luce, *White House Years*, 1979
Andrew Preston, *Nixon in the World: American Foreign Relations, 1969-1977*, 2008
Asaf Siniver, *Nixon, Kissinger, and U.S. Foreign Policy Making: The Machinery of Crisis*, 2008
Richard C. Thornton, *Nixon-Kissinger Years: The Re-Shaping of American Foreign Policy*, 2001

698

WILLIAM DALRYMPLE

The Last Mughal: The Fall of a Dynasty: Delhi, 1857

(New York: Alfred A. Knopf, 2007)

Subject(s): Indians (Asian people); Mughal Empire, 1526-1857; Colonialism

Summary: In *The Last Mughal: The Fall of a Dynasty: Delhi, 1857*, acclaimed author William Dalrymple recounts India's Great Mutiny and its unofficial leader, Bahadur Shah II (also known as Zafar). Dalrymple reconstructs the final days of the Mughal city of Delhi before its annihilation during the fighting between the native Indians and the colonial British. *The Last Mughal* contains a wealth of supplementary information, including maps, illustrations, notes on the text, a bibliography, and a full index.

Where it's reviewed:
Foreign Affairs, November/December 2007, page 81
Harper's Magazine, August 2007, page 81
New Statesman, October 30, 2006, page 56
New Yorker, May 14, 2007, page 149
Publishers Weekly, February 19, 2007

Other books by the same author:
White Mughals: Love and Betrayal in Eighteenth-Century India, 2004
City of Djinns: A Year in Delhi, 2003
From the Holy Mountain: A Journey Among the Christians of the Middle East, 1999

Other books you might like:
Abraham Eraly, *The Mughal Throne: The Saga of India's Great Emperors*, 2003
J.J.L. Gomans, *Mughal Warfare: Indian Frontiers and Highroads to Empire 1500-1700*, 2002
John Keay, *India; A History*, 2000
Ruby Lal, *Domesticity and Power in the Early Mughal World*, 2005
John F. Richards, *The Mughal Empire*, 1993

699

JOHN DARWIN

After Tamerlane: The Global History of Empire Since 1405

(New York: Bloomsbury Press, 2008)

Subject(s): History; International relations; Mongol Empire, 1206-1502

Summary: In *After Tamerlane: The Global History of Empire Since 1405*, John Darwin presents a scholarly study of the history of globalization during the past 600 years. Tamerlane, a 14th-century leader, was the last to conquer all of Europe and Asia, bringing them under a single rule. In this text, Darwin considers how smaller subsequent empires impacted the modern organization of the world. Darwin grounds the discussion in the present with his analysis of the United States as a "hyperpower" and his description of how China and India are influencing economic and political policies.

Where it's reviewed:
American Historical Review, October 2008, page 1114
CHOICE: Current Reviews for Academic Libraries, December 2008, page 751
History Today, August 2008, page 3
Publishers Weekly, October 15, 2007
Times Literary Supplement, December 21, 2007, page 34

Other books by the same author:
After Tamerlane: The Rise and Fall of Global Empires, 1400-2000, 2009
The Empire Project: The Rise and Fall of the British World-System, 1830-1970, 2006
The End of the British Empire: The Historical Debate, 2006

Other books you might like:
William J. Bernstein, *A Splendid Exchange: How Trade Shaped the World*, 2008
Jane Burbank, *Empires in World History: Power and the Politics of Difference*, 2010
Niall Ferguson, *Empire: The Rise and Demise of the British World Order and the Lessons for Global Power*, 2002
Timothy Parsons, *The Rule of Empires: Those Who Built Them, Those Who Endured Them, and Why They Always Fail*, 2010
John E. Wills, *1688: A Global History*, 2001

700

J.P. DAUGHTON

An Empire Divided: Religion, Republicanism and the Making of French Colonialism, 1880-1914

(New York: Oxford University Press, 2006)

Subject(s): Religion; Politics; Colonialism

Summary: In *An Empire Divided: Religion, Republicanism*

and the Making of French Colonialism, 1880-1914 J.P. Daughton considers the inextricable connections between Catholic missionaries and the Third Republic campaign to expand French territory. The French missionaries traveled to most of the same locations as the republicans. Although there was a great deal of conflict inherent in these initial interactions, it eventually became clear that a compromise was necessary. Daughton explores three regions where the two groups converged: Indochina, Polynesia, and Madagascar. While French colonialism was once considered a secular by-product of the Enlightenment, it was in fact linked quite closely with religious ideals. Daughton considers how the actions of the missionaries and republicans changed not just colonial rule but European ideas as well.

Where it's reviewed:
American Historical Review, June 2008, page 923
Catholic Historical Review, July 2010, page 505
CHOICE: Current Reviews for Academic Libraries, July 2007, page 1976
The Historian, Spring 2009, page 149
Journal of Modern History, September 2008, page 675

Other books you might like:
Pierre Brocheux, *Indochina: An Ambiguous Colonization, 1858-1954*, 2010
Alice Conklin, *A Mission to Civilize: The Republican Idea of Empire in France and West Africa, 1895-1930*, 1997
Madeleine Dobie, *Trading Places: Colonization and Slavery in Eighteenth-Century French Culture*, 2010
Laurent Dubois, *A Colony of Citizens: Revolution and Slave Emancipation in the French Caribbean, 1787-1804*, 2006
Daniel Hemery, *Indochina: An Ambiguous Colonization, 1858-1954*, 2010
David Prochaska, *Making Algeria French: Colonialism in Bone, 1870-1920*, 1990

701

JOHN A. DAVIS

Naples and Napoleon: Southern Italy and the European Revolutions, 1780-1860

(New York: Oxford University Press, 2006)

Subject(s): History; Italy; Revolutions

Summary: In *Naples and Napoleon: Southern Italy and the European Revolutions, 1780-1860*, John A. Davis considers southern Italy during the time period surrounding the Napoleonic Wars, focusing most specifically on the years between 1806 and 1815. Though southern Italy is not often considered in revolutionary and unification analyses, Davis argues that this state was one of the more significant sources of political and economic unrest. He considers how southern Italy came to be unified with neighboring states, also discussing European revolutions occurring in 1799 and then in Naples and Sicily in 1820. All of these subjects are considered in relation to Italian history as a whole, and the differences that led to such divisions in politics and reform between northern and southern Italy.

Where it's reviewed:
American Historical Review, February 2009, page 240
Catholic Historical Review, April 2008, page 388
CHOICE: Current Reviews for Academic Libraries, October 2007, page 349
Journal of European Studies, June 2007, page 232

Other books by the same author:
The Jews of San Nicandro, 2010
Conflict and Control: Law and Order in Nineteenth-Century Italy, 1988

Other books you might like:
Carlo Giuseppe G. Botta, *History of Italy During the Consulate and the Empire of Napoleon Buonoparte*, 2009
John A. Davis, *Italy in the Nineteenth Century: 1796-1900*, 2000
Spencer M. Di Scala, *Italy: From Revolution to Republic, 1700 to the Present*, 2004
John A. Marino, *Early Modern Italy: 1550-1796*, 2002
Frederick C. Schneid, *Napoleon's Italian Campaigns: 1805-1815*, 2002

702

KATHY DAVIS

The Making of Our Bodies, Ourselves: How Feminism Travels Across Borders

(Durham, North Carolina: Duke University Press, 2007)

Subject(s): Books; Women; Feminism

Summary: In *The Making of Our Bodies, Ourselves: How Feminism Travels Across Borders*, Kathy Davis examines the impact that the original book *Our Bodies, Ourselves*, first published in 1970, has had on women around the world. Davis argues that the book's message of empowerment to women, which encouraged them to make use of their experiences and firsthand knowledge about their own bodies, made it so successful and popular. She gathers information from interviews with the Boston Women's Health Book Collective, the group responsible for the initial publication, as well as individuals who have translated the book into other languages.

Where it's reviewed:
American Journal of Sociology, May 2009, page 1901
Canadian Journal of History, Spring/Summer 2010, page 204
CHOICE: Current Reviews for Academic Libraries, July 2008, page 1986
Contemporary Sociology, July 2008, page 384
Library Journal, October 2, 2007, page 83

Other books by the same author:
Dubious Equalities and Embodied Difference: Cultural Studies on Cosmetic Surgery, 2004
Reshaping the Female Body: The Dilemma of Cosmetic Surgery, 1994

Other books you might like:
Boston Women's Health Collective, *Our Bodies Ourselves for the New Century*, 1998
Kimberly Christenson, *Beyond Reproduction: Women's Health, Activism and Public Policy*, 2009
Mary E. Hawkesworth, *Globalization and Feminist Activism*, 2006
Sandra Morgen, *Into Our Own Hands: The Women's Health Movement in the United States, 1969-1990*, 2002
Aili Tripp, *Global Feminism: Transnational Women Activism*, 2006

703

KENNETH C. DAVIS

America's Hidden History: Untold Tales of the First Pilgrims, Fighting Women, and Forgotten Founders Who Shaped a Nation

(New York: Smithsonian Books, 2008)

Subject(s): United States history; United States history, 1600-1775 (Colonial period); History

Summary: In *America's Hidden History: Untold Tales of the First Pilgrims, Fighting Women, and Forgotten Founders Who Shaped a Nation*, New York Times bestselling author Kenneth C. Davis compiles a collection of little-known historic events that helped to shape the United States. Beginning with Spain's arrival in America and ending with the inauguration of George Washington, each story is comprised of intriguing facts that the average American has most likely never learned. Readers discover the identity of the first Pilgrims—French Huguenots who enjoyed drinking wine. Readers also learn interesting information concerning the Pilgrims and the Native Americans—a relationship that was far from friendly. Readers learn how pigs spread disease to the Native Americans and how George Washington was a hot-headed soldier responsible for the start of a war.

Where it's reviewed:
Library Journal, May 1, 2008, page 80
Publishers Weekly, March 24, 2008, page 64

Other books by the same author:
Don't Know Much About Mythology: Everything You Need to Know About the Greatest Stories in Human History But Never Learned, 2006
Don't Know Much About History: Everything You Need to Know About American History but Never Learned, 2004
Don't Know Much About the Universe: Everything You Need to Know About Outer Space but Never Learned, 2002

Other books you might like:
Thomas Ayres, *That's Not in My American History Book: A Compilation of Little Known Events and Forgotten Heroes*, 2000
Rick Beyer, *The Greatest Stories Never Told: 100 Tales*

from History to Astonish, Bewilder, and Stupefy,
2003
James W. Loewen, *Lies My Teacher Told Me:*
Everything Your American History Textbook Got
Wrong, 1995
Richard Shenkman, *Legends, Lies, and Cherished Myths*
of American History, 1988
Howard Zinn, *A People's History of the United States,*
1995

704

MICHAEL DOBBS

One Minute to Midnight: Kennedy, Khrushchev, and Castro on the Brink of Nuclear War

(New York: Knopf, 2008)

Subject(s): History; Cold War, 1945-1991; Cuban history

Summary: In *One Minute to Midnight: Kennedy, Khrush-chev, and Castro on the Brink of Nuclear War,* Michael Dobbs tells the story of the 1962 Cuban missile crisis. During that crisis, which pitted the United States against Cuba and its Russian allies, the leaders of the involved nations came frighteningly close to starting a nuclear war. The book focuses mainly on the 13 days in October when a crisis seemed imminent. In the book, Dobbs tries to explain the motivations behind the leaders' decisions, and he gives insight into the behind-the-scenes dealings that helped prevent major military action. Dobbs is also the author of *Saboteurs: The Nazi Raid on America.*

Where it's reviewed:
American Heritage, Winter 2009, page 62
Journal of American History, June 2009, page 294
Reviews in American History, December 2008, page 610
Times Literary Supplment, October 3, 2008, page 27
World Affairs, Summer 2009, page 99

Other books by the same author:
Saboteurs: The Nazi Raid on America, 2005
Madeleine Albright: A Twentieth-Century Odyssey, 2000
Down with Big Brother: The Fall of the Soviet Empire,
1998

Other books you might like:
Aleksandr Fursenko, *"One Hell of a Gamble":*
Khrushchev, Castro, and Kennedy, 1958-1964, 1997
Robert F. Kennedy, *Thirteen Days: A Memoir of the*
Cuban Missile Crisis, 1969
Ernest R. May, *The Kennedy Tapes: Inside the White*
House During the Cuban Missile Crisis, 1997
Don Munton, *The Cuban Missile Crisis: A Concise*
History, 2006
Timothy Naftali, *"One Hell of a Gamble": Khrushchev,*
Castro, and Kennedy, 1958-1964, 1997
Sheldon M. Stern, *The Week the Earth Stood Still:*
Inside the Secret Cuban Missile Crisis, 2004
Philip D. Zelikow, *The Kennedy Tapes: Inside the White*
House During the Cuban Missile Crisis, 1997

705

ERIC JAY DOLIN

Leviathan: The History of Whaling in America

(New York: W.W. Norton & Co., 2007)

Subject(s): Whaling; United States history; Economics

Summary: In *Leviathan: The History of Whaling in America,* Eric Jay Dolin provides a detailed account of the practices of whaling off the Atlantic coast and explains how whaling helped shape the country. Whaling and the subsequent products created from the process led to economic success in the various New England states. Whaling first began in the 17th century and, despite dropping off during the Revolutionary War, the practice continued through the middle of the 19th century. Dolin also considers issues related to the European settlers' colonization of Native American territories, and the way whaling affected slavery. Although some slaves were able to escape on whaling ships, some whaling ships were converted into slave ships. Dolin uses extensive research and a number of illustrations to share the importance of the whaling industry history without advocating for the practice in a contemporary context.

Where it's reviewed:
American Historical Review, December 2008, page
1518
CHOICE: Current Reviews for Academic Libraries,
December 2007, page 688
New England Quarterly, June 2009, page 379
The New Yorker, July 23, 2007, page 64

Technology and Culture, July 2010, page 745

Other books by the same author:
Fur, Fortune, and Empire: The Epic History of the Fur
Trade in America, 2010
Political Waters: The Long, Dirty, Contentious,
Incredibly Expensive but Eventually Triumphant
History of Boston Harbor, a Unique Environmental
Success Story, 2008
The Duck Stamp Story, 2000

Other books you might like:
John Braginton-Smith, *Cape Cod Shore Whaling:*
America First Whalemen, 2008
Stephen Currie, *Thar She Blows: American Whaling in*
the Nineteenth Century, 2001
Andrew Darby, *Harpoon: Into the Heart of Whaling,*
2008
Daniel Francis, *History of World Whaling,* 1990
A.O. Johnsen, *The History of Modern Whaling,* 1982
Duncan Oliver, *Cape Cod Shore Whaling: America*
First Whalemen, 2008
J.N. Tonnesson, *The History of Modern Whaling,* 1982

706

BARBARA DONAGAN

War in England 1642-1649

(New York: Oxford University Press, 2008)

Subject(s): England; Revolutions; Civil war

Summary: In *War in England 1642-1649*, Barbara Donagan tells the story of the English Civil War between the royalists and the parliamentarians from a more personal perspective, considering how it affected individuals fighting in the war and explaining what conditions were like at that time. Many of the soldiers knew each other prior to the beginning of the war, which made fighting especially challenging. Donagan considers topics such as the English view of war prior to the fighting in 1642, the way armies operated, and the accepted rules of conduct during battle. Donagan then provides a section focusing on two specific battles, providing military and civilian perspectives of both skirmishes.

Where it's reviewed:
American Historical Review, April 2009, page 480
History: Journal of the American Historical Society, October 2009, page 535
Renaissance Quarterly, Spring 2009, page 294
Times Literary Supplement, April 10, 2009, page 9.

Other books you might like:
M.J. Braddick, *God's Fury, England's Fire: A New History of the English Civil Wars*, 2009
Richard Cust, *Charles I: A Political Life*, 2005
Peter Gaunt, *The English Civil Wars 1642-1651*, 2003
Diane Purkiss, *The English Civil War: Papists, Gentlewomen, Soldiers, and Witchfinders in the Birth of Modern Britain*, 2006
Stuart Reid, *All the King''s Armies: A Military History of the English Civil War*, 1998

707

JAMES DONOVAN

A Terrible Glory: Custer and Little Bighorn—The Last Great Battle of the American West

(New York: Little, Brown and Co., 2008)

Subject(s): Native Americans; Wars; United States history

Summary: In *A Terrible Glory: Custer and Little Bighorn—The Last Great Battle of the American West*, James Donovan provides a comprehensive account of the 1876 massacre at Little Bighorn in the southern Montana territory, also known as Custer's Last Stand. Commander Philip Sheridan ordered the attack when a number of American Indians refused to relocate to reservations. The charge was led by General George Custer, but his soldiers were relatively unprepared for the fight. Donovan describes the entire battle in detail, explaining how Custer and his men were eventually defeated. The United States government wanted to blame Custer for this

failure, but the survivors of the battle would not allow the general to take the fall.

Where it's reviewed:
American Heritage, Winter 2009, page 64
CHOICE: Current Reviews for Academic Libraries, March 2009, page 1384
Journal of Southern History, May 2010, page 523
Publishers Weekly, November 12, 2007

Other books by the same author:
Custer and Little Big Horn: The Man, the Mystery, the Myth, 2001
The Dallas Cowboys Encyclopedia, 1996
Dallas: Shining Star of Texas, 1994

Other books you might like:
Joseph Agonito, *Buffalo Calf Road Woman: The Story of a Warrior of the Little Bighorn*, 2005
    Rosemary Agonito, co-author
Paul Andrew Hutton, *The Custer Reader*, 1992
Joseph Marshall III, *The Day the World Ended at Little Bighorn: A Lakota History*, 2007
Nathaniel Philbrick, *The Last Stand: Custer, Sitting Bull and the Battle of the Little Bighorn*, 2010
Paul Stekler, *Killing Custer*, 1994
    James Welch, co-author

708

THOMAS DUBLIN
WALTER LICHT , Co-Author

The Face of Decline: The Pennsylvania Anthracite Region in the Twentieth Century

(Ithaca, New York: Cornell University Press, 2005)

Subject(s): Natural resources; United States history; Economics

Summary: Historians Thomas Dublin and Walter Licht investigate the rise and fall of the once-thriving anthracite coal region of Pennsylvania. *The Face of Decline: The Pennsylvania Anthracite Region in the Twentieth Century* analyzes how the industry affected the area economically, socially, environmentally, and politically. The authors have culled information from a variety of sources—everything from oral accounts and photographs to coal company documentation, censuses, and newspapers—to give readers a comprehensive analysis of what transpired in the Pennsylvania anthracite district throughout the 20th century. This detailed text aims to illuminate the economic life of the area to provide both a history lesson and an important perspective on contemporary economic crises.

Where it's reviewed:
American Historical Review, April 2007, page 548
Journal of American History, December 2006, page 895
Journal of Social History, Winter 2007, page 472
Oral History Review, Winter/Spring 2008, page 82
Technology and Culture, January 2007, page 205

Other books by the same author:

When the Mines Closed: Stories of Struggles in Hard Times, 1998

Transforming Women's Work: New England Lives in the Industrial Revolution, 1995

Women and Power in American History: A Reader, Volume I to 1880, 1990

Other books you might like:

Richard G. Healey, *The Pennsylvania Anthracite Coal Industry, 1860-1802*, 2007

Joseph M. Leonard, *Anthracite Roots: Generations of Coal Mining in Schuykill County, Pennsylvania*, 2005

Barry P. Michrina, *Pennsylvania Mining Families: The Search for Dignity in the Coalfields*, 2004

Joan Quigley, *The Day the Earth Caved In: Am American Mining Tragedy*, 2009

James Moore Swank, *Introduction to a History of Ironmaking and Coal Mining in Pennsylvania*, 2009

709

LAURA F. EDWARDS

The People and Their Peace: Legal Culture and the Transformation of Inequality in the Post-Revolutionary South

(Chapel Hill, North Carolina: University of North Carolina Press, 2009)

Subject(s): United States history; Politics; Law

Summary: In *The People and Their Peace: Legal Culture and the Transformation of Inequality in the Post-Revolutionary South*, Laura F. Edwards considers a period in the history of the United States following the American Revolution, from approximately 1780 to 1840. In this time period, local governments wielded great power and often had the final word in many issues. These governments were focused on maintaining what they considered to be the "peace" in local communities, which tended to mean a patriarchal system that placed women and, of course, slaves at a much lower level. Over time, this patriarchal system expanded to the more centralized state governments. Edwards considers how all of these events helped to shape the American legal system and the development of laws.

Where it's reviewed:

American Historical Review, December 2009, page 1454

CHOICE: Current Reviews for Academic Libraries, September 2009, page 182

Journal of American History, December 2009, page 182

Journal of Interdisciplinary History, Spring/Summer 2010, page 618

Other books by the same author:

Scarlett Doesn't Live Here Anymore, 2004

Gendered Strife and Confusion: The Political Culture of Reconstruction, 1997

Other books you might like:

William Byrd, *The Commonplace Book of William Byrd II of Westover*, 2000

Drew Gilpin Faust, *The Ideology of Slavery: Proslavery Thought in the Antebellum South, 1830-1860*, 1981

Lawrence M. Friedman, *Law in America: A Brief History*, 2002

Stephanie McCurry, *Masters of Small Worlds: Yeoman Households, Gender Relations, and the Political Culture of the Antebellum South Carolina Low Country*, 1995

David Waldstreicher, *Slavery's Constitution: From Revolution to Ratification*, 2009

710

ROBERT EDWARDS

The Winter War: Russia's Invasion of Finland, 1939-40

(New York: Pegasus Books, 2007)

Subject(s): Wars; Russian history; World War II, 1939-1945

Summary: *The Winter War: Russia's Invasion of Finland, 1939-40* is a history written by Robert Edwards. In November 1939, the former Soviet Union invaded Finland expecting a quick and easy battle to acquire additional territory. Instead, a 105-day war ensued, in which the woefully unprepared Soviet army was held off by a much smaller yet much more efficient Finnish army led by Baron Carl Mannerheim. The Finnish soldiers would often travel on skis and attack the Soviet army at night, leading to panic and high casualties while keeping their own numbers up. Eventually the two armies reached a standstill, but Finland's resources were so depleted that they were forced to surrender a small part of their territory to the Soviets. The author argues that this battle significantly affected the Soviet Union in World War II, comparing it to the battle of Thermopylae between the Spartans and the Persian Army. A number of black-and-white photographs are also included in this book.

Where it's reviewed:

Booklist, March 1, 2008, page 46

Publishers Weekly, April 21, 2008, page 47

Other books you might like:

Allen F. Chew, *The White Death: The Epic of Soviet-Finnish Winter War*, 2002

Eloise Engle, *The Winter War: The Soviet Attack on Finland 1939-1940*, 1992

Philip Jowett, *Finland at War 1939-45*, 2006

William Trotter, *A Frozen Hell: The Russo-Finnish Winter War of 1939-1940*, 2000

William R. Trotter, *Winter Fire*, 1993

711

TIMOTHY EGAN

The Worst Hard Time: The Untold Story of Those Who Survived the Great American Dust Bowl
(New York: Mariner Press, 2005)

Subject(s): American History; American West; Depression (Economic)

Summary: The intersection of Kansas, Colorado, New Mexico, Texas, and Oklahoma was parceled off for homesteading and the promise of land and prosperity brought people to the region. Initially, their dreams were fulfilled; then the stock market crashed in 1929 and the first dust storm appeared in Texas in 1931. By 1935, the drought-ridden area became known as the Dust Bowl and many were forced to leave. Using survivor interviews and political and historical records, Egan creates a complete and personal picture of the rapid rise to success and the even quicker fall into tragedy that took place on the Plains. In the stories of six families who stayed and endured starvation, poverty, rising debt, failure, and the deaths of family members during the Dust Bowl, Egan also recounts great courage and heroism.

Where it's reviewed:
Earth Island Journal, Autumn 2006, page 47
The New Yorker, February 6, 2006, page 83
Publishers Weekly, November 28, page 42
Smithsonian, March 2006, page 110
Washington Monthly, April 2006, page 49

Other books by the same author:
The Big Burn: Teddy Roosevelt and the Fire That Saved America, 2010
The Winemaker's Daughter, 2005
The Good Rain: Across Time and Terrain in the Pacific Northwest, 19991

Other books you might like:
Michael L. Cooper, *Dust to Eat: Drought and Depression in the 1930s*, 2004
Timothy Egan, *The Big Burn: Teddy Roosevelt and the Fire that Saved America*, 2009
Albert Marrin, *Years of Dust: The Story of the Dust Bowl*, 2009
Alison Swan, *Fresh Water: Women Writing on the Great Lakes*, 2006
William T. Vollmann, *Imperial*, 2009

712

A. ROGER EKIRCH

At Day's Close: A History of Nighttime
(London: Weidenfeld & Nicolson, 2005)

Story type: Collection
Subject(s): Literature; Crime; Dance

Summary: In *At Day's Close: A History of Nighttime*, A. Roger Ekrich reminds readers that a sunset used to signal the end of the day. When it was dark outside, people would go inside to sleep. However, sometime between the 18th and 21st centuries, nights came alive. People left their homes to go to bars and taverns. They attended masquerade balls and danced late into the night. They even traveled by moonlight, making their way down deserted paths at quick, undisturbed speeds. At the same time people used the nighttime to enjoy themselves, others used it to mask criminal activities. Assassinations and thefts increased as people learned how to move through the darkness. In *At Day's Close*, Ekrich explains how the literature from these periods reflected what was happening at night.

Where it's reviewed:
American Historical Review, December 15, 2005, page 1480
Discover, January 2006, page 74
Harper's, June 2005, page 81
The Nation, August 29, 2005, page 38
Times Literary Supplement, October 28, 2005, page 29

Other books by the same author:
Birthright: The True Story That Inspired Kidnapped, 2010
Bound for America: The Transportation of British Convicts to the Colonies, 1718-1775, 1990
Poor Carolina: Politics and Society in Colonial North Carolina, 1729-1776, 1981

Other books you might like:
Paul Bogard, *Let There Be Night: Testimony on Behalf of the Dark*, 2008
Christopher Dewdney, *Acquainted with the Night: Excursions Through the World After Dark*, 2004
Bryan D. Palmer, *Cultures of Darkness: Night Travels in the History of Transgression*, 2001
Eluned Summers-Bremner, *Insomnia: A Cultural History*, 2008
Lawrence Wright, *Warm and Snug: The History of the Bed*, 2004

713

MARK ELLIOTT

Color-Blind Justice: Albion Tourgee and the Quest for Racial Equality from the Civil War to "Plessy v. Ferguson"
(New York: Oxford University Press USA, 2006)

Subject(s): Biographies; Civil rights; Law

Summary: *Color Blind Justice: Albion Tourgee and the Quest for Racial Equality from the Civil War to "Plessy v. Ferguson"* is a detailed biography of a lesser known Civil Rights advocate from the north. Albion Tourgee was raised in Ohio and served as a Union soldier during the Civil War. After the war, he became a lawyer and started a practice in North Carolina, helping to advocate for former slaves rights during the Reconstruction period.

Tourgee wrote prolifically on the subjects of race and injustice, authoring 15 novels, eight nonfiction books, and countless newspaper and magazine articles. He founded the National Citizen's Rights Association in 1891, wrote the first law against lynching in Ohio, and was the lawyer in the first Supreme Court case to challenge segregation.

Where it's reviewed:

American Historical Review, December 2007, page 1545

Modern Philology, November 2008, page 315

Publishers Weekly, October 16, 2005, page 47

Other books you might like:

Mark Elliott, *Undaunted Radical: The Selected Writings and Speeches of Albion W. Tourgee*, 2010

Erik Foner, *Forever Free: The Story of Emancipation and Reconstruction*, 2005

Keith Weldon Medley, *We as Freeman: Plessy v. Ferguson*, 2003

John David Smith, *Undaunted Radical: The Selected Writings and Speeches of Albion W. Tourgee*, 2010

Brook Thomas, *Plessy v. Ferguson*, 1996

James E. Wise, *Murder in the Courthouse: Reconstruction and Redemption in the North Carolina Piedmont*, 2010

714

JEFFREY A. ENGEL

Cold War at 30,000 Feet: The Anglo-American Fight for Aviation Supremacy

(Cambridge, Massachusetts: Harvard University Press, 2007)

Subject(s): International relations; Technology; Airplanes

Summary: In *Cold War at 30,000 Feet: The Anglo-American Fight for Aviation Supremacy*, author Jeffrey A. Engel examines the relationship between Great Britain and the United States after World War II. As the two nations most qualified to meet the aircraft demands of other global powers in the Cold War era, England and the United States found themselves in heated opposition. Though the nations shared a relationship of collaboration in the areas of diplomacy and world politics, they became adversaries in the quest for profits and power represented by the aircraft industry. As the author demonstrates, the effects of this struggle for supremacy impacted international relations around the world.

Where it's reviewed:

American Historical Review, February 2008, page 151

The Atlantic, October 2008, page 117

Journal of American History, December 2007, page 985

Journal of American Studies, February 2008, page 364

New York Times Book Review, August 16, 2007, page 51

Other books by the same author:

The Fall of the Berlin Wall: The Revolutionary Legacy of 1989, 2009

Other books you might like:

Tom D. Crouch, *Wings: A History of Aviation from Kites to the Space Age*, 2004

Steve Darlow, *Victory Fighters: Winning the Battle for Supremacy in the Skies Over Western Europe, 1941-1945*, 2005

James Fallows, *Free Flight: Inventing the Future of Travel*, 2001

E. Gordon, *Soviet Strategic Aviation in the Cold War*, 2009

R.G. Grant, *Flight: 100 Years of Aviation*, 2007

715

T.J. ENGLISH

Havana Nocturne

(New York: William Morrow, 2008)

Subject(s): Crime; Criminals; Cuban Revolution, 1953-1959

Summary: Before the revolution in 1958, Havana was known as a town full of fun: exotic night life, great music, as much cocaine and alcohol as a person could consume, and, of course, the occasional mob-related slaying, quickly hushed-up. This book describes the organization that controlled Havana, led by legendary mobster Meyer Lansky. The mafia owned the government of dictator Fulgencio Batista as well as the hotels, nightclubs, brothels, and drug dealers. So consumed was the Mafia by the enormous profits being made on this Caribbean island, it was taken by surprise by the rebels, led by the Castro brothers, who were intent on cleaning up the city forever.

Where it's reviewed:

Booklist, April 1, 2008, page 20

Library Journal, April 1, 2008, page 92

The Nation, June 29, 2009, page 23

Publishers Weekly, February 4, 2008, page 50

Other books by the same author:

Paddy Whacked: The Untold Story of the Irish American Gangster, 2006

The Westies: Inside New York's Irish Mob, 2006

Old Bones and Shallow Graves, 2005

Other books you might like:

Enrique Cirules, *The Mafia in Cuba*, 2003

Scott M. Deitch, *The Silent Don: The Criminal Underworld of Santo Trafficante Jr.*, 2007

Rosa Lowinger, *Tropicana Nights: The Life and Times of the Legendary Cuban Nightclub*, 2005

John Paul Rathbone, *The Sugar King of Havana: The Rise and Fall of Julio Cobo, Cuba's Last Tycoon*, 2010

Peter D. Russo, *Offshore Vegas: How the Mob Brought Revolution to Cuba*, 2007

716

RICHARD J. EVANS

The Third Reich at War

(New York: Penguin Press, 2009)

Subject(s): History; World War II, 1939-1945; Holocaust, 1933-1945

Summary: *The Third Reich at War* is the third book in Richard J. Evans's trilogy about the Third Reich, from its early beginnings to its collapse at the conclusion of World War II. Evans does not focus strictly on events of the war, but also covers the Nazi occupation of Poland, the concentration camps and the Holocaust, and the future impact of the Third Reich on German society. The author discusses the unbelievable amount of violence enacted by the Nazis at the beginning of occupation, and their spread throughout Europe, along with the weaknesses inherent in Germany from the beginning that made it seem inevitable that the country would lose the war. Points are illustrated in the book using statistics and numerous first-person accounts that provide varying perspectives.

Where it's reviewed:
Booklist, February 1, 2009, page 14
History Today, November 2008, page 66
Library Journal, January 1, 2009, page 104
Publishers Weekly, January 5, 2009, page 40

Other books by the same author:
Death in Hamburg: Society and Politics in the Cholera Years, 1830-1910, 2005
Lying About Hitler: History, Holocaust, and the David Irving Trial, 2002
Deng Xiaoping and the Making of Modern China, 1995

Other books you might like:
Michael Burleigh, *The Third Reich: A New History*, 2000
Peter Fritzsche, *Life and Death in the Third Reich*, 2008
William Shirer, *The Rise and Fall of the Third Reich*, 1960
Albert Speer, *Inside the Third Reich*, 2009
Michael Veranov, *The Third Reich at War: The Rise and Fall of Hitler's Awesome Military Machine*, 2004

717

DREW GILPIN FAUST

This Republic of Suffering: Death and the American Civil War

(New York: Knopf, 2008)

Subject(s): Civil war; Death; Grief

Summary: Historian Drew Gilpin Faust examines the aftermath of the Civil War and its impact on Americans. Faust argues that it was the first time in American history that people were exposed to that kind of death. She discusses the ways in which Americans learned to cope with the deaths of thousands of soldiers and bystanders,

whose passing was often horrific, senseless, or unknown. She asserts that the modern concept of respect for a military death and the ceremony of the military burial began with Americans' reactions to death after the Civil War. Using artifacts from historical archives, she provides a survey of the nation's letters, poems, funeral sermons, and so on.

Where it's reviewed:
American Historical Review, October 2008, page 1108
The New Republic, April 23, 2008, page 48
New York Review of Books, April 17, 2008, page 78
The New Yorker, January 21, 2008, page 77
Newsweek, January 21, 2008, page 76

Other books by the same author:
Mothers of Invention: Women of the Slaveholding South in the American Civil War, 2004
Creation of Confederate Nationalism: Ideology and Identity in the Civil War South, 1990
A Sacred Circle: The Dilemma of the Intellectual in the Old South, 1840-1860, 1986

Other books you might like:
Michael Fellman, *This Terrible War: The Civil War and Its Aftermath*, 2002
Lesley J. Gordon, co-author
William Marvel, *Andersonville: The Last Depot*, 2006
Richard Masterson, *Salisbury: Civil War Death Camp in North Carolina*, 2005
Andrew Roy, *Fallen Soldier: Memoir of a Civil War Casualty*, 2008
Mark S. Schantz, *Awaiting the Heavenly Country: The Civil War and America's Culture of Death*, 2008
Daniel E. Sutherland, *This Terrible War: The Civil War and Its Aftermath*, 2002

718

GREGORY FEIFER

The Great Gamble: The Soviet War in Afghanistan

(New York: HarperCollins, 2009)

Subject(s): Wars; Assassination; Ethnicity

Summary: *The Great Gamble: The Soviet War in Afghanistan* explores the failed war the Soviet Union waged against Afghanistan in the 1980s. Using firsthand accounts, journalist and Russian correspondent Gregory Feifer compares the Soviet invasion and overthrow of the Afghani government to the United States' invasion of Iraq. In 1979, Premier Leonid Brezhnev reacted to the ousting and execution of the first communist president in Afghanistan by quickly invading the country and setting up his own political regime. The Soviets invaded with little thought about the political or cultural composition of the region. The mighty Russian armies soon found their superior military forces being beaten by the guerrilla tactics of the smaller ethnic factions. The war discouraged the troops and helped precipitate the eventual downfall of the Soviet Union. After Gorbachev was elected, he started the slow withdrawal from Afghanistan that took four years to complete. The Soviet invasion is considered as much a failure as the United States' occupation in Vietnam, with its cost measured in the horrific loss of human life.

Where it's reviewed:
Booklist, December 1, 2008, page 14
Far Eastern Economic Review, March 2009, page 72
Foreign Affairs, May/June 2009, page 178
Washington Monthly, March-April 2009, page 48

Other books by the same author:
Spy Handler: Memoir of a KGB Officer: The True Story of the Man Who Recruited Robert Hanssen and Aldrich Ames, 2005

Other books you might like:
Svetlana Alexievich, *Zinky Boys: Soviet Voices from the Afghanistan War*, 1992
Steve Coll, *Ghost Wars: The Secret History of the CIA, Afghanistan, and Bin Laden, from the Soviet Invasion to September 10, 2001*, 2004
Lester W. Grau, *The Soviet-Afghan War: How a Superpower Fought and Lost*, 2002
    Michael A. Gress, co-author
Milan Hauner, *The Soviet War in Afghanistan*, 1992
Larry Heinemann, *Zinky Boys: Soviet Voices from the Afghanistan War*, 1992
Mohammed Hassan Kakar, *Afghanistan: The Soviet Invasion and the Afghan Response, 1979-1982*, 1995

719

BRUCE FEILER

Where God Was Born: A Journey by Land to the Roots of Religion
(New York: HarperCollins, 2005)

Subject(s): Bible; Christianity; Current Affairs

Summary: This book is a blend: a description of modern-day Israel, Iraq, and Iran, and a survey of the Holy Land of antiquity to be found in the prophetic books of the Old Testament. As he discusses the events of the Bible—Joshua's conquest of Canaan, David's battles with the Philistines, the wanderings of the prophets and the exile of the Jews—he also revisits the very places where these events took place, describing the way they look now. He also struggles with the question that comes constantly to mind on his visits to these blood-soaked and war-torn regions: can the three faiths of the land ever live in harmony here?

Where it's reviewed:
America,, November 7, 2005, page 32
Booklist, August 2005, page 1972
Christian Century, July 11, 2006, page 39
Library Journal, September 1, 2005, page 148
Publishers Weekly, August 2005, page 1972

Other books by the same author:
The Council of Dads: My Daughters, My Illness, and the Men Who Could Be Me, 2010
America's Prophet: Moses and the American Story, 2009

Abraham: A Journey to the Heart of Three Faiths, 2005

Other books you might like:
Meron Benvenisti, *Sacred Landscape: The Buried History of the Holy Land Since 1948*, 2002
Richard A. Freund, *Digging Through the Bible: Understanding Biblical People, Places, and Controversies Through Archaeology*, 2009
Duane Garrett, *Archeological Study Bible: An Illustrated Walk Through Biblical History and Culture*, 2006
    Walter C. Kaiser Jr., co-author
Rodney Stark, *Discovering God: The Origins of the Great Religions and the Evolution of Belief*, 2007
Robert Louis Wilken, *This Land Called Holy: Palestine in Christian History and Thought*, 2009

720

NIALL FERGUSON

The War of the World: Twentieth-Century Conflict and the Descent of the West
(New York: Penguin Press, 2006)

Subject(s): History; Military science; Wars

Summary: In *The War of the World: Twentieth-Century Conflict and the Descent of the West*, author Niall Ferguson examines the parallel increase in international conflict and socioeconomic improvement. Attributing much of the world's armed conflict to ethnic turbulence, the author argues that societies are prone to outbreaks of violence during periods of financial instability—regardless if the economic change represents a positive or negative shift. In demonstrating his theory, Ferguson cites 20th-century events in Germany, Turkey, Bosnia, Rwanda, and other nations affected by war. This book was originally published in the United Kingdom as *The War of the World: History's Age of Hatred*.

Where it's reviewed:
American Historical Review, June 2008, page 797
American Scholar, Winter 2007, page 141
Commentary, March 2008, page 74
Harper's, June 2007, page 83
New York Review of Books, November 2, 2006, page 23

Other books by the same author:
The Ascent of Money: A Financial History of the World, 2009
Empire: The Rise and Demise of the British World Order and the Lessons for Global Power, 2004
The Pity of War: Explaining World War I, 2000

Other books you might like:
Blaine Terry Brown, *Uncertain Alliances: The World in the Twentieth Century*, 2002
    Robert Charles Cottrell, co-author
Leslie Derfler, *An Age of Conflict: Readings in Twentieth-Century European History*, 2001
Felix Gilbert, *The End of the European Era: 1890 to the Present*, 2008

Richard B. Miller, *War in the Twentieth Century*, 2004
Oswald Spengler, *The Decline of the West*, 1945

721

CAROLE FINK

Defending the Rights of Others: The Great Powers, the Jews, and International Minority Protection, 1878-1938

(New York: Cambridge University Press, 2004)

Story type: Political

Subject(s): Politics; History; Law

Summary: In *Defending the Rights of Others: The Great Powers, the Jews, and International Minority Protection, 1878-1938*, historian Carole Fink examines the initiation of global efforts to supervise unstable areas of Europe. Exhaustively researched from archival and previously published sources, this important volume analyzes the origins of the global human rights initiative. As Fink explains, the first 60 years of international minority protection were marked by a range of challenges, including competition among the governing political bodies and the influences of nationalism, imperialism, and fascism. Carole Fink is a professor of European History at Ohio State University.

Where it's reviewed:
American Historical Review, June 2005, page 763
Canadian Journal of History, Autumn 2006, page 470
Central European History, Fall 2005, page 667
The Historian, Fall 2005, page 564
Journal of Modern History, June 2006, page 470

Other books by the same author:
The Genoa Conference: European Diplomacy, 1921-1922, 1993
Marc Bloch: A Life in History, 1991

Other books you might like:
Gustavo Corni, *Peoples on the Move: Population Transfers and Ethnic Cleansing Policies During World War II and Its Aftermath*, 2008
Roland Hsu, *Ethnic Europe: Mobility, Identity, and Conflict in a Globalized World*, 2010
Beate Kosmala, *Facing the Catastrophe: Jews and Non-Jews in Europe During World War II*, 2011
Margaret MacMillan, *Paris 1919: Six Months That Changed the World*, 2002
Panikos Panayi, *Outsiders: A History of European Minorities*, 2003
Georgi Verbeeck, *Facing the Catastrophe: Jews and Non-Jews in Europe During World War II*, 2011

722

THOMAS FLEMING

Washington's Secret War: The Hidden History of Valley Forge

(New York: Smithsonian Books/Collins, 2005)

Subject(s): History; Military science; Politics

Summary: In *Washington's Secret War: The Hidden History of Valley Forge*, historian Thomas Fleming studies the development of George Washington's military and political prowess during the Continental Army's encampment of 1777 to 1778. While the author recognizes the military significance of Valley Forge, he also describes Washington's growth as a statesman during that time, detailing the general's ability to overcome the criticism of the Congress and the challenge of brazen underlings to his brilliant diplomatic negotiations. The author asserts that Washington's successes were due in part to his determination to distance himself from political infighting.

Where it's reviewed:
Booklist, October 15, 2005, page 22
CHOICE: Current Reviews for Academic Libraries, September 2006, page 180
Library Journal, September 1, 2005, page 157
Publishers Weekly, August 15, 2005, page 47

Other books by the same author:
The Secret Trial of Robert E. Lee, 2010
The Intimate Lives of the Founding Fathers, 2009
The Perils of Peace: America's Struggle for Survival After Yorktown, 2008

Other books you might like:
Benson Bobrick, *Angel in the Whirlwind: The Triumph of the American Revolution*, 1998
Wayne K. Bodle, *The Valley Forge Winter: Civilians and Soldiers in War*, 2004
John Ferlin, *Almost a Miracle: The American Victory in the War of Independence*, 2007
Richard Norton Smith, *Patriarch: George Washington and the New American Nation*, 1997
W.J. Wood, *Battles of the Revolutionary War: 1775-1781*, 1990

723

JULIE FLINT
ALEX DE WAAL , Co-Author

Darfur: A New History of a Long War

(New York: Zed Books, 2008)

Subject(s): History; Civil war; Politics

Summary: In *Darfur: A New History of a Long War*, authors Julie Flint and Alex de Waal explore the history and complexities of Sudan's ongoing humanitarian crisis. First examining the roots of the Darfur tragedy in the actions of rebel groups such as Janjawiid, the Sudan Liberation Army, and the Justice and Equality Movement, Flint and de Waal go on to evaluate the varied responses of the governments of Africa and the world. *Darfur* also considers how the horrors of the region's refugee camps and rampant violence have gradually attracted the attention of politicians and celebrities from around the globe.

Where it's reviewed:
New York Review of Books, February 9, 2006, page 14

Other books you might like:
Jon Alter, *Darfur: Twenty Years of War and Genocide in Sudan*, 2008
    Leora Kahn, co-author
Mahmood Mamdani, *Saviors and Survivors: Darfur, Politics, and the War on Terror*, 2010
Jen Marlowe, *Darfur Diaries: Stories of Survival*, 2006
Gerard Prunier, *Darfur: A 21st Century Genocide*, 2008
Brian Steidle, *The Devil Came on Horseback: Bearing Witness to the Genocide in Darfur*, 2008
    Gretchen Steidle Wallace, co-author

724

RICHARD B. FRANK

MacArthur

(New York: Palgrave Macmillan, 2007)

Subject(s): Military life; World War I, 1914-1918; World War II, 1939-1945

Summary: Author Richard B. Frank investigates the life and work of celebrated—and feared—military commander Douglas MacArthur. *MacArthur* follows the subject's adventures, from his birth and upbringing in the fold of a military family to his West Point experiences, from his World War I service to his pivotal role in the waging of the Second World War. Frank also examines the legendary figure's notorious hard-edged approach to politics, combat, and life, and how this made him both a beloved and reviled figure in American history. *MacArthur* includes a bibliography and an index, as well as a foreword by Army general Wesley K. Clark.

Where it's reviewed:
Booklist, June 1, 2007, page 28
Library Journal, May 1, 2007, page 85

Other books by the same author:
Downfall: The End of the Imperial Japanese Empire, 2001
Guadalcana: The Definitive Account of the Landmark Battle, 1992

Other books you might like:
Jean Darby, *Douglas Macarthur*, 1989
Donna Kinni, *No Substitute for Victory: Lessons in Strategy and Leadership from General Douglas MacArthur*, 2005
    Theodore Kinni, co-author
William Manchester, *American Caesar, Douglas MacArthur, 1880-1964*, 1978
Michael D. Pearlman, *Truman and MacArthur: Policy,*

Politics, and the Hunger for Honor and Renown, 2008
Geoffrey Perret, *Old Soldiers Never Die: The Life of Douglas Macarthur*, 1997

725

GREGORY FREEMAN

Troubled Water: Race, Mutiny, and Bravery on the U.S.S. Kitty Hawk

(New York: Palgrave Macmillan, 2009)

Subject(s): History; African Americans; United States. Navy

Summary: In *Troubled Water: Race, Mutiny, and Bravery on the U.S.S. Kitty Hawk*, author Gregory Freeman chronicles the devastating riot aboard an American warship during the Vietnam conflict. With a crew of 5,000—fewer than 300 of them African Americans—the *Kitty Hawk* had already been at sea for almost 250 days when it was ordered to the Gulf of Tonkin in October of 1972. En route, a riot erupted among the crewmen, which according to reports was instigated by the black minority. Categorized by many witnesses as a true mutiny, the tragedy injured dozens of sailors, destroyed military careers, and precipitated an overhaul of naval race relations policies.

Other books by the same author:
Fixing Hell: An Army Psychologist Confronts Abu Ghraib, 2008
The Forgotten 500: The Untold Story of the Men Who Risked All for the Greatest Rescue Mission of World War II, 2007
Sailors to the End: The Deadly Fire on the USS Forrestal and the Heroes Who Fought It, 2004

Other books you might like:
Edward J. Marolda, *The U.S. Navy in the Vietnam War: An Illustrated History*, 2002
Richard F. Miller, *A Carrier at War: On Board the USS Kitty Hawk in the Iraq War*, 2007
Ron Rypel, *Your Signal Is Charley*, 2007
John Darrell Sherwood, *Black Sailor, White Navy: Racial Unrest in the Fleet During the Vietnam War Era*, 2007
James E. Wise, *The Navy Cross: Extraordinary Heroism in Iraq, Afghanistan and Other Conflicts*, 2007

726

DAVID M.P. FREUND

Colored Property: State Policy and White Racial Politics in Suburban America

(Chicago: University of Chicago Press, 2007)

Subject(s): Race relations; History; African Americans
Summary: In *Colored Property: State Policy and White*

Racial Politics in Suburban America, author David M.P. Freund examines the divide between civil rights rhetoric and the realities of integration in 20th-century America. In the first part of the book, "The Political Economy of Suburban Development and the Race of Economic Value, 1910-1970," Freund studies the growth of suburban America and the governmental policies that subtly but effectively limited the inclusion of blacks. In the book's second part, "Race and Development in Metropolitan Detroit, 1940-1970," the author describes how the "politics of exclusion" impacted the communities of Royal Oak and Dearborn.

Where it's reviewed:
Choice, October 2009, page 322
Library Journal, December 2, 2008, page 133
Publishers Weekly, October 13, 2008, page 50

Other books by the same author:
Biographical Supplement and Index (Young Oxford History of African Americans, V. 11), 1997

Other books you might like:
Arnold R. Hirsch, *Making the Second Ghetto: Race and Housing in Chicago 1940-1960*, 1983
Mary Pattillo, *Black on the Block: The Politics of Race and Class in the City*, 2007
Beryl Satter, *Family Properties: How the Struggle Over Race and Real Estate Transformed Chicago and Urban America*, 2009
Thomas J. Sugrue, *The Origins of the Urban Crisis: Race and Inequality in Postwar Detroit*, 1995
William Julius Wilson, *There Goes the Neighborhood: Racial, Ethnic, and Class Tensions in Four Chicago Neighborhoods and Their Meaning for America*, 2006

727

RICHARD A. FREUND

Digging Through the Bible: Understanding Biblical People, Places, and Controversies Through Archaeology

(Lanham, Maryland: Rowman and Littlefield, 2009)

Subject(s): Archaeology; Christianity; Religion

Summary: In *Digging Through the Bible: Understanding Biblical People, Places, and Controversies Through Archeology*, author Richard A. Freund shows how archaeological finds present new insights into faith and religion. This volume profiles the traditions and figures of a variety of religious cultures and what modern archaeology has unearthed in regard to these historical people and places. The result is a linkage of the religious figures and events of the past with the modes and practices of contemporary faith. *Digging Through the Bible* includes a bibliography and an index.

Where it's reviewed:
Choice, October 2009, page 322
Library Journal, December 1, 2008, page 133

Publishers Weekly, October 13, 2008, page 50

Other books by the same author:
Secrets of the Cave of Letters: Rediscovering a Dead Sea Mystery, 2004

Other books you might like:
Don C. Benjamin, *Stones and Stories: An Introduction to Archeology and the Bible*, 2009
Gaalyah Cornfeld, *Archeology of the Bible: Book by Book*, 1982
Bruce Feiler, *Where God Was Born: A Journey by Land to the Roots of Religion*, 2005
David N. Freedman, *Archeology of the Bible: Book by Book*, 1982
Duane Garrett, *Archeological Study Bible: An Illustrated Walk Through Biblical History and Culture*, 2006
Walter C. Kaiser Jr., co-author
Moshe Pearlman, *Digging Up the Bible: The Stories Behind the Great Archeological Discoveries in the Holy Land*, 1980

728

RACHEL FUCHS

Contested Paternity: Constructing Families in Modern France

(Baltimore: Johns Hopkins University Press, 2008)

Subject(s): History; Sociology; Law

Summary: In *Contested Paternity: Constructing Families in Modern France*, author Rachel Fuchs studies the role of fatherhood in French social and legal culture. For this insightful study, Fuchs researched legal records from the late 19th century through the first decade of the 21st century pertaining to a variety of paternity issues. The author reveals the evolution of the definition of paternity in France and the ramifications the changes in interpretation held for each generation. In tracing the history of paternity issues from France's old regime to the present, Fuchs considers the political, legal, cultural, and personal aspects of the subject.

Where it's reviewed:
Choice, June 2009, page 2013

Other books by the same author:
Gender and Poverty in Nineteenth-Century Europe, 2005
Women in Nineteenth-Century Europe, 2005
Abandoned Children: Foundlings and Child Welfare in Nineteenth-Century France, 1984

Other books you might like:
William Beik, *A Social and Cultural History of Early Modern France*, 2009
Robin Briggs, *Early Modern France 1560-1715*, 1998
Christophe Charle, *A Social History of France in the Nineteenth Century*, 1994
Natalie Zemon Davis, *Society and Culture in Early Modern France: Eight Essays*, 1975
Miriam Kochen, *A Social History of France in the Nineteenth Century*, 1994

Robert A. Nye, *Masculinity and Male Codes of Honor in Modern France*, 1998

729

JOHN LEWIS GADDIS

The Cold War: A New History
(New York: Penguin Press, 2005)

Subject(s): Cold War, 1945-1991; Politics; History

Summary: In *The Cold War: A New History*, historian John Lewis Gaddis presents a concise and perceptive study of international relations in the post-World War II era. Though the author acknowledges the existence of the capitalism vs. communism conflict before the war, he cites the development of nuclear arms as a pivotal factor in United States-Soviet Union relations. With both nations recognizing the potential not only for defeat but also for mutual annihilation, several world leaders—British Prime Minister Margaret Thatcher, President Ronald Reagan, Soviet president Mikhail Gorbachev, Pope John Paul II, and others—were able to assert an influential diplomatic voice.

Where it's reviewed:
New York Review of Books, March 23, 2006, page 11

Other books by the same author:
Surprise, Security, and the American Experience, 2005
The Age of Terror: America and the World After September 11, 2002
The Landscape of History: How Historians Map the Cold War, 2002

Other books you might like:
Jussi M. Hanhimaki, *The Cold War: A History in Documents and Eyewitness Accounts*, 2004
Melvyn P. Leffler, *For the Soul of Mankind: The United States, the Soviet Union, and the Cold War*, 2007
Robert J. McMahon, *The Cold War: A Very Short Introduction*, 2003
Ronald E. Powaski, *The Cold War: The United States and the Soviet Union, 1917-1991*, 1997
Martin Walker, *The Cold War: A History*, 1995
Odd Arne Westad, *The Cold War: A History in Documents and Eyewitness Accounts*, 2004

730

JONAH GOLDBERG

Liberal Fascism: The Secret History of the American Left from Mussolini to the Politics of Meaning
(New York: Doubleday, 2008)

Subject(s): Government; History; Politics

Summary: *National Review* contributing editor Jonah Goldberg traces the recent history of the modern politi-

cal left. He argues cogently that the modern left grew out of the same intellectual movements that fostered liberalism, socialism, and fascism. Goldberg identifies the central guiding philosophy of fascism as a rejection of individual decision making in favor of state action for the purported common good. This philosophy stands in conflict against the founding beliefs of the United States. Goldberg provides a wide range of information about actual fascist governmental policies, observes their similarity to many progressive policies, and documents the popularity that fascist ideas enjoyed among progressives in the early 20th century. In a more modest fashion, Goldberg criticizes some self-identified conservatives for their embrace of the same philosophy.

Where it's reviewed:
Booklist, December 15, 2007, page 8

Other books by the same author:
Proud to be Right: Voices of the Next Conservative Generation, 2010

Other books you might like:
David Coates, *Answering Back: Liberal Responses to Conservative Arguments*, 2009
David T. Courtwright, *No Right Turn: Conservative Politics in a Liberal America*, 2010
George Lakoff, *Moral Politics: How Liberals and Conservatives Think*, 2002
Douglas C. Rossinow, *Visions of Progress: The Left-Liberal Tradition in America*, 2009
Phil Valentine, *The Conservative's Handbook: Defining the Right Position on Issues from A to Z*, 2008

731

ANNE GOLDGAR

Tulipmania: Money, Honor, and Knowledge in the Dutch Golden Age
(Chicago: University of Chicago Press, 2007)

Subject(s): Flowers; Social conditions; History

Summary: In *Tupilmania: Money, Honor, and Knowledge in the Dutch Golden Age*, author Anne Goldgar disputes popularly held descriptions of the speculative tulip-bulb market of 1630s Netherlands. According to prevalent historic accounts, the "tulipmania" of the Dutch Golden Age was marked by outrageous investments, greed, financial ruin, and scandal. Through her thorough research of archival documents, Goldgar reveals that the myth of tulipmania was much exaggerated. According to Goldgar, while trade in tulip bulbs did increase in the early 17th century, the excessive claims about the market and its impact tell more about the national mindset of the era than the realities of its economy.

Where it's reviewed:
Times Literary Supplement, September 14, 2007, page 12

Other books by the same author:
Institutional Culture in Early Modern Society (co-author), 2004

Impolite Learning: Conduct and Community in the Republic of Letters, 1680-1750, 1995

Other books you might like:

Mike Dash, *Tulipomania: The Story of the World's Most Coveted Flower and the Extraordinary Passion It Aroused*, 2000

Rosalind Laker, *The Golden Tulip*, 1991

J.L. Price, *The Dutch Republic in the Seventeenth Century*, 1998

Simon Schama, *The Embarrassment of Riches: An Interpretation of Dutch Culture in the Golden Age*, 1997

Amy Stewart, *Flower Confidential: The Good, the Bad, and the Beautiful*, 2007

732

ADRIAN GOLDSWORTHY

How Rome Fell: Death of a Superpower

(New Haven, Connecticut: Yale University Press, 2009)

Subject(s): Ancient Roman civilization; History; Roman Empire, 30 BC-476 AD

Summary: In *How Rome Fell: Death of a Superpower*, noted historical scholar Adrian Goldsworthy explores the people and events that led to the downfall of the most powerful empire in the ancient world. Covering the third through sixth centuries, this volume provides an in-depth look at the fall of Rome, refuting the popular belief that the great city collapsed under attack from foreign military factions. Goldsworthy provides evidence that Rome self-destructed under the suffocating, corrupt power of its own dictatorship and offers a glimpse of life under Roman rule. *How Rome Fell* includes maps, illustrations, a chronology of notable events, a glossary of commonly used terms, bibliographical references, and an index.

Where it's reviewed:

Choice, March 2010, page 1349

Library Journal, May 1, 2009, page 88

Publishers Weekly, March 30, 2009, page 39

Other books by the same author:

Ceasar: Life of a Colossus, 2008

The Fall of Carthage: The Punic Wars 265-146 BC, 2008

In the Name of Rome: The Men Who Won the Roman Empire, 2004

Other books you might like:

Simon Baker, *Ancient Rome: The Rise and Fall of an Empire*, 2006

Edward Gibbon, *The History of the Decline and Fall of the Roman Empire*, 1788

P.J. Heather, *Empires and Barbarians: The Fall of Rome and the Birth of Europe*, 2010

P.J. Heather, *The Fall of the Roman Empire: A New History of Rome and the Barbarians*, 2007

Bryan Ward-Perkins, *The Fall of Rome: And the End of Civilization*, 2006

David P. Womersley, *The History of the Decline and Fall of the Roman Empire*, 1788

733

LAURA GOTKOWITZ

A Revolution for Our Rights: Indigenous Struggles for Land and Justice in Bolivia, 1880-1952

(Durham, North Carolina: Duke University Press, 2007)

Subject(s): History; South Americans; Social history

Summary: In *A Revolution for Our Rights: Indigenous Struggles for Land and Justice in Bolivia, 1880-1952*, author Laura Gotkowitz offers an alternative account of Bolivia's 1952 revolution. Countering popularly held beliefs about the revolution's basis as lying with class conflicts of the 1930s, Gotkowitz asserts that the nation's unrest actually took root in the early 1900s among the rural indigenous population. In analyzing the struggle of Bolivia's indigenous peoples, the author considers the topics of national unity, land and labor rights, populism, politics, and the rights of the individual. As Gotkowitz demonstrates, an understanding of the 1952 revolution facilitates an understanding of Bolivia's 21st-century issues. First book.

Where it's reviewed:

Choice, February 2009, page 1165

The Historian, February 2009, page 599

Other books you might like:

James Dunkerley, *Bolivia: Revolution and the Power of History in the Present: Essays*, 2007

Herbert S. Klein, *Bolivia: The Evolution of a Multi-Ethnic Society*, 1992

Herbert S. Klein, *A Concise History of Bolivia*, 2003

Herbert S. Klein, *Haciendas and Ayllus: Rural Society in the Bolivian Andes in the Eighteenth and Nineteenth Centuries*, 1993

Sinclair Thomson, *We Alone Will Rise: Native Andean Politics in the Age of Insurgency*, 2003

734

MARIE GOTTSCHALK

The Prison and the Gallows: The Politics of Mass Incarceration in America

(New York: Cambridge University Press, 2006)

Subject(s): Prisons; Politics; Law

Summary: In *The Prison and the Gallows: The Politics of Mass Incarceration in America*, author Marie Gottschalk examines the state of the U.S. penal system. According to the author, America has the highest per capital

History

incarceration rate in the world, with almost one in every 50 adults imprisoned. Though the U.S. has traditionally based its criminal justice system on the practice of punishment by imprisonment, Gottschalk contends that four relatively recent movements in America's culture (organized by groups promoting the rights of victims, women, and prisoners, and those opposed to capital punishment) caused the dramatic increase in the nation's incarceration rate.

Where it's reviewed:
Choice, April 2007, page 1419
The Nation, August 27, 2007, page 29

Other books by the same author:
The Shadow Welfare State: Labor, Business and the Politics of Health Care in the United States, 2000

Other books you might like:
Michelle Alexander, *The New Jim Crow: Mass Incarceration in the Age of Colorblindness*, 2010
Laura Bufano Edge, *Locked Up: A History of the U.S. Prison System*, 2009
David Garland, *The Culture of Control: Crime and Social Order in Contemporary Society*, 2001
Norval Morris, *The Oxford History of the Prison: The Practice of Punishment in Western Society*, 1997
John W. Roberts, *Reform and Retribution: An Illustrated History of American Prisons*, 1996
David J. Rothman, *The Oxford History of the Prison: The Practice of Punishment in Western Society*, 1997

735

JULIE GREENE

The Canal Builders: Making America's Empire at the Panama Canal
(New York: Penguin Press, 2009)

Subject(s): Panama Canal; History; Construction

Summary: In *The Canal Builders: Making America's Empire at the Panama Canal*, historian Julie Greene chronicles the construction of the 20th-century engineering marvel. Rather than focusing on the details of the enormous construction project in the tropics, Greene considers the men who built the canal and the complex social structure that grew among them. As the author examines the building of the canal from the viewpoint of the labor force that populated the canal zone, she discusses the related topics of progressivism and empire building, revealing the disputes, disparate pay practices, and racial discrimination that characterized the undertaking.

Where it's reviewed:
Library Journal, February 15, 2009, page 116
New York Times Book Review, March 29, 2009, page 11

Other books by the same author:
Pure and Simple Politics: The American Federation of Labor and Political Activism, 1881-1917, 1998

Other books you might like:
Ulrich Keller, *The Building of the Panama Canal in Historic Photographs*, 1984
John Lindsay-Poland, *Emperors in the Jungle: The Hidden History of the U.S. in Panama*, 2003
Noel Maurer, *The Big Ditch: How America Took, Built, Ran, and Ultimately Gave Away the Panama Canal*, 2010
David G. Mccullough, *The Path between the Seas: The Creation of the Panama Canal, 1870-1914*, 1977
Matthew Parker, *Panama Fever: The Epic Story of One of the Greatest Human Achievements of All Time—the Building of the Panama Canal*, 2008
Carlos Yu, *The Big Ditch: How America Took, Built, Ran, and Ultimately Gave Away the Panama Canal*, 2010

736

KARL TARO GREENFELD

China Syndrome: The True Story of the 21st Century's First Great Epidemic
(New York: HarperCollins, 2006)

Subject(s): History; Diseases; Health

Summary: In *China Syndrome: The True Story of the 21st Century's First Great Epidemic*, journalist Karl Taro Greenfeld provides a first-hand account of the emergence of severe acute respiratory syndrome (SARS). As editor for *Time Asia* in 2002, Greenfeld was familiar with the animal markets common on the streets of "Wild Flavor" era China—markets that served as virus incubators. When cases of "atypical pneumonia" were identified in the country, the author found himself on the front line of an avian flu epidemic. But unlike Greenfeld, the Chinese media and citizens did not have access to the same information due to the dangerous censorship of the government.

Where it's reviewed:
Booklist, February 1, 2006, page 14
Library Journal, February 1, 2006, page 99
New Statesman, September 4, 2006, page 56
Publishers Weekly, January 2, 2006, page 44

Other books by the same author:
Boy Alone: A Brother's Memoir, 2010
Standard Deviations: Growing Up and Coming Down in the New Asia, 2002
Speed Tribes: Days and Nights with Japan's Next Generation, 1995

Other books you might like:
Thomas Abraham, *Twenty-First Century Plague: The Story of SARS*, 2004
Madeline Drexler, *Emerging Epidemics: The Menace of New Infections*, 2002
Laurie Garrett, *The Coming Plague: Newly Emerging Diseases in a World out of Balance*, 1994

Arno Karlen, *Man and Microbes: Disease and Plagues in History and Modern Times*, 1995

Michael Oldstone, *Viruses, Plagues, and History*, 1998

737

RAMACHANDRA GUHA

India After Gandhi: The History of the World's Largest Democracy
(New York: Ecco, 2007)

Subject(s): History; Indian history; Politics

Summary: In *India After Gandhi: The History of the World's Largest Democracy*, historian Ramachandra Guha describes the fascinating story of India's rise as a worldwide democratic power. As Guha examines India's long history of religious, ethnic, and caste divisions and civil war, he examines the nation's amazing transformation to a unified democracy against seemingly insurmountable odds. The players in the story include famous public figures as well as India's commoners, tribe members, peasants, and women. In this balanced account, Guha details the country's surprising political successes in addition to the painful setbacks and continuing challenges it faces as it secures a stronghold in the modern world economy.

Where it's reviewed:
The Economist, June 23, 2007, page 93
Harper's Magazine, August 2007, page 81
The Nation, August 24, 2007, page 10
New York Times Book Review, August 26, 2007, page 16
Times Literary Supplement, August 24, 2007, page 10

Other books by the same author:
How Much Should a Person Consume?: Environmentalism in India and the United States, 2006
A Corner of a Foreign Field: The Indian History of a British Sport, 2003
Environmentalism: A Global History, 1999

Other books you might like:
Gucharan Das, *India Unbound: The Social and Economic Revolution from Independence to the Global Information Age*, 2002
Edward Luce, *In Spite of the Gods: The Strange Rise of Modern India*, 2007
Barbara D. Metcalf, *A Concise History of Modern India*, 2006
   Thomas R. Metcalf, co-author
Nandan Nilekani, *Imagining India: The Idea of a Renewed Nation*, 2009
Amartya Sen, *The Argumentative Indian: Writings on Indian History, Culture, and Identity*, 2005

738

S. C. GWYNNE

Empire of the Summer Moon: Quanah Parker and the Rise and Fall of the Comanches, the Most Powerful Indian Tribe in American History
(New York: Scribner, 2010)

Subject(s): Native Americans; History; Native American captivities

Summary: *Empire of the Summer Moon: Quanah Parker and the Rise and Fall of the Comanches, the Most Powerful Indian Tribe in American History* is a historical account from author S. C. Gwynne. In the book, Gwynne recounts the exciting and heartbreaking history of the Comanche tribe. He tells the story of Cynthia Ann Parker, a young girl kidnapped by the Comanches at nine years old, and her son, Quanah Parker, who became a great Comanche chief. *Empire of the Summer Moon* gives readers a comprehensive knowledge of the Comanches' military strategy and the history of their long battle with white settlers for the domination of western America.

Where it's reviewed:
Booklist, April 15, 2010, page 20
The Economist, June 17, 2010, page 85
Library Journal, February 15, 2010, page 104
New York Times Book Review, June 13, 2010, page 1
Publishers Weekly, February 1, 2010, page 41

Other books by the same author:
The Outlaw Bank: A Wild Ride Into the Secret Heart of BCCI (co-author), 1993
Selling Money: A Year, 1987

Other books you might like:
T.R. Fehrenbach, *Comanches: The History of a People*, 2003
Pekka Hamalainen, *The Comanche Empire*, 2008
Thomas W. Kavanagh, *The Comanches: A History, 1706-1875*, 1999
Nelson Lee, *Three Years Among the Comanches: The Narrative of Nelson Lee, the Texas Ranger*, 2001
Bill Neeley, *The Last Comanche Chief: The Life and Times of Quanah Parker*, 2009

739

DAVID HAGBERG
BORIS GINDIN , Co-Author

Mutiny: The True Events that Inspired the Hunt for Red October
(New York: Forge, 2008)

Subject(s): Mutiny; History; Military science

Summary: In *Mutiny: The True Events That Inspired the*

Hunt for Red October, author David Hagberg and former Soviet naval officer Boris Gindin describe the real story of the *FFG Storozhevoy*. On a mission in 1975, the *Storozhevoy*, a Russian warship, became the site of a mutiny staged by Captain Valery Sablin, who was determined to gain attention for the anti-Kremlin movement. Gindin, who maintained his loyalty to the Kremlin, was detained on board during the tense but relatively short-lived revolt. The mutiny fell apart when Brezhnev ordered the destruction of the ship to stop the revolt and suppress the mutineers' subversive message.

Where it's reviewed:
Booklist, May 1, 2008, page 59
Library Journal, June 1, 2008, page 107
Publishers Weekly, March 17, 2008, page 64

Other books by the same author:
The Cabal, 2010
Allah's Scorpion, 2007
Joshua's Hammer, 2006

Other books you might like:
Nate Brader, *The Last Sentry: The True Story That Inspired the Hunt for Red October*, 2005
John Pina Craven, *The Silent War: The Cold War Battle Beneath the Sea*, 2001
Christopher Drew, *Blind Man's Bluff: The Untold Story of American Submarine Espionage*, 1998
Peter Sasgen, *Stalking the Red Bear: The True Story of a U.S. Cold War Submarine's Covert Operations Against the Soviet Union*, 2009
Kenneth Sewell, *All Hands Down: The True Story of the Soviet Attack on the USS Scorpion*, 2008
Sherry Sontag, *Blind Man's Bluff: The Untold Story of American Submarine Espionage*, 1998
Gregory D. Young, *The Last Sentry: The True Story That Inspired the Hunt for Red October*, 2005

740

DAVID HALBERSTAM

The Coldest Winter: America and the Korean War
(New York: Hyperion, 2007)

Subject(s): Korean War

Summary: "The Coldest Winter" refers specifically to one campaign of the Korean War fought in November of 1950, a campaign that General Douglas MacArthur lost. Halberstam covers the politics behind this battle and the war in general, as well as the egos of the men in charge of both sides. He describes miscalculations and incorrect assumptions of leaders. He includes interviews of many soldiers involved in the war.

Where it's reviewed:
The Atlantic, January-February 2008, page 133
New York Review of Books, October 25, 2007, page 48

Other books by the same author:
Playing for Keeps: Michael Jordan the World He Made, 2000

The Best and the Brightest, 1994
The Fifties, 1994

Other books you might like:
Steven Casey, *Selling the Korean War: Propaganda, Politics, and Public Opinion in the United States, 1950-1953*, 2008
Bruce Cumings, *The Korean War: A History*, 2010
T.R. Fehrenbach, *This Kind of War: A Study in Unpreparedness*, 1963
Max Hastings, *The Korean War*, 1987
Michael Varhola, *Fire and Ice: The Korean War, 1950-1953*, 2000

741

PEKKA HAMALAINEN

The Comanche Empire
(New Haven, Connecticut: Yale University Press, 2008)

Story type: Historical - American West
Subject(s): Native Americans; History; Frontier life

Summary: In *The Comanche Empire*, author Pekka Hamalainen takes an in-depth look at the Comanche, a once powerful Native American tribe in the southwestern United States. Hamalainen explores the history of the Comanche from the time their existence was first noted in Spanish records in 1706 to their eventual defeat by American forces in 1874. Documenting the Comanche's rapid expansion in population, wealth, and power, Hamalainen demonstrates how this tribe grew to become one of the most dominant in all of western Texas and New Mexico. Hamalainen also explores the inner workings of Comanche society and the aggressive tactics that established their unique reputation in the American frontier.

Where it's reviewed:
New York Review of Books, May 29, 2008, page 155

Other books by the same author:
Uniting Germany: Actions and Reactions, 1994
In Time of Storm: Revolution, Civil War, and the Ethnolinguistic Issue in Finland, 1984

Other books you might like:
T.R. Fehrenbach, *Comanches: The History of a People*, 2003
S. C. Gwynne, *Empire of the Summer Moon: Quanah Parker and the Rise and Fall of the Comanches, the Most Powerful Indian Tribe in American History*, 2010
Thomas W. Kavanagh, *The Comanches: A History, 1706-1875*, 1999
Nelson Lee, *Three Years Among the Comanches: The Narrative of Nelson Lee, the Texas Ranger*, 2001
Bill Neeley, *The Last Comanche Chief: The Life and Times of Quanah Parker*, 2009

742

MARTHA HANNA

Your Death Would Be Mine: Paul and Marie Pireaud in the Great War

(Cambridge, Massachusetts: Harvard University Press, 2006)

Subject(s): World War I, 1914-1918; Armed forces; Letters (Correspondence)

Summary: Paul and Marie Pireaud were not famous or wealthy, nor were their lives rocked by scandal or drama. They were a simple couple from the French countryside who endured the pain of separation when Paul was called to fight in the First World War. In *Your Death Would Be Mine: Paul and Marie Pireaud in the Great War*, historian Martha Hanna compiles the correspondence of these two young people, who endured the chaos of war to carve out a loving, fruitful union in the midst of a world seemingly bent on collapse. Their letters to one another—which encompass everything from talk of love and desire to the daily workings of a rural French farm—paint a powerful portrait of World War I, peasant life, and the challenges of living in wartime. *Your Death Would Be Mine* includes a bibliography and an index.

Where it's reviewed:
Booklist, September 15, 2006, page 18

Other books by the same author:
John Massey: The House That Jack Built, 2004
The Mobilization of Intellect: French Scholars and Writers During the Great War, 1996

Other books you might like:
Alan Bishop, *Letters from a Lost Generation: First World War Letters of Vera Brittain and Four Friends*, 1999
    Mark Bostridge, co-author
John Graham Gillis, *A Lovely Letter from Cecie: The 1907-1915 Vancouver Diary and World War I Letters of Wallace Chambers*, 1998
W. Stull Holt, *The Great War at Home and Abroad: The World War I Diaries of W. Stull Holt*, 1998
G.J. Meyer, *A World Undone: The Story of the Great War, 1914 to 1918*, 2007
Robert J. Young, *Under Siege: Portraits of Civilian Life in France During World War I*, 2000

743

MAX HASTINGS

Retribution: The Battle for Japan, 1944-45

(New York: Alfred A. Knopf, 2008)

Subject(s): History; War; World War II

Summary: In *Retribution: The Battle for Japan, 1944-45*, author Max Hastings describes the last 12 months of the war in the Pacific. Hastings details the battles fought

across Asia, provides portraits of military and political leaders, and explores the lives of ordinary soldiers. Hastings examines Japan's war against China, MacArthur's difficulties in the Philippines, and the Soviet bombardment of Manchuria. He examines the decision-making process that led to the bombing of Hiroshima and Nagasaki and argues that using the atom bombs ultimately saved lives. Finally, Hastings considers the wartime mind-set of the Japanese, which contributed to much of the violence carried out in the Pacific.

Where it's reviewed:
Booklist, March 1, 2008, page 213
Choice, August 2008, page 2214
New York Review of Books, May 1, 2008, page 24

Other books by the same author:
Winston's War: Churchill, 1940-1945, 2010
Overlord: D-Day and the Battle for Normandy, 2006
The Battle for the Falklands, 1984

Other books you might like:
Haruko Taya Cook, *Japan at War: An Oral History*, 1995
    Theodore F. Cook, co-author
Michael D. Gordin, *Five Days in August: How World War II Became a Nuclear War*, 2007
Robert Leckie, *Okinawa: The Last Battle of World War II*, 1996
Bill Sloan, *The Ultimate Battle: Okinawa 1945—the Last Epic Struggle of World War II*, 2008
Barrett Tillman, *Whirlwind: The Air War Against Japan, 1942-1945*, 2010

744

MAUREEN HEALY

Vienna and the Fall of the Habsburg Empire: Total War and Everyday Life in World War I

(New York: Cambridge University Press, 2004)

Subject(s): World War I, 1914-1918; Social conditions; Military science

Summary: In *Vienna and the Fall of the Habsburg Empire: Total War and Everyday Life in World War I*, author Maureen Healy chronicles the challenges faced by the wartime residents of Austria's capital. As the able-bodied men of the Habsburg Empire battled in faraway lands, Healy explains, the women, children, and men not fit for duty dealt with unbearable circumstances in the streets of Vienna. In a diverse society increasingly impacted by shortages of food and supplies as a result of the war, stores, schools, and even homes became places of struggle and conflict. A full-blown revolt preceded the empire's fall in 1918.

Other books you might like:
Roger Chickering, *The Great War and Urban Life in Germany: Freiburg, 1914-1918*, 2009
Deborah R. Coen, *Vienna in the Age of Uncertainty: Science, Liberalism, and Private Life*, 2007
Belinda Joy Davis, *Home Fires Burning: Food, Politics,*

and Everyday Life in World War I Berlin, 2000
Jonathan E. Gumz, *The Resurrection and Collapse of Empire in Habsburg Serbia, 1914-1918*, 2009
Holger H. Herwig, *The First World War: Germany and Austria-Hungary 1914-1918*, 2009

745

SHARON A. ROGER HEPBURN

Crossing the Border: A Free Black Community in Canada

(Urbana, Illinois: University of Illinois Press, 2007)

Subject(s): History; Blacks; Pioneers

Summary: In *Crossing the Border: A Free Black Community in Canada*, author Sharon A. Roger Hepburn chronicles the history of Buxton, Ontario. Founded in 1849 by Reverend William King on a 9000-acre site in Ontario, Buxton—populated exclusively by former slaves—demonstrated a groundbreaking model of community life. Though the town encountered some resistance from whites in the region, Buxton enjoyed the support of the Presbyterian Church of Canada and a number of benefactors. Peaking at a population of 700 residents, Buxton's economy was based in agriculture. The town also sustained a post office and hotel as well as numerous churches and school.

Other books you might like:

George Hendrick, *Black Refugees in Canada: Accounts of Escape During the Era of Slavery*, 2010
James Oliver Horton, *In Hope of Liberty: Culture, Community and Protest Among Northern Free Blacks, 1700-1860*, 1998
    Lois E. Horton, co-author
Sarah-Jane Mathieu, *North of the Color Line: Migration and Black Resistance in Canada, 1870-1955*, 2010
Harvey Amani Whitfield, *Blacks on the Border: The Black Refugees in British North America, 1815-1860*, 2006
Robin W. Winks, *The Blacks in Canada: A History*, 1997

746

WILLIAM I. HITCHCOCK

The Bitter Road to Freedom: A New History of the Liberation of Europe

(New York: Free Press, 2008)

Subject(s): World War II, 1939-1945; History; Military science

Summary: In *The Bitter Road to Freedom: A New History of the Liberation of Europe*, historian William I. Hitchcock explores the impact of World War II liberation on affected civilians. Though popular accounts about the liberation of Europe portray the Allies as saviors, Hitch-

cock reveals truths about the era that are not always flattering. Through meticulous research, the author describes a painful process in which the number of French civilian deaths at Normandy matched U.S. military fatalities, displaced citizens had to be reintroduced to their own homelands, and the starving victims of Nazi camps relied on the inconsistent efforts of relief organizations for food and medical care.

Where it's reviewed:
Booklist, September 1, 2008, page 27
Choice, October 2009, page 27
Times Literary Supplment, April 17, 2009, page 27

Other books by the same author:
The Struggle for Europe: The Turbulent History of a Divided Continent, 1945 to the Present, 2004
France Restored: Cold War Diplomacy and the Search for Leadership, 1998

Other books you might like:
Antony Beevor, *Paris After the Liberation 1944-1949: Revised Edition*, 2004
Richard Bessel, *Germany 1945: From War to Peace*, 2009
Artemis Cooper, *Paris After the Liberation 1944-1949: Revised Edition*, 2004
Giles MacDonough, *After the Reich: the Brutal History of the Allied Occupation*, 2009
James J. Sheehan, *Where Have All the Soldiers Gone? The Transformation of Modern Europe*, 2008
David Stafford, *Endgame, 1945: The Missing Final Chapter of World War II*, 2007

747

ADAM HOCHSCHILD

Bury the Chains: Prophets and Rebels in the Fight to Free an Empire's Slaves

(Boston, Massachusetts: Houghton Mifflin Harcourt, 2005)

Subject(s): British history, 1714-1815; Slavery; Abolition of slavery

Summary: Adam Hochschild's *Bury the Chains: Prophets and Rebels in the Fight to Free an Empire's Slaves* chronicles the antislavery movement in Great Britain. In addition to describing the movement, Hochschild presents the logistics of the slave trade and its fundamental role in the British economy. Hochschild then describes the small group of visionaries who first met in 1787 with the hope of abolishing slavery. He shows how the movement spread throughout the British Empire, to the United States, and to the rest of the world. The book also provides an up-close look at the historical persons that shaped abolition—persons such as movement leader Granville Sharp, ex-slave Olaudah Equiano, and investigative journalist Thomas Clarkson. Finally, Hoschild delineates the House of Lords proceedings that ultimately ended slavery in the British Empire.

Where it's reviewed:
The Nation, February 14, 2005, page 23

New York Times Book Review, April 16, 2006, page 24
Publishers Weekly, January 3, 2005, page 48

Other books by the same author:
The Unquiet Ghost: Russians Remember Stalin, 2006
King Leopold's Ghost: A Story of Greed, Terror, and
   Heroism in Colonial Africa, 1999
Half the Way Home: A Memoir of Father and Son, 1986

Other books you might like:
Christopher Leslie Brown, Moral Capital: Foundations
   of British Abolitionism, 2006
Brycchan Carey, British Abolitionism and the Rhetoric
   of Sensibility: Writing, Sentiment and Slavery,
   1760-1807, 2005
Seymour Drescher, The Mighty Experiment: Free Labor
   versus Slavery in British Emancipation, 2004
Derek R. Peterson, Abolitionism and Imperialism in
   Britain, Africa and the Atlantic, 2010
C. Peter Ripley, The Black Abolitionist Papers: Vol. I:
   The British Isles, 1830-1865, 1985

748

DAVID L. HOLMES

The Faiths of the Founding Fathers

(New York: Oxford University Press, 2006)

Subject(s): Biographies; History; Religion

Summary: In The Faiths of the Founding Fathers, author
David L. Holmes examines the religious practices of
Benjamin Franklin, George Washington, John Adams,
Thomas Jefferson, James Madison, and James Monroe.
Though the author admits from the start that a person's
thoughts and intentions cannot definitively be known by
another, he uses the Founding Fathers' writings, as well
as anecdotal sources, to create a spiritual profile of each
man. As Holmes delves into the religious practices of
the Founders and their families, he discovers not a unified philosophy of Christian fundamentalism, as popularly thought, but a variety of beliefs ranging from deism
to agnosticism.

Where it's reviewed:
Booklist, April 1, 2006, page 7

Other books by the same author:
A Brief History of the Episcopal Church, 1993

Other books you might like:
David Barton, Separation of Church and State: What
   the Founders Meant, 2007
Peter A. Lillback, George Washington's Sacred Fire,
   2006
Jon Meacham, American Gospel: God, the Founding
   Fathers, and the Making of a Nation, 2006
Michael Novak, Washington's God: Religion, Liberty,
   and the Father of Our Country, 2006
Steven Waldman, Founding Faith: How Our Founding
   Fathers Forged a Radical New Approach to
   Religious Liberty, 2008

749

RICHARD HOLMES

The Age of Wonder: How the Romantic Generation Discovered the Beauty and Terror of Science

(New York: Pantheon Books, 2009)

Subject(s): Science; History

Summary: Author Richard Holmes chronicles the stories
of several scientists who changed the way we view the
universe in The Age of Wonder: How the Romantic
Generation Discovered the Beauty and Terror of Science.
Holmes's book focuses on the work of William and
Caroline Herschel and Humphry Davy. William Herschel
was a composer who took up astronomy as a hobby.
Eventually, William's sister Caroline began studying the
stars with him. The siblings' major contributions to the
field of astronomy included the discovery of Uranus and
several comets. Humphry Davy was a British chemist
who discovered chlorine, iodine, and several alkaline
earth metals. Throughout the book, Holmes explains
how these scientific discoveries fascinated both scientists
and artists.

Where it's reviewed:
Times Literary Supplement, February 6, 2009, page 12

Other books by the same author:
The Romantic Poets and Their Circle, 2006
Shelley: The Pursuit, 2003
Coleridge: Early Visions, 1772-1804, 1999

Other books you might like:
Alan Bewell, Wordsworth and the Enlightenment:
   Nature, Man, and Society in the Experimental
   Poetry, 1989
Tim Fulford, Literature, Science and Exploration in the
   Romantic Era: Bodies of Knowledge, 2007
David M. Knight, Science in the Romantic Era, 1998
Diane Moser, The History of Science in the Eighteenth
   Century, 1993
Alan Richardson, British Romanticism and the Study of
   the Mind, 2001
Ray Spangenburg, The History of Science in the
   Eighteenth Century, 1993

750

MICHAEL HONEY

Going Down Jericho Road: The Memphis Strike, Martin Luther King's Last Campaign

(New York: W. W. Norton & Company, 2007)

Subject(s): History; Assassination; Strikes

Summary: In Going Down Jericho Road: The Memphis
Strike, Martin Luther King's Last Campaign, author
Michael Honey examines the little known sanitation
worker strike that brought Martin Luther King, Jr., to

History

Memphis, Tennessee, in 1968, the scene of his eventual assassination. In January 1968, black sanitation workers in the city of Memphis began a work stoppage over mistreatment and discrimination. The situation came to a head after several days of inclement weather, when sanitation workers were sent home, but only white workers were paid. The work stoppage soon turned into a strike, and before long, became an entire civil rights campaign that drew King's attention. Honey thoroughly explores the strike, King's assassination, and the bloody aftermath of these events.

Where it's reviewed:
Booklist, February 1, 2007, page 25
The Historian, Summer 2010, page 436
Library Journal, December 1, 2006, page 139
Publishers Weekly, December 4, 2006, page 48

Other books by the same author:
Black Workers Remember: An Oral History of Segregation, Unionism, and the Freedom Struggle, 2002
Southern Labor and Black Civil Rights: Organizing Memphis Workers, 1993

Other books you might like:
Joan Beifuss, *At the River I Stand*
Laurie B. Green, *Battling the Plantation Mentality: Memphis and the Black Freedom Struggle*, 2007
Dick Gregory, *Murder in Memphis: The FBI and the Assassination of Martin Luther King*, 1993
Sherry L. Hoppe, *Maxine Smith's Unwilling Pupils: Lessons Learned in the Memphis Civil Rights Classroom*, 2007
Mark Lane, *Murder in Memphis: The FBI and the Assassination of Martin Luther King*, 1993
Kimberly K. Little, *You Must Be from the North: Southern White Women in the Memphis Civil Rights Movement*, 2009
Bruce W. Speck, *Maxine Smith's Unwilling Pupils: Lessons Learned in the Memphis Civil Rights Classroom*, 2007

751

DANIEL WALKER HOWE

What Hath God Wrought: The Transformation of America, 1815-1848

(New York: Oxford University Press, 2007)

Subject(s): History; Economics; Social history

Summary: Professor Daniel Walker Howe's *What Hath God Wrought: The Transformation of America, 1815-1848*, gives a social perspective to this important time in the American past. Howe writes in depth about the temperance and women's rights movements. Although most historians are interested in the economic conditions during this time of industrialization, Howe provides more descriptions of changes in religion, education, and the arts in early 19th century America. *What Hath God*

Wrought is a title in the Oxford History of United States series.

Where it's reviewed:
The Atlantic, December 2007, page 114

Other books by the same author:
Making the American Self: Jonathan Edwards to Abraham Lincoln, 2009
The Unitarian Conscience: Harvard Moral Philosophy, 1988
The Political Culture of the American Whigs, 1984

Other books you might like:
William Dudley, *Antebellum America: 1784-1850, Vol. 4*, 2003
William H. Goetzmann, *When the Eagle Screamed: The Romantic Horizon in American Expansionism, 1800-1860*, 2000
Walter Licht, *Industrializing America: The Nineteenth Century*, 1995
Gordon S. Wood, *Empire of Liberty: A History of the Early Republic, 1789-1815*, 2009
Howard Zinn, *A People's History of the United States*, 1995

752

DANIEL J. HULSEBOSCH

Constituting Empire: New York and the Transformation of Constitutionalism in the Atlantic World, 1664-1830

(Chapel Hill: University of North Carolina Press, 2008)

Subject(s): History; Law; Politics

Summary: In *Constituting Empire: New York and the Transformation of Constitutionalism in the Atlantic World, 1664-1830*, author Daniel J. Hulsebosch chronicles the development of New York state's governing system in the Colonial period. As Hulsebosch studies New York from its days as an imperial province to a post-Revolutionary state governed by constitution, he examines the state's varied periods of evolution, including an era of multiple constitutions, a search for imperial law, provincial resistance, the state constitution of 1777, the ratification and creation of constitutional law, and the convention of 1821. Hulsebosch discusses the contributions of Alexander Hamilton, James Kent, Sir William Johnson, and William Smith Jr.

Where it's reviewed:
Harvard Law Review, January 2007, page 754

Other books you might like:
Jill Lepore, *New York Burning: Liberty, Slavery, and Conspiracy in Eighteenth-Century Manhattan*, 2005
Donald Odell, *Union and Liberty: A Documentary History of American Constitutionalism*, 1969
Robert C. Ritchie, *Duke's Province: A Study of New York Politics and Society, 1664-1691*, 1977
James G. Wilson, *The Imperial Republic: A Structural History of American Constitutionalism from the*

Colonial Era to the Beginning of the Twentieth
Century, 2002
Serena R. Zabin, *Dangerous Economies: Status and
Commerce in Imperial New York*, 2009

753

THOMAS JACKSON

*From Civil Rights to Human
Rights: Martin Luther King, Jr.
and the Struggle for Economic
Justice*

(Philadelphia: University of Pennsylvania Press, 2006)

Subject(s): History; Human rights; African Americans

Summary: In *From Civil Rights to Human Rights: Martin
Luther King, Jr. and the Struggle for Economic Justice*,
author Thomas Jackson examines the broad scope of Dr.
King's causes. Noted for his heroic civil rights efforts on
behalf of black Americans, Martin Luther King, Jr.—the
"American Gandhi"—also sought equal rights and
economic status for the nation's poor. Inspired by a
philosophy that combined democracy, socialism, liberalism, internationalism, and African-American Christianity, King used peaceful means to secure his goals. Based
on archival research, *From Civil Rights to Human Rights*
gives perspective to Dr. King's crusade for justice in the
mid-20th century. First book.

Where it's reviewed:
The Nation, May 19, 2008, page 36

Other books you might like:
Claud Anderson, *Black Labor, White Wealth: The
Search for Power and Economic Justice*, 1994
Paul Le Blanc, *Black Liberation and the American
Dream: The Struggle for Racial and Economic
Justice: Analyis, Strategy, Readings*, 2003
Taylor Branch, *Parting the Waters: America in the King
Years, 1954-63*, 1988
Marshall Frady, *Martin Luther King, Jr.: A Life*, 2005
Juan Williams, *Eyes on the Prize: America's Civil
Rights Years, 1954-1965*, 1987

754

KARL JACOBY

*Shadows at Dawn: A Borderlands
Massacre and the Violence of
History*

(New York: Penguin Press, 2008)

Subject(s): History; Native Americans; Social sciences

Summary: In *Shadows at Dawn: A Borderlands Massacre
and the Violence of History*, historian Karl Jacoby
recounts the events surrounding the Camp Grant Massacre of 1871. In the early hours of April 30 of that year,
a band of Americans, Mexicans, and Tohono O'odham

Indians attacked an Arizona Apache camp, killing almost
150 as they slept. The massacre—launched against a
camp that was under government protection—
precipitated disputes among American politicians and
citizens. Though the country had initiated an Indian
peace policy, unrest among the factions persisted and the
perpetrators of the massacre maintained that they were
protecting themselves from the Apaches.

Other books by the same author:
*Continental Crossroads: Remapping U.S.-Mexico
Borderlands History*, 2004
*Crimes Against Nature: Squatters, Poachers, Thieves,
and the Hidden History of American Conservation*,
2003

Other books you might like:
Chip Colwell-Chanthaphonh, *Massacre at Camp Grant:
Forgetting and Remembering Apache History*, 2007
Brian DeLay, *War of a Thousand Deserts: Indian Raids
and the U.S.-Mexican War*, 2008
Rosemary A. King, *Border Confluences: Borderland
Narratives from the Mexican War to the Present*,
2004
Ian W. Record, *Big Sycamore Stands Alone: The
Western Apaches, Aravaipa, and the Struggle for
Place*, 2008
Cecil Robinson, *No Short Journeys: The Interplay of
Cultures in the History and Literature of the
Borderlands*, 1992

755

EUGENE JARECKI

*The American Way of War: Guided
Missiles, Misguided Men, and a
Republic in Peril*

(New York: Free Press, 2008)

Subject(s): History; Military science; International relations

Summary: In *The American Way of War: Guided Missiles,
Misguided Men, and a Republic in Peril*, author Eugene
Jarecki explains the governmental power shifts that have
given U.S. presidents dangerous control of the war-
making process. Though the declaration of war lies under
the constitutional jurisdiction of Congress, all war
declarations since World War II have been made by sitting presidents with the support of Congress understood.
Jarecki traces the political, economic, and military factors that have contributed to this imbalance and its
implications. The author uses examples from recent history to demonstrate the need to restore the power of war
declaration to Congress.

Where it's reviewed:
Library Journal, August 18, 2008, page 56
Publishers Weekly, August 18, 2008, page 56

Other books you might like:
Tariq Ali, *The Obama Syndrome: Surrender at Home,
War Abroad*, 2010

Andrew J. Bacevich, *Washington Rules: America's Path to Permanent War*, 2010

Chalmers Johnson, *Dismantling the Empire: America's Last Best Hope*, 2010

John Robb, *Brave New War: The Next Stage of Terrorism and the End of Globalization*, 2007

Bob Woodward, *Obama's Wars*, 2010

756

JOAN M. JENSEN

Calling This Place Home: Women on the Wisconsin Frontier, 1850-1925

(St. Paul: Minnesota Historical Society Press, 2006)

Subject(s): History; Women; Social sciences

Summary: In *Calling This Place Home: Women on the Wisconsin Frontier, 1850-1925*, historian Joan Jensen shares profiles of a diverse group of female Native Americans, pioneers, and immigrants from Wisconsin history. Included in this insightful study are Emina Johnson, a Swedish housekeeper who survived the 1871 fire at Peshtigo that claimed over 1000 lives; Isabella Wolfe, a Cherokee woman who worked on the Lac du Flambeau reservation as a nurse; Matilda Schopp, the author's grandmother, an immigrant to Wisconsin's cutover region; and others involved in the region's logging and dairy history. Jensen's inspiring and insightful study features personal correspondence, first-hand accounts, and period photographs.

Where it's reviewed:
Choice, November 2006, page 547

Other books by the same author:
One Foot on the Rockies, 1995
With These Hands: Women Working on the Land, 1993
Loosening the Bonds: Mid-Atlantic Farm Women, 1750-1850, 1988

Other books you might like:
Richard Current, *Wisconsin: A History*, 2001
Oestreich Lurie, *Wisconsin Indians*, 1987
Linda Peavy, *Pioneer Women: The Lives of Women on the Frontier*, 1998
Susan Sessions Rugh, *Our Common Country: Family Farming, Culture, and Community in the Nineteenth-Century Midwest*, 2001
Joanna Stratton, *Pioneer Women: Voices from the Kansas Frontier*, 1981

757

PAUL CHRISTOPHER JOHNSON

Diaspora Conversions: Black Carib Religion and the Recovery of Africa

(Berkeley: University of California Press, 2007)

Subject(s): History; Ethnicity; Religion

Summary: In *Diaspora Conversions: Black Carib Religion and the Recovery of Africa*, historian Paul Christopher Johnson examines the phenomenon of Central American and Caribbean emigration. Through a diaspora, the author explains, a group may redefine itself by altering its perception of its past. In tracing the migration of the Garifuna sect (the Black Caribs), Johnson compares the group's religious rituals as practiced in the native land and in their adopted home. With a large population of Garifuna coming to the U.S. over the past five decades, the author explains, the group's identity and practices have remained rooted in the Caribbean while adapting to a new society.

Where it's reviewed:
Choice, February 2008, page 1018

Other books by the same author:
Secrets, Gossip, and Gods: The Transformation of Brazilian Candomble, 2005

Other books you might like:
Patrick Bellegarde-Smith, *Voudou in Haitian Life and Culture: Invisible Powers*, 2006
Hemchand Gossai, *Religion, Culture and Tradition in the Caribbean*, 2000
Claudine Michel, *Voudou in Haitian Life and Culture: Invisible Powers*, 2006
Mozella G. Mitchell, *Crucial Issues in Caribbean Religions*, 2006
Nathaniel Samuel Murrell, *Religion, Culture and Tradition in the Caribbean*, 2000
Margarite Fernandez Olmos, *Healing Cultures: Art and Religion as Curative Practices in the Caribbean and Its Diaspora*, 2001
Lizabeth Paravisini-Gebert, co-author
Patrick Taylor, *Nation Dance: Religion, Identity and Cultural Differences in the Caribbean*, 2001

758

TONY JUDT

Postwar: A History of Europe Since 1945

(New York: Penguin, 2005)

Subject(s): Cold War; Diplomacy; Economics

Summary: Tony Judt is the director of New York University's Remarque Institute and a highly respected historian of 20th century Europe. In this magisterial volume, he shows how the events of World War II continued to affect politics, diplomacy, and economics in Europe for the next 55 years. He describes the way Europe was divided into blocs: the eastern bloc dominated by the might of the Soviet Union, the western influenced by American democracy, and several nations ideologically torn between the two. The author treats the continent as a whole and tracks broad trends, rather than focusing upon minutia in individual nations.

Where it's reviewed:
Harper's Magazine, May 2006, page 81
The Nation, May 2006, page 81
New York Review of Books, November 3, 2005, page 16

The New Yorker, November 28, 2005, page 16

Other books by the same author:
The Memory Chalet, 2010
Reappraisals: Reflections on the Forgotten Twentieth Century, 2008
With Us or Against Us: Studies in Global Anti-Americanism, 2007

Other books you might like:
P.M.H. Bell, *Twentieth-Century Europe*, 2006
William I. Hitchcock, *The Struggle for Europe: The Turbulent History of a Divided Continent, 1945 to the Present*, 2003
Harold James, *Europe Reborn: A History, 1914-2000*, 2003
Mark Mazower, *Dark Continent: Europe's Twentieth Century*, 1999
Robert O. Paxton, *Europe in the Twentieth Century*, 2001

759

MOON-HO JUNG

Coolies and Cane: Race, Labor, and Sugar in the Age of Emancipation

(Baltimore, Maryland: Johns Hopkins University Press, 2006)

Subject(s): History; Asian Americans; Immigrants

Summary: In *Coolies and Cane: Race, Labor, and Sugar in the Age of Emancipation*, author Moon-Ho Jung discusses the issue of Asian labor in the context of American history. While the subject of African slavery in the United States was eventually recognized as a violation of human rights, the author explains that the use of "coolies"—Asian day laborers—has drawn conflicting opinions. While some argue that the coolies represent the nation's increasing acceptance of immigrants, others cite the 19th-century Asian worker as an extension of slave labor. The questionable position of the coolie was further complicated in the aftermath of the Civil War when Asians joined blacks on Louisiana's plantations.

Other books you might like:
Richard Follett, *The Sugar Masters: Planters and Slaves in Louisiana's Cane World, 1820-1860*, 2005
Dr. Donald S. Frazier, *Fire in the Cane Field: The Federal Invasion of Louisiana and Texas, January 1861-January 1863*, 2009
Arnold J. Meagher, *The Coolie Trade: The Traffic in Chinese Laborers to Latin America*, 2008
Gary Okihiro, *Margins and Mainstreams: Asians in American History and Culture*, 1994
Lisa Yun, *The Coolie Speaks: Chinese Indentured Laborers and African Slaves in Cuba*, 2008

760

SEBASTIAN JUNGER

War

(New York: Twelve, 2010)

Subject(s): United States; Wars; Military life

Summary: Written by bestselling author Sebastian Junger, *War* is an eye-opening firsthand glimpse into the daily lives of soldiers in combat in Afghanistan. To gather material for *War*, reporter Sebastian Junger spent 14 months observing a platoon fighting in one of the most dangerous regions of Afghanistan. As Junger witnessed their courageous actions, brushes with death, and moments of complete terror, he also recognized their deeply rooted sense of loyalty, patriotism, service, love, and honor. *War* follows the highs and lows of this single platoon over the course of 14 months, beginning in 2007, and tells the story of the brave soldiers who serve the United States in times of war.

Where it's reviewed:
Booklist, August 1, 2010, page 67
Library Journal, April 15, 2010, page 96
Library Journal, Sept 1, 2010, page 76
Mother Jones, Sept-Oct 2010, page 75
Publishers Weekly, August 30, 2010, page 48

Other books by the same author:
A Death in Belmont, 2007
Tod in Belmont, 2007
The Perfect Storm: A True Story of Men Against the Sea, 2004
Fire, 2002

Other books you might like:
Eric Blehm, *The Only Thing Worth Dying For: How Eleven Green Berets Forged a New Afghanistan*, 2010
Seth G. Jones, *In the Graveyard of Empires: America's War in Afghanistan*, 2010
Robert Leckie, *Helmet for My Pillow: From Parris Island to the Pacific*, 2010
Anthony Shaffer, *Operation Dark Heart: Spycraft and Special Ops on the Frontlines of Afghanistan—and the Path to Victory*, 2010
Benjamin Tupper, *Greetings from Afghanistan, Send More Ammo: Dispatches from Taliban Country*, 2010

761

FRED KAPLAN

1959: The Year Everything Changed

(Hoboken, New Jersey: J. Wiley & Sons, 2009)

Subject(s): History; Culture

Summary: In *1959: The Year Everything Changed*,

journalist Fred Kaplan asserts that it was 1959—not the 1960s—that heralded a revolution in American society and culture. Kaplan focuses on three pivotal events of 1959 as the basis for his groundbreaking argument—the FDA's approval of the birth control pill, the invention of the microchip, and the first U.S. military deaths in Vietnam. In addition to medical, scientific, and political developments, the author considers the year's cultural landmarks, namely the release of Miles Davis's jazz album *Kind of Blue*, the publication of William Burroughs's controversial *Naked Lunch*, and the opening of New York's Guggenheim Museum, designed by Frank Lloyd Wright.

Where it's reviewed:
New York Times, August 18, 2009, page C4
Publishers Weekly, May 4, 2009, page 43

Other books by the same author:
Lincoln: The Biography of a Writer, 2010
Gore Vidal: A Biography, 2000
Henry James: The Imagination of Genius, A Biography, 1999

Other books you might like:
Andrew J. Dunar, *America in the Fifties*, 2006
David Halberstam, *The Fifties*, 1993
Rob Kirkpatrick, *1969: The Year Everything Changed*, 2009
Lewis MacAdams, *Birth of the Cool: Beat, Bebop, and the American Avant-Garde*, 2001
John Super, *The Fifties in America*, 2005

762

AMALIA D. KESSLER

A Revolution in Commerce: The Parisian Merchant Court and the Rise of Commercial Society in Eighteenth-century France

(New Haven, Connecticut: Yale University Press, 2007)

Subject(s): History; Business; Economics

Summary: In *A Revolution in Commerce: The Parisian Merchant Court and the Rise of Commercial Society in Eighteenth-century France*, author Amalia Kessler examines the dramatic changes experienced in the French commerce system of the 1700s. This exhaustively researched volume covers the topics of institutional structure and jurisdictional conflict; relational contracting and community-based approach to procedure; the court's resolution of sales, employment, and marital disputes; the changing structure of business associations; the problem of merchant relations; and the challenges of negotiability. The author also describes the role merchants played in redefining the era's commercial operations.

Other books you might like:
Paul Burton Cheney, *Revolutionary Commerce: Globalization and the French Monarchy*, 2010
Michael Kwass, *Privilege and the Politics of Taxation*

in Eighteenth-Century France: Liberte, Egalite, Fiscalite, 2006
J.G.A. Pocock, *Virtue, Commerce, and History: Essays on Political Thought and History, Chiefly in the Eighteenth Century*, 1985
Andrew P. Trout, *City on the Seine: Paris in the Time of Richelieu and Louis XIV, 1614-1715*, 1996
Jan de Vries, *The Industrious Revolution: Consumer Behavior and the Household Economy, 1650 to the Present*, 2008

763

STEPHEN KINZER

Overthrow: America's Century of Regime Change from Hawaii to Iraq

(New York: Times Books, 2006)

Subject(s): Wars; History; United States history

Summary: In *Overthrow: America's Century of Regime Change from Hawaii to Iraq*, author Stephen Kinzer poses the question, "Why does a strong nation strike against a weaker one?" Kinzer shows readers the motivations that have driven world leaders, military personnel, double agents, and corporate executives to topple foreign regimes. Kinzer begins with the 1893 overthrow of the Hawaiian monarchy and investigates all of America's takeover maneuvers between then and now, including the invasion of Iraq in 2003. The years of the Cold War, which saw countries such as Honduras, Nicaragua, and Puerto Rico held under America's thumb, and the deposing of government systems in places like Grenada and Afghanistan are also scrutinized. Kinzer goes on to explain why so many of the United States' attempts at foreign regime change have had devastating costs, providing solid proof of his assertion that no nation in modern history has toppled foreign regimes so consistently and so far from home.

Where it's reviewed:
New York Review of Books, May 11, 2006, page 25
New York Times Book Review, April 16, 2006, page 25

Other books by the same author:
Reset: Iran, Turkey and America's Future, 2010
All the Shah's Men: An American Coup and the Roots of Middle East Terror, 2008
A Thousand Hills: Rwanda's Rebirth and the Man Who Dreamed It, 2008

Other books you might like:
Tom Coffman, *Nation Within: The History of the American Occupation of Hawaii*, 2003
Camille Eiss, *Reshaping Rogue States: Preemption, Regime Change, and US Policy Toward Iran, Iraq, and North Korea*, 2004
Jane Franklin, *The U.S. Invasion of Panama: The Truth Behind Operational*, 1999
Alexander T. Lennon, *Reshaping Rogue States: Preemption, Regime Change, and US Policy Toward Iran, Iraq, and North Korea*, 2004

Robert Litwak, *Regime Change: U.S. Strategy Through the Prism of 9/11*, 2007

Mauricio Solaun, *U.S. Intervention and Regime Change in Nicaragua*, 2005

764

MATTHEW KLINGLE

Emerald City: An Environmental History of Seattle

(New Haven, Connecticut: Yale University Press, 2007)

Subject(s): Environmental history; Geography; Urban life

Summary: In *Emerald City: An Environmental History of Seattle*, author and professor Matthew Klingle uses the city of Seattle as a case study to prove a larger point about cities in general—that they should have an "ethic of place" that respects both the natural environment and the people who live there. Klingle shows how land development has destroyed natural habitats as he explains the effects of development from both an environmental and urban perspective. He shows how development not only affects wildlife, but also harms the city's poorest citizens. Klingle's work on this subject was awarded the 2009 Ray Allen Billington Prize, given by the Organization of American Historians.

Other books you might like:
William Cronon, *Native Seattle: Histories from the Crossing-Over Place*, 2007
William Dietrich, *The Final Forest: The Battle for the Last Great Trees of the Pacific Northwest*, 1992
Dale D. Goble, *Northwest Lands, Northwest Peoples: Readings in Environmental History*, 1999
    Paul W. Hirt, co-author
Clark Humphrey, *Vanishing Seattle*, 2006
Steve Pomper, *It Happened in Seattle: Remarkable Events That Shaped History*, 2009
Coll Thrush, *Native Seattle: Histories from the Crossing-Over Place*, 2007

765

DOROTHY KO

Cinderella's Sisters: A Revisionist History of Footbinding

(Berkeley, California: University of California Press, 2005)

Subject(s): History; Social sciences; Women

Summary: In *Cinderella's Sisters: A Revisionist History of Footbinding*, historian Dorothy Ko examines the complex issue of female footbinding as practiced throughout Chinese history. As the author explains, the binding of girls' and women's feet was an integral part of Chinese culture for almost a millennium. A physical representation of status, beauty, and fashion, footbinding has been commonly viewed as an example of oppression, but Ko considers the female viewpoint of the practice. Through her study of journals and writings of

the period, Ko reveals the surprising sense of self-worth that Chinese women associated with bound feet.

Where it's reviewed:
Choice, November 2006, page 54
The Historian, Fall 2007, page 572

Other books by the same author:
Women and Confucian Cultures, 2003
Every Step a Lotus: Shoes for Bound Feet, 2001
Teachers of the Inner Chambers: Women and Culture in Seventeenth-Century China, 1995

Other books you might like:
Pang-Mei Natasha Chang, *Bound Feet and Western Dress: A Memoir*, 1996
Hong Fan, *Footbinding, Feminism and Freedom: The Liberation of Women's Bodies in Modern China*, 1997
Jicai Feng, *The Three-Inch Golden Lotus*, 1994
Beverley Jackson, *Splendid Slippers: A Thousand Years of an Erotic Tradition*, 2000
Ping Wang, *Aching for Beauty: Footbinding in China*, 2000

766

MICHAEL KORDA

With Wings Like Eagles: A History of the Battle of Britain

(New York: Harper, 2009)

Subject(s): World War II, 1939-1945; Battle of Britain, 1940; Armed forces

Summary: In the summer of 1940, the United States had not yet entered World War II, and Hitler's forces had overtaken much of Western Europe. As German forces came closer and closer to taking Britain, that country's armed forces valiantly fought to protect their homeland. The Battle of Britain was the effort that kept the Germans from invading Britain, and it served as a turning point in the war. In his book *With Wings Like Eagles: A History of the Battle of Britain* author Michael Korda gives a detailed history of this war-changing battle. The battle was between the German and British air forces. In the book, Korda gives information about the leaders and airmen in the British Royal Air Force, and he discusses how their valiant efforts helped to save their country. Korda also explores the social, scientific, and political developments from the previous decade that led to Battle of Britain.

Where it's reviewed:
Booklist, November 15, 2008, page 16
Library Journal, April 15, 2009, page 68
New York Times Book Review, February 15, 2009, page 26
Publishers Weekly, October 13, 2008, page 47

Other books by the same author:
Ulysses S. Grant: The Unlikely Hero, 2009
Ike: An American Hero, 2008
Journey to a Revolution: A Personal Memoir and History of the Hungarian Revolution of 1956, 2007

History

Other books you might like:

Patrick Bishop, *Battle of Britain: A Day-by-Day Chronicle: 10 July 1940 to 31 October 1940*, 2009

Patrick Bishop, *Fighter Boys: The Battle of Britain, 1940*, 2003

Stephen Bungay, *The Most Dangerous Enemy: The Definitive History of the Battle of Britain*, 2000

David E. Fisher, *A Summer Bright and Terrible: Winston Churchill, Lord Dowding, Radar, and the Impossible Triumph of the Battle of Britain*, 2005

Richard Overy, *The Battle of Britain: The Myth and the Reality*, 2001

767

PAUL A. KRAMER

The Blood of Government: Race, Empire, the United States, and the Philippines

(Chapel Hill: University of North Carolina Press, 2006)

Subject(s): United States history; Wars; Politics

Summary: *The Blood of Government: Race, Empire, The United States, and the Philippines* chronicles the history of relations between The United States and the Philippines, beginning in 1899 and continuing through the next 50 years. The book argues that the United States military forces waged an "imperialist" war against the Philippines in order to expand its "empire," and used race as a means to divide the people and justify their actions. Filipino citizens were separated into two categories, Christian and Muslim. Christians were rewarded with self-government if they proved their worth, but not the Muslims.

Other books you might like:

Julian Go, *American Empire and the Politics of Meaning: Elite Political Cultures in the Philippines and Puerto Rico during U.S. Colonialism*, 2008

E. San Juan, *U.S. Imperialism and Revolution in the Philippines*, 2007

Stanley Karnow, *In Our Image: America's Empire in the Philippines*, 1989

Stuart Creighton Miller, *Benevolent Assimiliation: The American Conquest of the Philippines, 1899-1903*, 1982

David J. Silbey, *A War of Frontier and Empire: The Philippine-American War, 1899-1902*, 2007

768

MICHAEL KRANISH

Flight from Monticello: Thomas Jefferson at War

(Oxford; New York: Oxford University Press, 2010)

Subject(s): American Revolution, 1775-1783; Presidents (Government); United States history

Summary: During the waning years of the American Revolution, Virginia governor Thomas Jefferson fled the state to avoid capture by British troops. In *Flight from Monticello: Thomas Jefferson at War*, journalist Michael Kranish investigates this often-maligned period in Jefferson's life. Kranish puts Jefferson's actions in a historical perspective, presenting the very real dangers the governor faced during this turbulent time in American history. *Flight from Monticello* includes illustrations, a map, notes on the text, and a full index.

Where it's reviewed:

Library Journal, December 2009, page 119

Newsweek, February 1, 2010, page 51

Publishers Weekly, November 2, 2009, page 44

Other books by the same author:

John F. Kerry: The Complete Biography by the Boston Globe Reporters Who Know Him Best, 2004

Other books you might like:

R.B. Bernstein, *Thomas Jefferson*, 2005

Joseph J. Ellis, *American Sphinx: The Character of Thomas Jefferson*, 1997

Kevin J. Hayes, *The Road to Monticello: The Life and Mind of Thomas Jefferson*, 2008

Robert Middlekauff, *The Glorious Cause*, 1981

Jack Rakove, *Revolutionaries: A New History of the Invention of America*, 2010

769

THOMAS KUEHN

Heirs, Kin, and Creditors in Renaissance Florence

(Cambridge; New York: Cambridge University Press, 2008)

Subject(s): Law; Inheritance and succession; History

Summary: In *Heirs, Kin, and Creditors in Renaissance Florence*, Thomas Kuehn explores the practices of inheritance in Florence, Italy, during the Renaissance. The denial of inheritance was relatively common at that time. Individuals had a number of different reasons for refusing inheritance—many people were trying to engineer a certain social status or to avoid the "strings" that came with inheritances, such as unpaid debts. Others used the strategy as a tool to essentially discipline other family members or to ensure that inheritances would be directed to someone else of the heir's choosing, helping the family to meet certain objectives for each generation. Kuehn follows the legal history of the practice of repudiation of inheritance during this time period, discussing its somewhat unexpected use in society.

Other books by the same author:

Illegitimacy in Renaissance Florence, 2002

Law, Family, and Women: Toward a Legal Anthropology of Renaissance Italy, 1994

Emancipation in Late Medieval Florence, 1982

Other books you might like:

Gene A. Brucker, *Renaissance Florence, Updated Edition*, 1974

Roger J. Crum, *Renaissance Florence: A Social History*, 2006

Lauro Martines, *An Italian Renaissance Sextet: Six Tales in Historical Context*, 1995

John T. Paoletti, *Renaissance Florence: A Social History*, 2006

Tim Parks, *Medici Money: Banking, Metaphysics and Art in Fifteenth-century Florence*, 2005

Richard C. Trexler, *Public Life in Renaissance Florence*, 1981

770

SCOTT KURASHIGE

The Shifting Grounds of Race: Black and Japanese Americans in the Making of Multiethnic Los Angeles

(Princeton, New Jersey: Princeton University Press, 2010)

Subject(s): History; United States; Civil rights

Summary: In *The Shifting Grounds of Race: Black and Japanese Americans in the Making of Multiethnic Los Angeles*, Scott Kurashige considers the history of the city of Los Angeles in the 20th century. The author begins by considering large events such as the civil rights movement and the Japanese internment camps, then narrowing the focus to issues of segregation and resisted integration in the city of Los Angeles itself, which was historically considered a "white city." Racism was extremely prevalent in LA at the time, and Japanese Americans and African Americans often lived together in smaller communities within the urban landscape. Kurashige then considers the 1965 Watts Rebellion as an example of the ways in which African Americans were blamed for many of the problems in the city, while Japanese Americans were considered the "model minority." This led to unique relationships, sometimes positive and sometimes antagonistic, between various ethnic groups.

Where it's reviewed:
The Nation, June 30, 2008, page 42

Other books you might like:
Sung Hak Choi, *Trouble City: Korean-Black Conflict in Post-Insurrection Los Angeles*, 2007

Darnell Hunt, *Black Los Angeles: American Dreams and Racial Realities*, 2010

Lon Kurashige, *Japanese American Celebration and Conflict: A History of Ethnic Identity and Festival, 1934-1990*, 2002

John B. Orr, *Politics and the Spirit: Religion and Multiethnicity in Los Angeles*, 1994

Laura Pulido, *Black, Brown, Yellow, and Left: Radical Activism in Los Angeles*, 2006

Ana-Christina Ramon, *Black Los Angeles: American Dreams and Racial Realities*, 2010

771

ERIK LARSON

Thunderstruck

(New York: Crown, 2006)

Subject(s): Communication; History; Inventions

Summary: In this reconstruction of a historic manhunt, the story of inventor Guglielmo Marconi's wireless communication alternates with that of suspected murderer Dr. Hawley Harvey Crippen, who fled England on an ocean liner with his lover after killing his wife. Having outdone numerous scientists when he perfected the wireless, Marconi needed a means to prove the success and worth of his invention. The two-day chase after Crippen from Europe to Canada was all the world needed to embrace Marconi's invention: it transmitted news of the escaped murderer to the ship's captain, who, in turn, reported the suspect's presence on his ship. In response, an officer from Scotland Yard was dispatched on a faster ship and Crippen was caught.

Where it's reviewed:
Booklist, July 1, 2006, page 5
Bookmarks, January/February 2007, page 60
Library Journal, August 1, 2006, page 102
Newsweek, October 30, 2006, page 60
Publishers Weekly, August 14, 2006, page 191

Other books by the same author:
In the Garden of Beasts: Love, Terror, and an American Family in Hitler's Berlin, 2011

The Devil in the White City: Murder, Magic, and Madness at the Fair That Changed America, 2004

Isaac's Storm: A Man, A Time, and the Deadliest Hurricane in History, 2000

Lethal Passage: The Story of a Gun, 1995

Naked Consumer: How Our Private Lives Become Public Commodities, 1994

Other books you might like:
Tom A. Cullen, *The Mild Murderer: The True Story of the Dr. Crippen Case*, 1977

David James Smith, *Supper with the Crippens: A New Investigation into One of the Most Notorious Domestic Murders in History*, 2006

Calvin D. Trowbridge Jr., *Marconi: Father of Wireless, Grandfather of Radio, Great-Grandfather of the Cell Phone, The Story of the Race to Control Long-Distance Wireless*, 2010

Gavin Weightman, *Signor Marconi's Magic Box: The Most Remarkable Invention of the 19th Century and the Amateur Inventor Whose Genius Sparked a Revolution*, 2003

Filson Young, *The Trial of Dr. Hawley Hervey Crippen*, 2008

772

MARK ATWOOD LAWRENCE

Assuming the Burden: Europe and the American Commitment to War in Vietnam

(Berkeley, California: University of California Press, 2005)

Subject(s): History; Vietnam War, 1959-1975; United States history

Summary: In *Assuming the Burden: Europe and the American Commitment to War in Vietnam*, Mark Atwood Lawrence traces the history of America's connection to Vietnam, arguing that the United States first became involved with the nation in the 1940s. Lawrence first considers the decision of the US government to send military assistance to France in 1950, which he argues cemented the United States' position in Indochina conflicts. Lawrence also considers these actions in the larger concept of colonialism, discussing differing perspectives of the American, French, and British governments from the 1940s until the 1960s. The ways in which the Vietnam War was "sold," which included showcasing the fight as a Cold War battle between democracy and communism, illustrates how the three governments came to work together to commit to the war and persuade citizens to follow.

Other books by the same author:
The Vietnam War: A Concise International History, 2010

Other books you might like:
Peter Busch, *All the Way with JFK? Britain, the US and the Vietnam War*, 2003
Bernard B. Fall, *Street Without Joy: The French Debacle in Vietnam*, 1994
Stanley Karnow, *Vietnam: A History*, 1983
Thomas Alan Schwartz, *Lyndon Johnson and Europe: In the Shadow of Vietnam*, 2003
Marilyn Young, *Vietnam Wars*, 1991

773

EUGENIA LEAN

Public Passions: The Trial of Shi Jianqiao and the Rise of Popular Sympathy in Republican China

(Berkeley, California: University of California Press, 2007)

Subject(s): History; Social sciences; China

Summary: In *Public Passions: The Trial of Shi Jianqiao and the Rise of Popular Sympathy in Republican China*, Eugenia Lean analyzes an event that occurred in 1935 in China. Shi Jianqiao, a Chinese woman, murdered Sun Chuanfang, a warlord, in a Buddhist temple to get revenge for the death of her father. Once she was on trial, Shi used the media to garner public support. Public sympathy, which was a foreign concept to the Chinese at this time, built quickly, leading to Shi's eventual

exoneration. Lean uses these events to discuss topics such as the significance of gender and emotions on politics and the media, the different types of influence that the media has on public opinion, and contemporary law in China.

Other books you might like:
Paul John Bailey, *China in the Twentieth Century*, 2001
Yomi Braester, *Witness Against History: Literature, Film, and Public Discourse in Twentieth-Century China*, 2003
Elizabeth J. Perry, *Chinese Society: Change, Conflict and Resistance*, 2010
Mark Selden, co-author
Jonathan D. Spence, *The Search for Modern China*, 1990
Xiaoqun Xu, *Trial of Modernity: Judician Reform in Early Twentieth-Century China, 1901-1937*, 2008

774

MELVYN P. LEFFLER

For the Soul of Mankind: The United States, the Soviet Union, and the Cold War

(New York: Hill and Wang, 2007)

Subject(s): History; Cold War, 1945-1991; Russian history

Summary: In *For the Soul of Mankind: The United States, the Soviet Union, and the Cold War*, Melvyn P. Leffler presents a critical analysis of the Cold War and the complex political interactions that took place during the 50 years of conflict. While Leffler believes that Stalin and his totalitarian governmental rule were responsible for starting the Cold War, he also theorizes that it was unnecessary for the conflict to continue for such an extended period and that the United States is at least partly to blame for prolonging the conflict. The author explains why it was possible for Reagan and Gorbachev to end the war when many other leaders—including Truman, Eisenhower, Kennedy, Johnson, Malenkov, and Khrushchev—could not. Leffler describes the five instances during which the Cold War could have come to an end and explains why various governmental decisions delayed peace.

Where it's reviewed:
The Economist, September 15, 2007, page 101
Publishers Weekly, May 28, 2007, page 47

Other books by the same author:
Elusive Quest: America's Pursuit of Stability and French Security, 1919-1933, 2009
The Specter of Communism: The United States and the Origins of the Cold War, 1917-1953, 1994
A Preponderance of Power: National Security, the Truman Administration, and the Cold War, 1993

Other books you might like:
John Lewis Gaddis, *The Cold War: A New History*, 2005
Jussi M. Hanhimaki, *The Cold War: A History in Documents and Eyewitness Accounts*, 2004

Robert J. McMahon, *The Cold War: A Very Short Introduction*, 2003

Ronald E. Powaski, *The Cold War: The United States and the Soviet Union, 1917-1991*, 1997

Martin Walker, *The Cold War: A History*, 1995

Odd Arne Westad, *The Cold War: A History in Documents and Eyewitness Accounts*, 2004

775

JILL LEPORE

New York Burning: Liberty, Slavery, and Conspiracy in Eighteenth-Century Manhattan

(New York: Alfred A. Knopf, 2005)

Subject(s): Slavery; United States history, 1600-1775 (Colonial period); Murder

Summary: Jill Lepore's *New York Burning: Liberty, Slavery, and Conspiracy in Eighteenth-Century Manhattan* is a historical account of the horrendous crimes that took place against black slaves in 1741 in Manhattan, New York. A white woman named Mary Burton testified that slaves were conspiring to overthrow the local government, burn down the city, murder all the white men, and rape the white women. Over 200 slaves were accused and sent to trial. Almost 80 of them were forced to confess and implicate others. After the trial, 13 black men were burned at the stake, 17 were hanged along with four white men accused of conspiracy, and 70 were exiled to the Caribbean. Lepore bases much of the book on a 1744 journal written by a New York Supreme Court Justice. She questions if there was ever a conspiracy or if fear of a slave revolt was to blame for the heinous acts.

Where it's reviewed:
America, January 2, 2006, page 24
The Nation, November 21, 2005, page 37
The New Republic, January 30, 2006, page 29
New York Times Book Review, October 2, 2005, page 28

Other books by the same author:
The Whites of Their Eyes: The Tea Party's Revolution and the Battle Over American History, 2010
A is for American: Letters and Other Characters in the Newly United States, 2003
The Name of War: King Philip's War and the Origins of American Identity, 1999

Other books you might like:
Edwin G. Burrows, *Gotham: A History of New York City to 1898*, 1998
Edward Robb Ellis, *The Epic of New York City: A Narrative History*, 1990
Peter Charles Hoffer, *The Great New York Conspiracy of 1741: Slavery, Crime, and Colonial Law*, 2003
Mat Johnson, *The Great Negro Plot: A Tale of Conspiracy and Murder in Eighteenth-Century New York*, 2007
C.S. Manegold, *Ten Hills Farm: The Forgotten History of Slavery in the North*, 2009

Mike Wallace, *Gotham: A History of New York City to 1898*, 1998

776

PETER A. LILLBACK

George Washington's Sacred Fire

(Bryn Mawr, Pennsylvania: Providence Forum Press, 2006)

Subject(s): United States history; Military life; Faith

Summary: In *George Washington's Sacred Fire*, author Peter A. Lillback offers a voluminous portrait of the first president, focusing on his ideologies and inner drive. While chronicling the life and times of Washington, Lillback provides probing insights into the mind and heart of the courageous leader, which the author has drawn from tireless research conducted on Washington's private diaries and letters. This volume presents another perspective on America's first president, portraying a man who was much more than a brave leader and military figure: he was man of the utmost faith. *George Washington's Sacred Fire* includes a bibliography and a full index.

Other books by the same author:
Wall of Misconception, 2007
Binding of God: The Calvins' Role in the Development of Covenant Theology, 2001

Other books you might like:
Ron Chernow, *Washington: A Life*, 2010
Gaston Espinosa, *Religion and the American Presidency: George Washington to George W. Bush with Commentary and Primary Sources*, 2009
Michael Novak, *Washington's God: Religion, Liberty, and the Father of Our Country*, 2006
Mary V. Thompson, *In the Hands of a Good Providence: Religion in the Life of George Washington*, 2008

777

DEBORAH E. LIPSTADT

History on Trial: My Day in Court with David Irving

(New York: Ecco, 2005)

Subject(s): Law; Holocaust, 1933-1945; History

Summary: Author Deborah E. Lipstadt reconstructs author David Irving's libel suit against her in *History on Trial: My Day in Court with David Irving*. Irving sued Lipstadt, a historian, saying that she had defamed him by accusing him of being a Holocaust denier. This is Lipstadt's story about her own attempt to discredit Irving in the public arena and why she felt it was so important to fight back. Courtroom scenes fill the book, which also deconstructs Irving's research. Although some in the press questioned whether historical fact should be established in court, Lipstadt argues that, when it comes to the Holocaust, debunking attempts to deny it were essential.

History

Where it's reviewed:
Booklist, January 1, 2005, page 809
Kirkus Reviews, December 1, 2004, page 1134
Library Journal, January 1, 2005, page 128
Publishers Weekly, January 10, 2005, page 51

Other books by the same author:
The Eichmann Trial, 2011
Denying the Holocaust: The Growing Assault on Truth and Memory, 1994
Beyond Belief: The American Press and the Coming of the Holocaust, 1933-1945, 1993

Other books you might like:
Stephen E. Atkins, *Holocaust Denial as an International Movement*, 2009
Richard J. Evans, *In Defense of History*, 1999
Alex Grobman, *Denying History: Who Says the Holocaust Never Happened and Why Do They Say It?*, 2000
D.D. Guttenplan, *The Holocaust on Trial*, 2001
Gary Nash, *Lying About Hitler: History, Holocaust, and the David Irving Trial*, 2001
Michael Shermer, *Denying History: Who Says the Holocaust Never Happened and Why Do They Say It?*, 2000

778

JAMES W. LOEWEN

Sundown Towns: A Hidden Dimension of Segregation in America

(New York: Norton, 2005)

Subject(s): History; African Americans; Blacks

Summary: It's a different world when the sun sets, darkness sets in, and shadows fall. This scenario is especially true in small towns spread throughout the country, known as "sundown towns," in which African-Americans are banned from town after sunset. Such "sundown policies" were implemented and enforced through threats, intimidation, and other violent means. The aim was to evict African-Americans from small towns and send them into big cities so that whites could live in the small towns without the African-American presence. Sundown towns were found especially in the South and West—some even exist today. In *Sundown Towns: A Hidden Dimension of Segregation in America*, author James Loewen studies the history of these towns and rules and the reasons why they continue.

Where it's reviewed:
Library Journal, October 1, 2005, page 55
The Nation, February 27, 2006, page 30
Publishers Weekly, July 25, 2005, page 55

Other books by the same author:
Teaching What Really Happened: How to Avoid the Tyranny of Textbooks and Get Students Excited About Doing History, 2009

Lies Across America: What Our Historic Sites Get Wrong, 2007
Lies My Teacher Told Me: Everything Your American History Textbook Got Wrong, 1995

Other books you might like:
Nate Blakeslee, *Tulia: Race, Cocaine, and Corruption in a Small Texas Town*, 2005
Eduardo Bonilla-Silva, *Racism Without Racists: Color-Blind Racism and the Persistence of Racial Inequality in America*, 2006
Mark Nathan Cohen, *Culture of Intolerance: Chauvinism, Class and Racism in the United States*, 1998
Alexnder Polikoff, *Waiting for Gautreaux: A Story of Segregation, Housing, and the Black Ghetto*, 2006
Beverly Daniel Tatum, *Assimiliation Blues: Black Families in White Communities, Who Succeeds and Why*, 1987

779

DAVID LOYN

In Afghanistan: Two Hundred Years of British, Russian and American Occupation

(New York: Palgrave Macmillan, 2009)

Subject(s): Afghanistan Conflict, 2001-; History; Middle East

Summary: David Loyn's *In Afghanistan: Two Hundred Years of British, Russian and American Occupation* is a discussion of the myriad ways in which Afghanistan has remained a difficult or impossible conquest for invaders from different regions for more than two centuries. Loyn considers the challenges faced by British, Soviet, and, most recently, American forces as they entered Afghanistan. Loyn attributes the failed conquests to the country's constantly shifting alliances and religious uprisings that tend toward violence. In addition, he considers notable historical figures who helped influence the country and its evasive abilities, including Mountstuart Elphinstone, Abdur Habibullah, and Charlie Wilson, who directed funds to the mujahideen as the Soviets invaded the country.

Where it's reviewed:
Library Journal, June 1, 2009, page 111
Publishers Weekly, May 4, 2009, page 41

Other books by the same author:
Butcher and Bolt: Two Hundred Years of Foreign Engagement in Afghanistan, 2009
Frontline: The True Story of the Mavericks Who Changed the Face of War Reporting, 2005

Other books you might like:
Martin Ewans, *Afghanistan: A Short History of Its People and Politics*, 2002
Gregory Fremont-Barnes, *The Anglo-Afghan Wars 1839-1919*, 2009

Seth G. Jones, *In the Graveyard of Empires: America's War in Afghanistan*, 2010

Mohammed Hassan Kakar, *Afghanistan: The Soviet Invasion and the Afghan Response, 1979-1982*, 1995

Stephen Tanner, *Afghanistan: A Military History from Alexander the Great to the War against the Taliban*, 2009

780

JOHN D. LUKACS

Escape from Davao: The Forgotten Story of the Most Daring Prison Break of the Pacific War

(New York: Simon and Schuster, 2010)

Story type: Historical - World War II

Subject(s): History; World War II, 1939-1945; Prisoners of war

Summary: Written by historian John D. Lukacs, *Escape from Davao: The Forgotten Story of the Most Daring Prison Break of the Pacific War* is a true account of the brave escape of twelve men from a Japanese prison camp. In April of 1943, ten American prisoners of war and two Filipino convicts worked together to make a daring escape from Davao Penal Colony, a Japanese prison camp that was deemed impossible to escape from. They were the only group in history to successfully break out of Davao, and this is the first time their full story is being told. After the soldiers returned to America, they were silenced and censored by the government and military. Drawing on extensive research, personal letters, and interviews with survivors, Lukacs presents the complete account of this heroic and monumental escape.

Where it's reviewed:
Booklist, May 1, 2010, page 68

Other books by the same author:
The Legacy of the Second World War, 2010
Churchill: Visionary, Statesman, Historian, 2004
The Hitler of History, 1998

Other books you might like:
William E. Dyess, *Bataan Death March: A Survivor's Account*, 2002

Damon Gause, *The War Journal of Major Damon Rocky Gause: The Firsthand Account of One of the Greatest Escapes of World War II*, 1999

Bruce Henderson, *Hero Found: The Greatest POW Escape of the Vietnam War*, 2010

Elizabeth M. Norman, *Tears in the Darkness: The Story of the Bataan Death March and Its Aftermath*, 2009
Michael Norman, co-author

Hampton Sides, *Ghost Soldiers: The Forgotten Epic Story of World War II's Most Dramatic Mission*, 2001

781

SABINE MACCORMACK

On the Wings of Time: Rome, The Incas, Spain, and Peru

(Princeton, New Jersey: Princeton University Press, 2006)

Subject(s): South Americans; History; Incas

Summary: In *On the Wings of Time: Rome, The Incas, Spain, and Peru*, Sabine MacCormack considers how classical and Roman literature shaped Peru following the Spanish invasion and conquest of the Incan empire. MacCormack first considers the influence that Rome had on the Spanish people and the way the Spanish used that influence in South America. The Spanish invaders had a desire to understand the culture they had just invaded. Spanish attempts to contextualize their experiences were often filtered through their knowledge of Roman literature, which may be seen in writings from that time. Conversely, MacCormack also considers how the people of Peru interpreted that knowledge and how it influenced the formation of cities and language.

Other books by the same author:
The Shadows of Poetry: Vergil in the Mind of Augustine, 1998
Religion in the Andes, 1993
Art and Ceremony in Late Antiquity, 1990

Other books you might like:
Jon Cowans, *Early Modern Spain: A Documentary History*, 2003

Kim MacQuarrie, *The Last Days of the Incas*, 2007

R. Conrad Stein, *The Conquistadores: Building a Spanish Empire in the Americas*, 2004

Steve J. Stern, *Peru's Indian Peoples and the Challenge of Spanish Conquest: Huamanga to 1640*, 1993

Hugh Thomas, *Rivers of Gold: The Rise of the Spanish Empire, from Columbus to Magellan*, 2004

782

G. CALVIN MACKENZIE
ROBERT WEISBROT , Co-Author

The Liberal Hour: Washington and the Politics of Change in the 1960s

(New York: Penguin Press, 2008)

Subject(s): Politics; United States history; Social sciences

Summary: In *The Liberal Hour: Washington and the Politics of Change in the 1960s*, authors G. Calvin Mackenzie and Robert Weisbrot present their theory that the most significant force for social change in the United States during the 1960s was the liberal government in power—not the counterculture. Their theory turns the typical portrayal of this decade, in which the government is seen as an unwilling respondent to the voice of the people, on its head. The authors focus on presidents John F. Kennedy and Lyndon B. Johnson and a number of senators and congressmen in office at the time. They argue that the government was just as ready for change as the rest of the country. They give examples of economic, environmental, and civil policy reforms that occurred. Among the explanations the authors offer to explain these policy changes are the shift in power from the cities to the suburbs, which led to a change in the types of politicians found in government, and the prosperity in the country after the war.

Where it's reviewed:
Booklist, July 1, 2008, page 31
Library Journal, June 1, 2008, page 108
New York Times, August 13, 2008, page E2
Publishers Weekly, May 5, 2008, page 55

Other books by the same author:
Scandal Proof: Do Ethics Laws Make Government Ethical (Mackenzie), 2002
Bucking the Deficit: Economic Policymaking in America (Mackenzie), 1996
The Irony of Reform: Roots of American Political Disenchantment (Mackenzie), 1996
Marching Toward Freedom 1957-1965: From the Founding of the Southern Christian Leadership Conference to the Assassination of Malcom X (Weisbrot), 1994

Other books you might like:
Michael W. Flamm, *Debating the 1960s: Liberal, Conservative, and Radical Perspectives*, 2007
Peter B. Levy, *America in the Sixties—Right, Left, and Center: A Documentary History*, 1998
Mark Hamilton Lytle, *America's Uncivil Wars: The Sixties Era from Elvis to the Fall of Richard Nixon*, 2005
Allen J. Matusow, *The Unraveling of America: A History of Liberalism in the 1960s*, 2009
David Steigerwald, *Debating the 1960s: Liberal, Conservative, and Radical Perspectives*, 2007
Brian Ward, *The 1960s: A Documentary Reader*, 2009

783

MARGARET MACMILLAN

Nixon and Mao: The Week That Changed the World

(New York: Random House, 2007)

Subject(s): Government; History; International Relations

Summary: Margaret MacMillan presents a thorough and interesting account of the 1972 meeting between President Richard Nixon and Chairman Mao Zedong of China. MacMillan asserts that, while this meeting did not affect many of the issues discussed, it did lay the groundwork for later relations between China and the U.S. She pays considerable attention to the roles Henry Kissinger and Chinese Premier Chou En-Lai played in the negotiations. She also provides some details about Pat Nixon and Jiang Qing. The book gives many behind-the-scenes details and background information on the principal players, as well as a valuable understanding of Chinese and American history.

Where it's reviewed:
New York Review of Books, June 28, 2007, page 67
New York Times Book Review, February 25, 2007, page 14

Other books by the same author:
Dangerous Games: The Uses and Abuses of History, 2010
Women of the Raj: The Mothers, Wives, and Daughters of the British Empire in India, 2007
Paris 1919: Six Months That Changed the World, 2003

Other books you might like:
R. David Arkush, *Land Without Ghosts: Chinese Impressions of America from the Mid-Nineteenth Century to the Present*, 1989
Warren I. Cohen, *America's Response to China: A History of Sino-American Relations*, 1990
Frederik Logevall, *Nixon in the World: American Foreign Relations, 1969-1977*, 2008
Jim Mann, *About Face: A History of America's Curious Relationship with China, from Nixon to Clinton*, 1998
Andrew Preston, *Nixon in the World: American Foreign Relations, 1969-1977*, 2008
Ezra F. Vogel, *Living with China: U.S.-China Relations in the Twenty-First Century*, 1997

784

PAULINE MAIER

Ratification: The People Debate the Constitution, 1787-1788

(New York: Simon & Schuster, 2010)

Subject(s): United States history; Social sciences; Politics

Summary: *Ratification: The People Debate the Constitution, 1787-1788* by Pauline Maier explores the history of the development of the United States Constitution, from its initial birth at Philadelphia's 1787 Constitutional Convention through the ratification process. Maier's work explains the meticulous review process that often led to battles over inclusions as the document was presented at ratifying conventions. The author particularly focuses on four states' roles in the ratification of the U.S. Constitution: Pennsylvania, Massachusetts, Virginia, and New York.

Where it's reviewed:
Library Journal, September 15, 2010, page 85
Publishers Weekly, August 23, 2010, page 43

Other books by the same author:
American Scripture: Making the Declaration of Independence, 1998
From Resistance to Revolution: Colonial Radicals and the Development of American Opposition to Britain, 1765-1776, 1992
Old Revolutionaries, 1990

Other books you might like:
Michael Les Benedict, *The Blessings of Liberty: A*

Concise History of the Constitution of the United States, 2005

Carol Berkin, *A Brilliant Solution: Inventing the American Constitution*, 2003

Catherine Drinker Brown, *Miracle at Philadelphia: The Story of the Constitutional Convention, May-September 1787*, 1986

Christopher Collier, *Decision in Philadelphia: The Constitutional Convention of 1787*, 1986
James Lincoln Collier, co-author

David Stewart, *The Summer of 1787: The Men Who Invented the Constitution*, 2007

785

DANIEL R. MANDELL

Tribe, Race, History: Native Americans in Southern New England, 1780-1880

(Baltimore, Maryland: Johns Hopkins University Press, 2007)

Subject(s): Native Americans; United States history; Social sciences

Summary: *Tribe, Race, History: Native Americans in Southern New England, 1780-1880* by Daniel R. Mandell is a title in The Johns Hopkins University Studies in Historical and Political Science series. This extensively researched, comprehensive text covers the history of Native American peoples in Southern New England over the century between the American Revolution and the Reconstruction Era. Mandell considers how most Native Americans lived in communities separate from whites, but that there were a great deal of interracial marriages taking place, leading this into a longer discussion of ethnic boundaries. In addition, Mandell discusses topics such as land ownership, government, and religion in the context of similarities and differences between whites and American Indians; the way these Indians were portrayed by Europeans in art and literature; and the way the Civil War had a drastic and lasting impact on the future of tribes in the New England region.

Other books by the same author:

King Philip's War: Colonial Expansion, Native Resistance, and the End of Indian Sovereignty, 2010

King Philip's War: The Conflict Over New England, 2007

Behind the Frontier: Indians in Eighteenth-Century Eastern Massachusetts, 2000

Other books you might like:

Kathleen Joan Bragdon, *Native People of Southern New England, 1650-1775*, 2009

Colin G. Calloway, *After King Philip's War: Presence and Persistence in Indian New England*, 1997

D.E. Jarvis, *The Brothertown Nation of Indians: Land Ownership and Nationalism in Early America, 1740-1840*, 2010

David J. Silverman, *Red Brethren: The Brothertown and Stockbridge Indians and the Problem of Race in Early America*, 2010

William Scranton Simmons, *Spirit of the New England*

Tribes: Indian History and Folklore, 1620-1984, 1986

786

CHARLES C. MANN

1491: New Revelations of the Americas Before Columbus

(New York: Vintage, 2005)

Subject(s): American History; Anthropology; Archaeology

Summary: Traditional American history teaches that the people inhabiting the Western Hemisphere when Christopher Columbus landed lived mainly in small nomadic bands, in what was still a vast wilderness. Based on new archaeological evidence and thorough research, this groundbreaking study by Charles Mann challenges popular beliefs about this period of time. According to the study, native populations were often much larger than previously believed, and it is even likely that more people were living in the Americas before 1492 than in Europe. Rather than discovering a wilderness, Mann avows, Columbus arrived to find a land already transformed by sophisticated methods of farming. The book also takes an in-depth look at the environmental consequences of colonization.

Where it's reviewed:

Discover, January 2006, page 73

New York Review of Books, December 1, 2005, page 43

New York Times Book Review, October 9, 2005, page 21

Science, June 2, 2006, page 1313

Other books by the same author:

Before Columbus: The Americas of 1491, 2009

Noah's Choice: The Future of Endangered Species, 1995

The Aspirin Wars: Money, Medicine and 100 Years of Rampant Competition, 1993

Other books you might like:

Manuel Aguilar-Moreno, *Handbook to Life in the Aztec World*, 2005

Susan Alt, *Ancient Complexities: New Perspectives in Pre-Columbian North America*, 2010

Clarissa W. Confer, *Daily Life in Pre-Columbian Native America*, 2007

Lynn V. Foster, *Handbook to Life in the Ancient Maya World*, 2002

Stacy Kowtko, *Nature and the Environment in Pre-Columbian American Life*, 2006

Peter Mathews, *Handbook to Life in the Ancient Maya World*, 2002

787

SUSAN MANN

The Talented Women of the Zhang Family

(Berkeley, California: University of California Press, 2007)

Subject(s): Women; China; Literature

Summary: In *The Talented Women of the Zhang Family*, Susan Mann studies three generations of Chinese women from the 19th-century Zhang family; these are Tang Yao-qing, her daughter, and her granddaughter, all three being the eldest females in their respective generations. Each of these women were prolific poets and writers of their own memoirs, and Mann studies these writings as well as other documentation from the time period in order to get a complete picture of what life was like in imperialist China, during a transitional political period. She considers the personal lives of these three women as well as their own values and hopes for the future, but she also discusses the blossoming of their political awareness in a heavily male-dominated society.

Where it's reviewed:
The Historian, February 2009, page 629
Times Literary Supplement, June 13, 2008, page 28

Other books by the same author:
East Asia (China, Japan, Korea), 1999
Precious Records: Women in China's Long Eighteenth Century, 1997
Local Merchants and the Chinese Bureaucracy, 1986

Other books you might like:
Hong Fan, *Footbinding, Feminism and Freedom: The Liberation of Women's Bodies in Modern China*, 1997
Grace S. Fong, *Herself an Author: Gender, Agency, and Writing in Late Imperial China*, 2008
Dorothy Ko, *Teachers of the Inner Chambers: Women and Culture in Seventeenth-Century China*, 1995
Susan Mann, *Precious Records: Women in China's Long Eighteenth Century*, 1997
Ellen Widmer, *The Beauty and the Book: Women and Fiction in Nineteenth-Century China*, 2006

788

CHANDRA MANNING

What This Cruel War Was Over: Soldiers, Slavery, and the Civil War

(New York: Alfred A. Knopf, 2008)

Subject(s): Abolition of slavery; Abolitionists; African Americans

Summary: Historian Chandra Manning makes her literary debut with this social history purporting that the predominant basis for the American Civil War was indeed the institution of slavery, in contrast to suppositions that the war was fought on one side as a defense of Southern liberty against Northern incursions, or on the other for the preservation of the Union, or for a multitude of other causes for both. To this end, Manning eschews the somewhat capricious viewpoints of post-facto chronicles from the contemporary opinion-makers and goes right to the ground level, culling archival reports from over a thousand soldiers from both sides, including their personal firsthand accounts in journals and letters. Manning incorporates the perspectives of a wide array of soldiers: the particular struggles and motivations of immigrants and African Americans in the Union ranks, and the fear of both slaveholding and non-slaveholding Confederate soldiers that losing the war would bring the loss of the status, privilege, and safety of their lands and families that being a white man guaranteed in the South. Manning also contends that Union soldiers returned from their encounters with slavery so dismayed by the abominable practice that they helped create a ground-swell of sentiment that influenced the course of the Lincoln Administration, leading to the issuance of the Emancipation Proclamation. Ultimately, Manning's assertion is that the Civil War indeed relied heavily upon the personal convictions of the soldiers who fought in it.

Where it's reviewed:
Booklist, February 1, 2007, page 26
Library Journal, March 15, 2007, page 81
Publishers Weekly, January 8, 2007, page 41

Other books you might like:
David W. Blight, *Race and Reunion: The Civil War in American Memory*, 2001
Eric Foner, *A Short History of Reconstruction*, 1990
Michael P. Johnson, *Abraham Lincoln, Slavery, and the Civil War*, 2000
James M. McPherson, *For Cause and Comrades: Why Men Fought in the Civil War*, 1997
Andrew Ward, *The Slaves' War: The Civil War in the Words of Former Slaves*, 2008

789

PATRICK MANNING

The African Diaspora: A History Through Culture

(New York: Columbia University Press, 2009)

Subject(s): Culture; Africans; History

Summary: In *The African Diaspora: A History Through Culture*, Patrick Manning provides a comprehensive history of African peoples from the 15th century to modern times. A great deal of the book is focused on slavery, and the impact that slavery had on the African diaspora and the way communities and culture were formed. Manning considers the different areas of the world in which the African community has traveled and settled, either by choice or forcefully during the slave trade. The author also discusses the questions that often arose after slavery ended, when people of African descent considered whether they would return to Africa or stay in the new locations. Manning considers these movements and how they reflect changing attitudes of people around the world.

Where it's reviewed:
Foreign Affairs, March/April 2010, page 174

Other books by the same author:
Migration in World History, 2005
Slavery, Colonialism and Economic Growth in Dahomey, 1640-1960, 2004
Navigating World History: Historians Create a Global Past, 2003

Other books you might like:

Michael L. Conniff, *Africans in the Americas: A History of the Black Diaspora*, 1994
  Thomas J. Davis, co-author

Henry Louis Gates Jr., *Tradition and the Black Atlantic: Critical Theory in the African Diaspora*, 2009

Michael Angelo Gomez, *Reversing Sail: A History of the African Diaspora*, 2004

Joseph E. Harris, *Africans and Their History: Second Revised Edition*, 1998

Isidore Okpewho, *The African Diaspora: African Origins and New World Identities*, 2001

790

MARIA-ELENA MARTINEZ

Geneaological Fictions: Limpieza de Sangre, Religion, and Gender in Colonial Mexico

(Stanford, California: Stanford University Press, 2008)

Subject(s): Mexican history; Spain; History

Summary: In *Geneaological Fictions: Limpieza de Sangre, Religion, and Gender in Colonial Mexico*, Maria-Elena Martinez considers the topic of limpieza de sangre, or purity of blood, which she states is the basis for the sistema de castas in Mexico. This is a social class system based on ancestry and lineage of one's family. She considers this system as it first began in Spain until it was seen in colonial Mexico in the seventeenth century, and the way such a system was used to exclude Jewish or Muslim individuals who chose to convert to Christianity. Martinez discusses how the purity of blood concept contributed to a sense of identity among Mexican people, as well as how it was used in institutions such as the church and state in colonial Mexico, and how this came to shape the long-term values in much of the area.

Where it's reviewed:
Journal of Latin American Studies, November 2009, page 798

Other books you might like:

Richard Boyer, *Colonial Lives: Documents on Latin American History, 1550-1850*, 1999

Mark A. Burkholder, *Colonial Latin America*, 1997

Andrew Fisher, *Imperial Subjects: Race and Identity in Colonial Latin America*, 2009

Patricia Seed, *To Love, Honor, and Obey in Colonial Mexico: Conflicts Over Marriage Choice, 1574-1821*, 1992

Susan Migden Socolow, *The Women of Colonial Latin America*, 2000

791

JOHN MATTHEWS

The Journey of Theophanes: Travel, Business, and Daily Life in the Roman East

(New Haven, Connecticut: Yale University Press, 2006)

Story type: Historical - Pre-history
Subject(s): Roman Empire, 30 BC-476 AD; Rome (Ancient state); Travel

Summary: In the days before Constantine—in the early fourth century—a Roman lawyer named Theophanes went on a journey. He left the city of Hermopolis, which sat comfortably along the Nile River, and six months later reached the city of Antioch, where he would conduct very important business. Along the way, he recorded the activities of his daily travels on rolls of papyrus. *The Journey of Theophanes: Travel, Business, and Daily Life in the Roman East* contains the translation of those records. Every day, Theophanes noted where he was, who he spoke with, what he ate, and how he felt. For six months, he kept track of every hour of his life. In addition to the translation of Theophanes' records, this book contains information about Roman culture and history to help readers put Theophanes' work into the correct context.

Where it's reviewed:
Choice, August 2007, page 2155

Other books by the same author:
Roman Perspectives: Studies on Political and Cultural History, from the First to the Fifth Century, 2010
The Roman Empire of Ammianus, 2008
Western Aristocracies and Imperial Court, A.D. 364-425, 1990

Other books you might like:
Alan K. Bowman, *Life and Letters on the Roman Frontier*, 1998

John Haldon, *The Palgrave Atlas of Byzantine History*, 2005

Edward Luttwak, *The Grand Strategy of the Byzantine Empire*, 2009

Theophanes Confessor Theophanes Confessor, *The Chronicle of Theophanes Confessor: Byzantine and Near Eastern History, A.D. 284-813*, 1997

Paul Veyne, *A History of Private Life, Volume 1: From Pagan Rome to Byzantium*, 1992

792

MARK MAZOWER

Hitler's Empire: How the Nazis Ruled Europe

(New York: Penguin Press, 2008)

Subject(s): History; World War II, 1939-1945; Germans

Summary: *Hitler's Empire: How the Nazis Ruled Europe*

provides readers with a chilling glimpse into the organization, vision, and ultimate disbandment of the Nazi regime. Author Mark Mazower uses a vast number of resources to examine the Nazi party, their political, racial, and economic philosophies, and their actions. Mazower recounts the ways that the Nazis established and expanded their rule throughout much of Europe and how their rapid rise to power and short-sighted vision ultimately led to their demise. Comparing their regime to others throughout history, Mazower sheds light on what might have come of Europe had the Nazis been able to continue their reign.

Where it's reviewed:
Booklist, August 1, 2008, page 28
Library Journal, September 15, 2008, page 72
Publishers Weekly, July 7, 2008, page 49

Other books by the same author:
No Enchanted Palace: The End of Empire and the Ideological Origins of the United Nations, 2009
The Balkans: A Short History, 2002
Dark Continent: Europe's Twentieth Century, 2000

Other books you might like:
Philip W. Blood, *Hitler's Bandit Hunters: The SS and the Nazi Occupation of Europe*, 2006
Catherine Epstein, *Model Nazi: Arthur Greiser and the Occupation of Western Poland*, 2010
Pieter Lagrou, *The Legacy of Nazi Occupation: Patriotic Memory and National Recovery in Western Europe, 1945-1965*, 1999
Wendy Lower, *Nazi Empire-Building and the Holocaust in Ukraine*, 2005
Allan Mitchell, *Nazi Paris: The History of an Occupation, 1940-1944*, 2008

793

DAVID G. MCCULLOUGH

1776

(New York: Simon & Schuster, 2005)

Subject(s): American History; American Revolution; History

Summary: As this book opens, it is October of 1775, and King George III moves to pit the forces of his mighty empire against the colonists of America. The Americans are few, and are widely assumed by their opponents to be a cowardly, ill-bred, and degenerate race. In this book, which details the 12 months of 1776, esteemed historian David McCullough shows how those outnumbered and supposedly inferior men managed to fight off the world's greatest army. They did it, McCullough argues, primarily through luck. He also shows how ingenuity, courage, toughness, and a willingness to endure hardship contributed to victory.

Where it's reviewed:
The Historian, Spring 2007, page 120
Library Journal, April 15, 2005, page 878
Newsweek, May 23, 2005, page 42

Other books by the same author:
John Adams, 2008

Truman, 1993
Mornings on Horseback: The Story of an Extraordinary Family, a Vanished Way of Life and the Unique Child Who Became Theodore Roosevelt, 1982

Other books you might like:
Benson Bobrick, *Angle in the Whirlwind: The Triumph of the American Revolution*, 1997
Joseph J. Ellis, *Founding Brothers: The Revolutionary Generation*, 2002
Pauline Maier, *American Scripture: Making the Declaration of Independence*, 1997
Robert Middlekauff, *The Glorious Cause*, 1981
Gordon S. Wood, *The Radicalism of the American Revolution*, 1991

794

REBECCA M. MCLENNAN

The Crisis of Imprisonment: Protest, Politics, and the Making of the American Penal State, 1776-1941

(New York: Cambridge University Press, 2008)

Subject(s): Prisoners; History; Law

Summary: In *The Crisis of Imprisonment: Protest, Politics, and the Making of the American Penal State, 1776-1941*, Rebecca M. McLennan considers the history of forced servitude as punishment for crimes committed in the United States, beginning in 1776. McLennan uses this example of the treatment of prisoners and forced labor as an example of fights for freedom in the United States. She considers how this system originated and how it impacted the penal system in the country. McLennan also discusses reforms, which came about largely due to arguments that it was unethical, contributed to governmental corruption, and negatively affected the rest of the work force. The author also considers important questions that still have contemporary value. These include how prisoners should be treated, how much freedom prisoners should retain, and whether prisoners should work.

Where it's reviewed:
American Historical Review, April 2009, page 415

Other books you might like:
David Garland, *The Culture of Control: Crime and Social Order in Contemporary Society*, 2001
Marie Gottschalk, *The Prison and the Gallows: The Politics of Mass Incarceration in America*, 2006
Paul W. Keve, *Prisons and the American Conscience: A History of U.S. Federal Corrections*, 1991
Norval Morris, *The Oxford History of the Prison: The Practice of Punishment in Western Society*, 1997
John W. Roberts, *Reform and Retribution: An Illustrated History of American Prisons*, 1996
David J. Rothman, *The Oxford History of the Prison: The Practice of Punishment in Western Society*, 1997

795

JON MEACHAM

American Gospel: God, the Founding Fathers, and the Making of a Nation

(New York: Random House, 2006)

Subject(s): American History; American Revolution; Christianity

Summary: The religious leanings of America's founding fathers are fraught with political controversy even today. As Americans struggle with issues of church and state, the question of how Jefferson, Adams, Hamilton, and Madison truly felt about God's role in politics is frequently raised. This book describes how the founding fathers, though they were men who were raised in a solidly Christian tradition, were passionately devoted to the ideals of religious tolerance and that they instituted the separation of church and state for that reason. He argues that the modern-day attempts to place Christianity at the center of government are antithetical to the purposes of the drafters of the Constitution.

Where it's reviewed:
America, July 3, 2006, page 22
New York Times Book Review, May 7, 2006, page 26

Other books by the same author:
American Lion: Andrew Jackson in the White House, 2009
Franklin and Winston: An Intimate Portrait of an Epic Friendship, 2004

Other books you might like:
David Barton, *Separation of Church and State: What the Founders Meant*, 2007
David L. Holmes, *The Faiths of the Founding Fathers*, 2006
Peter A. Lillback, *George Washington's Sacred Fire*, 2006
Michael Novak, *Washington's God: Religion, Liberty, and the Father of Our Country*, 2006
Steven Waldman, *Founding Faith: How Our Founding Fathers Forged a Radical New Approach to Religious Liberty*, 2008

796

MARGARET MESERVE

Empires of Islam in Renaissance Historical Thought

(Cambridge, Massachusetts: Harvard University Press, 2008)

Subject(s): Renaissance; Islam; History

Summary: In *Empires of Islam in Renaissance Historical Thought*, Margaret Meserve considers how historical studies of Islam have influenced contemporary thoughts regarding the religion. Meserve analyzes and discusses the methods that European historians used to research and interpret Islam and how the ideals of humanism and a desire for objective, scholarly research frequently competed with deeply ingrained political and Christian prejudices. Some of the topics discussed in this volume include the Crusades, as well as the Ottoman Empire. Meserve considers the different portrayals of Islam, both positive and negative, using historical documents, speeches, and propaganda to support her arguments.

Where it's reviewed:
American Historical Review, February 2009, page 201
Times Literary Supplement, August 1, 2008,, page 25

Other books by the same author:
Commentaries, Volume 2: Books III-IV (co-author), 2007
Commentaries, Volume 1: Books I-II, 2004

Other books you might like:
Nancy Bisaha, *Creating East and West: Renaissance Humanists and the Ottoman Turks*, 2004
Eric R. Dursteler, *Venetians in Constantinople: Nation, Identity and Coexistence in the Early Modern Mediterranean*, 2006
Molly Greene, *A Shared World: Christians and Muslims in the Early Modern Mediterranean*, 2000
Benjamin J. Kaplan, *Divided by Faith: Religious Conflict and the Practice of Toleration in Early Modern Europe*, 2007
David Levering Lewis, *God's Crucible: Islam and the Making of Europe*, 2008

797

TIYA MILES

Ties That Bind: The Story of an Afro-Cherokee Family in Slavery and Freedom

(Berkeley, California: University of California Press, 2005)

Subject(s): Native North Americans; African Americans; Slavery

Summary: In *Ties That Bind: The Story of an Afro-Cherokee Family in Slavery and Freedom*, author Tiya Miles uses historical and literary sources to recreate the life and times of the Shoe Boots family. Shoe Boots was a Cherokee warrior and farmer who, in the late 1790s, purchased a slave named Doll. The two lived together first as master and slave, but over time their relationship grew into a marriage-like partnership. Doll and Shoe Boots shared a home together for 30 years, and their union resulted in children and grandchildren. Their story, however, is not portrayed as purely idyllic. Despite her unique relationship with Shoe Boots, Doll must, after his death, petition the state to gain rights as Shoe Boots's widow. In this unique family portrait, Miles delves into a rarely discussed aspect of history—the dynamics of slavery within Native American communities.

Where it's reviewed:
American Historical Review, October 2006, page 1171
American Studies, Spring 2006, page 168

Other books by the same author:
The House on Diamond Hill: A Cherokee Plantation Story, 2010
Crossing Waters, Crossing Worlds: The African Diaspora in Indian Country, 2005

Other books you might like:
Jack D. Forbes, *Africans and Native Americans: The Language of Race and the Evolution of Red-Black Peoples*, 1993
William Loren Katz, *Black Indians: A Hidden Heritage*, 1986
Katja May, *African Americans and Native Americans in the Cherokee and Creek Nations, 1830s-1920s Collision and Collusion*, 1996
Theda Perdue, *Slavery and the Evolution of Cherokee Society: 1540-1866*, 1979
Gabrielle Tayac, *IndiVisible: African-Native American Lives in the Americas*, 1999

798

DALIA TSUK MITCHELL

Architect of Justice: Felix S. Cohen and the Founding of American Legal Pluralism

(Ithaca, New York: Cornell University Press, 2007)

Subject(s): Law; History; Native Americans

Summary: *Architect of Justice: Felix S. Cohen and the Founding of American Legal Pluralism* is a biography written by Dalia Tsuk Mitchell. Felix S. Cohen earned a law degree from Columbia University and Ph.D. in philosophy from Harvard University, going on to spend much of his career working on new laws to protect and assist Native Americans. He created the Indian Reorganization Act of 1934, the Indian Claims Commission Act of 1946, and wrote *The Handbook of Federal Indian Law*. Mitchell considers Cohen's work in the larger context of legal pluralism. The author discusses Cohen's own influences and the reasons he was so determined to protect the rights of Native Americans.

Where it's reviewed:
Harvard Law Review, December 2007, page 684

Other books by the same author:
Transformations in American Legal History: Essays in Honor of Professor Morton J. Horwitz, 2009

Other books you might like:
Mireille Delmas-Marty, *Towards a Truly Common Law: Europe as a Laboratory for Legal Pluralism*, 2002
Lawrence Meir Freidman, *A History of American Law, Third Edition*, 2007
Morton J. Horowitz, *The Transformation of American Law, 1870-1960: The Crisis of Legal Orthodoxy*, 1992
William E. Nelson, *The Legalist Reformation: Law, Politics, and Ideology in New York, 1920-1980*, 2000
Naomi Norberg, *Towards a Truly Common Law: Europe as a Laboratory for Legal Pluralism*, 2002

Leon Shaskolsky Sheleff, *The Future of Tradition: Customary Law, Common Law and Legal Pluralism*, 2000

799

PABLO R. MITCHELL

Coyote Nation: Sexuality, Race, and Conquest in Modernizing New Mexico, 1880-1920

(Chicago, Illinois: University Of Chicago Press, 2005)

Subject(s): United States history; Racism; Sex roles

Summary: Part of the Worlds of Desire: The Chicago Series on Sexuality, Gender, and Culture, Pablo R. Mitchell's *Coyote Nation: Sexuality, Race, and Conquest in Modernizing New Mexico, 1880-1920* explores how multi-ethnic New Mexico developed over a 40-year span. When the transcontinental railroad arrived in New Mexico in 1880, it allowed a wide milieu of people to travel the rails to the western United States. As Native Americans, Mexican immigrants, native Hispanics, blacks, and whites intermingled, previously unaddressed questions of racial interaction were investigated and explored. As racial identities were often difficult to distinguish, personal habits and tendencies often provided the clues to an individual's race. Social cues such as attire, speaking habits, hairstyle, and shopping tendencies pointed to differentiation between the races.

Where it's reviewed:
American Historical Review, February 2008, page 191
Journal of American History, March 2006, page 1451

Other books you might like:
Deana J. Gonzalez, *Refusing the Favor: The Spanish-Mexican Women of Santa Fe, 1820-1880*, 1999
Peter Iverson, *Dine : A History of the Navajos*, 2002
Peggy Pascoe, *What Comes Naturally: Miscegenation Law and the Making of Race in America*, 2009
Andres Resendez, *Changing National Identities at the Frontier, Texas and New Mexico, 1800-1850*, 2004
Monty Roessel, *Dine : A History of the Navajos*, 2002
Marta Weigle, *Telling New Mexico: A New History*, 2009

800

JOEL MOKYR

The Enlightened Economy: An Economic History of Britain, 1700-1850

(New Haven, Connecticut: Yale University Press, 2009)

Subject(s): Industrial Revolution, ca. 1750-1900; Enlightenment (Cultural movement); Economics

Summary: In *The Enlightened Economy: An Economic History of Britain, 1700-1850*, author Joel Mokyr dissects the state of the British economy between the years of the Glorious Revolution and the Crystal Palace Exhibition. Grasping the events of this Age of Enlightenment, Mokyr asserts, leads to a fuller understanding of the Industrial Revolution. This volume provides an in-depth analysis of the economic and political atmosphere of the time, and it describes how this environment set the stage for Britain's role as the European leader of the Industrial Revolution. *The Enlightened Economy* contains bibliographical references and an index.

Where it's reviewed:
Choice, June 2010, page 1979
History Today, May 2010, page 56

Other books by the same author:
Why Ireland Starved: A Quantitative and Analytical History of the Irish Economy, 1800-1850, 2011
The Gifts of Athena: Historical Origins of the Knowledge Economy, 2004
The Lever of Riches: Technological Creativity and Economic Progress, 1992

Other books you might like:
K.N. Chaudhuri, *Trade and Civilisation in the Indian Ocean: An Economic History from the Rise of Islam to 1750*, 1985
Laurence Hanson, *Contemporary Printed Sources for British and Irish Economic History 1701-1750*, 2011
P.J. Marshall, *The Oxford History of the British Empire: Volume II: The Eighteenth Century*, 1998
John V.C. Nye, *War, Wine, and Taxes: The Political Economy of Anglo-French Trade, 1689-1900*, 2007
Carmen M. Reinhart, *This Time Is Different: Eight Centuries of Financial Folly*, 2009
   Kenneth Rogoff, co-author

801

BETHANY MORETON

To Serve God and Wal-Mart: The Making of Christian Free Enterprise

(Cambridge, Massachusetts: Harvard University Press, 2009)

Subject(s): Business; Business enterprises; Christianity

Summary: Historian Bethany Moreton explores the relationship between Christianity and capitalism, focusing her study on the powerful retail chain Wal-Mart. *To Serve God and Wal-Mart: The Making of Christian Free Enterprise* tells the stories of individuals who, brought together by the groundbreaking retail store, forever changed the landscape of American economics and free enterprise. While most big business was centered in the North, Sam Walton built his empire in the South, with a strong basis of Christian ethics. This drew a completely new workforce, those who challenged the status quo and helped build the largest retail chain in the world. First book.

Where it's reviewed:
American Historical Review, June 2010, page 870
New York Times Book Review, August 2, 2009, page 15

Other books you might like:
Charles Fishman, *The Wal-Mart Effect: How the World's Most Powerful Company Really Works—and How It's Transforming the American Economy*, 2006
Thomas Frank, *One Market Under God: Extreme Capitalism, Market Populism, and the End of Economic Democracy*, 2000
Thomas Frank, *What's the Matter with Kansas?: How Conservatives Won the Heart of America*, 2004
Nelson Lichtenstein, *The Retail Revolution: How Wal-Mart Created a Brave New World of Business*, 2009
Don Soderquist, *The Wal-Mart Way: The Inside Story of the Success of the World's Largest Company*, 2005

802

BENNY MORRIS

1948: A History of the First Arab-Israeli War

(New Haven, Connecticut: Yale University Press, 2008)

Subject(s): Wars; Arab-Israeli wars; Politics

Summary: Benny Morris's *1948: A History of the First Arab-Israeli War* is an informational text that presents an unbiased and fair history of the first war between the Arabs and the Israelis. Morris explores the reasons behind the initial attack of Palestine and describes the methods each side used throughout the entire war. He also explains the roles the United States, Great Britain, and the Soviet Union played in supporting, and later helping to end, the battle. Morris also discusses the politics involved in beginning and ending the war, while drawing attention to the embarrassment each side felt once the air was clear.

Where it's reviewed:
History Today, July 2008, page 64
New York Review of Books, May 28, 2009, page 38
New York Times Book Review, May 4, 2008, page 19
New Yorker, May 5, 2008, page 72

Other books by the same author:
One State, Two States: Resolving the Israel/Palestine Conflict, 2010
Righteous Victims: A History of the Zionist-Arab Conflict, 1881-2001, 2001
Israel's Secret Wars: A History of Israel's Intelligence Services, 1992

Other books you might like:
Trevor N. Dupuy, *Elusive Victory: The Arab-Israeli Wars, 1947-1974*, 1978
Shlomo Gazit, *The Arab-Israeli Wars: War and Peace in the Middle East*, 2005
   Chaim Herzog, co-author
Michael B. Oren, *Six Days of War: June 1967 and the Making of the Modern Middle East*, 2003
Itamar Rabinovich, *Waging Peace: Israel and the Arabs, 1948-2003*, 2004

Dennis Ross, *The Missing Peace: The Inside Story of the Fight for Middle East Peace*, 2004

803

NOEL MOSTERT

The Line Upon a Wind: The Great War at Sea, 1793-1815

(New York: W.W. Norton & Co., 2008)

Subject(s): Napoleonic Wars, 1800-1815; History; Weapons

Summary: In *The Line Upon a Wind: The Great War at Sea, 1793-1815*, Noel Mostert considers the Napoleonic and Revolutionary battles that occurred at sea after France declared war on Britain in 1793. Mostert examines the strategies used for naval battles and considers the relatively new weapons such as torpedoes and submarines and the effects these had on the sea skirmishes. He discusses specific naval battles that took place from the Mediterranean to Scandinavia in addition to the pivotal Battle of Trafalgar. Furthermore, Mostert profiles Napoleon Bonaparte and Admiral Horatio Nelson and provides highly detailed information about daily life onboard one of the battleships as well as various aspects of ship construction.

Where it's reviewed:
Booklist, June 1, 2008, page 26
Publishers Weekly, May 5, 2008, page 54

Other books by the same author:
Supership, 1976

Other books you might like:
Roy Adkins, *The War for All the Oceans: From Nelson at the Nile to Napoleon at Waterloo*, 2007
David Cordingly, *Cochrane: The Real Master and Commander*, 2007
Robert Gardiner, *Frigates of the Napoleonic Wars*, 2000
N.A.M. Rodger, *The Command of the Ocean: A Naval History of Britain, 1649-1815*, 2005
Richard Woodman, *The Victory of Seapower: Winning the Napoleonic War 1806-1814*, 1998

804

KLAUS MUHLHAHN

Criminal Justice in China: A History

(Cambridge, Massachusetts: Harvard University Press, 2009)

Subject(s): Law; China; History

Summary: In *Criminal Justice in China: A History*, Klaus Muhlhahn presents a history of criminal law and the justice system in China, over the changes in governmental rule. Muhlhahn begins in late imperialist China, when methods such as torture were used to coerce confessions and punishments included beatings, tattoos, servitude, or public executions. This changed in 1905, when the legal system began holding trials in open courts where evidence for conviction was required, and people convicted of crimes were fined, imprisoned, or executed in the worst cases. Criminal justice shifted again in 1949 with the rise of communism, leading to convictions in people's tribunals and often sentences to labor camps. Muhlhahn traces this history and discusses its significance in China and around the world.

Where it's reviewed:
American Historical Review, April 2010, page 516
Foreign Affairs, November/December 2009, page 171

Other books you might like:
Hungdah Chiu, *Criminal Justice in Post-Mao China: Analysis and Documents*, 1985
Robert E. Hegel, *True Crimes in Eighteenth-Century China: Twenty Case Histories*, 2009
Shao-Chuan Leng, *Criminal Justice in Post-Mao China: Analysis and Documents*, 1985
Yonghong Lu, *China's Legal Awakening: Legal Theory and Criminal Justice in Deng's Era*, 1995
Matthew Sommer, *Sex, Law, and Society in Late Imperial China*, 2000
Kam C. Wong, *Chinese Policing: History and Reform*, 2009

805

CHRIS MYERS ASCH

The Senator and the Sharecropper: The Freedom Struggles of James O. Eastland and Fannie Lou Hamer

(New York: New Press, 2008)

Subject(s): Civil rights movements; Race relations; United States history

Summary: In *The Senator and the Sharecropper: The Freedom Struggles of James O. Eastland and Fannie Lou Hamer*, author Chris Myers Asch shares the stories of two powerful individuals who worked on either side of the civil rights struggle in America. James O. Eastland was a rigid proponent of segregation at any cost, while sharecropper's daughter Fannie Lou Hamer worked tirelessly for equal rights. Though both hailed from the same region, their journeys and ideologies couldn't have been more different. Through their stories, Asch presents a gripping portrait of the civil rights movement and those who shaped it. *The Senator and the Sharecropper* includes a bibliography and an index.

Where it's reviewed:
Booklist, May 1, 2008, page 60

Other books you might like:
John Dittmer, *Local People: The Struggle for Civil Rights in Mississippi*, 1994
Henry Louis Gates, *The African-American Century: How Black Americans Have Shaped Our Country*, 2000
Steven F. Lawson, *Running for Freedom: Civil Rights and Black Politics in America Since 1941*, 2000

Chana Kai Lee, *For Freedom's Sake: The Life of Fannie Lou Hamer*, 2000

J. Todd Moye, *Let the People Decide: Black Freedom and White Resistance Movements in Sunflower County, Mississippi, 1945-1986*, 2003

Cornel West, *The African-American Century: How Black Americans Have Shaped Our Country*, 2000

806

ANDREW NAGORSKI

The Greatest Battle: Stalin, Hitler, and the Desperate Struggle for Moscow That Changed the Course of World War II

(New York: Simon & Schuster, 2007)

Subject(s): World War II, 1939-1945; Russian history; History

Summary: In *The Greatest Battle: Stalin, Hitler, and the Desperate Struggle for Moscow That Changed the Course of World War II*, Andrew Nagorski considers the battle for Moscow that took place from September 1941 until April 1942, over an extremely harsh Russian winter. Nagorski argues that this was one of the most merciless, deadly, and brutal battles, and one of the more important skirmishes of World War II. He considers the armies led by Stalin and Hitler and elucidates mistakes made on each side, ultimately concluding that it was Stalin's decision to keep the army in the city that led to the Soviet victory.

Where it's reviewed:
Booklist, August 2007, page 27
The Historian, Winter 2009, page 911
Library Journal, July 1, 2007, page 102
New York Review of Books,, October 25, 2007, page 34
Publishers Weekly, June 25, 2007, page 47

Other books by the same author:
Last Stop Vienna, 2003
Birth of Freedom, Shaping Lives and Societies in the New Eastern Europe, 1993
Reluctant Farewell, 1983

Other books you might like:
Rodric Braithwaite, *Moscow 1941: A City and Its People at War*, 2006
Robert Forczyk, *Moscow 1941: Hitler's First Defeat*, 2006
  Howard Gerrard, co-author
David M. Glantz, *When Titans Clashed: How the Red Army Stopped Hitler*, 1995
Richard Overy, *Russia's War: A History of the Soviet Effort: 1941-1945*, 1998
Albert Seaton, *The Battle for Moscow*, 2002

807

JOHN A. NAGY

Rebellion in the Ranks: Mutinies of the American Revolution

(Yardley, Pennsylvania: Westholme Publishing, 2007)

Subject(s): United States history; American Revolution, 1775-1783; Wars

Summary: In *Rebellion in the Ranks: Mutinies of the American Revolution*, John A. Nagy gives detailed descriptions of and explanations for the frequent mutinies that occurred during the Revolutionary War. Described by George Washington as more dangerous to the American fight for independence than the British themselves, mutinies most often occurred due to the living conditions present during the Revolution, including drastic food shortages, lack of income, and lack of proper clothing or shelter from the elements. Nagy provides descriptions of mutinies, the outcome, and the way the army recovered from these events to go on to win the war against the British.

Where it's reviewed:
Journal of American History, December 2008, page 819

Other books by the same author:
Invisible Ink: Spycraft of the American Revolution, 2009

Other books you might like:
T.H. Breen, *American Insurgents, American Patriots: The Revolution of the People*, 2010
Gregory Freeman, *Troubled Water: Race, Mutiny, and Bravery on the U.S.S. Kitty Hawk*, 2009
Webb Garrison, *Mutiny in the Civil War*, 2001
Robert Middlekauff, *The Glorious Cause*, 1981
Robert J. Richey, *Mutiny in the United States Navy in World War II: A True Story*, 2009

808

AFSANEH NAJMABADI

Women with Mustaches and Men Without Beards: Gender and Sexual Anxieties of Iranian Modernity

(Berkeley, California: University of California Press, 2005)

Subject(s): Middle East; History; Women

Summary: In *Women with Mustaches and Men Without Beards: Gender and Sexual Anxieties of Iranian Modernity*, Afsaneh Najmabadi considers Iranian history, beginning in the relatively recent nineteenth century, from the perspective of gender and sexuality. Najmabadi argues that analyzing history in this way can illustrate previously unconsidered perspectives. For example, the author considers how the idea of beauty was not a uniquely male or female trait and how this fluid concept affected social issues such as marriage, love, citizenship, and education for women and men. Najmabadi also includes a discussion of contemporary feminism and its significant and continued impact on Iranian culture.

Where it's reviewed:
American Historical Review, October 2006, page 1287
The Historian, Spring 2007, page 89

Other books by the same author:
The Story of the Daughters Quchan: Gender and National History in Iranian History, 1998
Women's Autobiography in Contemporary Iran, 1991
Land Reform and Social Change in Iran, 1988

Other books you might like:
Leila Ahmed, *Women and Gender in Islam: Historical Roots of a Modern Debate*, 1992
Kathryn Babayan, *Islamicate Sexualities: Translations Across Temporal Geographies of Desire*, 2008
Khaled El-Rouayheb, *Before Homosexuality in the Arab-Islamic World*, 2005
Stephen Murray, *Islamic Homosexualities: Culture, History, and Literature*, 1997
Dror Ze'evi, *Producing Desire: Changing Sexual Discourse in the Ottoman Middle East, 1500-1900*, 2006

809

LINDA NASH

Inescapable Ecologies: A History of Environment, Disease, and Knowledge

(Berkeley, California: University of California Press, 2007)

Subject(s): Environmental history; History; Health

Summary: In *Inescapable Ecologies: A History of Environment, Disease, and Knowledge*, Linda Nash considers the connection between public health and the public's relation to the surrounding environment and the recent acknowledgment that humans are just as much a part of surrounding ecosystems as wildlife and plants. Nash discusses the history of connecting one's health to the environment and the way that people began blaming places for certain illnesses or diseases, using examples of toxic pollution, smog, and chemicals found in the environment known to cause cancer. These issues in the environment that cause illness are primarily anthropogenic in origin, and Nash discusses the public's response to such knowledge in addition to other topics such as the response to expanding scientific discoveries.

Where it's reviewed:
Isis, March 2008, page 202
Reviews in American History, December 2007, page 565

Other books you might like:
Robert A. Aronowitz, *Unnatural History: Breast Cancer and American Society*, 2007
Riley Dunlap, *American Environmentalism: The US Environmental Movement, 1970-1990*, 1992
Barry L. Johnson, *Environmental Policy and Public Health*, 2006
Benjamin Kline, *First Along the River: A Brief History*

of the U.S. Environmental Movement, 2007
Angela G. Mertig, *American Environmentalism: The US Environmental Movement, 1970-1990*, 1992
Conevery Valencius, *The Health of the Country: How American Settlers Understood Themselves and Their Land*, 2002

810

MICHAEL S. NEIBERG

Fighting the Great War: A Global History

(Cambridge, Massachusetts: Harvard University Press, 2005)

Subject(s): World War I, 1914-1918; History; Wars

Summary: In *Fighting the Great War: A Global History*, Michael S. Neiberg provides a comparatively brief, single-volume account of World War I, managing to touch on most of the significant battles and issues surrounding the first World War. Neiberg provides a comprehensive discussion of the opposing forces during the war. He also examines the tactical strategies and the horrors of trench warfare, suggesting that defense was the real issue for most generals leading their troops in the war. Neiberg analyzes the reasons why the war continued past 1914, attributing its continuance to the subsequent failures of a number of campaign plans designed prior to the start of the war. A number of illustrations and annotated maps add to the information offered in the text.

Where it's reviewed:
The Historian, Summer 2007, page 405
Times Literary Supplement, June 16, 2006, page 3

Other books by the same author:
Soldier's Lives Through History: The Nineteenth Century, 2006
Warfare and Society in Europe: 1898 to the Present, 2003

Other books you might like:
Martin Gilbert, *First World War*, 1994
Reg Grant, *The First World War (How Did It Happen?)*, 2005
John Keegan, *The First World War*, 1999
G.J. Meyer, *A World Undone: The Story of the Great War, 1914 to 1918*, 2007
Hew Strachan, *The First World War*, 2004

811

SCOTT REYNOLDS NELSON

Steel Drivin' Man: John Henry: the Untold Story of an American Legend

(New York: Oxford University Press, USA, 2006)

Subject(s): Biographies; History; Race relations

Summary: John Henry is, according to legend, a railroad

worker who raced a machine to show that man was better than the new technology of the industry. Henry supposedly won, proving his point, but he immediately died from the strain. Historian and writer Scott Reynolds Nelson found that there was an actual John Henry working on the railroads in the late 1800s, and *Steel Drivin' Man: John Henry: the Untold Story of an American Legend* is his story in conjunction with the legend and the history of the American railroad industry of this time period. The real John Henry was a prisoner who was sentenced to work on the railroads. Nelson found that Henry did not have the larger-than-life stature of the man of the legend, and he didn't race a machine head-to-head. The facts, however, show that works of this time period used the legend to remind themselves that slowing down at work was very dangerous. In addition, this book looks at the racial tensions that defined this era and how that translated to working on the railroads.

Where it's reviewed:
American Historical Review, October 2007, page 1199
Journal of American History, September 2007, page 569
Reviews in American History, September 2007, page 399

Other books by the same author:
A People at War: Civilians and Soldiers in America's Civil War, 2008
Ain't Nothing But a Man: My Quest to Find the Real John Henry, 2007
Iron Confederacies: Southern Railways, Klan Violence, and Reconstruction, 1999

Other books you might like:
Stephen E. Ambrose, *Nothing Like It in the World: The Men Who Built the Transcontinental Railroad 1863-1869*, 2000
Ted Gioia, *Work Songs*, 2006
Matthew J. Mancini, *One Dies, Get Another*, 1996
Colson Whitehead, *John Henry Days*, 2001
Kai Wright, *The African American Experience: Black History and Culture through Speeches, Letters, Co-Editorials, Poems, Songs, and Stories*, 2009

812

MICHAEL NEUFELD

Von Braun: Dreamer of Space, Engineer of War

(New York: A.A. Knopf, 2007)

Subject(s): Space exploration; Space flight; Germans

Summary: Michael Neufeld, who runs the Smithsonian's space history division, is the author of *Von Braun: Dreamer of Space, Engineer of War*, the biography of Wernher von Braun, the creator of Nazi German rockets and the American rocket program. He was responsible for the satellite launching that placed America in a league with the Soviet Union in the space race. The book explains von Braun's Nazi past, his politics, and life in America. The book explores the morality that led him to make rockets, despite the source of financing. His goal was to become a pioneering explorer of space.

Where it's reviewed:
International History Review, December 2008, page 881
Isis, March 2009, page 182
New York Review of Books, November 17, 2008, page 8
New York Times Book Review, November 18, 2007, page 17
Technology and Culture, April 2009, page 464

Other books by the same author:
The Rocket and the Reich: Peenemunde and the Coming of the Ballistic Missile Era, 1996
The Skilled Metalworkers of Nuremburg: Craft and Class in the Industrial Revolution, 1989

Other books you might like:
James Harford, *Dark Side of the Moon: Wernher Von Braun, the Third Reich, and the Space Race*, 2009
Dennis Piszkiewicz, *The Nazi Rocketeers: Dreams of Space and Crimes of War*, 1995
Dennis Piszkiewicz, *Wernher von Braun: The Man Who Sold the Moon*, 1998
Wernher von Braun, *The Voice of Dr. Wernher von Braun: An Anthology*, 2007
Bob Ward, *Dr. Space: The Life of Wernher Von Braun*, 2005

813

TIM NEWARK

Highlander: The History of the Legendary Highland Soldier

(New York: Skyhorse Publishing, 2010)

Subject(s): Scotland; Military life; History

Summary: In *Highlander: The History of the Legendary Highland Soldier*, military historian Tim Newark provides an extensively researched history of the Scottish Highlanders. Originally commanded by Highland Chiefs, these men became part of the British army during the Napoleonic Wars and were quickly recognized and feared for their brutality, bravery, and fierceness in battle. Newark discusses specific battles in which the Highlanders played a significant role, including instances in World War I and World War II. The author also discusses and analyzes the way the Highlanders have been portrayed in popular culture and considers certain legends of Highlander soldiers.

Where it's reviewed:
Publishers Weekly, February 15, 2010, page 126

Other books by the same author:
Lucky Luciano: The Real and Fake Gangster, 2010
Mafia Allies: The True Story of America's Secret Alliance with the Mob in World War II, 2007
Turning the Tide of War: 50 Battles That Changed the Course of Modern History, 2006

Other books you might like:
Margaret Bennett, *Scottish Customs: From the Cradle to the Grave*, 2005
Collin G. Calloway, *White People, Indians, and Highlanders: Tribal People and Colonial Encounters*

in Scotland and America, 2008

Arthur Herman, *How the Scots Invented the Modern World: The True Story of How Western Europe's Poorest Nation Created Our World & Everything in It*, 2001

John Macleod, *Highlanders: A History of the Gaels*, 1996

Alistair Moffat, *The Highland Clans*, 2010

814

ADAM NICOLSON

Seize the Fire: Heroism, Duty, and the Battle of Trafalgar

(New York: HarperCollins, 2005)

Subject(s): Battle of Trafalgar, 1805; Napoleonic Wars, 1800-1815; Psychology

Summary: In *Seize the Fire: Heroism, Duty, and the Battle of Trafalgar*, Adam Nicolson analyzes the Battle of Trafalgar that took place in 1805 during the Napoleonic Wars, in which the British navy, led by Admiral Nelson, was able to defeat the Spanish and French navies. Nicolson chooses to analyze the battle from a psychological perspective, considering what it was about the culture and societies—as well as Nelson's leadership—that led to a British victory. Since he did not come from the aristocracy, Nelson would not have been permitted to become a naval commander in France or Spain, but Britain's differing social customs paved the way for Nelson's fame. Nicolson also considers the motivations of all three nations, concluding that Britain, most driven by trade, was able to muster the most support among its citizens and their desire for wealth and material possessions by leveraging higher taxes and using the income to fund the navy. In addition, the author spends a great deal of the text focusing on Nelson himself, his personal behavior and motivations, and the way he commanded the navy.

Where it's reviewed:
The Atlantic, August 2005, page 1985
Kirkus Reviews, June 1, 2005, page 627
New York Times Book Review, September 4, 2005, page 26
Publishers Weekly, June 20, 2005, page 71

Other books by the same author:
Quarrel with the King: The Story of an English Family on the High Road to Civil War, 2008
Sea Room: An Island Life in the Hebrides, 2007
God's Secretaries: The Making of the King James Bible, 2005

Other books you might like:
Mark Adkin, *The Trafalgar Companion: The Complete Guide to History's Most Famous Sea Battle and the Life of Admiral Lord Nelson*, 2005
Roy A. Adkins, *Nelson's Trafalgar: The Battle that Changed the World*, 2005
Richard Harding, *A Great and Glorious Victory: New Perspectives on the Battle of Trafalgar*, 2008
Roger Knight, *The Pursuit of Victory: The Life and

Achievement of Horatio Nelson, 2005
Alan Schom, *Trafalgar: Countdown to Battle, 1803-1805*, 1990

815

MICHAEL NORMAN
ELIZABETH M. NORMAN , Co-Author

Tears in the Darkness: The Story of the Bataan Death March and Its Aftermath

(New York: Farrar, Straus, and Giroux, 2009)

Subject(s): World War II, 1939-1945; History; Wars

Summary: *Tears in the Darkness: The Story of the Bataan Death March and Its Aftermath* is a historical account written by Michael and Elizabeth M. Norman. The book begins with a discussion of the battle for the Bataan peninsula in the Philippines in 1942, which led 76,000 Americans and Filipinos to surrender to the Japanese. The subsequent march by the prisoners to the labor camps is known as the Bataan Death March, but it was only the beginning of the brutality and starvation that the prisoners would have to endure for the next three years. Though the generals from both sides are discussed, POW Ben Steele, a soldier from Montana, is often the personal focus of the historical account, and some of his drawings are included in the text.

Where it's reviewed:
American Heritage, Winter 2010, page 104
Journal of Military History, January 2010, page 288

Other books by the same author:
These Good Men, 2010

Other books you might like:
William E. Dyess, *Bataan Death March: A Survivor's Account*, 2002
Damon Gause, *The War Journal of Major Damon Rocky Gause: The Firsthand Account of One of the Greatest Escapes of World War II*, 1999
Donald Knox, *Death March: The Survivors of Bataan*, 1961
Manny Lawton, *Some Survived: An Eyewitness Account of the Bataan Death March and the Men Who Lived through It*, 1984
Elizabeth M. Norman, *We Band of Angels: The Untold Story of American Nurses Trapped on Bataan by the Japanese*, 1999
John Toland, *Some Survived: An Eyewitness Account of the Bataan Death March and the Men Who Lived through It*, 1984

816

SUSAN EVA O'DONOVAN

Becoming Free in the Cotton South

(Cambridge, Massachusetts: Harvard University Press, 2007)

Subject(s): Race relations; Racism; American Reconstruction, 1865-1877

Summary: In *Becoming Free in the Cotton South*, writer and historian Susan Eva O'Donovan explores a time period that is often ignored—the transition from slavery to a free America. O'Donovan tells the story of slaves who suddenly found themselves on their own, surrounded by Southerners who saw the end of slavery as a threat to their unique way of life. Reconstruction promises from the government gave these former slaves hope for a better life, but O'Donovan points out that many blacks found themselves in situations that were almost as bad as slavery. In this book, the author shows readers the challenges that these people faced every day and explains how hatred marred their hard-won freedom.

Where it's reviewed:
American Historical Review, April 2010, page 543
Journal of American History, March 2008, page 1270
Reviews in American History, March 2008, page 38

Other books by the same author:
Freedom: A Documentary History of Emancipation, 1861-1867: Series 3, Vol. 1: Land and Labor, 1865, 2008

Other books you might like:
Ira Berlin, *Remembering Slavery: African Americans Talk about Their Personal Experiences of Slavery and Freedom*, 1998
    Marc Favreau, co-editor
Michael W. Fitzgerald, *Splendid Failure: Postwar Reconstruction in the American South*, 2008
Eric Foner, *A Short History of Reconstruction*, 1990
Erik Foner, *Forever Free: The Story of Emancipation and Reconstruction*, 2005
Tera W. Hunter, *To Joy My Freedom: Southern Black Women's Lives and Labors After the Civil War*, 1997

817

LYNNE OLSON

Troublesome Young Men: The Rebels Who Brought Churchill to Power and Helped Save England

(New York: Farrar, Straus and Giroux, 2007)

Subject(s): England; History; Politics

Summary: In *Troublesome Young Men: The Rebels Who Brought Churchill to Power and Helped Save England*, Lynne Olson discusses the members of Parliament who were opposed in the 1930s to England's appeasement tactic for dealing with Hitler and were determined to get Neville Chamberlain out of office. She provides brief biographies for a number of these individuals from the House of Commons, including, of course, Winston Churchill—who was serving in Chamberlain's cabinet though he vehemently disagreed with his approach to Nazi Germany. Olson provides texts of speeches in Parliament made by the anti-appeasers, and Olson uses this text to illustrate the careful plot to force Chamberlain's resignation and insert Churchill in his place. Further discussion—though a somewhat limited analysis—of Churchill's subsequent years as prime minister is included.

Where it's reviewed:
Biography, Summer 2007, page 420
New York Review of Books, May 29, 2008, page 4
New York Times Book Review, April 29, 2007, page 15
Times Literary Supplement, August 3, 2007, page 27

Other books by the same author:
Citizens of London: The Americans Who Stood with Britain in Its Darkest, Finest Hour, 2010
Freedom's Daughters: The Unsung Heroines of the Civil Rights Movement from 1830 to 1970, 2002
The Murrow Boys: Pioneers on fthe Front Lines of Broadcast Journalism, 1997

Other books you might like:
Simon Ball, *The Guardsmen: Harold Macmillan, Three Friends and the World They Made*, 2004
Max Hastings, *Winston's War: Churchill, 1940-1945*, 2009
Paul Johnson, *Churchill*, 2009
Richard Toye, *Churchill's Empire: The World That Made Him and the World He Made*, 2010
Peter Wilby, *Eden*, 2006

818

DAVID OSHINSKY

Polio: An American Story

(New York: Oxford University Press, 2005)

Subject(s): Medicine; Medical care; History

Summary: In *Polio: An American Story*, historian David Oshinsky examines the events and controversies surrounding the polio epidemic of the 1940s and 1950s. Oshinsky articulates how Franklin Delano Roosevelt raised public awareness about polio, and how The March of Dimes further spread this awareness. The book then focuses largely on the rivalry between Jonas Salk, who advocated a killed-virus vaccine, and Albert Sabin, who favored a live-virus vaccine. In depicting this rivalry, Oshinsky manages to capture the personalities of these men, as well as the way their feud polarized the medical community. Oshinsky concludes his documentation with the nationwide inoculations of 1954, but he clarifies that Sabin's oral vaccine was adopted on a global scale. In making this point, Oshinsky provokes the notion that the story of polio is, perhaps, ongoing.

Where it's reviewed:
American Historical Review, June 2006, page 865
The Economist, June 18, 2005, page 79
New York Times Book Review, April 10 2005, page 28
Reviews in American History, December 2005, page 566

Other books by the same author:
Capital Punishment on Trial: Furman v. Georgia and the Death Penalty in Modern America, 2010
A Conspiracy So Immense: The World of Joe McCarthy, 2005
Worse Than Slavery: Parchman Farm and the Ordeal of Jim Crow Justice, 1997

Other books you might like:

John M. Barry, *The Great Influenza: The Epic Story of the Deadliest Plague in History*, 2004

Kathryn Black, *In the Shadow of Polio: A Personal and Social History*, 1997

Anne Finger, *Elegy for a Disease: A Personal and Cultural History of Polio*, 2006

J.K. Silver, *Polio Voices: An Oral History from the American Polio Epidemics and Worldwide Eradication Efforts*, 2007

Heather Green Wooten, *The Polio Years in Texas: Battling a Terrifying Unknown*, 2009

819

CHRIS OTTER

The Victorian Eye: A Political History of Light and Vision in Britain, 1800-1910

(Chicago, Illinois: University of Chicago Press, 2008)

Subject(s): England; History; Technology

Summary: In *The Victorian Eye: A Political History of Light and Vision in Britain, 1800-1910*, Chris Otter considers how the development of lighting in Britain impacted and changed the existing Victorian culture and eventually led to the development of a very liberal culture, despite the fact that Britain monitors its citizens constantly through video surveillance. Otter considers such topics such as urban planning and governmental decision-making in the context of light and perception, providing a history of lighting in Britain. At first, lights were gas-powered; they were first powered by electricity in 1878. Scientific topics such as the actual science and technology behind various types of lighting are also discussed in this comprehensive and extensively re-searched text.

Where it's reviewed:
American Historical Review, February 2010, page 288
Technology and Culture, January 2010, page 246

Other books you might like:

Jane Brox, *Brilliant: The Evolution of Artificial Light*, 2010

Paul J. Nahn, *Oliver Heaviside: The Life, Work and Times of an Electrical Genius of the Victorian Age*, 2002

Dale H. Porter, *The Thames Embankment: Environment, Technology, and Society in Victorian London*, 1997

J.D. Poulter, *An Early History of Electricity Supply: The Story of the Electric Light in Victorian Leeds*, 1986

Wolfgang Schivelbusch, *Disenchanted Night: The Industrialization of Light in the Nineteenth Century*, 1988

820

GEORGE PACKER

The Assassins' Gate: America in Iraq

(New York: Farrar, Straus and Giroux, 2005)

Subject(s): Government; Middle East; Politics

Summary: Titled after the entrance to the post-Saddam American sector in Baghdad, this book begins with an examination of "neoconservative" versus "realist" intellectual positions on "regime change," followed by analysis of the George W. Bush administration's political argument for invading Iraq. It concludes with an account of the war's consequences for both Americans and Iraqis—GIs on the ground, a bereaved family back home, and beleaguered Arab civilians. Author George Packer, who covered Iraq for *The New Yorker* magazine, also devotes one chapter to the northern city of Kirkuk, which he uses as an illustration of the complex ethnic, tribal, and religious divisions in Iraqi society.

Where it's reviewed:
Booklist, September 15, 2005, page 22
The Economist, October 15, 2005, page 89
Spectator, November 12, 2005, page 48

Other books by the same author:
Interesting Times: Writings from a Turbulent Decade, 2010
Betrayed, 2009
Blood of the Liberals, 2001

Other books you might like:

Ali A. Allawi, *The Occupation of Iraq: Winning the War, Losing the Peace*, 2007

James DeFronzo, *The Iraq War: Origins and Consequences*, 2009

Steven Metz, *Iraq in Transition: The Legacy of Dictatorship and the Prospects for Democracy*, 2009

Bobby Muller, *What Was Asked of Us: An Oral History of the Iraq War by the Soldiers Who Fought It*, 2006

Peter J. Munson, *Iraq in Transition: The Legacy of Dictatorship and the Prospects for Democracy*, 2009

Thomas E. Ricks, *Fiasco: The American Military Adventure in Iraq*, 2006

Trish Wood, *What Was Asked of Us: An Oral History of the Iraq War by the Soldiers Who Fought It*, 2006

821

PEGGY PASCOE

What Comes Naturally: Miscegenation Law and the Making of Race in America

(Oxford; New York: Oxford University Press, 2009)

Subject(s): Law; History; Social sciences

Summary: In *What Comes Naturally: Miscegenation Law and the Making of Race in America*, Peggy Pascoe provides a comprehensive history of the miscegenation law in the United States against interracial marriage, showing readers how this law was used to maintain white power after the end of the Civil War. Pascoe discusses a number of individual cases where this law was put into action and evaluates the Supreme Court ruling in 1967 that found the law unconstitutional under the Fourteenth Amendment. Pascoe then relates the issue to the debate surrounding gay marriage in the United States, arguing that such laws only continue to promote discrimination.

Where it's reviewed:
The New Yorker, March 2, 2009, page 71

Other books by the same author:
Relations of Rescue: The Search for Female Moral Authority in the American West, 1874-1939, 1993

Other books you might like:
Tim Hashaw, *Children of Perdition: Melungeons and the Struggle of Mixed America*, 2006
K. Paul Johnson, *Pell Mellers: Race and Memory in a Carolina Pocosin*, 2008
Elise Virginia Lemire, *Miscegenation: Making Race in America*, 2009
Alex Lubin, *Romance and Rights: The Politics of Interracial Intimacy, 1945-1954*, 2004
Joel Williamson, *New People: Miscegenation and Mulattoes in the United States*, 1995

822

JOEL RICHARD PAUL

Unlikely Allies: How a Merchant, a Playwright, and a Spy Saved the American Revolution

(New York: Riverhead Books, 2009)

Subject(s): American Revolution, 1775-1783; History; Biographies

Summary: In *Unlikely Allies: How a Merchant, a Playwright, and a Spy Saved the American Revolution*, Joel Richard Paul tells the little known story of three influential men who contributed to the success of the American Revolution. These men include merchant Silas Deane, playwright Pierre-Augustin Caron de Beaumarchais, and spy Chevalier d'Eon. Silas Deane was an emissary from America sent to France to engineer an alliance and secure additional weapons for the army. Meanwhile, Chevalier d'Eon was a cross-dresser and a spy who used his employment with Louis XV to intimidate the French government. He threatened to start a war with England after Louis XVI became king, claiming that he had a number of letters that would set the conflict off. Louis XVI then asked Beaumarchais to get those letters back, refusing to offer an arms treaty to Deane until the task was completed. When Beaumarchais succeeded, he and Deane worked together to trade arms and other useful goods under the nose of the British government. The author explains how these events had a significant impact on the outcome of the Revolutionary War.

Where it's reviewed:
Booklist, October 15, 2009, page 19
Library Journal, October 15, 2009, page 91
Publishers Weekly, February 22, 2010, page 62

Other books you might like:
George L. Clark, *Silas Deane: A Connecticut Leader in the American Revolution*, 2008
Maurice Lever, *Beaumarchais: A Biography*, 2009
Andro Linklater, *An Artist in Treason: The Extraordinary Double Life of General James Wilkinson*, 2009
Jack Rakove, *Revolutionaries: A New History of the Invention of America*, 2010
Laura Charlotte Sheldon, *France and the American Revolution, 1763-1788*, 2010

823

NATHANIEL PHILBRICK

Mayflower: A Story of Courage, Community, and War

(New York: Viking, 2006)

Subject(s): American History; History; Indians of North America

Summary: In 1620, a small group of English men and women journeyed thousands of miles from home, in a little ship called the *Mayflower*, to start a new life in a new, strange, and dangerous land. In this book, historian Nathaniel Philbrick examines these people and explores their motivations in launching such a perilous venture. He describes the religious conflict that caused them to leave their homes and the burning religious faith that drew them on; the incredible hardships they suffered once they reached Plymouth Colony that November, low on supplies and with no experience of wilderness living. He also describes the bitter strife between the white settlers and the Indian inhabitants of Massachusetts.

Where it's reviewed:
American History, October 2006, page 72
New York Times Book Review, June 4, 2006, page 10
The New Yorker, April 24, 2006, page 164
Newsweek, May 1, 2006, page 63

Other books by the same author:
The Last Stand: Custer, Sitting Bull and the Battle of the Little Bighorn, 2010
The Revenge of the Whale: The True Story of the Whaleship Essex, 2004
Sea of Glory: America's Voyage of Discovery, The U.S. Exploring Expedition, 1838-1842, 2004

Other books you might like:
Peter Arenstam, *Mayflower 1620: A New Look at a Pilgrim Voyage*, 2003
Nick Bunker, *Making Haste from Babylon: The Mayflower Pilgrims and Their World*, 2010
Patricia Scott Deatz, *The Times of Their Lives: Life, Love, and Death in Plymouth Colony*, 2001
James Deetz, co-author

Christopher Hilton, *Mayflower: The Voyage that Changed the World*, 2005

Caleb H. Johnson, *The Mayflower and Her Passengers*, 2006

CHARLES POSTEL

The Populist Vision

(New York: Oxford University Press, USA, 2007)

Subject(s): History; United States history, 1865-1901; Politics

Summary: In the late 1800s, the American Populist Movement was seen at the time as a challenge to the country's ability to move forward. Today, many see this movement as irrational and idealistic, but Charles Postel argues that the men and women who defined themselves as Populists during this time period weren't uneducated farmers try to get revenge on an elite upper class. Rather, this group of people saw a new, yet traditional, approach to progress—one that embraced the common person's goals to help create a more equal and fair America. Postel's nonfiction snapshot of this era in American history celebrates the efforts of the downtrodden who felt they were being left behind during the industrialization of their country. He reviews their battle for better election policies, voice against immigration, and work for a better postal system, among other things. Today, their efforts still have an impact on U.S. politics, with popular politicians such as John Edwards and Ralph Nadar describing themselves as Populists.

Where it's reviewed:
The Historian, Summer 2009, page 380

Other books you might like:
Rebecca Edwards, *New Spirits: Americans in the Gilded Age, 1865-1905*, 2005
Matthew Hild, *Greenbackers, Knights of Labor and Populists: Farmer-labor Insurgency in the Late-Nineteenth-Century South*, 2007
Michael Kazin, *The Populist Persuasion: An American History*, 1998
T.J. Jackson Lears, *Rebirth of a Nation: The Making of Modern America, 1877-1920*, 2009
Robert C. McMath, *American Populism: A Social History 1877-1898*, 1992

JOHN PAUL RATHBONE

The Sugar King of Havana: The Rise and Fall of Julio Cobo, Cuba's Last Tycoon

(New York: Penguin Group, 2010)

Subject(s): Cuban history; Cuban Revolution, 1953-1959; Business

Summary: Author John Paul Rathbone details the life of Cuban sugar baron Julio Lobo in his book *The Sugar King of Havana: The Rise and Fall of Julio Lobo, Cuba's Last Tycoon*. Lobo, a sugar trader and wealthy speculator who was often called El Veneno, "the poisonous one," by his friends, was one of the last great sugar tycoons and an important part of prerevolutionary Cuba. Rathbone explores Lobo's colorful business and personal lives, discussing everything from his business practices to his personal relationships and his exile and death following the rise of Fidel Castro. Rathbone also offers his own personal memories of Lobo when from their families were entwined among the Cuban social elite.

Where it's reviewed:
Booklist, July 1, 2010, page 23
Library Journal, July 2010, page 94
New York Times, August 13, 2010, page C22
The New Yorker, October 4, 2010, page 95
Publishers Weekly, May 17, 2010, page 36

Other books by the same author:
Ecuador, the Galapagos, & Columbia, 1991

Other books you might like:
T.J. English, *Havana Nocturne*, 2008
Tom Gjelten, *Bacardi and the Long Fight for Cuba: The Biography of a Cause*, 2008
Rosa Lowinger, *Tropicana Nights: The Life and Times of the Legendary Cuban Nightclub*, 2005
Manuel Marquez-Sterling, *Cuba 1952-1959: The True Story of Castro's Rise to Power*, 2009
Peter Moruzzi, *Havana Before Castro: When Cuba Was a Tropical Playground*, 2008

MARCUS REDIKER

The Slave Ship: A Human History

(New York: Viking, 2007)

Subject(s): Slavery; History; Transportation

Summary: Marcus Rediker's *The Slave Ship: A Human History* explores the day-to-day lives of those involved in the horrors of the slave trade, from the brutal and callous ship owners to the human cargo who faced unthinkable conditions below the decks. He also touches on the lives of the working sailors tasked with the operation of the ships. Rediker utilizes both written records as well stories passed down from generation to generation to give voice to the individuals who did not survive the perilous overseas voyage. The author shows readers every aspect of the experience, describing how the miserable journey served to indoctrinate its victims into the lifestyle that awaited them on American shores.

Where it's reviewed:
The Nation, February 4, 2008, page 23
New York Times Book Review, October 21, 2007, page 15

Other books by the same author:
Villains of All Nations: Atlantic Pirates in the Golden Age, 2005
Between the Devil and the Deep Blue Sea: Merchant

Seamen, Pirates and the Anglo-American Maritime World, 1700-1750, 1989

Other books you might like:
David Brion Davis, *Inhuman Bondage: The Rise and Fall of Slavery in the New World,* 2006
Walter Johnson, *Soul by Soul: Life Inside the Antebellum Slave Market,* 1999
Bruce L. Mouser, *A Slaving Voyage to Africa and Jamaica: The Log of the Sandown, 1793-1794,* 2002
Stephanie E. Smallwood, *Saltwater Slavery: A Middle Passage from Africa to the American Diaspora,* 2007
Hugh Thomas, *The Slave Trade: The Story of the Atlantic Slave Trade, 1440-1870,* 1997

827

CARMEN M. REINHART
KENNETH ROGOFF , Co-Author

This Time Is Different: Eight Centuries of Financial Folly

(Princeton, New Jersey: Princeton University Press, 2009)

Subject(s): Economic depressions; Economics; Finance

Summary: *This Time Is Different: Eight Centuries of Financial Folly* is a guide to financial crises around the world from economists Carmen M. Reinhart and Kenneth Rogoff. Throughout history, societies and governments have struggled through economic hardships and financial difficulties. Although these financial crashes happen with some regularity, most governments believe that their financial difficulties are different from—and more serious than—others that came before. Reinhart and Rogoff shed light on the economic woes of 66 countries over 800 years to show how similar each financial crisis is to the preceding one. The authors use specific facts and figures to analyze and identify patterns and cycles of financial crises.

Where it's reviewed:
Foreign Affairs, March/April 2010, page 156
Foreign Policy, May/June 2009, page 165
New Statesman, January 4, 2010, page 42

Other books by the same author:
Money, Crises, and Transitions: Essays in Honor of Guillermo A. Calvo (Reinhart), 2008
Ratings, Rating Agencies and the Global Financial System (Reinhart), 2002
Assessing Financial Vulnerability: An Early Warning System for Emerging Markets, 2000
Foundations of International Macroeconomics (Rogoff), 1996

Other books you might like:
Gregory Clark, *A Farewell to Alms: A Brief Economic History of the Western World,* 2007
Kevin Dowd, *Alchemists of Loss: How Modern Finance and Government Intervention Crashed the Financial System,* 2010
  Martin Hutchinson, co-author

Charles P. Kinderberger, *Manias, Panics, and Crashes: A History of Financial Crises,* 2005
Paul Krugman, *The Return of Depression Economics and the Crisis of 2008,* 2009
Douglass C. North, *Structure and Change in Economic History,* 1981

828

THOMAS E. RICKS

The Gamble: General David Petraeus and the American Military Adventure in Iraq, 2006-2008

(New York: Penguin Press, 2009)

Subject(s): Wars; Military bases; Middle East

Summary: In *The Gamble: General David Petraeus and the American Military Adventure in Iraq, 2006-2008,* Pulitzer Prize winning author Thomas E. Ricks focuses on "the surge." In this book, Ricks spotlights three men: General David Petraeus, Lieutenant General Ray Odierno, and retired General Jack Keene. He explains that the insurgency happened only because these men were willing to take risks. Ricks then goes on to state what this plan actually entailed and why he believes it worked. He shows how everything done by military personnel helped bring about some semblance of peace and protection in a place where none was evident before. It also ensured that all parts of the military in this country were working toward a common goal. Although Ricks presents this account in an optimistic way, he is also quick to note that he does not believe the war is close to being over.

Where it's reviewed:
Biography, Spring 2009, page 433
The New Republic, April 30, 2009, page 41
New York Times, February 10, 2009, page C1
Time, February 23, 2009, page 13

Other books by the same author:
Making the Corps: 10th Anniversary Edition with a New Afterword by the Author, 2007
Fiasco: The American Military Adventure in Iraq, 2006
A Soldier's Duty: A Novel, 2002

Other books you might like:
Ali A. Allawi, *The Occupation of Iraq: Winning the War, Losing the Peace,* 2007
Christopher Cerf, *The Iraq War Reader: History, Documents, Opinions,* 2003
Dexter Filkins, *The Forever War,* 2008
David Finkel, *The Good Soldiers,* 2009
Williamson Murray, *Iraq War: A Military History,* 2003
  Robert H. Scales, co-author
Micah L. Sifry, *The Iraq War Reader: History, Documents, Opinions,* 2003

829

COKIE ROBERTS

Ladies of Liberty: The Women Who Shaped Our Nation

(New York: William Morrow, 2008)

Subject(s): United States history; Women; Biographies

Summary: *Ladies of Liberty: The Women Who Shaped Our Nation* picks up the story begun by journalist Cokie Roberts in *Founding Mothers: The Women Who Raised Our Nation*, exploring the contributions of post-revolutionary women to the formation of American society. Focusing on the presidencies of John Adams, Thomas Jefferson, James Madison, and James Monroe, Roberts relates the stories of the women behind the men—the wives, sisters, and daughters who carried on a social and political revolution of their own. The letters and diaries of Abigail Adams, Martha Jefferson, Dolley Madison, Elizabeth Monroe, and other prominent women of the late 18th and early 19th centuries provide a historical account of the shaping of the nation and a personal glimpse into their daily lives. Roberts emphasizes the impact these "Ladies of Liberty" had on their husband's careers and the decisions they made. With determination and poise, they fulfilled their duties as wives, mothers, and supporters while establishing new roles for their gender in the political world.

Where it's reviewed:
American Heritage, August 2008, page 65
Biography, Summer 2008, page 547

Other books by the same author:
Founding Mothers: The Women Who Raised Our Nation, 2005
From This Day Forward, 2001
We Are Our Mothers' Daughters, 1998

Other books you might like:
Catherine Allgor, *A Perfect Union: Dolley Madison and the Creation of the American Nation*, 2006
Carol Berkin, *Revolutionary Mothers: Women in the Struggle for America's Independence*, 2005
Melissa Lukeman Bohrer, *Glory, Passion, and Principle: The Story of Eight Remarkable Women at the Core of the American Revolution*, 2003
Patricia Brady, *Martha Washington: An American Life*, 2005
Woody Holton, *Abigail Adams*, 2009

830

GENE ROBERTS
HANK KLIBANOFF , Co-Author

The Race Beat: The Press, the Civil Rights Struggle, and the Awakening of a Nation

(New York: Knopf, 2006)

Subject(s): American History; Civil Rights Movement; History

Summary: This work traces how print and broadcast media brought the mistreatment of African Americans in the South into the national spotlight and, in doing so, helped fuel the Civil Rights movement. Journalists Roberts and Klibanoff were reporters during that time and use interviews, memoirs, news stories, correspondence, and editorials to create a picture of journalism in the mid-twentieth century. Race issues and the condition of African Americans were reported by the black press only, while the national and mainstream news did not address these issues. It took the brutal killing of young African American Emmett Till in Mississippi in 1955 and the acquittal of his white killers for the mainstream media to begin conveying such events. By simply writing about the facts of injustice and abuse, Roberts and Klibanoff argue, the media provided the publicity that African Americans needed to gain national support for the Civil Rights movement. Coverage of other critical events, such as the march on Selma, the desegregation of the University of Alabama, the church bombing in Birmingham, and the Montgomery bus boycott, are highlighted.

Where it's reviewed:
America, February 12, 2007, page 20
The Nation, January 8, 2007, page 10
New York Times Book Review, January 21, 2007, page 22

Other books you might like:
Raymond Arsenault, *The Changing South of Gene Patterson: Journalism and Civil Rights, 1960-1968*, 2002
Taylor Branch, *At Canaan's Edge: America in the King Years, 1965-1968*, 2006
Clayborne Carson, *Reporting Civil Rights: Part One: American Journalism 1941-1963*, 2003
Roy Peter Clark, *The Changing South of Gene Patterson: Journalism and Civil Rights, 1960-1968*, 2002
David J. Garrow, *Reporting Civil Rights: Part One: American Journalism 1941-1963*, 2003
  Bill Kovach, co-editor
  Carol Polsgrove, co-editor
Leigh Raiford, *The Civil Rights Movement in American Memory*, 2006
  Renee Christine Romano, co-author
Susan Weill, *In a Madhouse's Din: Civil Rights Coverage by Mississippi's Daily Press, 1948-1968*, 2002

831

N.A.M. RODGER

The Command of the Ocean: A Naval History of Britain, 1649-1815

(New York: W. W. Norton, 2005)

Subject(s): British history, 1714-1815; Armed forces; England

Summary: *The Command of the Ocean: A Naval History of Britain, 1649-1815* is a guide to the powerful history of the British Navy from author and scholar N.A.M

Rodger. Thoroughly researched, this book gives readers a comprehensive history of Britain's naval activity and rise to power, beginning with the establishment of the English Commonwealth. Rodger outlines the major successes and failures of the British Navy, including significant battles, voyages, and cruises, while also recounting the inner workings of the navy, and its influence, leadership, and funding. *The Command of the Ocean* includes a detailed history on the men who served during Britain's naval domination.

Where it's reviewed:
American History Review, December 2006, page 1592
The Atlantic, May 2005, page 112
London Review of Books, February 3, 2005, page 14

Other books by the same author:
The Safeguard of the Sea: A Naval History of Britain 660-1649, 1999
The Wooden World: An Anatomy of the Georgian Navy, 1996
The Insatiable Earl: A Life of John Mantagu, Fourth Earl of Sandwich 1718-1792, 1994

Other books you might like:
Gregory Fremont-Barnes, *The Royal Navy 1793-1815*, 2007
Arthur Herman, *To Rule the Waves: How the British Navy Shaped the Modern World*, 2004
Timothy Jenks, *Naval Engagements: Patriotism, Cultural Politics, and the Royal Navy 1793-1815*, 2006
Roger Knight, *The Pursuit of Victory: The Life and Achievement of Horatio Nelson*, 2005
Margarette Lincoln, *Naval Wives and Mistresses*, 2007

832

BARNABY ROGERSON

The Last Crusaders: The Hundred-Year Battle for the Center of the World

(New York: Overlook Press, 2010)

Subject(s): Crusades; History; Christianity

Summary: In *The Last Crusaders: The Hundred-Year Battle for the Center of the World*, Islamic scholar and author Barnaby Rogerson examines the lesser-known Crusades and their impact on the world. Although the Crusades that occurred between 1095 and 1291 are more widely known and studied, Rogerson contends that the later Crusades, a series of conflicts between Christians and Muslims from 1415 to 1578, were more significant and widespread. In *The Last Crusaders*, Rogerson examines these deadly skirmishes, which had a more far-reaching effect than the earlier battles. As the conflict spread along trade routes and the North African shore, the Crusades went global, impacting cultures and nations and spawning colonialism around the world.

Where it's reviewed:
Contemporary Review, Winter 2009, page 535
Library Journal, March 1, 2010, page 92

Other books by the same author:
The Heirs of Muhammed: Islam's First Century and the Origins of the Sunni-Shia Split, 2008
The Heirs of the Prophet Muhammed: The Two Paths of Islam, 2006
The Prophet Muhammed: A Biography, 2003

Other books you might like:
Thomas Asbridge, *The Crusades: The Authoritative History of the War for the Holy Land*, 2010
Diarmaid MacCulloch, *Christianity: The First Three Thousand Years*, 2010
Jonathan Philips, *Holy Warriors: A Modern History of the Crusades*, 2010
Jonathan Riley-Smith, *The Crusades: A History*, 1987
Rodney Stark, *Gods Battalions: The Case for the Crusades*, 2009

833

HANNAH ROSEN

Terror in the Heart of Freedom: Citizenship, Sexual Violence, and the Meaning of Race in the Postemancipation South

(Chapel Hill, North Carolina: University of North Carolina Press, 2009)

Subject(s): African Americans; Rape; Slavery

Summary: University of Michigan professor Hannah Rosen examines the ties between race and gender during the Reconstruction Era in the American South. *Terror in the Heart of Freedom: Citizenship, Sexual Violence, and the Meaning of Race in the Postemancipation South* shows how, during this tumultuous time in American history, issues of race gave way to unprecedented incidents of sexual violence. Using this history as a backdrop, Rosen explores the ways these incidents shaped future American attitudes toward race and equality. *Terror in the Heart of Freedom* contains a bibliography and an index.

Where it's reviewed:
Choice, January 2010, page 964

Other books you might like:
Canter Brown Jr., *The Varieties of Women's Experiences: Portraits of Southern Women in the Post-Civil War Century*, 2010
Crystal N. Feimster, *Southern Horrors: Women and the Politics of Rape and Lynching*, 2009
Erik Foner, *Forever Free: The Story of Emancipation and Reconstruction*, 2005
Leon Litwack, *Been in the Storm So Long: The Aftermath of Slavery*, 1979
Susan Eva O'Donovan, *Becoming Free in the Cotton South*, 2007

Larry Eugene Rivers, *The Varieties of Women's Experiences: Portraits of Southern Women in the Post-Civil War Century*, 2010

834

ANNE SARAH RUBIN

A Shattered Nation: The Rise & Fall of the Confederacy, 1861-1868

(Chapel Hill: University of North Carolina Press, 2006)

Subject(s): History; Civil war; Presidents (Government)

Summary: Some historians say the American Civil War was a battle fought for the freedom of African-American slaves. Others argue that the fight between the Union and Confederacy was rooted in other factors. Anne Sarah Rubin's *A Shattered Nation: The Rise & Fall of the Confederacy, 1861-1868* explores how half of a nation wanted a new way of life and how that desire still affects people today. Rubin's opinion of the Confederacy differs from that of many experts. She claims that the Southerners' patriotism started after the war with the Union. It was then that they formed for a cause. The author also highlights the symbols that are still displayed today. People exhibit and feel fondness for Confederate signs because they have been separated from the political side of the war. They no longer stand for a fight over slavery, but about the independence that the Southerners felt. Rubin also notes why the Confederacy had a hard time reconnecting with the rest of the country.

Where it's reviewed:
History, October 2006, page 596
Journal of American History, March 2006, page 1443
Reviews in American History, September 2005, page 366

Other books you might like:
Edward Porter Alexander, *Fighting for the Confederacy: The Personal Recollections of General Edward Porter Alexander*, 1998
D. Appleton, *The Carlyles: A Story of the Fall of the Confederacy*, 2010
Eugene D. Genovese, *A Consuming Fire: The Fall of the Confederacy in the Mind of the White Christian South*, 2009
John Remington Graham, *Principles of Confederacy: The Vision and the Dream and the Fall of the South*, 1992
Burton Harrison, *The Carlyles: A Story of the Fall of the Confederacy*, 2010
Ethan Sepp Rafuse, *Robert E. Lee and the Fall of the Confederacy 1863-1865*, 2009
James Van Treese, *Principles of Confederacy: The Vision and the Dream and the Fall of the South*, 1992

835

EDWARD B. RUGEMER

The Problem of Emancipation: The Caribbean Roots of the American Civil War

(Baton Rouge, Louisiana: Louisiana State University Press, 2008)

Subject(s): Slavery; United States Civil War, 1861-1865; Abolition of slavery

Summary: In *The Problem of Emancipation: The Caribbean Roots of the American Civil War*, Edward B. Rugemer explores the causes of the Civil War in the context of the British abolition of slavery in 1834, as well as three violent rebellions that occurred prior to that. Rugemer references the Haitian Revolution as well as rebellions against slavery that occurred in the West Indies; these events were published in American newspapers, which led Americans to fear that the same types of events would occur in the United States. Rugemer considers the actions of abolitionist newspapers, the way they enraged and frightened slaveholders, and the way this affected the American's response to abolitionists. The author discusses specific events as well as abolitionist leaders William Lloyd Garrison, Frederick Douglass, Lydia Maria Child, and William Ellery Channing and describes what they learned from British emancipation and carried those lessons to the beginnings of the Civil War in 1861.

Where it's reviewed:
Journal of Social History, Summer 2010, page 1109

Other books you might like:
Hilary Beckles, *Caribbean Slavery in the Atlantic World: A Student Reader*, 2009
Selwyn H.H. Carrington, *The Sugar Industry and the Abolition of Slave Trade, 1775-1810*, 2002
Seymour Drescher, *Abolition: A History of Slavery and Antislavery*, 2009
Herbert S. Klein, *African Slavery in Latin America and the Caribbean*, 2007
Verene Shepherd, *Caribbean Slavery in the Atlantic World: A Student Reader*, 2009
Verene Shepherd, *Working Slavery, Pricing Freedom: The Caribbean and the Atlantic World*, 2003
Ben Vinson III, *African Slavery in Latin America and the Caribbean*, 2007

836

GONZAGUE SAINT BRIS

Lafayette: Hero of the American Revolution

(New York: Pegasus Books, 2010)

Story type: Historical - American Revolution; Historical - French Revolution
Subject(s): French Revolution, 1789; American Revolution, 1775-1783; Biographies
Summary: Written by Gonzague Saint Bris, *Lafayette:*

Hero of the American Revolution is a detailed biography of French aristocrat Marquis Gilbert de Lafayette and the significant role he played during the American and French revolutions. During the American Revolution, Lafayette traveled from France to America to assist George Washington and the other Founding Fathers in their efforts. Saint Bris recounts the close personal friendship that Lafayette shared with Washington and the impact that the American Revolution had on the young politician. Lafayette later played a vital role in the French Revolution, during which he utilized the lessons and values he had learned during his time in America to impact his native land. *Lafayette* details the importance of French allies during the American Revolution and the pivotal role that Lafayette played in the shaping of two nations.

Where it's reviewed:
Library Journal, April 15, 2010, page 90

Other books you might like:
David A. Clary, *Adopted Son: Washington, Lafayette, and the Friendship That Saved the Revolution*, 2007
Russell Freedman, *Lafayette and the American Revolution*, 2010
James R. Gaines, *For Liberty or Glory: Washington, Lafayette, and Their Revolutions*, 2007
Jason Lane, *General and Madam de Lafayette: Partners in Liberty's Cause in the American and French Revolutions*, 2003
Harlow G. Unger, *Lafayette*, 2003

837

JAMES B. SALAZAR

Bodies of Reform: The Rhetoric of Character in Gilded Age America

(New York: New York University Press, 2010)

Subject(s): Literature; History; United States

Summary: *Bodies of Reform: The Rhetoric of Character in Gilded Age America* is a literary examination of the difficult-to-define idea of character in the United States, from author James B. Salazar. In an effort to better understand the prevalence of character and importance of building character during the 19th century, Salazar examines the written works of popular novelists such as Herman Melville, Mark Twain, and Charlotte Perkins Gilman as well as a number of other printed works such as parenting resources, Scout handbooks, success guides, health articles, and texts about how to build strong character. His findings highlight the role that character played in shaping literature, culture, politics, and philosophy in America during the mid 19th and early 20th centuries.

Other books you might like:
Susan Castillo, *American Literature in Context to 1865*, 2010
Elizabeth Duquette, *Loyal Subjects: Bonds of Nation, Race, and Allegiance in Nineteenth-Century America*, 2010
Michael T. Gilmore, *The War on Words: Slavery, Race,*

and Free Speech in American Literature, 2010
Alan Trachtenberg, *The Incorporation of America: Culture and Society in the Gilded Age*, 2007
Johannes Voelz, *Transcendental Resistance: The New Americanists and Emerson's Challenge*, 2010

838

MARTHA A. SANDWEISS

Passing Strange: A Gilded Age Tale of Love and Deception Across the Color Line

(New York: Penguin Press, 2009)

Subject(s): Biographies; History; African Americans

Summary: *Passing Strange: A Gilded Age Tale of Love and Deception Across the Color Line* by Martha A. Sandweiss is a biography of Clarence King, a well-known white geologist in 1880s' America who was a key player in the mapping of the American West. King traveled around much of the world, but eventually returned to New York where he met and fell in love with Ada Copeland, an African American woman. This is where his double life began. King introduced himself to Ada as James Todd, a Pullman porter with black ancestry, despite his blond hair and blue eyes. She believed him, and the two were married for seventeen years and had five children, though King managed to keep her, and his double identity, a secret until he was near death. Sandweiss explores this love story, the deception it entailed, and the larger subjects of cultural perceptions of race and identity in turn-of-the-century America.

Where it's reviewed:
Biography, Spring 2009, page 417
Library Journal, January 1, 2009, page 108
New York Times Book Review, March 8, 2009, page 11
The New Yorker, March 9, 2009, page 70

Other books by the same author:
Print the Legend: Photography and the American West, 2004
The Oxford History of the American West, 1996
Laura Gilpin: An Enduring Grace, 1986

Other books you might like:
Bliss Broyard, *One Drop: My Father's Hidden Life — A True Story of Family, Race, and Secrets*, 2007
Kent Anderson Leslie, *Woman of Color, Daughter of Privilege: Amanda America Dickson, 1849-1893*, 1995
Gloria Moldow, *Women Doctors in Gilded Age Washington: Race, Gender, and Professionalization*, 1987
James Gregory Moore, *King of the 40th Parallel: Discovery in the American West*, 2007
Robert Wilson, *The Explorer King: Adventure, Science, and the Great Diamond Hoax: Clarence King in the Old West*, 2007

839

PRIYA SATIA

Spies in Arabia: The Great War and the Cultural Foundations of Britain's Covert Empire in the Middle East

(Oxford; New York: Oxford University Press, 2009)

Story type: Historical - World War I

Subject(s): Wars; World War I, 1914-1918; United Kingdom. Army

Summary: In *Spies in Arabia: The Great War and the Cultural Foundations of Britain's Covert Empire in the Middle East*, author Priya Satia the various reasons that British spies entered Arab territories in the early 1900s. These agents were primarily concerned with finding a direct course to India and studying the different forms of spirituality within the area. But as time went on, these goals began to conflict with one another; what started out as a peaceful mission to learn about another region turned into violence as tension grew. Satia recreates the events that led up to violence in the Middle East and, ultimately, the First World War.

Where it's reviewed:
American Historical Review, April 2009, page 518
History, July 2010, page 358
Journal of British Studies, April 2009, page 543
Journal of Interdisciplinary History, Winter 2010, page 451
Middle East Journal, Winter 2009, page 156

Other books you might like:
James Barr, *Setting the Desert on Fire: T.E. Lawrence and Britain's Secret War in Arabia, 1916-1918*, 2008
Shareen Blair Brysac, *Kingmakers: The Invention of the Modern Middle East*, 2009
  Karl E. Meyer, co-author
Bernard Porter, *The Absent-Minded Imperialists: Empire, Society, and Culture in Britain*, 2005
Martin Thomas, *Empires of Intelligence: Security Services and Colonial Disorder after 1914*, 2007
Bruce C. Westrate, *The Arab Bureau: British Policy in the Middle East, 1916-1920*, 1992

840

LONDA SCHIEBINGER

Plants and Empire: Colonial Bioprospecting in the Atlantic World

(Cambridge, Massachusetts: Harvard University Press, 2004)

Story type: Historical

Subject(s): Botany; History; Native Americans

Summary: In *Plants and Empire: Colonial Bioprospecting in the Atlantic World*, author Londa Schiebinger looks at the role plants play from historian's perspective. Since the dawn of time, plants have been useful to human beings in some way. In this volume, readers are brought back to a time when America was still new. During this time, Europeans believed that the plants from the New World would help decrease starvation and prevent disease in their homelands. Within this work, Schiebinger reminds readers of the many ways that plants are used and explains why some explorers were willing to put everything on the line in their quest to locate some of the world's most exotic flora.

Where it's reviewed:
International History Review, March 2006, page 142
Natural History, April 2005, page 58
Times Literary Supplement, April 1, 2005, page 30

Other books by the same author:
Nature's Body: Gender in the Making of Modern Science, 2004
Has Feminism Changed Science?, 2001
The Mind Has No Sex? Women in the Origins of Modern Science, 1991

Other books you might like:
William Beinart, *Environment and Empire*, 2009
James Delbourgo, *Science and Empire in the Atlantic World*, 2007
  Nicholas Dew, co-author
Mark Harrison, *Medicine in an Age of Commerce and Empire: Britain and Its Tropical Colonies 1660-1830*, 2010
Lotte Hughes, *Environment and Empire*, 2009
Susan Scott Parrish, *American Curiosity: Cultures of Natural History in the Colonial British Atlantic World*, 2006
Laurelyn Whitt, *Science, Colonialism, and Indigeneous Peoples: The Cultural Politics of Law and Knowledge*, 2009

841

STACY SCHIFF

A Great Improvisation: Franklin, France, and the Birth of America

(New York: Henry Holt, 2005)

Subject(s): American Revolution, 1775-1783; French (European people); United States

Summary: Written by Pulitzer Prize winning author Stacy Schiff, *A Great Improvisation: Franklin, France, and the Birth of America* is a discussion about the eight-year diplomatic visit Benjamin Franklin made to France shortly after the United States was founded. Only months after America declared independence in December of 1776, 70-year old Benjamin Franklin embarked on a dangerous journey to secure an alliance between the United States and France. After spending 30 days at sea, Franklin arrived in France. During his visit, Franklin tried to convince the French government to support America's efforts to be independent from Britain. *A Great Improvisation* chronicles Franklin's trip, his accomplishments, and the long-standing bond that was formed between America and France.

Where it's reviewed:
American Heritage, April-May 2005, page 18
Booklist, March 1, 2005, page 1121
Harper's, October 2005, page 88
Newsweek, March 28, 2005, page 53

Other books by the same author:
Cleopatra: A Life, 2010
Saint Exupery: A Biography, 1997

Other books you might like:
Ron Chernow, *Washington: A Life*, 2010
Benjamin Franklin, *The Autobiography of Benjamin Franklin*, 2002
Walter Isaacson, *Benjamin Franklin: An American Life*, 2003

842

ROBERT J. SCHNELLER JR.

Breaking the Color Barrier: The U.S. Naval Academy's First Black Midshipmen and the Struggle for Racial Equality

(New York City, New York: NYU Press, 2005)

Subject(s): Military academies; Military life; Race relations

Summary: Robert J. Schneller's examination of the racist policies of the U.S. Naval Academy in Annapolis, Maryland, focuses on Wesley Brown, the first of five black men who entered the academy in 1949, and graduated from the academy as a midshipman. Brown's struggle was wrought with oppression both institutional and individual, as numerous policies sought to discourage black men from entering the academy and graduating. Schneller's historical analysis includes the influence of World War II on the naval academy's policies and the changing attitudes about race and culture in America.

Where it's reviewed:
American Historical Review, February 2007, page 240
Journal of Military History, January 2007, page 273

Other books by the same author:
Cushing: Civil War SEAL, 2003
Farragut: America's First Admiral, 2003
A Quest for Gold: A Biography of Rear Admiral John A. Dahlgren, 1995

Other books you might like:
Gerald Astor, *The Right to Fight: A History of African-Americans in the Military*, 1998
Gail Buckley, *American Patriots: The Story of Blacks in the Military from the Revolution to Desert Storm*, 2001
Mary Pat Kelly, *Proudly We Served: The Men of the U.S.S. Mason*, 1995
Richard E. Miller, *The Messman Chronicles: African-Americans in the U.S. Navy, 1932-1943*, 2004

J. Todd Moye, *Freedom Flyers: The Tuskegee Airmen of World War II*, 2010

843

STEPHEN SCHWAB

Guantanamo, USA: The Untold History of America's Cuban Outpost

(Lawrence, Kansas: University Press of Kansas, 2009)

Subject(s): Cuban history; Military bases; History

Summary: In *Guantanamo, USA: The Untold History of America's Cuban Outpost*, author Stephen Schwab discusses the history of one of the United States' most famous military bases. Located in Cuba, a country that has a tenuous relationship with the United States, the base has been the source of much controversy over the years. However, Schwab argues that this wasn't always the case. The book offers readers the complete history of Guantanamo Bay. From the base's foundation to its current status and functions, author Stephen Schwab covers all significant events involving Guantanamo Bay. Author Stephen Schwab was formerly employed by the CIA as the senior analyst. He now works as a professor of history.

Where it's reviewed:
CHOICE: Current Reviews for Academic Libraries, April 2010, page 1553
Publishers Weekly, September 28, 2009, page 56

Other books you might like:
Gordon Cucullo, *Inside Gitmo: The True Story Behind the Myths of Guantanamo Bay*, 2009
Mark Danner, *Torture and Truth: America, Abu Ghraib, and the War on Terror*, 2004
Jonathan Hafetz, *The Guantanamo Lawyers: Inside a Prison Outside the Law*, 2009
Murat Kurnaz, *Five Years of My Life: An Innocent Man in Guantanamo*, 2008
Andy Worthington, *The Guantanamo Files: The Stories of the 774 Detainees in America's Illegal Prison*, 2007

844

STUART B. SCHWARTZ

All Can Be Saved: Religious Tolerance and Salvation in the Iberian Atlantic World

(New Haven, Connecticut: Yale University Press, 2008)

Story type: Religious
Subject(s): Religion; History; Inquisition

Summary: In *All Can Be Saved: Religious Tolerance and Salvation in the Iberian Atlantic World*, historian Stuart Schwartz examines religious attitudes during the Spanish

Inquisition. In the book, Schwartz argues that, although Catholic zealots wanted to eradicate all other religious during this time, most common people were open-minded about religion. Schwartz describes the differences in religious idea throughout Europe and the New World. He also discusses the effects religion had on culture and vice-versa.

Where it's reviewed:

American Historical Review, June 2009, page 716

Hispanic Review, Winter 2010, page 123

New York Review of Books, August 13, 2009, page 38

Renaissance Quarterly, Summer 2009, page 568

William and Mary Quarterly, April 2009, page 409

Other books you might like:

Jorge Canizares-Esguerra, *Puritan Conquistadores: Iberianizing the Atlantic, 1550-1700*, 2006

Jerrilynn D. Dodds, *The Arts of Intimacy: Christians, Jews, and Muslims in the Making of Castilian Culture*, 2008

Benjamin J. Kaplan, *Divided by Faith: Religious Conflict and the Practice of Toleration in Early Modern Europe*, 2007

Chris Lowney, *A Vanished World: Muslims, Christians, and Jews in Medieval Spain*, 2005

Maria Rosa Menocal, *The Ornament of the World: How Muslims, Jews, and Christians Created a Culture of Tolerance in Medieval Spain*, 2002

845

M.G. SHEFTALL

Blossoms in the Wind: Human Legacies of the Kamikaze

(New York: NAL Trade, 2005)

Story type: Military

Subject(s): Japanese history; World War II, 1939-1945; Military life

Summary: *Blossoms in the Wind: Human Legacies of the Kamikaze* follows the history of the Japanese Kamikaze bombers during World War II. Kamikaze fighters were soldiers who would willingly kill themselves to directly attack their enemies. Japanese Kamikazes were the first fighters to use these tactics in battle. In the book, author M.G. Sheftall shares with readers the history of these bombers and explores the fighters' mentality. The author also describes his visit to camp where soldiers who lived through their Kamikaze attacks currently live.

Where it's reviewed:

Booklist, July 2005, page 1895

Far Eastern Economic Review, January/February 2006, page 72

Journal of Military History, April 2007, page 581

Publishers Weekly, July 2005, page 47

Other books you might like:

Albert Axell, *Kamikaze: Japan's Suicide Gods*, 2002

John Dower, *War Without Mercy: Race and Power in the Pacific War*, 1986

Rikihei Inoguchi, *The Divine Wind: Japan Kamikaze Force in World War II*, 1978

Yasuo Kuwahara, *Kamikaze: A Japanese Pilot's Own Spectacular Story of the Famous Suicide Squadrons*, 1978

Emiko Ohnuki-Tierney, *Kamikaze Diaries: Reflections of Japanese Student Soldiers*, 2006

846

TODD SHEPARD

The Invention of Decolonization: The Algerian War and the Remaking of France

(Ithaca, New York: Cornell University Press, 2006)

Subject(s): French (European people); Wars; Politics

Summary: Todd Shepard's *The Invention of Decolonization: The Algerian War and the Remaking of France* discusses France before, during, and after the Algerian War, during which Algeria separated from France. This war and the ensuing separation caused a number of dilemmas both in Algeria, which had not been its own country in many years, and in the French government. This book explores the process of decolonization and describes the changes that occur due to decolonization. Shepard also describes the negative effects decolonization can have.

Where it's reviewed:

American Historical Review, December 2009, page 1579

French Politics, Culture and Society, Spring 2008, page 137

International History Review, August 2008, page 356

International Review of Social History, August 2008, page 356

Journal of Peace Research, September 2008, page 717

Other books you might like:

Pierre Bourdieu, *Uncivil War: Intellectuals and Identity Politics During the Decolonization of Algeria, Second Edition*, 2005

Abdelmajid Hannoum, *Violent Modernity: France in Algeria*, 2011

Alistair Horne, *A Savage War of Peace: Algeria 1954-1962*, 2002

James D. LeSueur, *Uncivil War: Intellectuals and Identity Politics During the Decolonization of Algeria, Second Edition*, 2005

Patricia M. Lorcin, *Algeria and France, 1800-2000: Identity, Memory, Nostalgia*, 2006

Paul A. Silverstein, *Algeria in France: Transpolitics, Race, and Nation*, 2004

847

RICHARD B. SHER

The Enlightenment and the Book: Scottish Authors and Their Publishers in Eighteenth-Century Britain, Ireland, and America

(Chicago: University Of Chicago Press, 2006)

Subject(s): Scotland; Scottish history; Enlightenment (Cultural movement)

Summary: During the 1700s, the world saw an explosion in all things literary, philosophical, and scientific; this surge of knowledge came to be known as "The Enlightenment." Author Richard B. Sher invites readers back to the Enlightenment period in *The Enlightenment and the Book: Scottish Authors and Their Publishers in Eighteenth-Century Britain, Ireland, and America*. Within this piece, Sher focuses on Scottish writers and thinkers, including Robert Burns, Adam Smith, David Hume, and James Boswell, who depended on publishers to disseminate their ideas and words throughout the world. Sher explains how the publishing industry flourished during the Enlightenment and reflects upon the interdependent relationship that existed between writers and publishers during this important literary period.

Where it's reviewed:
The Atlantic, April 2008, page 106
English Historical Review, April 2009, page 435
Journal of Modern History, June 2009, page 405
London Review of Books, April 5, 2007, page 13
Times Literary Supplement, July 20, 2007, page 25

Other books by the same author:
The Glasgow Enlightenment, 1997
Sociability and Society in Eighteenth Century Scotland, 1993
Scotland and America in the Age of Enlightenment, 1990

Other books you might like:
Alexander Broadie, *The Scottish Enlightenment: The Historical Age of the Historical Nation*, 2007
James Buchan, *Crowded with Genius: The Scottish Enlightenment: Edinburgh's Moment of the Mind*, 2003
Arthur Herman, *How the Scots Invented the Modern World: The True Story of How Western Europe's Poorest Nation Created Our World & Everything in It*, 2001
Ernest Campbell Mossner, *The Life of David Hume*, 2001
Nicholas Phillipson, *Adam Smith: An Enlightened Life*, 2010

848

STEFANIE SIEGMUND

The Medici State and the Ghetto of Florence: The Construction of an Early Modern Jewish Community

(Stanford, California: Stanford University Press, 2006)

Subject(s): Jews; Jewish history; Italian history

Summary: The creation of the Florentine ghetto in the 16th century is the subject of this scholarly work by history and Judaic studies expert Stefanie Siegmund. *The Medici State and the Ghetto of Florence: The Construction of an Early Modern Jewish Community* looks at the political and religious maneuverings that led to the formation of the ghetto, which housed the Jews of Tuscany. Siegmund then delves into the rich history, culture, and traditions the Tuscan Jews created in the face of such hardship and discrimination. *The Medici State and the Ghetto of Florence* includes a bibliography and an index.

Where it's reviewed:
American Historical Review, February 2007, page 302
Journal of Religious History, September 2007, page 324
Renaissance Quarterly, Winter 2007, page 1327
Shofar, February 2008, page 181
Sixteenth Century Journal, Fall 2007, page 897

Other books you might like:
Robert Bonfil, *Jewish Life in Renaissance Italy*, 1994
Leone Modena, *The Autobiography of a Seventeenth-Century Venetian Rabbi*, 1988
David B. Ruderman, *Early Modern Jewry: A New Cultural History*, 2010
Michael Stuhlbarg, *The Jew in the Medieval World: A Source Book, 315-1791*, 1975
Ariel Toaff, *Love, Work, and Death: Jewish Life in Medieval Umbria*, 1995

849

MRINALINI SINHA

Specters of Mother India: The Global Restructuring of an Empire

(Durham, North Carolina: Duke University Press, 2006)

Subject(s): Sex roles; Indians (Asian people); Social sciences

Summary: *Specters of Mother India: The Global Restructuring of an Empire* examines the social and political transformation of India brought about by a controversial publication entitled *Mother India*, written by American journalist Katherine Mayo in 1927 that exposed a number of social ills and gender inequalities within India at that time. Author Mrinalini Sinha elucidates the positive political and social reforms that took place in India since the time of Mayo's expose, particularly concerning the identity and role of women within society.

History

Where it's reviewed:
Foreign Affairs, January-February 2007, page 176
International History Review, December 2007, page 892
Journal of British Studies, July 2007, page 726
Journal of Women's History, Winter 2008, page 177
Women's History Review, October 2008, page 1110

Other books you might like:
Gucharan Das, *India Unbound: The Social and Economic Revolution from Independence to the Global Information Age*, 2002
Ramachandra Guha, *India After Gandhi: The History of the World's Largest Democracy*, 2007
Edward Luce, *In Spite of the Gods: The Strange Rise of Modern India*, 2007
Gita Mehta, *Snakes and Ladders: Glimpses of Modern India*, 1998
Nandan Nilekani, *Imagining India: The Idea of a Renewed Nation*, 2009

850

CARROLL SMITH-ROSENBERG

This Violent Empire: The Birth of an American National Identity

(Chapel Hill, North Carolina: The University of North Carolina Press, 2010)

Story type: Historical - American Revolution
Subject(s): Violence; Sexism; Racism

Summary: In *This Violent Empire: The Birth of an American National Identity*, author Caroll Smith-Rosenberg travels back through U.S. history to reveal the thread of violence the lead to the construction of a nation. Smith-Rosenberg takes readers back to the foundation of the United States and pinpoints exactly when and why the violent mind frame took over; our forefathers, having little to nothing historically and culturally in common with one another, found themselves united in the shared hatred of certain sectors of the population. This hate united them—and arguably the country as well—within a circle of hate, violence, and prejudice. In addition to violence, Smith-Rosenburg also discusses racism, sexism, and paranoia.

Where it's reviewed:
Library Journal, April 15, 2010, page 95

Other books by the same author:
Disorderly Conduct: Visions of Gender in Victorian America, 1986
Religion and the Rise of the American City: New York City Mission Movement, 1812-70, 1972

Other books you might like:
Tony Judt, *Ill Fares the Land*, 2010
Jill Lepore, *The Name of War: King Philip's War and the Origins of American Identity*, 1998
Jon Pahl, *Empire of Sacrifice: The Religious Origins of American Violence*, 2010
Jack Rakove, *Revolutionaries: A New History of the Invention of America*, 2010
Audrey Smedley, *Race in North America: Origins and*

Evolution of a Worldview, 2007

851

FRANK N. SNOWDEN

The Conquest of Malaria: Italy 1900-1962

(New Haven, Connecticut: Yale University Press, 2006)

Story type: Historical
Subject(s): Italy; Italian history; Medicine

Summary: *The Conquest of Malaria: Italy 1900-1962* spans the time period in Italian history when the malaria outbreak exploded and ran rampant through the country, causing chaos, health deficiencies, and a number of economic, political, and social problems. Author Frank N. Snowden covers the topic fully from its onset to its final break in the late 1900s, revealing the measures taken to prevent the disease from spreading further. Snowden also discusses World War II and presents information regarding the malaria outbreak being an act of bioterrorism.

Where it's reviewed:
History Today, April 2006, page 91
Nature, June 22, 2006, page 933

Other books by the same author:
The Fascist Revolution in Tuscany, 1919-22, 2004
Violence and the Great Estates in the South of Italy: Apulia, 1900-1922, 2004
Naples in the Time of Cholera, 2002

Other books you might like:
Robert S. Desowitz, *The Malaria Capers: More Tales of Parasites and People, Research and Reality*, 1991
Randall M. Packard, *The Making of a Tropical Disease: A Short History of Malaria*, 2007
Sonia Shah, *The Fever: How Malaria Has Ruled Humankind for 500,000 Years*, 2010
Sheldon Watts, *Epidemics and History: Disease, Power and Imperialism*, 1997
James L.A. Webb, Jr., *Humanity's Burden: A Global History of Malaria*, 2008

852

JONATHAN D. SPENCE

Return to Dragon Mountain: Memories of a Late Ming Man

(New York: Viking, 2007)

Subject(s): Biographies; China; Chinese history

Summary: *Return to Dragon Mountain: Memories of a Late Ming Man* by author Jonathan D. Spence is a historical and biographical perspective of Zhang Dai, a Chinese writer and historian. Zhang Dai's life spanned significant points in China's history during the Ming

Dynasty. Spence takes a look at Zhang's life as derived from the subject's own writings and provides an overview of the history of the Ming. Spence is also the author of *The Death of Woman Wang* and *The Memory Palace of Matteo Ricci*.

Where it's reviewed:
American Historical Review, October 2008, page 1135
Far Eastern Economic Review, June 2008, page 74
New Republic, October 22, 2007, page 49
New York Review of Books, December 20, 2007, page 8
New York Times Book Review, October 7, 2007, page 20

Other books by the same author:
Mao Zedong: A Life, 2006
The Search for Modern China, 1999
God's Chinese Son: The Taiping Heavenly Kingdom of Hong Xiuquan, 1996

Other books you might like:
Timothy Brook, *The Troubled Empire: China in the Yuan and Ming Dynasties*, 2010
Jonathan Clements, *Coxinga and the Fall of the Ming Dynasty*, 2004
Bamber Gascoigne, *The Dynasties of China: A History*, 2003
Ray Huang, *1587, A Year of No Significance: The Ming Dynasty in Decline*, 1982
Sarah Schneewind, *A Tale of Two Melons: Emperor and Subject in Ming China*, 2006

853

MEGAN K. STACK

Every Man in This Village Is a Liar: An Education in War

(New York: Doubleday, 2010)

Subject(s): Biographies; Middle East; History

Summary: In *Every Man in This Village Is a Liar: An Education in War*, journalist Megan K. Stack chronicles the impact of war and oppression in the post-9/11 Middle East. First dispatched to cover the war in Afghanistan, Stack witnesses the horrors suffered by the civilians in the region caused by attacks by the United States and Israel. From there, Stack travels to a Palestinian uprising in Israel, Baghdad under occupation by U.S. and coalition forces, and Lebanon amidst the Hezbollah-Israeli conflict there. In detailing the political and military climate of the Middle East, the author also considers how social and cultural factors affect each region.

Where it's reviewed:
Booklist, April 15, 2010, page 20
Library Journal, April 1, 2010, page 85
National Interest, July/August 2010, page 66
Publishers Weekly, February 8, 2010, page 36
Sunday Times (London, England), August 1, 2010, page 52

Other books you might like:
Philip Caputo, *Means of Escape*, 1991
Ari Folman, *Waltz with Bashir: A Lebanon War Story*, 2009
Seth G. Jones, *In the Graveyard of Empires: America's War in Afghanistan*, 2010
John Miller, *Inside Israel: The Faiths, the People, and the Modern Conflicts of the World's Holiest Land*, 2002
Anthony Shadid, *Night Draws Near: Iraq's People in the Shadow of America's War*, 2005

854

TOM STANDAGE

An Edible History of Humanity

(New York: Walker & Co., 2009)

Summary: In *Every Man in This Village Is a Liar: An Education in War*, journalist Megan K. Stack chronicles the impact of war and oppression in the post-9/11 Middle East. First dispatched to cover the war in Afghanistan, Stack witnesses the horrors suffered by the civilians in the region caused by attacks by the United States and Israel. From there, Stack travels to a Palestinian uprising in Israel, Baghdad under occupation by U.S. and coalition forces, and Lebanon amidst the Hezbollah-Israeli conflict there. In detailing the political and military climate of the Middle East, the author also considers how social and cultural factors affect each region.

Where it's reviewed:
The Humanist, September/October 2009, page 46
Journal of Popular Culture, October 2010, page 1143
Journal of World History, June 2008, page 235
Library Journal, April 1, 2009, page 86
New Scientist, May 16, 2009, page 49

Other books by the same author:
The Victorian Internet: The Remarkable Story of the Telegraph and the Nineteenth Century's On-Line Pioneers, 2007
A History of the World in Six Glasses, 2006
The Neptune File: A Story of Astronomical Rivalry and the Pioneers of Planet Hunting, 2001

Other books you might like:
Linda Civitello, *Cuisine and Culture: A History of Food and People*, 2007
Felipe Fernandez-Armesto, *Near a Thousand Tables: A History of Food*, 2002
Sharman Apt Russell, *Hunger: An Unnatural History*, 2005
Maguelonne Toussaint-Samat, *A History of Food*, 2008
Margaret Visser, *Much Depends on Dinner: The Extraordinary History and Mythology, Allure and Obsessions, Perils and Taboos of an Ordinary Meal*, 1988

855

DOUG STANTON

Horse Soldiers: The Extraordinary Story of a Band of US Soldiers Who Rode to Victory in Afghanistan

(New York: Scribner, 2009)

Subject(s): Middle East; Horses; Wars

Summary: Author Doug Stanton tells the riveting true life story of the Horse Soldiers and their fearless attempts to protect human lives in Afghanistan. In *Horse Soldiers: The Extraordinary Story of a Band of US Soldiers Who Rode to Victory in Afghanistan*, Stanton recounts how, in the wake of September 11, a small band of American soldiers rode into the Middle Eastern country on horseback. Their aim was to bring down the Taliban, but a sudden surprise attack caught them unaware. The group fought nobly to protect all they had gained, and this volume chronicles their thrilling adventure. Includes a list of sources and a bibliography.

Where it's reviewed:
Biography, Summer 2009, page 590
Library Journal, June 15, 2009, page 84
New York Times Book Review, May 17, 2009, page 1
Publishers Weekly, May 25, 2009, page 54

Other books by the same author:
In Harm's Way: The Sinking of the USS Indianapolis and the Extraordinary Story of Its Survivors, 2003

Other books you might like:
Eric Blehm, *The Only Thing Worth Dying For: How Eleven Green Berets Forged a New Afghanistan*, 2010
Lou DiMarco, *War Horse: A History of the Military Horse and Rider*, 2008
Sebastian Junger, *War*, 2010
David Loyn, *In Afghanistan: Two Hundred Years of British, Russian and American Occupation*, 2009
Sean Naylor, *Not a Good Day to Die: The Untold Story of Operation Anaconda*, 2005

856

KEVIN STARR

Golden Dreams: California in an Age of Abundance, 1950-1963

(New York: Oxford University Press, 2009)

Subject(s): United States history; Sociology; Economics

Summary: In this sweeping historical, economic, and societal study, history professor and acclaimed author Kevin Starr examines life in California during the post World War II era. *Golden Dreams: California in an Age of Abundance, 1950-1963* chronicles the creation of suburbia and the building of urban life in The Golden State. This volume further explores issues surrounding

political change, art, and the erection of the freeways that would become a trademark of California life. Starr also provides insight into the state's race relations and chronicles the end of Jim Crow laws. *Golden Dreams*, an installment in the Americans and the California Dream series, contains illustrations, bibliographical references, and a full index.

Where it's reviewed:
California History, Winter 2009, page 73
The Economist, August 8, 2009, page 68
Washington Monthly, July/August 2009, page 61

Other books by the same author:
Golden Gate: The Life and Times of America's Greatest Bridge, 2010
Americans and the California Dream, 1850-1915, 1986
Inventing the Dream: California Through the Progressive Era, 1986

Other books you might like:
Robert M. Fogelson, *The Fragmented Metropolis: Los Angeles, 1850-1930*, 1993
Peter Moruzzi, *Palm Springs Holiday*, 2009
Charles Phoenix, *Southern California in the 50s: Sun, Fun, and Fantasy*, 2001
Richard B. Rice, *The Elusive Eden: A New History of California*, 1988
Richard B. Stolley, *The American Dream: The 50s*, 2000
Times Life Books Times Life Books, co-author

857

ALEX STOROZYNSKI

The Peasant Prince: Thaddeus Kosciuszko and the Age of Revolution

(New York: St. Martin's Press, 2009)

Subject(s): Biographies; American Revolution, 1775-1783; History

Summary: In *The Peasant Prince: Thaddeus Kosciuszko and the Age of Revolution*, biographer Alex Storozynski provides an overview of Kosciuszko's life and contributions to the United States. Born in Poland, Kosciuszko immigrated to the New World at the dawn of the American Revolution. He contributed his talents as an engineer to the colonists' quest for independence when the Continental Congress appointed him as colonel of engineers. He was responsible for buttressing the Philadelphia waterfront against British attacks, and he went on to serve as chief engineer of West Point Academy as well as Brigadier General of the Continental Army. In this book, the author takes a look at Kosciuszko's personal and professional accomplishments.

Where it's reviewed:
Booklist, April 1, 2009, page 17
Library Journal, April 15, 2009, page 101
Publishers Weekly, March 30, 2009, page 40

Other books you might like:

Anthony Walton White Evans, *Memoir of Thaddeus Kosciuszko, Poland's Hero and Patriot, an Officer in the American Army of the Revolution*, 2009

Graham Russell Gao Hodges, *Friends of Liberty: A Tale of Three Patriots, Two Revolutions, and the Betrayal That Divided a Nation: Thomas Jefferson, Thaddeus Kosciuszko, and Agrippa Hull*, 2008

Francis C. Kajencki, *Thaddeus Kosciuszko: Military Engineer of the American Revolution*, 1998

Gary Nash, *Friends of Liberty: A Tale of Three Patriots, Two Revolutions, and the Betrayal That Divided a Nation: Thomas Jefferson, Thaddeus Kosciuszko, and Agrippa Hull*, 2008

James S. Pula, *Thaddeus Kosciuszko: The Purest Son of Liberty*, 1998

Adam Zamoyski, *The Polish Way: A Thousand-Year History of the Poles and Their Culture*, 1993

858

THOMAS J. SUGRUE

Sweet Land of Liberty: The Forgotten Struggle for Civil Rights in the North

(New York: Random House, 2008)

Subject(s): Civil rights; United States history; Racism

Summary: In *Sweet Land of Liberty: The Forgotten Struggle for Civil Rights in the North*, author Thomas J. Sugrue looks at the civil rights movement as it was fought on the other side of the Mason-Dixon line. As Sugrue explains, much of the historical work about the American Civil War and subsequent civil rights movement focuses on the southern portion of the United States, where slavery was most prevalent. However, as the author contends, many struggles and triumphs on behalf of the African American population occurred in northern states. Sugrue looks at specific northern activists and organizations that underline the continued fight for civil rights in America and the progress that has been made thus far.

Where it's reviewed:
Library Journal, November 1, 2008, page 88
Publishers Weekly, September 22, 2008, page 55
Wilson Quarterly, Winter 2009, page 89

Other books by the same author:
Not Even Past: Barack Obama and the Burden of Race, 2010
The Origins of the Urban Crisis: Race and Inequality in Postwar Detroit, 2005
W.E.B. DuBois, Race, and the City, 1998

Other books you might like:
Taylor Branch, *At Canaan's Edge: America in the King Years, 1965-1968*, 2006

Patrick D. Jones, *The Selma of the North: Civil Rights Insurgency in Milwaukee*, 2010

David Kairys, *Philadelphia Freedom: Memoir of a Civil Rights Lawyer*, 2008

David Kushner, *Levittown: Two Families, One Tycoon, and the Fight for Civil Rights in America's Legendary Suburb*, 2009

James R. Ralph Jr., *Northern Protest: Martin Luther King, Jr., Chicago, and the Civil Rights Movement*, 1993

859

JAMES L. SWANSON

Manhunt: The 12-Day Chase for Lincoln's Killer

(New York: HarperCollins, 2006)

Subject(s): American History; Assassination; Civil War, U.S.

Summary: On April 14, 1865, one of the most daring and tragic crimes of American history was committed. John Wilkes Booth shot and killed President Abraham Lincoln in a crowded theater, and then escaped in the confusion. That night, Secretary of War Edwin Stanton launched a manhunt. This book tells the story of the ensuing 12 days, during which Booth was at large and cavalry troops hunted him. The search for Booth was complicated by the recent Civil War, as Confederate sympathizers sheltered and abetted Booth. On April 26, trapped in a barn and surrounded by cavalry troops, Booth refused to surrender and was killed.

Where it's reviewed:
The American Spectator, April 2006, page 63
Kirkus Reviews, December 1, 2005, page 1270
Library Journal, January 1, 2006, page 135
New York Times, March 9, 2006, page E9
Publishers Weekly, December 12, 2005, page 51

Other books by the same author:
Bloody Crimes: The Chase for Jefferson Davis and the Death Pageant for Lincoln's Corpse, 2010
Chasing Lincoln's Killer, 2009
Lincoln's Assassins: Their Trial and Execution, 2008

Other books you might like:
Thomas J. Craughwell, *Stealing Lincoln's Body*, 2007
Timothy S. Good, *We Saw Lincoln Shot: One Hundred Eyewitness Accounts*, 1996
Michael W. Kauffman, *American Brutus: John Wilkes Booth and the Lincoln Conspiracies*, 2004
Gordon Samples, *Lust for Fame: The Stage Career of John Wilkes Booth*, 1983
Edward Steers Jr., *Blood on the Moon: The Assassination of Abraham Lincoln*, 2010

860

STEPHAN TALTY

Empire of Blue Water: Captain Morgan's Great Pirate Army, the Epic Battle for the Americas, and the Catastrophe That Ended the Outlaws' Bloody Reign

(New York: Crown Publishing, 2007)

Subject(s): Pirates; Biographies; History

Summary: In *Empire of Blue Water: Captain Morgan's Great Pirate Army, the Epic Battle for the Americas, and the Catastrophe That Ended the Outlaws' Bloody Reign*, author Stephan Talty looks at the history of privateering and specifically the reign of Henry Morgan, one of the most famous pirates of the Caribbean. Commissioned by Britain's King Charles II, Morgan's quest was to end the Spaniards' control of the Caribbean and establish the British Empire in the Western world. Captain Morgan swiftly defeated the Spanish empire on several fronts, earning himself tremendous wealth, British knighthood, and eventually the position of deputy governor of Jamaica.

Where it's reviewed:
Biography, Summer 2007, page 436
Kirkus Reviews, February 1, 2007, page 117
Library Journal, April 1, 2007, page 100
New York Times Book Review, June 3, 2007, page 28
Publishers Weekly, February 5, 2007, page 51

Other books by the same author:
Escape from the Land of Snows: The Young Dalai Lama's Harrowing Flight to Freedom and the Making of a Spiritual Hero, 2011
The Illustrious Dead: The Terrifying Story of How Typhus Killed Napoleon's Greatest Army, 2010
Mulatto America: At the Crossroads of Black and White Culture: A Social History, 2004

Other books you might like:
Terry Breverton, *Admiral Sir Henry Morgan: King of the Buccaneers*, 2005
Peter Earle, *The Sack of Panama: Captain Morgan and the Battle for the Caribbean*, 2007
Dan Perry, *Blackbeard: The Real Pirate of the Caribbean*, 2006
Richard Sanders, *If a Pirate I Must Be...: The True Story of 'Black Bart,' King of the Caribbean Pirates*, 2007
Colin Woodward, *The Republic of Pirates: Being the True and Surprising Story of the Caribbean Pirates and the Man Who Brought Them Down*, 2009

861

JOHN TAYMAN

The Colony: The Harrowing True Story of the Exiles of Molokai

(New York: Scribner, 2006)

Subject(s): Medical care; History; Diseases

Summary: In *The Colony: The Harrowing True Story of the Exiles of Molokai*, author John Tayman tells the story of the most famous leper colony in the world, which was located on the Hawaiian island of Molokai. Chosen because of its remote site, the colonization of Molokai marked the first time that outside illnesses would set foot on Hawaiian land. Tayman looks at the history of the colony from its inception in 1866 until it was dismantled in 1969 and the social and mental effects it had on those who lived there.

Where it's reviewed:
Booklist, November 1, 2005, page 10
JAMA: Journal of American Medical Association, June 21, 2006, page 2793
Kirkus Reviews, October 1, 2005, page 1071
New England Journal of Medicine, September 7, 2006, page 1075
New York Times Book Review, January 22, 2006., page 12

Other books you might like:
Milton Bloombaum, *The Separating Sickness, Mai Ho'oka'wale: Interviews with Exiled Leprosy Patients at Kalaupapa, Hawaii*, 1996
Alan Brennert, *Moloka'i*, 2003
Gavan Daws, *Holy Man: Father Damien of Molokai*, 1989
Ted Gugelyk, *The Separating Sickness, Mai Ho'oka'wale: Interviews with Exiled Leprosy Patients at Kalaupapa, Hawaii*, 1996
Henry Kalalahilimoku, *No Footprints in the Sand: A Memoir of Kalaupapa*, 2006
Michelle Therese Moran, *Colonizing Leprosy: Imperialism and the Politics of Public Health in the United States*, 2007

862

EVAN THOMAS

Sea of Thunder: Four Commanders and the Last Great Naval Campaign 1941-1945

(New York: Simon & Schuster, 2006)

Subject(s): History; War; World War II

Summary: *Newsweek* assistant editor Evan Thomas recounts the story of the Battle of Leyte Gulf from the viewpoints of four naval officers: Americans Admiral William Halsey and Commander Ernest Evans, and Japanese Admirals Takeo Kurita and Matome Ugaki.

Thomas interviewed Imperial Japanese Navy veterans who survived the battle as well as friends and family of the admirals.

Where it's reviewed:
Booklist, November 15, 2006, page 22
Library Journal, November 1, 2006, page 88
Publishers Weekly, August 7, 2006, page 41

Other books by the same author:
The War Lovers: Roosevelt, Lodge, Hearst, and the Rush to Empire, 1898, 2010
The Very Best Men: The Daring Early Years of the CIA, 2006
John Paul Jones: Sailor, Hero, Father of the American Navy, 2004

Other books you might like:
Alan Burn, *The Fighting Commodores: The Convoy Commanders in the Second World War*, 1999
William Donald, *Stand by for Action: The Memoirs of a Small Ship Commander in World War II*, 2009
Samuel Eliot, *Two-Ocean War: A Short History of the United States Navy in the Second World War*, 2007
James D. Hornfischer, *The Last Stand of the Tin Can Sailors:The Extraordinary World War II Story of the U.S. Navy's Finest Hour*, 2005
John F. Wukovits, *Admiral Bull Halsey: The Life and Wars of the Navy's Most Controversial Commanders*, 2010

863

IAN W. TOLL

Six Frigates: The Epic History of the Founding of the U.S. Navy
(New York: W.W. Norton & Co., 2009)

Subject(s): United States. Navy; Military life; Shipbuilding

Summary: In *Six Frigates: The Epic History of the Founding of the U.S. Navy*, author Ian Toll looks at the very beginning of naval military history in the United States. Toll begins with the dawn of the Navy in the 1770s and continues until the War of 1812, when the U.S. Navy was well and fully established. The author also reviews the expense of constructing and maintaining a navy as well as the historical figures who played majors roles in the Navy's formation. Toll particularly examines the political divide that existed between Republicans and Federalists at the cost of building such a military defense.

Where it's reviewed:
The Economist, November 4, 2006, page 94
Journal of the Early Republic, Summer 2007, page 365
Kirkus Reviews, August 15, 2006, page 831
Library Journal, September 15, 2006, page 73
Naval War College Review, Winter 2008, page 129

Other books you might like:
James C. Bradford, *Quarterdeck and Bridge: Two Centuries of American Naval Leaders*, 1996
George C. Daughan, *If By Sea: The Forging of the*

American Navy, from the Revolution to the War of 1812, 2008
Stephen Howarth, *To Shining Sea: A History of the United States Navy, 1775-1998*, 1991
Nathan Miller, *The U.S. Navy: A History*, 1997
Craig Symonds, *The Naval Institute Historical Atlas of the U.S. Navy*, 1995

864

HARRY S. TRUMAN
DEAN ACHESON , Co-Author

Affection and Trust: The Personal Correspondence of Harry S. Truman and Dean Acheson, 1953-1971
(New York: Alfred A. Knopf, 2010)

Subject(s): Letters (Correspondence); United States history; Presidents (Government)

Summary: Edited by Dr. Ray Geselbracht and David C. Acheson, *Affection and Trust: The Personal Correspondence of Harry S. Truman and Dean Acheson, 1953-1971* is a collection of letters between the former United States president and his secretary of state. Following the end of their political terms, Truman and Acheson remained friends and kept in touch via written correspondence. The two men began corresponding shortly after leaving office and, over the course of nearly two decades, became close friends. These letters, published here for the first time, shed light on Truman and Acheson's opinions on major world events while describing the two men's personal experiences and family matters.

Where it's reviewed:
Publishers Weekly, October 4, 2010, page 40

Other books by the same author:
Defending the West: The Truman-Churchill Correspondence, 2004
Dear Bess: The Letters from Harry to Bess Truman, 1910-1959, 1998
Where the Buck Stops: The Personal and Private Writings of Harry S. Truman, 1990

Other books you might like:
Robert Dallek, *Harry S. Truman*, 2008
D.M. Giangreco, *Dear Harry...: Truman's Mailroom, 1945-1953: The Truman Administration Through Correspondence with*, 1999
David G. Mccullough, *Truman*, 1992
Kathryn Moore, *Dear Harry...: Truman's Mailroom, 1945-1953: The Truman Administration Through Correspondence with*, 1999
Harry S. Truman, *Defending the West: The Truman-Churchill Correspondence, 1945-1960*, 2004

Harry S. Truman, *Where the Buck Stops: The Personal and Private Writings of Harry S. Truman*, 1989

865

NICHOLAS WADE

Before the Dawn: Recovering the Lost History of Our Ancestors

(New York: Penguin Press, 2006)

Subject(s): Evolution (Biology); Human behavior; Archaeology

Summary: Nicholas Wade, a science reporter for the *New York Times*, uses recent genetic research to explore the origins of humanity in *Before the Dawn: Recovering the Lost History of Our Ancestors*. Wade chronicles Homo sapiens' early history, from their first appearance in Africa some 50,000 years ago to their conquest of the modern world. The author discusses early humans' relations with the Neanderthals and Homo erectus. Wade also describes how languages developed and explains how people eventually domesticated animals. The author examines the social behaviors, cultural beliefs, and practices of these people from an evolutionary viewpoint. This approach combines genetics with findings from linguistics, archaeology, and paleontology in an attempt to understand how humans developed.

Where it's reviewed:
American Scientist, September/October 2006, page 472
Discover, July 2006, page 64
New York Review of Books, September 21, 2006, page 18
New York Times Book Review, June 11, 2006, page 28
Science, July 14, 2006, page 174

Other books by the same author:
The Faith Instinct: How Religion Evolved and Why It Endures, 2009
Life Script: How the Human Genome Discoveries Will Transform Medicine and Enhance Your Health, 2002
Betrayers of the Truth, 1985

Other books you might like:
David W. Anthony, *The Horse, the Wheel, and Language: How Bronze-Age Riders from the Eurasian Steppes Shaped the Modern World*, 2007
Gregory Cochran, *The 10,000 Year Explosion: How Civilization Accelerated Human Evolution*, 2009
Steven Mithen, *After the Ice: A Global Human History, 20,000-5000 B.C.*, 2004
Linda Stone, *Genes, Culture, and Human Evolution: A Synthesis*, 2006
Spencer Wells, *Deep Ancestry: Inside the Genographic Project*, 2006

866

WENDY WALL

Inventing the "American Way": The Politics of Consensus from the New Deal to the Civil Rights Movement

(Oxford; New York: Oxford University Press, 2008)

Subject(s): Americana; Cultural identity; Politics

Summary: Wendy Wall's *Inventing the American Way: The Politics of Consensus from the New Deal to the Civil Rights Movement* describes the development of American ideals throughout the mid-20th century and explains how these ideals have become ingrained in the American conscience. Wall examines the patriotism that resulted after the Allies won World War II and the subsequent postwar prosperity. Although this was an important era for American ideology, Wall believes the principles that defined what it means to be a true American were established long before the United States' involvement in World War II. Wall provides a historical perspective of the changing traditions and cultural makeup of the United States throughout the 20th century and beyond.

Where it's reviewed:
American Historical Review, February 2010, page 248
Business History Review, Spring 2009, page 193
Journal of American History, June 2009, page 266
Reviews in American History, September 2008, page 449

Other books by the same author:
Study Guide: For Inventing America: A History of the United States, Second Edition (Vol. 2), 2006

Other books you might like:
Taylor Branch, *At Canaan's Edge: America in the King Years, 1965-1968*, 2006
Lizabeth Cohen, *A Consumers' Republic: The Politics of Mass Consumption in Postwar America*, 2003
Morris Dickstein, *Dancing in the Dark: A Cultural History of the Great Depression*, 2009
David Goldfield, *20th Century America: A Social and Political History*, 2004
Kim Phillips-Fein, *Invisible Hands: The Businessmen's Crusade Against the New Deal*, 2009

867

LAURA DASSOW WALLS

The Passage to Cosmos: Alexander von Humboldt and the Shaping of America

(Chicago: University of Chicago Press, 2009)

Subject(s): Science; Nature; Ecology

Summary: Alexander von Humboldt was a legendary

writer, scientist, and explorer whose ideas about the human relationship with nature influenced some of the world's greatest minds. In *The Passage to Cosmos: Alexander von Humboldt and the Shaping of America*, author Laura Dassow Walls recounts von Humboldt's journey to America in 1799, where he researched and laid the groundwork for his seminal book, *Cosmos*. This journey would forever alter attitudes about nature, ecology, and the role of humans in the natural world. *The Passage to Cosmos* includes a bibliography and a full index.

Where it's reviewed:
Biography, Spring 2010, page 443
Times Higher Education, December 31, 2009, page 56
Virginia Quarterly Review, Spring 2010, page 221

Other books by the same author:
Emerson's Life in Science: The Culture of Truth, 2003
Seeing New Worlds: Henry David Thoreau and Nineteenth-Century Natural Science, 1995

Other books you might like:
Gerard Helferich, *Humboldt's Cosmos: Alexander von Humboldt and the Epic Journey of Exploration through Latin America That Changed the Way We See the World*, 2004
Alexander von Humboldt, *Personal Narrative of a Journey to the Equinoctial Regions of the New Continent: Abridged Edition*, 1996
Daniel Kehlmann, *Measuring the World: A Novel*, 2006
Nicolaas A. Rupke, *Alexander von Humboldt: A Metabiography*, 2005
Aaron Sachs, *The Humboldt Current: Nineteenth-Century Exploration and the Roots of American Environmentalism*, 1995

868

LOUIS S. WARREN

Buffalo Bill's America: William Cody and the Wild West Show
(New York: Knopf, 2005)

Subject(s): Biographies; History; Wild west shows

Summary: *Buffalo Bill's America: William Cody and the Wild West Show* is Louis S. Warren's biography of the famous cowboy showman. Warren depicts Cody as a genius for using his shows to appeal to the public's sense of a changing America. While Warren concurs that Cody was a bit of an ego-driven showoff, he also provides another, more sympathetic, dimension to his personality by citing his genuine love of people and his generosity. In a series of essays, Warren argues a variety of theories that deal with Cody's connectedness to different aspects of culture. For example, Warren asserts that Cody influenced Bram Stroker's *Dracula*. He also explains that Cody's shows may have symbolized the growing conflict between labor and management in the early 20th century.

Where it's reviewed:
Biography, Winter 2006, page 208

Booklist, September 15, 2005, page 23
Kirkus Reviews, August 1, 2005, page 839
Library Journal, September 15, 2005, page 76
Publishers Weekly, August 1, 2005, page 54

Other books by the same author:
The Hunter's Game: Poachers and Conservationists in Twentieth-Century America, 1999

Other books you might like:
Robert A. Carter, *Buffalo Bill Cody: The Man Behind the Legend*, 2002
William F. Cody, *Buffalo Bill's Life Story: An Autobiography*, 2010
Chris Enss, *The Many Loves of Buffalo Bill: The True Story of Life on the Wild West Show*, 2010
Steve Friesen, *Buffalo Bill: Scout, Showman, Visionary*, 2010
Isabelle S. Sayers, *Annie Oakley and Buffalo Bill's Wild West*, 1981

869

RICK WARTZMAN

Obscene in the Extreme: The Burning and Banning of John Steinbeck's The Grapes of Wrath
(New York: PublicAffairs, 2008)

Subject(s): Literature; Censorship; Freedom of speech

Summary: In *Obscene in the Extreme: The Burning and Banning of John Steinbeck's* The Grapes of Wrath, author Rick Wartzman looks at the history of literary censorship in the United States. Wartzman especially examines this practice as it pertained to Steinbeck's literary classic *The Grapes of Wrath*, a novel that explored the impact of the Great Depression on an Oklahoman family fleeing the Dust Bowl. The banning of this book, Wartzman explains, was at the behest of California growers who were guilty of perpetrating the same exploitative measures Steinbeck described in his novel. According to Wartzman, these growers hid behind the coarse language of Steinbeck's narrative in an effort to quash the novel's message.

Where it's reviewed:
Booklist, September 15, 2008, page 13
Columbia Journalism Review, November/December 2008, page 65
Library Journal, September 15, 2008, page 56
Mother Jones, September/October 2008, page 97
Pacific Historical Review, November 2009, page 661

Other books you might like:
Paul S. Boyer, *Purity in Print: Book Censorship in America from the Gilded Age to the Computer Age*, 2002
Marjorie Heins, *Not in Front of the Children: 'Indecency,' Censorship, and the Innocence of Youth*, 2001
Nicholas J. Karolides, *120 Banned Books: Censorship Histories of World Literature*, 2005

Lucien X. Polastron, *Books on Fire: The Destruction of Libraries Throughout History*, 2007

John Steinbeck, *The Harvest Gypsies: On the Road to the Grapes of Wrath*, 1988
Charles Wollenberg, co-author

870

HARRIET A. WASHINGTON

Medical Apartheid: The Dark History of Medical Experimentation on Black Americans from Colonial Times to the Present

(New York: Doubleday, 2007)

Subject(s): African Americans; Science experiments (Education); Medicine

Summary: *Medical Apartheid: The Dark History of Medical Experimentation on Black Americans from Colonial Times to the Present* by scholar, author, and journalist Harriet A. Washington exposes a long history of questionable, unethical, and abusive medical experimentation on African Americans. Washington discusses particular instances throughout history and exposes a racial inequity based on class, economics, and education. Washington maintains that this type of cruelty toward people of color has a long history and is now branching out to communities in Africa and South America, where many people of color are considered prime subjects for medical experimentation.

Where it's reviewed:
Black Issues Book Review, January/February 2007, page 36
Journal of African American History, Winter 2009, page 101
New York Times Book Review, February 18, 2007, page 18
Newsweek, February 12, 2007, page 49
Reviews in American History, September 2009, page 386

Other books by the same author:
Living Healthy with Hepatitis C: Natural and Conventional Approaches to Recover Your Quality of Life, 2001

Other books you might like:
Fred D. Gray, *The Tuskegee Syphilis Study: The Real Story and Beyond*, 2005
James H. Jones, *Bad Blood: The Tuskegee Syphilis Experiment, New and Expanded Edition*, 1993
Thomas Alexis LaVeist, *Race, Ethnicity, and Health: A Public Health Reader*, 2002
Susan Reverby, *Examining Tuskegee: The Infamous Syphilis Study and Its Legacy*, 2009

Michael Winkelman, *Culture and Health: Applying Medical Anthropology*, 2008

871

BRUCE WATSON

Bread and Roses: Mills, Migrants, and the Struggle for the American Dream

(New York: Penguin, 2005)

Subject(s): Migrant labor; Labor movement; Immigrants

Summary: In *Bread and Roses: Mills, Migrants, and the Struggle for the American Dream*, author Bruce Watson explores the beginnings of the labor movement in the United States and the way one particular labor strike shaped that movement. In the book, Watson describes a 1912 strike that took place at a mill in Lawrence, Massachusetts. Watson describes the situation surrounding the strike, and he examines the motivations of the mill workers as well as the mill owners. Watson is also the author of *Freedom Summer: The Savage Season that Made Mississippi Burn and Made America a Democracy* and *Sacco and Vanzetti: The Men, the Murders, and the Judgment of Mankind*.

Where it's reviewed:
The Historian, Winter 2006, page 851
Journal of American History, June 2006, page 255
Kirkus Reviews, June 1, 2005, page 630
New England Quarterly, June 2006, page 339
New York Times Book Review, August 28, 2005, page 18

Other books by the same author:
Freedom Summer: The Savage Season That Made Mississippi Burn and Made America a Democracy, 2010
Sacco and Vanzetti: The Men, the Murders, and the Judgment of Mankind, 2007
Man Who Changed How Boys and Toys Were Made: The Life and Times of A.C. Gilbert, the Man Who Saved Christmas, 2002

Other books you might like:
Mary H. Blewitt, *The Last Generation: Work and Life in the Textile Mills of Lowell, Massachusetts, 1910-1960*, 1990
Benita Eisler, *The Lowell Offering: Writings by New England Mill Women (1840-1945)*, 1977
William Moran, *The Belles of New England: The Women of the Textile Mills and the Families Whose Wealth They Wove*, 2004
John A. Salmond, *Gastonia 1929: The Story of the Loray Mill Strike*, 1995
Philip Scranton, *Figured Tapestry: Production, Markets and Power in Philadelphia Textiles, 1855-1941*, 2002

872

TIM WEINER

Legacy of Ashes: The History of the CIA

(New York: Random House, 2007)

Subject(s): Cold War; Espionage; Government

Summary: *New York Times* correspondent Tim Weiner presents a complete history of the CIA from its formation by Harry Truman after World War II to its post-9/11 operations. This history is based on 50,000 documents, many of which are declassified CIA archives, and 300 interviews, including 10 with former CIA directors. In this account, Weiner argues that the CIA has repeatedly failed in its mission to understand the world, pointing out that the agency has not once anticipated a major world event, including the Korean War, the fall of the Soviet Union, and the attacks of 9/11. Often a lack of leadership, misdirected or misused resources, and arrogance were to blame; in other cases, the chief executive insisted on specific intelligence. Weiner maintains that the CIA's focus on covert activities has led the agency away from its purpose: to discover your adversary's intentions. The CIA should not be dismantled, he argues, but redirected.

Where it's reviewed:
American Spectator, September 2007, page 73
The Economist, August 18, 2007, page 72
Foreign Affairs, March/April 2008, page 138
The Nation, July 14, 2008, page 57
New York Times Book Review, July 22, 2007, page 11

Other books by the same author:
Betrayal: The Story of Aldrich Ames, an American Spy, 1995
Blank Check: The Pentagon's Black Budget, 1991

Other books you might like:
Steve Coll, *Ghost Wars: The Secret History of the CIA, Afghanistan, and Bin Laden, from the Soviet Invasion to September 10, 2001*, 2004
Charles Faddis, *Beyond Repair: The Decline and Fall of the CIA*, 2010
Ishmael Jones, *The Human Factor: Inside the CIA's Dysfunctional Intelligence Culture*, 2008
H. Keith Melton, *Spycraft: The Secret History of the CIA's Spytechs, from Communism to al-Qaeda*, 2008
    Henry Robert Schlesinger, co-author
    Robert Wallace, co-author

873

CHRIS WICKHAM

Framing the Early Middle Ages: Europe and the Mediterranean, 400-800

(New York: Oxford University Press USA, 2005)

Subject(s): Middle Ages; History; Roman Empire, 30 BC-476 AD

Summary: *Framing the Early Middle Ages: Europe and the Mediterranean, 400-800*, written by historian Chris Wickham, is a comprehensive analysis of the early Medieval period from 400 to 800 A.D. Wickham how this time period helped frame the Middle Ages. The author explores the social, physical, and economic changes that occurred after the Roman Empire fell and regions began to retain their own identities. Wickham is also the author of *The Inheritance of Rome: A History of Europe from 400 to 1000* and Early Medieval Italy; Central Power and Local Society, 400-1000.

Where it's reviewed:
Antiquity, March 2007, page 191
Economic History Review, May 2006, page 417
New Republic, July 30, 2008, page 42
Speculum: A Journal of Medieval Studies, April 2010, page 481
Women's Studies, March 2007, page 135

Other books by the same author:
The Inheritance of Rome: A History of Europe from 400 to 1000, 2010
Courts and Conflict in Twelfth-Century Tuscany, 2004
Constructing Heimat in Postwar Germany: Longing and Belonging, 1999

Other books you might like:
Peter Brown, *The Rise of Western Christendom: Triumph and Diversity, A.D. 200-1000*, 2003
P.J. Heather, *Empires and Barbarians: The Fall of Rome and the Birth of Europe*, 2010
Rosamond McKitterick, *The Early Middle Ages: Europe 400-1000*, 2001
Lynette Olson, *The Early Middle Ages: The Birth of Europe*, 2007
Julia Smith, *Europe After Rome: A New Cultural History, 500-1000*, 2005

874

TOM WIENER

Forever a Soldier: Unforgettable Stories of Wartime Service

(Washington, DC: National Geographic, 2005)

Subject(s): Wars; Military life; United States history

Summary: *Forever a Soldier: Unforgettable Stories of Wartime Service* is the second volume in the Library of Congress Veterans History Project, which also includes *Voice of War*. Written by Thomas Wiener, this volume discusses veterans who participated in military conflicts from the World War II era through to the Persian Gulf War of 1991. The author interviews such notable military figures as Rhonda Corum, a Prisoner of War during the Persian Gulf War, and Arizona Senator John McCain, a Prisoner of War during the Vietnam War. Wiener also features interviews with individuals who were innovative in their fields of expertise.

Where it's reviewed:
Booklist, November 1, 2005, page 7
Library Journal, November 1, 2005, page 99

Publishers Weekly, September 19, 2005, page 57

Other books by the same author:
The Off-Hollywood Film Guide: The Definitive Guide to Independent and Foreign Films on Video and DVD, 2002
Book of Video Lists 1991, Third Edition, 1990

Other books you might like:
Stephen E. Ambrose, *Band of Brothers: E Company, 506th Regiment, 101st Airborne: from Normandy to Hitler's Eagle's Nest*, 1992
Nathaniel Fick, *One Bullet Away: The Making of a Marine Officer*, 2005
Joseph L. Galloway, *We Were Soldiers Once...and Young: Ia Drang—The Battle That Changed the War in Vietnam*, 1992
Harold G. Moore, co-author
Craig M. Mullaney, *The Unforgiving Minute: A Soldier's Education*, 2009
Hampton Sides, *Ghost Soldiers: The Forgotten Epic Story of World War II's Most Dramatic Mission*, 2001

875

SEAN WILENTZ

The Rise of American Democracy: Jefferson to Lincoln

(New York: Norton, 2005)

Subject(s): United States history; Politics; American Revolution, 1775-1783

Summary: Author and historian Sean Wilentz chronicles the birth of democracy in the United States and its evolution from the years of the Revolutionary War to the Civil War. *The Rise of American Democracy: Jefferson to Lincoln* focuses on the defining political moments of these years, which instituted the framework for modern democratic thought and principles. Wilentz further probes the subject by looking at various social initiatives that advanced the cause of democracy to make it a cornerstone of American society. *The Rise of American Democracy* includes illustrations, notes on the text, and an index.

Where it's reviewed:
Journal of American History, September 2006, page 491
The Nation, October 31, 2005, page 23
New York Times, October 22, 2005, page 137
New York Times Book Review, November 13, 2005, page 10
Newsweek, October 31, 2005, page 56

Other books by the same author:
Bob Dylan in America, 2010
The Age of Reagan: A History, 1974-2008, 2008
Andrew Jackson, 2005

Other books you might like:
Daniel Walker Howe, *What Hath God Wrought: The Transformation of America, 1815-1848*, 2007
Gary B. Nash, *The Unknown American Revolution: The*

Unruly Birth of Democracy and the Struggle to Create America, 2005
David Waldstreicher, *In the Midst of Perpetual Fetes: The Making of American Nationalism, 1776-1820*, 1997
Harry L. Watson, *Liberty and Power: The Politics of Jacksonian America*, 1990
Gordon S. Wood, *Empire of Liberty: A History of the Early Republic, 1789-1815*, 2009

876

CALLIE WILLIAMSON

The Laws of the Roman People: Public Law in the Expansion and Decline of the Roman Republic

(Ann Arbor, Michigan: University of Michigan Press, 2005)

Subject(s): Roman Empire, 30 BC-476 AD; Law; History

Summary: In *The Laws of the Roman People: Public Law in the Expansion and Decline of the Roman Republic*, author Callie Williamson looks at the development of law and order in the Roman Empire. Williamson explores the public policies that helped shape the empire and the manner in which civil discourse helped the empire expand. In the book Williamson contends that the very end of the Roman Empire could be attributed to this quest for development as policies and laws contributed to the collapse of the Roman society.

Where it's reviewed:
American Historical Review, October 2006, page 1237
Classical Review, April 2007, page 170
Journal of Interdisciplinary History, Autumn 2006, page 265
Law and Social Inquiry, Winter 2006, page 114

Other books you might like:
George Willis Botsford, *The Roman Assemblies from Their Origin to the End of the Republic*, 2001
Cicero Cicero, *The Republic and the Laws*, 2009
Daniel J. Gargola, *Land, Laws, & Gods*, 1995
A.W. Lintott, *The Constitution of the Roman Republic*, 2003
Philip Matyszak, *Chronicle of the Roman Republic: The Rulers of Ancient Rome from Romulus to Augustus*, 2003

877

GARRY WILLS

Henry Adams and the Making of America

(New York: Houghton Mifflin Harcourt, 2005)

Subject(s): United States history; Biographies; United States

Summary: Garry Wills's *Henry Adams and the Making of*

America is a biography of American writer Henry Adams, who authored *The Education of Henry Adams*. This book explores Adams's influence on American history. Adams was the grandson of John Quincy Adams, the sixth president of the United States, and the great grandson of John Adams, the second president of the United States. With such a political history in his family's background, Henry Adams was destined to have a place in American history. Wills tells of how Adams brought internationalism into the public's conscience and introduced the United States to a new form of public policies.

Where it's reviewed:
American Scholar, Summer 2006, page 14
Foreign Affairs, January/February 2006, page 153
Kirkus Reviews, July 15, 2005, page 784
National Review, December 31, 2005, page 45
Parameters, Autumn 2007, page 125

Other books by the same author:
Outside Looking In: Adventures of an Observer, 2010
Nixon Agonistes: The Crisis of the Self-Made Man, 2002
Lincoln at Gettysburg: The Words That Remade America, 1992

Other books you might like:
Henry Adams, *The Jeffersonian Transformation: Passages from the 'History'*, 2006
Edward Chalfant, *Improvement of the World: A Biography of Henry Adams, His Last Life, 1891-1918*, 2001
David R. Contosta, *Henry Adams and His World*, 1993 Robert Muccigrosso, co-author
Ernest Samuels, *Henry Adams*, 1989
Natalie Fuehrer Taylor, *A Political Companion to Henry Adams*, 2010
Garry Wills, *The Jeffersonian Transformation: Passages from the 'History'*, 2006

878

JAY WINIK

The Great Upheaval: America and the Birth of the Modern World, 1788-1800

(New York: HarperCollins, 2007)

Subject(s): American History; French Revolution; Ottoman Empire

Summary: Evacuation Day, November 25, 1783, the final British troops ship out from New York harbor. Pandemonium breaks out in the streets. It is a new beginning for the now independent America. It is a time of great change elsewhere in the world too. The end of the century sees the world power, France, thrown into a bloody revolution of its own. Russia becomes a great power by defeating the Ottoman Empire. Winik does not describe these wars in isolation, but as critically related events that change the course of world history.

Where it's reviewed:
American History, February 2008, page 21
American Spectator, May 2008, page 68
Foreign Affairs, November/December 2007, page 43
New York Review of Books, November 18, 2007, page 32
New York Times Book Review, September 30, 2007, page 24

Other books by the same author:
April 1865: The Month That Saved America, 2006
On the Brink: The Dramatic Behind the Scenes Saga of the Reagan Era and the Men and Women Who Won the Cold War, 1996

Other books you might like:
Joseph J. Ellis, *American Creation: Triumphs and Tragedies at the Founding of the Republic*, 2007
Daniel Walker Howe, *What Hath God Wrought: The Transformation of America, 1815-1848*, 2007
David Stewart, *The Summer of 1787: The Men Who Invented the Constitution*, 2007
Sean Wilentz, *The Rise of American Democracy: Jefferson to Lincoln*, 2005
Gordon S. Wood, *Empire of Liberty: A History of the Early Republic, 1789-1815*, 2009

879

AMY LOUISE WOOD

Lynching and Spectacle: Witnessing Racial Violence in America, 1890-1940

(Chapel Hill, North Carolina: University of North Carolina Press, 2009)

Subject(s): United States history; Race relations; Violence

Summary: Racially motivated violence played a powerful, devastating role in American race relations in the 19th and early 20th centuries. In *Lynching and Spectacle: Witnessing Racial Violence in America, 1890-1940*, historian Amy Louise Wood explores this disturbing trend, which helped establish a white superiority and a culture of civil unrest. Wood's examination looks at the defining factors that instigated such violence as well as the painful legacy it has left on the nation. *Lynching and Spectacle* includes notes on the text, a bibliography, and a full index.

Where it's reviewed:
American Historical Review, December 2009, page 1473
CHOICE: Current Reviews for Academic Libraries, September 2009, page 187
Journal of American History, March 2010, page 1200
Journal of Interdisciplinary History, Autumn 2010, page 318

Other books you might like:
Dora Apel, *Imagery of Lynching: Black Men, White Women, and the Mob*, 2004
Philip Dray, *At the Hands of Persons Unknown: The Lynching of Black America*, 2002

Crystal N. Feimster, *Southern Horrors: Women and the Politics of Rape and Lynching*, 2009

James H. Madison, *A Lynching in the Heartland: Race and Memory in America*, 2003

Anne P. Rice, *Witnessing Lynching: American Writers Respond*, 2003

880

GORDON S. WOOD

Empire of Liberty: A History of the Early Republic, 1789-1815

(New York: Oxford University Press, 2009)

Subject(s): United States history; Politics; Law

Summary: In *Empire of Liberty: A History of the Early Republic, 1789-1815*, historian Gordon S. Wood describes the early years of the United States following the American Revolution. Wood documents the political, cultural, societal, and economical shifts that occurred during this period in history. He examines republican and federalist views, American expansion into the West, American involvement in the French Revolution, and, ultimately, the War of 1812 against the British. *Empire of Liberty* is part of the Pulitzer Prize-winning Oxford History of the United States series. Wood, author of the *The Radicalism of the American Revolution*, also a Pulitzer Prize winner, is one of the United States' most renowned historians.

Where it's reviewed:

History: Review of New Books, July 2010, page 84

The Nation, February 1, 2010, page 33

New York Review of Books, March 25, 2010, page 29

New York Times Book Review, November 29, 2009, page 12

Other books by the same author:

The Americanization of Benjamin Franklin, 2005

The Creation of the American Republic, 1776-1787, 1998

The Radicalism of the American Revolution, 1993

Other books you might like:

Joseph J. Ellis, *American Creation: Triumphs and Tragedies at the Founding of the Republic*, 2007

Daniel Walker Howe, *What Hath God Wrought: The Transformation of America, 1815-1848*, 2007

Reeve Huston, *The Early American Republic: A History in Documents*, 2010

Gary B. Nash, *The Unknown American Revolution: The Unruly Birth of Democracy and the Struggle to Create America*, 2005

David Waldstreicher, *In the Midst of Perpetual Fetes: The Making of American Nationalism, 1776-1820*, 1997

881

STEVEN E. WOODWORTH

Nothing But Victory: The Army of the Tennessee, 1861-1865

(New York: Knopf, 2005)

Story type: Historical - American Civil War

Subject(s): Civil war; United States Civil War, 1861-1865; United States history

Summary: In *Nothing But Victory: The Army of the Tennessee, 1861-1865*, author and historian Steven E. Woodworth shares details about one of the armies that helped win the Civil War. The Army of Tennessee was formed in the summer of 1861 under the direction of Ulysses S. Grant. From the start, the army was strong and won many battles, defeating the Confederates at Fort Henry, Shiloh, Vicksburg, and even Fort Donelson. In *Nothing But Victory*, Woodworth explains how the army survived the brutal winter of 1863 and went on to ultimately win the Civil War for the North.

Where it's reviewed:

Booklist, October 1, 2005, page 21

New York Review of Books, December 15, 2005, page 46

Publishers Weekly, September 5, 2005, page 46

Other books by the same author:

Manifest Destinies: America's Westward Expansion and the Road to the Civil War, 2010

Beneath a Northern Sky: A Short History of the Gettysburg Campaign, 2008

A Scythe of Fire: A Civil War Story of the Eighth Georgia Infantry Regiment, 2002

Other books you might like:

Peter Cozzens, *This Terrible Sound: The Battle of Chickamauga*, 1992

Edward Cunningham, *Shiloh and the Western Campaign of 1862*, 2007

Larry J. Daniel, *Days of Glory: The Army of the Cumberland, 1861-1865*, 2004

Stephen W. Sears, *Chancellorsville*, 1996

Noah Andre Trudeau, *Southern Storm: Sherman's March to the Sea*, 2008

882

LAWRENCE WRIGHT

The Looming Tower: Al-Qaeda and the Road to 9/11

(New York: Vintage, 2006)

Subject(s): Current Affairs; Islam; Politics

Summary: *New Yorker* staff writer Lawrence Wright presents a history of Islamic fundamentalism and terrorism through five years of interviews and research. He draws portraits of four men linked to the 9/11 attacks: Osama bin Laden, Ayman al-Zawahiri, FBI agent John

O'Neill, and Prince Turki al-Faisal, former head of Saudi intelligence. He presents the early days of Al-Qaeda through the bombings of the U.S. embassies in Tanzania and Kenya and the *U.S.S. Cole*, events that led to an influx of money and recruits for the organization. Wright also demonstrates that the 9/11 attacks could have been prevented had federal agencies worked together. Finally, Wright concludes that although bin Laden's influence has faded, several imitators have appeared since 9/11.

Where it's reviewed:
Commonweal, December 1, 2006, page 24
National Review, September 11, 2006, page 46
New York Review of Books, October 19, 2006, page 12
New York Times, August 1, 2006, page E6
New York Times Book Review, August 6, 2006, page 1

Other books by the same author:
God's Favorite: A Novel, 2007
Twins: And What They Tell Us About Who We Are, 1999
Remembering Satan: A Tragic Case of Recovered Memory, 1995

Other books you might like:
Stephen E. Atkins, *The 9/11 Encyclopedia*, 2008
Arnaud Blin, *The History of Terrorism: From Antiquity to Al Qaeda*, 2007
Gerard Chaliand, co-author
Steve Coll, *Ghost Wars: The Secret History of the CIA, Afghanistan, and Bin Laden, from the Soviet Invasion to September 10, 2001*, 2004
Bruce Hoffman, *Inside Terrorism*, 1998
Donald F. Kettl, *System Under Stress: Homeland Security and American Politics, 2nd Edition*, 2007

883

ROBERT E. WRIGHT

One Nation Under Debt: Hamilton, Jefferson, and the History of What We Owe

(Columbus, Ohio: McGraw-Hill, 2008)

Story type: Historical - Colonial America
Subject(s): United States history; Presidents (Government); Money

Summary: According to author Robert E. Wright, the United States has been in debt since day one. In *One Nation Under Debt: Hamilton, Jefferson, and the History of What We Owe*, Wright explains why the country has always been financially dependent on other countries. He offers insight into what past presidents, including Thomas Jefferson and Alexander Hamilton thought about debt; of these two, one believed debt was evil, while the other thought debt would only make the nation stronger. Wright tracks the country's debt from the eighteenth century to the current financial crisis and shows how it has increased and decreased in various ways.

Where it's reviewed:
American Historical Review, April 2009, page 439
Business History Review, Summer 2009, page 391
Journal of American History, December 2008, page 827

Journal of Interdisciplinary History, Summer 2009, page 114

Other books by the same author:
Bailouts: Public Money, Private Profit, 2010
Fubarnomics: A Lighthearted, Serious Look at America's Economic Ills, 2010
Financial Founding Fathers: The Men Who Made America Rich, 2006

Other books you might like:
Jeremy Atack, *A New Economic View of American History: From Colonial Times to 1940*, 1994
Ron Chernow, *Alexander Hamilton*, 2004
John Steele Gordon, *Hamilton's Blessing: The Extraordinary Life and Times of Our National Debt*, 1997
Douglass C. North, *The Economic Growth of the United States: 1790-1860*, 1966
Ronald E. Seavoy, *An Economic History of the United States: From 1607 to the Present*, 2006

884

MARILYN YALOM

The American Resting Place: Four Hundred Years of History Through Our Cemeteries and Burial Grounds

(Boston: Houghton Mifflin Harcourt, 2008)

Story type: Historical
Subject(s): United States history; Cemeteries; Death

Summary: In *The American Resting Place: Four Hundred Years of History Through Our Cemeteries and Burial Grounds*, author Marilyn Yalom and her son, Reid, explore four centuries of history found among United States' cemeteries. Featuring more than 80 photographs of gravestones and inscriptions, this book contains information about men and women from many cultures. Yalom shows how the graves of Native American descendants differ from those of Czech and African descent, for example. She compares the headstones of females and males of the 1700s to those of the 1900s. Studying the inscriptions allows Yalom to draw important connections between members of America's forgotten neighborhoods and settlements.

Where it's reviewed:
Biography, February 2008, page 812
Booklist, April 15, 2008, page 21
Library Journal, March 1, 2008, page 94
Newsweek, June 9, 2008, page 61
Publishers Weekly, March 31, 2008, page 51

Other books by the same author:
Birth of the Chess Queen: A History, 2005
History of the Breast, 1998
Blood Sisters: The French Revolution in Women's Memory, 1995

Other books you might like:
Meg Greene, *Rest in Peace: A History of American Cemeteries*, 2007
Douglas Keister, *Stories in Stone: The Complete Guide to Cemetery Symbolism*, 2004
Gary Laderman, *Rest in Peace: A Cultural History of Death and the Funeral Home in Twentieth-Century America*, 2003
Minda Powers-Douglas, *Cemetery Walk: Journey into the Art, History and Society of the Cemetery and Beyond*, 2005

885

MADELEINE ZELIN

The Merchants of Zigong: Industrial Entrepeneurship in Early Modern China

(West Sussex, England: Columbia University Press, 2006)

Subject(s): Chinese Revolution, 1911-1912; Chinese (Asian people); Business

Summary: In *The Merchants of Zigong: Industrial Entrepreneurship in Early Modern China*, Madeleine Zelin provides details about the salt trade in China from approximately 1900 to 1930. During this time, Chinese entrepreneurs built successful salt businesses and dominated trade within their own country. In this book, Zelin explores the marketing and business strategies of these merchants and the techniques they used to develop new technology to help their trade. The Sino-Japanese War halted salt production in Zigong in 1930. She is also the author of *The Magistrate's Tael: Rationalizing Fiscal Reform in Eighteenth Century Ch'ing China*.

Where it's reviewed:
American Historical Review, December 2007, page 1514
China Review International, February 2007, page 603
Far Eastern Economic Review, May 2006, page 66
Harvard Journal of Asiatic Studies, December 2007, page 485
Journal of Economic History, March 2007, page 242

Other books by the same author:
Empire, Nation, and Beyond: Chinese History in Late Imperial and Modern Times, 2006
Contract and Proptery in Early Modern China, 2004
The Magistrate's Tael: Rationalizing Fiscal Reform in Eighteenth Century Ch'ing China, 1992

Other books you might like:
Craig Clunas, *Superfluous Things: Material Culture and Social Status in Early Modern China*, 2004
Mark Elliott, *Emperor Qianlong: Son of Heaven, Man of the World*, 2009
Man Bun Kwan, *The Salt Merchants of Tianjin: State-Making and Civil Society in Late Imperial China*, 2001
Peter Allan Lorge, *War, Politics, and Society in Early Modern China, 900-1795*, 2005
F.W. Mote, *Imperial China, 900-1800*, 2000

Pop Culture

886

DIANE ACKERMAN

The Zookeeper's Wife: A War Story
(New York: W.W. Norton & Co., 2007)

Subject(s): Anti-Semitism; History; Nazis

Summary: Diane Ackerman relates the story of Warsaw Zoo director Jan Zabinski and his family during World War II. In the 1930s the Warsaw Zoo was one of the best in Europe, and Jan and Antonina Zabinski were devoted to the animals in their care. When Poland fell to the Nazis, the zoo was badly damaged. The Nazis displayed an interest in the zoo, however, because they were seeking rare animals and they wanted to resurrect extinct species. This afforded the Zabinskis some measure of protection and enabled Jan to work with the Polish Resistance. They were able to use the zoo grounds and their villa to hide three hundred Jews and to help others escape.

Where it's reviewed:
Booklist, January 1, 2008, page 6
Library Journal, September 1, 2007, page 147
Newsweek, March 3, 2008, page 213

Other books by the same author:
Dawn Light: Dancing with Cranes and Other Ways to Start the Day, 2010
An Alchemy of Mind: The Marvel and Mystery of the Brain, 2004
The Rarest of the Rare: Vanishing Animals, Timeless Worlds, 1997
A Natural History of the Senses, 1991

Other books you might like:
Diane Ackerman, *Dawn Light: Dancing with Cranes and Other Ways to Start the Day*, 2009
Michael Benanav, *Joshua and Isadora: A True Story of Love and Lost in the Holocaust*, 2008
Tatiana de Rosnay, *Sarah's Key*, 2007
Peter Duffy, *The Bielski Brothers: The True Story of Three Men Who Defied the Nazis, Built a Village in the Forest, and Saved 1,200 Jews*, 2010
Maryann Meyerhoff, *Four Girls from Berlin: The True Story of a Friendship That Defied the Holocaust*, 2007

Kathryn Stockett, *The Help*, 2009
Jack Sutin, *Jack and Rochelle: A Holocaust Story of Love and Resistance*, 1995
Rochelle Sutin, co-author
Markus Zusak, *The Book Thief*, 2006

887

JULIE ANDREWS

Home: A Memoir of My Early Years
(New York: Hyperion, 2008)

Subject(s): Autobiographies; Family relations; Theater

Summary: *Home: A Memoir of My Early Years* by Julie Andrews begins with her birth in 1935 and ends in 1962, when Walt Disney cast her as Mary Poppins. In between those years, Andrews reveals details about her difficult upbringing, which began with the divorce of her parents, living through World War II, and her mother's re-marriage to Canadian tenor Ted Andrews, and the difficult and tumultuous relationship that followed. Andrews also discusses her early acting career, her first marriage to Tony Walton, and the birth of their daughter, Emma. Her memoir details a somewhat surprising depth of tragic experiences for a woman most well known for her light and optimistic character portrayals of Mary Poppins and Maria. Andrews also shares funny anecdotes from her experiences working with actors such as Rex Harrison and Richard Burton.

Where it's reviewed:
Library Journal, March 1, 2008, page 83
Publishers Weekly, January 14, 2008, page 48

Other books by the same author:
The Very Fairy Princess, 2010
Julie Andrews' Collection of Poems, Songs, and Lullabies, 2009

Other books you might like:
Lucille Ball, *Love, Lucy*, 1996
Carol Burnett, *This Time Together: Laughter and Reflection*, 2010
Betty Hannah Hoffman, *Love, Lucy*, 1996
Mary Tyler Moore, *Growing Up Again: Life, Loves, and Oh Yeah, Diabetes*, 2009

Richard Stirling, *Julie Andrews: An Intimate Biography*, 2009

Barbara Walters, *Audition: A Memoir*, 2008

888

TARA ARIANO
SARAH D. BUNTING , Co-Author

Television Without Pity: 752 Things We Love to Hate (and Hate to Love) About TV

(Philadelphia, Pennsylvania: Quirk Books, 2006)

Subject(s): Television; Television programs; Entertainment industry

Summary: *Television Without Pity: 752 Things We Love to Hate (and Hate to Love) About TV* is written by Tara Ariano and Sarah D. Bunting, editors of the Web site TelevisionWithoutPity.com. In this book, the authors create humorous encyclopedia-style entries about popular television shows and characters, gleefully pointing out flaws and including various trivia facts for everything from popular prime-time shows to local news broadcasts. Entries such as "how to tell if you're watching a bad sitcom" and "show killers" are included as well. This book is designed for fans of snarky, irreverent humor.

Other books by the same author:
Hey! It's That Guy!, 2005
Untitled: A Bad Teen Novel, 2002

Other books you might like:
Heather Cocks, *Go Fug Yourself: The Fug Awards*, 2008
Justin Halpern, *Sh*t My Dad Says*, 2010
Christian Lander, *Stuff White People Like*, 2008
Jessica Morgan, *Go Fug Yourself: The Fug Awards*, 2008
The Onion, *Our Dumb World: The Onion's Atlas of the Planet Earth, 73rd Edition*, 2007

889

MARK BARROWCLIFFE

The Elfish Gene: Dungeons, Dragons and Growing Up Strange

(New York: Soho Press, 2008)

Subject(s): Role playing; Games; Adolescence

Summary: In *The Elfish Gene: Dungeons, Dragons and Growing Up Strange*, Mark Barrowcliffe recalls the summer of 1976, when he chose to give up sports and girls and dedicate his life to Dungeons and Dragons, the famed role-playing game. Instead of expanding his knowledge of the opposite sex, learning how to throw a ball, or exploring the streets of Britain, Barrowcliffe and a handful of friends locked themselves in bedrooms and basements and learned how write spells and roll dice. In this book, Barrowcliffe remarks on the greatest memories of his youth and some of the most awkward moments he wishes he could take back. Barrowcliffe uses the material in his book for many of his stand-up comedy skits.

Where it's reviewed:
Booklist, November 15, 2008, page 13
Entertainment Weekly, November 21, 2008, page 123
School Library Journal, February 2009, page 130

Other books by the same author:
Lucky Dog, 2006
Infidelity for First-Time Fathers, 2003
Girlfriend 44, 2000

Other books you might like:
John C. Beck, *The Kids Are Alright: How the Gamer Generation Is Changing the Workplace*, 2006
Ethan Gilsdorf, *Fantasy Freaks and Gaming Geeks: An Epic Quest for Reality Among Role Players, Online Gamers, and Other Dwellers of Imaginary Realms*, 2010
Ursula K. Le Guin, *A Wizard of Earthsea*, 1968
Shelly Mazzanoble, *Confessions of a Part-Time Sorceress: A Girl's Guide to the Dungeons & Dragons Game*, 2007
Brian Tinsman, *The Game Inventor's Guidebook: How to Invent and Sell Board Games, Card Games, Role-Playing Games, & Everything in Between!*, 2008
Mitchell Wade, *The Kids Are Alright: How the Gamer Generation Is Changing the Workplace*, 2006

890

MARIO BATALI

Spain: A Culinary Road Trip

(New York: Ecco, 2008)

Subject(s): Food; Cooking; Culture

Summary: *Spain: A Culinary Road Trip* follows celebrity chef Mario Batali and culinary extraordinaire Mark Bittman on a journey through Spain, a country rich in delicious dishes and delectable desserts. Accompanying the chefs on the trip are actresses Gwyneth Paltrow and Claudia Bassols, who share a love of food and the Spanish culture. This book includes hundreds of colorful photographs of the places the crew visited and the foods they ate as well as the scenes and people they passed and met along the way. In addition to information about Spain's landscapes and culture, this book contains more than 70 of Batali's recipes to recreate at home.

Where it's reviewed:
Entertainment Weekly, October 10, 2008, page 75

Other books by the same author:
Italian Grill, 2008
Molto Italiano, 2005
The Babbo Cookbook, 2002

Other books you might like:
Penelope Casas, *The Foods and Wines of Spain*, 1982
Matt McGinn, *Roadie: My Life on the Road with Coldplay*, 2010

891

PIERRE BAYARD

How to Talk about Books You Haven't Read

(New York: Bloomsbury USA, 2007)

Subject(s): Literature; Books; Humor

Summary: French literary professor and psychoanalyst Pierre Bayard shows readers how to hold intelligent conversations about texts they've never perused in *How to Talk about Books You Haven't Read.* Bayard explains that while reading is an important part of life, even the most devoted readers can only read so many books. Using a mixture of humor and social insight, the author explains that it is possible to understand the impact of many important texts without actually having read them. Bayard argues that knowing the details of a book, the characters' names, or the setting is not as important as understanding the role the text plays in our society. Professor Jeffery Mehlman translated Bayard's bestseller into English.

Where it's reviewed:
School Library Journal, January 2008, page 157

Other books by the same author:
Sherlock Holmes Was Wrong, 2008
Who Killed Roger Ackroyd?, 2000

Other books you might like:
Harry Frankfurt, *On Truth*, 2006
Harry G. Frankfurt, *On Bullshit*, 2005
Gary L. Hardcastle, *Bullshit and Philosophy (Popular Culture and Philosophy)*, 2006
Justine Larbalestier, *Liar*, 2009
George A. Reisch, *Bullshit and Philosophy (Popular Culture and Philosophy)*, 2006
Lauren Slater, *Lying: A Metaphorical Memoir*, 2000

892

SAMANTHA BEE

I Know I Am, but What Are You?

(New York: Gallery Books, 2010)

Subject(s): Humor; Autobiographies; Childhood

Summary: In *I Know I Am, but What Are You?* author and comedian Samantha Bee presents a series of essays that chronicle her hilarious adventures through life. From her Canadian childhood to her current role as a correspondent for *The Daily Show*, this volume charts Bee's outrageous journey, which includes a brief stint as a teenage car thief and an acting gig for which she portrayed an anime character. *I Know I Am, but What Are You?* is written with biting wit and a deep understanding of the foibles that make us human.

Where it's reviewed:
Entertainment Weekly, June 4, 2010, page 125

Other books you might like:
John Hodgman, *The Areas of My Expertise: An*

Almanac of Complete World Knowledge Compiled with Instructive Annotation and Arranged in Useful Order, 2005
John Hodgman, *More Information Than You Require*, 2009
David Rakoff, *Don't Get Too Comfortable: The Indignities of Coach Class, The Torments of Low Thread Count, The Never-Ending Quest for Artisanal Olive Oil, and Other First World Problems*, 2005
David Sedaris, *Me Talk Pretty One Day*, 2000
Eric Spitznagel, *You're a Horrible Person, but I Like You: The Believer Book of Advice*, 2010

893

MIKE BENDER
DOUG CHERNACK , Co-Author

Awkward Family Photos

(New York: Three Rivers Press, 2010)

Subject(s): Family; Humor; Photography

Summary: In *Awkward Family Photos*, Mike Bender and Dough Chernack present a collection of America's funniest and weirdest home photographs. An expansion on the popular website AwkwardFamilyPhotos.com, this book arranges its subject matter by category—family portraits, parents, kids, brothers and sisters, grandparents, pets, vacation, celebrations, and holidays. A chapter titled "Strange not Awkward" compiles the most bizarre submissions. From dated hairstyles to bad wardrobe choices, and tasteless poses to inappropriate props, each photo captures the quirkier aspects of life in the American family. Each chapter opens with a brief introduction, but for the most part, the authors have allowed the pictures speak for themselves.

Where it's reviewed:
The Bookseller, July 9, 2010, page 25

Other books you might like:
Ben Bator, *Texts From Last Night: All the Texts No One Remembers Sending*, 2010
Justin Halpern, *Sh*t My Dad Says*, 2010
Chelsea Handler, *My Horizontal Life: A Collection of One-Night Stands*, 2005
Matt Kuhn, *The Playbook: Suit up. Score Chicks. Be Awesome.*, 2010
Lauren Leto, *Texts From Last Night: All the Texts No One Remembers Sending*, 2010
John Lindsay, *Emails from an Asshole: Real People Being Stupid*, 2010
Barney Stinson, *The Playbook: Suit up. Score Chicks. Be Awesome.*, 2010

894

PETER BISKIND

Star: How Warren Beatty Seduced America

(New York: Simon and Schuster, 2010)

Subject(s): Biographies; Movie industry; Actors

Summary: In *Star: How Warren Beatty Seduced America*, entertainment journalist and celebrity biographer Peter Biskind offers readers a detailed examination of the public and private lives of one of the modern world's most celebrated movie stars. Warren Beatty has long been considered one of Hollywood's great Casanovas—a fact that has sometimes overshadowed his remarkable achievements in film. A celebrated actor, an Academy Award-winning director, and a virtuoso PR man, Beatty has made stunning contributions to the moviemaking world. This volume explores the life and times of Warren Beatty: the man, the myth, and the mogul. *Star* contains photographs, a bibliography, and an index.

Where it's reviewed:
Entertainment Weekly, January 8, 2010, page 75

Other books by the same author:
Down and Dirty Pictures: Miramax, Sundance, and the Rise of Independent Film, 2004
Seeing Is Believing: How Hollywood Taught Us to Stop Worrying and Love the Fifties, 2000
Easy Riders, Raging Bulls: How the Sex-Drugs-and-Rock 'N' Roll Generation Saved Hollywood, 1998

Other books you might like:
Rich Cohen, *When I Stop Talking, You'll Know I'm Dead: Useful Stories from a Persuasive Man*, 2010
Dennis Davern, *Goodbye Natalie, Goodbye Splendour*, 2009
A.E. Hotchner, *Paul and Me: Fifty-three Years of Adventures and Misadventures with My Pal Paul Newman*, 2010
Sam Kashner, *Furious Love: Elizabeth Taylor, Richard Burton, and the Marriage of the Century*, 2010
Nicole LaPorte, *The Men Who Would Be King: An Almost Epic Tale of Moguls, Movies and a Company Called DreamWorks*, 2010
Marti Rulli, *Goodbye Natalie, Goodbye Splendour*, 2009
Nancy Schoenberger, *Furious Love: Elizabeth Taylor, Richard Burton, and the Marriage of the Century*, 2010
Jerry Weintraub, *When I Stop Talking, You'll Know I'm Dead: Useful Stories from a Persuasive Man*, 2010

895

LEWIS BLACK

Me of Little Faith

(New York: Riverhead Hardcover, 2008)

Subject(s): Religion; Spirituality; Faith

Summary: Comedian Lewis Black, a frequent contributor to *The Daily Show with Jon Stewart*, gets angry about religion in his book *Me of Little Faith*. Black uses his particular brand of angry comedy to discuss his personal opinions about religion in general—and in specifics—because, as he states in the book, "anything that takes itself too seriously is open to ridicule." Raised as a non-practicing Jew, Black explores his personal experiences with matters of faith throughout his life. Comprised of more than two dozen essays of varying lengths, *Me of*

Little Faith pokes fun at all religions—no one is safe.

Where it's reviewed:
Kirkus Reviews, March 15, 2008, page 277-278
Publishers Weekly, April 21, 2008, page 54

Other books by the same author:
I'm Dreaming of a Black Christmas, 2010
Nothing's Sacred, 2005

Other books you might like:
Anthony Bozza, *Too Fat to Fish*, 2008
George Carlin, *Last Words*, 2009
   Tony Hendra, co-author
Artie Lange, *Too Fat to Fish*, 2008
Denis Leary, *No Cure for Cancer*, 1992
Dr. Denis Leary, *Why We Suck: A Feel Good Guide to Staying Fat, Loud, Lazy and Stupid*, 2008
Bill Maher, *New Rules: Polite Musings from a Timid Observer*, 2005

896

ANTHONY BOURDAIN

Medium Raw: A Bloody Valentine to the World of Food and the People Who Cook

(New York: Ecco Press, 2010)

Subject(s): Autobiographies; Cooking; Food

Summary: *Medium Raw: A Bloody Valentine to the World of Food and the People Who Cook* by Anthony Bourdain is a follow-up to 2001's *Kitchen Confidential*. Primarily autobiographical in nature, this book explores the changes in Bourdain's life, from his days as a cook to a world traveler and television personality, as well as a father. Bourdain also writes about significant current chefs such as David Chang and Alice Waters, as well as his opinions on winners of the television show *Top Chef*. The book is also full of Bourdain's trademark rants and essays, as well as investigations and interrogations similar in nature to the first book.

Other books by the same author:
Kitchen Confidential, 2007
The Nasty Bits, 2007
A Cook's Tour: In Search of the Perfect Meal, 2002

Other books you might like:
John Layman, *Chew Volume 2: International Flavor*, 2010
Food Network, *Food Network Favorites: Recipes from Our All-Star Chefs*, 2007
Jamie Oliver, *The Naked Chef*, 2000

897

RUSSELL BRAND

My Booky Wook: A Memoir of Sex, Drugs, and Stand-Up

(London: Hodder & Stoughton, 2007)

Subject(s): Autobiographies; Drug abuse; Sexuality

Summary: In *My Booky Wook: A Memoir of Sex, Drugs,*

and Stand-Up, comedian Russell Brand chronicles his unhappy childhood, his addiction to sex and drugs, and his eventual rise to comedic stardom. Born in England, Brand used comedy to cope with his parents' divorce and his lonely life as an only child. An unsuccessful school career led to drug abuse, bulimia, and sex addiction. Brand leaves nothing out of this humorous tell-all. The comedian recounts his most painful and embarrassing moments, including his introduction to prostitutes during a father-son vacation and his firing from MTV after dressing up as Osama Bin Laden on September 12, 2001. Brand also offers his views on everything from celebrity to depression to drama school.

Where it's reviewed:
Entertainment Weekly, March 20, 2009, page 68

Other books by the same author:
Articles of Faith, 2008

Other books you might like:
Kathy Griffin, *Official Book Club Selection: A Memoir According to Kathy Griffin*, 2009
Chelsea Handler, *Are You There, Vodka? It's Me, Chelsea*, 2008
Chelsea Handler, *Chelsea Chelsea Bang Bang*, 2010
Chelsea Handler, *My Horizontal Life: A Collection of One-Night Stands*, 2005
Heather McDonald, *You'll Never Blue Ball in This Town Again: One Woman's Painfully Funny Quest to Give It Up*, 2010

898

MAX BROOKS

The Zombie Survival Guide: Recorded Attacks

(New York: Three Rivers Press, 2009)

Subject(s): History; Monsters; Fear

Summary: In *The Zombie Survival Guide: Recorded Attacks*, author Max Brooks takes readers on a terrifying journey into zombie assaults throughout history. From ancient Africa to feudal Japan, from the Soviet Union of the 1960s to modern-day California, this volume offers nonstop chills as it shows the many ways humans have taken on the undead. *The Zombie Survival Guide* contains illustrations by Ibraim Roberson.

Other books by the same author:
World War Z: An Oral History of the Zombie War, 2007
The Zombie Survival Guide: Complete Protection from the Living Dead, 2003

Other books you might like:
Roger Ma, *The Zombie Combat Manual: A Guide to Fighting the Living Dead*, 2010
David P. Murphy, *Zombies for Zombies: Advice and Etiquette for the Living Dead*, 2009
Don Roff, *Zombies: A Record of the Year of Infection*, 2009

899

RHONDA BYRNE

The Secret

(New York: Atria Books/Beyond Words, 2006)

Subject(s): Conduct of Life; Philosophy; Relationships

Summary: In *The Secret*, Rhonda Byrne, producer of the popular movie of the same name, outlines the concept of The Secret, a philosophical and spiritual mode of thought that can be applied to any aspect of one's life. Byrne relates the stories of numerous people who have used the concept to achieve success and happiness in their lives, and instructs the reader on how to master the power of The Secret.

Where it's reviewed:
Cosmopolitan, June 2007, page 45

Other books by the same author:
The Power, 2010
The Secret Daily Teachings, 2008
The Secret Gratitude Book, 2007

Other books you might like:
Dale Carnegie, *How To Win Friends And Influence People*, 1937
Elizabeth Gilbert, *Eat, Pray, Love: One Woman's Search for Everything Across Italy, India and Indonesia*, 2006
Ed Gungor, *There is More to the Secret*, 2007
Michael J. Losier, *Law of Attraction: The Science of Attracting More of What You Want and Less of What You Don't*, 2010

900

JOHN CAPOUYA

Gorgeous George: The Outrageous Bad-Boy Wrestler Who Created American Pop Culture

(New York: Harper Entertainment, 2008)

Subject(s): Sports; Wrestling; United States

Summary: *Gorgeous George: The Outrageous Bad-Boy Wrestler Who Created American Pop Culture*, written by John Capouya, tells the life story of professional wrestler Gorgeous George Wagoner. Born in 1915, Wagoner wrestled on his high school team before joining a carnival, where he worked during the 1930s. It wasn't until the late 1940s and 1950s that wrestling became popular as television viewing increased, and Wagoner made the sport even more theatrical by creating the persona that would later influence American pop culture. His wife, Betty, helped him dye his hair and create elaborate outfits that gave Wagoner his signature look. Although more a figure of controversy than a hero, Wagoner is rumored to have influenced a large number of singers (James Brown and Bob Dylan), sports figures (Muhammad Ali), and other professional wrestlers. Near the end of his life, Wagoner turned to drinking. He died in 1963, but this book shows that his influences still exist today.

Where it's reviewed:
Booklist, September 1, 2008, page 34
Publishers Weekly, July 7, 2008, page 52

Other books by the same author:
Real Men Do Yoga, 2003

Other books you might like:
Freddie Blassie, *The Legends of Wrestling: "Classy" Freddie Blassie: Listen, You Pencil Neck Geeks (WWE)*, 2004
    Keith Elliot Greenberg, co-author
Ron Hall, *Sputnik, Masked Men, & Midgets: The Early Days of Memphis Wrestling*, 2009
Tim Hornbaker, *National Wrestling Alliance: The Untold Story of the Monopoly that Strangled Pro Wrestling*, 2007
Jeff Leen, *The Queen of the Ring: Sex, Muscles, Diamonds, and the Making of an American Legend*, 2009
Larry Matysik, *Drawing Heat the Hard Way: How Wrestling Really Works*, 2009
Sherman Willmott, *Sputnik, Masked Men, & Midgets: The Early Days of Memphis Wrestling*, 2009

901

GEORGE CARLIN
TONY HENDRA , Co-Author

Last Words

(New York: Free Press, 2009)

Subject(s): Autobiographies; Comedians; Comedy

Summary: George Carlin's comedy and observations always made an impact. Some people found him hilarious or ingenious; others thought he was crude or disrespectful. Regardless, for fifty years, Carlin presented stand-up routines that got people listening to his every word. In 1993, Carlin asked his friend Tony Hendra to collaborate on a memoir. Carlin died in 2008 before the book was completed, but Hendra decided to honor his friend by finishing the work and presenting it to the world. In *Last Words*, Hendra draws from many years of conversations with Carlin to describe the famous comic's long and accomplished life. Carlin grew up in a gritty part of New York where he observed class conflicts that made him think critically about how people acted. Then, family troubles and substance abuse gave him even more perspective on life. Carlin's observations would ultimately fuel comedic routines, including the infamous "Seven Words You Can Never Say On Television" skit.

Where it's reviewed:
Los Angeles Times, November 28, 2009, page D.1.
New York Times Book Review, January 31, 2010, page 13
The Washington Post, December 29, 2009, page C.5

Other books by the same author:
Three Times Carlin: An Orgy of George, 2006
When Will Jesus Bring the Pork Chops?, 2004

Brain Droppings, 1997

Other books you might like:
Lewis Black, *Me of Little Faith*, 2008
Anthony Bozza, *Too Fat to Fish*, 2008
George Carlin, *Brain Droppings*, 1997
George Carlin, *When Will Jesus Bring the Pork Chops?*, 2004
Artie Lange, *Too Fat to Fish*, 2008
Denis Leary, *No Cure for Cancer*, 1992

902

MICHAEL CHABON

Manhood for Amateurs: The Pleasures and Regrets of a Husband, Father, and Son

(New York: Harper, 2009)

Subject(s): Men; Fathers; Marriage

Summary: In *Manhood for Amateurs: The Pleasures and Regrets of a Husband, Father, and Son*, Pulitzer Prize-winning author Michael Chabon presents a series of essays examining what it means to be a man. Blending memoir and philosophy, Chabon fearlessly explores the role he has played in the lives of his family members: as a spouse, a father, and a son. In recounting his own childhood experiences, his parents' divorce, his youthful adventures and coming of age, Chabon crafts a universal investigation into the nature of manhood.

Where it's reviewed:
People, October 19, 2009, page 69

Other books by the same author:
Maps and Legends: Reading and Writing Along the Borderlands, 2008
The Amazing Adventures of Kavalier & Clay: A Novel, 2000
Wonder Boys, 1995

Other books you might like:
Bill Bryson, *The Life and Times of the Thunderbolt Kid: A Memoir*, 2006
Michael Chabon, *The Yiddish Policemen's Union: A Novel*, 2007
Michael Lewis, *Home Game: An Accidental Guide to Fatherhood*, 2009
Dan Savage, *The Commitment: Love, Sex, Marriage, and My Family*, 2005
Ayelet Waldman, *Bad Mother: A Chronicle of Maternal Crimes, Minor Calamities, and Occasional Moments of Grace*, 2009

903

MICHAEL CHABON

Maps and Legends: Reading and Writing Along the Borderlands

(New York: McSweeney's, 2008)

Subject(s): Writing; Writers

Pop Culture (sidebar)

Summary: Michael Chabon is the author of many popular works including the novels *The Yiddish Policemen's Union: A Novel* and *The Mysteries of Pittsburgh*. In his book *Maps and Legends: Reading and Writing Along the Borderlands*, Chabon gives readers a collection of nonfiction essays, many of which deal with writers and writing in the modern age. Chabon believes that too much of a gap exists between literature and writing that people enjoy. He also explores many of the genres that he most enjoys, including comic books and mysteries. Other essays in the collection discuss Chabon's own writing experiences. *Maps and Legends* contains sixteen entries.

Where it's reviewed:
Booklist, March 1, 2008, page 28
Library Journal, March 15, 2008, page 72
Publishers Weekly, January 21, 2008, page 163

Other books by the same author:
Manhood for Amateurs: The Pleasures and Regrets of a Husband, Father, and Son, 2009

Other books you might like:
Michael Chabon, *The Amazing Adventures of Kavalier & Clay: A Novel*, 2000
Ayelet Waldman, *Bad Mother: A Chronicle of Maternal Crimes, Minor Calamities, and Occasional Moments of Grace*, 2009

904

LAURA CLARIDGE

Emily Post: Daughter of the Gilded Age, Mistress of American Manners

(New York: Random House, 2008)

Subject(s): Biographies; Etiquette; Ethics

Summary: Laura Claridge's *Emily Post: Daughter of the Gilded Age, Mistress of American Manners* is the first authorized biography of one of the most influential women in American history. In this book, Claridge offers information about Emily Post's wondrous childhood, her proper upbringing, and her hopeless marriage. After divorcing Edwin Post, a man who regularly appeared on the front page of New York's newspapers, Post struggled to find a life of her own. She wrote novels, attended conferences, and critiqued the work of up-and-coming authors such as Mark Twain, but she was not happy. With the publication of *Etiquette*, Post took the world by storm. Her guide to acting respectably and graciously in public showed Americans exactly what they were doing wrong and taught them how to correct their behaviors. More than 50 years after *Etiquette*'s original publication, Post's greatest work is still being re-released and read across the world.

Other books by the same author:
Norman Rockwell: A Life, 2001

Other books you might like:
Meryl Gordon, *Mrs. Astor Regrets: The Hidden Betrayals of a Family Beyond Reproach*, 2008

Donna M. Lucey, *Archie and Amelie: Love and Madness in the Gilded Age*, 2007
Peggy Post, *Emily Post's Etiquette, 17th Edition*, 2004
Edith Wharton, *The Age of Innocence*, 1920
Edith Wharton, *The House of Mirth*, 1905

905

AV CLUB

Inventory: 16 Films Featuring Manic Pixie Dream Girls, 10 Great Songs Nearly Ruined by Saxophone, and 100 More Obsessively Specific Pop-Culture Lists

(New York: Scribner Publishing, 2009)

Subject(s): Popular culture; Entertainment industry; Movie industry

Summary: *Inventory: 16 Films Featuring Manic Pixie Dream Girls, 10 Great Songs Nearly Ruined by Saxophone, and 100 More Obsessively Specific Pop-Culture Lists* is a book written by the AV Club, a pop culture Web site and newspaper published by the satirical news group *The Onion*. The book includes more than 100 humorous lists about pop culture including "Whoa!: 6 Keanu Reeves Movies Somehow Not Ruined by Keanu Reeves," "Dancing about Architecture: 5 Essential Books about Popular Music," and "Not Dead Yet: 8 Great Films Made by Directors after They Turned 70." The book also includes "guest lists" from comedians and actors such as Robert Ben Garant (of the television show *Reno 911*), Amy Sedaris (of the television show *Strangers with Candy*), and Patton Oswalt (of the television show *King of Queens*).

Other books by the same author:
My Year of Flops: The A.V. Club Presents One Man's Journey Deep into the Heart of Cinematic Failure, 2010

Other books you might like:
John Hodgman, *The Areas of My Expertise: An Almanac of Complete World Knowledge Compiled with Instructive Annotation and Arranged in Useful Order*, 2005
Nathan Rabin, *The Big Rewind: A Memoir Brought to You by Pop Culture*, 2009
Nathan Rabin, *My Year of Flops: The A.V. Club Presents One Man's Journey Deep into the Heart of Cinematic Failure*, 2010
Rob Sheffield, *Talking to Girls about Duran Duran: One Young Man's Quest for True Love and a Cooler Haircut*, 2010
Claire Zulkey, *An Off Year*, 2009

906

HEATHER COCKS

JESSICA MORGAN , Co-Author

Go Fug Yourself: The Fug Awards

(New York: Simon Spotlight Entertainment, 2008)

Subject(s): Fashion; Humor; Actors

Summary: For more than five years, Heather Cocks and Jessica Morgan have posted brutal yet entertaining comments about the world's biggest celebrities and their fashion sense on GoFugYourself.com. Cocks and Morgan's Web site has caught the attention of *Time*, *Entertainment Weekly*, and millions of viewers throughout the years. In *Go Fug Yourself: The Fug Awards*, the authors take the greatest fashion disasters and train wrecks from their Web site and honor them with awards such as The Sag Award, The Peldon Prize, The Errstyle, and The Dr. Noooo! Fergie, Lindsay Lohan, and Hilary Duff all appear on the pages of this book.

Where it's reviewed:
Chicago Tribune, March 26, 2008, page 1

Other books you might like:
Tara Ariano, *Hey! It's That Guy!*, 2005
Tara Ariano, *Television Without Pity: 752 Things We Love to Hate (and Hate to Love) About TV*, 2006
Victoria Beckham, *Learning to Fly*, 2001
Sarah D. Bunting, *Television Without Pity: 752 Things We Love to Hate (and Hate to Love) About TV*, 2006
Ashley Olsen, *Influence*, 2008
    Mary-Kate Olsen, co-author
The Onion, *Our Dumb World: The Onion's Atlas of the Planet Earth, 73rd Edition*, 2007

907

STEPHEN COLBERT

I Am America (and So Can You!)

(New York: Grand Central Publishing, 2007)

Subject(s): Comedy; Entertainment; Humor

Summary: Talk show host Stephen Colbert, of *The Colbert Report*, presents *I Am America*. In the book he writes about everything he believes is attempting to destroy America as he knows it—from terrorists to Kashi breakfast cereal and offers opinions on the American family, sports, and religion. He includes charts and illustrations.

Where it's reviewed:
Variety, November 5, 2007, page 5

Other books by the same author:
Stephen Colbert and Philosophy: I Am Philosophy (And So Can You!), 2009
Stephen Colbert's Tek Jansen, 2007
Wigfield: The Can-Do Town That Just May Not, 2004

Other books you might like:
Jason Holt, *The Daily Show and Philosophy: Moments of Zen in the Art of Fake News*, 2007
Ben Karlin, *America (The Book): A Citizen's Guide to Democracy Inaction*, 2004
Aaron Allen Schiller, *Stephen Colbert and Philosophy: I Am Philosophy (And So Can You!)*, 2009
The Daily Show, *The Daily Show with Jon Stewart Presents America (The Book) Teacher's Edition: A Citizen's Guide to Democracy Inaction*, 2006
Jon Stewart, *America (The Book): A Citizen's Guide to Democracy Inaction*, 2004
Jon Stewart, *The Daily Show with Jon Stewart Presents America (The Book) Teacher's Edition: A Citizen's Guide to Democracy Inaction*, 2006
Jon Stewart, *The Daily Show with Jon Stewart Presents Earth (The Book): A Visitor's Guide to the Human Race*, 2010

908

ADRIAN COLESBERRY

How to Make Love to Adrian Colesberry

(New York: Gotham Books, 2009)

Subject(s): Sex education; Comedians; Humor

Summary: In *How to Make Love to Adrian Colesberry*, the comedian tells how to attract, romance, and sexually satisfy a man—specifically, him. Colesberry also shares his sexual and nonsexual proclivities in this memoir of his life both in and out of bed. Colesberry is a stand-up comic in Los Angeles, California, who has appeared as an extra in the film *Melvin Goes to Dinner*. He is also the author of *Costa Rica: The Last Country the Gods Made*.

Other books you might like:
Rich Blomquist, *Sexy Book of Sexy Sex*, 2010
Sharon Moalem, *How Sex Works: Why We Look, Smell, Taste, Feel, and Act the Way We Do*, 2009
Mary Roach, *Bonk: The Curious Coupling of Sex and Science*, 2008
Peter Sagal, *The Book of Vice: Very Naughty Things (and How to Do Them)*, 2007
Dan Savage, *The Commitment: Love, Sex, Marriage, and My Family*, 2005
Kristen Schaal, *Sexy Book of Sexy Sex*, 2010

909

JENNET CONANT

The Irregulars: Roald Dahl and the British Spy Ring in Wartime Washington

(New York: Simon and Schuster, 2008)

Subject(s): World War II, 1939-1945; Espionage; England

Summary: *The Irregulars: Roald Dahl and the British Spy Ring in Wartime Washington* is a historical account of espionage and political propaganda during World War II from bestselling author Jennet Conant. After being injured while serving as an RAF pilot, Roald Dahl was assigned to work at the British Embassy in Washington DC, where his chief task was to rub elbows with elite American politicians and gather intelligence for his country. During his time in the United States, Dahl played a major part in a political campaign, masterminded by William "Intrepid" Stephenson, to use propaganda to encourage American support of British policy and the nation's involvement in the war against Germany. *The Irregulars* recounts, in great detail, the hidden life of one of the world's most beloved children's authors.

Where it's reviewed:
TLS. Times Literary Supplement, August 21, 2009, page 10

Other books by the same author:
109 East Palace: Robert Oppenheimer and the Secret City of Los Alamos, 2005
Tuxedo Park: A Wall Street Tycoon and the Secret Palace of Science That Changed the Course of World War II, 2002

Other books you might like:
Roald Dahl, *The Best of Roald Dahl*, 1990
F.H. Hinsley, *Codebreakers: The Inside Story of Bletchley Park*, 1993
William Stevenson, *A Man Called Intrepid: The Secret War*, 1976
Alan Stripp, *Codebreakers: The Inside Story of Bletchley Park*, 1993

| 910 |

TOM DAVIS

Thirty-Nine Years of Short-Term Memory Loss: The Early Days of SNL from Someone Who Was There
(New York: Grove Press, 2009)

Subject(s): Autobiographies; Television programs; Humor

Summary: *Thirty-Nine Years of Short-Term Memory Loss: The Early Days of SNL from Someone Who Was There* is written by Tom Davis with a foreword by Al Franken, who was close friends with Davis while they were part of *Saturday Night Live*. Though the book purports to be a history of the early years of *Saturday Night Live*, it is more accurately an autobiography of Davis's life. He begins the book by discussing his childhood in Minneapolis and the events that led to his relocation to San Francisco and eventually to New York City. He also discusses the parties he would frequently attend, as well as his fairly regular drug use. Portions of the book are also devoted to SNL and the people who worked on the show.

Where it's reviewed:
Entertainment Weekly, March 6, 2009, page 75

Other books you might like:
Tanner Colby, *Belushi*, 2005
Al Franken, *The Truth (with Jokes)*, 2005
Steve Martin, *Born Standing Up: A Comic's Life*, 2007
James Andrew Miller, *Live from New York: An Uncensored History of Saturday Night Live*, 2002
Judy Belushi Pisano, *Belushi*, 2005
David Ritz, *We'll Be Here for the Rest of Our Lives: A Swingin' Show-Biz Saga*, 2009
    Paul Shaffer, co-author
Tom Shales, *Live from New York: An Uncensored History of Saturday Night Live*, 2002

| 911 |

RICHARD DAWKINS

The God Delusion
(New York: Houghton Mifflin Harcourt, 2006)

Subject(s): Atheism; Christianity; Religion

Summary: In *The God Delusion*, biologist Richard Dawkins offers a compelling argument against religious belief. He regards religion as an irrational and destructive delusion. Because of what Dawkins sees as the nature of religious belief, disagreements cannot be settled by reason and often become violent. He asserts that religion causes harm through encouraging a lack of conservation, religious war, intolerance, child abuse, resistance to scientific truth, and other things. He argues that religion is not a source for morality and points out that the gods of various religions often behave in patently immoral ways. He argues strongly in favor of evolution and against intelligent design.

Where it's reviewed:
The New Yorker, May 21, 2007, page 75

Other books by the same author:
The Greatest Show on Earth: The Evidence for Evolution, 2009
The Selfish Gene, 2006
The Ancestor's Tale: A Pilgrimage to the Dawn of Evolution, 2004

Other books you might like:
Deborah Heiligman, *Charles and Emma: The Darwins' Leap of Faith*, 2009
Christopher Hitchens, *God Is Not Great: How Religion Poisons Everything*, 2007
Christopher Hitchens, *Hitch-22*, 2010
Rebecca Newberger Goldstein, *36 Arguments for the Existence of God: A Work of Fiction*, 2010
Rebecca Skloot, *The Immortal Life of Henrietta Lacks*, 2009

| 912 |

TOM DE HAVEN

Our Hero: Superman on Earth
(New Haven, Connecticut: Yale University Press, 2010)

Subject(s): Comic books; History; Popular culture
Summary: Tom De Haven's *Our Hero: Superman on Earth*

considers the lasting legacy of the character of Super-man and the ways in which the character is still relevant today. De Haven provides biographical sketches of the individuals who created comic books and other Super-man texts. The book also includes information about the actors who played the character and the different ways they chose to portray him and define his identity. Discussions of the character as found in film and television are also included.

Where it's reviewed:
Entertainment Weekly, March 19, 2010, page 95

Other books by the same author:
It's Superman!: A Novel, 2005
Masters of American Comics, 2005

Other books you might like:
Michael Chabon, *The Amazing Adventures of Kavalier & Clay: A Novel*, 2000
Mike Madrid, *The Supergirls: Fashion, Feminism, Fantasy, and the History of Comic Book Heroines*, 2009
Richard Reynolds, *Super Heroes: A Modern Mythology*, 1992
Rikke Schubart, *Super Bitches and Action Babes: The Female Hero in Popular Cinema, 1970-2006*, 2007
Josh Wilker, *Cardboard Gods: An All-American Tale Told Through Baseball Cards*, 2010

913

MAX DECHARNE

Hardboiled Hollywood: The True Crime Stories Behind The Classic Noir Films

(Pegasus, 2010)

Subject(s): Movie industry; Crime; Movies

Summary: In *Hardboiled Hollywood: The True Crime Stories Behind the Classic Noir Films*, Max Decharne reveals the real facts behind Hollywood's most popular crime movies. Movies such as *Psycho* and *The Godfather* were inspired by real-life events, many of which were much more gruesome than the movies let on. In this book, Decharne recalls information about the real crimes and then explains how they were incorporated into some of Hollywood and Great Britain's most recognized noir films. Decharne includes information about 11 unforgettable and some not-so-well-known classics, including *Little Caesar* and *Hell is a City*. This book was originally published in Great Britain in 2003.

Where it's reviewed:
Library Journal, February 1, 2010, page 78
Publishers Weekly, November 30, 2009, page 39

Other books by the same author:
A Rocket in My Pocket, 2010
King's Road, 2005
Straight from the Fridge, Dad, 2000

Other books you might like:
Graydon Carter, *Vanity Fair's Tales of Hollywood: Rebels, Reds, and Graduates and the Wild Stories Behind the Making of 13 Iconic Films*, 2008
James Ellroy, *The Black Dahlia*, 1987
James Ellroy, *L.A. Confidential*, 1990
Marilee Strong, *Erased: Missing Women, Murdered Wives*, 2009
Jack Webb, *The Badge: True and Terrifying Crime Stories That Could Not Be Presented on TV, from the Creator and Star of Dragnet*, 2005

914

MICHAEL DEELEY

Blade Runners, Deer Hunters, and Blowing the Bloody Doors Off: My Life in Cult Movies

(New York: Pegasus Publishing, 2009)

Subject(s): Movie industry; Problem solving; Actors

Summary: As the producer of some of the most popular cult movies in the world, Michael Deeley knows what it's like to provide much-needed balance on a movie set. In *Blade Runners, Deer Hunters, and Blowing the Bloody Doors Off: My Life in Cult Movies*, Deeley recalls amusing and dangerous events that occurred on the set of movies such as *The Italian Job*, *The Deer Hunter*, *Don't Look Now*, *The Wicker Man*, and *Blade Runner*. He describes his role as producer and his responsibilities to the cast and crews of each movie. He includes many details about working with young actors such as Robert DeNiro and Harrison Ford. Deeley won an Academy Award for his work on *The Deer Hunter*.

Where it's reviewed:
Entertainment Weekly, April 24, 2009, page 109
Library Journal, March 15, 2009, page 107

Other books you might like:
Graydon Carter, *Vanity Fair's Tales of Hollywood: Rebels, Reds, and Graduates and the Wild Stories Behind the Making of 13 Iconic Films*, 2008
Rich Cohen, *When I Stop Talking, You'll Know I'm Dead: Useful Stories from a Persuasive Man*, 2010
Peter Hanson, *Tales from the Script: 50 Hollywood Screenwriters Share Their Stories*, 2010
Paul Robert Herman, co-editor
Nicole LaPorte, *The Men Who Would Be King: An Almost Epic Tale of Moguls, Movies and a Company Called DreamWorks*, 2010
Robert Sellers, *Hellraisers: The Life and Inebriated Times of Richard Burton, Richard Harris, Peter O'Toole, and Oliver Reed*, 2009
Jerry Weintraub, *When I Stop Talking, You'll Know I'm Dead: Useful Stories from a Persuasive Man*, 2010

915

ELIZABETH EDWARDS

Resilience: Reflections on the Burdens and Gifts of Facing Life's Adversities

(New York: Broadway Books, 2009)

Subject(s): Autobiographies; Cancer; Grief

Summary: Political personality Elizabeth Edwards presents an inspirational memoir looking back at the ups and downs of her rich and varied life. In *Resilience: Reflections on the Burdens and Gifts of Facing Life's Adversities*, Edwards examines the impact of tragedy on her life, what she has learned from it, and how she has grown because of it. From the death of her teenage son in a car accident to her husband's scandalous infidelity, Edwards fearlessly explores the cruel blows life can deal. But her greatest personal battle came when she was diagnosed with cancer, a war she waged with courage, strength, and quiet dignity.

Where it's reviewed:
Los Angeles Times, May 8, 2009, page D.1.

Other books by the same author:
Saving Graces: Finding Solace and Strength from Friends and Strangers, 2006

Other books you might like:
Mark Halperin, *Game Change: Obama and the Clintons, McCain and Palin, and the Race of a Lifetime*, 2010
John Heilemann, co-author
Meghan McCain, *Dirty Sexy Politics*, 2010
Jenny Sandford, *Staying True*, 2010
Jennifer Weiner, *Fly Away Home*, 2010
Andrew Young, *The Politician: An Insider's Account of John Edwards's Pursuit of the Presidency and the Scandal That Brought Him Down*, 2010

916

DAVE EGGERS

Zeitoun

(San Francisco, California: McSweeney's Books, 2009)

Subject(s): Biographies; Hurricanes; Natural disasters

Summary: *Zeitoun* by Dave Eggers is an examination of the War on Terror as well as the United States government's response to Hurricane Katrina in 2005, through a biographical account of the Zeitoun family. The Zeitouns were originally from Syria, but were living in New Orleans after Abdulrahman Zeitoun became a painting contractor. Abdulrahman stayed behind after the evacuation in order to protect his property. He went around the city in a canoe helping others until he was picked up and summarily arrested on suspicion of being a terrorist. Through this personal account, it becomes clear just how poor the government's response was to the people living

in New Orleans, and the many injustices they were forced to endure.

Where it's reviewed:
Library Journal, January 2010, page 63
New Statesman, March 8, 2010, page 52

Other books by the same author:
What is the What, 2006
You Shall Know Our Velocity, 2002
A Heartbreaking Work of Staggering Genius, 2001

Other books you might like:
Jay Allison, *This I Believe: The Personal Philosophies of Remarkable Men and Women*, 2006
Dave Eggers, *A Heartbreaking Work of Staggering Genius*, 2000
Dave Eggers, *What Is the What*, 2006
Dan Gediman, *This I Believe: The Personal Philosophies of Remarkable Men and Women*, 2006
Josh Neufeld, *A.D.: New Orleans After the Deluge*, 2009
Chris Rose, *1 Dead in Attic: After Katrina*, 2007

917

NORA EPHRON

I Feel Bad about My Neck: And Other Thoughts on Being a Woman

(New York: Vintage, 2006)

Subject(s): Aging; Fashion; Humor

Summary: In 15 essays, screenwriter and director Nora Ephron explores life as a woman—an aging woman, to be exact—and shares anecdotes, advice, and observations about being a woman. The title essay, "I Feel Bad about My Neck," describes the inevitability of aging and opens the book. "Considering the Alternative," Ephron's musings about death, closes the collection. In between, she describes the cost and effort of appearing young in "On Maintenance," shares "The Story of My Life in 3,500 Words or Less," and devotes an entire chapter to how much she hates her purse and the chaos and character flaws that it reflects.

Where it's reviewed:
The New York Review of Books, November 16, 2006, page 12
People, May 12, 2008, page 61

Other books by the same author:
Heartburn, 1983
Crazy Salad, 1975
Wallflower at the Orgy, 1970

Other books you might like:
Carrie Fisher, *Wishful Drinking*, 2008
Jodi Hills, *Slap on a Little Lipstick...You'll Be Fine*, 2006
Laurie Notaro, *The Idiot Girl and the Flaming Tantrum of Death: Reflections on Revenge, Germophobia, and Laser Hair Removal*, 2008
Laurie Notaro, *We Thought You Would Be Prettier: True*

Tales of the Dorkiest Girl Alive, 2005
Patricia Volk, *To My Dearest Friends*, 2007

918

TOM FARLEY
TANNER COLBY , Co-Author

The Chris Farley Show: A Biography in Three Acts
(New York: Viking, 2008)

Subject(s): Alcoholism; Comedians; Drug Abuse

Summary: Older brother Tom teams up with comedian, writer, and author of the biography *Belushi*, Tanner Colby, to present this candid biography of Chris Farley. It chronicles his life growing up in Wisconsin, his college days at Marquette University, his rise to fame, and his life of excess that lead to an overdose. Farley's life is told humorously and often poignantly through interviews with family, friends, and those who were there. While Tom Farley provides much of the back story, many famous celebrities share some of their favorite stories about Chris, including David Spade, Chris Rock, Molly Shannon and Mike Meyers.

Where it's reviewed:
Entertainment Weekly, May 9, 2008, page 66
People, May 12, 2008, page 61

Other books you might like:
Tanner Colby, *Belushi*, 2005
Steve Martin, *Born Standing Up: A Comic's Life*, 2007
James Andrew Miller, *Live from New York: An Uncensored History of Saturday Night Live*, 2002
Jay Mohr, *Gasping for Airtime: Two Years in the Trenches of Saturday Night Live*, 2004
Judy Belushi Pisano, *Belushi*, 2005
Tom Shales, *Live from New York: An Uncensored History of Saturday Night Live*, 2002
Bob Woodward, *Wired: The Short Life and Fast Times of John Belushi*, 1984

919

CRAIG FERGUSON

American on Purpose: The Improbable Adventures of an Unlikely Patriot
(New York: Harper, 2009)

Subject(s): Comedians; Scots (British people); Autobiographies

Summary: In *American on Purpose: The Improbable Adventures of an Unlikely Patriot*, Scottish-born comedian and talk show host Craig Ferguson recounts the ups and down of his life, as well as his adventures as a newly minted American citizen. A product of the rough streets of Glasgow, Ferguson dreamed of making it big as a comedian. He struggled long and hard to find his

niche, and along the way sought refuge in alcohol and drugs. When he finally came to America, he was clean and sober and soon landed a gig on *The Drew Carey Show*. This role made him a recognizable face in the pop culture landscape, leading to his current position as host of *The Late Late Show*. Interspersed with his own story are Ferguson's observations on American life and politics.

Other books by the same author:
Between the Bridge and the River, 2006

Other books you might like:
Russell Brand, *My Booky Wook: A Memoir of Sex, Drugs, and Stand-Up*, 2007
Chelsea Handler, *Chelsea Chelsea Bang Bang*, 2010
Dr. Denis Leary, *Why We Suck: A Feel Good Guide to Staying Fat, Loud, Lazy and Stupid*, 2008
Bill Maher, *New Rules: Polite Musings from a Timid Observer*, 2005
Jon Stewart, *The Daily Show with Jon Stewart Presents Earth (The Book): A Visitor's Guide to the Human Race*, 2010

920

CARRIE FISHER

Wishful Drinking
(New York: Simon & Schuster, 2008)

Subject(s): Autobiographies; Movie industry; Family

Summary: In *Wishful Drinking*, consummate Hollywood insider Carrie Fisher reveals the truth about her life and times. The book begins after Fisher has undergone electroshock therapy to help ease her bipolar disorder. Her memories, which disappeared for a while, are now flooding back, and she writes them down to help remember them. Born to stars Debbie Reynolds and Eddie Fisher, the author recounts the bizarre nature of growing up in the limelight, including having a mother who presented her with a sexual toy as gift at the age of 15. Fisher delves into her twisted romantic life, which included marrying, then divorcing, then dating Paul Simon, as well as being left by her daughter's father for another man. One tale involves the author going through her entire family tree to make sure her daughter's date wasn't, in fact, a relative. Fisher also delves into her years as a *Star Wars* icon, whose face was on every product imaginable, her years as an alcoholic and drug addict, her recovery, and the time she woke to find a close friend dead in her bed. Writing everything with a witty and humorous style, Fisher brings her life into focus again.

Where it's reviewed:
Library Journal, June 1, 2009, page 59
Publishers Weekly, March 31, 2009, page 48

Other books by the same author:
The Best Awful, 2004
Delusions of Grandma, 1994
Postcards from the Edge, 1987

Other books you might like:
David Patrick Columbia, *Debbie: My Life*, 1988

David Fisher, *Been There, Done That: An Autobiography*, 1999
  Eddie Fisher, co-author
Tatum O'Neal, *A Paper Life*, 2004
Mackenzie Phillips, *High on Arrival*, 2009
Debbie Reynolds, *Debbie: My Life*, 1988
Marlo Thomas, *Growing Up Laughing: My Story and the Story of Funny*, 2010

921

JONATHAN SAFRAN FOER

Eating Animals
(New York: Little, Brown and Company, 2009)

Subject(s): Food; Ethics; Agriculture

Summary: In *Eating Animals*, celebrated novelist Jonathan Safran Foer turns his attentions to the world of nonfiction and the moral and ethical implications of consuming animal products. As Foer anticipated the birth of his first child, he began wondering about the effects of eating meat. His pondering led him on a probing investigation of the meat and dairy industries, where he visited factory farms and witnessed firsthand the unsavory conditions animals were forced to endure. This volume also charts the role of meat in popular culture, storytelling, and philosophy. *Eating Animals* contains a list of bibliographical references and a full index.

Where it's reviewed:
TLS. Times Literary Supplement, March 5, 2010, page 3

Other books by the same author:
Extremely Loud & Incredibly Close: A Novel, 2006
Everything Is Illuminated, 2003

Other books you might like:
Susan Bourette, *Meat: A Love Story: My Year in Search of the Perfect Meal*, 2008
Steven Hopp, *Animal, Vegetable, Miracle: A Year of Food Life*, 2007
  Barbara Kingsolver, co-author
  Camille Kingsolver, co-author
Michael Pollan, *In Defense of Food: An Eater's Manifesto*, 2008
Michael Pollan, *The Omnivore's Dilemma: A Natural History of Four Meals*, 2006
Eric Schlosser, *Fast Food Nation: The Dark Side of the All-American Meal*, 2001

922

MICHAEL J. FOX

Always Looking Up: The Adventures of an Incurable Optimist
(New York: Hyperion, 2009)

Subject(s): Actors; Diseases; Autobiographies
Summary: In *Always Looking Up: The Adventures of an*

Incurable Optimist, Emmy Award-winning actor Michael J. Fox reflects on his time out of the spotlight after he was diagnosed with Parkinson's disease. Upon leaving the hit television show *Spin City*, Fox steered clear of the public eye and devoted his time to learning about his illness and reconnecting with his loved ones and himself. By exploring themes of work, politics, family, and faith, this volume charts the journey of a man who had always been defined by his achievements in the popular consciousness—but found he was actually so much more.

Where it's reviewed:
Library Journal, June 15, 2009, page 43
Publishers Weekly, June 29, 2009, page 126

Other books by the same author:
A Funny Thing Happened on the Way to the Future: Twists and Turns and Lessons Learned, 2010
Lucky Man: A Memoir, 2002

Other books you might like:
Elizabeth Edwards, *Resilience: Reflections on the Burdens and Gifts of Facing Life's Adversities*, 2009
Gary David Goldberg, *Sit, Ubu, Sit: How I Went from Brooklyn to Hollywood with the Same Woman, the Same Dog, and a Lot Less Hair*, 2008
Anthony E. Lang, *Parkinson's Disease: A Complete Guide for Patients and Families, Second Edition*, 2006
Christopher Reeve, *Nothing Is Impossible: Reflections on a New Life*, 2002
Christopher Reeve, *Still Me*, 1998
Lisa M. Shulman, *Parkinson's Disease: A Complete Guide for Patients and Families, Second Edition*, 2006
  William J. Weiner, co-author

923

HARRY G. FRANKFURT

On Bullshit
(Princeton, New Jersey: Princeton University Press, 2005)

Subject(s): Advertising; Dishonesty; Philosophy

Summary: According to Harry G. Frankfurt, the problem with modern society—a problem which everyone acknowledges, takes for granted, and adds to—is that there is so much bullshit. Bullshit is not a lie, he argues: it is a complete disregard for lies or for truth; an attitude that whether or not a statement is true or false is irrelevant. Truth, to the bullshitter, is not an issue; and this makes bullshit more insidious than deliberate untruth. He traces the problem of bullshit to a philosophical skepticism that pervades society; a cynical distrust of sincerity, a preference for the slick and the unreal. The author is a professor of philosophy emeritus at Princeton University.

Where it's reviewed:
Ethics, January 2006, page 416

Other books by the same author:
On Truth, 2006

The Reasons of Love, 2004
Necessity, Volition, and Love, 1998

Other books you might like:
Pierre Bayard, *How to Talk about Books You Haven't Read*, 2007
Harry Frankfurt, *On Truth*, 2006
Gary L. Hardcastle, *Bullshit and Philosophy (Popular Culture and Philosophy)*, 2006
Justine Larbalestier, *Liar*, 2009
George A. Reisch, *Bullshit and Philosophy (Popular Culture and Philosophy)*, 2006
Lauren Slater, *Lying: A Metaphorical Memoir*, 2000

924

THOMAS FRENCH

Zoo Story: Life and Death in the Garden of Captives

(New York: Hyperion, 2010)

Subject(s): Animals; Zoos; Wildlife conservation

Summary: Award-winning writer Thomas French explores life for the animal inhabitants and human workers of the Lowry Park Zoo in Tampa, Florida. *Zoo Story: Life and Death in the Garden of Captives* charts the experiences of a variety of animals—including chimpanzees, elephants, and tigers—as they adjust to zoo life and the human caretakers who look after them. French also examines the inherent contradiction zoos represent: wildlife conservation in exchange for money and, some would argue, the exploitation of animals. First book.

Where it's reviewed:
Library Journal, June 1, 2010, page 101

Other books you might like:
Temple Grandin, *Animals Make Us Human: Creating the Best Life for Animals*, 2009
Elizabeth Hess, *Nim Chimpsky: The Chimp Who Would Be Human*, 2008
Geoff Hosey, *Zoo Animals: Behaviour, Management and Welfare*, 2009
Michael Hutchins, *Second Nature: Environmental Enrichment for Captive Animals*, 1998
Catherine Johnson, *Animals Make Us Human: Creating the Best Life for Animals*, 2009
Vicky Melfi, *Zoo Animals: Behaviour, Management and Welfare*, 2009
Jill D. Mellen, *Second Nature: Environmental Enrichment for Captive Animals*, 1998
Sheila Pankhurst, *Zoo Animals: Behaviour, Management and Welfare*, 2009
David J. Shepherdson, *Second Nature: Environmental Enrichment for Captive Animals*, 1998
Vanessa Woods, *Bonobo Handshake: A Memoir of Love and Adventure in the Congo*, 2010

925

THOMAS L. FRIEDMAN

The World Is Flat: A Brief History of the Twenty-First Century

(New York: Ferrar, Straus, Giroux, 2005)

Subject(s): Business; Current Affairs; Economics

Summary: When Thomas L. Friedman says that the world is flat, he means that it is interconnected: at the opening of the 21st century, it is possible to communicate, inform, educate, and do business with billions of other people, instantaneously. Friedman's approach to the rapidly changing world is optimistic and excited; unlike many writers who describe the present and look to the future, he does not warn that the sky is falling. In this book, he explores the technological wonders of the present day: globalization means that individuals and small companies can get big results. He also notes that such small organizations as Al-Qaeda can also get big results, for the same reasons.

Where it's reviewed:
Time, April 18, 2005, page 153

Other books by the same author:
Hot, Flat, and Crowded, 2008
The World Is Flat: Further Updated and Expanded, Release 3.0: A Brief History of the Twenty-first Century, 2007
Longitudes and Attitudes, 2002
The Lexus and the Olive Tree, 2000

Other books you might like:
Thomas L. Friedman, *Hot, Flat, and Crowded*, 2008
Steven Hopp, *Animal, Vegetable, Miracle: A Year of Food Life*, 2007
Barbara Kingsolver, co-author
Camille Kingsolver, co-author
Michael Pollan, *The Omnivore's Dilemma: A Natural History of Four Meals*, 2006
Pietra Rivoli, *The Travels of a T-Shirt in the Global Economy: An Economist Examines the Markets, Power, and Politics of World Trade*, 2005
Christopher Steiner, *$20 Per Gallon: How the Inevitable Rise in the Price of Gasoline Will Change Our Lives for the Better*, 2009

926

THOMAS L. FRIEDMAN

Hot, Flat, and Crowded

(New York: Farrar Straus Giroux, 2008)

Subject(s): Economics; Energy conservation

Summary: Thomas L. Friedman, author of *The World is Flat*, says the growing global middle class, the flattening of the world, is both a blessing and a curse. On the one hand, a healthy middle class brings political stability and increased buying power to energize the world's economy. The dangerous flip side is an expanding demand for resources resulting in excessive pollution and other environmental hazards which will tax the earth's reserves to a point of catastrophic exhaustion. The only hope for American economic renewal and resurgence as a world leader is to invest, develop, and implement energy technology on a wide scale and do it now. A "green revolution" will come at a cost as all revolutions must. Companies who cannot convert to a new renewably based system will perish. Friedman makes his most convincing and succinct case yet for a brave new American path where sacrifice and ingenuity will lead to a triumph in American innovation the likes of which history has never seen before.

Where it's reviewed:
Newsweek, September 22, 2008, page 18

Other books by the same author:
The World Is Flat: A Brief History of the Twenty-First Century, 2006
Longitudes & Attitudes: The World in the Age of Terrorism, 2002
The Lexus and the Olive Tree, 2000

Other books you might like:
Thomas L. Friedman, *The World Is Flat: A Brief History of the Twenty-First Century*, 2005
Steven Hopp, *Animal, Vegetable, Miracle: A Year of Food Life*, 2007
  Barbara Kingsolver, co-author
  Camille Kingsolver, co-author
Michael Pollan, *The Omnivore's Dilemma: A Natural History of Four Meals*, 2006
Pietra Rivoli, *The Travels of a T-Shirt in the Global Economy: An Economist Examines the Markets, Power, and Politics of World Trade*, 2005
Christopher Steiner, *$20 Per Gallon: How the Inevitable Rise in the Price of Gasoline Will Change Our Lives for the Better*, 2009

927

MARTIN GARDNER

When You Were a Tadpole and I Was a Fish: And Other Speculations About This and That
(New York: Hill and Wang, 2009)

Subject(s): Science; Philosophy; Mathematics
Summary: In *When You Were a Tadpole and I Was a Fish: And Other Speculations About This and That*, Martin Gardner exposes the truth to many of science's biggest mysteries or tallest tales. Some of these border the name of science while others cause Gardner to delve deep into cells, bonds, and living systems. Some rumors are humorous while other tales turn out to be strictly fact. Gardner takes on the existence of Santa Claus, logical fallacies, the game of chess, and extrasensory perception. The topics in this book fall within seven categories: Mathematics, Logic, Religion/Philosophy, Science, Literature, Bogus Science, and Politics.

Other books by the same author:
Did Adam and Eve Have Navels?: Debunking Pseudoscience, 2001

The Whys of a Philosophical Scrivener, 1999
My Best Mathematical and Logic Puzzles, 1994
Perplexing Puzzles and Tantalizing Teasers, 1988
Other books you might like:
Richard Dawkins, *The God Delusion*, 2006
Christopher Hitchens, *God Is Not Great: How Religion Poisons Everything*, 2007
Christopher Hitchens, *Hitch-22*, 2010

928

ROSE GEORGE

The Big Necessity: The Unmentionable World of Human Waste and Why It Matters
(New York: Metropolitan Books, 2008)

Subject(s): Health; Medicine; Sanitation
Summary: In *The Big Necessity: The Unmentionable World of Human Waste and Why It Matters*, author Rose George discusses the awkward—but important—topic of human waste. In the book George explains that in many places throughout the world, human waste is becoming a big problem, but few people want to talk about the problem or take action to solve it. According to George, even industrialized nations have problems dealing with waste, and the author believes nothing will be done to solve problem before people feel free to talk openly about it.

Where it's reviewed:
Library Journal, September 1, 2008, page 157
School Library Journal, November 2008, page 158
Other books by the same author:
A Life Removed, 2004
Other books you might like:
Maggie Black, *The Last Taboo: Opening the Door on the Global Sanitation Crisis*, 2008
  Ben Fawcett, co-author
Morna E. Gregory, *Toilets of the World*, 2009
  Sian James, co-author
Steven Johnson, *The Ghost Map: The Story of London's Most Terrifying Epidemic—and How It Changed Science, Cities, and the Modern World*, 2006
Dave Praeger, *Poop Culture: How America Is Shaped by Its Grossest National Product*, 2007
  Paul Provenza, co-author
Elizabeth Royte, *Garbage Land: Land on the Secret Trail of Trash*, 2005

929

ELIZABETH GILBERT

Eat, Pray, Love: One Woman's Search for Everything Across Italy, India and Indonesia
(New York: Viking, 2006)

Subject(s): Food; Meditation; Spiritualism

Summary: Upon moving to the suburbs with her new husband, ready to start a family, author Elizabeth Gilbert realized that, although she had everything, she did not have what she wanted. This book recounts the healing trip that she took following a drawn-out divorce. Gilbert gave up her job and her belongings and dedicated a year to travel. Each destination was chosen to address a part of her being: Italy for pleasure; India for spiritualism; and Indonesia to balance the two. Her first stop, Rome, includes delicious pizza, generous amounts of wine, and new friends. Outside of Mumbai, India, she practices yoga and meditation. In Bali, she studies with a medicine man and—unexpectedly—falls in love.

Where it's reviewed:
Booklist, June 1-June 15, 2006, page 106
Kirkus Reviews, January 1, 2006, page 27
Library Journal, November 15, 2006, page 105

Other books by the same author:
Committed: A Skeptic Makes Peace with Marriage, 2010
Pilgrims, 2007
Stern Men, 2000

Other books you might like:
Frances Mayes, *Under the Tuscan Sun: At Home in Italy*, 1996
Audrey Niffenegger, *The Time Traveler's Wife*, 2003
Julie Powell, *Cleaving: A Story of Marriage, Meat, and Obsession*, 2009
Rima Rudner, *Choose To Be Happy: A Guide to Total Happiness*, 2008
Nicholas Sparks, *Nights in Rodanthe*, 2002

930

MALCOLM GLADWELL

Outliers

(New York: Little, Brown and Company, 2008)

Subject(s): Success; Culture; Social class

Summary: Malcolm Gladwell has a knack for looking at things from a different perspective. In *Outliers*, he takes a new look at what makes someone successful. Most think successful people possess common traits, habits, or philosophies. Gladwell suggests we look deeper at heritage and culture as the basis of accomplishment. By looking at famous, successful people he shows their achievements are due to certain advantages in their lives. Advantages that others with similar talents have not had, and therefore have not succeeded. There are many examples throughout the book to illustrate the point of "Outliers". Such as how a large portion of the descendants of Jewish immigrant garment workers have become high power attorneys, or how the hard work of growing rice in East Asia for generations has made children there more adept at math.

Where it's reviewed:
Booklist, Novemer 15, 2008, page 8
Bookmarks, Jan/Feb 2009, page 53
Library Journal, October 1, 2008, page 86
Library Journal, February 1, 2009, page 45

Publishers Weekly, January 26, 2009, page 117

Other books by the same author:
What the Dog Saw: And Other Adventures, 2009
Blink: The Power of Thinking Without Thinking, 2005
The Tipping Point: How Little Things Can Make a Big Difference, 2000

Other books you might like:
Cathy Birkenstein, *They Say/I Say: The Moves That Matter in Academic Writing*, 2009
Stephen J. Dubner, *Superfreakonomics: Global Cooling, Patriotic Prostitutes and Why Suicide Bombers Should Buy Life Insurance*, 2009
Stephen J. Dubner, *Freakonomics: A Rogue Economist Explores the Hidden Side of Everything. Rev. and Expanded Ed.*, 2006
Atul Gawande, *The Checklist Manifesto: How to Get Things Right*, 2009
Gerald Graff, *They Say/I Say: The Moves That Matter in Academic Writing*, 2009
Tony Hsieh, *Delivering Happiness: A Path to Profits, Passion, and Purpose*, 2010
Steven D. Levitt, *Superfreakonomics: Global Cooling, Patriotic Prostitutes and Why Suicide Bombers Should Buy Life Insurance*, 2009
Steven D. Levitt, *Freakonomics: A Rogue Economist Explores the Hidden Side of Everything. Rev. and Expanded Ed.*, 2006

931

MALCOLM GLADWELL

Blink: The Power of Thinking Without Thinking

(New York: Little, Brown and Co., 2005)

Subject(s): Neuroscience; Self-Perception

Summary: This book is about how people make decisions. Everyone is familiar with the phenomenon of the gut reaction: you make up your mind about something in a split second. Your first impressions are often accurate. Gladwell delves into this process, showing that the split-second decision is more complicated, and more precise, than is usually assumed. In the process, he goes into the nature of perception, and argues that, if properly trained, people can make their gut reactions more accurate than ever before. However, he also discusses some of the drawbacks to the split-second decision. For instance, in the fatal shooting of Amadou Dialo, the inaccurate gut reactions of the police had tragic results.

Where it's reviewed:
Booklist, September 1, 2004, page 2
Kirkus Reviews, October 1, 2004, page 948
Library Journal, November 15, 2004, page 75
Publishers Weekly, November 1, 2004, page 52

Other books by the same author:
What the Dog Saw: And Other Adventures, 2009
Outliers, 2008
The Tipping Point, 2000

Other books you might like:

Cathy Birkenstein, *They Say/I Say: The Moves That Matter in Academic Writing*, 2009

Stephen J. Dubner, *Freakonomics: A Rogue Economist Explores the Hidden Side of Everything. Rev. and Expanded Ed.*, 2006

Malcolm Gladwell, *Outliers*, 2008

Malcolm Gladwell, *The Tipping Point: How Little Things Can Make a Big Difference*, 2000

Malcolm Gladwell, *What the Dog Saw: And Other Adventures*, 2009

Gerald Graff, *They Say/I Say: The Moves That Matter in Academic Writing*, 2009

Steven D. Levitt, *Freakonomics: A Rogue Economist Explores the Hidden Side of Everything. Rev. and Expanded Ed.*, 2006

932

DANNY GOLDBERG

Bumping into Geniuses: My Life inside the Rock and Roll Business

(New York: Gotham Publishing, 2008)

Subject(s): Popular culture; Music; Rock music

Summary: In *Bumping into Geniuses: My Life inside the Rock and Roll Business*, author Danny Goldberg tells of his experience as a music journalist, publicist, and record label executive. His career spanned more than four decades, during which time he met many musical legends including Greg Allman, Kurt Cobain, Jimmy Page, and Robert Plant. Goldberg's book is divided into three chapters: Woodstock Nation's Brief State of Grace, which details the years from 1969 until 1976; Corporate Rock, which discusses rock and roll from 1976 through to 1989; and Rock and Roll's Middle Age, which deals with 1989 through until 2004. Goldberg is also the author of *How the Left Lost Teen Spirit* and *Dispatches from the Culture Wars*.

Where it's reviewed:

Booklist, September 1, 2008, page 24

Library Journal, August 1, 2008, page 85

Publishers Weekly, June 30, 2008, page 175

Other books by the same author:

How the Left Lost Teen Spirit: (And how they're getting it back!), 2005

Other books you might like:

Cameron Crowe, *Almost Famous*, 2000

Fred Goodman, *The Mansion on the Hill: Dylan, Young, Geffen, Springsteen, and the Head-on Collision of Rock and Commerce*, 1997

Bill Graham, *Bill Graham Presents: My Life Inside Rock And Out*, 2004

Robert Greenfield, co-author

Al Kooper, *Backstage Passes and Backstabbing Bastards: Memoirs of a Rock 'N' Roll Survivor*, 2008

Chris Salewicz, *Redemption Song: The Ballad of Joe Strummer*, 2008

933

GARY DAVID GOLDBERG

Sit, Ubu, Sit: How I Went from Brooklyn to Hollywood with the Same Woman, the Same Dog, and a Lot Less Hair

(New York: Harmony, 2008)

Subject(s): Entertainment industry; Dogs; Television

Summary: Producer and scriptwriter Goldberg is the creator of the memorable television series the Bob Newhart Show and the Tony Randal Show. His production company UBU (named after his dog) produced shows like Family Ties and Spin City. Goldberg retraces his humble beginnings in Brooklyn to his hard-won successes in the television industry, thanking many people along the way and relying on the humor that made his television shows great successes.

Where it's reviewed:

Library Journal, November 15, 2007, page 61

People, February 25, 2008, page 53

Publishers Weekly, October 15, 2007, page 49

Other books you might like:

Barbara Roisman Cooper, *Anna Lee: Memoir of a Career on General Hospital and in Film*, 2007

Michael J. Fox, *Always Looking Up: The Adventures of an Incurable Optimist*, 2009

Melissa Gilbert, *Prairie Tale: A Memoir*, 2009

Anna Lee, *Anna Lee: Memoir of a Career on General Hospital and in Film*, 2007

Garry Marshall, *Wake Me When It's Funny: How to Break into Show Business and Stay There*, 1997

Lori Marshall, co-author

Betty White, *Here We Go Again: My Life In Television*, 2010

934

TEMPLE GRANDIN
CATHERINE JOHNSON , Co-Author

Animals Make Us Human: Creating the Best Life for Animals

(New York: Houghton Mifflin Harcourt, 2009)

Subject(s): Animals; Human behavior; Human-animal relationships

Summary: Author Temple Grandin—an autistic person who has worked for more than a decade to make the treatment of livestock on the way to slaughter more humane—focuses on other creatures, domestic and wild, such as dogs, cats, pigs, cows, poultry, and zoo animals in *Animals Make Us Human: Creating the Best Life for Animals*. She shares her unique insight into the animal world, explaining what animals need from humans and the qualities that humans and animals have in common, so that the relationships between the two can be enriched

Pop Culture

through a common understanding. She also discusses the best and most humane ways to treat domestic farm animals and the most beneficial methods for training animals. Catherine Johnson, coauthor of *Animals Make Us Human*, also cowrote *Animals in Translation*.

Other books by the same author:
The Way I See It, 2008
Thinking in Pictures: And Other Reports from My Life with Autism, 2006
Animals in Translation: Using the Mysteries of Autism to Decode Animal Behavior, 2004

Other books you might like:
Sean Barron, *The Unwritten Rules of Social Relationships: Decoding Social Mysteries through the Unique Perspectives of Autism*, 2005
Temple Grandin, *Animals in Translation: Using the Mysteries of Autism to Decode Animal Behavior*, 2005
Temple Grandin, *Emergence: Labeled Autistic*, 1986
Temple Grandin, *Humane Livestock Handling: Understanding Livestock Behavior and Building Facilities for Healthier Animals*, 2008
Temple Grandin, *The Unwritten Rules of Social Relationships: Decoding Social Mysteries through the Unique Perspectives of Autism*, 2005
Temple Grandin, *The Way I See It: A Personal Look at Autism and Asperger's*, 2008
Catherine Johnson, *Animals in Translation: Using the Mysteries of Autism to Decode Animal Behavior*, 2005
Margaret M. Scariano, *Emergence: Labeled Autistic*, 1986

935

DAVID GRANN

The Devil and Sherlock Holmes: Tales of Murder, Madness, and Obsession

(New York: Doubleday, 2010)

Subject(s): Mental disorders; Human behavior; Murder

Summary: *The Devil and Sherlock Holmes: Tales of Murder, Madness, and Obsession* by David Grann is a collection of 12 journalistic narratives dealing with the dark side of the human mind. Each story carries a theme of obsessive or violent behavior, mystery, perversity, or some other dangerous trait. In one story, a scientist becomes preoccupied with finding a giant squid, regardless of dangers to himself or his sailing crew. In another, a racist gang spreads its message and recruits new members in the prison system. Other stories involve dangerous jobs, crime mysteries, and bizarre occurrences. Grann is also a writer for the New Yorker.

Where it's reviewed:
Booklist, February 15, 2010, page 7
Library Journal, March 15, 2010, page 110

Other books by the same author:
The Lost City of Z: A Tale of Deadly Obsession in the Amazon, 2009

Other books you might like:
Evan L. Balkan, *Vanished!: Explorers Forever Lost*, 2007
Sir Arthur Conan Doyle, *The Complete Sherlock Holmes*, 1953
Martin Dugard, *Into Africa: The Epic Adventures of Stanley and Livingstone*, 2003
Percy Fawcett, *Exploration Fawcett: Journey to the Lost City of Z*, 2010
Graham Moore, *The Sherlockian*, 2010

936

KATHY GRIFFIN

Official Book Club Selection: A Memoir According to Kathy Griffin

(New York: Ballantine Books, 2009)

Subject(s): Autobiographies; Comedians; Actors

Summary: In her autobiography *Official Book Club Selection: A Memoir According to Kathy Griffin*, the Emmy Award-winning comedian offers up the remarkable story of her life and career. Told with Kathy's signature humor and unwavering honesty, this volume charts the comic's moving—and hysterical—journey: a troubled Midwestern family, the L.A. comedy circuit of the 1980s, her brother's death, her own divorce, celebrity run-ins, and plastic surgery challenges. Filled with Kathy's hilarious perspectives on life and love, as well as a surprising sensitivity to the people and challenges she's encountered, *Official Book Club Selection* is ideal for Griffin fans old and new.

Where it's reviewed:
Entertainment Weekly, September 18, 2009, page 133

Other books you might like:
Russell Brand, *My Booky Wook: A Memoir of Sex, Drugs, and Stand-Up*, 2007
Chelsea Handler, *Are You There, Vodka? It's Me, Chelsea*, 2008
Chelsea Handler, *Chelsea Chelsea Bang Bang*, 2010
Chelsea Handler, *My Horizontal Life: A Collection of One-Night Stands*, 2005
Heather McDonald, *You'll Never Blue Ball in This Town Again: One Woman's Painfully Funny Quest to Give It Up*, 2010

937

JOHN GROGAN

Marley & Me: Life and Love with the World's Worst Dog

(New York: HarperCollins, 2005)

Subject(s): Dogs; Family Life; Friendship
Summary: When journalist John Grogan and his wife,

Jenny, were first married, they decided to get a dog, partly to practice their "parenting" skills. They were totally unprepared for their sweet and cuddly little puppy to turn into 97 pounds of undisciplined exuberance. Marley was expelled from obedience school, frequently cleared coffee tables with his tail, crashed through screen doors, affectionately knocked down little children, and ate everything in sight—including furniture and an 18-kt. solid gold necklace. His boundless energy was matched by his boundless love and affection, and he quickly won a permanent place in the hearts of the entire Grogan family. This memoir is one that will resonate with everyone who has ever loved a dog.

Where it's reviewed:
Booklist, October 1, 2005, page 12
Library Journal, July 1, 2005, page 108
Publishers Weekly, September 19, 2005, page 13

Other books by the same author:
The Longest Trip Home: A Memoir, 2008

Other books you might like:
Mitch Albom, *The Five People You Meet in Heaven*, 2003
Mitch Albom, *Tuesdays with Morrie: An Old Man, a Young Man, and Life's Greatest Lesson*, 1997
Michael J. Fox, *Always Looking Up: The Adventures of an Incurable Optimist*, 2009
Vicki Myron, *Dewey: The Small-Town Library Cat Who Touched the World*, 2008
Nicholas Sparks, *Nights in Rodanthe*, 2002
Bret Witter, *Dewey: The Small-Town Library Cat Who Touched the World*, 2008

938

CINDY GUIDRY

The Last Single Woman in America
(New York: Dutton Publishing, 2009)

Subject(s): Dating (Social customs); Humor; Interpersonal relations

Summary: *The Last Single Woman in America* by Cindy Guidry is a series of essays about being single in America among a seemingly endless sea of couples. Guidry declares herself "The Last Single Woman" in the country after realizing she was the only single woman at a wedding she attended. In the book's 24 essays, Guidry provides her own personal insight into and perspective on being unattached in a couple's world, and she explains how she has learned to cope with it. Guidry is a native of New Orleans and a former Hollywood studio executive.

Where it's reviewed:
Library Journal, January 1, 2008, page 110
Publishers Weekly, November 19, 2007, page 49

Other books you might like:
Jane Austen, *Pride and Prejudice*, 1813
Helen Fielding, *Bridget Jones's Diary*, 1996
Ben Karlin, *Things I've Learned from Women Who've Dumped Me*, 2008

Judy McGuire, *How Not to Date*, 2007
Jennifer Weiner, *Good in Bed*, 2001

939

MALU HALASA
RANA SALAM , Co-Author

The Secret Life of Syrian Lingerie: Intimacy and Design
(San Francisco, California: Chronicle Books, 2008)

Subject(s): Clothing; Culture; Tradition

Summary: *The Secret Life of Syrian Lingerie: Intimacy and Design* focuses on a part of Syria's culture that is often overlooked: the country's deep traditional ties to lingerie. In this volume, authors Malu Halasa and Rana Salam take an in-depth look at this phenomenon through a series of essays and memorable photographs. Celebrating the little-known Syrian custom, the authors explore the role of lingerie in the country's traditions and rituals, as well as the wealth of unique lingerie styles and innovations created there. *The Secret Life of Syrian Lingerie* includes bibliographical references, a full index, and biographical information on the contributors.

Other books you might like:
Rebecca Apsan, *The Lingerie Handbook*, 2006
Sami Moubayed, *Steel & Silk: Men and Women Who Shaped Syria 1900-2000*, 2005
Ali Salem, *A Drive to Israel: An Egyptian Meets His Neighbors*, 2003
Elyse Semerdjian, *Off the Straight Path: Illicit Sex, Law, and Community in Ottoman Aleppo*, 2008
Sarah Stark, *The Lingerie Handbook*, 2006
Richard Tapper, *A Taste of Thyme: Culinary Cultures of the Middle East*, 2001
Sami Zubaida, co-editor

940

JUSTIN HALPERN

Sh*t My Dad Says
(New York: It Books, 2010)

Subject(s): Father-son relations; Humor; Coming of age

Summary: Humorist Justin Halpern has made a name for himself as the creator of the Twitter phenomenon *Sh*t My Dad Says*. Now, in the book version of the social media sensation, Halpern draws fans even further into the wit and wisdom of his opinionated father, Sam. Interspersed with Sam's classic nuggets of wisdom is the story of Justin's upbringing, from baseball games to disastrous family vacations, written with laugh-out-loud wit and surprising sensitivity.

Other books you might like:
Ben Bator, *Texts From Last Night: All the Texts No One Remembers Sending*, 2010
Chelsea Handler, *My Horizontal Life: A Collection of One-Night Stands*, 2005

Pop Culture

Matt Kuhn, *The Playbook: Suit up. Score Chicks. Be Awesome.*, 2010

Lauren Leto, *Texts From Last Night: All the Texts No One Remembers Sending*, 2010

John Lindsay, *Emails from an Asshole: Real People Being Stupid*, 2010

Tucker Max, *I Hope They Serve Beer in Hell*, 2006

Barney Stinson, *The Playbook: Suit up. Score Chicks. Be Awesome.*, 2010

941

PATRICIA HAMPL

The Florist's Daughter

(New York: Harcourt, 2007)

Subject(s): Family; Childhood; Coming of age

Summary: In *The Florist's Daughter*, Patricia Hampl observes, "Nothing is harder to grasp than the relentlessly modest life." Hampl, author of several critically acclaimed autobiographies, opens this memoir with the death of her mother. The death marks the end of several years as a caretaker and faithful daughter and brings forth the desire to recall and reflect upon the ordinary lives of her parents, Stan and Mary Hampl. The aesthetic sensibility of a Czech father, who earned his living as a florist, and the love of words and archiving of an Irish mother, who was employed as a library file clerk, help to inform Hampl's prose style and metaphoric vision of the world. The opening of the memoir begins with the question of why she never left her birthplace of St. Paul, Minnesota, and ultimately concludes that there was work required of her, beyond her responsibilities as a daughter, to serve the relentlessness of modest life.

Where it's reviewed:
Booklist, September 1, 2007, page 38
Library Journal, September 1, 2007, page 144

Other books by the same author:
Blue Arabesque, 2006
I Could Tell You Stories: Sojourns in the Land of Memory, 1999
A Romantic Education, 1981

Other books you might like:
Joan Didion, *The Year of Magical Thinking*, 2005
Patricia Hampl, *I Could Tell You Stories: Sojourns in the Land of Memory*, 1999
Patricia Hampl, *A Romantic Education*, 1999
Kathryn Stockett, *The Help*, 2009
Virginia Woolf, *A Room of One's Own*, 1929

942

CHELSEA HANDLER

Are You There, Vodka? It's Me, Chelsea

(New York: Simon Spotlight Entertainment, 2008)

Subject(s): Humor; Family; Culture

Summary: Chelsea Handler, a well-known comedian, gives readers a follow-up to her earlier collection of essays called *My Horizontal Life* with her book *Are You There, Vodka? It's Me, Chelsea*. In this collection, Handler tells stories from her past to explore the topics of family, friendships, work, and society. The stories are told in a humorous, lighthearted style. Whether she is trying to convince her classmates that she is starring in a Hollywood film or babysitting someone two years older than herself, Handler often winds up in awkward, but hilarious, situations. Handler does not hold anything back in her irreverent, personal, and comical book.

Where it's reviewed:
Library Journal, May 15, 2008, page 101
Publishers Weekly, April 21, 2008, page 42

Other books by the same author:
Chelsea Chelsea Bang Bang, 2010
My Horizontal Life: A Collection of One-Night Stands, 2006

Other books you might like:
Russell Brand, *My Booky Wook: A Memoir of Sex, Drugs, and Stand-Up*, 2007
Kathy Griffin, *Official Book Club Selection: A Memoir According to Kathy Griffin*, 2009
Chelsea Handler, *Chelsea Chelsea Bang Bang*, 2010
Chelsea Handler, *My Horizontal Life: A Collection of One-Night Stands*, 2005
Heather McDonald, *You'll Never Blue Ball in This Town Again: One Woman's Painfully Funny Quest to Give It Up*, 2010

943

CHELSEA HANDLER

Chelsea Chelsea Bang Bang

(New York: Grand Central Publishing, 2010)

Subject(s): Humor; Modern Life; Family

Summary: Chelsea Handler is a popular comic who talks about her life and experiences from a humorous perspective. *Chelsea Chelsea Bang Bang* is a collection of short humorous essays by Handler. These tales cover her life from her youth—dealing with her family, pondering over politics, and trying to acquire Cabbage Patch dolls—to her adulthood. She talks about relationships, show business, jokes and pranks, and fun times with her friends. Handler also wrote *Are You There, Vodka? It's Me, Chelsea*.

Where it's reviewed:
Publishers Weekly, March 8, 2010, page 52

Other books by the same author:
Are You There, Vodka? It's Me, Chelsea, 2008
My Horizontal Life: A Collection of One-Night Stands, 2006

Other books you might like:
Russell Brand, *My Booky Wook: A Memoir of Sex, Drugs, and Stand-Up*, 2007
Kathy Griffin, *Official Book Club Selection: A Memoir According to Kathy Griffin*, 2009
Heather McDonald, *You'll Never Blue Ball in This Town*

Again: One Woman's Painfully Funny Quest to Give It Up, 2010

Sarah Silverman, *The Bedwetter: Stories of Courage, Redemption, and Pee*, 2010

Stefanie Wilder-Taylor, *It's Not Me, It's You: Subjective Recollections from a Terminally Optimistic, Chronically Sarcastic and Occasionally Inebriated Woman*, 2009

944

CHELSEA HANDLER

My Horizontal Life: A Collection of One-Night Stands

(New York: Bloomsbury Publishing, 2005)

Subject(s): Humor; Interpersonal relations

Summary: In *My Horizontal Life*, author and comedian Chelsea Handler explores the allure of the one-night stand through a series of stories about her encounters with various men. This humorous collection of essays chronicles Handler's experiences with sex: from catching her parents in the act as a child to making out with a little person while on vacation in Mexico to dating a male stripper called Thunder. The outgoing comedian isn't ashamed to share her most embarrassing tales of first-date disasters and family dysfunctions with readers. As she approaches her thirties, Handler questions whether the one-night stand is really all that its cracked up to be.

Where it's reviewed:
Kirkus Reviews, March 15, 2005, page 334
Library Journal, April 15, 2005, pages 99-100
Publishers Weekly, April 18, 2005, page 53

Other books by the same author:
Chelsea Chelsea Bang Bang, 2010
Are You There, Vodka? It's Me, Chelsea, 2008

Other books you might like:
Russell Brand, *My Booky Wook: A Memoir of Sex, Drugs, and Stand-Up*, 2007
Kathy Griffin, *Official Book Club Selection: A Memoir According to Kathy Griffin*, 2009
Chelsea Handler, *Are You There, Vodka? It's Me, Chelsea*, 2008
Chelsea Handler, *Chelsea Chelsea Bang Bang*, 2010
Heather McDonald, *You'll Never Blue Ball In This Town Again: One Woman's Painfully Funny Quest to Give It Up*, 2010

945

EVAN HANDLER

It's Only Temporary: The Good News and the Bad News of Being Alive

(New York: Riverhead Books, 2008)

Subject(s): Autobiographies; Cancer; Interpersonal relations

Summary: *It's Only Temporary: The Good News and the Bad News of Being Alive* is a series of autobiographical essays written by actor Evan Handler. Though his first book, *Time on Fire*, focused predominantly on his struggles with leukemia, this book touches not only on his illness, but also on his recovery. He considers the years of his life lost to leukemia, as well as the often poor quality of his healthcare. In addition, Handler discusses his time spent attempting to grow as a person and become more mature, often turning the spotlight on his relationships with women and the way they often end in drama when he refuses to stay committed. In these essays, Handler searches for his own identity, recognizing that he still has some work to do to become the person he wishes to be.

Where it's reviewed:
Publishers Weekly, March 31, 2008, page 49

Other books by the same author:
Time on Fire: My Comedy of Terrors, 1997

Other books you might like:
Rob Ballister, *God Does Have a Sense of Humor*, 2005
Candace Bushnell, *Sex and the City*, 2002
Fran Di Giacomo, *I'd Rather Do Chemo Than Clean Out the Garage: Choosing Laughter over Tears*, 2003
Alec Kalla, *57 Good Things About Chemotherapy*, 2001

946

BOB HARRIS

Prisoner of Trebekistan: A Decade in Jeopardy!

(New York: Crown Publishing, 2006)

Subject(s): Games; Television programs; Entertainment industry

Summary: In 1998, *Jeopardy!* contestant and stand-up comedian Bob Harris won five games in a row—the most possible at that time—and was subsequently invited to partake in the television game show's "Tournament of Champions." In *Prisoner of Trebekistan: A Decade in Jeopardy!*, Harris reveals the legacy that his accomplishment left behind and the impact that his success on the show has had on his personal life. The book also contains information about the show's history since its inception in 1963, and it describes some tips and strategies players use on the game. Harris is also the author of *Who Hates Whom* and *Steal This Book: And Get Life without Parole*.

Where it's reviewed:
Booklist, September 1, 2006, page 34
Publishers Weekly, July 17, 2006, page 153

Other books by the same author:
Who Hates Whom: Well-Armed Fanatics, Intractable Conflicts, and Various Things Blowing Up A Woefully Incomplete Guide, 2007
Steal This Book: And Get Life Without Parole, 1999

Other books you might like:
Peter Barsocchini, *The Jeopardy! Book: The Answers, the Questions, the Facts, and the Stories of the*

Pop Culture

Greatest Game Show in History, 1990

Michael Dupee, *How to Get on Jeopardy! and Win: Valuable Information from a Champion*, 1998

Trevor Homer, *The Book of Origins: Discover the Amazing Origins of the Clothes We Wear, the Food We Eat, the People We Know, the Languages We Speak, and the Things We Use*, 2007

Ken Jennings, *Brainiac: Adventures in the Curious, Competitive, Compulsive World of Trivia*, 2006

Ken Jennings, *Ken Jennings's Trivia Almanac: 8,888 Questions in 365 Days*, 2008

Alex Trebek, *The Jeopardy! Book: The Answers, the Questions, the Facts, and the Stories of the Greatest Game Show in History*, 1990

947

STEVE HARVEY

Act Like a Lady, Think Like a Man: What Men Really Think About Love, Relationships, Intimacy, and Commitment

(New York: Amistad, 2009)

Subject(s): Interpersonal relations; Dating (Social customs); Human behavior

Summary: *Act Like A Lady, Think Like A Man: What Men Really Think About Love, Relationships, Intimacy, and Commitment* by Steve Harvey sets women straight on what men are all about and how to get what they want from them. Harvey, a comedian, a radio show host, and an author, provides insight into what makes men tick and states that it is surprisingly simple. He notes the differences between the way women love and the way men love to help women better understand the men in their lives. He also develops guidelines for how women should act to get the best results from the men that they love, want to date, or want to marry. His straightforward words of advice and explanation are intended to help women achieve the happiness they want and deserve in their relationships with men.

Other books by the same author:
Straight Talk, No Chaser: How to Find, Keep, and Understand a Man, 2010

Other books you might like:
Sherry Argov, *Why Men Love Bitches: From Doormat to Dreamgirl—A Woman's Guide to Holding Her Own in a Relationship*, 2002

Maria Bustillos, *Act Like a Gentleman, Think Like a Woman: A Woman's Response to Steve Harvey's Act Like a Lady, Think Like a Man*, 2009

Hill Harper, *The Conversation: How Black Men and Women Can Build Loving, Trusting Relationships*, 2009

Sister Souljah, *No Disrespect*, 1994

948

ELIZABETH HESS

Nim Chimpsky: The Chimp Who Would Be Human

(New York: Bantam Books, 2008)

Subject(s): Animals; Chimpanzees; Human-animal relationships

Summary: Elizabeth Hess writes about the friendship between animals and humans in *Nim Chimpsky: The Chimp Who Would Be Human*. During the 1970s, chimpanzee Nim Chimpsky was part of an experiment at the University of Oklahoma, where researchers wanted to determine if a chimp could learn sign language. Nim was sent to live with a family in New York City. The family raised him and taught him sign language. The experiment was both a success and a failure, as Nim lived between the human world and the animal world, bouncing from home to home to various facilities across the United States.

Where it's reviewed:
Booklist, February 1, 2008, page 12
Fortune, March 17, 2008, page 58
Science News, June 21, 2008, page 30

Other books by the same author:
Lost and Found: Dogs, Cats, and Everyday Heroes at a Country Animal Shelter, 2000

Other books you might like:
Noam Chomsky, *On Language: Chomsky's Classic Works*, 1998

Roger Fouts, *Next of Kin: My Conversations with Chimpanzees*, 1998

Christine Kenneally, *The First Word: The Search for the Origins of Language*, 2008

Roger Lewin, *Kanzi: The Ape at the Brink of the Human Mind*, 1996

Stephen Tukel Mills, *Next of Kin: My Conversations with Chimpanzees*, 1998

Sue Savage-Rumbaugh, *Kanzi: The Ape at the Brink of the Human Mind*, 1996

Lauren Slater, *Opening Skinner's Box: Great Psychological Experiments of the Twentieth Century*, 2005

949

CHRISTOPHER HITCHENS

God Is Not Great: How Religion Poisons Everything

(New York: Twelve, 2007)

Subject(s): Atheism; Religion; Bible stories

Summary: Christopher Hitchens's *God is Not Great: How Religion Poisons Everything* speaks out against all organized religion and in support of atheism. Using readings from the Bible and other religious texts, Hitchens finds support for anti-religious ideas that claim that religion is man-made and its only purpose is to create a sex-less society. He speaks of better, more fulfilling lives filled with science and rationale instead of lives of sacrifice and dedication to a faceless and nameless God. Hitchens doesn't spend time shooting down on specific religion within this text—he takes on all of them. Hitchens often appears on television and radio shows to promote his atheistic view along with his own political ideals.

Other books by the same author:
Hitch-22, 2010
The Portable Atheist: Essential Readings for the Nonbeliever, 2007

Other books you might like:
Richard Dawkins, *The God Delusion*, 2006
Deborah Heiligman, *Charles and Emma: The Darwins' Leap of Faith*, 2009
William Lobdell, *Losing My Religion: How I Lost My Faith Reporting on Religion in America—and Found Unexpected Peace*, 2009
Rebecca Newberger Goldstein, *36 Arguments for the Existence of God: A Work of Fiction*, 2010
Rebecca Skloot, *The Immortal Life of Henrietta Lacks*, 2009

950

CHRISTOPHER HITCHENS

Hitch-22
(New York: Twelve, 2010)

Subject(s): Journalism; Politics; Immigrants

Summary: Journalist and author Christopher Hitchens takes readers on a rollicking ride through his life, work, and worldly adventures. *Hitch-22* spans the globe as Hitchens recounts his days spent working in such places as Afghanistan, Cuba, The Czech Republic, and Iraq. Always willing to go the limit for a story, he even subjects himself to some surprising challenges (including being waterboarded) in his quest for truth. Woven throughout stories of his career and escapades around the world are tales of Hitchens's personal life and history, and how these aspects of his story shaped both the man and the writer.

Other books by the same author:
God is Not Great: How Religion Poisons Everything, 2007
The Portable Atheist: Essential Readings for the Nonbeliever, 2007

Other books you might like:
Richard Dawkins, *The God Delusion*, 2006
Deborah Heiligman, *Charles and Emma: The Darwins' Leap of Faith*, 2009
Rebecca Newberger Goldstein, *36 Arguments for the Existence of God: A Work of Fiction*, 2010
Salman Rushdie, *Imaginary Homelands: Essays and Criticism, 1981-1991*, 1991
Rebecca Skloot, *The Immortal Life of Henrietta Lacks*, 2009

951

JOHN HODGMAN

The Areas of My Expertise: An Almanac of Complete World Knowledge Compiled with Instructive Annotation and Arranged in Useful Order
(New York: Dutton Adult, 2005)

Subject(s): Humor; Homeless persons; History

Summary: *The Areas of My Expertise: An Almanac of Complete World Knowledge Compiled with Instructive Annotation and Arranged in Useful Order* is a collection of 55 amusing, yet informative, articles written by John Hodgman. As a literary agent, comedian, and professional writer, Hodgman has been around the block a few times. His travels and research have allowed him to become a self-proclaimed expert in numerous areas including utopias, monsters, deformities, submarines, and hobos. *The Areas of My Expertise* is Hodgman's first book. He's best known as a correspondent on *The Daily Show with Jon Stewart*.

Where it's reviewed:
Library Journal, October 1, 2005, page 75
Publishers Weekly, July 25, 2005, page 58

Other books by the same author:
More Information Than You Require, 2008

Other books you might like:
The Onion, *Our Dumb World: The Onion's Atlas of the Planet Earth, 73rd Edition*, 2007
David Rakoff, *Don't Get Too Comfortable: The Indignities of Coach Class, The Torments of Low Thread Count, The Never-Ending Quest for Artisanal Olive Oil, and Other First World Problems*, 2005
David Sedaris, *Me Talk Pretty One Day*, 2000
Eric Spitznagel, *You're a Horrible Person, but I Like You: The Believer Book of Advice*, 2010
Larry Wilmore, *I'd Rather We Got Casinos, and Other Black Thoughts*, 2009

952

JOHN HODGMAN

More Information Than You Require
(New York: Dutton, 2009)

Subject(s): Humor; United States; Autobiographies

Summary: *More Information Than You Require* by John Hodgman, which comes on the heels of *The Areas of My Expertise*, Hodgman continues his patented brand of truth-stretching and absurdity to get a laugh, while still maintaining a shred of truth in each of his stories. An extensive discussion of mole-men can be found in this book, as well as a number of pieces of trivia and interesting photos. Specific sections include "How to Tell the Future Using a Pig's Spleen," "How to Deal With Some Common Infestations," and "How to Be Famous," based on his own experiences in moving from a career as a writer and literary agent to a television personality, among a number of other humorous advice sections.

Other books by the same author:
The Areas of My Expertise: An Almanac of Complete World Knowledge Compiled with Instructive Annotation and Arranged in Useful Order, 2005

Other books you might like:
Samantha Bee, *I Know I Am, but What Are You?*, 2010
David Rakoff, *Don't Get Too Comfortable: The Indignities of Coach Class, The Torments of Low Thread Count, The Never-Ending Quest for Artisanal Olive Oil, and Other First World Problems*, 2005
David Sedaris, *Me Talk Pretty One Day*, 2000
Eric Spitznagel, *You're a Horrible Person, but I Like You: The Believer Book of Advice*, 2010
Larry Wilmore, *I'd Rather We Got Casinos, and Other Black Thoughts*, 2009

953

TREVOR HOMER

The Book of Origins: Discover the Amazing Origins of the Clothes We Wear, the Food We Eat, the People We Know, the Languages We Speak, and the Things We Use

(London: Portrait, 2007)

Subject(s): Reference works; Inventions; Biographies

Summary: *The Book of Origins: Discover the Amazing Origins of the Clothes We Wear, the Food We Eat, the People We Know, the Languages We Speak, and the Things We Use* is a collection of trivia and brief entries written by Trevor Homer. The book covers an extremely extensive range of topics, and most topics are covered in concise summaries. In addition to the origins of things such as food, clothing, and technology, other topics covered in the book include religions, languages, inventions, crimes, and notable people. Homer is also the author of *Born in the USA: The American Book of Origins*.

Where it's reviewed:
Library Journal, July 1, 2007, page 118

Other books by the same author:
Born in the USA: The American Book of Origins, 2009

Other books you might like:
Peter Barsocchini, *The Jeopardy! Book: The Answers, the Questions, the Facts, and the Stories of the Greatest Game Show in History*, 1990
Michael Dupee, *How to Get on Jeopardy! and Win: Valuable Information from a Champion*, 1998
Bob Harris, *Prisoner of Trebekistan: A Decade in Jeopardy!*, 2006

Ken Jennings, *Brainiac: Adventures in the Curious, Competitive, Compulsive World of Trivia*, 2006
Ken Jennings, *Ken Jennings's Trivia Almanac: 8,888 Questions in 365 Days*, 2008
Alex Trebek, *The Jeopardy! Book: The Answers, the Questions, the Facts, and the Stories of the Greatest Game Show in History*, 1990

954

A.E. HOTCHNER

Paul and Me: Fifty-three Years of Adventures and Misadventures with My Pal Paul Newman

(New York: Bantam Books, 2010)

Subject(s): Biographies; Entertainment industry; Movie industry

Summary: In *Paul and Me: Fifty-three Years of Adventures and Misadventures with My Pal Paul Newman*, American playwright and biographer A.E. Hotchner discusses his friendship with actor Paul Newman, who passed away in September, 2008. Hotchner and Newman first met on the set of a television play that Hotchner wrote, which was based on a story by Ernest Hemingway. What followed was a friendship that spanned more than five decades and included various movies, television appearances, and even a charitable business enterprise called Newman's Own. In this biography of Newman, Hotchner describes the personal and professional man he grew to know and love.

Where it's reviewed:
Library Journal, March 1, 2010, page 84

Other books by the same author:
Papa Hemingway, 2005
Louisiana Purchase, 1997
Blown Away: the Rolling Stones and the Death of the Sixties, 1990

Other books you might like:
Peter Biskind, *Star: How Warren Beatty Seduced America*, 2010
Rich Cohen, *When I Stop Talking, You'll Know I'm Dead: Useful Stories from a Persuasive Man*, 2010
Yann-Brice Dherbier, *Paul Newman: A Life in Pictures*, 2006
A.E. Hotchner, *In Pursuit of the Common Good: Twenty-Five Years of Improving the World, One Bottle of Salad Dressing at a Time*, 2008
Sam Kashner, *Furious Love: Elizabeth Taylor, Richard Burton, and the Marriage of the Century*, 2010
Paul Newman, *In Pursuit of the Common Good: Twenty-Five Years of Improving the World, One Bottle of Salad Dressing at a Time*, 2008
Nancy Schoenberger, *Furious Love: Elizabeth Taylor, Richard Burton, and the Marriage of the Century*, 2010

Pierre-Henri Verlhac, *Paul Newman: A Life in Pictures*, 2006

Jerry Weintraub, *When I Stop Talking, You'll Know I'm Dead: Useful Stories from a Persuasive Man*, 2010

955

YUNTE HUANG

Charlie Chan: The Untold Story of the Honorable Detective and his Rendezvous with American History

(New York: W. W. Norton & Company, 2010)

Subject(s): Asian Americans; Detective fiction; Americana

Summary: *Charlie Chan: The Untold Story of the Honorable Detective and his Rendezvous with American History* provides readers insight into the persona and history of Asian-American icon Charlie Chan. Yunte Huang provides the biography of Chang Apana, a real-life, Hawaiian-born detective who served as the inspiration for fictional character Charlie Chan. Huang also investigates and presents details about the popular character of books and movies who helped define the stereotype of Asians living in America. For over a decade, Huang researched movies, novels, and scholarship to write a comprehensive portrait of an Asian-American icon and to tell the story of his influence on American and Asian culture.

Where it's reviewed:
Booklist, July 1, 2010, page 12
Library Journal, July 2010, page 90
Publishers Weekly, June 28, 2010, page 122

Other books by the same author:
Transpacific Imaginations, 2008
Transpacific Displacement, 2002

Other books you might like:
Howard M. Berlin, *The Charlie Chan Film Encyclopedia*, 2000
Earl Derr Biggers, *Charlie Chan: Five Complete Novels*, 1981
Glen David Gold, *Sunnyside: A Novel*, 2009
Glen David Gold, *Carter Beats the Devil*, 2001
Isabel Wilkerson, *The Warmth of Other Suns: The Epic Story of America's Great Migration*, 2010

956

A.J. JACOBS

The Year of Living Biblically: One Man's Humble Quest to Follow the Bible as Literally as Possible

(New York: Simon & Schuster, 2007)

Subject(s): Judaism; Christianity; Bible

Summary: A.J. Jacobs decides to live one year of his life based on the teachings of the Bible. He vows to obey the Ten Commandments, to love his neighbor and adhere to various other teachings, including some of the lesser known rules such as to play a ten-string harp. *A Year of Living Biblically* is the result of this journey. Throughout the book, Jacobs details his interactions with people of different religions, learns how each interprets the Bible, and reveals how it all has helped to shape his life.

Where it's reviewed:
Booklist, July 1, 2007, page 6
Bookmarks, Jan-Feb 2008, Page 60
Books & Culture, Nov-Dec 2007, page 9
Library Journal, Sept 15, 2007, page 65
Publishers Weekly, June 25, 2007, page 49

Other books by the same author:
My Life as an Experiment: One Man's Humble Quest to Improve Himself by Living as a Woman, Becoming George Washington, Telling No Lies, and Other Radical Tests, 2010
The Guinea Pig Diaries: My Life as an Experiment, 2009
The Guinea Pig Diaries: My Life as an Experiment, 2009
The Know-It-All: One Man's Humble Quest to Become the Smartest Person in the World, 2005
Fractured Fairy Tales, 1999
America Off-Line: The Complete Outernet Starter Kit, 1996
The Two Kings: Jesus & Elvis, 1996

Other books you might like:
Susan E. Isaacs, *Angry Conversations with God: A Snarky but Authentic Spiritual Memoir*, 2009
A.J. Jacobs, *The Guinea Pig Diaries: My Life as an Experiment*, 2009
Jen Lancaster, *My Fair Lazy: One Reality Television Addict's Attempt to Discover If Not Being A Dumb Ass Is the New Black, or, a Culture-Up Manifesto*, 2010
Robyn Okrant, *Living Oprah: My One-Year Experiment to Walk the Walk of the Queen of Talk*, 2010
David Plotz, *Good Book: The Bizarre, Hilarious, Disturbing, Marvelous, and Inspiring Things I Learned When I Read Every Single Word of the Bible*, 2009

957

DANA JENNINGS

Sing Me Back Home: Love, Death, and Country Music

(New York: Faber & Faber, 2008)

Subject(s): Popular culture; Country music; Music

Pop Culture

Summary: In *Sing Me Back Home: Love, Death, and Country Music*, author Dana Jennings provides a historical perspective on country music and its impact on Americana. In this book, Jennings looks closely at a time period that is widely considered to be the heyday of country music: the 1950s through the 1970s. The author states that, as a man who grew up in rural America, he understands the viewpoints of many country songs and the hardscrabble life they portray. Jennings is also the author of *What a Difference a Dog Makes: Big Lessons on Life, Love and Healing from a Small Pooch*.

Where it's reviewed:
Booklist, May 1, 2008, page 63
Kirkus Reviews, March 1, 2008, page 231
Library Journal, March 1, 2008, page 84

Other books by the same author:
What a Difference a Dog Makes: Big Lessons on Life, Love and Healing from a Small Pooch, 2010
Me, Dad, & Number 6, 1997
Lonesome Standard Time, 1996

Other books you might like:
Patrick Carr, *Cash: The Autobiography*, 1997
Tom Carter, *I Lived to Tell It All*, 1996
Tom Carter, *Merle Haggard's My House of Memories: For the Record*, 1999
Johnny Cash, *Cash: The Autobiography*, 1997
Merle Haggard, *Merle Haggard's My House of Memories: For the Record*, 1999
Waylon Jennings, *Waylon: An Autobiography*, 1996
George Jones, *I Lived to Tell It All*, 1996
Lenny Kaye, *Waylon: An Autobiography*, 1996
Willie Nelson, *Willie: An Autobiography*, 1988
    Bud Shrake, co-author

958

KEN JENNINGS

Brainiac: Adventures in the Curious, Competitive, Compulsive World of Trivia

(New York: Villard, 2006)

Subject(s): Contests; Games; Popular Culture

Summary: The history of trivia as a past time and recurring fad is recounted by Ken Jennings, *Jeopardy!*'s longest-running and best-known champion. A former computer programmer, Jennings tells of his long-standing love for trivia and reveals the behind-the-scenes action of *Jeopardy!* In retelling his rise to trivia fame, Jennings traces the trivia subculture from London cafes of the 17th century through mid-20th century TV game shows to the emergence of Trivial Pursuit and the Internet. He also explores current trivia events, including college quiz-bowl tournaments and the World's Largest Trivia Contest held in Steven Points, Wisconsin each year. In describing the world of trivia, Jennings also wonders what purpose these contests serve in our culture. Trivia questions are interwoven into the text, with answers provided at the end of each chapter.

Where it's reviewed:
Library Journal, September 15, 2006, page 77
Publishers Weekly, May 29, 2006, page 45
Time, September 25, 2006, page 83

Other books by the same author:
Ken Jennings's Trivia Almanac: 8,888 Questions in 365 Days, 2008

Other books you might like:
Peter Barsocchini, *The Jeopardy! Book: The Answers, the Questions, the Facts, and the Stories of the Greatest Game Show in History*, 1990
Michael Dupee, *How to Get on Jeopardy! and Win: Valuable Information from a Champion*, 1998
Bob Harris, *Prisoner of Trebekistan: A Decade in Jeopardy!*, 2006
Trevor Homer, *The Book of Origins: Discover the Amazing Origins of the Clothes We Wear, the Food We Eat, the People We Know, the Languages We Speak, and the Things We Use*, 2007
Alex Trebek, *The Jeopardy! Book: The Answers, the Questions, the Facts, and the Stories of the Greatest Game Show in History*, 1990
Matt Weiland, *State by State: A Panoramic Portrait of America*, 2008
    Sean Wilsey, co-editor

959

STEVEN JOHNSON

The Ghost Map: The Story of London's Most Terrifying Epidemic—and How It Changed Science, Cities, and the Modern World

(New York: Riverhead, 2006)

Subject(s): Science; Medicine; Diseases

Summary: In *The Ghost Map: The Story of London's Most Terrifying Epidemic—and How It Changed Science, Cities, and the Modern World*, author Steven Johnson chronicles the events that led to a deadly outbreak of cholera in London in 1854. Physician John Snow emerges as the heroic scientist who discovers that the outbreak is caused by contaminated water and not by noxious gases in the air. He met with resistance from the government and the medical community, but ultimately won through meticulous scientific proof. His groundbreaking work transformed the medical and scientific communities as well as the cities are constructed around the world.

Where it's reviewed:
The New York Review of Books, June 28, 2007, page 41

Other books by the same author:
The Invention of Air, 2008
Everything Bad is Good for You, 2006
Mind Wide Open, 2004

Other books you might like:
Maggie Black, *The Last Taboo: Opening the Door on*

the *Global Sanitation Crisis*, 2008
  Ben Fawcett, co-author
Rose George, *The Big Necessity: The Unmentionable World of Human Waste and Why It Matters*, 2008
Morna E. Gregory, *Toilets of the World*, 2009
  Sian James, co-author
Dave Praeger, *Poop Culture: How America Is Shaped by Its Grossest National Product*, 2007
  Paul Provenza, co-author
Elizabeth Royte, *Garbage Land: Land on the Secret Trail of Trash*, 2005

960

BEN JONES

Redneck Boy in the Promised Land
(New York: Crown Publishing, 2008)

Subject(s): Autobiographies; Entertainment industry; Television programs

Summary: In *Redneck Boy in the Promised Land*, author, actor, and former politician Ben Jones discusses his life including his childhood upbringing in rural Virginia, his civil rights activism, his stint as a Hollywood actor, and his time as a Georgia congressman. Jones is probably best known for playing the role of Cooter Davenport, the mechanic on the popular television show *The Dukes of Hazzard*. Although the show was popular in the 1980s, Jones's own career was marred by alcoholism and addiction. In the book, Jones talks about how he struggled with addiction and how he got back on track to have a successful career in politics.

Where it's reviewed:
Publishers Weekly, April 14, 2008, page 51

Other books you might like:
Alison Arngrim, *Confessions of a Prairie Bitch: How I Survived Nellie Oleson and Learned to Love Being Hated*, 2010
James Best, *Best in Hollywood: The Good, the Bad, and the Beautiful*, 2009
  Jim Clark, co-author
Melissa Gilbert, *Prairie Tale: A Memoir*, 2009
Chris Kreski, *Growing Up Brady: I Was a Teenage Greg*, 1992
Mackenzie Phillips, *High on Arrival*, 2009
Barry Williams, *Growing Up Brady: I Was a Teenage Greg*, 1992

961

SAM KASHNER
NANCY SCHOENBERGER , Co-Author

Furious Love: Elizabeth Taylor, Richard Burton, and the Marriage of the Century
(New York: Harper, 2010)

Subject(s): Biographies; Entertainment industry; Marriage
Summary: *Furious Love: Elizabeth Taylor, Richard Bur-*

ton, and the Marriage of the Century* is a dual biography written by journalist Sam Kashner and biographer Nancy Schoenberger. The authors closely examine the relationship and marriage of the two actors, basing the biography on private diary entries and letters between the two, as well as interviews with other actors, producers, and directors who worked directly with the couple. This biography provides extensive details about the couple's notoriously riotous relationship.

Where it's reviewed:
Booklist, June 1, 2010, page 21
Variety, June 21, 2010, page 2

Other books by the same author:
When I was Cool, 2004
The Bad and the Beautiful, 2002
A Talent for Genius, 1994

Other books you might like:
Edward Albee, *Who's Afraid of Virginia Woolf?*, 1962
Peter Biskind, *Star: How Warren Beatty Seduced America*, 2010
A.E. Hotchner, *Paul and Me: Fifty-three Years of Adventures and Misadventures with My Pal Paul Newman*, 2010
William J. Mann, *How to Be a Movie Star: Elizabeth Taylor in Hollywood*, 2009
Michael Munn, *Richard Burton: Prince of Players*, 2008

962

STEPHEN KENDRICK
ALEX KENDRICK , Co-Author

The Love Dare
(Nashville, Tennessee: B&H Books, 2008)

Subject(s): Marriage; Love

Summary: *The Love Dare* first appeared in the Christian movie *Fireproof*, in which a couple headed for divorce uses the book as a last effort to save their failing marriage. Couples using the *The Love Dare* undergo a forty-day journey in which they read a daily quote from Scripture and a short lesson. They are then given a challenge—a dare—in which they must do something nice for their partner such as buy a special gift or write a renewal of their marriage vows. The book contends that most marital problems stem from a lack of understanding about the meaning of unconditional true love.

Other books you might like:
Dr. Gary Chapman, *The Five Love Languages: How to Express Heartfelt Commitment to Your Mate*, 1995
Jennifer Dion, *Fireproof Your Marriage Couple's Kit*, 2008
Emerson Eggerichs, *Love & Respect: The Love She Most Desires; The Respect He Desperately Needs*, 2004
Nina Roesner, *The Respect Dare*, 2009
Mitch Temple, *The Marriage Turnaround: How Thinking Differently About Your Relationship Can Change Everything*, 2009

963

CHIP KIDD
MIKE ESSL , Co-Author
DAVID GIBBONS , Co-Author

Watching the Watchmen

(London: Titan Books, 2008)

Subject(s): Comic books; Movie industry; Entertainment industry

Summary: *Watching the Watchmen* is a companion guide for movie buffs to use while watching *Watchmen*, a film that was released in 2009 and was based on the popular graphic novel series by the name. The series and film revolve around an alternate universe in which former superheroes must solve the murder of one of their own kind. In this book, series illustrator David Gibbons—along with co-authors Chip Kidd and Mike Essl—provides insight into the characters and the storyline of the film.

Other books by the same author:
The Life and Times of Martha Washington in the Twenty-First Century, 2009
Green Lantern: Tales of the Sinestro Corps, 2008

Other books you might like:
Neil Gaiman, *The Sandman, Volume One: Preludes and Nocturnes*, 1993
Alan Moore, *From Hell*, 2000
Alan Moore, *V for Vendetta*, 2005
Alan Moore, *Watchmen*, 1986
Brian K. Vaughan, *Y: The Last Man: Unmanned*, 2003

964

TRACY KIDDER

Strength in What Remains

(New York: Random House, 2009)

Subject(s): Biographies; Genocide; Emigration and immigration

Summary: *Strength in What Remains* is a biography by Tracy Kidder of Deogratias, known as Deo. Deo was still a young man when he fled his home in the African nation of Burundi in 1993 after civil war broke out. Deo traveled through Rwanda, surviving the genocide taking place there, and eventually wound up in New York City, struggling to survive on very meager wages. Through the help of strangers who reached out to him, Deo was able to attend Columbia University and get his medical degree along with his American citizenship. Despite the fact that Deo would never need to return to Burundi, he still travels there regularly to work on creating a public health system and open medical clinics. Deo was able to turn the horrors of his young life into something positive for many people in his country of Burundi, and continues to make the country a better place with his strength.

Where it's reviewed:
Booklist, May 1, 2009, page 4

Other books by the same author:
My Detachment: A Memoir, 2006
Mountains Beyond Mountains, 2003
Among Schoolchildren, 1990

Other books you might like:
Dave Eggers, *Zeitoun*, 2009
William Kamkwamba, *The Boy Who Harnessed the Wind: Creating Currents of Electricity and Hope*, 2009
Bryan Mealer, co-author
Greg Mortenson, *Stones into Schools: Promoting Peace with Books, Not Bombs, in Afghanistan and Pakistan*, 2009
Greg Mortenson, *Three Cups of Tea: One Man's Mission to Fight Terrorism and Build Nations...One School at a Time*, 2006
David Oliver Relin, co-author
Rebecca Skloot, *The Immortal Life of Henrietta Lacks*, 2009

965

BARBARA KINGSOLVER
STEVEN HOPP , Co-Author
CAMILLE KINGSOLVER , Co-Author

Animal, Vegetable, Miracle: A Year of Food Life

(New York: Harper Collins, 2007)

Subject(s): Agriculture; Ecology; Food

Summary: In *Animal, Vegetable, Miracle: A Year of Food Life*, popular novelist Barbara Kingsolver turns to nonfiction to reflect on a year in her family's life as locavores, which means they only ate food grown or raised locally. Kingsolver, her husband, and their two daughters moved from Arizona to Virginia to create a farm that could feed them for an entire year. What was not on their farm—meat, poultry, and apples—they purchased from other local farms. Kingsolver explains in the book how they planted, harvested, and prepared their food. Her daughter Camille contributes recipes while her husband offers facts about ecology and industrial farming.

Where it's reviewed:
The Christian Century, July 24, 2007, page 36
Times Literary Supplement, September 7, 2007, page 7

Other books you might like:
Bill Bryson, *A Walk in the Woods*, 1998
Novella Carpenter, *Farm City: The Education of an Urban Farmer*, 2009
Manny Howard, *My Empire of Dirt: How One Man Turned His Big-City Backyard into a Farm*, 2010
Michael Pollan, *In Defense of Food: An Eater's Manifesto*, 2008
Michael Pollan, *The Omnivore's Dilemma: A Natural History of Four Meals*, 2006
Tristram Stuart, *Waste: Uncovering the Global Food Scandal*, 2009

`966`

CHUCK KLOSTERMAN

Eating the Dinosaur

(New York: Scribner, 2009)

Subject(s): Popular culture; Entertainment industry; Music

Summary: In *Eating the Dinosaur*, bestselling author Chuck Klosterman examines the world of pop culture with his trademark style and wit. The 13 essays of this volume explore subjects of entertainment, politics, and the human obsession with fame and fortune. Whether investigating the lasting influences of ABBA's music or plumbing the murky depths of the Branch Davidian cult, Klosterman outlines the unique and incisive similarities that bind humanity's fascination with popular culture. From a treatise on the influence of a media-brainwashed society to a piece probing the intentions of the Unabomber, this volume covers the gamut of cultural attraction. *Eating the Dinosaur* contains a full index.

Where it's reviewed:
Kirkus Reviews, September 15, 2009, page 56

Other books by the same author:
Downtown Owl, 2008
Sex, Drugs, and Cocoa Puffs, 2003
Fargo Rock City: A Heavy Metal Odyssey in Rural North Dakota, 2001

Other books you might like:
AV Club, *Inventory: 16 Films Featuring Manic Pixie Dream Girls, 10 Great Songs Nearly Ruined by Saxophone, and 100 More Obsessively Specific Pop-Culture Lists*, 2009
Douglas Coupland, *Generation A*, 2009
Nathan Rabin, *The Big Rewind: A Memoir Brought to You by Pop Culture*, 2009
Nathan Rabin, *My Year of Flops: The A.V. Club Presents One Man's Journey Deep into the Heart of Cinematic Failure*, 2010
Rob Sheffield, *Love Is a Mix Tape: Life and Loss, One Song at a Time*, 2007

`967`

JEFFREY KOTERBA

Inklings

(Boston: Houghton Mifflin Harcourt, 2009)

Subject(s): Artists; Family; Drawing

Summary: In *Inklings*, cartoonist Jeffrey Koterba shares the story of his unique journey through life and the challenges he's faced. As a child, Koterba found escape in drawing cartoons, a skill he would develop into a fruitful career as an adult. But growing up, Koterba had to deal with a bizarre, unpredictable father, a house bursting with clutter, and the unusual effects of Tourette's syndrome. His story is a refreshing glimpse into a creative mind, the forces that shaped it, and the life events that lead one to forgiveness and self-discovery.

Where it's reviewed:
Booklist, November 1, 2009, page 17
Publishers Weekly, August 10, 2009, page 43

Other books you might like:
Phoebe Gloeckner, *A Child's Life and Other Stories*, 2000
Marjane Satrapi, *The Complete Persepolis*, 2007
Craig Thompson, *Blankets*, 2003
Adrian Tomine, *Shortcomings*, 2007
Chris Ware, *Jimmy Corrigan: The Smartest Kid on Earth*, 2000

`968`

STEVEN KURUTZ

Like a Rolling Stone: The Strange Life of a Tribute Band

(New York: Broadway Books, 2008)

Subject(s): Music; Bands (Music); Biographies

Summary: In *Like a Rolling Stone: The Strange Life of a Tribute Band*, journalist Steven Kurutz examines the history of tribute bands, beginning with Beatlemania on Broadway in 1977. He then spends the rest of the book focusing on two of the most popular Rolling Stones tribute bands: Sticky Fingers and the Blushing Brides. Kurutz provides biographical information on Glen Carroll and Maurice Raymond, the heads of the rival bands. The author also offers behind-the-scenes information on what it is like to be part of a tribute band, which involves performing everywhere from colleges to seedy bars.

Where it's reviewed:
Entertainment Weekly, April 25, 2008, page 123
Publishers Weekly, February 25, 2008, page 67

Other books you might like:
Marley Brant, *Tales from the Rock 'n' Roll Highway*, 2004
Sam Cutler, *You Can't Always Get What You Want: My Life with the Rolling Stones, the Grateful Dead and Other Wonderful Reprobates*, 2008
Pamela Des Barres, *I'm with the Band: Confessions of a Groupie*, 1987
Shane Homan, *Access All Eras: Tribute Bands and Global Pop Culture*, 2006
Jessica Pallington West, *What Would Keith Richards Do?: Daily Affirmations from a Rock 'N' Roll Survivor*, 2009

`969`

CHRISTIAN LANDER

Stuff White People Like

(New York: Random House Trade Paperbacks, 2008)

Subject(s): Humor; Popular culture

Summary: This book is based upon a popular comedy blog of the same title, which does exactly what it says—it describes all the stuff that white people like. Stuff like free-trade coffee and gourmet fruit juice, films by Wes Anderson and radio commentary by David Sedaris, Ikea, yoga, and Che Guevara. The irony of the book's subtitle ("the unique taste of millions") is deliberate, for more than anything else, the thing white people most like is uniqueness and yet, somehow, they all seem to like the same things. This is a satire of white upper-middle-class liberal hip culture, by a white upper-middle-class liberal hipster, for white upper-middle-class liberal hipsters.

Where it's reviewed:
The Atlantic, October 2008, page 91

Other books you might like:
Mike Bender, *Awkward Family Photos*, 2010
    Doug Chernack, co-author
Kathy Griffin, *Official Book Club Selection: A Memoir According to Kathy Griffin*, 2009
Justin Halpern, *Sh*t My Dad Says*, 2010
Heather McDonald, *You'll Never Blue Ball in This Town Again: One Woman's Painfully Funny Quest to Give It Up*, 2010
Jen Yates, *Cake Wrecks: When Professional Cakes Go Hilariously Wrong*, 2009

970

ARTIE LANGE
ANTHONY BOZZA, Co-Author

Too Fat to Fish

(New York: Spiegel & Grau, 2008)

Subject(s): Autobiographies; Comedians; Actors

Summary: In *Too Fat to Fish*, comedian and actor Artie Lange talks about his outrageous life. Famous for his role as shock jock Howard Stern's assistant on "The Howard Stern Show," Lange is known for his crude humor and daring antics. This autobiography not only includes the funny side of this comedian, but also touches on his relationship with his father, his suicide attempts, and the time he spent in rehab for heroin addiction. Chapter titles include "Mr. October," "Driving Miss Wasted," and "Greetings from Sunny Kandahar." Filled with Lange's typical wit, this memoir offers an in-depth look into the author's private life.

Where it's reviewed:
Booklist, March 15, 2009, page 74
Publishers Weekly, December 22, 2008, page 49

Other books you might like:
Gary Dell'Abate, *They Call Me Baba Booey*, 2010
    Chad Millman, co-author
Robin Quivers, *Quivers: A Life*, 1995
Sarah Silverman, *The Bedwetter: Stories of Courage, Redemption, and Pee*, 2010
Howard Stern, *Miss America*, 1995
Howard Stern, *Private Parts*, 1993

971

DR. DENIS LEARY

Why We Suck: A Feel Good Guide to Staying Fat, Loud, Lazy and Stupid

(New York: Viking, 2008)

Subject(s): Comedy; Comedians; Culture

Summary: If you like your comedy sarcastic and biting, then Dr. Denis Leary's *Why We Suck* is for you. Leary was bestowed a doctorate by his old school, Emerson College, which he claims is a sure sign that he's a celebrity. He has made a career of being cynical and is known for his brash stand up. Leary applies his own brand of common sense to poke fun at the politically correct and the social norms of our society. From his Irish-Catholic upbringing, to his family life, to why America is so messed up, Leary doesn't hold back. The book reads like a stand up routine. His diatribes are intelligent, witty, and sure to leave fans laughing.

Where it's reviewed:
Publishers Weekly, September 15, 2008, page 59

Other books by the same author:
No Cure for Cancer, 1992

Other books you might like:
Lewis Black, *Me of Little Faith*, 2008
Anthony Bozza, *Too Fat to Fish*, 2008
George Carlin, *Last Words*, 2009
    Tony Hendra, co-author
Artie Lange, *Too Fat to Fish*, 2008
Denis Leary, *No Cure for Cancer*, 1992
Bill Maher, *New Rules: Polite Musings from a Timid Observer*, 2005

972

STEVEN D. LEVITT
STEPHEN J. DUBNER, Co-Author

Superfreakonomics: Global Cooling, Patriotic Prostitutes and Why Suicide Bombers Should Buy Life Insurance

(New York: William Morrow, 2009)

Subject(s): Humor; Economics; Popular culture

Summary: *Superfreakonomics: Global Cooling, Patriotic Prostitutes, and Why Suicide Bombers Should Buy Life Insurance*, by Steven D. Levitt and Stephen J. Dubner, is the follow-up to the widely popular *Freakonomics*. The authors combine fact and fiction while investigating humorous, thought-provoking questions. Some of the topics explored in this edition are doctors and hand washing techniques, prostitutes and Santa Claus, terrorism, child car seat effectiveness, kangaroo as a delicacy, greenhouse gases, Al Gore, economics, and cable television.

Other books by the same author:
Freakonomics: A Rogue Economist Explores the Hidden Side of Everything. Rev. and Expanded Ed., 2006

Other books you might like:
Stephen J. Dubner, *Freakonomics: A Rogue Economist Explores the Hidden Side of Everything*, 2005
Malcolm Gladwell, *Blink: The Power of Thinking Without Thinking*, 2005
Malcolm Gladwell, *The Tipping Point: How Little Things Can Make a Big Difference*, 2000
Malcolm Gladwell, *What the Dog Saw: And Other Adventures*, 2009
Steven D. Levitt, *Freakonomics: A Rogue Economist Explores the Hidden Side of Everything*, 2005
Michael Lewis, *The Big Short: Inside the Doomsday Machine*, 2010

973

MARK LEYNER
BILLY GOLDBERG , Co-Author

Why Do Men Have Nipples?: Hundreds of Questions You'd Only Ask a Doctor After Your Third Martini

(New York: Three Rivers Press, 2005)

Subject(s): Humor; Medicine

Summary: Mark Leyner is a humorist and a frequent contributor to such magazines as *The New Yorker*. Billy Goldberg is an emergency room doctor who works and lives in New York. They collaborated to produce this collection of questions and answers about the human body—questions that many people have wondered about, but few have asked. Some of the issues they confront are: why do people get headaches when they eat ice cream or other cold foods quickly? Is it really a good idea to try to suck the poison out of a snake bite? Are toilet seats dangerously germ-ridden? And is it possible to lose one's contact lens inside one's eye-socket forever?

Where it's reviewed:
The Bookseller, November 18, 2005, page 12

Other books by the same author:
Let's Play Doctor: The Instant Guide to Walking, Talking, and Probing Like a Real M.D., 2008
Why Do Men Fall Asleep After Sex?: More Questions You'd Only Ask a Doctor After Your Third Whiskey Sour, 2006

Other books you might like:
Billy Goldberg, *Why Do Men Fall Asleep After Sex?: More Questions You'd Only Ask a Doctor After Your Third Whiskey Sour*, 2006
Justin Halpern, *Sh*t My Dad Says*, 2010
Mark Leyner, *Why Do Men Fall Asleep After Sex?: More Questions You'd Only Ask a Doctor After Your Third Whiskey Sour*, 2006
John Lloyd, *The Book of Animal Ignorance: Everything*

You Think You Know Is Wrong, 2007
John Lloyd, *The Book of General Ignorance*, 2007
John Mitchinson, *The Book of Animal Ignorance: Everything You Think You Know Is Wrong*, 2007
John Mitchinson, *The Book of General Ignorance*, 2007
New Scientist, *Does Anything Eat Wasps?: And 101 Other Unsettling, Witty Answers to Questions You Never Thought You Wanted to Ask*, 2005

974

JOHN LINDSAY

Emails from an Asshole: Real People Being Stupid

(New York: Sterling Publishing, 2010)

Subject(s): Communications; Human behavior; Humor

Summary: In 2009, John Lindsay began emailing people who had posted amusing classified ads online. Originally pretending to be interested in what they were selling, Lindsay soon steered the conversations toward inappropriate—yet hilarious—subjects and offers. To let the world in on the joke, Lindsay created DontEvenReply. com, a website showcasing his most amusing conversations. Soon came *Emails from an Asshole: Real People Being Stupid*, a book filled with conversations that Lindsay kept from the website specifically for readers of the book. These emails show exactly how gullible some people can truly be and what they'll say when they're pushed to their limits.

Other books you might like:
Ben Bator, *Texts From Last Night: All the Texts No One Remembers Sending*, 2010
Justin Halpern, *Sh*t My Dad Says*, 2010
Chelsea Handler, *My Horizontal Life: A Collection of One-Night Stands*, 2005
Matt Kuhn, *The Playbook: Suit up. Score Chicks. Be Awesome.*, 2010
Lauren Leto, *Texts From Last Night: All the Texts No One Remembers Sending*, 2010
Tucker Max, *I Hope They Serve Beer in Hell*, 2006
Barney Stinson, *The Playbook: Suit up. Score Chicks. Be Awesome.*, 2010

975

MIKE MADRID

The Supergirls: Fashion, Feminism, Fantasy, and the History of Comic Book Heroines

(Minneapolis, Minnesota: Exterminating Angel Press, 2009)

Subject(s): Comic books; Cartoons; Supernatural

Summary: In *The Supergirls: Fashion, Feminism, Fantasy, and the History of Comic Book Heroines*, Mike Madrid discusses the role of female superheroes in comics of the past, present, and possibly the future. As he examines each supergirl, Madrid discusses how the readers of the world reacted to her emergence on the pages of their favorite comics. He speaks of what was happening around the world when artists and authors decided a woman was necessary if a few male superheroes were going to defeat a handful of evil characters. Heroines that appear in this book include Wonder Woman, Supergirl, Scarlet Witch, Marvel Girl, and Black Canary.

Where it's reviewed:
Entertainment Weekly, October 16, 2009, page 62

Other books you might like:
Alison Bechdel, *Fun Home: A Family Tragicomic*, 2006
Michael Chabon, *The Amazing Adventures of Kavalier & Clay: A Novel*, 2000
Robert Greenberger, *Wonder Woman: Amazon. Hero. Icon*, 2010
Brian K. Vaughan, *Y: The Last Man: Unmanned*, 2003
Emilie Zaslow, *Feminism, Inc.: Coming of Age in Girl Power Media Culture*, 2009

976

STEVE MARTIN

Born Standing Up: A Comic's Life
(New York: Scribner, 2007)

Subject(s): Autobiography; Comedy; Comics

Summary: Actor and comedian Steve Martin chronicles his personal and professional development through the first phase of his career in his book *Born Standing Up: A Comic's Life*. His father was a frustrated actor turned businessman, and Martin's relationship with him was strained. He recounts his working for Disneyland in a variety of capacities as a teenager, his early interest in magic, his enjoyment of philosophy and aspiration to teach, and his panic attacks. He traces his career as a comic, appearances as a guest on Johnny Carson's television show, writing for the Smothers Brothers, and working on *Saturday Night Live*. Martin also discusses a comedic epiphany he had in a college psychology class that contributed to his unique style.

Where it's reviewed:
Publishers Weekly, December 31, 2007, page 39

Other books by the same author:
Late for School, 2010
Shopgirl, 2001
Pure Drivel, 1998

Other books you might like:
George Carlin, *Last Words*, 2009
Tanner Colby, *The Chris Farley Show: A Biography in Three Acts*, 2008
Tom Davis, *Thirty-Nine Years of Short-Term Memory Loss: The Early Days of SNL from Someone Who Was There*, 2009
Tom Farley, *The Chris Farley Show: A Biography in Three Acts*, 2008
Craig Ferguson, *American on Purpose: The Improbable Adventures of an Unlikely Patriot*, 2009
Tony Hendra, *Last Words*, 2009

James Andrew Miller, *Live from New York: An Uncensored History of Saturday Night Live*, 2002
Tom Shales, co-author

977

RUE MCCLANAHAN

My First Five Husbands...and the Ones Who Got Away
(New York: Broadway Books, 2007)

Subject(s): Biographies; Popular culture; Acting

Summary: Actress Rue McClanahan, best known for her role as Blanche Devereaux on *The Golden Girls*, shares her experiences in her professional and personal life in the memoir *My First Five Husbands... and the One's Who Got Away*. From her early years in Hollywood to her big screen debuts, from husband number one all the way to husband number six, McClanahan shares wit and wisdom between inspiring life lessons. McClanahan reflects on all of the events in her life with humor as she explains why her marriages ended and how she eventually landed the role of a lifetime. Readers will enjoy chronicling the actress's rise to fame as McClanahan discusses the fascinating people she met along the way.

Where it's reviewed:
Entertainment Weekly, April 27, 2007, page 143
Publishers Weekly, February 26, 2007, page 71

Other books you might like:
Carol Burnett, *This Time Together: Laughter and Reflection*, 2010
Michael D. Craig, *Thank You for Being a Friend: A Golden Girls Trivia Book*, 2005
Sam Kashner, *Furious Love: Elizabeth Taylor, Richard Burton, and the Marriage of the Century*, 2010
Cloris Leachman, *Cloris: My Autobiography*, 2009
Nancy Schoenberger, *Furious Love: Elizabeth Taylor, Richard Burton, and the Marriage of the Century*, 2010
Betty White, *Here We Go Again: My Life In Television*, 2010

978

JULIE METZ

Perfection: A Memoir of Betrayal and Renewal
(New York: Hyperion, 2009)

Subject(s): Autobiographies; Marriage; Infidelity

Summary: After Julie Metz's husband passed away, she struggled to get used to the idea of life without him in it. As a widower, she was unsure she could raise their six-year-old daughter by herself. In *Perfection: A Memoir of Betrayal and Renewal*, Metz realizes the perfect life she lead while her husband was alive wasn't as wonderful as she'd once thought. From the outside, their marriage was flawless, but months after her husband's death, Metz realized that he was hiding things—people—from her. As she uncovered evidence that her husband had been unfaithful for the duration of their 12-year marriage, her world fell apart all over again. The only way she can cope with this new information is to confront the women her husband was seeing. In *Perfection*, Metz discusses how she rebuilt her life after her husband's death and betrayal.

Where it's reviewed:
Publishers Weekly, April 27, 2009, page 124

Other books you might like:
Elizabeth Edwards, *Resilience: Reflections on the Burdens and Gifts of Facing Life's Adversities*, 2009
Isabel Gillies, *Happens Every Day: An All-Too-True Story*, 2009
Stacy Morrison, *Falling Apart in One Piece: One Optimist's Journey Through the Hell of Divorce*, 2010
Jenny Sandford, *Staying True*, 2010
Jennifer Weiner, *Fly Away Home*, 2010

979

DAVID N. MEYER

Twenty Thousand Roads: The Ballad of Gram Parsons and His Cosmic American Music
(New York: Villard, 2007)

Subject(s): Biographies; Music; Musicians

Summary: David N. Meyer explores the life of musician Gram Parsons in *Twenty Thousand Roads: The Ballad of Gram Parsons and His Cosmic American Music*. During the 1960s and 1970s, Parsons was a legend playing with one band and then departing for another. He was known for his musical abilities as much as for the sequined cowboy suits he wore on stage. Parsons played on the Byrds' album, *Sweetheart of the Rodeo* and collaborated with the Rolling Stones' Keith Richards. He was at the height of his career when he died of a drug and alcohol overdose at just twenty-six years old.

Where it's reviewed:
TLS. Times Literary Supplement, October 17, 2008, page 31

Other books by the same author:
A Girl and a Gun: The Complete Guide to Film Noir on Video, 1998
The 100 Best Films to Rent You've Never Heard Of: Hidden Treasures, Neglected Classics, and Hits From By-Gone Eras, 1996

Other books you might like:
Patrick Carr, *Cash: The Autobiography*, 1997
Tom Carter, *I Lived to Tell It All*, 1996
Tom Carter, *Merle Haggard's My House of Memories: For the Record*, 1999
Johnny Cash, *Cash: The Autobiography*, 1997
Merle Haggard, *Merle Haggard's My House of*

Memories: For the Record, 1999
Waylon Jennings, *Waylon: An Autobiography*, 1996
George Jones, *I Lived to Tell It All*, 1996
Lenny Kaye, *Waylon: An Autobiography*, 1996
Willie Nelson, *Willie: An Autobiography*, 1988
   Bud Shrake, co-author

980

BEN MEZRICH

The Accidental Billionaires: The Founding of Facebook: A Tale of Sex, Money, Genius and Betrayal
(New York: Doubleday, 2009)

Subject(s): Business; Internet; Biographies

Summary: In *The Accidental Billionaires: The Founding of Facebook: A Tale of Sex, Money, Genius and Betrayal*, Ben Mezrich approaches the founding of the social networking site Facebook from a non-technical standpoint. Mezrich was never able to get an interview with Mark Zuckerberg, the founder of the site, and was only able to speak with Eduardo Saverin, the co-founder of the company who was forced out. Mezrich embellishes the facts with fictional, imagined scenarios. The basic information about the founding of the company and its unlikely success is accurate, but many of the stories of fancy parties and sexual encounters are made up by Mezrich for dramatic effect.

Where it's reviewed:
The New York Review of Books, Feb 25, 2010, page 8

Other books by the same author:
Rigged: The True Story of an Ivy League Kid Who Changed the World of Oil, from Wall Street to Dubai, 2007
Ugly Americans: The True Story of the Ivy League Cowboys Who Raided the Asian Markets for Millions, 2004
21: Bringing Down the House: The Inside Story of Six M.I.T. Students Who Took Vegas for Millions, 2003

Other books you might like:
Bret Easton Ellis, *American Psycho: A Novel*, 1991
David Kirkpatrick, *The Facebook Effect: The Inside Story of the Company That Is Connecting the World*, 2010
Michael Lewis, *The Big Short: Inside the Doomsday Machine*, 2010

981

ALYSSA MILANO

Safe at Home: Confessions of a Baseball Fanatic
(New York: William Morrow, 2009)

Subject(s): Autobiographies; Sports; Baseball
Summary: In *Safe at Home: Confessions of a Baseball*

Pop Culture

Fanatic, author Alyssa Milano reveals her lifelong affection for baseball and how it has shaped her life. Born in Brooklyn as the daughter of an embittered Dodgers fan who could never forgive the team for leaving New York, Milano was reunited with her father's home team once the family moved to Los Angeles to support her acting career. There she learned that in baseball, just as in life, one cannot deny his or her true self. Milano is an American actress best known for her roles in the sitcom *Who's the Boss?* and the television drama *Charmed*.

Other books you might like:

Michael Duca, *The Baseball Codes: Beanballs, Sign Stealing, and Bench-Clearing Brawls: The Unwritten Rules of America's Pastime*, 2010

Jane Heller, *Confessions of a She-Fan: The Course of True Love with the New York Yankees*, 2009

Larry King, *Why I Love Baseball*, 2004

Michael Lewis, *Moneyball: The Art of Winning an Unfair Game*, 2003

Julie McCarron, *Why I Love Baseball*, 2004

Cait Murphy, *Crazy '08: How a Cast of Cranks, Rogues, Boneheads, and Magnates Created the Greatest Year in Baseball History*, 2007

Jason Turbow, *The Baseball Codes: Beanballs, Sign Stealing, and Bench-Clearing Brawls: The Unwritten Rules of America's Pastime*, 2010

982

LISA MILLER

Heaven: Our Enduring Fascination with the Afterlife

(New York: Harper, 2010)

Subject(s): Heaven; Afterlife; Religion

Summary: Author Lisa Miller, a specialist in religious journalism, offers a probing investigation into humanity's collective attraction to life after death. *Heaven: Our Enduring Fascination with the Afterlife* looks at the topic from a wide array of perspectives, including Jewish, Christian, and Muslim beliefs; the influence of literature, movies, and music; and the legacy of Mormon leader Joseph Smith. Miller's study provides an all-encompassing examination of the factors that form popular views of heaven and how these factors shape believers' everyday lives. *Heaven* includes a bibliography, notes on the text, and an index. First book.

Where it's reviewed:
Library Journal, March 15, 2010, page 108

Other books you might like:

John Casey, *After Lives: A Guide to Heaven, Hell, and Purgatory*, 2009

Joan Didion, *The Year of Magical Thinking*, 2005

Kenneth Kramer, *The Sacred Art of Dying: How the World Religions Understand Death*, 1988

Sherwin B. Nuland, *How We Die: Reflections on Life's Final Chapter*, 1993

Studs Terkel, *Will the Circle Be Unbroken?: Reflections on Death, Rebirth, and Hunger for a Faith*, 2001

983

WES MOORE

The Other Wes Moore: One Name, Two Fates

(New York: Spiegel & Grau, 2010)

Subject(s): Autobiographies; Race relations; Social sciences

Summary: *The Other Wes Moore: One Name, Two Fates* is an autobiography written by Wes Moore, an investment banker from Baltimore who was once an aide to Condoleezza Rice. Moore was surprised to learn one day that another Wes Moore from Baltimore was wanted for killing a police officer. Intrigued, the author chose to look into this other Wes. He was surprised to learn of the similarities between them. Both are African Americans of the same age from the same area of Baltimore, both grew up without fathers, and both briefly dealt drugs as a way to obtain money and status. The author, however, managed to turn his life around, avoiding the criminal path of the other Wes Moore. Throughout the book, the author examines how two men who lead very similar early lives ended up with such drastically different outcomes.

Where it's reviewed:
Booklist, May 1, 2010, page 69
Entertainment Weekly, May 14, 2010, page 79
People, May 17, 2010, page 65

Other books you might like:

John Green, *Will Grayson, Will Grayson*, 2009

bell hooks, *Where We Stand: Class Matters*, 2000

David Levithan, *Will Grayson, Will Grayson*, 2009

Greg Mortenson, *Three Cups of Tea: One Man's Mission to Fight Terrorism and Build Nations...One School at a Time*, 2006
   David Oliver Relin, co-author

Jacob A. Riis, *How the Other Half Lives*, 1890

Rebecca Skloot, *The Immortal Life of Henrietta Lacks*, 2009

984

GREG MORTENSON
DAVID OLIVER RELIN , Co-Author

Three Cups of Tea: One Man's Mission to Fight Terrorism and Build Nations...One School at a Time

(New York: Penguin, 2006)

Subject(s): Autobiography; Conduct of Life; Inspirational

Summary: Greg Mortenson is nursed back to health in a small, rural Pakistani village after failing in his attempt to climb the second highest mountain in the world, K2. Learning about these people and grateful for their assistance to him, Mortenson pledges to build a school in their village. After the founding of the Central Asia Institute and 55 schools later, Mortenson and his co-author, journalist David Oliver Relin, recount the details of living in this dangerous region amidst Taliban supporters hostile toward Americans. This inspirational story attests to the remarkable contribution that can be made by one man.

Where it's reviewed:
The Christian Century, July 29, 2008, page 35

Other books by the same author:
Listen to the Wind, 2009
Stones into Schools, 2009

Other books you might like:
Chinua Achebe, *Things Fall Apart*, 1958
Khaled Hosseini, *The Kite Runner*, 2003
Khaled Hosseini, *A Thousand Splendid Suns*, 2007
Jaume Sanllorente, *Bombay Smiles: The Trip that Changed My Life*, 2009
Peter Singer, *Practical Ethics*, 1999

985

CAIT MURPHY

Crazy '08: How a Cast of Cranks, Rogues, Boneheads, and Magnates Created the Greatest Year in Baseball History

(Washington, DC: Smithsonian Publications, 2007)

Subject(s): Sports; Baseball; United States history

Summary: In *Crazy '08: How a Cast of Cranks, Rogues, Boneheads, and Magnates Created the Greatest Year in Baseball History*, author Cait Murphy reveals how the 1908 World Series, which pitted the Chicago Cubs against the New York Giants, changed baseball and ushered the sport into its modern-day incarnation. In the book, Murphy looks at how the game of baseball that existed more than a century ago was infused with heroes (such as Christy Mathewson), villains (such as the racist and raucous Ty Cobb), and rabid fans who were known to become violent as the result of a bad call or a missed play. This book features a foreword from sportswriter Robert Creamer.

Where it's reviewed:
Booklist, February 1, 2007, page 16
Publishers Weekly, February 5, 2007, page 53

Other books by the same author:
Scoundrels in Law: The Trials of Howe and Hummel, Lawyers to the Gangsters, Cops, Starlets, and Rakes Who Made the Gilded Age, 2010

Other books you might like:
Eliot Asinof, *Eight Men Out: The Black Sox and the 1919 World Series*, 1963
Sean Deveney, *The Original Curse: Did the Cubs Throw the 1918 World Series to Babe Ruth's Red Sox and Incite the Black Sox Scandal?*, 2010
John Heidenry, *The Gashouse Gang: How Dizzy Dean, Leo Durocher, Branch Rickey, Pepper Martin, and*

Their Colorful, Come-from-Behind Ball Club Won the World Series—and America's Heart—During the Great Depression, 2007
Alyssa Milano, *Safe at Home: Confessions of a Baseball Fanatic*, 2009
Lawrence Ritter, *The Glory of Their Times: The Story of the Early Days of Baseball Told by the Men Who Played It*, 1966

986

VICKI MYRON
BRET WITTER , Co-Author

Dewey: The Small-Town Library Cat Who Touched the World

(New York: Grand Central Publishing, 2008)

Subject(s): Libraries; Economics; Alcoholism

Summary: On a cold day in 1988, Spencer Public Library in Iowa got a special delivery. Vicki Myron, the library's director, found a nearly frozen ball of orange fur in the overnight drop box. That orange fur ball was a kitten that ended up not only changing the library, but the town and eventually went on to touch the whole world. The cat became known as Dewey Readmore Books and acted as a mascot for the library. He seemed to have an innate sense of who needed a little bit of the love he was always eager to share, and could soften the most cantankerous patron. Intermixed with tales about Dewey exploits are stories about Vicki Myron and her life, her struggles, and successes. The book will make you laugh, cry, and find inspiration from a little ginger cat that touched everyone's life.

Where it's reviewed:
Booklist, August 1, 2008, page 20
Library Journal, July 1, 2008, page 101
Publishers Weekly, August 11, 2008, page 9

Other books by the same author:
Dewey's Christmas at the Library, 2010
Dewey's Nine Lives, 2010
Dewey: There's a Cat in the Library!, 2009

Other books you might like:
Gwen Cooper, *Homer's Odyssey: A Fearless Feline Tale, or How I Learned About Love and Life With a Blind Wonder Cat*, 2009
David Dosa, *Making Rounds with Oscar: The Extraordinary Gift of an Ordinary Cat*, 2010
Vicki Myron, *Dewey's Nine Lives: The Legacy of the Small-Town Library Cat Who Inspired Millions*, 2010
Stacey O'Brien, *Wesley the Owl: The Remarkable Love Story of an Owl and His Girl*, 2008
Brad Steiger, *Cat Miracles: Inspirational True Stories of Remarkable Felines*, 2003
    Sherry Hansen Steiger, co-author
Bret Witter, *Dewey's Nine Lives: The Legacy of the Small-Town Library Cat Who Inspired Millions*, 2010

Pop Culture

987

NATHAN NEDOROSTEK
ANTHONY PAPPALARDO , Co-Author

Radio Silence: A Selected Visual History of American Hardcore Music

(New York: MTV Press, 2008)

Subject(s): Music; Musicians; Reference works

Summary: In the book *Radio Silence: A Selected Visual History of American Hardcore Music*, authors Nathan Nedorostek and Anthony Pappalardo show the transition from the punk-rock music scene to the hardcore music scene and the simultaneous changes in the music's audience. This volume not only discusses the changes in the sound and rhythm of the music, but it also shows the changes among the people who listened to the music. The book shows the way the clothing, the style, and the attitudes of hardcore music listeners changed over time as hardcore music become more widely listened to and a larger part of the mainstream.

Other books you might like:
Norman Brannon, *The Anti-Matter Anthology: A 1990s Post-Punk & Hardcore Reader*, 2007
Stevie Chick, *Spray Paint the Walls: The Story of Black Flag*, 2009
Brian Peterson, *Burning Fight: The Nineties Hardcore Revolution in Ethics, Politics, Spirit, and Sound*, 2009
Henry Rollins, *Get in the Van: On the Road with Black Flag*, 1994
Chris Salewicz, *Redemption Song: The Ballad of Joe Strummer*, 2008

988

ADAM NIMOY

My Incredibly Wonderful, Miserable Life

(New York: Simon & Schuster, 2008)

Subject(s): Writers; Drug abuse; Addiction

Summary: *My Incredibly Wonderful, Miserable Life* is an anti-memoir by Adam Nimoy, son of Star Trek actor Leonard Nimoy. The younger Nimoy grew up beneath his father's shadow, and in this book he tells of his struggle to get out from under it. Nimoy survived a severe drug addiction that lasted for nearly three decades, as well as a divorce and, worst of all, swarms of Trekkies at sci-fi conventions, only to find himself a substitute teacher and single father navigating the tenuous L.A. dating scene.

Where it's reviewed:
Booklist, July 1, 2008, page 25
Publishers Weekly, May 26, 2008, page 55

Other books you might like:
Chris Kreski, *Star Trek Memories*, 1993

Leonard Nimoy, *I Am Not Spock*, 1979
Leonard Nimoy, *I Am Spock*, 1995
Leonard Nimoy, *A Lifetime of Love: Poems on the Passages of Life*, 2002
Leonard Nimoy, *Shekhina*, 2002
William Shatner, *Star Trek Memories*, 1993

989

LAURIE NOTARO

The Idiot Girl and the Flaming Tantrum of Death: Reflections on Revenge, Germophobia, and Laser Hair Removal

(New York: Villard, 2008)

Subject(s): Autobiographies; Humor; Family

Summary: *The Idiot Girl and the Flaming Tantrum of Death: Reflections on Revenge, Germophobia, and Laser Hair Removal* by Laurie Notaro is a humorous essay collection inspired by a variety of events in the author's own life. In this book, Notaro discusses her ridiculous fear of illnesses on airplanes and other enclosed areas, her fascination of laser hair removal, her obsession with the sex offender who has moved in down the street, and hilarious encounters with questionable family members. Essays in this collection include "Stink Bomb," "Love Thy Neighbor," "Happy Birthday and the Element of Surprise," and "Blue-Light Special."

Other books by the same author:
Spooky Little Girl, 2010
An Idiot Girl's Christmas: True Tales from the Top of the Naughty List, 2005
We Thought You Would Be Prettier: True Tales of the Dorkiest Girl Alive, 2005

Other books you might like:
Nora Ephron, *I Feel Bad about My Neck: And Other Thoughts on Being a Woman*, 2006
Chelsea Handler, *Are You There, Vodka? It's Me, Chelsea*, 2008
Chelsea Handler, *Chelsea Chelsea Bang Bang*, 2010
Heather McDonald, *You'll Never Blue Ball in This Town Again: One Woman's Painfully Funny Quest to Give It Up*, 2010
Celia Rivenbark, *Stop Dressing Your Six-Year-Old Like a Skank: And Other Words of Delicate Southern Wisdom*, 2006

990

LAURIE NOTARO

We Thought You Would Be Prettier: True Tales of the Dorkiest Girl Alive

(New York: Villard, 2005)

Subject(s): Autobiographies; Writing; Humor

Summary: In *We Thought You Would Be Prettier: True*

Tales of the Dorkiest Girl Alive, author Laurie Notaro describes the moment she realized she'd lost her patience for dumb people. Beginning with an entertaining description of her life while touring the country to promote one of her previous books, Notaro explains what made her realize that she was starting to lose her mind. She describes the small things that started to irritate her and the human behaviors she could no longer tolerate. She had hoped that she could keep her cool for a few more years, but in *We Thought You'd Be Prettier*, she becomes certain her time has come. Now, Notaro struggles to deal with the fact that she has officially become a crotchety, insane old lady.

Where it's reviewed:
USA TODAY, June 1, 2005, page D.11.

Other books by the same author:
Spooky Little Girl, 2010
The Idiot Girl and the Flaming Tantrum of Death: Reflections on Revenge, Germophobia, and Laser Hair Removal, 2009
An Idiot Girl's Christmas: True Tales from the Top of the Naughty List, 2005

Other books you might like:
Nora Ephron, *I Feel Bad about My Neck: And Other Thoughts on Being a Woman*, 2006
Chelsea Handler, *Are You There, Vodka? It's Me, Chelsea*, 2008
Chelsea Handler, *Chelsea Chelsea Bang Bang*, 2010
Heather McDonald, *You'll Never Blue Ball in This Town Again: One Woman's Painfully Funny Quest to Give It Up*, 2010

991

LAURIE NOTARO

An Idiot Girl's Christmas: True Tales from the Top of the Naughty List

(New York: Villard, 2005)

Subject(s): Holidays; Christmas; Shopping

Summary: *An Idiot Girl's Christmas: True Tales from the Top of the Naughty List* is a collection of entertaining holiday-themed essays by Laurie Notaro. Although Notaro is a fan of the Christmas season, she doesn't necessarily love everything that comes with it. Family parties are either over-the-top or annoyingly dull and Christmas shopping with her penny-pinching grandmother drives her a little crazy. This collection contains 13 essays, including "Have Yourself a Kmart Little Christmas," "O Holy Night, or The Year I Ruined Christmas," and "Jingle Hell." *An Idiot Girl's Christmas: True Tales from the Top of the Naughty List* is Laurie Notaro's fifth book.

Where it's reviewed:
Entertainment Weekly, December 16, 2005, page 88

Other books by the same author:
Spooky Little Girl, 2010

The Idiot Girl and the Flaming Tantrum of Death: Reflections on Revenge, Germophobia, and Laser Hair Removal, 2009
We Thought You Would Be Prettier: True Tales of the Dorkiest Girl Alive, 2005

Other books you might like:
Chelsea Handler, *Are You There, Vodka? It's Me, Chelsea*, 2008
Chelsea Handler, *Chelsea Chelsea Bang Bang*, 2010
Heather McDonald, *You'll Never Blue Ball in This Town Again: One Woman's Painfully Funny Quest to Give It Up*, 2010

992

JENNIFER O'CONNELL

Everything I Needed to Know About Being a Girl I Learned from Judy Blume

(New York: Pocket Books, 2007)

Subject(s): Women; Writers; Adolescence

Summary: *Everything I Needed to Know About Being a Girl I Learned from Judy Blume* is an essay collection, edited by Jennifer O'Connell and written in tribute of famed author Judy Blume. In this collection, more than twenty female writers recall the time they spent reading Blume's work as children and young women. They reflect on what Blume taught them about their bodies, their friends, and their loves, and they take the time to thank her for writing works such as *Are You There God? It's Me Margaret*, *Otherwise Known as Sheila the Great*, and *Tales of a Fourth Grade Nothing*. Authors who contributed to this collection include Meg Cabot, Laura Ruby, Erica Orloff, and Elise Juska.

Where it's reviewed:
Booklist, June 1, 2007, page 20
Library Journal, June 1, 2007, page 116
Publishers Weekly, February 26, 2007, page 72

Other books by the same author:
Local Girls, 2008
Rich Boys, 2008
Plan B, 2006

Other books you might like:
Andrea J. Buchanan, *The Daring Book for Girls*, 2007
Suzanne Collins, *The Hunger Games*, 2008
Kara Jesella, *How Sassy Changed My Life: A Love Letter to the Greatest Teen Magazine of All Time*, 2007
    Marisa Meltzer, co-author
Miriam Peskowitz, *The Daring Book for Girls*, 2007
Lizzie Skurnick, *Shelf Discovery: The Teen Classics We Never Stopped Reading*, 2009

993

ROSIE O'DONNELL

Celebrity Detox (The Fame Game)

(New York: Grand Central Publishing, 2007)

Subject(s): Actors and Actresses; Entertainment; Relationships

Summary: In her book *Celebrity Detox (The Fame Game)*, author and television personality Rosie O'Donnell gives an account of her withdrawing from celebrity life. In 2002 O'Donnell walked away from her famous television show. The book talks about why the star decided to leave the limelight and how she believes fame is like a drug. O'Donnell explains that she felt addicted to fame and, much like any other addict, she was afraid she might relapse. O'Donnell returned to television in 2006 when she cohosted on ABC's *The View*. The book also discusses her experiences on that show and how her experiences changed her outlook on life.

Where it's reviewed:
Booklist, July 1, 2007, page 10
Entertainment Weekly, October 19, 2007, page 131

Other books by the same author:
Rosie O'Donnell's Crafty U: 100 Easy Projects the Whole Family Can Enjoy All Year Long, 2008
Find Me, 2002
Kids Are Punny, 1997

Other books you might like:
Lance Bass, *Out of Sync: A Memoir*, 2007
Ellen DeGeneres, *My Point...and I Do Have One*, 1995
Kathy Griffin, *Official Book Club Selection: A Memoir According to Kathy Griffin*, 2009
Barbara Walters, *Audition: A Memoir*, 2008

994

ROBYN OKRANT

Living Oprah: My One-Year Experiment to Walk the Walk of the Queen of Talk

(New York: Center Street, 2010)

Subject(s): Biographies; Culture; Popular culture

Summary: In her debut book *Living Oprah: My One-Year Experiment to Walk the Walk of the Queen of Talk*, author Robyn Okrant recounts her experiences from the year she spent following Oprah Winfrey's rules for living a better life. In 2008 Okrant modified her diet, exercise routines, and reading habits, and more when she decided to dedicate the year to Oprah's set of rules. Okrant used Oprah's television, magazine, and Web site for the rules she followed. In her book, Okrant shares with readers how these changes affected her physically and emotion-

ally and how her views have changed from the experience.

Where it's reviewed:
People, January 11, 2010, page 51
Publishers Weekly, October 19, 2009, page 45

Other books you might like:
Benyamin Cohen, *My Jesus Year: A Rabbi's Son Wanders the Bible Belt in Search of His Own Faith*, 2008
Ed Gungor, *There is More to the Secret*, 2007
A.J. Jacobs, *The Guinea Pig Diaries: My Life as an Experiment*, 2009
A.J. Jacobs, *The Know-It-All: One Man's Humble Quest to Become the Smartest Person in the World*, 2004
A.J. Jacobs, *The Year of Living Biblically: One Man's Humble Quest to Follow the Bible as Literally as Possible*, 2007

995

MARY-KATE OLSEN
ASHLEY OLSEN , Co-Author

Influence

(New York: Razorbill, 2008)

Subject(s): Actors; Fashion; Fashion design

Summary: *Influence*, by Mary-Kate and Ashley Olsen, is a book about the people who have influenced the Olsen twins in their careers as fashion designers. Together they have two fashion lines, The Row and Elizabeth and James, along with their occasional acting work. This book is focused on their work in the fashion industry and is primarily based on interviews with the designers and artists who have influenced them. Mary-Kate and Ashley have different interviewing styles and ask different types of questions, which adds a great deal of variation to the text. Numerous photographs are included. The book is available with two different covers: one with Mary-Kate on the cover, and another with Ashley. The two books are otherwise identical.

Other books by the same author:
Mary-Kate & Ashley's Passport to Paris Scrapbook, 2000

Other books you might like:
Rose Apodaca, *Style A to Zoe: The Art of Fashion, Beauty, & Everything Glamour*, 2007
Victoria Beckham, *That Extra Half an Inch: Hair, Heels and Everything in Between*, 2006
Nina Garcia, *The Little Black Book of Style*, 2007
Tim Gunn, *Tim Gunn: A Guide to Quality, Taste, and Style*, 2007
Kate Moloney, co-author
Nicole Richie, *The Truth about Diamonds*, 2005

Rachel Zoe, *Style A to Zoe: The Art of Fashion, Beauty, & Everything Glamour*, 2007

996

THE ONION

Our Dumb World: The Onion's Atlas of the Planet Earth, 73rd Edition

(New York: Little, Brown & Company, 2007)

Subject(s): Politics; Culture; Social conditions

Summary: After their triumph with *Our Dumb Century*, the staff of *The Onion* returns in book form with a blunt and satirical look at our planet. The sardonic staff of the weekly fake news program offers their intelligent, absurd, and fabricated observations of the world. Inside, readers can find out why Afghanistan is also known as "Allah's Cat Box," which countries have the highest Bono activity, and why the Ukraine has the reputation as "the Bridebasket of Europe." Even though *The Onion* is unsure of how many countries exist, facts to inform and offend are provided for all of them. The atlas includes reference tools to help make sense of it all including; a life-size map of the world, a chart to help determine which country you would have the best chance of launching a successful invasion against, flag designs that didn't make the cut, and which crafts are the most irritating.

Where it's reviewed:
Library Journal, December 1, 2007, page 119
Publishers Weekly, December 31, 2007, page 41

Other books by the same author:
Our Front Pages: 21 Years of Greatness, Virtue, and Moral Rectitude from America's Finest News Source, 2009
Our Dumb Century, 2004
The Tenacity of the Cockroach, 2002

Other books you might like:
John Hodgman, *The Areas of My Expertise: An Almanac of Complete World Knowledge Compiled with Instructive Annotation and Arranged in Useful Order*, 2005
The Onion, *Our Front Pages: 21 Years of Greatness, Virtue, and Moral Rectitude from America's Finest News Source*, 2009
Nathan Rabin, *My Year of Flops: The A.V. Club Presents One Man's Journey Deep into the Heart of Cinematic Failure*, 2010
David Ritz, *We'll Be Here for the Rest of Our Lives: A Swingin' Show-Biz Saga*, 2009
 Paul Shaffer, co-author
Claire Zulkey, *An Off Year*, 2009

997

THE ONION

Our Front Pages: 21 Years of Greatness, Virtue, and Moral Rectitude from America's Finest News Source

(New York: Scribner, 2009)

Subject(s): Humor; Newspapers; Satire

Summary: *Our Front Pages: 21 Years of Greatness, Virtue, and Moral Rectitude from America's Finest News Source* comes from the people behind the satire news source The Onion. The book is a collection of many of the best and funniest front-page stories featured on The Onion, including such headlines as "War, Come On, Let's Have One," "Loveless Union Ends in Baby," or "Bush: 'Our Long National Nightmare of Peace and Prosperity is Finally Over'," just to name a few. Though many of the humorous headline news stories are political in nature, many are simply irreverent and designed to produce a laugh.

Where it's reviewed:
New York Times Book Review, December 6, 2009, page 40

Other books by the same author:
Our Dumb World: The Onion's Atlas of the Planet Earth, 73rd Edition, 2007
Our Dumb Century, 2004
The Tenacity of the Cockroach, 2002

Other books you might like:
AV Club, *Inventory: 16 Films Featuring Manic Pixie Dream Girls, 10 Great Songs Nearly Ruined by Saxophone, and 100 More Obsessively Specific Pop-Culture Lists*, 2009
John Hodgman, *The Areas of My Expertise: An Almanac of Complete World Knowledge Compiled with Instructive Annotation and Arranged in Useful Order*, 2005
Nathan Rabin, *My Year of Flops: The A.V. Club Presents One Man's Journey Deep into the Heart of Cinematic Failure*, 2010
Claire Zulkey, *An Off Year*, 2009

998

JOHN ORTVED

The Simpsons: An Uncensored, Unauthorized History

(London: Faber and Faber, 2009)

Subject(s): Cartoons; Television programs; Criticism

Summary: The first family of Springfield gets the royal treatment in *The Simpsons: An Uncensored, Unauthorized History*. Author John Ortved examines the story behind the popular animated program, charting the

Pop Culture

show's journey from filler material on *The Tracey Ullman Show* to its current place as one of the longest-running sitcoms in television history. Ortved also provides information on the show's creators and those working behind the scenes, as well as analysis and commentary on selected episodes. *The Simpsons* includes a foreword by author Douglas Coupland.

Where it's reviewed:
Entertainment Weekly, October 23, 2009, page 61

Other books you might like:
Michael Davis, *Street Gang: The Complete History of Sesame Street*, 2008
Matt Groening, *The Simpsons One Step Beyond Forever : A Complete Guide to Our Favorite Family...Continued Yet Again*, 2005
Steven Keslowitz, *The World According to The Simpsons: What Our Favorite TV Family Says about Life, Love, and the Pursuit of the Perfect Donut*, 2006
James Andrew Miller, *Live from New York: An Uncensored History of Saturday Night Live*, 2002
Tom Shales, co-author
Chris Turner, *Planet Simpson: How a Cartoon Masterpiece Defined a Generation*, 2004

999

DOUGLAS PERRY

The Girls of Murder City: Fame, Lust, and the Beautiful Killers Who Inspired *Chicago*

(New York: Viking Adult, 2010)

Subject(s): Murder; Biographies; Women

Summary: Desperate to make a name for herself as a journalist or playwright in the bustling city of Chicago, Maurine Watkins embraced the idea of reporting on something exciting, like murder. In *The Girls of Murder City: Fame, Lust, and the Beautiful Killers Who Inspired* Chicago, Douglas Perry examines Watkins's actions as she jumped to cover two specific murder cases in 1924. These cases were sure to garner attention from the start, as their defendants were attractive females. That fact, along with Watkins's colorful writing, drew more interest than predicted and Watkins soon saw her name in print and in lights.

Where it's reviewed:
Booklist, June 1, 2010, page 8
Publishers Weekly, April 12, 2010, page 39

Other books you might like:
Karen Abbott, *Sin in the Second City: Madams, Ministers, Playboys, and the Battle for America's Soul*, 2007
Michael Harvey, *The Chicago Way*, 2007
Erik Larson, *The Devil in the White City: Murder, Magic, and Madness at the Fair That Changed America*, 2003
Cait Murphy, *Scoundrels in Law: The Trials of Howe

and Hummel, Lawyers to the Gangsters, Cops, Starlets, and Rakes Who Made the Gilded Age*, 2010
Geoffrey O'Brien, *The Fall of the House of Walworth: A Tale of Madness and Murder in Gilded Age America*, 2010

1000

MICHAEL POLLAN

The Omnivore's Dilemma: A Natural History of Four Meals

(New York: Penguin, 2006)

Subject(s): Agriculture; Food; Health

Summary: Michael Pollan is a naturalist whose former books have been on the topic of botany and natural history. In this book, he discusses a fact that most Americans like to ignore—all food, including the much-maligned Twinkie, is made from previously-living organisms. He describes four meals and traces them backwards to the species that made them up. The MacDonald's lunch, for instance, begins as corn in a cornfield. Corn is fed to cows which become the beef patties; corn is made into oil to fry the McNuggets and the fries; corn is made into the syrup that flavors the shakes and the soda pop. Later he dissects, in somewhat the same way, a meal prepared from ingredients bought from a grocery store; a chicken dinner prepared from animals and plants raised on an organic farm; and finally, a meal prepared entirely from foods hunted and foraged by the author himself.

Where it's reviewed:
Booklist, October 15, 2009, page 51

Other books by the same author:
The Botany of Desire: A Plant's-Eye View of the World, 2010
Food Rules: An Eater's Manual, 2009
In Defense of Food: An Eater's Manifesto, 2008

Other books you might like:
Bill Bryson, *A Walk in the Woods*, 1998
Steven Hopp, *Animal, Vegetable, Miracle: A Year of Food Life*, 2007
Barbara Kingsolver, co-author
Barbara Kingsolver, *The Poisonwood Bible*, 1998
Camille Kingsolver, *Animal, Vegetable, Miracle: A Year of Food Life*, 2007
Michael Pollan, *In Defense of Food: An Eater's Manifesto*, 2008
Eric Schlosser, *Fast Food Nation: The Dark Side of the All-American Meal*, 2001

1001

MICHAEL POLLAN

In Defense of Food: An Eater's Manifesto

(New York: Penguin, 2008)

Subject(s): Food; Health; Nutrition

Summary: In this follow-up to *The Omnivore's Dilemma*, Michael Pollan attempts to answer the question, "What should we eat?" Pollan advocates for a return to traditional foods, for a diet weighted toward green vegetables, for consuming small portions, and for avoiding processed foods. He advises skepticism toward processed foods that are touted as having nutritional virtues. Pollan observes that real foods are being removed from the American diet, and that this change has corresponded to increases in diabetes, obesity, and cancer. He objects to a flawed philosophy he labels "nutritionism" and argues that we need to change our relationship to the food we eat.

Where it's reviewed:
London Review of Books, March 20, 2008, page 26

Other books by the same author:
Food Rules: An Eater's Manual, 2009
The Omnivore's Dilemma: A Natural History of Four Meals, 2006
The Botany of Desire: A Plant's-Eye View of the World, 2001

Other books you might like:
Jonathan Bloom, *American Wasteland: How America Throws Away Nearly Half of Its Food (and What We Can Do About It)*, 2010
Bill Bryson, *A Walk in the Woods*, 1998
Steven Hopp, *Animal, Vegetable, Miracle: A Year of Food Life*, 2007
Barbara Kingsolver, co-author
Camille Kingsolver, co-author
Marion Nestle, *What to Eat*, 2006
Eric Schlosser, *Fast Food Nation: The Dark Side of the All-American Meal*, 2001

1002

JULIE POWELL

Julie & Julia: 365 Days, 524 Recipes, 1 Tiny Apartment Kitchen: How One Girl Risked Her Marriage, Her Job, & Her Sanity to Master the Art of Living

(New York: Little, Brown and Company, 2005)

Subject(s): Cooking; Cooks

Summary: Twenty-nine-year-old Julie Powell was dissatisfied with her life. She worked as a secretary at a government agency, lived in a small apartment in Queens, and pondered over health concerns. While taking an emotional time-out at her parents' house in Austin, Texas, the author found her mother's worn copy of Julia Child's *Mastering the Art of French Cooking*. To distract her from her workday life, Powell decided to prepare all 524 recipes in the cookbook in one year. While her husband Eric endured dishes with long ingredient lists and even longer preparation times, Powell bore through recipes containing calves' hooves, kidneys, and brains. Throughout the cooking process, the author blogged about her successes and failures and her life. Even though Powell

never met her inspiration, Julia Child, she was encouraged to infuse some of Child's zest into her own life. The book has also been made into a movie.

Where it's reviewed:
TLS. Times Literary Supplement, March 10, 2006, pages 28-29

Other books by the same author:
Cleaving, 2009

Other books you might like:
Julia Child, *Mastering the Art of French Cooking, vol. 1*, 1961
Julia Child, *Mastering the Art of French Cooking, vol. 2*, 1970
Julia Child, *My Life in France*, 2006
Elizabeth Gilbert, *Eat, Pray, Love: One Woman's Search for Everything Across Italy, India and Indonesia*, 2006
Alex Prud'homme, *My Life in France*, 2006
Mort Rosenblum, *A Goose in Toulouse: And Other Culinary Adventures in France*, 2000

1003

JULIE POWELL

Cleaving: A Story of Marriage, Meat, and Obsession

(New York: Little, Brown and Company, 2009)

Subject(s): Autobiographies; Marriage; Infidelity

Summary: Julie Powell, of *Julie and Julia* fame, offers up another memoir of her life in *Cleaving: A Story of Marriage, Meat, and Obsession*. This follow-up autobiography, in addition to detailing Powell's stint as a butcher's apprentice, describes the affairs—her own and her husband's—that almost led to their divorce. Learning the art of cutting meat at Fleisher's, a butcher shop in upstate New York, proved therapeutic for Powell, however, and gave her time and space to reflect on her life and her decisions. In *Cleaving*, Powell provides detailed accounts of animals going to slaughter and separating meat from bone, but mixes in stories about her sexual escapades with her lover, "D.," and her eventual reunion with her husband.

Where it's reviewed:
TLS. Times Literary Supplement, October 16, 2009, page 28

Other books by the same author:
Julie & Julia: 365 Days, 524 Recipes, 1 Tiny Apartment Kitchen: How One Girl Risked Her Marriage, Her Job, & Her Sanity to Master the Art of Living, 2005

Other books you might like:
Bill Buford, *Heat: An Amateur's Adventures as Kitchen Slave, Line Cook, Pasta-Maker, and Apprentice to a Dante-Quoting Butcher in Tuscany*, 2006
Julia Child, *Mastering the Art of French Cooking, vol. 1*, 1961
Julia Child, *Mastering the Art of French Cooking, vol. 2*, 1970

Pop Culture

Julia Child, *My Life in France*, 2006

Elizabeth Gilbert, *Eat, Pray, Love: One Woman's Search for Everything Across Italy, India and Indonesia*, 2006

Alex Prud'homme, *My Life in France*, 2006

1004

NATHAN RABIN

The Big Rewind: A Memoir Brought to You by Pop Culture

(New York: Scribner, 2009)

Subject(s): Biographies; Memory; Culture

Summary: Writer Nathan Rabin recounts stories from his childhood in the memoir *The Big Rewind: A Memoir Brought to You by Pop Culture*. Rabin, growing up with no parents, jumped from place to place trying to find some semblance of home. He shares stories from the different and strange places he's lived, and he discusses variety of experiences that helped him evolve as a person. Throughout the book, Rabin relates his stories, experiences, and encounters back to the pop culture of the time and the elements of culture he enjoyed during his youth. Rabin is currently a writer for the online news Web site *The Onion*.

Where it's reviewed:
Booklist, June 1, 2009, page 10
Publishers Weekly, April 27, 2009, page 121

Other books by the same author:
My Year of Flops: The A.V. Club Presents One Man's Journey Deep into the Heart of Cinematic Failure, 2010

Other books you might like:
AV Club, *Inventory: 16 Films Featuring Manic Pixie Dream Girls, 10 Great Songs Nearly Ruined by Saxophone, and 100 More Obsessively Specific Pop-Culture Lists*, 2009

John Hodgman, *The Areas of My Expertise: An Almanac of Complete World Knowledge Compiled with Instructive Annotation and Arranged in Useful Order*, 2005

Chuck Klosterman, *Eating the Dinosaur*, 2009

Rob Sheffield, *Talking to Girls about Duran Duran: One Young Man's Quest for True Love and a Cooler Haircut*, 2010

Claire Zulkey, *An Off Year*, 2009

1005

LOREE RACKSTRAW

Love as Always, Kurt: Vonnegut as I Knew Him

(Cambridge, Massachusetts: Da Capo Press, 2009)

Subject(s): Writers; Friendship; Love

Summary: Loree Rackstraw knew famed author Kurt Von-

negut before he had written a best seller and had garnered much literary respect. She knew him when he was simply a professor teaching a writing workshop in Iowa. As a student who admired her instructor's work, Rackstraw pursued a relationship with Vonnegut. What began as a romance became a complex and lasting friendship, kept alive through letters and visits for many years. In *Love as Always, Kurt: Vonnegut as I Knew Him*, Rackstraw describes Vonnegut's life as the unknown author transformed into a literary sensation. In this book, Rackstraw includes many of the letters Vonnegut wrote to her throughout the years.

Where it's reviewed:
Kirkus Reviews, February 1, 2009, page 62
Library Journal, April 15, 2009, page 93

Other books you might like:
William Rodney Allen, *Conversations with Kurt Vonnegut*, 1988

Todd F. Davis, *Kurt Vonnegut's Crusade: Or, How a Postmodern Harlequin Preaches a New Kind of Humanism*, 2006

Jerome Klinkowitz, *Kurt Vonnegut's America*, 2010

Lee Stringer, *Like Shaking Hands With God: A Conversation About Writing*, 2000
Kurt Vonnegut, co-author

Kurt Vonnegut, *Palm Sunday: An Autobiographical Collage*, 1981

1006

DAVID RAKOFF

Don't Get Too Comfortable: The Indignities of Coach Class, The Torments of Low Thread Count, The Never-Ending Quest for Artisanal Olive Oil, and Other First World Problems

(New York: Broadway Books, 2005)

Subject(s): Greed; Humor; Popular Culture

Summary: This collection of autobiographical essays by *GQ* writer-at-large David Rakoff takes readers on a grand tour of cultural excess, where no one is safe from his scathing wit. Rakoff's journalistic assignments place him everywhere from a luxurious flight on the Concorde to a chicken-wing-studded jaunt on Hooters Air. On the runways of a Paris fashion show, at a soft-core *Playboy* shoot off the coast of Belize, and in a Beverly Hills plastic surgeon's office, he witnesses firsthand the greed, privilege, pretentiousness, and narcissism that characterize the North American penchant for over-consumption. Rakoff is also the author of *Fraud* and a contributor to programs on National Public Radio.

Where it's reviewed:
Booklist, August 2005, page 1969
Publishers Weekly, May 30, 2005, page 47

Other books by the same author:
Fraud: Essays, 2001

Other books you might like:
John Hodgman, *The Areas of My Expertise: An Almanac of Complete World Knowledge Compiled with Instructive Annotation and Arranged in Useful Order*, 2005
John Hodgman, *More Information Than You Require*, 2009
David Sedaris, *Me Talk Pretty One Day*, 2000
Eric Spitznagel, *You're a Horrible Person, but I Like You: The Believer Book of Advice*, 2010
Larry Wilmore, *I'd Rather We Got Casinos, and Other Black Thoughts*, 2009

1007

DAVID RITZ
GRANDMASTER FLASH , Co-Author

The Adventures of Grandmaster Flash: My Life, My Beats
(New York: Broadway Books, 2008)

Subject(s): Autobiographies; Biographies; Music

Summary: *The Adventures of Grandmaster Flash: My Life, My Beats* is a memoir as told by hip-hop artist Grandmaster Flash to writer David Ritz. Grandmaster Flash tells the story of his childhood in Barbados in the 1960s, and of first being drawn to music when he heard a James Brown record. He became a DJ well known for his "scratching" techniques, eventually becoming a rap artist in New York with the group Furious Five, who were later inducted to the Rock and Roll Hall of Fame. He discusses his frequent struggles in New York City, as well as his issues with other recording artists and producers throughout his career. This book also considers how Grandmaster Flash, as a pioneer of rap music, influenced a number of other musicians as well.

Where it's reviewed:
Booklist, June 1, 2008, page 28

Other books you might like:
Michael Eric Dyson, *Between God and Gangsta Rap: Bearing Witness to Black Culture*, 1997
Nelson George, *Hip Hop America*, 1998
Fred L. Johnson, *Tupac Shakur: The Life and Times of an American Icon*, 2010
Johan Kugelberg, *Born in the Bronx: A Visual Record of the Early Days of Hip Hop*, 2007
Tayannah Lee McQuillar, *Tupac Shakur: The Life and Times of an American Icon*, 2010
Cathy Scott, *The Murder of Biggie Smalls*, 2000

1008

CELIA RIVENBARK

Stop Dressing Your Six-Year-Old Like a Skank: And Other Words of Delicate Southern Wisdom
(New York: St. Martin's Press, 2006)

Subject(s): Popular culture; Humor; Modern Life

Summary: In *Stop Dressing Your Six-Year-Old Like a Skank: And Other Words of Delicate Southern Wisdom*, newspaper columnist and author Celia Rivenbark provides words of wisdom on pop culture dilemmas such as the tendency for tweens to wear revealing clothes, the obsession families have with Disney World despite its cost, and the celebrity baby boom's affect on fashion trends. The book contains more than 30 essays, all of which are full of Rivenbark's rapier observations and Southern wit. Rivenbark is also the author of *You Can't Drink All Day If You Don't Start in the Morning* and *We're Just Like You, Only Prettier*.

Where it's reviewed:
Publishers Weekly, June 12, 2006, page 41

Other books by the same author:
You Can't Drink All Day If You Don't Start in the Morning, 2009
Belle Weather: Mostly Sunny with a Chance of Scattered Hissy Fits, 2008
We're Just Like You, Only Prettier: Confessions of a Tarnished Southern Belle, 2005

Other books you might like:
Samantha Bee, *I Know I Am, but What Are You?*, 2010
Sloane Crosley, *I Was Told There'd Be Cake*, 2008
Chelsea Handler, *My Horizontal Life: A Collection of One-Night Stands*, 2005
Laurie Notaro, *The Idiot Girl and the Flaming Tantrum of Death: Reflections on Revenge, Germophobia, and Laser Hair Removal*, 2008
David Sedaris, *Me Talk Pretty One Day*, 2000

1009

MARY ROACH

Packing for Mars: The Curious Science of Life in the Void
(New York: W.W. Norton, 2010)

Subject(s): Space exploration; Space flight; Science

Summary: In *Packing for Mars: The Curious Science of Life in the Void*, author Mary Roach investigates the bizarre ways modern science is preparing for the possibility of human habitation in outer space. Roach answers a series of questions about how human life could possibly be sustained in a world without gravity or basic necessities and conveniences. Her curiosity leads her to some surprising—and oftentimes humorous—findings, including a space shuttle "training toilet" and a strange

Pop Culture

NASA crash test. *Packing for Mars* contains a listing of bibliographical references.

Where it's reviewed:
Booklist, July 1, 2010, page 16
Library Journal, July 2010, page 106
Time, August 9, 2010, page 16

Other books by the same author:
Bonk: The Curious Coupling of Science and Sex, 2009
Spook: Science Tackles the Afterlife, 2006
Stiff: The Curious Lives of Human Cadavers, 2004

Other books you might like:
Bill Bryson, *A Short History of Nearly Everything*, 2003
Colin Burgess, *In the Shadow of the Moon: A Challenging Journey to Tranquility, 1965-1969*, 2007
    Francis French, co-author
George Friedman, *The Next 100 Years: A Forecast for the 21st Century*, 2009
Jeff Kanipe, *Chasing Hubble's Shadows: The Search for Galaxies at the Edge of Time*, 2006
Charles Seife, *Decoding the Universe: How the New Science of Information Is Explaining Everything in the Cosmos, from Our Brains to Black Holes*, 2006

1010

MARY ROACH

Bonk: The Curious Coupling of Sex and Science

(New York: W. W. Norton, 2008)

Subject(s): Sexual behavior; Science; Sexuality

Summary: Written by Mary Roach, *Bonk: The Curious Coupling of Sex and Science* is a humorous and scientific book all about sex. Bonk spent two years researching sexual physiology and presents her findings in this nonfiction work. In *Bonk*, she gives readers a greater understanding of lust, attraction, sexual arousal, orgasm, and sexual intercourse from a scientific, and often humorous, approach. Studying everything from the effects of Viagra on animals to the power that the mind plays in orgasm, Roach presents a comprehensive guide to all things sex-related. *Bonk* provides readers with the facts about sex and how understanding the science behind it can actually make the act more enjoyable for couples.

Other books by the same author:
Packing for Mars: the Curious Science of Life in the Void, 2010
Spook: Science Tackles the Afterlife, 2005
Stiff: The Curious Lives of Human Cadavers, 2004

Other books you might like:
Bill Bryson, *A Short History of Nearly Everything*, 2003
Mary Roach, *Packing for Mars: The Curious Science of Life in the Void*, 2010
Mary Roach, *Spook: Science Tackles the Afterlife*, 2006
Mary Roach, *Stiff: The Curious Lives of Human Cadavers*, 2003
Tom Wolfe, *The Right Stuff*, 1979

1011

DAVY ROTHBART

Requiem for a Paper Bag: Celebrities and Civilians Tell Stories of the Best Lost, Tossed, and Found Items from Around the World

(Whitby, Ontario, Canada: Fireside Publishing, 2009)

Subject(s): Entertainment industry; Writers; Comedians

Summary: Since 2001, Davy Rothbart and his friends have been publishing FOUND Magazine, a publication featuring notes, drawings, grocery lists, and other interesting items people find on the street. *Requiem for a Paper Bag: Celebrities and Civilians Tell Stories of the Best Lost, Tossed, and Found Items from Around the World* is a spin-off of Rothbart's magazine and its Web site. For this book, Rothbart asked famous writers, comedians, artists, and musicians for items they found that inspired them to produce a particular piece of work. If the celebrities no longer had the item, they instead gave Rothbart the jokes, short stories, illustrations, or songs the items inspired. Rothbart is also the editor of *FOUND* and *FOUND II*.

Where it's reviewed:
Library Journal, April 1, 2009, page 76

Other books by the same author:
Found II: More of the Best Lost, Tossed, and Forgotten Items from Around the World, 2006
The Lone Surfer of Montana, Kansas: Stories, 2005
Found: The Best Lost, Tossed, and Forgotten Items from Around the World, 2004

Other books you might like:
Mike Bender, *Awkward Family Photos*, 2010
    Doug Chernack, co-author
Justin Halpern, *Sh*t My Dad Says*, 2010
David Nadelberg, *Mortified: Real Words. Real People. Real Pathetic.*, 2006

1012

MARJANE SATRAPI

The Complete Persepolis

(New York: Pantheon Books, 2007)

Subject(s): Autobiographies; Comic books; Women

Summary: *The Complete Persepolis* combines both of Marjane Satrapi's autobiographical graphic "novels" in a single volume. In comic-book style, Satrapi recounts the early years of her life in Tehran—the joy and support provided by her close-knit family, and the increasing oppression suffered amidst the Islamic Revolution. Sent away to Vienna by her parents during her teenage years to get an education, Satrapi adapts to a new culture as she deals with the pain of separation from the home she knows. When she finally come back to Tehran, however, the experience is bittersweet, leading Satrapi eventually to leave her motherland with a vow never to return.

Other books by the same author:
Chicken with Plums, 2006
Monsters are Afraid of the Moon, 2006
Embroideries, 2005

Other books you might like:
Alison Bechdel, *Fun Home: A Family Tragicomic*, 2006
Phoebe Gloeckner, *A Child's Life and Other Stories*, 2000
Craig Thompson, *Blankets*, 2003
Adrian Tomine, *Shortcomings*, 2007
Chris Ware, *Jimmy Corrigan: The Smartest Kid on Earth*, 2000

1013

MARJANE SATRAPI

Embroideries

(New York: Pantheon, 2005)

Subject(s): Women; Men; Storytelling

Summary: Author Marjane Satrapi continues in the vein of her other celebrated works, interweaving memoir and fiction. In *Embroideries*, her grandmother, her mother, her aunt, and several friends from their neighborhood in Iran gather for afternoon tea, where the conversation quickly turns to love, sex, and the trouble with men. Marjane listens to three generations of her family tell humorous stories about the things they have done for the love and attention of the men in their lives and for the ability to continue to live with them. The title comes from a term used to describe an operation that is performed on women to give them the sensation of being a virgin again.

Where it's reviewed:
Booklist, April 1, 2005, page 1351
Entertainment Weekly, April 22, 2005, page 68
Library Journal, May 15, 2005, page 102

Other books by the same author:
The Complete Persepolis, 2007
Chicken with Plums, 2006
Monsters are Afraid of the Moon, 2006

Other books you might like:
Alison Bechdel, *Fun Home: A Family Tragicomic*, 2006
Phoebe Gloeckner, *A Child's Life and Other Stories*, 2000
Craig Thompson, *Blankets*, 2003
Adrian Tomine, *Shortcomings*, 2007
Chris Ware, *Jimmy Corrigan: The Smartest Kid on Earth*, 2000

1014

HAROLD SCHECHTER

True Crime: An American Anthology

(New York: Library of America, 2008)

Subject(s): Crime; United States history; Murder

Summary: Professor and true crime author Harold Schechter brings together 50 stories showcasing the best in American crime writing. Since the first Europeans arrived in North America, true crime reportage has been a popular and captivating form of literature, and *True Crime: An American Anthology* chronicles both the history of American crime and the powerful writing that has been created around it. Authors in this volume run the gamut from historical figures to modern-day literary powerhouses, including Cotton Mather, Benjamin Franklin, Nathaniel Hawthorne, Abraham Lincoln, Mark Twain, Edna Ferber, Truman Capote, Jimmy Breslin, Ann Rule, and Dominck Dunne. Schechter provides an introduction to the volume.

Other books by the same author:
The Serial Killer Files, 2003
Deranged, 1998
Deviant, 1998

Other books you might like:
Thomas H. Cook, *The Best American Crime Reporting 2009*, 2009
James Ellroy, *The Black Dahlia*, 1987
James Ellroy, *L.A. Confidential*, 1990
Charlaine Harris, *Real Murders*, 1990
Erik Larson, *The Devil in the White City: Murder, Magic, and Madness at the Fair That Changed America*, 2003
Otto Penzler, *The Best American Crime Reporting 2009*, 2009

1015

JOAN SCHENKAR

The Talented Miss Highsmith: The Secret Life and Serious Art of Patricia Highsmith

(New York: St. Martin's Press, 2009)

Subject(s): Writers; Alcoholism; Sexuality

Summary: In *The Talented Miss Highsmith: The Secret Life and Serious Art of Patricia Highsmith*, biographer and playwright Joan Schenkar explores the turbulent life and career of the acclaimed mystery novelist. Highsmith is world-renowned for her Tom Ripley series of mysteries as well as the iconic novel *Strangers on a Train*, but her private life was filled with just as many ups and downs as those of her characters. From a Texas childhood to the New York literary circuit, from doomed love affairs to a volatile relationship with the bottle, Schenkar leaves no aspect of Highsmith's life unexplored. The result is this all-encompassing work that captures the complicated mind of one of the 20th century's greatest writers.

Where it's reviewed:
Booklist, December 1, 2009, page 11
Library Journal, November 15, 2009, page 64
Publishers Weekly, October 26, 2009, page 1

Other books by the same author:
Signs of Life: Six Comedies of Menace, 1997

Pop Culture

Other books you might like:
Harry M. Benshoff, *Queer Cinema: The Film Reader*, 2004
Charlotte Chandler, *It's Only a Movie: Alfred Hitchcock, a Personal Biography*, 2005
Katherine V. Forrest, *Lesbian Pulp Fiction: The Sexually Intrepid World of Lesbian Paperback Novels, 1950-1965*, 2005
Sean Griffin, *Queer Cinema: The Film Reader*, 2004
Patricia Highsmith, *Strangers on a Train*, 1950
Patricia Highsmith, *The Talented Mr. Ripley*, 1955

1016

WILLIAM SHATNER
DAVID FISHER , Co-Author

Up Till Now: The Autobiography
(New York: St. Martin's Press, 2008)

Subject(s): Acting; Actors and Actresses; Growing Up

Summary: Although Shatner has written before about his Star Trek career, this is the first book to encompass Shatner's entire life...up till now. Shatner takes us through his childhood in Montreal, his career in theater and television, as well as his writing and directing. His writing is honest, as he chronicles his successes and failures in life. You may know Shatner as the dashing captain of the Enterprise, the hard working cop, TJ Hooker, a frisky lawyer in Boston Legal, or even the goofy Priceline Investigator. Come meet the man behind it all. This is an enjoyable read for any Shatner fan.

Where it's reviewed:
Library Journal, April 15, 2008, page 88
Publishers Weekly, March 3, 2008, page 41

Other books by the same author:
Collision Course, 2008
Captain's Blood, 2003
Star Trek Memories, 1993

Other books you might like:
Justin Halpern, *Sh*t My Dad Says*, 2010
Chris Kreski, *Star Trek Memories*, 1993
Leonard Nimoy, *I Am Not Spock*, 1979
Leonard Nimoy, *I Am Spock*, 1995
William Shatner, *Get a Life!*, 1999
William Shatner, *Star Trek Memories*, 1993

1017

ROB SHEFFIELD

Talking to Girls about Duran Duran: One Young Man's Quest for True Love and a Cooler Haircut
(New York: Penguin, 2010)

Subject(s): Music; Rock music; Coming of age
Summary: Author and *Rolling Stone* contributing editor

Rob Sheffield came of age in the 1980s, when his love of music and popular culture was formed. In *Talking to Girls about Duran Duran: One Young Man's Quest for True Love and a Cooler Haircut*, Sheffield recounts his adolescent years and the music that played a pivotal role in shaping his youthful escapades. As he tries to understand girls, make it through high school, and endure a horrible summer job, Sheffield displays the wit, wisdom, and music savvy that have made him famous within the music industry.

Where it's reviewed:
Booklist, June 1, 2010, page 27
Library Journal, June 15, 2010, page 76
Publishers Weekly, May 3, 2010, page 38

Other books by the same author:
Love Is a Mix Tape: Life and Loss, One Song at a Time, 2007

Other books you might like:
AV Club, *Inventory: 16 Films Featuring Manic Pixie Dream Girls, 10 Great Songs Nearly Ruined by Saxophone, and 100 More Obsessively Specific Pop-Culture Lists*, 2009
John Hodgman, *The Areas of My Expertise: An Almanac of Complete World Knowledge Compiled with Instructive Annotation and Arranged in Useful Order*, 2005
Nathan Rabin, *The Big Rewind: A Memoir Brought to You by Pop Culture*, 2009
Nathan Rabin, *My Year of Flops: The A.V. Club Presents One Man's Journey Deep into the Heart of Cinematic Failure*, 2010
Claire Zulkey, *An Off Year*, 2009

1018

JUDY SHEPARD

The Meaning of Matthew: My Son's Murder in Laramie, and a World Transformed
(New York: Hudson Street Press, 2009)

Subject(s): Homosexuality; Murder; Mother-son relations

Summary: In October 1998, Matthew Shepard was severely beaten, hung on a fence, and left to die by Aaron McKinney and Russell Henderson. Shepard died two weeks later, and McKinney and Henderson were arrested and later found guilty of felony murder. The men testified that they targeted and killed Shepard because he was a homosexual. In *The Meaning of Matthew: My Son's Murder in Laramie, and a World Transformed*, Matthew's mother, Judy Shepard, discusses her son's death and the affect the murder trial had on the world. She writes about Matthew's life before his death, how she survived the tragedy of his death, and how it motivated her to start the Matthew Shepard Foundation and push for the passing of the Matthew Shepard Act.

Where it's reviewed:
Kirkus Reviews, June 1, 2009, page 600

Other books you might like:

Leroy Aarons, *Prayers for Bobby: A Mother's Coming to Terms with the Suicide of Her Gay Son*, 1996

Mindy Drucker, *Crisis: 40 Stories Revealing the Personal, Social, and Religious Pain and Trauma of Growing Up Gay in America*, 2008
Mitchell Gold, co-editor

Patrick Hinds, *The Whole World Was Watching: Living in the Light of Matthew Shepard*, 2005

Moises Kaufman, *The Laramie Project*, 2001

Beth Loffreda, *Losing Matt Shepard: Life and Politics in the Aftermath of Anti-Gay Murder*, 2000

Romaine Patterson, *The Whole World Was Watching: Living in the Light of Matthew Shepard*, 2005

Tectonic Theater Project, *The Laramie Project*, 2001

1019

SARAH SILVERMAN

The Bedwetter: Stories of Courage, Redemption, and Pee

(New York: Harper, 2010)

Subject(s): Autobiographies; Humor

Summary: In *The Bedwetter: Stories of Courage, Redemption, and Pee*, comedienne Sarah Silverman looks back at her childhood growing up in New Hampshire, followed by her successful standup career. Silverman tackles both the humorous and the serious, using her trademark acerbic wit to relay the tale of her chronic bedwetting problem while peppering in reflections on her bout with teenage depression. Silverman is the star of Comedy Central's *The Sarah Silverman Program*.

Where it's reviewed:
Booklist, March 15, 2010, page 4
The New Yorker, June 14, 2010, page 137
Publishers Weekly, March 29, 2010, page 48

Other books you might like:

David Cross, *I Drink for a Reason*, 2010

Kathy Griffin, *Official Book Club Selection: A Memoir According to Kathy Griffin*, 2009

Justin Halpern, *Sh*t My Dad Says*, 2010

David Rakoff, *Don't Get Too Comfortable: The Indignities of Coach Class, The Torments of Low Thread Count, The Never-Ending Quest for Artisanal Olive Oil, and Other First World Problems*, 2005

Eric Spitznagel, *You're a Horrible Person, but I Like You: The Believer Book of Advice*, 2010

1020

LIZZIE SKURNICK

Shelf Discovery: The Teen Classics We Never Stopped Reading

(New York: Avon, 2009)

Subject(s): Adolescence; Reading; Adolescent interpersonal relations

Summary: In *Shelf Discovery: The Teen Classics We Never Stopped Reading*, Lizzie Skurnick evaluates the young adult novels of the 1960s through 1980s. During this time, the teen novel underwent significant changes. Instead of perfect, obedient narrators and main characters, the protagonists in these stories experienced real-life issues such as dealing with puberty, divorce, sexual abuse, drug abuse, and death. Skurnick discusses how this shift in literature for teens affected an entire generation of readers. This collection, discussing works by writers such as Joan Aiken, Judy Blume, Beverly Cleary, Louise Fitzhugh, and Norma Klein, is divided into sections including "Still Checked Out: YA Heroines We'll Never Return," "She's at That Age: Girls on the Verge," and "Him She Loves: Romanced, Rejected, Affianced, Dejected."

Where it's reviewed:
Library Journal, June 15, 2009, page 74

Other books you might like:

Andrea J. Buchanan, *The Daring Book for Girls*, 2007

Kara Jesella, *How Sassy Changed My Life: A Love Letter to the Greatest Teen Magazine of All Time*, 2007
Marisa Meltzer, co-author

Jennifer O'Connell, *Everything I Needed to Know About Being a Girl I Learned from Judy Blume*, 2007

Miriam Peskowitz, *The Daring Book for Girls*, 2007

Anita Silvey, *Everything I Need to Know I Learned from a Children's Book*, 2009

Eileen Spinelli, *Today I Will: A Year of Quotes, Notes, and Promises to Myself*, 2009
Jerry Spinelli, co-author

1021

DAVID SMALL

Stitches: A Memoir

(New York: Norton, 2009)

Subject(s): Autobiographies; Cancer; Father-son relations

Summary: In *Stitches: A Memoir*, author David Small uses illustrations in the style of a graphic novel in order to create an account of his young life. Small's life story is both sad and remarkable because of the obstacles he had to overcome. Small, who was the son of a radiologist, was exposed to unnecessary x-ray treatments for a variety of illnesses that did not call for such excessive action. Later, Small developed cancer because of the overexposure to radiology, and he remained untreated for a long period of time. In pictures and sparse prose, Small recounts the ordeal for readers.

Where it's reviewed:
The Christian Century, December 15, 2009, page 25

Other books by the same author:
Imogene's Antlers, 2010
So You Want to be President?, 2004

Other books you might like:

Phoebe Gloeckner, *A Child's Life and Other Stories*, 2000

Marjane Satrapi, *The Complete Persepolis*, 2007

Craig Thompson, *Blankets*, 2003
Adrian Tomine, *Shortcomings*, 2007
Chris Ware, *Jimmy Corrigan: The Smartest Kid on Earth*, 2000

1022

PATTI SMITH
Just Kids
(New York: HarperCollins Publishers, 2010)

Subject(s): Autobiographies; Art; Friendship

Summary: Before Patti Smith became a famous singer, she met her longtime friend Robert Mapplethorpe. As a young woman, Patti Smith left her life and her family in Philadelphia and moved to New York in hopes of finding a different type of life. After a short time in the city, Smith met Robert Mapplethorpe. The twosome immediately hit it off, and they soon become lovers. When Mapplethorpe realized that he was gay, he and Smith became great friends. Smith and Mapplethorpe lived among other artists in New York, and they met people such as Jimmi Hendrix, Allen Ginsberg, and Janis Joplin while they lived at the Hotel Chelsea. Together, Smith and Mapplethorpe created art and survived on what little money they scraped together. Eventually, Smith became famous for her music, but she and Mapplethorpe remained close friends. Mapplethorpe died of AIDS in 1989. *Just Kids* is a memoir by Patti Smith.

Where it's reviewed:
Entertainment Weekly, January 15, 2010, page 75
New Statesman, March 1, 2010, page 47
Publishers Weekly, December 7, 2009, page 43

Other books by the same author:
Patti Smith, Land 250, 2008
Patti Smith Complete 1975-2006: Lyrics, Reflections & Notes for the Future, 2006

Other books you might like:
David Byrne, *CBGB and OMFUG: Thirty Years from the Home of Underground Rock*, 2005
Veronica Kofman, *Lobotomy: Surviving the Ramones*, 2000
Hilly Kristal, *CBGB and OMFUG: Thirty Years from the Home of Underground Rock*, 2005
Patricia Morrisroe, *Mapplethorpe: A Biography*, 1997
Dee Dee Ramone, *Lobotomy: Surviving the Ramones*, 2000
Gary Valentine, *New York Rocker: My Life in the Blank Generation with Blondie, Iggy Pop, and Others, 1974-1981*, 2006

1023

ZADIE SMITH
Changing My Mind: Occasional Essays
(New York: Penguin Press, 2009)

Subject(s): Literature; Movies; Politics

Summary: In *Changing My Mind: Occasional Essays*, award-winning novelist Zadie Smith presents a series of nonfiction pieces that explore the worlds of literature, art, film, politics, and philosophy. Smith shares her experiences and insights on a vast array of topics, including the Academy Awards, Barack Obama, the literary legacy of the late David Foster Wallace, British comedy, and actresses Anna Magnani and Katharine Hepburn. Told with Smith's trademark style and fierce intelligence, this volume heralds the arrival of a unique new voice in contemporary nonfiction. *Changing My Mind* includes a list of bibliographical references and a full index.

Where it's reviewed:
Library Journal, October 1, 2009, page 78

Other books by the same author:
On Beauty, 2005
The Autograph Man, 2002
White Teeth, 2001

Other books you might like:
Dave Eggers, *A Heartbreaking Work of Staggering Genius*, 2000
Salman Rushdie, *Imaginary Homelands: Essays and Criticism, 1981-1991*, 1991
Salman Rushdie, *Step Across This Line: Collected Nonfiction 1992-2002*, 2002
David Shields, *Reality Hunger: A Manifesto*, 2010
David Foster Wallace, *A Supposedly Fun Thing I'll Never Do Again: Essays and Arguments*, 1997

1024

TORI SPELLING
HILARY LIFTIN , Co-Author
Mommywood
(New York: Simon Spotlight Entertainment, 2009)

Subject(s): Actors; Mothers; Parenthood

Summary: Actress Tori Spelling recounts her experiences as a Hollywood mom in the memoir *Mommywood*. Born the heir to an entertainment dynasty, Spelling grew up in the spotlight. Fame had its ups and down, but Spelling wanted to shield her own children from the trappings of life in Beverly Hills. This book explains how she and her husband, Dean McDermott, try to make their home life as normal as possible. Along the way, she learns valuable lessons about the nature of parenthood as she comes to terms with her own parents' fault, experiences the less-glamorous aspects of parenting (i.e. changing dirty diapers), and attempts to deal with the inescapable pressures of notoriety. Blending humor, advice, and surprising insight, *Mommywood* shows readers that Spelling is a lot like other working mothers.

Where it's reviewed:
Library Journal, September 15, 2009, page 35

Other books by the same author:
uncharted terriTORI, 2010
sTORI Telling, 2008

Other books you might like:
Kate Gosselin, *I Just Want You to Know: Letters to My Kids on Love, Faith, and Family*, 2010

Kathy Griffin, *Official Book Club Selection: A Memoir According to Kathy Griffin*, 2009

Jenny McCarthy, *Baby Laughs: The Naked Truth about Mommyhood*, 2005

Heather McDonald, *You'll Never Blue Ball in This Town Again: One Woman's Painfully Funny Quest to Give It Up*, 2010

Kendra Wilkinson, *Sliding into Home*, 2010

▮1025

TORI SPELLING

Uncharted terriTORI

(New York: Gallery Books, 2010)

Subject(s): Actors; Autobiographies; Movie industry

Summary: Tori Spelling has made a name for herself as an actress, author, reality television star, and entrepreneur. But in *Uncharted terriTORI*, Spelling's essays show that her greatest role is just being herself. She charts the rocky terrain of marriage and motherhood, her unsteady relationship with her mother, her not-always-lauded standing in pop culture, and much more. With the wit and candor that made her previous two books bestsellers, Spelling takes on contemporary Hollywood—and her strange, hilarious place in it.

Other books by the same author:
Mommywood, 2010
sTORI Telling, 2008

Other books you might like:
Kathy Griffin, *Official Book Club Selection: A Memoir According to Kathy Griffin*, 2009

Chelsea Handler, *Are You There, Vodka? It's Me, Chelsea*, 2008

Heather McDonald, *You'll Never Blue Ball in This Town Again: One Woman's Painfully Funny Quest to Give It Up*, 2010

Candy Spelling, *Stories from Candyland*, 2009

Kendra Wilkinson, *Sliding into Home*, 2010

▮1026

TORI SPELLING

Stori Telling

(New York: Simon Spotlight Entertainment, 2008)

Subject(s): Family; Wealth; Television programs

Summary: *Stori Telling* is the autobiography of television actress Tori Spelling. As the daughter of famed producer Aaron Spelling, Tori became famous by starring on her father's show *Beverly Hills 90210*. When the show ended, Tori found it impossible to get any acting job. In *Stori Telling*, Tori reveals behind-the-scenes details about her life and the Spelling family, most notably her strained relationship with her parents. Tori makes a point of dispelling rumors about her life, such as the suggestion that her mother took away her inheritance. She tells what is was like to grow up rich in Hollywood and

become a teen star. Readers can find out who Tori Spelling really is.

Where it's reviewed:
Entertainment Weekly, January 30, 2009, page 102

Other books by the same author:
uncharted terriTORI, 2010
Mommywood, 2009

Other books you might like:
Kathy Griffin, *Official Book Club Selection: A Memoir According to Kathy Griffin*, 2009

Hilary Liftin, *Mommywood*, 2009

Heather McDonald, *You'll Never Blue Ball in This Town Again: One Woman's Painfully Funny Quest to Give It Up*, 2010

Tori Spelling, *Mommywood*, 2009

Tori Spelling, *Uncharted terriTORI*, 2010

Kendra Wilkinson, *Sliding into Home*, 2010

▮1027

ERIC SPITZNAGEL

You're a Horrible Person, but I Like You: The Believer Book of Advice

(New York: Vintage Press, 2010)

Subject(s): Humor; Comedians; Self help books

Summary: *You're a Horrible Person, but I Like You: The Believer Book of Advice* is a compilation of stories that have appeared in *The Believer* magazine, selected and edited by Eric Spitznagel. This satirical self-help book features anecdotes by comedians such as Sarah Silverman, Zach Galifianakis, Judd Apatow, Michael Ian Black, and Martha Plimpton. Spitznagel is a contributor to magazines such as *Playboy*, *Esquire*, and *Maxim*.

Where it's reviewed:
Library Journal, February 15, 2010, page 96

Other books you might like:
John Hodgman, *The Areas of My Expertise: An Almanac of Complete World Knowledge Compiled with Instructive Annotation and Arranged in Useful Order*, 2005

David Sedaris, *Me Talk Pretty One Day*, 2000

David Sedaris, *When You Are Engulfed in Flames*, 2008

Sarah Vowell, *Assassination Vacation*, 2005

Larry Wilmore, *I'd Rather We Got Casinos, and Other Black Thoughts*, 2009

▮1028

BARNEY STINSON

The Bro Code

(New York: Fireside, 2008)

Subject(s): Humor; Dating (Social customs); Sexual behavior

Summary: *The Bro Code* is written from the perspective of Barney Stinson, a fictional character played by actor Neil-Patrick Harris on the television sitcom *How I Met Your Mother*. In the book, womanizer Barney expounds on what it means to be a "bro." Barney explains that all bros must follow a certain code in order to maintain their standing with other bros. Now, for the first time, Barney explains the rules of the code. In the text Barney explains the origins of the code, amendments that have been adopted over the years, and what to do when a bro violates the code.

Other books by the same author:
The Playbook: Suit up. Score chicks. Be Awesome., 2010

Other books you might like:
Ben Bator, *Texts From Last Night: All the Texts No One Remembers Sending*, 2010
Justin Halpern, *Sh*t My Dad Says*, 2010
Chelsea Handler, *My Horizontal Life: A Collection of One-Night Stands*, 2005
Lauren Leto, *Texts From Last Night: All the Texts No One Remembers Sending*, 2010
Tucker Max, *I Hope They Serve Beer in Hell*, 2006

1029

HANK STUEVER

Tinsel: A Search for America's Christmas Present

(New York: Houghton Mifflin Harcourt, 2009)

Subject(s): Christmas; Christian life; Decorative arts

Summary: In *Tinsel: A Search for America's Christmas Present*, Hank Stuever documents three consecutive Christmas seasons in Fresco, Texas. The people of Fresco are known for going over the top during the holidays. In fact, the city's celebration is so big that part of it can be seen from space. Throughout this book, Stuever describes the efforts of seasonal business owners who help Fresco's residents decorate their large homes with millions of lights and yards of tinsel every year. He details the trials and tribulations of homeowners Jeff and Bridgette Trykoski as they prepare their yard for the spectacular light show that has garnered international attention in years past. Stuever dives deep into the lives of these Christmas fanatics to find out why they spend so much time and money celebrating the holiday.

Where it's reviewed:
Booklist, November 1, 2009, page 15
The New Yorker, December 21, 2009, page 139

Other books by the same author:
Off Ramp: Adventures and Heartache in the American Elsewhere, 2004

Other books you might like:
Michele Clarke, *The Dreaded Feast: Writers on Enduring the Holidays*, 2009
Rebecca Mead, *One Perfect Day: The Selling of the American Wedding*, 2007
Taylor Plimpton, *The Dreaded Feast: Writers on*

Enduring the Holidays, 2009
Susan Waggoner, *Christmas Memories: Gifts, Activities, Fads, and Fancies, 1920s-1960s*, 2009
Joel Waldfogel, *Scroogenomics: Why You Shouldn't Buy Presents for the Holidays*, 2009

1030

CHESLEY SULLENBERGER
JEFFREY ZASLOW , Co-Author

Highest Duty: My Search for What Really Matters

(New York: William Morrow, 2009)

Subject(s): Aviation; Rescue work; Family life

Summary: In January 2009, one news story captivated the nation. It was a story about an airline pilot who managed to save the lives of all the passengers on his plane by making an emergency landing in the Hudson River. The image of the plane floating in the water as passengers were evacuated filled newspapers and televisions. That pilot, Captain Chesley "Sully" Sullenberger, became an acclaimed national hero, and he tells his story in *Highest Duty: My Search for What Really Matters*. This book explains Sullenberger's upbringing from his early days flying a crop duster to his career in the U.S. Air Force. Along the way, he shows how his highest ideals formed. Sullenberger discusses his beliefs about the American spirit, the "can-do" attitude that makes people act in brave and helpful ways, and the importance of family. Despite his public accomplishments, Sullenberger reveals, he is most fulfilled by his role as father and husband. That, he believes, is what really matters.

Where it's reviewed:
Booklist, September 15, 2009, page 5
Library Journal, February 1, 2010, page 42
Publishers Weekly, December 21, 2009, page 58

Other books you might like:
Joseph Balzer, *Flying Drunk: The True Story of a Northwest Airlines Flight, Three Drunk Pilots, and One Man's Fight for Redemption*, 2009
Dorothy Firman, *Brace for Impact: Miracle on the Hudson Survivors Share Their Stories of Near Death and Hope for New Life*, 2010
William Langewiesche, *Fly by Wire: The Geese, the Glide, the Miracle on the Hudson*, 2009
The Survivors of Flight 1549, *Miracle on the Hudson: The Survivors of Flight 1549 Tell Their Extraordinary Stories of Courage, Faith, and Determination*, 2009
Laura Parker, co-author
Richard Phillips, *A Captain's Duty: Somali Pirates, Navy SEALS, and Dangerous Days at Sea*, 2010
William Prochnau, *Miracle on the Hudson: The Survivors of Flight 1549 Tell Their Extraordinary Stories of Courage, Faith, and Determination*, 2009
Kevin Quirk, *Brace for Impact: Miracle on the Hudson Survivors Share Their Stories of Near Death and Hope for New Life*, 2010

Stephan Talty, *A Captain's Duty: Somali Pirates, Navy SEALS, and Dangerous Days at Sea*, 2010

1031

STUDS TERKEL

P.S.: Further Thoughts from a Lifetime of Listening

(New York: New Press, 2008)

Subject(s): History; Writers; Literature

Summary: *P.S.: Further Thoughts from a Lifetime of Listening* is a collection of essays and interviews from oral historian Studs Terkel. All of the pieces in this book are previously unpublished. Some of the essays are more personal and are about the author's life growing up in Chicago. One of the most notable interviews in the book took place with James Baldwin in 1961, in which the two discussed politics, music, and what it was like to be an African American in the country at that time. Other important inclusions are "A Gathering of Survivors," which is written about the Great Depression, and an interview with E.Y. Harburg, who wrote "Brother, Can You Spare a Dime?"

Where it's reviewed:
Booklist, October 1, 2008, page 11
Library Journal, October 15, 2008, page 70

Other books by the same author:
Will the Circle Be Unbroken?: Reflections on Death, Rebirth, and Hunger for a Faith, 2001
Race: How Blacks and Whites Think and Feel about the American Obsession, 1992
Working: People Talk about What They Do All Day and How They Feel about What They Do, 1972
Hard Times, 1970
Division Street America, 1966

Other books you might like:
F. Richard Ciccone, *Royko: A Life in Print*, 2001

1032

KATE TORGOVNICK

Cheer!: Inside the Secret World of College Cheerleaders

(New York: Simon & Schuster, 2008)

Subject(s): Sports; Universities and colleges; Women

Summary: Journalist Kate Torgovnick takes readers behind the scenes of contemporary cheerleading—and all the suspense and drama it holds. *Cheer!: Inside the Secret World of College Cheerleaders* centers on the journeys of three highly respected teams as they take part in one tumultuous season, battling it out for the national championship title. Torgovnick immerses herself in the secret society of the sport, profiling the memorable characters and the unique challenges they face as they

set out to win a cutthroat competition. *Cheer!* includes a dictionary of commonly used terms.

Where it's reviewed:
Booklist, December 15, 2007, page 15
Library Journal, January 1, 2008, page 122

Other books you might like:
Natalie Guice Adams, *Cheerleader!: An American Icon*, 2003
  Pamela Jean Bettis, co-author
Mary Ellen Hanson, *Go! Fight! Win!: Cheerleading in American Culture*, 1995
James T. McElroy, *We've Got Spirit: The Life and Times of America's Greatest Cheerleading Team*, 2000
Joan Ryan, *Little Girls in Pretty Boxes: The Making and Breaking of Elite Gymnasts and Figure Skaters*, 1995
Leslie Wilson, *The Ultimate Guide to Cheerleading: For Cheerleaders and Coaches*, 2003

1033

SARAH VOWELL

Assassination Vacation

(New York: Simon & Schuster, 2005)

Subject(s): American History; Assassination; History

Summary: Sarah Vowell is fascinated by the first three presidential assassinations in American history, those of presidents Abraham Lincoln, James A. Garfield, and William McKinley. So, for vacation, she makes a pilgrimage to the sites of the homes, assassinations, and graves of these three men. This book is the result of her research and her travels. She gives the biographies of these presidents, as well as their assassins, spending considerable effort in trying to find common characteristics among the three, to understand the nature of a person who would murder a president. She also investigates the way the monuments of assassination have become cultural icons and even tourist traps.

Where it's reviewed:
Publishers Weekly, December 19, 2005, page 8

Other books by the same author:
The Wordy Shipmates, 2008
The Partly Cloudy Patriot, 2002
Take the Cannoli: Stories from the New World, 2000
Radio On: A Listener's Diary, 1997

Other books you might like:
David Sedaris, *Me Talk Pretty One Day*, 2000
David Sedaris, *When You Are Engulfed in Flames*, 2008
Hampton Sides, *Hellhound on His Trail: The Stalking of Martin Luther King, Jr. and the International Hunt for His Assassin*, 2009
Eric Spitznagel, *You're a Horrible Person, but I Like You: The Believer Book of Advice*, 2010

1034

SARAH VOWELL

The Wordy Shipmates

(New York: Riverhead Books, 2008)

Subject(s): Puritans; Biblical studies; Colonialism

Summary: In *The Wordy Shipmates*, author Sarah Vowell suggests that many American problems are the result of our country's Puritan origins. In an engaging and modern tone, Vowell tells the story of the English colonists who settled in the Massachusetts Bay Colony and named John Winthrop as their governor. Vowell asserts that these colonists laid the groundwork for many of the problems our country would suffer in its future. Vowell compares historical stories with anecdotes about present-day culture to support her thesis. She also compares several notable Puritans to their counterparts in current times. Vowell ultimately suggests that the Puritans' obsession with the Bible and their belief that they were exceptional created a nation of individualistic readers and writers.

Where it's reviewed:
Details, November 2008, page 44

Other books by the same author:
Assassination Vacation, 2005
The Partly Cloudy Patriot, 2002
Radio On: A Listener's Diary, 1997

Other books you might like:
David Sedaris, *Me Talk Pretty One Day*, 2000
Sarah Vowell, *Assassination Vacation*, 2005
Sarah Vowell, *The Partly Cloudy Patriot*, 2003
Sarah Vowell, *Radio On: A Listener's Diary*, 1997
Sarah Vowell, *Take the Cannoli: Stories from the New World*, 2000

1035

AYELET WALDMAN

Bad Mother: A Chronicle of Maternal Crimes, Minor Calamities, and Occasional Moments of Grace

(New York: Doubleday, 2009)

Subject(s): Mothers; Love; Marriage

Summary: *Bad Mother: A Chronicle of Maternal Crimes, Minor Calamities, and Occasional Moments of Grace* is a collection of 18 essays by Ayelet Waldman, a mother of four who once confessed to loving her husband more than her children. In the essays, Waldman writes about feminism, her childhood, her close relationship with her husband and their family dynamics, and her children, with the overarching theme that it is impossible to be a "good" mother in today's society, and that women are constantly made to feel guilty. She makes honest confessions about her personal life in the book, including aborting a fetus with a genetic defect, and states that women need to do the best they can and learn to forgive

themselves for everything else.

Where it's reviewed:
Booklist, April 15, 2009, page 14
Publishers Weekly, March 16, 2009, page 52

Other books by the same author:
Red Hook Road, 2010
Love and Other Impossible Pursuits, 2007
Daughter's Keeper, 2004

Other books you might like:
Laura Bennett, *Didn't I Feed You Yesterday?: A Mother's Guide to Sanity in Stilettos*, 2010
Michael Chabon, *Manhood for Amateurs: The Pleasures and Regrets of a Husband, Father, and Son*, 2009
Randi Hutter Epstein, *Get Me Out: A History of Childbirth from the Garden of Eden to the Sperm Bank*, 2010
Jonathan Franzen, *Freedom*, 2010
Dave Isay, *Mom: A Celebration of Mothers from StoryCorps*, 2010

1036

FRANK WARREN

PostSecret: Confessions on Life, Death, and God

(New York: William Morrow, 2009)

Subject(s): Art; Psychology; Self knowledge

Summary: In *PostSecret: Confessions on Life, Death, and God*, Frank Warren presents a thought-provoking collection of postcards he's received from individuals around the world who reveal their most personal beliefs. In the early 2000s, the author began soliciting hand-designed postcards from strangers. Each postcard would contain a well-guarded secret or belief. Those messages have appeared in Warren's previous books, his touring art show, and on his Web site. This volume offers a glimpse into people's most private thoughts—their innermost feelings about the nature (or nonexistence) of God, their life philosophies, and their concepts of what happens at the moment of death and beyond.

Where it's reviewed:
Kirkus Reviews, October 1, 2009, page 8

Other books by the same author:
The Secret Lives of Men and Women: A PostSecret Book, 2007
PostSecret: Extraordinary Confessions from Ordinary Lives, 2005

Other books you might like:
Mike Bender, *Awkward Family Photos*, 2010
Doug Chernack, co-author
Kathy Griffin, *Official Book Club Selection: A Memoir According to Kathy Griffin*, 2009
Justin Halpern, *Sh*t My Dad Says*, 2010
Heather McDonald, *You'll Never Blue Ball in This Town Again: One Woman's Painfully Funny Quest to Give It Up*, 2010

Jen Yates, *Cake Wrecks: When Professional Cakes Go Hilariously Wrong*, 2009

1037

MATT WEILAND
SEAN WILSEY , Co-Editor

State by State: A Panoramic Portrait of America

(New York: Ecco, 2008)

Subject(s): Travel; United States; Americana

Summary: *State by State: A Panoramic Portrait of America* aims to help readers gain a deeper understanding of each of the United States. The editors, who previously put together *The Thinking Fan's Guide to the World Cup*, have collected the writings of 50 authors to analyze the American Guide series of the Federal Writers Project that was produced in the 1930s. In the American Guide series, 6,000 writers attempted to create a portrait of the American states through writing. *State by State: A Panoramic Portrait of America* contains passages by 50 different contemporary authors, including Dave Eggars, William T. Vollman, and Alison Bechdel. Unlike the 1930s series by the Federal Writers Project, the essays in this collection share the writers' personal feelings about each state. The book also compares and contrasts various strange statistics for each state.

Other books by the same author:
The Thinking Fan's Guide to the World Cup, 2006
Commodify Your Dissent, 1997

Other books you might like:
Ken Jennings, *Brainiac: Adventures in the Curious, Competitive, Compulsive World of Trivia*, 2006
Ken Jennings, *Ken Jennings's Trivia Almanac: 8,888 Questions in 365 Days*, 2008
J. Stephen Lang, *The Big Book of American Trivia*, 1997
Mark Stein, *How the States Got Their Shapes*, 2008
Mark Usler, *Hometown Revelations: How America's Cities, Towns, and States Acquired Their Names*, 2006

1038

STEFANIE WILDER-TAYLOR

It's Not Me, It's You: Subjective Recollections from a Terminally Optimistic, Chronically Sarcastic and Occasionally Inebriated Woman

(New York: Simon Spotlight Entertainment, 2009)

Subject(s): Biographies; Television; Adventure

Summary: In *It's Not Me, It's You: Subjective Recollections from a Terminally Optimistic, Chronically Sarcastic*

and Occasionally Inebriated Woman , writer, producer, and comedian Stefanie Wilder-Taylor shares with readers a number of essays about her life and experiences in the entertainment industry. She writes about how she left her home in New York at a young age, and moved to fabulous Los Angeles with little money in hand. Wilder-Taylor takes readers on a truly unconventional journey and shares the adventures, mishaps, and lessons that eventually led to her life as a happy wife and mother. *It's not Me, It's You* shows readers how bizarre yet rewarding life can be and demonstrates how taking random turns can lead to unexpected but wonderful places.

Where it's reviewed:
Entertainment Weekly, July 24, 2009, page 63

Other books by the same author:
Naptime is the New Happy Hour, 2008
Sippy Cups are not for Chardonnay, 2006

Other books you might like:
Russell Brand, *My Booky Wook: A Memoir of Sex, Drugs, and Stand-Up*, 2007
Kathy Griffin, *Official Book Club Selection: A Memoir According to Kathy Griffin*, 2009
Chelsea Handler, *Chelsea Chelsea Bang Bang*, 2010
Chelsea Handler, *My Horizontal Life: A Collection of One-Night Stands*, 2005
Heather McDonald, *You'll Never Blue Ball in This Town Again: One Woman's Painfully Funny Quest to Give It Up*, 2010

1039

KENDRA WILKINSON

Sliding into Home

(New York: Gallery Books, 2010)

Subject(s): Autobiographies; Entertainment industry; Television programs

Summary: *Sliding into Home* is an autobiography by Kendra Wilkinson, who worked as a *Playboy* model, lived at the Playboy Mansion, and who co-starred on the reality television show *The Girls Next Door*. In the book, Kendra discusses her childhood and difficult teenage years after her father left. She openly reveals how she struggled with—and ultimately overcame—drug addiction. After graduating from high school, Wilkinson was discovered by Hugh Hefner, *Playboy*'s founder. She candidly discusses her experience of living in the Playboy Mansion and filming the television show. Kendra also shares how she met her husband, NFL player Hank Baskett, and her new experiences as a wife and mother.

Other books you might like:
Kathy Griffin, *Official Book Club Selection: A Memoir According to Kathy Griffin*, 2009
Hilary Liftin, *Mommywood*, 2009
Heather McDonald, *You'll Never Blue Ball in This Town Again: One Woman's Painfully Funny Quest to Give It Up*, 2010
Tori Spelling, *Mommywood*, 2009

Tori Spelling, *Stori Telling*, 2008
Tori Spelling, *Uncharted terriTORI*, 2010

1040

LARRY WILMORE

I'd Rather We Got Casinos, and Other Black Thoughts

(New York: Hyperion, 2009)

Subject(s): African Americans; Racism; United States

Summary: *I'd Rather We Got Casinos, and Other Black Thoughts* is a collection of comedian Larry Wilmore's ideas on race relations, the media, and America in general. Fake radio transcripts, letters, and essays provide continuous laughs while at the same time pinpointing very real issues that Americans face. Wilmore works as the "Senior Black Correspondent" on Jon Stewart's *The Daily Show*, which airs on Comedy Central, and is renowned for his sarcastic, often caustic wit. *I'd Rather We Got Casinos* provides funny insights into Black History Month and why black audiences talk back to horror movies. Wilmore also ponders why black people never see UFOs. Wilmore's dive into the politically incorrect serves to entertain and introduce readers to his own unique brand of humor and perspective.

Where it's reviewed:
Booklist, February 1, 2009, page 16

Other books you might like:
John Hodgman, *The Areas of My Expertise: An Almanac of Complete World Knowledge Compiled with Instructive Annotation and Arranged in Useful Order*, 2005
John Hodgman, *More Information Than You Require*, 2009
David Rakoff, *Don't Get Too Comfortable: The Indignities of Coach Class, The Torments of Low Thread Count, The Never-Ending Quest for Artisanal Olive Oil, and Other First World Problems*, 2005
David Sedaris, *Me Talk Pretty One Day*, 2000
Eric Spitznagel, *You're a Horrible Person, but I Like You: The Believer Book of Advice*, 2010

1041

MISHNA WOLFF

I'm Down: A Memoir

(New York: St. Martin's Press, 2009)

Subject(s): Race relations; Childhood; Father-daughter relations

Summary: In *I'm Down: A Memoir*, Mishna Wolff, an author, a humorist, and a former model, chronicles her childhood as a minority in an all-black suburb of Seattle, Washington. Wolff's father, who grew up in a similar neighborhood, urges his children to embrace the many aspects of African American culture prevalent in their community. Wolff's desire to please her father is thwarted by the simple fact that she is not black and, as much as she might try, cannot fit in with the neighborhood girls. Wolff's attempts are made more difficult when her mother decides to enroll her in an all-white school for gifted children. The disconnect between her home life and her school life is detailed in many humorous anecdotes.

Where it's reviewed:
School Library Journal, June 2009, page 154

Other books you might like:
Quinn Cummings, *Notes from the Underwire: Adventures from My Awkward and Lovely Life*, 2009
Danny Evans, *Rage Against the Meshugenah: Why It Takes Balls to Go Nuts*, 2009
Justin Halpern, *Sh*t My Dad Says*, 2010
Chelsea Handler, *Chelsea Chelsea Bang Bang*, 2010
Rhoda Janzen, *Mennonite in a Little Black Dress: A Memoir of Going Home*, 2009

1042

CRYSTAL ZEVON

I'll Sleep When I'm Dead: The Dirty Life and Times of Warren Zevon

(New York: Ecco, 2007)

Subject(s): Biographies; Music; Musicians

Summary: *I'll Sleep When I'm Dead: The Dirty Life and Times of Warren Zevon* is a biography of musician and songwriter Warren Zevon. Written by his ex-wife and friend Crystal Zevon, the book collects a series of 87 oral histories from Warren's friends and family, which are interspersed with Zevon's own narrative of her ex-husband's life. People interviewed for the book include Jackson Browne, Bruce Springsteen, Billy Bob Thornton, Stephen King, and others, as well as the people who were especially close to Warren, such as his band-mates. The interviewees share honest stories about Warren's life: the way he wrote his lyrical, complex songs; his drug and alcohol addictions; his eventual sobriety; his often questionable behavior as a father and husband; and his eventual death from lung cancer in 2003. All of the stories are told with love and respect for Warren and his influential music.

Where it's reviewed:
Booklist, May 1, 2007, page 62
Library Journal, April 15, 2007, page 93
Publishers Weekly, December 31, 2007, page 47

Other books you might like:
Pamela Des Barres, *I'm with the Band: Confessions of a Groupie*, 1987
Tom Petty, *Conversations with Tom Petty*, 2005
Brian Sweet, *Steely Dan: Reelin in the Years*, 1994
Jessica Pallington West, *What Would Keith Richards Do?: Daily Affirmations from a Rock 'N' Roll Survivor*, 2009
Paul Zollo, *Conversations with Tom Petty*, 2005

Science

1043

AMIR D. ACZEL

Uranium Wars: The Scientific Rivalry That Created the Nuclear Age

(New York: Palgrave Macmillan, 2009)

Story type: Historical
Subject(s): Science; Nuclear warfare; Nuclear physics

Summary: Written by bestselling author Amir D. Aczel, *Uranium Wars: The Scientific Rivalry That Created the Nuclear Age* is a historical examination of the race to harness nuclear energy. Although uranium is an ordinary natural element, it has become more important than gold to scientists. It holds a remarkable power that is both dangerous and controversial. In *Uranium Wars*, Aczel recounts the history surrounding the study of uranium, including the competition between scientists to discover its untapped nuclear power. Marie Curie first identified radioactivity and Otto Hahn and Lise Meitner made incredible discoveries in fission. Aczel discusses the importance of these discoveries and explains how they contribute to the threat of nuclear war today.

Where it's reviewed:
Booklist, August 1, 2009, page 19
History Magazine, December 2009, page 48
Library Journal, July 1, 2009, page 119

Other books by the same author:
Present at the Creation: The Story of CERN and the Large Hadron Collider, 2010
Fermat's Last Theorem: Unlocking the Secret of an Ancient Mathematical Problem, 2007
Pendulum: Leon Foucault and the Triumph of Science, 2004
The Riddle of the Compass: The Invention that Changed the World, 2002
God's Equation: Einstein, Relativity, and the Expanding Universe, 200

Other books you might like:
Marcia Bartusiak, *The Day We Found the Universe*, 2010
Franz J. Dahlkamp, *Uranium Deposits of the World*, 2010

James Mahaffey, *Atomic Awakening*, 2010
Gerhardt H. Wolfe, *Uranium: Compounds, Isotopes and Applications*, 2008
Tom Zoellner, *Uranium: War, Energy and the Rock That Shaped the World*, 2009

1044

SYED NAEEM AHMED

Physics and Engineering of Radiation Detection

(Boston, Massachusetts: Academic Press, 2007)

Subject(s): Science; Physics; Engineering

Summary: *Physics and Engineering of Radiation Detection* is a textbook by Syed Naeem Ahmed. The book provides students with a comprehensive understanding of radiation-detection methods and devices, including the origins and properties of radiation, how it's detected and measured, and various methods employed to protect individuals and communities from the adverse effects of radiation. Ahmed explains the experimental procedures and modern technologies utilized in radiation detection, problem-solving methods for measuring radiation, and different media used in detection, including gases, liquids, liquefied gases, semiconductors, and scintillators. Using straightforward language, Ahmed provides students with easy-to-understand information, statistics, and practical examples.

Where it's reviewed:
Choice, October 2007, page 314

Other books you might like:
Claus Grupen, *Introduction to Radiation Protection*, 2010
Krzysztof Iniewski, *Electronics for Radiation Detection*, 2010
Glenn F. Knoll, *Radiation Detection and Measurement: 4th Edition*, 2010
K. Muraleedhara Varier, *Nuclear Radiation Detection: Measurements and Analysis*, 2009

1045

SUSAN ALDRIDGE

Magic Molecules: How Drugs Work, Second Edition

(Cambridge, United Kingdom; New York: Cambridge University Press, 2007)

Subject(s): Drugs; Medicine; Science

Summary: In *Magic Molecules: How Drugs Work, Second Edition*, author Susan Aldridge explains the ways drugs—both medicinal and recreational—function in the human body. This authoritative volume looks at just how various medicines work in conjunction with natural processes to alleviate pain, cure illness, and provide relief or escape. Aldridge also explores how drugs are created, the future of pharmaceuticals, and even how drugs end up in foods as additives and fillers. *Magic Molecules* includes a bibliography and a full index.

Other books by the same author:
Cloning, 2010

Other books you might like:
William R. Clark, *In Defense of Self: How the Immune System Really Works*, 2008
Jessica Snyder Sachs, *Good Germs, Bad Germs: Health and Survival in a Bacterial World*, 2007
Lauren M. Sompayrac, *How the Immune System Works*, 2008

1046

JOHN ALLEN

Student Atlas of World Geography

(Boston, Massachusetts: McGraw-Hill, 2009)

Subject(s): Encyclopedias and dictionaries; Science; Geography

Summary: *Student Atlas of World Geography* is a comprehensive guide to the discipline of geography and its relationship with other fields of study, including politics, ecology, and economics. This sixth edition contains full-colored illustrations of charts, maps, and other information to help readers identify shifts within each particular area of the world. Maps include data about rural and agrarian regions and industrialized regions as well as the economy and politics of each region. Each map includes detailed text that describes the purpose of the data depicted within that map. This atlas is written by John L. Allen.

Other books by the same author:
Me and the Biospheres, 2009

Other books you might like:
Nathaniel Harris, *Atlas of the Worlds Deserts*, 2007
Rand McNally, *Goode's World Atlas, 22nd Edition*, 2009

1047

DAVID ARCHER

The Long Thaw: How Humans Are Changing the Next 100,000 Years of Earth's Climate

(Princeton, New Jersey: Princeton University Press, 2010)

Subject(s): Science; Weather; Ecology

Summary: *The Long Thaw: How Humans Are Changing the Next 100,000 Years of Earth's Climate* by David Archer is an accessible, concise explanation of the ways that humans contribute to climate change. Archer has divided the text into three sections: past, present, and future. He considers how data from the past and present can help scientists predict the future of life on Earth. The author feels that the warming that will most likely take place during the next thousand years could wipe out the human species. Archer uses analogies to explain more complex scientific terms and discusses what can be done to begin reversing the effects of climate change.

Where it's reviewed:
The American Prospect, Jan-Feb 2009, page 30
Choice, April 2009, page 1535

Other books by the same author:
The Global Carbon Cycle, 2010
Global Warming: Understanding the Forecast, 2006

Other books you might like:
Dianne Dumanoski, *The End of the Long Summer: Why We Must Remake Our Civilization to Survive on a Volatile Earth*, 2010
Gwynne Dyer, *The Climate Wars*, 2008
Dennis Klocek, *Climate: Soul of the Earth*, 2010
William F. Ruddiman, *Earth's Climate: Past and Future*, 2007
Spencer Weart, *The Discovery of Global Warming: (New Histories of Science, Technology, and Medicine)*, 2003

1048

IOANNIS S. ARVANITOYANNIS

HACCP and ISO 22000: Application to Foods of Animal Origin

(Chichester, United Kingdom: Wiley-Blackwell, 2009)

Subject(s): Science; Safety; Food

Summary: In *HACCP and ISO 22000: Application to Foods of Animal Origin*, editor Ioannis S. Arvanitoyannis presents a guide to the two most commonly used food safety management systems for professionals, researchers, and students in the field. After an introduction that compares the two systems, the text explains the implementation of HACCP and ISO 22000 in the production and manufacture of such animal foods as dairy, meat, poultry, seafood, and eggs, giving special attention to the topic of food catering operations. Ioannis Arvanitoyannis is a professor in the Department of Agriculture, Ichthyology, and Aquatic Environment at the University of Thessaly, Greece.

Other books by the same author:
Irradiation of Food Commodities: Techniques, Applications, Detection, Legislation, Safety and Consumer Opinion, 2010
Waste Management for the Food Industries, 2007

Other books you might like:
Phyllis Entis, *Food Safety: Old Habits and New Perspectives*, 2007
Guillermo Etienne, *Principles of Cleaning and Sanitation in the Food and Beverage Industry*, 2006
Marion Nestle, *Safe Food: The Politics of Food Safety*, 2010
Jeffrey M. Smith, *Genetic Roulette: The Documented Health Risks of Genetically Engineered Foods*, 2007
Frank Yiannas, *Food Safety Culture: Creating a Behavior-Based Food Safety Management System*, 2008

1049

VADIM ASTAKHOV

Biomedical Informatics

(New York: Humana Press, 2009)

Subject(s): Biology; Engineering; Technology

Summary: *Biomedical Informatics*, edited by Vadim Astakhov, is a textbook intended for students and active researchers using biomedical informatics. The topics covered in this text include new developments in the field of biotechnology, with perspectives from researchers around the world. The researchers discuss the current methods used in bioinformatics and potential avenues for collaboration on a larger scale. They also consider the software challenges that are presented with biomedical informatics on a large scale. Each chapter in the text is formatted the same way, with an introduction followed by a detailed section on biomedical informatics methods as well as common errors that can be located and avoided.

Other books you might like:
Jules J. Berman, *Ruby Programming for Medicine and Biology*, 2007
David Dagan Feng, *Biomedical Information Technology*, 2007
William R. Hersh, *Information Retrieval: A Health and Biomedical Perspective*, 2008
Ira J. Kalet, *Principles of Biomedical Informatics*, 2008
Athina Lazakidou, *Biocomputation and Biomedical Informatics: Case Studies and Applications*, 2009

1050

R.A. BAILEY

Design of Comparative Experiments

(Cambridge; New York: Cambridge University Press, 2008)

Subject(s): Research; Reference works; Science

Summary: *Design of Comparative Experiments* is a textbook by R.A. Bailey intended for upper-level undergraduate students or graduate students, as well as practicing statisticians. Bailey presents comprehensive explanations for the design of experiments, focusing primarily on the use of Hasse diagrams. These are "used to elucidate structure, calculate degrees of freedom and allocate treatment sub-spaces to appropriate strata," according to the publisher. The concept is based on the premise that units and treatments should first be considered, then treatments allocated to units, allowing different considerations of factors and frameworks used. Bailey created this text based on a course taught in experimental design since 1989.

Where it's reviewed:
Choice, Feb 2009, page p1140
Technometrics, May 2010, page p261

Other books by the same author:
Association Schemes: Designed Experiments, Algebra and Combinatorics, 2004

Other books you might like:
Michael J. Crawley, *The R Book*, 2007
Richard Gonzalez, *Data Analysis for Experimental Design*, 2008
Douglas C. Montgomery, *Design and Analysis of Experiment*, 2009
Phil Spector, *Data Manipulation with R*, 2008
Ivan Valiela, *Doing Science: Design, Analysis, and Communication of Scientific Research*, 2009

1051

ROBERT G. BAILEY

Ecosystem Geography: From Ecoregions to Sites

(New York: Springer, 2009)

Subject(s): Geography; Ecology; Science

Summary: In *Ecosystem Geography: From Ecoregions to Sites*, author Robert G. Bailey examines the Earth's environmental ecosystems and classifies them in hierarchical order. The guide is of particular use to foresters and environmental engineers who require further information on the subject of ecosystem management. Bailey outlines a three-point system in which each individual environment is subdivided and charted according to various conditions and factors. Originally published in 1995, the 2009 edition includes updated graphs, maps, and information on the subject matter. Bailey is also the author of *Ecoregions: The Ecosystem*

Science

Geography of the Oceans and Continents and *Ecoregion-Based Design for Sustainability*.

Where it's reviewed:
Choice, July 2010 v47 i11, page p2127

Other books you might like:
Joseph M. Craine, *Resource Strategies of Wild Plants*, 2009
Adam Markham, *Potential Impacts of Climate Change on Tropical Forest Ecosystems*, 2010

1052

MICHAEL E. BAKICH

1,001 Celestial Wonders to See Before You Die

(New York: Springer-Verlag, 2010)

Subject(s): Astronomy; Science; Education

Summary: In *1,001 Celestial Wonders to See Before You Die: The Best Sky Objects for Star Gazers*, author Michael E. Bakich provides a comprehensive handbook for readers to identify what he calls the "best and brightest" of the night sky's objects. Bakich particularly details deep sky objects such as star clusters, constellations, and other phenomena that are difficult to locate with the naked eye. The book is laid out on a month-to-month basis to provide readers with an accurate timeline of when each celestial body is best viewed. The author also supplements this work with more than 250 full-color telescopic photographs.

Where it's reviewed:
Choice, April 2008 v45 i8, page p136

Other books by the same author:
Atlas of the Stars, 2006

Other books you might like:
Peter Grego, *Astronomical Cybersketching*, 2009
Philip S. Harrington, *Cosmic Challenge: The Ultimate Observing List for Amateurs*, 2010
Roger W. Sinnott, *Sky & Telescope's Pocket Sky Atlas*, 2006

1053

EDUARDO BANQUERI

The Night Sky

(New York: Enchanted Lion, 2007)

Story type: Young Readers
Subject(s): Astronomy; Science; Nature

Summary: *The Night Sky* by Eduardo Banqueri is presented in the form of a picture book, but features vocabulary that is more advanced for older children. Written in the form of a field journal with full-color photographs annotated by handwritten notes and additional sketches for explanation, this text provides a basic introduction to star-gazing. Diagrams and lists of facts are included as well for quick reference. A number of charts at the end

of the text also provide reference information for viewing meteor showers or for learning the location of other stars, planets, and galaxies in space.

Where it's reviewed:
Booklist, May 15, 2007, page p44
School Library Journal, Sept 2007, page p214

Other books by the same author:
Weather, 2006

Other books you might like:
Sue French, *Celestial Sampler*, 2007
Ken Hewitt-White, *Patterns in the Sky*, 2007
Paul E. Kinzer, *Stargazing Basics: Getting Started in Recreational Astronomy*, 2008
Becky Ramotowski, *Secrets of Stargazing*, 2007
Roger W. Sinnott, *Sky & Telescope's Pocket Sky Atlas*, 2006

1054

CHARLES B. BECK

An Introduction to Plant Structure and Development: Plant Anatomy for the Twenty-First Century

(New York: Cambridge University Press, 2006)

Subject(s): Trees (Plants); Reference works; Nature

Summary: *An Introduction to Plant Structure and Development: Plant Anatomy for the Twenty-First Century* by Charles B. Beck is a textbook suitable for use by both graduate and undergraduate students studying plant science. The book focuses mainly on cellular and molecular biology as pertaining to plant development, as well as other highly specific topics such as integrative significance of plasmodesmata, the concepts of the symplast and multicellularity, the function of the cytoskeleton in growth and development, signal transduction, and evolution, among others. Controversies and opposing viewpoints in the field of plant anatomy are also considered in this work.

Where it's reviewed:
Quarterly Review of Biology, Sept 2006, page p284

Other books by the same author:
Origin and Evolution of Gymnosperms, 1988

Other books you might like:
Nafees A. Khan, *Ethylene Action in Plants*, 2010
Jennifer W. MacAdam, *Structure and Function of Plants*, 2009
James D. Mauseth, *Plant Anatomy*, 2008
Park S. Nobel, *Physicochemical and Environmental Plant Physiology*, 2009
Paula Rudall, *Anatomy of Flowering Plants: An Introduction to Structure and Development*, 2007

1055

DAVID BEERLING

The Emerald Planet: How Plants Changed Earth's History

(New York: Oxford University Press, 2008)

Subject(s): Nature; Botany; Evolution (Biology)

Summary: In *The Emerald Planet: How Plants Changed Earth's History*, David Beerling considers the concept of climate change within the context of botany and paleobotany, which describes the way plants have changed and evolved throughout the history of the planet. The author also describes what these evolutionary changes indicate about the future of the planet. Beerling especially focuses on changes in the composition of the atmosphere and the way these changes affected the plants in existence on the planet. For example, plants needed to evolve in order to grow leaves; this indicates a significant atmospheric shift that occurred long before humans roamed the earth. The author also considers topics such as the growth of forests on Antarctica and the enormous size of prehistoric insects, both of which indicate the many ways that plant evolution changed the course of life on Earth.

Where it's reviewed:

American Scientist, May-June 2008, page p254
Quarterly Review of Biology, March 2008, page p117

Other books you might like:

Douglas H. Erwin, *Extinction: How Life on Earth Nearly Ended 250 Million Years Ago*, 2008
Richard Fortey, *Earth: An Intimate History*, 2004
Nick Lane, *Life Ascending: The Ten Great Inventions of Evolution*, 2010
Oliver Morton, *Eating the Sun*, 2008
Ted Nield, *Supercontinent: Ten Billion Years in the Life of Our Planet*, 2007

1056

JIM BELL

Postcards from Mars: The First Photographer on the Red Planet

(New York: Dutton, 2010)

Subject(s): Photography; Astronomy; Mars (Planet)

Summary: In *Postcards from Mars: The First Photographer on the Red Planet*, author Jim Bell depicts the "Red Planet" through photographs taken by the first real Martian explorers. In 2003, NASA initiated the Mars Exploration Rover Mission and sent two space rovers, Spirit and Opportunity, to investigate the planet and record findings. Many of the resulting photographs from this space mission, which was ongoing at the time of the book's publication, are compiled within this book. Bell supplements these photographs with facts, figures, and personal anecdotes. Bell is also the author of *Mars 3-D: A Rover's Eye View of the Red Planet* and *The Martian Surface: Composition, Mineralogy and Physical Properties*.

Where it's reviewed:

Sky & Telescope, April 2007 v113 i4, page p81

Other books by the same author:

Moon 3-D: The Lunar Surface Comes to Life, 2009
Mars 3-D: A Rover's-Eye View of the Red Planet, 2008
The Martian Surface: Composition, Mineralogy and Physical Properties, 2008

Other books you might like:

K. Maria D. Lane, *Geographies of Mars: Seeing and Knowing the Red Planet*, 2011
Nancy Loewen, *Seeing Red: The Planet Mars*, 2008
Donald Rapp, *Human Missions to Mars: Enabling Technologies for Exploring the Red Planet*, 2010

1057

PIERRE BELY

The Design and Construction of Large Optical Telescopes

(New York: Springer-Verlag, 2010)

Subject(s): Science; Astronomy; Engineering

Summary: *The Design and Construction of Large Optical Telescopes*, edited by Pierre Bely, is a comprehensive guide to large-scale optical telescopes and how those telescopes are made. The book discusses such topics as telescopes' intensity, refraction, and other design mechanisms, as well as particular utilizations of such instruments, including design principles, costs, and materials. The book also includes chapters on Astronomical Observations, Instruments, Design Methods and Project Management, Telescope Optics, Stray Light Control, Telescope Structure and Mechanisms, Pointing and Control, Active and Adaptive Optics, Thermal Control, Integration and Verification, Observatory Enclosure, Observatory Sites, and more.

Other books you might like:

Harold Richard Suiter, *Star Testing Astronomical Telescopes: A Manual for Optical Evaluation and Adjustment*, 2009
Robert Zimmerman, *The Universe in a Mirror: The Saga of the Hubble Space Telescope and the Visionaries Who Built It*, 2010

1058

MICHAEL BENSON

Beyond: Visions of the Interplanetary Probes, Paperback Edition

(New York: Harry N. Abrams, 2003)

Subject(s): Photography; Space exploration; Science

Summary: Armchair astronauts and space exploration

enthusiasts can finally get an up close and personal look at the unmanned satellites filling the skies. In *Beyond: Visions of the Interplanetary Probes, Paperback Edition,* author, journalist, and filmmaker Michael Benson presents the definitive collection of images spotlighting satellites in action. The vibrant photos of this volume are accompanied by individual essays profiling the unique contributions and stories behind the featured probes. Renowned author Arthur C. Clarke provides a foreword to this volume, and award-winning journalist Lawrence Weschler contributes the afterword in this updated edition. First book.

Other books by the same author:
Beyond: A Solar System Voyage, 2009
Far Out: A Space-Time Chronicle, 2009

Other books you might like:
Paul Dickson, *A Dictionary of the Space Age,* 2009
Kenneth R. Lang, *The Sun from Space,* 2008

1059

JEREMY BERNSTEIN

Nuclear Weapons: What You Need to Know

(Cambridge, England: Cambridge University Press, 2010)

Story type: Historical
Subject(s): Nuclear weapons; Science; History

Summary: *Nuclear Weapons: What You Need to Know* is a detailed history of nuclear bombs from author and professor, Jeremy Bernstein. The book provides a thorough account of nuclear weaponry and the people associated with it throughout the years. Bernstein begins with background on the origins of nuclear weapons, starting in the early 20th century, and takes readers through to the present day advancements and developments. In each section of the book, Bernstein offers a scientific explanation of nuclear weaponry at each stage of its evolution. He also profiles the scientists involved, many of which he had personal interaction with. In addition to providing an exhaustive historical account, *Nuclear Weapons* also sheds light on the power of nuclear bombs and their threat to the world today.

Where it's reviewed:
Choice, April 2008 v45 i8, page p1368
The International History Review, Dec 2008 v30 i4, page p932-934
New York University Journal of International Law and Politics, Spring 2008 v40 i3, page p894-897
Physics Today, April 2008 v61 i4, page p67
Survival, August-Sept 2008 v50 i4, page p212-213

Other books by the same author:
Plutonium: A History of the World's Most Dangerous Element, 2009
Quantum Leaps, 2009

Other books you might like:
Amir D. Aczel, *Uranium Wars: The Scientific Rivalry That Created the Nuclear Age,* 2009

Joseph Cirincione, *Bomb Scare: The History and Future of Nuclear Weapons,* 2007
Stephen P. Depoe, *Nuclear Legacies: Communication, Controversy, and the U.S. Nuclear Weapons Complex,* 2008
George N. Schulte, *Dismantlement and Destruction of Chemical, Nuclear and Conventional Weapons,* 2010

1060

KARIN BIJSTERVELD

Mechanical Sound: Technology, Culture, and Public Problems of Noise in the Twentieth Century

(Cambridge, Massachusetts: MIT Press, 2008)

Story type: Historical
Subject(s): Science; Technology; History

Summary: Written by Karin Bijsterveld, *Mechanical Sound: Technology, Culture, and Public Problems of Noise in the Twentieth Century* is an examination of the impact that technological sounds have had on communities around the globe from 1875 to 1975. With every technological advance comes a barrage of new noises and sounds. Since the late 19th century, sounds from technology have been a source of frustration and complaint in Europe and the United States. Individuals have fought against noises created by factories, automobiles, aircraft, steam trains, and gramophones. Bijsterveld documents the public's opposition to noise throughout the 19th and 20th centuries, paying special attention to disputes over industrial noise, traffic noise, noise from neighborhood radios and gramophones, and aircraft noise.

Where it's reviewed:
Contemporary Sociology, July 2009, page 375
Isis, December 2009, page 942

Other books you might like:
Joanna Demers, *Listening through the Noise,* 2010
Colin H. Hansen, *The Effects of Low-Frequency Noise and Vibration on People,* 2007
Bart Kosko, *Noise,* 2006
Brandon LaBelle, *Acoustic Territories: Sound Culture and Everyday Life,* 2010
David Toop, *Sinister Resonance: The Mediumship of the Listener,* 2010

1061

ARNOLD J. BLOOM

Global Climate Change: Convergence of Disciplines

(Sunderland, Massachusetts: Sinauer Associates, 2009)

Subject(s): Science; Weather; Meteorology

Summary: In *Global Climate Change: Convergence of Disciplines,* Arnold J. Bloom presents a ground-breaking text on the disputed phenomenon of global change. As the author explains, civilization has impacted the earth's weather, despite political and scientific arguments to the contrary. Informative and accessible, this volume provides information on the causes of climate change and describes the impact that such change will have on the planet and its populations. In addition to discussion of the scientific aspects of the climate change problem, Bloom considers the challenges that await world leaders as they discern the best course of action.

Other books you might like:

Robert Henson, *The Rough Guide to Climate Change*, 2008

Edmond A. Mathez, *Climate Change: The Science of Global Warming and Our Energy Future*, 2009

Frank Princiotta, *Global Climate Change - The Technology Challenge*, 2011

Burton Richter, *Beyond Smoke and Mirrors: Climate Change and Energy in the 21st Century*, 2010

Nicholas Stern, *The Economics of Climate Change: The Stern Review*, 2007

1062

GORDON B. BONAN

Ecological Climatology: Concepts and Applications, Second Edition

(Cambridge, United Kingdom: Cambridge University Press, 2008)

Subject(s): Ecology; Nature; Geography

Summary: *Ecological Climatology: Concepts and Applications, Second Edition* by Gordon B. Bonan is a textbook for upper-level undergraduate students or graduate students studying the natural sciences. Throughout the text, the author seeks to explore and define the connection between ecology and climate. Specifically, Bonan focuses on the way terrestrial ecosystems affect climate change and, conversely, the way climate change affects the environment. The author considers how the life cycles of vegetation alter the climate and explains how human land use impacts the natural world. These concepts are discussed on different scales and lengths of time to provide the most complete picture. This updated edition contains additional illustrations, study questions, summaries, and extensive references for further study.

Where it's reviewed:
Choice, June 2009, page p1962

Other books you might like:

Julie Kerr Casper, *Global Warming Trends: Ecological Footprint*, 2009

Jonathan Cowie, *Climate Change: Biological and Human Aspects*, 2007

Ashraf M.T. Elewa, *Migration of Organisms*, 2010

Gillian Judson, *A New Approach to Ecological Education*, 2010

Linda O. Mearns, *Issues in the Impacts of Climate Variability and Change on Agriculture*, 2010

1063

GARY E. BOWMAN

Essential Quantum Mechanics

(Oxford; New York: Oxford University Press, 2008)

Subject(s): Physics; Science; Mathematics

Summary: In *Essential Quantum Mechanics*, physicist and professor Gary E. Bowman offers a detailed explanation of the key elements of quantum theory. Bowman aims to arm readers with both a practical and mathematical comprehension of the subject, illustrating the ideas, framework, and modalities of contemporary quantum mechanics. This volume includes appendices, a bibliography, and a full index. First book.

Other books you might like:

Bipin R. Desai, *Quantum Mechanics with Basic Field Theory*, 2009

David J. Griffiths, *Introduction to Elementary Particles*, 2008

Paul A. Klevgard, *Einstein's Method: A Fresh Approach to Quantum Mechanics and Relativity*, 2008

David A. B. Miller, *Quantum Mechanics for Scientists and Engineers*, 2008

Henry P. Stapp, *Mind, Matter and Quantum Mechanics*, 2009

1064

RICHARD N. BOYD

An Introduction to Nuclear Astrophysics

(Chicago: University of Chicago Press, 2008)

Subject(s): Science; Astronomy; Physics

Summary: In *An Introduction to Nuclear Astrophysics*, scientist Richard N. Boyd explains the complicated topic with fresh insight and a new approach to the basics of the science. Boyd discusses the fundamental aspects of astrophysics and how these aspects have branched out into other arenas, including the study of astronomy and cosmology, to name a few. This volume further investigates the subject by examining advanced stellar evolution, the beginnings of the universe, and hydrogen burning. *An Introduction to Nuclear Astrophysics* contains an appendix, a bibliography, and an index. First book.

Where it's reviewed:
Choice, Dec 2008, page p712

Other books you might like:

Francis LeBlanc, *An Introduction to Stellar Astrophysics*, 2010

Fulvio Melia, *High-Energy Astrophysics*, 2009

Peter Meszaros, *The High Energy Universe: Ultra-High Energy Events in Astrophysics and Cosmology*, 2010

Donald Perkins, *Particle Astrophysics*, 2009

Science

1065

LINDELL BROMHAM

Reading the Story in DNA: A Beginner's Guide to Molecular Evolution

(Oxford; New York: Oxford University Press, 2008)

Subject(s): Genetics; Biology; Science

Summary: Professor Lindell Bronham arms readers with the fundamental knowledge essential to understanding deoxyribonucleic acid, or DNA. To fully grasp the role of DNA, Bronham insists, students and teachers alike must possess a thorough knowledge of how molecular evolution works. In this volume, the author makes this sometimes-daunting topic approachable for readers, outlining the ways to harness molecular data to glean an all-encompassing insight into the functions and characteristics of DNA. *Reading the Story in DNA: A Beginner's Guide to Molecular Evolution* includes illustrations, three appendices, a glossary, a bibliography, and an index. First book.

Where it's reviewed:
Quarterly Review of Biology, June 2010, page p223
Times Higher Education, May 28, 2009, page pX

Other books you might like:
Sean B. Carroll, *The Making of the Fittest: DNA and the Ultimate Forensic Record of Evolution*, 2006
Lawrence Hunter, *The Processes of Life: An Introduction to Molecular Biology*, 2009
Durdica Ugarkovic, *Centromere: Structure and Evolution*, 2009

1066

ROBERT J. BROOKER

Genetics: Analysis and Principles, Third Edition

(New York: McGraw-Hill, 2008)

Subject(s): Genetics; Genetic research; Science

Summary: In *Genetics: Analysis and Principles, Third Edition*, author Robert J. Brooker offers a detailed examination of the fundamentals of genetic science. This third edition is fully revised and updated with the latest findings in the field. Brooker probes each topic by discussing various genetic experiments and how these experiments illustrate the principles of genetic understanding. *Genetics* contains a bibliography and an index.

Other books by the same author:
Chemistry, Cell Biology and Genetics: Volume One, 2010
Evolution, Diversity and Ecology: Volume Two, 2010
Plants and Animals:Volume Three, 2010

Other books you might like:
Daniel L. Hartl, *Essential Genetics: A Genomics*

Perspective, Fifth Edition, 2009
Ricki Lewis, *Human Genetics: Concepts and Applications*, 2009
Desmond S. T. Nicholl, *An Introduction to Genetic Engineering, Third Edition*, 2008
Benjamin Pierce, *Genetics Essentials: Concepts and Connections*, 2009

1067

EDWARD BRYANT

Tsunami: The Underrated Hazard, 2nd Edition

(New York: Springer, 2010)

Subject(s): Natural disasters; Science; Nature

Summary: Written by tsunami researcher and climatology professor, Edward Bryant, *Tsunami: The Underrated Hazard, 2nd Edition* is a comprehensive guide to the catastrophic natural disasters. Bryant gives readers a thorough explanation of tsunamis, what causes them, their unique characteristics, and their historical impact. Divided into four sections, *Tsunami* relies on fieldwork, historical information, case studies, and recent findings to explain the nature of tsunamis. The first section addresses historical records of tsunamis and explains the dynamics and principles of the natural disasters. The second section examines landscapes shaped by tsunamis and compares damage done by various types. In the third section, Bryant identifies the causes of tsunamis before evaluating the present-day risk in the fourth section.

Where it's reviewed:
Choice, Sept 2008 v46 i1, page p130
Pure and Applied Geophysics, Nov 2009 v166 i12, page p2115

Other books by the same author:
Climate Process and Change, 2010
Natural Hazards, 2005

Other books you might like:
Roy Chester, *Furnace of Creation, Cradle of Destruction: A Journey to the Birthplace of Earthquakes, Volcanoes, and Tsunamis*, 2008
Bruce B. Parker, *The Power of the Sea: Tsunamis, Storm Surges, Rogue Waves, and Our Quest to Predict Disasters*, 2010
Linda Tagliaferro, *How Does An Earthquake Become A Tsunami?*, 2009

1068

FRED BUNZ

Principles of Cancer Genetics

(Dordrecht: Springer, 2008)

Subject(s): Cancer; Genetics; Genetic research

Summary: Author Fred Bunz examines the cancer gene theory in order to offer students a more thorough comprehension of the genetic foundations of the deadly disease. *Principles of Cancer Genetics* looks at the roles of oncogenes and tumor suppressor genes, as well as the effects of genetic instability and alterations. This volume also explores cancer gene pathways and cancer genetics from a clinical perspective. *Principles of Cancer Genetics* contains an appendix and an index. First book.

Other books you might like:

Anne M. Bowcock, *Breast Cancer: Molecular Genetics, Pathogenesis, and Therapeutics*, 2010

Paul B. Fisher, *Cancer Genomics and Proteomics: Methods and Protocols*, 2010

Lewis J. Kleinsmith, *Principles of Cancer Biology*, 2005

Raymond W. Ruddon, *Cancer Biology, Fourth Edition*, 2007

Wolfgang Arthur Schulz, *Molecular Biology of Human Cancers: An Advanced Student's Textbook*, 2007

1069

WILLIAM JAMES BURROUGHS

Climate Change: A Multidisciplinary Approach, 2nd Edition

(Cambridge, England: Cambridge University Press, 2007)

Subject(s): Weather; Science; Education

Summary: *Climate Change: A Multidisciplinary Approach, 2nd Edition* is a textbook about the many facets of climate change from award-winning science writer William James Burroughs. The second edition provides the latest information and research on global climate change for students of meteorology, oceanography, environmental science, earth science, geography, history, agriculture, and social science. *Climate Change* presents detailed information on the physical principles of the world's climate and an overview of past climate change. Burroughs examines the possible causes of climate change, methods for measuring and analyzing climate, and predictions for future change.

Where it's reviewed:
Choice, June 2008, page 1798

Other books by the same author:
Climate Change in Prehistory: The End of the Reign of Chaos, 2008
Does the Weather Really Matter?: The Social Implications of Climate Change, 2005
Weather Cycles: Real or Imaginary?, 2004

Other books you might like:

Heidi Cullen, *The Weather of the Future: Heat Waves, Extreme Storms, and Other Scenes from a Climate-Changed Planet*, 2010

Robert Henson, *The Rough Guide to Climate Change*, 2008

Mike Hulme, *Why We Disagree About Climate Change: Understanding Controversy, Inaction and Opportunity*, 2009

Edmond A. Mathez, *Climate Change: The Science of*

Global Warming and Our Energy Future, 2009
Fred Pearce, *With Speed and Violence: Why Scientists Fear Tipping Points in Climate Change*, 2008

1070

CHRISTOPHER C. BURT

Extreme Weather: A Guide and Record Book

(New York: W.W. Norton, 2007)

Subject(s): Science; Weather; Meteorology

Summary: In *Extreme Weather: A Guide and Record Book*, Christopher C. Burt presents a compendium of weather facts and trivia. Each chapter focuses on a specific aspect of weather—heat, cold, snow, rain, drought, thunderstorms, tornadoes, hurricanes, and windstorms—listing extreme examples of each in the United States and the world. Weather buffs will learn about heat bursts, makeshift Alaskan thermometers, ice storms, mud showers, superbolts, luminous tornadoes, el nino, la nina, and other weather phenomena. The author also weighs in on the debate over climate change and global warming. Supplementary graphics include dozens of maps, informative tables, and over 100 color photographs.

Where it's reviewed:
Science Books & Films, Nov-Dec 2007, page p270

Other books you might like:
Peter Bunyard, *Extreme Weather: The Cataclysmic Effects of Climate Change*, 2006
Paul Douglas, *Restless Skies*, 2007
Clive Gifford, *Chasing the World's Most Dangerous Storms*, 2010
H. Michael Mogil, *Extreme Weather*, 2007
Chris Mooney, *Storm World: Hurricanes, Politics, and the Battle over Global Warming*, 2007

1071

JOHN M. BUTLER

Forensic DNA Typing: Biology, Technology, and Genetics of STR Markers, Second Edition

(Burlington, Massachusetts: Elsevier Academic Press, 2007)

Subject(s): Biology; Technology; Reference works

Summary: *Forensic DNA Typing: Biology, Technology, and Genetics of STR Markers, Second Edition* by John M. Butler is a textbook for students studying forensic DNA analysis. Butler provides extensive discussion of the new technologies used for forensic DNA typing, as well as of the biological and genetic scientific advances that have made this possible, such as genealogy markers. Charts and graphs are also included to make the information more easily understood by students. Advantages and disadvantages of different pieces of equipment or forensic DNA typing methods are also discussed, making this text practical for those who are working or planning to work in crime labs. Case studies as well as a discussion of ethical issues are included as well.

Where it's reviewed:
Jurimetrics Journal of Law, Science and Technology, Winter 2007, page p245-249

Other books by the same author:
Improved analysis of DNA short tandem repeats with time-of-flight mass spectrometry, 2001

Other books you might like:
Suzanne Bell, *Forensic Chemistry,* 2005
Angel Carracedo, *Forensic DNA Typing Protocols,* 2010
Adrian Linacre, *Forensic Science in Wildlife Investigations,* 2009
J. Thomas McClintock, *Forensic DNA Analysis: A Laboratory Manual,* 2008
Colin J. Sanderson, *Understanding Genes and GMOs,* 2007

1072

SEAN B. CARROLL

The Making of the Fittest: DNA and the Ultimate Forensic Record of Evolution

(New York: W.W. Norton & Co, 2006)

Subject(s): Evolution (Biology); Science

Summary: In *The Making of the Fittest: DNA and the Ultimate Forensic Record of Evolution,* author Sean B. Carroll points out that even as natural selection encourages beneficial change in organisms, it leaves behind genes for earlier characteristics in the organism's DNA. These fossilized genes can be used to trace the development of the species and sometimes to interpret changes in the environment as well. The examples in this book include colobus monkeys, dolphins, and an Antarctic ice fish that has no red blood cells. Carrol is a professor of genetics at the University of Wisconsin-Madison.

Where it's reviewed:
Journal of Clinical Investigation, July 2007, page p1737
Quarterly Review of Biology, Sept 2007, page p271
Science Books & Films, May-June 2007, page p122
Times Higher Education, Feb 7, 2008, page p45

Other books by the same author:
Remarkable Creatures: Epic Adventures in the Search for the Origins of Species, 2009
Into The Jungle: Great Adventures in the Search for Evolution, 2008
Endless Forms Most Beautiful: The New Science of Evo Devo, 2006

Other books you might like:
Peter Bugert, *DNA and RNA Profiling in Human Blood,* 2008
Brian Innes, *DNA and Body Evidence,* 2007
Nick Lane, *Life Ascending: The Ten Great Inventions of Evolution,* 2010

J. Thomas McClintock, *Forensic DNA Analysis: A Laboratory Manual,* 2008

1073

GEORGE CASELLA

Statistical Design

(New York: Springer, 2008)

Subject(s): Science; Mathematics

Summary: In *Statistical Design,* author and statistics professor George Casella presents a comprehensive overview of the fundamentals of statistical study and design theory. The chapters of this volume cover topics such as randomization, layout, replication, complete block designs, split block designs, and much more. Casella's approach is a highly functional one, illustrating the myriad ways statistics and design theory fit into several key aspects of life and business. *Statistical Design* includes a bibliography and author and subject indexes.

Other books you might like:
R.A. Bailey, *Design of Comparative Experiments,* 2008
John W. Creswell, *Research Design: Qualitative, Quantitative, and Mixed Methods Approaches, Third Edition,* 2008
John Lawson, *Design and Analysis of Experiments with SAS,* 2010

1074

RANDY CERVENY

Weather's Greatest Mysteries Solved!

(Amherst, New York: Prometheus Books, 2009)

Subject(s): Weather; Meteorology; Science

Summary: Written by award-winning climatologist Randy Cerveny, *Weather's Greatest Mysteries Solved!* is an examination of fascinating and inexplicable climate phenomena in the past and present. Cerveny sets out to answer intriguing questions about various weather happenings including the extinction of the dinosaurs, the parting of the Red Sea, the end of the Mayan civilization, and the Great American Dustbowl. Cerveny gives readers a basic understanding of climate study and the techniques utilized in it, as well as the impact that weather has had on humans throughout all stages of history. *Weather's Greatest Mysteries Solved!* also offers predictions for weather patterns over the next 10,000 years.

Where it's reviewed:
Choice, October 2009, page 337
Science News, July 18, 2009, page 30
The Science Teacher, October 2009, page 72

Other books by the same author:
Freaks of the Storm, 2006
Freaks of the Storm: From Flying Cows to Stealing

Thunder: The World's Strangest True Weather Stories, 2005

Other books you might like:
Stefan Bechtel, *Roar of the Heavens*, 2007
Peter Bunyard, *Extreme Weather: The Cataclysmic Effects of Climate Change*, 2006
Christopher C. Burt, *Extreme Weather: A Guide and Record Book*, 2007
Clive Gifford, *Chasing the World's Most Dangerous Storms*, 2010
Jeff Kanipe, *Cosmic Connection: How Astronomical Events Impact Life on Earth*, 2009

1075

NICOLAS CHEETHAM

Earth: A Journey Through Time

(London: Quercus, 2009)

Subject(s): Photography; Geography; Earth

Summary: In *Earth: A Journey Through Time*, author Nicolas Cheetham provides a photographic essay of artistic images depicting the Earth throughout its evolution. The book is dividing into four complete chapters according to the elements: Fire, Water, Air, and Earth. Each chapter shows geological features as well as other features such as weather formations and natural disasters. The author also includes in this book written text that details the phenomena in each image. Cheetham is also the author of *Universe: A Journey to the Edge of the Cosmos*.

Other books by the same author:
Universe, 2008
Universe: A Journey to the Edge of the Cosmos, 2008

Other books you might like:
Gregory L. Vogt, *Landscapes of Mars: A Visual Tour*, 2008

1076

ROY CHESTER

Furnace of Creation, Cradle of Destruction: A Journey to the Birthplace of Earthquakes, Volcanoes, and Tsunamis

(New York: AMACOM, 2008)

Subject(s): Science; Earth; Natural disasters

Summary: Written by oceanographer Roy Chester, *Furnace of Creation, Cradle of Destruction: A Journey to the Birthplace of Earthquakes, Volcanoes, and Tsunamis* is a comprehensive examination of earth science and the cause of natural disasters. In recent years, hundreds of thousands of people have been killed by deadly tsunamis off the coast of the Indian Ocean, and scientists predict that even more of these fatal natural disasters will strike California, Hawaii, and Oregon in the coming years.

Chester explains what's causing this swell in tsunamis, earthquakes, and volcanos: plate tectonics, a shifting of Earth's plates. *Furnace of Creation, Cradle of Destruction* gives readers a thorough history on the discovery of plate tectonics, as well as details about the creation of the earth's surface and its evolution.

Where it's reviewed:
Choice, January 2009, page 934
Kliatt, November 2008, page 63
Perspectives on Science and Christian Faith, June 2009, page 130
Science Books & Films, Nov-Dec 2008, page 236

Other books by the same author:
Marine Geochemistry, 2003

Other books you might like:
Damon P. Coppola, *Introduction to International Disaster Management*, 2006
Wildred D. Iwan, *Earthquake Spectra*, 2006
Terry J. Jennings, *Earthquakes and Tsunamis*, 2009
David A. Rothery, *Volcanoes, Earthquakes and Tsunamis*, 2011
Linda Tagliaferro, *How Does An Earthquake Become A Tsunami?*, 2009

1077

DANIEL CHIRAS

Environmental Science

(Boston, Massachusetts: McGraw-Hill Science, 2009)

Subject(s): Education; Science; Environmental history

Summary: *Environmental Science* by Daniel Chiras is an educational textbook that deals with the disciplines of physical and biological science as they relate to the Earth's environment. In this book, Chiras examines the connection between derivative disciplines within the realm of the field of study, such as geology, ecology, and other related fields. The author also explores the history of the environment as well as economical and political impacts on the environment. Originally published in 2001, the updated 2009 edition includes "Go Green" tips to offer advice for students on environmental awareness and ecological stewardship.

Other books by the same author:
Human Biology, 2011
Green Home Improvement: 65 Projects That Will Cut Utility Bills, Protect Your Health & Help the the Environment, 2008
Study Guide to Accompany Human Biology, 2005

Other books you might like:
Thomas A. Easton, *Environmental Issues: Taking Sides - Clashing Views on Environmental Issues*, 2008
Emilio F. Moran, *Environmental Social Science: Human - Environment interactions and Sustainability*, 2010
Richard T. Wright, *Environmental Science: Toward A Sustainable Future*, 2007

1078

JOSEPH CIRINCIONE

Bomb Scare: The History and Future of Nuclear Weapons

(New York: Columbia University Press, 2007)

Subject(s): Nuclear weapons; Nuclear warfare; History

Summary: In *Bomb Scare: The History and Future of Nuclear Weapons*, Joseph Cirincione provides a history of the development of nuclear weapons and explains why various nations choose to possess the destructive devices. He first provides a brief explanation of nuclear weapons. Cirincione then considers the proliferation of nuclear weapons around the world and the steps that have been taken to control these devices. The author explains the Nonproliferation Project and various arms control agreements since the 1970s, which aim to prevent the further spread of nuclear weapons and to reduce the number of nuclear weapons in existing nations. An extensive discussion of the politics of nonproliferation is included as well.

Where it's reviewed:
Air & Space Power Journal, Fall 2009, page p122
Arms Control Today, March 2007, page p52

Other books by the same author:
Repairing the Regime: Preventing the Spread of Weapons of Mass Destruction, 2000

Other books you might like:
Alexander V. Avakov, *Quality of Life, Balance of Powers, and Nuclear Weapons*, 2009
Jeremy Bernstein, *Nuclear Weapons: What You Need to Know*, 2010
Stephen P. Depoe, *Nuclear Legacies: Communication, Controversy, and the U.S. Nuclear Weapons Complex*, 2008
Samuel Glasstone, *The Effects of Nuclear Weapons*, 2006
Kedar N. Prasad, *Bio-Shield, Antioxidants Against Radiological, Chemical and Biological Weapons*, 2008

1079

WILLIAM R. CLARK

In Defense of Self: How the Immune System Really Works

(New York: Oxford University Press, 2008)

Subject(s): Health; Science; Anatomy

Summary: *In Defense of Self: How the Immune System Really Works* is a comprehensive overview of the human immune system from professor and author William R. Clark. In this book, Clark offers straightforward and easy-to-understand information on the inner workings of the immune system and how it protects humans from disease. The immune system is the body's main line of defense, blocking harmful bacteria, parasites, viruses, and mold from starting diseases. However, the immune system can often turn against healthy cells and cause autoimmune disorders or reject organ transplants intended to save lives. Clark explains how the immune system works, how the body distinguishes good microbes from bad ones, and how the immune system would react to bioterrorism. He also offers the latest information on vaccinations.

Where it's reviewed:
Choice, November 2008, page 548

Other books by the same author:
A Means to an End: The Biological Basis of Aging and Death, 2002

Other books you might like:
Daisuke Kitamura, *How the Immune System Recognizes Self and Nonself*, 2010
Lorrie Klosterman, *Immune System*, 2008
W. Ivan Morrison, *The Ruminant Immune System in Health and Disease*, 2009
Robert B. Northrop, *Introduction to Complexity and Complex Systems*, 2010
Lauren M. Sompayrac, *How the Immune System Works*, 2008

1080

MARK CLUTE

Food Industry Quality Control Systems

(Boca Raton: CRC Press, 2008)

Subject(s): Food; Cooking; Cooks

Summary: In *Food Industry Quality Control Systems*, author Mark Clute, a veteran food management specialist, offers readers a comprehensive guide to the standard modern guidelines for food preparation and quality control. Utilizing a system of top-down management commitment, Clute explores the entire information collection process and touches on the key parts of the system, such as supplier certification, lot coding, sanitation programs, pest control, organizational charts, and more. He also includes an outline of various subprograms, like HACCP, which is special system that helps food manufacturers to ensure effective, continuing food safety. Using *Food Industry Quality Control Systems* as a guide, foodservice professionals can create their own quality control programs.

Other books you might like:
Ioannis S. Arvanitoyannis, *HACCP and ISO 22000: Application to Foods of Animal Origin*, 2009
Frank Yiannas, *Food Safety Culture: Creating a Behavior-Based Food Safety Management System*, 2008

1081

MICHAEL COLLIER

Over the Coasts: An Aerial View of Geology

(New York: Mikaya Press, 2009)

Subject(s): Photography; Geology; Geography

Summary: *Over the Coasts: An Aerial View of Geology* is a photo essay by geological photographer Michael Collier, who is also author of the companion books *Over the Rivers* and *Over the Rivers*. In this book, Collier's photography examines geological formations and how their appearances and details reveal their relationship to their surrounding environs. The author explores various regions of the world, including Alaska, the Gulf of Mexico, the Southern and Northern Atlantic, and the Pacific Ocean. This book contains information about the natural geological shifts as well as the manmade formations such as beach mansions, artificial reefs, beach erosion, and other impacts of human development on the coasts of the Earth.

Where it's reviewed:
Science News, Dec 19, 2009, page p30

Other books by the same author:
Over the Rivers (An Aerial View of Geology), 2008
Over the Mountains (An Aerial View of Geology), 2007

Other books you might like:
Yann Arthus-Bertrand, *The New Earth from Above: 365 Days*, 2009
W. Kenneth Hamblin, *Anatomy of the Grand Canyon: Panoramas of the Canyon's Geology*, 2008

1082

RUTH SCHWARTZ COWAN

Heredity and Hope: The Case for Genetic Screening

(Cambridge, Massachusetts: Harvard University Press, 2008)

Subject(s): Genetics; Genetic research; Medicine

Summary: In *Heredity and Hope: The Case for Genetic Screening*, author and science history professor Ruth Schwartz Cowan offers a timely exploration of medical genetics and its important role in the health of humankind. In presenting a thorough history of genetic research, Cowan charts the effects of both genetics and eugenics, illuminating the challenges and choices faced by patients, caregivers, and scientists. *Heredity and Hope* contains notes on the text, a bibliography, and an index.

Where it's reviewed:
Commonweal, Nov 7, 2008, page p21
Nature, May 22, 2008, page p452
Nature Genetics, Jan 2009, page p3

Other books you might like:
Dena S. Davis, *Genetic Dilemmas: Reproductive Technology, Parental Choices, and Children's Futures*, 2009

Aviad E. Raz, *Community Genetics and Genetic Alliances*, 2009
Doris Teichler-Zallen, *To Test or Not to Test: A Guide to Genetic Screening and Risk*, 2008
Carlos Valverde, *Genetic Screening of Newborns: An Ethical Inquiry*, 2010

1083

DANIEL COYLE

The Talent Code: Greatness Isn't Born. It's Grown. Here's How

(New York: Bantam Books, 2009)

Subject(s): Science; Gifted persons; Biology

Summary: Written by bestselling author Daniel Coyle, *The Talent Code: Greatness Isn't Born. It's Grown. Here's How* is an examination of myelin in the human brain and how it contributes to the development of skills and talent. Recent studies have shown that myelin serves as more than a brain-cell insulator. It is actually a major contributor to a person's ability to acquire skills. Coyle gives readers an overview of myelin and the various ways it grows and develops. *The Talent Code* reveals the types of exercises, practice, motivation, and coaching that cause the greatest surge in myelin development. Coyle relies on the latest scientific research and interviews with the world's greatest musicians, skateboarders, artists, athletes, fighter pilots, and bank robbers to offer readers information on ways to reach their full potential.

Where it's reviewed:
Journal of Sports Sciences, February 15, 2010, page 451

Other books by the same author:
Lance Armstrong's War: One Man's Battle Against Fate, Fame, Love, Death, Scandal, and a Few Other Rivals on the Road to the Tour de France, 2010

Other books you might like:
Ruth C. Clark, *Building Expertise: Cognitive Methods for Training and Performance Improvement*, 2008
Ruth Colvin Clark, *Evidence-Based Training Methods: A Guide for Training Professionals*, 2010
Geoff Colvin, *Talent Is Overrated: What Really Separates World-Class Performers from Everybody Else*, 2010
Carol Dweck, *Mindset*, 2007
Thomas M. Sterner, *The Practicing Mind*, 2006

1084

JOSEPH M. CRAINE

Resource Strategies of Wild Plants

(Princeton, New Jersey: Princeton University Press, 2009)

Subject(s): Science; Ecology; Botany

Summary: In *Resource Strategies of Wild Plants*, Joseph

Science

M. Craine discusses the various methods seed-bearing land plants have developed over the millennia to survive in less than ideal environments. As the author explains, wild plants deal with such stresses as competition for resources, the threat of herbivores, and climactic changes. In this fascinating study, Craine examines a variety of resource strategies, including the low-nutrient strategy, the high-resource strategy, the low-light strategy, and the low-water and low-carbon dioxide strategy. Through each of these mechanisms, plants adapt to the conditions at hand to thrive and produce seeds to establish another generation.

Where it's reviewed:
Choice, Jan 2010, page p915
Quarterly Review of Biology, June 2010, page p233

Other books you might like:
Peter Del Tredici, *Wild Urban Plants of the Northeast*, 2010
John Kallas, *Edible Wild Plants*, 2010
Jim Meuninck, *Basic Essentials Edible Wild Plants and Useful Herbs*, 2007
Samuel Thayer, *The Forager's Harvest: A Guide to Identifying, Harvesting, and Preparing Edible Wild Plants*, 2006
Frank Tozer, *The Uses of Wild Plants*, 2007

1085

JOHN W. CRESWELL

Research Design: Qualitative, Quantitative, and Mixed Methods Approaches, Third Edition

(Thousand Oaks, California: Sage Publications, 2008)

Subject(s): Science; Social sciences

Summary: In *Research Design: Qualitative, Quantitative, and Mixed Methods Approaches, Third Edition*, John W. Creswell updates his text for undergraduate and post-graduate students of social and behavioral sciences. The first part of the book explains the selection of a research design, reviewing related literature, the use of theory, writing strategies, and ethical considerations. The book's second part addresses the process of research presentation, including developing a purpose statement, the role of research questions and hypotheses, quantitative methods, qualitative procedures, as well as mixed methods procedures. Additional resources are available on companion websites for teachers and students.

Other books by the same author:
Qualitative Inquiry and Research Design, 2006
Educational Research, 2004

Other books you might like:
Dana Dunn, *The Practical Researcher*, 2009
Richard Gonzalez, *Data Analysis for Experimental Design*, 2008
Scott Menard, *Handbook of Longitudinal Research*, 2007
Douglas C. Montgomery, *Design and Analysis of Experiment*, 2009

Ivan Valiela, *Doing Science: Design, Analysis, and Communication of Scientific Research*, 2009

1086

BRIAN CUDNIK

Lunar Meteoroid Impacts and How to Observe Them

(New York: Springer, 2009)

Subject(s): Astronomy; Science; Space exploration

Summary: The subject of LTPs—lunar transient phenomena—is the subject of this authoritative volume by author and meteor expert Brian Cudnik. Though it's common knowledge that the moon's surface is etched with the fallout from meteor collisions, Cudnik reveals this phenomenon is still occurring on a regular basis. His practical advice and expert guidance show amateur astronomers how to identify these meteor impacts on the lunar surface and how this identification can inform one's perspective on the history of the galaxy. *Lunar Meteoroid Impacts and How to Observe Them* includes eight appendices and a full index. First book.

Where it's reviewed:
Choice, August 2010, page 2347

Other books you might like:
Martin Beech, *Meteors and Meteorites: Origins and Observations*, 2006
Walter T. Brown, *In the Beginning*, 2008
Jane Kelley, *Comets and Meteors*, 2009
Michel Maurette, *Micrometeorites and the Mysteries of Our Origins*, 2006
Steve Parker, *Comets, Asteroids and Meteors*, 2007

1087

GUY DAUNCEY

The Climate Challenge: 101 Solutions to Global Warming

(Gabriola Island, British Columbia: New Society Publishers, 2009)

Subject(s): Science; Weather; Nature

Summary: One of the biggest potential problems faced today by people around the world is global warming. In *The Climate Challenge: 101 Solutions to Global Warming*, author Guy Dauncey offers readers an array of through-provoking solutions that could play an important role in answering the question of what to do about global warming once and for all. In offering his 101 solutions, Dauncey portrays us all as a group of soldiers preparing to fight in the war against global warming, the most important battle of our lives. In addition to laying out the battle plan, Dauncey riles up the troops with the promise of a better future that could be attainable if we make our stand today.

Other books you might like:
David Archer, *The Long Thaw: How Humans Are*

Changing the Next 100,000 Years of Earth's Climate, 2010

Greg Craven, *What's the Worst That Could Happen?: A Rational Response to the Climate Change Debate*, 2009

Albert Gore, *Our Choice: A Plan to Solve the Climate Crisis*, 2009

Spencer Weart, *The Discovery of Global Warming: (New Histories of Science, Technology, and Medicine)*, 2003

1088

THOMAS M. DEVLIN

Textbook of Biochemistry with Clinical Correlations

(Hoboken, New Jersey: John Wiley & Sons, 2010)

Subject(s): Science; Biology; Chemistry

Summary: In *Textbook of Biochemistry: With Clinical Correlations*, editor Thomas M. Devlin presents a comprehensive textbook for medical students and professionals concerning the biochemistry of cells in mammals. Organized into five parts—"Structure of Macromolecules," "Transmission of Information," "Functions of Proteins," "Metabolic Pathways and Their Control," and "Physiological Processes"—this volume examines the relationship between cellular biochemical activity and the physiology of the body as a whole. Topics covered include eukaryotic cell structure, regulation of gene suppression, fundamentals of signal transduction, metabolic interrelationships, and the digestion and absorption of basic nutritional constituents. Thomas Devlin is professor emeritus of biochemistry at Drexel University's School of Medicine.

Other books you might like:

Nessar Ahmed, *Clinical Biochemistry*, 2011

Gerald Litwack, *Human Biochemistry and Disease*, 2008

Vassilis Mougios, *Exercise Biochemistry*, 2006

David Sheehan, *Physical Biochemistry: Principles and Applications*, 2009

Donald Voet, *Biochemistry: 4th Edition*, 2010
    Judith G. Voet, co-author

1089

JAMES A. DEWAR

To the End of the Solar System: The Story of the Nuclear Rocket, Second Edition

(Lexington, Kentucky: The University Press of Kentucky, 2008)

Subject(s): Science; Technology; Engineering

Summary: In *To the End of the Solar System: The Story of the Nuclear Rocket*, James A. Dewar (formerly of the Department of Energy) chronicles the development of the nuclear rocket propulsion system. Dewar focuses specifically on the 1950s, 60s, and 70s—the decades during which the United States focused on the application of the rocket to its space program, specifically the Rover and NERVA programs. The author also looks to the future, considering the practical and political issues associated with further development of nuclear rockets for extended space missions. Appendices include information on the Russian nuclear rocket program and fuel element development.

Where it's reviewed:
Ad Astra, Summer 2008, page p54

Other books by the same author:
The Nuclear Rocket: Making Our Planet Green, Peaceful and Prosperous, 2009

Other books you might like:

Charles L. Bradshaw, *Rockets, Reactors, and Computers Define the Twentieth Century*, 2007

Clayton K. S. Chun, *Thunder over the Horizon: From V-2 Rockets to Ballistic Missiles*, 2006

James A. Dewar, *The Nuclear Rocket: Making Our Planet Green, Peaceful and Prosperous*, 2009

Chris Gainor, *To a Distant Day: The Rocket Pioneers*, 2008

1090

PAUL DICKSON

A Dictionary of the Space Age

(Baltimore, Maryland: Johns Hopkins University Press, 2009)

Subject(s): Science; Reference works; Space exploration

Summary: *A Dictionary of the Space Age* is a collection of space-related phrases and their meanings from author Paul Dickson. The Space Age officially began in 1957 with the launch of Sputnik 1. As America and Russia competed with one another in the space race, their citizens became enthralled with each country's developments and advancements. New words and phrases were introduced to the world, including many acronyms coined by NASA. In *A Dictionary of the Space Age*, Dickson offers definitions of the words, acronyms, and phrases of the era, including the meanings and origins of sayings such as "spam in a can," "the Eagle has landed," and "tickety-boo."

Where it's reviewed:
Choice, November 2009, page 474

Other books by the same author:
Sputnik: The Shock of the Century, 2007
Sputnik: The Launch of the Space Race, 2002

Other books you might like:
Colin Burgess, *Footprints in the Dust*, 2010

Jay Gallentine, *Ambassadors from Earth*, 2009

Christopher Hallpike, *How We Got Here: From Bows and Arrows to the Space Age*, 2008

Christopher Mari, *The Next Space Age*, 2008

Robert Zimmerman, *The Universe in a Mirror: The Saga of the Hubble Space Telescope and the Visionaries Who Built It*, 2010

Science

1091

BRIAN M. FAGAN

The Complete Ice Age: How Climate Change Shaped the World

(New York: Thames and Hudsons, 2009)

Subject(s): Environmental history; Natural resource conservation; Ecology

Summary: *The Complete Ice Age: How Climate Change Shaped the World* is an overview of the first documented instance of global climate change in the history of Earth: the Ice Age. In this book, editor Brian Fagan has compiled information and data on the turbulent climate shifts and changes during the Ice Age, and how certain species were able to endure it while others could not. The book also reveals data that shows information about the evolutionary periods of humans and the animals that co-existed with them. Predictions about future global climate shifts, which may occur with or without human interference, are also made. Contributors to the book include John F. Hoffecker, Mark Maslin, and Hannah O'Regan.

Where it's reviewed:
Choice, March 2010, page p1315
Geographical, Nov 2009, page p59
School Science Review, June 2010, page p129

Other books by the same author:
Ancient Lives: An Introduction to Archaeology and Prehistory, 2009
Archaeology: A Brief Introduction, 2008
Discovery!: Unearthing the New Treasures of Archaeology, 2007

Other books you might like:
Clive Finlayson, *The Humans Who Went Extinct: Why Neanderthals Died Out and We Survived*, 2009
Douglas Palmer, *Origins: Human Evolution Revealed*, 2010

1092

JEFF A. FARINACCI

Guide to Observing Deep-Sky Objects: A Complete Global Resource for Astronomers

(New York: Springer Science and Business Media, 2007)

Subject(s): Astronomy; Reference works; Science

Summary: *Guide to Observing Deep-Sky Objects: A Complete Global Resource for Astronomers* by Jeff A. Farinacci is a guide for students or amateur astronomers. Charts for 88 constellations are provided. Each chart features a list of the brightest objects in the constellation, the Bayer labels, specific coordinates and magnitudes for each, tables for additional objects located in the constellation, and graphs that provide detailed time descriptions. Though the text is oriented to the northern hemisphere, a CD-ROM is also included to allow the

user to specify a location and time of night anywhere in the world. The program then displays the constellations that can be viewed in that specified location.

Where it's reviewed:
Choice, June 2008, page 1791

Other books you might like:
Mark A. Garlick, *Astronomy: A Visual Guide*, 2004
Jacqueline Mitton, *Cambridge Illustrated Dictionary of Astronomy*, 2008
Dinah L. Moche, *Astronomy*, 2009
Roger W. Sinnott, *Sky & Telescope's Pocket Sky Atlas*, 2006

1093

JOHN FARRELL

Stargazer's Alphabet: Night-Sky Wonders from A to Z

(Honesdale, Pennsylvania: Boyds Mills Press, 2009)

Subject(s): Astronomy; Rhyme; Space exploration

Summary: *Stargazer's Alphabet: Night-Sky Wonders from A to Z* is a book for young readers about the stars and planets that can be found in the night sky. Written in rhyme, the book contains full-page photographs, and each letter of the alphabet corresponds to something found in space. For example, A is for Andromeda, and B is for Big Dipper. Topics such as the constellations that make up the zodiac, the influence of the moon on Earth's tides, and methods of locating other planets or the North Star in the sky are addressed in these rhymed, alphabetized topics. Though not truly a reference book on space, this text provides a good introduction for young readers.

Where it's reviewed:
Booklinks, March 2009, page p46

Other books by the same author:
The Day Without Yesterday: Lemaitre, Einstein, and the Birth of Modern Cosmology, 2005

Other books you might like:
Sue French, *Celestial Sampler*, 2007
Ken Hewitt-White, *Patterns in the Sky*, 2007
Paul E. Kinzer, *Stargazing Basics: Getting Started in Recreational Astronomy*, 2008
Becky Ramotowski, *Secrets of Stargazing*, 2007
Roger W. Sinnott, *Sky & Telescope's Pocket Sky Atlas*, 2006

1094

MICHAEL D. FAYER

Absolutely Small: How Quantum Theory Explains Our Everyday World

(New York: AMACOM, 2010)

Subject(s): Physics; Science; Mathematics
Summary: In *Absolutely Small: How Quantum Theory*

Explains Our Everyday World, Michael D. Fayer provides an accessible, comprehensive discussion of quantum mechanics for anyone with an interest in science. Fayer discusses important theories of quantum mechanics succinctly and clearly without making use of complex mathematical equations, choosing instead to use the theories to explain the natural world around us. This allows Fayer to address such questions as why fruits are a certain color, why molecules have unique shapes, and what makes carbon dioxide a greenhouse gas. Diagrams are provided to illustrate difficult concepts, but Fayer primarily focuses on explaining the influence of quantum theory on life on Earth in a narrative way.

Other books by the same author:
Elements of Quantum Mechanics, 2001

Other books you might like:
John Gribbin, *In Search of the Multiverse*, 2010
Charles Nash, *Relativistic Quantum Fields*, 2010
Tai-Kai Ng, *Introduction to Classical and Quantum Field Theory*, 2009
Richard Panek, *The 4 Percent Universe: Dark Matter, Dark Energy, and the Race To Discover the Rest of Reality*, 2010
Anton Zeilinger, *Dance of the Photons: From Einstein to Quantum Teleportation*, 2010

1095

CORDELIA FINE

A Mind of Its Own: How Your Brain Distorts and Deceives

(New York: W.W. Norton & Co., 2008)

Subject(s): Neurosciences; Psychology; Depression (Mood disorder)

Summary: In *A Mind of Its Own: How Your Brain Distorts and Deceives*, Cordelia Fine examines how the brain affects our perception of the world and can tend to cast our self-perception in a more positive light than our perceptions of those around us, in a "distorting prism of self-knowledge." For example, people primarily believe that other people are to blame for our failures, but that our successes are a result of our own superiority; that we are more attractive than those around us; and that we are more moral, more skilled, behave better, and simply above-average. Fine explains how this skewed perception contributes to an optimistic worldview and allows humans to continue to function in the world despite criticism or failures. Fine considers specific responses in the brain such as "retroactive pessimism," in which people will consider all the ways that the odds were stacked against them to begin with, in an attempt to find an acceptable excuse for failing. Fine advises developing better self-awareness to prevent this distortion, while cautioning that those people with the most realistic level of perception also tend to be clinically depressed.

Where it's reviewed:
Skeptic, Summer 2008, page p62

Other books by the same author:
Delusions of Gender: The Real Science Behind Sex Differences, 2010
The Britannica Guide To The Brain, 2008

Other books you might like:
John S. Allen, *The Lives of the Brain: Human Evolution and the Organ of Mind*, 2009
Louis J. Cozolino, *The Neuroscience of Human Relationships*, 2006
Stanislas Dehaene, *Reading in the Brain*, 2009
Norman Doidge, *The Brain That Changes Itself: Stories of Personal Triumph from the Frontiers of Brain Science*, 2007
John Nolte, *Essentials of the Human Brain*, 2007

1096

CLIVE FINLAYSON

The Humans Who Went Extinct: Why Neanderthals Died Out and We Survived

(New York: Oxford University Press, 2009)

Subject(s): Science; Evolution (Biology); Biology

Summary: In *The Humans Who Went Extinct: Why Neanderthals Died Out and We Survived*, Clive Finlayson, director of the Gibraltar Museum, examines the rise and decline of the species that most closely resembled modern man. The Neanderthals thrived in various regions of Europe, but eventually died out approximately 28,000 years ago. One of the last known sites of Neanderthal occupation is believed to be a cave in Gibraltar. According to Finlayson, the cause of the species' extinction was not lack of intelligence but more likely infection and changes in the environment. Homo sapiens survived more by good fortune than by physical or mental superiority.

Where it's reviewed:
Choice, May 2010, page p1713
Quarterly Review of Biology, Sept 2010, page p347

Other books by the same author:
Neanderthals and Modern Humans, 2009

Other books you might like:
Ann Gibbons, *The First Human: The Race to Discover Our Earliest Ancestors*, 2007
Richard G. Klein, *The Human Career: Human Biological and Cultural Origins*, 2009
Nick Lane, *Life Ascending: The Ten Great Inventions of Evolution*, 2010
Charles Lockwood, *The Human Story: Where We Come From & How We Evolved*, 2008
Ian Tattersall, *The Fossil Trail*, 2008

Science

1097

JOHN FLECK

The Tree Rings' Tale: Understanding Our Changing Climate

(Albuquerque: University of New Mexico Press, 2009)

Subject(s): Trees (Plants); Nature; Rivers

Summary: In *The Tree Rings' Tale: Understanding Our Changing Climate*, author John Fleck introduces young readers to the scientific study of tree rings, known as dendroclimatology. Fleck explains how the science of tree rings began with John Wesley Powell, an early explorer of the American West. He recounts how Powell, during his first expedition in 1869, noticed a particular tree along the banks of the Colorado River in southwest Colorado. Wesley saw that tree had a modest-sized ring. During his second expedition in 1871, Powell found the same tree and observed that its ring had become very thin. On another trip the following year, Powell again located the tree and noted that its ring had grown fat. This and later findings showed that one could estimate how much water had flowed down the river in a given year based on how thin or fat a tree's rings were. This information proved to be vital for the pioneers who were attempting to established settlements nearby. Fleck demonstrates the importance of tree ring science and shows how it is connected with many other areas of science.

Where it's reviewed:
The Horn Book Guide, Spring 2010, page p140

Other books you might like:
Albert Gore, *Our Choice: A Plan to Solve the Climate Crisis*, 2009
James H. Speer, *Fundamentals of Tree Ring Research*, 2010
Spencer Weart, *The Discovery of Global Warming: (New Histories of Science, Technology, and Medicine)*, 2003

1098

CHRIS FRITH

Making up the Mind: How the Brain Creates Our Mental World

(Malden, Massachusetts: Wiley-Blackwell, 2007)

Subject(s): Neurosciences; Human behavior; Psychology

Summary: The human brain offers endless mysterious processes that help shape how people perceive the world around them. In *Making up the Mind: How the Brain Creates Our Mental World*, neuroscientist Chris Frith explores the various methods the brain uses to construct the inner landscapes of the mind. Frith draws from a variety of sources, including case studies, psychological testing, and brain scans, to illustrate the symbiotic connection between the mind and the brain. *Making up the*

Mind contains illustrations and an index.

Where it's reviewed:
Choice, March 2008, page p1183
New Scientist, April 21, 2007, page p50
Quarterly Review of Biology, Dec 2007, page p438

Other books you might like:
Daniel Coyle, *The Talent Code: Greatness Isn't Born. It's Grown. Here's How*, 2009

1099

JIBAMITRA GANGULY

Thermodynamics in Earth and Planetary Sciences

(New York: Springer, 2008)

Subject(s): Science; Geology; Physics

Summary: Author Jibamitra Ganguly investigates thermodynamics and its relationship to various and sundry geochemical, geological, and geophysical quandaries. *Thermodynamics in Earth and Planetary Sciences* illuminates the role of thermodynamics in numerous natural structures. Topics in this volume include in-depth analyses of the nature and scope of thermodynamics, equations of states, thermal pressure, surface effects, and much more. Three appendices, a bibliography, and two indexes are also included. First book.

Where it's reviewed:
Physics of Life Reviews, Dec 2008, page p225

Other books you might like:
Caleb A. Scharf, *Extrasolar Planets and Astrobiology*, 2008
Youxue Zhang, *Geochemical Kinetics*, 2008
Haibo Zou, *Quantitative Geochemistry*, 2007

1100

WILL GATER

The Practical Astronomer

(New York: DK Publishing, 2010)

Subject(s): Astronomy; Science; Physics

Summary: *The Practical Astronomer*, published by DK Publishing, is a guidebook for amateur as well as experienced astronomers to the night sky, galaxy, and constellations. This book includes information on stellar formations and space phenomena that can be seen without aid, through simply viewing the night sky with one's eyes, to viewing distant objects. The book also includes full-color illustrations, photos, and graphics of celestial bodies and phenomena to help readers identify and locate various entities in the night sky.

Other books by the same author:
The Cosmic Keyhole: How Astronomy Is Unlocking the Secrets of the Universe, 2009

Other books you might like:
Jeff A. Farinacci, *Guide to Observing Deep-Sky Objects:*

A Complete Global Resource for Astronomers, 2007
Mike Inglis, *Astrophysics is Easy!: An Introduction for the Amateur Astronomer*, 2007
Jeff Lashley, *The Radio Sky and How to Observe It*, 2010

1101

JEFF GILLMAN

How Trees Die: The Past, Present, and Future of our Forests

(Yardley, Pennsylvania: Westholme Publishing, 2009)

Subject(s): Trees (Plants); Ecology; Forestry

Summary: *How Trees Die: The Past, Present, and Future of our Forests* is an environmental perspective on the contributions that trees make to the geography, geology, and ecology of the world around them. In this book, author Jeff Gillman outlines the importance of trees and how their existence and health is interdependent with the Earth's environment. Gillman details the natural, and in some cases unnatural, process of a tree's life and, more importantly, a tree's death, and the implications and impact that process has on surrounding environments. The author also explores how changing infrastructure and industrialization impacts tree ecosystems and what can be done to curb that impact.

Where it's reviewed:
Choice, Jan 2010, page p916
Library Journal, July 1, 2009, page p119

Other books by the same author:
The Truth About Garden Remedies, 2008
The Truth about Organic Gardening: Benefits, Drawnbacks, and the Bottom Line, 2008

Other books you might like:
James B. Nardi, *Life in the Soil: A Guide for Naturalists and Gardeners*, 2007
David Allen Sibley, *The Sibley Guide to Trees*, 2009
Simon Toomer, *Planting and Maintaining a Tree Collection*, 2010

1102

BEVERLY GLOVER

Understanding Flowers and Flowering: An Intergrated Approach

(New York: Oxford University Press, USA, 2008)

Subject(s): Flowers; Ecology; Evolution (Biology)

Summary: In *Understanding Flowers and Flowering: An Intergrated Approach*, author Beverly Glover provides readers with an in-depth and comprehensive look at the nature and science of flowers. Glover argues that the key to understanding the concept of plant development is understanding why a flower's unique appearance is so important. In examining the science of flowers, Glover

discusses both the molecular genetics and ecology of these beautiful floral forms of life. Readers will learn about the evolution of flowers, the processes that ultimately produce flowers in model plants, the wide range of physical properties of different kinds of flowers, the role of floral biology in the attraction of animals that assist in pollination, and more.

Where it's reviewed:
BioScience, Dec 2008, page p1089

Other books you might like:
David Beerling, *The Emerald Planet: How Plants Changed Earth's History*, 2008
Park S. Nobel, *Physicochemical and Environmental Plant Physiology*, 2009
Michael G. Simpson, *Plant Systematics*, 2005

1103

DONALD F. GLUT

Dinosaurs: The Encyclopedia, Supplement 4

(Jefferson, North Carolina: McFarland & Co., 2006)

Subject(s): Reference works; Dinosaurs; Science

Summary: Author Donald F. Glut offers the fourth installment and updating of his famed 1998 academic volume *Dinosaurs: The Encyclopedia*. Here Glut tackles the scientific findings and dinosaur discoveries made since the publication of the previous installment. This scholarly work is wide-ranging in perspective, examining everything from physical characteristics to the intelligence levels of various dinosaurs. *Dinosaurs: The Encyclopedia, Supplement 4* is presented as a series of alphabetical entries and includes illustrations and a glossary.

Where it's reviewed:
SciTech Book News, March 2004, page p59

Other books you might like:
Phillip J. Currie, *Encyclopedia of Dinosaurs*, 1997
Dougal Dixon, *World Encyclopedia of Dinosaurs and Prehistoric Creatures*, 2008
Chris Marshall, *Dinosaurs*, 2008
Kevin Padlan, *Encyclopedia of Dinosaurs*, 1997

1104

JOHN M. GOODMAN

Space Weather and Telecommunications

(New York: Springer-Verlag, 2010)

Subject(s): Weather; Space exploration; Telecommunications

Summary: *Space Weather and Telecommunications* by John M. Goodman is an educational textbook that details the interdependent relationship between the weather conditions in space and telecommunications technologies. In this text, Goodman examines that relationship and the various components that contribute to such interdependency. The author explores solar activity and the implications that activity has within the ionosphere, and how those implications impact technologies. Goodman also details frequencies of telecommunications and how space weather affects those frequencies. The book provides a technical and scientific as well as a historical perspective on the field of study and subject matter.

Other books you might like:

Jean Lilensten, *Space Weather: Research Towards Applications in Europe*, 2007

Mark Moldwin, *An Introduction to Space Weather*, 2008

1105

ALBERT GORE

Our Choice: A Plan to Solve the Climate Crisis

(Emmaus, Pennsylvania: Rodale, 2009)

Subject(s): Energy conservation; Natural resource conservation; Environmental history

Summary: Al Gore is renowned for his work regarding the world's climate crisis. In 2007, he, along with the UN's Intergovernmental Panel on Climate Change, won the Nobel Peace Prize, and his documentary *An Inconvenient Truth*, which brought the issue of climate change to the forefront, garnered two Academy Awards. With *Our Choice: A Plan to Solve the Climate Crisis*, Gore continues his mission to inform the world about climate change, global warming, and the greenhouse effect. Unlike *An Inconvenient Truth*, however, *Our Choice* focuses more on solutions to correct the problem than on the problem itself. The goal of the book, according to Gore in the "Introduction," is "to depoliticize the issue as much as possible and inspire readers to take action."

Where it's reviewed:

African Business, January 2010, page 64
AudioFile Magazine, April-May 2010, page 49
The National Interest, March-April 2010, page 75
School Library Journal, February 2010, page 131

Other books by the same author:

The Assault on Reason, 2008
Our Purpose: The Nobel Peace Prize Lecture 2007, 2008
An Inconvenient Truth: The Crisis of Global Warming, 2007
Earth in the Balance: Ecology and the Human Spirit, 2006
An Inconvenient Truth: The Planetary Emergency of Global Warming and What We Can Do About It, 2006

Other books you might like:

John Authers, *The Fearful Rise of Markets: Global Bubbles, Synchronized Meltdowns, and How To Prevent Them in the Future*, 2010

James Hansen, *Storms of My Grandchildren: The Truth About the Coming Climate Catastrophe and Our Last Chance to Save Humanity*, 2009

William F. Ruddiman, *Earth's Climate: Past and Future*, 2007

Vaclav Smil, *Energy at the Crossroads: Global Perspectives and Uncertainties*, 2005

Tom Wessels, *The Myth of Progress: Toward a Sustainable Future*, 2006

1106

DAVID F. GRAY

The Observation and Analysis of Stellar Photospheres, Third Edition

(Cambridge, United Kingdom: Cambridge University Press, 2008)

Subject(s): Astronomy; Science; Space exploration

Summary: Astronomer David F. Gray takes readers into the intricate details surrounding stellar photospheres. Stellar physics aficionados are given a comprehensive tour of the latest equipment, modes of observation, and methods of technical analysis. Chapters cover such topics as fourier transforms, spectroscopic tools, radiation terms and definitions, and the behavior of spectral lines. *The Observation and Analysis of Stellar Photospheres, Third Edition*, fully revised and updated, contains six appendices and a full index.

Other books you might like:

Jack Martin, *A Spectroscopic Atlas of Bright Stars: A Pocket Field Guide*, 2009

1107

ALAN GUNN

Essential Forensic Biology: Second Edition

(Hoboken, New Jersey: Wiley, 2009)

Subject(s): Science; Biology; Crime

Summary: *Essential Forensic Biology: Second Edition* is an educational textbook on the use of biology in crime scene investigations from author Alan Gunn. The second edition includes updated information on forensics and the ways that biology is applied to legal investigations, including new coverage of bioterrorism and wildlife forensics. Gunn provides students with an overview of forensic biology, including details on the decay process, the organisms that can be used as evidence in an investigation, and the importance of human fluids and tissues, including blood cells, bloodstain pattern analysis, hair, teeth, bones, and wounds. The book also addresses ethical concerns relating to forensics. *Essential Forensic Biology* includes full-color illustrations, review questions, case studies, and test questions.

Other books you might like:

Bradley J. Adams, *Forensic Anthropology*, 2007

Andrea Baxter, *Forensic Biology: The Science of Trace Evidence in Serious Crimes*, 2011

Angel Carracedo, *Forensic DNA Typing Protocols*, 2010

Caroline Wilkinson, *Forensic Facial Reconstruction*, 2008

Return of the California Condor to the Grand Canyon Region, 2007
James Lawrence Powell, *Grand Canyon: Solving Earth's Grandest Puzzle*, 2006
Dave Thayer, *An Introduction to Grand Canyon Fossils*, 2009
Jonathan Waterman, *Running Dry: A Journey From Source to Sea Down the Colorado River*, 2010

1108

ALAN HALL

The Wild Food Trailguide, New Edition

(Charleston, South Carolina: BookSurge Publishing, 2008)

Subject(s): Botany; Food; Science

Summary: Journalist and wild plant expert Alan Hall offers readers an authoritative manual featuring the most widely available edible plants in North America. *The Wild Food Trailguide, New Edition* profiles more than 80 plants found throughout the continent, all of which can be consumed for both sustenance and deliciousness. Hall also presents identification methods and various preparation styles, including salads, jams, and even desserts. This volume includes an illustrated glossary and an index.

Other books you might like:

Linda Runyon, *The Essential Wild Food Survival Guide*, 2009
Samuel Thayer, *The Forager's Harvest: A Guide to Identifying, Harvesting, and Preparing Edible Wild Plants*, 2006

1109

W. KENNETH HAMBLIN

Anatomy of the Grand Canyon: Panoramas of the Canyon's Geology

(Grand Canyon, Arizona: Grand Canyon Association, 2008)

Subject(s): Geology; Science; Photography

Summary: Written by geologist and author W. Kenneth Hamblin, *Anatomy of the Grand Canyon: Panoramas of the Canyon's Geology* focuses on the geology and beauty of the Grand Canyon. The book provides readers with an in-depth examination of the natural wonder from end to end. Beginning at Lees Ferry and traveling the 277 miles to the Grand Canyon's other edge at the Grand Wash Cliffs, *Anatomy of the Grand Canyon* features panoramic photographs that highlight the various geological aspects of the chasm. Hamblin includes detailed maps, texts, and illustrations to educate readers on the natural formation of the Grand Canyon and give them a visual tour of the Colorado River and the canyon itself.

Other books by the same author:
Introduction to Physical Geology, 1994

Other books you might like:
Arthur J. Gordon, *Geologic Guide to Grand Canyon National Park*, 2010
Sophie A.H. Osborn, *Condors in Canyon Country: The*

1110

SUE L. HAMILTON

DNA Analysis: Forensic Fluids and Follicles

(Edina, Minnesota: ABDO Publishing Company, 2008)

Subject(s): Science; Genetics; Biology

Summary: In *DNA Analysis: Forensic Fluids and Follicles*, Sue Hamilton presents a history of DNA analysis in the field of criminal justice. Written for an intermediate grade audience, this accessible guide covers the discovery of DNA, the first use of DNA evidence in a legal setting, and the application of DNA fingerprinting and profiling. Later chapters explore the legal applications of DNA analysis, from the collection of evidence to the use of DNA in convicting the guilty and exonerating the innocent. The author includes a discussion of the Simpson/Goldman murder case to demonstrate the methods and theories described. Photographs, graphics, and a glossary supplement the text.

Where it's reviewed:
School Library Journal, June 2008, page p161

Other books you might like:
Terry Brown, *Gene Cloning and DNA Analysis*, 2010
Peter Bugert, *DNA and RNA Profiling in Human Blood*, 2008
Brian Innes, *DNA and Body Evidence*, 2007

1111

JAMES RALPH HANSON

Chemistry in the Garden

(Cambridge, United Kingdom: RSC Publishing, 2007)

Subject(s): Chemistry; Ecology; Gardens

Summary: A standard backyard garden is a veritable treasure trove for amateur chemists. In *Chemistry in the Garden*, author James Ralph Hanson celebrates this unique source of scientific inquiry, offering readers with an interest in either gardening or chemistry a hands-on guide to the chemical goings-on of the average garden. Chapters explore such topics as the chemical diversity of plant life, plant biochemistry, and an examination of soil makeup. Hanson also discusses the chemical components of fungi and insects. *Chemistry in the Garden* includes a bibliography, a glossary, and a subject index.

Where it's reviewed:
Chemistry and Industry, March 24, 2008, page p27

Science

Other books you might like:
Brian Capon, *Botany for Gardeners*, 2010
Eric Grissell, *Insects and Gardens: In Pursuit of a Garden Ecology*, 2006
Jeff Lowenfels, *Teaming with Microbes*, 2010
James B. Nardi, *Life in the Soil: A Guide for Naturalists and Gardeners*, 2007
Jessica Walliser, *Good Bug Bad Bug*, 2008

1112

DAVID M. HARLAND

Exploring the Moon: The Apollo Expeditions, Second Edition

(New York: Springer, 2007)

Subject(s): Space exploration; Science; Astronomy

Summary: In *Exploring the Moon: The Apollo Expeditions, Second Edition*, author David M. Harland examines the contributions made by the Apollo astronauts during their series of expeditions to the moon. Harland first focuses on the legendary landing of Apollo 11 and how this landmark event paved the way for future Apollo journeys, which unearthed startling new information about the lunar surface. This special commemorative reissuing features a foreword by one of the Apollo astronauts as well as never-before-seen photographs.

Other books by the same author:
Apollo 12 - On the Ocean of Storms, 2010
How NASA Learned to Fly in Space, 2010
NASA's Moon Program: Paving the Way for Apollo 11, 2009
The First Men on the Moon: The Story of Apollo 11, 2006

Other books you might like:
William David Compton, *Where No Man Has Gone Before: A History of NASA's Apollo Lunar Expeditions*, 2010
Edgar M. Cortright, *Apollo Expeditions to the Moon: The NASA History*, 2009
Robert Godwin, *Project Apollo: Exploring the Moon*, 2008

1113

DANIEL C. HARRIS

Quantitative Chemical Analysis, Eighth Edition

(New York: W. H. Freeman and Company, 2010)

Subject(s): Science; Chemistry; Reference works

Summary: *Quantitative Chemical Analysis, Eighth Edition* is an educational textbook for students on analytic chemistry from author Daniel C. Harris. The book instructs students on the principles of analytic chemistry and how those theories affect chemistry and other fields of study, particularly life sciences and environmental

studies. The book's 29 chapters cover a wide variety of related topics, including laboratory operations, statistics, volumetric and gravimetric analysis, chemical and electrochemical equilibrium, acid- base chemistry, complex formation, electrochemical measurements, spectrophotometry, atomic spectroscopy, chromatography, and sample preparation. Additional resources, such as spreadsheets, test questions, review problems, and supplementary information, are included in the 8th edition.

Other books by the same author:
Exploring Chemical Analysis, 2008

Other books you might like:
George Chapman Caldwell, *Elements of Qualitative and Quantitative Chemical Analysis—1892*, 2009
John Charles Olsen, *A Text-Book of Quantitative Chemical Analysis by Gravimetric, Electrolytic, Volumetric and Gasometric Methods*, 2009
Thomas Bliss Stillman, *Engineering Chemistry: A Manual of Quantitative Chemical Analysis, for the Use of Students, Chemists and Engineers*, 2009
Henry Paul Talbot, *An Introductory Course of Quantitative Chemical Analysis: With Explanatory Notes and Stoichiometrical Problems*, 2010

1114

DANIEL L. HARTL

Essential Genetics: A Genomics Perspective, Fifth Edition

(Sudbury, Massachusetts: Jones and Bartlett Publishers, 2009)

Subject(s): Science; Genetics; Medicine

Summary: In *Essential Genetics: A Genomics Perspective, Fifth Edition*, Daniel L. Hartl updates his introductory text on the field of genetics. Written for the undergraduate student, this volume covers a range of topics pertinent to the genetic mechanism, including the chromosomal basis of heredity, genetic mapping, the structure of DNA, gene expression and regulation, genetic engineering, the genetics of bacteria and viruses, and molecular genetics of the cell cycle and cancer. The fifth edition includes new information on genetic analysis and probability and pathogenicity. Students can access supplemental materials, including self-evaluative tools and activities on the associated website.

Other books by the same author:
Genetics, 2008
Genetics: Analysis of Genes and Genomes, 2001
A Primer of Population Genetics, 2000

Other books you might like:
Robert J. Brooker, *Genetics: Analysis and Principles, Third Edition*, 2008
William D. Fixsen, *Introduction to Genetic Analysis Solutions MegaManual*, 2007
Matthew B. Hamilton, *Population Genetics*, 2009
Ricki Lewis, *Human Genetics: Concepts and Applications*, 2009
Eberhard Passarge, *Color Atlas of Genetics*, 2006

1115

WILLIAM M. HAYNES

CRC Handbook of Chemistry and Physics, 91st Edition

(Boca Raton, Florida: CRC Press, 2010)

Subject(s): Science; Reference works; Chemistry

Summary: Edited by scientist emeritus, Dr. William M. Haynes, *CRC Handbook of Chemistry and Physics, 91st Edition* is a highly esteemed educational textbook on science, chemistry, and physics. A new edition of the authoritative scientific reference guide is published every year to give students and educators the most updated and reliable information on the subject matter. The 91st edition includes an electronic version on CD-ROM and online to give readers a more interactive experience with the content. The 91st edition also includes new tables and updated information on fluid properties, analytical chemistry, polymer properties, molecular structure and spectroscopy, and properties of solids.

Where it's reviewed:
Choice, March 2010, page 1251
Journal of the American Chemical Society, Sept 9, 2009, page 12862

Other books by the same author:
Handbook of Chemistry and Physics, 2006

Other books you might like:
Francis T. Farago, *Handbook of Dimensional Measurement*, 2007
Nouredine Zettili, *Quantum Mechanics: Concepts and Applications, Second Edition*, 2009

1116

J. MARVIN HERNDON

Maverick's Earth and Universe

(Victoria, British Columbia, Canada: Trafford, 2008)

Subject(s): Science; Astronomy; Discovery and exploration

Summary: In *Maverick's Earth and Universe*, author and geophysicist J. Marvin Herndon presents his revolutionary theories on the earth, the galaxy, and the big bang hypothesis. By exposing elemental errors in widely accepted arenas of astrophysics and other areas of science, Herndon offers concrete alternatives to the long-held myths that have captivated scientists for so long. The result is a groundbreaking new perspective on the formation of the earth and stars—and the processes by which such theories were reached. *Maverick's Earth and Universe* includes photos, figures, a bibliography, and an index. First book.

Other books you might like:
Nicolas Cheetham, *Universe: A Journey from Earth to the Edge of the Cosmos*, 2009

Robert Dinwiddie, *Space: From Earth to the Edge of the Universe*, 2010
David A. Weintraub, *How Old Is the Universe?*, 2011

1117

KEVIN HILE

The Handy Weather Answer Book

(Canton, Mississippi: Visible Ink Press, 2009)

Subject(s): Weather; Meteorology; Science

Summary: If you have a question about weather, *The Handy Weather Answer Book* has the answer. Author Kevin Hile presents this useful guide to all things weather and weather-related. Hile touches on a wide variety of weather topics that include everything from modern meteorology technology to unique weather phenomena, oceanography, geology, and space science. He also includes a special section devoted to global warming and the resulting climate change. *The Handy Weather Answer Book* includes over 1,000 weather related questions and answers and is designed to be a practical reference resource for students, teachers, or anyone interested learning about weather.

Where it's reviewed:
Library Journal, Sept 15, 2009, page p83

Other books by the same author:
Dams and Levees, 2007

Other books you might like:
Christopher C. Burt, *Extreme Weather: A Guide and Record Book*, 2007
Randy Cerveny, *Weather's Greatest Mysteries Solved!*, 2009
Jack Williams, *The AMS Weather Book: The Ultimate Guide to America's Weather*, 2009

1118

SHIRL J. HOFFMAN

Introduction to Kinesiology: Studying Physical Activity

(Champaign, Illinois: Human Kinetics, 2009)

Subject(s): Science; Exercise

Summary: In *Introduction to Kinesiology: Studying Physical Activity*, editor Shirl J. Hoffman examines the emerging field of kinesiology—the scientific study of human movement. This volume considers kinesiology beyond its usual applications to physical education. Shirl Hoffman is a professor in the Department of Exercise and Sport Sciences at the University of North Carolina at Greensboro.

Where it's reviewed:
Applied Physiology, Nutrition, and Metabolism, August 2009, page p803

Other books you might like:
Lynn Lippert, *Clinical Kinesiology and Anatomy*, 2006
Joseph E. Muscolino, *Kinesiology: The Skeletal System and Muscle Function*, 2010

Donald A. Neumann, *Kinesiology of the Musculoskeletal System: Foundations for Rehabilitation, Second Edition*, 2009

1119

JAY B. HOLBERG

Sirius: Brightest Diamond in the Night Sky

(New York: Springer, 2007)

Subject(s): Science; Astronomy; Space exploration

Summary: Written by historian and astrophysicist Jay B. Holberg, *Sirius: Brightest Diamond in the Night Sky* is an in-depth study of Sirius, also known as "Dog Star," the brightest fixed star in the sky. The book takes both an astrophysical and a cultural approach in examining the history and importance of Sirius. Throughout history, people created myths and legends about Sirius, many of which Holberg includes in this book. Holberg also provides readers with details surrounding historical studies of Sirius and scientific research discovered about the star. He explains how studies of Sirius have affected the study of stars as a whole and the significance that Sirius has had on a wide variety of cultures and communities, including the ancient Egyptians.

Where it's reviewed:
Choice, September 2007, page 121
Journal for the History of Astronomy, August 2007, page 386
Sky & Telescope, December 2007, page 45

Other books you might like:
Marcia Bartusiak, *Archives of the Universe*, 2006
Noah Brosch, *Sirius Matters*, 2010
Alan Hirshfeld, *Astronomy Activity and Laboratory Manual*, 2008
W.S. Merwin, *The Shadow of Sirius*, 2008
Fred Schaaf, *The 50 Best Sights in Astronomy and How to See Them*, 2007

1120

SUSAN HOUGH

Predicting the Unpredictable: The Tumultuous Science of Earthquake Prediction

(Princeton, New Jersey: Princeton University Press, 2009)

Subject(s): Earthquakes; Natural disasters; Geology

Summary: In *Predicting the Unpredictable: The Tumultuous Science of Earthquake Prediction*, geologist Susan Hough provides a historical as well as scientific perspective on the process of earthquake prediction. Hough looks at the discipline beginning in the 1960s, when geologists still believed that earthquake prediction could be made an exact science, and follows through to the next four decades prior to the book's publication to detail the

realizations made about the science within that time. The author looks at specific disasters and the geological data surrounding those earthquakes, and explains why even with 21st century technology, predicting such geological turbulence is a onerous task.

Where it's reviewed:
American Scientist, March-April 2010 v98 i2, page p160
Choice, July 2010 v47 i11, page p2136
Civil Engineering, Feb 2010 v80 i2, page p80
Nature, Feb 11, 2010 v463 i7282, page p735
Times Higher Education, June 17, 2010, page p52

Other books by the same author:
Richter's Scale: Measure of an Earthquake, Measure of a Man, 2007

Other books you might like:
David S. Brumbaugh, *Earthquakes: Science & Society*, 2009
Earl V. Leary, *Earthquakes: Risk, Monitoring and Research*, 2009
Christopher D. Monahan, *The Big Shake: Implications of a Major Earthquake in California*, 2010
Ragnar Stefansson, *Advances in Earthquake Prediction: Seismic Research and Risk Mitigation*, 2010
Seth Stein, *Disaster Deferred: How New Science Is Changing our View of Earthquake Hazards in the Midwest*, 2010

1121

SUSAN HOUGH

Richter's Scale: Measure of an Earthquake, Measure of a Man

(Princeton, New Jersey: Princeton University Press, 2007)

Subject(s): Science; Earthquakes; Biographies

Summary: Written by seismologist Susan Elizabeth Hough, *Richter's Scale: Measure of an Earthquake, Measure of a Man* is a detailed biography on the life and career of Charles Richter and a history of seismology. Due to his invention of the scale to measure the intensity of earthquakes, Richter has become a household name, but not much is known about his life. Hough presents a comprehensive narrative on the seismologist, relying on his personal papers and interviews with his family, friends, and colleagues. *Richter's Scale* gives readers an insider's glimpse into the life, relationships, upbringing, academic success, and career achievements of Richter, including little-known details about his artistic aspirations, life as a nudist, and unconventional relationship with his wife.

Where it's reviewed:
Choice, August 2007, page 2126
Civil Engineering, May 2007, page 68
Physics Today, January 2008, page 60
Science Books & Films, July-August 2007, page 165
Times Literary Supplement, June 22, 2007, page 25

Other books by the same author:
Finding Fault in California: An Earthquake Tourist's Guide, 2004

Other books you might like:
Jacques Betbeder-Matibet, *Seismic Engineering*, 2007
Charles Davison, *Origin of Earthquakes*, 2009
Cliff Frohlich, *Deep Earthquakes*, 2010
Tienfuan Kerh, *Seismic Data Analysis by Using Computational Intelligence*, 2010
Valentin L. Popov, *Contact Mechanics and Friction: Physical Principles and Applications*, 2010

1122

MICHAEL E. HOUSTON

Biochemistry Primer for Exercise Science, Third Edition

(Champaign, Illinois: Human Kinetics, 2006)

Subject(s): Biology; Chemistry; Exercise

Summary: *Biochemistry Primer for Exercise Science, Third Edition* by Michael E. Houston is intended for advanced undergraduates or graduate students studying biochemistry, nutrition, exercise science, and anatomy and physiology. This text focuses on the understanding of theoretical concepts as well as their practical applications in the field of exercise science. Biochemistry studies are broken down into four concepts including molecular biology, chemistry, metabolism, and transcription regulation. In addition, review questions and answers are provided for each section to assess understanding. This new edition includes sections on oxidative stress, signal transduction, bioenergetics and energy systems and explains how this applies to exercise science. Considerations for future research in the field are also included.

Where it's reviewed:
Applied Physiology, Nutrition, and Metabolism, Feb 2007, page p155

Other books you might like:
Nessar Ahmed, *Clinical Biochemistry*, 2011
Donald MacLean, *Biochemistry for Sport and Exercise Science*, 2011
Vassilis Mougios, *Exercise Biochemistry*, 2006
David Sheehan, *Physical Biochemistry: Principles and Applications*, 2009
R. Bruce Wilcox, *High-Yield Biochemistry*, 2009

1123

LAWRENCE HUNTER

The Processes of Life: An Introduction to Molecular Biology

(Cambridge, Massachusetts: MIT Press, 2009)

Subject(s): Biology; Education; Science

Summary: Written by Lawrence Hunter, *The Processes of*

Life: An Introduction to Molecular Biology is an educational textbook for students and professionals that explains how living organisms function. The book provides an introductory overview on molecular biology, covering the basics of the complex field. Hunter begins with a brief history on molecular biology and an explanation of the diversity of living creatures. *The Processes of Life* then moves on to explain evolutionary theory, biochemistry, universal life processes, molecular structures of living things, the role of proteins and nucleic acids in life, structures and processes in eukaryotes, multicellular organisms, the anatomy and physiology of animals, human disease and treatment, biotechnology, and bioethics.

Where it's reviewed:
Choice, June 2009, page 1959
JAMA, The Journal of the American Medical Association, July 1, 2009, page 94

Other books by the same author:
Artificial Intelligence and Molecular Biology, 1993

Other books you might like:
Bruce Alberts, *Molecular Biology of the Cell*, 2007
Lizabeth Ann Allison, *Fundamental Molecular Biology*, 2007
David P. Clark, *Molecular Biology*, 2009
Gerald Karp, *Cell and Molecular Biology*, 2007
Robert Franklin Weaver, *Molecular Biology*, 2007

1124

DON IHDE

Listening and Voice: Phenomenologies of Sound, Second Edition

(Albany: State University of New York Press, 2007)

Subject(s): Science; Philosophy; Music

Summary: In 1976, philosophy professor Don Ihde published his trailblazing volume *Listening and Voice: Phenomenologies of Sound*. This revised and updated edition expands upon the facts, findings, and theories of that original work, encompassing up-to-date data and further information on the topic. Ihde explores the role of sound from such perspectives as language, music, and religious practice, bringing clarity to the powerful role of sound in the human auditory experience. *Listening and Voice: Phenomenologies of Sound, Second Edition* includes a bibliography, an index, and a new introduction by the author.

Where it's reviewed:
Choice, May 2008, page p1552

Other books by the same author:
Embodied Technics, 2010
Ironic Technics, 2008

Other books you might like:
Karin Bijsterveld, *Mechanical Sound: Technology, Culture, and Public Problems of Noise in the Twentieth Century*, 2008
Jean-Luc Nancy, *Listening*, 2007

Science

George Prochnik, *In Pursuit of Silence: Listening for Meaning in a World of Noise*, 2010

1125

MIKE INGLIS

Astrophysics is Easy!: An Introduction for the Amateur Astronomer

(London: Springer, 2007)

Subject(s): Astronomy; Physics; Science

Summary: *Astrophysics is Easy!: An Introduction for the Amateur Astronomer* by Mike Inglis is a concise guide for astronomers who enjoy viewing the night sky and wish to learn more about the science behind what they are seeing. Rather than presenting daunting mathematical concepts, Inglis explains the basic tenets of astrophysics in a narrative manner. He discusses topics such as the interstellar medium stars, different types of galaxies, and Hubble's law, among others. He provides a number of examples for various concepts that amateur astronomers can go outside and observe for themselves in the night sky using non-professional equipment. Illustrations and photographs are also included in this text.

Where it's reviewed:
Choice, February 2008, page 1000

Other books by the same author:
Astronomy of the Milky Way, 2004
Observer's Guide to Stellar Evolution, 2003
Field Guide to Deep-Sky Objects, 2001

Other books you might like:
Hale Bradt, *Astrophysics Processes*, 2008
Judith A. Irwin, *Astrophysics: Decoding the Cosmos*, 2007
Francis LeBlanc, *An Introduction to Stellar Astrophysics*, 2010
Dan Maoz, *Astrophysics in a Nutshell*, 2007
Steven L. Weinberg, *Cosmology*, 2008

1126

IRA J. KALET

Principles of Biomedical Informatics

(Amsterdam; Boston: Academic Press/Elsevier, 2008)

Subject(s): Information science; Medicine; Science

Summary: Biomedical informatics is the practice of utilizing, storing, and retrieving information regarding pertinent biomedical data. In *Principles of Biomedical Informatics*, author Ira J. Kalet explains this process as it relates to biology, scientific medicine, and public health. Kalet examines the subject through studies of information access, data demonstration, and decision-making as they cooperate with various practices of biomedical informatics. This volume includes an appendix, a

bibliography, and a full index. First book.

Where it's reviewed:
Journal of Biomedical Science, May 2008, page p317

Other books you might like:
Vadim Astakhov, *Biomedical Informatics*, 2009
Francisco Azuaje, *Bioinformatics and Biomarker Discovery*, 2010
Athina Lazakidou, *Biocomputation and Biomedical Informatics: Case Studies and Applications*, 2009

1127

KUNIHIKO KANEKO

Life: An Introduction to Complex Systems Biology

(New York: Springer, 2010)

Subject(s): Science; Biology; Reference works

Summary: Written by Kunihiko Kaneko, *Life: An Introduction to Complex Systems Biology* is an academic textbook for college students on the science of living systems. The book challenges the traditional theories and principles of molecular biology to explain the universal nature of all living systems and how living organisms should be studied. Kaneko identifies the commonalities between living systems in an effort to understand the phenomena responsible for evolution, differentiation, and the development of complex processes like reproductive cellular systems. Designed for non-scientists and students from various fields, *Life* presents information in a clear, concise, and straightforward manner, avoiding an abundance of technical jargon.

Where it's reviewed:
Choice, March 2007 v44 i7, page p1192

Other books you might like:
Pierre Pontarotti, *Evolutionary Biology: Concept, Modeling, and Application*, 2009

1128

GLENN F. KNOLL

Radiation Detection and Measurement: 4th Edition

(Hoboken, New Jersey: Wiley, 2010)

Subject(s): Science; Reference works; Nuclear physics

Summary: Written by Glenn F. Knoll, *Radiation Detection and Measurement: 4th Edition* is a comprehensive guide on the various processes and technologies used to detect ionizing radiation. The book, now in its 4th edition, serves as a resource guide for both engineers and college students alike. The reference work begins with a basic overview of radiation detection before providing detailed information on modern applications, radiation interactions, technological advancements, error predictions, and the various methods and tools used to detect and measure radiation. The 4th edition includes updated information on ROC curves, micropattern gas detectors, scintillation light sensors, the excess noise factor, cryogenic spectrometers, and the VME standard.

Other books you might like:

Syed Naeem Ahmed, *Physics and Engineering of Radiation Detection*, 2007

Gul Asiye Aycik, *New Techniques for the Detection of Nuclear and Radioactive Agents*, 2009

K. Muraleedhara Varier, *Nuclear Radiation Detection: Measurements and Analysis*, 2009

1129

ELIZABETH KOLBERT

Field Notes from a Catastrophe: Man, Nature, and Climate Change

(London: Bloomsbury Publishing PLC, 2006)

Subject(s): Environmental history; Ecology; Science

Summary: In *Field Notes from a Catastrophe: Man, Nature, and Climate Change*, journalist and author Elizabeth Kolbert compiles research from scientists around the world who are studying the effects of climate change to assess the severity of the situation. She contends that within in the United States, scientists are either working on projects to improve environmental conditions or preparing to deal with the consequences of what has already been set in motion. The book chronicles the follies of governments, such as the United States, that she believes have not taken the effects of global warming seriously enough and urges them to act now.

Where it's reviewed:
Choice, December 2006, page 680
Planning, August-Sept 2007, page 63

Other books by the same author:
The Arctic - An Anthology, 2008

Other books you might like:

Van Jones, *The Green Collar Economy: How One Solution Can Fix Our Two Biggest Problems*, 2008

Laura Lee, *Blame It on the Rain: How the Weather Has Changed History*, 2006

Bill McKibben, *The End of Nature*, 2006

Heather Rogers, *Gone Tomorrow: The Hidden Life of Garbage*, 2005

William F. Ruddiman, *Plows, Plagues, and Petroleum*, 2010

1130

MANJIT KUMAR

Quantum: Einstein, Bohr, and the Great Debate about the Nature of Reality

(New York: Fourth Estate, 2007)

Subject(s): Biographies; Science; Technology

Summary: In *Quantum: Einstein, Bohr, and the Great Debate about the Nature of Reality*, science journalist

---

Manjit Kumar chronicles the revolutionary contest of the early 1900s between the world's most respected physicists and their conflicting theories. After the discovery of quanta by Max Planck in 1900, Niels Bohr used these particles—tiny parcels of electromagnetic radiation and light energy—to explain the behavior of electrons. But Bohr's resultant theory of quantum mechanics was soundly disputed by another physics giant—Albert Einstein. In recounting this ground-breaking debate, Kumar reveals an exciting era of scientific discovery that changed man's understanding of reality. Includes 16 pages of photos.

Other books you might like:
Florian Scheck, *Quantum Physics*, 2007

1131

KENNETH R. LANG

The Cambridge Guide to the Solar System: 2nd Edition

(Cambridge, England: Cambridge University Press, 2010)

Subject(s): Science; Space exploration; Astronomy

Summary: *The Cambridge Guide to the Solar System: 2nd Edition* is a comprehensive guide to the sun, moon, planets, and stars from author and astronomy professor, Kenneth R. Lang. The book serves as an academic textbook and solar system encyclopedia, providing readers with in-depth knowledge of the history and science surrounding outer space. Lang begins by providing a detailed background on the solar system, as well as an overview of the recent scientific findings and understanding. The book then focuses on individual topics, including the moon, Earth, the other planets and their moons, and asteroids and comets. Filled with vivid illustrations and photographs, *The Cambridge Guide to the Solar System* is an authoritative guide on outer space.

Where it's reviewed:
Booklist, May 15, 2004 v100 i18, page p1652
Library Journal, April 1, 2004 v129 i6, page p86

Other books by the same author:
The Sun from Space, 2008
Sun, Earth and Sky, 2006

Other books you might like:
Michael Benson, *Beyond: A Solar System Voyage*, 2009
Michael A. Seeds, *The Solar System*, 2010
Giles Sparrow, *The Planets: A Journey Through the Solar System*, 2009

1132

KENNETH R. LANG

The Sun from Space

(New York: Springer, 2008)

Subject(s): Science; Space exploration; Astronomy

Summary: Written by Kenneth R. Lang, *The Sun from Space* is a comprehensive examination of the sun's 11-

year cycle of magnetic activity, as documented by nine solar missions. Lang begins with a historical overview of previous solar studies and an explanation of the scientific purposes of the nine missions before discussing the advances that have been made in studying the sun. The information included in *The Sun from Space* was collected by three solar spacecraft: SOHO, Ulysses, and Yohkoh. Lang relays the findings of the nine solar missions, including details on the solar interior, the solar corona, which is the sun's outer atmosphere where the temperature reaches a million degrees, solar winds, explanations regarding solar flares, and the space-weather relationship between the sun and the earth.

Where it's reviewed:
Choice, June 2009, page 1957

Other books by the same author:
A Companion to Astronomy and Astrophysics: Chronology and Glossary with Data Tables, 2006
Parting the Cosmic Veil, 2006
Sun, Earth and Sky, 2006
The Cambridge Guide to the Solar System, 2003
The Cambridge Encyclopedia of the Sun, 2001

Other books you might like:
David R. Brooks, *Bringing the Sun Down to Earth: Designing Inexpensive Instruments for Monitoring the Atmosphere*, 2010
Stephen Eales, *Planets and Planetary Systems*, 2009
Jamey L. Jenkins, *The Sun and How to Observe It*, 2009
Dermott J. Mullan, *Physics of the Sun*, 2009
Claudio Vita-Finzi, *The Sun: A User's Manual*, 2010

1133

ERVIN LASZLO

Quantum Shift in the Global Brain

(Rochester, Vermont: Inner Traditions, 2008)

Subject(s): Science; Prophecy; Futuristic society

Summary: Written by *World Futures* editor Ervin Laszlo, *Quantum Shift in the Global Brain* is a prophetic book about the imminent changes happening around the world. According to Laszlo, the world is in the midst of a Macroshift, a major change that's altering everyone's view of reality. With growing global organizations and a barrage of new issues, ranging from global warming to industrialized agriculture, the globe is in the process of shifting to a completely new reality. Laszlo examines these global shifts and encourages readers to change as quickly as the world around them to survive. The book presents a "map" for readers to navigate through the new reality and world around them.

Where it's reviewed:
Perspectives on Science and Christian Faith, March 2009, page 50

Other books by the same author:
You Can Change the World: The Global Citizen's Handbook for Living on Planet Earth, 2010
The Akashic Experience: Science and the Cosmic Memory Field, 2009

The Connectivity Hypothesis, 2003
The Systems View of the World, 1996

Other books you might like:
Linda Howe, *How to Read the Akashic Records: Accessing the Archive of the Soul and Its Journey*, 2009
Ervin Laszlo, *The Akashic Experience: Science and the Cosmic Memory Field*, 2009
Lynne McTaggart, *The Intention Experiment*, 2008
Dean Radin, *Entangled Minds: Extrasensory Experiences in a Quantum Reality*, 2006
Rupert Sheldrake, *Morphic Resonance: The Nature of Formative Causation*, 2009

1134

ERIC LAX

The Mold in Dr. Florey's Coat: The Story of the Penicillin Miracle

(New York: H. Holt, 2004)

Subject(s): Medicine; Medical care; Science

Summary: Penicillin is one of the most widely used drugs in the world, treating a number of otherwise deadly illnesses each year. In *The Mold in Dr. Florey's Coat: The Story of the Penicillin Miracle*, author Eric Lax explores the history behind this remarkable medical discovery. Scottish scientist Alexander Fleming discovered penicillin in 1928, but it took Oxford researchers Howard Florey, Ernst Chain, and Norman Heatley more than ten years to develop the antibiotic used today. The collaborative efforts of these men brought relief to sufferers of pneumonia, gonorrhea, and scarlet fever. Interestingly, none of these scientists ever received compensation for their brilliant work. Lax follows the scientists' tale, explaining how the pressures of drug development affected each man.

Where it's reviewed:
Booklist, Jan 1, 2005, page p767
Discover, Jan 2005, page p82

Other books you might like:
Paul A. Offit, *Vaccinated: One Man's Quest to Defeat the World's Deadliest Diseases*, 2007

1135

LAURA LEE

Blame It on the Rain: How the Weather Has Changed History

(New York: Harper, 2006)

Subject(s): Weather; Culture; History

Summary: Weather conditions have had a profound effect on countless key events in the history of humankind. In *Blame It on the Rain: How the Weather Has Changed History*, author Laura Lee presents a series of essays examining the impact weather has had on history and culture throughout the world. From the flood that inspired Noah to build an ark to the election of Harry Truman as president, this volume captures the randomness, drama, and even the humor of changes in the atmosphere. *Blame It on the Rain* contains a listing of bibliographical references.

Where it's reviewed:
Choice, May 2007, page p1568
Kirkus Reviews, May 15, 2006, page p507
Publishers Weekly, June 19, 2006, page p55
Science News, August 12, 2006, page p111

Other books you might like:
Elizabeth Kolbert, *Field Notes from a Catastrophe: Man, Nature, and Climate Change*, 2006
Eugene Linden, *The Winds of Change: Climate, Weather, and the Destruction of Civilizations*, 2007
Spencer Weart, *The Discovery of Global Warming: (New Histories of Science, Technology, and Medicine)*, 2003

1136

TREVOR LETCHER

Climate Change: Observed Impacts on Planet Earth

(Oxford, United Kingdom: Elsevier Science, 2009)

Subject(s): Ecology; Environmental history; Natural resource conservation

Summary: *Climate Change: Observed Impacts on Planet Earth* is an educational perspective on global climate shifts and the perceived consequences of those shifts. More than 30 contributors give data and information on the global changes, from the history of the issue to its stance from a 21st century perspective. Authorities on the subject matter delve beyond the hot button issues of human environmental impact to reveal other contributing factors such as natural changes in the environment. The book also includes 30 full-color photographs of global climate phenomena.

Where it's reviewed:
Chemistry International, Sept-Oct 2009, page p21
Choice, Dec 2009, page p713

Other books by the same author:
Future Energy: Improved, Sustainable and Clean Options for our Planet, 2008
Developments and Applications in Solubility, 2007
Thermodynamics, Solubility and Environmental Issues, 2007

Other books you might like:
Arnold J. Bloom, *Global Climate Change: Convergence of Disciplines*, 2009
William James Burroughs, *Climate Change: A Multidisciplinary Approach, 2nd Edition*, 2007
Mike Hulme, *Why We Disagree About Climate Change: Understanding Controversy, Inaction and Opportunity*, 2009

1137

DANIEL J. LEVITIN

This Is Your Brain on Music: The Science of a Human Obsession

(New York: Plume/Penguin, 2006)

Subject(s): Music; Science

Summary: Author Daniel J. Levitin, a musician turned cognitive neuroscientist, takes readers on a journey showing how music affects both the emotional and physiological responses of the human body in *This Is Your Brain on Music*. He illustrates these findings via brain imaging and easy-to-understand terminology describing how the brain is stimulated by music.

Where it's reviewed:
Book World, Sept 16, 2007, page p12
Books In Canada, Nov 2007, page p11
Guitar Player, April 2007, page p69
Technical Communication, August 2007, page p373
University of Toronto Quarterly, Winter 2009, page p160-161

Other books by the same author:
Foundations of Cognitive Psychology: Core Readings, 2010
The World in Six Songs: How the Musical Brain Created Human Nature, 2008

Other books you might like:
Philip Ball, *The Music Instinct: How Music Works and Why We Can't Do Without It*, 2010
Aniruddh D. Patel, *Music, Language, and the Brain*, 2007
Oliver Sacks, *Musicophilia: Tales of Music and the Brain*, 2007
Michael Thaut, *Rhythm, Music, and the Brain: Scientific Foundations and Clinical Applications*, 2007
William Forde Thompson, *Music, Thought, and Feeling: Understanding the Psychology of Music*, 2008

1138

DAVID H. LEVY

David Levy's Guide to Observing Meteor Showers

(Cambridge; New York: Cambridge University Press, 2007)

Subject(s): Astronomy; Science; Reference works

Summary: *David Levy's Guide to Observing Meteor Showers* is an accessible guide written by David H. Levy for anyone interested in viewing meteors and meteor showers from their own backyards. Levy states that meteors can be seen in the night sky every night of the year when a clear viewing field is available. People can view these meteors even before it is completely dark outside, often without the aid of a telescope. Levy explains basic science using common terminology, but stays away from difficult concepts, preferring instead to focus on the basic

Science

steps for viewing and enjoying meteor showers. The author's excitement and enthusiasm for the topic is evident throughout the text.

Where it's reviewed:
Choice, Jan 2009, page p926
Sky & Telescope, May 2009, page p40

Other books by the same author:
David Levy's Guide to Eclipses, Transits, and Occultations, 2010
Star Trails: 50 Favorite Columns from Sky & Telescope, 2007
David Levy's Guide to Variable Stars, 2006
Shoemaker by Levy: The Man Who Made an Impact, 2002
David Levy's Guide to the Night Sky, 2001

Other books you might like:
Martin Beech, *Meteors and Meteorites: Origins and Observations*, 2006
F. S. Kim, *Meteor Showers*, 2009
Charles P. Olivier, *Meteors*, 2007
Fred Schaaf, *The 50 Best Sights in Astronomy and How to See Them*, 2007

1139

RICHARD LI

Forensic Biology: Identification and DNA Analysis of Biological Evidence

(Boca Raton, Florida: CRC Press, 2008)

Subject(s): Biology; Science; Reference works

Summary: *Forensic Biology: Identification and DNA Analysis of Biological Evidence* by Richard Li is a textbook intended for students of forensic biology. The author first provides a general background of the most important scientific principles used in this field, and then focuses on application of these principles when examining biological evidence. The text is divided into two sections. The first is focused on identification techniques for blood, semen, and saliva, and the different types of tests that may be used to confirm the presence of DNA evidence. The second section focuses on methods of individualizing evidence through forensic DNA analysis techniques. Comprehensive explanations for "extraction methods, quantization methods, DNA profiling analysis, and interpretation of results" are included, as well as study questions and a reference guide for each chapter.

Other books you might like:
Terry Brown, *Gene Cloning and DNA Analysis*, 2010
Peter Bugert, *DNA and RNA Profiling in Human Blood*, 2008
Alan Gunn, *Essential Forensic Biology: Second Edition*, 2009
Brian Innes, *DNA and Body Evidence*, 2007
J. Thomas McClintock, *Forensic DNA Analysis: A Laboratory Manual*, 2008

1140

EUGENE LINDEN

The Winds of Change: Climate, Weather, and the Destruction of Civilizations

(New York: Simon & Schuster Paperbacks, 2007)

Subject(s): Science; Weather; Meteorology

Summary: In *The Winds of Change: Climate, Weather, and the Destruction of Civilizations*, environmental writer Eugene Linden examines the historical relationship between humans and the forces of the weather. The author considers a range of meteorological events and the effect they had on civilization, including the "Little Ice Age" of the 1300s that obliterated Norse settlements in Greenland, the el nino of the late 19th century that precipitated devastating droughts, and Hurricane Katrina, which brought enormous loss of life and property to the American Gulf coast. As Linden asserts, global warming and climate change have begun and their impact on the modern world has yet to be seen.

Where it's reviewed:
Journal of College Science Teaching, May-June 2007, page p74
Science News, Sept 22, 2007, page p191

Other books by the same author:
The Ragged Edge of the World, 2011

Other books you might like:
Peter Bunyard, *Extreme Weather: The Cataclysmic Effects of Climate Change*, 2006
Laura Lee, *Blame It on the Rain: How the Weather Has Changed History*, 2006
Mark Lynas, *Six Degrees: Our Future on a Hotter Planet*, 2008
Bill McKibben, *The End of Nature*, 2006
William F. Ruddiman, *Plows, Plagues, and Petroleum*, 2010

1141

GERALD LITWACK

Human Biochemistry and Disease

(Amsterdam; Boston: Elsevier, 2008)

Subject(s): Diseases; Medicine; Science

Summary: In *Human Biochemistry and Disease*, Dr. Gerald Litwack guides students through the inner workings of human biochemistry. Aimed at students who have no formal training in the subject, this volume approaches biochemistry through in-depth profiles of proteins, amino acids, carbohydrates, lipids, nucleic acids, hormones, and much more. Litwack also explains biochemistry by showing its role in certain medical conditions. *Human Biochemistry and Disease* includes three appendices, a glossary, and an index. First book.

Where it's reviewed:
Biochemistry (Moscow), Nov 2008, page p1269

Other books you might like:
Florian Lang, *Encyclopedia of Molecular Mechanisms of Disease*, 2009
Heinz-Peter Nasheuer, *Genome Stability and Human Diseases*, 2009

1142

MALCOLM S. LONGAIR

Galaxy Formation

(New York: Springer-Verlag, 2008)

Subject(s): Astronomy; Science; Physics

Summary: *Galaxy Formation* by Malcolm S. Longair, is the second edition of a textbook that examines the creation of the galaxy. The first edition was published in 1998; this new edition includes updated information about astrophysics, classic views of cosmology, and the Universe's beginnings. The author is a British physicist who served as the Jacksonian Professor of Natural Philosophy at Cambridge University's Cavendish Laboratory from 1991 until 2008, at the time that both the first and second edition of these books were published. Longair is also the author of *The Cosmic Century: A History of Astrophysics and Cosmology* and *High Energy Astrophysics*.

Where it's reviewed:
Choice, June 2008, page 1791

Other books by the same author:
High Energy Astrophysics, 2011
The Cosmic Century: A History of Astrophysics and Cosmology, 2006
The Cosmic Century: A History of Astrophysics and Cosmology, 2006
Theoretical Concepts in Physics: An Alternative View of Theoretical Reasoning in Physics, 2003
Our Evolving Universe, 1997

Other books you might like:
Immo Appenzeller, *High-Redshift Galaxies: Light from the Early Universe*, 2009
F. Combes, *Mysteries of Galaxy Formation*, 2010
William C. Keel, *The Road to Galaxy Formation*, 2010
Ian Ridpath, *Stars and Planets: The Most Complete Guide to the Stars, Planets, Galaxies, and the Solar System*, 2008
Hyron Spinrad, *Galaxy Formation and Evolution*, 2010

1143

AMY LUNDEBREK

Under the Night Sky

(Gardiner, Maine: Tilbury House, 2009)

Story type: Young Readers
Subject(s): Astronomy; Mother-son relations; Family

Summary: Written by Amy Lundebrek and illustrated by Anna Rich, *Under the Night Sky* is a picture story for young readers. In the story, a young boy is getting ready to go to bed when his mother gets home from work. She tells him to get up and get dressed to go outside. At first he is confused and worried, but then he sees his neighbors outside as well. Soon, both families gather on top of their cars to watch the aurora borealis, or northern lights. He can't believe how beautiful the graceful lights in the sky are, as they twist and spin. At the same time, his mother tells him that she will always be there for him, even when they disagree about things.

Where it's reviewed:
Library Media Connection, Jan-Feb 2009, page p66

Other books you might like:
Robert Buchheim, *The Sky is Your Laboratory*, 2007
Mark A. Garlick, *Astronomy: A Visual Guide*, 2004
Jacqueline Mitton, *Cambridge Illustrated Dictionary of Astronomy*, 2008
Dinah L. Moche, *Astronomy*, 2009
Ian Ridpath, *Stars and Planets: The Most Complete Guide to the Stars, Planets, Galaxies, and the Solar System*, 2008

1144

ROBERT LUNSFORD

Meteors and How to Observe Them

(New York: Springer, 2009)

Subject(s): Science; Astronomy; Space exploration

Summary: Author and expert Robert Lunsford offers readers a practical guide to viewing and understanding meteors. *Meters and How to Observe Them* discusses the best ways to view these celestial objects, no matter where on Earth an observer may be located. Filled with hands-on advice and an insider's tricks of the trade, this volume contains photographs and a calendar of annual meteor showers. Also included is a listing of bibliographical references and a full index.

Where it's reviewed:
Science News, Sept 2007, page p205

Other books you might like:
Brian Cudnik, *Lunar Meteoroid Impacts and How to Observe Them*, 2009
David H. Levy, *David Levy's Guide to Observing Meteor Showers*, 2007
Charles P. Olivier, *Meteors*, 2007

1145

DOUG MACDOUGALL

Nature's Clocks: How Scientists Measure the Age of Almost Everything

(Los Angeles: University of California Press, 2009)

Subject(s): Earth; Geology; Science

Summary: In *Nature's Clocks: How Scientists Measure the Age of Almost Everything.* author Doug Macdougall

Science

examines how scientists and researchers employ various methods to determine the age and date of artifacts. Macdougall explores the process of carbon dating, which he explains is only effective for carbon-based life forms newer than 50,000 years, but also introduces readers to other dating forms. For example, certain types of artifacts can be accurately dated through potassium-argon dating, while others are dated through other radiometric dating systems. The book includes black and white photographs, illustrations, and mapping to supplement the author's work.

Where it's reviewed:
Book World, Sept 7, 2008 v38 i36, page p9
Choice, Nov 2008 v46 i3, page p545
Civil Engineering, Oct 2008 v78 i10, page p76
Isis, Sept 2009 v100 i3, page p674
Library Journal, July 1, 2008, page p104

Other books by the same author:
Why Geology Matters: Decoding the Past, Anticipating the Future, 2011
Frozen Earth: The Once and Future Story of Ice Ages, 2006

Other books you might like:
Hugh MacMillan, *The Clock Of Nature*, 2007
M.Paul Smith, *Telling the Evolutionary Time: Molecular Clocks and the Fossil Record*, 2007

1146

LOIS N. MAGNER

A History of Infectious Diseases and the Microbial World

(Westport, Connecticut: Praeger, 2009)

Story type: Historical
Subject(s): Science; Diseases; Medical care

Summary: Written by professor and author Lois N. Magner, *A History of Infectious Diseases and the Microbial World* is a detailed overview of the background and impact of major infectious diseases. The book is part of the Healing Society: Disease, Medicine, and History series. Magner analyzes the spread of infectious diseases throughout history, including malaria, leprosy, bubonic plague, tuberculosis, syphilis, diphtheria, cholera, yellow fever, poliomyelitis, HIV/AIDS, and influenza. She examines the causes of the illnesses, their transmission, and their profound impact on different populations. The book also explores the methods developed to treat, prevent, and control the diseases.

Where it's reviewed:
Choice, October 2009, page 344

Other books by the same author:
A History of Medicine, 2005

Other books you might like:
Mark S. Dworkin, *Outbreak Investigations Around the World: Case Studies in Infectious Disease Field Epidemiology*, 2009
Richard L. Kradin, *Diagnostic Pathology of Infectious Disease*, 2010

David Schlossberg, *Clinical Infectious Disease*, 2008
Frederick Southwick, *Infectious Diseases*, 2007

1147

DAN MAOZ

Astrophysics in a Nutshell

(Princeton, New Jersey: Princeton University Press, 2007)

Subject(s): Astronomy; Physics; Reference works

Summary: Dan Maoz's *Astrophysics in a Nutshell* is a concise yet very comprehensive volume for advanced undergraduate students of astronomy. The author is able to strike a balance between observation and theoretical concepts. Mathematical concepts discussed in this text are simple and straightforward. Discussions of observations from the most current research in the field, such as research into black holes and dark energy are also included, as well as standard discussions of galaxies and stellar remnants and life cycles. Charts and diagrams are also provided for further explanation of challenging concepts. This text is recommended for students with a background in physics.

Where it's reviewed:
Choice, Oct 2007, page p305

Other books you might like:
Hale Bradt, *Astrophysics Processes*, 2008
Judith A. Irwin, *Astrophysics: Decoding the Cosmos*, 2007
K. Maria D. Lane, *Geographies of Mars: Seeing and Knowing the Red Planet*, 2011
Francis LeBlanc, *An Introduction to Stellar Astrophysics*, 2010
Steven L. Weinberg, *Cosmology*, 2008

1148

BERNARD MARCUS

Tropical Forests

(Sudbury, Massachusetts: Jones & Bartlett Publishers, 2008)

Subject(s): Rain forests; Ecology; Biology

Summary: Author Bernard Marcus' *Tropical Forests* is a simple guide to tropical forests, one of the many different types of biomes found here on Earth. Designed to serve as supplemental reading for those enrolled in beginning environmental science, biology, and ecology classes, *Tropical Forests* offers a basic, yet complete overview of tropical forest ecosystems and their unique climates, weather, geology, and plant and animal life. With its information presented in an evolutionary context and accompanied by numerous illustrations and diagrams, *Tropical Forests* makes learning about tropical forests informative and entertaining for students or any other readers interested in the life sciences.

Other books by the same author:
Evolution That Anyone Can Understand, 2011

Other books you might like:
N. Myers, *Tropical Forests and Climate*, 2010
K. S. S. Nair, *Tropical Forest Insect Pests: Ecology, Impact, and Management*, 2007
Lars H. Schmidt, *Tropical Forest Seed*, 2007
John Sessions, *Forest Road Operations in the Tropics*, 2010
Ian Mark Turner, *The Ecology of Trees in the Tropical Rain Forest*, 2008

1149

JAMES D. MAUSETH

Botany: An Introduction to Plant Biology

(Sudbury, Massachusetts: Jones & Bartlett Publishers, 2008)

Subject(s): Botany; Biology; Genetics

Summary: *Botany: An Introduction to Plant Biology*, by author James D. Mauseth, provides a comprehensive overview of the basic elements of botany. Uniquely, Mauseth organizes his chapters in order of difficulty, beginning with the simplest and most familiar topics and moving progressively through the more difficult and least familiar ones. He covers everything from basic plant structures to plant metabolisms, evolution, genetics, ecology, and more. Mauseth writes with a strong emphasis on natural selection, consistently demonstrating the importance of this concept to all forms of plant life. Students and teacher alike will find *Botany: An Introduction to Plant Biology* to be a useful and educational classroom tool.

Other books by the same author:
Plant Anatomy, 2008

Other books you might like:
H. S. Chawla, *Introduction to Plant Biotechnology*, 2009
Park S. Nobel, *Physicochemical and Environmental Plant Physiology*, 2009
Keith Roberts, *Handbook of Plant Science*, 2008
Michael G. Simpson, *Plant Systematics*, 2005

1150

JAMES CLERK MAXWELL

Matter and Motion

(Amherst, New York: Prometheus Books, 2010)

Subject(s): Physics; Mathematics; Science

Summary: Written by legendary and pioneering physician and mathematician, James Clerk Maxwell, *Matter and Motion* is a guide to the basic principles and theories of physics. The book was first published in 1888 following the death of Maxwell, the first Cavendish Professor of Physics at Cambridge University. Maxwell relies on Sir Isaac Newton's theories to explain the properties of mass, motion, and energy. *Mass and Motion* gives readers a comprehensive overview and basic understanding of the

mathematical and physical principles behind common processes and reactions such as force, energy, gravitational pull, and the center mass of a material.

Where it's reviewed:
SciTech Book News, March 2003 v27, page p43

Other books by the same author:
An Elementary Treatise on Electricity, 2010

Other books you might like:
Desmond Ayim-Aboagye, *Matter Man and Motion: Scientific Theories on Modern Man and Adaptation*, 2008
Robert M. Mazo, *Brownian Motion: Fluctuations, Dynamics, and Applications*, 2009
Ubbo F. Wiersema, *Brownian Motion Calculus*, 2008

1151

J. THOMAS MCCLINTOCK

Forensic DNA Analysis: A Laboratory Manual

(Boca Raton: CRC Press, 2008)

Subject(s): Science; Genetics; Medicine

Summary: Modern criminal investigations have been transformed by the use of forensics. In *Forensic DNA Analysis: A Laboratory Manual*, author J. Thomas McClintock presents a trove of hands-on information vital to any expert working in the field. In addition to a thorough background on criminal forensics, this volume includes a detailed overview of DNA analysis and how to properly work with scientific findings to solve crimes. McClintock also includes a series of exercises aimed to challenge students and more fully illustrate the complexities of this fascinating subject. *Forensic DNA Analysis* contains a bibliography and an index. First book.

Where it's reviewed:
Journal of Forensic Sciences, Sept 2008, page p1238

Other books you might like:
John M. Butler, *Fundamentals of Forensic DNA Typing*, 2009
Sue L. Hamilton, *DNA Analysis: Forensic Fluids and Follicles*, 2008
Brian Innes, *DNA and Body Evidence*, 2007
Richard Li, *Forensic Biology: Identification and DNA Analysis of Biological Evidence*, 2008

1152

BRENDA C. MCCOMB

Wildlife Habitat Management: Concepts and Applications in Forestry

(Boca Raton, Florida: CRC Press, 2007)

Subject(s): Nature; Forestry; Wildlife conservation

Summary: *Wildlife Habitat Management: Concepts and Applications in Forestry* by Brenda C. McComb is a textbook based on the relatively new concepts of conservation biology, in which economic goals in forestry need to be considered alongside ecological goals and consideration for habitat management of wildlife. Sustainable forestry and maintenance of biodiversity are two of the common tenets of this area of conservation biology. McComb offers solutions for economically beneficial forest planning and resource management while considering such topics as forest composition and age, the manner in which forest changes influence habitat, techniques for assessing and monitoring forests and habitats, ways to ensure biodiversity, and ethical and legal considerations. A glossary of scientific terms is also provided.

Where it's reviewed:
Choice, December 2007, page 655

Other books you might like:
Malcolm Ausden, *Habitat Management for Conservation*, 2008
Michael J. Manfredo, *Who Cares About Wildlife?*, 2010
L. Scott Mills, *Conservation of Wildlife Populations: Demography, Genetics and Management*, 2006
    L. Scott Mills, co-author
David R. Patton, *Forest Wildlife Ecology and Habitat Management*, 2010

1153

RAND MCNALLY

Goode's World Atlas, 22nd Edition
(Skokie, Illinois: Rand McNally, 2009)

Subject(s): Maps (Geography); Geography; Reference works

Summary: *Goode's World Atlas, 22nd Edition* comes from Rand McNally publishers and is edited by Howard Veregin. This premier atlas features hundreds of reference maps for locations around the world. The maps are divided into sections based on physical, political, and thematic definitions. These include maps based on climate change and changes in sea level. A number of charts and tables are provided as well as a pronunciation guide and extensive index. This edition features additional coverage of certain regions including Africa, Asia, and South and Central America and a number of new maps that have been digitally produced.

Other books you might like:
John Allen, *Student Atlas of World Geography*, 2009
Robert W. Christopherson, *Geosystems: An Introduction to Physical Geography*, 2008
Nick Constable, *World Atlas of Archaeology*, 2009
Andrew Morton, *The Pocket Book of the World*, 2006
Peter Stalker, *A Guide to Countries of the World*, 2009

1154

FULVIO MELIA

High-Energy Astrophysics
(Princeton, New Jersey: Princeton University Press, 2009)

Subject(s): Science; Physics; Mathematics

Summary: *High-Energy Astrophysics* by Fulvio Melia is a textbook intended for graduate students studying astrophysics, as well as researchers and professionals in the field. The book delves into observational and mathematical theories for high-energy astrophysics, covering a number of topics in a comprehensive manner. The author discusses observational techniques and important topics in this field, including pulsars, black holes, active galactic nuclei, gamma-ray bursts, neutron stars, and galaxy clusters, among others. The text is written in a concise yet accessible manner.

Where it's reviewed:
Choice, Sept 2009, page p132

Other books by the same author:
The Galactic Supermassive Black Hole, 2007
The Black Hole at the Center of Our Galaxy, 2003
The Edge of Infinity: Supermassive Black Holes in the Universe, 2003
Electrodynamics, 2001

Other books you might like:
Hale Bradt, *Astrophysics Processes*, 2008
Judith A. Irwin, *Astrophysics: Decoding the Cosmos*, 2007
Francis LeBlanc, *An Introduction to Stellar Astrophysics*, 2010
Homer Edward Newell, *Beyond the Atmosphere: Early Years of Space Science*, 2010
Steven L. Weinberg, *Cosmology*, 2008

1155

JIM MEUNINCK

Medicinal Plants of North America
(Guilford, Connecticut: FalconGuides, 2008)

Subject(s): Medicine; Botany; Healing

Summary: Jim Meuninck's *Medicinal Plants of North America* is a comprehensive field guide to the healing flora of the United States, Canada, and Mexico. This resource manual takes readers into the wild and presents a series of tools for easy identification of helpful plants. Meuninck explains how these various plants work to heal the body and provides recipes, toxicity data, and gardening advice. *Medicinal Plants of North America* contains a bibliography and a full index.

Other books by the same author:
Basic Essentials Edible Wild Plants and Useful Herbs, 2007

Other books you might like:
Daniel E. Moerman, *Native American Medicinal Plants: An Ethnobotanical Dictionary*, 2009
Louis Hermann Pammel, *A Manual of Poisonous Plants*, 2009
Robert Rogers, *The Fungal Pharmacy: Medicinal Mushrooms and Lichens of North America*, 2011
Natural Standard, *Natural Standard Herb and Supplement Guide: An Evidence-Based Reference*, 2010

Matthew Wood, *The Earthwise Herbal: A Complete Guide to New World Medicinal Plants*, 2009

1156

WILLIAM MILLER III

Trace Fossils: Concepts, Problems, Prospects

(Amsterdam; Boston: Elsevier, 2007)

Subject(s): Fossils; Geology; Science

Summary: The study of ichnology is the focus of this academic volume edited by William Miller III. *Trace Fossils: Concepts, Problems, Prospects* is comprised of a series of essays on the subject, written by some of the foremost scholars in the field. Topics cover the gamut of scientific inquiry, from the history and fundamentals of ichnology to research challenges and the future of the science. Contributors to this volume include John E. Pollard, James A. MacEachern, and Dixie L. West. *Trace Fossils* contains a bibliography and an index.

Where it's reviewed:
Choice, August 2008, page 2187

Other books you might like:
Richard Fortey, *Fossils: The History of Life*, 2009
Margaret Hynes, *Rocks and Fossils*, 2006
Steve Parker, *Fossil Hunting*, 2009
Adolf Seilacher, *Trace Fossil Analysis*, 2007

1157

DAVID A. MINDELL

Digital Apollo: Human and Machine in Spaceflight

(Cambridge, Massachusetts: MIT Press, 2010)

Subject(s): Space flight; Technology; Engineering

Summary: In *Digital Apollo: Human and Machine in Spaceflight*, David A. Mindell considers the six Apollo lunar landings and the interactions between the astronauts commanding the spacecrafts and the computers providing directional control and guidance. Mindell begins with the story of Neil Armstrong's pivotal moon landing, in which the navigational computer displayed an error that nearly caused the mission to be aborted. Instead, Armstrong chose to assume manual control and land the spacecraft successfully that way. Similar events occurred in the following five Apollo moon landings; each saw the astronaut taking manual command rather than allowing the computer to make the landing, though the computers were still in use. Mindell considers the relationship between technology and human ability, and what this means for future space flights.

Where it's reviewed:
Choice, July 2009, page 2139
Civil Engineering, March 2009, page 78
Isis, June 2009, page 441

Other books by the same author:
The Evolving World: Evolution in Everyday Life, 2007
Between Human and Machine: Feedback, Control, and Computing before Cybernetics, 2004
Avian Molecular Evolution and Systematics, 1997

Other books you might like:
Robert Godwin, *Surveyor: Lunar Exploration Program: The NASA Mission Reports*, 2010
Thomas J. Kelly, *Moon Lander*, 2009
Frank O'Brien, *The Apollo Guidance Computer*, 2010
W. David Woods, *How Apollo Flew to the Moon*, 2008

1158

EDGAR MITCHELL
DWIGHT WILLIAMS , Co-Author

The Way of the Explorer: An Apollo Astronaut's Journey Through the Material and Mystical Worlds

(New York: G.P. Putnam's Sons, 1996)

Subject(s): Science; Religion; Space exploration

Summary: In *The Way of the Explorer: An Apollo Astronaut's Journey Through the Material and Mystical Worlds*, human consciousness expert, paranormal investigator, and astronaut Dr. Edgar Mitchell blends memoir and scientific inquiry to craft a wholly unique odyssey into the human mind. On his journey to the moon in the 1970s, Mitchell experienced an insightful realization that changed his life. He was deeply affected by a sense of interconnectedness among all people, and he devoted the next few decades to studying this idea. With a scientist's passion, a journalist's curiosity, and an astronaut's scientific know-how, this volume takes readers into the depths of human consciousness—and the ties that connect each and every one of us. Written with Dwight Williams, *The Way of the Explorer* includes notes on the text, a bibliography, and an index.

Other books by the same author:
The Way of the Explorer: An Apollo Astronaut's Journey Through the Material and Mystical Worlds, 2009

Other books you might like:
Ervin Laszlo, *Quantum Shift in the Global Brain*, 2008
Lynne McTaggart, *The Field: The Quest for the Secret Force of the Universe*, 2008

1159

DANIEL E. MOERMAN

Native American Medicinal Plants: An Ethnobotanical Dictionary

(Portland, Oregon: Timber Press, 2009)

Subject(s): Botany; Alternative medicine; Reference works

Summary: *Native American Medicinal Plants: An Ethnobotanical Dictionary* by Daniel E. Moerman is an extensively detailed resource that specifies the medicinal uses of approximately 2,700 plants, based on the research of 218 Native American tribes. The indexes that make up the text are organized by tribe, determined medicinal usage, and the common name of the plant. The plants are further broken down into pain relievers, sedatives, contraceptives, and aids for digestion, just to name a few. This reference work is recommended for anyone who with an interest in plants or Native American medicinal practices.

Where it's reviewed:
Choice, April 2010, page 1450

Other books by the same author:
Meaning, Medicine and the 'Placebo Effect', 2002
Native American Ethnobotany, 1998

Other books you might like:
Ken Cohen, *Honoring the Medicine: The Essential Guide to Native American Healing*, 2006
James A. Duke, *Duke's Handbook of Medicinal Plants of the Bible*, 2007
Jim Meuninck, *Medicinal Plants of North America*, 2008
Samuel Thayer, *The Forager's Harvest: A Guide to Identifying, Harvesting, and Preparing Edible Wild Plants*, 2006

1160

JOHN W. MOFFAT

Reinventing Gravity: A Physicist Goes Beyond Einstein
(New York: Smithsonian Books, 2008)

Subject(s): Science; Spacetime; Physics

Summary: John W. Moffat is the professor emeritus of physics at the University of Toronto. In *Reinventing Gravity: A Physicist Goes Beyond Einstein*, Moffat presents his theory of Modified Gravity (MOG), which he developed in response to the many overly complicated theories being developed today: black holes, dark matter, and dark energy, among them. These theories are explained by Moffat as objectionable, and Einstein's general theory of relativity, as wrong. Moffat presents MOG as a much more streamlined theory, one which can account for the observations of the universe without theoretical dark matter. Moffat's calculations also predict the existence of grey stars, massive objects very similar to black holes. Written for the layperson, Moffat's work presents these complex theories of astrophysics in easy-to-understand language.

Where it's reviewed:
Discover, November 2008, page 71
Publishers Weekly, July 21, 2008, page 149

Other books you might like:
Martin Bojowald, *Canonical Gravity and Applications*, 2011
David Darling, *Gravity's Arc: The Story of Gravity,*

from Aristotle to Einstein and Beyond, 2006
George Gamow, *Gravity*, 2009
Richard Hammond, *The Unknown Universe*, 2008
Daniele Oriti, *Approaches to Quantum Gravity*, 2009

1161

MARK MOLDWIN

An Introduction to Space Weather
(Cambridge, England: Cambridge University Press, 2008)

Subject(s): Science; Earth; Technology

Summary: Written by professor Mark Moldwin, *An Introduction to Space Weather* is a textbook for students of space physics. The book presents non-science majors with a basic understanding of the relationship between the sun and the earth and how this relationship affects technology. The sun significantly impacts the earth's space environment and can cause errors with certain technologies. When the sun releases electromagnetic energy and particle radiation, satellite, navigation, communication and power distribution systems are often damaged or destroyed. In *An Introduction to Space Weather*, Moldwin also offers straightforward, easy-to-understand information on space physics and provides definitions for space physics terms.

Where it's reviewed:
Choice, May 2009, page 1723

Other books you might like:
Volker Bothmer, *Space Weather*, 2006
Norma Crosby, *Interplanetary Travel and Space Weather: Scientific, Technological and Biological Issues*, 2011
Arnold Hanslmeier, *The Sun and Space Weather*, 2010
Peter Meischner, *Weather Radar: Principles and Advanced Applications*, 2010
Vincent L. Webber, *Environmental Satellites: Weather and Environmental Information Systems*, 2009

1162

EMILIO F. MORAN

People and Nature: An Introduction to Human Ecological Relations
(Oxford: Blackwell, 2008)

Subject(s): Ecology; Environmental history; Anthropology

Summary: In *People and Nature: An Introduction to Human Ecological Relations*, Emilio F. Moran provides an anthropological history of the interactions between humans and nature, and the way this has led to the issues of today. Moran presents a number of contemporary environmental problems and then examines ways in which humans have used and abused nature throughout history. Instead, he suggests that hunter-gatherer or early agricultural peoples were more successful at living simple lives in harmony with the surrounding natural world. The author notes current environmental challenges, but he also provides advice and hope for the future. Discussions of planning and environmental law and policy, as well as previous environmental trends and what they might mean for the future, are also included.

Where it's reviewed:
Journal of the Royal Anthropological Institute, Dec 2008, page p908-909

Other books by the same author:
Human Adaptability: An Introduction to Ecological Anthropology, 2007
Through Amazonian Eyes: The Human Ecology of Amazonian Populations, 1993
The Ecosystem Approach in Anthropology: From Concept to Practice, 1991

Other books you might like:
Fikret Berkes, *Sacred Ecology*, 2008
W. Penn Handwerker, *The Origin of Cultures: How Individual Choices Make Cultures Change*, 2009
Clive Ponting, *A New Green History of the World*, 2007
Patricia Townsend, *Environmental Anthropology*, 2008
Nicholas Wade, *Before the Dawn: Recovering the Lost History of Our Ancestors*, 2006

1163

JACK MORAN

An Introduction to Theoretical and Computational Aerodynamics

(Hoboken, New Jersey: John Wiley & Sons, 2010)

Subject(s): Science; Physics; Astronomy

Summary: *An Introduction to Theoretical and Computational Aerodynamics*, written by author Jack Moran, is a comprehensive guide to the introduction of the field of aerodynamics. In this book, Moran provides for readers an outline of principles applied within the field of study, and describes both traditional or classic theories within the subject matter as well as modern, updated hypotheses. Originally published in 1984, this book has been revised in a 2010 edition to include updated material. Moran supplements the text with illustrations and graphics that enhance the subject matter.

Other books you might like:
Tuncer Cebeci, *An Engineering Approach to the Calculation of Aerodynamic Flows*, 2010
Kirill V. Rozhdestvensky, *Aerodynamics of a Lifting System in Extreme Ground Effect*, 2010

1164

A.J. NAIR

Introduction to Biotechnology and Genetic Engineering

(Hingham, Massachusetts: Infinity Science Press, 2008)

Subject(s): Genetic engineering; Biology; Science

Summary: *Introduction to Biotechnology and Genetic Engineering* by A. J. Nair is a textbook for students in various scientific disciplines, but it is also designed to be accessible for those interested in independent study who do not have extensive knowledge of biology or genetic research. The topics covered include genetic principles and bioethics, among others. The text also comes with a CD-ROM that includes some mathematical explanations and additional resources, including simulations of practical applications of the topics discussed in the text, such as DNA mapping.

Other books by the same author:
Basics of Biotechnology, 2005

Other books you might like:
Clair Hope Cummings, *Uncertain Peril: Genetic Engineering and the Future of Seeds*, 2008
S. Harisha, *Biotechnology Procedures and Experiments Handbook*, 2007
Russ Hodge, *Genetic Engineering*, 2009
Harvey Lodish, *Molecular Cell Biology Solutions Manual*, 2007
Desmond S. T. Nicholl, *An Introduction to Genetic Engineering, Third Edition*, 2008

1165

JEAN-LUC NANCY

Listening

(New York: Fordham University Press, 2007)

Subject(s): Music; Hearing; Philosophy

Summary: *Listening* is a philosophical examination of the effect that sound has on the body from author and professor, Jean-Luc Nancy. The book analyzes the differences between listening and hearing, what listening includes, and how humans react differently to what is heard as opposed to what is seen. Nancy contends that sound has a much greater impact than visual art because of its long-lasting consequences in the body. Humans react to sound and music both inwardly and outwardly. They also have no natural way to block out sound; therefore, they are constantly engaging themselves in a continued state of listening which includes hearing sound and interpreting it. Throughout *Listening*, Nancy encourages readers to meditate on the mysterious ways that sound affects them.

Where it's reviewed:
Current Musicology, Fall 2008, page 157

Other books you might like:
Mark Brady, *Right Listening*, 2008
Colin H. Hansen, *The Effects of Low-Frequency Noise and Vibration on People*, 2007
Bart Kosko, *Noise*, 2006
Anne D. Le Claire, *Listening Below the Noise: A Meditation on the Practice of Silence*, 2009

1166

JAMES B. NARDI

Life in the Soil: A Guide for Naturalists and Gardeners

(Chicago, Illinois: University of Chicago Press, 2007)

Subject(s): Nature; Gardening; Biology

Summary: *Life in the Soil: A Guide for Naturalists and Gardeners* by James B. Nardi is a text intended for anyone wishing to learn more about soil ecosystems and the creatures found in them. Nardi first provides an overview of soil ecosystems and the types of soil found around the world, and then delves into a discussion of the different organisms found within the soil and the ways in which they use nutrients and affect the makeup of the soil. The book is organized by taxon and includes information about bacteria, fungi, mites, insects, worms, snails, and vertebrates, among many others, with a number of surprising and interesting facts about soil biology. The book also includes more than 300 illustrations and sketches and offers suggestions for observing some of the organisms and ecosystems detailed in the text.

Where it's reviewed:
The American Gardener, July-August 2008, page p54
Choice, March 2008, page p1184
Science News, Nov 10, 2007, page p303

Other books by the same author:
The World Beneath Our Feet: A Guide to Life in the Soil, 2003

Other books you might like:
Brian Capon, *Botany for Gardeners*, 2010
William Bryant Logan, *Dirt: The Ecstatic Skin of the Earth*, 2007
Jeff Lowenfels, *Teaming with Microbes*, 2010
David R. Montgomery, *Dirt: The Erosion of Civilizations*, 2007

1167

BERNARD J. NEBEL

Building Foundations of Scientific Understanding: A Science Curriculum for K-2

(Denver: Outskirts Press, 2007)

Subject(s): Science; Teaching; Education

Summary: A thorough understanding of scientific frameworks is essential to the teaching of science and associated subjects. In *Building Foundations of Scientific Understanding: A Science Curriculum for K-2*, author Bernard J. Nebel offers teachers an all-encompassing syllabus for effectively presenting scientific concepts to children in their first years of elementary school. With more than 40 lesson plans, this volume instructs teachers on the best methods of generating interest in the sciences and incorporates elements of reading, creative writing,

and more. *Building Foundations of Scientific Understanding* includes an appendix. First book.

Where it's reviewed:
The Psychological Record, Fall 2009, page p679

Other books you might like:
Daniel A. Griffith, *Spatial Autocorrelation and Spatial Filtering: Gaining Understanding Through Theory and Scientific Visualization*, 2010
Barbara A. Somervill, *What Do You Want to Prove?: Planning Investigations*, 2007
Barbara A. Somervill, *What's the Big Idea?: Forming Hypotheses*, 2007

1168

ROBIN NELSON

The Night Sky

(Minneapolis, Minnesota: Lerner Publishing Group, 2010)

Story type: Young Readers
Subject(s): Science; Astronomy; Education

Summary: *The Night Sky* by Robin Nelson is a First Step Nonfiction: Discovering Nature's Cycles book from Lerner Publishing Group. This book teaches young readers how the night sky evolves and progresses from month to month and year to year, and what those changes mean. Readers will learn about the waxing and waning of the moon and how that activity controls certain bodies of water, about the star formations, and about the changes in appearance in the entire sky. Nelson is also the author of *Hibernation*, *Where is My Continent*, and *From Kernel to Corn*.

Where it's reviewed:
Sky & Telescope, May 2008 v115 i5, page p41

Other books by the same author:
Soil, 2005

Other books you might like:
Eduardo Banqueri, *The Night Sky*, 2007
Jay B. Holberg, *Sirius: Brightest Diamond in the Night Sky*, 2007
Patrick Moore, *The Sky at Night*, 2010

1169

FRANK H. NETTER

Atlas of Human Anatomy, 5th Edition

(Philadelphia: Saunders/Elsevier, 2010)

Subject(s): Anatomy; Reference works; Science

Summary: The *Atlas of Human Anatomy, 5th Edition* by Frank H. Netter is a single-volume reference guide to the complete anatomy of the human body, featuring color illustrations throughout the text. The atlas is composed entirely of detailed drawings with labels, illustrating each section of the human body and often cross-sections as well, such as for the spinal cord. It also includes a 36-page index to help the reader easily locate information on specific sections of body. This text is recommended for all medical students or those who need to study human anatomy.

Other books by the same author:
Interactive Atlas of Human Anatomy, 2002
Musculoskeletal System, 1994

Other books you might like:
Robin Kelly, *The Human Antenna*, 2010
Jon Mallatt, *A Brief Atlas of the Human Body*, 2006
Werner Platzer, *Color Atlas of Human Anatomy*, 2008
Kenneth S. Saladin, *Human Anatomy*, 2010

1170

DONALD A. NEUMANN

Kinesiology of the Musculoskeletal System: Foundations for Rehabilitation, Second Edition

(St. Louis, Missouri: Mosby/Elsevier, 2009)

Subject(s): Science; Medicine

Summary: In *Kinesiology of the Musculoskeletal System: Foundations for Rehabilitation, Second Edition*, editor Donald A. Neumann updates his text on the study of physical activity. This comprehensive volume first introduces students to the components of the musculoskeletal system, discussing the structure and biomechanical principles of the shoulder, elbow and forearm, wrist, hand, hip, knee, ankle, and foot. The role of muscle in joint stability and skeletal movement and the interactions of muscle and joint are also discussed. Chapters on the kinesiology of mastication and ventilation provide practical demonstrations of the principles introduced. Hundreds of illustrations supplement the text.

Other books by the same author:
Kinesiology of the Musculoskeletal System, 2002

Other books you might like:
Roger M. Enoka, *Neuromechanics of Human Movement*, 2008
Lynn Lippert, *Clinical Kinesiology and Anatomy*, 2006
Joseph E. Muscolino, *Kinesiology: The Skeletal System and Muscle Function*, 2010
James Watkins, *Structure and Function of the Musculoskeletal System*, 2009

1171

DESMOND S. T. NICHOLL

An Introduction to Genetic Engineering, Third Edition

(Cambridge, United Kingdom; New York: Cambridge University Press, 2008)

Subject(s): Genetics; Genetic engineering; Science
Summary: Biology professor Desmond S.T. Nicholl guides students through the basics of genetic engineering. This

volume covers such fields of study as an introduction to molecular biology, how genes are manipulated, and the various uses of genetic technology. The third edition includes up-to-date information on recent breakthroughs in the study of genetics. *An Introduction to Genetic Engineering, Third Edition* contains a bibliography, a list of helpful web resources, a glossary, and an index. First book.

Other books you might like:
William D. Fixsen, *Introduction to Genetic Analysis Solutions MegaManual*, 2007
David Hyde, *Introduction to Genetic Principles*, 2008
A.J. Nair, *Introduction to Biotechnology and Genetic Engineering*, 2008
A. Rashid, *Introduction to Genetic Engineering of Crop Plants: Aims and Achievements*, 2009

1172

CHRISTIANE NUSSLEIN-VOLHARD

Coming to Life: How Genes Drive Development

(San Diego: Kales Press, 2008)

Subject(s): Genetics; Evolution (Biology); Science
Summary: The worlds of genetics and evolution are explored with expert insight by Nobel Prize-winning geneticist Christiane Nusslein-Volhard. *Coming to Life: How Genes Drive Development* takes readers into the inner life of cells, illustrating how these pivotal building blocks initiate a variety of processes integral to human development. Informed by the author's years of work and her unrivaled enthusiasm for the subject, this volume makes a complex topic accessible and entertaining for a lay readership. *Coming to Life* includes illustrations, a bibliography, and an index.

Where it's reviewed:
BioEssays, Oct 2007, page p1064
Choice, Nov 2006, page p505
Quarterly Review of Biology, Dec 2007, page p417
Science, April 20, 2007, page p373

Other books you might like:
Sean B. Carroll, *The Making of the Fittest: DNA and the Ultimate Forensic Record of Evolution*, 2006
Lawrence Hunter, *The Processes of Life: An Introduction to Molecular Biology*, 2009
Durdica Ugarkovic, *Centromere: Structure and Evolution*, 2009

1173

STEPHEN JAMES O'MEARA

Stephen James O'Meara's Observing the Night Sky with Binoculars: A Simple Guide to the Heavens

(Cambridge, United Kingdom: Cambridge University Press, 2008)

Subject(s): Astronomy; Science; Mythology

Summary: In *Stephen James O'Meara's Observing the Night Sky with Binoculars: A Simple Guide to the Heavens*, science journalist O'Meara takes fellow stargazers on a guided tour of the heavens. The author points out various spots of interest on a month by month basis, describing the mythology and history of each star or constellation before discussing its scientific prominence. Aimed at the amateur stargazer, this volume offers practical advice for identifying and enjoying the glittering night sky. *Stephen James O'Meara's Observing the Night Sky with Binoculars* includes three appendices and an index.

Where it's reviewed:
Sky & Telescope, March 2009, page p66

Other books by the same author:
Exploring the Solar System with Binoculars, 2010
Observing the Night Sky with Binoculars: A Simple Guide to the Heavens, 2008
Deep-Sky Companions: Hidden Treasures, 2007
Steve O'Meara's Herschel 400 Observing Guide, 2007
Deep-Sky Companions: The Messier Objects, 2000

Other books you might like:
Paul E. Kinzer, *Stargazing Basics: Getting Started in Recreational Astronomy*, 2008
Becky Ramotowski, *Secrets of Stargazing*, 2007
Gary Seronik, *Binocular Highlights: 99 Celestial Sights for Binocular Users*, 2007
Roger W. Sinnott, *Sky & Telescope's Pocket Sky Atlas*, 2006
Anton Vamplew, *Simple Stargazing*, 2006

1174

CAROL A. OATIS

Kinesiology: The Mechanics and Pathomechanics of Human Movement, Second Edition

(Baltimore: Lippincott Williams and Wilkins, 2008)

Subject(s): Science; Medicine; Medical care

Summary: Author Carol A. Oatis offers the quintessential reference guide to all things related to the study and treatment of human movement. *Kinesiology: The Mechanics and Pathomechanics of Human Movement, Second Edition* looks at the basic principles of biomechanics and how these principles fit into the overall understanding of how the body functions and moves. Chapters explore the kinesiology of the upper and lower extremities, the head and spine, as well as issues relating to posture and gait. This volume, fully updated and revised in a second edition, includes a full index. First book.

Other books you might like:
Blandine Calais-Germain, *Anatomy of Movement*, 2007
Roger M. Enoka, *Neuromechanics of Human Movement*, 2008
Shirl J. Hoffman, *Introduction to Kinesiology: Studying Physical Activity*, 2009

Joseph E. Muscolino, *Kinesiology: The Skeletal System and Muscle Function*, 2010
Donald A. Neumann, *Kinesiology of the Musculoskeletal System: Foundations for Rehabilitation, Second Edition*, 2009
Jane Thurnell-Read, *Health Kinesiology*, 2009

1175

PAUL A. OFFIT

Vaccinated: One Man's Quest to Defeat the World's Deadliest Diseases

(Washington, District of Columbia: Smithsonian Books, 2007)

Story type: Historical
Subject(s): Science; Diseases; Medicine

Summary: Written by doctor and professor Paul A. Offit, *Vaccinated: One Man's Quest to Defeat the World's Deadliest Diseases* is a comprehensive narrative on the life and career of Maurice Hilleman, the father of modern vaccinations. Hilleman's personal goal was to develop vaccinations for all deadly diseases that threaten children. He didn't quite reach his goal, but with the development of nine major vaccinations, he came close. He's best known for developing the vaccinations for previously deadly diseases, such as mumps, rubella, and measles. Offit interweaves the tale of Hilleman's scientific research and accomplishments with a thorough medical history on vaccines, covering a period of 200 years.

Where it's reviewed:
Book World, November 25, 2007, page 11
Booklist, August 2007, page 20
Choice, December 2007, page 662
Nature Medicine, February 2008, page 113
The New England Journal of Medicine, October 25, 2007, page 1785

Other books by the same author:
Autism's False Prophets: Bad Science, Risky Medicine, and the Search for a Cure, 2010
Deadly Choices: How the Anti-Vaccine Movement Threatens Us All, 2010
The Cutter Incident: How America's First Polio Vaccine Led to the Growing Vaccine Crisis, 2007

Other books you might like:
Arthur Allen, *Vaccine: The Controversial Story of Medicine's Greatest Lifesaver*, 2008
Molly Caldwell Crosby, *The American Plague*, 2007
D. A. Henderson, *Smallpox: The Death of a Disease*, 2009
Jeffrey Kluger, *Splendid Solution: Jonas Salk and the Conquest of Polio*, 2005
David Oshinsky, *Polio: An American Story*, 2005

1176

CALLY OLDERSHAW

Guide to Gems

(Toronto: Firefly Books, 2009)

Subject(s): Geology; Mineralogy; Science

Summary: In *Guide to Gems*, author Cally Oldershaw provides a comprehensive handbook to semi-precious minerals. Oldershaw prefaces the guidebook's detailed photographs and tables with an overview of geological processes as well as the various features of gems and stones, including structural makeup. The author also includes data on collectible gems, cut and shape, proper weights and measures, and storage. Each gem featured in this book is described through text and is depicted in photographs of the gem in its natural state as well as in jewelry settings. Oldershaw is also the author of *Rock and Minerals* and *Gems of the World*.

Other books by the same author:
Gems of the World, 2009
Gemstones, 2006

Other books you might like:
Rick Hudson, *A Field Guide to Gold, Gemstones and Minerals*, 2008
Shelley A. Kaehr, *Gemstone Enlightenment*, 2007
Walter Schumann, *Gemstones of the World, Revised Edition*, 1997
Arthur Thomas, *Gemstones: Properties, Identification and Use*, 2009

1177

DOUGLAS PALMER

Origins: Human Evolution Revealed

(London, England: Mitchell Beazley, 2010)

Subject(s): Science; Evolution (Biology); Human behavior

Summary: Science writer Douglas Palmer's *Origins: Human Evolution Revealed* is a scientific history on *Homo sapiens* and evolution. Palmer takes readers through history to see the primate ancestors of humans, including the Proconsul, ape-like creatures that resided in Africa 17 million years ago, and *Homo floresiensis*, a species of Indonesian dwarves from 18,000 years ago. He sheds light on their lifestyles, including specifics about their diets, clothing, behavior, language, and habitats. The information is accompanied by detailed artwork and facial reconstruction to give readers a picture of what these creatures might have looked like. Palmer continues with a comprehensive timeline of evolution and theories about the development and spread of the human race.

Where it's reviewed:
Publishers Weekly, October 4, 2010, page 39

Other books by the same author:
The Complete Earth, 2009
Fortune & Glory: Tales of History's Greatest

Archaeological Adventurers, 2008
Fossils, 2006
Fossil Revolution: The Finds That Changed Our View of the Past, 2004
Atlas of the Prehistoric World, 1999

Other books you might like:
Derek Bickerton, *Adam's Tongue: How Humans Made Language, How Language Made Humans*, 2010
Ann Gibbons, *The First Human: The Race to Discover Our Earliest Ancestors*, 2007
Richard G. Klein, *The Human Career: Human Biological and Cultural Origins*, 2009
Charles Lockwood, *The Human Story: Where We Come From & How We Evolved*, 2008
Carl Zimmer, *Smithsonian Intimate Guide to Human Origins*, 2007

1178

TAO PANG

An Introduction to Computational Physics: 2nd Edition

(Cambridge, England: Cambridge University Press, 2010)

Subject(s): Science; Computers; Physics

Summary: *An Introduction to Computational Physics: 2nd Edition* is an academic textbook on scientific computing from author and physics professor, Tao Pang. The book gives college students a general overview on the theories and methods of computational physics. The revised 2nd edition includes updated information on technological advances made in the area of scientific computing. Filled with step-by-step instruction, program listings in JavaTM, and interactive exercises, *An Introduction to Computational Physics* is a reference guide for under-grad or graduate students of computational physics or scientific computation. Topics covered in the textbook include numerical calculus, ordinary differential equations, spectral analysis, Monte Carlo simulations, and genetic algorithm and programming.

Where it's reviewed:
Choice, Oct 2006 v44 i2, page p332

Other books you might like:
Hans Petter Langtangen, *Python Scripting for Computational Science*, 2010
Joseph Marie Thijssen, *Computational Physics*, 2007

1179

BRUCE B. PARKER

The Power of the Sea: Tsunamis, Storm Surges, Rogue Waves, and Our Quest to Predict Disasters

(New York: Palgrave Macmillan, 2010)

Subject(s): Science; Weather; Natural disasters

Summary: In *The Power of the Sea: Tsunamis, Storm*

Science

Surges, Rogue Waves, and Our Quest to Predict Disasters, Bruce Parker, a former scientist with the National Oceanic and Atmospheric Administration, examines the historic relationship between the forces of the ocean and human society. Acknowledging that man's best defense against tsunamis, storm surges, waves, and tides is accurate prediction, Parker discusses specific events in history that were affected or defined by ocean events. From Napoleon's battles at sea and the D-Day invasion at Normandy to the Indian tsunami of 2004 and Hurricane Katrina's impact on America's Gulf region, the author provides an intriguing study of man's continued battle against nature's greatest force.

Where it's reviewed:
Publishers Weekly, Sept 13, 2010, page p35

Other books by the same author:
Tidal Hydrodynamics, 1991

Other books you might like:
Mohamed Gad-el-Hak, *Large-Scale Disasters: Prediction, Control, and Mitigation*, 2008
Earl V. Leary, *Earthquakes: Risk, Monitoring and Research*, 2009
Maureen A. Miller, *Rogue Wave*, 2010

1180

ANIRUDDH D. PATEL

Music, Language, and the Brain

(New York: Oxford University Press, 2007)

Subject(s): Music; Neurosciences; Science

Summary: Neuroscientist Aniruddh D. Patel investigates the interaction between music, language, and neuroscience. *Music, Language, and the Brain* draws on the latest scientific findings to illuminate just how the human brain is able to process, interpret, and utilize the intricacies of music and language. Patel looks at several different key aspects of the cognitive process, including the precise implications of pitch, timbre, melody, and rhythm. *Music, Language, and the Brain* contains a bibliography and an index. First book.

Where it's reviewed:
Music Perception, Feb 2009, page p287-288
Nature Neuroscience, April 2008, page p377
Notes, Sept 2009, page p59
Times Higher Education, May 13, 2010, page p51

Other books you might like:
David Huron, *Sweet Anticipation: Music and the Psychology of Expectation*, 2008
Daniel J. Levitin, *This Is Your Brain on Music: The Science of a Human Obsession*, 2006
Daniel J. Levitin, *The World in Six Songs: How the Musical Brain Created Human Nature*, 2008
Michael Thaut, *Rhythm, Music, and the Brain: Scientific Foundations and Clinical Applications*, 2007

1181

LAUREN PECORINO

Molecular Biology of Cancer: Mechanisms, Targets, and Therapeutics, Second Edition

(Oxford; New York: Oxford University Press, 2008)

Subject(s): Cancer; Biology; Science

Summary: Lauren Pecorino's *Molecular Biology of Cancer: Mechanisms, Targets, and Therapeutics, Second Edition* examines the various cellular breakdowns that can result in a cancer diagnosis. Updated with the latest scientific findings and additional materials for teachers and students, this volume looks at the molecular structures of cancer and how these structures affect healthy cell division. *Molecular Biology of Cancer* includes two appendices, a glossary of commonly used terms, and an index. First book.

Other books you might like:
Elizabeth H. Chen, *Cell Fusion: Overviews and Methods*, 2010
Paul B. Fisher, *Cancer Genomics and Proteomics: Methods and Protocols*, 2010
Raymond W. Ruddon, *Cancer Biology, Fourth Edition*, 2007
Wolfgang Arthur Schulz, *Molecular Biology of Human Cancers: An Advanced Student's Textbook*, 2007

1182

BENJAMIN PIERCE

Genetics: A Conceptual Approach, Third Edition

(New York: W. H. Freeman and Co., 2008)

Subject(s): Genetics; Genetic research; Science

Summary: Benjamin Pierce's *Genetics: A Conceptual Approach, Third Edition* includes the latest scientific breakthroughs in the study of genetics and associated disciplines. Pierce examines the topics essential to gaining a thorough understanding of the topic. He discusses the principles of classic genetics, the details of modern genetic research, and the inner workings of DNA. *Genetics* includes a bibliography and a full index.

Other books by the same author:
Transmission and Population Genetics, 2010
Genetics Essentials: Concepts and Connections, 2009
Genetics Essentials: Concepts and Connections & Solutions and Problem Solving Manual, 2009

Other books you might like:
Robert J. Brooker, *Genetics: Analysis and Principles, Third Edition*, 2008
Daniel L. Hartl, *Essential Genetics: A Genomics Perspective, Fifth Edition*, 2009
Ricki Lewis, *Human Genetics: Concepts and Applications*, 2009

Desmond S. T. Nicholl, *An Introduction to Genetic Engineering, Third Edition*, 2008

Benjamin Pierce, *Genetics Essentials: Concepts and Connections*, 2009

1183

EDWARD PLASTER

Soil Science and Management

(Florence, Kentucky: Delmar Cengage Learning, 2008)

Subject(s): Ecology; Agriculture; Science

Summary: Where most environmental science books approach soil as an independent element, *Soil Science and Management* focuses on our interactions with and effects on soil. Author Edward Plaster provides a simple overview of the important concepts of soil as it relates to agriculture, horticulture, and environmentalism. Emphasizing the proper use and management of precious soil and water resources, Plaster examines various types of soils, how they function, and how we can use them most effectively. In addition to the scientific fundamentals of soil, Plaster also looks at the various legal concepts and government programs associated with soils. *Soil Science and Management* also includes color illustrates that make learning about soils even easier.

Other books you might like:

Eldor Alvin Paul, *Soil Microbiology, Ecology and Biochemistry*, 2007

Alexia Stokes, *The Supporting Roots of Trees and Woody Plants Form, Function and Physiology*, 2010

1184

GAVIN PRETOR-PINNEY

The Cloud Collector's Handbook

(London: Sceptre, 2009)

Subject(s): Meteorology; Weather; Science

Summary: If you have ever spent a lazy summer day staring up at the sky, looking for shapes and figures in the clouds, you just might enjoy author Gavin Pretor-Pinney's *The Cloud Collector's Handbook*. In this unique, handy guidebook, Pretor-Pinney explores all the different types of clouds, including the ones we see every day and those that appear only very rarely. He provides a full description and photos of each type. In addition to serving as a useful guide for cloud lovers, *The Cloud Collector's Handbook* also makes it possible for readers to engage in competitive cloud spotting. With a point system and place to mark the clouds you have seen, *The Cloud Collector's Handbook* allows you to compete against your friends to see who can earn the most points by spotting the rarest clouds. Simply put, if you love a cloudy day, *The Cloud Collector's Handbook* is for you.

Other books by the same author:

The Cloudspotter's Guide: The Science, History, and Culture of Clouds, 2007

Other books you might like:

John A. Day, *The Book of Clouds*, 2003

Richard Hamblyn, *Extraordinary Clouds*, 2009

1185

FRED H. PREVIC

The Dopaminergic Mind in Human Evolution and History

(Cambridge; New York: Cambridge University Press, 2009)

Subject(s): Neurosciences; Psychology; Medical care

Summary: *The Dopaminergic Mind in Human Evolution and History*, Fred H. Previc presents his theory on human behavior and evolution. Previc believes that a drastic increase in dopamine 80,000 years ago led to the evolution of modern man. The author argues that these higher levels of dopamine are what accounts for our personalities and the unique abilities possessed only by humans. He attributes the increase in dopamine levels throughout human evolution to epigenetic factors rather than genetic factors and goes on to argue that the dopaminergic mind, with continuously increasing dopamine levels, could actually be detrimental to society.

Where it's reviewed:

Choice, July 2010, page 2129

Other books you might like:

Antonio Damasio, *Self Comes to Mind: Constructing the Conscious Brain*, 2010

Marco Iacoboni, *Mirroring People: The Science of Empathy and How We Connect with Others*, 2009

Gary Marcus, *Kluge: The Haphazard Evolution of the Human Mind*, 2009

Daniel J. Siegel, *Mindsight: The New Science of Personal Transformation*, 2010

1186

GEORGE PROCHNIK

In Pursuit of Silence: Listening for Meaning in a World of Noise

(New York: Doubleday, 2010)

Subject(s): Architecture; Psychology; Social sciences

Summary: George Prochnik discusses the importance of finding silence in the busy world we live in today, in his book *In Pursuit of Silence: Listening for Meaning in a World of Noise*. Prochnik argues that with the ever-present noise in elevators, waiting rooms, department stores, subways, and trains, it's difficult to find peace and quiet anywhere outside of one's own home. Even at home, Prochnik argues, the furniture and appliances make unnecessary noise. As he travels the world, speaking with people who feel the same, Prochnik comes across many who have entered the battle between noise and silence. For example, Prochnik speaks to an architect with blueprints for quiet buildings. In this book, Prochnik shows why silence is so important to society as a whole.

Science

Where it's reviewed:
The American Conservative, August 2010, page p48
Library Journal, May 15, 2010, page p93
The Wilson Quarterly, Summer 2010, page p100

Other books by the same author:
Putnam Camp: Sigmund Freud, James Jackson Putnam, and the Purpose of American Psychology, 2006

Other books you might like:
George M. Foy, *Zero Decibels: The Quest for Absolute Silence*, 2010
Garret Keizer, *The Unwanted Sound of Everything We Want: A Book About Noise*, 2010
Brandon LaBelle, *Acoustic Territories: Sound Culture and Everyday Life*, 2010
Anne D. Le Claire, *Listening Below the Noise: A Meditation on the Practice of Silence*, 2009
Alex Ross, *Listen to This*, 2010

1187

DONALD RAPP

Human Missions to Mars: Enabling Technologies for Exploring the Red Planet

(New York: Springer, 2010)

Subject(s): Mars (Planet); Space exploration; Science

Summary: Written by Donald Rapp, *Human Missions to Mars: Enabling Technologies for Exploring the Red Planet* is an examination of the likelihood of Mars exploration by people in the future. Rapp discusses the possibility of human missions to Mars, in place of exploration by spacecraft. Rapp's information offers readers with a realistic prediction as to whether the many ambitious space programs will succeed in their quest. Rapp also dissects NASA's current program and contends that, unless major changes are made, human missions will not make it to Mars before 2080.

Where it's reviewed:
Choice, May 2008, page 1563

Other books by the same author:
Assessing Climate Change: Temperatures, Solar Radiation and Heat Balance, 2010
Ice Ages and Interglacials: Measurements, Interpretation and Models, 2009

Other books you might like:
Pat Duggins, *Trailblazing Mars: NASA's Next Giant Leap*, 2010
K. Maria D. Lane, *Geographies of Mars: Seeing and Knowing the Red Planet*, 2011
Ronald Mak, *The Martian Principles for Successful Enterprise Systems*, 2006
Erik Seedhouse, *Martian Outpost: The Challenges of Establishing a Human Settlement on Mars*, 2009

1188

LUCY ROGERS

It's ONLY Rocket Science: An Introduction in Plain English

(New York: Springer Science+Business Media, 2008)

Subject(s): Science; Technology; Astronomy

Summary: In *It's ONLY Rocket Science: An Introduction in Plain English*, Lucy Rogers attempts to present the basic aspects of aeronautics in layman's terms. Though Rogers is an engineer discussing the mechanics of space flight, virtually no mathematical concepts are discussed in depth. Specific topics include designing the rocket, planning the flight, navigating space, communicating with Earth, and tracking satellites. The text also includes a glossary, as well as a few charts or graphs to explain more difficult concepts.

Where it's reviewed:
Choice, September 2008, page 122
Professional Engineering Magazine, May 7, 2008, page 76

Other books you might like:
Michael Belfiore, *Rocketeers: How a Visionary Band of Business Leaders, Engineers, and Pilots Is Boldly Privatizing Space*, 2007
Piers Bizony, *How to Build Your Own Spaceship*, 2009
Graham Swinerd, *How Spacecraft Fly*, 2008
Travis S. Taylor, *Introduction to Rocket Science and Engineering*, 2009

1189

WILLIAM K ROSE

Astrophysics

(Mineola, New York: Dover Publications, 2010)

Subject(s): Astronomy; Physics; Science

Summary: *Astrophysics* is a comprehensive guide and educational resource on the physics of stars and astronomical entities from author William K. Rose. Originally published in 1973, the book examines all facets of a star's origins, its development, and final stages before death. An exhaustive resource on astrophysics, the book covers a wide variety of related topics including the formation of stars, protostars, variable stars, red giants, planetary nebulae, novae and galactic x-ray sources, white dwarfs, and supernovae and the formation of heavy elements. Rose also provides readers with detailed information on pulsars, neutron stars, galaxies, and cosmology.

Other books you might like:
M. S. Longair, *High Energy Astrophysics*, 2011
Dan Maoz, *Astrophysics in a Nutshell*, 2007
Peter Meszaros, *The High Energy Universe: Ultra-High Energy Events in Astrophysics and Cosmology*, 2010

1190

RAYMOND W. RUDDON

Cancer Biology, Fourth Edition

(New York: Oxford University Press, 2007)

Subject(s): Biology; Cancer; Medicine

Summary: In *Cancer Biology, Fourth Edition*, Raymond Ruddon updates his comprehensive text about the biological aspects of human cancer and advances made in the field of cancer study. Presented in nine in-depth chapters, this volume discusses a range of cancer topics, including characteristics, causes, epidemiology, biochemistry, cell biology, molecular genetics, tumor immunology, diagnosis, treatment, and prevention. Ruddon explains the process by which normal cells become malignant, and how those cells then metastasize to affect other cells, tissues, and the body as a whole. Illustrations and diagrams supplement the text. Raymond Ruddon is a professor at the University of Michigan Medical School.

Where it's reviewed:
Quarterly Review of Biology, Dec 2009, page p427

Other books you might like:
Sadhan Majumder, *Stem Cells and Cancer*, 2009
Lauren Pecorino, *Molecular Biology of Cancer: Mechanisms, Targets, and Therapeutics, Second Edition*, 2008
Wolfgang Arthur Schulz, *Molecular Biology of Human Cancers: An Advanced Student's Textbook*, 2007
Edwin Wang, *Cancer Systems Biology*, 2010

1191

JESSICA SNYDER SACHS

Good Germs, Bad Germs: Health and Survival in a Bacterial World

(New York: Hill and Wang, 2007)

Subject(s): Biology; Medicine; Medical care

Summary: In her book *Good Germs, Bad Germs: Health and Survival in a Bacterial World*, author Jessica Snyder Sachs examines the modern use of microbial life forms in medicine. Sachs observes that antibiotics, which were once highly effective forms of medical treatment, are quickly becoming weaker and weaker as our bodies build greater resistance to these medications. She argues that after many years of antibiotic usage in agriculture and a rampant over-prescription of medical antibiotics, we have reached a level of tolerance that could easily become dangerous, and perhaps deadly. Sachs says that our disregard for microbial life has led to a potentially catastrophic health hazard that could lead to an epidemic of auto-immune diseases. She suggests that we might avoid this problem if we work to cultivate strong and resilient microbes that can do their intended job without disrupting the delicate balance of the microbial world.

Where it's reviewed:
Booklist, Sept 15, 2007, page p12
Books & Culture, July-August 2008, page 12

Choice, July 2008, page 1970
Library Journal, July 1, 2007, page p112
Science News, Nov 17, 2007, page p319

Other books by the same author:
Corpse, 2002

Other books you might like:
Anthony D. Barnosky, *Heatstroke: Nature in an Age of Global Warming*, 2010
Dorothy H. Crawford, *Deadly Companions: How Microbes Shaped Our History*, 2009
Anne E. Maczulak, *Allies and Enemies: How the World Depends on Bacteria*, 2010
Lois N. Magner, *A History of Infectious Diseases and the Microbial World*, 2009
Carl Zimmer, *Parasite Rex: Inside the Bizarre World of Nature's Most Dangerous Creatures*, 2000

1192

MENDEL SACHS

Quantum Mechanics and Gravity

(New York: Springer-Verlag, 2010)

Subject(s): Physics; Astronomy; Science

Summary: *Quantum Mechanics and Gravity* by Mendel Sachs is an educational perspective on the philosophical and mathematical differences between the science of quantum theory as opposed to that of the theory of general relativity. Sachs examines these differences through several different viewpoints, including the historical evolution of the theories applied to quantum physics as well as the rational or idealistic implications of such a theory. The author particularly explores the epistemological shift in modern physics theory as the discipline progresses from a positivist approach to a more comprehensive and constructivist viewpoint. Sachs is also the author of *Physics of the Universe* and *Relativity in Our Time*.

Other books by the same author:
Physics of the Universe, 2010
Concepts of Modern Physics: The Haifa Lectures, 2007

Other books you might like:
Claus Kiefer, *Quantum Gravity*, 2007
John W. Moffat, *Reinventing Gravity: A Physicist Goes Beyond Einstein*, 2008

1193

CALEB A. SCHARF

Extrasolar Planets and Astrobiology

(Sausalito, California: University Science Books, 2008)

Subject(s): Science; Biology; Chemistry

Summary: *Extrasolar Planets and Astrobiology* is a textbook intended for advanced undergraduate or graduate students, written by astrophysicist Caleb A. Scharf. Although this field of study is relatively young, Scharf

Science

provides a great deal of background on various sciences including biology, chemistry, physics, astronomy, mathematics, astrophysics, and geophysics. Practical mathematical applications are included in this text as well and numerous examples are provided to illustrate the concepts of astrobiology in actual applications. Practice exercises are found at the end of each chapter. Students may also access a corresponding website that provides supplemental information.

Where it's reviewed:
Astrobiology, April 2010, page p257
Choice, May 2009, page p1723

Other books you might like:
Joseph Gale, *Astrobiology of Earth*, 2009
Chris Impey, *Talking about Life: Conversations on Astrobiology*, 2010
Lucas John Mix, *Life in Space: Astrobiology for Everyone*, 2009
Andrew M. Shaw, *Astrochemistry: From Astronomy to Astrobiology*, 2006
Peter Ulmschneider, *Intelligent Life in the Universe*, 2010

1194

FLORIAN SCHECK

Quantum Physics

(Berlin: Springer, 2007)

Subject(s): Physics; Science; History

Summary: Physicist Florian Scheck provides students a detailed initiation into the world of quantum physics. This volume approaches the multifaceted subject from an array of angles, encompassing the fundamentals of quantum theory, the various applications of quantum mechanics, the elements of quantum electrodynamics, and much more. *Quantum Physics* contains an abundance of additional resources, including eight appendices, historical notes, a list of exercises and tips, a bibliography, and an index.

Where it's reviewed:
Choice, Oct 2007, page p321

Other books by the same author:
Mechanics: From Newton's Laws to Deterministic Chaos, 2010

Other books you might like:
Gary E. Bowman, *Essential Quantum Mechanics*, 2008
Michael D. Fayer, *Absolutely Small: How Quantum Theory Explains Our Everyday World*, 2010
Manjit Kumar, *Quantum: Einstein, Bohr, and the Great Debate about the Nature of Reality*, 2007
David McMahon, *Quantum Field Theory Demystified*, 2008
Fred Wolf, *Taking the Quantum Leap: The New Physics for Nonscientists*, 1981

1195

HOWARD SCHNEIDER
PATRICIA DANIELS , Co-Author

Backyard Guide to the Night Sky

(Washington, D.C.: National Geographic Society, 2009)

Subject(s): Astrology; Astronomy; Science

Summary: In *National Geographic*'s *Backyard Guide to the Night Sky*, authors Howard Schneider and Patricia Daniels take an easy approach to astrology that everyone from amateur stargazers to professional astronomers can understand. In ten chapters, readers learn basic facts about what they see when they look into the sky at night. They also learn how to improve their stargazing techniques so they can see more of the sky by using telescopes and constellation maps. This book includes hundreds of detailed photographs, illustrations, fact boxes, and sidebars with additional information about stars, planets, and constellations. Both Schneider and Daniels are experienced science writers.

Other books you might like:
Paul E. Kinzer, *Stargazing Basics: Getting Started in Recreational Astronomy*, 2008
Michael A. Seeds, *Foundations of Astronomy*, 2007
Thomas Nelson, Inc., *The Heavens Proclaim His Glory: A Spectacular View of Creation Through the Lens of the NASA Hubble Telescope*, 2010
Robert Bruce Thompson, *Illustrated Guide to Astronomical Wonders*, 2007
Stephen F. Tonkin, *Binocular Astronomy*, 2006

1196

WALTER SCHUMANN

Gemstones of the World, Revised Edition

(New York: Sterling Publishing, 1997)

Subject(s): Geology; Science; Hobbies

Summary: Walter Schumann's *Gemstones of the World, Revised Edition* is the definitive reference guide to locating and identifying precious minerals. With more than 1000 entries, this volume encompasses all the pertinent data any gem-seeker will need to know, including notable characteristics, color and luster, and geographic information. *Gemstones of the World* contains a bibliography and an index for easier look-up.

Other books by the same author:
Minerals of the World, 2008

Other books you might like:
Judith Crowe, *The Jeweler's Directory of Gemstones*, 2006
Rick Hudson, *A Field Guide to Gold, Gemstones and Minerals*, 2008
Shelley A. Kaehr, *Gemstone Enlightenment*, 2007
Antoinette L. Matlins, *Colored Gemstones*, 2005
Cally Oldershaw, *Guide to Gems*, 2009

Arthur Thomas, *Gemstones: Properties, Identification and Use*, 2009

Keith Wallis, *Gemstones: Understanding, Identifying, Buying*, 2006

1197

ERIK SEEDHOUSE

Prepare for Launch: The Astronaut Training Process

(New York: Springer, 2010)

Subject(s): Astronomy; Space exploration; Physics

Summary: In *Prepare for Launch: The Astronaut Training Process*, author Erik Seedhouse examines in detail the process of becoming an astronaut, and how that career path has seen increasing interest in recent years. Seedhouse explores the requirements of various space exploration programs, including NASA, the European Space Agency, and the Canadian Space Agency, and the rigorous regiments that candidates of such programs endure. The author has firsthand experience on the subject matter as a final candidate for the CSA; through interviews and personal anecdotes, Seedhouse reveals his findings through that experience.

Other books by the same author:
Martian Outpost: The Challenges of Establishing a Human Settlement on Mars, 2010
The New Space Race: China vs. USA, 2010
Lunar Outpost: The Challenges of Establishing a Human Settlement on the Moon, 2008

Other books you might like:
Philip Baker, *The Story of Manned Space Stations: An Introduction*, 2007
David A. Mindell, *Digital Apollo: Human and Machine in Spaceflight*, 2010
David Shayler, *Space Rescue: Ensuring the Safety of Manned Spacecraft*, 2009

1198

ADOLF SEILACHER

Trace Fossil Analysis

(Berlin, Germany: Springer, 2007)

Subject(s): Fossils; Science; Paleontology

Summary: The textbook *Trace Fossil Analysis* is written by trace fossil expert Adolf Seilacher. Trace fossils, also known as ichnofossils, are records that indicate how and where animals lived and behaved on the earth millions of years ago. They provide researchers and scientists with helpful information regarding paleoenvironmental reconstructions, basin analyses, and petroleum explorations. The textbook covers a wide array of information regarding trace fossils, including examples found on various landscapes and environments such as the deep sea and continental habitats. In addition to its vast information, *Trace Fossil Analysis* also includes

detailed illustrations from Seilacher and a glossary of key terms.

Where it's reviewed:
Choice, October 2007, page 313

Other books by the same author:
Morphodynamics of Invertebrate Skeletons, 2010

Other books you might like:
Friedrich Christian Accum, *A Practical Essay On the Analysis of Minerals*, 2010
Susan Cachel, *Primate and Human Evolution*, 2009
Anna Meyer, *The DNA Detectives*, 2009
Stephen Weiner, *Microarchaeology*, 2010
Bernard A. Wood, *Human Evolution*, 2006

1199

DAVID SHAYLER

Space Rescue: Ensuring the Safety of Manned Spacecraft

(New York: Springer, 2009)

Subject(s): Space exploration; Space flight; Science

Summary: In *Space Rescue: Ensuring the Safety of Manned Spacecraft*, David Shayler examines the history of safety measures that have been taken on various manned space flights and describes the way technology and escape measures have changed. Some of the current escape measures include escape towers, ejection seats, abort profiles, and extensively detailed contingency plans, including evacuation plans from the International Space Station. The author discusses the training methods used to prepare astronauts for unplanned situations, such as abort simulations and wilderness training. Shayler also considers ideas for escape methods and crew rescue proposals for future manned space flights, such as future expeditions to Mars.

Where it's reviewed:
Choice, July 2009, page 2140

Other books by the same author:
Apollo, 2002
Disasters and Accidents in Manned Spaceflight, 2002
Gemini Steps to the Moon, 2001
Skylab: America's Space Station, 2001

Other books you might like:
Bob Fish, *Hornet Plus Three: The Story of the Apollo 11 Recovery*, 2009
Chris Gainor, *To a Distant Day: The Rocket Pioneers*, 2008
David M. Harland, *NASA's Moon Program: Paving the Way for Apollo 11*, 2009
Stephen J. Pyne, *Voyager: Seeking Newer Worlds in the Third Great Age of Discovery*, 2010
Erik Seedhouse, *Lunar Outpost: The Challenges of Establishing a Human Settlement on the Moon*, 2008

Science

1200

PETER M. SHEARER

Introduction to Seismology
(New York: Cambridge University Press, 2009)

Subject(s): Geography; Geology; Earthquakes

Summary: *Introduction to Seismology* is an undergraduate-level college textbook that examines the field of seismology, a discipline that measures movement within the earth. Written by Peter M. Shearer and originally published in 1999, the 2009 edition includes additional material on earthquake data, source theory, and other related subject matter in the field of study. The book also includes end-of-chapter questions to help readers practice the methods and theories described within the chapter. Additionally, the author provides a Website for students to apply their knowledge. An index is included at the back of the book to help readers navigate the text.

Other books you might like:

Muneo Hori, *Introduction to Computational Earthquake Engineering*, 2010
Susan Hough, *Richter's Scale: Measure of an Earthquake, Measure of a Man*, 2007
J.R. Kayal, *Microearthquake Seismology and Seismotectonics of South Asia*, 2008

1201

SARA J. SHETTLEWORTH

Cognition, Evolution, and Behavior
(New York: Oxford University Press, 2009)

Subject(s): Evolution (Biology); Animals; Ecology

Summary: *Cognition, Evolution, and Behavior* by Sara J. Shettlesworth is an educational text for the disciplines of behaviorism, psychology, ecology, and biology. Shettlesworth provides for readers an overview of these inter-related fields of study as they pertain to the manner in which animals behave and think. The author includes case studies and examples of various species including bees, rats, and even humans to portray animal thought processes. The final product of the book illustrates the interconnected relationship between biology and psychology, and how each discipline can supplement the other. Originally published in 1988, the 2009 edition includes further studies and information about the subject matter.

Where it's reviewed:

Choice, June 2010 v47 i10, page p1952
Contemporary Psychology, June 2000 v45, page p292
Nature, April 8, 2010 v464 i7290, page p835

Other books you might like:

Fred H. Previc, *The Dopaminergic Mind in Human Evolution and History*, 2009
Alice D. Travis, *Cognitive Evolution: The Biological Imprint of Applied Intelligence*, 2007

1202

DAVID ALLEN SIBLEY

The Sibley Guide to Trees
(New York: Knopf, 2009)

Subject(s): Reference works; Trees (Plants); Nature

Summary: In the authoritative *The Sibley Guide to Trees*, author David Allen Sibley identifies and illustrates more than 600 tree species found in North America. Each page in the book shares the same design, which makes it easy to look for information; in addition, the tree species are arranged taxonomically. Sibley illustrates each tree to show its life cycle, paying special attention to the similarities and differences between species of trees by focusing on details such as bark, leaves, needles, flowers, fruit, and silhouettes. More than 400 maps indicate the locations of the trees and accompany essays on conservation, preservation, and environmental health.

Where it's reviewed:

The American Gardener, Nov-Dec 2009, page 54
Birder's World, December 2009, page 40
Choice, February 2010, page 1098
Globe & Mail, March 20, 2010, page F12

Other books by the same author:

Sibley's Raptors of North America, 2010
The Sibley Guide to Bird Life and Behavior, 2009
Sibley Field Guide to Birds of Western North America, 2003
Sibley's Birding Basics, 2002
The Sibley Guide to Birds, 2000

Other books you might like:

Hormoz BassiriRad, *Nutrient Acquisition by Plants: An Ecological Perspective*, 2009
Bryan G. Bowes, *Trees and Forests — A Color Guide*, 2010
Robert H. Mohlenbrock, *This Land: A Guide to Eastern National Forests*, 2006
Bob Watson, *Trees: Their Use, Management, Cultivation and Biology*, 2006
Tom Wessels, *Forest Forensics*, 2010

1203

JIM SNOOK

Ice Age Extinction: Cause and Human Consequences
(New York: Algora Publishing, 2007)

Subject(s): Geology; Paleontology; Evolution (Biology)

Summary: In *Ice Age Extinction: Cause and Human Consequences*, geologist Jim Snook considers atmospheric carbon dioxide as both causal and indicative of global climate change, taking his research back to previous ice ages that led to mass extinction of megaflora and megafauna. Snook first argues that a sudden and sustained decrease in temperature led to an equally sudden decrease in carbon dioxide in the atmosphere, which led to the mass extinctions. As the planet warmed, carbon dioxide increased, allowing life to flourish once again. Snook believes these atmospheric and temperature changes are cyclical and similar events could take place in the next few centuries. The author backs up his theories with facts and extensive explanations.

Where it's reviewed:
Choice, April 2008, page 1367

Other books you might like:
Julie Kerr Casper, *Global Warming Cycles: Ice Ages and Glacial Retreat*, 2009
Brian M. Fagan, *Cro-Magnon: How the Ice Age Gave Birth to the First Modern Humans*, 2010
Brian M. Fagan, *The Complete Ice Age: How Climate Change Shaped the World*, 2009
Sharon Levy, *Once and Future Giants: What Ice Age Extinctions Tell Us About the Fate of Earth's Largest Animals*, 2011

1204

STEVEN E. SONDERGARD

Climate Balance: A Balanced and Realistic View of Climate Change

(Mustang, Oklahoma: Tate Publishing, 2009)

Subject(s): Weather; Earth; Pollution

Summary: Author Steven E. Sondergard offers an unbiased and comprehensive look at the looming environmental issues of global warming and climate change in his book, *Climate Balance: A Balanced and Realistic View of Climate Change*. In many cases, the information we receive about global warming and climate change is presented with a heavy political slant that always seems to favor one side or the other. Sondergard offers readers a balanced, impartial take on this important subject. With this approach in mind, Sondergard introduces readers to many of the basic concepts involved with global warming, including climate, fossil fuels, and greenhouse gases. He also explores more complex issues like what we can do about global warming and climate change, how we can cut down on greenhouse gases, what the future holds for fossil fuels, and more.

Other books you might like:
David Archer, *The Long Thaw: How Humans Are Changing the Next 100,000 Years of Earth's Climate*, 2010
Greg Craven, *What's the Worst That Could Happen?: A Rational Response to the Climate Change Debate*, 2009
Jim Snook, *Ice Age Extinction: Cause and Human Consequences*, 2007

1205

HYRON SPINRAD

Galaxy Formation and Evolution

(New York: Springer-Verlag, 2010)

Subject(s): Evolution (Biology); Science; Astronomy

Summary: *Galaxy Formation and Evolution*, written by Hyron Spinrad, is a textbook based around the subjects of astronomy, planetary evolution, and galaxy formation. In this text, Spinrad compiles evidence about the creation and configuration of the Milky Way galaxy, and how its structure has contributed to the overall development of the entire universe. The author also examines, through assessments of nearby galaxies as well as hypotheses about distant ones, how other galaxies have contributed to this development. Spinrad also reviews the system of galaxy morphology, which involves the categorizations of galaxies according to their appearances.

Other books you might like:
F. Combes, *Mysteries of Galaxy Formation*, 2010
William C. Keel, *The Road to Galaxy Formation*, 2010
Malcolm S. Longair, *Galaxy Formation*, 2008

1206

ROBERT SPLINTER

Handbook of Physics in Medicine and Biology

(Boca Raton, Florida: CRC Press, 2010)

Story type: Medical
Subject(s): Science; Physics; Biology

Summary: Edited by Robert Splinter, *Handbook of Physics in Medicine and Biology* is an academic textbook that examines the role that physics play in medical advancements and natural biological processes. Divided into seven sections, *Handbook of Physics in Medicine and Biology* features more than 40 chapters written by experts in the field. The book details how physics principles and theories can be applied to basic biological features, such as the five senses present in humans, organ functions, cell makeup, cardiovascular processes, and respiration. Also covered is the crucial role that physics have played in medical and technological advancements, including ultrasound imaging, optics, x-rays, prosthetic devices, and artificial organs.

Other books by the same author:
An Introduction to Biomedical Optics, 2006

Other books you might like:
Paul Davidovits, *Physics in Biology and Medicine*, 2007
Matteo Santin, *Strategies in Regenerative Medicine: Integrating Biology with Materials Design*, 2009

1207

GARRISON SPOSITO

The Chemistry of Soils, Second Edition

(Oxford; New York: Oxford University Press, 2008)

Subject(s): Chemistry; Ecology; Science

Summary: When Garrison Sposito's *The Chemistry of Soils* was first published in 1989, it pioneered the study of soil chemistry. In this expanded and updated edition of the original trailblazing volume, Sposito again covers the basics of soil chemistry utilizing a strictly physical method. He also expounds upon the role of soil chemistry in ecological change, illuminating the far-ranging impact of this powerful course of study. *The Chemistry of Soils, Second Edition* includes an appendix and a full index.

Other books you might like:
W. F. Bleam, *Soil and Environmental Chemistry*, 2011
James Ralph Hanson, *Chemistry in the Garden*, 2007
Eldor Alvin Paul, *Soil Microbiology, Ecology and Biochemistry*, 2007
D. Max Roundhill, *Extraction of Metals from Soils and Waters*, 2010
Robert E. White, *Understanding Vineyard Soils*, 2009

1208

BRUCE L. STINCHCOMB

Paleozoic Fossils

(Atglen, Pennsylvania: Schiffer Publishing, 2008)

Subject(s): Paleontology; Fossils; Science

Summary: The Paleozoic Era produced some of the most astonishing fossils ever unearthed. In *Paleozoic Fossils*, author Bruce L. Stinchcomb examines the various paleontological remnants of the successive periods which encompassed the Paleozoic Era. The author's findings provide an insightful investigation of a time period steeped in mystery, shedding light on the world's first plant and animal life forms. This volume includes a bibliography and a full index.

Where it's reviewed:
Rocks & Minerals, Nov-Dec 2009, page p564

Other books by the same author:
Cenozoic Fossils 1: Paleogene, 2010
Cenozoic Fossils II The Neogene, 2010
Mesozoic Fossils II: The Cretaceous Period, 2009
Mesozoic Fossils I: Triassic & Jurassic Periods, 2008
World's Oldest Fossils, 2007

Other books you might like:
Loren E. Babcock, *Visualizing Earth History*, 2008
William Miller III, *Trace Fossils: Concepts, Problems, Prospects*, 2007
Adolf Seilacher, *Trace Fossil Analysis*, 2007
Steven M. Stanley, *Earth System History*, 2008

1209

HAROLD H. STOWELL

Geology of Southeast Alaska: Rock and Ice in Motion

(Fairbanks, Alaska: University of Alaska Press, 2006)

Subject(s): Geology

Summary: Southeast Alaska's fiercely beautiful landscape attracts travelers and geologists from every continent.

Harold H. Stowell, professor of geology at the University of Alabama, has written *Geology of Southeast Alaska: Rock and Ice in Motion* as a guidebook through Southeast Alaska's geological events. In illustrations and photographs, Stowell demonstrates how Alaska's geological activity—earthquakes, ice ages, violent shifts in the earth's tectonic plates—formed the mountain ranges, bays, and islands to create one of the world's most spectacular landscapes.

Where it's reviewed:
Arctic, Dec 2006, page p435
Choice, Sept 2006, page p143
Geotimes, Dec 2006, page p64

Other books you might like:
Montana Hodges, *Rockhounding Alaska: A Guide to 75 of the State's Best Rockhounding Sites*, 2010
James R. Mitchell, *The Rockhound's Handbook*, 2008

1210

BILL STREEVER

Cold: Adventures in the World's Frozen Places

(New York: Little, Brown and Co., 2009)

Subject(s): Weather; Ecology; Geography

Summary: *Cold: Adventures in the World's Frozen Places* is written by Bill Streever, a scientist and chair of the North Slope Science Initiative's Science Technical Advisory Panel. Streever writes about the importance of cold-weather systems to life on Earth, describing his many travels to the Arctic and other subzero regions where he works and performs research. Streever explores topics including mysteries from the Ice Age, the building of igloos, weather topics such as permafrost and hailstorms, bird migration, and the way scientists determine what the climate was like in ancient history based on data of today. The book is written in an interesting narrative style rather than a formal, factual structure.

Where it's reviewed:
Library Journal, May 1, 2009, page 97
Nature Conservancy, Summer 2010, page 77
Publishers Weekly, April 27, 2009, page 121

Other books by the same author:
Saving Louisiana? The Battle for Coastal Wetlands, 2001
Bringing Back the Wetlands, 1999

Other books you might like:
Sean Callery, *Frozen World: Polar Meltdown*, 2009
Bernd Heinrich, *Winter World: The Ingenuity of Animal Survival*, 2009
Steve House, *Beyond the Mountain*, 2009
Sara L. Latta, *Ice Scientist: Careers in the Frozen Antarctic*, 2009

1211

THOMAS F. TASCIONE

Introduction to the Space Environment

(Malabar, Florida: Krieger Publishing Company, 2010)

Subject(s): Weather; Space exploration; Astronomy

Summary: *Introduction to the Space Environment* by Thomas F. Tascione is a comprehensive guide to the stars, constellations, planets, solar systems, and galaxies that make up the Universe, as well as the tools and theories that scientists use to explore it. Originally published in 1988, the newest edition published in 2010 includes new information about space weather and services. Tascione provides readers, most of whom are expected to have some knowledge of astrophysics, with an overview of relevant topics within the field of study. Other subject matter includes plasma physics, solar physics, solar wind processes, radiowaves, and the effects that space's environment has on exploration crafts.

Other books you might like:
William E. Wiesel, *Spaceflight Dynamics*, 2010

1212

DORIS TEICHLER-ZALLEN

To Test or Not to Test: A Guide to Genetic Screening and Risk

(New Brunswick, New Jersey: Rutgers University Press, 2008)

Story type: Medical
Subject(s): Science; Genetics; Genetic disorders

Summary: *To Test or Not to Test: A Guide to Genetic Screening and Risk* is a guide to genetic testing from author Doris Teichler-Zallen. With modern advances in medicine, individuals can now undergo genetic testing to gain a better understanding of their likelihood of contracting certain diseases and illnesses. While the testing is controversial, it is often helpful. In *To Test or Not to Test*, Teichler-Zallen interviews genetic specialists, doctors, and researchers to provide answers to the tough questions surrounding genetic screening, including how the process works and the risks associated with it. The book includes more than 100 true stories of individuals who faced genetic testing for breast/ovarian cancer, colon cancer, Alzheimer's disease, and hereditary hemochromatosis.

Where it's reviewed:
Choice, May 2009, page 1739

Other books you might like:
Michela Betta, *The Moral, Social, and Commercial Imperatives of Genetic Testing and Screening*, 2010
Elizabeth Boskey, *America Debates Genetic DNA Testing*, 2007
Robert Kolb, *The Ethics of Genetic Commerce*, 2007
Sandra R. Pupecki, *Focus on Genetic Screening Research*, 2006

Aviad E. Raz, *Community Genetics and Genetic Alliances*, 2009

1213

SAMUEL THAYER

The Forager's Harvest: A Guide to Identifying, Harvesting, and Preparing Edible Wild Plants

(Ogema, Wisconsin: Forager's Harvest, 2006)

Subject(s): Agriculture; Ecology; Botany

Summary: *The Forager's Harvest: A Guide to Identifying, Harvesting, and Preparing Edible Wild Plants* by Samuel Thayer is a field guide for those interested in learning to locate, identify, and prepare edible plants. Thayer first provides detailed methods for finding and correctly identifying edible plants based on their locations, harvest seasons and detailed color photographs for each plant showcasing it at different stages of growth. Information on collecting, harvesting, and safely preparing or preserving the edible plants is then provided. This text also includes a reference index, illustrated glossary, and calendar to indicate harvest seasons. It is often recommended for people who are just beginning to learn about foraging and harvesting wild plants, but may also be used by those who are more experienced.

Other books by the same author:
Nature's Garden: A Guide to Identifying, Harvesting, and Preparing Edible Wild Plants, 2010

Other books you might like:
Jane Eastoe, *Wild Food*, 2008
Alan Hall, *The Wild Food Trailguide, New Edition*, 2008
John Kallas, *Edible Wild Plants*, 2010
Richard Mabey, *Food for Free*, 2007
Frank Tozer, *The Uses of Wild Plants*, 2007

1214

THOMAS NELSON, INC.

The Heavens Proclaim His Glory: A Spectacular View of Creation Through the Lens of the NASA Hubble Telescope

(Nashville: Thomas Nelson, Inc., 2010)

Subject(s): Photography; Christianity; Space exploration

Summary: The publishing team at Thomas Nelson, Inc., marries a series of photos taken by the Hubble Telescope with a collection of musings, commentary, and Bible verses. *The Heavens Proclaim His Glory: A Spectacular View of Creation Through the Lens of the NASA Hubble Telescope* celebrates each photograph as proof of God's divine hand playing a role in the creation of Heaven and Earth. Full color photos are accompanied by quotations or Bible passages. Contributors to this volume include Kirk Cameron, Mike Huckabee, and Henry and Richard Blackaby.

Other books you might like:

Leo Marriott, *Universe: Images from the Hubble Telescope*, 2007

Martin Ratcliffe, *State of the Universe 2008: New Images, Discoveries, and Events*, 2007

Edward John Weiler, *Hubble: A Journey through Space and Time*, 2010

1215

KAREN C. TIMBERLAKE

Lab Manual for General, Organic, and Biological Chemistry: 2nd Edition

(Boston, Massachusetts: Prentice Hall, 2010)

Subject(s): Science; Science experiments (Education); Biology

Summary: Written by textbook author and professor emeritus of chemistry, Karen C. Timberlake, *Lab Manual for General, Organic, and Biological Chemistry: 2nd Edition* is a supplementary educational resource for students of chemistry. The book includes 42 experiments for students to complete during times in the laboratory to complement the material being learned in general, organic, or biological chemistry courses. The projects in the lab manual are divided into three sections: Dry Labs, General Chemistry, and Organic and Biological Chemistry. The experiments cover a wide range of subject matter including properties of organ compounds; measuring length, volume, and mass; nuclear radiation; gas laws; hydrocarbon reactions; and DNA components.

Other books by the same author:

Basic Chemistry, 2010

MasteringChemistry Student Access Kit for Chemistry: An Introduction to General, Organic, & Biological Chemistry, 2009

Chemistry: An Introduction to General, Organic, & Biological Chemistry, 2008

Basic Chemistry Study Guide, 2007

Chemistry: Study Guide and Selected Solutions - An Introduction to General, Organic, and Biological Chemistry, 2005

Other books you might like:

Charles H. Corwin, *Introductory Chemistry: Concepts & Connections*, 2007

H. Stephen Stoker, *Lab Manual for Stoker's General, Organic, and Biological Chemistry*, 2008

1216

WIL TIRION

The Cambridge Star Atlas: 4th Edition

(Cambridge, England: Cambridge University Press, 2010)

Subject(s): Science; Astronomy; Maps (Geography)

Summary: *The Cambridge Star Atlas: 4th Edition* is a comprehensive map to stars, galaxies, and clusters from uranographer Wil Tirion. The 4th edition includes up-to-date information on the location and visibility of constellations and stars for novice and seasoned astronomers alike. The full-color illustrated maps show readers the exact location of various stars that can be viewed using binoculars or telescopes. *The Cambridge Star Atlas* features details about constellation boundaries, the Milky Way, and other fascinating astronomical sights. The revised edition includes a new Moon map, featuring craters, a new mirror-reversed Moon map, constellation index charts, and updated data on planetary systems.

Other books you might like:

Erich Karkoschka, *The Observer's Sky Atlas: With 50 Star Charts Covering the Entire Sky*, 2007

Jack Martin, *A Spectroscopic Atlas of Bright Stars: A Pocket Field Guide*, 2009

1217

IKUO TOWHATA

Geotechnical Earthquake Engineering

(Berlin: Springer, 2008)

Subject(s): Earthquakes; Engineering; Geology

Summary: The gamut of earthquake risks and the reasons for those risks are the subject of this authoritative volume. In *Geotechnical Earthquake Engineering*, author Ikuo Towhata explores the myriad causes of earthquakes from a geotechnical perspective, examining such topics as soil and ground conduct and how to utilize this information to predict earth movement. Culled from hands-on data obtained from tremors large and small, this comprehensive study includes charts, graphs, sample exercises, and test questions. First book.

Where it's reviewed:

Choice, Oct 2008, page 334

Other books you might like:

Michael N. Fardis, *Advances in Performance-Based Earthquake Engineering*, 2010

Ruwan Rajapakse, *Geotechnical Engineering Calculations and Rules of Thumb*, 2008

Milutin Srbulov, *Geotechnical Earthquake Engineering: Simplified Analyses with Case Studies and Examples*, 2008

Andreas Stark, *Seismic Methods and Applications*, 2010

1218

MARIO F. TRIOLA

Essentials of Statistics, Third Edition

(Boston: Pearson/Addison Wesley, 2006)

Subject(s): Science; Mathematics

Summary: The world of statistics can be a daunting field of study, but in *Essentials of Statistics, Third Edition*, mathematics professor Mario F. Triola dispels much of the mystery surrounding the subject. Through practical insight and straightforward discussions, Triola presents such topics as summarizing and graphing data, correlation and regression, and analysis of variance. Triola offers his findings through real-life examples that further illustrate the various functions and importance of statistical research. *Essentials of Statistics* includes a full index.

Other books by the same author:
Elementary Statistics Using Excel, 2010
Student Solutions Manual for Elementary Statistics Using Excel, 2009

Other books you might like:
Teresa Bradley, *Essential Statistics for Economics, Business and Management*, 2007
Joseph F. Healey, *The Essentials of Statistics: A Tool for Social Research*, 2009
David S. Moore, *Essential Statistics*, 2009

1219

MARTIN J. L. TURNER

Rocket and Spacecraft Propulsion: Principles, Practice and New Developments

(New York: Springer-Verlag, 2010)

Subject(s): Science; Space exploration; Space flight

Summary: *Rocket and Spacecraft Propulsion: Principles, Practice and New Developments* is a comprehensive text detailing the development and advancement of rocket propulsion and astrophysics, and the principles that lie within the field of study. Initially published in 2000, this new edition examines later developments in space launch crafts that are up-to-date with the publication of the text, and describes innovations within the field. Author Martin J. L. Turner uses detailed graphics and charts as well as full-color photographs to illustrate the subject matter. Turner is also the author of *Expedition Mars*.

Other books by the same author:
Mars Base One: Creating a Permanent Presence on the Red Planet, 2008

Other books you might like:
Matthew A. Bentley, *Spaceplanes: From Airport to Spaceport*, 2008
James A. Dewar, *To the End of the Solar System: The Story of the Nuclear Rocket, Second Edition*, 2008

Raymond Friedman, *A History of Jet Propulsion, Including Rockets*, 2010

1220

DANIEL J. VELLEMAN

How to Prove It: A Structured Approach, Second Edition

(Cambridge, United Kingdom; New York: Cambridge University Press, 2006)

Subject(s): Mathematics; Science; Students

Summary: Both seasoned mathematicians and novice students have long encountered trouble when it comes to proving mathematical theorems. In *How to Prove It: A Structured Approach, Second Edition*, author and math whiz Daniel J. Velleman presents the fundamentals of set theory and how this theory can be applied to mathematics. This second edition is fully expanded with more than 200 hands-on exercises in which students are challenged to establish proof of their mathematical findings. *How to Prove It* includes two appendices, a bibliography, and an index. First book.

Where it's reviewed:
SIAM Review, Dec 2006, page 808

Other books you might like:
Antonella Cupillari, *The Nuts and Bolts of Proofs*, 2005
Gordon Mackay, *Comparative Metamathematics*, 2010
Paul Zeitz, *The Art and Craft of Problem Solving*, 2006

1221

MARIO VIETRI

Foundations of High-Energy Astrophysics

(Chicago, Illinois: University of Chicago Press, 2008)

Subject(s): Physics; Astronomy; Science

Summary: *Foundations of High-Energy Astrophysics* by astrophysicist Mario Vietri provides an introduction to space science from both the mathematical and physical process perspectives, though Vietri chooses to focus more intently on the physical processes than on the mathematical concepts of astrophysics. Some of the topics presented in this text include magnetohydrodynamics, hydrodynamics, radiative processes, and the electrodynamics of neutron stars and black holes. The book is recommended for individuals studying both astronomy and astrophysics.

Where it's reviewed:
Choice, Nov 2008, page 535

Other books you might like:
Hale Bradt, *Astrophysics Processes*, 2008
Judith A. Irwin, *Astrophysics: Decoding the Cosmos*, 2007
Francis LeBlanc, *An Introduction to Stellar Astrophysics*, 2010

Science

Steven L. Weinberg, *Cosmology*, 2008
Georg Wolschin, *Lectures on Cosmology*, 2010

1222

ROBERTO VILLAVERDE

Fundamental Concepts of Earthquake Engineering

(Boca Raton, Florida: CRC Press, 2009)

Subject(s): Earthquakes; Environmental engineering; Science

Summary: In *Fundamental Concepts of Earthquake Engineering*, author Roberto Villaverde provides for readers an overview of the principles that apply to structural engineering in earthquake zones. While the author concedes that the prevention of seismic disturbances may never be plausible, he illustrates how destruction caused by an earthquake can be minimized through various engineering techniques. Villaverde delves into the discipline of seismology to explain its interrelationship with structural engineering, and how the designs of buildings and other structures are impacted by seismography. The author also looks into scientific principles that apply to the study of earthquake engineering.

Other books you might like:

Muneo Hori, *Introduction to Computational Earthquake Engineering*, 2010
Susan Hough, *Richter's Scale: Measure of an Earthquake, Measure of a Man*, 2007
J.R. Kayal, *Microearthquake Seismology and Seismotectonics of South Asia*, 2008

1223

DONALD VOET
JUDITH G. VOET , Co-Author

Biochemistry: 4th Edition

(New York: J. Wiley & Sons, 2010)

Subject(s): Science; Biology; Chemistry

Summary: Written by Donald Voet and Judith G. Voet, *Biochemistry: 4th Edition* is an academic textbook on biochemical theory. Designed for college students who have completed general chemistry and biology courses, *Biochemistry* provides a more in-depth, comprehensive evaluation of the subject matter. The book provides detailed information on biochemical theories and principles, as well as updated research on the latest scientific discoveries and developments. The 4th edition has been revised to include more extensive facts about molecular biological techniques, greater detail about human disease, and new advances made with nucleic acid and protein structure. The book also includes detailed illustrations and review questions.

Other books you might like:

Rodney F. Boyer, *Biochemistry Laboratory: Modern Theory and Techniques*, 2006

Rodney F. Boyer, *Concepts in Biochemistry*, 2005
Thomas M. Devlin, *Textbook of Biochemistry with Clinical Correlations*, 2010
Michael E. Houston, *Biochemistry Primer for Exercise Science, Third Edition*, 2006
R. Bruce Wilcox, *High-Yield Biochemistry*, 2009

1224

GREGORY L. VOGT

Landscapes of Mars: A Visual Tour

(New York: Springer Science, 2008)

Subject(s): Mars (Planet); Photography; Space exploration

Summary: *Landscapes of Mars: A Visual Tour* is a collection of photographs of the Red Planet from Gregory L. Vogt. Every area of Mars is covered in the book, which includes extended captions offering information on the planet. Vogt gives readers a photographic tour of Mars, including details on topographical areas of the planet, the martian uplands, giant volcanos, the grand canyon of Mars, craters, erosion, sand dunes, dust devils, and wind shadows. The book provides a thorough examination of the planet's landscape, allowing readers to see how it differs in all the major regions. *Landscapes of Mars* also features conversation regarding the quest for water on Mars, the Viking Mission search for life, Mars meteorite fossil bacteria, and ways to protect the planet in the future.

Where it's reviewed:
Choice, June 2009, page 1957

Other books by the same author:
Exploring Space, 2003
Living on Other Worlds, 2003
Comets, 2002
The Galaxy, 2002
Jupiter, 2000

Other books you might like:
Jim Bell, *Mars 3-D: A Rover's-Eye View of the Red Planet*, 2008
Pat Duggins, *Trailblazing Mars: NASA's Next Giant Leap*, 2010
K. Maria D. Lane, *Geographies of Mars: Seeing and Knowing the Red Planet*, 2011
Steven W. Squyres, *Roving Mars: Spirit, Opportunity, and the Exploration of the Red Planet*, 2006
Frederic W. Taylor, *The Scientific Exploration of Mars*, 2010

1225

ALEXEY A. VOINOV

Systems Science and Modeling for Ecological Economics

(Amsterdam; Boston: Elsevier, 2008)

Subject(s): Science; Ecology; Mathematics
Summary: In *Systems Science and Modeling for Ecologi-*

cal Economics, author Alexey A. Voinov examines the fundamentals of modeling as it relates to key areas of modern science and ecology. Voinov guides readers through the various methods of inspection that can be utilized to glean solid information from scientific and mathematical models. Using actual examples and straightforward explanations, this volume illustrates the revolutionary role of modeling in fields as diverse as management, sustainability theory, and oil production. *Systems Science and Modeling for Ecological Economics* includes a full index.

Where it's reviewed:
Ecological Economics, August 2009, page 2498

Other books you might like:
Nino Boccara, *Modeling Complex Systems*, 2010
Andrew Ford, *Modeling the Environment*, 2009
Donella H. Meadows, *Thinking in Systems*, 2008
Robert A. Meyers, *Encyclopedia of Complexity and Systems Science*, 2009

▐1226▌

EDWARD JOHN WEILER

Hubble: A Journey through Space and Time

(New York: Abrams, 2010)

Subject(s): Astronomy; Photography; Space exploration

Summary: Edward John Weiler's *Hubble: A Journey through Space and Time* is a photobook produced by NASA to celebrate 20 years of photography and research through the use of the Hubble telescope. More than 100 images have been chosen for this book and reproduced in full-page, high-resolution photographs. Twenty of these photographs, determined to be the most scientifically relevant, feature accompanying explanations or commentary from premier scientists who have worked on the project, as well as a number of astronauts sent to perform work on the telescope itself.

Where it's reviewed:
USA Today, May 2010, page 81

Other books you might like:
Alan Boss, *The Crowded Universe: The Search for Living Planets*, 2009
Heather Couper, *Universe: Stunning Satellite Imagery from Outer Space*, 2006
Jerome Drexler, *Discovering Postmodern Cosmology*, 2008
Jean-Pierre Luminet, *The Wraparound Universe*, 2010
Georg Wolschin, *Lectures on Cosmology*, 2010

▐1227▌

DAVID A. WEINTRAUB

How Old Is the Universe?

(Princeton, New Jersey: Princeton University Press, 2011)

Subject(s): Astronomy; History; Science
Summary: In *How Old Is the Universe?* David A. Wein-

traub explains the science behind the dating of the universe, showing readers how scientists concluded that the universe is about 13.7 billion years old. Weintraub begins with a discussion of the way astronomers first studied our solar system and were able to date lunar rocks and meteorites to determine that the solar system is about 4.5 billion years old. Then, the work of Edwin Hubble allowed astronomers to determine that other galaxies in the universe were moving away from our own solar system, which led scientists to determine that the universe was about 13.5 billion years old. The study of concepts such as dark matter, dark energy, weakly interacting massive particles, and massive compact halo objects allowed further refinement of that number. Weintraub provides readable explanations of the different methods used to date the universe, which is ongoing.

Where it's reviewed:
Library Journal, Oct 1, 2010, page 96

Other books by the same author:
Is Pluto a Planet?: A Historical Journey through the Solar System, 2008

Other books you might like:
Martin Bojowald, *Once Before Time: A Whole Story of the Universe*, 2010
Evalyn Gates, *Einstein's Telescope: The Hunt for Dark Matter and Dark Energy in the Universe*, 2010
Brian Greene, *The Hidden Reality: Parallel Universes and the Deep Laws of the Cosmos*, 2011
John Gribbin, *In Search of the Multiverse*, 2010
Anton Zeilinger, *Dance of the Photons: From Einstein to Quantum Teleportation*, 2010

▐1228▌

P.C. WHITE

Crime Scene to Court: The Essentials of Forensic Science, 3rd Edition

(Cambridge, England: Royal Society of Chemistry, 2005)

Subject(s): Science; Crime; Criminal law

Summary: Written by forensic science consultant, P.C. White, *Crime Scene to Court: The Essentials of Forensic Science, 3rd Edition* is an educational guide to using forensic science in crime scene investigations. The book provides a basic overview on forensic science and how it is utilized in crime scenes, laboratories, and court. Written for non-scientists or students with limited scientific background, *Crime Scene to Court* offers straightforward and easy-to-understand information about what forensic science is, how it's utilized in criminal investigations, and the principles and practices of forensic science in the United Kingdom. The book includes updated information on accident reconstruction, as well as details about DNA testing, courtroom procedures, technology based crimes, bloodstain pattern analysis, and professional requirements.

Other books you might like:
Vernard Irvine Adams, *Guidelines for Reports by Autopsy Pathologists*, 2010

Science

Maciej J. Bogusz, *Quality Assurance in the Pathology Laboratory: Forensic, Technical, and Ethical Aspects*, 2011

Susanne Hummel, *Ancient DNA Typing: Methods, Strategies and Applications*, 2010

Patrick Jones, *Practical Forensic Digital Imaging: Applications and Techniques*, 2011

David Pierce, *Mechanics of Impression Evidence*, 2011

1229

JACK WILLIAMS

The AMS Weather Book: The Ultimate Guide to America's Weather

(Chicago, Illinois: University of Chicago Press, 2009)

Subject(s): Meteorology; Weather; Science

Summary: In *The AMS Weather Book: The Ultimate Guide to America's Weather*, Jack Williams and the American Meteorological Society provide an accessible guide to individuals interested in learning more about weather and climatology. Topics include daily weather patterns, air pollution, wind and precipitation, atmospheric changes, the oceans, climate patterns and climate change, and an extensive discussion of severe weather, such as how and why hurricanes and tornadoes form and why they rotate in certain directions. Williams explains why weather patterns vary so much over the continental United States and the rest of the world. In addition, the book includes charts, graphs, and illustrations to explain concepts more fully.

Where it's reviewed:
Choice, Oct 2009, page 338

Other books by the same author:
East 40 Degrees: An Interpretive Atlas, 2007

Other books you might like:
Donald Ahrens, *Meteorology Today*, 2008
Paul Douglas, *Restless Skies*, 2007
Michael Hodgson, *Basic Essentials Weather Forecasting*, 2007
Joseph M. Moran, *Weather Studies: Introduction to Atmospheric Science*, 2006
Thomas T. Warner, *Numerical Weather and Climate Prediction*, 2010

1230

SAUL WISCHNITZER

Atlas and Dissection Guide for Comparative Anatomy, Sixth Edition

(New York: W. H. Freeman and Co., 2006)

Subject(s): Anatomy; Science; Science experiments (Education)

Summary: For students studying the anatomies of various vertebrate animals, Saul Wischnitzer's *Atlas and Dissection Guide for Comparative Anatomy, Sixth Edition* provides a valuable roadmap to the entire process. Filled with predominantly black and white illustrations, this volume guides readers through the dissection procedure involving several different animals. Specimens covered include a cat, a dogfish shark, a lamprey, and a mud puppy. This laboratory manual comes equipped with a bibliography and a full index.

Other books you might like:
Blandine Calais-Germain, *Anatomy of Movement*, 2007
Sharon Colacino, *Atlas of Human Anatomy*, 1989
Dale W. Fishbeck, *Comparative Anatomy*, 2008
Duane V. Knudson, *Fundamentals of Biomechanics*, 2007
Frank Netter, *Atlas of Human Anatomy*, 1989

1231

NOUREDINE ZETTILI

Quantum Mechanics: Concepts and Applications, Second Edition

(Chichester, United Kingdom: Wiley, 2009)

Subject(s): Science; Mathematics; Reference works

Summary: *Quantum Mechanics: Concepts and Applications, Second Edition* by Nouredine Zettili is a textbook for undergraduate and graduate students, divided into four sections. The first section focuses on mathematics for quantum mechanics, followed by fundamental postulates, angular momentum theory, time independent and dependent approximation application, and solutions of the Schrodinger equation in one and three dimensional potentials. Each concept includes sample problems with the solution provided with a detailed explanation and step-by-step problem-solving process. This text is recommended for intermediate students with knowledge of physics and linear algebra.

Other books you might like:
Bipin R. Desai, *Quantum Mechanics with Basic Field Theory*, 2009
David J. Griffiths, *Introduction to Elementary Particles*, 2008
Paul A. Klevgard, *Einstein's Method: A Fresh Approach to Quantum Mechanics and Relativity*, 2008
David A. B. Miller, *Quantum Mechanics for Scientists and Engineers*, 2008
Henry P. Stapp, *Mind, Matter and Quantum Mechanics*, 2009

1232

YOUXUE ZHANG

Geochemical Kinetics

(Princeton, New Jersey: Princeton University Press, 2008)

Subject(s): Science; Chemistry; Geology

Summary: Written by geology professor Youxue Zhang, *Geochemical Kinetics* is an educational textbook about the practical and theoretical application of chemical kinetics to geological issues. Zhang begins with a broad introduction to the basic principles of geochemical kinetics before diving into more complex theories and practices including details on nonisothermal kinetics and inverse theories, geochronology, thermochronology, geospeedometry, homogeneous reactions, mass and heat transfer, and heterogeneous reactions. The book is filled with examples, review questions and problems, reference lists, and appendices to help students with their comprehension and understanding of the material.

Where it's reviewed:
Choice, May 2009, page 1732
Physics Today, September 2009, page 53

Other books you might like:
Craig Bethke, *Geochemical and Biogeochemical Reaction Modeling*, 2008
Shun-ichiro Karato, *Deformation of Earth Materials: An Introduction to the Rheology of Solid Earth*, 2008
Haibo Zou, *Quantitative Geochemistry*, 2007

1233

ROBERT ZIMMERMAN

The Universe in a Mirror: The Saga of the Hubble Space Telescope and the Visionaries Who Built It

(Princeton, New Jersey: Princeton University Press, 2010)

Story type: Historical
Subject(s): Science; Astronomy; Space exploration

Summary: Written by Robert Zimmerman, *The Universe in a Mirror: The Saga of the Hubble Space Telescope*

and the Visionaries Who Built It is a detailed history of the construction of the Hubble telescope and the controversy surrounding it. The Hubble Space Telescope has captured amazing photographs of the universe, allowing individuals to gain a greater understanding of the cosmos and advancing the scientific study of astronomers, but it almost failed completely. Zimmerman gives readers a rich history on the construction of the telescope, which began shortly after World War II. Zimmerman vividly recounts the lobbying, funding, design, construction, delays, and errors encountered along the way, including a major setback in 1990 when it was discovered that the main mirror was flawed. *The Universe in a Mirror* showcases the challenging struggle that scientists faced and the ultimate reward they received for their hard work.

Where it's reviewed:
American Scientist, Jan-Feb 2009, page 75
Choice, December 2008, page 713
Journal for the History of Astronomy, November 2009, page 474
Sky & Telescope, April 2009, page 40

Other books by the same author:
Leaving Earth: Space Stations, Rival Superpowers, and the Quest for Interplanetary Travel, 2006
The Chronological Encyclopedia of Discoveries in Space, 2000
Genesis: The Story Of Apollo 8, 1999

Other books you might like:
Geoff Andersen, *The Telescope: Its History, Technology, and Future*, 2007
John D. Barrow, *Cosmic Imagery: Key Images in the History of Science*, 2008
Tim Furniss, *A History of Space Exploration*, 2006
Norman K. Glendenning, *Our Place in the Universe*, 2007
Ian S. McLean, *Electronic Imaging in Astronomy*, 2008

Social Sciences

1234

KAREN ABBOTT

Sin in the Second City: Madams, Ministers, Playboys, and the Battle for America's Soul

(New York: Random House, 2007)

Subject(s): American History; History; Prostitution

Summary: Journalist Karen Abbott explores the rise and fall of America's most famous brothel: the Everleigh Club. The club was open from 1900 to 1911 in the Levee district of Chicago. It catered to wealthy men, and the 30 prostitutes it housed were not only beautiful, but were well fed, well paid, dressed in expensive gowns, educated in literature, and received regular medical care. The brothel was owned and operated by Ada and Minna Everleigh, sisters who bribed city officials to remain open. Despite the efforts of rival madams to implicate the Everleigh Club and the minister who preached outside its doors each night, it was the force of social reform that eventually closed the famous brothel.

Where it's reviewed:
Booklist, July 1, 2007, page 15
Booklist, July 1, 2007, page 15
Library Journal, June 15, 2007, page 79
Library Journal, June 15, 2007, page 79
Publishers Weekly, April 16, 2007, page 41

Other books by the same author:
American Rose: A Nation Laid Bare: The Life and Times of Gypsy Rose Lee, 2010

Other books you might like:
Erik Larson, *The Devil in the White City: Murder, Magic, and Madness at the Fair That Changed America*, 2003
Michael Lesy, *Murder City: The Bloody History of Chicago in the Twenties*, 2008
Daniel Okrent, *Last Call: The Rise and Fall of Prohibition*, 2010
Douglas Perry, *The Girls of Murder City: Fame, Lust, and the Beautiful Killers Who Inspired Chicago*, 2010
Mark Wahlgren Summers, *The Gilded Age: Or the Hazard of New Functions*, 1997

1235

GEETA ANAND

The Cure: How a Father Raised $100 Million — and Bucked the Medical Establishment — in a Quest to Save His Children

(New York: HarperCollins, 2006)

Summary: In *Mom: A Celebration of Mothers from Story-corps*, editor Dave Isay presents a collection of essays honoring the diverse experience of American motherhood. Culled from interviews conducted through Isay's Storycorps project—a national effort that gathers personal oral histories from every corner of the country—*Mom* shares diverse stories of mothers and children, from an immigrant mother's dreams of securing a good education for her family to an aging mother who now relies on the care of her grown children. Each narrative in *Mom* is a universal and unique contribution to our understanding of the maternal experience.

Where it's reviewed:
Booklist, September 15, 2006, page 7

Other books you might like:
John F. Crowley, *Chasing Miracles: The Crowley Family Journey of Strength, Hope, and Joy*, 2010
Ken Kurson, co-author
Alex O'Meara, *Chasing Medical Miracles: The Promise and Perils of Clinical Trials*, 2009
David Oshinsky, *Polio: An American Story*, 2005
Gary P. Pisano, *Science Business: The Promise, the Reality, and the Future of Biotech*, 2006
Sonia Shah, *The Body Hunters: Testing New Drugs on the World's Poorest Patients*, 2006

1236

DAN ARIELY

The Upside of Irrationality: The Unexpected Benefits of Defying Logic at Work and at Home

(New York: Harper, 2010)

Subject(s): Human behavior; Psychology; Science

Summary: Dan Ariely, an expert in psychology in behavioral economics, explores the consequences of irrationality on everyday life. *The Upside of Irrationality: The Unexpected Benefits of Defying Logic at Work and at Home* offers a variety of case studies that show the long-ranging impact of human behavior. But Ariely goes one step further, providing readers with practical advice on how to make realistic, enduring changes that have a positive outcome on the lives of one and all. *The Upside of Irrationality* includes notes on the text, a bibliography, and a full index.

Where it's reviewed:
New York Times Book Review, June 6, 2010, page 31

Other books by the same author:
Predictably Irrational: The Hidden Forces That Shape Our Decisions, 2009

Other books you might like:
Elliot Aronson, *Mistakes Were Made (But Not by Me): Why We Justify Foolish Beliefs, Bad Decisions, and Hurtful Acts*, 2007
Clay Shirky, *Here Comes Everybody: The Power of Organizing Without Organizations*, 2008
Cass R. Sunstein, *Nudge: Improving Decisions about Health, Wealth, and Happiness*, 2009
Don Tapscott, *Wikinomics: How Mass Collaboration Changes Everything*, 2006
Carol Tavris, *Mistakes Were Made (But Not by Me): Why We Justify Foolish Beliefs, Bad Decisions, and Hurtful Acts*, 2007
Richard H. Thaler, *Nudge: Improving Decisions about Health, Wealth, and Happiness*, 2009
Anthony D. Williams, *Wikinomics: How Mass Collaboration Changes Everything*, 2006

1237

STEPHEN ASMA

On Monsters: An Unnatural History of Our Worst Fears

(Oxford University Press: Oxford; New York, 2009)

Subject(s): Monsters; Fear; Psychology

Summary: Stephen Asma's *On Monsters: An Unnatural History of Our Worst Fears* explores humankind's strange obsession with the creatures that frighten us most. This investigation of the history of monsters, both real and fictional, covers a wide variety of frightening fiends from around the world. The author describes how stories of monsters tend to change over time, serving as a snapshot of a society's collective fears at a particular point in history. In the book, Asma discusses everything from ghosts and vampires to murderers and modern-day terrorists as he attempts to figure out why people enjoy watching movies or reading novels about the things that scare them. The author believes that the ways in which people deal with these monsters provides great insight into cultural values, revealing hopes and fears that they never knew they had.

Where it's reviewed:
Booklist, October 1, 2009, page 10

Publishers Weekly, August 10, 2009, page 46
Skeptical Inquirer, July-August 2010, page 61

Other books by the same author:
Why I Am a Buddhist: No-Nonsense Buddhism with Red Meat and Whiskey, 2010
Buddha: A Beginners Guide, 2009
The God Question: Freud and C. S. Lewis Reconsidered, 2008
How to Survive the Apocalypse, 2008
Dinosaurs on the Ark: the Creation Museum, 2007
The Gods Drink Whiskey: Stumbling Toward Enlightenment in the Land of the Tattered Buddha, 2006
Stuffed Animals and Pickled Heads: The Culture and Evolution of Natural History Museums, 2003

Other books you might like:
Mark S. Blumberg, *Freaks of Nature: What Anomalies Tell Us About Development and Evolution*, 2008
Christopher Dell, *Monsters: A Bestiary of the Bizarre*, 2010
Ernest Drake, *Monsterology: The Complete Book of Monstrous Beasts*, 2008
Niall Scott, *Monsters and the Monstrous: Myths and Metaphors of Enduring Evil*, 2007

1238

KEN AULETTA

Googled: The End of the World as We Know It

(New York: Penguin Press HC, 2009)

Subject(s): Technology; Internet; Biographies

Summary: In *Googled: The End of the World as We Know It*, author Ken Auletta provides in-depth information about the founders of Google, the creation of the search engine, and the questionable future of the multibillion dollar company. Auletta includes plenty of information about the ways in which Google was influenced the world since its creation. He focuses on how media outlets such as newspapers, magazines, and television programming, and advertising have changed since the inception of Google. Although Larry Page and Sergey Brin are typically quiet men who don't share much of their personal lives with the media, they open up to Auletta about their plans for Google, YouTube, and the company's new line of cell phones.

Where it's reviewed:
Booklist, September 1, 2009, page 4
Kirkus Reviews, September 15, 2009, page 988
Library Journal, October 15, 2009, page 86
Publishers Weekly, February 22, 2010, page 62

Other books by the same author:
Media Man: Ted Turner's Improbable Empire, 2005
Backstory: Inside the Business of News, 2004
Greed and Glory on Wall Street: The Fall of the House of Lehman, 2001

World War 3.0: Microsoft and Its Enemies, 2001

The Underclass, 1999

The Highwaymen, 1998

Three Blind Mice: How the TV Networks Lost Their Way, 1992

The Art of Corporate Success, 1985

Other books you might like:

John Battelle, *The Search: How Google and Its Rivals Rewrote the Rules of Business and Transformed Our Culture*, 2005

Bernard Girard, *The Google Way: How One Company is Revolutionizing Management As We Know It*, 2009

David Kirkpatrick, *The Facebook Effect: The Inside Story of the Company That Is Connecting the World*, 2010

Randall Stross, *Planet Google: One Company's Audacious Plan to Organize Everything We Know*, 2008

1239

ALBERT-LASZLO BARABASI

Bursts: The Hidden Pattern Behind Everything We Do

(New York: Dutton, 2010)

Subject(s): Psychology; Human behavior; Technology

Summary: In *Bursts: The Hidden Pattern Behind Everything We Do*, author and professor Albert-Laszlo Barabasi sets out to answer the age-old question of whether human beings can utilize science to foresee the future. Barabasi bases his investigation on people's habits concerning modern technology. Through his studies, he finds that all humans follow an eerily similar pattern of behavior—a pattern that could very well help predict the future of the human race. *Bursts* contains a bibliography and a full index.

Other books by the same author:

The Structure and Dynamics of Networks, 2006

Linked: How Everything Is Connected to Everything Else and What It Means, 2003

Fractal Concepts in Surface Growth, 1995

Other books you might like:

Len Fisher, *The Perfect Swarm: The Science of Complexity in Everyday Life*, 2004

Herb Sorensen, *Inside the Mind of the Shopper: The Science of Retailing*, 2009

Cass Sunstein, *Going to Extremes: How Like Minds Unite and Divide*, 2009

Cass R. Sunstein, *Nudge: Improving Decisions about Health, Wealth, and Happiness*, 2009

    Richard H. Thaler, co-author

1240

JEFF BENEDICT

Little Pink House: A True Story of Defiance and Courage

(New York: Grand Central Publishing, 2009)

Subject(s): Law; Housing

Summary: *Little Pink House: A True Story of Defiance and Courage* tells the true story of Susette Kelo's struggle to fight an injustice done to her and her neighborhood. In 1997, Susette moved to Connecticut to begin a new chapter in her life. In 1998, she was being told she would have to evacuate her home in order for a pharmaceutical company to begin building in her neighborhood. Having spent so long rebuilding her house, Susette put her foot down. She and her fellow neighbors refused to give up their homes; in return, the town condemned their houses. But Susette refused to give in. Soon, the case was brought to court, and it helped raise awareness of eminent domain issues across the country.

Where it's reviewed:

Biography, Spring 2009, page 416

Commentary, May 2009, page 75

Publishers Weekly, October 13, 2008, page 43

Other books by the same author:

How to Build a Business Warren Buffett Would Buy: The R. C. Willey Story, 2009

The Mormon Way of Doing Business: How Eight Western Boys Reached the Top of Corporate America, 2008

Out of Bounds: Inside the NBA's Culture of Rape, Violence, and Crime, 2005

No Bone Unturned: The Adventures of a Top Smithsonian Forensic Scientist and the Legal Battle for America's Oldest Skeletons, 2003

Without Reservation: The Making of America's Most Powerful Indian Tribe and Foxwoods the World's Largest Casino, 2000

Public Heroes, Private Felons: Athletes and Crimes Against Women, 1999

Athletes and Acquaintance Rape, 1998

Pros and Cons: The Criminals Who Play in the NFL, 1998

Other books you might like:

Jean Boggio, *Stolen Fields: A Story of Eminent Domain and the Death of the American Dream*, 2008

Don Corace, *Government Pirates: The Assault on Private Property Rights—and How We Can Fight It*, 2008

Carla T. Main, *Bulldozed: "Kelo," Eminent Domain, and the American Lust for Land*, 2007

1241

JEFF BIGGERS

Reckoning at Eagle Creek: The Secret Legacy of Coal in the Heartland

(New York: Nation Books, 2010)

Story type: Family Saga

Subject(s): Mining; Family; Mountain life

Summary: In *Reckoning at Eagle Creek: The Secret Legacy of Coal in the Heartland* cultural historian Jeff Biggers takes readers to the abandoned coal mines of Eagle Creek, Illinois. It was here, within the Shawnee National Forest, where the men of his family spent most of their time, slaving away for money and developing health problems that would eventually result in their premature deaths. In recent years, however, Biggers' relatives have sold the coal mines outside Appalachia to men more interested in strip mines. In this book, Biggers discusses how his family used the mines in the past and compares it to the work men and women are doing with it presently.

Where it's reviewed:

Booklist, February 1, 2010, page 8

Kirkus Reviews, November 15, 2009, page 1185

Library Journal, February 1, 2010, page 87

Publishers Weekly, November 9, 2009, page 37

Other books by the same author:

In the Sierra Madre, 2007

The United States of Appalachia: How Southern Mountaineers Brought Independence, Culture, and Enlightenment to America, 2007

Other books you might like:

Barbara Freese, *Coal: A Human History*, 2003

Jeff Goodell, *Big Coal: The Dirty Secret Behind America's Energy Future*, 2006

Silas House, *Something's Rising: Appalachians Fighting Mountaintop Removal*, 2009
    Jason Howard, co-author

Erik Reece, *Lost Mountain: A Year in the Vanishing Wilderness: Radical Strip Mining and the Devastation of Appalachia*, 2006

Michael Shnayerson, *Coal River*, 2008

1242

JENNIFER BLOCK

Pushed: The Painful Truth About Childbirth and Modern Maternity Care

(Cambridge, Massachusetts: Da Capo Press, 2007)

Summary: *Denialism: How Irrational Thinking Hinders Scientific Progress, Harms the Planet, and Threatens Our Lives* is a thought-provoking book from science writer and journalist Michael Specter. Despite the major scientific and medical advances made in the past two centuries, many individuals are growing more wary and skeptical of scientific institutions. This has resulted in the protesting of vaccinations for children, stem cell research, and the use of genetically altered grain in African countries, among other advancemants that are being refuted by modern society. In *Denialism*, Specter presents a compelling argument for trusting and utilizing scientific advancements and the dangers associated with refuting them.

Where it's reviewed:

Conscience, Autumn 2007, page 45

Publishers Weekly, December 31, 2007, page 52

The Women's Review of Books, July-August 2007, page 3

Other books you might like:

Tina Cassidy, *Birth: The Surprising History of How We Are Born*, 2007

Randi Hutter Epstein, *Get Me Out: A History of Childbirth from the Garden of Eden to the Sperm Bank*, 2010

Susan Kim, *Flow: The Cultural Story of Menstruation*, 2009

Rachel Kauder Nalebuff, *My Little Red Book*, 2009

Elissa Stein, *Flow: The Cultural Story of Menstruation*, 2009

Marsden Wagner, *Born in the USA: How a Broken Maternity System Must Be Fixed to Put Women and Children First*, 2006

1243

JONATHAN BLOOM

American Wasteland: How America Throws Away Nearly Half of Its Food (and What We Can Do About It)

(Cambridge, Massachusetts: Da Capo Press, 2010)

Subject(s): Food; United States; Ethics

Summary: Why is it that so much of the American food supply ends up in the trash bin? In *American Wasteland: How America Throws Away Nearly Half of Its Food (and What We Can Do About It)*, journalist Jonathan Bloom examines this disturbing phenomena, which has only increased with the advancement of modern American society. Bloom utilizes both economics and ethics to probe the motivations of such behavior and discusses what every American can do to ensure that no food goes unwasted. *American Wasteland* includes notes on the text, an appendix, a list of resources, and an index. First book.

Where it's reviewed:

Booklist, Oct 1, 2010, page 17

Publishers Weekly, Sept 27, 2010, page 48

Other books you might like:

Jonathan Safran Foer, *Eating Animals*, 2009

Scott Kilman, *Enough: Why the World's Poorest Starve in an Age of Plenty*, 2009

Raj Patel, *Stuffed and Starved: The Hidden Battle for*

the World Food System, 2008
Michael Pollan, *In Defense of Food: An Eater's Manifesto*, 2008
Tristram Stuart, *Waste: Uncovering the Global Food Scandal*, 2009
Roger Thurow, *Enough: Why the World's Poorest Starve in an Age of Plenty*, 2009

1244

PAUL BLOOM

How Pleasure Works: The New Science of Why We Like What We Like

(New York: W.W. Norton and Company, 2010)

Subject(s): Psychology; Neurosciences; Counseling

Summary: *How Pleasure Works: The New Science of Why We Like What We Like*, by Yale psychologist Paul Bloom, examines the reasons and emotions behind pleasure and certain preferences based on psychological and neurological studies. Bloom challenges the idea that pleasure is nothing more than a basic sensory response based on favorable stimuli; instead, his research suggests that pleasure is a much more complex emotion that stems from the true nature or "essence" of a particular person or thing. The book is written in a witty, straightforward manner that makes complicated concepts easy to understand. For instance, Bloom explores why people enjoy movies that make them cry, why they prefer genuine accessories or pieces of art rather than knock-offs, and even why they choose a mate in life.

Where it's reviewed:
New York Times Book Review, June 27, 2010, page 6

Other books by the same author:
Descartes' Baby: How the Science of Child Development Explains What Makes Us Human, 2005
How Children Learn the Meanings of Words (Learning, Development, and Conceptual Change), 2002

Other books you might like:
Denis Dutton, *The Art Instinct: Beauty, Pleasure, and Human Evolution*, 2008
Daniel Miller, *Stuff*, 2009
Gene Wallenstein, *The Pleasure Instinct: Why We Crave Adventure, Chocolate, Pheromones, and Music*, 2008
Semir Zeki, *Splendors and Miseries of the Brain: Love, Creativity, and the Quest for Human Happiness*, 2008

1245

DEREK BOK

The Politics of Happiness: What Government Can Learn from the New Research on Well-Being

(Princeton, New Jersey: Princeton University Press, 2010)

Story type: Political
Subject(s): Politics; Presidents (Government); Psychology

Summary: *The Politics of Happiness: What Government Can Learn from the New Research on Well-Being* is a scientific examination on the correlation between happiness and politics, written by former president of Harvard University Derek Bok. Using the research of "happiness scholars," Bok addresses politicians about the importance of creating policies that would increase the well-being of their citizens. Bok relies on psychological research on happiness and well-being to craft an argument that policies should be determined that would impact the quality of life for citizens. Outlining the findings of happiness research, Bok details political issues, including unemployment, retirement, health care, economic growth, and education, that could be shaped based on these surveys.

Where it's reviewed:
Library Journal, March 15, 2010, page 113
New York Times Book Review, February 21, 2010, page 16
Publishers Weekly, January 25, 2010, page 104
Washington Monthly, March-April 2010, page 39

Other books by the same author:
Our Underachieving Colleges: A Candid Look at How Much Students Learn and Why They Should Be Learning More, 2007
The Trouble with Government, 2004
Universities in the Marketplace: The Commercialization of Higher Education, 2004
The Cost of Talent: How Executives And Professionals Are Paid And How It Affects America, 2002
The State of the Nation: Government and the Quest for a Better Society, 1998
Universities and the Future of America, 1994
Higher Learning, 1988
Beyond the Ivory Tower: Social Responsibilities of the Modern University, 1984

Other books you might like:
Ed Diener, *Happiness: Unlocking the Mysteries of Psychological Wealth*, 2008
Daniel Gilbert, *Stumbling on Happiness*, 2006
Carol Graham, *Happiness Around the World: The Paradox of Happy Peasants and Miserable Millionaires*, 2009
Gretchen Craft Rubin, *The Happiness Project: Or, Why I Spent a Year Trying to Sing in the Morning, Clean My Closets, Fight Right, Read Aristotle, and Generally Have More Fun*, 2009

1246

ORI BRAFMAN
ROM BRAFMAN , Co-Author

Sway: The Irresistible Pull of Irrational Behavior

(New York: Doubleday, 2008)

Subject(s): Human Behavior; Identity; Peer Pressure

Summary: The book combines empirical research with real life stories to explain why people think the way they do, and how outside factors often influence decision making. The brothers combine talents from their individual professions (Ori is a business expert and Rom is a psychologist) to create an insightful theory on human behavior. The book explains why people are afraid of failure or won't give up on a bad situation. It also delves into how the human psyche will involuntarily pick up on certain attributes that society assigns to them, and how once a person forms an opinion, it is very hard to change. The book could very well change how you think, and the way you think.

Where it's reviewed:
Booklist, April 15, 2008, page 7
Inc., May 2008, page 26
Library Journal, May 1, 2008, page 86

Other books by the same author:
Click: The Magic of Instant Connections, 2010
Kopflos, 2008
The Starfish and the Spider: The Unstoppable Power of Leaderless Organizations, 2008

Other books you might like:
Ori Brafman, *Click: The Magic of Instant Connections*, 2010
 Rom Brafman, co-author
Robert Burton, *On Being Certain: Believing You Are Right Even When You're Not*, 2008
Malcolm Gladwell, *Blink: The Power of Thinking Without Thinking*, 2005
Rob Walker, *Buying In: The Secret Dialogue Between What We Buy and Who We Are*, 2008

1247

JANE BROX

Brilliant: The Evolution of Artificial Light

(Boston, Massachusetts: Houghton Mifflin Harcourt, 2010)

Story type: Historical
Subject(s): Electricity; History; Inventions

Summary: *Brilliant: The Evolution of Artificial Light* is a historical account of the pursuit of light from award-winning author, Jane Brox. Artificial light has always been of utmost importance to civilization, whether it was stone lamps in prehistoric caves or Edison's invention of the light bulb. People have always needed and searched for new forms of artificial light regardless of their station in life or point in history. In *Brilliant*, Brox takes readers on a journey throughout centuries of history to witness the ever-evolving world of light and its many complications. From the quest for whale oil to the invention of gas street lamps to the present-day struggle over environmentally conscious electricity, Brox showcases the various ways that light impacted the world throughout history.

Where it's reviewed:
Booklist, July 1, 2010, page 16
Entertainment Weekly, July 9, 2010, page 121
Library Journal, May 15, 2010, page 93
New York Times Book Review, August 1, 2010, page 14

Publishers Weekly, May 10, 2010, page 37

Other books by the same author:
Clearing Land: Legacies of the American Farm, 2005
Here and Nowhere Else: Late Seasons of a Farm and Its Family, 2004
Five Thousand Days Like This One: An American Family History, 2000

Other books you might like:
Nicholas Carr, *The Big Switch: Rewiring the World, from Edison to Google*, 2008
Michael Hiltzik, *Colossus: Hoover Dam and the Making of the American Century*, 2010
Jill Jonnes, *Empires of Light: Edison, Tesla, Westinghouse, and the Race to Electrify the World*, 2003
William Kamkwamba, *The Boy Who Harnessed the Wind: Creating Currents of Electricity and Hope*, 2009
 Bryan Mealer, co-author
Chris Otter, *The Victorian Eye: A Political History of Light and Vision in Britain, 1800-1910*, 2008

1248

JEB BRUGMANN

Welcome to the Urban Revolution: How Cities are Changing the World

(New York: Bloomsbury Press, 2009)

Subject(s): Urban life; Social sciences; Revolutions

Summary: Written by urban development expert Jeb Brugman, *Welcome to the Urban Revolution: How Cities are Changing the World* is a critical examination of the technological, social, political, economic, and cultural impact of urbanization on the world. As of the beginning of the 21st century, more than 50% of the planet's population resides in cities. Brugman draws on decades of social research and studies to explain the powerful impact that cities have on the world at large. The work being done in cities, in every field, influences politics, cultural trends, technological advances, social issues, and economics. *Welcome to the Urban Revolution* explores major cities around the world.

Where it's reviewed:
Booklist, April 15, 2009, page 8
Publishers Weekly, April 6, 2009, page 40

Other books you might like:
Robert A. Beauregard, *When America Became Suburban*, 2006
Stephen DeStefano, *Coyote at the Kitchen Door: Living with Wildlife in Suburbia*, 2010
Joan Fitzgerald, *Emerald Cities: Urban Sustainability and Economic Development*, 2010
Jeff Mapes, *Pedaling Revolution: How Cyclists Are Changing American Cities*, 2009
Mario Polese, *Wealth and Poverty of Regions: Why Cities Matter*, 2010

1249

BILL BRYSON

At Home: A Short History of Private Life

(New York: Doubleday, 2010)

Subject(s): History; Housing; Food

Summary: Celebrated author Bill Bryson undertakes a completely new adventure—this time, without ever leaving home. In *At Home: A Short History of Private Life*, Bryson explores his own house and opens up fresh worlds of discovery. Each room is a new land: the bathroom offers up the history of hygiene, the kitchen an account of spices and their fragrant past, and the bedroom a study of sex and death. With his trademark style and fearlessness, Bryson plumbs the depths of the everyday and unearths the miracles living under one's own roof.

Where it's reviewed:
The Economist, September 4, 2010, page 92
Library Journal, September 1, 2010, page 118
London Times, May 30, 2010, page 33
New York Times Book Review, October 10, 2010, page 21
Publishers Weekly, August 9, 2010, page 41

Other books by the same author:
Seeing Further: The Story of Science, Discovery, and the Genius of the Royal Society, 2010
A Short History of Nearly Everything: Special Illustrated Edition, 2010
Shakespeare (The Illustrated and Updated Edition), 2009
The Life and Times of the Thunderbolt Kid: A Memoir, 2007
A Walk in the Woods: Rediscovering America on the Appalachian Trail, 2006
Bryson's Dictionary of Troublesome Words: A Writer's Guide to Getting It Right, 2004
Bill Bryson's African Diary, 2002
In a Sunburned Country, 2001
Neither Here nor There: Travels in Europe, 2001
I'm a Stranger Here Myself: Notes on Returning to America After 20 Years Away, 2000
Made in America: An Informal History of the English Language in the United States, 1996

Other books you might like:
Bill Bryson, *Seeing Further: The Story of Science, Discovery, and the Genius of the Royal Society*, 2010
Bill Bryson, *Shakespeare: The World as Stage*, 2007
Phil Mason, *Napoleon's Hemorrhoids: And Other Small Events That Changed History*, 2010
Ian Mortimer, *The Time Traveler's Guide to Medieval England: A Handbook for Visitors to the Fourteenth Century*, 2008
Marlene Wagman-Geller, *Eureka!: The Surprising Stories Behind the Ideas That Shaped the World*, 2010

1250

HANK CARDELLO
DOUG GARR , Co-Author

Stuffed: An Insider's Look at Who's (Really) Making America Fat

(New York: HarperCollins, 2009)

Subject(s): Food; Marketing; Health

Summary: Hank Cardello and Doug Garr examine the food industry and its effect on Americans. This nonfiction piece opens with a story about "A Boxcar Full of Turkeys," recalling the birth of the TV dinner that came about in 1953, and with it the advent of quick, convenient, non-nutritional food choices. The authors explain how the industry has convinced people to buy food that is more convenient, less healthy, and bland, in order to strengthen its bottom-line. Cardello and Garr contend that America now appears to have the mindset that quick, easy food is better because it allows for more time. However, this same fare is causing a large outbreak of obesity and other health issues. Although Cardello and Garr do not provide a quick fix to this problem, the authors do offer solutions to how corporations can offer better food selections, and how consumers can make better, nutritious choices.

Where it's reviewed:
Booklist, January 1, 2009, page 29
Publishers Weekly, December 15, 2008, page 44

Other books you might like:
Barry Popkin, *The World Is Fat: The Fads, Trends, Policies, and Products That Are Fattening the Human Race*, 2008
Eric Schlosser, *Chew on This: Everything You Don't Want to Know About Fast Food*, 2006
Michele Simon, *Appetite for Profit: How the Food Industry Undermines Our Health and How to Fight Back*, 2006
Karl Weber, *Food, Inc.: How Industrial Food Is Making Us Sicker, Fatter, and Poorer—and What You Can Do About It*, 2009
Charles Wilson, *Chew on This: Everything You Don't Want to Know About Fast Food*, 2006

1251

NICHOLAS CARR

The Shallows: What the Internet Is Doing to Our Brains

(New York: W.W. Norton and Company, 2010)

Subject(s): Psychology; Neurosciences; Technology

Summary: In his book *The Shallows: What the Internet Is Doing to Our Brains*, Nicholas Carr uses neuroscience to explore the Internet's effects on the human brain. Carr explains that humans today receive information in different ways than they did in the past. In the past, humans

Social Sciences

received written information mainly through long passages of books; however, humans now receive small pieces of information in the form of text messages, images, videos, and more. These constant interruptions, Carr claims, prevent the retention of information and impede deep understanding. Carr argues that through modern technology, humans are reconfiguring their brains and developing what he calls a "new intellectual ethic," a phenomenon with both positive and negative results.

Where it's reviewed:
Booklist, May 1, 2010, page 62
Business Week Number, June 7, 2010, page 90
Fortune, June 14, 2010, page 26
Library Journal, April 15, 2010, page 104

Other books by the same author:
The Big Switch: Rewiring the World, from Edison to Google, 2009
Does IT Matter? Information Technology and the Corrosion of Competitive Advantage, 2004

Other books you might like:
Mark Bauerlein, *The Dumbest Generation: How the Digital Age Stupefies Young Americans and Jeopardizes Our Future (Or, Don't Trust Anyone Under 30)*, 2008
Dalton Conley, *Elsewhere, U.S.A.: How We Got From the Company Man, Family Dinners, and the Affluent Society to the Home Office, BlackBerry Moms, and Economic Anxiety*, 2009
Maggie Jackson, *Distracted: The Erosion of Attention and the Coming Dark Age*, 2008
Gary Small, *IBrain: Surviving the Technological Alteration of the Modern Mind*, 2008
  Gigi Vorgan, co-author

1252

LIBBY CATALDI

Stay Close: A Mother's Story of Her Son's Addiction
(New York: St. Martin's Griffin, 2009)

Story type: Contemporary
Subject(s): Addiction; Family; Mother-son relations

Summary: *Stay Close: A Mother's Story of Her Son's Addiction* is a true story about a mother's love and courage as she tries to help her son overcome his drug addiction. Mother and author Libby Cataldi didn't notice the signs of her son Jake's struggle until it was too late. Before Libby realized her son was in trouble, he had already experimented with numerous drugs, and he was an addict. After learning about her son's problem, Libby quickly took action to help her son through this hardship. Throughout the painful journey, Libby stayed steadfast in her role as a parent and kept her love for her son strong.

Where it's reviewed:
Publishers Weekly, March 16, 2009, page 52

Other books you might like:
Beverly Conyers, *Everything Changes: Help for Families of Newly Recovering Addicts*, 2009
Carrie Fisher, *Wishful Drinking*, 2008
James Frey, *My Friend Leonard*, 2005
William Cope Moyers, *Broken: My Story of Addiction and Redemption*, 2006
David Sheff, *Beautiful Boy: A Father's Journey through His Son's Addiction*, 2008

1253

THOMAS CATHCART
DANIEL M. KLEIN , Co-Author

Plato and a Platypus Walk into a Bar: Understanding Philosophy through Jokes
(New York: Abrams Image, 2007)

Subject(s): Humor; Philosophy
Summary: In *Plato and a Platypus Walk into a Bar*, authors Thomas Cathcart and Daniel Klein provide readers with a humorous and light-hearted look at philosophy and its various concepts. Ideas covered include existentialism, language, and feminism. The book teaches readers to not get overwhelmed by all of the philosophical "deep thinking."

Where it's reviewed:
Artforum International, December 2007, page 105
Kliatt, May 2008, page 53
New York Times Book Review, July 29, 2007, page 18
Publishers Weekly, July 14, 2008, page 15

Other books by the same author:
Heidegger and a Hippo Walk Through Those Pearly Gates: Using Philosophy (and Jokes!) to Explore Life, Death, the Afterlife, and Everything in Between, 2010
Aristotle and an Aardvark Go to Washington: Understanding Political Doublespeak Through Philosophy and Jokes, 2008

Other books you might like:
Jay Allison, *This I Believe: The Personal Philosophies of Remarkable Men and Women*, 2006
Julian Baggini, *The Pig That Wants to Be Eaten: 100 Experiments for the Armchair Philosopher*, 2006
Thomas Cathcart, *Aristotle and an Aardvark Go to Washington: Understanding Political Doublespeak Through Philosophy and Jokes*, 2008
Thomas Cathcart, *Heidegger and a Hippo Walk Through Those Pearly Gates: Using Philosophy (and Jokes!) to Explore Life, Death, the Afterlife, and Everything in Between*, 2009
Dan Gediman, *This I Believe: The Personal Philosophies of Remarkable Men and Women*, 2006
Daniel Klein, *Heidegger and a Hippo Walk Through Those Pearly Gates: Using Philosophy (and Jokes!) to Explore Life, Death, the Afterlife, and Everything in Between*, 2009
Daniel M. Klein, *Aristotle and an Aardvark Go to*

Washington: Understanding Political Doublespeak Through Philosophy and Jokes, 2008

John Lloyd, *The Book of General Ignorance*, 2007

John Mitchinson, co-author

1254

CHRISTOPHER CHABRIS
DANIEL SIMONS , Co-Author

The Invisible Gorilla: And Other Ways Our Intuitions Deceive Us
(New York: Crown, 2010)

Story type: Psychological
Subject(s): Psychology; Blindness; Human psychological experimentation

Summary: In *The Invisible Gorilla: And Other Ways Our Intuitions Deceive Us*, Christopher Chabris and Daniel Simons examine the human mind and how it works. Chabris and Simons are best known for their psychological experiment on inattentional blindness, or how often humans will miss significant or unusual behaviors or activities happening right in front of them because their focus is elsewhere. The authors reveal how faulty human intuition can be in a variety of circumstances. Using their own psychological experiment as a basis and drawing on other research about memory, perception, and reason, Chabris and Simons explore everyday illusions. They also offer explanations for unusual circumstances, including why measles are returning and why companies spend billions on products they know will fail.

Where it's reviewed:
Library Journal, April 15, 2010, page 96
Science News, July 3, 2010, page 30

Other books you might like:
Robert Burton, *On Being Certain: Believing You Are Right Even When You're Not*, 2008
Anil Gaba, *Dance with Chance: Making Luck Work for You*, 2009
 Robin Hogarth, co-author
 Spyros Makridakis, co-author
Rob Walker, *Buying In: The Secret Dialogue Between What We Buy and Who We Are*, 2008

1255

CRAIG CHILDS

Finders Keepers: A Tale of Archaeological Plunder and Obsession
(New York: Little, Brown and Company, 2010)

Subject(s): Archaeology; Science; Culture

Summary: In *Finders Keepers: A Tale of Archaeological Plunder and Obsession*, author and ecologist Craig Childs probes questions of ownership and ethical responsibility in regard to the unearthing of archeologi-

cal treasures. This volume blends Childs's own adventures in the field with matters of science, philosophy, and sociology, as he questions the customary habit of removing ancient objects from their natural environments. *Finders Keepers* includes notes on the text and an index.

Where it's reviewed:
Library Journal, Sept 1, 2010, page 118
New York Times Book Review, August 29, 2010, page 8
Publishers Weekly, May 24, 2010, page 43

Other books by the same author:
The Animal Dialogues: Uncommon Encounters in the Wild, 2009
House of Rain: Tracking a Vanished Civilization Across the American Southwest, 2008
The Way Out: A True Story of Ruin and Survival, 2006
Soul of Nowhere, 2003
The Desert Cries: A Season of Flash Floods in a Dry Land, 2002
The Secret Knowledge of Water : Discovering the Essence of the American Desert, 2001
The Southwest's Contrary Land: Forever Changing Between Four Corners and the Sea of Cortes, 2001
Stone Desert: A Naturalist's Exploration of Canyonlands National Park, 2001
Grand Canyon: Time Below the Rim, 1999
Crossing Paths: Uncommon Encounters With Animals in the Wild, 1997

Other books you might like:
Guy Deutscher, *Through the Language Glass: Why the World Looks Different in Other Languages*, 2010
Percy Fawcett, *Exploration Fawcett: Journey to the Lost City of Z*, 2010
David Grann, *The Lost City of Z: A Tale of Deadly Obsession in the Amazon*, 2009
Christopher Heaney, *Cradle of Gold: The Story of Hiram Bingham, a Real-Life Indiana Jones, and the Search for Machu Picchu*, 2010
Sharon Waxman, *Loot: The Battle over the Stolen Treasures of the Ancient World*, 2008

1256

RICHARD A. CLARKE
ROBERT KNAKE , Co-Author

Cyber War: The Next Threat to National Security and What to Do About It
(New York: Ecco, 2010)

Subject(s): Safety; Computers; Politics

Summary: National security experts Richard A. Clark and Robert Knake offer an examination of "cyber warfare," what it means, and the threats it poses to the national security landscape. *Cyber War: The Next Threat to National Security and What to Do About It* explores the rise of cyberspace criminal activity and how it has become a major challenge to the country's safety. Written in straightforward prose, this volume also explains the risks of cyber warfare on issues of military science and economics and what can be done to avoid the dangers. *Cyber War* includes a glossary of terms.

Where it's reviewed:
Booklist, May 1, 2010, page 60
Library Journal, May 15, 2010, page 84
Publishers Weekly, June 28, 2010, page 122

Other books by the same author:
Your Government Failed You: Breaking the Cycle of National Security Disasters, 2009
Breakpoint, 2007
The Scorpion's Gate, 2007
The Forgotten Homeland: A Century Foundation Task Force Report, 2006
Against All Enemies: Inside America's War on Terror, 2004
Defeating The Jihadists: A Blueprint For Action, 2004

Other books you might like:
Jack Goldsmith, *Who Controls the Internet: Illusions of a Borderless World*, 2006
Joseph Menn, *Fatal System Error: The Hunt for the New Crime Lords Who are Bringing Down the Internet*, 2010
Don Tapscott, *Grown Up Digital: How the Net Generation is Changing Your World*, 2008
John Viega, *The Myths of Security: What the Computer Security Industry Doesn't Want You to Know*, 2004
Tim Wu, *Who Controls the Internet: Illusions of a Borderless World*, 2006
Jonathon Zittrain, *The Future of the Internet—And How to Stop It*, 2008

1257

MATTHEW B. CRAWFORD

Shop Class as Soulcraft: An Inquiry into the Value of Work

(New York: Penguin Press, 2009)

Subject(s): Work environment; Working conditions; Philosophy

Summary: While U.S. universities crank out candidates for white-collar, knowledge-based jobs, enrollment in high school vocational education programs continues to slide. In *Shop Class as Soulcraft: An Inquiry into the Value of Work*, Matthew B. Crawford makes a convincing case for the value of the manual trades over office occupations. Uniquely qualified to author such a study, Crawford (Ph.D. in political philosophy from the University of Chicago and owner and operator of a motorcycle repair shop) invites readers to rethink the current American education/employment model. In addition to the reality of the necessity for mechanics, electricians, and builders, Crawford cites other advantages of manual labor—pride in tangible accomplishments and a healthy connection between thinking and doing.

Where it's reviewed:
Library Journal, May 1, 2009, page 94
Publishers Weekly, April 20, 2009, page 45

Time, June 8, 2009, page 18

Other books you might like:
Matthew Crawford, *Case for Working with Your Hands: Or Why Office Work Is Bad for Us and Fixing Things Feels Good*, 2010
Ken Denmead, *Geek Dad: Awesomely Geeky Projects and Activities for Dads and Kids to Share*, 2010
Mark Frauenfelder, *Made by Hand: Searching for Meaning in a Throwaway World*, 2010
Megan Hustad, *How to Be Useful: A Beginner's Guide to Not Hating Work*, 2008
Julie Jansen, *I Don't Know What I Want, But I Know It's Not This: A Step-by-Step Guide to Finding Gratifying Work*, 2010

1258

LAUREN GOLDSTEIN CROWE
SAGRA MACEIRA DE ROSEN , Co-Author

The Towering World of Jimmy Choo: A Glamorous Story of Power, Profits, and the Pursuit of the Perfect Shoe

(New York: Bloomsbury, 2009)

Subject(s): Fashion; Shopping; Economics

Summary: In *The Towering World of Jimmy Choo: A Glamorous Story of Power, Profits, and the Pursuit of the Perfect Shoe*, Lauren Goldstein Crowe, a fashion journalist for Portfolio.com, and Sagra Maceira de Rosen, president of the Luxury and Retail Division at the investment company Reig Capital Group, examine the effect a flailing economy has on the purchase of expensive goods—specifically Jimmy Choos, a high-end shoe brand. Crowe and de Rosen look at the brand's history and seemingly constant state of flux, especially in terms of ownership. The book also examines how this instability could ultimately affect the brand. Crowe is also the author of *Isabella Blow: A Life in Fashion*.

Where it's reviewed:
Booklist, April 15, 2009, page 9
Library Journal, March 1, 2009, page 80
Publishers Weekly, February 2, 2009, page 41

Other books by the same author:
Isabella Blow: A Life in Fashion, 2010

Other books you might like:
Deborah Ball, *House of Versace: The Untold Story of Genius, Murder, and Survival*, 2010
Peter McNeil, *Shoes: A History from Sandals to Sneakers*, 2006
Renata Molho, *Being Armani: A Biography*, 2008
Design Museum, *Fifty Shoes That Changed the World*, 2009
Georgio Riello, *Shoes: A History from Sandals to Sneakers*, 2006
Michael Tonello, *Bringing Home the Birkin: My Life in*

Hot Pursuit of the World's Most Coveted Handbag, 2009

1259

KATHERINE CROWLEY
KATHI ELSTER , Co-Author

Working With You is Killing Me: Freeing Yourself from Emotional Traps at Work
(New York: Warner Books, 2006)

Subject(s): Business; Work environment; Employment

Summary: *Working With You is Killing Me: Freeing Yourself from Emotional Traps at Work*, written by Katherine Crowley and Kathi Elster, is a guide to help workers deal with employers, coworkers, and employees that tax others' patience and work productivity. Crowley and Elster offer advice and insight into managing interpersonal relationships in the workplace. They also discuss how to avoid the pitfalls of emotional work traps and how to get out of sticky situations in the workplace that are created by toxic colleagues. Crowley and Elster are also the authors of *Working for You Isn't Working for Me.*

Where it's reviewed:
Booklist, February 1, 2006, page 11
Harvard Business Review, April 2006, page 30
Publishers Weekly, December 19, 2005, page 53
USA Today, March 20, 2006, page 04B

Other books by the same author:
Working for You Isn't Working for Me: The Ultimate Guide to Managing Your Boss, 2009

Other books you might like:
Katherine Crowley, *Working for You Isn't Working for Me: The Ultimate Guide to Managing Your Boss*, 2009
  Kathi Elster, co-author
Elizabeth Holloway, *Toxic Workplace!: Managing Toxic Personalities and Their Systems of Power*, 2009
Julie Jansen, *You Want Me to Work with Who?: Eleven Keys to a Stress-Free, Satisfying, and Successful Work Life . . . No Matter Who You Work With*, 2006
Mitchell Kusy, *Toxic Workplace!: Managing Toxic Personalities and Their Systems of Power*, 2009
Vicky Oliver, *Bad Bosses, Crazy Coworkers & Other Office Idiots: 201 Smart Ways to Handle the Toughest People*, 2008
Robert Sutton, *The No Asshole Rule: Building a Civilized Workplace and Surviving One That Isn't*, 2007

1260

DAVE CULLEN
Columbine
(New York: Twelve, 2009)

Subject(s): Weapons; Massacres; Schools

Summary: In *Columbine*, journalist Dave Cullen presents a true account of the events surrounding the school shooting at Columbine High School in Littleton, Colorado, on April 20, 1999. Using videotapes and diaries left by the perpetrators of the violence, Eric Harris and Dylan Klebold, in combination with police records, interviews, and media coverage, Cullen shows how two ordinary high school students transformed into psychopathic killers. In addition, Cullen examines falsities reported by the media; reports the effects of the shootings on victims, survivors, and their families; and presents psychological analyses of Harris and Klebold.

Where it's reviewed:
Booklist, May 1, 2009, page 9
Kirkus Reviews, February 15, 2009, page 180
Library Journal, March 15, 2009, page 117

Other books you might like:
Jonas Beiler, *Think No Evil: Inside the Story of the Amish Schoolhouse Shooting...and Beyond*, 2009
Jonathan Fast, *Ceremonial Violence: A Psychological Explanation of School Shootings*, 2008
Jeff Kass, *Columbine: A True Crime Story, a Victim, the Killers and the Nation's Search for Answers*, 2009
Peter Langman, *Why Kids Kill: Inside the Minds of School Shooters*, 2009
Lucinda Roy, *No Right to Remain Silent: The Tragedy at Virginia Tech*, 2009
Shawn Smucker, *Think No Evil: Inside the Story of the Amish Schoolhouse Shooting...and Beyond*, 2009

1261

IVO H. DAALDER
I.M. DESTLER , Co-Author

In the Shadow of the Oval Office: Profiles of the National Security Advisers and the Presidents They Served—From JFK to George W. Bush
(New York: Simon and Schuster, 2009)

Subject(s): Presidents (Government); United States history; Politics

Summary: Authors Ivo Daalder and I.M. Destler examine the histories, responsibilities, and personalities of the presidential national security advisers from the Kennedy Era through George W. Bush. *In the Shadow of the Oval Office: Profiles of the National Security Advisers and the Presidents They Served—From JFK to George W. Bush* explores the variety of ways the national security adviser works with the president to ensure the safety and security of the American people. Zbigniew Brzezinski, McGeorge Bundy, Henry Kissinger, Colin Powell, and Condoleezza Rice have all played pivotal roles in the nation's security, and this volume chronicles their unique contributions. *In the Shadow of the Oval Office* includes a list of bibliographical references and a full index.

Where it's reviewed:
Booklist, January 1, 2009, page 28

Social Sciences

Library Journal, January 1, 2009, page 104
Publishers Weekly, November 24, 2008, page 44

Other books by the same author:
America Unbound: The Bush Revolution in Foreign Policy, 2005
Winning Ugly: Nato's War to Save Kosovo, 2001
Getting to Dayton: The Making of America's Bosnia Policy, 2000

Other books you might like:
Fred I. Greenstein, *Presidential Difference: Leadership Style from FDR to Barack Obama*, 2009
David Rothkopf, *Running the World: The Inside Story of the National Security Council And the Architects of America's Power*, 2005
Robert Schlesinger, *White House Ghosts: Presidents and Their Speechwriters*, 2008
Nicholas Thompson, *The Hawk and the Dove: Paul Nitze, George Kennan, and the History of the Cold War*, 2009
Julian Zelizer, *Arsenal of Democracy: The Politics of National Security — From World War II to the War on Terrorism*, 2009

1262

WADE DAVIS

The Wayfinders: Why Ancient Wisdom Matters in the Modern World

(Toronto, Ontario, Canada: Anansi, 2009)

Subject(s): Culture; Nature; Indigenous peoples

Summary: Wade Davis explores the vanishing languages and cultures across the globe in *The Wayfinders: Why Ancient Wisdom Matters in the Modern World*. Davis says that while people are aware that animals and plants face extinction, not many know much about the disappearance of cultural diversity. He says that biologists estimate that 18 percent of animals and 8 percent of plants will be lost during our lifetimes. But Davis states that 50 percent of the languages present throughout the world today will be gone tomorrow. He also gives an overview of the different indigenous cultures that may not be around for our children's and grandchildren's lifetimes.

Where it's reviewed:
Alternatives Journal, May 2010, page 36
Booklist, October 1, 2009, page 12
New Internationalist, April 2010, page 34

Other books by the same author:
Shadows in the Sun: Travels to Landscapes of Spirit and Desire, 2010
Book of Peoples of the World: A Guide to Cultures, 2008
Light at the Edge of the World: A Journey Through the Realm of Vanishing Cultures, 2007
One River, 1997

Passage of Darkness: The Ethnobiology of the Haitian Zombie, 1988
The Serpent and the Rainbow: A Harvard Scientist's Astonishing Journey into the Secret Societies of Haitian Voodoo, Zombis, and Magic, 1985

Other books you might like:
Leah Bendavid-Val, *National Geographic: The Photographs*, 2008
Nayan Chanda, *Bound Together: How Traders, Preachers, Adventurers, and Warriors Shaped Globalization*, 2008
Wade Davis, *Book of Peoples of the World: A Guide to Cultures*, 2008
Wade Davis, *Light at the Edge of the World: A Journey Through the Realm of Vanishing Cultures*, 2001
H.J. de Blij, *Human Geography: People, Place, and Culture, Ninth Edition*, 2009
Erin H. Fouberg, co-author
K. David Harrison, *Book of Peoples of the World: A Guide to Cultures*, 2008
Alexander B. Murphy, *Human Geography: People, Place, and Culture, Ninth Edition*, 2009

1263

STEPHANIE DOLGOFF

My Formerly Hot Life: Dispatches from the Other Side of Young

(New York: Ballantine Books, 2010)

Subject(s): Women; Aging (Biology); Humor

Summary: In *My Formerly Hot Life: Dispatches from the Other Side of Young*, author and blogger Stephanie Dolgoff describes her views about aging in modern society. Dolgoff first explained her ideas about aging through her Web site Formerly Hot. In the book, Dolgoff goes into even more detail about being a "Formerly," which is the term she uses to describe women who are past their 20s and unsure of where they fit in life. Dolgoff explains that although aging includes many pitfalls—such as wrinkles and sagging body parts—aging also brings wisdom, wit, and patience, which can make life more interesting and appealing.

Where it's reviewed:
Library Journal, April 1, 2010, page 60
New York Times, August 8, 2010, page 1L
Publishers Weekly, June 28, 2010, page 122

Other books you might like:
Jill Conner Browne, *American Thighs: Sweet Potato Queens' Guide to Preserving Your Assets*, 2009
Meghan Daum, *Life Would Be Perfect If I Lived in That House*, 2010
Lisa Kogan, *Someone Will Be with You Shortly: Notes from a Perfectly Imperfect Life*, 2010
Pamela Redmond Satran, *How Not to Act Old: 185 Ways to Pass for Phat, Sick, Hot, Dope, Awesome, or at Least Not Totally Lame*, 2009

Wendy Shanker, *Are You My Guru?: How Medicine, Meditation, and Madonna Saved My Life*, 2010

1264

GREGG EASTERBROOK

Sonic Boom: Globalization at Mach Speed

(New York: Random House, 2009)

Subject(s): Economics; Business; Politics

Summary: In *Sonic Boom: Globalization at Mach Speed*, *Atlantic Monthly* and *New Republic* contributing editor Gregg Easterbrook discusses how the rapid pace of the globalization phenomenon will impact daily life in the decades to come. As Easterbrook explains, globalization is already underway and its speed and reach will increase with each passing year. Although the effects of globalization will generally be beneficial (increased access to information and wealth), Easterbrook predicts that the unprecedented changes will also bring stress. In building his argument, Easterbrook looks at cities in the United States, Europe, Asia, and South America already profoundly impacted by globalization.

Where it's reviewed:
Booklist, January 1, 2010, page 30
National Review, February 8, 2010, page 47

Other books by the same author:
Beside Still Waters: Searching for Meaning in an Age of Doubt, 2004
The Progress Paradox: How Life Gets Better While People Feel Worse, 2004
The Here and Now: A Novel, 2002
Tuesday Morning Quarterback: Haiku and Other Whimsical Observations to Help You Understand the Modern Game, 2001
A Moment on the Earth: The Coming Age of Environmental Optimism, 1996

Other books you might like:
Sara Bongiorni, *A Year Without 'Made in China': One Family's True Life Adventure in the Global Economy*, 2007
Stephen S. Cohen, *The End of Influence: What Happens When Other Countries Have the Money*, 2010
Bradford De Long, co-author
John Elkington, *The Power of Unreasonable People: How Social Entrepreneurs Create Markets That Change the World*, 2008
Pamela Hartigan, co-author
Joseph E. Stiglitz, *Making Globalization Work*, 2006

1265

BARBARA EHRENREICH

Bait and Switch: The (Futile) Pursuit of the American Dream

(New York: Metropolitan Books, 2005)

Subject(s): Careers; Economics; Work

Summary: Barbara Ehrenreich is a journalist and activist whose books about the working poor and the lower classes have earned her a passionate following. In this book, she turns her attention to white-collar workers who have lost their jobs and are struggling to find new ones. She posed as one such job-seeker, arming herself with a plausible resume and references. She expected to get a job and to be able to write a book about the human side of the corporate experience. Instead, she found herself writing about not getting a job, about the fruitless search. One of the things she discovered was how much hirers rely upon personality tests, rather than on actual skills and experience.

Where it's reviewed:
Booklist, September 15, 2005, page 14
Kirkus Reviews, July 1, 2005, page 717
Library Journal, September 1, 2005, page 164
Publishers Weekly, July 11, 2005, page 72

Other books by the same author:
Bright-Sided: How Positive Thinking Is Undermining America, 2010
Witches, Midwives, and Nurses: A History of Women Healers, 2010
This Land Is Their Land: Reports from a Divided Nation, 2009
Dancing in the Streets: A History of Collective Joy, 2007
Global Woman: Nannies, Maids, and Sex Workers in the New Economy, 2004
Nickel and Dimed: On (Not) Getting By in America, 2002

Other books you might like:
Barbara Ehrenreich, *This Land Is Their Land: Reports from a Divided Nation*, 2008
Robert H. Frank, *Falling Behind: How Rising Inequality Harms the Middle Class*, 2007
Jacob S. Hacker, *The Great Risk Shift: The Assault on American Jobs, Families, Health Care, and Retirement — and How You Can Fight Back*, 2006
Gary Rivlin, *Broke, USA: From Pawnshops to Poverty, Inc.: How the Working Poor Became Big Business*, 2010
Stuart Vyse, *Going Broke: Why Americans Can't Hold On to Their Money*, 2008

1266

JONATHAN EIG

Get Capone: The Secret Plot That Captured America's Most Wanted Gangster

(New York: Simon and Schuster, 2010)

Subject(s): Criminals; Organized crime; Law enforcement

Summary: The name "Al Capone" has become synonymous with organized crime and merciless gangster activity. *Get Capone: The Secret Plot That Captured America's Most Wanted Gangster* charts the epic story

Social Sciences

of this unforgettable figure, from his initial ventures into the world of crime to the fantastic events that led to his downfall and capture. Bestselling author Jonathan Eig has uncovered previously untapped sources to bring stunning new information to this chronicle of Capone's life and times. *Get Capone* includes a listing of bibliographical references and a full index.

Where it's reviewed:
Kirkus Reviews, February 15, 2010, page 117
Library Journal, March 1, 2010, page 93
New York Times Book Review, May 2, 2010, page 16
Publishers Weekly, February 22, 2010, page 54

Other books by the same author:
Opening Day: The Story of Jackie Robinson's First Season, 2008
Luckiest Man: The Life and Death of Lou Gehrig, 2006

Other books you might like:
Scott M. Burnstein, *Family Affair: Treachery, Greed, and Betrayal in the Chicago Mafia*, 2010
  Sam Giancana, co-author
Daniel Okrent, *Last Call: The Rise and Fall of Prohibition*, 2010
John Partington, *The Mob and Me: Wiseguys and the Witness Protection Program*, 2010
Douglas Perry, *The Girls of Murder City: Fame, Lust, and the Beautiful Killers Who Inspired Chicago*, 2010
Greg B. Smith, *Nothing But Money: How the Mob Infiltrated Wall Street*, 2009
Arlene Violet, *The Mob and Me: Wiseguys and the Witness Protection Program*, 2010

1267

BETH FERTIG

Why Can't U Teach Me 2 Read?: Three Students and a Mayor Put Our Schools to the Test

(New York: Farrar, Straus and Giroux, 2009)

Story type: Contemporary
Subject(s): Schools; Students; Student protests

Summary: In *Why Can't U Teach Me 2 Read?: Three Students and a Mayor Put Our Schools to the Test*, author Beth Fertig explains how modern educators are struggling to teach children to read. Throughout the book, Fertig follows three students, all of whom are in high school but cannot read. In addition to their journey, readers also follow Mayor Michael Bloomberg's quest to improve the education and reading standards of New York. Fertig gives readers an in-depth look at education in the city of New York, shows where learning and education stand currently, and questions what can be done to improve learning throughout the country.

Where it's reviewed:
Booklist, September 1, 2009, page 18
Kirkus Reviews, August 15, 2009, page 857
Publishers Weekly, July 27, 2009, page 56

Other books by the same author:
Covering Catastrophe, 2002

Other books you might like:
Linda Darling-Hammond, *The Flat World and Education: How America's Commitment to Equity Will Determine Our Future*, 2009
Rafe Esquith, *Teach Like Your Hair's on Fire: The Methods and Madness Inside Room 56*, 2007
Erin Gruwell, *Teach with Your Heart: Lessons I Learned from the Freedom Writers*, 2007
Diane Ravitch, *The Death and Life of the Great American School System: How Testing and Choice Are Undermining Education*, 2010
Tony Wagner, *Global Achievement Gap: Why Even Our Best Schools Don't Teach the New Survival Skills Our Children Need — and What We Can Do about It*, 2008

1268

ERIC A. FINKELSTEIN
LAURIE ZUCKERMAN, Co-Author

The Fattening of America: How The Economy Makes Us Fat, If It Matters, and What to Do about It

(Hoboken, New Jersey: Wiley Publishing, 2008)

Subject(s): Health; Economics; Food

Summary: In *The Fattening of America: How The Economy Makes Us Fat, If It Matters, and What To Do About It*, authors Eric Finkelstein and Laurie Zuckerman examine the growing obesity epidemic in America during the 21st century. The authors take a look at how industry and technology lowered the activity level of Americans and how convenience foods increased the average American's fat intake. Finkelstein and Zuckerman also discuss how economists, healthcare providers, nutritionists, and the general public could best deal with that epidemic.

Where it's reviewed:
The Financial Times, February 16, 2008, page 34
Health & Medicine Week, February 25, 2008, page 3252
Library Journal, January 1, 2008, page 112
Publishers Weekly, December 3, 2007, page 62

Other books by the same author:
Incidence and Economic Burden of Injuries in the United States, 2006

Other books you might like:
Paul Hawken, *Blessed Unrest: How the Largest Movement in the World Came into Being and Why No One Saw It Coming*, 2007
Raj Patel, *Stuffed and Starved: The Hidden Battle for the World Food System*, 2008
Barry Popkin, *The World Is Fat: The Fads, Trends, Policies, and Products That Are Fattening the Human Race*, 2008
Michele Simon, *Appetite for Profit: How the Food*

Industry Undermines Our Health and How to Fight Back, 2006

Jonathan Weiner, *Long for This World: The Strange Science of Immortality*, 2010

1269

TED C. FISHMAN

Shock of Gray: The Aging of the World's Population and How It Pits Young Against Old, Child Against Parent, Worker Against Boss, Company Against Rival and Nation Against Nation

(New York: Scribner, 2010)

Subject(s): Aging (Biology); Social sciences

Summary: In *Shock of Gray: The Aging of the World's Population and How It Pits Young Against Old, Child Against Parent, Worker Against Boss, Company Against Rival and Nation Against Nation*, Ted C. Fishman attributes a number of current and future problems in the United States to an aging population coupled with overall declining birth rates. He bases these determinations on visits to retirement communities and nursing homes around the world, where he often finds a neglected, unhappy population of elderly individuals who barely scrape by on pension funds due to ever-increasing health care costs. In addition, Fishman notes the lack of people to care for the elderly in these locations. Fishman links these issues with larger social issues such as problems in the global economy, the lack of an industrial economy in America, environmental issues, falling employment rates, and immigration, to name a few. He does not offer solutions but sheds light on an issue that often goes ignored.

Where it's reviewed:
Publishers Weekly, August 16, 2010, page 44

Other books by the same author:
China, Inc.: How the Rise of the Next Superpower Challenges America and the World, 2006

Other books you might like:
Ann Clurman, *Generation Ageless: How Baby Boomers Are Changing the Way We Live Today . . . And They're Just Getting Started*, 2007
Richard Croker, *The Boomer Century, 1946-2046: How America's Most Influential Generation Changed Everything*, 2007
Lynne C. Lancaster, *The M-Factor: How the Millennial Generation Is Rocking the Workplace*, 2010
J. Walker Smith, *Generation Ageless: How Baby Boomers Are Changing the Way We Live Today . . . And They're Just Getting Started*, 2007
David Stillman, *The M-Factor: How the Millennial Generation Is Rocking the Workplace*, 2010
Jean Twenge, *Generation Me: Why Today's Young Americans are More Confident, Assertive, Entitled—and More Miserable than Ever Before*, 2006

1270

DONNA FOOTE

Relentless Pursuit: A Year in the Trenches with Teach for America

(New York: Alfred A. Knopf, 2008)

Subject(s): United States; Education; Teachers

Summary: In *Relentless Pursuit: A Year in the Trenches with Teach for America*, author Donna Foote chronicles the experiences of four Teach for America recruits in a Los Angeles high school. As an organization, Teach for America strives to close the achievement gap between whites and minorities in the United States by sending 2,000 college graduates out into the teaching workforce. With only a summer of training under their belt, these new teachers are usually thrown into the some of the worst-performing schools. Foote's four subjects are no exception. They face hardships from all sides, even from some of their colleagues, but they manage to maintain their youthful enthusiasm and the belief that their small effort will make a large difference in the lives of their students.

Where it's reviewed:
Booklist, April 15, 2008, page 11
Education Next, Fall 2008, page 82

Other books you might like:
Coleen Armstrong, *The Truth about Teaching: What I Wish the Veterans Had Told Me*, 2009
Linda Darling-Hammond, *The Flat World and Education: How America's Commitment to Equity Will Determine Our Future*, 2009
Rafe Esquith, *Teach Like Your Hair's on Fire: The Methods and Madness Inside Room 56*, 2007
Erin Gruwell, *Teach with Your Heart: Lessons I Learned from the Freedom Writers*, 2007
Barbara Torre Veltri, *Learning on Other People's Kids: Becoming a Teach for America Teacher*, 2007

1271

JOHN FREEMAN

The Tyranny of E-mail: The Four-Thousand-Year Journey to Your Inbox

(New York: Scribner, 2009)

Subject(s): Communications; Internet; Interpersonal relations

Summary: Author John Freeman attempts to convince readers to decrease the number of e-mails they send and increase the number of people they physically interact with on a day-to-day basis, in *The Tyranny of E-mail: The Four-Thousand-Year Journey to Your Inbox*. Freeman begins his argument with the evaluation of com-

Social Sciences

munication thousands of years ago. He examines the use of clay tablets and telegrams, and eventually tracks the first e-mail sent in the 1980s. In a time when people receive, check, and reply to dozens of e-mails daily, Freeman reminds people to embrace face-to-face communication whenever possible.

Where it's reviewed:
Booklist, September 1, 2009, page 21
Kirkus Reviews, September 15, 2009, page 993
Library Journal, October 1, 2009, page 92
Publishers Weekly, August 24, 2009, page 54
Time, November 2, 2009, page 18

Other books you might like:
Gordon Bell, *Total Recall: How the E-Memory Revolution Will Change Everything*, 2009
Nicholas Carr, *The Shallows: What the Internet Is Doing to Our Brains*, 2010
Nicholas A. Christakis, *Connected: The Surprising Power of Our Social Networks and How They Shape Our Lives*, 2009
Jim Gemmell, *Total Recall: How the E-Memory Revolution Will Change Everything*, 2009
Maggie Jackson, *Distracted: The Erosion of Attention and the Coming Dark Age*, 2008
Jaron Lanier, *You Are Not a Gadget: A Manifesto*, 2010

1272

GEORGE FRIEDMAN

The Next 100 Years: A Forecast for the 21st Century

(New York: Doubleday, 2009)

Subject(s): Futuristic society; Politics; Space exploration

Summary: Using facts and figures related to such topics as population cycles and the state of natural resources, author George Friedman predicts the geopolitical future of the world over the course of the century in *The Next 100 Years: A Forecast for the 21st Century*. Friedman is the founder of an independent forecasting company, Stratfor, which helps nations around the world and Fortune 500 companies assess their futures by predicting political events, natural disasters, population booms, and other geopolitical occurrences. The book includes many of Friedman's broad predictions for the future, including space wars between Japan, Turkey, and the United States in the middle of the century and the domination of American influence on culture, science, and art around the world, leading to a golden age for the United States near the end of the century.

Where it's reviewed:
Booklist, January 1, 2009, page 28
Publishers Weekly, December 15, 2008, page 46

Other books by the same author:
The Next Decade: Where We've Been . . . and Where We're Going, 2011
America's Secret War: Inside the Hidden Worldwide Struggle between America and Its Enemies, 2005
The Future of War: Power, Technology and American

World Dominance in the Twenty-first Century, 1998
The Coming War With Japan, 1992

Other books you might like:
Jacques Attali, *A Brief History of the Future: A Brave and Controversial Look at the Twenty-First Century*, 2009
James Canton, *Extreme Future: The Top Trends That Will Reshape the World for the Next 5, 10, and 20 Years*, 2006
Bill Emmott, *Rivals: How the Power Struggle between China, India, and Japan will Shape Our Next Decade*, 2008
Andrew Krepinevich, *7 Deadly Scenarios: A Military Futurist Explores War in the 21st Century*, 2009
Mark J. Penn, *Microtrends: The Small Forces Behind Tomorrow's Big Changes*, 2007
E. Kinney Zalesne, co-author

1273

THOMAS L. FRIEDMAN

The World Is Flat: Updated and Expanded: A Brief History of the Twenty-First Century

(New York: Ferrar, Straus, Giroux, 2006)

Subject(s): Business; Business Enterprises; Current Affairs

Summary: The original edition of *The World Is Flat* presented a world in which the playing fields of economics and power were leveled and individuals of all kinds, rather than just corporations, were strong competitors. The changes were possible through technological advances that allow global communications and business to occur instantaneously. The updated edition includes 100 additional pages and addresses the impact of blogs, podcasts, and other information sharing driven by individuals. The expanded material also includes advice about how to compete in the new world, such as recommended technical training for individuals, and what governments must do to accommodate current global changes.

Where it's reviewed:
Booklist, April 15, 2005, page 1412
Kirkus Reviews, March 15, 2005, page 332
Publishers Weekly, March 28, 2005, page 68
School Library Journal, November 2005, page 184

Other books by the same author:
Hot, Flat, and Crowded, 2008
Longitudes & Attitudes: The World in the Age of Terrorism, 2003
The Lexus and the Olive Tree, 1999
From Beirut to Jerusalem, 1989

Other books you might like:
Stephen J. Dubner, *Freakonomics: A Rogue Economist Explores the Hidden Side of Everything*, 2005
William Kamkwamba, *The Boy Who Harnessed the Wind: Creating Currents of Electricity and Hope*, 2009

Steven D. Levitt, *Freakonomics: A Rogue Economist Explores the Hidden Side of Everything*, 2005

Bryan Mealer, *The Boy Who Harnessed the Wind: Creating Currents of Electricity and Hope*, 2009

Pietra Rivoli, *The Travels of a T-Shirt in the Global Economy: An Economist Examines the Markets, Power, and Politics of World Trade*, 2005

Rachel Louise Snyder, *Fugitive Denim: A Moving Story of People and Pants in the Borderless World of Global Trade*, 2007

1274

RANDY O. FROST

GAIL STEKETEE , Co-Author

Stuff: Compulsive Hoarding and the Meaning of Things

(Boston: Houghton Mifflin Harcourt, 2010)

Subject(s): Psychology; Mental disorders; Mental health

Summary: In *Stuff: Compulsive Hoarding and the Meaning of Things*, authors and experts Randy O. Frost and Gail Steketee present a series of cases centering on the psychology of hoarding. Through these studies, the authors reveal the underlying causes of hoarding and how this compulsion can easily take control of a person's life. This volume also offers advice on how to identify hoarding and what to do if you or someone you love is a hoarder. *Stuff* includes a list of references.

Where it's reviewed:
Booklist, March 15, 2010, page 12
Library Journal, February 15, 2010, page 107
Publishers Weekly, February 8, 2010, page 39

Other books by the same author:
Buried in Treasures: Help for Compulsive Acquiring, Saving, and Hoarding, 2007
Compulsive Hoarding and Acquiring: Therapist Guide, 2006
Cognitive Approaches to Obsessions and Compulsions: Theory, Assessment, and Treatment, 2002

Other books you might like:
Cecile Andrews, *Less is More: Embracing Simplicity for a Healthy Planet, a Caring Economy and Lasting Happiness*, 2009
Duane Elgin, *Voluntary Simplicity: Toward a Way of Life that is Outwardly Simple, Inwardly Rich*, 2010
Hal Friedman, *Against Medical Advice*, 2008
Annie Leonard, *Story of Stuff: How Our Obsession with Stuff is Trashing the Planet, Our Communities, and Our Health — and a Vision for Change*, 2010
Howie Mandel, *Here's the Deal: Don't Touch Me*, 2009
James Patterson, *Against Medical Advice*, 2008

1275

TIM GAYNOR

Midnight on the Line: The Secret Life of the U.S.- Mexico Border

(New York: Thomas Dunne Books, 2009)

Subject(s): Illegal immigrants; United States history; Social sciences

Summary: In *Midnight on the Line: The Secret Life of the U.S.-Mexico Border*, author and journalist Tim Gaynor provides an inside look at illegal immigration and other issues on the boarder U.S.-Mexico boarder. Gaynor and his photographer gained firsthand knowledge about crossing the boarder when they attempted to cross it themselves, only to be intercepted by boarder patrol agents. In the book, Gaynor also examines the illegal drug trade from Mexico, the use of drug mules to get drugs across the boarder, and human trafficking. The book describes the ways boarder patrol agents protect the boarder and deal with these alarming problems.

Where it's reviewed:
Booklist, February 1, 2009, page 8
Kirkus Reviews, January 1, 2009, page 22
Library Journal, March 1, 2009, page 88
Publishers Weekly, December 8, 2008, page 53

Other books you might like:
Peter Andreas, *Border Games: Policing the U.S.-Mexico Divide*, 2009
Clark Kent Ervin, *Open Target: Where America Is Vulnerable to Attack*, 2007
Kathryn Ferguson, *Crossing with the Virgin: Stories from the Migrant Trail*, 2010
Lee Morgan, *Reaper's Line: Life and Death on the Mexican Border*, 2006
Ted Parks, *Crossing with the Virgin: Stories from the Migrant Trail*, 2010
Norma A. Price, co-author
Luis Alberto Urrea, *The Devil's Highway: A True Story*, 2004

1276

ROBERT GLENNON

Unquenchable: America's Water Crisis and What To Do About It

(Washington, District of Columbia: Island Press, 2009)

Subject(s): Natural resource conservation; Natural resources; United States

Summary: *Unquenchable: America's Water Crisis and What to Do about It* is an account of American water use by author Robert Glennon. Each year in the United States, trillions of gallons of water are flushed down toilets and billions of gallons are used for entertainment purposes such as water fountains, indoor waterways, and lagoons. Meanwhile, small towns across the nation are suffering and trucking in water from other areas. In

Unquenchable, Glennon confronts the wastefulness of the American population and outlines the impending water crisis that looms for the nation if water use isn't curbed quickly.

Where it's reviewed:
Arizona Attorney, February 2010, page 36
Audubon, July-August 2009, page 70
Booklist, May 1, 2009, page 51
Independent Review, Spring 2010, page 616

Other books by the same author:
Water Follies: Groundwater Pumping And The Fate Of America's Fresh Waters, 2004
The Iconoclast As Reformer: Jerome Frank's Impact on American Law, 1985

Other books you might like:
Maude Barlow, *Blue Covenant: The Global Water Crisis and the Coming Battle for the Right to Water*, 2008
Paul Hawken, *Blessed Unrest: How the Largest Movement in the World Came into Being and Why No One Saw It Coming*, 2007
Robert D. Morris, *The Blue Death: Disease, Disaster, and the Water We Drink*, 2007
Fred Pearce, *When the Rivers Run Dry: Water—The Defining Crisis of the Twenty-First Century*, 2006

1277

GREG GRANDIN

Fordlandia: The Rise and Fall of Henry Ford's Forgotten Jungle City

(New York: Metropolitan Books, 2009)

Subject(s): Automobiles; Rain forests; Business

Summary: In *Fordlandia: The Rise and Fall of Henry Ford's Forgotten Jungle City*, renowned author Greg Grandin investigates the famed automobile mogul's attempts to build an idyllic settlement in the Amazon jungle. It was 1927 when Ford purchased land in remote Brazil with the hope of establishing a rubber plantation. But the tycoon's attentions soon turned to bigger things: developing the plantation into a corporate-driven community. Through photographs and Grandin's probing storytelling, this little-known aspect of Ford's life is brought to vivid life. *Fordlandia* contains notes on the text, bibliographical references and a full index.

Where it's reviewed:
Booklist, June 1, 2009, page 13
Library Journal, May 1, 2009, page 88
New Yorker, August 10, 2009, page 81
Publishers Weekly, May 4, 2009, page 44
Time, June 22, 2009, page 107

Other books by the same author:
Who Is Rigoberta Menchu?, 2010
Empire's Workshop: Latin America, the United States, and the Rise of the New Imperialism, 2006
The Last Colonial Massacre: Latin America in the Cold War, 2004

The Blood of Guatemala: A History of Race and Nation, 2000

Other books you might like:
William J. Bernstein, *A Splendid Exchange: How Trade Shaped the World*, 2008
Henry Ford, *My Life and Work: An Autobiography of Henry Ford*, 2008
Joe Jackson, *The Thief at the End of the World: Rubber, Power, and the Seeds of Empire*, 2008
John Soluri, *Banana Cultures: Agriculture, Consumption, and Environmental Change in Honduras and the United States*, 2006
Steven Watts, *The People's Tycoon: Henry Ford and the American Century*, 2006

1278

JOHN GRISHAM

The Innocent Man: Murder and Injustice in a Small Town

(New York: Doubleday, 2006)

Subject(s): Crime and Criminals; Government; History

Summary: John Grisham's first nonfiction book chronicles the story of Ron Williamson. Out of high school, Williamson was drafted to play professional baseball, but a shoulder injury ended his career. He returned to his hometown of Ada, Oklahoma, where he struggled with drug and alcohol abuse and mental illness. In 1982, Debbie Carter, a young cocktail waitress, was brutally raped and murdered. In 1987, Williamson was accused and convicted of the crime; he was sentenced to death. The case against Williamson was mostly circumstantial, and he was arguably not competent to stand trial. The prosecutor used false testimony to convict Williamson and a co-conspirator; the prosecutor also withheld exculpatory evidence from the defense. After spending 11 years on death row, Williamson was exonerated by DNA evidence. He died soon after being released from prison.

Where it's reviewed:
Bookmarks, Jan/Feb 2007, page 51
Entertainment Weekly, October 13, 2006, page 134
People Weekly, October 23, 2006, page 53

Other books by the same author:
The Confession: A Novel, 2010
The Partner, 2005
The Summons, 2002
The Testament, 1999
The Partner, 1997
The Runaway Jury, 1996
The Rainmaker, 1995
The Client, 1993
The Pelican Brief, 1992
The Firm, 1991
A Time to Kill, 1989

Other books you might like:
Kerry Max Cook, *Chasing Justice: My Story of Freeing Myself After Two Decades on Death Row for a*

Crime I Didn't Commit, 2006

Steven Drizin, *True Stories of False Confessions*, 2009

Dave Eggers, *Surviving Justice: America's Wrongfully Convicted and Exonerated*, 2005

Dennis Fritz, *Journey Toward Justice*, 2006

Lola Vollen, *Surviving Justice: America's Wrongfully Convicted and Exonerated*, 2005

Rob Warden, *True Stories of False Confessions*, 2009

Tom Wells, *The Wrong Guys: Murder, False Confessions, and the Norfolk Four*, 2008

1279

JEFF GUINN

Go Down Together: The True, Untold Story of Bonnie and Clyde

(New York: Simon and Schuster, 2009)

Subject(s): Biographies; Crime; Love

Summary: The story of Bonnie and Clyde is one that's been told and retold in books, movies, and television shows. In *Go Down Together: The True, Untold Story of Bonnie and Clyde*, Jeff Guinn finally reveals the truth about this infamous twosome. Guinn explains that Bonnie and Clyde were very different from the way that the media portrayed them. Instead of the glamorous and cunning criminals the media made them out to be, Guinn proves that they were clumsy, awkward, and highly unsuccessful in most of their endeavors. The author, however, concedes that the story of Bonnie and Clyde is truly a tale of love and excitement.

Where it's reviewed:

Booklist, February 15, 2009, page 8

Bookmarks, May/June 2009, page 62

Kirkus Reviews, January 1, 2009, page 23

Publishers Weekly, January 19, 2009, page 51

Other books by the same author:

The Christmas Chronicles, 2008

The Autobiography of Santa Claus, 2006

How Mr. Claus Saved Christmas, 2006

Our Land Before We Die, 2005

Something in the Blood: The Underground World of Today's Vampires, 1997

Other books you might like:

Elliott J. Gorn, *Dillinger's Wild Ride: The Year That Made America's Public Enemy Number One*, 2009

Nate Hendley, *Bonnie and Clyde: A Biography*, 2007

Laurent Marechaux, *Outlaws!: Adventures of Pirates, Scoundrels, and Other Rebels*, 2009

Alston Purvis, *Vendetta: Special Agent Melvin Purvis, John Dillinger, and Hoover's FBI in the Age of Gangsters*, 2009

Paul Schneider, *Bonnie and Clyde: The Lives Behind the Legend*, 2009

1280

ANNABELLE GURWITCH
JEFF KAHN , Co-Author

You Say Tomato, I Say Shut Up: A Love Story

(New York: Crown, 2010)

Subject(s): Marriage; Love; Parenthood

Summary: Marriage isn't easy—just ask Annabelle Gurwitch and Jeff Kahn, authors of *You Say Tomato, I Say Shut Up: A Love Story*. In this sordid and wildly comical piece, the married couple reveal the ins and outs of their marriage and how they've made it through all the ordeals. Their journey spans difficulties with each other, problems with their children, and a huge family medical crisis. They discuss times when they've annoyed each other—and even downright hated each other—and how but they've managed to survive thirteen years of marriage and raising their children.

Where it's reviewed:

People Weekly, February 22, 2010, page 49

Psychology Today, March/April 2010, page 31

Publishers Weekly, December 14, 2009, page 49

Other books you might like:

Paula Butturini, *Keeping the Feast: One Couple's Story of Love, Food, and Healing in Italy*, 2010

Ellen Graf, *Natural Laws of Good Luck: A Memoir of an Unlikely Marriage*, 2009

Ellen Greene, *Remember the Sweet Things: One List, Two Lives, and Twenty Years of Marriage*, 2009

Lisa Kogan, *Someone Will Be with You Shortly: Notes from a Perfectly Imperfect Life*, 2010

1281

ANDREW HACKER
CLAUDIA DREIFUS , Co-Author

Higher Education?: How Colleges Are Wasting Our Money and Failing Our Kids—-and What We Can Do About It

(New York: Times Books, 2010)

Subject(s): Education; Universities and colleges; Sociology

Summary: In *Higher Education?: How Colleges Are Wasting Our Money and Failing Our Kids—-and What We Can Do About It*, sociologist Andrew Hacker and author Claudia Dreifus join forces to explore the current landscape of secondary education. This volume sets out to expose the gross inadequacies of the modern university and tackles everything from skyrocketing tuition costs to archaic institutions and teachers' shortfalls. Hacker and Dreifus also instruct readers on how to go about combating this seemingly insurmountable system to attain the best, most cost-effective education. *Higher Education?*

includes a bibliography and an index.

Where it's reviewed:
Booklist, August 1, 2010, page 12
The New York Times, August 19, 2010, page C6

Other books by the same author:
Mismatch: The Growing Gulf Between Women and Men, 2007
Two Nations : Black and White, Separate, Hostile, Unequal, 2003
Money: Who Has How Much and Why, 1998

Other books you might like:
Frank Donoghue, *The Last Professors: The Corporate University and the Fate of the Humanities*, 2008
Christopher Newfield, *Unmaking the Public University: The Forty-Year Assault on the Middle Class*, 2008
Gaye Tuchman, *Wannabe U: Inside the Corporate University*, 2009
Jennifer Washburn, *University, Inc: The Corporate Corruption of Higher Education*, 2005

1282

JOHN R. HALE

Lords of the Sea: The Epic Story of the Athenian Navy and the Birth of Democracy
(New York: Viking, 2009)

Subject(s): History; Politics; Greek history, to 330 (Ancient period)

Summary: In *Lords of the Sea: The Epic Story of the Athenian Navy and the Birth of Democracy*, author John R. Hale examines the Athenian Navy and the part it played in introducing and maintaining the idea of democracy in Ancient Greece. Hale examines the beginnings of the naval fleet as well as some of the campaigns it embarked on in the name of preserving the empire. The book also explores the tentative relationship between freedom and elitism as he explains how free men from Greek civilization were required to participate in naval endeavors during times of battle, yet members of the aristocracy controlled the navy.

Where it's reviewed:
Booklist, April 1, 2009, page 9
New York Times, August 7, 2009, page C23
Publishers Weekly, April 27, 2009, page 123

Other books you might like:
Victor Davis Hanson, *A War Like No Other: How the Athenians and Spartans Fought the Peloponnesian War*, 2005
Donald Kagan, *Thucydides: The Reinvention of History*, 2009
Michael Scott, *From Democrats to Kings: The Brutal Dawn of a New World from the Downfall of Athens to the Rise of Alexander the Great*, 2009
Barry Strauss, *The Battle of Salamis: The Naval Encounter That Saved Greece—and Western Civilization*, 2005

Stephen V. Tracy, *Pericles: A Sourcebook and Reader*, 2009

1283

MORTEN T. HANSEN

Collaboration: How Leaders Avoid the Traps, Create Unity, and Reap Big Results
(Boston, Massachusetts: Harvard Business School Press, 2009)

Subject(s): Business; Management; Employment

Summary: In *Collaboration: How Leaders Avoid the Traps, Create Unity, and Reap Big Results*, author Morten T. Hansen examines the importance of teamwork and cooperation in the workplace. Hansen outlines strategies to help group leaders implement better collaborative efforts in a business environment, no matter what industry or profession that business is. The author uses studies and research, as well as anecdotal evidence, to help support his claims. Hansen is also the co-author of *How Organizations Get Smart and Stay Smart* and *What's Your Strategy for Managing Knowledge?*.

Where it's reviewed:
Financial Executive, November 2009, page 68
People Management, June 18, 2009, page 42
Research-Technology Management, Jan-Feb 2010, page 70

Other books by the same author:
The Innovation Value Chain, 2007
How Organizations Get Smart—and Stay Smart, 2004
Introducing T-Shaped Managers: Knowledge Management's Next Generation, 2001
What's Your Strategy for Managing Knowledge?, 2000

Other books you might like:
Peter J. Denning, *The Innovator's Way: Essential Practices for Successful Innovation*, 2010
  Robert P. Dunham, co-author
Jean Gomes, *The Way We're Working Isn't Working: The Four Forgotten Needs that Energize Great Performance*, 2010
  Catherine McCarthy, co-author
Richard Pascale, *The Power of Positive Deviance: How Unlikely Innovators Solve the World's Toughest Problems*, 2010
Keith Sawyer, *Group Genius: The Creative Power of Collaboration*, 2007
Tony Schwartz, *The Way We're Working Isn't Working: The Four Forgotten Needs that Energize Great Performance*, 2010
Clay Shirky, *Here Comes Everybody: The Power of Organizing Without Organizations*, 2008
Jerry Sternin, *The Power of Positive Deviance: How Unlikely Innovators Solve the World's Toughest Problems*, 2010
  Monique Sternin, co-author

1284

RUTH HARRIS

Dreyfus: Politics, Emotion, and the Scandal of the Century

(New York: Metropolitan Books, 2010)

Story type: Historical
Subject(s): History; Antisemitism; Espionage

Summary: In *Dreyfus: Politics, Emotion, and the Scandal of the Century*, author Ruth Harris presents a historical account of the Dreyfus affair and its far-reaching impact on France at the turn of the 20th century. In 1894, Jewish French officer Alfred Dreyfus was wrongfully accused and convicted of selling French secrets to the German army. The sentence for his alleged crimes was a life of solitary confinement on Devil's Island. Dreyfus's wrongful conviction sparked nationwide controversy as his sympathizers tried to free him and anti-Semites fought to keep the truth hidden. In *Dreyfus*, Harris highlights key players in the incident, including Alfred's wife, Lucie Dreyfus, who fought for his freedom, and Colonel Georges Picquart, the man in charge of the investigation. Harris presents a comprehensive narrative about the actions and beliefs of individuals on both sides of the controversy.

Where it's reviewed:
Booklist, June 1, 2010, page 17
New York Times Book Review, July 25, 2010, page 17
Publishers Weekly, May 24, 2010, page 49

Other books by the same author:
Lourdes: Body and Spirit in the Secular Age, 2000
Murders and Madness: Medicine, Law, and Society in the Fin de Si[e8636c]e, 1989

Other books you might like:
Louis Begley, *Why the Dreyfus Affair Matters*, 2009
Frederick Brown, *For the Soul of France: Culture Wars in the Age of Dreyfus*, 2010
Michael Goldfarb, *Emancipation: How Liberating Europe's Jews from the Ghetto Led to Revolution and Renaissance*, 2009

1285

SHANE HARRIS

The Watchers: The Rise of America's Surveillance State

(New York: Penguin Press, 2010)

Subject(s): United States history; Politics; Social sciences

Summary: In *The Watchers: The Rise of America's Surveillance State*, debut author Shane Harris provides a perspective on the increase in national security in the United States, as a result of the 1983 attacks on a U.S. Marine base in Lebanon and the World Trade Center and Pentagon attacks on September 11, 2001. Because of these threats to American security, then National Security Advisor John Poindexter made it his goal to develop

technologies that help experts track and find terrorists. Harris looks at how these security endeavors affect Americans, since such initiatives walk a fine line between ensuring safety and limiting freedom. Harris is a journalist for *National Journal*. First book.

Where it's reviewed:
Kirkus Reviews, December 1, 2009, page 1227
Publishers Weekly, November 9, 2009, page 37

Other books you might like:
Matthew M. Aid, *The Secret Sentry: The Untold History of the National Security Agency*, 2009
Patrick Radden Keefe, *Chatter: Dispatches from the Secret World of Global Eavesdropping*, 2005
Frederick S. Lane, *American Privacy: The 400-Year History of Our Most Contested Right*, 2009
James B. Rule, *Privacy in Peril: How We Are Sacrificing a Fundamental Right in Exchange for Security and Convenience*, 2007
Gabriel Schoenfeld, *Necessary Secrets: National Security, the Media, and the Rule of Law*, 2010

1286

CHIP HEATH
DAN HEATH , Co-Author

Switch: How to Change Things When Change Is Hard

(New York: Broadway Books, 2010)

Subject(s): Psychology; Business; Human behavior

Summary: Brothers and business experts Chip and Dan Heath offer a practical guide to successfully implementing change in the workplace and at home. *Switch: How to Change Things When Change Is Hard* examines the two polarizing states of mind—rational and emotional—and how to marry the needs of the two to create a positive impact on any person, situation, or business model. Chapters in this volume explore such topics as employee motivation, the importance of a positive work/home environment, and building beneficial habits. Through case studies and meticulous research, *Switch* provides a road map for any individual or business seeking a way out of a slump.

Where it's reviewed:
The Futurist, July-August 2010, page 64
Library Journal, February 1, 2010, page 77
Publishers Weekly, January 4, 2010, page 40
Time, February 15, 2010, page C2
The Wall Street Journal Eastern Edition, February 19, 2010, page A13

Other books by the same author:
Made to Stick: Why Some Ideas Survive and Others Die, 2007
Rumor Mills (Social Problems and Social Issues), 2005

Other books you might like:
Scott Belsky, *Making Ideas Happen: Overcoming the Obstacles Between Vision and Reality*, 2010
Atul Gawande, *The Checklist Manifesto: How to Get Things Right*, 2009

Malcolm Gladwell, *Blink: The Power of Thinking Without Thinking*, 2005

Chip Heath, *Made to Stick: Why Some Ideas Survive and Others Die*, 2007
Dan Heath, co-author

Daniel H. Pink, *A Whole New Mind: Why Right-Brainers Will Rule the Future*, 2006

1287

CHIP HEATH
DAN HEATH , Co-Author

Made to Stick: Why Some Ideas Survive and Others Die

(New York: Random House, 2007)

Subject(s): Communications; Memory; Self help books

Summary: *Made to Stick*, written by brothers Chip and Dan Heath, explores the use of effective communication to make ideas or stories unforgettable. They use the term "stickiness," which they define as the art of making ideas unforgettable, to lay out six principles they say make a lasting impression: simplicity, unexpectedness, concreteness, credibility, emotions and stories (mnemonic is SUCCES). Examples given by the Heaths to prove their point include everything from urban legends about organ-harvesting rings to advertisements to President Kennedy's speeches to the American public. In addition to explaining the techniques for effective storytelling and persuasive communication, the book contains exercises to help readers learn to apply these lessons.

Where it's reviewed:
Business Horizons, Jan-Feb 2008, page 75
Leadership, Sept-Oct 2007, page 27
Library Journal, February 1, 2007, page 83
Psychology Today, Jan-Feb 2007, page 32
School Library Journal, March 2007, page 246

Other books by the same author:
Switch: How to Change Things When Change is Hard, 2010
Rumor Mills (Social Problems and Social Issues), 2005

Other books you might like:
Chip Heath, *Switch: How to Change Things When Change Is Hard*, 2010
Dan Heath, co-author

Sheena Iyengar, *The Art of Choosing*, 2010

Richard Pascale, *The Power of Positive Deviance: How Unlikely Innovators Solve the World's Toughest Problems*, 2010

Daniel H. Pink, *Drive: The Surprising Truth About What Motivates Us*, 2009

Erik Qualman, *Socialnomics: How Social Media Transforms the Way We Live and Do Business*, 2009

Jerry Sternin, *The Power of Positive Deviance: How Unlikely Innovators Solve the World's Toughest Problems*, 2010
Monique Sternin, co-author

1288

GORDON HEMPTON
JOHN GROSSMANN , Co-Author

One Square Inch of Silence: One Man's Search for Natural Silence in a Noisy World

(New York: Free Press, 2009)

Subject(s): Nature; Environmental history; Science

Summary: In *One Square Inch of Silence: One Man's Search for Natural Silence in a Noisy World*, authors Gordon Hempton and John Grossman show readers how valuable silence is in a world where it's nearly impossible to find it. Gordon Hempton, an acoustic ecologist, wanted to try to find one spot in the country where noise from human beings could not be heard. Although Hempton traveled to the most secluded areas, he couldn't escape human-made noise for at least 15 minutes. The noise of airplanes, traffic, and more can be heard in even the most serene national parks. In the book, Hempton discusses the effects of noise on wildlife and suggests that humans attempt to reduce noise for nature and for themselves.

Where it's reviewed:
Booklist, March 15, 2009, page 33
Kirkus Reviews, February 1, 2009, page 129
Library Journal, March 1, 2009, page 95

Other books you might like:
George M. Foy, *Zero Decibels: The Quest for Absolute Silence*, 2010

Garret Keizer, *The Unwanted Sound of Everything We Want: A Book About Noise*, 2010

Anne D. Le Claire, *Listening Below the Noise: A Meditation on the Practice of Silence*, 2009

George Prochnik, *In Pursuit of Silence: Listening for Meaning in a World of Noise*, 2010

1289

RONALD A. HOWARD
CLINTON D. KORVER , Co-Author

Ethics for the Real World: Creating a Personal Code to Guide Decisions in Work and Life

(Boston, Massachusetts: Harvard Business Press, 2008)

Subject(s): Ethics; Work environment; Interpersonal relations

Summary: *Ethics for the Real World: Creating a Personal Code to Guide Decisions in Work and Life* by Ronald A. Howard and Clinton D. Korver is intended to help guide individuals in creating ethical codes and "rules to live by." Much of the information is focused on behaving ethically in the workplace, though the advice may also be applied to interpersonal relationships as well. The authors use examples of situations in which an ethical decision might be more difficult based on certain factors or when the "right" choice is not immediately evident. Creating ethical plans in advance, taking time to stop and consider ethical behavior, and coming up with creative solutions to problems are also discussed.

Where it's reviewed:
CHOICE: Current Reviews for Academic Libraries, December 2008, page 701
Financial Executive, September 2008, page 18
Publishers Weekly, April 21, 2008, page 49
U.S. News & World Report, July 21, 2008, page 112

Other books you might like:
Dick Couch, *A Tactical Ethic: Moral Conduct in the Insurgent Battlespace*, 2010
Paul Hersey, *The Ethical Executive: Becoming Aware of the Root Causes of Unethical Behavior: 45 Psychological Traps That Every One of Us Falls Prey To*, 2008
    Robert Hoyk, co-author
John C. Maxwell, *Ethics 101: What Every Leader Needs to Know*, 2005
Jonathan Tasini, *The Audacity of Greed: Free Markets, Corporate Thieves, and the Looting of America*, 2009

1290

RANYA IDLIBY
SUZANNE OLIVER , Co-Author
PRISCILLA WARNER , Co-Author

The Faith Club: A Muslim, a Christian, a Jew—Three Women Search for Understanding

(New York: Free Press, 2006)

Subject(s): Faith; Christian life; Islam

Summary: Following the devastation and cultural turmoil of the aftermath of September 11th, Muslim Ranya Idliby decided to write a children's book that would encompass the common grounds of the three major world religions. She enlisted the aid and experience of two other American mothers, Christian Suzanne Oliver and Jew Priscilla Warner. Before they could find their similarities, however, the three women had to hash out their differences. Christian Oliver began with the Jewish involvement in the crucifixion of Jesus Christ, which came as a direct assault upon Warner. Idliby found herself in a familiar position: as a Muslim woman with a sense of not having a seat at the table. The women eventually formed a club devoted to the understanding and strengthening of one another's respective traditions.

Where it's reviewed:
Booklist, September 1, 2006, page 25
Kirkus Reviews, July 1, 2006, page 664
Library Journal, September 1, 2006, page 153
Publishers Weekly, August 14, 2006, page 198

Other books you might like:
Karen Armstrong, *Tent of Abraham: Stories of Hope and Peace for Jews, Christians, and Muslims*, 2006
    Saadi Shakur Chishti, co-author

Joan Chittister, co-author
Bruce Feiler, *America's Prophet: Moses and the American Story*, 2009
Bruce Feiler, *Where God Was Born: A Daring Adventure through the Bible's Greatest Stories*, 2005
Gregory C. V. Johnson, *Bridging the Divide: The Continuing Conversation between a Mormon and an Evangelical*, 2007
    Robert L. Millett, co-author
Greg Mortenson, *Three Cups of Tea: One Man's Mission to Fight Terrorism and Build Nations...One School at a Time*, 2006
    David Oliver Relin, co-author
Arthur Waskow, *Tent of Abraham: Stories of Hope and Peace for Jews, Christians, and Muslims*, 2006

1291

DAVE ISAY

Mom: A Celebration of Mothers from StoryCorps

(New York: Penguin Press, 2010)

Subject(s): Mothers; Mother-daughter relations; Mother-son relations

Summary: In *Mom: A Celebration of Mothers from Story-corps*, editor Dave Isay presents a collection of essays honoring the diverse experience of American motherhood. Culled from interviews conducted through Isay's Storycorps project—a national effort that gathers personal oral histories from every corner of the country—*Mom* shares diverse stories of mothers and children, from an immigrant mother's dreams of securing a good education for her family to an aging mother who now relies on the care of her grown children. Each narrative in *Mom* is a universal and unique contribution to our understanding of the maternal experience.

Where it's reviewed:
Booklist, April 1, 2010, page 8
Publishers Weekly, March 8, 2010, page 43

Other books by the same author:
Listening Is an Act of Love: A Celebration of American Life from the StoryCorps Project, 2007
12 American Voices: An Authentic Listening and Integrated-Skills Text, 2001
Flophouse: Life on the Bowery, 2001
Our America: Life and Death on the South Side of Chicago, 1998
Holding on: Dreamers, Visionaries, Eccentrics, and Other American Heroes, 1995

Other books you might like:
Jay Allison, *This I Believe II: More Personal Philosophies of Remarkable Men and Women*, 2008
Jay Allison, *This I Believe: The Personal Philosophies of Remarkable Men and Women*, 2006
Patti Davis, *The Lives Our Mothers Leave Us: Prominent Women Discuss the Complex, Humorous,*

and Ultimately Loving Relationships They Have with Their Mothers, 2009

Dan Gediman, *This I Believe II: More Personal Philosophies of Remarkable Men and Women*, 2008

Dan Gediman, *This I Believe: The Personal Philosophies of Remarkable Men and Women*, 2006

David Isay, *Listening Is an Act of Love: A Celebration of American Life from the StoryCorps Project*, 2007

Oprah Magazine Editors, *Words That Matter: A Little Book of Life Lessons*, 2010

StoryCorps, *Listening Is an Act of Love: A Celebration of American Life from the StoryCorps Project*, 2007

1292

JANE ISAY

Mom Still Likes You Best: The Unfinished Business Between Siblings

(New York: Doubleday, 2010)

Story type: Contemporary
Subject(s): Family; Sibling rivalry; Psychology

Summary: Many people assume that the bond between siblings is one that is unchanging and everlasting—how wrong that assumption is. In *Mom Still Likes You Best: The Unfinished Business Between Siblings*, author Jane Isay shows readers the obstacles and hardships many siblings go through in order to achieve a close-knit bond. By interviewing hundreds of subjects, Isay examines the powerful interconnectedness between siblings throughout their lives. Isay is also the author of *Walking on Eggshells: Navigating the Delicate Relationship Between Adult Children and Parents*.

Where it's reviewed:
Library Journal, April 1, 2010, page 90

Other books by the same author:
Walking on Eggshells: Navigating the Delicate Relationship Between Adult Children and Parents, 2006

Other books you might like:
Jane Isay, *Walking on Eggshells: Navigating the Delicate Relationship between Adult Children and Parents*, 2007

Dorothy Rowe, *My Dearest Enemy, My Dangerous Friend: Making and Breaking Sibling Bonds*, 2007

Deborah Tannen, *You Were Always Mom's Favorite!: Sisters in Conversation Throughout Their Lives*, 2009

Ayelet Waldman, *Bad Mother: A Chronicle of Maternal Crimes, Minor Calamities, and Occasional Moments of Grace*, 2009

Beth Whitehouse, *Match: 'Savior Siblings' and One Family's Battle to Heal Their Daughter*, 2010

1293

SHEENA IYENGAR

The Art of Choosing

(New York: Twelve, 2010)

Subject(s): Human behavior; Psychology; Sociology

Summary: The power of making choices can be both a gift and a curse, but it remains an integral part of the human experience. In *The Art of Choosing*, social psychologist Sheena Iyengar studies the impacts of decision-making on our everyday lives and how these decisions can positively or negatively affect the chooser. With the modern world ever-changing and growing more interlocked, one's choices can have a profound influence on the rest of the world. In this approachable volume, Dr. Iyengar shows why this is so. *The Art of Choosing* contains notes on the text, a bibliography, and an index. First book.

Where it's reviewed:
Booklist, March 1, 2010, page 33
Maclean's, August 23, 2010, page 80
Money, June 2010, page 111
Time, March 22, 2010, page 19

Other books you might like:
Stephen S. Hall, *Wisdom: From Philosophy to Neuroscience*, 2010

Chip Heath, *Made to Stick: Why Some Ideas Survive and Others Die*, 2007
Dan Heath, co-author

Michael J. Mauboussin, *Think Twice: Harnessing the Power of Counterintuition*, 2009

Cass R. Sunstein, *Nudge: Improving Decisions about Health, Wealth, and Happiness*, 2009
Richard H. Thaler, co-author

1294

A.J. JACOBS

The Year of Living Biblically: One Man's Humble Quest to Follow the Bible as Literally as Possible

(New York: Simon & Schuster, 2007)

Subject(s): Bible; Christianity; Judaism

Summary: A.J. Jacobs decides to live one year of his life based on the teachings of the Bible. He vows to obey the Ten Commandments, to love his neighbor and adhere to various other teachings, including some of the lesser known rules such as to play a ten-string harp. *A Year of Living Biblically* is the result of this journey. Throughout the book, Jacobs details his interactions with people of different religions, learns how each interprets the Bible, and reveals how it all has helped to shape his life.

Where it's reviewed:
Booklist, July 1, 2007, page 6
Bookmarks, Jan-Feb 2008, Page 60

Books & Culture, Nov-Dec 2007, page 9
Library Journal, Sept 15, 2007, page 65
Publishers Weekly, June 25, 2007, page 49

Other books by the same author:

My Life as an Experiment: One Man's Humble Quest to Improve Himself by Living as a Woman, Becoming George Washington, Telling No Lies, and Other Radical Tests, 2010

The Guinea Pig Diaries: My Life as an Experiment, 2009

The Guinea Pig Diaries: My Life as an Experiment, 2009

The Know-It-All: One Man's Humble Quest to Become the Smartest Person in the World, 2005

Fractured Fairy Tales, 1999

America Off-Line: The Complete Outernet Starter Kit, 1996

The Two Kings: Jesus & Elvis, 1996

Other books you might like:

Susan E. Isaacs, *Angry Conversations with God: A Snarky but Authentic Spiritual Memoir*, 2009

A.J. Jacobs, *The Guinea Pig Diaries: My Life as an Experiment*, 2009

Jen Lancaster, *My Fair Lazy: One Reality Television Addict's Attempt to Discover If Not Being A Dumb Ass Is the New Black, or, a Culture-Up Manifesto*, 2010

Robyn Okrant, *Living Oprah: My One-Year Experiment to Walk the Walk of the Queen of Talk*, 2010

David Plotz, *Good Book: The Bizarre, Hilarious, Disturbing, Marvelous, and Inspiring Things I Learned When I Read Every Single Word of the Bible*, 2009

1295

MARTIN JACQUES

When China Rules the World: The End of the Western World and the Birth of a New Global Order

(New York: Penguin Press, 2009)

Subject(s): China; Economics; Politics

Summary: In *When China Rules the World: The End of the Western World and the Birth of a New Global Order*, author Martin Jacques analyzes China's expanding influence in the international arena and offers his predictions of a future world with the Asian power in the leading role. Basing his arguments on the commonly accepted projection that China will dominate the world economy by 2050, Jacques explains how the nation's culture and politics will make a global impact while China itself will retain its own identity. According to Jacques, America's response to China's rise will set the tone of international diplomacy in the 21st century and beyond.

Where it's reviewed:

Booklist, October 15, 2009, page 11
Kirkus Reviews, September 1, 2009, page 930
Library Journal, September 1, 2009, page 129
New York Times Book Review, January 3, 2010, page 14

Publishers Weekly, August 31, 2009, page 43

Other books by the same author:
The Menace of the Monopolies, 1970

Other books you might like:

Lawrence L. Allen, *Chocolate Fortunes: The Battle for the Hearts, Minds, and Wallets of China's Consumers*, 2009

Zachary Karabell, *Superfusion: How China and America Became One Economy and Why the World's Prosperity Depends on It*, 2009

Mark Leonard, *What Does China Think?*, 2008

Doris Naisbitt, *China's Megatrends: The 8 Pillars of a New Society*, 2010
    John Naisbitt, co-author

Susan L. Shirk, *China: Fragile Superpower*, 2007

1296

EAMON JAVERS

Broker, Trader, Lawyer, Spy: The Secret World of Corporate Espionage

(New York: Harper, 2010)

Subject(s): Business; Spies; Politics

Summary: Corporate espionage is a well-concealed aspect of the international business world. In *Broker, Trader, Lawyer, Spy: The Secret World of Corporate Espionage*, journalist Eamon Javers dives into the sordid history of this big-business undercover work, which has its roots in 18th century Washington politics. From the stateroom to the boardroom, this volume follows the trajectory of corporate spy maneuvers and how these maneuvers have affected everything from business and profit to politics and international relations. *Broker, Trader, Lawyer, Spy* contains notes on the text and a full index. First book.

Where it's reviewed:

Booklist, Feb 15, 2010, page 14
The New York Times, March 7, 2010, page 9
Publishers Weekly, Feburary 22, 2010, page 58

Other books you might like:

Richard A. Clarke, *Cyber War: The Next Threat to National Security and What to Do About It*, 2010
    Robert Knake, co-author

Michael Lewis, *The Big Short: Inside the Doomsday Machine*, 2010

Harry Markopolos, *No One Would Listen: A True Financial Thriller*, 2010

H. Keith Melton, *Spycraft: The Secret History of the CIA's Spytechs, from Communism to al-Qaeda*, 2008

Scott Patterson, *The Quants: How a New Breed of Math*

Whizzes Conquered Wall Street and Nearly Destroyed It, 2010

Henry Robert Schlesinger, *Spycraft: The Secret History of the CIA's Spytechs, from Communism to al-Qaeda*, 2008
Robert Wallace, co-author

1297

MARILYN JOHNSON

This Book Is Overdue!: How Librarians and Cybrarians Can Save Us All

(New York: Harper, 2010)

Subject(s): Libraries; Information science; Technology

Summary: *This Book Is Overdue!: How Librarians and Cybrarians Can Save Us All* is a humorous, yet thought-provoking, book from author Marilyn Johnson. In this well-researched work, Johnson presents an argument for the importance of information professionals, such as librarians, in our modern world. Despite the fact that information is so readily available through technological advances, Johnson makes a compelling case for human help and interaction. *This Book Is Overdue!* features profiles on unique, eccentric, and hilarious men and women around the world who are providing helpful services to those in need of information while breaking stereotypes about information specialists.

Where it's reviewed:
Booklist, January 1, 2010, page 26
Information Today, May 2010, page 30
Library Journal, February 1, 2010, page 5
New York Times Book Review, March 7, 2010, page 8

Other books by the same author:
The Dead Beat: Lost Souls, Lucky Stiffs, and the Perverse Pleasures of Obituaries, 2006

Other books you might like:
Scott Douglas, *Quiet, Please: Dispatches from a Public Librarian*, 2008
Vicki Myron, *Dewey: The Small-Town Library Cat Who Touched the World*, 2008
Audrey Niffenegger, *The Night Bookmobile*, 2010
Mary Roach, *Bonk: The Curious Coupling of Sex and Science*, 2008
Avi Steinberg, *Running the Books: The Adventures of an Accidental Prison Librarian*, 2010
Bret Witter, *Dewey: The Small-Town Library Cat Who Touched the World*, 2008

1298

MEAGAN JOHNSON
LARRY JOHNSON , Co-Author

Generations, Inc.: From Boomers to Linksters — Managing the Friction Between Generations at Work

(New York: AMACOM, 2010)

Story type: Contemporary
Subject(s): Work environment; Employment; Social conditions

Summary: In *Generations, Inc.: From Boomers to Linksters—Managing the Friction Between Generations at Work*, authors Meagan Johnson and Larry Johnson delve into the topic of generational gaps and help employers see eye-to-eye with every generation. Johnson and Johnson reveal ways to keep the lines of communication open, and they show how to push differences aside to keep employees working to their best and fullest potential. The book includes tips and strategies managers can use to deal with employees of every age.

Where it's reviewed:
Library Journal, May 15, 2010, page 82

Other books you might like:
Jeff Gordinier, *X Saves the World: How Generation X Got the Shaft but Can Still Keep Everything from Sucking*, 2008
Lynne C. Lancaster, *The M-Factor: How the Millennial Generation Is Rocking the Workplace*, 2010
Jeanne C. Meister, *2020 Workplace: How Innovative Companies Attract, Develop, and Keep Tomorrow's Employees Today*, 2010
Robin Rask, *Work Ethics and the Generation Gap: Which Ethical Track Are You On?*, 2008
David Stillman, *The M-Factor: How the Millennial Generation Is Rocking the Workplace*, 2010
Jean Twenge, *Generation Me: Why Today's Young Americans are More Confident, Assertive, Entitled—and More Miserable than Ever Before*, 2006
Karie Willyerd, *2020 Workplace: How Innovative Companies Attract, Develop, and Keep Tomorrow's Employees Today*, 2010

1299

SEBASTIAN JUNGER

A Death in Belmont

(New York: Norton, 2006)

Subject(s): Murder; United States history; Crime

Summary: In *A Death in Belmont*, acclaimed author Sebastian Junger investigates the 1963 murder of a Belmont, Massachusetts, woman. One autumn morning, Bessie Goldberg hired African American handyman Roy

Smith to do a few chores for her. Later, after Goldberg's body was found, Smith was convicted of murder and imprisoned. But at the same time, Albert DeSalvo, a.k.a. The Boston Strangler, was also in Belmont, a fact widely known; though after his apprehension, DeSalvo never confessed to Goldberg's murder. Junger launches his own examination of the crime, and his findings paint a revealing portrait of a city, an era, and a crime spree that changed American history.

Where it's reviewed:
Booklist, February 15, 2006, page 4
Kirkus Reviews, March 1, 2006, page 221
Library Journal, April 1, 2006, page 110
Publishers Weekly, February 13, 2006, page 70

Other books by the same author:
War, 2010
The Perfect Storm: A True Story of Men Against the Sea, 2009
Tod in Belmont, 2007
Fire, 2002

Other books you might like:
John Heidenry, *Zero at the Bone: The Playboy, the Prostitute, and the Murder of Bobby Greenlease*, 2009
Laura James, *The Love Pirate and the Bandit's Son: Murder, Sin, and Scandal in the Shadow of Jesse James*, 2009
William Landay, *The Strangler*, 2007
Gary M. Pomerantz, *The Devil's Tickets: A Night of Bridge, a Fatal Hand, and a New American Age*, 2009
Terry Weston, *America's Bloodiest Serial Killers: From Jeffrey Dahmer to the Boston Strangler*, 2010

1300

SEBASTIAN JUNGER

War
(New York: Twelve, 2010)

Subject(s): Military life; Wars; United States

Summary: Written by bestselling author Sebastian Junger, *War* is an eye-opening firsthand glimpse into the daily lives of soldiers in combat in Afghanistan. To gather material for *War*, reporter Sebastian Junger spent 14 months observing a platoon fighting in one of the most dangerous regions of Afghanistan. As Junger witnessed their courageous actions, brushes with death, and moments of complete terror, he also recognized their deeply rooted sense of loyalty, patriotism, service, love, and honor. *War* follows the highs and lows of this single platoon over the course of 14 months, beginning in 2007, and tells the story of the brave soldiers who serve the United States in times of war.

Where it's reviewed:
Booklist, August 1, 2010, page 67
Library Journal, April 15, 2010, page 96
Library Journal, Sept 1, 2010, page 76
Mother Jones, Sept-Oct 2010, page 75
Publishers Weekly, August 30, 2010, page 48

Other books by the same author:
A Death in Belmont, 2007
Tod in Belmont, 2007
The Perfect Storm: A True Story of Men Against the Sea, 2004
Fire, 2002

Other books you might like:
Eric Blehm, *The Only Thing Worth Dying For: How Eleven Green Berets Forged a New Afghanistan*, 2010
Seth G. Jones, *In the Graveyard of Empires: America's War in Afghanistan*, 2010
Robert Leckie, *Helmet for My Pillow: From Parris Island to the Pacific*, 2010
Anthony Shaffer, *Operation Dark Heart: Spycraft and Special Ops on the Frontlines of Afghanistan—and the Path to Victory*, 2010
Benjamin Tupper, *Greetings from Afghanistan, Send More Ammo: Dispatches from Taliban Country*, 2010

1301

SAM KEAN

The Disappearing Spoon: And Other True Tales of Madness, Love, and the History of the World from the Periodic Table of the Elements
(New York: Little, Brown and Company, 2010)

Subject(s): Chemistry; Science; History

Summary: Science writer Sam Kean presents a volume of true stories and sketches centering on the elements of the periodic table. *The Disappearing Spoon: And Other True Tales of Madness, Love, and the History of the World from the Periodic Table of the Elements* contains 19 pieces that examine the role of various chemical elements in the fields of politics, history, art, and economics. From the idiosyncrasies of the Lewis and Clark expedition to the creation of the silicon transistor, this volume offers surprising and witty insights into the seemingly mundane world of the periodic table. *The Disappearing Spoon* contains illustrations, notes on the text, and a full index.

Where it's reviewed:
Booklist, July 1, 2010, page 15
Library Journal, May 1, 2010, page 90
Publishers Weekly, May 10, 2010, page 37
Science News, October 9, 2010, Page 30

Other books you might like:
Patrick Coffey, *Cathedrals of Science: The Personalities and Rivalries That Made Modern Chemistry*, 2008
Thomas Hager, *The Alchemy of Air: A Jewish Genius, a Doomed Tycoon, and the Scientific Discovery That Fed the World but Fueled the Rise of Hitler*, 2008
David R. Montgomery, *Dirt: The Erosion of Civilizations*, 2007
Herve This, *Building a Meal: From Molecular Gastronomy to Culinary Constructivism (Arts and*

Traditions of the Table: Perspectives on Culinary History), 2009

Herve This, *Kitchen Mysteries: Revealing the Science of Cooking (Arts and Traditions of the Table: Perspectives on Culinary History)*, 2007

1302

JOHN KEAY

The Spice Route: A History

(Los Angeles, California: University of California Press, 2006)

Subject(s): History; Politics; Discovery and exploration

Summary: *The Spice Route: A History* by John Keay looks at the history of spices and how humans' need for flavorful recipes and exotic dishes has encouraged explorers to traverse rocky terrain and perilous oceans in order to obtain spices. In fact, Keay argues that this very need for flavor has forced globalization upon the modern world. The author looks at explorers such as Marco Polo whose job it was to seek out spice routes during the Age of Discovery, as the Ottoman Empire blocked routes to Asia. Keay is also the author of *China: A History* and *India: A History*.

Other books by the same author:
China: A History, 2009
Gilgit Game, 2003
The Mammoth Book of Explorers, 2002
Explorers Extraordinary, 2001
The Great Arc: The Dramatic Tale of How India Was Mapped and Everest Was Named, 2001
India Discovered: The Recovery of a Lost Civilization, 2001
India: A History, 2001
The Honourable Company: A History of the English East India Company, 1993
Sowing the Wind, 1980

Other books you might like:
Paul Freedman, *Out of the East: Spices and the Medieval Imagination*, 2008
Priscilla Galloway, *Adventures on the Ancient Silk Road*, 2009
   Dawn Hunter, co-author
Michael Krondl, *The Taste of Conquest: The Rise and Fall of the Three Great Cities of Spice*, 2007
Dirk Meier, *Seafarers, Merchants and Pirates in the Middle Ages*, 2006
Sarah Rose, *For All the Tea in China: How England Stole the World's Favorite Drink and Changed History*, 2010

1303

PIPER KERMAN

Orange Is the New Black: My Year in a Women's Prison

(New York: Spiegel & Grau, 2010)

Subject(s): Prisons; Women; Autobiographies

Summary: In *Orange Is the New Black: My Year in a Women's Prison*, Piper Kerman recounts the 13 months she spent in prison for a crime she committed as a college graduate. At the age of 34, with a career and a comfortable Manhattan lifestyle, Kerman was surprised to find that her previous involvement with a drug-dealing operation 10 years ago had finally caught up with her. In serving her sentence, Kerman found a unique society behind the walls of the women's prison with its own system of conduct and justice. While enduring head counts and strip searches, Kerman met a wide range of fellow inmates, each with her own story. Kerman now works as a communications executive for a nonprofit organization.

Where it's reviewed:
Booklist, March 15, 2010, page 10
Columbia Journalism Review, May-June 2010, page 55
Entertainment Weekly, April 16, 2010, page 76
Publishers Weekly, March 8, 2010, page 48

Other books you might like:
Nell Bernstein, *All Alone in the World*, 2005
Erin George, *A Woman Doing Life: Notes from a Prison for Women*, 2010
Christina Rathbone, *A World Apart: Women, Prison, and Life Behind Bars*, 2004
Silia J.A. Talvi, *Women Behind Bars: The Crisis of Women in the U.S. Prison System*, 2007

1304

ANNE KINGSTON

The Meaning of Wife: A Provocative Look at Women and Marriage in the Twenty-First Century

(New York: Ferrar, Straus, Giroux, 2005)

Summary: In *The Beauty Bias: The Injustice of Appearance in Life and Law*, Deborah L. Rhode examines discrimination based on appearance. Rhode focuses primarily on discrimination in hiring practices, and she cites specific examples of people from a range of social classes and various professions who may have been treated unfairly based on appearance issues such as weight problems or hairstyles. She examines how appearance subtly affects hiring practices, even in professions where appearance-related discrimination in the workplace is illegal. *The Beauty Bias* also focuses on women in the workplace and the discrimination women face when they choose not to conform to traditional standards of beauty.

Where it's reviewed:
Kirkus Reviews, December 15, 2004, page 1184
Library Journal, December 1, 2004, page 145
Psychology Today, March-April 2005, page 36
Publishers Weekly, January 17, 2005, page 45
Sunday Times, February 27, 2005, page 45

Other books you might like:
Nora Ephron, *I Feel Bad about My Neck: And Other Thoughts on Being a Woman*, 2006

Elizabeth Gilbert, *Committed: A Skeptic Makes Peace with Marriage*, 2010

Ariel Levy, *Female Chauvinist Pigs: Women and the Rise of Raunch Culture*, 2005

Mary Roach, *Bonk: The Curious Coupling of Sex and Science*, 2008

1305

LAURA KIPNIS

How to Become a Scandal: Adventures in Bad Behavior

(New York: Metropolitan Books, 2010)

Subject(s): Scandals; Current events; History

Summary: *How to Become a Scandal: Adventures in Bad Behavior* by Laura Kipnis is a satirical guide to becoming a household name the wrong way: through scandal. Kipnis examines four scandals that shocked the public: the disgrace of astronaut Lisa Nowak, who drove from Texas to Florida wearing a diaper in order to confront her ex-lover's new girlfriend; the breakdown of Sol Wachtler, former Chief Judge of the New York Court of Appeals, who was jailed for threatening the life of a former lover; Linda Tripp, whose admissions caused the impeachment of President Clinton; and James Frey, who gained notoriety after his autobiography *A Million Little Pieces* was exposed to be a fake.

Where it's reviewed:
Library Journal, April 1, 2010, page 60
Publishers Weekly, August 2, 2010, page 38

Other books by the same author:
The Female Thing: Dirt, Envy, Sex, Vulnerability, 2006
Against Love: A Polemic, 2004
Bound and Gagged: Pornography and the Politics of Fantasy in America, 1998

Other books you might like:
Jay Allison, *This I Believe: The Personal Philosophies of Remarkable Men and Women*, 2006
Jeff Burbank, *Las Vegas Babylon: True Tales of Glitter, Glamour, and Greed*, 2005
Dan Gediman, *This I Believe: The Personal Philosophies of Remarkable Men and Women*, 2006
Laura Kipnis, *Female Thing: Dirt, Sex, Envy, Vulnerability*, 2006
Keith Olbermann, *Worst Person in the World: And 202 Strong Contenders*, 2006
Ellyn Spragins, *What I Know Now: Letters to My Younger Self*, 2006

1306

DAVID KIRKPATRICK

The Facebook Effect: The Inside Story of the Company That Is Connecting the World

(New York: Simon & Schuster, 2010)

Subject(s): Internet; Business; Economics

Summary: In *The Facebook Effect: The Inside Story of the Company That Is Connecting the World*, David Kirkpatrick (senior writer for *Fortune* magazine), takes readers behind the scenes at the social networking Web site that has revolutionized the way people communicate. Researched with the support of Facebook founder Mark Zuckerberg and other company officials, Kirkpatrick's book chronicles the growth of the Internet entity from its birth in a dormitory at Harvard University to its status as the most successful Internet site of its kind, with over 350 million accounts worldwide. Kirkpatrick also considers Facebook's effect on societal and privacy issues.

Where it's reviewed:
Booklist, July 1, 2010, page 23
Kirkus Reviews, June 1, 2010, page 507
Library Journal, May 15, 2010, page 80
Publishers Weekly, April 19, 2010, page 47

Other books you might like:
Shel Israel, *Twitterville: How Businesses Can Thrive in the New Global Neighborhoods*, 2009
Shama Hyder Kabani, *The Zen of Social Media Marketing: An Easier Way to Build Credibility, Generate Buzz, and Increase Revenue*, 2010
Ben Mezrich, *The Accidental Billionaires: The Founding of Facebook: A Tale of Sex, Money, Genius and Betrayal*, 2009
David Pogue, *The World According to Twitter*, 2009
Jesse Rice, *The Church of Facebook: How the Hyperconnected Are Redefining Community*, 2009

1307

NICHOLAS D. KRISTOF
SHERYL WUDUNN , Co-Author

Half the Sky: Turning Oppression into Opportunity for Women Worldwide

(New York: Alfred A. Knopf, 2009)

Subject(s): Women; Women's rights; Economics

Summary: In *Half the Sky: Turning Oppression into Opportunity for Women Worldwide*, the Pulitzer Prize-winning, husband-and-wife writing team of Nicholas D. Kristof and Sheryl WuDunn probes the problems faced by women around the world and how to put an end to these injustices. From the seedy streets of Cambodia to the lackluster medical world of remote Africa, this volume charts the experiences of a variety of women who transformed their oppression into success and freedom. The authors single out economic factors as being the key cause for the subjugation of females, and they examine the ways in which economic development could radically alter the lives and opportunities for women around the globe. *Half the Sky* includes bibliographical references and an index.

Where it's reviewed:
Booklist, July 1, 2009, page 14
Library Journal, June 15, 2010, page S14(
The Nation, October 5, 2009, page 10

New York Times Book Review, November 19, 2009, page 33

Publishers Weekly, August 17, 2009, page 57

Other books by the same author:
Thunder from the East: Portrait of a Rising Asia, 2001
The Japanese economy at the millennium: Correspondents' insightful views, 1999
China Wakes: The Struggle for the Soul of a Rising Power, 1995

Other books you might like:
Mike Davis, *Planet of Slums*, 2006
Kathleen Gerson, *The Unfinished Revolution: How a New Generation is Reshaping Family, Work, and Gender in America*, 2009
Greg Mortenson, *Three Cups of Tea: One Man's Mission to Fight Terrorism and Build Nations...One School at a Time*, 2006
Anne Firth Murray, *From Outrage to Courage: The Unjust and Unhealthy Situation of Women in Poor Countries and What They are Doing about It*, 2007
David Oliver Relin, *Three Cups of Tea: One Man's Mission to Fight Terrorism and Build Nations...One School at a Time*, 2006
Lisa Shannon, *A Thousand Sisters: My Journey into the Worst Place to be a Woman*, 2010

1308

SHARON LAMB
MARK TAPPAN , Co-Author
LYN MIKEL BROWN , Co-Author

Packaging Boyhood: Saving Our Sons from Superheroes, Slackers, and Other Media Stereotypes

(New York: St. Martin's Press, 2009)

Subject(s): Children; Psychology; Social conditions

Summary: Authors and experts Lyn Mikel Brown, Sharon Lamb, and Mark Tappan offer parents a roadmap into the minds of their sons. *Packaging Boyhood: Saving Our Sons from Superheroes, Slackers, and Other Media Stereotypes* examines the barrage of unhealthy messages boys absorb from the media and the ways these messages can have negative impacts on healthy self-esteem and growth. The authors include advice for communicating with boys on this sensitive subject, they give tips about how to best to help boys better understand themselves. *Packaging Boyhood* includes notes on the text, a bibliography, and a full index.

Where it's reviewed:
Booklist, September 1, 2009, page 17

Other books by the same author:
Packaging Girlhood: Rescuing Our Daughters from Marketers' Schemes, 2007
Sex, Therapy, and Kids: Addressing Their Concerns Through Talk and Play, 2006
The Secret Lives of Girls: What Good Girls Really Do—Sex Play, Aggression, and Their Guilt, 2002

The Trouble with Blame: Victims, Perpetrators, and Responsibility, 1999

Other books you might like:
Ken Corbett, *Boyhoods: Rethinking Masculinities*, 2009
Michael Kimmel, *Guyland: The Perilous World Where Boys Become Men*, 2008
Leonard Sax, *Boys Adrift: The Five Factors Driving the Growing Epidemic of Unmotivated Boys and Underachieving Young Men*, 2007
Peg Tyre, *The Trouble with Boys: A Surprising Report Card on Our Sons, Their Problems at School, and What Parents and Educators Must Do*, September 9, 2008
Richard Whitmire, *Why Boys Fail: Saving Our Sons from an Educational System That's Leaving Them Behind*, 2010

1309

SARA LAWRENCE-LIGHTFOOT

The Third Chapter: Passion, Risk, and Adventure in the 25 Years after 50

(New York: Farrar, Straus and Giroux, 2009)

Story type: Contemporary
Subject(s): Aging (Biology); Psychology; Retirement

Summary: In her guide to life after age 50, which is titled *The Third Chapter: Passion, Risk, and Adventure in the 25 Years after 50*, author Sara Lawrence-Lightfoot introduces readers to different ways to keep things exciting and enjoyable in life's later years. In the book, the author looks critically at the way society views aging, and she explains how most people's notions about being middle aged are misguided and even wrong. She believes that life after age 50 can be fulfilling and exhilarating. To book also includes personal stories of people who have learned to enjoy and cherish life after the age of 50.

Where it's reviewed:
Library Journal, February 1, 2009, page 84
Publishers Weekly, October 20, 2008, page 45

Other books by the same author:
The Essential Conversation: What Parents and Teachers Can Learn from Each Other, 2004
The Art and Science of Portraiture, 2002
Respect: An Exploration, 2000
Balm in Gilead: Journey of a Healer, 1995
The Good High School: Portraits of Character and Culture, 1985

Other books you might like:
Sara Davidson, *Leap!: What Will We Do with the Rest of Our Lives?*, 2007
Howard Massey, *When I'm 64: Planning for the Best of Your Life*, 2009
Sherwin Nuland, *Art of Aging: A Doctor's Prescription for Well-Being*, 2007

Lillian B. Rubin, *60 on Up: The Truth about Aging in America*, 2007

Marvin Tolkin, *When I'm 64: Planning for the Best of Your Life*, 2009

Andrew Weil, *Healthy Aging: A Lifelong Guide to Your Physical and Spritual Well-Being*, 2005

1310

JUDITH LEVINE

Not Buying It: My Year without Shopping

(New York: Free Press, 2006)

Story type: Contemporary
Subject(s): Money; Shopping; Business

Summary: In her book *Not Buying It: My Year without Shopping* author Judith Levine describes the experiences she had during the year she stopped shopping. Like most people, Levine was struggling with saving money, so she decided to do away with extraneous shopping. Through the experience, she's gained insight into her own spending habits and the national economy. For a year, Levine only bought the basic necessities, questioned if even these "necessities" were necessary, and learned a minimalist lifestyle. In *Not Buying It: My Year without Shopping*, she shares with readers all her experiences and what she's learned from them.

Where it's reviewed:
Booklist, February 15, 2006, page 29
Kirkus Reviews, December 15, 2005, page 1313
Library Journal, February 1, 2006, page 97
Publishers Weekly, January 2, 2006, page 48

Other books by the same author:
Do You Remember Me?: A Father, a Daughter, and a Search for the Self, 2004
Harmful to Minors: The Perils of Protecting Children from Sex, 2003
My Enemy, My Love: Women, Masculinity, and the Dilemmas of Gender, 2003

Other books you might like:
Andrew Benett, *Consumed: Rethinking Business in the Era of Mindful Spending*, 2010
    Ann O'Reilly, co-author
Lauren Weber, *In Cheap We Trust: The Story of a Misunderstood American Virtue*, 2009
Ronald T. Wilcox, *Whatever Happened to Thrift?: Why Americans Don't Save and What to Do About It*, 2008
Joshua Yates, *Thrift in America: Capitalism and Moral Order from the Puritans to the Present*, 2010
Jeff Yeager, *The Cheapskate Next Door: The Surprising Secrets of Americans Living Happily Below Their Means*, 2010

1311

MICHAEL LEWIS

The Big Short: Inside the Doomsday Machine

(New York: W. W. Norton & Company, 2010)

Subject(s): Economic depressions; Economics; Money
Summary: Starting around 2008, the United States economy suffered a series of losses and crashes that, many believe, were the worst since the Great Depression. *The Big Short: Inside the Doomsday Machine* by Michael Lewis explains these crashes and just how they happened. Lewis explains the roots of the trouble, largely in people's greed for easy money and luxury. In addition, Lewis examines the people in this so-called "Doomsday Machine:" Wall Street insiders, government leaders, and financial officials who lied, blundered, and grabbed, causing the economy to spiral into disaster. Lewis is also the author of *Liar's Poker*.

Where it's reviewed:
Bookmarks, March-April 2010, page 6
Fortune, March 22, 2010, page 18
Library Journal, April 15, 2010, page 91
The New York Review of Books, June 10, 2010, page 37
Publishers Weekly, December 21, 2009, page 26

Other books by the same author:
The Money Culture, 2011
Home Game: An Accidental Guide to Fatherhood, 2010
Panic: The Story of Modern Financial Insanity, 2009
Coach: Lessons on the Game of Life, 2008
The Blind Side, 2006
Moneyball: The Art of Winning an Unfair Game, 2003
The New New Thing: A Silicon Valley Story, 2001
Losers: The Road to Everyplace but the White House, 1998
Liar's Poker: Rising through the Wreckage of Wall Street, 1989

Other books you might like:
George A. Akerlof, *Animal Spirits: How Human Psychology Drives the Economy, and Why It Matters for Global Capitalism*, 2010
Bret Easton Ellis, *American Psycho: A Novel*, 1991
David Kirkpatrick, *The Facebook Effect: The Inside Story of the Company That Is Connecting the World*, 2010
Michael Lewis, *Liar's Poker: Rising through the Wreckage of Wall Street*, 1989
Ben Mezrich, *Bringing Down the House: The Inside Story of Six M.I.T. Students Who Took Vegas for Millions*, 2002
Ben Mezrich, *Ugly Americans: The True Story of the Ivy League Cowboys Who Raided the Asian Markets for Millions*, 2004
Scott Patterson, *The Quants: How a New Breed of Math Whizzes Conquered Wall Street and Nearly Destroyed It*, 2010
Carmen M. Reinhart, *This Time Is Different: Eight Centuries of Financial Folly*, 2009

Social Sciences

Kenneth Rogoff, co-author

Robert J. Shiller, *Animal Spirits: How Human Psychology Drives the Economy, and Why It Matters for Global Capitalism*, 2010

Joseph E. Stiglitz, *Freefall: America, Free Markets, and the Sinking of the World Economy*, 2010

Gregory Zuckerman, *The Greatest Trade Ever: The Behind-the-Scenes Story of How John Paulson Defied Wall Street and Made Financial History*, 2009

1312

MICHAEL LEWIS

Home Game: An Accidental Guide to Fatherhood

(New York: W.W. Norton and Co., 2009)

Subject(s): Fathers; Parent-child relations; Family history

Summary: In *Home Game: An Accidental Guide to Fatherhood*, Michael Lewis, a sports and finance writer, details his experiences as a father of three and relates them to the experiences of his own father, noting the differences between the generations. Lewis asserts that he is not the best father, but he is trying to come closer to that ideal. The book is filled with humorous anecdotes about his children and his interactions—of lack of interactions—with them. Lewis grapples with the idea of being a "hands-on" father, unlike his own, and distancing himself from his children to have a life of his own.

Where it's reviewed:
Commonweal, September 11, 2009, page Sept 11, 2009
New York Times Book Review, June 28, 2009, page 17
Publishers Weekly, April 13, 2009, Page 38

Other books by the same author:
The Money Culture, 2011
The Big Short: Inside the Doomsday Machine, 2010
Liar's Poker, 2010
The Blind Side, 2009
Panic: The Story of Modern Financial Insanity, 2009
Coach: Lessons on the Game of Life, 2008
Moneyball: The Art of Winning an Unfair Game, 2004
Next: The Future Just Happened, 2002
The New New Thing: A Silicon Valley Story, 2001
Losers: The Road to Everyplace but the White House, 1998
Pacific Rift: Why Americans and Japanese Don't Understand Each Other, 1993

Other books you might like:
Michael Chabon, *Manhood for Amateurs: The Pleasures and Regrets of a Husband, Father, and Son*, 2009
Ben Karlin, *Things I've Learned from Women Who've Dumped Me*, 2008
Michael Lewis, *Coach: Lessons on the Game of Life*, 2005
Rob Sheffield, *Talking to Girls about Duran Duran: One Young Man's Quest for True Love and a Cooler Haircut*, 2010
Robert Wilder, *Daddy Needs a Drink: An Irreverent Look at Parenting from a Dad Who Truly Loves His Kids—Even When They're Driving Him Nuts*, 2006

1313

FARHAD MANJOO

True Enough: Learning to Live in a Post-Fact Society

(Hoboken, New Jersey, Wiley, 2008)

Summary: *Denialism: How Irrational Thinking Hinders Scientific Progress, Harms the Planet, and Threatens Our Lives* is a thought-provoking book from science writer and journalist Michael Specter. Despite the major scientific and medical advances made in the past two centuries, many individuals are growing more wary and skeptical of scientific institutions. This has resulted in the protesting of vaccinations for children, stem cell research, and the use of genetically altered grain in African countries, among other advancemants that are being refuted by modern society. In *Denialism*, Specter presents a compelling argument for trusting and utilizing scientific advancements and the dangers associated with refuting them.

Where it's reviewed:
Booklist, February 15, 2008, page 15
CHOICE: Current Reviews for Academic Libraries, August 2008, page 2138
Columbia Journalism Review, July-August 2008, page 59
Publishers Weekly, January 28, 2008, page 56
Survival, Feb-March 2010, page 232

Other books you might like:
Maggie Jackson, *Distracted: The Erosion of Attention and the Coming Dark Age*, 2008
Frank I. Luntz, *Words That Work: It's Not What You Say, It's What People Hear*, 2007
Charles P. Pierce, *Idiot America: How Stupidity Became a Virtue in the Land of the Free*, 2009
Michael Specter, *Denialism: How Irrational Thinking Hinders Scientific Progress, Harms the Planet, and Threatens Our Lives*, 2009

1314

REBECCA MEAD

One Perfect Day: The Selling of the American Wedding

(New York: Penguin, 2007)

Subject(s): Weddings; Marriage; Business enterprises

Summary: In the last few decades, wedding ceremonies have gone from small rituals of commitment to lavish spectacles that have spawned a billion-dollar industry. In *One Perfect Day: The Selling of the American Wedding*, journalist Rebecca Mead examines the phenomenon of the contemporary wedding, describes how it has evolved, and explains what it says about modern society. Mead goes behind the veil to show the inner workings of the wedding industry and illustrates how this industry has influenced the recent trend of "bridezillas." *One Perfect Day* includes a full index.

Where it's reviewed:

Booklist, March 1, 2007, page 46
The Christian Century, November 27, 2007, page 30
Entertainment Weekly, May 25, 2007, page 87
Library Journal, May 15, 2007, page 107
Publishers Weekly, February 19, 2007, page 155

Other books you might like:

Colleen Curran, *Altared: Bridezillas, Bewilderment, Big Love, Breakups, and What Women Really Think About Contemporary Weddings*, 2007
Vicki Howard, *Brides, Inc.: American Weddings and the Business of Tradition*, 2006
Dan Savage, *The Commitment: Love, Sex, Marriage, and My Family*, 2005
Kamy Wicoff, *I Do but I Don't: Walking Down the Aisle Without Losing Your Mind*, 2006

`1315`

DANIEL MENAKER

A Good Talk: The Story and Skill of Conversation

(New York: Twelve Publishers, 2010)

Subject(s): Communications; Speech; Interpersonal relations

Summary: *A Good Talk: The Story and Skill of Conversation* by Daniel Menaker delves into the art, history, and process of human interpersonal communication. Menaker mixes a historical perspective of the formation of language with the biological development of speech communication, then adds a sociological angle about conversational interaction. Menaker also includes a transcript from one of his own conversations in order to give the reader a glimpse at the informal and formal interview process. Menaker is a former senior editor of the *New Yorker* and a literary editor for Random House Publishing. He is also the author of *The Old Left and Other Stories* and *The Treatment*.

Where it's reviewed:

Booklist, January 1, 2010, page 25
Kirkus Reviews, October 15, 2009, page 1106
Library Journal, November 15, 2009, page 75
Publishers Weekly, November 16, 2009, page 47

Other books by the same author:

The Treatment, 1999
The Old Left and other stories, 1988
Friends and Relations: A Collection of Stories, 1976

Other books you might like:

Henry Alford, *How to Live: A Search for Wisdom from Old People*, 2009
Mike Bechtle, *Confident Conversation: How to*

Communicate Successfully in Any Situation, 2008
Catherine Blyth, *The Art of Conversation: A Guided Tour of a Neglected Pleasure*, 2008
Jeanne Martinet, *The Art of Mingling: Proven Techniques for Mastering Any Room*, 2006
Jacqueline Olds, *The Lonely American: Drifting Apart in the Twenty-first Century*, 2009

`1316`

CHRIS MOONEY
SHERIL KIRSHENBAUM , Co-Author

Unscientific America: How Scientific Illiteracy Threatens our Future

(Philadelphia, Pennsylvania: Perseus Book Group, 2009)

Subject(s): Science; Education; Knowledge

Summary: Chris Mooney and Sheril Kirshenbaum's *Unscientific America: How Scientific Illiteracy Threatens our Future* explores the implications of the average American's lack of scientific knowledge and the ways this ignorance could affect the future of the nation. The authors point to the often-negative portrayal of scientists in the media and the suspicions that exists between the scientific and nonscientific communities as reasons why scientific ignorance exists. They also discuss the possible outcomes of this ignorance. Mooney is the author of *The Republican War on Science*, and Kirshenbaum is the author of *The Science of Kissing*.

Where it's reviewed:

American Scientist, Nov-Dec 2009, page 509
The Futurist, Nov-Dec 2009, page 63
The Humanist, Jan-Feb 2010, page 40
Publishers Weekly, May 25, 2009, page 50

Other books by the same author:

Storm World: Hurricanes, Politics, and the Battle Over Global Warming, 2008
The Republican War on Science, 2006

Other books you might like:

Mark Bauerlein, *The Dumbest Generation: How the Digital Age Stupefies Young Americans and Jeopardizes Our Future (Or, Don't Trust Anyone Under 30)*, 2008
Elaine Howard Ecklund, *Science vs. Religion: What Scientists Really Think*, 2010
David H. Freedman, *Wrong: Why Experts* Keep Failing Us—and How to Know When Not to Trust Them: *Scientists, Finance Wizards, Doctors, Relationship Gurus, Celebrity CEOs, High-Powered Consultants, Health Officials and More*, 2010
David Goodstein, *On Fact and Fraud: Cautionary Tales from the Front Lines of Science*, 2010
Chris Hedges, *Empire of Illusion*, 2009

Social Sciences

1317

GREG MORTENSON

Stones into Schools: Promoting Peace with Books, Not Bombs, in Afghanistan and Pakistan
(New York: Viking, 2009)

Subject(s): Education; Human rights; Islam

Summary: In this follow-up to *Three Cups of Tea*, humanitarian Greg Mortenson uses first person narrative to recount his ongoing efforts to build schools in the remote regions of Pakistan and Afghanistan. Just as his previous work focused on his promise to build a school in Korphe, Pakistan, this work begins with the promise he makes to the Kirghiz horsemen in the Wakhan corridor of Afghanistan to build a school. Mortenson describes how his organization, Central Asia Institute (CAI), supported the efforts of these nomadic people to build a school on their own in the village of Bozai Gumbaz. He recounts how his organization responded to the 2005 earthquake in Azad Kashmir and Pakistan, how he works with Islamic clerics, war lords, and militia commanders alike, and how he survived an eight-day abduction by the Taliban. Throughout, Mortenson promotes the principle that simply teaching a girl to read and write sets off a chain reaction of positive changes.

Where it's reviewed:
Booklist, December 1, 2009, page 4
Bookmarks, Mar/Apr 2010, page 50
Kirkus Reviews, November 1, 2009, page 1150
People Weekly, December 14 2009, page 75

Other books by the same author:
Listen to the Wind, 2009
Three Cups of Tea: One Man's Mission to Fight Terrorism and Build Nations...One School at a Time, 2007

Other books you might like:
Greg Barrett, *The Gospel of Father Joe: Revolutions and Revelations in the Slums of Bangkok*, 2008
Leon Hesser, *The Man Who Fed the World: Nobel Peace Prize Laureate Norman Borlaug and His Battle to End World Hunger*, 2006
Ranya Idliby, *The Faith Club: A Muslim, a Christian, a Jew—Three Women Search for Understanding*, 2006
Twesigye Jackson Kaguri, *The Price of Stones: Building a School for My Village*, 2010
Greg Mortenson, *Three Cups of Tea: One Man's Mission to Fight Terrorism and Build Nations...One School at a Time*, 2006
Suzanne Oliver, *The Faith Club: A Muslim, a Christian, a Jew—Three Women Search for Understanding*, 2006
David Oliver Relin, *Three Cups of Tea: One Man's Mission to Fight Terrorism and Build Nations...One School at a Time*, 2006
Susan Urbanek Linville, *The Price of Stones: Building a School for My Village*, 2010
Priscilla Warner, *The Faith Club: A Muslim, a*
Christian, a Jew—Three Women Search for Understanding*, 2006

1318

DAMBISA MOYO

Dead Aid: Why Aid Is Not Working and How There Is a Better Way for Africa
(New York: Farrar, Straus and Giroux, 2009)

Subject(s): Economics; Africa; International relations

Summary: Zambian-born economist Dambisa Moyo examines the effects of international aid on African countries and the way this aid has delayed, and not inspired, economic growth. *Dead Aid: Why Aid Is Not Working and How There Is a Better Way for Africa* explores the differences between nations that have utilized foreign monies and those who have not and points out the various traps that international aid creates. Moyo then lays out a detailed plan for a more economically-secure Africa. In addition to a bibliography, notes on the text, and a full index, this volume also includes an introduction by financial and economic historian Niall Ferguson.

Where it's reviewed:
Africa Today, Fall 2009, page 115
Booklist, March 15, 2009, page 31
Library Journal, April 1, 2009, page 88

Other books you might like:
Robert Calderisi, *Trouble with Africa: Why Foreign Aid Isn't Working*, 2006
Paul Collier, *The Bottom Billion: Why the Poorest Countries Are Failing and What Can Be Done about It*, 2007
William Esterly, *White Man's Burden: Why the West's Efforts to Aid the Rest Have Done So Much Ill and So Little Good*, 2006
William Kamkwamba, *The Boy Who Harnessed the Wind: Creating Currents of Electricity and Hope*, 2009
Bryan Mealer, co-author
Michela Wrong, *It's Our Turn to Eat: The Story of a Kenyan Whistle-Blower*, 2009

1319

KEVIN O'KEEFE

Average American: The Extraordinary Search for the Nation's Most Ordinary Citizen
(New York: PublicAffairs, 2005)

Summary: In *Mom: A Celebration of Mothers from Story-corps*, editor Dave Isay presents a collection of essays honoring the diverse experience of American motherhood. Culled from interviews conducted through

Isay's Storycorps project—a national effort that gathers personal oral histories from every corner of the country—*Mom* shares diverse stories of mothers and children, from an immigrant mother's dreams of securing a good education for her family to an aging mother who now relies on the care of her grown children. Each narrative in *Mom* is a universal and unique contribution to our understanding of the maternal experience.

Where it's reviewed:
Booklist, November 15, 2005, page 9

Other books you might like:
Claude S. Fischer, *Made in America: A Social History of American Culture and Character*, 2010
Malcolm Gladwell, *Outliers*, 2008
Sarah E. Igo, *The Averaged American: Surveys, Citizens, and the Making of a Mass Public*, 2007
David Isay, *Listening Is an Act of Love: A Celebration of American Life from the StoryCorps Project*, 2007
Frank I. Luntz, *What Americans Really Want... Really: The Truth About Our Hopes, Dreams, and Fears*, 2009
StoryCorps, *Listening Is an Act of Love: A Celebration of American Life from the StoryCorps Project*, 2007

1320

DANIEL OKRENT

Last Call: The Rise and Fall of Prohibition

(New York: Scribner, 2010)

Subject(s): Prohibition; Organized crime; United States history

Summary: In *Last Call: The Rise and Fall of Prohibition*, author Daniel Okrent chronicles America's brief encounter with alcohol prohibition in the 1920s and '30s. First examining the national atmosphere and political battle that led up to the passage of the 18th Amendment, Okrent goes on to explore the broad impact prohibition had on American culture. From the speakeasy society embodied by Manhattan's infamous 21 Club to rabbis who used religious exemptions from the law to access—and distribute—wine, Okrent reveals an era defined by overwhelmed law enforcement agencies and mobsters ready to turn bootlegging into a profitable and violent business.

Where it's reviewed:
Booklist, March 1, 2010, page 34
Library Journal, January 2010, page 120
New York Times Book Review, May 23, 2010, page 20
Publishers Weekly, January 11, 2010, page 40
Vanity Fair, May 2010, page 122

Other books by the same author:
Public Editor #1: The Collected Columns (with Reflections, Reconsiderations, and Even a Few Retractions) of the First Ombudsman of The New York Times, 2008
Great Fortune: The Epic of Rockefeller Center, 2003
Baseball Anecdotes, 1989

Way We Were: New England Then New England Now, 1989
Nine Innings, 1985

Other books you might like:
Karen Abbott, *Sin in the Second City: Madams, Ministers, Playboys, and the Battle for America's Soul*, 2007
Edward Behr, *Prohibition: Thirteen Years That Changed America*, 1996
Jonathan Eig, *Get Capone: The Secret Plot That Captured America's Most Wanted Gangster*, 2010
Lucy Moore, *The Thieves' Opera*, 1998
Garrett Peck, *The Prohibition Hangover: Alcohol in America from Demon Rum to Cult Cabernet*, 2009

1321

SUZE ORMAN

Women and Money: Owning the Power to Control Your Destiny

(New York: Spiegel and Grau, 2007)

Story type: Contemporary
Subject(s): Money; Women; Business

Summary: Suze Orman, renowned for her financial knowledge, addresses the concerns women have about money in *Women and Money: Owning the Power to Control Your Destiny*. In this book, Orman discusses the power struggle between women and money. Without being critical, Orman shows women how to manage their money successfully and take control of their financial futures. She even includes a five-month plan for financial security. Suze Orman is the best-selling author of *The 9 Steps to Financial Freedom*, *The Money Book for the Young, Fabulous & Broke*, and *Suze Orman's Financial Guidebook*.

Where it's reviewed:
New York Times Magazine, February 25, 2007, page 19
Publishers Weekly, March 5, 2007, page 56

Other books by the same author:
The Road to Wealth - Revised, 2010
Suze Orman's Action Plan: New Rules for New Times, 2010
The Money Book for the Young, Fabulous & Broke, 2007
The 9 Steps to Financial Freedom: Practical and Spiritual Steps So You Can Stop Worrying, 2006
Suze Orman's Financial Guidebook: Put the 9 Steps to Work, 2006
The Laws of Money: 5 Timeless Secrets to Get Out and Stay Out of Financial Trouble, 2004
The Courage to be Rich: Creating a Life of Material and Spiritual Abundance, 2001

Other books you might like:
Eleanor Blayley, *Women's Worth: Finding Your Financial Confidence*, 2010

Jean Chatzky, *Difference: How Anyone Can Prosper in Even The Toughest Times*, 2009

Susan L. Hirshman, *Does This Make My Assets Look Fat? A Woman's Guide to Finding Financial Empowerment and Success*, 2010

Manisha Thakor, *On My Own Two Feet: A Modern Girl's Guide to Personal Finance*, 2007

Wynne A. Whitman, *Smart Women Protect Their Assets: Essential Information for Every Woman About Wills, Trusts, and More*, 2008

1322

GORDON PATZER

Looks: Why They Matter More Than You Ever Imagined

(New York: AMACOM, 2008)

Subject(s): Beauty; Social sciences; Psychology

Summary: In *Looks: Why They Matter More Than You Ever Imagined*, author Gordon Patzer examines the impact that attraction and beauty has on a person's life. Patzer uses scientific studies as well as personal anecdotes compiled during his 30 years of researching the subject to show how people with more appealing appearances tend to achieve more and do better in life. Patzer is also the author of *The Power and Paradox of Physical Attractiveness*.

Where it's reviewed:

CHOICE: Current Reviews for Academic Libraries, January 2009, page 952

Publishers Weekly, November 26, 2007, page 43

Other books by the same author:

Why Physically Attractive People Are More Successful: The Scientific Explanation, Social Consequences And Ethical Problems, 2007

The Power and Paradox of Physical Attractiveness, 2006

Experiment-Research Methodology in Marketing: Types and Applications, 1996

Using Secondary Data in Marketing Research: United States and Worldwide, 1995

The Physical Attractiveness Phenomena (Perspectives in Social Psychology), 1985

Other books you might like:

Geoffrey Jones, *Beauty Imagined: A History of the Global Beauty Business*, 2010

Stacy Malkan, *Not Just a Pretty Face: The Ugly Side of the Beauty Industry*, 2007

Gordon L. Patzer, *The Power and Paradox of Physical Attractiveness*, 2006

Julia Savacool, *The World Has Curves: The Global Quest for the Perfect Body*, 2009

1323

PAUL E. PETERSON

Saving Schools: From Horace Mann to Virtual Learning

(Cambridge, Massachusetts: Belknap Press of Harvard University Press, 2010)

Story type: Contemporary
Subject(s): Schools; History; Reformation

Summary: In *Saving Schools: From Horace Mann to Virtual Learning*, author Paul E. Peterson examines the evolution of schooling and education in the United States. He follows the efforts of six important figures in the development of schooling—Horace Mann, John Dewey, Martin Luther King Jr., Albert Shanker, William Bennett, and James Coleman—and reveals the ups and downs of American education, both in the past and in the present. He also discusses the current state of education, where it's headed in the future with initiatives such as virtual learning, and what should be done to improve schooling to help it reach its full potential.

Where it's reviewed:

American History, October 2010, page 12

Education Next, Spring 2010, page 24

Library Journal, March 1, 2010, page 90

Other books by the same author:

America's New Democracy (5th Edition), 2008

School Money Trials: The Legal Pursuit of Educational Adequacy, 2007

The Education Gap: Vouchers And Urban Schools, 2006

Generational Change: Closing the Test Score Gap, 2006

Choice and Competition in American Education, 2005

No Child Left Behind?: The Politics and Practice of School Accountability, 2003

Earning and Learning: How Schools Matter, 1999

Classifying by Race, 1995

The Price of Federalism, 1995

Can the Government Govern?, 1989

City Limits, 1981

Race and Authority in Urban Politics: Community Relations and the War on Poverty, 1976

Other books you might like:

Linda Darling-Hammond, *The Flat World and Education: How America's Commitment to Equity Will Determine Our Future*, 2009

Susan Eaton, *Children in Room E4: American Education on Trial*, 2007

Diane Ravitch, *The Death and Life of the Great American School System: How Testing and Choice Are Undermining Education*, 2010

Susan S. Sullivan, *Building Effective Learning Communities: Strategies for Leadership, Learning, & Collaboration*, 2005

Bernie Trilling, *21st Century Skills: Learning for Life in Our Times*, 2009

1324

CHARLES P. PIERCE

Idiot America: How Stupidity Became a Virtue in the Land of the Free

(New York: Doubleday, 2009)

Subject(s): Social sciences; Popular culture; Politics

Summary: *Idiot America: How Stupidity Became a Virtue in the Land of the Free* is a treatise by Charles P. Pierce, author *Moving the Chains* and *Hard to Forget*, on the dumbing down of America and how political and pop cultural debates have succeeded only in appealing to the stupidity of the masses. To frame his argument, Pierce uses the example of his visit to Kentucky's Creation Museum, where he witnessed a dinosaur wearing a saddle as the creationists' attempt to "take back the dinosaurs from the evolutionists." Pierce laments the corrosion of critical, intelligent thought in America, which he contends has been replaced by a nation more likely to vote on reality show contestants than on political candidates.

Where it's reviewed:
Esquire, November 2005, page 180
Library Journal, June 1, 2009, page 112
Publishers Weekly, March 30, 2009, page 38
Skeptical Inquirer, March-April 2010, page 57
Time, June 22, 2009, page 18

Other books by the same author:
Moving the Chains: Tom Brady and the Pursuit of Everything, 2007
Hard to Forget: An Alzheimer's Story, 2000
Sports Guy: In Search of Corkball, Warroad Hockey, Hooters Golf, Tiger Woods, and the Big, Big Game, 2000

Other books you might like:
Mark Bauerlein, *The Dumbest Generation: How the Digital Age Stupefies Young Americans and Jeopardizes Our Future (Or, Don't Trust Anyone Under 30)*, 2008
Chris Hedges, *Empire of Illusion*, 2009
Susan Jacoby, *The Age of American Unreason*, 2008
Rick Shenkman, *Just How Stupid Are We?: Facing the Truth About the American Voter*, 2008
Matt Taibbi, *The Great Derangement: A Terrifying True Story of War, Politics, and Religion at the Twilight of the American Empire*, 2008

1325

DENNIS POWERS

Sentinel of the Seas: Life and Death at the Most Dangerous Lighthouse Ever Built

(New York: Kensington Publishing Corporation, 2009)

Subject(s): Architecture; Lighthouses; Boats
Summary: In *Sentinel of the Seas: Life and Death at the Most Dangerous Lighthouse Ever Built*, author Dennis Powers relates the story of the construction and operation of the St. George's Reef Lighthouse. Built off the coast of northern California, St. George's Reef Lighthouse was constructed at the request of the United States Congress in response to many deadly shipping accidents that occurred in the area. The St. George's Reef Lighthouse was approximately 12 miles from the nearest harbor, and it took workers ten years to build. The book explores the men and women who bravely manned the lighthouse during its 75 years of operation and the dangers and hazards they endured. Powers is also the author of *The Raging Sea* and *Treasure Ship*.

Where it's reviewed:
Booklist, June 1, 2007, page 11

Other books by the same author:
Tales of the Seven Seas: The Escapades of Captain Dynamite Johnny O'Brien, 2010
Taking the Sea: Perilous Waters, Sunken Ships, and the True Story of the Legendary Wrecker Captains, 2009
Treasure Ship: The Legend And Legacy of the S.S. Brother Jonathan, 2006
The Raging Sea: The Powerful Account of the Worst Tsunami in U.S. History, 2005
The Internet Legal Guide: Everything You Need to Know When Doing Business Online, 2001

Other books you might like:
Bella Bathurst, *The Wreckers: A Story of Killing Seas and Plundered Shipwrecks, from the 18th-Century to the Present Day*, 2005
Dennis M. Powers, *Taking the Sea: Perilous Waters, Sunken Ships, and the True Story of the Legendary Wrecker Captains*, 2009
Dennis M. Powers, *Treasure Ship: The Legend and Legacy of the S.S. Brother Jonathan*, 2006
Michael Schumacher, *Mighty Fitz: The Sinking of the Edmund Fitzgerald*, 2005
Michael J. Tougias, *The Finest Hours: The True Story of the U.S. Coast Guard's Most Daring Sea Rescue*, 2009

1326

DOUGLAS PRESTON
MARIO SPEZI , Co-Author

The Monster of Florence

(New York: Grand Central Publishing, 2008)

Subject(s): Murder; Police Procedural; Serial Killers

Summary: Author Douglas Preston became interested in the serial killer dubbed "The Monster of Florence" when he moved to Florence, Italy in 2000 and learned that a murder had been committed in the olive grove near his home. From 1974 to 1985, seven couples were viciously killed while parked in their cars in isolated areas near Florence, and the murderer has never been brought to justice. Joined by Italian journalist Mario Spezi, who believed he had identified the true killer, Preston began an investigation to prove—and locate—the killer's identity. They were met not only with missing evidence and conspiracy theories, but harassment by the local authorities. Preston was accused of planting evidence and told to leave Italy; Spezi was arrested, jailed, and accused of being the murderer. Although the authors located and interviewed their prime suspect, this true crime piece is more about the trials of Preston and Spezi's investigation than proving the identity of the killer.

Where it's reviewed:
Booklist, June 1, 2008, page 14
Library Journal, May 1, 2008, page 83
Publishers Weekly, March 10, 2008, page 67

Other books by the same author:
Cemetary Dance (Pendergast, Book 9), 2010
Fever Dream, 2010
Impact, 2010
The Book of the Dead (Pendergast, Book 7), 2007
Dance of Death, 2006
Brimstone (Pendergast, Book 5), 2005
Still Life With Crows (Pendergast, Book 4), 2004
The Cabinet of Curiosities (Pendergast, Book 3), 2003
The Ice Limit, 2001
Thunderhead, 2000
Riptide, 1999
Reliquary (Pendergast, Book 2), 1998
Relic (Pendergast, Book 1), 1996

Other books you might like:
Benjamin Blech, *The Sistine Secrets: Michelangelo's Forbidden Message in the Heart of the Vatican*, 2008
Nigel Cawthorne, *Jack the Ripper's Secret Confession: The Hidden Testimony of Britain's First Serial Killer*, 2009
Roy Doliner, *The Sistine Secrets: Michelangelo's Forbidden Message in the Heart of the Vatican*, 2008
Dorothy Hoobler, *The Crimes of Paris: A True Story of Murder, Theft, and Detection*, 2009
    Thomas Hoobler, co-author
David Monaghan, *Jack the Ripper's Secret Confession: The Hidden Testimony of Britain's First Serial Killer*, 2009
Timothy Riordan, *Prince of Quacks: The Notorious Life of Dr. Francis Tumblety, Charlatan and Jack the Ripper Suspect*, 2009
R.A. Scotti, *Basilica: The Splendor and the Scandal: Building St. Peter's*, 2006

1327

DIANE RAVITCH

The Death and Life of the Great American School System: How Testing and Choice Are Undermining Education

(New York: Basic Books, 2010)

Subject(s): Education; Educational tests; Educational environment

Summary: *The Death and Life of the Great American School System: How Testing and Choice Are Undermining Education* is a critical examination of the U.S. education system from award-winning author and former assistant secretary of education Diane Ravitch. In this book, Ravitch analyzes many facets of the American education system, including the privatization of schools, standardized testing, teacher salaries, the charter school system, and disciplinary measures. In her address of each issue plaguing the education system in the U.S., Ravitch also offers solutions and suggestions based on her more than 40 years of experience working in education reform. In *The Death and Life of the Great American School System*, Ravitch argues that decisions regarding schools should be made by educators not politicians, and that the standards of learning should be increased and adhered to nationwide.

Where it's reviewed:
Education Week, March 10, 2010, page 1
National Review, March 22, 2010, page 49
New York Times Book Review, May 16, 2010, page 14
Washington Monthly, March-April 2010, page 46

Other books by the same author:
EdSpeak: A Glossary of Education Terms, Phrases, Buzzwords, and Jargon, 2007
The English Reader: What Every Literate Person Needs to Know, 2006
The Language Police: How Pressure Groups Restrict What Students Learn, 2004
Left Back: A Century of Battles over School Reform, 2001
The Great School Wars: A History of the New York City Public Schools, 2000
National Standards in American Education: A Citizen's Guide, 1995
The American Reader: Words That Moved a Nation, 1990
The Schools We Deserve, 1987

Other books you might like:
Linda Darling-Hammond, *The Flat World and Education: How America's Commitment to Equity Will Determine Our Future*, 2009
Todd Farley, *Making the Grades: My Misadventures in the Standardized Testing Industry*, 2009
Daniel M. Koretz, *Measuring Up: What Educational Testing Really Tells Us*, 2008
Mike Rose, *Why School?*, 2008
Larry D. Rosen, *Rewired: Understanding the iGeneration and the Way They Learn*, 2010

1328

DEBORAH L. RHODE

The Beauty Bias: The Injustice of Appearance in Life and Law

(New York: Oxford University Press, 2010)

Subject(s): Beauty; Fashion; Law

Summary: In *The Beauty Bias: The Injustice of Appear-

ance in Life and Law, Deborah L. Rhode examines discrimination based on appearance. Rhode focuses primarily on discrimination in hiring practices, and she cites specific examples of people from a range of social classes and various professions who may have been treated unfairly based on appearance issues such as weight problems or hairstyles. She examines how appearance subtly affects hiring practices, even in professions where appearance-related discrimination in the workplace is illegal. *The Beauty Bias* also focuses on women in the workplace and the discrimination women face when they choose not to conform to traditional standards of beauty.

Where it's reviewed:
New York Times Book Review, May 23, 2010, page 8
Newsweek, June 14, 2010, page 20
Publishers Weekly, June 21, 2010, page 44

Other books by the same author:
Legal Ethics (University Casebook), 2008
Women and Leadership: The State of Play and Strategies for Change, 2007
In Pursuit of Knowledge: Scholars, Status, and Academic Culture, 2006
Professional Responsibility and Regulation, 2006
Legal Ethics: Law Stories, 2005
The Difference 'Difference' Makes: Women and Leadership, 2003
Ethics in Practice: Lawyers' Roles, Responsibilities, and Regulation, 2003
In the Interests of Justice: Reforming the Legal Profession, 2003
Speaking of Sex: The Denial of Gender Inequality, 1999
Theoretical Perspectives on Sexual Difference, 1992
Justice and Gender: Sex Discrimination and the Law, 1991

Other books you might like:
Barbara J. Berg, *Sexism in America: Alive, Well, and Ruining Our Future*, 2009
Stacy Malkan, *Not Just a Pretty Face: The Ugly Side of the Beauty Industry*, 2007
Gordon Patzer, *Looks: Why They Matter More Than You Ever Imagined*, 2008
Gordon L. Patzer, *The Power and Paradox of Physical Attractiveness*, 2006

1329

MATT RIDLEY

The Rational Optimist: How Prosperity Evolves

(New York: Harper, 2010)

Subject(s): Wealth; Ethics; Science

Summary: Award-winning science writer Matt Ridley turns his attention to the current state of humanity—and arrives at some surprising conclusions. In *The Rational Optimist: How Prosperity Evolves*, Ridley unearths a wealth of scientific data, which suggests that there is much to celebrate in a seemingly downtrodden world.

By focusing on the positive aspects of the human race (namely, the innate capacities for intelligence and compassion each person possesses), this volume offers a grounded—though uplifting—treatise on the future of civilization. *The Rational Optimist* includes a bibliography and an index.

Where it's reviewed:
Booklist, May 1, 2010, page 62
The Bookseller, June 18, 2010, page 37
Library Journal, April 1, 2010, page 82
National Review, August 16, 2010, page 46
New York Times Book Review, June 13, 2010, page 20

Other books by the same author:
Francis Crick: Discoverer of the Genetic Code, 2006
Genome: The Autobiography of a Species in 23 Chapters, 2006
The Agile Gene: How Nature Turns on Nurture, 2004
The Red Queen: Sex and the Evolution of Human Nature, 2003
The Future of Disease: Predictions, 1999
The Origins of Virtue: Human Instincts and the Evolution of Cooperation, 1998

Other books you might like:
William J. Bernstein, *A Splendid Exchange: How Trade Shaped the World*, 2008
Barbara Ehrenreich, *Bright-Sided: How the Relentless Promotion of Positive Thinking Has Undermined America*, 2009
Richard Florida, *The Great Reset: How New Ways of Living and Working Drive Post-Crash Prosperity*, 2010

1330

GARY RIVLIN

Broke, USA: From Pawnshops to Poverty, Inc.: How the Working Poor Became Big Business

(New York: HarperCollins, 2010)

Subject(s): Economics; Economic depressions; United States

Summary: Written by award-winning author and journalist Gary Rivlin, *Broke, USA: From Pawnshops to Poverty, Inc.: How the Working Poor Became Big Business* is a critical examination of how American businesses were affected by the recent economic downturn. While the recession of 2008 left many Americans in the throes of financial ruin and loss, some businesses began thriving, making a profit from the poor and financially strained. In *Broke, USA*, Rivlin showcases the major success and financial profit to be made through businesses that cater to the poor, including pawn shops, loan services, and cash checking operations. Filled with true success stories and relevant anecdotes, *Broke, USA* offers readers a glimpse into the business of poverty.

Where it's reviewed:
Booklist, June 1, 2010, page 8
Publishers Weekly, April 26, 2010, page 103

Social Sciences

Time, June 28, 2010, page 18

Other books by the same author:
The Godfather of Silicon Valley: Ron Conway and the Fall of the Dot-coms, 2001
The Plot to Get Bill Gates: An Irreverent Investigation of the World's Richest Man... and the People Who Hate Him, 2000
Drive By, 1996
Fire on the Prairie: Chicago's Harold Washington and the Politics of Race, 1993

Other books you might like:
Daryl Collins, *Portfolios of the Poor: How the World Poor Live on $2 Per Day*, 2009
Mike Davis, *Planet of Slums*, 2006
Richard C. Longworth, *Caught in the Middle: America's Heartland in the Age of Globalism*, 2007
Jonathon Morduch, *Portfolios of the Poor: How the World Poor Live on $2 Per Day*, 2009
Raghuram Rajan, *Fault Lines: How Hidden Fractures Still Threaten the World Economy*, 2010
Pietra Rivoli, *The Travels of a T-Shirt in the Global Economy: An Economist Examines the Markets, Power, and Politics of World Trade*, 2005
Orlando Ruthven, *Portfolios of the Poor: How the World Poor Live on $2 Per Day*, 2009

1331

MARY ROACH

Spook: Science Tackles the Afterlife

(New York: W.W. Norton, 2006)

Subject(s): Religion; Science; Parapsychology

Summary: In *Spook: Science Tackles the Afterlife*, best-selling author Mary Roach sets out to test a range of theories and beliefs about what happens to the human soul after death. With scientific precision and a sharp sense of humor, Roach describes man's search for the soul or spirit in the microscopic structures of the body. As she identifies the diverse beliefs ascribed to the activities of the soul at the instant of death and beyond, she shares anecdotes of her own research into the afterlife. From ectoplasm to electromagnetism, soul-weighing to seances, Roach explores the afterlife with equal parts cynicism and reverence.

Where it's reviewed:
Booklist, September 1, 2005, Page 23
Kirkus Reviews, August 1, 2005, page 835
Library Journal, September 1, 2005, page 174
Publishers Weekly, August 22, 2005, page 54

Other books by the same author:
Packing for Mars: The Curious Science of Life in the Void, 2010
Bonk: The Curious Coupling of Science and Sex, 2009
Stiff: The Curious Lives of Human Cadavers, 2004

Other books you might like:
Concetta Bertoldi, *Do Dead People Watch You Shower?: And Other Questions You've Been All but*

Dying to Ask a Medium, 2007
Mary Roach, *Bonk: The Curious Coupling of Sex and Science*, 2008
Mary Roach, *Packing for Mars: The Curious Science of Life in the Void*, 2010
Will Storr, *Will Storr vs. The Supernatural: One Man's Search for the Truth About Ghosts*, 2006

1332

ALEXANDRA ROBBINS

The Overachievers: The Secret Lives of Driven Kids

(New York: Hyperion, 2006)

Subject(s): Adolescence; Colleges and Universities; Competition

Summary: Author Alexandra Robbins takes readers back to high school in *The Overachievers*. She follows the lives of eight students at Walt Whitman High School in Bethesda, Maryland. These students are dealing with extreme pressure to get straight A's, take as many AP classes as possible, and obtain leadership roles in various extracurricular activities, all to get into Ivy League colleges. The students suffer from emotional breakdowns, come to school while seriously ill, and resort to cheating. Robbins provides suggestions for what parents and the education system can do to take some of the pressure off of students.

Where it's reviewed:
Booklist, July 1, 2006, page 14
Kirkus Reviews, June 1, 2006, page 564
Library Journal, July 1, 2006, page 14
Publishers Weekly, May 22, 2006, page 42

Other books by the same author:
Pledged: The Secret Life of Sororities, 2005
Conquering Your Quarterlife Crisis: Advice from Twentysomethings Who Have Been There and Survived, 2004
Secrets of the Tomb: Skull and Bones, the Ivy League, and the Hidden Paths of Power, 2003
Quarterlife Crisis: The Unique Challenges of Life in Your Twenties, 2001

Other books you might like:
Michael Bamberger, *Wonderland: A Year in the Life of an American High School*, 2004
Madeline Levine, *The Price of Privilege: How Parental Pressure and Material Advantage Are Creating a Generation of Disconnected and Unhappy Kids*, 2006
David L. Marcus, *Acceptance: A Legendary Guidance Counselor Helps Seven Kids Find the Right Colleges—and Find Themselves*, 2009
Liz Murray, *Breaking Night: A Memoir of Forgiveness, Survival, and My Journey from Homeless to Harvard*, 2010

1333

WILLIAM ROSEN

The Most Powerful Idea in the World: A Story of Steam, Industry, and Invention

(New York: Random House, 2010)

Subject(s): Industrial Revolution, ca. 1750-1900; Inventions; Inventors

Summary: Acclaimed author William Rosen explores the history of the Industrial Revolution and the pivotal role the steam engine played in the development of modern industry. *The Most Powerful Idea in the World: A Story of Steam, Industry, and Invention* examines the contributions of such luminaries as Thomas Newcomen, James Watt, Adam Smith, and Joseph Black, all of whom contributed to the scientific, social, and philosophical climate of the era. Rosen presents both scientific data and historical analysis in a straightforward manner, offering a comprehensive look at the modernization of the West.

Where it's reviewed:
Booklist, May 15, 2010, page 18
The Economist, August 14, 2010, page 70
Library Journal, May 1, 2010, page 83
London Times, June 13, 2010, page 38
New York Times Book Review, August 29, 2010, page 20

Other books by the same author:
Justinian's Flea: Plague, Empire, and the Birth of Europe, 2007

Other books you might like:
Alice Sparberg Alexiou, *The Flatiron: The New York Landmark and the Incomparable City That Arose with It*, 2010
Nicholas Carr, *The Big Switch: Rewiring the World, from Edison to Google*, 2008
Michael Hiltzik, *Colossus: Hoover Dam and the Making of the American Century*, 2010
Jill Jonnes, *Eiffel's Tower: And the World's Fair Where Buffalo Bill Beguiled Paris, the Artists Quarreled, and Thomas Edison Became a Count*, 2009
Maury Klein, *The Power Makers: Steam, Electricity, and the Men Who Invented Modern America*, 2008

1334

ROGER ROSENBLATT

Making Toast

(New York: Ecco, 2010)

Subject(s): Family; Grandparents; Death

Summary: In *Making Toast*, Roger Rosenblatt works his way through the most heartbreaking challenge of his life—the death of his daughter Amy. With her unexpected death comes a new set of responsibilities for Roger and his wife, Ginny. They immediately pack their things and leave their home on Long Island to move in with Amy's husband. Harris needs all the help he can get raising his and Amy's three children, all under the age of six. Although Ginny and Roger are out of practice, they quickly get back into the swing of raising and caring for children again. As Roger writes, he reflects on the process and how it helped him accept Amy's death.

Where it's reviewed:
Booklist, March 1, 2010, page 34
Kirkus Reviews, November 15, 2009, page 1193
Publishers Weekly, September 28, 2009, page 51

Other books by the same author:
Beet: A Novel, 2009
Where We Stand: 30 Reasons for Loving Our Country, 2002
Rules for Aging: A Wry and Witty Guide to Life, 2001
Coming Apart: A Memoir of the Harvard Wars of 1969, 1997
The Man in the Water: And Other Essays, 1994
Children of War, 1992

Other books you might like:
Nancy G. Brinker, *Promise Me: How a Sister's Love Launched the Global Movement to End Breast Cancer*, 2010
Gail Caldwell, *Let's Take the Long Way Home: A Memoir of Friendship*, 2010
Zoe Fitzgerald Carter, *Imperfect Endings: A Daughter's Tale of Life and Death*, 2010
Joni Rodgers, *Promise Me: How a Sister's Love Launched the Global Movement to End Breast Cancer*, 2010
Katherine Rosman, *If You Knew Suzy: A Mother, a Daughter, a Reporter's Notebook*, 2010
Phyllis Theroux, *Journal Keeper: A Memoir*, 2010

1335

PETER SAGAL

The Book of Vice: Very Naughty Things (and How to Do Them)

(New York: HarperEntertainment, 2007)

Subject(s): Conduct of life; Pornography; Gambling

Summary: NPR personality Peter Sagal examines America's obsession with the world of the illicit. In *The Book of Vice: Very Naughty Things (and How to Do Them)*, Sagal delves into the secret societies of the country's fringe, from sex clubs and pornography studios to gambling halls and strippers' dens. With a comedian's wit and a journalist's sensibilities, Sagal leads readers through these scenes and shows the error, folly, and splendor of America's appetite for wickedness.

Where it's reviewed:
Publishers Weekly, July 30, 2007, page 64

Other books by the same author:
Denial: A drama in two acts, 1999

Other books you might like:

Adrian Colesberry, *How to Make Love to Adrian Colesberry*, 2009

Anne Coyle, *Undateable: 311 Things Guys Do That Guarantee They Won't Be Dating or Having Sex*, 2010

Joe Quirk, *Sperm are from Men, Eggs are from Women*, 2006

Ellen Rakieten, *Undateable: 311 Things Guys Do That Guarantee They Won't Be Dating or Having Sex*, 2010

Mary Roach, *Bonk: The Curious Coupling of Sex and Science*, 2008

Andrew Trees, *Decoding Love: Why It Takes Twelve Frogs to Find a Prince, and Other Revelations from the Science of Attraction*, 2009

1336

LANEY SALISBURY
ALY SUJO , Co-Author

Provenance: How a Con Man and a Forger Rewrote the History of Modern Art

(New York: Penguin Press, 2009)

Subject(s): Biographies; Forgery; Art

Summary: In *Provenance: How a Con Man and a Forger Rewrote the History of Modern Art*, journalists Laney Salisbury and Aly Sujo recount the fantastic but true exploits of John Drewe and John Myatt. Purveyors of bold acts of art fraud in the 1980s and '90s, Drewe, a seasoned con man, and Myatt, an artist, devised an ingenious scheme of fraud and forgery that impacted some of Europe's greatest museums. So convincing were Myatt's brilliant counterfeits—and so ingenious was Drewe's con—that decades after the pair's initial crime spree, some of their fakes remain on display in museums, undetected.

Where it's reviewed:
Booklist, July 1, 2009, page 15
Kirkus Reviews, May 15, 2009, page 542
Publishers Weekly, May 18, 2009, page 1

Other books by the same author:
The Conman: The Extraordinary Story How One Amateur with a Pot of Emulsion Paint Mixed with KY Jelly Fooled the Art Experts, 2010
The Conman: How One Man Fooled Britain's Modern-Art Establishment, 2009

Other books you might like:

Ulrich Boser, *The Gardner Heist: The True Story of the World's Largest Unsolved Art Theft*, 2009

Edward Dolnick, *Rescue Artist: A True Story of Art, Thieves, and the Hunt for a Missing Masterpiece*, 2005

Jonathan Lopez, *The Man Who Made Vermeers: Unvarnishing the Legend of Master Forger Han van Meegeren*, 2008

Philip Mould, *The Art Detective: Fakes, Frauds, and Finds and the Search for Lost Treasures*, 2010

John Shiffman, *Priceless: How I Went Undercover to Rescue the World's Stolen Treasures*, 2010
Robert K. Wittman, co-author

1337

JAUME SANLLORENTE

Bombay Smiles: The Trip that Changed My Life

(Philadelphia: Paul Dry Books, 2009)

Summary: Authors Ivo Daalder and I.M. Destler examine the histories, responsibilities, and personalities of the presidential national security advisers from the Kennedy Era through George W. Bush. *In the Shadow of the Oval Office: Profiles of the National Security Advisers and the Presidents They Served—From JFK to George W. Bush* explores the variety of ways the national security adviser works with the president to ensure the safety and security of the American people. Zbigniew Brzezinski, McGeorge Bundy, Henry Kissinger, Colin Powell, and Condoleezza Rice have all played pivotal roles in the nation's security, and this volume chronicles their unique contributions. *In the Shadow of the Oval Office* includes a list of bibliographical references and a full index.

Where it's reviewed:
Booklist, November 15, 2009, page 4

Other books you might like:

Ishmael Beah, *A Long Way Gone: Memoirs of a Boy Soldier*, 2007

Mark Bixler, *Lost Boys of Sudan: An American Story of the Refugee Experience*, 2005

David Grant, *Beyond the Soiled Curtain — Project Rescue's Fight for the Victims of the Sex-Slave Industry*, 2008

Melissa Fay Greene, *There Is No Me without You*, 2006

Greg Mortenson, *Three Cups of Tea: One Man's Mission to Fight Terrorism and Build Nations...One School at a Time*, 2006
David Oliver Relin, co-author

1338

DAN SAVAGE

The Commitment: Love, Sex, Marriage, and My Family

(New York: Dutton, 2005)

Subject(s): Marriage; Family; Homosexuality

Summary: Author, advice columnist, and media personality Dan Savage reveals the story behind his family and the commitment that holds it together. *The Commitment: Love, Sex, Marriage, and My Family* describes Savage's decision to marry his longtime partner, Terry. But, despite the fact the two had been together for more than a decade and had adopted a son together, same-sex marriage remained illegal in their state of residence. This inspired Savage to chronicle exactly what makes a family, leading him on an enlightening journey of personal and societal discovery.

Where it's reviewed:
Entertainment Weekly, October 7, 2005, page 82
The Gay & Lesbian Review Worldwide, March-April 2006, page 42
Kirkus Reviews, August 1, 2005, page 836
Library Journal, October 1, 2005, page 98
Publishers Weekly, July 25, 2005, page 63

Other books by the same author:
Skipping Towards Gomorrah, 2003
The Kid: What Happened After My Boyfriend and I Decided to Go Get Pregnant, 2000
Savage Love: Straight Answers from America's Most Popular Sex Columnist, 1998

Other books you might like:
Kate Braestrup, *Marriage and Other Acts of Charity: A Memoir*, 2010
Michael Chabon, *Manhood for Amateurs: The Pleasures and Regrets of a Husband, Father, and Son*, 2009
Adrian Colesberry, *How to Make Love to Adrian Colesberry*, 2009
Elizabeth Gilbert, *Committed: A Skeptic Makes Peace with Marriage*, 2010
David Sedaris, *When You Are Engulfed in Flames*, 2008

1339

KATHRYN SCHULZ

Being Wrong: Adventures in the Margin of Error

(New York: HarperCollins, 2010)

Story type: Psychological
Subject(s): Psychology; Human behavior; Self perception

Summary: *Being Wrong: Adventures in the Margin of Error* is a critical examination of the failures and mistakes of humans from author Kathryn Schulz. Most people in the world are convinced that they're right about what they believe, feel, and do. Although humans are fallible and making errors is expected, most people are convinced that the way they think and act is right. In *Being Wrong*, Schulz examines why it's so important for people to be right and what it means to be incorrect, mistaken, or just plain wrong about things. Relying on wisdom from sources as diverse as Groucho Marx and Charles Darwin, Schulz makes an argument for the importance of wrongness and explains how it can positively affect a person's life, future, and relationships.

Where it's reviewed:
Booklist, April 15, 2010, page 6
Library Journal, March 15, 2010, page 113
Mother Jones, July-August 2010, page 67
New York Times Book Review, July 25, 2010, page 16
Publishers Weekly, March 22, 2010, page 60

Other books you might like:
Elliot Aronson, *Mistakes Were Made (But Not by Me): Why We Justify Foolish Beliefs, Bad Decisions, and Hurtful Acts*, 2007
David H. Freedman, *Wrong: Why Experts* Keep Failing Us—and How to Know When Not to Trust Them: *Scientists, Finance Wizards, Doctors, Relationship Gurus, Celebrity CEOs, High-Powered Consultants, Health Officials and More*, 2010
Malcolm Gladwell, *Blink: The Power of Thinking Without Thinking*, 2005
Zachary Shore, *Blunder: Why Smart People Make Bad Decisions*, 2008
Carol Tavris, *Mistakes Were Made (But Not by Me): Why We Justify Foolish Beliefs, Bad Decisions, and Hurtful Acts*, 2007

1340

AMY SEDARIS

I Like You: Hospitality under the Influence

(New York: Grand Central Publishing, 2006)

Subject(s): Entertaining; Food; Humor

Summary: Actor and comedian Amy Sedaris provides a funny and sarcastic collection of entertaining tips for almost all situations: what not to say at a funeral; cooking under the influence; the need to engage elderly guests to avoid "the express train to nappy-land"; cutting off the inebriated; inappropriate introductions; and removing vomit stains. Sedaris offers more than 100 recipes, including ones for spanikopita and pastistio. She also gives quirky craft and decorating tips—such as a calf-stretcher and a mini-pantyhose plant hanger—and offbeat, themed party ideas. *I Like You* has a scrapbook feel with stained recipe cards and numerous photos.

Where it's reviewed:
Booklist, August 1, 2006, page 5
Library Journal, October 1, 2006, page 101
Publishers Weekly, July 17, 2006, page 144
Time, December 4, 2006, page 126

Other books by the same author:
Simple Times: Crafts for Poor People, 2010
Wigfield: The Can-Do Town That Just May Not, 2004

Other books you might like:
Samantha Bee, *I Know I Am, but What Are You?*, 2010
Stephen Colbert, *Wigfield: The Can-Do Town That Just May Not*, 2003
David Cross, *I Drink for a Reason*, 2010
Paul Dinello, *Wigfield: The Can-Do Town That Just May Not*, 2003
    Amy Sedaris, co-author
Sarah Silverman, *The Bedwetter: Stories of Courage, Redemption, and Pee*, 2010
Eric Spitznagel, *You're a Horrible Person, but I Like You: The Believer Book of Advice*, 2010

Social Sciences

1341

SCOTT ANDREW SELBY
GREG CAMPBELL , Co-Author

Flawless: Inside the Largest Diamond Heist in History

(New York: Sterling Publishing Co., 2010)

Story type: Historical
Subject(s): Crime; Theft; Journalism

Summary: In the winter of 2003, a group of men broke into an airtight vault in Belgium and stole more than $100 million worth of diamonds. In *Flawless: Inside the Largest Diamond Heist in History*, authors Scott Andrew Selby and Greg Campbell explain how the thieves made it into and out of the vault undetected—their presence was not detected by security guards or alarms. Despite the perfect execution of the theft, the group's getaway was not as flawless and they were quickly caught. Although the thieves were apprehended, they never spoke of how they were able to enter the vault and escape with the jewels. In this book, Selby and Campbell sort through rumor and fact to put together the story of how these thieves almost got away with the perfect crime.

Where it's reviewed:
Booklist, February 1, 2010, page 11
Kirkus Reviews, January 1, 2010, page 35
Publishers Weekly, December 14, 2009, page 50

Other books you might like:
Ulrich Boser, *The Gardner Heist: The True Story of the World's Largest Unsolved Art Theft*, 2009
Paul Doherty, *Great Crown Jewels Robbery of 1303: The Extraordinary Story of the First Big Bank Raid in History*, 2005
Lee Gruenfeld, *Confessions of a Master Jewel Thief*, 2005
   Bill Mason, co-author
Adam Shand, *King of Thieves: The Adventures of Arthur Delaney and the Kangaroo Gang*, 2010
John Shiffman, *Priceless: How I Went Undercover to Rescue the World's Stolen Treasures*, 2010
   Robert K. Wittman, co-author

1342

TOM SHACHTMAN

Rumspringa: To Be or Not to Be Amish

(New York: North Point Press, 2006)

Subject(s): Amish; Adolescence; Coming of age

Summary: In *Rumspringa: To Be or Not to Be Amish*, Tom Shachtman, author and documentary filmmaker of *The Devil's Playground*, expounds upon concepts and characters that he researched for the making of that documentary. Rumspringa is an Amish practice that encourages adolescents at the age of 16 or older to go out into the modern world and explore it in order to decide whether or not they want to continue to live in the Amish community. Shachtman allows teenagers participating in Rumspringa to tell their own stories of their experiences. He uses the construct as a way to open up a discussion of coming of age in the United States and of the Amish lifestyle.

Where it's reviewed:
Booklist, April 1, 2006, page 7
Bookmarks, Sept/Oct 2006, page 49
Kirkus Reviews, March 15, 2006, page 281
School Library Journal, August 2006, page 146
Wilson Quarterly, Autumn 2006, page 107

Other books by the same author:
Airlift to America: How Barack Obama, Sr., John F. Kennedy, Tom Mboya, and 800 East African Students Changed Their World and Ours, 2009
Dead Center: Behind the Scenes at the World's Largest Medical Examiner's Office, 2007
The Gilded Leaf: Triumph, Tragedy, and Tobacco: Three Generations of the R. J. Reynolds Family and Fortune, 2006
25 to Life: The Truth, the Whole Truth, and Nothing But the Truth, 2002
Skyscraper Dreams: The Great Real Estate Dynasties of New York, 2001
Absolute Zero and the Conquest of Cold, 2000
The Most Beautiful Villages of New England, 1997
The FBI-KGB War, 1995
Whoever Fights Monsters: My Twenty Years Tracking Serial Killers for the FBI, 1993

Other books you might like:
Anne Beiler, *Twist of Faith: The Story of Anne Beiler, Founder of Auntie Anne's Pretzels*, 2008
Jonas Beiler, *Think No Evil: Inside the Story of the Amish Schoolhouse Shooting...and Beyond*, 2009
Peter C. Hill, *Psychology of Religious Fundamentalism*, 2005
   Ralph W. Hood, co-author
Joe Mackall, *Plain Secrets: An Outsider among the Amish*, 2007
Anna Dee Olson, *Growing Up Amish: Insider Secrets from One Woman's Inspirational Journey*, 2008
Shawn Smucker, *Think No Evil: Inside the Story of the Amish Schoolhouse Shooting...and Beyond*, 2009
W. Paul Williamson, *Psychology of Religious Fundamentalism*, 2005

1343

ROB SHEFFIELD

Love Is a Mix Tape: Life and Loss, One Song at a Time

(New York: Crown Publishers, 2007)

Subject(s): Autobiographies; Music; Love

Summary: *Love Is a Mix Tape: Life and Loss, One Song at a Time* is the story of *Rolling Stone* journalist Rob Sheffield's relationship with the woman he loved and the music they enjoyed together. Using the track lists of 15 mix tapes he made throughout the course of his life, Sheffield recalls special moments from summer camp, high school, and the day he met Renee, his wife of eight years. From Elvis Presley to the Red Hot Chili Peppers, Nirvana to Missy Elliott, Sheffield draws connections between his favorite songs and the events they correspond to in his life. Music is invaluable to Sheffield, as it brought him and Renee together—and kept him from falling apart when she died suddenly.

Where it's reviewed:
Booklist, December 15, 2006, page 11
Kirkus Reviews, October 15, 2006, page 1060
Library Journal, November 15, 2006, page 73
Publishers Weekly, December 18, 2006, page 59

Other books by the same author:
Talking to Girls About Duran Duran: One Young Man's Quest for True Love and a Cooler Haircut, 2010

Other books you might like:
Michael Chabon, *Manhood for Amateurs: The Pleasures and Regrets of a Husband, Father, and Son*, 2009
Anne Coyle, *Undateable: 311 Things Guys Do That Guarantee They Won't Be Dating or Having Sex*, 2010
Chuck Klosterman, *Eating the Dinosaur*, 2009
Ellen Rakieten, *Undateable: 311 Things Guys Do That Guarantee They Won't Be Dating or Having Sex*, 2010
Rob Sheffield, *Talking to Girls about Duran Duran: One Young Man's Quest for True Love and a Cooler Haircut*, 2010
Jeffrey Zaslow, *The Girls from Ames: A Story of Women and a Forty-Year Friendship*, 2009

1344

HAMPTON SIDES

Hellhound on His Trail: The Stalking of Martin Luther King, Jr. and the International Hunt for His Assassin
(New York: Doubleday, 2009)

Subject(s): Assassination; United States history; Criminals

Summary: In *Hellhound on His Trail: The Stalking of Martin Luther King, Jr. and the International Hunt for His Assassin*, acclaimed author Hampton Sides tells the story of the civil rights leader's assassination and the exhaustive search for the man responsible. After James Earl Ray escaped from prison, he drifted across the country in search of purpose—a purpose he felt he found in the racist ranting of politician George Wallace. When he shot and killed Martin Luther King Jr., Ray fled with the authorities in hot pursuit, embarking upon a 65-day manhunt that spanned the world. This volume tells the story of that hunt, focusing on Ray's perverse determination and the FBI's tireless drive. *Hellhound on His Trail* includes notes on the text and a listing of bibliographic references.

Where it's reviewed:
American Scholar, Summer 2010, page 108
Booklist, April 1, 2010, page 8
Library Journal, March 1, 2010, page 92
Publishers Weekly, February 8, 2010, page 37

Other books by the same author:
Blood and Thunder: The Epic Story of Kit Carson and the Conquest of the American West, 2007
Americana: Dispatches from the New Frontier, 2004
Ghost Soldiers: The Epic Account of World War II's Greatest Rescue Mission, 2002
Stomping Grounds: A Pilgrim's Progress Through Eight American Subcultures, 1992

Other books you might like:
David Aaronovitch, *Voodoo Histories: The Role of the Conspiracy Theory in Shaping Modern History*, 2010
Vincent Bugliosi, *Reclaiming History: The Assassination of President John F. Kennedy*, May 15, 2007
Dave Cullen, *Columbine*, 2009
Shane O'Sullivan, *Who Killed Bobby?: The Unsolved Murder of Robert F. Kennedy*, 2008
David Talbot, *Brothers: The Hidden History of the Kennedy Years*, 2007

1345

LENORE SKENAZY

Free-Range Kids: How to Raise Safe, Self-Reliant Children (Without Going Nuts with Worry)
(San Francisco, California: Jossey-Bass, 2009)

Subject(s): Children; Parenthood; Parent-child relations

Summary: In *Free-Range Kids: How to Raise Safe, Self-Reliant Children (Without Going Nuts with Worry)*, Lenore Skenazy describes her theory that people in the world are basically good and that children should be allowed a great deal more freedom to explore and discover the world on their own. Skenazy drew criticism when she announced in 2008 that she allowed her nine-year-old son to ride the subway alone, but she argues that this has made him much more self-reliant and able to handle challenges. The author argues that a bit more trust and a little less control can go a long way when raising a child.

Where it's reviewed:
The Christian Century, November 3, 2009, page 43
National Catholic Reporter, November 27, 2009, page 1a

Other books by the same author:
Who's the Blonde That Married What's-His-Name?: The Ultimate Tip-of-the-Tongue Test of Everything You Know You Know—But Can't Remember Right Now, 2009

Other books you might like:
Po Bronson, *NurtureShock: New Thinking About Children*, 2009
Warwick Cairns, *How to Live Dangerously: The*

Social Sciences

Hazards of Helmets, the Benefits of Bacteria, and the Risks of Living Too Safe, 2009

Alfie Kohn, *The Homework Myth: Why Our Kids Get Too Much of a Bad Thing*, 2006

Hara Estroff Marano, *A Nation of Wimps: The High Cost of Invasive Parenting*, 2008

Ashley Merryman, *NurtureShock: New Thinking About Children*, 2009

Ayelet Waldman, *Bad Mother: A Chronicle of Maternal Crimes, Minor Calamities, and Occasional Moments of Grace*, 2009

1346

STEVEN SOLOMON

Water: The Epic Struggle for Wealth, Power, and Civilization

(New York: HarperCollins Publishing, 2010)

Subject(s): Politics; Ecology; Human behavior

Summary: *Water: The Epic Struggle for Wealth, Power, and Civilization* by Steven Solomon describes the historical impact that water has had on the planet and how nations and tribes have fought and warred for control of water sources for centuries. In the book, Solomon also explores how water sources have shaped the development of civilizations and how its depleting supply could result in world domination for those nations with ample resources. Solomon is also the author of *The Confidence Game* and *Small Business USA*.

Where it's reviewed:
Booklist, December 1, 2009, page 20
The Economist, January 2, 2010, page 64EU
The National Interest, March-April 2010, page 75
Publishers Weekly, October 26, 2009, page 41

Other books by the same author:
Confidence Game, 1995
Small Business USA, 1986

Other books you might like:
Maude Barlow, *Blue Covenant: The Global Water Crisis and the Coming Battle for the Right to Water*, 2008
Peter H. Gleick, *Bottled and Sold: The Story Behind Our Obsession with Bottled Water*, 2010
Thomas M. Kostigen, *You Are Here: Exposing the Vital Link Between What We Do and What That Does to Our Planet*, 2008
Robert D. Morris, *The Blue Death: Disease, Disaster, and the Water We Drink*, 2007

1347

DANIEL J. SOLOVE

The Future of Reputation: Gossip, Rumor, and Privacy on the Internet

(New Haven, Connecticut: Yale University Press, 2007)

Summary: Starting around 2007, the United States was rocked by a series of financial crises that, together,

caused more damage to the economy than any troubles since the Stock Market Crash of 1929. This latest crisis, compared by many to the Great Depression, was largely the result of greed and overinflated egos, a sense of being "too big to fail." In *Too Big to Fail: The Inside Story of How Wall Street and Washington Fought to Save the Financial System from Crisis—and Lost*, New York Times reporter Andrew Ross Sorkin reconstructs the actions and events that led up to the economic disaster. He uses real names and inside information to show the drama and the tension that quickly spread from company boardrooms to the White House and then all around the world. Business, politics, and personalities all come together in this book in which Sorkin shows that nothing—no business or individual—is truly too big to fail.

Where it's reviewed:
American Lawyer, December 2007, page 97
Law and Politics Book Review, December 2007, page 909
Maclean's, November 19, 2007, page 168
University of Chicago Law Review, Summer 2009, page 1407-1448
Utne Reader, Jan-Feb 2008, page 33

Other books by the same author:
Nothing to Hide: The False Tradeoff between Privacy and Security, 2011
Understanding Privacy, 2010
Information Privacy: Statutes & Regulations, 2010-2011, 2009
Information Privacy Law, 2008
Privacy and the Media, 2008
The Digital Person: Technology and Privacy in the Information Age, 2006

Other books you might like:
Ken Auletta, *Googled: The End of the World as We Know It*, 2009
Gordon Bell, *Total Recall: How the E-Memory Revolution Will Change Everything*, 2009
    Jim Gemmell, co-author
Viktor Mayer-Schonberger, *Delete: The Virtue of Forgetting in the Digital Age*, 2009
Cass R. Sunstein, *Infotopia: How Many Minds Produce Knowledge*, 2006
Cass R. Sunstein, *On Rumors: How Falsehoods Spread, Why We Believe Them, What Can Be Done*, 2009

1348

ANDREW ROSS SORKIN

Too Big to Fail: The Inside Story of How Wall Street and Washington Fought to Save the Financial System from Crisis—and Lost

(New York: Viking, 2009)

Subject(s): Economic depressions; Economics; Business enterprises

Summary: Starting around 2007, the United States was

rocked by a series of financial crises that, together, caused more damage to the economy than any troubles since the Stock Market Crash of 1929. This latest crisis, compared by many to the Great Depression, was largely the result of greed and overinflated egos, a sense of being "too big to fail." In *Too Big to Fail: The Inside Story of How Wall Street and Washington Fought to Save the Financial System from Crisis—and Lost*, New York Times reporter Andrew Ross Sorkin reconstructs the actions and events that led up to the economic disaster. He uses real names and inside information to show the drama and the tension that quickly spread from company boardrooms to the White House and then all around the world. Business, politics, and personalities all come together in this book in which Sorkin shows that nothing—no business or individual—is truly too big to fail.

Where it's reviewed:
The American Prospect, Jan-Feb 2010, page 33
The Financial Times, November 19, 2009, page 10
New York Times Book Review, November 8, 2009, page 34

Other books you might like:
Adam Gopnik, *Angels and Ages: A Short Book about Darwin, Lincoln, and Modern Life*, 2009
Roger Lowenstein, *The End of Wall Street*, 2010
Erwann Michel-Kerjan, *The Irrational Economist: Making Decisions in a Dangerous World*, 2010
Scott Patterson, *The Quants: How a New Breed of Math Whizzes Conquered Wall Street and Nearly Destroyed It*, 2010
Carmen M. Reinhart, *This Time Is Different: Eight Centuries of Financial Folly*, 2009
  Kenneth Rogoff, co-author
Paul Slovic, *The Irrational Economist: Making Decisions in a Dangerous World*, 2010

1349

MICHAEL SPECTER

Denialism: How Irrational Thinking Hinders Scientific Progress, Harms the Planet, and Threatens Our Lives

(New York: Penguin Press, 2009)

Subject(s): Science; Medicine; Trust (Psychology)

Summary: *Denialism: How Irrational Thinking Hinders Scientific Progress, Harms the Planet, and Threatens Our Lives* is a thought-provoking book from science writer and journalist Michael Specter. Despite the major scientific and medical advances made in the past two centuries, many individuals are growing more wary and skeptical of scientific institutions. This has resulted in the protesting of vaccinations for children, stem cell research, and the use of genetically altered grain in African countries, among other advancemants that are being refuted by modern society. In *Denialism*, Specter presents a compelling argument for trusting and utilizing

scientific advancements and the dangers associated with refuting them.

Where it's reviewed:
Booklist, October 15, 2009, page 8
Kirkus Reviews, October 1, 2009, page 1062
Library Journal, October 15, 2009, page 100
New York Times Book Review, November 29, 2009, page 26
Publishers Weekly, September 14, 2009, page 36

Other books you might like:
Erik Conway, *Merchants of Doubt: How a Handful of Scientists Obscured the Truth on Issues from Tobacco Smoke to Global Warming*, 2010
Elaine Howard Ecklund, *Science vs. Religion: What Scientists Really Think*, 2010
Adam Gopnik, *Angels and Ages: A Short Book about Darwin, Lincoln, and Modern Life*, 2009
Farhad Manjoo, *True Enough: Learning to Live in a Post-Fact Society*, 2008
Naomi Oreskes, *Merchants of Doubt: How a Handful of Scientists Obscured the Truth on Issues from Tobacco Smoke to Global Warming*, 2010
Charles P. Pierce, *Idiot America: How Stupidity Became a Virtue in the Land of the Free*, 2009

1350

ROBERT SPECTOR

The Mom and Pop Store: How the Unsung Heroes of the American Economy Are Surviving and Thriving

(New York: Walker & Company, 2009)

Subject(s): Business; Small business; Economics

Summary: Author Robert Spector introduces readers to the world of small, family-owned businesses in *The Mom and Pop Store: How the Unsung Heroes of the American Economy Are Surviving and Thriving*. Through a series of interviews with other small business owners, Spector shows how these businesses operate and stay afloat even in a world that seems to revolve around big corporations. He also discusses customers—how their continued support keeps local shops alive and the factors that keep customers coming back. *The Mom and Pop Store: How the Unsung Heroes of the American Economy Are Surviving and Thriving* was republished under the title *The Mom and Pop Store: Stories from the Heart of America*.

Where it's reviewed:
Booklist, September 1, 2009, page 19
Kirkus Reviews, July 15, 2009, page 750
Library Journal, November 1, 2009, page 84
Publishers Weekly, June 29, 2009, page 119

Other books by the same author:
Category Killers: The Retail Revolution and Its Impact on Consumer Culture, 2005
The Nordstrom Way to Customer Service Excellence: A

Handbook For Implementing Great Service in Your Organization, 2005

Anytime, Anywhere: How the Best Bricks-and-Clicks Businesses Deliver Seamless Service to Their Customers, 2003

Amazon.com: Get Big Fast, 2002

The Ale Master: How I Pioneered America's Craft Brewing Industry, Opened the First Brewpub, Bucked Trends, and Enjoyed Every Minute of It, 1998

Other books you might like:

Sara Bongiorni, *A Year Without 'Made in China': One Family's True Life Adventure in the Global Economy*, 2007

Donna Fenn, *Alpha Dogs: How Your Small Business Can Become a Leader of the Pack*, 2005

Bill Geist, *Way Off the Road: Discovering the Peculiar Charms of Small Town America*, 2007

Michael H. Shuman, *Small-Mart Revolution: How Local Businesses Are Beating the Global Competition*, 2006

1351

HILARY SPURLING

Matisse the Master: A Life of Henri Matisse: The Conquest of Colour, 1909-1954

(New York: Knopf, 2005)

Subject(s): Art; Artists and Art; Biography

Summary: Following *The Unknown Matisse: A Life of Henri Matisse: The Early Years, 1869-1908* in a two-part biography, this volume draws heavily on documentary sources to present a very complete picture of Matisse's later years as an established artist. Spurling explores how this change in status affected his artistic career (he nevertheless continued to experiment) and personal life (though they accepted his time-consuming vocation for decades, the family eventually withdrew their support and wife Amelie requested a divorce). Spurling also shows that, contrary to the wild emotion and vivid colors of the paintings he created, Matisse lived a disciplined life. Along with expert analysis of her subject's paintings and unprecedented use of color, the biographer discusses his health (especially how he coped with illness in old age), political views (she counters charges that he collaborated with Nazi occupiers during World War II), and relationships with the women who were important in his life.

Where it's reviewed:

Booklist, July 2005, page 1887

Harper's Bazaar, December 2005, page 90

Publishers Weekly, May 9, 2005, page 53

Vogue, September 2005, page 579

Other books by the same author:

Pearl Buck in China: Journey to The Good Earth, 2010

The Unknown Matisse, 2005

The Girl from the Fiction Department: A Portrait of Sonia Orwell, 2004

Other books you might like:

Barbara Hess, *Willem de Koonig: 1904-1997*, 2004

Steven Naifeh, *Jackson Pollock: An American Saga*, 1998

Cecile Shapiro, *Abstract Expressionism: A Critical Record*, 1990

David Shapiro, co-author

Gregory Smith, *Jackson Pollock: An American Saga*, 1998

Mark Stevens, *de Kooning: An American Master*, 2004

Annalyn Swan, co-author

1352

TRISTRAM STUART

Waste: Uncovering the Global Food Scandal

(New York: W. W. Norton & Company, 2009)

Subject(s): Food; Economics

Summary: A major problem in the world today is food—whether people lack it or have an overabundance of it. In *Waste: Uncovering the Global Food Scandal*, author Tristram Stuart exposes food wasters, revealing which countries waste the most food. He also discusses which nations lack not only food but also the means of keeping and rearing crops. Stuart introduces a number of different changes that people can implement to stop throwing away the food and money that so many nations lack. Stuart is also the author of *The Bloodless Revolution*.

Where it's reviewed:

Booklist, October 15, 2009, page 10

Kirkus Reviews, August 15, 2009, page 864

Library Journal, October 1, 2009, page 96

Publishers Weekly, August 24 2009, page 56

Other books by the same author:

The Bloodless Revolution: A Cultural History of Vegetarianism: From 1600 to Modern Times, 2008

Other books you might like:

Steven Hopp, *Animal, Vegetable, Miracle: A Year of Food Life*, 2007

Scott Kilman, *Enough: Why the World's Poorest Starve in an Age of Plenty*, 2009

Barbara Kingsolver, *Animal, Vegetable, Miracle: A Year of Food Life*, 2007

Camille Kingsolver, co-author

Raj Patel, *Stuffed and Starved: The Hidden Battle for the World Food System*, 2008

Carlo Petrini, *Slow Food Nation: Why Our Food Should Be Good, Clean, and Fair*, 2007

Carlo Petrini, *Terra Madre: Forging a New Global Network of Sustainable Food Communities*, 2010

Roger Thurow, *Enough: Why the World's Poorest Starve in an Age of Plenty*, 2009

1353

KATE SUMMERSCALE

The Suspicions of Mr. Whicher: A Shocking Murder and the Undoing of a Great Victorian Detective

(New York: Walker & Company, 2009)

Story type: Historical - Victorian; Mystery
Subject(s): Crime; History; England

Summary: *The Suspicions of Mr. Whicher: A Shocking Murder and the Undoing of a Great Victorian Detective* is an intriguing true story from author Kate Summerscale. In 1860, after the horrific murder of a three-year-old boy in London, Scotland Yard Inspector Jonathan Whicher was assigned to investigate the case. At the time, there were only eight detectives in all of England, and Whicher was considered to be the best. The case garnered a great public following, as individuals across the country grew intrigued and fascinated by detection as a whole. Whicher's suspicions that a family member was responsible for the crime were dismissed, until years later when his theory was finally proven correct.

Where it's reviewed:
Bookseller, May 23, 2008, page 24
Library Journal, February 1, 2008, page 85
Publishers Weekly, November 19, 2007, page 46
Sunday Times (London, England), April 6, 2008, page 50
Time, April 28, 2008, page 83

Other books by the same author:
The Queen of Whale Cay: The Eccentric Story of 'Joe' Carstairs, Fastest Woman on Water, 1999

Other books you might like:
Giles Fowler, *Deaths on Pleasant Street: The Ghastly Enigma of Colonel Swope and Doctor Hyde*, 2009
David Grann, *The Devil and Sherlock Holmes: Tales of Murder, Madness, and Obsession*, 2010
David Grann, *The Lost City of Z: A Tale of Deadly Obsession in the Amazon*, 2009
Richard Jones, *Jack the Ripper: The Casebook*, 2009
Jonathan Lopez, *The Man Who Made Vermeers: Unvarnishing the Legend of Master Forger Han van Meegeren*, 2008

1354

ROBERT I. SUTTON

Good Boss, Bad Boss: How to Be the Best...and Learn from the Worst

(New York: Business Plus, 2010)

Subject(s): Business; Employment; Management

Summary: Dr. Robert Sutton composed *Good Boss, Bad Boss: How to Be the Best...and Learn from the Worst* for those who struggle to get their employees to produce high-quality work while holding managerial or supervisory positions. In this book, he defines what makes a "good" boss and the qualities that make a "bad" boss. He then gives tips to avoid being the type of boss that employees typically avoid. Sutton uses real stories from satisfied and miserable employees alike to show the difference between company morale and profit when employees enjoy working with their superiors and when they fear or don't respect their employers. Sutton is also the author of *The No Asshole Rule*.

Where it's reviewed:
Fortune, Sept 27, 2010, page 22
Publishers Weekly, Sept 6, 2010, page 35
Risk Management, Oct 2010, page 42

Other books by the same author:
The No Asshole Rule: Building a Civilized Workplace and Surviving One That Isn't, 2007
Hard Facts, Dangerous Half-Truths And Total Nonsense: Profiting From Evidence-Based Management, 2006

Other books you might like:
Paul Babiak, *Snakes in Suits: When Psychopaths Go to Work*, 2006
    Robert D. Hare, co-author
Elizabeth Holloway, *Toxic Workplace!: Managing Toxic Personalities and Their Systems of Power*, 2009
Marvin Karlins, *What Every BODY is Saying: An Ex-FBI Agent's Guide to Speed-Reading People*, 2008
Mitchell Kusy, *Toxic Workplace!: Managing Toxic Personalities and Their Systems of Power*, 2009
Joe Navarro, *What Every BODY is Saying: An Ex-FBI Agent's Guide to Speed-Reading People*, 2008
Christine Pearson, *The Cost of Bad Behavior: How Incivility Is Damaging Your Business and What to Do About It*, 2009
    Christine Porath, co-author
Robert Sutton, *The No Asshole Rule: Building a Civilized Workplace and Surviving One That Isn't*, 2007

1355

MATT TAIBBI

The Great Derangement: A Terrifying True Story of War, Politics, and Religion at the Twilight of the American Empire

(New York: Spiegel & Grau, 2008)

Subject(s): Conspiracies; Politics; Religion

Summary: As National Affairs Correspondent for *Rolling Stone* magazine, Matt Taibbi has covered national and international news events—always with an edgy, editorial opinion. In *The Great Derangement*, Taibbi writes about the current American populace with a scathing perspective that he is most commonly associated with. Whether he is discussing the time he spent with the

Social Sciences

congregation of the Corner Stone church in San Antonio under the direction of televangelist John Hagee, or the time he joined the 9/11 Truth Movement, nothing is free from his characteristic cynicism and disapproval. However, he also endeavors to relate to the different groups and relates his understanding of why they hold the beliefs they do.

Where it's reviewed:
Publishers Weekly, March 17, 2008, page 60

Other books by the same author:
Griftopia: Bubble Machines, Vampire Squids, and the Long Con That Is Breaking America, 2010
Smells Like Dead Elephants: Dispatches from a Rotting Empire, 2007
Spanking the Donkey: Dispatches from the Dumb Season, 2006

Other books you might like:
Dave Eggers, *Zeitoun*, 2009
George Lakoff, *The Political Mind: Why You Can't Understand 21st-Century American Politics with an 18th-Century Brain*, 2008
Matt Taibbi, *Smells Like Dead Elephants: Dispatches from a Rotting Empire*, 2007
Matt Taibbi, *Spanking the Donkey: Dispatches from the Dumb Season*, 2005

1356

NASSIM NICHOLAS TALEB

The Black Swan: The Impact of the Highly Improbable
(New York: Random House, 2007)

Subject(s): Philosophy; Business; History

Summary: In *The Black Swan: The Impact of the Highly Improbable*, author Nassim Nicholas Taleb discusses the use of induction by social scientists today and explores the idea of structure versus randomness. According to Taleb, solely witnessing an event once does not mean that it will reoccur in the future. Using the title of his book, he creates a simple anecdote that is reinforced throughout the entire text—if a person only sees hundreds of white swans, it does not mean that a black swan does not exist somewhere. Whether it is in hiding or on the other side of the world, there is a still a chance that the black swan exists. Taleb examines governmental, economical, and social ideas and decisions of the past and applies the Black Swan theory to each in order to test their claims.

Where it's reviewed:
Booklist, March 15, 2007, page 9
Books & Culture, Sept-Oct 2007, page 23
Library Journal, April 15, 2007, page 94
National Review, June 25, 2007, page 46

Other books by the same author:
The Bed of Procrustes: Philosophical and Practical Aphorisms, 2010
Fooled by Randomness: The Hidden Role of Chance in Life and in the Markets, 2008

Dynamic Hedging: Managing Vanilla and Exotic Options, 1997

Other books you might like:
Albert-Laszlo Barabasi, *Bursts: The Hidden Pattern Behind Everything We Do*, 2010
Leonard Mlodinow, *The Drunkard's Walk: How Randomness Rules Our Lives*, 2008
Kenneth A. Posner, *Stalking the Black Swan: Research and Decision Making in a World of Extreme Volatility*, 2010
Nassim Nicholas Taleb, *Fooled by Randomness: The Hidden Role of Chance in Life and in the Markets*, 2008

1357

HELEN THORPE

Just Like Us: The True Story of Four Mexican Girls Coming of Age in America
(New York: Scribner, 2009)

Story type: Coming-of-Age
Subject(s): Illegal immigrants; Mexican Americans; Education

Summary: In *Just Like Us: The True Story of Four Mexican Girls Coming of Age in America*, journalist Helen Thorpe documents the lives of four Mexican girls with hopes of achieving similar American dreams. Although they are all good students and respectable young women, the group of close friends is split in half for a very distinct reason. Elissa and Clara are legal, either born in the United States or in possession of a green card, while Marisela and Yadira are not. Marisela and Yadira wish to attend college and pursue ground-breaking careers, but without green cards or social security numbers, they cannot. Instead, they sit on the sidelines and watch Elissa and Clara achieve their dreams. When controversy over illegal immigration rises to a new level in Denver, Marisela and Yadira fear that even though they've lived the majority of their lives in America, they will soon have to leave the country they call home.

Where it's reviewed:
Booklist, August 1, 2009, page 14
Kirkus Reviews, July 15, 2009, page 751
Library Journal, July 1, 2009, page 114
New Yorker, January 4, 2010, page 73
Publishers Weekly, May 25, 2009, page 48

Other books you might like:
David Bacon, *Communities Without Borders: Images and Voices from the World of Migration*, 2006
Tim Gaynor, *Midnight on the Line: The Secret Life of the U.S.- Mexico Border*, 2009
Tomas Jimenez, *Replenished Ethnicity: Mexican Americans, Immigration, and Identity*, 2009
Peter Orner, *Underground America: Narratives of Undocumented Lives*, 2008

William Perez, *We ARE Americans: Undocumented Students Pursuing the American Dream*, 2009

`1358`

JEAN TWENGE
W. KEITH CAMPBELL , Co-Author

The Narcissism Epidemic: Living in the Age of Entitlement
(New York: Free Press, 2009)

Subject(s): Psychology; Self love; Self perception

Summary: In *The Narcissism Epidemic: Living in the Age of Entitlement*, authors Jean M. Twenge and W. Keith Campbell explore the 21st-century epidemic of narcissism. According to the authors, new technology and media fuel the general public's narcissism by providing avenues in which the average person can practice self-adulation. Twenge and Campbell also discuss materialism and how it may have resulted in the economic crisis of the early 21st century. Twenge is also the author of *Generation Me: Why Today's Young Americans Are More Confident, Assertive, Entitled—and More Miserable than Ever.*

Where it's reviewed:
Booklist, April 1, 2009, page 6
Newsweek, April 27, 2009, page 48
Publishers Weekly, January 26, 2009, page 109

Other books by the same author:
Generation Me: Why Today's Young Americans Are More Confident, Assertive, Entitled—and More Miserable Than Ever Before, 2007

Other books you might like:
Wendy T. Behary, *Disarming the Narcissist: Surviving & Thriving with the Self-Absorbed*, 2008
Jake Halpern, *Fame Junkies: The Hidden Truths Behind America's Favorite Addiction*, 2006
Cooper Lawrence, *The Cult of Celebrity: What Our Fascination with the Stars Reveals About Us*, 2009
Martha Stout, *The Sociopath Next Door: The Ruthless Versus the Rest of Us*, 2005

`1359`

JUSTIN VAISSE

Neoconservatism: The Biography of a Movement
(Cambridge, Massachusetts: Belknap Press of Harvard, 2010)

Story type: Political
Subject(s): Politics; History; Philosophy

Summary: Written by Justin Vaisse and translated by Arthur Goldhammer, *Neoconservatism: The Biography of a Movement* is a comprehensive history on the origins, evolution, and practices of neoconservatives. In this detailed narrative, Vaisse divides the neoconservatism movement into three distinct eras. The first is the start of

neoconservatism in the 1960s when scholars countered left-wing extremists. In the 1970s and 1980s, neoconservatism evolved to focusing strictly on anticommunist activities and supporting President Ronald Reagan. In the 1990s and 2000s, neoconservatism changed yet again during the presidency of George W. Bush. The movement was absorbed as part of the Republican Party to utilize military force and spread democracy. In *Neoconservatism*, Vaisse provides a detailed history of the movement, as well as profiles on key players like Norman Podhoretz, Daniel Patrick Moynihan, and William Kristol.

Where it's reviewed:
New York Times Book Review, June 13, 2010, page 22
Publishers Weekly, March 22, 2010, page 62

Other books you might like:
Yaron Brook, *Neoconservatism: An Obituary for an Idea*, 2010
Murray Friedman, *The Neoconservative Revolution: Jewish Intellectuals and the Shaping of Public Policy*, 2005
Douglas Murray, *NeoConservatism: Why We Need It*, 2006
C. Bradley Thompson, *Neoconservatism: An Obituary for an Idea*, 2010

`1360`

JESSICA VALENTI

The Purity Myth: How America's Obsession with Virginity Is Hurting Young Women
(Berkeley, California: Perseus Books Group, 2009)

Subject(s): Women; Women's rights; Sexuality

Summary: In *The Purity Myth: How America's Obsession with Virginity Is Hurting Young Women*, author Jessica Valenti argues that the predominant belief that exists in America about girls "saving themselves," as well as recent campaigns for "abstinence only," serve merely to confuse and harm young women. Furthermore, Valenti contends that these beliefs affect women's rights by over-sexualizing women instead of recognizing them as humans. Valenti is also the author of *He's a Stud, She's a Slut, and 49 Other Double Standards Every Woman Should Know* and *Full Frontal Feminism: A Young Woman's Guide to Why Feminism Matters.*

Where it's reviewed:
Booklist, April 15, 2009, page 7
CHOICE: Current Reviews for Academic Libraries, February 2010, page 1177
Curve, Jan-Feb 2010, page 57
Ms. Magazine, Spring 2009, page 79
Vanity Fair, May 2009, page 60

Other books by the same author:
He's a Stud, She's a Slut, and 49 Other Double Standards Every Woman Should Know, 2008
Yes Means Yes: Visions of Female Sexual Power and A World Without Rape, 2008

Full Frontal Feminism: A Young Woman's Guide to Why Feminism Matters, 2007

Other books you might like:
Hanne Blank, *Virgin: The Untouched History*, 2007
Kathleen Bogle, *Hooking Up: Sex, Dating, and Relationships on Campus*, 2008
Laura Carpenter, *Virginity Lost: An Intimate Portrait of First Sexual Experiences*, 2005
Laura Sessions Stepp, *Unhooked: How Young Women Pursue Sex, Delay Love and Lose at Both*, 2008
Jessica Valenti, *He's a Stud, She's a Slut, and 49 Other Double Standards Every Woman Should Know*, 2008

1361

SHANKAR VEDANTAM

The Hidden Brain: How Our Unconscious Minds Elect Presidents, Control Markets, Wage Wars, and Save Our Lives

(New York: Spiegel & Grau, 2010)

Story type: Psychological
Subject(s): Psychology; Human behavior; Philosophy

Summary: Shankar Vedantam's *The Hidden Brain: How Our Unconscious Minds Elect Presidents, Control Markets, Wage Wars, and Save Our Lives* examines the ways that unconscious thoughts, opinions, and biases affect a person's conscious decisions, attitudes, and behaviors. Vedantam contends that a great deal of brain activity is controlled by a subconscious philosophy and belief system that might be contradictory to a person's conscious values and beliefs. When confronted with major decisions like who to vote for, who to fall in love with, and how to respond in an emergency, the brain relies on an unconscious set of principles which Vedantam calls "the hidden brain." Using psychological research and experiments, Vedantam sheds light on how the hidden parts of the mind affect decisions and how people can counteract their subconscious influence.

Where it's reviewed:
Booklist, December 1, 2009, page 6
Publishers Weekly, October 26, 2009, page 44

Other books by the same author:
The Ghosts of Kashmir, 2006

Other books you might like:
Gregory Berns, *Iconoclast: A Neuroscientist Reveals How to Think Differently*, 2008
Torkel Klingberg, *The Overflowing Brain: Information Overload and the Limits of Working Memory*, 2008
Michael LeGault, *Think!: Why Crucial Decisions Can't be Made in the Blink of an Eye*, 2006
Martin Lindstrom, *Buyology: Truth and Lies About Why We Buy*, 2008

1362

SUDHIR VENKATESH

Gang Leader for a Day: A Rogue Sociologist Takes to the Streets

(New York: Penguin Press, 2008)

Subject(s): Gangs; Crime; Criminals
Summary: Sudhir Venkatesh, a Columbia University professor, spent seven years studying and following the Black Kings, a Chicago street gang that deals crack cocaine. He wrote about his experiences in *Gang Leader for a Day: A Rogue Sociologist Takes to the Streets*. Venkatesh was allowed into the gang's inner structure, its decision-making process, and its daily existence. His account is rich with anecdote and filled with humanity, as he recounts his own struggles with morality while dealing with the gang's activities. The book debunks some of the myths about street gangs, such as their members are all uneducated and poverty stricken.

Where it's reviewed:
Books & Culture, July-August 2008, page 29
The Nation, February 4, 2008, page 28
Publishers Weekly, November 5, 2007, page 59
School Library Journal, April 2009, page S46
Washington Monthly, April 2008, page 43

Other books by the same author:
Off the Books: The Underground Economy of the Urban Poor, 2009
American Project: The Rise and Fall of a Modern Ghetto, 2002

Other books you might like:
Jay Dobyns, *No Angel: My Harrowing Undercover Journey to the Inner Circle of the Hells Angels*, 2009
Nils Johnson-Shelton, co-author
Jeannette Walls, *The Glass Castle: A Memoir*, 2005
William Julius Wilson, *More than Just Race: Being Black and Poor in the Inner City*, 2009
Sharon Zukin, *Naked City: The Death and Life of Authentic Urban Places*, 2009

1363

MARGARET VISSER

The Gift of Thanks: The Roots and Rituals of Gratitude

(New York: Houghton Mifflin Harcourt, 2009)

Story type: Historical
Subject(s): Culture; History; Parent-child relations

Summary: In *The Gift of Thanks: The Roots and Rituals of Gratitude*, Margaret Vesser examines how people of different cultural backgrounds have shown their gratitude throughout history. Vesser explains the many ways people say "thank you," from offering a handshake to showing appreciation with gifts and verbal thanks. In this book, Vesser provides details about everything from 16th century thankfulness to the way parents currently teach their children to show their appreciation for the positive events and people in their lives. Vesser is also the author of *The Rituals of Dinner: The Origins, Evolution, Eccentricities, and Meaning of Table Manners.*

Where it's reviewed:
Kirkus Reviews, October 1, 2009, page 1063
Library Journal, September 15, 2009, page 63
Publishers Weekly, September 21, 2009, page 50

Other books by the same author:
Much Depends on Dinner: The Extraordinary History and Mythology, Allure and Obsessions, Perils and Taboos of an Ordinary Meal, 2010
The Rituals of Dinner, 1992

Other books you might like:
Walter Green, *This Is the Moment!: How One Man's Yearlong Journey Captured the Power of Extraordinary Gratitude,* 2010
Todd Aaron Jensen, *On Gratitude,* 2010
John Kralik, *365 Thank Yous: How Simple Acts of Daily Gratitude Changed a Life,* 2010
Nina Lesowitz, *Living Life as a Thank You: The Transformative Power of Gratitude,* 2009
M.J. Ryan, *Attitudes of Gratitude: How to Give and Receive Joy Every Day of Your Life,* 2009
Mary Beth Sammons, *Living Life as a Thank You: The Transformative Power of Gratitude,* 2009

1364

CLARENCE E. WALKER

Mongrel Nation: The America Begotten by Thomas Jefferson and Sally Hemings

(Charlottesville, Virginia: University of Virginia Press, 2009)

Subject(s): United States history, 1600-1775 (Colonial period); Presidents (Government); Racially mixed people

Summary: In *Mongrel Nation: The America Begotten by Thomas Jefferson and Sally Hemings,* author Clarence E. Walker offers a historical perspective on race relations in America, and the important part that historical figures—especially Thomas Jefferson—played in these relations. Walker contrasts Jefferson's writings on race and his now widely known relationship with Sally Hemings, his former slave with whom he allegedly fathered several children, to present the contradictions between America's historical views on racism and its practices regarding race relations. Walker contends that, until the country accepts these contrasts, the United States will not be able to truly cross its racial divide. Walker is also the author of *The Preacher and the Politician: Jeremiah Wright, Barack Obama, and Race in America.*

Where it's reviewed:
Booklist, February 1, 2009, page 20
Journal of Southern History, August 2010, page 708
Library Journal, February 15, 2009, page 117

Other books by the same author:
The Preacher and the Politician: Jeremiah Wright, Barack Obama, and Race in America, 2009
We Can't Go Home Again: An Argument about Afrocentrism, 2001
Breaking Strongholds in the African-American Family, 1996
Biblical Counseling With African-Americans: Taking a Ride in the Ethiopian's Chariot, 1992
Deromanticizing Black History: Critical Essays Reappraisals, 1991

Other books you might like:
Andrew Burstein, *Madison and Jefferson,* 2010
Eric Foner, *The Fiery Trial: Abraham Lincoln and American Slavery,* 2010
Annette Gordon-Reed, *The Hemingses of Monticello: An American Family,* 2008
William G. Hyland Jr., *In Defense of Thomas Jefferson: The Sally Hemings Sex Scandal,* 2009
Nancy Isenberg, *Madison and Jefferson,* 2010
Andrew Levy, *The First Emancipator: The Forgotten Story of Robert Carter, the Founding Father Who Freed His Slaves,* 2005

1365

BILL WASIK

And Then There's This: How Stories Live and Die in Viral Culture

(New York: Viking, 2009)

Subject(s): Internet; Journalism; Technology

Summary: *And Then There's This: How Stories Live and Die in Viral Culture* is an examination of the creation and spreading of news stories since the development and rise of the Internet. Journalist Bill Wasik explores the ways that media technology has changed the world. Conducting many wild Internet experiments of his own, Wasik attempts to understand and explain the ways in which the World Wide Web impacts cultural trends, news stories, and individual perspectives on world issues. Presenting research on phenomena such as the rise and fall of pop bands, the power of online marketing, and the exploding popularity of political, environmental, or social blogs, Wasik reveals how influential the Internet can be in nearly every area of life. *And Then There's This* examines the consequences of living in a world where every potentially newsworthy story is available at one's fingertips immediately.

Where it's reviewed:
Booklist, June 1, 2009, page 7
Kirkus Reviews, May 15, 2009, page 544
Psychology Today, May/June 2009, page 30

Other books you might like:
Eric Boehlert, *Bloggers on the Bus: How the Internet Changed Politics and the Press,* 2009
Nicholas Carr, *The Shallows: What the Internet Is Doing to Our Brains,* 2010

Martin Howard, *We Know What You Want: How They Change Your Mind*, 2005

Scott Rosenberg, *Say Everything: How Blogging Began, What It's Becoming, and Why It Matters*, 2010

Clay Shirky, *Here Comes Everybody: The Power of Organizing Without Organizations*, 2008

1366

BRUCE WATSON

Freedom Summer: The Savage Season That Made Mississippi Burn and Made America a Democracy

(New York: Viking, 2010)

Subject(s): United States history; Civil rights movements; African Americans

Summary: With Jim Crow laws firmly in place, 1964 Mississippi didn't seem like a hotbed of social action and civil rights advancement. But that's exactly what happened in the summer of that year, when the state saw a surge in racial intolerance and violence, bringing the attentions of activists, artists, and leaders from around the nation. In *Freedom Summer: The Savage Season That Made Mississippi Burn and Made America a Democracy*, author Bruce Watson investigates the history of that tumultuous summer, the people and politics involved, and how it laid the groundwork for civil rights in America. This volume includes a bibliography and an index.

Where it's reviewed:
Booklist, May 1, 2010, page 60
The Economist, June 12, 2010, page 92
Publishers Weekly, May 3, 2010, page 40

Other books by the same author:
Sacco and Vanzetti: The Men, the Murders, and the Judgment of Mankind, 2007
Bread and Roses: Mills, Migrants, and the Struggle for the American Dream, 2006
Man Who Changed How Boys and Toys Were Made: The Life and Times of A.C. Gilbert, the Man Who Saved Christmas, 2002

Other books you might like:
Michelle Alexander, *The New Jim Crow: Mass Incarceration in the Age of Colorblindness*, 2010
James N. Gregory, *The Southern Diaspora: How the Great Migrations of Black and White Southerners Transformed America*, 2007
Alex Heard, *The Eyes of Willie McGee: A Tragedy of Race, Sex, and Secrets in the Jim Crow South*, 2010
Nelson Mandela, *Conversations with Myself*, 2010
Isabel Wilkerson, *The Warmth of Other Suns: The Epic Story of America's Great Migration*, 2010

1367

ISABEL WILKERSON

The Warmth of Other Suns: The Epic Story of America's Great Migration

(New York: Random House, 2010)

Subject(s): African Americans; United States history; Travel

Summary: In *The Warmth of Other Suns: The Epic Story of America's Great Migration*, Pulitzer Prize-winning author Isabel Wilkerson tells the story of six million black men, women, and children who escaped their lives in the South for better opportunities and treatment in northern states between 1915 and 1970. By chronicling the lives of three specific people—Ida Mae Gladney from Mississippi, George Starling from Florida, and Robert Foster from Lousiana—Wilkerson is able to paint a picture of the lives of millions who chose to travel by foot or automobile. Wilkerson incorporates details about the journey itself, what happened when these citizens got to their respective cities, and how the migration of black citizens to the north changed the United States forever.

Where it's reviewed:
Booklist, September 15, 2010, page 8
Library Journal, June 15, 2010, page 9
New York Times Book Review, September 5, 2010, page 1
Publishers Weekly, July 26, 2010, page 65

Other books you might like:
Philip Dray, *There is Power in a Union: The Epic Story of Labor in America*, 2010
James N. Gregory, *The Southern Diaspora: How the Great Migrations of Black and White Southerners Transformed America*, 2007
Yunte Huang, *Charlie Chan: The Untold Story of the Honorable Detective and his Rendezvous with American History*, 2010
Peter M. Rutkoff, *Fly Away: The Great African American Cultural Migrations*, 2010
William B. Scott, co-author
Bruce Watson, *Freedom Summer: The Savage Season That Made Mississippi Burn and Made America a Democracy*, 2010

1368

VALERIE PLAME WILSON

Fair Game: How a Top CIA Agent Was Betrayed by Her Own Government

(New York: Simon & Schuster, 2007)

Story type: Historical
Subject(s): Autobiographies; Political crimes; Journalism

Summary: In July 2003, journalist Robert Novak revealed

Valerie Plame Wilson's top secret occupation to the world. As an operative for the CIA, Wilson had sworn to keep the details of her job from the public. In fact, many of her closest family and friends weren't even aware of her vocation until Novak published his infamous newspaper column in *The New York Times*. Many speculated about the missions Wilson had been responsible for, and rumors flew throughout the United States. In *Fair Game: How a Top CIA Agent Was Betrayed by Her Own Government*, Wilson reveals what she can about her job with the CIA and what happened after her identity was compromised.

Where it's reviewed:
Biography, Winter 2008, page 211
New York Times Book Review, July 6, 2008, page 20

Other books you might like:
Matthew M. Aid, *The Secret Sentry: The Untold History of the National Security Agency*, 2009
Charles Faddis, *Beyond Repair: The Decline and Fall of the CIA*, 2010
Charles S. Faddis, *Willful Neglect: The Dangerous Illusion of Homeland Security*, 2010
Ishmael Jones, *The Human Factor: Inside the CIA's Dysfunctional Intelligence Culture*, 2008
Reza Kahlili, *A Time to Betray: The Astonishing Double Life of a CIA Agent Inside the Revolutionary Guards of Iran*, 2010

1369

LIZ WISEMAN
GREG MCKEOWN , Co-Author

Multipliers: How the Best Leaders Make Everyone Smarter
(New York: HarperBusiness, 2010)

Subject(s): Business; Management; Success

Summary: Business leader Liz Wiseman and contributing author Greg Mckeown highlight the two different kinds of leaders in the business world and how to harness this insight to make smarter leadership decisions. *Multipliers: How the Best Leaders Make Everyone Smarter* identifies two types of managers: multipliers, who are employee-focused and inspirational, and diminishers, who rule with an iron fist and have little or no regard for employees. In distinguishing these two, Wiseman and Mckeown show readers how to become multipliers by generating ideas, supporting workers, and constantly advancing the livelihood and profits of a business. First book.

Where it's reviewed:
American Executive, September 2010, page 6
Library Journal, May 15, 2010), page 83
Publishers Weekly, April 26, 2010, page 104

Other books by the same author:
The No Asshole Rule: Building a Civilized Workplace and Surviving One That Isn't, 2010
Weird Ideas That Work: How to Build a Creative Company, 2007

Hard Facts, Dangerous Half-Truths And Total Nonsense: Profiting From Evidence-Based Management, 2006
The Knowing-Doing Gap: How Smart Companies Turn Knowledge into Action, 2000
Readings in Organizational Decline: Frameworks, Research, and Prescriptions, 1988

Other books you might like:
Chip Heath, *Switch: How to Change Things When Change Is Hard*, 2010
Dan Heath, co-author
Richard Pascale, *The Power of Positive Deviance: How Unlikely Innovators Solve the World's Toughest Problems*, 2010
Daniel H. Pink, *Drive: The Surprising Truth About What Motivates Us*, 2009
Keith Sawyer, *Group Genius: The Creative Power of Collaboration*, 2007
Jerry Sternin, *The Power of Positive Deviance: How Unlikely Innovators Solve the World's Toughest Problems*, 2010
Monique Sternin, co-author
Don Tapscott, *Wikinomics: How Mass Collaboration Changes Everything*, 2006
Anthony D. Williams, co-author

1370

ANTHONY WOLF

Why Can't You Shut Up?: How We Ruin Relationships—How Not To
(New York: Ballantine Books, 2006)

Subject(s): Interpersonal relations; Psychology; Self help books

Summary: In *Why Can't You Shut Up?: How We Ruin Relationships—How Not To* Anthony Wolf claims that by being more aware of communication habits and intentions during arguments, people can improve their relationships. Wolf argues that each of us possesses a "baby self" that is irrational, wants instant gratification, and resorts to insults and anger when disagreeing with someone. The book says that recognizing and curbing the instincts of this "baby self" will lead to compromise and can curb confrontations that can destroy relationships. Wolf provides a number of example conversations between couples and provides specific advice on what people should and should not say during disagreements.

Where it's reviewed:
Library Journal, January 1, 2006, page 139
Psychology Today, July-August 2006, page 33
Publishers Weekly, November 7, 2005, page 64

Other books by the same author:
"Mom, Jason's Breathing on Me!": The Solution to Sibling Bickering, 2003
Get Out of My Life, but First Could You Drive Me & Cheryl to the Mall: A Parent's Guide to the New Teenager, Revised and Updated, 2002

The Secret of Parenting: How to Be in Charge of Today's Kids—from Toddlers to Preteens—Without Threats or Punishment, 2000

Why Did You Have to Get a Divorce? And When Can I Get a Hamster?: A Guide to Parenting Through Divorce, 1998

It's Not Fair, Jeremy Spencer's Parents Let Him Stay Up All Night!: A Guide to the Tougher Parts of Parenting, 1994

I'll Be Home Before Midnight and I Won't Get Pregnant, 1988

Other books you might like:

Po Bronson, *NurtureShock: New Thinking About Children*, 2009

Po Bronson, *Why Do I Love These People?: Understanding, Surviving, and Creating Your Own Family*, 2005

Cheryl Dellasega, *Mean Girls Grown Up: Adult Women Who Are Still Queen Bees, Middle Bees, and Afraid-to-Bees*, 2005

Ashley Merryman, *NurtureShock: New Thinking About Children*, 2009

Jeannette Walls, *The Glass Castle: A Memoir*, 2005

SAM WYLY

1,000 Dollars and an Idea: Entrepreneur to Billionaire
(New York: Newmarket Press, 2009)

Subject(s): Business; Money

Summary: In his book, *1,000 Dollars and an Idea: Entrepreneur to Billionaire*, businessman Sam Wyly explains how he transformed from a boy working in the fields into a one of the most successful people in America. Wyly grew up in Louisiana, where he worked in the cotton fields. His childhood motivated him to work hard and succeed. After attending college, Wyly worked in a few different companies before starting his own ventures. In the book, Wyly explains how his determination and a bit of good luck helped him become a billionaire. He also discusses his experiences in business and his passion for the environment.

Where it's reviewed:
Library Journal, September 15, 2008, page 67
Publishers Weekly, June 2, 2008, page 36

Other books you might like:
Bill Burke, *Call Me Ted*, 2008
Wes Moss, *Starting from Scratch: Secrets from 22 Ordinary People Who Made the Entrepreneurial Leap*, 2005
T. Boone Pickens, *The First Billion is the Hardest*, 2008
Alice Schroeder, *The Snowball: Warren Buffett and the Business of Life*, 2008
William L. Simon, *iCon Steve Jobs: The Greatest Second Act in the History of Business*, 2005
Ted Turner, *Call Me Ted*, 2008

Jeffrey S. Young, *iCon Steve Jobs: The Greatest Second Act in the History of Business*, 2005

1372

XINRAN XINRAN

China Witness: Voices from a Silent Generation
(New York: Pantheon Books, 2009)

Subject(s): Biographies; History; China

Summary: *China Witness: Voices from a Silent Generation* by Xinran is a collection of interviews and oral histories from Xinran's travels across China for two years in 2005 and 2006. Approximately 20 stories are included, most from people in their 70s. Chinese people are inherently reticent, but Xinran was able to get them to tell her their stories about their lives in Communist China under Mao. She spoke to people from all walks of life, including an acrobat and a policeman, among many others, collecting intensely personal and varied stories on topics such as family life, the Long March, labor camps, prisons, and the universal suffering yet enduring hope of so many.

Where it's reviewed:
Booklist, February 15, 2009, page 18
New York Times Book Review, March 8, 2009, page 13
Publishers Weekly, December 1, 2008, page 41

Other books by the same author:
Message from an Unknown Chinese Mother: Stories of Loss and Love, 2010
Miss Chopsticks, 2008
Motherbridge of Love, 2007
What the Chinese Don't Eat, 2006
Sky Burial: An Epic Love Story of Tibet, 2004
The Good Women of China: Hidden Voices, 2003

Other books you might like:
Kay Bratt, *Silent Tears: A Journey of Hope in a Chinese Orphanage*, 2010
Jeff Gammage, *China Ghosts: My Daughter's Journey to America, My Passage to Fatherhood*, 2008
Xinran, *Message from an Unknown Chinese Mother: Stories of Loss and Love*, 2010
Xianhui Yang, *Woman from Shanghai: Tales of Survival from a Chinese Labor Camp*, 2009
Liao Yiwu, *The Corpse Walker: Real Life Stories, China from the Bottom Up*, 2008

1373

JEFFREY ZASLOW

The Girls from Ames: A Story of Women and a Forty-Year Friendship
(New York: Gotham Books, 2009)

Subject(s): Friendship; Women; Rural life
Summary: Eleven girls come of age in the small Midwest-

ern college town of Ames, Iowa. After graduation, they go their separate ways, scattering across the country, yet they keep up an enduring friendship that sees them through life's triumphs and tragedies. In *The Girls from Ames: A Story of Women and a Forty-Year Friendship*, author Jeffrey Zaslow tells the inspiring tales of these amazing women as they support one another. Filled with photographs and testimonies from the girls themselves, this volume is a unique celebration of female friendship and its awesome power.

Where it's reviewed:

Kirkus Reviews, February 23, 2009, page 244
New York Times Book Review, May 16, 2010, page 32
People Weekly, May 4, 2009, page 47

Other books by the same author: page 47

Other books by the same author:

Take It from Us: Advice from 262 Celebrities on Everything That Matters-To Them and to You, 1994
Tell Me All About It: A Personal Look at the Advice Business by "the Man Who Replaced Ann Landers", 1989

Other books you might like:

Jennifer Baggett, *The Lost Girls: Three Friends. Four Continents. One Unconventional Detour Around the World*, 2010
Stephanie Congdon Barnes, *Year of Mornings: 3191 Miles Apart*, 2008
Holly C. Corbett, *The Lost Girls: Three Friends. Four Continents. One Unconventional Detour Around the World*, 2010
Nancy Lindmeyer, *My First Best Friend: Thirty Stories, Lifetime Memories*, 2010
Mariana Pasternak, *Best of Friends: Martha and Me*, 2010
Brenda Poinsett, *Friendship Factor: Why Women Need Other Women*, 2010
Amanda Pressner, *The Lost Girls: Three Friends. Four Continents. One Unconventional Detour Around the World*, 2010
Maria Alexandra Vettese, *Year of Mornings: 3191 Miles Apart*, 2008

Social Sciences

Author Index

This index is an alphabetical listing of the authors of books featured in entries and those listed within entries under the rubrics "Other books by the same author" and "Other books you might like." For each author, the titles of books described or listed in this edition and their entry numbers appear. Bold numbers indicate a featured main entry; light-face numbers refer to books recommended for further reading.

A

Aaronovitch, David
Voodoo Histories: The Role of the Conspiracy Theory in Shaping Modern History 1344

Aarons, Leroy
Prayers for Bobby: A Mother's Coming to Terms with the Suicide of Her Gay Son 1018

Abadinsky, Howard
Drug Use and Abuse: A Comprehensive Introduction 546

Abarbanel, Karin
Birthing the Elephant: The Woman's Go-For-It! Guide to Overcoming the Big Challenges of Launching a Business 335

Abbott, Karen
American Rose: A Nation Laid Bare: The Life and Times of Gypsy Rose Lee 1234
Sin in the Second City: Madams, Ministers, Playboys, and the Battle for America's Soul 54, 999, **1234**, 1320

Abbott, Stacey
Angel 1
Celluloid Vampires 1
Falling in Love Again 1
Reading Angel 1

Abel, Robert Jr.
The Eye Care Revolution: Prevent and Reverse Common Vision Problems **460**
Lethal Hindsight 460

Abman, Steven H.
Bronchopulmonary Dysplasia 598, 600

Abraham, Thomas
Twenty-First Century Plague: The Story of SARS 736

Abramson, Jill
Obama: The Historic Journey 191

Abramson, Jon Stuart
Inside the 2009 Influenza Pandemic 547, 595

Abu-Lughod, Lila
Media Worlds: Anthropology on New Terrain 49

Accum, Friedrich Christian
A Practical Essay On the Analysis of Minerals 1198

Acevedo-Munoz, Ernesto R.
Bunuel and Mexico: The Crisis of National Cinema 38

Acham, Christine
Revolution Televised: Prime Time and the Struggle for Black Power 63

Achebe, Chinua
Things Fall Apart 984

Acheson, Dean
Affection and Trust: The Personal Correspondence of Harry S. Truman and Dean Acheson, 1953-1971 207, **864**

Ackerman, Diane
An Alchemy of Mind: The Marvel and Mystery of the Brain 886
Dawn Light: Dancing with Cranes and Other Ways to Start the Day 886, 886
A Natural History of the Senses 886
The Rarest of the Rare: Vanishing Animals, Timeless Worlds 886
The Zookeeper's Wife: A War Story **886**

Acosta, Phyllis B.
Nutrition Management of Patients with Inherited Metabolic Diseases **461**, 533

Aczel, Amir D.
Fermat's Last Theorem: Unlocking the Secret of an Ancient Mathematical Problem 1043
God's Equation: Einstein, Relativity, and the Expanding Universe 1043
Pendulum: Leon Foucault and the Triumph of Science 1043
Present at the Creation: The Story of CERN and the Large Hadron Collider 1043
The Riddle of the Compass: The Invention that Changed the World 1043
Uranium Wars: The Scientific Rivalry That Created the Nuclear Age **1043**, 1059

Adams, Bradley J.
Forensic Anthropology 1107

Adams, Casey
Arthritis — The Botanical Solution: Nature's Answer to Rheumatoid Arthritis, Osteoarthritis, Gout and Other Forms of Arthritis 555
Oral Probiotics: The Newest Way to Prevent Infection, Boost the Immune System and Fight Disease 625

Adams, Doug
The Music of The Lord of the Rings Films: A Comprehensive Account of Howard Shore's Scores 62, 107

Adams, Francis V.
The Asthma Sourcebook 566

Adams, Henry
The Jeffersonian Transformation: Passages from the 'History' 877

Adams, Natalie Guice
Cheerleader!: An American Icon 1032

Adams, Vernard Irvine
Guidelines for Reports by Autopsy Pathologists 1228

Adamson, Allen P.
BrandDigital: Simple Ways Top Brands Succeed in the Digital World 336
BrandSimple: How the Best Brands Keep It Simple and Succeed 336, 421

Adderley, Rosanne Marion
New Negroes from Africa: Slave Trade Abolition and Free African Settlement in the Nineteenth-Century Caribbean **651**, 669

Adkin, Mark
The Trafalgar Companion: The Complete Guide to History's Most Famous Sea Battle and the Life of Admiral Lord Nelson 814

Adkins, Roy
The War for All the Oceans: From Nelson at the Nile to Napoleon at Waterloo 803

Adkins, Roy A.
Nelson's Trafalgar: The Battle that Changed the World 814

Adler, Bill
The Uncommon Wisdom of Oprah Winfrey: A Portrait in Her Own Words 248

Adler, Frances Payne
Fire and Ink: An Anthology of Social Action Writing **2**
The Making of A Matriot 2
Raising the Tents 2
When the Bough Breaks: Pregnancy and the Legacy of Addiction 2

Adler, Steven
My Appetite for Destruction: Sex, and Drugs, and Guns N' Roses 293

Agassi, Andre
Open: An Autobiography **161**

Agatston, Arthur
The South Beach Heart Health Revolution: Cardiac Prevention That Can Reverse Heart Disease and Stop Heart Attacks and Strokes 594

Agawu, Kofi
Representing African Music: Postcolonial Notes, Queries, Positions 150

Agee, James
Let Us Now Praise Famous Men: Three Tenant Families 111

Agonito, Joseph
Buffalo Calf Road Woman: The Story of a Warrior of the Little Bighorn 707

Agonito, Rosemary
Buffalo Calf Road Woman: The Story of a Warrior of the Little Bighorn 707

Aguilar-Moreno, Manuel
Handbook to Life in the Aztec World 786

Ahamed, Liaquat
Lords of Finance: The Bankers Who Broke the World 652

Ahmadi, Farah
The Story of My Life: An Afghan Girl on the Other Side of the Sky 310

Ahmed, Leila
Women and Gender in Islam: Historical Roots of a Modern Debate 808

Ahmed, Nessar
Clinical Biochemistry 1088, 1122

A Song Flung Up to Heaven 162

Anker, Steve
Radical Light: Alternative Film and Video in the San Francisco Bay Area, 1945-2000 **9**, 79

Ansary, Tamim
West of Kabul, East of New York: An Afghan American Story 310

Anthony, Carl Sferrazza
Nellie Taft: The Unconventional First Lady of the Ragtime Era 52

Anthony, David W.
The Horse, the Wheel, and Language: How Bronze-Age Riders from the Eurasian Steppes Shaped the Modern World 865

Anthony, Susan B.
Failure Is Impossible: Susan B. Anthony in Her Own Words 68

Anton, Maggie
Rashi's Daughters, Book II: Miriam: A Novel of Love and the Talmud in Medieval France 117

Apel, Dora
Imagery of Lynching: Black Men, White Women, and the Mob 879

Apodaca, Rose
Style A to Zoe: The Art of Fashion, Beauty, & Everything Glamour 995

Appenzeller, Immo
High-Redshift Galaxies: Light from the Early Universe 1142

Applegate, Debby
The Most Famous Man in America: The Biography of Henry Ward Beecher **163**

Appleton, D.
The Carlyles: A Story of the Fall of the Confederacy 834

Apsan, Rebecca
The Lingerie Handbook 939

Arab American National Museum
Telling Our Story: The Arab American National Museum **10**

Arana, Marie
The Writing Life: Writers on How They Think and Work 141

Archer, David
The Global Carbon Cycle 1047
Global Warming: Understanding the Forecast 1047
The Long Thaw: How Humans Are Changing the Next 100,000 Years of Earth's Climate **1047**, 1087, 1204

Archuleta, David
Chords of Strength: A Memoir of Soul, Song and the Power of Perseverance **164**

Arenstam, Peter
Mayflower 1620: A New Look at a Pilgrim Voyage 823

Argov, Sherry
Why Men Love Bitches: From Doormat to Dreamgirl—A Woman's Guide to Holding Her Own in a Relationship 947

Ariano, Tara
Hey! It's That Guy! 888, 906
Television Without Pity: 752 Things

We Love to Hate (and Hate to Love) About TV **888**, 906
Untitled: A Bad Teen Novel 888

Arias, Kathleen Meehan
Outbreak Investigation, Prevention, and Control in Health Care Settings: Critical Issues in Patient Safety 496, 574

Ariely, Dan
Predictably Irrational, Revised and Expanded Edition: The Hidden Forces That Shape Our Decisions **339**, 357
Predictably Irrational: The Hidden Forces That Shape Our Decisions 1236
The Upside of Irrationality: The Unexpected Benefits of Defying Logic at Work and at Home 339, 450, **1236**

Aristophanes, Aristophanes
Classical Comedy 138

Arkush, R. David
Land Without Ghosts: Chinese Impressions of America from the Mid-Nineteenth Century to the Present 783

Arloski, Michael
Wellness Coaching for Lasting Lifestyle Change 525, 639

Armstrong, Coleen
The Truth about Teaching: What I Wish the Veterans Had Told Me 1270

Armstrong, Karen
The Bible: A Biography 653
Buddha 274
The Case for God 653
The Great Transformation: The Beginning of Our Religious Traditions **653**
A History of God: The 4,000-Year Quest of Judaism, Christianity and Islam. 653
Muhammad: A Prophet for Our Time 274
A Short History of Myth 653
Tent of Abraham: Stories of Hope and Peace for Jews, Christians, and Muslims 1290

Arnell, Peter
Shift: How to Reinvent Your Business, Your Career, and Your Personal Brand **340**

Arngrim, Alison
Confessions of a Prairie Bitch: How I Survived Nellie Oleson and Learned to Love Being Hated 222, 960

Arnold, Peri E.
Remaking the Presidency: Roosevelt, Taft, and Wilson, 1901-1916 52

Aronowitz, Robert A.
Unnatural History: Breast Cancer and American Society 809

Aronson, Elliot
Mistakes Were Made (But Not by Me): Why We Justify Foolish Beliefs, Bad Decisions, and Hurtful Acts 1236, 1339

Aronson, Marc
Robert F. Kennedy: A Twentieth-Century Life 691

Arp, Robert
South Park and Philosophy: You Know, I Learned Something Today 148

Arsenault, Raymond
The Changing South of Gene Patterson: Journalism and Civil Rights, 1960-1968 830

Arthus-Bertrand, Yann
The New Earth from Above: 365 Days 1081

Arvanitoyannis, Ioannis S.
HACCP and ISO 22000: Application to Foods of Animal Origin **1048**, 1080
Irradiation of Food Commodities: Techniques, Applications, Detection, Legislation, Safety and Consumer Opinion 1048
Waste Management for the Food Industries 1048

Asbridge, Thomas
The Crusades: The Authoritative History of the War for the Holy Land 832

Ash, Lorraine
Life Touches Life: A Mother's Story of Stillbirth and Healing 267

Ash, Stephen V.
Firebrand of Liberty: The Story of Two Black Regiments That Changed the Course of the Civil War **654**
Middle Tennessee Society Transformed, 1860-1870: War and Peace in the Upper South 654
A Year in the South: 1865: The True Story of Four Ordinary People Who Lived Through the Most Tumultuous Twelve Months in American History 654

Ashby, Justine
British Cinema, Past and Present 94

Ashenburg, Katherine
The Dirt on Clean: An Unsanitized History **655**
The Mourner's Dance: What We Do When People Die 655

Ashton, Paul
Etched in Hope: A Weekly Journal for Those Living with or Affected by HIV/AIDS 483

Asinof, Eliot
Eight Men Out: The Black Sox and the 1919 World Series 985

Asma, Stephen
Buddha: A Beginners Guide 1237
Dinosaurs on the Ark: the Creation Museum 1237
The God Question: Freud and C. S. Lewis Reconsidered 1237
The Gods Drink Whiskey: Stumbling Toward Enlightenment in the Land of the Tattered Buddha 1237
How to Survive the Apocalypse 1237
On Monsters: An Unnatural History of Our Worst Fears 16, **1237**
Stuffed Animals and Pickled Heads: The Culture and Evolution of Natural History Museums 1237
Why I Am a Buddhist: No-Nonsense Buddhism with Red Meat and Whiskey 1237

Astakhov, Vadim
Biomedical Informatics **1049**, 1126

Astor, Gerald
The Right to Fight: A History of African-Americans in the Military 842

Atack, Jeremy
A New Economic View of American History: From Colonial Times to 1940 883

Atkins, Stephen E.
The 9/11 Encyclopedia 882

Atkins, Stephen E.
Holocaust Denial as an International Movement 777

Atkinson, Brooks
The Essential Writings of Ralph Waldo Emerson 113

Atkinson, Jacqueline M.
Advance Directives in Mental Health: Theory, Practice and Ethics 618

Atkinson, Mary
Healing Touch for Children: Massage, Acupressure and Reflexology Routine for Children Aged 4-12 557

Atkinson, Rick
An Army at Dawn: The War in North Africa, 1942-1943 656
Crusade: The Untold Story of the Persian Gulf War 656
The Day of Battle: The War in Sicily and Italy, 1943-1944 **656**
In the Company of Soldiers: A Chronicle of Combat 656

Attali, Jacques
A Brief History of the Future: A Brave and Controversial Look at the Twenty-First Century 1272

Attwood, Janet
The Passion Test: The Effortless Path to Discovering Your Destiny 423

Auerbach, Nina
Forbidden Journeys: Fairy Tales and Fantasies by Victorian Women Writers 132

Augenbraum, Harold
The Latino Reader: An American Literary Tradition from 1542 to the Present 93

Auletta, Ken
The Art of Corporate Success 1238
Backstory: Inside the Business of News 1238
Googled: The End of the World as We Know It 343, **1238**, 1347
Greed and Glory on Wall Street: The Fall of the House of Lehman 1238
The Highwaymen 1238
Media Man: Ted Turner's Improbable Empire 1238
Three Blind Mice: How the TV Networks Lost Their Way 1238
The Underclass 1238
World War 3.0: Microsoft and Its Enemies 1238

Ausden, Malcolm
Habitat Management for Conservation 1152

Auslander, Shalom
Beware of God: Stories 165

Taking Charge of Adult ADHD **467**, 589, 633

Barlow, Maude

Blue Covenant: The Global Water Crisis and the Coming Battle for the Right to Water 1276, 1346

Barnes, Djuna

Nightwood 119

Barnes, Julian

Arthur & George 168

Flaubert's Parrot 168

The Lemon Table 168

Nothing to Be Frightened Of **168**

Barnes, Justyn

The Official Michael Jackson Opus **124**

Barnes, Stephanie Congdon

Year of Mornings: 3191 Miles Apart 1373

Barnett, LeRoy

Makin' Music: Michigan's Rock and Roll Legacy 27, 53

Barney, Richard A.

David Lynch: Interviews 80

Barnosky, Anthony D.

Heatstroke: Nature in an Age of Global Warming 1191

Barr, James

Setting the Desert on Fire: T.E. Lawrence and Britain's Secret War in Arabia, 1916-1918 839

Barral, J. P.

Manual Therapy for the Prostate 543

Barrett, Greg

The Gospel of Father Joe: Revolutions and Revelations in the Slums of Bangkok 1317

Barrier, Michael

The Animated Man: A Life of Walt Disney 373

Barron, Sean

The Unwritten Rules of Social Relationships: Decoding Social Mysteries through the Unique Perspectives of Autism 934

Barrow, John D.

Cosmic Imagery: Key Images in the History of Science 1233

Barrowcliffe, Mark

The Elfish Gene: Dungeons, Dragons and Growing Up Strange **889**

Girlfriend 44 889

Infidelity for First-Time Fathers 889

Lucky Dog 889

Barry, John M.

The Great Influenza: The Epic Story of the Deadliest Plague in History 818

Barsocchini, Peter

The Jeopardy! Book: The Answers, the Questions, the Facts, and the Stories of the Greatest Game Show in History 946, 953, 958

Barthelme, Donald

Not-Knowing: The Essays and Interviews 210

Sixty Stories 210

Bartlett, Robert H.

Critical Care Physiology 561

Bartollas, Clemens F.

Women and the Criminal Justice System 88

Barton, David

Separation of Church and State: What the Founders Meant 748, 795

Barton, Ruth

Keeping it Real: Irish Film and Television 101

Bartusiak, Marcia

Archives of the Universe 1119

The Day We Found the Universe 1043

Bass, Lance

Out of Sync: A Memoir 164, **169**, 993

BassiriRad, Hormoz

Nutrient Acquisition by Plants: An Ecological Perspective 1202

Batali, Mario

The Babbo Cookbook 890

Italian Grill 890

Molto Italiano 890

Spain: A Culinary Road Trip **890**

Bathurst, Bella

The Lighthouse Stevensons: The Extraordinary Story of the Building of the Scottish Lighthouses by the Ancestors of Robert Louis Stevenson 664

Special: A Novel 664

The Wreckers: A Story of Killing Seas and Plundered Shipwrecks, from the 18th-Century to the Present Day **664**, 1325

Batmanghelidj, F.

Your Body's Many Cries for Water 554

Bator, Ben

Texts From Last Night: All the Texts No One Remembers Sending 893, 940, 974, 1028

Battelle, John

The Search: How Google and Its Rivals Rewrote the Rules of Business and Transformed Our Culture 338, **343**, 1238

Bauer, Larry A.

Applied Clinical Pharmacokinetics 648

Bauer, Susan Wise

The History of the Ancient World: From the Earliest Accounts to the Fall of Rome 661

Bauerlein, Mark

The Dumbest Generation: How the Digital Age Stupefies Young Americans and Jeopardizes Our Future (Or, Don't Trust Anyone Under 30) 1251, 1316, 1324

Baughman, James L.

The Republic of Mass Culture: Journalism, Filmmaking, and Broadcasting in America Since 1941 12

Same Time, Same Station 12

Same Time, Same Station: Creating American Television, 1948-1961 126

Baum, Dan

Nine Lives: Mystery, Magic, Death, and Life in New Orleans 30

Baumann, Leslie

Cosmetic Dermatology: Principles and Practice, 2nd Edition **468**, 650

The Skin Type Solution 468

Baxter, Andrea

Forensic Biology: The Science of Trace Evidence in Serious Crimes 1107

Bayard, Pierre

How to Talk about Books You Haven't Read **891**, 923

Sherlock Holmes Was Wrong 891

Who Killed Roger Ackroyd? 891

Bayles, Sheri

Laugh and Learn About Childbirth 479

Bayoumi, Moustafa

How Does It Feel to Be a Problem?: Being Young and Arab in America 288

Bazzana, Kevin

Wondrous Strange: The Life and Art of Glenn Gould 251

Beach, Christopher

ABC of Influence 13

Class, Language, and American Film Comedy 13

The Films of Hal Ashby **13**

Poetic Culture 13

Beacham, Richard C.

The Roman Theatre and Its Audience 139

Beachey, Will

Respiratory Care Anatomy and Physiology: Foundations for Clinical Practice 561

Beah, Ishmael

A Long Way Gone: Memoirs of a Boy Soldier **170**, 1337

Beals, Katharine

Raising a Left-Brain Child in a Right-Brain World: Strategies for Helping Bright, Quirky, Socially Awkward Children to Thrive at Home and at School 619

Bean, Annemarie

Inside the Minstrel Mask: Readings in Nineteenth-Century Blackface Minstrelsy 57

Beatles, The

The Beatles Anthology 280, 306

Beauchamp, Cari

Without Lying Down: Frances Marion and the Powerful Women of Early Hollywood 15

Beauregard, Robert A.

When America Became Suburban 1248

Beazley, Sara A.

A Brief Guide To The U.S. Health Care Delivery System: Facts, Definitions, and Statistics 500

Bechdel, Alison

Dykes and Sundry Other Carbon-Based Life Forms to Watch Out For 171

The Essential Dykes to Watch Out For 171

Fun Home: A Family Tragicomic **171**, 975, 1012, 1013

Hot, Throbbing Dykes to Watch Out for 171

Bechtel, Stefan

Roar of the Heavens 1074

Bechtle, Mike

Confident Conversation: How to Communicate Successfully in Any Situation 1315

Beck, Charles B.

An Introduction to Plant Structure and Development: Plant Anatomy for the Twenty-First Century **1054**

Origin and Evolution of Gymnosperms 1054

Beck, Glenn

Arguing with Idiots: How to Stop Small Minds and Big Government 281

Beck, John C.

The Kids Are Alright: How the Gamer Generation Is Changing the Workplace 889

Beck, Mark

Theory and Practice of Therapeutic Massage 564

Beck, Randy W.

Functional Neurology for Practitioners of Manual Therapy 516

Beckerleg, Tracey

Fun with Messy Play: Ideas and Activities for Children With Special Needs 578

Beckett, Sandra L.

Crossover Fiction 14

Recycling Red Riding Hood 14

Red Riding Hood for All Ages: A Fairy-Tale Icon in Cross-Cultural Contexts **14**, 18

Beckham, Victoria

Learning to Fly 906

That Extra Half an Inch: Hair, Heels and Everything in Between 995

Beckles, Hilary

Caribbean Slavery in the Atlantic World: A Student Reader 835

Beckwith, Harry

You, Inc.: The Art of Selling Yourself 417

Bee, Samantha

I Know I Am, but What Are You? 205, **892**, 952, 1008, 1340

Beech, Martin

Meteors and Meteorites: Origins and Observations 1086, 1138

Beerling, David

The Emerald Planet: How Plants Changed Earth's History **1055**, 1102

Beevor, Antony

D-Day: The Battle for Normandy **665**

The Fall of Berlin 1945 665

The Mystery of Olga Chekhova 665

Paris After the Liberation 1944-1949: Revised Edition 746

Stalingrad: The Fateful Siege 1942-1943 665

Begam, Richard

Modernism and Colonialism: British and Irish Literature, 1899, 1939 119

Bratt, Kay

Silent Tears: A Journey of Hope in a Chinese Orphanage 1372

Braun, J. W.

The Lord of the Films: The Unofficial Guide to Tolkien's Middle-Earth on the Big Screen 135

Braun, Thomas

On Stage: Flip Wilson 133

Bredesen, Phil

Fresh Medicine: How to Fix Reform and Build a Sustainable Health Care System 582

Bredeson, Carmen

The Spindletop Gusher: The Story of the Texas Oil Boom 685

Breen, T.H.

American Insurgents, American Patriots: The Revolution of the People 807

Brennert, Alan

Moloka'i 861

Breverton, Terry

Admiral Sir Henry Morgan: King of the Buccaneers 860

Brewster, Bill

Last Night a DJ Saved My Life: The History of the Disc Jockey 121

Bridge, Rachel

My Big Idea: 30 Successful Entrepreneurs Reveal How They Found Inspiration 397

Briggs, Robin

Early Modern France 1560-1715 728

Brighton, Terry

Patton, Montgomery, Rommel: Masters of War 657

Brill, Lesley

Crowds, Power and Transformation in Cinema 23

The Hitchcock Romance 23

John Huston's Filmmaking 23

Brinker, Nancy G.

Promise Me: How a Sister's Love Launched the Global Movement to End Breast Cancer 1334

Brinkley, Douglas

The Boys of Pointe du Hoc: Ronald Reagan, D-Day, and the U.S. Army 2nd Ranger Battalion 177

Fear and Loathing in America: The Brutal Odyssey of an Outlaw Journalist 679

The Great Deluge: Hurricane Katrina, New Orleans, and the Mississippi Gulf Coast **679**, 177

The Reagan Diaries 177

Wheels for the World: Henry Ford, His Company, and a Century of Progress 177

The Wilderness Warrior: Theodore Roosevelt and the Crusade for America **177**

Brinner, Benjamin Elon Brinner

Playing Across a Divide: Israeli-Palestinian Musical Encounters 61

Britton, Andrew

Katharine Hepburn: Star as Feminist 55

Broadie, Alexander

The Scottish Enlightenment: The Historical Age of the Historical Nation 847

Brocheux, Pierre

Indochina: An Ambiguous Colonization, 1858-1954 700

Brodsky, Norm

The Knack: How Street-Smart Entrepreneurs Learn to Handle Whatever Comes Up **350**, 367, 419, 442

Broe, Mary Lynn

The Gender of Modernism: A Critical Anthology 119

Brogan, Chris

Social Media 101: Tactics and Tips to Develop Your Business Online 351

Trust Agents: Using the Web to Build Influence, Improve Reputation, and Earn Trust **351**, 366, 378, 394, 438

Brogan, Hugh

Alexis de Tocqueville: A Life **178**

The Penguin History of the USA 178

Bromham, Lindell

Reading the Story in DNA: A Beginner's Guide to Molecular Evolution **1065**

Bronson, Po

NurtureShock: New Thinking About Children 1345, 1370

Why Do I Love These People?: Understanding, Surviving, and Creating Your Own Family 1370

Bronson, Rachel

Thicker than Oil: America's Uneasy Partnership with Saudi Arabia 201

Brook, Timothy

The Troubled Empire: China in the Yuan and Ming Dynasties 852

Brook, Yaron

Neoconservatism: An Obituary for an Idea 1359

Brooker, Robert J.

Chemistry, Cell Biology and Genetics: Volume One 1066

Evolution, Diversity and Ecology: Volume Two 1066

Genetics: Analysis and Principles, Third Edition **1066**, 1114, 1182

Plants and Animals:Volume Three 1066

Brooks, Arthur C.

The Battle: How the Fight Between Free Enterprise and Big Government Will Shape America's Future 352

Gifts of Time and Money: The Role of Charity in America's Communities 352

Gross National Happiness: Why Happiness Matters for America—and How We Can Get More of It 352

Social Entrepreneurship: A Modern Approach to Social Value Creation 352

Who Really Cares: The Surprising Truth About Compasionate Conservatism Who Gives, Who Doesn't, and Why It Matters 352

Brooks, David R.

Bringing the Sun Down to Earth: Designing Inexpensive Instruments for Monitoring the Atmosphere 1132

Brooks, Jennifer

Embracing An Aching Heart 649

Brooks, Max

World War Z: An Oral History of the Zombie War 898

The Zombie Survival Guide: Complete Protection from the Living Dead 898

The Zombie Survival Guide: Recorded Attacks **898**

Brosch, Noah

Sirius Matters 1119

Broughton, Frank

Last Night a DJ Saved My Life: The History of the Disc Jockey 121

Brown, Blaine Terry

Uncertain Alliances: The World in the Twentieth Century 720

Brown, Canter Jr.

The Varieties of Women's Experiences: Portraits of Southern Women in the Post-Civil War Century 833

Brown, Catherine Drinker

Miracle at Philadelphia: The Story of the Constitutional Convention, May-September 1787 784

Brown, Christopher Leslie

Arming Slaves: From Classical Times to the Modern Age 680

Moral Capital: Foundations of British Abolitionism **680**, 747

Brown, David H.

Santeria Enthroned: Art, Ritual, and Innovation in an Afro-Cuban Religion 102

Brown, Don

Ruth Law Thrills a Nation 327

Brown, Frederick

Flaubert: A Biography **179**

For the Soul of France: Culture Wars in the Age of Dreyfus 179, 1284

Zola: A Life 179

Brown, Howard G.

Ending the French Revolution: Violence, Justice, and Repression from the Terror to Napoleon **681**

War, Revolution, and the Bureaucratic State: Politics and Army Administration in France, 1791-1799 681

Brown, Iesha

The Story Of The Beginning and End Of The First Hip Hop Female MC...Luminary Icon Sha-Rock 115

Brown, John Russell

The Routledge Companion to Directors' Shakespeare 158

Brown, Judith E.

Nutrition Now 472

Nutrition through the Life Cycle, 3rd Edition **472**, 568

Brown, Julie K.

Contesting Images: Photography and the World's Columbian Exposition 54

Brown, Leslie

Upbuilding Black Durham: Gender, Class, and the Black Community Development in the Jim Crow South 682

Brown, Lyn Mikel

Packaging Boyhood: Saving Our Sons from Superheroes, Slackers, and Other Media Stereotypes **1308**

Brown, Mary Beth

Condi: The Life of a Steel Magnolia 185

Brown, Peter

The Rise of Western Christendom: Triumph and Diversity, A.D. 200-1000 873

Brown, Terry

Gene Cloning and DNA Analysis 1110, 1139

Brown, Tim

Change by Design: How Design Thinking Transforms Organizations and Inspires Innovation 410

Brown, Tina

The Diana Chronicles **180**

Brown, Walter T.

In the Beginning 1086

Brown Taylor, Barbara

Leaving Church: A Memoir of Faith 308

Browne, Jill Conner

American Thighs: Sweet Potato Queens' Guide to Preserving Your Assets 1263

Browne-Umar, S. D.

HIV/AIDS Treatment Strategies 544

Brownlee, Shannon

Overtreated: Why Too Much Medicine Is Making Us Sicker and Poorer 531

Brox, Jane

Brilliant: The Evolution of Artificial Light 819, **1247**

Clearing Land: Legacies of the American Farm 1247

Five Thousand Days Like This One: An American Family History 1247

Here and Nowhere Else: Late Seasons of a Farm and Its Family 1247

Broyard, Bliss

One Drop: My Father's Hidden Life — A True Story of Family, Race, and Secrets 838

Brubaker, Susan Howell

Workbook for Cognitive Skills: Exercises for Thought-processing and Word Retrieval 504

Bruce, Harry

Maud: The Life of L.M. Montgomery 321

Bruce, Robert B.

Fighting Techniques of the Napoleonic Age 1792-1815: Equipment, Combat Skills, and Tactics 666

Brucker, Gene A.

Renaissance Florence, Updated Edition 769

Brugmann, Jeb
Welcome to the Urban Revolution: How Cities are Changing the World **1248**

Bruinius, Harry
Better for All the World: The Secret History of Forced Sterilization and America's Quest for Racial Purity **683**

Brumbaugh, David S.
Earthquakes: Science & Society 1120

Brunette, Peter
Michael Haneke 108

Bruni, Frank
Ambling Into History: The Unlikely Odyssey of George W. Bush 181
Born Round: The Secret History of a Full-Time Eater 172, **181**
A Gospel of Shame: Children, Sexual Abuse, and the Catholic Church 181
Italy: The Best Travel Writing from the New York Times 181

Bryant, Edward
Climate Process and Change 1067
Natural Hazards 1067
Tsunami: The Underrated Hazard, 2nd Edition **1067**

Bryant, Howard
The Last Hero: A Life of Henry Aaron 319

Bryant, Jen
Kaleidoscope Eyes 182
Ringside 1925: Views from the Scopes Trial 182
A River of Words: The Story of William Carlos Williams **182**

Brysac, Shareen Blair
Kingmakers: The Invention of the Modern Middle East 839

Bryson, Bill
At Home: A Short History of Private Life 24, **1249**
Bill Bryson's African Diary 103, 1249
Bryson's Dictionary of Troublesome Words 24
Bryson's Dictionary of Troublesome Words: A Writer's Guide to Getting It Right 1249
I'm a Stranger Here Myself: Notes on Returning to America After 20 Years Away 103, 1249
In a Sunburned Country 1249
The Life and Times of the Thunderbolt Kid: A Memoir 902, 1249
Made in America: An Informal History of the English Language in the United States 1249
The Mother Tongue: English & How It Got That Way 24
Neither Here nor There: Travels in Europe 103, 1249
Seeing Further: The Story of Science, Discovery, and the Genius of the Royal Society 1249
Shakespeare (The Illustrated and Updated Edition) 1249
Shakespeare: The World as Stage **24**, 1249
A Short History of Nearly Everything 1009, 1010

A Short History of Nearly Everything: Special Illustrated Edition 24, 1249
A Walk in the Woods 103, 134, 965, 1000, 1001
A Walk in the Woods: Rediscovering America on the Appalachian Trail 24, 1249

Brzezinksi, Mika
All Things at Once **183**, 299

Buchan, James
Crowded with Genius: The Scottish Enlightenment: Edinburgh's Moment of the Mind 847

Buchanan, Andrea J.
The Daring Book for Girls **25**, 992, 1020
The Double-Daring Book for Girls 25
The Pocket Daring Book for Girls: Wisdom & Wonder 25

Buchanan, Patrick J.
Churchill, Hitler and the Unnecessary War: How Britain Lost Its Empire and the West Lost the World **684**
Day of Reckoning: How Hubris, Ideology, and Greed Are Tearing America Apart 684
The Death of the West: How Dying Populations and Immigrant Invasions Imperil Our Country and Civilization 684
Where the Right Went Wrong: How Neoconservatives Subverted the Reagan Revolution and Hijacked the Bush Presidency 684

Buchheim, Robert
The Sky is Your Laboratory 1143

Buck, Jari Holland
24/7 or Dead: A Handbook for Families with a Loved One in the Hospital 473
Hospital Stay Handbook: A Guide to Becoming a Patient Advocate for Your Loved Ones **473**, 500, 618

Buckholtz, Charlie
In Heaven Everything Is Fine: The Unsolved Life of Peter Ivers and the Lost History of the New Wave Theatre **46**

Buckley, Gail
American Patriots: The Story of Blacks in the Military from the Revolution to Desert Storm 842

Budd, John M.
The Changing Academic Library: Operations, Culture, Environments 387

Budgazad, Sari
The Cardiac Recovery Cookbook: Heart Healthy Recipes for Life After Heart Attack or Heart Surgery 463, **490**

Buford, Bill
Among the Thugs 184
Heat: An Amateur's Adventures as Kitchen Slave, Line Cook, Pasta-Maker, and Apprentice to a Dante-Quoting Butcher in Tuscany 181, **184**, 1003

Bugert, Peter
DNA and RNA Profiling in Human Blood 1072, 1110, 1139

Bugliosi, Vincent
Reclaiming History: The Assassination of President John F. Kennedy 1344

Buhle, Paul
The Art of Harvey Kurtzman: The Mad Genius of Comics **72**

Bumiller, Elisabeth
Condoleezza Rice: An American Life: A Biography **185**
For Women Only, Revised Edition: A Revolutionary Guide to Reclaiming Your Sex Life 185
May You Be the Mother of a Hundred Sons: A Journey Among the Women of India 185

Bumsted, J.M.
A History of the Canadian Peoples 251

Bungay, Stephen
The Most Dangerous Enemy: The Definitive History of the Battle of Britain 766

Bunker, Nick
Making Haste from Babylon: The Mayflower Pilgrims and Their World 823

Bunting, Josiah
Ulysses S. Grant: The American Presidents Series: The 18th President, 1869-1877 204

Bunting, Sarah D.
Television Without Pity: 752 Things We Love to Hate (and Hate to Love) About TV **888**, 906

Bunyard, Peter
Extreme Weather: The Cataclysmic Effects of Climate Change 1070, 1074, 1140

Bunz, Fred
Principles of Cancer Genetics **1068**

Burbank, Jane
Empires in World History: Power and the Politics of Difference 699

Burbank, Jeff
Las Vegas Babylon: True Tales of Glitter, Glamour, and Greed 1305

Burden, Wendy
Dead End Gene Pool 303

Burg, Bob
The Go-Giver: A Little Story about a Powerful Business Idea **353**

Burgess, Colin
Footprints in the Dust 1090
In the Shadow of the Moon: A Challenging Journey to Tranquility, 1965-1969 1009

Burgess, Glenda
The Geography of Love 212

Burke, Bill
Call Me Ted 1371

Burke, Louise
Clinical Sports Nutrition 484, 602

Burke, Roland
Decolonization and the Evolution of International Human Rights 674

Burkholder, Mark A.
Colonial Latin America 790

Burleigh, Michael
The Third Reich: A New History 716

Burleigh, Robert
Flight: The Journey of Charles Lindbergh 327

Burlingame, Michael
Abraham Lincoln: A Life, Volumes 1 and 2 **186**, 329
Abraham Lincoln: The Observations of John G. Nicolay and John Hay 186
The Inner World of Abraham Lincoln 186

Burlingham, Bo
The Knack: How Street-Smart Entrepreneurs Learn to Handle Whatever Comes Up **350**, 367, 419, 442

Burn, Alan
The Fighting Commodores: The Convoy Commanders in the Second World War 862

Burnett, Arthur
Johns Hopkins Patients' Guide to Prostate Cancer 501, 540, 543, 553, 567

Burnett, Carol
One More Time: A Memoir 187
This Time Together: Laughter and Reflection **187**, 213, 324, 887, 977

Burnett, James Compton
Curability of Cataract with Medicines 460, 494

Burnett, Tamy
The Literary Angel: Essays on Influences and Traditions Reflected in the Joss Whedon Series 1

Burns, Jennifer
Goddess of the Market: Ayn Rand and the American Right 236

Burnstein, Scott M.
Family Affair: Treachery, Greed, and Betrayal in the Chicago Mafia 1266

Burr, Eric
Ski Trails and Wildlife : Toward Snow Country Restoration 235

Burrell, Paul
The Way We Were: Remembering Diana 180

Burrough, Bryan
Barbarians at the Gate: The Fall of RJR Nabisco 685
The Big Rich: The Rise and Fall of the Greatest Texas Oil Fortunes **685**
Dragonfly: NASA and the Crisis Aboard Mir 685
Public Enemies: The True Story of America's Greatest Crime Wave 685

Burroughs, Augusten
Dry: A Memoir 194, 247, 686
Magical Thinking: True Stories 686
Possible Side Effects 686
Running with Scissors: A Memoir 203, 323, 686
A Wolf at the Table: A Memoir of My Father **686**

Burroughs, William James
Climate Change in Prehistory: The End of the Reign of Chaos 1069
Climate Change: A Multidisciplinary Approach, 2nd Edition **1069**, 1136

Clark, David P.
Molecular Biology 1123

Clark, Gary
Live Forever or Your Money Back: How We Age, How We Die and How Not To! The Ultimate Anti Aging Solution 513, 515, 527

Clark, George L.
Silas Deane: A Connecticut Leader in the American Revolution 822

Clark, Gregory
A Farewell to Alms: A Brief Economic History of the Western World 827

Clark, Jim
Best in Hollywood: The Good, the Bad, and the Beautiful 222, 960

Clark, Ken
The Pocket Idiot's Guide to the FairTax 349

Clark, Nancy
Food Guide for Soccer: Tips & Recipes from the Pros 484
Nancy Clark's Food Guide for Marathoners: Tips for Everyday Champions 484
Nancy Clark's Food Guide for New Runners: Getting It Right from the Start 484
Nancy Clark's Sports Nutrition Guidebook: 2nd Edition **484**, 498

Clark, Roy Peter
The Changing South of Gene Patterson: Journalism and Civil Rights, 1960-1968 830

Clark, Ruth C.
Building Expertise: Cognitive Methods for Training and Performance Improvement 1083

Clark, Ruth Colvin
Evidence-Based Training Methods: A Guide for Training Professionals 1083

Clark, William R.
In Defense of Self: How the Immune System Really Works 591, 1045, **1079**
A Means to an End: The Biological Basis of Aging and Death 1079

Clarke, Jane
Yummy Baby: The Essential First Nutrition Bible and Cookbook 593, 617

Clarke, Joe T. R.
A Clinical Guide to Inherited Metabolic Diseases 461, 533

Clarke, Michele
The Dreaded Feast: Writers on Enduring the Holidays 1029

Clarke, Richard A.
Against All Enemies: Inside America's War on Terror 1256
Breakpoint 1256
Cyber War: The Next Threat to National Security and What to Do About It **1256**, 1296
Defeating The Jihadists: A Blueprint For Action 1256
The Forgotten Homeland: A Century Foundation Task Force Report 1256
The Scorpion's Gate 1256

Your Government Failed You: Breaking the Cycle of National Security Disasters 1256

Clarke, Thurston
Ask Not: The Inauguration of John F. Kennedy and the Speech That Changed America 691
The Last Campaign: Robert F. Kennedy and 82 Days That Inspired America 691
Pearl Harbor Ghosts: A Journey to Hawaii Then and Now 691
Searching for Paradise: A Grand Tour of the World's Unspoiled Islands 691

Clarkson, Adrienne
Heart Matters 199, 292
Norman Bethune **199**, 251, 292, 321

Clary, David A.
Adopted Son: Washington, Lafayette, and the Friendship That Saved the Revolution 836

Claxton, Melvin
Uncommon Valor: A Story of Race, Patriotism, and Glory in the Final Battles of the Civil War 654

Clemens, Paul
Made in Detroit: A South of 8 Mile Memoir **200**
Punching Out: One Year in a Closing Auto Plant 200

Clements, Jonathan
Coxinga and the Fall of the Ming Dynasty 852

Clinton, Bill
My Life 188, 331

Clinton, Catherine
Mrs. Lincoln: A Life 329

Clinton, Hillary Rodham
Living History 189

Clipinger, Karen
Dance Anatomy and Kinesiology 529

Clough, John D.
Arthritis 485
The Cleveland Clinic Guide to Arthritis **485**
To Act as a Unit : The Story of the Cleveland Clinic 485

Cloutier, George
Profits Aren't Everything, They're the Only Thing: No-Nonsense Rules from the Ultimate Contrarian and Small Business Guru **358**

Club, AV
Inventory: 16 Films Featuring Manic Pixie Dream Girls, 10 Great Songs Nearly Ruined by Saxophone, and 100 More Obsessively Specific Pop-Culture Lists **905**, 966, 997, 1004, 1017
My Year of Flops: The A.V. Club Presents One Man's Journey Deep into the Heart of Cinematic Failure 905

Clunas, Craig
Superfluous Things: Material Culture and Social Status in Early Modern China 885

Clurman, Ann
Generation Ageless: How Baby Boomers Are Changing the Way

We Live Today . . . And They're Just Getting Started 1269

Clute, Mark
Food Industry Quality Control Systems **1080**

Coates, David
Answering Back: Liberal Responses to Conservative Arguments 730

Cobb, Charles E.
Radical Equations: Math Literacy and Civil Rights 695

Cochran, Gregory
The 10,000 Year Explosion: How Civilization Accelerated Human Evolution 865

Cockayne, Emily
Hubbub: Filth, Noise, and Stench in England, 1600-1770 655

Cocks, Heather
Go Fug Yourself: The Fug Awards 888, **906**

Codevilla, Angelo M.
The Ruling Class: How They Corrupted America and What We Can Do About It 430

Codrescu, Andrei
The Blood Countess 30
New Orleans, Mon Amour: Twenty Years of Writings from the City **30**
The Poetry Lesson 30
The Posthuman Dada Guide 30

Cody, William F.
Buffalo Bill's Life Story: An Autobiography 868

Coen, Deborah R.
Vienna in the Age of Uncertainty: Science, Liberalism, and Private Life 744

Coffey, Patrick
Cathedrals of Science: The Personalities and Rivalries That Made Modern Chemistry 1301

Coffman, Tom
Nation Within: The History of the American Occupation of Hawaii 763

Cogliano, Francis D.
American Maritime Prisoners in the Revolutionary War: The Captivity of William Russell 687

Cohan, Wendy
The Better Bladder Book: A Holistic Approach to Healing Interstitial Cystitis and Chronic Pelvic Pain 597

Cohan, William D.
House of Cards: A Tale of Hubris and Wretched Excess on Wall Street **359**
The Last Tycoons: The Secret History of Lazard Frères & Co. 359

Cohen, Barbara J.
Medical Terminology: An Illustrated Guide 528

Cohen, Benyamin
My Jesus Year: A Rabbi's Son Wanders the Bible Belt in Search of His Own Faith 994

Cohen, Dan S.
The Heart of Change Field Guide:

Tools and Tactics for Leading Change in Your Organization 403

Cohen, Deborah
Braceros: Migrant Citizens and Transnational Subjects in the Postwar United States and Mexico 692
Household Gods: The British and Their Possessions **692**
The War Come Home: Disabled Veterans in Britain and Germany, 1914-1939 692

Cohen, Jeffrey Jerome
Monster Theory: Reading Culture 16

Cohen, Ken
Honoring the Medicine: The Essential Guide to Native American Healing 1159

Cohen, Kerry
Loose Girl: A Memoir of Promiscuity 333

Cohen, Leah Hager
Train Go Sorry: Inside a Deaf World 263

Cohen, Lizabeth
A Consumers' Republic: The Politics of Mass Consumption in Postwar America 866

Cohen, Mark Nathan
Culture of Intolerance: Chauvinism, Class and Racism in the United States 778

Cohen, Rich
When I Stop Talking, You'll Know I'm Dead: Useful Stories from a Persuasive Man 74, 894, 914, 954

Cohen, Richard M.
Strong at the Broken Places: Voices of Illness, a Chorus of Hope 503, 526

Cohen, Sheldon S.
Yankee Sailors in British Gaols: Prisoners of War at Forton and Mill, 1777-1783 687

Cohen, Stephen S.
The End of Influence: What Happens When Other Countries Have the Money 1264

Cohen, Warren I.
America's Response to China: A History of Sino-American Relations 783

Colacino, Sharon
Atlas of Human Anatomy 1230

Colbert, Stephen
I Am America (and So Can You!) **907**
Stephen Colbert and Philosophy: I Am Philosophy (And So Can You!) 907
Stephen Colbert's Tek Jansen 907
Wigfield: The Can-Do Town That Just May Not 907, 1340

Colby, Tanner
Belushi 910, 918
The Chris Farley Show: A Biography in Three Acts **918**, 976

Coleman, Mary
The Neurology of Autism 516

Colesberry, Adrian
How to Make Love to Adrian Colesberry **908**, 1335, 1338

Methods to Preserve Brain Function and Prevent Dementia 590

Desai, Bipin R.

Quantum Mechanics with Basic Field Theory 1063, 1231

Desai, Samir P.

250 Biggest Mistakes 3rd Year Medical Students Make And How to Avoid Them 493

Clinician's Guide to Laboratory Medicine, 3rd Edition **493**

The Successful Match: 200 Rules to Succeed in the Residency Match 493

DeSaix, Deborah Durland

The Grand Mosque of Paris: A Story of How Muslims Rescued Jews During the Holocaust 175

Desi, Thomas

The New Music Theater: Seeing the Voice, Hearing the Body 26

Desowitz, Robert S.

The Malaria Capers: More Tales of Parasites and People, Research and Reality 851

DeStefano, Stephen

Coyote at the Kitchen Door: Living with Wildlife in Suburbia 1248

Destler, I.M.

In the Shadow of the Oval Office: Profiles of the National Security Advisers and the Presidents They Served—From JFK to George W. Bush **1261**

Deutscher, Guy

Through the Language Glass: Why the World Looks Different in Other Languages 1255

Deveney, Sean

The Original Curse: Did the Cubs Throw the 1918 World Series to Babe Ruth's Red Sox and Incite the Black Sox Scandal? 985

Devgan, Uday

Cataract Surgery: A Patient's Guide to Cataract Treatment **494**

Devinsky, Orrin

Complementary and Alternative Therapies for Epilepsy 495

Epilepsy: Patient and Family Guide, 3rd Edition **495**

Devlin, Thomas M.

Textbook of Biochemistry with Clinical Correlations **1088**, 1223

Dew, Nicholas

Science and Empire in the Atlantic World 840

Dewar, James A.

The Nuclear Rocket: Making Our Planet Green, Peaceful and Prosperous 1089, 1089

To the End of the Solar System: The Story of the Nuclear Rocket, Second Edition **1089**, 1219

Dewdney, Christopher

Acquainted with the Night: Excursions Through the World After Dark 712

Dherbier, Yann-Brice

Paul Newman: A Life in Pictures 954

Di Giacomo, Fran

I'd Rather Do Chemo Than Clean Out the Garage: Choosing Laughter over Tears 945

Di Scala, Spencer M.

Italy: From Revolution to Republic, 1700 to the Present 701

Diamant, Anita

Choosing a Jewish Life: A Handbook for People Converting to Judaism and for Their Family and Friends 160

Day After Night 160

Living a Jewish Life: A Guide for Starting, Learning, Celebrating, and Parenting 160

Pitching My Tent 160

The Red Tent 160

Diaz, Monica

Indigenous Writings from the Convent: Negotiating Ethnic Autonomy in Colonial Mexico 85

Dickman, Andrew

Drugs in Palliative Care 648

Dickson, Paul

A Dictionary of the Space Age 1058, **1090**

Sputnik: The Launch of the Space Race 1090

Sputnik: The Shock of the Century 1090

Dickstein, Morris

Dancing in the Dark: A Cultural History of the Great Depression 866

Didion, Joan

Play It as It Lays 212

Slouching Towards Bethlehem 212

The White Album: Essays 212

The Year of Magical Thinking **212**, 941, 982

Dieken, Connie

Talk Less, Say More: Three Habits to Influence Others and Make Things Happen 411, 445

Diener, Ed

Happiness: Unlocking the Mysteries of Psychological Wealth 1245

Dierenfield, Bruce J.

The Civil Rights Movement: Revised Edition 677

Dietrich, Thomas K.

The Origin of Culture and Civilization: The Cosmological Philosophy of the Ancient Worldview Regarding Myth, Astrology, Science and Religion 672

Dietrich, William

The Final Forest: The Battle for the Last Great Trees of the Pacific Northwest 764

DiJulius, John R.

What's the Secret: To Providing a World-Class Customer Experience 348

DiLauri, Jonathan

Physical Therapy Musculoskeletal Examination 470

Diller, Phyllis

The Joys of Aging 213

Like a Lampshade In a Whorehouse: My Life In Comedy **213**

DiMarco, Lou

War Horse: A History of the Military Horse and Rider 855

Dinello, Paul

Wigfield: The Can-Do Town That Just May Not 1340

Dines, Gail

Gender, Race, and Class in Media: A Text-Reader 63

Dinwiddie, Robert

Space: From Earth to the Edge of the Universe 1116

Dion, Jennifer

Fireproof Your Marriage Couple's Kit 962

DiPucchio, Kelly

Grace for President 312

Dittmer, John

Local People: The Struggle for Civil Rights in Mississippi 695, 805

Dixon, Dougal

World Encyclopedia of Dinosaurs and Prehistoric Creatures 1103

Dobard, Raymond G.

Hidden in Plain View: A Secret Story of Quilts and the Underground Railroad 673

Dobbs, Michael

Down with Big Brother: The Fall of the Soviet Empire 704

Madeleine Albright: A Twentieth-Century Odyssey 704

One Minute to Midnight: Kennedy, Khrushchev, and Castro on the Brink of Nuclear War **704**

Saboteurs: The Nazi Raid on America 704

Dobie, Madeleine

Trading Places: Colonization and Slavery in Eighteenth-Century French Culture 700

Dobyns, Jay

No Angel: My Harrowing Undercover Journey to the Inner Circle of the Hells Angels 1362

Dodds, Jerrilynn D.

The Arts of Intimacy: Christians, Jews, and Muslims in the Making of Castilian Culture 844

Dodge, Bryan

The Good Life Rules: 8 Keys to Being Your Best as Work and at Play 387

Doherty, Paul

Great Crown Jewels Robbery of 1303: The Extraordinary Story of the First Big Bank Raid in History 1341

Doidge, Norman

The Brain That Changes Itself: Stories of Personal Triumph from the Frontiers of Brain Science 626, 1095

Doland, Erin R.

Unclutter Your Life in One Week 337

Dolgoff, Stephanie

My Formerly Hot Life: Dispatches from the Other Side of Young **1263**

Dolin, Eric Jay

The Duck Stamp Story 705

Fur, Fortune, and Empire: The Epic History of the Fur Trade in America 705

Leviathan: The History of Whaling in America **705**

Political Waters: The Long, Dirty, Contentious, Incredibly Expensive but Eventually Triumphant History of Boston Harbor, a Unique Environmental Success Story 705

Doliner, Roy

The Sistine Secrets: Michelangelo's Forbidden Message in the Heart of the Vatican 1326

Dolislager, Phyllis Porter

Who Hit the Down Button: Life with a Chronic Illness or Disability 503

Dollaghan, Christine A.

Handbook for Evidence-Based Practice in Communication Disorders 580

Dolnick, Edward

Rescue Artist: A True Story of Art, Thieves, and the Hunt for a Missing Masterpiece 1336

Donagan, Barbara

War in England 1642-1649 **706**

Donald, David Herbert

Lincoln 226

Donald, David

Lincoln 270

Donald, William

Stand by for Action: The Memoirs of a Small Ship Commander in World War II 862

Donaldson, Frances

P.G. Wodehouse: A Biography 268

Donoghue, Frank

The Fame Machine: Book Reviewing and Eighteenth-Century Literary Careers 39

The Last Professors: The Corporate University and the Fate of the Humanities **39**, 1281

Donovan, James

Custer and Little Big Horn: The Man, the Mystery, the Myth 707

The Dallas Cowboys Encyclopedia 707

Dallas: Shining Star of Texas 707

A Terrible Glory: Custer and Little Bighorn—The Last Great Battle of the American West **707**

Dosa, David

Making Rounds with Oscar: The Extraordinary Gift of an Ordinary Cat 986

Dougherty, Dorothy P.

Teach Me How to Say It Right: Helping Your Child With Articulation Problems 504

Douglas, Ann

Trying Again: A Guide to Pregnancy After Miscarriage, Stillbirth, and Infant Loss 267

Douglas, Paul

Restless Skies 1070, 1229

Douglas, Scott

Quiet, Please: Dispatches from a Public Librarian 1297

Douglass, Frederick

Narrative of the Life of Frederick Douglass, an American Slave 671

Dowd, Kevin

Alchemists of Loss: How Modern Finance and Government Intervention Crashed the Financial System 827

Dower, John

War Without Mercy: Race and Power in the Pacific War 845

Dowling, Robert M.

Critical Companion to Eugene O'Neill 40

Slumming in New York: From the Waterfront to Mythic Harlem **40**

Downs, Frederick Jr.

The Killing Zone: My Life in the Vietnam War 317

Downs, Linda Bank

Diego Rivera: The Detroit Industry Murals 91

Doyle, Sir Arthur Conan

The Complete Sherlock Holmes 935

Doyle, William

The Oxford History of the French Revolution 208, 681

Draelos, Zoe Diana

Cosmetic Dermatology: Principles and Practice 468

Drake, Ernest

Monsterology: The Complete Book of Monstrous Beasts 1237

Draper, Robert

Dead Certain: The Presidency of George W. Bush 188

Dray, Philip

At the Hands of Persons Unknown: The Lynching of Black America 214, 879

Capitol Men: The Epic Story of Reconstruction through the Lives of the First Black Congressmen **214**

Stealing God's Thunder: Benjamin Franklin's Lightning Rod and the Invention of America 214

There is Power in a Union: The Epic Story of Labor in America 1367, 214

Dreifus, Claudia

Higher Education?: How Colleges Are Wasting Our Money and Failing Our Kids—and What We Can Do About It 39, 47, 100, **1281**

Drescher, Seymour

Abolition: A History of Slavery and Antislavery 835

Capitalism and Antislavery: British Mobilization in Comparative Perspective 680

The Mighty Experiment: Free Labor versus Slavery in British Emancipation 747

Drew, Christopher

Blind Man's Bluff: The Untold Story of American Submarine Espionage 739

Drexler, Jerome

Discovering Postmodern Cosmology 1226

Drexler, Madeline

Emerging Epidemics: The Menace of New Infections 736

Drizin, Steven

True Stories of False Confessions 1278

Drucker, Malka

Portraits of Jewish-American Heroes 175

Drucker, Mindy

Crisis: 40 Stories Revealing the Personal, Social, and Religious Pain and Trauma of Growing Up Gay in America 1018

Du Bois, W.E.B.

Black Reconstruction in America 214

The Souls of Black Folk 220

Duarte, Nancy

Slide:ology: The Art and Science of Creating Great Presentations 432

Dublin, Thomas

The Face of Decline: The Pennsylvania Anthracite Region in the Twentieth Century **708**

Transforming Women's Work: New England Lives in the Industrial Revolution 708

When the Mines Closed: Stories of Struggles in Hard Times 708

Women and Power in American History: A Reader, Volume I to 1880 708

Dubner, Stephen J.

Superfreakonomics: Global Cooling, Patriotic Prostitutes and Why Suicide Bombers Should Buy Life Insurance 930, **972**

Dubner, Stephen J.

Freakonomics: A Rogue Economist Explores the Hidden Side of Everything 384, 972, 1273

Freakonomics: A Rogue Economist Explores the Hidden Side of Everything. Rev. and Expanded Ed. **405**, 930, 931

Dubois, Laurent

A Colony of Citizens: Revolution and Slave Emancipation in the French Caribbean, 1787-1804 700

Duca, Michael

The Baseball Codes: Beanballs, Sign Stealing, and Bench-Clearing Brawls: The Unwritten Rules of America's Pastime 981

Duchamp, Marcel

Marcel Duchamp: Works, Writings, Interviews 69

Dudden, Faye E.

Women in the American Theatre: Actresses and Audiences, 1790-1870 139

Dudley, William

Antebellum America: 1784-1850, Vol. 4 751

Due, Casey

The Captive Woman's Lament in Greek Tragedy 138

Duffy, Peter

The Bielski Brothers: The True Story of Three Men Who Defied the Nazis, Built a Village in the Forest, and Saved 1,200 Jews 886

Dugard, Martin

Into Africa: The Epic Adventures of Stanley and Livingstone 245, 935

Duggins, Pat

Trailblazing Mars: NASA's Next Giant Leap 1187, 1224

Duis, Perry R.

Challenging Chicago: Coping with Everyday Life, 1837-1920 54

Duke, James A.

Duke's Handbook of Medicinal Plants of the Bible 1159

Dumanoski, Dianne

The End of the Long Summer: Why We Must Remake Our Civilization to Survive on a Volatile Earth 1047

Dumas, Firoozeh

Funny in Farsi: A Memoir of Growing Up Iranian in America 215

Dunar, Andrew J.

America in the Fifties 761

Duncan, Paul

The Art of Bollywood 41

Cinema Now 41

The Godfather Family Album 41

The Ingmar Bergman Archives **41**

Duncan, Randy

The Power of Comics: History, Form and Culture 78

Dunford, Marie

Sports Nutrition: A Practice Manual for Professionals 484, 602

Dunham, Robert P.

The Innovator's Way: Essential Practices for Successful Innovation 1283

Dunkerley, James

Bolivia: Revolution and the Power of History in the Present: Essays 733

Dunlap, Riley

American Environmentalism: The US Environmental Movement, 1970-1990 809

Dunn, Dana

The Practical Researcher 1085

Dupee, Michael

How to Get on Jeopardy! and Win: Valuable Information from a Champion 946, 953, 958

Dupuy, Trevor N.

Elusive Victory: The Arab-Israeli Wars, 1947-1974 802

Duquette, Elizabeth

Loyal Subjects: Bonds of Nation, Race, and Allegiance in Nineteenth-Century America 837

Durand, Kevin K.

Buffy Meets the Academy: Essays on the Episodes and Scripts as Texts 1

Dursteler, Eric R.

Venetians in Constantinople: Nation, Identity and Coexistence in the Early Modern Mediterranean 796

Dutton, Denis

The Art Instinct: Beauty, Pleasure, and Human Evolution 64, 1244

Dweck, Carol

Mindset 1083

Dworkin, Mark S.

Cases in Field Epidemiology: A Global Perspective 565, 496

Outbreak Investigations Around the World: Case Studies in Infectious Disease Field Epidemiology 482, **496**, 519, 1146

Dye, Robin

Testament: My Survival and Conquest of Breast Cancer 506, 562

Dyer, Gwynne

The Climate Wars 1047

Dyer, Richard

Nino Rota: Music, Film and Feeling 62, 107

Dyess, William E.

Bataan Death March: A Survivor's Account 780, 815

Dyson, Michael Eric

Between God and Gangsta Rap: Bearing Witness to Black Culture 1007

E

Eales, Stephen

Planets and Planetary Systems 1132

Earle, David M.

All Man!: Hemingway, 1950s Men's Magazines, and the Masculine Persona 42

Re-Covering Modernism: Pulps, Paperbacks, and the Prejudice of Form **42**

Earle, Peter

The Sack of Panama: Captain Morgan and the Battle for the Caribbean 860

Easterbrook, Gregg

Beside Still Waters: Searching for Meaning in an Age of Doubt 1264

The Here and Now: A Novel 1264

A Moment on the Earth: The Coming Age of Environmental Optimism 1264

The Progress Paradox: How Life Gets Better While People Feel Worse 1264

Sonic Boom: Globalization at Mach Speed 443, **1264**

Tuesday Morning Quarterback: Haiku and Other Whimsical Observations to Help You Understand the Modern Game 1264

Eastoe, Jane

Wild Food 1213

Easton, Thomas A.

Environmental Issues: Taking Sides - Clashing Views on Environmental Issues 1077

Eaton, Susan

Children in Room E4: American Education on Trial 1323

Eaves, Ted

The Practical Guide to Athletic Training **497**, 602

Ebadi, Shirin

Honeymoon in Tehran: Two Years of Love and Danger in Iran 215

Iran Awakening: A Memoir of Revolution and Hope **215**

Lipstick Jihad: A Memoir of Growing up Iranian in America and American in Iran 215

Eberle, Suzanne Girard

Endurance Sports Nutrition: 2nd Edition 484, **498**, 602

The Pleasure Principal: Can You Really Have Your Cake and Eat It, Too? 498

Eberwein, Robert T.

Armed Forces: Masculinity and Sexuality in the American War Film 48, 77, 147

EBONY Magazine

Ebony Special Tribute: Michael Jackson In His Own Words 124

Eccles, W.J.

The Canadian Frontier, 1534-1760 219

Ecklund, Elaine Howard

Science vs. Religion: What Scientists Really Think 1316, 1349

Edberg, Mark Cameron

Essential Readings in Health Behavior: Theory and Practice 536

Essentials of Health Behavior 536

Essentials of Health Behavior: Social and Behavioral Theory in Public Health 634

Edelman, Julia Schlam

Menopause Matters: Your Guide to a Long and Healthy Life **499**, 630

Edge, Laura Bufano

Locked Up: A History of the U.S. Prison System 734

Edlund, Matthew

The Power of Rest 559

Edwards, Elizabeth

Resilience: Reflections on the Burdens and Gifts of Facing Life's Adversities 299, 331, **915**, 922, 978

Saving Graces: Finding Solace and Strength from Friends and Strangers 915, 299

Edwards, Justin D.

Gothic Passages: Racial Ambiguity and the American Gothic 32

Edwards, Laura F.

Gendered Strife and Confusion: The Political Culture of Reconstruction 709

The People and Their Peace: Legal Culture and the Transformation of Inequality in the Post-Revolutionary South **709**

Scarlett Doesn't Live Here Anymore 709

Edwards, Rebecca

New Spirits: Americans in the Gilded Age, 1865-1905 824

Edwards, Robert

The Winter War: Russia's Invasion of Finland, 1939-40 **710**

Egan, Eric

Films of Makhmalbaf: Cinema, Politics and Culture in Iran 34

Egan, Timothy

The Big Burn: Teddy Roosevelt and the Fire That Saved America 711

The Big Burn: Teddy Roosevelt and the Fire that Saved America 177, 711

The Good Rain: Across Time and Terrain in the Pacific Northwest 711

The Winemaker's Daughter 711

The Worst Hard Time: The Untold Story of Those Who Survived the Great American Dust Bowl 134, **711**

Eggerichs, Emerson

Love & Respect: The Love She Most Desires; The Respect He Desperately Needs 962

Eggers, Dave

A Heartbreaking Work of Staggering Genius 275, 916, 1023

Surviving Justice: America's Wrongfully Convicted and Exonerated 105, 1278

What Is the What 170

What is the What 916

You Shall Know Our Velocity 916

Zeitoun 6, 256, 679, **916**, 964, 1355

Ehrenclou, Martine

Critical Conditions: The Essential Hospital Guide to Get Your Loved One Out Alive 473, **500**

Ehrenreich, Barbara

Bait and Switch: The (Futile) Pursuit of the American Dream **1265**

Bright-Sided: How Positive Thinking Is Undermining America 1265

Bright-Sided: How the Relentless Promotion of Positive Thinking Has Undermined America 1329

Dancing in the Streets: A History of Collective Joy 1265

Global Woman: Nannies, Maids, and Sex Workers in the New Economy 1265

Nickel and Dimed: On (Not) Getting by in America 275

Nickel and Dimed: On (Not) Getting By in America 1265

This Land Is Their Land: Reports from a Divided Nation 1265, 1265

Witches, Midwives, and Nurses: A History of Women Healers 1265

Eidem, William Kelley

The Doctor Who Cures Cancer 570

Eig, Jonathan

Get Capone: The Secret Plot That Captured America's Most Wanted Gangster **1266**, 1320

Luckiest Man: The Life and Death of Lou Gehrig 239, 1266

Opening Day: The Story of Jackie Robinson's First Season 1266

Eigner, Saeb

Art of the Middle East: Modern and Contemporary Art of the Arab World and Iran 10

Einstein, Albert

Ideas and Opinions 241

The World As I See It 241

Eisen, Tim

Renal Cancer 586

Eisenberg, Bryan

Always Be Testing: The Complete Guide to Google Website Optimizer 365

Call to Action: Secret Formulas to Improve Online Results **365**

Waiting for Your Cat to Bark?: Persuading Customers When They Ignore Marketing 365

Eisenberg, Jeffrey

Call to Action: Secret Formulas to Improve Online Results **365**

Eisler, Benita

Byron: Child of Passion, Fool of Fame 125

The Lowell Offering: Writings by New England Mill Women (1840-1945) 871

Eisner, Will

Will Eisner's Shop Talk 72

Eiss, Camille

Reshaping Rogue States: Preemption, Regime Change, and US Policy Toward Iran, Iraq, and North Korea 763

Eitzen, D. Stanley

Solutions to Social Problems from the Bottom Up: Successful Social Movements 2

Ekirch, A. Roger

At Day's Close: A History of Nighttime **712**

Birthright: The True Story That Inspired Kidnapped 712

Bound for America: The Transportation of British Convicts to the Colonies, 1718-1775 712

Poor Carolina: Politics and Society in Colonial North Carolina, 1729-1776 712

El-Rouayheb, Khaled

Before Homosexuality in the Arab-Islamic World 808

Elbow, Peter

Being a Writer: A Community of Writers Revisited 252

Elewa, Ashraf M.T.

Migration of Organisms 1062

Elgin, Duane

Voluntary Simplicity: Toward a Way of Life that is Outwardly Simple, Inwardly Rich 1274

Eliot, Samuel

Two-Ocean War: A Short History of the United States Navy in the Second World War 862

Elkington, John

The Power of Unreasonable People: How Social Entrepreneurs Create Markets That Change the World 1264

Elliot-Wright, Susan

Living with Heart Failure 622

Elliott, Mark

Color-Blind Justice: Albion Tourgee and the Quest for Racial Equality from the Civil War to "Plessy v. Ferguson" 713

Emperor Qianlong: Son of Heaven, Man of the World 885

Undaunted Radical: The Selected Writings and Speeches of Albion W. Tourgee 713

Ellis, Bret Easton

American Psycho: A Novel 980, 1311

Ellis, Edward Robb

The Epic of New York City: A Narrative History 775

Ellis, Joseph J.

American Creation: Triumphs and Tragedies at the Founding of the Republic 878, 880

American Sphinx: The Character of Thomas Jefferson 768

Founding Brothers: The Revolutionary Generation 793

Ellis, Markman

The History of Gothic Fiction 32

Ellison, Ralph

The Collected Essays of Ralph Ellison 289

Invisible Man 289

Ellison, Sarah

War at the Wall Street Journal: Inside the Struggle To Control an American Business Empire 74

Ellmann, Richard

James Joyce 210

Ellroy, James

The Black Dahlia 913, 1014

L.A. Confidential 913, 1014

Ellsworth, Pamela

100 Q and A About Prostate Cancer, Second Edition **501**, 567

The Little Black Book of Urology 501

Questions and Answers about Overactive Bladder and Urinary Incontinence 501

Elster, Kathi

Working for You Isn't Working for Me: The Ultimate Guide to Managing Your Boss 1259

Working With You is Killing Me: Freeing Yourself from Emotional Traps at Work **1259**

Elton, Kat

A Resilient Life: Learning to Thrive, Not Just Survive With Rheumatoid Arthritis 485

Emerson, Chad Denver

Project Future: The Inside Story Behind the Creation of Disney World 373

Emerson, Ralph Waldo

The Essential Writings of Ralph Waldo Emerson 113

Eminem

Angry Blonde 216

The Way I Am 53, **216**

Emmott, Bill

Rivals: How the Power Struggle between China, India, and Japan will Shape Our Next Decade 1272

Engel, Jeffrey A.

Cold War at 30,000 Feet: The Anglo-American Fight for Aviation Supremacy **714**

The Fall of the Berlin Wall: The Revolutionary Legacy of 1989 714

Galassi, Peter
Henri Cartier-Bresson: The Modern Century 227

Galbraith, Patrick W.
The Otaku Encyclopedia: An Insider's Guide to the Subculture of Cool Japan 35

Gale, Joseph
Astrobiology of Earth 1193

Gallagher, John
AIA Detroit: The American Institute of Architects Guide to Detroit Architecture 95, 137
Great Architecture of Michigan 95, 137

Gallant, Joel E.
100 Questions and Answers About HIV and AIDS 483, **511**
Global HIV/AIDS Medicine 511
Johns Hopkins Poc-It Center Hiv Guide 2011 511
Medical Management of HIV Infection 511

Gallardo-C., Ximena
Alien Woman: The Making of Lt. Ellen Ripley 70

Gallena, Sally K.
Voice and Laryngeal Disorders: A Problem-Based Clinical Guide with Voice Samples 504

Gallentine, Jay
Ambassadors from Earth 1090

Galloway, Joseph L.
We Were Soldiers Once...and Young: Ia Drang—The Battle That Changed the War in Vietnam 874

Galloway, Patrick
Asia Shock: Horror and Dark Cinema from Japan, Korea, Hong Kong, and Thailand 86

Galloway, Priscilla
Adventures on the Ancient Silk Road 1302

Galt, John
The Life of Lord Byron 125

Gammage, Jeff
China Ghosts: My Daughter's Journey to America, My Passage to Fatherhood 1372

Gamow, George
Gravity 1160

Ganda, Kanchan M.
Dentist's Guide to Medical Conditions and Complications **512**

Ganeri, Anita
Alive: The Living, Breathing, Human Body Book 474

Ganeva, Mila
Women in Weimar Fashion: Discourses and Displays in German Culture, 1918-1933 44

Ganguly, Jibamitra
Thermodynamics in Earth and Planetary Sciences **1099**

Gannon, Michael
Operation Drumbeat: The Dramatic True Story of Germany's First U-boat Attacks Along the American Coast in World War II 238

Ganz, Caryn
Fool the World: The Oral History of a Band Called Pixies 46

Garabedian, Helen
Itsy Bitsy Yoga for Toddlers and Preschoolers: 8-Minute Routines to Help Your Child Grow Smarter, Be Happier, and Behave Better 557

Garavaglia, Jan
How Not to Die: Surprising Lessons on Living Longer, Safer, and Healthier from America's Favorite Medical Examiner **513**, 527, 628

Garber, Marjorie
Shakespeare and Modern Culture 158

Garcia, Diana
Fire and Ink: An Anthology of Social Action Writing **2**

Garcia, Nina
The Little Black Book of Style 995

Garcia Marquez, Gabriel
The Autumn of the Patriarch 297
Collected Stories 262
Memories of My Melancholy Whores 262
Of Love and Other Demons 157

Gardiner, Robert
Frigates of the Napoleonic Wars 803

Gardner, Donald E.
Toxicology of the Lung 598, 600

Gardner, Howard
Changing Minds: The Art and Science of Changing Our Own and Other People's Minds 49
Five Minds for the Future 409, 425

Gardner, Martin
Did Adam and Eve Have Navels?: Debunking Pseudoscience 927
My Best Mathematical and Logic Puzzles 927
Perplexing Puzzles and Tantalizing Teasers 927
When You Were a Tadpole and I Was a Fish: And Other Speculations About This and That **927**
The Whys of a Philosophical Scrivener 927

Gargola, Daniel J.
Land, Laws, & Gods 876

Garland, David
The Culture of Control: Crime and Social Order in Contemporary Society 734, 794

Garland, David Siteman
Smarter, Faster, Cheaper: Non-Boring, Fluff-Free Strategies for Marketing and Promoting Your Business 374, 376, 402

Garland, Joseph E.
Unknown Soldiers: Reliving World War II in Europe 656

Garlick, Mark A.
Astronomy: A Visual Guide 1092, 1143

Garofano, Jane Schultz
SUCCESS! in Massage Therapy 470

Garr, Doug
Stuffed: An Insider's Look at Who's (Really) Making America Fat **1250**

Garrett, Chris
ProBlogger: Secrets for Blogging Your Way to a Six-Figure Income 341, **436**

Garrett, Duane
Archeological Study Bible: An Illustrated Walk Through Biblical History and Culture 719, 727

Garrett, Laurie
The Coming Plague: Newly Emerging Diseases in a World out of Balance 736

Garrett, Mary
Remapping the Humanities: Identity, Community, Memory, (Post)Modernity **47**

Garrison, Cheryl
The Iron Disorders Institute Guide to Anemia, 2nd Edition **514**

Garrison, Webb
Mutiny in the Civil War 807

Garro, Elena
Recollections of Things to Come 157

Garrow, David J.
Reporting Civil Rights: Part One: American Journalism 1941-1963 830

Garza, Armida De la
Mexico On Film: National identity and International Relations 38

Gascoigne, Bamber
The Dynasties of China: A History 852

Gasparino, Charles
Blood on the Street: The Sensational Inside Story of How Wall Street Analysts Duped a Generation of Investors **375**
Bought and Paid For: The Unholy Alliance Between Barack Obama and Wall Street 375
King of the Club: Richard Grasso and the Survival of the New York Stock Exchange 375
The Sellout: How Three Decades of Wall Street Greed and Government Mismanagement Destroyed the Global Financial System 375

Gater, Will
The Cosmic Keyhole: How Astronomy Is Unlocking the Secrets of the Universe 1100
The Practical Astronomer **1100**

Gates, Evalyn
Einstein's Telescope: The Hunt for Dark Matter and Dark Energy in the Universe 1227

Gates, Henry Jr. Louis
The Future of the Race 220

Gates, Henry Louis
The African-American Century: How Black Americans Have Shaped Our Country 805
The Classic Slave Narratives 671

Gates, Henry Louis Jr.
Tradition and the Black Atlantic: Critical Theory in the African Diaspora 789

Gateward, Frances
Cinema and Modernity 48

From Hobbits to Hollywood: Essays on Peter Jackson's Lord of the Rings 48
Popping Culture: 4th Edition 48
Where the Boys Are: Cinemas of Masculinity and Youth **48**, 56, 77, 147

Gaunt, Peter
The English Civil Wars 1642-1651 706

Gause, Damon
The War Journal of Major Damon Rocky Gause: The Firsthand Account of One of the Greatest Escapes of World War II 780, 815

Gavigan, Christopher
Healthy Child Healthy World: Creating a Cleaner, Greener, Safer Home 541

Gawande, Atul
The Checklist Manifesto: How to Get Things Right 405, 409, 425, 930, 1286

Gay, Kathlyn
Epilepsy: The Ultimate Teen Guide 495

Gay, Timothy M.
Satch, Dizzy, and Rapid Robert: The Wild Saga of Interracial Baseball Before Jackie Robinson 319

Gaynor, Tim
Midnight on the Line: The Secret Life of the U.S.- Mexico Border **1275**, 1357

Gazit, Shlomo
The Arab-Israeli Wars: War and Peace in the Middle East 802

Gediman, Dan
Edward R. Murrow's This I Believe: Selections from the 1950s Radio Series 6
This I Believe II: More Personal Philosophies of Remarkable Men and Women 6, 1291
This I Believe: The Personal Philosophies of Remarkable Men and Women **6**, 256, 916, 1253, 1291, 1305

Gediman, Mary Jo
Edward R. Murrow's This I Believe: Selections from the 1950s Radio Series 6

Gegax, Tom
The Big Book of Small Business: You Don't Have to Run Your Business by the Seat of Your Pants 449

Geiger, James Tad
The Sweet Smell of Success 554

Geist, Bill
Way Off the Road: Discovering the Peculiar Charms of Small Town America 1350

Geist, Mary Ellen
Measure of the Heart: Caring for a Parent with Alzheimer's 478, 592

Gemmell, Jim
Total Recall: How the E-Memory Revolution Will Change Everything 1271, 1347

Geniesse, Jane Fletcher
Passionate Nomad: The Life of Freya Stark 240

Greenberg, Judith E.
Helen Herron Taft: 1861-1943 52

Greenberg, Keith Elliot
The Legends of Wrestling: "Classy" Freddie Blassie: Listen, You Pencil Neck Geeks (WWE) 900

Greenberg, Lynne A.
The Body Broken: A Memoir 572, 579, 588

Greenberg, Riva
50 Diabetes Myths That Can Ruin Your Life: And the 50 Diabetes Truths That Can Save It 471, 487, **521**
The ABCs of Loving Yourself with Diabetes 521

Greenberger, Robert
Wonder Woman: Amazon. Hero. Icon 975

Greenblatt, Stephen
Will in the World: How Shakespeare Became Shakespeare 233

Greene, Brian
The Hidden Reality: Parallel Universes and the Deep Laws of the Cosmos 1227

Greene, Christina
Our Separate Ways: Women and the Black Freedom Movement in Durham, North Carolina 682

Greene, Ellen
Remember the Sweet Things: One List, Two Lives, and Twenty Years of Marriage 1280

Greene, Julie
The Canal Builders: Making America's Empire at the Panama Canal **735**
Pure and Simple Politics: The American Federation of Labor and Political Activism, 1881-1917 735

Greene, Meg
Rest in Peace: A History of American Cemeteries 884

Greene, Melissa Fay
Praying for Sheetrock: A Work of Nonfiction 231
The Temple Bombing 231
There Is No Me without You **231**, 1337

Greene, Molly
A Shared World: Christians and Muslims in the Early Modern Mediterranean 796

Greene, Valerie
Conquering Stroke: How I Fought My Way Back and How You Can Too 477, **522**, 523, 560, 628

Greenfeld, Karl Taro
Boy Alone: A Brother's Memoir 736
China Syndrome: The True Story of the 21st Century's First Great Epidemic **736**
Speed Tribes: Days and Nights with Japan's Next Generation 736
Standard Deviations: Growing Up and Coming Down in the New Asia 736

Greenfield, Robert
Bill Graham Presents: My Life Inside Rock And Out 932

Greenhouse, Linda
Becoming Justice Blackmun: Harry Blackmun's Supreme Court Journey 232

Greenstein, Fred I.
The Hidden-Hand Presidency: Eisenhower as Leader 232
Presidential Difference: Leadership Style from FDR to Barack Obama 1261

Greenwald, Bruce C. N.
Competition Demystified: A Radically Simplified Approach to Business Strategy **382**
Globalization: n. the irrational fear that someone in China will take your job 382

Greer, David M.
Acute Ischemic Stroke: An Evidence-Based Approach **523**
Pocket Neurology 523

Greer, Germaine
The Female Eunuch 233
Shakespeare's Wife **233**
Shakespeare: A Brief Insight 233
The Whole Woman 233

Greer, Julia B.
The Anti-Cancer Cookbook 613

Gregg, Michael
Field Epidemiology 496, 574

Gregg, Robert
Sparks from the Anvil of Oppression: Philadelphia's African Methodists and Southern Migrants, 1890-1940 693

Grego, Peter
Astronomical Cybersketching 1052

Gregory, Dick
Murder in Memphis: The FBI and the Assassination of Martin Luther King 750

Gregory, James N.
The Southern Diaspora: How the Great Migrations of Black and White Southerners Transformed America 1366, 1367

Gregory, John
Edward R. Murrow's This I Believe: Selections from the 1950s Radio Series 6

Gregory, Morna E.
Toilets of the World 928, 959

Gregory, Philippa
The Other Boleyn Girl 325

Grenny, Joseph
Influencer: The Power to Change Anything 379

Gress, Michael A.
The Soviet-Afghan War: How a Superpower Fought and Lost 718

Gribbin, John
In Search of the Multiverse 1094, 1227

Griffin, Kathy
Official Book Club Selection: A Memoir According to Kathy Griffin 897, **936**, 942, 943, 944, 969, 993, 1019, 1024, 1025, 1026, 1036, 1038, 1039

Griffin, Sean
Queer Cinema: The Film Reader 1015

Griffith, Daniel A.
Spatial Autocorrelation and Spatial Filtering: Gaining Understanding Through Theory and Scientific Visualization 1167

Griffiths, Andrew
101 Secrets to Building a Winning Business 383
101 Ways to Build a Successful Network Marketing Business 383
101 Ways to Market Your Business: Building a Successful Business with Creative Marketing 383
Bulletproof Your Business Now **383**
Me Myth: What do you mean it's not all about me? 383
Organizational Change for Corporate Sustainability: A Guide for Leaders and Change Agents of the Future (Understanding Organizational Change) 383

Griffiths, David J.
Introduction to Elementary Particles 1063, 1231

Grimes, Jill
The 5-Minute Clinical Consult 2010 524
Seductive Delusions: How Everyday People Catch STDs **524**, 569

Grimes, Nikki
Talkin' about Bessie: The Story of Aviator Elizabeth Coleman 327

Grisham, John
The Client 1278
The Confession: A Novel 1278
The Firm 1278
The Innocent Man: Murder and Injustice in a Small Town **1278**
The Partner 1278
The Pelican Brief 1278
The Rainmaker 1278
The Runaway Jury 1278
The Summons 1278
The Testament 1278
A Time to Kill 1278

Grissell, Eric
Insects and Gardens: In Pursuit of a Garden Ecology 1111

Griswold, Eliza
The Tenth Parallel: Dispatches from the Fault Line Between Christianity and Islam 653

Grobman, Alex
Denying History: Who Says the Holocaust Never Happened and Why Do They Say It? 777

Groening, Matt
The Simpsons One Step Beyond Forever : A Complete Guide to Our Favorite Family...Continued Yet Again 998

Groensteen, Thierry
The System of Comics 78

Grogan, John
The Longest Trip Home: A Memoir 937
Marley & Me: Life and Love with the World's Worst Dog **937**

Gross, Paul M.
Superfruits 614

Grossman, Edith
Living to Tell the Tale 262
Memories of My Melancholy Whores 262

Grossmann, John
One Square Inch of Silence: One Man's Search for Natural Silence in a Noisy World **1288**

Gruenberg, Bonnie Urquhart
Birth Emergency Skills Training 534

Gruenfeld, Lee
Confessions of a Master Jewel Thief 1341

Grundmann, Roy
A Companion to Michael Haneke 108

Grupen, Claus
Introduction to Radiation Protection 1044

Gruwell, Erin
Teach with Your Heart: Lessons I Learned from the Freedom Writers 1267, 1270

Gualtieri, Sarah
Between Arab and White: Race and Ethnicity in the Early Syrian American Diaspora 92, 104

Guarneri, Mimi
The Heart Speaks: A Cardiologist Reveals the Secret Language of Healing 525

Guenther-Pal, Alison
German Essays on Film 44

Gugelyk, Ted
The Separating Sickness, Mai Ho'oka'wale: Interviews with Exiled Leprosy Patients at Kalaupapa, Hawaii 861

Guha, Ramachandra
A Corner of a Foreign Field: The Indian History of a British Sport 737
Environmentalism: A Global History 737
How Much Should a Person Consume?: Environmentalism in India and the United States 737
India After Gandhi: The History of the World's Largest Democracy **737**, 849

Guidry, Cindy
The Last Single Woman in America **938**

Guillebeau, Chris
The Art of Non-Conformity: Set Your Own Rules, Live the Life You Want, and Change the World 360, 369, 370, 376, 393, 396, 442, 448

Guinn, Jeff
The Autobiography of Santa Claus 1279
The Christmas Chronicles 1279
Go Down Together: The True, Untold Story of Bonnie and Clyde **1279**
How Mr. Claus Saved Christmas 1279
Our Land Before We Die 1279
Something in the Blood: The Underground World of Today's Vampires 1279

Time on Fire: My Comedy of Terrors 945

Handley, Ann
Content Rules: How to Create Killer Blogs, Podcasts, Videos, Ebooks, Webinars (and More) That Engage Customers and Ignite Your Business 374, 448

Handlin, Mimi
Living With ADD When You're Not the One Who Has It: A Workbook For Partners 589

Handwerker, W. Penn
The Origin of Cultures: How Individual Choices Make Cultures Change 1162

Hanhimaki, Jussi M.
The Cold War: A History in Documents and Eyewitness Accounts 729, 774

Hanley, Richard
South Park and Philosophy: Bigger, Longer, and More Penetrating 148

Hanna, Martha
John Massey: The House That Jack Built 742
The Mobilization of Intellect: French Scholars and Writers During the Great War 742
Your Death Would Be Mine: Paul and Marie Pireaud in the Great War **742**

Hannan, Daniel
The New Road to Serfdom: A Letter of Warning to America 352

Hannigan, Steve
Inherited Metabolic Diseases: A Guide to 100 Conditions 461, **533**

Hannoum, Abdelmajid
Violent Modernity: France in Algeria 846

Hansen, Colin H.
The Effects of Low-Frequency Noise and Vibration on People 1060, 1165

Hansen, Heine
Textbook of Lung Cancer 570

Hansen, James
Storms of My Grandchildren: The Truth About the Coming Climate Catastrophe and Our Last Chance to Save Humanity 1105

Hansen, Morten T.
Collaboration: How Leaders Avoid the Traps, Create Unity, and Reap Big Results **1283**
How Organizations Get Smart—and Stay Smart 1283
The Innovation Value Chain 1283
Introducing T-Shaped Managers: Knowledge Management's Next Generation 1283
What's Your Strategy for Managing Knowledge? 1283

Hanslmeier, Arnold
The Sun and Space Weather 1161

Hansmann, Georg
Neonatal Emergencies **534**, 557

Hanson, Helen
Hollywood Heroines: Women in Film Noir and the Female Gothic Film 142

Hanson, James Ralph
Chemistry in the Garden **1111**, 1207

Hanson, Laurence
Contemporary Printed Sources for British and Irish Economic History 1701-1750 800

Hanson, Mary Ellen
Go! Fight! Win!: Cheerleading in American Culture 1032

Hanson, Peter
Tales from the Script: 50 Hollywood Screenwriters Share Their Stories 914

Hanson, Ralph E.
Mass Communication: Living in a Media World 12

Hanson, Victor Davis
A War Like No Other: How the Athenians and Spartans Fought the Peloponnesian War 1282

Harcombe, Zoe
The Obesity Epidemic: What Caused It? How Can We Stop It? 538

Hardberger, Max
Seized: A Sea Captain's Adventures Battling Scoundrels and Pirates While Recovering Stolen Ships in the World's Most Troubled Waters 664

Hardcastle, Gary L.
Bullshit and Philosophy (Popular Culture and Philosophy) 891, 923

Harding, Richard
A Great and Glorious Victory: New Perspectives on the Battle of Trafalgar 814

Hardy, Thomas
Thomas Hardy: The Complete Poems 316

Hare, Robert D.
Snakes in Suits: When Psychopaths Go to Work 1354

Harford, James
Dark Side of the Moon: Wernher Von Braun, the Third Reich, and the Space Race 812

Harford, Tim
Dear Undercover Economist: Priceless Advice on Money, Work, Sex, Kids, and Life's Other Challenges 384
The Logic of Life: The Rational Economics of an Irrational World 384
The Undercover Economist: Exposing Why the Rich Are Rich, the Poor Are Poor—And Why You Can Never Buy a Decent Used Car! 384

Hargrove, Hondon B.
Buffalo Soldiers in Italy: Black Americans in World War II 656

Harisha, S.
Biotechnology Procedures and Experiments Handbook 1164

Harland, David M.
NASA's Moon Program: Paving the Way for Apollo 11 1199

Harland, David M.
Apollo 12 - On the Ocean of Storms 1112

Exploring the Moon: The Apollo Expeditions, Second Edition **1112**
The First Men on the Moon: The Story of Apollo 11 1112
How NASA Learned to Fly in Space 1112
NASA's Moon Program: Paving the Way for Apollo 11 1112

Harness, Cheryl
George Washington 295

Harnish, Verne
Mastering the Rockefeller Habits: What You Must Do to Increase the Value of Your Growing Firm **385**

Harper, Hill
The Conversation: How Black Men and Women Can Build Loving, Trusting Relationships 947

Harper, Peter S.
First Years of Human Chromosomes: The Beginnings of Human Cytogenetics 535
A Short History of Medical Genetics 464, 469, 533, **535**, 596

Harrington, Jill
The Lupus Recovery Diet 637

Harrington, Philip S.
Cosmic Challenge: The Ultimate Observing List for Amateurs 1052

Harris, Bill
Birth of a Notion; Or, the Half Ain't Never Been Told: A Narrative Account with Entertaining Passages of the State of Minstrelsy and of America and the True Relation Thereof 57
The Ringmaster's Array 57, 57
Yardbird Suite: Side One : 1920-1940 57, 57

Harris, Bob
Motor City Rock and Roll: The 1960's and 1970's 53
Prisoner of Trebekistan: A Decade in Jeopardy! **946**, 953, 958
Steal This Book: And Get Life Without Parole 946
Who Hates Whom: Well-Armed Fanatics, Intractable Conflicts, and Various Things Blowing Up A Woefully Incomplete Guide 946

Harris, Charlaine
Real Murders 1014

Harris, Daniel C.
Exploring Chemical Analysis 1113
Quantitative Chemical Analysis, Eighth Edition **1113**

Harris, Joseph E.
Africans and Their History: Second Revised Edition 789

Harris, Mark
Pictures at a Revolution: Five Movies and the Birth of the New Hollywood 334

Harris, Mike
Find Your Lightbulb: How to Make Millions from Apparently Impossible Ideas 386

Harris, Nathaniel
Atlas of the Worlds Deserts 1046

Harris, Ruth
Dreyfus: Politics, Emotion, and the Scandal of the Century **1284**

Lourdes: Body and Spirit in the Secular Age 1284
Murders and Madness: Medicine, Law, and Society in the Fin de Siècle 1284

Harris, Shane
The Watchers: The Rise of America's Surveillance State **1285**

Harrison, Burton
The Carlyles: A Story of the Fall of the Confederacy 834

Harrison, Charles
Art in Theory 1900-2000: An Anthology of Changing Ideas 64

Harrison, George
I, Me, Mine 280, 306

Harrison, K. David
Book of Peoples of the World: A Guide to Cultures 1262

Harrison, Kathryn
The Kiss 203

Harrison, Mark
Medicine in an Age of Commerce and Empire: Britain and Its Tropical Colonies 1660-1830 840

Harrison, Rebecca
Deep, Dark and Dangerous: On the Bottom with the Northwest Salvage Divers 664

Hart, Archibald D.
Sleep, It Does a Family Good: How Busy Families Can Overcome Sleep Deprivation 507, 556

Hartigan, Pamela
The Power of Unreasonable People: How Social Entrepreneurs Create Markets That Change the World 1264

Hartl, Daniel L.
Essential Genetics: A Genomics Perspective, Fifth Edition 1066, **1114**, 1182
Genetics 1114
Genetics: Analysis of Genes and Genomes 1114
A Primer of Population Genetics 1114

Hartman, Saidiya
Lose Your Mother: A Journey Along the Atlantic Slave Route 154

Harvey, Michael
The Chicago Way 999

Harvey, Steve
Act Like a Lady, Think Like a Man: What Men Really Think About Love, Relationships, Intimacy, and Commitment **947**
Straight Talk, No Chaser: How to Find, Keep, and Understand a Man 947

Hashaw, Tim
Children of Perdition: Melungeons and the Struggle of Mixed America 821

Haskell, Molly
Frankly, My Dear: "Gone with the Wind" Revisited 127

Hastings, Max
The Battle for the Falklands 743
The Korean War 740

Overlord: D-Day and the Battle for Normandy 743

Retribution: The Battle for Japan, 1944-45 **743**

Winston's War: Churchill, 1940-1945 743, 684, 817

Hatley, Flora J.

History of African Americans in North Carolina 682

Hatmaker, Mark

No Holds Barred Fighting: The Ultimate Guide to Conditioning 497

Hauner, Milan

The Soviet War in Afghanistan 718

Hausladen, Gary J.

Western Places, American Myths: How We Think About The West 128

Havers, Richard

Rolling with the Stones 293

Hawken, Paul

Blessed Unrest: How the Largest Movement in the World Came into Being and Why No One Saw It Coming 1268, 1276

Hawkesworth, Mary E.

Globalization and Feminist Activism 702

Hawks, Melanie

Influencing Without Authority 387
Life-Work Balance **387**

Hayashi, Robert T.

Haunted by Waters: A Journey through Race and Place in the American West 128

Hayden, Joanna

Introduction to Health Behavior Theory 536

Haye, Amy de la

Lucile: London, Paris, New York and Chicago 118

Hayes, A. Wallace

Principles and Methods of Toxicology, Fifth Edition **537**

Hayes, Bill

The Anatomist: A True Story of Gray's Anatomy 513, 527

Hayes, Kevin J.

The Road to Monticello: The Life and Mind of Thomas Jefferson 768

Haynes, William M.

CRC Handbook of Chemistry and Physics, 91st Edition **1115**
Handbook of Chemistry and Physics 1115

Hays, J. N.

The Burdens of Disease: Epidemics and Human Response in Western History 595

Hayt, Charles W.

Obstetrics: A Manual for Students and Practitioners 502

Healey, Joseph F.

The Essentials of Statistics: A Tool for Social Research 1218

Healey, Richard G.

The Pennsylvania Anthracite Coal Industry, 1860-1802 708

Healy, Maureen

Vienna and the Fall of the Habsburg

Empire: Total War and Everyday Life in World War I **744**

Heaney, Christopher

Cradle of Gold: The Story of Hiram Bingham, a Real-Life Indiana Jones, and the Search for Machu Picchu 1255

Heap, Chad

Slumming: Sexual and Racial Encounters in American Nightlife, 1885-1940 40, 131

Heard, Alex

The Eyes of Willie McGee: A Tragedy of Race, Sex, and Secrets in the Jim Crow South 1366

Heath, Chip

Made to Stick: Why Some Ideas Survive and Others Die 378, 434, 1286, **1287**, 1293, 1286

Rumor Mills (Social Problems and Social Issues) 1286, 1287

Switch: How to Change Things When Change Is Hard 379, 409, 425, 447, **1286**, 1287, 1369

Switch: How to Change Things When Change is Hard 1287

Heath, Dan

Made to Stick: Why Some Ideas Survive and Others Die 378, 434, 1286, **1287**, 1293

Switch: How to Change Things When Change Is Hard 379, 409, 425, 447, **1286**, 1287, 1369

Heather, P.J.

Empires and Barbarians: The Fall of Rome and the Birth of Europe 732, 873

The Fall of the Roman Empire: A New History of Rome and the Barbarians 661, 732

Hecht, Roger W.

The Erie Canal Reader, 1790-1950 668

Hedges, Chris

Empire of Illusion 1316, 1324

Hedrick, Joan

Harriet Beecher Stowe: A Life 163

Hegel, Robert E.

True Crimes in Eighteenth-Century China: Twenty Case Histories 804

Heidenry, John

The Gashouse Gang: How Dizzy Dean, Leo Durocher, Branch Rickey, Pepper Martin, and Their Colorful, Come-from-Behind Ball Club Won the World Series—and America's Heart—During the Great Depression 985

Zero at the Bone: The Playboy, the Prostitute, and the Murder of Bobby Greenlease 1299

Heier, Jeffrey S.

100 Questions and Answers About Macular Degeneration 460, 494

Heilemann, John

Game Change: Obama and the Clintons, McCain and Palin, and the Race of a Lifetime 298, 331, 915

Heiligman, Deborah

Charles and Emma: The Darwins' Leap of Faith 911, 949, 950

Heine, Peter

From Mesopotamia to Iraq: A Concise History 659

Heinemann, Larry

Zinky Boys: Soviet Voices from the Afghanistan War 718

Heinemeier Hansson, David

Rework 344, 345, 364, 367, 393

Heinrich, Bernd

Summer World: A Season of Bounty 235

Winter World: The Ingenuity of Animal Survival **235**, 1210

Heins, Marjorie

Not in Front of the Children: 'Indecency,' Censorship, and the Innocence of Youth 869

Helferich, Gerard

Humboldt's Cosmos: Alexander von Humboldt and the Epic Journey of Exploration through Latin America That Changed the Way We See the World 867

Heller, Anne C.

Ayn Rand and the World She Made **236**

Heller, Jane

Confessions of a She-Fan: The Course of True Love with the New York Yankees 981

Hemery, Daniel

Indochina: An Ambiguous Colonization, 1858-1954 700

Hemingway, Ernest

The Nick Adams Stories 43

Hempton, Gordon

One Square Inch of Silence: One Man's Search for Natural Silence in a Noisy World **1288**

Hendel, Amy

Fat Families, Thin Families: How to Save Your Family from the Obesity Trap **538**, 541

Henderson, Bill

Cancer-Free: Your Guide to Gentle, Non-toxic Healing 558

Henderson, Bruce

Hero Found: The Greatest POW Escape of the Vietnam War 780

Henderson, D. A.

Smallpox: The Death of a Disease 1175

Hendler, Glenn

Keywords for American Cultural Studies 66

Hendley, Nate

Bonnie and Clyde: A Biography 1279

Hendra, Tony

Last Words 895, **901**, 971, 976

Hendrick, George

Black Refugees in Canada: Accounts of Escape During the Era of Slavery 745

Hendrix, John

Abe Lincoln Crosses a Creek: A Tall, Thin Tale (Introducing His Forgotten Frontier Friend) 237

The Giant Rat of Sumatra: Or Pirates Galore 237

*How to Save Your Tail: *if You Are a*

Rat Nabbed by Cats Who Really Like Stories about Magic Spoons, Wolves with Snout-warts, Big, Hairy Chimney Trolls . . . and Cookies, Too 237

John Brown: His Fight for Freedom **237**

Henrich, William L.

Principles and Practice of Dialysis, Fourth Edition 491, **539**, 586

Henson, Robert

The Rough Guide to Climate Change 1061, 1069

Hepburn, Sharon A. Roger

Crossing the Border: A Free Black Community in Canada **745**

Herman, Arthur

How the Scots Invented the Modern World: The True Story of How Western Europe's Poorest Nation Created Our World & Everything in It 813, 847

To Rule the Waves: How the British Navy Shaped the Modern World 831

Herman, Dsvid

The Cambridge Companion to Narrative 21

Herman, Paul Robert

Tales from the Script: 50 Hollywood Screenwriters Share Their Stories 914

Herman, Richard T.

Immigrant, Inc.: Why Immigrant Entrepreneurs Are Driving the New Economy (and how they will save the American worker) **388**

Herndon, J. Marvin

Maverick's Earth and Universe **1116**

Herodotus

The Histories 98

Hersey, Paul

The Ethical Executive: Becoming Aware of the Root Causes of Unethical Behavior: 45 Psychological Traps That Every One of Us Falls Prey To 1289

Hersh, Seymour M.

The Price of Power: Kissinger in the Nixon White House 697

Hersh, William R.

Information Retrieval: A Health and Biomedical Perspective 1049

Herwig, Holger H.

The First World War: Germany and Austria-Hungary 1914-1918 744

Herzog, Chaim

The Arab-Israeli Wars: War and Peace in the Middle East 802

Herzog, Elizabeth

Life Is with People: The Culture of the Shtetl 73

Hess, Barbara

Willem de Koonig: 1904-1997 309, 1351

Hess, Elizabeth

Lost and Found: Dogs, Cats, and Everyday Heroes at a Country Animal Shelter 948

Nim Chimpsky: The Chimp Who Would Be Human 924, **948**

Hesser, Leon
The Man Who Fed the World: Nobel Peace Prize Laureate Norman Borlaug and His Battle to End World Hunger 1317

Hewitt-White, Ken
Patterns in the Sky 1053, 1093

Heylin, Clinton
Bob Dylan: Behind the Shades Revisited 58
Despite the System: Orson Welles Versus the Hollywood Studios **58**
Revolution in the Air 58
So Long as Men Can Breathe 58

Hickey, Anthony J.
Inhalation Aerosols: Physical and Biological Basis for Therapy 598, 600

Hickman, Roger
Reel Music: Exploring 100 Years of Film Music 62, 107

Higgins, Ilona Laszlo
Creating Life Against the Odds: The Journey from Infertility to Parenthood 508

Higham, William
The Next Big Thing: Spotting and Forecasting Consumer Trends for Profit 452

Highsmith, Patricia
Strangers on a Train 1015
The Talented Mr. Ripley 1015

Higson, Andrew
British Cinema, Past and Present 94

Hild, Matthew
Greenbackers, Knights of Labor and Populists: Farmer-labor Insurgency in the Late-Nineteenth-Century South 824

Hile, Kevin
Dams and Levees 1117
The Handy Weather Answer Book **1117**

Hill, Eric J.
AIA Detroit: The American Institute of Architects Guide to Detroit Architecture 95, 137

Hill, John
National Cinemas And World Cinema (Studies in Irish Film) 101

Hill, Marc Lamont
Beats, Rhymes, and Classroom Life: Hip-Hop Pedagogy and the Politics of Identity 28, 99, 156

Hill, Peter C.
Psychology of Religious Fundamentalism 1342

Hill, Robert
Dead Men Don't Have Sex: A Guy's Guide to Surviving Prostate Cancer **540**, 543, 567

Hillenbrand, Laura
Seabiscuit: An American Legend 238
Unbroken: A World War II Story of Survival, Resilience, and Redemption **238**

Hillenbrand, Will
Louie! 290

Hilliard, Brian
Networking Like a Pro: Turning Contacts into Connections 392, **417**

Hills, Jodi
Slap on a Little Lipstick...You'll Be Fine 917

Hilton, Christopher
Mayflower: The Voyage that Changed the World 823

Hiltzik, Michael
Colossus: Hoover Dam and the Making of the American Century 1247, 1333

Hinds, Patrick
The Whole World Was Watching: Living in the Light of Matthew Shepard 1018

Hines, Melissa
Brain Gender 577

Hinsley, F.H.
Codebreakers: The Inside Story of Bletchley Park 909

Hinton, Stephen
Kurt Weill: The Threepenny Opera 26

Hirsch, Arnold R.
Making the Second Ghetto: Race and Housing in Chicago 1940-1960 726

Hirsch, Foster
The Dark Side of the Screen: Film Noir 142

Hirsch, James S.
Cheating Destiny: Living with Diabetes 239
Hurricane: The Miraculous Journey of Rubin Carter 239
Willie Mays: The Life, the Legend **239**, 319

Hirsch, James S.
Hurricane: The Miraculous Journey of Rubin Carter 239

Hirshfeld, Alan
Astronomy Activity and Laboratory Manual 1119

Hirshman, Susan L.
Does This Make My Assets Look Fat? A Woman's Guide to Finding Financial Empowerment and Success 1321

Hirt, Paul W.
Northwest Lands, Northwest Peoples: Readings in Environmental History 764

Hitchcock, William I.
The Bitter Road to Freedom: A New History of the Liberation of Europe 746
France Restored: Cold War Diplomacy and the Search for Leadership 746
The Struggle for Europe: The Turbulent History of a Divided Continent, 1945 to the Present 758, 746

Hitchens, Christopher
God Is Not Great: How Religion Poisons Everything 911, 927, **949**
God is Not Great: How Religion Poisons Everything 950
Hitch-22 911, 927, **950**, 949
The Portable Atheist: Essential Readings for the Nonbeliever 949, 950

Hoagland, Ken
The FairTax Solution: Financial Justice for All Americans 349

Hochschild, Adam
Bury the Chains: Prophets and Rebels in the Fight to Free an Empire's Slaves **747**
Half the Way Home: A Memoir of Father and Son 747
King Leopold's Ghost: A Story of Greed, Terror, and Heroism in Colonial Africa 747
The Unquiet Ghost: Russians Remember Stalin 747

Hockenhull, Stella
Neo-Romantic Landscapes: An Aesthetic Approach to the Films of Powell and Pressburger 90, 130

Hodge, Russ
Genetic Engineering 1164

Hodges, Graham Russell Gao
Friends of Liberty: A Tale of Three Patriots, Two Revolutions, and the Betrayal That Divided a Nation: Thomas Jefferson, Thaddeus Kosciuszko, and Agrippa Hull 857

Hodges, Montana
Rockhounding Alaska: A Guide to 75 of the State's Best Rockhounding Sites 1209

Hodgman, John
The Areas of My Expertise: An Almanac of Complete World Knowledge Compiled with Instructive Annotation and Arranged in Useful Order 302, 892, 905, **951**, 996, 997, 1004, 1006, 1017, 1027, 1040, 952
More Information Than You Require 892, **952**, 1006, 1040, 951

Hodgson, Ernest
A Textbook of Modern Toxicology 537, 552, 599

Hodgson, Michael
Basic Essentials Weather Forecasting 1229

Hoffer, Peter Charles
The Great New York Conspiracy of 1741: Slavery, Crime, and Colonial Law 775

Hoffman, Betty Hannah
Love, Lucy 187, 887

Hoffman, Bruce
Inside Terrorism 882

Hoffman, Shirl J.
Introduction to Kinesiology: Studying Physical Activity **1118**, 1174

Hofler, Robert
Party Animals: A Hollywood Tale of Sex, Drugs, and Rock 'n' Roll Starring the Fabulous Allan Carr 46, 74

Hogan, Kevin
Covert Persuasion: Psychological Tactics and Tricks to Win the Game 357

Hogarth, Robin
Dance with Chance: Making Luck Work for You 1254

Hogshead, Sally
Fascinate: Your 7 Triggers to Persuasion and Captivation 391, 414

Hohnsbeen, Roger
Amyotrophic Lateral Sclerosis 526

Holberg, Jay B.
Sirius: Brightest Diamond in the Night Sky **1119**, 1168

Holden, James Herschel
A History of Horoscopic Activity 672

Holden, Reed
Pricing with Confidence: 10 Ways to Stop Leaving Money on the Table 418

Holland, James
Italy's Sorrow: A Year of War, 1944-1945 656

Holland, Jesse J.
Black Men Built the Capitol: Discovering African-American History In and Around Washington, D.C. 214

Holland, Peter
The Performing Century: Nineteenth-Century Theatre's History 114

Holler, Teresa
Cardiology Essentials 541
Holler for Your Health: Be the Key to a Healthy Family **541**

Hollingsworth, Cristopher
Alice Beyond Wonderland: Essays for the Twenty-First Century 59
Poetics of the Hive: Insect Metaphor in Literature 59

Holloway, Elizabeth
Toxic Workplace!: Managing Toxic Personalities and Their Systems of Power 1259, 1354

Holmes, Chet
The Ultimate Sales Machine: Turbocharge Your Business with Relentless Focus on 12 Key Strategies 360

Holmes, David L.
A Brief History of the Episcopal Church 748
The Faiths of the Founding Fathers **748**, 795

Holmes, Richard
The Age of Wonder: How the Romantic Generation Discovered the Beauty and Terror of Science **749**
Coleridge: Early Visions, 1772-1804 749
The Romantic Poets and Their Circle 749
Shelley: The Pursuit 749

Holohan, Conn
Cinema on the Periphery: Contemporary Irish and Spanish Film 101

Holsoe, Svend E.
African-American Exploration in West Africa: Four Nineteenth-Century Diaries 688, 689

Holt, Jason
The Daily Show and Philosophy: Moments of Zen in the Art of Fake News 907

Holt, W. Stull
The Great War at Home and Abroad: The World War I Diaries of W. Stull Holt 742

Holton, Woody
Abigail Adams 829

Hummel, Susanne
Ancient DNA Typing: Methods, Strategies and Applications 1228

Humphrey, Clark
Vanishing Seattle 764

Hundert, Gershon David
Jews in Poland-Lithuania in the Eighteenth Century: A Genealogy of Modernity 73

Hunt, Darnell
Black Los Angeles: American Dreams and Racial Realities 770

Hunt, Darnell M.
Channeling Blackness: Studies on Television and Race in America **63**
O. J. Simpson Facts and Fictions 63

Hunt, John Dixon
Art, Word and Image: 2,000 Years of Visual/Textual Interaction **64**
Garden History: Issues, Approaches, Methods 64
Gardens and the Picturesque: Studies in the History of Landscape Architecture 64
The Italian Garden: Art, Design and Culture 64

Hunt, Tara
The Whuffie Factor: Using the Power of Social Networks to Build Your Business 394

Hunter, Dawn
Adventures on the Ancient Silk Road 1302

Hunter, John O.
Inflammatory Bowel Disease 608

Hunter, Lawrence
Artificial Intelligence and Molecular Biology 1123
The Processes of Life: An Introduction to Molecular Biology 1065, **1123**, 1172

Hunter, Tera W.
To Joy My Freedom: Southern Black Women's Lives and Labors After the Civil War 816

Hurley, Dan
Diabetes Rising: How a Rare Disease Became a Modern Pandemic, and What to Do About It 521, 547

Huron, David
Sweet Anticipation: Music and the Psychology of Expectation 1180

Hurston, Zora Neale
Their Eyes Were Watching God 289

Hustad, Megan
How to Be Useful: A Beginner's Guide to Not Hating Work 1257

Huston, Reeve
The Early American Republic: A History in Documents 880

Hutcheon, Linda
A Theory of Adaptation 36

Hutchins, Michael
Second Nature: Environmental Enrichment for Captive Animals 924

Hutchinson, Martin
Alchemists of Loss: How Modern Finance and Government Intervention Crashed the Financial System 827

Hutton, Paul Andrew
The Custer Reader 707

Huwyler, Joseph S.
The Dancer's Body: A Medical Perspective on Dance and Dance Training 529

Huyssen, Andreas
After The Great Divide: Modernism, Mass Culture, Postmodernism 131

Hyde, David
Introduction to Genetic Principles 1171

Hyland, William Jr. G.
In Defense of Thomas Jefferson: The Sally Hemings Sex Scandal 229, 297, 1364

Hynes, Margaret
Rocks and Fossils 1156

I

Iacoboni, Marco
Mirroring People: The Science of Empathy and How We Connect with Others 1185

Idliby, Ranya
The Faith Club: A Muslim, a Christian, a Jew—Three Women Search for Understanding **1290**, 1317

Ifudu, Onyekachi
Renal Anemia: Conflicts and Controversies 465, 466

Iggulden, Conn
The Dangerous Book for Boys 25

Iggulden, Hal
The Dangerous Book for Boys 25

Igo, Sarah E.
The Averaged American: Surveys, Citizens, and the Making of a Mass Public 1319

Ihde, Don
Embodied Technics 1124
Ironic Technics 1124
Listening and Voice: Phenomenologies of Sound, Second Edition **1124**

Ikeno, Osamu
The Japanese Mind: Understanding Contemporary Japanese Culture 35

Impey, Chris
Talking about Life: Conversations on Astrobiology 1193

Inada, Lawson Fusao
Only What We Could Carry: The Japanese American Internment Experience 658

Incontrera, Kate
I.O.U.S.A. 457

Inge, M. Thomas
Charles M. Schulz: Conversations (Conversations with Comic Artists) 273

Inghilleri, Leonardo
Exceptional Service, Exceptional Profit: The Secrets of Building a Five-Star Customer Service Organization 348, 389

Inglis, Mike
Astronomy of the Milky Way 1125
Astrophysics is Easy!: An Introduction for the Amateur Astronomer 1100, **1125**
Field Guide to Deep-Sky Objects 1125
Observer's Guide to Stellar Evolution 1125

Iniewski, Krzysztof
Electronics for Radiation Detection 1044

Innes, Brian
DNA and Body Evidence 1072, 1110, 1139, 1151

Inness, Sherrie A.
Dinner Roles: American Women and Culinary Culture 8

Inoguchi, Rikihei
The Divine Wind: Japan Kamikaze Force in World War II 845

Irish, Sharon
Cass Gilbert, Architect 65
Suzanne Lacy: Spaces Between **65**

Irwin, Judith A.
Astrophysics: Decoding the Cosmos 1125, 1147, 1154, 1221

Irwin, Terri
Steve and Me 197

Irwin, William
Alice in Wonderland and Philosophy: Curiouser and Curiouser 59

Isaacs, Susan E.
Angry Conversations with God: A Snarky but Authentic Spiritual Memoir 956, 1294

Isaacson, Karen L. J.
Life in the Fast Brain: Keeping Up With Gifted Minds 619

Isaacson, Walter
American Sketches: Great Leaders, Creative Thinkers, and Heroes of a Hurricane 241, 242
Benjamin Franklin: An American Life 241, 841
Einstein: His Life and Universe 190, **242**
Einstein: The Life of a Genius **241**
Kissinger: A Biography 241, 242
The Wise Men: Six Friends and the World They Made 241, 242

Isay, Dave
12 American Voices: An Authentic Listening and Integrated-Skills Text 1291
Flophouse: Life on the Bowery 1291
Holding on: Dreamers, Visionaries, Eccentrics, and Other American Heroes 1291
Listening Is an Act of Love: A Celebration of American Life from the StoryCorps Project 1291
Mom: A Celebration of Mothers from StoryCorps 6, 243, 1035, **1291**
Our America: Life and Death on the South Side of Chicago 1291

Isay, David
Flophouse: Life on the Bowery 243
Listening Is an Act of Love: A Celebration of American Life from the StoryCorps Project **243**, 1291, 1319

Isay, Jane
Mom Still Likes You Best: The Unfinished Business Between Siblings **1292**
Walking on Eggshells: Navigating the Delicate Relationship Between Adult Children and Parents 1292

Isenberg, Nancy
Madison and Jefferson 1364

Ishay, Micheline
The Human Rights Reader: Major Political Essays, Speeches and Documents from Ancient Times to the Present, Second Edition 674

Israel, Shel
Naked Conversations: How Blogs Are Changing the Way Businesses Talk with Customers 413, **438**
Naked Conversations: How Blogs are Changing the Way Businesses Talk with Customers 390
Twitterville: How Businesses Can Thrive in the New Global Neighborhoods **390**, 406, 1306

Iverson, Peter
Dine : A History of the Navajos 799

Ivy, John
Nutrient Timing 614

Iwan, Wildred D.
Earthquake Spectra 1076

Iyengar, Sheena
The Art of Choosing 1287, **1293**

J

Jackson, Beverley
Splendid Slippers: A Thousand Years of an Erotic Tradition 765

Jackson, Carlos Francisco
Chicana and Chicano Art: ProtestArte 93

Jackson, Joe
The Thief at the End of the World: Rubber, Power, and the Seeds of Empire 230, 1277

Jackson, Maggie
Distracted: The Erosion of Attention and the Coming Dark Age 1251, 1271, 1313

Jackson, Thomas
From Civil Rights to Human Rights: Martin Luther King, Jr. and the Struggle for Economic Justice **753**

Jackson, Troy
Becoming King: Martin Luther King Jr. and the Making of a National Leader 112

Jacobs, A.J.
America Off-Line: The Complete Outernet Starter Kit 956, 1294
Fractured Fairy Tales 956, 1294
The Guinea Pig Diaries: My Life as an Experiment 956, 994, 1294
The Know-It-All: One Man's Humble Quest to Become the Smartest Person in the World 956, 994, 1294
My Life as an Experiment: One Man's Humble Quest to Improve Himself by Living as a Woman,

Kelton, Alan
The Fit Arthritic: Fighting Knee and Hip Arthritis with Exercise 485

Kelts, Roland
Japanamerica: How Japanese Pop Culture Has Invaded the U.S. 35

Kemp, Donna R.
Mental Health in America: A Reference Handbook 618

Kendrick, Alex
The Love Dare **962**

Kendrick, Stephen
The Love Dare **962**

Kenneally, Christine
The First Word: The Search for the Origins of Language 948

Kennedy, Dan
No B.S. Marketing to the Affluent: The No Holds Barred, Kick Butt, Take No Prisoners Guide to Getting Really Rich 377

Kennedy, Dan S.
The Ultimate Marketing Plan: Find Your Hook. Communicate Your Message. Make Your Mark. 377
The Ultimate Sales Letter: Attract New Customers. Boost Your Sales 377

Kennedy, Edward M.
America Back on Track 250
True Compass: A Memoir 191, **250**

Kennedy, John Fitzgerald
A Nation of Immigrants 250

Kennedy, John F.
Profiles in Courage 250

Kennedy, Maxwell Taylor
Make Gentle the Life of This World: The Vision of Robert F. Kennedy 691

Kennedy, Robert F.
Thirteen Days: A Memoir of the Cuban Missile Crisis 704

Kenny, Tom
The Nuts and Bolts of Cardiac Pacing, Second Edition **548**
The Nuts and Bolts of Cardiac Resynchronization Therapy 548
The Nuts and Bolts of ICD Therapy 548
The Nuts and bolts of Paced ECG Interpretation 489, 550, 631, 548

Kenrose, Stephanie
The Reactive Hypoglycemia Cookbook 487

Keough, Donald R.
The Ten Commandments for Business Failure 395

Keough, Kelly
Sugar-Free Gluten-Free Baking and Desserts 520, 605

Kerh, Tienfuan
Seismic Data Analysis by Using Computational Intelligence 1121

Kerman, Piper
Orange Is the New Black: My Year in a Women's Prison **1303**

Keslowitz, Steven
The World According to The Simpsons: What Our Favorite TV Family Says about Life, Love, and the Pursuit of the Perfect Donut 998

Kessler, Amalia D.
A Revolution in Commerce: The Parisian Merchant Court and the Rise of Commercial Society in Eighteenth-century France **762**

Kessler, David
A Question of Intent: A Great American Battle with a Deadly Industry 678

Kessler, Lauren
Finding Life in the Land of Alzheimer's: One Daughter's Hopeful Story 283, 478, **549**, 592

Kester, Grant H.
Conversation Pieces: Community and Communication in Modern Art 2

Ketchum, Ralph
James Madison: A Biography 272

Kettl, Donald F.
System Under Stress: Homeland Security and American Politics, 2nd Edition 882

Keve, Paul W.
Prisons and the American Conscience: A History of U.S. Federal Corrections 794

Key, Josephine
Back Pain: A Movement Problem 505

Khan, M. Gabriel
Encyclopedia of Heart Diseases 550
Rapid ECG Interpretation, Third Edition **550**

Khan, Nafees A.
Ethylene Action in Plants 1054

Khatib, Lina
Filming the Modern Middle East: Politics in the Cinemas of Hollywood and the Arab World 120

Kicinski, Carol
Simply . . . Gluten-Free Desserts: 150 Delicious Recipes for Cupcakes, Cookies, Pies, and More Old and New Favorites 520, 605

Kidd, Chip
Green Lantern: Tales of the Sinestro Corps 963
The Life and Times of Martha Washington in the Twenty-First Century 963
Watching the Watchmen **963**

Kidd, Parris M.
PS (PhosphatidylSerine) Nature's Brain Booster 478

Kidder, Tracy
Among Schoolchildren 964
Mountains Beyond Mountains 964
My Detachment: A Memoir 964
Strength in What Remains 246, **964**

Kiefer, Claus
Quantum Gravity 1192

Kilcoyne, Martha E.
Defeat Chronic Fatigue Syndrome 629

Kilman, Scott
Enough: Why the World's Poorest Starve in an Age of Plenty 1243, 1352

Kim, F. S.
Meteor Showers 1138

Kim, Richard
Going Rouge: An American Nightmare 281

Kim, Susan
Flow: The Cultural Story of Menstruation 1242

Kim, W. Chan
Blue Ocean Strategy: How to Create Uncontested Market Space and Make Competition Irrelevant 372, **400**

Kimball, Warren F.
Forged in War: Roosevelt, Churchill and the Second World War 684

Kimmel, Haven
A Girl Named Zippy: Growing Up Small in Mooreland, Indiana 183

Kimmel, Michael
Guyland: The Perilous World Where Boys Become Men 1308

Kinderberger, Charles P.
Manias, Panics, and Crashes: A History of Financial Crises 827

King, Dean
Skeletons on the Zahara: A True Story of Survival 245

King, Geoff
Science Fiction Cinema: From Outerspace to Cyberspace 70

King, John
Tribal Leadership: Leveraging Natural Groups to Build a Thriving Organization 389

King, Larry
My Remarkable Journey 324
Why I Love Baseball 981

King, Rosemary A.
Border Confluences: Borderland Narratives from the Mexican War to the Present 754

Kingsolver, Barbara
Animal, Vegetable, Miracle: A Year of Food Life 134, 921, 925, 926, **965**, 1000, 1001, 1352
The Poisonwood Bible 246, 1000

Kingsolver, Camille
Animal, Vegetable, Miracle: A Year of Food Life 134, 921, 925, 926, **965**, 1000, 1001, 1352

Kingston, Anne
The Meaning of Wife: A Provocative Look at Women and Marriage in the Twenty-First Century **1304**

Kingwell, Mark
Canada: Our Century 292
Concrete Reveries: Consciousness and the City 251
Glenn Gould 199, **251**, 258, 292
Nearest Thing to Heaven: The Empire State Building and American Dreams 251
Nothing For Granted: Tales of War, Philosophy, and Why the Right Was Mostly Wrong 251
Opening Gambits: Essays on Art and Philosophy 251

Kinni, Donna
No Substitute for Victory: Lessons in Strategy and Leadership from General Douglas MacArthur 724

Kinni, Theodore
No Substitute for Victory: Lessons in Strategy and Leadership from General Douglas MacArthur 724

Kinzer, Paul E.
Stargazing Basics: Getting Started in Recreational Astronomy 1053, 1093, 1173, 1195

Kinzer, Stephen
All the Shah's Men: An American Coup and the Roots of Middle East Terror 763
Overthrow: America's Century of Regime Change from Hawaii to Iraq 763
Reset: Iran, Turkey and America's Future 763
A Thousand Hills: Rwanda's Rebirth and the Man Who Dreamed It 763

Kipnis, Laura
Against Love: A Polemic 1305
Bound and Gagged: Pornography and the Politics of Fantasy in America 1305
The Female Thing: Dirt, Envy, Sex, Vulnerability 1305
Female Thing: Dirt, Sex, Envy, Vulnerability 1305
How to Become a Scandal: Adventures in Bad Behavior **1305**

Kirk, Russell
The Conservative Mind: From Burke to Eliot 84

Kirkby, Mary-Ann
I Am Hutterite: The Fascinating True Story of a Young Woman's Journey to Reclaim Her Heritage 244

Kirkpatrick, David
The Facebook Effect: The Inside Story of the Company That Is Connecting the World 980, 1238, **1306**, 1311

Kirkpatrick, Rob
1969: The Year Everything Changed 761

Kirn, Walter
Lost in the Meritocracy: The Undereducation of an Overachiever **252**
Mission to America: A Novel 252
Thumbsucker 252
Up in the Air 252

Kirshenbaum, Sheril
Unscientific America: How Scientific Illiteracy Threatens our Future **1316**

Kisor, Henry
What's That Pig Outdoors? A Memoir of Deafness 263

Kissinger, Henry
White House Years 697

Kitamura, Daisuke
How the Immune System Recognizes Self and Nonself 1079

Kitchen, Clyde K.
Fact and Fiction of Healthy Vision: Eye Care for Adults and Children 460, 494, **551**

Kitchen, Denis
The Art of Harvey Kurtzman: The Mad Genius of Comics **72**

McLoone, Martin
Irish Film: The Emergence of a Contemporary Cinema 101

McMahon, David
Quantum Field Theory Demystified 1194

McMahon, Robert J.
The Cold War: A Very Short Introduction 729, 774

McMath, Robert C.
American Populism: A Social History 1877-1898 824

McMillan, Alexander
Sexually Transmissible Infections in Clinical Practice: A Problem-Based Approach 488, 524, 581

McMillan, Kenneth
Tales from the Yankee Dugout: A Collection of the Greatest Yankee Stories Ever Told 259

McNab, Chris
Napoleon Wars: An Illustrated History 666

McNair, Amy
Donors of Longmen: Faith, Politics, And Patronage in Medieval Chinese Buddhist Sculpture 145

McNally, Rand
Goode's World Atlas, 22nd Edition 1046, **1153**

McNees, Kelly O'Connor
The Lost Summer of Louisa May Alcott 264

McNeil, Peter
Shoes: A History from Sandals to Sneakers 1258

McNiff, Shaun
Art as Medicine 144
Art Heals: How Creativity Cures the Soul 144

McPhail, Thomas L.
Development Communication: Reframing the Role of the Media 49

McPhee, Peter
The French Revolution, 1789-1799 681

McPherson, James M.
Abraham Lincoln **270**, 329
Battle Cry of Freedom: The Civil War Era 270
For Cause and Comrades: Why Men Fought in the Civil War 788
Hallowed Ground: A Walk at Gettysburg 270
Ordeal by Fire: The Civil War and Reconstruction 270

McQuillar, Tayannah Lee
Tupac Shakur: The Life and Times of an American Icon 1007

McRoy, Jay
Japanese Horror Cinema 86

McTaggart, Lynne
The Field: The Quest for the Secret Force of the Universe 1158
The Intention Experiment 1133

Meacham, Jon
American Gospel: God, the Founding Fathers, and the Making of a Nation 748, **795**, 271

American Lion: Andrew Jackson in the White House 795, **271**, 330
Franklin and Winston: An Intimate Portrait of an Epic Friendship 795, 271

Mead, Rebecca
One Perfect Day: The Selling of the American Wedding 1029, **1314**

Meadows, Donella H.
Thinking in Systems 1225

Meagher, Arnold J.
The Coolie Trade: The Traffic in Chinese Laborers to Latin America 759

Mealer, Bryan
The Boy Who Harnessed the Wind: Creating Currents of Electricity and Hope **246**, 964, 1247, 1273, 1318

Mearns, Linda O.
Issues in the Impacts of Climate Variability and Change on Agriculture 1062

Mears, Emira
The Boss of You: Everything A Woman Needs to Know to Start, Run, and Maintain Her Own Business 335

Medley, Keith Weldon
We as Freeman: Plessy v. Ferguson 713

Meek, Barbra A.
We Are Our Language: An Ethnography of Language Revitalization in a Northern Athabascan Community **85**

Mehta, Gita
Snakes and Ladders: Glimpses of Modern India 849

Meier, Dirk
Seafarers, Merchants and Pirates in the Middle Ages 1302

Meikle, Denis
A History of Horrors: The Rise and Fall of the House of Hammer 86
Johnny Depp: A Kind of Illusion 86
The Ring Companion **86**
Vincent Price: The Art of Fear 86

Meintjes, Louise
Sound of Africa: Making Music Zulu in a South African Studio 150

Meischner, Peter
Weather Radar: Principles and Advanced Applications 1161

Meister, Jeanne C.
2020 Workplace: How Innovative Companies Attract, Develop, and Keep Tomorrow's Employees Today 1298

Melanson, Philip H.
The Secret Service: The Hidden History of an Engimatic Agency 694

Melfi, Vicky
Zoo Animals: Behaviour, Management and Welfare 924

Melia, Fulvio
The Black Hole at the Center of Our Galaxy 1154
The Edge of Infinity: Supermassive Black Holes in the Universe 1154
Electrodynamics 1154

The Galactic Supermassive Black Hole 1154
High-Energy Astrophysics 1064, **1154**

Mellen, Jill D.
Second Nature: Environmental Enrichment for Captive Animals 924

Mellon, James
Bullwhip Days: The Slaves Remember 671

Meloy, Maile
Both Ways Is the Only Way I Want It 304

Melton, H. Keith
Spycraft: The Secret History of the CIA's Spytechs, from Communism to al-Qaeda 872, 1296

Meltzer, Marisa
How Sassy Changed My Life: A Love Letter to the Greatest Teen Magazine of All Time 25, 992, 1020

Menaker, Daniel
Friends and Relations: A Collection of Stories 1315
A Good Talk: The Story and Skill of Conversation **1315**
The Old Left and other stories 1315
The Treatment 1315

Menand, Louis
The Marketplace of Ideas: Reform and Resistance in the American University 68

Menander, Menander
Classical Comedy 138
The Plays and Fragments 138

Menard, Scott
Handbook of Longitudinal Research 1085

Mendelson, Scott D.
Beyond Alzheimer's: How to Avoid the Modern Epidemic of Dementia 283, 478, **573**, 592
Metabolic Syndrome and Psychiatric Illness: Interactions, Pathophysiology, Assessment & Treatment 573

Mendes, Valerie D.
Lucile: London, Paris, New York and Chicago 118
Twentieth-Century Fashion in Detail 118

Menn, Joseph
Fatal System Error: The Hunt for the New Crime Lords Who are Bringing Down the Internet 1256

Menocal, Maria Rosa
The Ornament of the World: How Muslims, Jews, and Christians Created a Culture of Tolerance in Medieval Spain 844

Meridith, Alan T.
Handbook of Prostate Cancer Cell Research: Growth, Signalling and Survival 501, 540, 553

Merrill, Ray M.
Environmental Epidemiology: Principles and Methods 486, **574**
Introduction to Epidemiology 519, 574
Principles of Epidemiology Workbook: Exercises and Activities 574
Reproductive Epidemiology: Principles and Methods 574

Merrill, Rebecca
Speed of Trust: The One Thing That Changes Everything **361**

Merry, Robert W.
A Country of Vast Designs: James K. Polk, The Mexican War, and the Conquest of the American Continent 204, **272**
Sands of Empire: Missionary Zeal, American Foreign Policy, and the Hazards of Global Ambition 272
Taking on the World: Joseph and Stewart Alsop, Guardians of the American Century 272

Merryman, Ashley
NurtureShock: New Thinking About Children 1345, 1370

Mertig, Angela G.
American Environmentalism: The US Environmental Movement, 1970-1990 809

Merwin, W.S.
The Shadow of Sirius 1119

Meserve, Margaret
Commentaries, Volume 1: Books I-II 796
Commentaries, Volume 2: Books III-IV (co-author) 796
Empires of Islam in Renaissance Historical Thought **796**

Messenger, Charles
The D-Day Atlas: Anatomy of the Normandy Campaign 665

Messer, Susan
Grand River and Joy: A Novel 200

Meszaros, Peter
The High Energy Universe: Ultra-High Energy Events in Astrophysics and Cosmology 1064, 1189

Metcalf, Barbara D.
A Concise History of Modern India 737

Metcalf, Thomas R.
A Concise History of Modern India 737

Metz, Julie
Perfection: A Memoir of Betrayal and Renewal **978**

Metz, Steven
Iraq in Transition: The Legacy of Dictatorship and the Prospects for Democracy 820

Metz, Walter
Bewitched 87
Engaging Film Criticism 87

Meuninck, Jim
Basic Essentials Edible Wild Plants and Useful Herbs 1084, 1155
Medicinal Plants of North America **1155**, 1159

Meyer, Anna
The DNA Detectives 1198

Meyer, Danny
Setting the Table: The Transforming Power of Hospitality in Business 451

Meyer, David N.
The 100 Best Films to Rent You've Never Heard Of: Hidden Treasures, Neglected Classics, and Hits From By-Gone Eras 979

Mitsumoto, Hiroshi

Amyotrophic Lateral Sclerosis: A Guide for Patients and Families, 3rd Edition 526, **576**

Mitton, Jacqueline

Cambridge Illustrated Dictionary of Astronomy 1092, 1143

Mix, Lucas John

Life in Space: Astrobiology for Everyone 1193

Mlodinow, Leonard

The Drunkard's Walk: How Randomness Rules Our Lives 1356

Mlotek, Chana

Pearls of Yiddish Poetry 89

Yiddish Folksongs from the Ruth Rubin Archive 89

Moalem, Sharon

How Sex Works: Why We Look, Smell, Taste, Feel, and Act the Way We Do 908

Moaveni, Azadeh

Iran Awakening: A Memoir of Revolution and Hope **215**

Lipstick Jihad: A Memoir of Growing Up Iranian in America and American in Iran 215

Moche, Dinah L.

Astronomy 1092, 1143

Modena, Leone

The Autobiography of a Seventeenth-Century Venetian Rabbi 848

Moehringer, J.R.

The Tender Bar **275**

Moerman, Daniel E.

Meaning, Medicine and the 'Placebo Effect' 1159

Native American Ethnobotany 1159

Native American Medicinal Plants: An Ethnobotanical Dictionary 1155, **1159**

Moffat, Alistair

The Highland Clans 813

Moffat, John W.

Reinventing Gravity: A Physicist Goes Beyond Einstein **1160**, 1192

Moffat, Wendy

A Great Unrecorded History: A New Life of E.M. Forster 313

Mogil, H. Michael

Extreme Weather 1070

Mohammed, Rafi

The 1% Windfall: How Successful Companies Use Price to Profit and Grow **418**

The Art of Pricing: How to Find the Hidden Profits to Grow Your Business 418

Mohlenbrock, Robert H.

This Land: A Guide to Eastern National Forests 1202

Mohr, Jay

Gasping for Airtime: Two Years in the Trenches of Saturday Night Live 918

Mokyr, Joel

The Enlightened Economy: An Economic History of Britain, 1700-1850 **800**

The Gifts of Athena: Historical Origins of the Knowledge Economy 800

The Lever of Riches: Technological Creativity and Economic Progress 800

Why Ireland Starved: A Quantitative and Analytical History of the Irish Economy, 1800-1850 800

Molderings, Herbert

Duchamp and the Aesthetics of Chance: Art as Experiment 69

Moldow, Gloria

Women Doctors in Gilded Age Washington: Race, Gender, and Professionalization 838

Moldwin, Mark

An Introduction to Space Weather 1104, **1161**

Molho, Renata

Being Armani: A Biography 1258

Molles, Manuel

Ecology: Concepts and Applications **276**

Molloy, Andrea

Stop Living Your Job, Start Living Your Life: 85 Simple Strategies to Achieve Work/Life Balance 387

Moloney, Kate

Tim Gunn: A Guide to Quality, Taste, and Style 995

Moltz, Barry

B-A-M! Bust A Myth: Delivering Customer Service in a Self-Service World 347, 419

Bounce!: Failure, Resiliency, and Confidence to Achieve Your Next Great Success 419

Momsen, Janet Henshall

Gender and Development 472, 568, **577**

Monaghan, David

Jack the Ripper's Secret Confession: The Hidden Testimony of Britain's First Serial Killer 1326

Monahan, Christopher D.

The Big Shake: Implications of a Major Earthquake in California 1120

Monem, Nadine

Art and Text 64

Montagu, Ewen

The Man Who Never Was: World War II's Boldest Counter-Intelligence Operation 257

Montanari, Massimo

Food Is Culture 7

Montgomery, David R.

Dirt: The Erosion of Civilizations 1166, 1301

Montgomery, Douglas C.

Design and Analysis of Experiment 1050, 1085

Montgomery, L.M.

Anne of Green Gables 321

Anne of Green Gables Series 321

Montgomery, Leslie

The Faith of Condoleezza Rice 185

Montgomery, Sy

Walking with the Great Apes 284

Mooney, Chris

The Republican War on Science 1316

Storm World: Hurricanes, Politics, and the Battle over Global Warming 1070

Storm World: Hurricanes, Politics, and the Battle Over Global Warming 1316

Unscientific America: How Scientific Illiteracy Threatens our Future **1316**

Moor, Andrew

Architectural Glass 90

Architectural Glass Art 90

Colours of Architecture 90

Michael Powell: International Perspectives on an English Filmmaker 90, 130

Powell and Pressburger: A Cinema of Magic Spaces **90**, 130

Moor, Julia

Playing, Laughing and Learning with Children on the Autism Spectrum: A Practical Resource of Play Ideas for Parents and Carers **578**, 587, 624

Moore, Alan

From Hell 963

V for Vendetta 963

Watchmen 963

Moore, Andrew

Andrew Moore: Detroit Disassembled 95, 137

Moore, Christopher

Canada: Our Century 292

Moore, David S.

Essential Statistics 1218

Moore, Donnica

Women's Health For Life 517

Moore, Graham

The Sherlockian 935

Moore, Harold G.

We Were Soldiers Once...and Young: Ia Drang—The Battle That Changed the War in Vietnam 874

Moore, James Gregory

King of the 40th Parallel: Discovery in the American West 838

Moore, John

Tribal Knowledge: Business Wisdom Brewed from the Grounds of Starbucks Corporate Culture 415

Moore, Judith

Fat Girl: A True Story 333

Moore, Kathryn

Dear Harry...: Truman's Mailroom, 1945-1953: The Truman Administration Through Correspondence with 864

Moore, Lucy

The Thieves' Opera 1320

Moore, Mary Tyler

Growing Up Again: Life, Loves, and Oh Yeah, Diabetes 887

Moore, Mary Tyler

After All 187

Moore, Patrick

The Sky at Night 1168

Dr. Moore, Peter

The Little Book of Pandemics 547

Moore, Russell D.

Adopted for Life: The Priority of Adoption for Christian Families and Churches 231

Moore, Thomas

Life of Lord Byron, Vol. 1: With His Letters and Journals 125

Moore, Wes

The Other Wes Moore: One Name, Two Fates **983**

Moorehead, Alan

The White Nile 245

Mora, Carl J.

Mexican Cinema: Reflections of a Society, 1896-1980 38

Moran, Emilio F.

The Ecosystem Approach in Anthropology: From Concept to Practice 1162

Environmental Social Science: Human - Environment interactions and Sustainability 1077

Human Adaptability: An Introduction to Ecological Anthropology 1162

People and Nature: An Introduction to Human Ecological Relations **1162**

Through Amazonian Eyes: The Human Ecology of Amazonian Populations 1162

Moran, Jack

An Introduction to Theoretical and Computational Aerodynamics **1163**

Moran, Joseph M.

Weather Studies: Introduction to Atmospheric Science 1229

Moran, Michelle Therese

Colonizing Leprosy: Imperialism and the Politics of Public Health in the United States 861

Moran, William

The Belles of New England: The Women of the Textile Mills and the Families Whose Wealth They Wove 871

Morduch, Jonathon

Portfolios of the Poor: How the World Poor Live on $2 Per Day 1330

Moreton, Bethany

To Serve God and Wal-Mart: The Making of Christian Free Enterprise **801**

Morgan, Jessica

Go Fug Yourself: The Fug Awards 888, **906**

Morgan, Lee

Reaper's Line: Life and Death on the Mexican Border 1275

Morgan, Tracy

I Am the New Black 133

Morgen, Sandra

Into Our Own Hands: The Women's Health Movement in the United States, 1969-1990 702

Morin, Christophe

Neuromarketing: Understanding the Buy Buttons in Your Customer's Brain 381, 407, **429**

O

O'Berry, Denise
Small Business Cash Flow: Strategies for Making Your Business a Financial Success 458

O'Brien, Cormac
Secret Lives of the First Ladies: What Your Teachers Never Told You About the Women of The White House 52

O'Brien, Frank
The Apollo Guidance Computer 1157

O'Brien, Geoffrey
The Fall of the House of Walworth: A Tale of Madness and Murder in Gilded Age America 999

O'Brien, Harvey
Keeping it Real: Irish Film and Television 101

O'Brien, Stacey
Wesley the Owl: The Remarkable Love Story of an Owl and His Girl 986

O'Brien, Susan
Gluten-free, Sugar-free Cooking: Over 200 Delicious Recipes to Help You Live a Healthier, Allergy-Free Life 520, 605

O'Brien, Tim
The Things They Carried 317, 323

O'Callaghan, Chris
Practical Paediatric Procedures 586
The Renal System at a Glance 491, **586**

O'Connell, Diog
New Irish Storytellers: Narrative Strategies in Film **101**

O'Connell, Jennifer
Everything I Needed to Know About Being a Girl I Learned from Judy Blume 25, **992**, 1020
Local Girls 992
Plan B 992
Rich Boys 992

O'Connor, Flannery
The Complete Stories 166
Flannery O'Connor : Collected Works : Wise Blood / A Good Man Is Hard to Find / The Violent Bear It Away / Everything that Rises Must Converge / Essays & Letters 225
The Habit of Being: Letters 225

O'Donnell, Rosie
Celebrity Detox (The Fame Game) 169, **993**
Find Me 993
Kids Are Punny 993
Rosie O'Donnell's Crafty U: 100 Easy Projects the Whole Family Can Enjoy All Year Long 993

O'Donovan, Susan Eva
Becoming Free in the Cotton South 816, 833
Freedom: A Documentary History of Emancipation, 1861-1867: Series 3, Vol. 1: Land and Labor, 1865 816

O'Hara, Maureen
'Tis Herself: A Memoir 318

O'Keefe, Kevin
Average American: The Extraordinary Search for the Nation's Most Ordinary Citizen 243, **1319**

O'Meara, Alex
Chasing Medical Miracles: The Promise and Perils of Clinical Trials 1235

O'Meara, Stephen James
Deep-Sky Companions: Hidden Treasures 1173
Deep-Sky Companions: The Messier Objects 1173
Exploring the Solar System with Binoculars 1173
Observing the Night Sky with Binoculars: A Simple Guide to the Heavens 1173
Stephen James O'Meara's Observing the Night Sky with Binoculars: A Simple Guide to the Heavens **1173**
Steve O'Meara's Herschel 400 Observing Guide 1173

O'Neal, Paul W.
Motivation of Health Behavior 536

O'Neal, Tatum
A Paper Life 265, 285, 920

O'Reilly, Ann
Consumed: Rethinking Business in the Era of Mindful Spending 1310

O'Reilly, Bill
A Bold Fresh Piece of Humanity 281, 298

O'Shea, Tara
Chicks Dig Time Lords: A Celebration of Doctor Who by the Women Who Love It 31, 76

O'Sullivan, Shane
Who Killed Bobby?: The Unsolved Murder of Robert F. Kennedy 1344

Oates, Stephen B.
With Malice Toward None: A Life of Abraham Lincoln 270

Oatis, Carol A.
Kinesiology: The Mechanics and Pathomechanics of Human Movement, Second Edition **1174**

Odell, Donald
Union and Liberty: A Documentary History of American Constitutionalism 752

of Flight 1549, The Survivors
Miracle on the Hudson: The Survivors of Flight 1549 Tell Their Extraordinary Stories of Courage, Faith, and Determination 1030

of Life, Editors
The Kennedys: End of a Dynasty 250

Offit, Paul A.
Autism's False Prophets: Bad Science, Risky Medicine, and the Search for a Cure **587**, 1175
The Cutter Incident: How America's First Polio Vaccine Led to the Growing Vaccine Crisis 1175
Deadly Choices: How the Anti-Vaccine Movement Threatens Us All 1175
Vaccinated: One Man's Quest to Defeat the World's Deadliest Diseases 1134, **1175**, 587
Vaccines 587

Vaccines and Your Child: Separating Fact from Fiction 587

Ohno, Kazuo
Kazuo Ohno's World: From Without and Within 45

Ohno, Yoshito
Kazuo Ohno's World: From Without and Within 45

Ohnuki-Tierney, Emiko
Kamikaze Diaries: Reflections of Japanese Student Soldiers 845

Okihiro, Gary
Margins and Mainstreams: Asians in American History and Culture 759

Okpewho, Isidore
The African Diaspora: African Origins and New World Identities 789

Okrant, Robyn
Living Oprah: My One-Year Experiment to Walk the Walk of the Queen of Talk 248, 956, **994**, 1294

Okrent, Daniel
Baseball Anecdotes 1320
Great Fortune: The Epic of Rockefeller Center 1320
Last Call: The Rise and Fall of Prohibition 1234, 1266, **1320**
Nine Innings 1320
Public Editor #1: The Collected Columns (with Reflections, Reconsiderations, and Even a Few Retractions) of the First Ombudsman of The New York Times 1320
Way We Were: New England Then New England Now 1320

Olbermann, Keith
Worst Person in the World: And 202 Strong Contenders 1305

Olderman, Rick
Fixing You: Back Pain 505, **588**
Fixing You: Back Pain During Pregnancy 588
Fixing You: Neck Pain and Headaches 588
Fixing You: Shoulder and Elbow Pain 588

Oldershaw, Cally
Gems of the World 1176
Gemstones 1176
Guide to Gems **1176**, 1196

Olds, Jacqueline
The Lonely American: Drifting Apart in the Twenty-first Century 1315

Oldstone, Michael
Viruses, Plagues, and History 736

Oleckno, William Anton
Epidemiology: Concepts and Methods 496, 519, 565, 574

Olfshski, Robert
Agendas and Decisions 193

Olien, Diana Davids
Oil in Texas: The Gusher Age, 1895-1945 685

Olien, Roger M.
Oil in Texas: The Gusher Age, 1895-1945 685
Wildcatters: Texas Independent Oilmen 685

Oliver, Duncan
Cape Cod Shore Whaling: America First Whalemen 705

Oliver, J. Eric
Fat Politics: The Real Story behind America's Obesity Epidemic 538

Oliver, Jamie
The Naked Chef 896

Oliver, Suzanne
The Faith Club: A Muslim, a Christian, a Jew—Three Women Search for Understanding **1290**, 1317

Oliver, Vicky
Bad Bosses, Crazy Coworkers & Other Office Idiots: 201 Smart Ways to Handle the Toughest People 1259

Olivier, Charles P.
Meteors 1138, 1144

Ollestad, Norman
Crazy for the Storm: A Memoir of Survival 230

Olmos, Margarite Fernandez
The Latino Reader: An American Literary Tradition from 1542 to the Present 93

Olmos, Margarite Fernandez
Healing Cultures: Art and Religion as Curative Practices in the Caribbean and Its Diaspora 757

Olsen, Ashley
Influence 906, **995**

Olsen, John Charles
A Text-Book of Quantitative Chemical Analysis by Gravimetric, Electrolytic, Volumetric and Gasometric Methods 1113

Olsen, Mary-Kate
Influence 906, **995**
Mary-Kate & Ashley's Passport to Paris Scrapbook 995

Olson, Anna Dee
Growing Up Amish: Insider Secrets from One Woman's Inspirational Journey 1342

Olson, Kent R.
Poisoning And Drug Overdose 552, 599

Olson, Lynette
The Early Middle Ages: The Birth of Europe 873

Olson, Lynne
Citizens of London: The Americans Who Stood with Britain in Its Darkest, Finest Hour 817
Freedom's Daughters: The Unsung Heroines of the Civil Rights Movement from 1830 to 1970 817, 695
The Murrow Boys: Pioneers on fthe Front Lines of Broadcast Journalism 817
Troublesome Young Men: The Rebels Who Brought Churchill to Power and Helped Save England **817**

Olupona, Jacob K.
Orisa Devotion as World Religion: The Globalization of Yoruba Religious Culture 102

Omari-Tunkara, Mikelle S.
Manipulating the Sacred: Yoruba Art, Ritual,and Resistance in Brazilian Candomble **102**

Parker, Laura
Miracle on the Hudson: The Survivors of Flight 1549 Tell Their Extraordinary Stories of Courage, Faith, and Determination 1030

Parker, Lewis K.
Cornelius Vanderbilt and the Railroad Industry 311

Parker, Matthew
Panama Fever: The Epic Story of One of the Greatest Human Achievements of All Time—the Building of the Panama Canal 735

Parker, Philip M.
Sickle Cell Anemia: A Bibliography and Dictionary for Physicians, Patients and Genome Researchers 465, 466

Parker, Steve
Comets, Asteroids and Meteors 1086
Fossil Hunting 1156

Parker, Trey
South Park Guide to Life 148

Parks, Ted
Crossing with the Virgin: Stories from the Migrant Trail 1275

Parks, Tim
Medici Money: Banking, Metaphysics and Art in Fifteenth-century Florence 769

Parles, Karen
100 Questions and Answers About Lung Cancer 570

Parrish, Susan Scott
American Curiosity: Cultures of Natural History in the Colonial British Atlantic World 840

Parsons, Timothy
The Rule of Empires: Those Who Built Them, Those Who Endured Them, and Why They Always Fail 699

Partington, John
The Mob and Me: Wiseguys and the Witness Protection Program 1266

Pascal, Cybele
Allergen-Free Baker's Handbook 520, 605

Pascale, Richard
The Power of Positive Deviance: How Unlikely Innovators Solve the World's Toughest Problems 1283, 1287, 1369

Pascoe, Peggy
Relations of Rescue: The Search for Female Moral Authority in the American West, 1874-1939 821
What Comes Naturally: Miscegenation Law and the Making of Race in America 799, **821**

Pasqualini, Jorge R.
Breast Cancer: Prognosis, Treatment, and Prevention 575

Passarge, Eberhard
Color Atlas of Genetics 1114

Pasternak, Mariana
Best of Friends: Martha and Me 1373

Patel, Aniruddh D.
Music, Language, and the Brain 1137, **1180**

Patel, Raj
Stuffed and Starved: The Hidden Battle for the World Food System 1243, 1268, 1352

Patten, Bernard M.
The Logic of Alice: Clear Thinking in Wonderland 59

Patterson, James
Against Medical Advice 1274

Patterson, Kerry
Influencer: The Power to Change Anything 379

Patterson, Romaine
The Whole World Was Watching: Living in the Light of Matthew Shepard 1018

Patterson, Scott
The Quants: How a New Breed of Math Whizzes Conquered Wall Street and Nearly Destroyed It 1296, 1311, 1348

Pattillo, Mary
Black on the Block: The Politics of Race and Class in the City 726

Patton, David R.
Forest Wildlife Ecology and Habitat Management 1152

Patton, George
War as I Knew It 657

Patzer, Gordon
Experiment-Research Methodology in Marketing: Types and Applications 1322
Looks: Why They Matter More Than You Ever Imagined **1322**, 1328
The Physical Attractiveness Phenomena (Perspectives in Social Psychology) 1322

Patzer, Gordon L.
The Power and Paradox of Physical Attractiveness 1322, 1328

Patzer, Gordon
The Power and Paradox of Physical Attractiveness 1322
Using Secondary Data in Marketing Research: United States and Worldwide 1322
Why Physically Attractive People Are More Successful: The Scientific Explanation, Social Consequences And Ethical Problems 1322

Paul, Eldor Alvin
Soil Microbiology, Ecology and Biochemistry 1183, 1207

Paul, Joel Richard
Unlikely Allies: How a Merchant, a Playwright, and a Spy Saved the American Revolution **822**

Pavlat, Leo
Jewish Folk Tales 4

Paxton, Robert O.
Europe in the Twentieth Century 758

Pearce, Fred
When the Rivers Run Dry: Water—The Defining Crisis of the Twenty-First Century 1276
With Speed and Violence: Why Scientists Fear Tipping Points in Climate Change 1069

Pearce, Nancy
Inside Alzheimer's: How to Hear and Honor Connections with a Person Who Has Dementia **592**

Pearlman, Michael D.
Truman and MacArthur: Policy, Politics, and the Hunger for Honor and Renown 724

Pearlman, Moshe
Digging Up the Bible: The Stories Behind the Great Archeological Discoveries in the Holy Land 727

Pearlman, Robb
The Q Guide to Sex and the City: Stuff You Didn't Even Know You Wanted to Know...about Carrie, Samantha, Miranda, and Charlotte...and Cosmos 67

Pearson, Christine
The Cost of Bad Behavior: How Incivility Is Damaging Your Business and What to Do About It 1354

Peate, Ian
Manual of Sexually Transmitted Infections 488, 524, 581
Men's Sexual Health 583

Peavy, Linda
Pioneer Women: The Lives of Women on the Frontier 756

Peck, Garrett
The Prohibition Hangover: Alcohol in America from Demon Rum to Cult Cabernet 1320

Peckenpaugh, Nancy J.
Nutrition Essentials and Diet Therapy, 11th Edition **593**, 604
Real Cowboys Eat Beans: For Cowboys and the Women Who Love 'Em 593

Pecorino, Lauren
Molecular Biology of Cancer: Mechanisms, Targets, and Therapeutics, Second Edition **1181**, 1190

Peebles Cookery, Peebles Cookery
The Ultimate Gout Cookbook 555

Pelzer, Dave
A Child Called "It": An Abused Child's Journey from Victim to Victor 326

Penenberg, Adam L.
Viral Loop: From Facebook to Twitter, How Today's Smartest Businesses Grow Themselves **424**

Penn, Mark J.
Microtrends: The Small Forces Behind Tomorrow's Big Changes 1272

Penzler, Otto
The Best American Crime Reporting 2009 1014
The Black Lizard Big Book of Pulps 42

Peppercorn, Mark A.
Contemporary Diagnosis and Management of Ulcerative Colitis and Proctitis 603

Pera, Gina
Is It You, Me, or Adult A.D.D.? 467, 589

Perdue, Theda
Slavery and the Evolution of Cherokee Society: 1540-1866 797

Perez, Louis A. Jr.
Hitler's Man in Havana: Heinz Luning and Nazi Espionage in Latin America 257

Perez, Venus
I'm Still Here 483

Perez, William
We ARE Americans: Undocumented Students Pursuing the American Dream 1357

Perkins, Donald
Particle Astrophysics 1064

Perlstein, Rick
Before the Storm: Barry Goldwater and the Unmaking of the American Consensus 282
Nixonland: The Rise of a President and the Fracturing of America 282
The Stock Ticker and the Super Jumbo: How the Democrats Can Once Again Become America's Dominant Political Party 282

Perret, Geoffrey
Old Soldiers Never Die: The Life of Douglas Macarthur 724

Perrucci, Dorianne
I.O.U.S.A. **457**

Perry, Dan
Blackbeard: The Real Pirate of the Caribbean 860

Perry, Dennis R.
Poe, "The House of Usher," and the American Gothic 32

Perry, Douglas
The Girls of Murder City: Fame, Lust, and the Beautiful Killers Who Inspired Chicago **999**, 1234, 1266

Perry, Elizabeth J.
Chinese Society: Change, Conflict and Resistance 773

Persico, Joseph
My American Journey 185

Pescatore, Fred
The Allergy and Asthma Cure: A Complete 8-Step Nutritional Program 566

Peskowitz, Miriam
The Daring Book for Girls **25**, 992, 1020

Petechuk, David
Organ Transplantation 606

Peters, John Douglas
Motor City Rock and Roll: The 1960's and 1970's 53

Petersen, Barry
Jan's Story: Love Lost to the Long Goodbye of Alzheimer's **283**, 549, 573

Peterson, Brian
Burning Fight: The Nineties Hardcore Revolution in Ethics, Politics, Spirit, and Sound 987

Peterson, Dale
Eating Apes 284

Porter, Lynnette

Lost's Buried Treasures, 3E: The Unofficial Guide to Everything Lost Fans Need to Know 153

Posner, Kenneth A.

Stalking the Black Swan: Research and Decision Making in a World of Extreme Volatility 1356

Posner, Michael

The Last Honest Man: Mordecai Richler: an Oral Biography 199

Post, Peggy

Emily Post's Etiquette, 17th Edition 904

Postel, Charles

The Populist Vision **824**

Postgate, J.N.

Early Mesopotamia: Society and Economy at the Dawn of History 659

Postman, Neil

Technopoly: The Surrender of Culture to Technology 159

Postolowski, Ellen

It's Just Personal: A Personal Chef's Essential Guide to Shopping, Cooking, and Eating Smarter 593, 617

Potter, David M.

Impending Crisis, 1848-1861 291

Potts, Jeanette M.

Genitourinary Pain and Inflammation: Diagnosis and Management **597**, 612

Potts, Joanna

Warlords: An Extraordinary Recreation of World War II Through the Eyes and Minds of Hitler, Churchill, Roosevelt and Stalin 684

Poulter, J.D.

An Early History of Electricity Supply: The Story of the Electric Light in Victorian Leeds 819

Poundstone, William

Priceless: The Myth of Fair Value (and How to Take Advantage of It) 418

Powaski, Ronald E.

The Cold War: The United States and the Soviet Union, 1917-1991 729, 774

Powell, Colin L.

My American Journey 185

Powell, James Lawrence

Grand Canyon: Solving Earth's Grandest Puzzle 1109

Powell, Julie

Cleaving 1002

Cleaving: A Story of Marriage, Meat, and Obsession 929, **1003**

Julie & Julia: 365 Days, 524 Recipes, 1 Tiny Apartment Kitchen: How One Girl Risked Her Marriage, Her Job, & Her Sanity to Master the Art of Living **1002**, 1003

Powell, Michael

A Life in Movies: An Autobiography 90, 130

Power, James IV D.

Satisfaction: How Every Great Company Listens to the Voice of the Customer **427**

Powers, Dennis

The Internet Legal Guide: Everything You Need to Know When Doing Business Online 1325

The Raging Sea: The Powerful Account of the Worst Tsunami in U.S. History 1325

Sentinel of the Seas: Life and Death at the Most Dangerous Lighthouse Ever Built 664, **1325**

Powers, Dennis M.

Taking the Sea: Perilous Waters, Sunken Ships, and the True Story of the Legendary Wrecker Captains 664, 1325

Powers, Dennis

Taking the Sea: Perilous Waters, Sunken Ships, and the True Story of the Legendary Wrecker Captains 1325

Tales of the Seven Seas: The Escapades of Captain Dynamite Johnny O'Brien 1325

Powers, Dennis M.

Treasure Ship: The Legend and Legacy of the S.S. Brother Jonathan 1325

Powers, Dennis

Treasure Ship: The Legend And Legacy of the S.S. Brother Jonathan 1325

Powers, Ron

Flags of Our Fathers 287

Last Flag Down: The Epic Journey of the Last Confederate Warship 287

Mark Twain: A Life **287**

Tom and Huck Don't Live Here Anymore 287

Powers-Douglas, Minda

Cemetery Walk: Journey into the Art, History and Society of the Cemetery and Beyond 884

Powrie, Phil

Changing Tunes: The Use of Pre-existing Music in Film **107**

French Cinema in the 1990s: Continuity and Difference 107

French Cinema: A Student's Guide 107

The Trouble with Men: Masculinities in European and Hollywood Cinema 107

Pradeep, A.K.

The Buying Brain: Secrets for Selling to the Subconscious Mind 429

Praeger, Dave

Poop Culture: How America Is Shaped by Its Grossest National Product 928, 959

Prager, Brad

The Collapse of the Conventional: German Film and Its Politics at the Turn of the Twenty-First Century **44**

Prasad, Kedar N.

Bio-Shield, Antioxidants Against Radiological, Chemical and Biological Weapons 1078

Pratt, Mary K.

Pandemics 547

Pressfield, Steven

Gates of Fire: An Epic Novel of the Battle of Thermopylae 690

Pressner, Amanda

The Lost Girls: Three Friends. Four Continents. One Unconventional Detour Around the World 1373

Preston, Andrew

Nixon in the World: American Foreign Relations, 1969-1977 697, 783

Preston, Douglas

The Book of the Dead (Pendergast, Book 7) 1326

Brimstone (Pendergast, Book 5) 1326

The Cabinet of Curiosities (Pendergast, Book 3) 1326

Cemetary Dance (Pendergast, Book 9) 1326

Dance of Death 1326

Fever Dream 1326

The Ice Limit 1326

Impact 1326

The Monster of Florence **1326**

Relic (Pendergast, Book 1) 1326

Reliquary (Pendergast, Book 2) 1326

Riptide 1326

Still Life With Crows (Pendergast, Book 4) 1326

Thunderhead 1326

Prestowitz, Clyde

Three Billion New Capitalists: The Great Shift of Wealth and Power to the East 433

Pretor-Pinney, Gavin

The Cloud Collector's Handbook 1184

The Cloudspotter's Guide: The Science, History, and Culture of Clouds 1184

Previc, Fred H.

The Dopaminergic Mind in Human Evolution and History **1185**, 1201

Price, Barbara Raffel

The Criminal Justice System and Women: Offenders, Prisoners, Victims and Workers 88

Price, Brian

On Michael Haneke **108**

Price, David A.

Love and Hate in Jamestown 109

The Pixar Touch **109**

Price, J.L.

The Dutch Republic in the Seventeenth Century 731

Price, Norma A.

Crossing with the Virgin: Stories from the Migrant Trail 1275

Price, Richard

Making Empire: Colonial Encounters and the Creation of Imperial Rule in Nineteenth-Century Africa 688

Maroon Societies: Rebel Slave Communities in the Americas 669

Princiotta, Frank

Global Climate Change - The Technology Challenge 1061

Prochaska, David

Making Algeria French: Colonialism in Bone, 1870-1920 700

Prochnau, William

Miracle on the Hudson: The Survivors of Flight 1549 Tell Their Extraordinary Stories of Courage, Faith, and Determination 1030

Prochnik, George

In Pursuit of Silence: Listening for Meaning in a World of Noise 1124, **1186**, 1288

Putnam Camp: Sigmund Freud, James Jackson Putnam, and the Purpose of American Psychology 1186

Project, Tectonic Theater

The Laramie Project 1018

Prothero, Stephen R.

God Is Not One: The Eight Rival Religions That Run the World—and Why Their Differences Matter 653

Proud, David

The Pulmonary Epithelium in Health and Disease **598**, 642

Provenza, Paul

Poop Culture: How America Is Shaped by Its Grossest National Product 928, 959

Prud'homme, Alex

My Life in France 1002, 1003

Prunier, Gerard

Darfur: A 21st Century Genocide 723

Pula, James S.

Thaddeus Kosciuszko: The Purest Son of Liberty 857

Pulido, Laura

Black, Brown, Yellow, and Left: Radical Activism in Los Angeles 770

Pullinger, Kate

The Piano 110

Puls, Mark

Uncommon Valor: A Story of Race, Patriotism, and Glory in the Final Battles of the Civil War 654

Pupecki, Sandra R.

Focus on Genetic Screening Research 1212

Purkiss, Diane

The English Civil War: Papists, Gentlewomen, Soldiers, and Witchfinders in the Birth of Modern Britain 706

Purvis, Alston

Vendetta: Special Agent Melvin Purvis, John Dillinger, and Hoover's FBI in the Age of Gangsters 1279

Pyne, Stephen J.

Voyager: Seeking Newer Worlds in the Third Great Age of Discovery 1199

Pyron, Darden Asbury

Liberace: An American Boy 318

Q

Qiang, Ning

Art, Religion, and Politics in Medi-

eval China: The Dunhuang Cave of the Zhai Family 145

Qualman, Erik
Socialnomics: How Social Media Transforms the Way We Live and Do Business 351, 1287

Queenan, Joe
Closing Time: A Memoir **288**
If You're Talking to Me, Your Career Must Be in Trouble: Movies, Mayhem, and Malice 288
Malcontents 288
Queenan Country: A Reluctant Anglophile's Pilgrimage to the Mother Country 288
Red Lobster, White Trash and the Blue Lagoon: Joe Queenan's America 288
True Believers: The Tragic Inner Life of Sports Fans 288

Queijo, Jon
Breakthrough!: How the 10 Greatest Discoveries in Medicine Saved Millions and Changed Our View of the World 464, 535, 596

Quigley, Joan
The Day the Earth Caved In: Am American Mining Tragedy 708

Quinn, Campion
100 Questions and Answers About Congestive Heart Failure 622

Quinn, Robert E.
Change the World : How Ordinary People Can Achieve Extraordinary Results 39, 47

Quintero del Rio, Ana I.
Lupus: A Patient's Guide to Diagnosis, Treatment, and Lifestyle 637

Quirk, Joe
Sperm are from Men, Eggs are from Women 1335

Quirk, Kevin
Brace for Impact: Miracle on the Hudson Survivors Share Their Stories of Near Death and Hope for New Life 1030

Quivers, Robin
Quivers: A Life 970

R

Rabin, Nathan
The Big Rewind: A Memoir Brought to You by Pop Culture 905, 966, **1004**, 1017
My Year of Flops: The A.V. Club Presents One Man's Journey Deep into the Heart of Cinematic Failure 905, 966, 996, 997, 1017, 1004

Rabinovich, Itamar
Waging Peace: Israel and the Arabs, 1948-2003 802

Rachlin, Nahid
Persian Girls: A Memoir 215

Rackstraw, Loree
Love as Always, Kurt: Vonnegut as I Knew Him **1005**

Radin, Dean
Entangled Minds: Extrasensory Experiences in a Quantum Reality 1133

Radner, Hilary
Cinema Genre 110
Jane Campion: Cinema, Nation, Identity **110**
Neo-Feminist Cinema: Girly Films, Chick Flicks, and Consumer Culture 110
Siegfried Sassoon: The Journey From The Trenches, A Biography (1918-1967) 110

Raeburn, John
Ben Shahn's American Scene 111
Fame Became of Him 111
A Staggering Revolution: A Cultural History of Thirties Photography **111**

Raengo, Alessandra
Literature and Film: A Guide to the Theory and Practice of Film Adaptation 36

Rafuse, Ethan Sepp
Robert E. Lee and the Fall of the Confederacy 1863-1865 834

Raiford, Leigh
The Civil Rights Movement in American Memory 830

Rains, Jessica
Claude Rains: An Actor's Voice 127

Rajan, Raghuram
Fault Lines: How Hidden Fractures Still Threaten the World Economy 1330

Rajapakse, Ruwan
Geotechnical Engineering Calculations and Rules of Thumb 1217

Rakieten, Ellen
Undateable: 311 Things Guys Do That Guarantee They Won't Be Dating or Having Sex 1335, 1343

Rakoff, David
Don't Get Too Comfortable: The Indignities of Coach Class, The Torments of Low Thread Count, The Never-Ending Quest for Artisanal Olive Oil, and Other First World Problems 892, 951, 952, **1006**, 1019, 1040
Fraud: Essays 1006

Rakove, Jack
Revolutionaries: A New History of the Invention of America 768, 822, 850

Ralph, James Jr. R.
Northern Protest: Martin Luther King, Jr., Chicago, and the Civil Rights Movement 858

Ralston, Aron
Between a Rock and a Hard Place 301

Ramon, Ana-Christina
Black Los Angeles: American Dreams and Racial Realities 770

Ramone, Dee Dee
Lobotomy: Surviving the Ramones 1022

Ramotowski, Becky
Secrets of Stargazing 1053, 1093, 1173

Rampersad, Arnold
Jackie Robinson: A Biography 289
The Life of Langston Hughes: Volume I: 1902-1941, I, Too, Sing America 289
Ralph Ellison: A Biography **289**

Ramsey, Sonya
Reading, Writing, and Segregation: A Century of Black Women Teachers in Nashville **112**

Rand, Ayn
Anthem 236
Atlas Shrugged 236
The Fountainhead 236

Rane, Abhay
Urinary Tract Infections: Questions and Answers 612

Rapaport, Brooke Kamin
Houdini: Art and Magic 123

Rapp, Donald
Assessing Climate Change: Temperatures, Solar Radiation and Heat Balance 1187
Human Missions to Mars: Enabling Technologies for Exploring the Red Planet 1056, **1187**
Ice Ages and Interglacials: Measurements, Interpretation and Models 1187

Rappaport, Doreen
Eleanor, Quiet No More 312
Freedom River 237

Rashid, A.
Introduction to Genetic Engineering of Crop Plants: Aims and Achievements 1171

Rask, Robin
Work Ethics and the Generation Gap: Which Ethical Track Are You On? 1298

Ratcliffe, Martin
State of the Universe 2008: New Images, Discoveries, and Events 1214

Ratey, Nancy A.
The Disorganized Mind: Coaching Your ADHD Brain to Take Control of Your Time, Tasks, and Talents 633

Rathbone, Christina
A World Apart: Women, Prison, and Life Behind Bars 1303

Rathbone, John Paul
Ecuador, the Galapagos, & Columbia 825
The Sugar King of Havana: The Rise and Fall of Julio Cobo, Cuba's Last Tycoon 715, **825**

Ravitch, Diane
The American Reader: Words That Moved a Nation 1327
The Death and Life of the Great American School System: How Testing and Choice Are Undermining Education 1267, 1323, **1327**
EdSpeak: A Glossary of Education Terms, Phrases, Buzzwords, and Jargon 1327
The English Reader: What Every Literate Person Needs to Know 1327

The Great School Wars: A History of the New York City Public Schools 1327
The Language Police: How Pressure Groups Restrict What Students Learn 1327
Left Back: A Century of Battles over School Reform 1327
National Standards in American Education: A Citizen's Guide 1327
The Schools We Deserve 1327

Rawlings, Deirdre
Food that Helps Win the Battle Against Fibromyalgia 629, 646

Ray, Deborah Kogan
Dinosaur Mountain: Digging into the Jurassic Age 290
Down the Colorado: John Wesley Powell, the One-Armed Explorer 290
Flying Eagle 290
To Go Singing Through the World: The Childhood of Pablo Neruda 290
Wanda Gag: The Girl Who Lived to Draw **290**

Rayman, Margaret
Healthy Eating for Prostate Care 501, 540, 553

Raz, Aviad E.
Community Genetics and Genetic Alliances 1082, 1212

Reay, Pauline
Music in Film: Soundtracks and Synergy 62, 107

Record, Ian W.
Big Sycamore Stands Alone: The Western Apaches, Aravaipa, and the Struggle for Place 754

Redden, Kenneth G.
My Song: Comatose Yet Aware 645

Rediker, Marcus
Between the Devil and the Deep Blue Sea: Merchant Seamen, Pirates and the Anglo-American Maritime World, 1700-1750 826
The Slave Ship: A Human History **826**
Villains of All Nations: Atlantic Pirates in the Golden Age 826

Redmond, Geoffrey
It's Your Hormones 616

Reece, Erik
Lost Mountain: A Year in the Vanishing Wilderness: Radical Strip Mining and the Devastation of Appalachia 1241

Reed, Betsy
Going Rouge: An American Nightmare 281

Reef, Catherine
Ernest Hemingway: A Writer's Life 43

Rees, Martin
Our Final Hour: A Scientist's Warning: How Terror, Error, and Environmental Disaster Threaten Humanity's Future in This Century 159

Reeve, Christopher
Nothing Is Impossible: Reflections on a New Life 922

Riis, Jacob A.
How the Other Half Lives 983

Riley-Smith, Jonathan
The Crusades: A History 832

Rilke, Ina
Balzac and the Little Chinese Seamstress 196

Rimmerman, Curtis M.
The Cleveland Clinic Guide to Heart Attack 509, 609

Rinear, David L.
Stage, Page, Scandals and Vandals: William E. Burton and Nineteenth-Century American Theatre 158

Ringel, Edward
Little Black Book of Pulmonary Medicine **600**, 642

Rio, Robin
Connecting Through Music with People with Dementia: A Guide for Caregivers 518, **601**

Riordan, Timothy
Prince of Quacks: The Notorious Life of Dr. Francis Tumblety, Charlatan and Jack the Ripper Suspect 1326

Ripley, C. Peter
The Black Abolitionist Papers: Vol. I: The British Isles, 1830-1865 680, 747

Ritchie, Jean
The Dulcimer Book 5
Folk Songs of the Southern Appalachians as Sung by Jean Ritchie 5

Ritchie, Robert C.
Duke's Province: A Study of New York Politics and Society, 1664-1691 752

Ritholtz, Barry
Bailout Nation: How Greed and Easy Money Corrupted Wall Street and Shook the World Economy **431**
Greenspans Bubbles- The Age of Ignorance at the Federal Reserve 431

Ritter, Lawrence
The Glory of Their Times: The Story of the Early Days of Baseball Told by the Men Who Played It 985

Ritz, David
The Adventures of Grandmaster Flash: My Life, My Beats **1007**
Journey of a Thousand Miles: My Story 253
Rickles' Book: A Memoir 213
We'll Be Here for the Rest of Our Lives: A Swingin' Show-Biz Saga 910, 996

Rivenbark, Celia
Belle Weather: Mostly Sunny with a Chance of Scattered Hissy Fits 1008
Stop Dressing Your Six-Year-Old Like a Skank: And Other Words of Delicate Southern Wisdom 989, **1008**
We're Just Like You, Only Prettier: Confessions of a Tarnished Southern Belle 1008
You Can't Drink All Day If You Don't Start in the Morning 1008

Rivera, Diego
Diego Rivera: The Detroit Industry Murals 91

Rivers, Joan
Men Are Stupid ... And They Like Big Boobs: A Woman's Guide to Beauty Through Plastic Surgery 213

Rivers, Larry Eugene
The Varieties of Women's Experiences: Portraits of Southern Women in the Post-Civil War Century 833

Rivlin, Gary
Broke, USA: From Pawnshops to Poverty, Inc.: How the Working Poor Became Big Business 1265, **1330**
Drive By 1330
Fire on the Prairie: Chicago's Harold Washington and the Politics of Race 1330
The Godfather of Silicon Valley: Ron Conway and the Fall of the Dot-coms 1330
The Plot to Get Bill Gates: An Irreverent Investigation of the World's Richest Man... and the People Who Hate Him 1330

Rivoli, Pietra
The Travels of a T-Shirt in the Global Economy: An Economist Examines the Markets, Power, and Politics of World Trade 925, 926, 1273, 1330

Roach, Mary
Bonk: The Curious Coupling of Science and Sex 1009, 1331
Bonk: The Curious Coupling of Sex and Science 908, **1010**, 1297, 1304, 1331, 1335
Packing for Mars: The Curious Science of Life in the Void **1009**, 1010, 1331
Packing for Mars: the Curious Science of Life in the Void 1010
Packing for Mars: The Curious Science of Life in the Void 1331
Spook: Science Tackles the Afterlife 1010, **1331**, 1009, 1010
Stiff: The Curious Lives of Human Cadavers 1009, 1010, 1331

Roam, Dan
The Back of the Napkin: Solving Problems and Selling Ideas with Pictures **432**
Unfolding the Napkin: The Hands-On Method for Solving Complex Problems with Simple Pictures 432

Robb, Brian J.
Timeless Adventures: How Doctor Who Conquered TV 31, 76

Robb, John
Brave New War: The Next Stage of Terrorism and the End of Globalization 755

Robbins, Alexandra
Conquering Your Quarterlife Crisis: Advice from Twentysomethings Who Have Been There and Survived 1332
The Overachievers: The Secret Lives of Driven Kids **1332**

Pledged: The Secret Life of Sororities 1332
Quarterlife Crisis: The Unique Challenges of Life in Your Twenties 1332
Secrets of the Tomb: Skull and Bones, the Ivy League, and the Hidden Paths of Power 1332

Roberts, Andrew
Hitler and Churchill: Secrets of Leadership 684

Roberts, Barbara H.
Treating And Beating Heart Disease: A Consumer's Guide To Cardiac Medicines 621

Roberts, Chris
Michael Jackson: The King of Pop 1958-2009 124

Roberts, Cokie
Founding Mothers: The Women Who Raised Our Nation 829
From This Day Forward 829
Ladies of Liberty: The Women Who Shaped Our Nation **829**
We Are Our Mothers' Daughters 829, 324

Roberts, Daniel L.
The First Year: Age-Related Macular Degeneration: An Essential Guide for the Newly Diagnosed 551

Roberts, Gene
The Race Beat: The Press, the Civil Rights Struggle, and the Awakening of a Nation **830**

Roberts, John W.
Reform and Retribution: An Illustrated History of American Prisons 734, 794

Roberts, Keith
Handbook of Plant Science 1149

Roberts, Patrick A.
Give 'Em Soul, Richard!: Race, Radio, and Rhythm and Blues in Chicago 33

Roberts, Randy
Joe Louis: Hard Times Man 261

Roberts, Russell
The Choice: A Fable of Free Trade and Protection, 3rd Edition **433**
The Price of Everything: A Parable of Possibility and Prosperity 401, 433
Tony Ray-Jones 433

Roberts, Steven V.
From Every End of This Earth: 13 Families and the New Lives They Made in America 388

Robinson, Cecil
No Short Journeys: The Interplay of Cultures in the History and Literature of the Borderlands 754

Robinson, Katrina
ALS: Lou Gehrig's Disease Patient Advocate 576

Robinson, Patrick
A Colossal Failure of Common Sense: The Inside Story of the Collapse of Lehman Brothers 359

Robson, Philip
Forbidden Drugs 546

Rock, Peter
My Abandonment 326

Rock, Sha
The Story Of The Beginning and End Of The First Hip Hop Female MC...Luminary Icon Sha-Rock 115

Rockett, Kevin
National Cinemas And World Cinema (Studies in Irish Film) 101

Rockwell, Anne
Big George: How a Shy Boy Became President Washington **295**
Clouds 295
My Preschool 295
Only Passing Through: The Story of Sojourner Truth 237
Presidents' Day 295
What's So Bad About Gasoline?: Fossil Fuels and What They Do 295

Rodger, Gillian M.
Champagne Charlie and Pretty Jemima: Variety Theater in the Nineteenth Century **114**

Rodger, N.A.M.
The Command of the Ocean: A Naval History of Britain, 1649-1815 803, **831**
The Insatiable Earl: A Life of John Mantagu, Fourth Earl of Sandwich 1718-1792 831
The Safeguard of the Sea: A Naval History of Britain 660-1649 831
The Wooden World: An Anatomy of the Georgian Navy 831

Rodgers, Joni
Promise Me: How a Sister's Love Launched the Global Movement to End Breast Cancer 1334

Rodgers, Tom
The Perfect Distance: Training for Long-Course Triathlons 497, **602**

Rodley, Chris
Lynch on Lynch, Revised Edition 80

Rodman, George R.
Mass Media in a Changing World 12

Rodriguez, Deborah
Kabul Beauty School: An American Woman Goes Behind the Veil 310

Rodriguez, Rachel Victoria
Building on Nature 296
Through Georgia's Eyes **296**

Roesner, Nina
The Respect Dare 962

Roessel, Monty
Dine : A History of the Navajos 799

Roff, Don
Zombies: A Record of the Year of Infection 898

Rogers, Douglas
The Last Resort: A Memoir of Mischief and Mayhem on a Family Farm in Africa 224, 242

Rogers, Heather
Gone Tomorrow: The Hidden Life of Garbage 1129

Rogers, Lucy
It's ONLY Rocket Science: An Introduction in Plain English **1188**

Rogers, Robert

The Fungal Pharmacy: Medicinal Mushrooms and Lichens of North America 1155

Rogerson, Barnaby

The Heirs of Muhammed: Islam's First Century and the Origins of the Sunni-Shia Split 832

The Heirs of the Prophet Muhammed: The Two Paths of Islam 832

The Last Crusaders: The Hundred-Year Battle for the Center of the World **832**

The Prophet Muhammed: A Biography 832

Rogoff, Kenneth

This Time Is Different: Eight Centuries of Financial Folly 652, 800, **827**, 1311, 1348

Rogovoy, Seth

The Essential Klezmer: A Music Lover's Guide to Jewish Roots and Soul Music, from the Old World to the Jazz Age to the Downtown Avant Garde 89

Roiphe, Anne

1185 Park Avenue: A Memoir 297

Epilogue: A Memoir **297**

An Imperfect Lens: A Novel 297

Water from the Well: Sarah, Rebekah, Rachel, and Leah 297

Roll, Jarred

Spirit of Rebellion: Labor and Religion in the New Cotton South 682

Rollins, Henry

Get in the Van: On the Road with Black Flag 987

Romano, Renee Christine

The Civil Rights Movement in American Memory 830

Romanowski, Patricia

Life Is Just What You Make It: My Story So Far 164

Romero, Brenda M.

Dancing across Borders: Danzas y Bailes Mexicanos **93**

Romney, Mitt

No Apology: The Case for American Greatness 298

Rooney, Kathleen

Reading with Oprah: The Book Club That Changed America 248

Rophie, Katie

Uncommon Arrangements: Seven Portraits of Married Life in London Literary Circles 1919-1939 174

Roscher, Brenda

How to Cook for Crohn's and Colitis: More Than 200 Healthy, Delicious Recipes the Whole Family Will Love **603**, 608

Rose, Chris

1 Dead in Attic: After Katrina 30, 679, 916

Rose, Mike

Why School? 1327

Rose, Sarah

For All the Tea in China: How England Stole the World's Favorite Drink and Changed History 1302

Rose, William K

Astrophysics **1189**

Rosen, Emanuel

The Anatomy of Buzz Revisited: Real-Life Lessons in Word-of-Mouth Marketing **434**

Rosen, Hannah

Terror in the Heart of Freedom: Citizenship, Sexual Violence, and the Meaning of Race in the Postemancipation South **833**

Rosen, Harry

The Consult Manual of Internal Medicine 597

Rosen, Larry D.

Rewired: Understanding the iGeneration and the Way They Learn 1327

Rosen, William

Justinian's Flea: Plague, Empire, and the Birth of Europe 1333

The Most Powerful Idea in the World: A Story of Steam, Industry, and Invention **1333**

Rosenbaum, Jonathan

Essential Cinema: On the Necessity of Film Canons 21

Rosenberg, Scott

Say Everything: How Blogging Began, What It's Becoming, and Why It Matters 1365

Rosenblatt, Roger

Beet: A Novel 1334

Children of War 1334

Coming Apart: A Memoir of the Harvard Wars of 1969 1334

Making Toast **1334**

The Man in the Water: And Other Essays 1334

Rules for Aging: A Wry and Witty Guide to Life 1334

Where We Stand: 30 Reasons for Loving Our Country 1334

Rosenblum, Mort

A Goose in Toulouse: And Other Culinary Adventures in France 1002

Rosenfeld, Jo Ann

Handbook of Women's Health 502

Rosenstein, Ann A.

Water Exercises for Rheumatoid Arthritis: The Effective Way to Reduce Pain and Inflammation While Increasing Flexibility and Mobility 485

Rosman, Katherine

If You Knew Suzy: A Mother, a Daughter, a Reporter's Notebook 1334

Ross, Alex

Listen to This 1186

The Rest Is Noise: Listening to the Twentieth Century 601

Ross, Dennis

The Missing Peace: The Inside Story of the Fight for Middle East Peace 802

Ross, Stephen

Fundamentals of Corporate Finance Standard Edition 444

Rossington, Michael

Theories of Memory: A Reader 154

Rossinow, Douglas C.

Visions of Progress: The Left-Liberal Tradition in America 730

Roth, Philip

Portnoy's Complaint 165

Roth, Ruth A.

Nutrition and Diet Therapy, Tenth Edition 584, 593, **604**

Rothbart, Davy

Found II: More of the Best Lost, Tossed, and Forgotten Items from Around the World 1011

Found: The Best Lost, Tossed, and Forgotten Items from Around the World 1011

The Lone Surfer of Montana, Kansas: Stories 1011

Requiem for a Paper Bag: Celebrities and Civilians Tell Stories of the Best Lost, Tossed, and Found Items from Around the World **1011**

Rothenberg, Gunther Erich

The Napoleonic Wars 666

Rothero, Christopher

The Armies of Agincourt 663

Rothery, David A.

Volcanoes, Earthquakes and Tsunamis 1076

Rothfeder, Jeffrey

McIlhenny's Gold: How a Louisiana Family Built the Tabasco Empire **435**

Rothkopf, David

Running the World: The Inside Story of the National Security Council And the Architects of America's Power 1261

Rothman, David J.

The Oxford History of the Prison: The Practice of Punishment in Western Society 734, 794

Roundhill, D. Max

Extraction of Metals from Soils and Waters 1207

Rousseau, Jean-Jacques

Confessions 208

Reveries of the Solitary Walker 208

The Social Contract and Discourses 208

Rove, Karl

Courage and Consequence: My Life as a Conservative in the Fight **298**

Rowe, Dorothy

My Dearest Enemy, My Dangerous Friend: Making and Breaking Sibling Bonds 1292

Rowse, Darren

ProBlogger: Secrets for Blogging Your Way to a Six-Figure Income 341, **436**

Roy, Andrew

Fallen Soldier: Memoir of a Civil War Casualty 717

Roy, Lucinda

No Right to Remain Silent: The Tragedy at Virginia Tech 1260

Royte, Elizabeth

Garbage Land: Land on the Secret Trail of Trash 928, 959

Rozhdestvensky, Kirill V.

Aerodynamics of a Lifting System in Extreme Ground Effect 1163

Rubin, Anne Sarah

A Shattered Nation: The Rise & Fall of the Confederacy, 1861-1868 **834**

Rubin, Gretchen Craft

The Happiness Project: Or, Why I Spent a Year Trying to Sing in the Morning, Clean My Closets, Fight Right, Read Aristotle, and Generally Have More Fun 404, 1245

Rubin, Lillian B.

60 on Up: The Truth about Aging in America 1309

Rubin, Rose

A Treasury of Jewish Folksong 89

Rubin, Ruth

Voices of a People 89

Rubin, Stacey H.

The ABCs of Breastfeeding 640

Rudall, Paula

Anatomy of Flowering Plants: An Introduction to Structure and Development 1054

Rudat, April

Oh Yes You Can Breastfeed Twins! 640

Rudden, Jane

If We Must Dance, Then I Will Lead: A Memoir of Breast Cancer Survival 506, 562

Ruddiman, William F.

Earth's Climate: Past and Future 1047, 1105

Ruddiman, William F.

Plows, Plagues, and Petroleum 1129, 1140

Ruddon, Raymond W.

Cancer Biology, Fourth Edition 1068, 1181, **1190**

Ruderman, David B.

Early Modern Jewry: A New Cultural History 848

Rudner, Rima

Choose To Be Happy: A Guide to Total Happiness 929

Rudnicki, Kelly

The Food Allergy Mama's Baking Book: Great Dairy-, Egg-, and Nut-Free Treats for the Whole Family 476, **605**, 635

Vegan Baking Classics: Delicious, Easy-to-Make Traditional Favorites 605

Ruell, Karen Gray

The Grand Mosque of Paris: A Story of How Muslims Rescued Jews During the Holocaust 175

Rugemer, Edward B.

The Problem of Emancipation: The Caribbean Roots of the American Civil War **835**

Rugh, Susan Sessions

Our Common Country: Family Farming, Culture, and Community in the Nineteenth-Century Midwest 756

Shiffman, John
Priceless: How I Went Undercover to Rescue the World's Stolen Treasures 1336, 1341

Shiller, Robert J.
Animal Spirits: How Human Psychology Drives the Economy, and Why It Matters for Global Capitalism 1311

Shilts, Randy
And the Band Played On: Politics, People, and the AIDS Epidemic 511, 644

Shirer, William
The Rise and Fall of the Third Reich 716

Shirk, Susan L.
China: Fragile Superpower 1295

Shirky, Clay
Cognitive Surplus: Creativity and Generosity in a Connected Age 398
Here Comes Everybody: The Power of Organizing Without Organizations 338, 343, 430, 450, 1236, 1283, 1365

Shlaes, Amity
The Forgotten Man: A New History of the Great Depression 177

Shnayerson, Michael
Coal River 1241

Shneerson, John
Sleep Medicine: A Guide to Sleep and its Disorders 556

Shore, Zachary
Blunder: Why Smart People Make Bad Decisions 1339

Shorvon, Simon D.
Handbook of Epilepsy Treatment 495

Shoskes, Daniel A.
Chronic Prostatitis/Chronic Pelvic Pain Syndrome 597

Show, The Daily
The Daily Show with Jon Stewart Presents America (The Book) Teacher's Edition: A Citizen's Guide to Democracy Inaction 907

Shrake, Bud
Willie: An Autobiography 957, 979

Shulman, Julius
No More Glasses: The Complete Guide to Laser Vision Correction 551

Shulman, Lisa M.
Parkinson's Disease: A Complete Guide for Patients and Families, Second Edition 922

Shuman, Michael H.
Small-Mart Revolution: How Local Businesses Are Beating the Global Competition 456, 1350

Shusterman, Richard
Body Consciousness: A Philosophy of Mindfulness and Somaesthetics 11

Sibbet, David
Visual Meetings: How Graphics, Sticky Notes and Idea Mapping Can Transform Group Productivity 432

Sibley, Brian
The Lord of the Rings: The Making of the Movie Trilogy 135
Peter Jackson: A Film-Maker's Journey 135

Sibley, David Allen
Sibley Field Guide to Birds of Western North America 1202
The Sibley Guide to Bird Life and Behavior 1202
The Sibley Guide to Birds 1202
The Sibley Guide to Trees 1101, **1202**
Sibley's Birding Basics 1202
Sibley's Raptors of North America 1202

Sicile-Kira, Chantal
41 Things to Know about Autism 481
Autism Life Skills 587, 624

Sicko, Dan
Techno Rebels: The Renegades of Electronic Funk **121**

Sides, Hampton
Americana: Dispatches from the New Frontier 1344
Blood and Thunder: The Epic Story of Kit Carson and the Conquest of the American West 1344
Ghost Soldiers: The Epic Account of World War II's Greatest Rescue Mission 1344
Ghost Soldiers: The Forgotten Epic Story of World War II's Most Dramatic Mission 665, 780, 874
Hellhound on His Trail: The Stalking of Martin Luther King, Jr. and the International Hunt for His Assassin 1033, **1344**
Stomping Grounds: A Pilgrim's Progress Through Eight American Subcultures 1344

Sidman, Joyce
This Is Just to Say: Poems of Apology and Forgiveness 182

Siebert, Al
The Resiliency Advantage: Master Change, Thrive Under Pressure, and Bounce Back from Setbacks 419

Siebert, Wilbur H.
Underground Railroad from Slavery to Freedom 673

Siegel, Daniel J.
Mindsight: The New Science of Personal Transformation 1185

Siegmund, Stefanie
The Medici State and the Ghetto of Florence: The Construction of an Early Modern Jewish Community **848**

Sifry, Micah L.
The Iraq War Reader: History, Documents, Opinions 828

Sijie, Dai
Balzac and the Little Chinese Seamstress 196

Sijll, Jennifer Van
Cinematic Storytelling: The 100 Most Powerful Film Conventions Every Filmmaker Must Know 22

Silberberg, Daniel Doen
Wonderland: The Zen of Alice 59

Silbey, David J.
A War of Frontier and Empire: The Philippine-American War, 1899-1902 767

Siler, Julia Flynn
The House of Mondavi: The Rise and Fall of an American Wine Dynasty 435

Silver, J.K.
Polio Voices: An Oral History from the American Polio Epidemics and Worldwide Eradication Efforts 818

Silver, Julie K.
After Cancer Treatment: Heal Faster, Better, Stronger 615
Essentials of Physical Medicine and Rehabilitation 615
Super Healing: The Clinically Proven Plan to Maximize Recovery from Illness or Injury 615
What Helped Get Me Through: Cancer Survivors Share Wisdom and Hope 506, 558, **615**

Silverman, David J.
Red Brethren: The Brothertown and Stockbridge Indians and the Problem of Race in Early America 785

Silverman, Sarah
The Bedwetter: Stories of Courage, Redemption, and Pee 943, 970, **1019**, 1340

Silverstein, Paul A.
Algeria in France: Transpolitics, Race, and Nation 846

Silverstone, Liesl
Art Therapy Exercises: Inspirational and Practical Ideas to Stimulate the Imagination 475, 571

Silvey, Anita
Everything I Need to Know I Learned from a Children's Book 1020

Simmons, William Scranton
Spirit of the New England Tribes: Indian History and Folklore, 1620-1984 785

Simon, Mayo
The Audience and The Playwright: How to Get the Most Out of Live Theatre 139

Simon, Michele
Appetite for Profit: How the Food Industry Undermines Our Health and How to Fight Back 1250, 1268

Simon, William L.
iCon Steve Jobs: The Greatest Second Act in the History of Business 1371

Simonds, Anika K.
Non Invasive Respiratory Support: A Practical Handbook 642

Simons, Daniel
The Invisible Gorilla: And Other Ways Our Intuitions Deceive Us **1254**

Simpson, Brian P.
Markets Don't Fail! 375, 405, 428

Simpson, Jeffrey
Chautauqua 29

Simpson, Kathryn R.
The Women's Guide to Thyroid Health: Comprehensive Solutions for All Your Thyroid Symptoms 610

Simpson, Michael G.
Plant Systematics 1102, 1149

Sinatra, Stephen T.
The Sinatra Solution: Metabolic Cardiology 490

Sinclair, Upton
The Flivver King 200

Sinek, Simon
Start with Why: How Great Leaders Inspire Everyone to Take Action 445

Singer, Irving
Ingmar Bergman, Cinematic Philosopher: Reflections on His Creativity 41

Singer, P.W.
Children at War 170

Singer, Peter
Practical Ethics 984

Singh, Gary
How To Boost Your Immune System Naturally? 591

Singleton, Kenneth B.
The Lyme Disease Solution 482

Sinha, Mrinalini
Specters of Mother India: The Global Restructuring of an Empire **849**

Siniver, Asaf
Nixon, Kissinger, and U.S. Foreign Policy Making: The Machinery of Crisis 697

Sinnott, Roger W.
Sky & Telescope's Pocket Sky Atlas 1052, 1053, 1092, 1093, 1173

Sire, James W.
The Universe Next Door: A Basic Worldview Catalog 653

Sisario, Ben
The Pixies' Doolittle (33 1/3) 46

Sisson, Mark
The Primal Blueprint 627

Sitney, P. Adams
Eyes Upside Down: Visionary Filmmakers and the Heritage of Emerson 131

Skal, David J.
Claude Rains: An Actor's Voice 127

Skenazy, Lenore
Free-Range Kids: How to Raise Safe, Self-Reliant Children (Without Going Nuts with Worry) **1345**
Who's the Blonde That Married What's-His-Name?: The Ultimate Tip-of-the-Tongue Test of Everything You Know You Know—But Can't Remember Right Now 1345

Sklenicka, Carol
D.H. Lawrence and the Child 304
Raymond Carver: A Writer's Life 304

Skloot, Rebecca
The Immortal Life of Henrietta Lacks 154, 911, 949, 950, 964, 983

Skolnik, Richard L.
Essentials of Global Health 634

Skurnick, Lizzie
Shelf Discovery: The Teen Classics We Never Stopped Reading 25, 992, **1020**

Slater, Lauren
Lying: A Metaphorical Memoir 891, 923

Opening Skinner's Box: Great Psychological Experiments of the Twentieth Century 948

Slater, Robert
No Such Thing as Over-Exposure: Inside the Life and Celebrity of Donald Trump **441**

Seizing Power: The Grab for Global Oil Wealth 441

Soros: The Life, Ideas, and Impact of the World's Most Influential Investor 441

Slaughter, Mark S.
Cardiac Surgery in Chronic Renal Failure 586

Slim, Pamela
Escape From Corporate Hell: Unlock Your Potential and Love Your Work 442

Escape From Cubicle Nation: From Corporate Prisoner to Thriving Entrepreneur 370, **442**

Sloan, Bill
The Ultimate Battle: Okinawa 1945—the Last Epic Struggle of World War II 743

Sloan, Mark
Birth Day: A Pediatrician Explores the Science, the History, and the Wonder of Childbirth 632

Slobin, Mark
Yiddish Folksongs from the Ruth Rubin Archive **89**

Sloman, Larry
The Secret Life of Houdini: The Making of America's First Superhero 123

Slovic, Paul
The Irrational Economist: Making Decisions in a Dangerous World 1348

Small, David
Imogene's Antlers 1021
So You Want to be President? 1021
Stitches: A Memoir 314, 326, **1021**

Small, Gary
IBrain: Surviving the Technological Alteration of the Modern Mind 1251

Smallwood, Stephanie E.
Saltwater Slavery: A Middle Passage from Africa to the American Diaspora 826

Smart, Bradford D.
Topgrading: How Leading Companies Win by Hiring, Coaching, and Keeping the Best People, Revised and Updated Edition 385

Smart, Geoff
Who: The A Method for Hiring 385

Smedley, Audrey
Race in North America: Origins and Evolution of a Worldview 850

Smick, David M.
The World Is Curved: Hidden Dangers to the Global Economy **443**

Smil, Vaclav
Energy at the Crossroads: Global Perspectives and Uncertainties 1105

Smith, A. Jr. Laurence
Integrated Healthcare Information Systems 493

Smith, Allan Lloyd
American Gothic Fiction: An Introduction 32

Smith, Carmen Gimenez
Bring Down the Little Birds: On Mothering, Art, Work and Everything Else **122**

David Smith: A Centennial 122
Odalisque in Pieces 50, 51, 122, 122

Smith, Charles R.
Black Jack: The Ballad of Jack Johnson 305
Chameleon 305
My People 305
Twelve Rounds to Glory: The Story of Muhammad Ali **305**
Winning Words 305

Smith, Claude Clayton
The Way of Kinship: An Anthology of Native Siberian Literature 85

Smith, David James
Supper with the Crippens: A New Investigation into One of the Most Notorious Domestic Murders in History 771

Smith, Greg B.
Nothing But Money: How the Mob Infiltrated Wall Street 1266

Smith, Gregory
Jackson Pollock: An American Saga 309, 1351

Smith, Huston
The World's Religions: Our Great Wisdom Traditions 653

Smith, J. Walker
Generation Ageless: How Baby Boomers Are Changing the Way We Live Today . . . And They're Just Getting Started 1269

Smith, Jason
Alien Woman: The Making of Lt. Ellen Ripley 70

Smith, Jean Edward
FDR 176

Smith, Jeffrey M.
Genetic Roulette: The Documented Health Risks of Genetically Engineered Foods 1048

Smith, John David
Undaunted Radical: The Selected Writings and Speeches of Albion W. Tourgee 713

Smith, Julia
Europe After Rome: A New Cultural History, 500-1000 873

Smith, Julien
Trust Agents: Using the Web to Build Influence, Improve Reputation, and Earn Trust 351, 366, 378, 394, 438

Smith, Lane
John, Paul, George and Ben 295
Madame President 312

Smith, M.Paul
Telling the Evolutionary Time: Molecular Clocks and the Fossil Record 1145

Smith, Matthew J.
The Power of Comics: History, Form and Culture 78

Smith, Pamela Wartian
Demystifying Weight Loss: A Concise Guide for Solving the Weight Loss Puzzle 616, 617

What You Must Know About Vitamins, Minerals, Herbs, and More: Choosing the Nutrients That Are Right for You 614, **617**, 616

What You Must Know About Women's Hormones: Your Guide to Natural Hormone Treatments for PMS, Menopause, Osteoporosis, PCOS, and More **616**, 617

Smith, Patti
Just Kids **1022**
Patti Smith Complete 1975-2006: Lyrics, Reflections & Notes for the Future 1022
Patti Smith, Land 250 1022

Smith, Richard Norton
Patriarch: George Washington and the New American Nation 722

Smith, Robert L.
Immigrant, Inc.: Why Immigrant Entrepreneurs Are Driving the New Economy (and how they will save the American worker) **388**

Smith, Shelley Ann
The Fibromyalgia Cookbook 646

Smith, Susan
Hitchcock: Suspense, Humour and Tone 155

Smith, Terry L.
Nutrition and Food Safety 568

Smith, Tom
A Balanced Life: 9 Strategies for Coping with the Mental Health Problems of a Loved One 473, **618**

The Tattered Tapestry: A Family's Search for Peace with Bipolar Disorder 618

Smith, Virginia
Clean: A History of Personal Hygiene and Purity 655

Smith, William Tyler
A Manual of Obstetrics: Theoretical and Practical 502

Smith, Zadie
The Autograph Man 1023
Changing My Mind: Occasional Essays **1023**
On Beauty 1023
White Teeth 1023

Smith-Rosenberg, Carroll
Disorderly Conduct: Visions of Gender in Victorian America 850

Religion and the Rise of the American City: New York City Mission Movement, 1812-70 850

This Violent Empire: The Birth of an American National Identity **850**

Smucker, Shawn
Think No Evil: Inside the Story of the Amish Schoolhouse Shooting...and Beyond 1260, 1342

Snook, Jim
Ice Age Extinction: Cause and Human Consequences **1203**, 1204

Snowden, Frank N.
The Conquest of Malaria: Italy 1900-1962 **851**

The Fascist Revolution in Tuscany, 1919-22 851

Naples in the Time of Cholera 851

Violence and the Great Estates in the South of Italy: Apulia, 1900-1922 851

Snyder, Lisa
Living Your Best With Early-Stage Alzheimer's: An Essential Guide 549, 573

Snyder, Rachel Louise
Fugitive Denim: A Moving Story of People and Pants in the Borderless World of Global Trade 1273

Sobchack, Vivian
Screening Space: The American Science Fiction Film 70

Socolow, Susan Migden
The Women of Colonial Latin America 790

Soderquist, Don
The Wal-Mart Way: The Inside Story of the Success of the World's Largest Company 801

Sokoloff, Natalie
The Criminal Justice System and Women: Offenders, Prisoners, Victims and Workers 88

Solaun, Mauricio
U.S. Intervention and Regime Change in Nicaragua 763

Solis, Brian
Engage: The Complete Guide for Brands and Businesses to Build, Cultivate, and Measure Success in the New Web 351, 448

Solnit, Rebecca
River of Shadows: Eadweard Muybridge and the Technological Wild West 9, 79

Solomon, Matthew
Disappearing Tricks: Silent Film, Houdini, and the New Magic of the Twentieth Century **123**

Solomon, Michael R.
The Truth about What Customers Want **444**

Solomon, Robert C.
Death and Philosophy 168

Solomon, Steven
Confidence Game 1346
Small Business USA 1346
Water: The Epic Struggle for Wealth, Power, and Civilization **1346**

Solomon, Tara A.
What Your Gynecologist Never Told You...And Your Mother Didn't Know 502

Solove, Daniel J.
The Digital Person: Technology and Privacy in the Information Age 1347

Stachowiak, Julie
The Diabetes Manifesto: Take Charge of Your Life 620
The Multiple Sclerosis Manifesto: Action to Take, Principles to Live By 510, **620**

Stack, Debbie Daino
Cruising America's Waterways: The Erie Canal 668

Stack, Megan K.
Every Man in This Village Is a Liar: An Education in War **853**

Stack, Pamela J.
Art Therapy Activities: A Practical Guide for Teachers, Therapists And Parents 475, 571

Stadiem, William
Don't Mind If I Do 318

Stafford, David
Endgame, 1945: The Missing Final Chapter of World War II 746

Stafford, Nikki
Finding Lost: The Unofficial Guide 153

Stahl, Stephen M.
Depression and Bipolar Disorder 621
The Prescriber's Guide, 3rd Edition **621**, 648
Stahl's Essential Psychopharmacology Online: Print and Online 621
Stahl's Illustrated Antipsychotics 621
Stahl's Illustrated Anxiety, Stress, and PTSD 621

Staiger, Janet
Authorship and Film 82, 83

Stalker, Peter
A Guide to Countries of the World 1153

Stam, Lawrence E.
100 Questions and Answers About Kidney Dialysis 539, 586

Stam, Robert
Literature and Film: A Guide to the Theory and Practice of Film Adaptation 36

Stamz, Richard E.
Give 'Em Soul, Richard!: Race, Radio, and Rhythm and Blues in Chicago 33

Stanberry, Lawrence R.
Understanding Herpes 488, 524, 581

Standage, Tom
An Edible History of Humanity **854**
A History of the World in Six Glasses 854
The Neptune File: A Story of Astronomical Rivalry and the Pioneers of Planet Hunting 854
The Victorian Internet: The Remarkable Story of the Telegraph and the Nineteenth Century's On-Line Pioneers 854

Standard, Natural
Natural Standard Herb and Supplement Guide: An Evidence-Based Reference 1155

Stanier, Michael Bungay
Do More Great Work. Stop the Busywork, and Start the Work That Matters 344, **447**

Stanley, Steven M.
Earth System History 1208

Stanton, Doug
Horse Soldiers: The Extraordinary Story of a Band of US Soldiers Who Rode to Victory in Afghanistan 238, **855**
In Harm's Way: The Sinking of the USS Indianapolis and the Extraordinary Story of Its Survivors 855, 238

Stanton, Lucia C.
Slavery at Monticello 229

Stapp, Henry P.
Mind, Matter and Quantum Mechanics 1063, 1231

Stark, Andreas
Seismic Methods and Applications 1217

Stark, Rodney
Discovering God: The Origins of the Great Religions and the Evolution of Belief 719
Gods Battalions: The Case for the Crusades 696, 832

Stark, Sarah
The Lingerie Handbook 939

Starkey, David
Six Wives: The Queens of Henry VIII 325

Starks, Lisa S.
The Reel Shakespeare: Alternative Cinema and Theory 9, 79

Starling, Randall C.
The Cleveland Clinic Guide to Heart Failure 594, **622**

Starr, Kevin
Americans and the California Dream, 1850-1915 856
Golden Dreams: California in an Age of Abundance, 1950-1963 **856**
Golden Gate: The Life and Times of America's Greatest Bridge 856
Inventing the Dream: California Through the Progressive Era 856

Starr, Paul
The Creation of the Media: Political Origins of Modern Communication 12

Staugaard-Jones, Jo Ann
The Anatomy of Exercise and Movement: For the Study of Dance, Pilates, Sport and Yoga 529

Stearns, Jean
Jazz Dance: The Story Of American Vernacular Dance 81

Stearns, Marshall
Jazz Dance: The Story Of American Vernacular Dance 81

Steegmuller, Francis
Flaubert and Madame Bovary 179

Steene, Birgitta
Ingmar Bergman: A Reference Guide 41

Steers, Edward Jr.
Blood on the Moon: The Assassination of Abraham Lincoln 859

Stefansson, Ragnar
Advances in Earthquake Prediction: Seismic Research and Risk Mitigation 1120

Steidle, Brian
The Devil Came on Horseback: Bearing Witness to the Genocide in Darfur 723

Steiger, Brad
Cat Miracles: Inspirational True Stories of Remarkable Felines 986

Steiger, Sherry Hansen
Cat Miracles: Inspirational True Stories of Remarkable Felines 986

Steigerwald, David
Debating the 1960s: Liberal, Conservative, and Radical Perspectives 782

Stein, Ben
The Little Book of Bulletproof Investing: Do's and Don'ts to Protect Your Financial Life 423

Stein, Elissa
Flow: The Cultural Story of Menstruation 1242

Stein, Gertrude
Picasso 294

Stein, Joel
Stroke Recovery and Rehabilitation 477

Stein, Mark
How the States Got Their Shapes 1037

Stein, R. Conrad
The Conquistadores: Building a Spanish Empire in the Americas 781

Stein, Seth
Disaster Deferred: How New Science Is Changing our View of Earthquake Hazards in the Midwest 1120

Steinbeck, John
The Harvest Gypsies: On the Road to the Grapes of Wrath 869

Steinberg, Avi
Running the Books: The Adventures of an Accidental Prison Librarian **307**, 1297

Steinberg, Samuel
The Physician's Survival Guide for the Hospital: Let the Hospital Work for You 500

Steiner, Christopher
$20 Per Gallon: How the Inevitable Rise in the Price of Gasoline Will Change Our Lives for the Better 246, 925, 926

Steingarten, Jeffrey
The Man Who Ate Everything: And Other Gastronomic Feats, Disputes and Pleasurable Pursuits 181, 184

Steinke, Darcey
Easter Everywhere: A Memoir **308**
Jesus Saves 308
Suicide Blonde 308

Steinmeyer, Jim
Magic 1400s-1950s 123

Steketee, Gail
Stuff: Compulsive Hoarding and the Meaning of Things **1274**

Stekler, Paul
Killing Custer 707

Stepp, Laura Sessions
Unhooked: How Young Women Pursue Sex, Delay Love and Lose at Both 524, 1360

Stern, Howard
Miss America 970
Private Parts 970

Stern, Nicholas
The Economics of Climate Change: The Stern Review 1061

Stern, Sheldon M.
The Week the Earth Stood Still: Inside the Secret Cuban Missile Crisis 704

Stern, Steve J.
Peru's Indian Peoples and the Challenge of Spanish Conquest: Huamanga to 1640 781

Sterner, Thomas M.
The Practicing Mind 1083

Sternin, Jerry
The Power of Positive Deviance: How Unlikely Innovators Solve the World's Toughest Problems 1283, 1287, 1369

Sternin, Monique
The Power of Positive Deviance: How Unlikely Innovators Solve the World's Toughest Problems 1283, 1287, 1369

Sterritt, David
The Films of Alfred Hitchcock 155

Stevens, Mark
All the Money in the World: How the Forbes 400 Make—and Spend—Their Fortunes 309
de Kooning: An American Master **309**, 1351

Stevens, Sharon McKenzie
A Place for Dialogue: Language, Land Use, and Politics in Southern Arizona **128**

Stevenson, William
A Man Called Intrepid: The Secret War 909

Stewart, Amy
Flower Confidential: The Good, the Bad, and the Beautiful 731

Stewart, David
The Summer of 1787: The Men Who Invented the Constitution 784, 878

Stewart, Donna E.
Menopause: A Mental Health Practitioner's Guide 499, 585

Stewart, Elizabeth A.
Uterine Fibroids: The Complete Guide 610, **623**

Stewart, Gary
Rumba on the River: A History of the Popular Music of the Two Congos 150

Stewart, James B.
DisneyWar 373

Stewart, Jon
America (The Book): A Citizen's Guide to Democracy Inaction 907
The Daily Show with Jon Stewart Presents America (The Book) Teacher's Edition: A Citizen's Guide to Democracy Inaction 907

Timberlake, Karen C.
Basic Chemistry 1215
Basic Chemistry Study Guide 1215
Chemistry: An Introduction to General, Organic, & Biological Chemistry 1215
Chemistry: Study Guide and Selected Solutions - An Introduction to General, Organic, and Biological Chemistry 1215
Lab Manual for General, Organic, and Biological Chemistry: 2nd Edition **1215**
MasteringChemistry Student Access Kit for Chemistry: An Introduction to General, Organic, & Biological Chemistry 1215

Timbrell, John A.
Principles of Biochemical Toxicology 537

Times Life Books, Times Life Books
The American Dream: The 50s 856

Tincknell, Estella
Viewing Jane Campion: Angels, Demons and Unsettling Voices 110

Tinsman, Brian
The Game Inventor's Guidebook: How to Invent and Sell Board Games, Card Games, Role-Playing Games, & Everything in Between! 889

Tirion, Wil
The Cambridge Star Atlas: 4th Edition **1216**

Tisch, Jonathan M.
Chocolates on the Pillow Aren't Enough: Reinventing the Customer Experience **451**
Citizen You: Doing Your Part to Change the World 451

Toaff, Ariel
Love, Work, and Death: Jewish Life in Medieval Umbria 848

Tobin, Jacqueline L.
Hidden in Plain View: A Secret Story of Quilts and the Underground Railroad 673

Tocqueville, Alexis de
Letters from America 178

Tocqueville, Alexis de
Democracy in America 178

Todd, Janet
Mary Wollstonecraft: A Revolutionary Life 228

Toibin, Colm
Brooklyn 244

Tolan, Sandy
The Lemon Tree: An Arab, a Jew, and the Heart of the Middle East 332

Toland, John
Some Survived: An Eyewitness Account of the Bataan Death March and the Men Who Lived through It 815

Tolkin, Marvin
When I'm 64: Planning for the Best of Your Life 1309

Toll, Ian W.
Six Frigates: The Epic History of the Founding of the U.S. Navy **863**

Tomalin, Claire
Jane Austen: A Life 316
The Life and Death of Mary Wollstonecraft 316
Samuel Pepys: The Unequalled Self 316
Thomas Hardy **316**

Tomine, Adrian
Shortcomings 171, 967, 1012, 1013, 1021

Tonello, Michael
Bringing Home the Birkin: My Life in Hot Pursuit of the World's Most Coveted Handbag 1258

Tonkin, Stephen F.
Binocular Astronomy 1195

Tonnesson, J.N.
The History of Modern Whaling 705

Toobin, Jeffrey
The Nine: Inside the Secret World of the Supreme Court 232

Toomer, Simon
Planting and Maintaining a Tree Collection 1101

Toop, David
Sinister Resonance: The Mediumship of the Listener 1060

Torgovnick, Kate
Cheer!: Inside the Secret World of College Cheerleaders **1032**

Tornetta, Giuditta
Painless Childbirth: An Empowering Journey Through Pregnancy and Childbirth 479, **632**

Torre, Joe
The Yankee Years 259

Torrence, Paul F.
Antiviral Drug Discovery for Emerging Diseases and Bioterrorism Threats 544

Torres, Sasha
Living Color: Race and Television in the United States 63

Tottis, James W.
The Guardian Building: Cathedral of Finance **137**

Tough, Paul
Whatever It Takes: Geoffrey Canada's Quest to Change Harlem and America 286

Tougias, Michael J.
The Finest Hours: The True Story of the U.S. Coast Guard's Most Daring Sea Rescue 1325

Toussaint-Samat, Maguelonne
A History of Food 854

Towhata, Ikuo
Geotechnical Earthquake Engineering **1217**

Townsend, Patricia
Environmental Anthropology 1162

Toye, Richard
Churchill's Empire: The World That Made Him and the World He Made 817

Tozer, Frank
The Uses of Wild Plants 1084, 1213

Trachtenberg, Alan
The Incorporation of America: Culture and Society in the Gilded Age 837
Reading American Photographs: Images As History, Mathew Brady to Walker Evans 111

Tracy, Stephen V.
Pericles: A Sourcebook and Reader 1282

Traill, Ariana
Women and the Comic Plot in Menander 138

Tratner, Michael
Crowd Scenes: Movies and Mass Politics 23

Travis, Alice D.
Cognitive Evolution: The Biological Imprint of Applied Intelligence 1201

Trebek, Alex
The Jeopardy! Book: The Answers, the Questions, the Facts, and the Stories of the Greatest Game Show in History 946, 953, 958

Trees, Andrew
Decoding Love: Why It Takes Twelve Frogs to Find a Prince, and Other Revelations from the Science of Attraction 1335

Treese, James Van
Principles of Confederacy: The Vision and the Dream and the Fall of the South 834

Trexler, Richard C.
Public Life in Renaissance Florence 769

Tribe, Steve
Doctor Who: Companions And Allies 76
Doctor Who: The TARDIS Handbook 31, 76

Trilling, Bernie
21st Century Skills: Learning for Life in Our Times 1323

Triola, Mario F.
Elementary Statistics Using Excel 1218
Essentials of Statistics, Third Edition **1218**
Student Solutions Manual for Elementary Statistics Using Excel 1218

Tripp, Aili
Global Feminism: Transnational Women Activism 702

Trombley, Laura Skandera
Mark Twain's Other Woman: The Hidden Story of His Final Years 287

Trotter, William
A Frozen Hell: The Russo-Finnish Winter War of 1939-1940 710

Trotter, William R.
Winter Fire 710

Troupe, Quincy
Miles, the Autobiography 249

Trout, Andrew P.
City on the Seine: Paris in the Time of Richelieu and Louis XIV, 1614-1715 762

Trowbridge, Calvin D. Jr.
Marconi: Father of Wireless, Grandfather of Radio, Great-Grandfather of the Cell Phone, The Story of the Race to Control Long-Distance Wireless 771

Trudeau, Noah Andre
Southern Storm: Sherman's March to the Sea 881

Truman, Harry S.
Affection and Trust: The Personal Correspondence of Harry S. Truman and Dean Acheson, 1953-1971 207, **864**
Dear Bess: The Letters from Harry to Bess Truman, 1910-1959 864
Defending the West: The Truman-Churchill Correspondence 864
Defending the West: The Truman-Churchill Correspondence, 1945-1960 864
Where the Buck Stops: The Personal and Private Writings of Harry S. Truman 864, 864

Trussoni, Danielle
Angelology: A Novel 317
Falling Through the Earth: A Memoir **317**

Trutnau, John-Paul
A One-Man Show? The Construction and Deconstruction of a Patriarchal Image in the Reagan Era: Reading the Audio-Visual Poetics of Miami Vice 116

Tsigdinos, Pamela Mahoney
Silent Sorority: A Barren Woman Gets Busy, Angry, Lost and Found 611

Tubesing, Andrew
Colitiscope: Living With Crohn's Disease and Ulcerative Colitis 608

Tuchman, Gaye
Wannabe U: Inside the Corporate University 1281

Tucker, Shelia
Nutrition and Diet Therapy for Nurses 604

Tuckman, Ari
Integrative Treatment for Adult ADHD: A Practical, Easy-to-Use Guide for Clinicians 467, 589, **633**
More Attention, Less Deficit: Success Strategies for Adults with ADHD 467, 589, 633

Tulloch, John
Doctor Who: The Unfolding Text 139
Risk and Everyday Life 139
Shakespeare and Chekhov in Production and Reception: Theatrical Events and Their Audiences **139**
Watching Television Audiences 139

Tupper, Benjamin
Greetings from Afghanistan, Send More Ammo: Dispatches from Taliban Country 760, 1300

Turbow, Jason
The Baseball Codes: Beanballs, Sign Stealing, and Bench-Clearing Brawls: The Unwritten Rules of America's Pastime 981

Turk, James
The Collapse of the Dollar and How

to Profit from It: Make a Fortune by Investing in Gold and Other Hard Assets 362

Turley, Richard Marggraf
The Monstrous Debt: Modalities of Romantic Influence in Twentieth-Century Literature **140**
Presences that Disturb: Models of Romantic Self-Definition in the Culture and Literature of the 1790s 140
Romanticism, History, Historicism: Essays on an Orthodoxy 140
Wales and the Romantic Imagination 140

Turnage, Wallace
A Slave No More: Two Men Who Escaped to Freedom, Including Their Own Narratives of Emancipation **671**

Turner, Chris
Planet Simpson: How a Cartoon Masterpiece Defined a Generation 998

Turner, Fred
From Counterculture to Cyberculture: Stewart Brand, the Whole Earth Network, and the Rise of Digital Utopianism 66

Turner, Graeme
Television Studies After TV: Understanding Television in the Post-Broadcast Era 126

Turner, Ian Mark
The Ecology of Trees in the Tropical Rain Forest 1148

Turner, Kathleen
Send Yourself Roses: Thoughts on My Life, Love, and Leading Roles **318**

Turner, Martin J. L.
Mars Base One: Creating a Permanent Presence on the Red Planet 1219
Rocket and Spacecraft Propulsion: Principles, Practice and New Developments **1219**

Turner, Steve
A Hard Day's Write: The Stories Behind Every Beatles Song 280, 306

Turner, Ted
Call Me Ted 1371

Turnock, Bernard J.
Essentials of Public Health **634**, 639
Public Health: Career Choices That Make a Difference 634
Public Health: What It Is and How It Works 634

Turtledove, Harry
366 Days in Abraham Lincoln's Presidency: The Private, Political, and Military Decisions of America's Greatest President 226

Twain, Mark
The Adventures of Huckleberry Finn 287
Autobiography of Mark Twain, Vol. 1 287

Twenge, Jean
Generation Me: Why Today's Young Americans are More Confident, Assertive, Entitled—and More Miserable than Ever Before 1269, 1298

Generation Me: Why Today's Young Americans Are More Confident, Assertive, Entitled—and More Miserable Than Ever Before 1358
The Narcissism Epidemic: Living in the Age of Entitlement **1358**

Tye, Larry
The Father of Spin: Edward L. Bernays and The Birth of Public Relations 319
Home Lands: Portraits of the New Jewish Diaspora 319
Rising from the Rails: Pullman Porters and the Making of the Black Middle Class 319
Satchel: The Life and Times of an American Legend 239, 260, **319**

Tyre, Peg
The Trouble with Boys: A Surprising Report Card on Our Sons, Their Problems at School, and What Parents and Educators Must Do 1308

Tyring, Stephen K.
Mucosal Immunology and Virology 598, 600

U

Ugarkovic, Durdica
Centromere: Structure and Evolution 1065, 1172

Uhlberg, Myron
Hands of My Father: A Hearing Boy, His Deaf Parents, and the Language of Love 263

Ulmschneider, Peter
Intelligent Life in the Universe 1193

Ulwick, Anthony
What Customers Want: Using Outcome-Driven Innovation to Create Breakthrough Products and Services 427

Underdown, David
Fire from Heaven: Life in an English Town in the Seventeenth Century 195

Underhill, Paco
Why We Buy: The Science of Shopping—Updated and Revised for the Internet, the Global Consumer, and Beyond 407

Unger, Harlow G.
Lafayette 836

Unger, Harlow Giles
A Call to Greatness 272

Unger, Jeff
Diabetes Management in Primary Care 471, 487

Updike, John
John Updike: The Early Stories 166

Urbanek Linville, Susan
The Price of Stones: Building a School for My Village 1317

Urofsky, Melvin I.
The American Presidents: Critical Essays 320
Louis D. Brandeis: A Life **320**
A March of Liberty: A Constitutional

History of the United States Volume II: From 1877 to the Present 320

Urquhart, Jane
L.M. Montgomery 199, 251, 292, **321**
A Map of Glass 321
Penguin Book of Canadian Short Stories 321
Sanctuary Line 321

Urquhart-Brown, Susan
The Accidental Entrepreneur: The 50 Things I Wish Someone Had Told Me About Starting a Business 350

Urrea, Luis Alberto
The Devil's Highway: A True Story 1275

Usler, Mark
Hometown Revelations: How America's Cities, Towns, and States Acquired Their Names 1037

V

Vaisse, Justin
Neoconservatism: The Biography of a Movement **1359**

Valdez, Joseph
Healing Back and Joint Injuries: A Proven Approach to Ending Chronic Pain and Avoiding Unnecessary Surgery 572, 579, 588

Valencius, Conevery
The Health of the Country: How American Settlers Understood Themselves and Their Land 809

Valente, Catherynne M.
In the Night Garden 14, 18, 19, 129, 136

Valenti, Jessica
Full Frontal Feminism: A Young Woman's Guide to Why Feminism Matters 1360
He's a Stud, She's a Slut, and 49 Other Double Standards Every Woman Should Know 1360, 1360
The Purity Myth: How America's Obsession with Virginity Is Hurting Young Women 1360
Yes Means Yes: Visions of Female Sexual Power and A World Without Rape 1360

Valentine, Gary
New York Rocker: My Life in the Blank Generation with Blondie, Iggy Pop, and Others, 1974-1981 1022

Valentine, Phil
The Conservative's Handbook: Defining the Right Position on Issues from A to Z 730

Valiela, Ivan
Doing Science: Design, Analysis, and Communication of Scientific Research 1050, 1085

Valverde, Carlos
Genetic Screening of Newborns: An Ethical Inquiry 1082

Vamplew, Anton
Simple Stargazing 1173

Van Dyke, Fred
Conservation Biology: Foundations, Concepts, Applications 276

Van Norman, Kay A.
Exercise and Wellness for Older Adults 530, 584

van Wormer, Katherine Stuart
Women and the Criminal Justice System 88

VanBurkleo, Sandra F.
Remapping the Humanities: Identity, Community, Memory, (Post)Modernity **47**

Vanderbilt, Arthur T.
Fortune's Children: The Fall of the House of Vanderbilt 311

Vanston, Carrie
Minitrends: Finding & Profiting from Emerging Business Opportunity Gems **452**

Vanston, John H.
Biotechnology: A Technology Forecast 452
Home Technology Integration: A Technology Forecast 452
Mechatronics: A Technology Forecast 452
Minitrends: Finding & Profiting from Emerging Business Opportunity Gems **452**

Varhola, Michael
Fire and Ice: The Korean War, 1950-1953 740

Varier, K. Muraleedhara
Nuclear Radiation Detection: Measurements and Analysis 1044, 1128

Vaschenko, Alexander
The Way of Kinship: An Anthology of Native Siberian Literature 85

Vaughan, Brian K.
Y: The Last Man: Unmanned 963, 975

Vaynerchuk, Gary
Crush It!: Why NOW Is the Time to Cash In on Your Passion 369, 383, 394
Viral Loop: From Facebook to Twitter, How Today's Smartest Businesses Grow Themselves **453**

Vedantam, Shankar
The Ghosts of Kashmir 1361
The Hidden Brain: How Our Unconscious Minds Elect Presidents, Control Markets, Wage Wars, and Save Our Lives 407, **1361**

Vee, Tesco
Touch and Go: The Complete Hardcore Punk Zine '79-'83 46

Vegas, Johnny
Keeping the British End Up: Four Decades of Saucy Cinema 94

Velleman, Daniel J.
How to Prove It: A Structured Approach, Second Edition **1220**

Veltri, Barbara Torre
Learning on Other People's Kids: Becoming a Teach for America Teacher 1270

Weber, Caroline
Queen of Fashion: What Marie Antoinette Wore to the Revolution 118

Weber, Karl
Chocolates on the Pillow Aren't Enough: Reinventing the Customer Experience **451**
Food, Inc.: How Industrial Food Is Making Us Sicker, Fatter, and Poorer—and What You Can Do About It 1250

Weber, Lauren
In Cheap We Trust: The Story of a Misunderstood American Virtue 1310

Weightman, Gavin
Signor Marconi's Magic Box: The Most Remarkable Invention of the 19th Century and the Amateur Inventor Whose Genius Sparked a Revolution 771

Weigle, Marta
Telling New Mexico: A New History 799

Weil, Andrew
Healthy Aging: A Lifelong Guide to Your Physical and Spritual Well-Being 1309
Healthy Aging: A Lifelong Guide to Your Well-Being 639
Life Over Cancer: The Block Center Program for Integrative Cancer Treatment 639
Why Our Health Matters: A Vision of Medicine That Can Transform Our Future **639**

Weiland, Matt
Commodify Your Dissent 1037
State by State: A Panoramic Portrait of America 958, **1037**
The Thinking Fan's Guide to the World Cup 1037

Weiler, Edward John
Hubble: A Journey through Space and Time 1214, **1226**

Weill, Susan
In a Madhouse's Din: Civil Rights Coverage by Mississippi's Daily Press, 1948-1968 830

Weinberg, Gerhard L.
Hitler's Foreign Policy 1933-1939: The Road to World War II 660

Weinberg, Steven L.
Cosmology 1125, 1147, 1154, 1221

Weinberg, Tamar
The New Community Rules: Marketing on the Social Web 351, **454**

Weiner, Arthur A.
The Fearful Dental Patient: A Guide to Understanding and Managing 512

Weiner, Howard L.
Curing MS: How Science Is Solving the Mysteries of Multiple Sclerosis 563, 620

Weiner, Jennifer
Fly Away Home 915, 978
Good in Bed 938

Weiner, Jonathan
Long for This World: The Strange Science of Immortality 1269

Weiner, Stephen
Microarchaeology 1198

Weiner, Tim
Betrayal: The Story of Aldrich Ames, an American Spy 872
Blank Check: The Pentagon's Black Budget 872
Legacy of Ashes: The History of the CIA **872**

Weiner, William J.
Parkinson's Disease: A Complete Guide for Patients and Families, Second Edition 922

Weinstein, Jodi Buckman
Tell Me What to Eat Before, During, and After Cancer Treatment: Nutritional Guidelines for Patients and Their Loved Ones 613

Weinstock, Jeffrey Andrew
Critical Approaches to the Films of M. Night Shyamalan: Spoiler Warnings 148
Scare Tactics: Supernatural Fiction by American Women 148
Spectral America: Phantoms and the National Imagination 148
Taking South Park Seriously **148**

Weintraub, David A.
How Old Is the Universe? 1116, **1227**
Is Pluto a Planet?: A Historical Journey through the Solar System 1227

Weintraub, Jerry
When I Stop Talking, You'll Know I'm Dead: Useful Stories from a Persuasive Man 74, 894, 914, 954

Weir, Alison
The Captive Queen: A Novel of Eleanor of Aquitaine 325
Innocent Traitor: A Novel of Lady Jane Grey 325
The Lady Elizabeth: A Novel 325
The Lady in the Tower: The Fall of Anne Boleyn **325**
Queen Isabella 325

Weisberger, Lauren
Last Night at Chateau Marmont 358, 363

Weisbrot, Robert
The Liberal Hour: Washington and the Politics of Change in the 1960s **782**

Weiss, Robin Elise
The Better Way to Breastfeed: The Latest, Most Effective Ways to Feed and Nurture Your Baby with Comfort and Ease **640**
The Complete Illustrated Pregnancy Companion 640
Everything Guide to Raising Adolescent Boys 640
Guarantee the Sex of Your Baby 640

Welch, Amanda
The Kids Are All Right: A Memoir 323, **326**

Welch, Cheryl B.
The Cambridge Companion to Tocqueville 178

Welch, Dan
The Kids Are All Right: A Memoir 323, **326**

Welch, Diana
The Kids Are All Right: A Memoir 323, **326**

Welch, H. Gilbert
Should I Be Tested for Cancer: Maybe Not and Here's Why 531

Welch, Jack
10-10-10: A Fast and Powerful Way to Get Unstuck in Love, at Work, and with Your Family 455
Winning 455
Winning: The Answers: Confronting 74 of the Toughest Questions in Business Today 455

Welch, James
Killing Custer 707

Welch, Liz
The Kids Are All Right: A Memoir 323, **326**

Welch, Suzy
Winning 455

Welles, Orson
This Is Orson Welles 17, 58

Wells, Rosemary
Wingwalker 327

Wells, Spencer
Deep Ancestry: Inside the Genographic Project 865

Wells, Tom
The Wrong Guys: Murder, False Confessions, and the Norfolk Four 1278

Welsh, Joe
The Cars of Pullman 371

Wengian, Gao
Zhou Enlai: The Last Perfect Revolutionary 196

Werner, Dan
Real Men Wear Pink: A Man's Guide to Surviving a Loved One's Breast Cancer 462

Werner, Ruth
Disease Handbook for Massage Therapists **641**
A Massage Therapist's Guide to Pathology 641

Weschler, Lawrence
Everything That Rises: A Book of Convergences **149**
Mr. Wilson's Cabinet of Wonder: Pronged Ants, Horned Humans, Mice on Toast and Other Marvels... 149, 149
Seeing Is Forgetting the Name of the Thing One Sees 149, 149
True to Life: Twenty-Five Years of Conversations with David Hockney 149, 149

Weschler, Tom
Travelin' Man: On the Road and Behind the Scenes with Bob Seger **53**, 216

Wesner, Erik
Success Made Simple: An Inside Look at Why Amish Businesses Thrive 456

Wessels, Tom
Forest Forensics 1202
The Myth of Progress: Toward a Sustainable Future 1105

West, Cornel
The African-American Century: How Black Americans Have Shaped Our Country 805
The Future of the Race 220

West, Darrell M.
Brain Gain: Rethinking U.S. Immigration Policy 388

West, Elliott
The Contested Plains: Indians, Goldseekers, and the Rush to Colorado 670

West, Jessica Pallington
What Would Keith Richards Do?: Daily Affirmations from a Rock 'N' Roll Survivor 968, 1042

West, John B.
High Altitude Medicine and Physiology 642
Pulmonary Pathophysiology: The Essentials, Seventh Edition **642**
Pulmonary Physiology and Pathophysiology 642
Pulmonary Physiology and Pathophysiology: An Integrated, Case-Based Approach 561
Respiratory Physiology: The Essentials 642

Westad, Odd Arne
The Cold War: A History in Documents and Eyewitness Accounts 729, 774

Weston, Terry
America's Bloodiest Serial Killers: From Jeffrey Dahmer to the Boston Strangler 1299

Westrate, Bruce C.
The Arab Bureau: British Policy in the Middle East, 1916-1920 839

Wexman, Virginia Wright
Film and Authorship 82, 83

Whalen, R. Christopher
Inflated: How Money and Debt Built the American Dream 431

Wharton, Edith
The Age of Innocence 904
A Backward Glance 255
The House of Mirth 904

Wheatley, Catherine
Michael Haneke Cinema: The Ethic of the Image 108

Wheelan, Charles
Naked Economics: Undressing the Dismal Science 384

Wheeler, Alina
Designing Brand Identity: An Essential Guide for the Whole Branding Team 336, 421

Whiffen, Leeann
A Child's Journey Out of Autism: One Family's Story of Living in Hope and Finding a Cure 587, 624, **643**

Whitaker, Suzanne George
The Daring Miss Quimby 327

White, Betty
Here We Go Again: My Life In Television 933, 977

White, Bob W.
Rumba Rules: The Politics of Dance Music in Mobutu's Zaire 150

Title Index

This index alphabetically lists all titles featured in entries and those listed within entries under "Other books by the same author" and "Other books you might like." Each title is followed by the author's name and the number of the entry where the book is described or listed. Bold numbers indicate featured main entries; light-face numbers refer to books recommended for further reading.

563

Title Index

Are You There, Vodka? It's Me, Chelsea

C

Title Index

H

Title Index

Monster Theory: Reading Culture
Cohen, Jeffrey Jerome 16

Monsterology: The Complete Book of Monstrous Beasts
Drake, Ernest 1237

Monsters and the Monstrous: Myths and Metaphors of Enduring Evil
Scott, Niall 1237

Monsters are Afraid of the Moon
Satrapi, Marjane 1012, 1013

Monsters: A Bestiary of the Bizarre
Dell, Christopher 1237

Monsters: Evil Beings, Mythical Beasts, and All Manner of Imaginary Terrors
Gilmore, David D. 16

The Monstrous Debt: Modalities of Romantic Influence in Twentieth-Century Literature
Turley, Richard Marggraf **140**

Moon 3-D: The Lunar Surface Comes to Life
Bell, Jim 1056

Moon Lander
Kelly, Thomas J. 1157

Moral Capital: Foundations of British Abolitionism
Brown, Christopher Leslie **680** , 747

Moral Politics: How Liberals and Conservatives Think
Lakoff, George 730

The Moral, Social, and Commercial Imperatives of Genetic Testing and Screening
Betta, Michela 1212

More Attention, Less Deficit: Success Strategies for Adults with ADHD
Tuckman, Ari 467, 589, 633

More Information Than You Require
Hodgman, John 892, **952** , 1006, 1040, 951

More than Just Race: Being Black and Poor in the Inner City
Wilson, William Julius 1362

More than Night: Film Noir in Its Contexts
Naremore, James 142

The Mormon Way of Doing Business: How Eight Western Boys Reached the Top of Corporate America
Benedict, Jeff 1240

Mornings on Horseback: The Story of an Extraordinary Family, a Vanished Way of Life and the Unique Child Who Became Theodore Roosevelt
Mccullough, David G. 793

Morphic Resonance: The Nature of Formative Causation
Sheldrake, Rupert 1133

Morphodynamics of Invertebrate Skeletons
Seilacher, Adolf 1198

Morrie: In His Own Words
Schwartz, Morrie 576

Mortified: Real Words. Real People. Real Pathetic.
Nadelberg, David 1011

Moscow 1941: A City and Its People at War
Braithwaite, Rodric 806

Moscow 1941: Hitler's First Defeat
Forczyk, Robert 806

Moses: When Harriet Tubman Led Her People to Freedom
Weatherford, Carole Boston 237

The Most American Thing in America: Circuit Chautauqua as Performance
Canning, Charlotte M. **29**

The Most Beautiful Villages of New England
Shachtman, Tom 1342

The Most Dangerous Enemy: The Definitive History of the Battle of Britain
Bungay, Stephen 766

The Most Exclusive Club: A History Of The Modern United States Senate
Gould, Lewis L. 52

The Most Famous Man in America: The Biography of Henry Ward Beecher
Applegate, Debby **163**

The Most of P.G. Wodehouse
Wodehouse, P.G. 268

The Most Powerful Idea in the World: A Story of Steam, Industry, and Invention
Rosen, William **1333**

The Most Successful Small Business in The World: The Ten Principles
Gerber, Michael E. 458

The Mother of Us All: A History of Queen Nanny, Leader of the Windward Jamaican Maroons
Gottlieb, Karla 651, 669

The Mother Tongue: English & How It Got That Way
Bryson, Bill 24

Mother: A Cradle to Hold Me
Angelou, Maya 162

Motherbridge of Love
Xinran, Xinran 1372

Mothers of Invention: Women of the Slaveholding South in the American Civil War
Faust, Drew Gilpin 717

Motivation of Health Behavior
O'Neal, Paul W. 536

Motor City Rock and Roll: The 1960's and 1970's
Harris, Bob 53

Mount Pleasant: My Journey from Creating a Billion-Dollar Company to Teaching at a Struggling Public High School
Poizner, Steve **286**

Mountains Beyond Mountains
Kidder, Tracy 964

The Mourner's Dance: What We Do When People Die
Ashenburg, Katherine 655

The Mourning Voice: An Essay on Greek Tragedy
Loraux, Nicole 138

Moving the Chains: Tom Brady and the Pursuit of Everything
Pierce, Charles P. 1324

Mr. Wilson's Cabinet of Wonder: Pronged Ants, Horned Humans, Mice on Toast and Other Marvels...
Weschler, Lawrence 149, 149

Mrs. Astor Regrets: The Hidden Betrayals of a Family Beyond Reproach
Gordon, Meryl 904

Mrs. Lincoln: A Life
Clinton, Catherine 329

Mrs. Vargas and the Dead Naturalist
Alcala, Kathleen 3

Much Depends on Dinner: The Extraordinary History and Mythology, Allure and Obsessions, Perils and Taboos of an Ordinary Meal
Visser, Margaret 854, 1363

Mucosal Immunology and Virology
Tyring, Stephen K. 598, 600

The Mughal Empire
Richards, John F. 698

The Mughal Throne: The Saga of India's Great Emperors
Eraly, Abraham 698

Mughal Warfare: Indian Frontiers and Highroads to Empire 1500-1700
Gomans, J.J.L. 698

Muhammad: A Prophet for Our Time
Armstrong, Karen 274

Mukiwa: A White Boy in Africa
Godwin, Peter 224, 242

Mulatto America: At the Crossroads of Black and White Culture: A Social History
Talty, Stephan 860

The Mulligan: A Parable of Second Chances
Blanchard, Ken 347

The Multiple Sclerosis Manifesto: Action to Take, Principles to Live By
Stachowiak, Julie 510, **620**

Multiple Sclerosis: 300 Tips for Making Life Easier
Schwarz, Shelley Peterman 563, 620

Multipliers: How the Best Leaders Make Everyone Smarter
Wiseman, Liz **1369**

Murder City: The Bloody History of Chicago in the Twenties
Lesy, Michael 1234

Murder in Memphis: The FBI and the Assassination of Martin Luther King
Lane, Mark 750

Murder in the Courthouse: Reconstruction and Redemption in the North Carolina Piedmont
Wise, James E. 713

The Murder of Biggie Smalls
Scott, Cathy 1007

Murders and Madness: Medicine, Law, and Society in the Fin de Siècle
Harris, Ruth 1284

The Murrow Boys: Pioneers on fthe Front Lines of Broadcast Journalism
Olson, Lynne 817

Musculoskeletal System
Netter, Frank H. 1169

Music in Film: Soundtracks and Synergy
Reay, Pauline 62, 107

The Music Instinct: How Music Works and Why We Can't Do Without It
Ball, Philip 1137

The Music of The Lord of the Rings Films: A Comprehensive Account of Howard Shore's Scores
Adams, Doug 62, 107

Music Therapy
Podolsky, Edward 518

Music Therapy Education and Training: From Theory to Practice
Goodman, Karen D. 518

Music Therapy Groupwork with Special Needs Children: The Evolving Process
Goodman, Karen D. 475, **518** , 601

Music, Language, and the Brain
Patel, Aniruddh D. 1137, **1180**

Music, Thought, and Feeling: Understanding the Psychology of Music
Thompson, William Forde 1137

Musichound Country: The Essential Album Guide
Graff, Gary 53

Musichound Rock: The Essential Album Guide
Graff, Gary 53

Musicophilia: Tales of Music and the Brain
Sacks, Oliver 518, **607** , 1137

Mustaine: A Heavy Metal Memoir
Mustaine, Dave 293

Mutiny in the Civil War
Garrison, Webb 807

Mutiny in the United States Navy in World War II: A True Story
Richey, Robert J. 807

Mutiny: The True Events that Inspired the Hunt for Red October
Hagberg, David **739**

My Abandonment
Rock, Peter 326

My American Journey
Powell, Colin L. 185

My Appetite for Destruction: Sex, and Drugs, and Guns N' Roses
Adler, Steven 293

My Best Mathematical and Logic Puzzles
Gardner, Martin 927

My Big Idea: 30 Successful Entrepreneurs Reveal How They Found Inspiration
Bridge, Rachel 397

My Booky Wook: A Memoir of Sex, Drugs, and Stand-Up
Brand, Russell **897** , 919, 936, 942, 943, 944, 1038

Title Index

Subject Index

This index lists subjects which are covered in the featured titles. Beneath each subject heading, titles are arranged alphabetically with the author names and entry numbers also indicated.

Shift: How to Reinvent Your Business, Your Career, and Your Personal Brand - Peter Arnell 340

Afghanistan Conflict, 2001-

In Afghanistan: Two Hundred Years of British, Russian and American Occupation - David Loyn 779

Africa

Blood River: A Journey to Africa's Broken Heart - Tim Butcher 190

Dead Aid: Why Aid Is Not Working and How There Is a Better Way for Africa - Dambisa Moyo 1318

Rumba Rules: The Politics of Dance Music in Mobutu's Zaire - Bob W. White 150

There Is No Me without You - Melissa Fay Greene 231

When a Crocodile Eats the Sun: A Memoir of Africa - Peter Godwin 224

African Americans

Birth of a Notion; Or, the Half Ain't Never Been Told: A Narrative Account with Entertaining Passages of the State of Minstrelsy and of America and the True Relation Thereof - Bill Harris 57

Channeling Blackness: Studies on Television and Race in America - Darnell M. Hunt 63

Colored Property: State Policy and White Racial Politics in Suburban America - David M.P. Freund 726

Condoleezza Rice: An American Life: A Biography - Elisabeth Bumiller 185

Firebrand of Liberty: The Story of Two Black Regiments That Changed the Course of the Civil War - Stephen V. Ash 654

Freedom Summer: The Savage Season That Made Mississippi Burn and Made America a Democracy - Bruce Watson 1366

From Civil Rights to Human Rights: Martin Luther King, Jr. and the Struggle for Economic Justice - Thomas Jackson 753

Gettin' Our Groove On: Rhetoric, Language, and Literacy for the Hip Hop Generation - Kermit E. Campbell 28

The Hemingses of Monticello: An American Family - Annette Gordon-Reed 229

I'd Rather We Got Casinos, and Other Black Thoughts - Larry Wilmore 1040

Keepin' It Hushed: The Barbershop and African American Hush Harbor Rhetoric - Vorris L. Nunley 99

A Little Taste of Freedom: The Black Freedom Struggle in Claiborne County, Mississippi - Emilye Crosby 695

Margaret, Circa 1834-1858 - Nagueyalti Warren 146

Medical Apartheid: The Dark History of Medical Experimentation on Black Americans from Colonial Times to the Present - Harriet A. Washington 870

Middle Passages: African American Journeys to Africa, 1787-2005 - James T. Campbell 689

Mirror to America: The Autobiography of John Hope Franklin - John Hope Franklin 220

Oprah: A Biography - Kitty Kelley 248

Passing Strange: A Gilded Age Tale of Love and Deception Across the Color Line - Martha A. Sandweiss 838

Reading, Writing, and Segregation: A Century of Black Women Teachers in Nashville - Sonya Ramsey 112

Sundown Towns: A Hidden Dimension of Segregation in America - James W. Loewen 778

Terror in the Heart of Freedom: Citizenship, Sexual Violence, and the Meaning of Race in the Postemancipation South - Hannah Rosen 833

Ties That Bind: The Story of an Afro-Cherokee Family in Slavery and Freedom - Tiya Miles 797

Troubled Water: Race, Mutiny, and Bravery on the U.S.S. Kitty Hawk - Gregory Freeman 725

The Warmth of Other Suns: The Epic Story of America's Great Migration - Isabel Wilkerson 1367

What This Cruel War Was Over: Soldiers, Slavery, and the Civil War - Chandra Manning 788

Willie Mays: The Life, the Legend - James S. Hirsch 239

Your Average Nigga: Performing Race, Literacy, and Masculinity - Vershawn Ashanti Young 156

Africans

The African Diaspora: A History Through Culture - Patrick Manning 789

Captives and Voyagers: Black Migrants Across the Eighteenth-Century British Atlantic World - Alexander X. Byrd 688

Middle Passages: African American Journeys to Africa, 1787-2005 - James T. Campbell 689

Afterlife

Heaven: Our Enduring Fascination with the Afterlife - Lisa Miller 982

Aging (Biology)

100 Simple Things You Can Do to Prevent Alzheimer's and Age-Related Memory Loss - Jean Carper 478

Fact and Fiction of Healthy Vision: Eye Care for Adults and Children - Clyde K. Kitchen 551

Health Promotion and Aging: Practical Applications for Health Professionals - David Haber 530

My Formerly Hot Life: Dispatches from the Other Side of Young - Stephanie Dolgoff 1263

Shock of Gray: The Aging of the World's Population and How It Pits Young Against Old, Child Against Parent, Worker Against Boss, Company Against Rival and Nation Against Nation - Ted C. Fishman 1269

The Third Chapter: Passion, Risk, and Adventure in the 25 Years after 50 - Sara Lawrence-Lightfoot 1309

Agriculture

Animal, Vegetable, Miracle: A Year of Food Life - Barbara Kingsolver 965

Eating Animals - Jonathan Safran Foer 921

The Forager's Harvest: A Guide to Identifying, Harvesting, and Preparing Edible Wild Plants - Samuel Thayer 1213

The Omnivore's Dilemma: A Natural History of Four Meals - Michael Pollan 1000

Soil Science and Management - Edward Plaster 1183

AIDS (Disease)

100 Questions and Answers About HIV and AIDS - Joel E. Gallant 511

HIV/AIDS Treatment Drugs - Brigid M. Kane 544

HIV/AIDS: A Very Short Introduction - Alan Whiteside 644

Living with HIV: A Patient's Guide - Mark Cichocki 483

There Is No Me without You - Melissa Fay Greene 231

Air travel

The Daring Miss Quimby - Suzanne George Whitaker 327

Airplanes

Cold War at 30,000 Feet: The Anglo-American Fight for Aviation Supremacy - Jeffrey A. Engel 714

Alcoholism

The Chris Farley Show: A Biography in Three Acts - Tom Farley 918

Dewey: The Small-Town Library Cat Who Touched the World - Vicki Myron 986

The Glass Castle: A Memoir - Jeannette Walls 323

Lit: A Memoir - Mary Karr 247

Smashed: Story of a Drunken Girlhood - Koren Zailckas 333

The Talented Miss Highsmith: The Secret Life and Serious Art of Patricia Highsmith - Joan Schenkar 1015

Allergy

Allergy and Asthma: Practical Diagnosis and Management - Massoud Mahmoudi 566

Allergy Free Desserts: Gluten-free, Dairy-free, Egg-free, Soy-free and Nut-free Delights - Elizabeth Gordon 520

Clinical Allergy: Diagnosis and Management - Gerald W. Volcheck 635

The Food Allergy Mama's Baking Book: Great Dairy-, Egg-, and Nut-Free Treats for the Whole Family - Kelly Rudnicki 605

Healthier Without Wheat: A New Understanding of Wheat Allergies, Celiac Disease, and Non-Celiac Gluten Intolerance - Stephen Wangen 638

Pediatric Allergy, Asthma and Immunology - Arnaldo Cantani 476

Alternative medicine

Anticancer: A New Way of Life - David Servan-Schreiber 613

Native American Medicinal Plants: An Ethnobotanical Dictionary - Daniel E. Moerman 1159

Alzheimer's disease

100 Simple Things You Can Do to Prevent Alzheimer's and Age-Related Memory Loss - Jean Carper 478

Finding Life in the Land of Alzheimer's: One Daughter's Hopeful Story - Lauren Kessler 549

Inside Alzheimer's: How to Hear and Honor Connections with a Person Who Has Dementia - Nancy Pearce 592

Jan's Story: Love Lost to the Long Goodbye of Alzheimer's - Barry Petersen 283

American History

1491: New Revelations of the Americas Before Columbus - Charles C. Mann 786

1776 - David G. Mccullough 793

American Gospel: God, the Founding Fathers, and the Making of a Nation - Jon Meacham 795

Assassination Vacation - Sarah Vowell 1033

Biography

Biology

Business Building

Business enterprises

Subject Index

Health Care

Hearing

Heart diseases

Heaven

Heroes and Heroines

Hispanic Americans

History

Innovation by Building on the Ideas of Others - David Kord Murray 420

BrandSimple: How the Best Brands Keep It Simple and Succeed - Allen P. Adamson 336

Citizen Marketers: When People Are the Message - Ben McConnell 413

The Fall of PR & the Rise of Advertising - Stefan Engeseth 366

Flip the Funnel: How to Use Existing Customers to Gain New Ones - Joseph Jaffe 391

I Love You More Than My Dog: Five Decisions That Drive Extreme Customer Loyalty in Good Times and Bad - Jeanne Bliss 348

In Pursuit of Elegance: Why the Best Ideas Have Something Missing - Matthew E. May 412

The Long Tail, Revised and Updated Edition: Why the Future of Business is Selling Less of More - Chris Anderson 338

Million Dollar Website: Simple Steps to Help You Compete with the Big Boys—Even on a Small Business Budget - Lori Culwell 363

Neuromarketing: Understanding the Buy Buttons in Your Customer's Brain - Patrick Renvoise 429

The New Community Rules: Marketing on the Social Web - Tamar Weinberg 454

The New Rules of Marketing and PR: How to Use News Releases, Blogs, Podcasting, Viral Marketing and Online Media to Reach Buyers Directly - David Meerman Scott 439

Outrageous Advertising That's Outrageously Successful: Created for the 99% of Small Business Owners Who Are Dissatisfied with the Results They Get from Their Current Advertising - Bill Glazer 377

Personality Not Included: Why Companies Lose Their Authenticity and How Great Brands Get It Back - Rohit Bhargava 346

Read This First: The Executive's Guide to New Media—from Blogs to Social Networks - Ron Ploof 426

Reality Check: The Irreverent Guide to Outsmarting, Outmanaging, and Outmarketing Your Competition - Guy Kawasaki 397

The Referral Engine: Teaching Your Business to Market Itself - John Jantsch 392

Satisfaction: How Every Great Company Listens to the Voice of the Customer - James D. Power IV 427

Shift: How to Reinvent Your Business, Your Career, and Your Personal Brand - Peter Arnell 340

Six Pixels of Separation: Everyone Is Connected. Connect Your Business to Everyone - Mitch Joel 394

Smarter, Faster, Cheaper: Non-Boring, Fluff-Free Strategies for Marketing and Promoting Your Business - David Siteman Garland 374

Stuffed: An Insider's Look at Who's (Really) Making America Fat - Hank Cardello 1250

The Truth about What Customers Want - Michael R. Solomon 444

UnMarketing: Stop Marketing. Start Engaging. - Scott Stratten 448

Upstarts!: How GenY Entrepreneurs are Rocking the World of Business and 8 Ways You Can Profit from Their Success - Donna Fenn 367

Marriage

The ADHD Effect on Marriage: Understand and Rebuild Your Relationship in Six Steps - Melissa Orlov 589

Bad Mother: A Chronicle of Maternal Crimes, Minor Calamities, and Occasional Moments of Grace - Ayelet Waldman 1035

Cleaving: A Story of Marriage, Meat, and Obsession - Julie Powell 1003

The Commitment: Love, Sex, Marriage, and My Family - Dan Savage 1338

Committed: A Skeptic Makes Peace with Marriage - Elizabeth Gilbert 221

Furious Love: Elizabeth Taylor, Richard Burton, and the Marriage of the Century - Sam Kashner 961

Leonard Woolf: A Biography - Victoria Glendinning 223

The Love Dare - Stephen Kendrick 962

Manhood for Amateurs: The Pleasures and Regrets of a Husband, Father, and Son - Michael Chabon 902

The Oldest We've Ever Been: Seven True Stories of Midlife Transitions - Maud Lavin 75

One Perfect Day: The Selling of the American Wedding - Rebecca Mead 1314

Perfection: A Memoir of Betrayal and Renewal - Julie Metz 978

Shakespeare's Wife - Germaine Greer 233

Spoken from the Heart - Laura Bush 189

Staying True - Jenny Sandford 299

The Year of Magical Thinking - Joan Didion 212

You Say Tomato, I Say Shut Up: A Love Story - Annabelle Gurwitch 1280

Mars (Planet)

Human Missions to Mars: Enabling Technologies for Exploring the Red Planet - Donald Rapp 1187

Landscapes of Mars: A Visual Tour - Gregory L. Vogt 1224

Postcards from Mars: The First Photographer on the Red Planet - Jim Bell 1056

Massacres

Columbine - Dave Cullen 1260

Mathematics

Absolutely Small: How Quantum Theory Explains Our Everyday World - Michael D. Fayer 1094

Essential Quantum Mechanics - Gary E. Bowman 1063

Essentials of Statistics, 3rd Edition - Mario F. Triola 1218

High-Energy Astrophysics - Fulvio Melia 1154

How to Prove It: A Structured Approach, 2nd Edition - Daniel J. Velleman 1220

Marvelous Geometry: Narrative and Metafiction in Modern Fairy Tale - Jessica Tiffin 136

Matter and Motion - James Clerk Maxwell 1150

Quantum Mechanics: Concepts and Applications, Second Edition - Nouredine Zettili 1231

Statistical Design - George Casella 1073

Systems Science and Modeling for Ecological Economics - Alexey A. Voinov 1225

When You Were a Tadpole and I Was a Fish: And Other Speculations About This and That - Martin Gardner 927

McCarthy Era

American Prometheus: The Triumph and Tragedy of J. Robert Oppenheimer - Kai Bird 173

Medical care

100 Q and A About Prostate Cancer, Second Edition - Pamela Ellsworth 501

100 Questions and Answers About HIV and AIDS - Joel E. Gallant 511

50 Diabetes Myths That Can Ruin Your Life: And the 50 Diabetes Truths That Can Save It - Riva Greenberg 521

Acute Ischemic Stroke: An Evidence-Based Approach - David M. Greer 523

Amyotrophic Lateral Sclerosis: A Guide for Patients and Families, 3rd Edition - Hiroshi Mitsumoto 576

Atlas of Brain Function, 2nd Edition - William W. Orrison Jr. 590

Autism and Its Medical Management: A Guide for Parents and Professionals - Michael G. Chez 481

Basic Clinical Pharmacokinetics, Fifth Edition - Michael E. Winter 648

Bates' Pocket Guide to Physical Examination and History Taking, Sixth Edition - Lynn S. Bickley 470

Beating Gout: A Sufferer's Guide to Living Pain Free, Second Edition - Victor Konshin 555

Beyond Alzheimer's: How to Avoid the Modern Epidemic of Dementia - Scott D. Mendelson 573

Born in the USA: How a Broken Maternity System Must Be Fixed to Put Women and Children First - Marsden Wagner 636

Caplan's Stroke: A Clinical Approach, Fourth Edition - Louis R. Caplan 477

Cataract Surgery: A Patient's Guide to Cataract Treatment - Uday Devgan 494

A Child in Pain: What Health Professionals Can Do to Help - Leora Kuttner 557

A Child's Journey Out of Autism: One Family's Story of Living in Hope and Finding a Cure - Leeann Whiffen 643

Choices in Breast Cancer Treatment: Medical Specialists and Cancer Survivors Tell You What You Need to Know - Kenneth D. Miller 575

The Cleveland Clinic Guide to Fibromyalgia - William S. Wilke 646

The Cleveland Clinic Guide to Heart Failure - Randall C. Starling 622

The Cleveland Clinic Guide to Lung Cancer - Peter Mazzone 570

The Cleveland Clinic Guide to Prostate Cancer - Eric Klein 553

Clinical Allergy: Diagnosis and Management - Gerald W. Volcheck 635

Clinician's Guide to Laboratory Medicine, 3rd Edition - Samir P. Desai 493

The Colony: The Harrowing True Story of the Exiles of Molokai - John Tayman 861

The Comatose Patient - Eelco F.M. Wijdicks 645

Comprehensive Medical Terminology, 3rd Edition - Betty Davis Jones 542

Connecting Through Music with People with Dementia: A Guide for Caregivers - Robin Rio 601

Conquering Stroke: How I Fought My Way Back and How You Can Too - Valerie Greene 522

Cosmetic Dermatology: Principles and Practice, 2nd Edition - Leslie Baumann 468

Crohn's Disease and Ulcerative Colitis: Everything You Need to Know, Revised Edition - Fred Saibil 608

Dead Men Don't Have Sex: A Guy's Guide to Surviving Prostate Cancer - Robert Hill 540

Dentist's Guide to Medical Conditions and Complications - Kanchan M. Ganda 512

Disease Handbook for Massage Therapists - Ruth Werner 641

Disease of the Kidney and Urinary Tract: 8th Edition - Robert W. Schrier 612

Do You Really Need Back Surgery?: A Surgeon's Guide to Back and Neck Pain and How to Choose Your Treatment - Aaron G. Filler 505

Meditation

Memory

Memory disorders

Men

Mennonites

Menopause

Mental disorders

Mental health

Meteorology

Mexican Americans

Rocket and Spacecraft Propulsion: Principles, Practice and New Developments - Martin J. L. Turner 1219

Sirius: Brightest Diamond in the Night Sky - Jay B. Holberg 1119

Soil Science and Management - Edward Plaster 1183

Space Rescue: Ensuring the Safety of Manned Spacecraft - David Shayler 1199

Spook: Science Tackles the Afterlife - Mary Roach 1331

Statistical Design - George Casella 1073

Stephen James O'Meara's Observing the Night Sky with Binoculars: A Simple Guide to the Heavens - Stephen James O'Meara 1173

The Strangest Man: The Hidden Life of Paul Dirac, Mystic of the Atom - Graham Farmelo 217

Student Atlas of World Geography - John Allen 1046

The Sun from Space - Kenneth R. Lang 1132

Systems Science and Modeling for Ecological Economics - Alexey A. Voinov 1225

The Talent Code: Greatness Isn't Born. It's Grown. Here's How - Daniel Coyle 1083

Textbook of Biochemistry with Clinical Correlations - Thomas M. Devlin 1088

Thermodynamics in Earth and Planetary Sciences - Jibamitra Ganguly 1099

This Is Your Brain on Music: The Science of a Human Obsession - Daniel J. Levitin 1137

To Test or Not to Test: A Guide to Genetic Screening and Risk - Doris Teichler-Zallen 1212

To the End of the Solar System: The Story of the Nuclear Rocket, Second Edition - James A. Dewar 1089

Trace Fossil Analysis - Adolf Seilacher 1198

Trace Fossils: Concepts, Problems, Prospects - William Miller III 1156

Tsunami: The Underrated Hazard, 2nd Edition - Edward Bryant 1067

Turning Blood Red: The Fight for Life in Cooley's Anemia - Arthur Bank 465

The Universe in a Mirror: The Saga of the Hubble Space Telescope and the Visionaries Who Built It - Robert Zimmerman 1233

Unscientific America: How Scientific Illiteracy Threatens our Future - Chris Mooney 1316

The Upside of Irrationality: The Unexpected Benefits of Defying Logic at Work and at Home - Dan Ariely 1236

Uranium Wars: The Scientific Rivalry That Created the Nuclear Age - Amir D. Aczel 1043

Vaccinated: One Man's Quest to Defeat the World's Deadliest Diseases - Paul A. Offit 1175

The Way of the Explorer: An Apollo Astronaut's Journey Through the Material and Mystical Worlds - Edgar Mitchell 1158

Weather's Greatest Mysteries Solved! - Randy Cerveny 1074

When You Were a Tadpole and I Was a Fish: And Other Speculations About This and That - Martin Gardner 927

The Wild Food Trailguide, New Edition - Alan Hall 1108

The Winds of Change: Climate, Weather, and the Destruction of Civilizations - Eugene Linden 1140

Science experiments (Education)

Atlas and Dissection Guide for Comparative Anatomy, 6th Edition - Saul Wischnitzer 1230

Lab Manual for General, Organic, and Biological Chemistry, 2nd Edition - Karen C. Timberlake 1215

Medical Apartheid: The Dark History of Medical

Experimentation on Black Americans from Colonial Times to the Present - Harriet A. Washington 870

Science fiction

British Science Fiction Television: A Hitchhiker's Guide - John R. Cook 31

From Alien to the Matrix: Reading Science Fiction Film - Roz Kaveney 70

Scotland

The Enlightenment and the Book: Scottish Authors and Their Publishers in Eighteenth-Century Britain, Ireland, and America - Richard B. Sher 847

Highlander: The History of the Legendary Highland Soldier - Tim Newark 813

Scots (British people)

American on Purpose: The Improbable Adventures of an Unlikely Patriot - Craig Ferguson 919

Scottish history

The Enlightenment and the Book: Scottish Authors and Their Publishers in Eighteenth-Century Britain, Ireland, and America - Richard B. Sher 847

Sea stories

The Wreckers: A Story of Killing Seas and Plundered Shipwrecks, from the 18th-Century to the Present Day - Bella Bathurst 664

Secrets

The Secret - Rhonda Byrne 899

Self awareness

The 4-Hour Workweek, Expanded and Updated: Escape 9-5, Live Anywhere, and Join the New Rich - Timothy Ferriss 369

Self confidence

The Business Devotional: 365 Inspirational Thoughts on Management, Leadership & Motivation - Lillian Hayes Martin 411

Self help books

The 4-Hour Workweek, Expanded and Updated: Escape 9-5, Live Anywhere, and Join the New Rich - Timothy Ferriss 369

The 7 Triggers to Yes: The New Science Behind Influencing People's Decisions - Russell Granger 381

The Brand Gap: Expanded Edition - Marty Neumeier 421

The Business Devotional: 365 Inspirational Thoughts on Management, Leadership & Motivation - Lillian Hayes Martin 411

Do More Great Work. Stop the Busywork, and Start the Work That Matters - Michael Bungay Stanier 447

Made to Stick: Why Some Ideas Survive and Others Die - Chip Heath 1287

Making It All Work: Winning at the Game of Work and Business of Life - David Allen 337

Networking Like a Pro: Turning Contacts into Connections - Ivan Misner 417

New Job, New You: A Guide to Reinventing Yourself in a Bright New Career - Alexandra Levit 404

The Secret Code of Success: 7 Hidden Steps to More Wealth and Happiness - Noah St. John 446

SNAP Selling: Speed Up Sales and Win More Business with Today's Frazzled Customers - Jill Konrath 402

Why Can't You Shut Up?: How We Ruin Relationships—How Not To - Anthony Wolf 1370

You're a Horrible Person, but I Like You: The Believer Book of Advice - Eric Spitznagel 1027

Self knowledge

PostSecret: Confessions on Life, Death, and God - Frank Warren 1036

Self love

The Narcissism Epidemic: Living in the Age of Entitlement - Jean Twenge 1358

Self perception

Being Wrong: Adventures in the Margin of Error - Kathryn Schulz 1339

Blink: The Power of Thinking Without Thinking - Malcolm Gladwell 931

The Narcissism Epidemic: Living in the Age of Entitlement - Jean Twenge 1358

Serial Killers

The Monster of Florence - Douglas Preston 1326

Sex education

How to Make Love to Adrian Colesberry - Adrian Colesberry 908

Seductive Delusions: How Everyday People Catch STDs - Jill Grimes 524

Sexually Transmitted Diseases - Leanne Currie-McGhee 488

Sex roles

Coyote Nation: Sexuality, Race, and Conquest in Modernizing New Mexico, 1880-1920 - Pablo R. Mitchell 799

Gender and Development - Janet Henshall Momsen 577

Pimps, Wimps, Studs, Thugs and Gentlemen: Essays on Media Images of Masculinity - Elwood Watson 147

Specters of Mother India: The Global Restructuring of an Empire - Mrinalini Sinha 849

Sexism

Self-Made Man: One Woman's Journey into Manhood and Back - Norah Vincent 322

This Violent Empire: The Birth of an American National Identity - Carroll Smith-Rosenberg 850

Sexual behavior

Bonk: The Curious Coupling of Sex and Science - Mary Roach 1010

The Bro Code - Barney Stinson 1028

City Boy: My Life in New York During the 1960s and '70s - Edmund White 328

The Secret Pleasures of Menopause - Christiane Northrup 585

making, and Broadcasting in America Since 1941 - James L. Baughman 12

Sex and the City - Deborah Jermyn 67

Sit, Ubu, Sit: How I Went from Brooklyn to Hollywood with the Same Woman, the Same Dog, and a Lot Less Hair - Gary David Goldberg 933

Television Without Pity: 752 Things We Love to Hate (and Hate to Love) About TV - Tara Ariano 888

This Time Together: Laughter and Reflection - Carol Burnett 187

TV by Design: Modern Art and the Rise of Network Television - Lynn Spigel 126

Television programs

Angel - Stacey Abbott 1
Bewitched - Walter Metz 87

Television Programs

Brainiac: Adventures in the Curious, Competitive, Compulsive World of Trivia - Ken Jennings 958

Television programs

British Science Fiction Television: A Hitchhiker's Guide - John R. Cook 31

Doctor Who - Jim Leach 76

The Flip Wilson Show - Meghan Sutherland 133

Here's the Story: Surviving Marcia Brady and Finding My True Voice - Maureen McCormick 265

Living Lost: Why We're All Stuck on the Island - J. Wood 153

Prisoner of Trebekistan: A Decade in Jeopardy! - Bob Harris 946

Redneck Boy in the Promised Land - Ben Jones 960

The Simpsons: An Uncensored, Unauthorized History - John Ortved 998

Sliding into Home - Kendra Wilkinson 1039

Stori Telling - Tori Spelling 1026

Taking South Park Seriously - Jeffrey Andrew Weinstock 148

Television Without Pity: 752 Things We Love to Hate (and Hate to Love) About TV - Tara Ariano 888

Thirty-Nine Years of Short-Term Memory Loss: The Early Days of SNL from Someone Who Was There - Tom Davis 910

Tennis

Open: An Autobiography - Andre Agassi 161

Terror

Son of Hamas: A Gripping Account of Terror, Betrayal, Political Intrigue, and Unthinkable Choices - Mosab Hassan Yousef 332

Theater

Acting in the Night: Macbeth and the Places of the Civil War - Alexander Nemerov 97

Champagne Charlie and Pretty Jemima: Variety Theater in the Nineteenth Century - Gillian M. Rodger 114

Home: A Memoir of My Early Years - Julie Andrews 887

The Making of Theatrical Reputations: Studies from the Modern London Theatre - Yael Zarhy-Levo 158

The Most American Thing in America: Circuit Chautauqua as Performance - Charlotte M. Canning 29

Shakespeare and Chekhov in Production and Reception: Theatrical Events and Their Audiences - John Tulloch 139

When Broadway Was the Runway: Theater, Fashion and American Culture - Marlis Schweitzer 118

Theft

Flawless: Inside the Largest Diamond Heist in History - Scott Andrew Selby 1341

Time

The 24-Hour Customer: New Rules for Winning in a Time-Starved, Always-Connected Economy - Adrian C. Ott 422

Making It All Work: Winning at the Game of Work and Business of Life - David Allen 337

Tradition

The Secret Life of Syrian Lingerie: Intimacy and Design - Malu Halasa 939

Transplantation

Handbook of Kidney Transplantation: 5th Edition - Gabriel M. Danovitch 491

Transportation

The Slave Ship: A Human History - Marcus Rediker 826

Travel

An American Map - Anne-Marie Oomen 103

Champlain's Dream - David Hackett Fischer 219

Even A Daughter Is Better Than Nothing - Mykel Board 20

Exploration Fawcett: Journey to the Lost City of Z - Percy Fawcett 218

Gertrude Bell: Queen of the Desert, Shaper of Nations - Georgina Howell 240

How Did You Get This Number - Sloane Crosley 205

The Journey of Theophanes: Travel, Business, and Daily Life in the Roman East - John Matthews 791

The Places in Between - Rory Stewart 310

Stanley: The Impossible Life of Africa's Greatest Explorer - Tim Jeal 245

State by State: A Panoramic Portrait of America - Matt Weiland 1037

Vanished!: Explorers Forever Lost - Evan L. Balkan 167

The Warmth of Other Suns: The Epic Story of America's Great Migration - Isabel Wilkerson 1367

Trees (Plants)

How Trees Die: The Past, Present, and Future of Our Forests - Jeff Gillman 1101

An Introduction to Plant Structure and Development: Plant Anatomy for the Twenty-First Century - Charles B. Beck 1054

The Sibley Guide to Trees - David Allen Sibley 1202

The Tree Rings' Tale: Understanding Our Changing Climate - John Fleck 1097

Tribalism

Tribes: We Need You to Lead Us - Seth Godin 378

Trust (Psychology)

Denialism: How Irrational Thinking Hinders Scientific Progress, Harms the Planet, and Threatens Our Lives - Michael Specter 1349

Speed of Trust: The One Thing That Changes Everything - Stephen M.R. Covey 361

Underground Railroad (Slave escape network)

Bound for Canaan: The Underground Railroad and the War for the Soul of America - Fergus M. Bordewich 673

United Kingdom. Army

Spies in Arabia: The Great War and the Cultural Foundations of Britain's Covert Empire in the Middle East - Priya Satia 839

United States

American Liberalism: An Interpretation for Our Time - John McGowan 84

American Wasteland: How America Throws Away Nearly Half of Its Food (and What We Can Do About It) - Jonathan Bloom 1243

Angeleno Days: An Arab American Writer on Family, Place, and Politics - Gregory Orfalea 104

Arab/American: Landscape, Culture, and Cuisine in Two Great Deserts - Gary Paul Nabhan 92

The Battle: How the Fight Between Free Enterprise and Big Government Will Shape America's Future - Arthur C. Brooks 352

Bodies of Reform: The Rhetoric of Character in Gilded Age America - James B. Salazar 837

Broke, USA: From Pawnshops to Poverty, Inc.: How the Working Poor Became Big Business - Gary Rivlin 1330

Canyon Cinema: The Life and Times of an Independent Film Distributor - Scott MacDonald 79

Courage and Consequence: My Life as a Conservative in the Fight - Karl Rove 298

Fresh Water: Women Writing on the Great Lakes - Alison Swan 134

Gorgeous George: The Outrageous Bad-Boy Wrestler Who Created American Pop Culture - John Capouya 900

A Great Improvisation: Franklin, France, and the Birth of America - Stacy Schiff 841

Helen Taft: Our Musical First Lady - Lewis L. Gould 52

Henry Adams and the Making of America - Garry Wills 877

I'd Rather We Got Casinos, and Other Black Thoughts - Larry Wilmore 1040

I.O.U.S.A. - Addison Wiggin 457

More Information Than You Require - John Hodgman 952

New Orleans, Mon Amour: Twenty Years of Writings from the City - Andrei Codrescu 30

Nixonland: The Rise of a President and the Fracturing of America - Rick Perlstein 282

A Place for Dialogue: Language, Land Use, and Politics in Southern Arizona - Sharon McKenzie Stevens 128

Radical Light: Alternative Film and Video in the San Francisco Bay Area, 1945-2000 - Steve Anker 9

Relentless Pursuit: A Year in the Trenches with Teach for America - Donna Foote 1270

Renaming the Earth: Personal Essays - Ray Gonzalez 50

The Shifting Grounds of Race: Black and Japanese Americans in the Making of Multiethnic Los Angeles - Scott Kurashige 770

Zoos